Agency, Partnerships and Limited Liability Companies

Agency, Partnerships and Limited Liability Companies

Gary S. Rosin
PROFESSOR OF LAW
SOUTH TEXAS COLLEGE OF LAW

Michael L. Closen
PROFESSOR OF LAW
THE JOHN MARSHALL LAW SCHOOL

CAROLINA ACADEMIC PRESS
Durham, North Carolina

ISBN 0-89089-903-7
LCCN 00-106267

CAROLINA ACADEMIC PRESS
700 Kent Street
Durham, NC 27701
Telephone (919) 489-7486
Fax (919) 493-5668
www.cap-press.com

Printed in the United States of America

Contents

Table of Cases

Preface

We are pleased to present this edition of our casebook. This casebook is unusual in that this is its *third* first edition. The first version of the book was authored by Professor Closen, and published by Butterworth Publishing. The second version was co-authored by Professors Closen and Rosin, and published by Carolina Academic Press. With this edition, we changed the name to reflect the addition of coverage of limited liability companies, as well as of limited liability partnerships and limited liability limited partnerships. We are appreciate the continued confidence of Carolina Academic Presses in the book.

Because agency law is the foundation on which the law of business firms is built, this edition retains substantial treatment of agency law in both its contract and tort aspects. We have reorganized the book so that the materials relating to the agency aspects of the various forms of business firms are grouped with the related agency materials. For example, this edition highlights the importance of fiduciary duties as an ever-present outgrowth of business relationships in all its aspects. The intent is to emphasize that the duties of owners and managers of business firms are related to, but often different from, the duties of agents and employees.

Where possible, we have organized the materials according to the functional characteristics of business firms, such as formation, management and conduct of firm business, firm property, interests in the firm, dissociation of owners, dissolution of the firm, etc. This allows students to compare and contrast the alternatives offered by the various forms of unincorporated businesses.

To facilitate teaching by the problem method, this edition integrates problems into the text. In addition to problems from the old Problems and Statutes supplement, we have added many new problems. Some of these are used to introduce note cases. Others ask students to structure transactions so as to achieve client goals while addressing the concerns raised in the materials.

Several acknowledgments are due for the assistance provided to us over the years that it has taken to complete this project. Professor Closen has had the full support and encouragement of Dean R. Gilbert Johnston, and of his colleagues on the faculty at The John Marshall Law School. Particular mention is deserved by his colleagues who teach agency and partnership law, for they offered considerable guidance and encouragement. They are Professors John Ingram and Randall Peterson, and Adjunct Professor Marc Ginsberg. The typing of these materials was accomplished by a group of very capable secretaries, Gwen Konigsfeld, Yolanda Aparicio, Diane Gordon and Christine Cotter.

Professor Rosin wishes to express his appreciation for the support and encouragement of Dean Frank T. Read and his colleagues on the faculty at South Texas College of Law, as well as that of Dean Harry J. Haynsworth and his colleagues on the faculty of William Mitchell College of Law, where he visited in the Spring of 2000. In preparing these materials he was assisted by Ms. Gloria Landrum, faculty secretary at South Texas College of Law, and Brad Jacobson, Administrative Assistant at William Mitchell College of Law. Particular thanks are owed to Professors Bruce A. McGovern and Val D. Ricks, and to the students at South Texas College of Law and William Mitchell College of Law, who used manuscript working-versions of this edition. Their comments and suggestions helped improve the edition before you.

We would also like to thank Professor Carol R. Goforth, of the University of Arkansas School of Law. Professor Goforth co-authored some of the supplements to the first edition. While Professor Goforth was unable to participate in this edition, it incorporates material that first appeared in those supplements.

Special thanks to Tim Colton of Carolina Academic Press for his thoroughness and attention to detail.

July 2000

Gary S. Rosin
Michael L. Closen

Preface to the First Edition

We are pleased to present this edition of our casebook on the law of agency and partnership. We sincerely appreciate the confidence displayed in us by Carolina Academic Press, and we must especially note our genuine indebtedness to the publishers of the first edition of the book for their continued cooperation and support. The first edition was authored by Professor Closen and published in 1984 by Butterworth Publishing.

As the title indicates, this book treats the closely related subjects of agency and partnership law. The significance of these subjects is readily apparent. Almost all commercial and many noncommercial activities are carried out by agents or servants—employees acting for their employers. Far more than one hundred million Americans serve as employees each year. More than a million businesses are operated as partnerships, and partnership law constitutes a special branch of the law of agency. Hence, these subjects are unquestionably worthy of study, and it is appropriate to consider them in a single law school course. This book reflects the belief of the authors that the course in agency–partnership provides essential foundation materials of a sound legal education in commercial/business law.

We share the concern that our students be prepared for the practice of law, and even for more advanced courses in law school, with materials that emphasize the modern law of agency and partnership. We have found that the fundamentals of this course can be comprehensively addressed in a contemporary fashion, principally from recent cases.

Virtually all principal cases in this volume were decided in the decades of the 1970s, 1980s, and 1990s and most since 1980. The recent decisions are more relevant and thus more interesting and instructive about the factual and legal contexts that today's students will later encounter. Additionally, the recency of these materials should help students to appreciate the continuing vitality of the subjects addressed in this book. *See* Closen, *Teaching with Recent Decisions: A Survey of Past and Present Practices*, 11 FLA. ST. U. L. REV. 289 (1983). Liberal reference has been made to the Restatement (Second) of Agency. Although we also refer to the Restatement (Second) of Torts, citations to the "Restatement" without differentiation refer to the Restatement (Second) of Agency. In the partnership portion of the materials, liberal reference has been made to the Uniform Partnership Act, the Uniform Limited Partnership Act, the Revised Uniform Limited Partnership Act, and the Revised Uniform Partnership Act. (All of these partnership statutes appear in the statutory supplement to this casebook.)

One of our major tasks has been to keep the materials down to manageable size for a single–volume casebook without sacrificing thoroughness of coverage. Consequently, we have had to be very selective. The materials chosen have been generously and liberally edited, usually without any indication. Almost all citations to authority and footnotes have been omitted, and the original footnote numbers from the cases appear on the footnotes that have been retained. Any reader wishing to conduct further research or to cite the material included here must, therefore, consult the original sources. We have abandoned almost entirely the use of ellipses. But, we should hasten to add that the accuracy and soundness of our final product has not been diminished.

Several acknowledgments are due for the assistance provided to us over the years that it has taken to complete this project. Professor Closen has had the full support and encouragement of Dean Howard Markey, Associate Dean R. Gilbert Johnston, and his colleagues on the faculty at The John Marshall Law School. Particular mention is deserved by his colleagues who teach agency and partnership law, for they offered considerable guidance and encouragement. They are Professors John Ingram and Randall Peterson. Over the years, several able student research assistants have made important contributions, including Cory Aronovitz, Grant Dixon, John Furnari, Michael Osty, and Anthony Perniciaro. The typing of these materials was accomplished by a group of very capable secretaries, Gwen Konigsfeld, Joanne Sorce, Yolanda Aparicio, and Nancy Ruberry.

Professor Rosin wishes to express his appreciation for the support and encouragement of Dean William L. Wilks and his colleagues on the faculty at South Texas College of Law. In preparing these materials he was assisted by Ms. Terry L. Velligan, his student research assistant. Special thanks to Ms. Diane Lee, faculty secretary, for her many long hours at the word processor.

Our grateful acknowledgment is hereby extended to the American Law Institute for permission to reprint selected portions of the Restatement (Second) of Agency and the Restatement (Second) of Torts, and to the National Conference of Commissioners on Uniform State Laws for permission to reprint the uniform partnership statutes.

The preparation of this casebook has been challenging, interesting, and rewarding for us, and we hope that readers who study this book will find it profitable as well.

April 1992

Michael L. Closen
Gary S. Rosin

Agency, Partnerships and Limited Liability Companies

Chapter 1

Introduction to Firms

A. Introduction

When you think of American businesses, you may tend to think in terms of corporations. Almost all of the largest business enterprises are organized as corporations, and public investment is focused on corporations. Certainly corporations are a tremendously important aspect of the American business landscape. However, there are a multitude of other business forms which are available to firms today, and these may be very like the corporation or very different from that form of business.

These other business forms range from the sole proprietorship, a very simple business form with a single owner, to publicly traded limited partnerships which may have dozens or even hundreds of passive investors scattered over the country or even other nations. They may be formed very informally, or they may have extensive organizational and operating agreements. Participants may be active in the management and affairs of the business, or purely passive investors. In fact, they need not even be investors. All sorts of business have "participants" who act as agents of the enterprise without being owners or investors.

The following material provides a brief overview of the most common forms of business available under state law, including an overview of applicable statutes and a brief discussion of how the entity is formed, who can "own" the entity, and default rules concerning issues such as management rights, allocation of profits and losses, distributions, and transferability of ownership interests. The summary below does not seek to take into account *every* similarity or difference between entity forms, but rather focuses on what will probably be the most significant factors when comparing one entity against another.

B. The Types of Firms

1. Sole Proprietorships

A sole proprietorship is a business owned by a single individual. While that individual may hire employees or other agents to assist him or her in conducting business operations, the proprietor is the sole owner of the business. Moreover, the business has no legal existence independent of the proprietor. There is no entity which can sue or be sued, or which can shield the proprietor from personal liability for debts arising out of the business.

Because there is no separate legal entity, there is no general statute which governs the formation and operation of a sole proprietorship. Instead, a sole proprietorship will be subject to general state laws and regulations such as those governing the operation of a business under a fictitious name and those requiring licenses and permits for the operation of certain types of business. It will also be governed by general principles of agency and employment law whenever the sole proprietor hires agents or employees to assist with business operations.

In general, the proprietor has sole control over the business and all decisions relating to its operation, unless that control has been delegated to agents. All debts of the business are also debts of the proprietor, and in fact, business assets can be seized to pay for personal debts of the proprietor.

Because the business has no legal existence apart from the proprietor, the proprietor will be able to use business assets for personal purposes and personal assets to meet business obligations. There need be no segregation of assets or income. All earnings or losses are attributed and taxed directly to the proprietor. There is no need for formal distributions from the business.

A sole proprietorship has no separate tax status. It is not an entity recognized under the Internal Revenue Code. Rather, it is treated as an extension of the owner (proprietor). The proprietor is required to report all items of income and expense on his or her personal tax return. There is a separate schedule on which to calculate profit and loss from a business, but there is no separate tax on income earned from such an enterprise. Instead, the income is added to any other taxable income attributable to the proprietor. Similarly, if there is a loss from the business, such loss can generally be deducted from other taxable income earned by the proprietor.

Notes and Problems

1. What kinds of business are most likely to choose the sole proprietorship form of operation? Are sole proprietors likely to seek legal advice in planning their businesses? What type of advice do you want to give to a client thinking about establishing a sole proprietorship? Are there special considerations such clients should be aware of?

2. Is there any way for a business to be established as a sole proprietorship if there are going to be multiple investors? If so, how might this be accomplished? Why might multiple investors want to choose the sole proprietorship form of enterprise?

2. Partnerships

A partnership—sometimes called a "general" partnership—is an association of two or more persons who have agreed to carry on as co-owners a business for profit. No particular formalities are required to form a partnership; there is no filing requirement, and the "agreement" to form a partnership need not be in writing and need not contain any particular language. It is possible to form a partnership without ever using the words "partner" or "partnership. " In fact, under the Uniform Partnership Act (UPA), an agreement to share profits is prima facie evidence that a partnership has been established, although there are ways of rebutting the presumption of partnership status created by such profit sharing. (UPA §§ 6 & 7.) The Uniform Partnership Act (1997) (RUPA)[A] has similar rules. (RUPA § 202.)

The partnership form of enterprise has been around for many decades, and is quite familiar to most business practitioners. In addition, there are a number of resources which can be relied upon for forms and research.

The partnership is a very flexible form of enterprise. State partnership statutes provide default rules (i.e., rules which will govern the relationship of the parties absent specific agreement to the contrary). These rules cover issues such as management rights and the way to calculate each partner's share of profits and losses, but the parties to a partnership agreement are often free to change these default provisions by agreement. For example, absent agreement to the contrary all partners have equal management authority and are entitled to share equally in the profits and losses of the enterprise (after a return of each partner's initial contribution). However, these provisions can be changed by agreement, and it is not at all unusual to see a general partnership with a managing partner or executive committee with full management powers, and with special allocations of profit and loss among the partners. Notes that under RUPA, the statutory provisions may appear at first glance to be mandatory (see, *i.e.*, RUPA § 401), but in fact a separate section lists the only provisions in the Act which are not subject to modification. (RUPA § 103.)

One of the biggest drawbacks to the traditional general partnership is that all partners have unlimited personal liability for all debts of the partnership. This means that if one partner in a professional service partnership engages in malpractice, all members of the firm are personally liable for the full amount of any judgment entered because of that malpractice. Personal liability for entity debts covers contractual obligations as well as tort liability. Under the UPA, liability might be joint or it might be joint and several (depending on the type of liability involved and on whether the particular jurisdiction modified the UPA rule). (UPA § 15.) RUPA makes all such liability joint and several, meaning that an "innocent" partner with a minimal interest in the partnership might wind up being liable for 100% of the partnership's excess debt. (RUPA § 306(a).)

Aside from the personal liability of partners for partnership obligations, another drawback to the partnership form of business has been that the partnership is an association of persons. Among other things, this meant that if any partner ceases to be a partner, for any reason, there was at least a technical dissolution of the first partnership. The remaining partners may have had the right to continue the business of the partnership, but one of the difficult issues in organizing a partnership was to provide what happened when a partner withdrew. It was not always easy to articulate the rights and obligations of both the remaining and the

---

A. During the drafting process, the Uniform Partnership Act (1997) was called the "Revised Uniform Partnership Act" and was commonly referred to as the "RUPA". This book continues that convention.

withdrawing partners. Under some state statutes, even partners withdrawing in violation of the partnership agreement had the right to be bought out at the time of withdrawal, and so dissolution provisions in a partnership agreement were extremely important. Although RUPA makes it clear that a partnership is to be considered an entity (RUPA § 201), it continues the presumption that dissociation of a partner triggers dissolution of the partnership, and thus many of the drafting challenges remain. (RUPA § 601). RUPA is, however, clearer on how the default rules are to work in the case of a partner who withdraws wrongfully, and somewhat clearer on the extent to which the partners can modify a withdrawing partner's right to be bought out.

On the other hand, one of the primary advantages of the partnership form of business is that there is no entity level tax imposed on partnerships. Each item of income and loss is passed through to the partners in accordance with either the default rules or the partnership agreement if the parties have agreed to a different allocation. Until quite recently, this result could not be avoided since a general partnership under state law would always be a tax partnership for income tax purposes. However, Congress recently enacted an elective scheme whereby partnerships under state law, while presumed to be tax partnerships for federal income tax purposes, can elect to be taxed as corporations. This possibility is of more theoretical interest than anything else, since it is widely recognized that partnership tax status is almost always preferable to being taxed as a corporation.

Notes and Problems

1. The foregoing materials talk about both the UPA and RUPA. In 1914, the Commissioners on Uniform State Laws adopted a Uniform Partnership Act (the UPA), a version of which was eventually adopted in every state, although many states did make at least minor modifications to the uniform act. Over time, however, there were criticisms of a number of UPA provisions, and in 1994 the Commissioners on Uniform State Laws approved a revised Uniform Partnership Act (RUPA). RUPA has already been amended once by the National Commissioners, to provide for limited liability partnerships (LLP's), which will be talked about later in these materials. As of this writing, more states still have the UPA, but RUPA is likely to be increasingly influential in the future. Given the controversy surrounding certain sections of RUPA, however, it is virtually certain that state will tinker with the statutory language, resulting in at least some variation in state laws.

3. Limited Partnerships

A limited partnership is formed by the filing a certificate of limited partnership with appropriate state officials. Obviously, this means that an oral agreement will not be sufficient to create a limited partnership. However, the information required to be in a certificate of limited partnership is quite limited. Typically, unless the parties wish to abide by the default rules contained in the relevant statutes, the bulk of the agreement between the partners in a limited partnership will be contained in a partnership agreement. (If they wish the default rules to control as to one or more issues, no agreement is technically necessary, although there may be practical reasons for repeating the statutory defaults in an actual partnership agreement.)

A limited partnership is a partnership with at least one general partner and at least one limited partner. A limited partnership is taxed as a partnership (unless an election to be taxed as a corporation is made by the partners) and is subject to many of the same rules as general partnerships. The biggest distinctions between general and limited partnerships have to do with management rights and limited liability of the limited partners.

Management of a limited partnership is vested in the general partners. Limited partners do not have management authority. They do, however, have a benefit that the general partners do not possess. Limited partners do not have the unlimited personal liability of general partners, provided that if they do assume management responsibilities and a third party assumes because of their actions that they are general partners, the limited partners will lose their limited liability as to such third party.

In addition, there are different default rules for limited partnerships than for general partnerships as to such issues as proper allocation of profits and losses absent agreement to the contrary, and for withdrawal rights of limited partners.

4. Limited Liability Partnerships

One of the two newest forms of business entity is the limited liability partnership (LLP). (The other is the limited liability limited partnership or LLLP, discussed below.) Wyoming was the last American state to enact LLP legislation. Because most of these statutes were written and adopted before RUPA was amended to suggest uniform LLP language, there is substantial variation from state to state. Therefore, the following description of LLP's is very general in nature. LLP statues typically appear in the form of amendments to state general partnership laws, and many of these differences may disappear as more and more states adopt RUPA, which does contain uniform language governing LLP's.

In essence, an LLP is a general partnership where all partners have limited liability as to certain of the partnership's debts. Except for a very few special provisions, it is subject to the same rules as a general partnership.

One difference between an LLP and a general partnership is that an LLP is formed only when a partnership files an application with the appropriate state officials (which means that it is impossible to form an LLP solely with an oral agreement). In some states there are minimum insurance or financial responsibility provisions in the statute. This is obviously procedural rather than operational differences between general partnerships and LLP's.

The most significant operational difference is that partners in LLP's have no liability for certain debts of the entity beyond their capital contribution. The reason for hedging on the description of limited liability in an LLP is that there are, as of this writing, two general models of liability in LLP's. The original LLP statutes provided that partners in an LLP would have no liability for obligations arising out of the misconduct of others. These statutes did not permit partners to avoid personal liability for business debts incurred in the course of ordinary partnership operations. Because partners in these LLP's continued to have personal liability for at least some entity-level debts, the liability provisions in this first wave or generation of statutes have often been described as providing a "partial-shield" from personal liability. On the other hand, a number of states, beginning with Minnesota and including such influential jurisdictions as New York, adopted a much broader limitation on personal liability for partners in LLP's. In these jurisdictions, a partner in an LLP has no personal liability for debts of the partnership, regardless of how such debts are incurred. Not surprisingly, this type of statute is often referred to as a "full-shield."

The National Commissioners on Uniform State Laws chose the full-shield model for RUPA in 1996, and since that time an increasing number of states have elected full-shield status. Even Texas, the state which enacted the original partial-shield statutes, recently amended its LLP provisions to authorize full-shield protections.

Other than these differences in how the LLP is formed and the limited liability feature, most rules applicable to general partnerships also apply to LLP's. All partners will have equal management authority unless otherwise agreed, and even with agreement to the contrary, all partners retain certain apparent authority. Absent agreement to the contrary, all partners have equal rights to share in profits and losses of the enterprise. Withdrawal of any member triggers at least a technical dissolution of the partnership.

As a practical matter, perhaps the most significant disadvantage to the LLP as compared to the general partnership form of business is the novelty and unfamiliarity of the LLP. This means that relatively little has been written about them. There are few form books or other resources to help a practitioner become familiar with the new entity, but over time this limitation is likely to disappear.

Another problem associated with the LLP is the lack of uniformity in LLP statutes. Although LLP's are authorized in every state, there is still considerable variation on essential issues. For example, statutes differ on how often a filing must be made in order to preserve a partnership's status as an LLP, whether an LLP has to maintain certain insurance or fiscal reserves, and the extent of partners' personal liability. This means that there is some uncertainty as to how partners in an LLP organized under the laws of a jurisdiction which has one set of rules will be treated in other jurisdictions with different rules. Although there is unlikely to be much of a problem when it comes to figuring out which rules to apply to the internal operations of the partnership, there might well be more of a problem when it comes to the issue of settling the liability of partners to third parties who deal with the partnership.

5. Limited Liability Limited Partnerships

A few states have also adopted statutes which expressly authorize the formation of limited liability limited partnerships (LLLP's). An LLLP is a limited partnership where the general partners have the same protections against personal liability that general partners in an LLP possesses.

There is an on-going debate as to whether a number of other states have authorized the formation of LLLP's by implication in their LLP statutes. Since LLP legislation generally takes the form of an amendment to existing partnership law, an argument can and has been made that statutory references which authorize "partnerships" to organize as limited liability entities should include implicit authorization for limited partnerships to make the same election. This argument is bolstered by provisions in state limited partnership laws which say that the law applicable to general partnerships will also apply to limited partnerships, except where there is a direct conflict between the general partnership provisions and the limited partnership statutes. However, until there is a judicial determination that such LLP legislation implicitly authorizes LLLP's, the legality of LLLP's is certain only in those states which expressly address this form of entity.

With the exception of registration requirements, the requirement that every LLLP contain some indication in its name that it is an LLLP, and the change in the personal liability of the general partner(s), an LLLP is virtually indistinguishable from a limited partnership under state law.

6. Limited Liability Companies

The limited liability company (LLC) is also a relatively new form of business. Only in the last decade have a significant number of jurisdictions enacted legislation authorizing the formation of LLC's. The last two states enacted LLC legislation in the Spring of 1996. There is a Uniform LLC Act, although it was promulgated after most states had already enacted LLC legislation. Because the Uniform law was approved so late in the game, it was not particularly influential. Only a few states have actually adopted the Uniform Act, although a number of state legislatures have considered or are considering bills which either call for the adoption of the Uniform LLC Act or would bring the state statute more into line with the uniform provisions.

Despite the fact that the LLC is a relatively new form of business enterprise, in the last few years a number of treatises and form books devoted to LLC's have been published to aid a practitioner in understanding, forming and organizing LLC's.

Generally speaking, an LLC is an entity formed by filing a very brief document usually referred to as articles of formation. The resulting LLC will be governed either by the default rules contained in the relevant state statutes or by agreement of the parties as reflected in an organizational document usually known as an operating agreement. In some states a written operating agreement is required by law; in other states no formal operating agreement is needed if the parties agree to be governed solely by the default rules of the state statute. In some states, an oral operating agreement may suffice, although it would almost certainly be less than ideal.

As with the general partnership, the LLC is a very flexible form of enterprise. While most statutes provide default rules governing such issues as management and sharing of profits and losses, the members of an LLC are generally free to change these default provisions by agreement. For example, most state LLC statutes provide that, absent agreement to the contrary, all members will have equal management authority. However, by including an appropriate provision in the articles of formation or possibly even in the operating agreement (depending on the statutory language), the LLC can elect to be managed by managers. Similar flexibility is allowed with regard to sharing of profits and losses, and in a growing number of jurisdictions, the withdrawal rights of members as well.

The biggest advantage to the LLC form of business enterprise when compared to general partnership is that members in an LLC do not have unlimited personal liability. This means that if limited liability is an important consideration, the LLC is preferable even to the limited partnership, because every limited partnership must have at least one general partner with unlimited personal liability.

When compared to an LLP or LLLP, the first consideration will have to be whether the LLP or LLLP statute in question provides for full-shield or partial-shield protection from personal liability. In partial-shield jurisdictions, the LLC may be preferable because it offers members more protection from the risk of personal liability. In full-shield states, however, a different basis for comparison will be needed.

In most states, LLC statutes are more flexible than partnership statutes. For example, it may be impossible to prevent a partner in an LLP from having at least apparent authority (and therefore the legal power) to bind the partnership in ways which are contrary to the actual agreement of the partners. However, an LLC can be formed in such a way that members are given little or no authority (actual or apparent) to bind their firm. Similarly, in most states it is impossible to prevent a general partner from withdrawing from a partnership, even if the withdrawal is in contravention of the partnership agreement. In many states, an LLC can be formed so that its members do not have the legal power to withdraw in violation of the agreement. The flexibility to create an LLC which conforms more precisely to the preferences of those involved in a particular enterprise may therefore make the LLC preferable even in comparison to the LLP or LLLP.

There are also advantages when comparing the LLC to the corporation. First, there is the question of tax status. An LLC which has at least 2 members is presumed to be a tax partnership, although the members do have the power to elect corporate tax status if they so desire. A corporation can be taxed only under subchapter C or subchapter S of the Internal Revenue Code. A C Corporation (the "C" refers to subchapter C of the tax code) will be subject to double taxation . In other words, corporate earnings are taxed once at the corporate level, and then again, when distributed as dividends to the shareholders. S Corporations are, in many ways, taxed like partnerships although there are some important differences between subchapter K of the Internal Revenue Code (which governs partnerships) and subchapter S. These differences are far beyond the scope of this book. One major problem with Subchapter S is that not all corporations are eligible to make the S election. For example, there are limitations on the number of shareholders and the type of shareholders permitted. Even more importantly, an S corporation may have only one class of stock, which severely restricts the ability of participants to structure differing rates of return or of sharing losses.

In addition to these tax concerns, however, there are also some advantages to the LLC form which are not available with corporations. For example, the LLC is often more flexible with regard to management options. Corporations are generally managed by or under the authority of a board of directors. Although state statutes may allow close corporations to opt-out of this arrangement in theory, few corporations take this route. Thus, the overwhelming majority of even close corporations continue to be run through a board of directors, even where a simpler management structure would be optimal. Similarly, corporate statutes generally require formal meetings and written or transcribable records of those proceedings. No such formality is mandated with the LLC. The flexibility and informality of the LLC will often make it more desirable from an operational standpoint than the corporation.

7. Corporations

The corporation is probably the form of business entity which comes most readily to mind for many people. It is formed by filing articles of incorporation (also called the corporate charter) with the appropriate state officials. To the extent desired, a corporation may also have written bylaws, which will govern how the corporation is run on a day to day basis.

The equity owners of a corporation are called shareholders. Shareholders, in their capacity as shareholders, have only very limited voting rights. They can elect the managers of the corporation (called directors), and they are entitled to vote on most decisions which would require an amendment to the articles of incorporation and on certain fundamental transactions involving a change in control such as mergers or mandatory share exchanges.

For the most part, in the traditional corporation, day-to-day management decisions are vested with a board of directors. However, because this level of complexity and formality is not particularly desirable or necessary in many small corporations, many state statutes allow smaller corporations to elect to have shareholders retain management authority by including a provision to that effect in the corporation's articles of incorporation. In the case of a small corporation with such an election, the shareholders would have direct management authority. Note that not all state statutes would permit or recognize such an election, and even in states where this is an option, very few corporations actually choose this route.

The right to share in the corporation's net profits depends on the amount of stock held by each shareholder. Every holder of the same class of stock is entitled to a pro rata proportion of any distribution, although different classes of stock can have different priorities and claims to distributions. For the most part, the actual distributions (typically in the form of dividends) depends on the board of directors, who generally have very broad discretion in declaring dividends. Shareholders are not liable for losses of the corporation, and therefore are not entitled to report any loss on their personal taxes as a result of losses at the corporate level, unless a valid "S" election is in effect for the company.

Absent agreement to the contrary, a shareholder may sell his or her shares at any time to any other legal person. While a shareholder who has control over the corporation cannot knowingly sell the control shares to someone who intends to come in and "loot" the corporation, there are very few limits on a shareholder's rights and ability to transfer shares.

The primary advantage to a corporation, aside from the fact the it is likely to be the entity with which practitioners and many business people have the greatest degree of familiarity and for which there are probably the greatest number of planning aids such a form books and treatises, is that all shareholders have limited liability for corporate debts. In other words, a shareholder stands to lose his or her investment in the corporation if the corporation acquires debts greater than its assets, but absent highly unusual circumstances, will not be compelled to pay additional sums to make good on those debts. Obviously, if the shareholder has signed a personal guarantee the shareholder will have personal liability, and equally obviously, if the shareholder has no significant personal assets, the risk that those assets might be subject to entity-level debt is no particularly significant. However, for many business owners, protection against personal liability for entity level debt is a significant advantage.

On the down-side, most corporations are subject to double taxation. In other words, in these enterprises, all corporate income is subject to a corporate income tax, paid by the corporation. Distributions to the shareholders can only be made out of amounts which are left over after this corporation income tax has been paid. That is the first level of tax. The second level of tax is assessed against the shareholders when they receive dividends from the corporation. These payments are income to the shareholders, and the shareholders must each pay individual income tax on such amounts. This is the "double taxation" of corporations about which you have already heard in these materials, and perhaps elsewhere.

Corporations with a limited number of shareholders, and having only one kind of stock, can sometimes elect to be taxed more-or-less like a partnership. These are known as "S" corporations, and as mentioned earlier, they are generally taxed like partnerships, although there are some significant differences between true partnership taxation and taxation of S Corporations.

Note

As mentioned earlier, some state statutes specifically allow smaller corporations (often referred to as "close corporations" or "closely held corporations") to elect to operate with greater informality, and perhaps without a board of directors. However, very few corporations actually elect to be subject to these special rules. Why is there such a reluctance to elect to be a close corporation in order to dispense with a board of directors, which may be operationally desirable for many smaller business? In some cases, the failure may be caused by ignorance , but there are also valid considerations which might support a decision to stick to the traditional management structure. For example, the business might feel pressure by lenders and other creditors to follow normal procedures, which would generally require that corporate decisions be verified by certified copies of directors' resolutions. Alternatively, some shareholders are likely to be concerned over the extent to which acting without aboard of directors magnifies the shareholders' risk of personal liability.

C. What Does This Book Have to Do with These Kinds of Firms?

This book seeks to integrate agency law into the business context. It involves a consideration of the non-corporate forms of business, including all of the partnership forms introduced in the preceding section, as well as the LLC. It integrates agency issues into the discussion, because it is impossible to understand how businesses really operate without understanding the foundations of agency law.

For example, take the case of the sole proprietorship. It is true that the sole proprietor might have the sole responsibility for managing and carrying on the day-to-day affairs of the business. A hot-dog vendor, for example, need not have any employees or agents, and might do all negotiation and contracting, as well as all selling, in her personal capacity. However, with the single exception of the sole proprietor with no employees or other persons who have been given responsibility or authority to act for the business, every other type of business acts through agents, at least some of the time. In fact, most businesses will act through agents *all of the time*.

A partnership, for example, is by definition an "association" of persons. It is those persons (the partners), or their designated agents or representatives, who must act on behalf of the association. "The partnership" cannot negotiate. It cannot sign a contract. Only partners, or other agents who have been given the authority to act on behalf of the partnership, can actually do these things.

Even LLC's and corporations, traditionally regarded as independent legal entities or persons under the law, cannot actually act, except through agents. A corporation will never shake your hand, but its agents (whether they be officers, employees or other agents) can certainly do so.

It is therefore obvious that the rules governing agency relationships are absolutely critical to an understanding of how firms act, since for the most part they act through agents and except for sole proprietorships, only through agents. The legal issues which this fact creates are numerous and complex.

How does one create an agency relationship? What is the extent of an agent's power to bind the firm (the principal in the agency relationship)? What are the consequences to the third person of dealing with an agent rather than the principal? What if the agent acts without authority? How do you terminate an agency relationship once it has been created?

For certain types of firms, there are special rules which supplement the common law of agency. For example, in the UPA, which governs partnerships, partners are made agents of the partnership for certain purposes. This relationship exists as a matter of law, and has certain consequences which might be different from the result under the traditional common law of agency. In many cases, however, the common law of agency will govern, and in any event provides an important backdrop for understanding the rights and liabilities of the various participants in firms.

This book does not cover in any detail the special rules applicable to corporations and corporate agents, such as directors and officers. However, many of the principles which are covered in this book, do apply to corporate agents. For the most part, this book focuses on agency relationships in other types of firms, and in particular on partnerships (including the traditional general and limited partnerships as well as the more recently authorized limited liability partnerships and limited liability limited partnerships), and limited liability companies.

The book discusses the rights and liabilities of the firm in both contractual dealing by agents and in the context of tortious conduct by agents. It also examines the rights and liabilities of the agents in such settings, and the liability of the owners of the firm as well. Obviously, in order to understand the liabilities of the agent and the firm, the rights of third parties will also have to be considered.

In addition to this focus on rights and liabilities, the book will also provide a more detailed analysis of firm organization than that which is given in this overview. Organization of the firm, ownership of property, transfer of ownership and dissolution of the firms will all be considered. We start, however, with a consideration of the notion of the firm and its agents. What does it take to establish an agency relationship? Are there different types of agency, and if there are, what are the consequences of having one type of relationship rather than another?

D. The Firm and Its Agents and Servants

Problem 1.1

While swimming behind a boat in Peaceful Valley Lake in Missouri, Bunting died of acute carbon monoxide poisoning. The boat's motor was manufactured by Mercury Marine, Inc. Under Missouri law, Mercury Marine may be sued either in the county in which the accident happened, or in any other county in which it "keeps an office or agent for the transaction of [its] usual and customary business." Mercury Marine has no office in St. Louis, but its boat motors are sold in that city by Dealer. Mercury Marine appointed Dealer as its "authorized dealer for the retail sale, display, and servicing" of its products. Under the agreement between them:

(a) Mercury Marine sells its products to Dealer for resale. Dealer is free to sell products made by other manufacturers.

(b) Dealer gives Mercury Marine's warranty to all buyers of Mercury Marine products.

(c) Dealer performs warranty service on Mercury Marine products. Mercury Marine honors warranty claims "made by purchaser through Dealer" and reimburses Dealer for warranty service it performs "on behalf of Mercury Marine."

Is Dealer Mercury Marine's agent for purposes of determining venue? *See State* ex rel. *Bunting v. Koehr,* 865 S.W.2d 351 (Mo. 1993) (*en banc*).

Green v. H & R Block, Inc.
355 Md. 488, 735 A.2d 1039 (1999)

CHASANOW, J.*

This case involves the tax preparation and refund services provided by H&R Block to thousands of Maryland residents. The primary issue for our consideration relates to whether H&R Block may have a duty to disclose to customers the

---

* Chasanow, J., now retired, participated in the hearing and conference of this case while an active member of this Court. After being recalled pursuant to the Constitution of Maryland, Article IV, § 3A, he participated in the decision and adoption of this opinion.

benefits it receives from lending institutions to which it refers customers who are seeking a bank loan in the amount of their anticipated tax refund. The trial court granted H&R Block's motion to dismiss, finding, *inter alia,* that H&R Block had no duty to disclose the benefits because no fiduciary obligation exists between H&R Block and its customers. For the reasons set forth below, we reverse, finding that sufficient facts have been alleged to warrant a factual determination regarding the existence of a principal-agent relationship that gives rise to a fiduciary duty to disclose any conflict of interest.

I. Factual Background
A.

This class action lawsuit was filed in the Circuit Court for Baltimore City on behalf of all those in Maryland for whom H&R Block prepared taxes and who participated in its "Rapid Refund" program by obtaining a "Rapid Anticipation Loan" (RAL) any time from January 1992 to present. The named plaintiff, Joyce A. Green, the appellant in this appeal, used H&R Block's tax preparation and filing services in 1993, 1994, and 1995. Because we are reviewing the trial court's dismissal of Green's complaint, we will assume the truth of the facts alleged in the complaint. *See* Part II, *infra.*

H&R Block's tax filing services allow customers to obtain faster tax refunds than would otherwise occur by simply mailing the return to the Internal Revenue Service (IRS). H&R Block offers two such services. A customer can pay $25 for H&R Block to file the return electronically, enabling the customer to obtain the refund in two weeks. For customers who want to obtain an even faster refund, H&R Block arranges bank loans in the amount of the customer's refund through its RAL program. H&R Block's RAL program lies at the center of this dispute, and so we describe it in detail.

Through its RAL program, H&R Block facilitates loans between its customers and a third-party bank that are secured by the taxpayer's anticipated refund. In Maryland, H&R Block arranges the loans through Beneficial National Bank (BNB). H&R Block informs the taxpayer of his or her eligibility for the loan after preparing a customer's return and learning that the taxpayer is entitled to a refund payment from the IRS. Interested customers then fill out a loan application. A paragraph on the reverse side of the loan application explains:

> Upon approval of your rapid Refund Anticipation Loan by Beneficial National Bank an account is opened in your name at Beneficial National Bank. This account is established to receive the Direct Deposit of your Federal Tax Refund from the IRS. When you endorse the Refund Anticipation Loan check you have authorized Beneficial National Bank to withdraw the amount deposited into this account by the IRS and apply this amount to your Refund Anticipation Loan balance. If your IRS refund is greater than your RAL, a check in such excess amount will be sent to you shortly after the bank receives your refund.

H&R Block transmits the loan application to the bank for the customer. H&R Block then files the refund electronically with the IRS, and the IRS is informed to send the customer's tax refund check directly to the bank. The customer picks up the loan check at H&R Block's offices within a day or two after filing. The service allows customers to obtain the amount of their refund in a loan within a few days rather than waiting approximately two weeks for the IRS to send the actual refunds that are electronically filed.

The cost of an RAL is described in the loan materials as a "finance charge" of BNB. For the tax years 1993-95, when Green used the RAL program, the finance charges ranged from $29 to $89. The finance charge is deducted directly from the taxpayer's refund by the bank. The annual percentage rate of interest that corresponds to the finance charge ranged from approximately 25% to 500%, depending on the amount of the refund and the amount of the finance charge to the particular customer.[1]

The loan application, entitled "A Refund Anticipation Loan Program Offered by Beneficial National Bank in Association with H&R Block," authorizes H&R Block to disclose to the bank the customer's federal income tax return "for the purpose of enabling BNB to determine whether or not to make a Refund Anticipation Loan ("RAL") to me in response to my application for such loan which is a part of this form." As a result of H&R Block's and the bank's screening of potential RAL customers, customers who for one reason or another may not receive their IRS refund are deemed ineligible for the RAL program. Because of this screening process, and because the IRS deposits the tax refunds directly into the customers' account at the lending bank which may then withdraw the proceeds to pay the loan, lenders take on few risks by lending money to the taxpayer.

The 1993 application requires the H&R Block customer to sign an "acknowledgment," stating:

> By signing below, I acknowledge that the FINANCE CHARGE for my RAL is $_____ and I further acknowledge that I have read and understand the important disclosures above and on the reverse side of this Loan Application form....

For each RAL that it arranges between the taxpayer and the bank, H&R Block benefits financially in at least one, and up to as many as three ways. First, for every RAL referred to a lending bank, H&R Block receives a "license fee" that is not disclosed to the H&R Block taxpayer/customer. The "license fee" is a payment by the lending bank to H&R Block for each loan customer referred to it by H&R Block. The fee has ranged from $3 to $9 per loan. Second, through its subsidiary, H&R Block Financial, H&R Block purchases about one-half of the RALs from the lender banks. This fact is also not disclosed to the H&R Block customer. Finally, H&R Block has arranged with Sears, Roebuck & Company (Sears) for H&R Block to receive 15% of the check-cashing fee that Sears charges for cashing BNB loan checks. Many H&R Block offices are located at Sears, and H&R Block encourages RAL customers to cash their RAL checks there. This arrangement with Sears is also not disclosed to H&R Block customers. Thus, for each RAL it procures, the lending banks effectively return a portion of the finance charge back to H&R Block, and H&R Block may addi-

---

1. The record shows that Joyce A. Green, the class representative, paid a $29 finance charge for the RAL service in 1993. For her 1994 and 1995 filings, however, the spaces in Green's loan applications where the amount of the finance charge is to be inserted were left blank. The reverse sides of the 1994 and 1995 loan application forms include disclosures for sample finance charges of $29, $34, and $89.

tionally benefit as a result of profits earned from its purchase of RALs through its subsidiary or from the RAL customer's cashing of the check at a Sears store.

B.

Green's claims turn on H&R Block's failure to disclose the various ways it may benefit from the RAL program. She labels these various benefits illegal "kickbacks" and asserts that they are in violation of the fiduciary obligations H&R Block owes to its customers as a result of an agency relationship. The complaint generally alleges that H&R Block's fiduciary obligations arise out of the contract by which H&R Block prepares and files the tax returns, H&R Block's role with respect to the loan application, H&R Block's advertising campaigns, and H&R Block's procedures for encouraging customers to use its RAL service.

According to the amended complaint, for consumers who contract with H&R Block for tax preparation and filing, H&R Block undertakes a fiduciary duty in the form of an agency relationship "to both explain and/or prepare...the various options, elections, forms and documents involved in an individual's tax preparation matters, including those involved with the taxpayer obtaining back any tax refund he or she was owed by the government." This duty pertains to all matters within the scope of the taxpayer/tax preparer relationship, including assuring that the amount of refund a customer receives is the maximum amount or the additional taxes required to be paid is the minimal amount. As evidence of the agency relationship, Green points out that H&R Block agrees to accompany the taxpayer to any IRS audit should one be required.[2] Further, H&R Block's tax preparers offer general tax advice for retirement and for the sale of residences. Regarding the RAL program, Green alleges that H&R Block acts as the customer's agent in preparing and explaining the loan application and forwarding the application to the lender bank.

As further support for her claim that a fiduciary relationship exists between H&R Block and its customers, Green emphasizes the context in which H&R Block offers and provides its services, particularly its promotional activities. H&R Block's advertising campaigns create "the impression that [H&R] Block and its tax preparation offices and personnel are trustworthy," Green alleges. These advertisements tell consumers to "[d]o what millions of Americans do. Trust H&R Block." H&R Block also advertises its ability to obtain tax refunds quickly. Green quotes H&R Block advertisements stating, "WHY WAIT? IT'S YOUR MONEY!" Signs placed at storefronts in Maryland declare: "RAPID REFUND. REFUND IN 2 DAYS," and "GET YOUR REFUND FAST!" Once these advertisements provoke interest in a consumer who wants a fast refund, H&R Block's goal is to get the consumer to participate in the loan program. The complaint asserts that

> [H&R Block e]mployees are instructed that, regardless of the reason for the customer's visit, if a return meets RAL Lender's loan requirements, offer the RAL first (*i.e.*, before other means of more quickly obtaining a refund back, including [H&R] Block's electronic filing service and direct deposit), and if the client says yes to that, go no further.

---

2. The documentation H&R Block gives to its customers states: "If your income tax return is audited, H&R Block will appear with you at that audit and explain how your refund was prepared, even though we cannot act as your legal representative."

Finally, Green alleges that the RALs are marketed as one of H&R Block's Rapid Refund products even though they are really loans secured by the recipient's anticipated tax refund.

Green concludes that these various advertisements and interactions create an agency relationship between H&R Block and its customers who participate in the RAL program. As discussed below, an agency relationship may carry with it a duty on the part of the agent to disclose information to the principal; it is this duty to disclose which Green asserts that H&R Block has breached. The alleged breaches include, *inter alia*, H&R Block's failure "to disclose the fact that [H&R] Block was receiving money, in the form of kickback payments, from the lenders for the refund anticipation loans entered into by Plaintiff and the Class and/or from Sears in connection with the cashing of the RAL checks"; its failure "to disclose the true nature of the [H&R] Block Defendants' relationship with the lenders as broker or agent for the lenders"; its representation "that obtaining a refund anticipation loan was the only or best means of receiving an expedited tax refund"; its failure to inform consumers that an expedited return would be available through electronic filing alone, and that an RAL is not in the consumer's best interest.

The amended complaint contained five claims, all of which were dismissed by the trial court on H&R Block's motion to dismiss. We are concerned with Green's appeal of the trial court's dismissal of three of those claims. Those three claims include: (1) breach of fiduciary duty based on an alleged agency relationship between Green and H&R Block; (2) violation of the Maryland Consumer Protection Act; and (3) fraudulent concealment. We granted the writ of certiorari on our own motion prior to consideration of the matter by the Court of Special Appeals.

II. Standard of Review

The trial court dismissed Green's complaint for failure to state a claim upon which relief may be granted. The granting of a motion to dismiss "is proper only if the facts alleged fail to state a cause of action." The granting of a motion of dismiss therefore depends solely on the adequacy of the plaintiff's complaint. The trial court's memorandum opinion, however, contains various references to materials outside of Green's complaint. For example, the trial court referred to exhibits filed with the court by H&R Block. Because the trial court referred to matters outside of the pleadings, the motion should have been treated as a motion for summary judgment.

*   *   *

When the court considers matters outside the pleading in ruling on a motion to dismiss and the motion, therefore, should be considered as one for summary judgment, there is a risk that the non-moving party will not be given a reasonable opportunity to present material that may be pertinent to the court's decision.... * * * [W]e shall treat the trial court's action as the grant of a motion for summary judgment.[3]

---

3. The trial court's ruling, however, took place prior to discovery. Thus, the trial court's granting of H&R Block's motion to dismiss deprived Green of the opportunity to produce additional information that may be relevant to her claims. However, given our ultimate conclusion, the prejudicial effect of entertaining an appeal of an order granting a motion to dismiss as one granting summary judgment is minimized. On remand, Green will have the opportunity to obtain discovery for further facts to support her claim.

* * * In determining whether summary judgment was properly granted in favor of H&R Block, we examine whether the trial court was legally correct, taking the facts in the light most favorable to the losing party. Our review is *de novo* since we have "the same information from the record and decide[] the same issues of law as the trial court." *[Heat & Power v. Air Products*, 320 Md. 584, 591-92, 578 A.2d 1202, 1206 (1990)]. Where multiple inferences may be drawn from the facts, they must be resolved in favor of the nonmoving party.

III. Principal-Agent Relationship
A.

The predominate issue in this appeal involves whether an agency relationship exists between H&R Block and its taxpayer customers, in particular those customers who choose to participate in H&R Block's RAL program. According to the Restatement (Second) of Agency, "Agency is the fiduciary relation which results from the manifestation of consent by one person to another that the other shall act on his behalf and subject to his control, and consent by the other so to act." Restatement (Second) of Agency § 1 (1958). The creation of an agency relationship ultimately turns on the parties' intentions as manifested by their agreements or actions.

While the agent and principal must both consent to the relationship, an agency relationship can be created by express agreement or by inference from the acts of the agent and principal. "The relation of principal and agent does not necessarily depend upon an express appointment and acceptance thereof, but it may be implied from the words and conduct of the parties and the circumstances." *Medical Mut. Liab. v. Mutual Fire*, 37 Md. App. 706, 712, 379 A.2d 739, 742-43 (1977).

In recent cases, courts applying Maryland agency law have considered three characteristics as having particular relevance to the determination of the existence of a principal-agent relationship: (1) the agent's power to alter the legal relations of the principal; (2) the agent's duty to act primarily for the benefit of the principal; and (3) the principal's right to control the agent. These factors derive from the Restatement (Second) of Agency §§ 12-14 (1958). *See* Restatement (Second) of Agency § 12 (1958) ("An agent or apparent agent holds a power to alter the legal relations between the principal and third persons and between the principal and himself."); Restatement (Second) of Agency § 13 (1958) ("An agent is a fiduciary with respect to matters within the scope of his agency."); Restatement (Second) of Agency § 14 (1958) ("A principal has the right to control the conduct of the agent with respect to matters entrusted to him.").

When a party asserts a claim that is dependent upon an agency relationship created by inference, that party has the burden of proving the existence of the principal-agent relationship, including its nature and its extent. In order to defeat a motion for summary judgment, the party's burden is to produce legally sufficient evidence of a principal-agent relationship.

When legally sufficient evidence is produced of an agency relationship, the question of the existence of the agency relationship is a factual matter and must be submitted to the jury. * * *

If the party alleging the existence of a principal-agent relationship fails to produce sufficient evidence to allow a reasonable fact finder to conclude that such a relationship exists, then summary judgment would be proper on the agency issue. Finally, where only one inference may be drawn from the evidence, it is proper for the court to find the existence of an agency relationship as a matter of law.

B.

The trial court determined that no agency relationship had been created between H&R Block and its customers as a matter of law. Citing *Schear [v. Motel Management Corp.*, 61 Md. App. 670, 487 A.2d 1240 (1985)], the trial court's written order stated that "three essential elements must be satisfied" in order to determine the existence of an agency relationship, including (1) the principal's right of control over the agent, (2) the agent's duty to act primarily for the benefit of the principal, and (3) the agent's power to alter the legal relations of the principal. Applying this three-part test and relying largely on decisions of trial courts in other states, the trial court held that Green failed to demonstrate the first and third elements. That holding provided the primary basis for the trial court's dismissal of each of the claims appealed to this Court.

We disagree, at least in part, with the trial court's agency analysis. Initially, as noted above, the primary determination of whether a principal-agent relationship exists involves ascertaining the parties' intent, as evidenced by their agreements and actions:

> There are two fundamental elements for the creation of the agency relationship: (1) some manifestation or indication by the principal to the agent that he consents to the agent's acting for his benefit; and (2) consent by the agent to act for the principal. In sum, the agency relationship can arise only when there is mutual consent between the two parties that it should arise. However, consent may be inferred from words or conduct, including acquiescence. Whereas, however, some manifestation of the principal's consent must actually come to the attention of the agent, the agent need not necessarily communicate his consent to the principal if, under the circumstances, embarking on the purpose of the agency is, itself, a sufficient indication of consent. (Footnotes omitted).

W. Edward Sell, Sell on Agency § 7, at 7-8 (1975).

The three factors adopted in *Schear* and used by the trial court in this case provide guidance to determining whether an agency relationship exists. The trial court, however, overstated the significance of the three factors when it labeled them "essential elements" of an agency relationship. The factors are proper considerations for determining agency, but rather than being determinative, the three factors should be viewed within the context of the entire circumstances of the transaction or relations. They are neither exclusive nor conclusive considerations in determining the existence of an agency relationship.

Nevertheless, contrary to the trial court's conclusions, as discussed next, we conclude that the evidence alleged concerning the "control" and "legal relations" factors supports a finding of agency. After considering those two factors, we examine some of the additional circumstances that would support a factual finding in favor of the existence of an agency relationship in this case.

1.

The trial court concluded that Green's allegations regarding H&R Block's efforts in "preparing their returns, checking the accuracy of their tax returns, electronically filing their tax returns and if necessary, accompany[ing] them to IRS audits" were insufficient to demonstrate that Green had the right to control H&R Block's conduct. The quoted text indicates that the trial court's emphasis was on H&R Block's activities as a tax preparer and tax filer, rather than its activities in procuring a loan for its customers secured by the anticipated tax refund. Although related to H&R Block's tax activities, the more pertinent question involves whether H&R Block was acting as Green's agent with respect to the RAL transaction. Indeed, at oral argument H&R Block conceded that it acts as an agent for its customers for the purposes of preparing the tax return and filing it with the IRS. The question we must address, however, is whether sufficient facts are alleged to support a reasonable inference that either H&R Block was Green's agent with respect to the RAL transaction, or that the scope of H&R Block's status as its customer's agent for preparing and filing the tax return is broad enough to encompass its role in the RAL process.

Green contends that the loan agreement provides the control element for a finding of an agency relationship between H&R Block and its customers with respect to the RAL. The loan application authorizes H&R Block to disclose to the bank the customer's federal income tax return "for the purpose of enabling BNB to determine whether or not to make a Refund Anticipation Loan ("RAL") to me in response to my application for such loan which is a part of this form." The authorization goes on to limit H&R Block's use of the information: "H&R Block may not use or disclose such tax return information or such other information for any purpose... other than as stated herein." H&R Block apparently concedes that the authorization clause may create an agency relationship between H&R Block and its customers for transmitting the RAL application but argues that "once [H&R] Block successfully transmitted the required information to the RAL lender, any agency relationship—and any corresponding liability for breach of fiduciary duty—was terminated."

H&R Block misconstrues the level of control necessary for establishing a principal-agent relationship. The control a principal must exercise over an agent in order to evidence an agency relationship is not so comprehensive. A principal need not exercise physical control over the actions of its agent in order for an agency relationship to exist; rather, the agent must be subject to the principal's control over the result or ultimate objectives of the agency relationship.

Often an agent is left free from direct supervisory control as he or she furthers the interest of the principal. As explained by Restatement (Second) of Agency § 14 cmt. a (1958), "The control of the principal does not... include control at every moment; its exercise may be very attenuated and... may be ineffective." Indeed, there are circumstances under which very little control is exercised by the principal.

If it is otherwise clear that there is an agency relation... the principal, although he has contracted with the agent not to exercise control and to permit the agent the free exercise of his discretion, nevertheless has the power to give lawful directions which the agent is under a duty to obey if he continues to act as such.

Restatement (Second) of Agency § 14 cmt. b (1958).

The level of control a principal must exercise over the agent becomes more clear when it is contrasted with the control exercised by the master in a master-servant relationship. In *Globe Indemnity Co. [v. Victill Corp.*, 208 Md. 573, 119 A.2d 423 (1956)], a hotel employee sought to hold vicariously liable the employer of a business guest who had assaulted him. We discussed the difference between the control a master has over a servant and the control a principal has over an agent:

> It is important to distinguish between a servant and an agent who is not a servant, because ordinarily a principal is not liable for the incidental acts of negligence in the performance of duties committed by an agent who is not a servant. An agent is a person who represents another in contractual negotiations or transactions akin thereto. *A servant is a person who is employed to perform personal services for another in his affairs, and who, in respect to his physical movements in the performance of the service, is subject to the other's control or right of control. Persons who render service but retain control over the manner of doing it are not servants.*
>
> We reaffirm the rule that a principal is not liable for any physical injury caused by the negligent conduct of his agent, who is not a servant, during the performance of the principal's business, unless the act was done in the manner authorized or directed by the principal, or the result was one authorized or intended by the principal. *A principal employing an agent to accomplish a result, but not having the right to control the details of his movements*, is not responsible for incidental negligence while such agent is conducting the authorized transaction. 1 *Restatement, Agency*, sec. 250. (Emphasis added).

Globe Indemnity Co., 208 Md. at 581-82, 119 A.2d at 427. As the emphasized text demonstrates, a principal who is not an employer need not "control the details" nor the "physical movements" of the agent.

More recently, in *Chevron, U.S.A., Inc. v. Lesch*, 319 Md. 25, 570 A.2d 840 (1990), we again discussed the control necessary to establish a master-servant relationship in the context of determining an alleged principal's liability to a third party for the purported agent's tort. The plaintiff, Lesch, alleged that Chevron, a national gasoline distributor, should be liable as a master for the actions of its alleged servant, a local service station. We explained:

> *One may be an agent of another, owing to his principal the fiduciary obligations of loyalty and general obedience, but at the same time not be sufficiently under the control of the principal to be considered a servant.* The relationship of master and servant exists only when the employer has the right to control and direct the servant in the performance of his work and in the manner in which the work is to be done.

>   *   *   *

> 'The decisive test in determining whether the relation of master and servant exists is whether the employer has the *right to control and direct the servant in the performance of his work and in the manner in*

which the work is to be done.' (Citations omitted) (emphasis added and supplied).

Chevron, U.S.A., Inc., 319 Md. at 32-33, 570 A.2d at 844 (quoting *Keitz v. National Paving Co.*, 214 Md. 479, 491, 134 A.2d 296, 301 (1957)).

These cases make clear that the level of control a principal exercises over an agent is less than the level of control a master has over a servant. Indeed, the level of control a master exercises over a servant is a key factor distinguishing the master-servant subset of the set of principal-agent relationships. In other words, all masters are principals and all servants are agents, but only when the level of control is sufficiently high does a principal become a master and an agent a servant. *See* Restatement (Second) of Agency § 2 cmt. a (1958) ("A master is a species of principal, and a servant is a species of agent."). Thus, principals who are not masters exercise a much lesser degree of control over their agents than masters do over their servants.

In sum, the control a principal exercises over its agent is not defined rigidly to mean control over the minutia of the agent's actions, such as the agent's physical conduct, as is required for a master-servant relationship. The level of control may be very attenuated with respect to the details. However, the principal must have ultimate responsibility to control the end result of his or her agent's actions; such control may be exercised by prescribing the agents' obligations or duties before or after the agent acts, or both.

Applying this analysis to the instant case, we conclude that it would be reasonable to infer that H&R Block's customers retain control over H&R Block's ultimate actions and representations with respect to filing the tax return and applying for the RAL. Viewed most favorably to Green, H&R Block's relationship with its customers is analogous to other principal-agent relationships, such as between an attorney and his or her client. An attorney who, for example, serves as his or her client's representative in negotiations to settle a lawsuit is generally not subject to the client's control over the best strategy to use in order to arrive at a good settlement, but the client controls the final decision as to whether to settle or not. The client/principal may have little knowledge of the law or negotiating strategies and so trusts the attorney/agent to further his or her interests in the settlement negotiations.

Similar to the client who is represented by an attorney in settlement negotiations, the H&R Block customer may be unknowledgeable in tax and financial matters, trusting H&R Block to further his or her interests. Like the attorney representing a client in settlement negotiations, H&R Block undertakes to file customer tax returns with the IRS and the loan application with the bank, but only at the direction of the customer, who ultimately controls whether H&R Block takes either action with respect to the third party. It is not dispositive, as the trial court implied, that H&R Block's customers do not generally exercise control over the manner in which H&R Block prepares the tax filings. Indeed, H&R Block conceded at oral argument that it serves as its customers' agent for the purpose of filing the tax return and transmitting the loan application to the lender. Thus, H&R Block's customers retain enough control over H&R Block to support a finding of an agency relationship. Our conclusion is in accord with the only other appellate opinion, of which we are aware, that has addressed the identical issue. *See Basile v. H&R Block, Inc.*, 729 A.2d 574 (Pa. Super. Ct. 1999) (holding in a similar lawsuit that H&R Block's customers exercise enough control to evidence an agency relationship).

2.

We also disagree with the trial court's analysis regarding H&R Block's ability to alter the legal relations of its customers. The trial court concluded that the complaint "fails to allege that Defendants had been granted or accepted or had the power to alter the legal relations of Plaintiff." Because H&R Block's customers actually sign the loan application, and not H&R Block, the trial court concluded that Green "fail[ed] to demonstrate that [H&R Block] had the authority to represent Plaintiff in her transactions with RAL lenders...."

When the facts otherwise demonstrate an agency relationship, that relationship cannot be negated simply because the principal's and not the agent's signature appears on a document otherwise prepared and negotiated by the agent. Such a result would create a legal fiction contrary to the substantive reality. For example, as noted above, an attorney may represent a client in a settlement negotiation as an agent of the client; if the client ultimately signs the settlement papers, that fact does not alter the attorney's status as an agent of his or her client. Similarly, a principal may hire a consultant to negotiate a business transaction; the principal's signing of the contract would not necessarily negate what is otherwise a principal-agent relationship.

In the instant case, Green alleges that a contract existed under which H&R Block would prepare and transmit her RAL application to the bank, obtain the bank's acceptance of the application, and then receive and deliver to her the proceeds of the loan. A reasonable inference is that, although it is the H&R Block customer's signature on the loan application, it is H&R Block's role in implicitly endorsing the contents of the application that lowers the perceived risk to the bank of providing the loan. Moreover, the RAL application expressly authorizes H&R Block to share the customer's tax return and related information, which H&R Block itself prepared admittedly as its customer's agent. Finally, the bank delivers the loan check to H&R Block, which holds it and turns it over to its customer. It is therefore reasonable to infer that H&R Block played an integral part in the customer's receipt of the bank loan, which indisputedly has legal ramifications for the H&R Block customer and the bank. Furthermore, as Green contends, discovery may disclose other means by which H&R Block affected its customers' legal relations with third-party lenders.

3.

Other circumstances alleged by Green provide further support for a jury to conclude that Green consented to H&R Block acting on her behalf and that H&R Block consented to act for Green, thus establishing the intent necessary to create an agency relationship. Through its national and local efforts advertising its tax preparation and refund services, H&R Block strives to convince potential customers that it can be "trusted" to obtain both the highest and fastest possible refunds for its customers. Its advertisements call on consumers to "Do what millions of Americans do. Trust H&R Block." H&R Block declares that it "watch[es] over" its customers and that "you can trust H&R Block." H&R Block promotes itself as having the expertise to achieve the maximum allowable tax return, with the customer secure in the knowledge that, if necessary, an experienced tax preparer "will appear with you at [an] audit and explain how your refund was prepared...." Finally, H&R Block's advertisements promoting its ability to secure a "Rapid Refund" constitute an integral part of its promotional efforts. *See Basile*, 729 A.2d at 581 (discussing H&R Block's media efforts and concluding that an agency relationship had been formed).

Customers who enter the doors of the local H&R Block office therefore may reasonably believe that H&R Block is acting on their behalf—to obtain the highest and fastest return possible—in the preparation and filing of the tax returns with the IRS and, in the case of the RAL, in acting as the intermediary to the transactions with the lending bank. The internal procedures H&R Block has established for its employees tell them to encourage those qualifying for RALs to pursue them. H&R Block's general advertising seeks to gain customer trust in not only filing tax returns, but also in obtaining a "Rapid Refund," and its RAL program is an integral part of its Rapid Refund program. Thus, both before they enter H&R Block's offices and while they are there, H&R Block customers are encouraged to trust H&R Block to help them get a maximum return more quickly than conventional filing methods.

Particularly in the context of its promotional efforts, it would be reasonable to conclude that H&R Block, as an agent, is seeking—and gaining—the consent of its customers to act on their behalf with respect to the transactions with the lending bank as well as the IRS. While H&R Block disputes that it has consented to act as its customers' agent in securing the loan, an "agent need not necessarily communicate his consent to the principal if, under the circumstances, embarking on the purpose of the agency is, itself, a sufficient indication of consent." W. Edward Sell, Sell on Agency § 7, at 8 (1975). H&R Block intended to create the circumstances under which customers would trust it to obtain the maximum refund fast, and it embarked on efforts to secure a loan in order to gain the refund quickly. In light of H&R Block's conduct, its customers may reasonably believe that H&R Block is acting as their agent.

Viewing the facts most favorably to Green, H&R Block's role is similar to that of an insurance broker who acts as the agent for its customers seeking insurance. In *[American Casualty Co. v.] Ricas*, we addressed whether an insurance broker who placed policies with a number of insurers and who was not employed by any single insurer was an agent of the insurer. We concluded that, if anything, the broker was an agent of the insured, not the insurer. We said that

> an insurance solicitor, or broker, is one who acts as a middle man between the assured and the insurer, and who solicits insurance from the public under no employment from any special company, but having secured an order, either places the insurance with a company selected by the assured, or in the absence of any selection by him, then with a company selected by the broker. *Ordinarily, the relation between the insured and the broker is that between principal and agent.* (Emphasis added).

[*American Casualty Co. v. Ricas*, 179 Md. 627, 631, 22 A.2d 484, 487 (1941).]

While in the instant case H&R Block apparently does not represent to customers that it will shop prospectively among banks for the best loan, customers may reasonably believe that H&R Block has already "shopped" to find the best loan package for its customers. It therefore would be reasonable to conclude that H&R Block customers reasonably believed that H&R Block is operating as their broker for a loan much as the broker in *Ricas*—finding for its customers the best loan package that fulfills H&R Block's twin commitments of maximizing tax refunds in terms of amount and speed.

Furthermore, as noted above, at oral argument H&R Block conceded that it operates as the customer's agent for the purposes of preparing and filing the tax returns. With respect to the RAL customer, H&R Block argued that instead of serving as the customer's agent to the bank, it serves as the bank's agent to the customer. Under H&R Block's analysis, the customer arrives at an H&R Block office for tax help, perhaps desiring a Rapid Refund. H&R Block then serves as the customer's agent for preparing the taxes. When it becomes known that the customer qualifies for an RAL, H&R Block instantaneously changes hats, becoming the agent *of the bank* and terminating its agency relationship with the customer, and then offering the customer the RAL service. H&R Block contends that these various transactions should be treated distinctly so as to avoid the conclusion that it is the agent of the customer for the loan transaction. Its role in facilitating the loan, H&R Block argues, is separate from its role as tax preparer and filer.

There are several problems with H&R Block's analysis. First, assuming that H&R Block is the bank's agent, H&R Block still may be the customer's agent, even though its dual agency status may create liability problems arising from divided loyalties, as discussed in Part IV.A, *infra*. Second, H&R Block concedes that it serves as its customers' agent to the lending bank for the limited purpose of transmitting the loan application and tax information to the bank, in light of the written form that its customers sign authorizing such transmission. Thus, even within the context of a single loan transaction, H&R Block serves two different principals without disclosing that fact. Third, it is not at all clear that H&R Block has completed its obligations as the agent of its customers prior to becoming the bank's agent. It would appear that H&R Block cannot file its customer's tax return until after the RAL has been approved by the bank, since the IRS must be told to deposit the taxpayer's refund directly into the bank account that the lending institution created for the H&R Block RAL customer in order to secure the loan. Thus, even under its own analysis, H&R Block begins acting as the bank's agent before it has completed its agency obligations for its customers.

We are unconvinced that, as a matter of law, H&R Block can so conveniently end one agency relationship and begin another simply by treating what may reasonably be construed as a package of related services as unrelated distinct transactions. H&R Block's attempt to break down its activities into individual transactions raises the very question that must be resolved by the jury—what is the scope of H&R Block's undertaking as the agent of its customers? The facts alleged allow for the reasonable inference that H&R Block and its customers, through their objective manifestations, mutually consented and intended to form a principal-agent relationship, the scope of which included obtaining the maximum amount of tax refund quickly, and that H&R Block was acting as its customers' agent in matters pertaining to the refund loan. The trial court therefore incorrectly concluded that as a matter of law there was no agency relationship between H&R Block and its customers.

*   *   *

V. Conclusion

The creation of an agency relationship ultimately turns on the parties' intentions as manifested by their agreements or actions. When legally sufficient evidence of an agency relationship is produced, the question of the existence of the agency relationship is a factual matter and must be submitted to the jury. In this case, the plaintiff has alleged sufficient facts supporting the existence of an agency relationship that would give rise to a duty of H&R Block to inform its customers of its financial stakes in the RAL program. Because the trial court dismissed all three claims for want of a duty to disclose, the case must be remanded for further consideration.

JUDGMENT OF THE CIRCUIT COURT FOR BALTIMORE CITY REVERSED, AND CASE REMANDED TO THAT COURT FOR FURTHER PROCEEDINGS CONSISTENT WITH THIS OPINION. COSTS TO BE PAID BY APPELLEE.

Notes

1. Problem 1.1 is based on *State ex rel. Bunting v. Koehr,* 865 S.W.2d 351 (Mo. 1993) *(en banc).* On the issue of whether Dealer was Mercury marine's agent because it sold Mercury Marine products, the court reasoned as follows:

> *State ex rel. Elson v. Koehr,* 856 S.W.2d 57, 60 (Mo. banc 1993), reached an important conclusion in construing the words "agent for the transaction of its usual and customary business" in the context of Section 508.040. *Koehr* holds that traditional rules of agency articulated in the Restatement of Law (Second) Agency determine the existence of agency for purposes of venue.
>
> There are three attributes of agency.[1] First, "[a]n agent...holds a power to alter legal relations between the principal and third persons and between the principal and himself." Restatement (Second) Agency, § 12. Second, "[a]n agent is a fiduciary with respect to matters within the scope of his agency." *Id.* § 13. Third, the "principal has the right to control the conduct of the agent with respect to matters entrusted to him." *Id.* § 14. The absence of any one of the three elements of agency defeats a claim that agency exists.
>
> Relator first asserts that the dealers are agents of Mercury Marine for the purpose of distributing and selling Mercury Marine products to the public. Relator claims that the agency relationship is established because Mercury Marine is in the business of manufacturing, selling and distributing its products and has entrusted the retail sale of those products to St. Louis dealers. Restatement (Second) Agency, § 14J provides:
>
> > One who receives goods from another for resale to a third person is not thereby the other's agent in the transaction: whether he is an agent for this purpose or is himself a buyer depends upon whether the parties agree that his duty is to act primarily for the benefit of one delivering the goods to him or is to act primarily for his own benefit. [Emphasis added.]
>
> "Primarily" means "principally." Webster's Third New International Dictionary, 1800 (1976). Although the agreement requires the dealer to

---

1. Cf. Restatement (Second) Agency, § 1. Agency is the fiduciary relation which results from the manifestation of consent by one person to another that the other shall act on his behalf and subject to his control, and consent by the other to so act.

conduct its business "in a manner that preserves and enhances the reputation of both Mercury Marine and Dealer for providing quality products and services," the dealer is independent of Mercury Marine, is permitted to sell products of competing companies, and purchases Mercury Marine motors primarily for the purpose of reselling them for its own profit. The dealer does not sell Mercury Marine products principally for the benefit of Mercury Marine. The relationship between the dealers and Mercury Marine for the sale of Mercury Marine products is, therefore, that of buyer and seller, not agent and principal.

Id. at 353-54

If Dealer was not acting as Mercury Marine's agent in selling its products, what was the relationship? What changes would be necessary to convert the relationship to that of principal and agent?

2. With respect to the provision of the warranty in connection with sale, the court in *State ex rel. Bunting v. Koehr* again held that there was no agency relationship:

Second, relator urges that a dealer's act of extending to and perfecting Mercury Marine's product warranty for the ultimate purchaser is a sufficient factual predicate to support the legal conclusion that the dealer is Mercury Marine's agent.

Agency does not exist unless the dealer has the "power to alter the legal relationship" between Mercury Marine and the ultimate purchaser. Restatement (Second) Agency § 12. In this case, the dealer purchases the boat motor from Mercury Marine. When the dealer purchases the motor, part of the bargain includes the manufacturer's warranty. The dealer agrees to extend that warranty to any subsequent purchaser of the motor and notify Mercury Marine of the new holder of the warranty. The manufacturer's warranty is an integral part of the product the dealer purchases for resale and the ultimate user purchases. For purposes of agency analysis, the warranty is no different than a spark plug or a piston within the motor.

The dealer's contractual obligation to inform the purchaser of the manufacturer's warranty and notify the manufacturer of the identity of the new holder of the warranty is not the same as a power to alter a legal relationship between the manufacturer and the purchaser. This is so because the manufacturer (1) sells the product to the dealer for resale; (2) unilaterally imposes the terms of the warranty prior to the sale to the dealer; (3) forbids the dealer from altering the terms of the warranty in any way; (4) requires the dealer to extend the warranty as part of the sale and notify the manufacturer of the new holder of the warranty: and (5) makes the warranty a part of the purchaser's bargain when he or she purchases the product. We hold that under these circumstances, there is no agency between the manufacturer and the dealer as there is no power in the dealer to alter the legal relationship between the manufacturer and the purchaser.

Id. at 354.

Do you agree with the *Koehr* court's conclusion? Under the court's reasoning, what role does Dealer play with respect to the warranty?

3. The court in *State ex rel. Bunting v. Koehr* also rejected the argument that dealer's obligation to provide warranty service made it Mercury Marine's agent:

> Nor do we believe that relator's final claim of agency — that a dealer's performance of warranty work on Mercury Marine products establishes agency — places in the dealer the power to alter Mercury Marine's legal relationship with third parties. Relator supports his argument with *State ex rel. Ford Motor Company v. Dierker,* 766 S.W.2d 691, 694 (Mo.App. 1989). *Dierker* holds that a Ford Motor Company dealership becomes an agent of Ford Motor Company when it performs warranty work on behalf of Ford. The court of appeals reasoned that Ford's extensive control over the dealer in the performance of the warranty work warranted a conclusion of agency. Control is one of the three attributes of agency. Restatement (Second) Agency § 14.
>
> In reaching its conclusion, the court of appeals in *Dierker* relied on the definition of agency found in *Wilson v. Sanders,* 745 S.W.2d 735, 737 (Mo.App. 1987). An agent is " 'a person authorized by another to act for him, one entrusted with another's business.' Black's Law Dictionary, p. 85 (4th ed. 1968)." *Koehr,* however, implicitly rejects the *Sanders* definition as insufficiently precise to determine the existence of an agency relationship.
>
> We assume for the sake of argument that Mercury Marine exercises substantial control over the dealers' warranty work. Nevertheless, agency does not exist unless both of the remaining elements of agency are also present.
>
> We conclude that no agency exists as a result of the dealers' performance of warranty work for Mercury Marine and the purchaser. This is because the dealers' obligation to perform warranty work is not tantamount to a power to alter Mercury Marine's legal relationship with a third party. The warranty that Mercury Marine sells with its product establishes the legal relationship between the manufacturer and the purchaser. The dealers do not alter that relationship when they undertake the repairs and/or replacements for which the warranty provides. To the extent that *Dierker* holds otherwise, it is overruled.

Id. at 354-55.

On whose behalf does Dealer do warranty work? Do you agree with the court's conclusion that Dealer's performance of warranty services does not alter Mercury Marine's legal relationship with the purchaser?

4. In *Green v. H & R. Block, Inc.,* the court contrasted the principal-agent and master-servant relationships. Only a minimal degree of control is necessary for a principal-agent relationship — the right to specify the object of the agency. A greater degree of control is necessary for a master-servant relationship — the right to control the details of the work. The nature of the relationship can be crucial in determining the consequences that grow out of the relationship. A significant focus of principal-agent questions is whether the principal is bound by contracts entered into by the agent on the principal's behalf. These questions will be considered in Chapters 2 through 5. The dominant issue in master-servant relationship is the master's liability in tort for incidental torts. A master is liable

without fault for torts committed by a servant within the scope of the servant's employment. A principal is generally not liable for the torts of a non-servant agent. These questions will be considered in Chapters 10 through 12.

Problem 1.2

ABC Corporation sold mobile homes and developed mobile home parks. ABC employed Agent, a licensed real estate broker, to acquire land for development as mobile home parks, at a weekly salary of $125. Agent told ABC that Parkacre was available for purchase. ABC asked Agent to purchase the land as a "straw man," and then to convey the land to ABC. Agent told ABC that the land would cost $30,000, and ABC gave Agent that amount.

Unknown to ABC, Agent had an interest in Parkacre. Before he had been employed by ABC, Agent had paid $1,000 for an option to buy Parkacre for $15,000. When ABC gave Agent the $30,000 he asked for, Agent exercised his option to buy Parkacre. Agent then used $14,000 of the $30,000 to complete the purchase, and kept the remaining $16,000.

ABC has now sued Agent for breach of fiduciary duty, asking that Agent be required to give ABC the entire $15,000 profit on the transaction. Agent argues that ABC's sole remedy is to rescind the transaction—return Parkacre in exchange for the $30,000 purchase price. *See Desfosses v. Notis,* 333 A.2d 83 (Me. 1975).

Note 6.

Green v. H & R Block, Inc. (Part 2)
355 Md. 488, 735 A.2d 1039 (1999)

This case involves the tax preparation and refund services provided by H&R Block to thousands of Maryland residents. The primary issue for our consideration relates to whether H&R Block may have a duty to disclose to customers the benefits it receives from lending institutions to which it refers customers who are seeking a bank loan in the amount of their anticipated tax refund. The trial court granted H&R Block's motion to dismiss, finding, *inter alia,* that H&R Block had no duty to disclose the benefits because no fiduciary obligation exists between H&R Block and its customers. For the reasons set forth below, we reverse, finding that sufficient facts have been alleged to warrant a factual determination regarding the existence of a principal-agent relationship that gives rise to a fiduciary duty to disclose any conflict of interest.

[Reread the facts printed above.]

* * *

* * * The facts alleged allow for the reasonable inference that H&R Block and its customers, through their objective manifestations, mutually consented and intended to form a principal-agent relationship, the scope of which included obtaining the maximum amount of tax refund quickly, and that H&R Block was acting as its customers' agent in matters pertaining to the refund loan. The trial court therefore incorrectly concluded that as a matter of law there was no agency relationship between H&R Block and its customers.

IV. Causes of Action

We now turn to Green's claims that were dismissed by the trial court and appealed to this Court. We accordingly address Green's claim for breach of the principal-agent relationship, the claim for violation of the Maryland Consumer Protection Act, and finally the fraudulent concealment claim.

A. Breach of the Principal-Agent Relationship

The duties an agent owes to his or her principal are well established. An agent has "a duty to his principal to act solely for the benefit of the principal in all matters connected with his agency." Restatement (Second) of Agency § 387 (1958). We have recognized the

> 'universal principle in the law of agency, that the powers of the agent are to be exercised for the benefit of the principal *only, and not of the agent or of third parties*. A power to do all acts that the principal could do, or all acts of a certain description, for and in the name of the principal, is limited to the doing of them for the use and benefit of the principal only, *as much as if it were so expressed*.' (Emphasis in original).

King v. Bankerd, 303 Md. 98, 108-09, 492 A.2d 608, 613 (1985) (quoting *Adams Express Co. v. Trego*, 35 Md. 47, 67 (1872)). Moreover, an agent is under a strict duty to avoid any conflict between his or her self-interest and that of the principal: "'It is an elementary principle that the fundamental duties of an agent are loyalty to the interest of his principal and the need to avoid any conflict between that interest and his own self-interest.'" *C-E-I-R, Inc. v. Computer Corp.*, 229 Md. 357, 366, 183 A.2d 374, 379 (1962) (quoting *Maryland Credit v. Hagerty*, 216 Md. 83, 90, 139 A.2d 230, 233 (1958)). As Professor Mechem has observed:

> It is the duty of the agent to conduct himself with the utmost loyalty and fidelity to the interests of his principal, and not to place himself or voluntarily permit himself to be placed in a position where his own interests or those of any other person whom he has undertaken to represent may conflict with the interests of his principal.

Philip Mechem, Mechem Outlines Agency § 500, at 345 (4th ed. 1952). *See also* Restatement (Second) of Agency § 389 cmt. a (1958) ("[A]n agent who is appointed to sell or to give advice concerning sales violates his duty if, without the principal's knowledge, he sells to himself....").

One of the primary obligations of an agent to his or her principal is to disclose any information the principal may reasonably want to know. The obligation to disclose is strongest when a principal has a conflicting interest in a transaction connected with the agency. *See* Restatement (Second) of Agency § 389 (1958) ("Unless otherwise agreed, an agent is subject to a duty not to deal with his principal as an adverse party in a transaction connected with his agency *without the principal's knowledge*.") (emphasis added). An agent's failure to disclose information material to the agency thus constitutes a breach of the principal-agent relationship.

Where an agent breaches a duty to the principal and profits from the breach, the principal may maintain an action to recover those profits for her or himself. *Nagel v. Todd*, 185 Md. 512, 517, 45 A.2d 326, 328 (1946) (An agent "cannot make a secret profit out of any transaction with his principal."); Restatement (Second) of Agency § 388 (1958) ("[A]n agent who makes a profit in connection with transactions conducted by him on behalf of the principal is under a duty to give such profit to the principal."). An example of such an action is found in *Gussin v. Shockey*, 725 F.Supp. 271 (D.Md. 1989), *aff'd* 933 F.2d 1001 (4th Cir. 1991). Frederic and Paul Gussin entered into an agreement with Richard Shockey who was to assist them in buying, maintaining, breeding, and selling thoroughbred horses. The Gussins had no experience in the horse business and relied on Shockey's 20 years of experience buying and selling horses. The Gussins were to pay Shockey 5% of the net proceeds on the sale of the horses. Without the Gussins' knowledge, in arranging the purchases of various horses, Shockey received commissions from the sellers by negotiating a base price above which the seller would pay him the proceeds. For example, for one horse Shockey arranged a base price of $525,000 and a total price of $650,000. He informed the Gussins that the price was $650,000, and upon the Gussins' payment, the seller issued a check of $125,000 to Shockey as a "commission"—or as the Gussins called it, a "kickback." Shockey never informed the Gussins about the "commission" arrangements he made with the various sellers.

Shockey contended that although the Gussins trusted him and relied on his advice, he was not obligated to get the best price on the horses for the Gussins. Applying Maryland agency law, the court rejected Shockey's argument, finding there was an agency relationship and that Shockey had breached it:

> If the agent is to receive any benefit from a transaction in which he is serving his principal, the agent must fully disclose any interest he has in the transaction and receive the consent of his principal to proceed, even if the principal ultimately was to benefit from the transaction. (Citation omitted).

Gussin, 725 F.Supp. at 275.

The instant case resembles *Gussin* in a number of ways. In essence, Green alleges that H&R Block advised her to take a loan that included benefits for H&R Block that H&R Block did not disclose. Green has identified three ways in which H&R Block benefits from the RALs—the "license fee" paid to H&R Block by the lending institution for each RAL, ranging from $3 to $9; H&R Block's profits from the purchase of the RALs through its subsidiary H&R Block Financial; and 15% of the check cashing charge if the loan check is cashed at Sears. Just as the Gussins paid for the horses at the price they were told by Shockey, H&R Block customers were informed that the "finance charge" was the bank's price for providing the loan. And just as Shockey breached his duty to the Gussins by failing to disclose his benefit from the transaction, so too did H&R Block breach its duty to disclose its secret benefits, assuming that Green succeeds in convincing the jury of the existence of an agency relationship.

H&R Block contends that its customers have not been harmed by the RAL program since they enter into the RAL transaction fully aware of the total "finance charge" which they must pay in order to obtain the loan based on their tax refund. The argument is similar to the one made by Shockey in *Gussin*, that since the Gussins agreed to pay the total price for the horse, the undisclosed commission received by Shockey did not result in any harm to the Gussins. Although the harm caused by H&R Block's failure to disclose may be much smaller for any individual H&R Block customer than in *Gussin*, the nature of the agent's alleged action is virtually identical in both cases, and there is no minimum value below which an agent may freely take undisclosed profits from his or her principal.

Furthermore, Green need not prove she was harmed at all in order to maintain an action based on a breach of the principal-agent relationship. The rule against dealing with a principal as an adverse party without the principal's knowledge

> is not based upon the existence of harm to the principal in the particular case. It exists to prevent a conflict of opposing interests in the minds of agents whose duty it is to act solely for the benefit of their principals. The rule applies, therefore, even though the transaction between the principal and the agent is beneficial to the principal.

Restatement (Second) of Agency § 389 cmt. c (1958).

In sum, H&R Block had several interests in the loan transaction by virtue of the license agreement, its purchase of loans from the banks, and its arrangement with Sears. These interests in the loan transaction posed a conflict between H&R Block's interests and those of its customers. Thus, assuming the existence of an agency relationship and viewing the facts in the light most favorable to Green, H&R Block was required to disclose those interests affecting its ability to act solely for the benefit of its customers.

[The Court also reversed the trial court's dismissal of Green's claims for violation of Maryland's Consumer Protection Act and for fraudulent concealment.]

V. Conclusion

The creation of an agency relationship ultimately turns on the parties' intentions as manifested by their agreements or actions. When legally sufficient evidence of an agency relationship is produced, the question of the existence of the agency relationship is a factual matter and must be submitted to the jury. In this case, the plaintiff has alleged sufficient facts supporting the existence of an agency relationship that would give rise to a duty of H&R Block to inform its customers of its financial stakes in the RAL program. Because the trial court dismissed all three claims for want of a duty to disclose, the case must be remanded for further consideration.

JUDGMENT OF THE CIRCUIT COURT FOR BALTIMORE CITY REVERSED, AND CASE REMANDED TO THAT COURT FOR FURTHER PROCEEDINGS CONSISTENT WITH THIS OPINION. COSTS TO BE PAID BY APPELLEE.

Notes

1. An agent is a fiduciary as to matters entrusted to the agent. Restatement § 13. Comment a to Restatement section 13 elaborates on what might be called *the fiduciary principle* and its implications:

> The agreement to act on behalf of the principal causes the agent to be a fiduciary, that is, *a person having a duty, created by his undertaking, to act primarily for the benefit of another* in matters connected with his undertaking. Among the agent's fiduciary duties to the principal is the duty to account for profits arising out of the employment, the duty not to act as, or on account of, an adverse party without the principal's consent, the duty not to compete with the principal on his own ac-

count or for another in matters relating to the subject matter of the agency, and the duty to deal fairly with the principal in all transactions between them.

Restatement § 13 comment a (emphasis added). As stated in Restatement section 387, an agent's duty as a fiduciary requires the agent (unless other wise agreed) "to act *solely* for the benefit of the principal in all matters connected with [the] agency." Restatement § 387 (emphasis added).

2. Under Restatement section 388, an agent has a duty to account to the principal for any profits received by the agent in connection with transactions conducted by the agent on the principal's behalf. Comment a to Restatement section 388 explains that the duty to account is grounded in the agent's duty to act solely for the benefit of the principal:

> Ordinarily, the agent's primary function is to make profits for the principal, and his duty to account includes accounting for any unexpected and incidental accretions whether or not received in violation of duty. Thus, an agent who, without the knowledge of the principal, receives something in connection with, or because of, a transaction conducted for the principal, has a duty to pay this to the principal even though otherwise he has acted with perfect fairness to the principal and violates no duty of loyalty in receiving the amount.

3. Section 403 of the Restatement provides that, where "an agent receives anything as a result of his violation of a duty of loyalty to the principal, he is subject to a liability to deliver it, its value, or its proceeds, to the principal." Restatement § 403. The traditional equitable remedy against the agent is the constructive trust. See Restatement section 403 comment d.

4. Perhaps the most famous and eloquent summary of the nature of a fiduciary's duty of loyalty is by Judge Cardozo in *Meinhard v. Salmon,* 249 N.Y. 458, 164 N.E. 545 (1928):

> Joint adventurers, like copartners, owe to one another the duty of finest loyalty while the enterprise continues. Many forms of conduct permissible in a workaday world for those acting at arm's length are forbidden to those bound by fiduciary ties. Not honesty alone but the punctilio of an honor most sensitive is the standard of behavior. There has developed a tradition about this standard that is unbending and inveterate. Uncompromising rigidity has been the attitude of courts of equity.

5. Restatement section 389 sets forth the duties of an agent dealing with the principal as an adverse party:

§ 389. Acting as Adverse Party without Principal's Consent

Unless otherwise agreed, an agent is subject to a duty not to deal with his principal as an adverse party in a transaction connected with [the agent's] agency without the principal's knowledge.

6. In *Desfosses v. Notis,* 333 A.2d 83 (Me. 1975), an agent realized a secret profit by dealing with the principal as an adverse party. The court rejected the argument that the principal's sole remedy was rescission:

> * * * The agent's fiduciary duties to his principal may be broadly phrased as duties of service and obedience, and duties of loyalty. Here,

plaintiff has satisfactorily established numerous breaches by defendant of his fiduciary duties, to wit: failure to fully disclose material facts; misrepresentations of matters within the scope of the agency; false inducements to obtain money from the principal; and misuse and wrongful retention of funds peculated by defendant from his principal. A fiduciary who commits a breach of his duty as fiduciary is guilty of tortious conduct and the beneficiary can obtain redress either at law or in equity for the harm done.

Here, plaintiff claims that he is damaged to the extent that defendant retained moneys given to him in excess of what was required to properly accomplish the agency. Defendant contends that plaintiff is at most entitled to a remedy in the form of recision [sic]; that plaintiff may receive back all of the money given to defendant if plaintiff will rescind the bargain and reconvey the land in question to defendant.

Even if we concede for the sake of argument that defendant's interest in the bond for a deed arrangement antedated the inception of the agency relation, we do not think plaintiff's remedy must be restricted on that account. Defendant urges that although he did not disclose his antecedent, independent interest in the land, plaintiff is without remedy unless he wants to rescind the sale altogether. The shortcoming of defendant's argument is that it fails to consider an additional aspect of the defendant's wrongful conduct, that defendant used plaintiff's money to complete defendant's own purchase of the property under the bond for a deed. Whatever the nature of defendant's antecedent interest in the property, his acquisition of the property was an indubitable incident of the agency. An agent who, in violation of his duty to his principal, uses for his own purposes or those of a third person assets of the principal's business is subject to liability to the principal for the value of the use. Restatement (Second) of Agency, § 404. If an agent has received a benefit as a result of violating his duty of loyalty, the principal is entitled to recover from him what he has so received, its value, or its proceeds, and also the amount of damage thereby caused. Id. § 407. Here, defendant applied his principal's assets in such a way as to obtain the land for his principal by using only a portion of the assets entrusted to him. On these facts it is unacceptable to suggest that defendant may retain his ill-gotten gains, originally entrusted to purchase the very same land. We think the above principles of the Restatement mandate a clear and decisive result. Defendant has misapplied his principal's assets, using them for his own benefit and manifestly violating his fiduciary duty of loyalty and fair dealing. He is liable to his principal for secret profits, in this case moneys wrongfully retained after the purpose of the agency was accomplished.

In simpler days, this Court has reached similar conclusions. When a principal gave an agent $80 to purchase a certain horse and instructed the agent to pay no more than the sum, and less if possible, it was held that the agent was not at liberty to make a profit for himself in the transaction. Thus, when the agent represented to his principal that the purchase had consumed the whole $80—though the agent had in fact paid only $72.50—it was further held that the sum remaining in the agent's hands was the money of his principal, which could be recovered in a proper action. *Bunker v. Miles,* 30 Me. 431, 432-33 (1849). There was no suggestion in *Bunker* that the principal was obliged to return the horse in order to recover the funds given to the agent. Rather the principal was entitled to retain the benefit of the agent's acting within the scope of his agency, while also recovering the excess money which the agent had duplicitously and wrongfully arrogated. It may be of interest to mention that according to the headnotes in the *Bunker* case, the agent had acquired a contractual interest in the horse in his own behalf before he entered into an agency relation with his principal and received his principal's funds.

We hold that plaintiff may retain the land and sue the agent to recover his profits, in this case money of the principal wrongfully retained by the agent. Whether plaintiff's remedy is viewed as an accounting of a fiduciary in equity or the recovery of damages at law is not material to our view of the case. On these facts, the exact and unfailing measure of plaintiff's damage is the difference between the sum entrusted to defendant, and the contract purchase price actually paid by defendant to acquire the property in his own name prior to the transfer to plaintiff in accordance with the agency relation. At that point the defendant had acquired the power to perfect his fiduciary obligation, and plaintiff is entitled to the full benefit of his agent's rightful duties. Defendant owed plaintiff a fiduciary obligation; defendant bought the land in his own name under a contract for $15,474.62; he conveyed the land to his principal, who had given him $32,400 to make the purchase. Defendant must now answer for the $16,925.38, together with interest and costs.

7. Presumably the principal in *Desfosses* (and in Problem 1.2) believed at the time of contracting that the land was worth what he paid for it. If that is so, why should the principal be entitled to keep the land *and* get a refund on the purchase price? How has the principal been harmed?

E. The Firm and Its Owners

The rules which govern the question of when an agency relationship is created will be further explored in Chapter 3. Similarly, the extent of a principal's liability for the acts of an agent will also be examined in more detail in later Chapters. We turn now to a consideration of the type of relationship created not be agency rules, but by the choice of persons to be associated with one another in a business. As we shall see, the consequences of this type of association turn largely on the form of business which is chosen.

1. Partnerships

Note on Entity versus Aggregate Theories of Business Forms

A recurring dispute in partnership law is the "nature" of a partnership. At common law, a partnership was generally viewed as a *relationship* among the partners. That is, "the partnership" was considered to be the *aggregate* of its partners. Unlike a corporation, "the partnership" was not generally regarded as an *entity*, a legal person separate from the partners. This dichotomy was never completely comfortable. For example, if the partnership is no a separate entity, how could it own property? Similarly, how could the partners own an interest "in" the partnership, if the partnership had no existence apart from the partners?

The competing concepts of the nature of a partnership have had a significant impact on the development of partnership law. Courts often have looked to the nature of a partnership in determining the substantive rights and obligations arising out of partnerships. For example, the early common law, with its aggregate concept of partnerships, tried to describe partnership rights and obligations *solely* in terms of existing concepts of ownership and liability. Unfortunately, many of those concepts did not work well in a partnership context. As a result, the early common law put too much emphasis on the *individual* rights and obligations of the partners and too little emphasis on the *collective* rights and obligations of all the partners. and too little emphasis on the individual rights and obligations of each partner.

Under the UPA, partnerships are part aggregate *and* part entity. In some contexts, it is better to treat the partners *separately* — as if the partnership were an aggregate — while in other contexts it is better to treat the partners *collectively* — as if the partnership were an entity. This compromise at least arguably reflects a realistic approach presented to the problem created by the partnership form of business.

The problem with a purely *conceptual* approach to partnership law is that it determines partnership rights and obligations *exclusively* on the basis of the perceived "true" nature of a partnership. As a result, conceptualism leaves partnership law too little flexibility. Instead, partnership law requires a *functional* approach that recognizes the *unique* nature of partnerships. Instead of adopting the legal person concept, the UPA retained the aggregate concept without being limited by it. In essence, it adopted a functional approach that allows either the individual or the collective rights of partners to be emphasized according to the particular factual and policy context.

Nevertheless, many commentators have argued that the only way to account for the UPA's treatment of partnership rights and obligations is by an implied adoption of the entity concept of a partnership. For additional discussion, *see* Rosin, *The Entity-Aggregate Dispute: Conceptualism and Functionalism in Partnership Law,* 42 Ark. L. Rev. 395 (1989).

On the other hand, RUPA specifies that a partnership is *"an entity resulting from the* association of two or more persons to carry on as co-owners a business for profit."* (RUPA § 201, emphasis added). Nevertheless, as the Prefatory Note to the RUPA makes clear, "RUPA does not require relentless application of the entity approach. The aggregate approach is retained for some purposes."

In reading partnership materials, the student should begin by looking at any applicable UPA (or RUPA) provisions. The student should then look at the particular *context* in which the courts are being asked to determine partnership-related rights and obligations. The student should then ask whether, in view of the provisions of the UPA (or RUPA) and the context, it is more appropriate to treat the partners separately (as an aggregate) or collectively (as an entity).

Once this basic context is understood, the courts' decisions may begin to make more sense. In the following case, the court is clearly concerned about the nature of the partnership relationship in the context of workers' compensation laws.

Problem 1.3

Costa and Head are partners in Costa and Head Land Company ("Land Company"). Land Company and Henry Tyler Construction Corporation ("HTCC") entered into a construction contract, under which HTCC was to be compensated on a time and material basis. During the course of construction, HTCC had submitted bills, all of which were paid. When HTCC submitted its final bill, Land Company paid only a portion of the bill, leaving an outstanding balance of $39,639.98. HTCC has filed suit for breach of contract against Land Company, and against Costa and Head, individually.

You have been engaged by Land Company, and by Costa and Head, to represent them in the litigation with HTCC. Please advise them as to the following:

a. May HTCC sue Land Company in its name?

b. Are Costa and Head liable for Land Company's obligations?

c. May HTCC sue Costa and Head with first exhausting remedies against Land Company?

See Head v. Henry Tyler Construction Corp., 539 So. 2d 196 (Ala. 1988) and Allgeier, Martin & Associates v. Ashmore, 508 S.W.2d 524 (Mo. App. 1974).

Swiezynski v. Civiello
489 A.2d 634 (N.H. 1985)

BATCHELDER, Justice.

The issue before us is whether a partnership employee who has received workers' compensation benefits for an injury received in the course of employment may maintain a negligence action against an individual partner who owns the work premises for this same injury. The resolution of this issue turns on whether an individual partner is an employer under the Workers' Compensation Law, and thereby is entitled to immunity from certain employee suits.

The plaintiff, Margaret Swiezynski, was employed as a grocery clerk at the Garden Street Superette in Milford. The grocery store was operated by the defendants, Rocco V. Civiello and William B. Crawford, as a partnership. The premises were owned by the defendants individually as tenants in common. On March 16, 1981, the plaintiff was injured when she fell in the store. The plaintiff subsequently received workers' compensation benefits for her injuries. She thereafter filed the instant action against the defendants, alleging that her injury resulted from a breach of a duty of care owed to her by each of the defendants as the landowners.

Without consulting the partnership agreement between the defendants, the Superior Court dismissed the plaintiff's suit, holding that the individual defendants are immune from the plaintiff's suit because they are employers within the meaning of the statute.

In *Holzworth v. Fuller*, 122 N.H. 643, 645, 448 A.2d 394, 395 (1982), we held that an employer's provision of workers' compensation insurance insulated the employer-landowner from a suit which alleged that the employee's injury had resulted from the employer's breach of his duty of care arising from his ownership of the premises. Whether the plaintiff may maintain her claims depends on whether the defendants are employers under the statute and thereby enjoy protection under *Holzworth*.

Under the Workers' Compensation Law, "employer" is defined as "a person, *partnership*, association, corporation, or legal representative of a person, *partnership*, association or corporation, who employs one or more persons." (emphasis added). We find that, for purposes relevant here, a partnership has no legal identity distinguishable from its partners who have retained their statutory rights of management and hence that such partners qualify as employers under the statute. Our holding is necessitated by the Workers' Compensation Law's conception of what constitutes an employment relationship and by the statute's underlying policy. Our conclusion that a partnership does not, in this context, constitute a legal entity distinguishable from its partners is consistent with New Hampshire partnership law, case law under the Workers' Compensation Law, and the decisions of the vast majority of the jurisdictions that have considered this question.

The Workers' Compensation Law refers to a private employment relationship as "any contract of hire, express or implied, oral or written." RSA 281:2, III (Supp. 1983). Such a contract confers on the employer a right to the labor of the employee and on the employee a corresponding right to compensation.

The dispositive characteristic of the employer's status is his right to control the employee's work performance. Under the Workers' Compensation Law, the distinguishing features of an employment relationship, therefore, are the employer's right to the employee's labor and his right to control the employee's performance and the employee's corresponding right to compensation.

Under New Hampshire law, these features are present in the relationship between a partner and a partnership employee. Unless the partnership agreement provides otherwise, partners by law have "equal rights in the management and conduct of the partnership business." [UPA § 18(e)]. Consequently, each partner has an equal right to control the work performance of a partnership employee. Partners are personally liable for partnership obligations, [UPA § 15], including an employee's claim for compensation.

As the Supreme Court of New Jersey stated in a similar case, "we cannot conceive of any incident of the employer-employee relationship which is here lacking." [*Mazzuchelli v. Silberberg*, 29 N.J. 15, 22, 148 A.2d 7, 11 (1959)]. Professor Larson is in accord:

> [I]n any ordinary partnership each partner has by law an equal share in management, and is therefore in actual possession of the powers of the employer. *Unless he has contracted away these powers*, which he can theoretically do, he is as much the employer as anyone can be, not as a matter of conceptual reasoning but as a matter of actual functions and rights.

1C A. Larson, [The Law of Workmen's Compensation § 54.32, at 9-202—9-203 (1982)] (emphasis added). Accordingly, we hold that a partner retaining his right of management is in an employment relationship with a partnership employee and, thus, constitutes an employer under the Workers' Compensation Law.

The Workers' Compensation Law balances the interests of the employee against those of the employers. The employee receives a right to receive insurance benefits for work-related injuries in exchange for his forfeiture of his corresponding rights of action against the employer; the employer receives statutory immunity from employee suits in exchange for his provision of insurance benefits. Under New Hampshire law, partners are personally liable for all debts of the partnership, [UPA § 15], including the liability for workers' compensation insurance.

To construe "employer" not to include individual partners would require partners to endure the liability for compensation insurance without the enjoyment of the corresponding benefit of immunity from employee suits. This construction would frustrate the policy underlying the Workers' Compensation Law. Where reasonably possible, a statute should be construed to effectuate its underlying policy. Construing the term "employer" to include individual partners, therefore, is preferable because it gives force to a policy central to the act.

The Uniform Partnership Act ("UPA"), which states the law governing partnerships in this State, is instructive on the issue before us. The UPA commingles the entity theory, which regards a partnership as an independent legal entity, with the aggregation theory, which holds that a partnership has no such independent status. The plaintiff asks us to extrapolate from the UPA's partial adoption of the entity theory the conclusion that a partnership is a distinct legal entity for the purposes relevant here. We are mindful, however, that "[u]ltimately it is not too important whether a specific result directed by the uniform law is dressed in garb of the entity concept, provided the fictional personification is confined to the specific result and is not used as a premise for syllogistic thrusts elsewhere." *Mazzuchelli v. Silberberg*, 29 N.J. at 21, 148 A.2d at 11.

A partnership is not considered an entity separate from its members, except in limited circumstances. The entity theory governs only in matters of procedure, *see, e.g.,* [UPA §§ 11, 12, 27, 28, 30], and in the holding and conveyancing of property, *see, e.g.,* [UPA §§ 10, 24-26], including the marshalling of assets, *see* [UPA § 40(h), (i)].

The aggregation theory controls in matters relating to the substantive liabilities and duties of the partners. Our statute defines a partnership as "an *association* of two or more persons to carry on as *co-owners* a business for profit." [UPA § 6] (emphasis added). "To state that partners are co-owners of a business is to state that they each have the power of *ultimate* control." [UPA § 6, comment (1)] (emphasis added). Partners accordingly "have equal rights in the management and conduct of the partnership business," [UPA § 18(e)], and are personally liable for partnership obligations, [UPA § 15]. In short, "[t]he Uniform Partnership Act does not make a legal partnership an independent juristic entity, and whatever recognition is given therein to the entity theory is solely for procedural or conveyancing purposes." *Carlson v. Carlson*, [346 N.W.2d 525, 527 (Iowa 1984)].

A number of jurisdictions have considered the precise issue before us; namely, whether a partner is an employer under a workers' compensation statute and thereby is entitled to immunity from employee suits. The vast majority of these jurisdictions has held that a partner is an employer.

A number of cases expressly considered the UPA. With but one exception, these cases held that under the act a partnership is not a legal entity distinct from its partners. Because we construe the UPA as enacted in New Hampshire "to make uniform the law of those states which [have] enact[ed] it," [UPA § 4(4)], we treat this majority rule as persuasive.

Where reasonably possible, statutes should be construed as consistent with each other. Construing the term "employer" in the Workers' Compensation Law not to include individual partners would frustrate a policy of the UPA and therefore should be avoided. The UPA expressly recognizes that title to real property owned by the partnership may be held in the names of all the partners. *See* [UPA § 10(4), (5)]. The plaintiff claims that she may maintain her negligence action against the defendants because they held title to the supermarket in their names as tenants in common and not in the name of the partnership. If we accept this argument, the defendants will be penalized for holding their property in a form expressly condoned by the UPA and members of other business partnerships will be discouraged from adopting this statutorily sanctioned form of partnership. This final circumstance further recommends our holding.

We remand for a determination as to whether the partnership agreement provided that the defendants did not retain their legal rights of management. Unless it so provided, the defendants are employers under the Workers' Compensation Law.

Order vacated, remanded.

Notes

1. Under RUPA section 201(a) "[a] partnership is an entity distinct from its partners." The comment to RUPA section 201 provides as follows:

> [The] RUPA embraces the entity theory of the partnership. In light of the UPA's ambivalence on the nature of partnerships, the explicit statement provided by subsection (a) is deemed appropriate as an expression of the *increased emphasis* on the entity theory as the *dominant model. But see* Section 306 (partners' liability joint and several...).

RUPA § 201 comment (emphasis added). To what extent does RUPA section 201(a) represent a political judgment that public policy requires that a partnership should be treated as an entity?

2. Would the adoption by New Hampshire change the result in *Swiezynski v. Civiello?* Consider the following extract from the Prefatory Note to the RUPA:

> The [RUPA] enhances the entity treatment of partnerships to achieve simplicity for state law purposes, particularly in matters concerning title to partnership property. [The] RUPA does not, however, relentlessly apply the entity approach. The aggregate approach is retained for some purposes, such as partners' joint and several liability.

3. At common law, a partnership could neither sue or be sued in partnership name. In *Allgeier, Martin & Associates v. Ashmore,* 508 S.W.2d 524 (Mo. App. 1974), a partnership filed suit in its own name. At first a default judgment was entered against the defendant. The trial court set aside the default judgment and allowed the defendant to file both an answer and a counterclaimed against the partnership.

Missouri follows the common law or aggregate theory of partnership rather than the entity theory. The Uniform Partnership Law did not transform a partnership into a separate or juristic entity and, generally, all partners are necessary parties-plaintiff in actions to enforce an obligation due the partnership. Absent statutory authority, a partnership cannot sue in the firm name and a judgment rendered for a partnership so suing will be reversed on appeal on the principle that a partnership has no legal existence apart from its members, but is a mere ideal entity.

To augment the confusion, in its order, the trial court not only set aside the default judgment but also granted defendants leave to file an answer and counterclaim or cross bill. Just as plaintiff may not maintain this suit in the partnership name, so too

> in a suit [or counterclaim] against a partnership in its firm name only, there is no legal entity before the court against which lawful judgment may be rendered, [which] constitutes a fatal defect not waived by failure to object, and a judgment against the partnership in its firm name alone is void.

Davison v. Farr, [273 S.W.2d 500, 503 (Mo. App. 1954)].

The situation presented is one in which plaintiff, by default or otherwise, cannot secure a valid judgment against the defendants or any of them, and where the defendants, singularly or collectively, cannot obtain a valid judgment against the plaintiff via a counterclaim or otherwise. In fine, the parties are but caponized litigants whose crowings will gain them neither success nor posterity. We have no choice but to direct the judgment which the trial court should have entered, and that is to dismiss the cause in its entirety. Therefore, the order and judgment appealed from is reversed and the cause is remanded with directions to enter a judgment dismissing the cause.

4. The common law rule that partnerships cannot sue and be sued in partnership name has been modified in many jurisdictions by so-called "common name" or "joint debtor" statutes authorizing suits *against the partners* in the partnership name. Consistent with the RUPA's dominant entity approach, RUPA section 301(a) expressly allows *partnerships* to sue and to be sued in partnership name. What is the difference between RUPA section 301(a) and the common name and joint debtor statutes?

5. Under UPA section 15, partners are *jointly* liable for all partnership obligations [§ 15(b)], except for wrongful acts and breaches of trust by partners, as to which partners are *jointly and severally* liable. Some of the differences between joint and joint and several liability are explained in *Head v. Henry Tyler Construction Corp.*, 539 So. 2d 196 (Ala. 1988):

> [The partners] concede in their brief that they are liable for the debt in question. However, they assert that under Alabama law a condition precedent exists to holding them liable. They maintain that a partnership creditor must first exhaust efforts to obtain payment from the partnership or prove that the partnership has no assets before proceeding directly against the individual partners and their assets. Therefore, the sole issue to be de-

cided in this case is whether the trial court was correct in its determination that no such condition precedent exists under Alabama law.

The general common law rule is that partnership contracts create only a joint liability among the partners. The partners are not individually liable for partnership contracts, unless assets of the partnership are inadequate to pay the partnership debts or there is no effective remedy without resort to the property of individual partners. The Uniform Partnership Act, § 15(b), provides that partners are jointly liable for all debts and obligations of a partnership, except those arising from a tort or breach of trust. This is a codification of the common law rule.

By statute, however, Alabama long ago abandoned this common law rule of imposing only joint liability on partners for partnership debts and obligations. In *Dollins & Adams v. Pollock & Co.*, 89 Ala. 351, 7 So. 904 (1890), this Court recognized that the Alabama Code of 1886 provided for *joint and several liability* on the partners for partnership obligations and permitted a creditor to sue them jointly or severally at his option. Likewise in *First National Bank v. Capps*, 208 Ala. 207, 94 So. 109 (1922), the Court conceded that, in the absence of a statutory provision to the contrary, partnership contracts are joint and not several and that under the common law, liability of partners was so treated. The Court then cited the Code of 1907, which authorized a creditor of the partnership to sue one partner for the obligation of all. This statute, the Court stated,

> gave the creditor of a partnership the right to sue any member of the firm, and by such suit to change the nature of the partnership obligation from joint to joint and several.

Consequently, when the Uniform Partnership Act was being proposed for adoption in Alabama, § 15(b), providing for only joint liability, was the subject of debate. In 1962, a subcommittee of the Alabama State Bar's Committee on Jurisprudence and Law Reform suggested that the section be changed to conform to existing Alabama law. The report of the subcommittee's findings states:

> Our committee has recommended only two changes in the terminology of the Uniform Partnership Act as originally drawn by the Commissioners. Section 15 provides that partners were jointly and severally liable for breaches of trust and wrongful acts and omissions causing loss or injury but that they are jointly liable only for all other debts and obligations of the partnership. This appears to be a statement of the common law rule as understood in most jurisdictions. However, Section 141, Title 7, *Code of Alabama*, expressly authorizes actions against one or more of the partners for the 'obligations' of the partnership, thus, in effect, converting the liability at the election of the party bringing the action to joint and several liability for all practical purposes except set-off and recoupment. In view of this situation, the subcommittee, with one member dissenting, felt that it would be more in keeping with the existing Alabama law and procedure to amend Section 15 by providing simply that all partners shall be

liable jointly and severally for all debts and obligations of the partnership.

Woolf, *New Partnership Act Proposed by Committee on Jurisprudence and Law Reform*, 24 Ala. Law. 115, 116 (1963).

The Alabama legislature eventually enacted the Alabama Partnership Act, patterned after the Uniform Partnership Act, but adopted the suggested change to § 15(b). The provision of the Act dealing with partner liability unequivocally states that partners are "jointly and severally" liable for all debts and obligations of the partnership. Appellant still contends, however, that a creditor must first exhaust any remedies against the partnership before initiating an action against individual partners. This argument is without merit because it does not recognize the legal impact, through the years, of Alabama's statutes making partners severally liable on partnership contracts in addition to the already existing common law joint liability.

The major impact of making partners not merely jointly liable but also severally liable is that if a creditor chooses to bring an action against one of the partners, that partner is liable for all of the partnership debts, regardless of whether the creditor first attempted to recover the debt from the partnership or prove that the partnership had no assets. Several liability is

> [l]iability *separate and distinct from liability of another* to the extent that an independent action may be brought without joinder of others.

Black's Law Dictionary (5th ed. 1979) at 1232. (Emphasis added.) The individual liability associated with partners that are jointly liable is not separate and distinct from the liability of all the partners jointly. Rather, the individual liability arises only after it has been shown that the partnership assets are inadequate. No direct cause of action may be maintained against the individual partners until the above condition is met. Several liability, on the other hand, imposes no such conditions precedent before one can be held individually liable. As stated in 59A Am. Jr. 2d *Partnerships*, § 709 at 590 (1987):

> Where partners are considered jointly and severally liable on partnership obligations, establishing personal unlimited liability of partners as individuals, each individual partner thus pursued must be made a party to the action without the necessity of joining all partners in the suit as indispensable parties, nor must the plaintiff bring a prior action against the partnership. A direct right of action exists against the partner.

Alabama has long recognized the legal effect of joint and several liability of partners for partnership debts:

> As a general rule, each individual partner is liable to creditors of the firm for the whole amount of every debt due therefrom. Nor is a creditor of the firm, except, perhaps, as to individual creditors of a member thereof, required to resort to the firm assets before looking to the individual property of the respective members of the said firm for the satisfaction of this debt.

Cleckler v. First National Bank of Anniston, 204 Ala. 268, 269, 85 So. 484, 484 (1920). (Emphasis added.) Likewise, other jurisdictions that have adopted joint and several liability provisions in their partnership acts hold that creditors of the partnership do not have to pursue partnership assets before looking to any of the individual partners for payment of the entire debt.

6. The RUPA makes two changes in the liability of partners. First, partners would be jointly and severally liable for *all* partnership debts and obligations. RUPA § 306. Second, notwithstanding the joint and several nature of the partners' liability, judgment creditors would generally be required to exhaust partnership assets before proceeding against the individual assets of partners. RUPA § 307(c).

2. Limited Partnerships

The Uniform Limited Partnership Act (1976) with 1985 amendments (RULPA)[A] defines a limited partnership as "a partnership formed by two or more persons…, having one or more general partners and one or more limited partners." (RULPA § 101(7)) Subject to certain limitations, a "general partner" in a limited partnership "has the rights and powers and is subject to the restrictions and liabilities of a partner in a partnership without limited partners." (RULPA § 404) Limited partners, on the other hand, have both limited rights and limited obligations. Limited partners generally are not personally liable for partnership obligations. (RULPA § 303) On the other hand, they have no general right to participate in the management of the business, but only such voting rights as given under the limited partnership agreement. (RULPA § 302) In fact, as discussed later in this book, limited partners who participate in the "control" of the limited partnership's business run the risk of becoming liable as general partners for obligations of the limited partnership. (RULPA § 303)

As discussed in the following extract from *Klein v. Weiss*, 284 Md. 36, 395 A.2d 126 (1978), the limited partnership form of business association began in the late 1700s and early 1800s:

> Limited partnerships were unknown at common law; they are exclusively a creature of statute, their main purpose being to permit a form of business enterprise, other than a corporation, in which persons could invest money without becoming liable as general partners for all debts of the partnership. "The general purpose of (limited partnership) acts was not to assist creditors, but was to enable persons to invest their money in partnerships and share in the profits without being liable for more than the amount of money they had contributed. The reason for this was to encourage investing." *Gilman Paint & Varnish Co. v. Legum*, 197 Md. 665, 670, 80 A.2d 906, 908 (1951).

A. The Uniform Limited Partnership Act (1976) with 1985 amendments was originally named the "Revised" Uniform Limited Partnership Act and was commonly referred to as "RULPA". This book will refer to Act using the original title and "RULPA".

The first limited partnership statute in the United States was enacted by New York in 1822; Maryland adopted a similar statute [in] 1836. These early statutes required the recording of a partnership certificate giving notice to the public of the exact terms of the partnership, including the amount of the capital contributions of the limited partners, so that the public could deal with the partnership "advisedly." *Lineweaver v. Slagle*, 64 Md. 465, 2 A. 693 (1886). The fundamental difference between the liability of general and limited partners under these statutes was "that the former are responsible *in solido* for the debts and obligations of the firm, as in the case of ordinary partnerships, without regard to the amounts contributed by them to the social capital; whilst the latter is not personally liable if the statute has been complied with, because his cash contribution is substituted for a personal liability." *Safe Deposit Co. v. Cahn*, 102 Md. 530, 546, 62 A. 819 (1906). Strict compliance with all statutory provisions was deemed essential to create a limited partnership under these early statutes, since they were in derogation of the common law. As a consequence, even minor or trivial infractions of the statute were held by some courts to subject the limited partners to unlimited liability as general partners. Because the strict construction of these statutes inhibited the effective accomplishment of the purpose for which they were intended, the National Conference of Commissioners on Uniform State Laws proposed the adoption in 1916 of a Uniform Limited Partnership Act [(ULPA)]. Maryland enacted the [ULPA in] 1918, and the statute with minor modifications is now in effect in every state in the country except Louisiana. The Act's provisions are intended to govern the determination of essentially all questions arising out of the formation and operation of limited partnerships. The rule that statutes in derogation of the common law are to be strictly construed is expressly made inapplicable to the [ULPA].

Decisions interpreting the [ULPA] recognize that a limited partnership consists of general partners who conduct the business and who have unlimited liability to creditors for its obligations, and of limited partners who have no right to participate in the management of the business, and whose liability is limited to the amount of their capital contribution. As the Official Comment to section 1 of the [ULPA] makes clear, a limited partner, though so called by custom, is not "in any sense" either a partner or a principal in the business or transactions of the partnership; his liability, except for known false statements in the certificate of partnership, is to the partnership, and not to its creditors. Succinctly put, a limited partnership interest in a business is in the nature of an investment. Section 17(a) of the [ULPA] delineates the extent of the limited partner's investment in the business; it makes him liable to the partnership:

(1) For the difference between his contribution as actually made and that stated in the certificate as having been made; and

(2) For any unpaid contribution which he agreed in the certificate to make in the future at the time and on the conditions stated in the certificate.

The creation of a limited partnership is not a mere private, informal, voluntary agreement as in the case of a general partnership, but is a public and formal proceeding which must follow the statutory requirements of the [ULPA]. [Section 2(2) of the ULPA] prescribes that a limited partnership is formed "if there has been substantial compliance in good faith" with the requirements contained in section 2(1). That subsection mandates that a certificate of a partnership be signed by the parties, acknowledged, and recorded with the clerk of the court. It requires that the certificate set forth designated partnership details, including the name of the partnership, the character and location of the business, the identity of the general and limited partners, the term of the partnership, the cash contributions made by the limited partners, and such additional contributions, if any, which the limited partners have agreed to make in the future. The certificate is a statutory prerequisite to creation of a limited partnership and until it is filed, the partnership is not formed as a limited partnership. The principal function of the certificate is to give third persons notice of the essential features of the limited partnership. Of course, whether a limited partnership has been formed is of particular importance in determining whether a person has achieved the status of a limited partner with the attendant limitation of his liability to third persons dealing with the partnership.

As noted in the foregoing excerpt, the ULPA, first promulgated in 1916, was eventually adopted by every state except for Louisiana. The ULPA has, however, now largely been supplanted by the RULPA. The RULPA, adopted by the National Conference of Commissioners on Uniform State Laws in 1976 and substantially amended in 1985, has now been adopted in forty-six states. The RULPA is now in the process of being revised by the National Conference.

For further information regarding the development of limited partnership law generally, and especially the 1985 RULPA, *see* Closen, *Limited Partnership Reform: A Commentary on the Proposed Illinois Statute and the 1976 and 1985 Versions of the Uniform Limited Partnership Act,* 6 N. ILL. L. REV. 205 (1986).

Life Care Centers of America, Inc. v. Charles Town Assoc. Ltd. Partnership
79 F.3d 496 (6th Cir. 1996)

JULIAN ABELE COOK, Jr., Chief District Judge.

For the reasons that have been set forth below, we affirm in part and reverse in part the decisions of the district court, and remand the case for a new trial in accordance with this opinion.

I.

On November 10, 1982, Life Care entered into a written management agreement with the then-owner of Jeffersonian Manor, a nursing home in Charles Town, West Virginia. In 1987, Charles Town Associates Limited Partnership

(Charles Town) acquired Jeffersonian Manor and retained Life Care as its managing agent. The management agreement contained a termination clause which, as a condition precedent, required Charles Town: (1) to notify Life Care of any perceived breaches of their contract, and (2) to provide Life Care with an opportunity to correct any of the claimed contractual violations.

In 1990, the limited partners of Charles Town voted to make LPIMC their new managing general partner. On July 10, 1991, Life Care initiated a bid among Charles Town's limited partners to replace LPIMC as their managing general partner. LPIMC, upon learning of this contact with the limited partners, advised Life Care that it considered this solicitation effort to constitute substantive violations of their management agreement and its fiduciary duties as a managing agent. LPIMC also warned Life Care that its employment tenure with Charles Town would be terminated unless this activity ceased immediately. However, when Life Care refused to do so, its services were terminated.

Notwithstanding the cessation of its formal relationship with LPIMC, Life Care continued its bid to become the new managing general partner of Charles Town. However, these efforts were stymied in the spring of 1992 when the limited partners voted to reject Life Care's application. Thereafter, Life Care filed a lawsuit against LPIMC, Charles Town and its general partners, charging them with breach of contract/wrongful termination, tortious interference with a contract, and inducement to breach a contract.

II.

There is no question that an agent owes a duty of loyalty and obedience to his principal, the breach of which provides a legal basis for the termination of the agency relationship. The Defendants [LPIMC, Charles Town and its general partners] correctly note that "[t]he relationship of a principal and agent is based on trust and confidence." *Thomson McKinnon Sec., Inc. v. Moore's Farm Supply, Inc.,* 557 F.Supp. 1004, 1011 (W.D.Tenn. 1983). Moreover,

[t]he relationship of principal and agent requires that friendly relations be maintained between the two, and an agent who owes a duty of service violates it by acting in such manner that this is impossible. He need not render cheerful obedience, but he must not be insubordinate in speech or by other manifestation, either to the principal or to third parties.

RESTATEMENT (SECOND) OF AGENCY § 380, comment b. Thus,

[w]hen the relationship of superior and subordinate is of such a personal and intimate nature that certain forms of public criticism of the superior by the subordinate would seriously undermine the effectiveness of the working relationship between them, the balance tips against the employee.

Goldwasser v. Brown, 417 F.2d 1169, 1177 (D.C.Cir. 1969), *cert. denied,* 397 U.S. 922, 90 S.Ct. 918, 25 L.Ed.2d 103 (1970) [additional citations omitted].

In the instant case, it is difficult to evaluate the merit of the Defendants' argument on this issue because the identity of the principal to whom Life Care owed a fiduciary duty is not clear. If Life Care's principals were the individual partners, then its fiduciary duties flowed to each of them. Under this theory, it is possible that Life Care's refusal to obey the general partners would warrant its dismissal. On the other hand, if Life Care's principal was Charles Town, then its fiduciary duty is quite clear. Under this alternative theory, it is possible that Life Care's refusal to obey the general partners' directives was in the best interest of Charles Town and, hence, its actions did not violate any fiduciary duties. Thus, the crux of the controversy in the instant case is not whether the termination of Life Care's service for being disobedient or disloyal to its principal was legally justifiable, but rather whether its fiduciary duties were violated.

Surprisingly, there is a virtual absence of case law around the country which discusses the identity of the principal in a limited partnership context. On the other hand, there is ample authority for the notion that an agent to a general partnership owes his fiduciary duties to the partnership. On its face, this concept would suggest that the partnership is the principal of the agent. However, there is also authority which suggests that the agent's principal in the partnership context is each partner. *See* RESTATEMENT (SECOND) OF AGENCY § 20, comment e (1957) ("A person acting for an unincorporated group of persons may be an agent either of all members of the group or certain of them. If the one who authorized him to act for all has also been authorized by all of the members or certain of them to appoint him, he is the agent of such persons. Thus, one appointed by a member of a partnership who has been authorized to act to the partnership is the agent of all the partners"). Therefore, it is clear that an agent to a general partnership owes a fiduciary duty to the partnership and the partners. However, it is not clear whether the same conclusion follows with respect to an agent's relationship with limited partnerships or how the fiduciary duty to multiple principals would play out in situations which, like this one, may involve a conflict of interest between the principals. A conceptual understanding of partnership theory is vital to formulating an answer to this question.

The reason why agents of partnerships owe individual partners a fiduciary duty lies in the distinct nature of the partnership as a business organization. Partnerships, unlike corporations, do not have a separate existence from the partners who form the partnership. *See Battista v. Lebanon Trotting Ass'n,* 538 F.2d 111, 116 (6th Cir. 1976) ("A corporation is generally recognized as a separate legal entity from its shareholders, officers and directors, but a partnership is not so considered"). Instead, partnerships have traditionally existed by virtue of their partners' existence. *See* UNIFORM PARTNERSHIP ACT § 4 (1914) (death of any partner terminates partnership under Tennessee law). However, this traditional view of partnerships as an "aggregate" of individuals is not always adequate in the context of limited partnerships.

The modus operandi of limited partnerships is an important reason why the "aggregate" theory of partnerships is not always applicable in this context. Limited partnerships are business organizations in which the limited partners are precluded by law from participating in the operation of the partnership. In exchange for their abstention from participating in the management of the business, the law provides limited investors with limited liability for the debts of the partnership. The operations of the business of the limited partnership are left to the general partner, who, unlike the limited partners, is personally liable for the operation of the partnership. A general partner accepts this unlimited form of liability as a trade-off for the limited partners' investment in the partnership's business.

Thus, in a typical situation, a general partner acts much like the management of a corporation, while the involvement of the limited partners is comparable to the shareholders of a corporation. In fact, the general partner has the primary responsibility of making the business successful in order to provide a satisfactory return for the partnership, including its limited partners. By contrast, the role of the limited partners is very passive, in that it consists of an investment in the partnership with the expectation of obtaining a profitable return. *See Klebanow v. New York Produce Exchange*, 344 F.2d 294, 297 (2nd Cir. 1965) (Friendly, J.) ("[A] limited partner is more like a shareholder, often expecting a share of the profits, subordinated to general creditors, having some control over direction of the enterprise by his veto on the admission of new partners, and able to examine books and have on demand true and full information of all things affecting the partnership...."). Not surprisingly, an alternative approach to partnerships — one which views them as "entities" with lives that are independent of their partners rather than mere "aggregates" of people — has a compelling appeal in the limited partnership context. *See generally* HAROLD GILL REUSCHLEIN AND WILLIAM A. GREGORY, THE LAW OF AGENCY AND PARTNERSHIP 264 (2d Ed. 1990) (discussing "aggregate" and "entity" theories of partnership).

Each theory of partnership is likely to produce a different result with respect to the issue of fiduciary duty in question. Under the "aggregate" theory of partnership, an agent's fiduciary duty would run first and foremost to the individual partners who compose the partnership. However, under the "entity" theory of partnership, an agent's fiduciary duty would run primarily to the partnership. The distinction of whether the fiduciary duty runs exclusively or primarily to the partners or the partnership becomes crucial when the interests between the partners and/or the partnership conflict. Under such circumstances, the agent will be required to act in the best interests of his "primary" principal, which in turn may require him to act against the best interests of the "subordinate" principal. Thus, the decision as to which partnership theory is "proper" and should be applied in a particular situation is a determinative one with respect to the issue of fiduciary duty.

Unfortunately, the common law provides little conclusive guidance on the subject inasmuch as the issue of the "proper" partnership theory is an ongoing debate: Some jurisdictions reached far toward an entity theory by not permitting creditors to reach the individual assets of partners until the partnership assets were first exhausted. The common law at the time of the drafting of the UPA essentially favored the aggregate approach although it created a number of serious problems. A very few jurisdictions and some scholars favored the entity approach. The law seemed to be slowly developing toward some version of the entity approach at the time. In fact, the first draft of the UPA was based clearly on an entity approach having been prepared by Dean Ames. This view was not favored and the ultimate version of the UPA as drafted by Dean Lewis adopted the aggregate approach with some modifications.... Further, the UPA as enacted was ambiguous enough so as not to cut off further judicial progress toward the entity approach. At least one jurisdiction [Arkansas] has determined that the UPA did not embrace the entity theory, but instead retains the common law aggregate theory. The entity approach tends to keep its attractiveness to courts and commentators mainly because it is realistic and closely in accord with the expectations of most businessmen. Unfortunately, Tennessee case law does not shed light on this issue. In fact, there are no reported Tennessee cases which have addressed the two competing theories of partnership or the specific issue of an agent's fiduciary responsibilities that is before the Court. Thus, in the absence of clear guidance on the subject, the counsel of Reuschlein and Gregory, both of whom advocate that the constraints and formalisms to which the courts have traditionally given rigid adherence be rejected and, instead, the realities of a specific situation be examined in order to fashion an appropriate remedy, is particularly appealing:

> A pragmatic approach to the controversy is to reject either theory and simply to solve problems of partnership law as they arise, with the solution being dictated not by legal formalism, but by the merits of particular solutions. This eclectic approach while inconsistent in terms of formal logic has much to recommend it.

The only case in the country, other than the instant one, in which the issue of fiduciary duty has been decided, embraced this "eclectic" approach. Ironically, that case involved virtually the same parties who are involved in this case.

In *Life Care Centers of America, Inc. v. East Hampden Assoc. Ltd. Partnership,* [a 1992 decision by the District Court for Colorado], Life Care sued LPIMC, Weinstein, Rosen, and Galston, among other persons, as the general partners of a limited partnership which owned several nursing homes. As in the instant case, Life Care had been dismissed as the managing agent of the nursing homes for soliciting the limited partners of the limited partnership in an attempt to oust the general partners.

The district court concluded that the agents of the limited partnerships, such as Life Care, not only owed a fiduciary duty to the partnership, but also to the partners. Through this holding, the district court implicitly rejected the dichotomy that is presented by the "aggregate" and "entity" theories of partnership, finding that the limited partnership at issue was a hybrid business structure with traditional "aggregate" aspects (i.e., the flow of fiduciary duty to the partners) and corporate-like "entity" aspects (i.e., the flow of fiduciary duty to the entity).

Having concluded that the agent owed a fiduciary duty to the partnership and the individual partners, the Colorado court dealt with the conflict of interest which arose between the agent's duty of loyalty to the partnership and the agent's duty of loyalty to the individual partners, including the general partners, in the following manner:

> [I]n the event that the interests of the partnership's incumbent management and its limited partners conflict, an agent, in an attempt to serve the best interests of the partnership and its limited partners, may take action which may not be in the best interest of present management. Just as a shareholder has the right to change incumbent management, so does the limited partner have such a right. Limited partnerships provide for such a change. It is not a breach of fiduciary duty to offer to the limited partners a change in general partner in a manner which is in accord with the provisions of the limited partnership agreement, especially in the belief that the general partner is not acting in the best interests of the limited partnership.

Id.

In *East Hampden,* the court, although determining that the collective interests of the limited partners and the interests of the partnership were basically identical, recognized that the collective interests of the limited partners and the partnership may conflict with those of the general partner. This premise is essentially correct. The interest of the general partner in the prosperity of the partnership could conflict with a competing interest in maintaining his position as the general partner even if a change of a leadership would be in the best interest of the partnership.

In dealing with the conflict of interest dilemma, the district court allowed the agent to act in the best interest of the partnership even if such acts were not in the best interest of the general partner. Thus, the court in Colorado clearly adopted the viewpoint that the individual interests of the partners, including those of the general partners, were subordinate to the collective interests of the limited partners and the partnership. Therefore, while the court implicitly embraced a hybrid approach to the business structure known as the limited partnership, it nevertheless recognized that, in the modern business world, the "entity" component of this hybrid business structure predominates over its "aggregate" counterpart.

By contrast, the approach of the district court in Tennessee [in this case] represented a total rejection of the "aggregate" theory of partnership and a complete endorsement of the "entity" theory counterpart. In deciding that Life Care had only a fiduciary duty toward Charles Town, the district court treated the partnership as a business entity that is indistinguishable from a corporation. *See* Order, June 29, 1993 ("[I]f Life Care owed a fiduciary duty, it was owed to the limited partnership and not to the individual partners. Defendants have not shown that a mere communication made in an effort to oust the incumbent general managing partner of the limited partnership, LPIMC, violated any duty owed to that limited partnership, Charles Town"). While the simplicity of this approach is seductive, it is misdirected.

Although a limited partnership does have many of the characteristics of a corporation, it is not only a "corporate" type of business entity, but it is also an "aggregate" of partners as it is underscored by certain aspects of the structure, such as the personal liability of general partners. Nevertheless, an analysis of the business reality of limited partnerships suggests that this business structure has a strong "entity" character, in that its identity and existence is separate and apart from its individual partners whose participation in the operation of the limited partnership is minimal. It is this "entity" character which requires that the management of the limited partnership be placed in a quasi-corporate light and subjected to special constraints. Therefore, while it is important to recognize that fiduciary duties flow to the individual partners of a limited partnership, it is also appropriate to subordinate those interests to those of the entity when a conflict of interest arises.

In order to comply with this standard, an agent who is accused of a breach of fiduciary duty must point to a specific divergence of interests between the individual partner and the limited partnership that would justify his conduct (*e.g.,* the wasting of corporate assets or an involvement of the general partner in self-serving transactions with the partnership). An agent can also discharge his burden by demonstrating that he had a justifiable belief which was well-grounded in fact and law that a specific divergence existed which warranted his decisions.

In the instant case, Life Care has made several accusations against the general partners, including their mismanagement of the limited partnership. If Life Care had a reasonable belief as to the accuracy of its allegations, then it was justified in soliciting the limited partners for the ouster of the general partners. However, the record is not conclusive as to whether Life Care's accusations were based on any reasonable belief. Quite the contrary, the general partners have denied the accuracy of these accusations, attributing them to Life Care's desire to become the general partner of Charles Town at any cost. Thus, a genuine issue of a material fact remains as to the reasonableness of Life Care's belief, if any, that the specific interests of the general partners and Charles Town were in conflict which, in turn, would warrant its solicitation of the limited partners notwithstanding its fiduciary duty to the general partners.[1] The district court erred in concluding otherwise.

BATCHELDER, Circuit Judge, concurring in part and dissenting in part.

I would affirm the district court in all respects. Even if I could agree with the majority's apparent conclusion that in Tennessee, as a matter of law, an agent's fiduciary duty runs to the individual limited partners, I cannot agree with its conclusion that the conduct of the agent in this case, i.e., soliciting the votes of the individual limited partners, could constitute a breach of fiduciary duty. As the district court correctly pointed out, "Life Care simply solicited the proxies of the limited partners who were required to make the decision whether to retain the incumbent general managing partner, LPIMC. Life Care had no control over the vote and could not force the elimination of [the] incumbent general partner." The district court went on to hold that if Life Care owed a fiduciary duty at all, that duty was to the limited partnership and not to the individual limited partners. I am hard-pressed to see how, even if the duty were to the limited partners, the agent's mere solicitation of those individuals' proxies, without at least some demonstrated power on the part of the agent to force the individuals to comply with the solicitation, could constitute a breach of that duty.

Although the majority opinion appears to overrule the district court's "total rejection of the 'aggregate' theory of partnership and...complete endorsement of the 'entity' theory," (pursuant to which the district court held that Life Care's duty, if any, was to the limited partnership), it does not clearly hold to whom Life Care owed a fiduciary duty. Rather, the majority opinion states, "while it is important to recognize that fiduciary duties flow to the individual partners of a

1. Importantly, the district court, anticipating that its conclusions on fiduciary duty would be dispositive of that defense, did not decide if Life Care was an agent of the Defendants or whether there was a genuine issue of a material fact as to the existence of the agency. Rather, it appears that the district court assumed arguendo that Life Care was in fact an agent of the Defendants. Clearly, this is a threshold question (i.e., whether Life Care is an agent of the Defendants or merely an independent contractor) that should be addressed on remand. It should be pointed out that the Defendants have submitted two additional arguments in opposition to the district court's conclusion that Life Care did not owe them a fiduciary duty. First, they have contended that Life Care should have been estopped from advancing its current position on the fiduciary duty issue because it had adopted the opposite view in the Colorado litigation. Second, they argued that, in striking their eighth affirmative defense pertaining to the breach of fiduciary duty issue, the district court improperly turned Life Care's motion to strike into a motion for summary judgment. They maintain that this decision by the district court wrongfully deprived them of an opportunity to demonstrate that a genuine issue of a material fact existed concerning the matter. In light of the conclusion by this Court that Life Care owed a fiduciary duty to the general partners, the issues of judicial estoppel and/or the procedural deficiencies, if any, are moot and, therefore, have not been addressed in this opinion.

limited partnership, it is also appropriate to subordinate those interests to those of the entity when a conflict of interest arises." The majority then holds that a genuine issue of fact remains as to whether Life Care's solicitation of proxies from the limited partners was warranted "notwithstanding its fiduciary duty to the general partners." (emphasis added).

Finally, the majority cites no authority (and I have found none) for its conclusion that Life Care's mere solicitation of proxies was a breach of its fiduciary duty unless Life Care could demonstrate the reasonableness of its basis for making the solicitation.

The district court's opinion is clear, its reasoning is cogent, and I would affirm.

Notes

1. In *Life Care Centers of America, Inc. v. Charles Town Associates Limited Partnership,* why does it matter to whom Life Care owes a fiduciary duty?

2. Is the reasoning of the court in *Life Care Centers of America, Inc.* consistent with that used in *Swiezynski v. Civiello?*

3. Under what circumstances does the court in *Life Care Centers of America, Inc.* require an agent to show a "specific divergence of interests between the individual partner and the limited partnership that would justify his conduct"? What purpose is served by imposing this standard and placing the burden of proof on the agent?

4. Consider the following extract from Rule 1.13 of the ABA Model Rules of Professional Conduct, dealing with the *ethical* responsibilities of lawyers representing business organizations, including unincorporated organizations. Does Rule 1.13 take an aggregate, entity or hybrid approach? How does Rule 1.13 balance the interests of a constituent who is managing the organization with that the organization and its other constituents?

RULE 1.13 Organization as Client

(a) A lawyer employed or retained by an organization represents the organization acting through its duly authorized constituents.

(b) If a lawyer for an organization knows that an officer, employee or other person associated with the organization is engaged in action, intends to act or refuses to act in a matter related to the representation that is a violation of a legal obligation to the organization, or a violation of law which reasonably might be imputed to the organization, and is likely to result in substantial injury to the organization, the lawyer shall proceed as is reasonably necessary in the best interest of the organization. In determining how to proceed, the lawyer shall give due consideration to the seriousness of the violation and its consequences, the scope and nature of the lawyer's representation, the responsibility in the organization and the apparent motivation of the person involved, the policies of the organization concerning such matters and any other relevant considerations. Any measures taken shall be designed to minimize disruption of the organization and the risk of revealing information relating to the representation to persons outside the organization. Such measures may include among others:

(1) asking reconsideration of the matter;

(2) that a separate legal opinion on the matter be sought for presentation to appropriate authority in the organization; and

(3) referring the matter to higher authority in the organization, including, if warranted by the seriousness of the matter, referral to the highest authority that can act in on behalf of the organization as determined by applicable law.

(c) If, despite the lawyer's efforts in accordance with paragraph (b), the highest authority that can act on behalf of the organization insists upon action, or a refusal to act, that is early a violation of law and is likely to result in substantial injury to the organization, the lawyer may resign in accordance with rule 1.16.

(d) In dealing with an organization's directors, officers, employees, members, shareholders or other constituents, a lawyer shall explain the identity of the client when it is apparent that the organization's interests are adverse to those of the constituents with whom the lawyer is dealing.

(e) A lawyer representing an organization may also represent any of its directors, officers, employees, members, shareholders or other constituents, subject to the provisions of rule 1.7. If the organization's consent to the dual representation is required by rule 1.7, the consent shall be given by an appropriate official of the organization other than the individual who is be represented, or by the shareholders.

COMMENT:

The Entity as the Client

[1] An organizational client is a legal entity, but it cannot act except through its officers, directors, employees, shareholders and other constituents.

[2] Officers, directors, employees and shareholders are the constituents of the corporate organizational client. The duties defined in this Comment apply equally to unincorporated associations. "Other constituents" as used in this Comment means the positions equivalent to officers, directors, employees and shareholders held by persons acting for organizational clients that are not corporations.

*   *   *

[4] When constituents of the organization make decisions for it, the decisions ordinarily must be accepted by the lawyer even if their utility or prudence is doubtful. Decisions concerning policy and operations, including ones entailing serious risk, are not as such in the lawyer's province. However, different considerations arise when the lawyer knows that the organization may be substantially injured by action of [a] constituent that is in violation of law. In such a circumstance, it may be reasonably necessary for the lawyer to ask the constituent to reconsider the matter. If that fails, or if the matter is of sufficient seriousness and importance to the organization, it may be reasonably necessary for the lawyer to take steps to have the matter re-

viewed by a higher authority in the organization. Clear justification should exist for seeking review over the head of the constituent normally responsible for it. The stated policy of the organization may define circumstances and prescribe channels for such review, and a lawyer should encourage the formulation of such a policy. Even in the absence of organization policy, however, the lawyer may have an obligation to refer a matter to higher authority, depending on the seriousness of the matter and whether the constituent in question has apparent motives to act at variance with the organization's interest. Review by the chief executive officer or by the board of directors may be required when the matter is of importance commensurate with their authority. At some point it may be useful or essential to obtain an independent legal opinion.

*   *   *

[5] In an extreme case, it may be reasonably necessary for the lawyer to refer the matter to the organization's highest authority. Ordinarily, that is the board of directors or similar governing body. However, applicable law may prescribe that under certain conditions highest authority reposes elsewhere; for example, in the independent directors of a corporation.

*   *   *

Clarifying the Lawyer's Role

[8] There are times when the organization's interest may be or become adverse to those of one or more of its constituents. In such circumstances the lawyer should advise any constituent, whose interest the lawyer finds adverse to that of the organization of the conflict or potential conflict of interest, that the lawyer cannot represent such constituent, and that such person may wish to obtain independent representation. Care must be taken to assure that the individual understands that, when there is such adversity of interest, the lawyer for the organization cannot provide legal representation for that constituent individual, and that discussions between the lawyer for the organization and the individual may not be privileged.

5. The issue raised in the principal case bears directly on the role of the attorney in representing general and limited partnerships. Keep in mind that the attorney is often retained by a general partner on behalf of the partnership. Do the attorney's duties run to the general partner, the limited partnership itself, the limited partners, or some combination of the foregoing?

Arpadi v. First MSP Corp, 68 Ohio St.3d 453, 628 N.E.2d 1335 (Ohio 1994), involved a malpractice claim brought against a lawyer who had been hired to represent a limited partnership. The court described the problem as follows:

> The present action involves whether the duty owed by an attorney to exercise due care in the provision of legal services to a partnership extends to the limited partners as well. Appellees contend that to so hold would create an ethical dilemma for the attorney. In support thereof, appellees cite the Code of Professional Responsibility for the proposition that no duty is owed to limited partners by an attorney representing the partnership. In this regard, EC 5-18 provides:

"A lawyer employed or retained by a corporation or similar entity owes his allegiance to the entity and not to a stockholder, director, officer, employee, representative, or other person connected with the entity. In advising the entity, a lawyer should keep paramount its interests and his professional judgment should not be influenced by the personal desires of any person or organization. Occasionally, a lawyer for an entity is requested by a stockholder, director, officer, employee, representative, or other person connected with the entity to represent him in an individual capacity; in such case the lawyer may serve the individual only if the lawyer is convinced that differing interests are not present." (Emphasis added.)

The foregoing argument, however, misperceives the nature of the partnership form of enterprise and, consequently, the meaning of EC 5-18. The statutory and decisional law of this state has consistently adhered to the principle that a partnership is an aggregate of individuals and does not constitute a separate legal entity.

Further, a partnership not only does not constitute an entity similar to a corporation for purposes of EC 5-18, it also lacks the attributes of a separate legal entity in most other respects.

* * * In a partnership, the partners of which it is composed owe a fiduciary duty to each other. Consequently, in a limited partnership, the general partner owes a fiduciary duty to the limited partners of the enterprise. * * *

Therefore, whether the duty arising from an attorney-client relationship is owed to the limited partnership itself or to the general partner thereof, it must be viewed as extending to the limited partners as well. Inasmuch as a limited partnership is indistinguishable from the partners which compose it, the duty arising from the relationship between the attorney and the partnership extends as well to the limited partners. Where such duty arises from the relationship between the attorney and the general partner, the fiduciary relationship between the general partner and the limited partners provides the requisite element of privity.... Such privity, in turn, extends the duty owed to the general partner to the limited partners regarding matters of concern to the enterprise.

6. While the foregoing opinion held that an attorney owes duties to all partners in a limited partnership, not all courts would agree. In fact, even in the context of general partners, there are a number of cases which have concluded that the partnership's attorney owes no independent duty to partners. For example, consider *Zimmerman v. Dan Kamphausen,* No. 96CA0946, 66 USLW 1907, 1998 WL 69140 (Colo.App. Feb. 19, 1998), *as modified on denial of rehearing* (April 2, 1998). *Zimmerman* actually involved a general partnership. One of the two partners brought a claim against the partnership's law firm, and sought summary judgment on the issue of whether that attorney owed a specific duty to the partner as well as the partnership. The court analyzed this issue as follows:

Jurisdictions that have considered this issue are split as to whether one's status as an attorney for a partnership creates an attorney-client relationship with each of the partners. *Compare Hopper v. Frank,* 16

F.3d 92 (5th Cir. 1994) (finding no attorney-client relationship between a general partner and the attorney for the partnership because,
as a general rule, an attorney represents the entity not the individual
partners); *Quintel Corp. v. Citibank,* 589 F.Supp. 1235 (S.D.N.Y.
1984) (limited partner not client of partnership's attorney in absence of
affirmative assumption of such by attorney); *Mursau Corp. v. Florida
Penn Oil & Gas, Inc.,* 638 F.Supp. 259 (W.D.Pa. 1986) (buyer of limited partnership did not have attorney-client relationship with attorney
for seller so as to find attorney liable for opinion letter); *Security Bank
v. Klicker,* 142 Wis.2d 289, 418 N.W.2d 27 (Wis.Ct.App. 1987) (attorney-client relationship between general partners and partnership's attorney is a question of fact and not a matter of law); *with Pucci v.
Santi,* 711 F.Supp. 916 (N.D.Ill. 1989) (attorney for limited partnership had fiduciary duty to all partners); *Wortham & Van Liew v. Superior Court,* 188 Cal.App.3d 927, 233 Cal.Rptr. 725 (1987) (attorney
for partnership represents all partners as to matters of partnership
business); and *Arpadi v. First MSP Corp.,* 68 Ohio St.3d 453, 628
N.E.2d 1335 (Ohio 1994) (attorney for limited partnership owes duty
to all partners).

In Colorado, the fact that an attorney represents a partnership does
not, standing alone, create an attorney-client relationship with each of
the partners. *See Glover v. Southard,* 894 P.2d 21 (Colo.App. 1994) (declining to impose duty of care in favor of beneficiaries named in testamentary documents drafted by attorney); *Schmidt v. Frankewich,* 819
P.2d 1074 (Colo.App. 1991) (attorney for corporation not liable to
shareholders or guarantors in absence of fraud or malicious conduct); *In
re Estate of Brooks,* 42 Colo.App. 333, 596 P.2d 1220 (1979) (trustee's
attorney not liable to alleged beneficiary for breach of trust). *See also
Holmes v. Young, supra* (attorney representing partnership was not
thereby attorney for limited partner).

Here, there was no showing in the summary judgment submissions
of any indication by the law firm to Kamphausen that it was representing
both the partnership and Kamphausen at the time the partnership agreement was prepared. Indeed, the law firm's letter to him enclosing copies
of the partnership agreement for signature merely states his father's intent to avoid probate. And, according to Kamphausen, he heard nothing
further about the partnership until plaintiff asserted a right to proceed
against Kamphausen's assets pursuant to the guaranty.

Under these circumstances, we agree with the trial court that Kamphausen failed to demonstrate, as a matter of law, the existence of any
attorney-client relationship between himself and the firm or Levy.

3. Limited Liability Partnerships (LLP's)

Note on the LLP and LLLP Forms of Business

Perhaps the best way of looking at LLP's is to understand that an LLP is basically a general partnership, with a few important modifications, all of which

are spelled out in the applicable statutes. Because there is no model or uniform LLP Act, there is considerable variation in statutory language from state to state, although there are some areas of agreement.

The first step in becoming an LLP is for the partnership to file an application with an appropriate state official, registering as an LLP. This filing requirement seems quite consistent with the general statutory approach taken with regard to other business forms that offer owners protection from unlimited personal liability. One major difference between the filing for an LLP and the filing required for other limited liability entities is that in many states, in order to continue LLP status, a renewal application must be filed annually. In these states, if an LLP neglects to file its annual renewal, the liability protections offered to partners by LLP status terminate. Not all states, however, require an annual filing, and the consequences of a late renewal on debts incurred while a registration was in effect are not at all certain..

Certain basic information is required in both the original application and every renewal. Typically, the original application must include such information as the name of the partnership (which generally must include some indication that the partnership in question is in fact an LLP or is seeking status as an LLP), the address of the partnership's principal office and/or registered office and service agent, and a brief statement of the business in which the partnership engages.

In addition to these informational requirements, both types of documents must be accompanied by a fee. The amount of the required filing fee varies significantly from state to state. In some states, a flat fee is imposed. In other states, the fee is tied to the number of partners in the LLC. In a few states, the filing fee may be based on different considerations, but most statutes use either the flat fee or a fee based on the number of partners.

Filing appropriate documents and paying the required fee is not always enough to insure that a partnership will qualify as an LLP. In several states, achieving LLP status is also conditioned upon maintaining certain required levels of insurance or being able to demonstrate a minimum level of financial responsibility. The type and amount of insurance or the minimum capitalization requirement depends on the jurisdiction. Some states require as little as $100,000 in insurance; others require $1,000,000; still others have a variable requirement dependent on the number of partners in the LLP. It should be noted that in some of these states, this insurance is not required if the LLP in question maintains the required amount of funds in a segregated account specifically designated for the satisfaction of judgments against the partnership or its partners based on the kinds of liability which is limited under the statute in question. However, in some states, the insurance requirement is absolute, and may not be met simply by showing that the partnership has retained funds in a segregated account. On the other hand, not all states have an insurance or financial responsibility requirement. The statutes in these states more closely mirror the modern capitalization provisions governing corporations or LLC's. In other words, there is no minimum capital or specific amount of malpractice insurance required for LLP's in these states.

The benefit of achieving LLP status is that partners in an LLP are protected from certain sorts of liability, whereas partners in an ordinary general partnership are liable for all debts of the partnership. We say that partners in an LLP are protected from "certain sorts of liability" because the type of liability from which partners are insulated depends greatly on the jurisdiction in which the LLP is formed.

The Delaware LLP legislation adopts one of the two approaches, creating a level of protection for owners which is somewhere between the relatively complete protection offered to shareholders in the traditional corporation and the complete absence of such protection offered to general partners in a traditional partnership. In Delaware:

> [A] partner in a registered limited liability partnership is not liable, either directly or indirectly, by way of indemnification, contribution, assessment or otherwise, for debts, obligations and liabilities of or chargeable to the partnership arising from negligence, wrongful acts or misconduct, whether characterized as tort, contract or otherwise, committed while the partnership is a registered limited liability partnership and in the course of the partnership business by another partner or an employee, agent or representative of the partnership.

Del. Code Ann. tit. 6 § 1515(b) (1994 Supp.). Because this protection is less than absolute, this type of statute is commonly referred to as a partial-shield statute. Because most of the earlier statutes took this approach, the partial shield statutes are also sometimes referred to as first-generation statutes.

In essence, in jurisdictions that follow this model, a partner in an LLP is relieved of liability for the negligence, wrongful acts and misconduct of another partner and of employees, agents and representatives of the partnership. In other words, a partner in such an LLP would be liable only for his or her own conduct, and in some states, the conduct of those under his or her direct supervision and control. Although it was an issue in a few of the very earliest LLP statutes, the statutory language was quickly amended to make it clear that partners were not to be liable for the misconduct of others, even if the claim was somehow framed in terms of a contractual duty rather than a tort. However, the partial shield statutes do not apply to ordinary business debts of the partnership.

Although the early LLP statutes all used this approach, a growing number of states have taken a very different approach. The Minnesota and New York legislation illustrate this alternative approach. In these jurisdictions, partners in an LLP are insulated from personal liability for any partnership debt, regardless of whether the obligation was incurred as a result of wrongful conduct.

The Minnesota statute specifies that:

> [a] partner of a limited liability partnership is not, merely on account of this status, personally liable for anything chargeable to the partnership [under specified sections of the partnership act] ... or for any other debts or obligations of the limited liability partnership, if the charge, debt, or obligation arose or accrued while the partnership had a registration in effect.

Minn. Stat. Ann. § 323.14.2 (West 1995 Supp.). The language of the New York statute is similar in effect:

> [N]o partner of a partnership which is a registered limited liability partnership is liable or accountable, directly or indirectly ... for any debts, obligations or liabilities or, or chargeable to, the registered limited liabil-

ity partnership or each other, whether arising in tort, contract or otherwise, which are incurred, created or assumed by such partnership which such partnership is a registered limited liability partnership, solely by reason of being such a partner.

N.Y. Partnership Law art. 3 § 26(b) (1995 Supp.). These statutes basically provide partners in an LLP with the same type of limited liability that shareholders of a corporation enjoy. Indications are that several states with liability provisions like those found in the Delaware statute are considering amendments which would result in increased protection from personal liability for partners, more along the lines of the Minnesota and New York legislation.

One reason to believe that the "full-shield" or "second-generation" LLP statutes may become more prevalent is the fact that the RUPA was recently amended to include this kind of language. As amended in 1996, RUPA takes provides that "[a]n obligation of a [LLP]...whether arising in contract, tort or otherwise, is solely the obligation of the partnership." RUPA (1994) § 306.

LLLP's are very similar to LLP's. In fact, the only significant difference is that the new provisions relating to filing, insurance, and limited liability for general partners apply to limited partnerships rather than general partnerships. Obviously, the name of an LLLP would be slightly different from the name of an LLP as well.

With regard to the effect of electing LLLP status, a limited partner in a limited partnership is already insulated against personal liability for debts of the partnership (unless the limited partner participates excessively in the control of the partnership), but a limited partnership must also have at least one general partner. The advantage of being an LLLP is therefore that the general partner(s) of the limited partnership will be insulated from personal liability, either arising out of the misconduct of others or from any entity level debt, depending on the statutory language used. Other than that, an LLLP is much like an LLP, except that the basic structure is that of a limited partnership rather than a general partnership.

The only other fact worth emphasizing with regard to LLLP's is that far fewer states explicitly recognize the LLLP than the LLP.

For most purposes, then, an LLP is a general partnership in which the limited partners are provided some protection against personal liability. Because the LLP is so new, however, we are only beginning to see cases discussing the issue of whether the relationship between partners in an LLP is precisely the same as that which would have been created had they formed a traditional general partnership.

Liberty Mutual Ins. Co. v. Gardere & Wynne, L.L.P.

C.A. NO. 94-10609-MLW, 1994 U.S. Dist.
LEXIS 17928 (D.Mass. Dec. 6, 1994)

MEMORANDUM AND ORDER***

KAROL, U.S.M.J.

I. INTRODUCTION

The defendant law firm, Gardere & Wynne ("G&W"), is a Registered Limited Liability Partnership created under the laws of the State of Texas and with a principal place of business in Dallas Texas. Defendant John C. Nabors ("Nabors") is an attorney licensed to practice law in the State of Texas and is a litigation partner in G&W. Defendant Gregory N. Woods ("Woods") is also an attorney licensed to practice law in the State of Texas. He formerly worked under Nabors at G&W but left the firm approximately one month after being elected an income partner in the spring of 1993. Plaintiffs, Liberty Mutual Insurance Company and Liberty Mutual Fire Insurance Company (collectively, "Liberty Mutual"), are insurance companies licensed to do business in Massachusetts and with principal places of business in Boston, Massachusetts. Liberty Mutual is often called upon by its insureds to defend lawsuits brought against them throughout the United States. Occasionally, Liberty Mutual must also defend against lawsuits brought against it directly. G&W has long-represented and currently represents Liberty Mutual in many such lawsuits brought against it and its insureds, primarily, but not exclusively, in Texas. In this case Liberty Mutual seeks injunctive relief and money damages against G&W, Nabors, and Woods for alleged breaches of fiduciary duty and conflicts of interest arising out of activities regarding Texas lawsuits taken by Nabors and Woods on behalf of clients whose interests are adverse to those of Liberty Mutual. ***

G&W's motion seeks dismissal…pursuant to Fed. R. Civ. P. 17(b) on the ground that G&W, who is sued here in its common name, is not an entity capable of being sued [or in the alternative to transfer the case]. ***

II. FACTS

*** Liberty Mutual has an office and a substantial presence in Texas, where, as might be expected, it frequently becomes involved in litigation on behalf of itself or its insureds. For more than forty years, when that has occurred, it has regularly turned to G&W to represent it. As a result, it has, over that period, paid G&W millions of dollars in legal fees, and it is presently represented by G&W in more than ten cases in Texas and elsewhere. As also might be expected, G&W attorneys have, over the years, paid frequent visits to Liberty Mutual in Boston to discuss pending cases and, presumably, the prospect of future business.

Nabors and Woods are both attorneys licensed to practice in Texas, the state in which they also live and work. Neither ever personally represented Liberty Mutual, ever had any professional dealings with it (until Nabors was confronted regarding the alleged conflict that is the subject of this lawsuit), or, with very few exceptions, ever set foot in Massachusetts, on business or otherwise. Prior to February 1992, Nabors was a partner and Woods was an associate in the Texas law firm of Liddell, Sapp, Zivley, Hill & LaBoon ("L&S"). Nabors then left L&S to become a partner in G&W, and, a few weeks later, Woods joined him at G&W as an associate. That is when the trouble began.

Nabors' principal client was and is a company named TransAmerican Natural Gas Corporation ("TANG"). For a number of years, TANG, represented by Nabors and Woods, had been involved in bitter litigation in Texas with one of Liberty Mutual's insureds, and, eventually, with Liberty Mutual itself. TANG, again represented by Nabors and Woods, was also a plaintiff in another lawsuit in Texas that threatened and still threatens to involve Liberty Mutual as an adverse party. When Nabors and Woods moved from L&S to G&W, they took all this pending litigation with them. In March 1992, approximately one month after the move, Liberty Mutual met with Nabors in Texas and confronted him with the conflict between, on the one hand, his representation of TANG and, on the other, his new partnership status in a firm that had long been Liberty Mutual's regular litigation counsel in Texas. Nabors immediately conceded the existence of a conflict and agreed to a way of resolving it that appeared to satisfy Liberty Mutual. The resolution was that he would promptly cause Liberty Mutual to be severed from the pending litigation and then withdraw as counsel to TANG in the separate case against Liberty Mutual. This in fact is what he did. Liberty Mutual alleges in the present case, however, that he and Woods nevertheless violated their duty of utmost loyalty to Liberty Mutual by (1) failing to disclose certain actions detrimental to Liberty Mutual which they had undertaken in connection with the pending cases in the interim period between their February 1992 move to G&W and their withdrawal from the severed case and (2) continuing, even after their withdrawal, to take actions on behalf of TANG that were detrimental to Liberty Mutual in the pending cases. Liberty Mutual seeks damages from them and G&W for their alleged breach of fiduciary duty, as well as a preliminary and permanent injunction enjoining them, among other things, from continuing to represent or assist TANG in any of the pending cases.

Later developments concerning Woods' employment at G&W have an important bearing on the pending motions. On or about April 1, 1993, or about a year prior to the commencement of this lawsuit, the equity partners of G&W voted to make Woods an income partner. Income partners at G&W have considerably less stature than equity partners. They receive fixed annual salaries, with the possibility of discretionary, year-end bonuses; they are not entitled to a share of firm profits; they do not sit on firm committees; they receive none of the perquisites that equity partners do, such as parking or furniture allowances; and they have only limited voting rights.

Within approximately one month of his election to income partnership, Woods resigned from G&W to accept a partnership at another law firm. Because his tenure at G&W as an income partner was so brief. Woods never signed G&W's partnership agreement. Nor is there any evidence that he otherwise formally accepted the offer of income partnership that G&W had extended to him. Furthermore, as far as the record reveals, the firm never held him out as a partner, either to clients generally or to Liberty Mutual in particular. Specifically, the record does not reflect that G&W ever sent out or published a professional announcement regarding Woods' elevation or showed his name (or anyone else's) as a partner on its letterhead. In light of all these factors, it is unclear whether Woods ever in fact was an income partner of G&W, let alone a "partner" for purposes of analyzing the difficult issues of personal jurisdiction and substantive liability which this lawsuit presents.

Other facts having a bearing on the analysis will be considered below.

III. ANALYSIS

***[I]t is first necessary to consider the difficult and unsettled issues of Texas law raised by [G&Ws motion to dismiss for lack a capacity to be sued].... Fed. R. Civ. P. 17(b) provides, with some exceptions not here applicable, that the capacity of a partnership to be sued is to be determined by the law of the state in which the district court sits. Therefore, to determine whether G&W is capable of being sued in its common name, the court, at least in the first instance, must look to the law of Massachusetts.

It is undisputed that Massachusetts law does not permit suit to be brought against a general partnership in its common name. Rather, the claim must be asserted against each of the general partners individually, and each general partner must be personally served. See *Shapira v. Budish, 275 Mass. 120, 175 N.E. 159, 161 (Mass. 1931)* ("With certain exceptions not here material, all partners must be parties to a suit involving partnership rights."); *Gorovitz v. Planning Bd. of Nantucket, 394 Mass. 246, 475 N.E.2d 377, 380 (1985)* (same). It is also undisputed that Texas law does permit suit to be brought against a general partnership in its common name. *See* Tex. R. Civ. P. 28 ("Any partnership...may sue or be sued in its partnership, assumed or common name for the purpose of enforcing for or against it a substantive right."). Therefore, in the absence of any complicating factor, Liberty Mutual's present suit against G&W in its common name would be subject to outright dismissal (without prejudice), and, presumably, the court could take into account in determining the motion to transfer the relative ease of suing a partnership in Texas. [4]

There is, however, a substantial complicating factor. G&W is not a general partnership, at least not in the traditional sense familiar to Massachusetts judges and lawyers. Rather, it is a Texas Registered Limited Liability Partnership ("RLLP"), pursuant to Tex. Rev. Civ. Stat. Ann. art. 6132b-3.08 (West 1994). Section 3.08, which has no counterpart in Massachusetts law, now provides in pertinent part as follows:

(a) Liability of Partners.

(1) A partner in a registered limited liability partnership is not individually liable for debts and obligations of the partnership arising from errors, omissions, negligence, incompetence, or malfeasance committed while the partnership is a registered limited liability partnership and in the course of the partnership business by another partner or a representative of the partnership not working under the supervision or direction of the first partner unless the first partner:

---

4. If the case were transferred to Texas, G&W might still argue, citing Van Dusen v. Barrack, that the case must still be dismissed, because the law of the transferor state would continue to govern with respect to the issue of capacity. *Van Dusen, 376 U.S. at 639, 84 S. Ct. at 821* ("The transferee district court must be obligated to apply the state law that would have been applied if there had been no change of venue."). It is not at all clear, however, that Van Dusen would require that result where the issue of capacity is not, as it was in Van Dusen itself, outcome determinative. Id. at n.40 ("We are only concerned here with those state laws of the transferor State which would significantly affect the outcome of the case."). In any event, G&W has made it quite clear that it is not now seeking transfer in order to raise this issue in a different venue. See Mem. in Support of Defs.' Mot. to Dismiss This Action as Against Gardere & Wynne L.L.P., or in the Alternative to Transfer Venue to Texas at 4 (stating that the issue of G&W's capacity to be sued would be "voided upon transfer of this matter to a more appropriate venue"). The instant order regarding transfer could be (and is) conditioned on G&W's express agreement to waive such argument.

(A) was directly involved in the specific activity in which the errors, omissions, negligence, incompetence or malfeasance were committed by the other partner or representative; or

(B) had notice or knowledge of the errors, omissions, negligence, incompetence, or malfeasance by the other partner or representative at the time of occurrence and then failed to take reasonable steps to prevent or cure the errors, omissions, negligence, incompetence, or malfeasance.

(2) Subsection (a)(1) does not affect:

(A) the joint and several liability of a partner for debts and obligations of the partnership arising from a cause other than the causes specified by Subsection (a)(1);

(B) the liability of a partnership to pay its debts and obligations out of partnership property; or

(C) the manner in which service of citation or other civil process may be served in an action against a partnership.

Thus, an RLLP is something of a hybrid. As is the case regarding a general partnership, all general partners of an RLLP are personally liable for general partnership debts and obligations such as lease obligations, as well as those resulting from errors, omissions, negligence, incompetence, or malfeasance as to which they had contemporaneous notice or knowledge and which they failed to take reasonable steps to prevent. On the other hand, however, an RLLP resembles a limited partnership, in that non-culpable partners generally are not personally liable for debts and obligations resulting from the mistakes of their partners, although the assets of the partnership appear to be available to satisfy debts arising from such mistakes.

The question of whether G&W is a limited partnership for purposes of Massachusetts law has potential procedural and substantive significance. Procedurally, a plaintiff may bring suit against a Massachusetts limited partnership by naming as defendants only its general partners. See, e.g., *Halleran v. Hoffman, 966 F.2d 45, 47 (1st Cir. 1992); Milton Commons Ass'n v. Board of Appeals of Milton, 14 Mass. App. Ct. 111, 436 N.E.2d 1236, 1236 n.l (Mass. App. Ct. 1982).* By analogy, if G&W is deemed to be a limited partnership, it might be possible to bring suit against it by naming only those partners who are personally liable for the type of claims that Liberty Mutual seeks to assert. If that is the case, Liberty Mutual might be able to bring this action in Massachusetts by naming as defendants only those G&W partners who would be liable for the breach of fiduciary duty that is the subject of its complaint. If not, Liberty Mutual must reinstitute this lawsuit, naming and serving each partner individually. This analysis, in turn, raises the substantive question whether a claim for breach of fiduciary duty is a claim of the type enumerated (i.e. one "arising from errors, omissions, negligence, incompetence, or malfeasance"), and, if it is, whether, "at the time of the occurrence," some or all of G&W's partners "had notice or knowledge of the errors, omissions, negligence, incompetence, or malfeasance" and "failed to take reasonable steps to prevent or cure" such acts.

A predecessor statute governing RLLP's, Tex. Rev. Civ. Stat. Ann. art. 6132(b), § 15, did not expressly excuse non-offending partners who had taken such "reasonable steps." In fact, the predecessor statute was entirely silent on the matter of "reasonable steps."

After the occurrence of the facts giving rise to this case, namely on January 1, 1994, the current statute took effect, providing that liability would not attach to partners who did have notice or knowledge, but who had taken "reasonable steps."

According to historical notes accompanying it, the new statute merely "clarifies" the older statute. Nonetheless, it is at least arguable whether the new language in the current statute applies to this case.

To the extent these questions arise in the context of G&W's motion to dismiss under Fed. R. Civ. P. 17(b), they all become moot if the case is transferred to Texas.[6] That is because Texas law permits G&W to be sued in its common name without regard to the type of partnership it is. Thus, if the case is transferred to Texas, it not only becomes unnecessary for this federal court sitting in Massachusetts to decide these difficult and unsettled issues of Texas law, but it becomes unnecessary, in the context of a motion to dismiss, for any court to do so. That does not necessarily mean that these issues will never have to be decided; if Nabors' or Woods' liability is ultimately established, it may well become necessary at some point for the court hearing the case to reach the substantive question of which of Nabors' partners may be vicariously liable for his or Woods' wrongdoing. But even in that case, it is preferable for the issue to be decided by a federal court in Texas, which is much more likely than a federal court in Massachusetts to be familiar with Texas law regarding the circumstances under which partners in RLLP's may be vicariously liable for the acts of other partners. See *Troyer*, 488 F. Supp. at 1207 ("A final factor which tips the balance decidedly in favor of transfer is that [plaintiffs'] causes of action...will apparently be governed by Ohio law. Resolution of the complex issues surrounding these claims is best reserved for courts familiar with Ohio substantive law.").[7]

[The Court ultimately concludes that so many difficult questions of Texas law would be presented by the cross-motions to dismiss, that, in the interest of justice, the case should be transferred to the Northern District of Texas.]* * *

Notes

Please review the following provisions from selected LLP statutes: The Texas LLP Act; Minnesota Statutes Ann. §§ 323.14 & .44; Calif. Corp. Code §§ 15002(g)

---

6. As discussed in note 4, *supra,* this assumes either that the capacity of G&W to be sued, not being outcome determinative, will be determined in accordance with the law of the transferee state, or that G&W will waive any argument to the contrary

7. The court assumes that, if this case were tried in a state or federal court in Massachusetts, the court would look to Texas substantive law to determine the liability of partners in a Texas RLLP for debts arising out of claims for breach of fiduciary duty by other partners. See Mass. Gen. L. ch. 109. § 48 (liability of limited partners of a foreign limited partnership "shall be governed by the laws of the state under which it is organized"); *Klaxon v. Stentor Elec. Mfg. Co., 313 U.S. 487, 496, 61 S. Ct. 1020, 1021-22, 85 L. Ed. 1477 (1941)* (federal court in diversity case applies choice of law principles of state in which federal court is located). Thus, Texas law will apply to this question whether or not the case is transferred, and this is not at all inconsistent with the holding of Van Dusen that the transferee forum must apply the same substantive law that the transferor forum would have applied if the case had not been transferred. *Van Dusen, 376 U.S. at 821-23.*

& (I), 15006, 15015, 15049, 15052 & 15-53. In addition, review section 306(c), and 1001 to 1003 of RUPA. (All of these provisions are included in the statutory supplement.)

1. Currently, all LLP statutes provide, either explicitly or implicitly, that a partner will continue to be liable for his or her own acts. There is, however, considerable variation in the language used to explain when a partner will be liable for the acts of others.

As originally written, the Texas statute dealt with this issue by specifying that the shield against personal liability for partners in an LLP prevents a partner from being liable the misconduct of others, so long as they are "not working under the supervision or direction of the first partner." The statute contains the caveat that first partner will be liable if that partner:

(A) was directly involved in the specific activity in which the errors, omissions, negligence, incompetence, or malfeasance were committed by the other partner or representative; or

(B) had notice or knowledge of the errors, omissions, negligence, incompetence, or malfeasance by the other partner or representative at the time of occurrence and then failed to take reasonable steps to prevent or cure the errors, omissions, negligence, incompetence, or malfeasance.

Texas LLP Act § 3.08(a).

In 1997, the statute was revised to extend the limited-liability shield to *almost* all obligations of the partnership. Although the current language is inartfully drafted, arguably the statute continues vicarious partner liability for the torts under the circumstances described above. *Id.* at §§ 3.08(a)(1) & 3.08(a)(2).

2. In most states with LLP statutes, the current statutory language provides that a partner will continue to liable for the misconduct of those under the partner's "direct supervision and control." *See, e.g.,* Ariz. Rev. Stat. Ann. § 29-215 (1995); Conn. Gen. Stat. § 34-53 (1995); Del. Code Ann. tit. 6 § 1515 (1994); Fla. Stat. ch. 620.782 (1996); Idaho Code § 53-315 (1995); Ill. Ann. Stat. ch. 805 para. 15 (Smith-Hurd 1995); Iowa Code § 486.15 (1995); Kan. Stat. Ann. § 56-315 (1994); Mich. Comp. Laws § 449.46 (1995); Mo. Rev. Stat. § 38.150 (1996); Nev. Rev. Stat. § 87.150.2 (1996); N.J. Rev. Stat. § 42:1-15 (1995); N.M. Stat. Ann. § 54-1-15 (1995); N.Y. Partnership Law art. 3 § 26 (1995); Ohio Rev. Code Ann. § 1775.14 (1995); 15 Pa. Cons. Stat. § 8204 (1995); S.C. Code Ann. § 33-41-370 (Law. Co-op. Supp. 1994); S.D. Codified Laws § 48-2-15 (1995); Tenn. Code Ann. § 61-1-114 (1996); Va. Code Ann. § 50-15 (1995); Wash. Rev. Code § 25.04.730 (1996).

Some of these states also impose additional requirements in order for the "direct supervision and control" language to apply. For example, the Kansas statute provides that the limitation of liability in an LLP does not extend to liability for misconduct of another if the partner was exercising "direct supervision and control at the time the negligence, malpractice, wrongful acts and omissions or misconduct occurred." Similarly, the Virginia statute requires that the "direct supervision and control" be in "the specific activity in which the negligence, malpractice, wrongful acts or misconduct occurred." The New York LLP Act provides that liability will exist if a partner was exercising "direct supervision and control while rendering professional services...."

One might ask whether this language is any different in effect from the language used in the Texas statute. The answer to this will depend on judicial interpretation of the statutory language.

3. A third group of state statutes omit any reference to potential liability for the acts of others. See Cal. Corp. Code § 151015 (1996); Colo. Rev. Stat. § 7-60-115 (1996); Ga. Code Ann. § 14-18-15 (1995); Ind. Code § 23-4-1-15 (1996); Ky. Rev. Stat. Ann. § 362.220 (Baldwin 1995); Ind. Code § 23-4-1-15 (1996); La. Rev. Stat. Ann. § 3431 (1995); Minn. Stat. § 323.14 (1995) (as amended by 1995 Minn. Sess. Law Serv. ch. 58 (S.F. 1042) (West); Utah Code Ann. § 48-1-12 (1995). See also RUPA (1994) § 306(c).

It would, however, be incorrect to assume that a partner in an LLP formed under any of these statutes will never have liability for the misconduct of others. Even in an LLP, partners retain liability for their own misconduct, and that should include negligent hiring or supervision of others. In addition, courts in a state where the statute is silent on the issue of liability for the misconduct of others, even those under the first partner's direct supervision and control, might be more likely to find an affirmative duty to monitor the behavior of other partners. Obviously, if such a duty is found to exist, breach of that duty could support an action for personal liability. For a detailed discussion of the issue of a partner's obligation to monitor the conduct of others, see Susan Saab Fortney, *Am I My Partner's Keeper? Peer Review in Law Firms*, 66 U. Colo. L. Rev. 329 (1995).

4. Let's take a more concrete example. Suppose you are a partner in a law firm organized as an LLP in Texas. A partner who happens to work in your area of expertise, and in the very next office, commits malpractice by failing to comply with the statute of limitations for filing an action.

a. Are you liable for your partner's acts on these facts?

b. Would it make any difference if you had also represented the same client on a related matter?

c. Would it make any difference if you were the billing attorney (i.e., you prepare and send out bills for the firm) for that client?

d. What if you are a senior partner, and the partner who committed malpractice is one of a number of junior partners whose work you are supposed to review when it is bonus time?

e. What if you are the chair of the litigation department?

f. What if you are on the firm's executive committee?

g. What if you are the firm's managing partner?

Unfortunately, the answers to these questions are quite uncertain. Until the courts interpret the relevant statutory language, we simply do not know the precise limits of the shield against personal liability in state LLP statutes.

4. Limited Liability Companies

The limited liability company (LLC) is a form of business entity which exists solely because of the adoption of statutes recognizing its existence. As described briefly in the introductory section of this chapter, it is a business form which blends the most desirable attributes of partnerships and corporations. Like a partnership formed under the applicable state statutes, it is extremely flexible and can avoid taxation at the entity level. As with a corporation, the owners are provided with limited liability for debts created by the entity. Unlike the limited partnership, which also combines certain partnership and corporate attributes, there is no requirement that at least one owner be subjected to unlimited personal liability, or prohibition on at least some members participating in control. Unlike the S corporation, another hybrid of partnership and corporations, there are no limitations on who can invest in an LLC and it is possible to achieve tax recognition of special allocations.

One point regarding terminology is worth making here. The federal tax code does not have a separate regime for LLC's. A business that involves as association of two or more persons engaged in a profit making venture will generally have to be an association taxable as a corporation or a tax partnership. Domestic LLC's are presumed to be tax partnerships, unless a specific election to be taxed as a corporation is made. Thus, we have the somewhat confusing system where for business purposes, the business is called an "LLC," but it is a tax "partnership."

Of course, tax considerations are not the only driving force behind the LLC. Aside from the benefits of avoiding double taxation while providing limited liability for investors, the biggest attraction of the LLC as a form of entity is the extreme flexibility offered by most state statutes. For example, state LLC statutes do not mandate any particular management structure. This stands in rather stark contrast to the detailed statutory requirements dealing with shareholders' and directors' authority in the corporate setting. The LLC is not prohibited from adopting an organizational structure which delegates management authority to others, who might then serve much as directors do in American corporations, but this is certainly not required by existing LLC statutes.

In some respects, it is hard to talk about LLC's in generalities, because there was no model or uniform LLC Act on which states could model their statute and there is considerable variation in the state statutes. In fact, on any given issue there are a number of possible approaches which have been taken.

Further complicating any general discussion of LLC's is the fact that most state statutes are themselves drafted for maximum flexibility. This means that even in a given state, there will probably be an almost infinite variety of forms which an LLC can take. In most states, there are statutory "default" rules which apply if the parties forming the LLC do not make an alternative arrangement, but alternatives to the default rules are also possible.

There are, of course, some basic characteristics or features common to all or most LLC's. All LLC's are formed upon the filing of an organizational document, most often called articles of organization. The owners, rather than being called shareholders or partners, are referred to as members. In the majority of jurisdictions, there must be at least two members in order to operate an LLC. The internal affairs of the LLC are managed in accordance with either the statutory default rules or with an operating agreement or internal regulations the provisions of which are agreed to by the members. Owners can contribute cash or property, and usually services to the LLC, in return for their membership interests. Absent agreement to the contrary, the owners have no personal liability for debts incurred by the LLC. Virtually all other attributes of LLC's vary depending on either the statute under which they are organized, or the agreement between the members.

Elf Atochem North America, Inc. v. Jaffari
727 A.2d 286 (Del. 1999)

Before **VEASEY**, Chief Justice, **WALSH** and **BERGER**, Justices.

VEASEY, Chief Justice:

This is a case of first impression before this Court involving the Delaware Limited Liability Company Act (the "Act"). The limited liability company ("LLC") is a relatively new entity that has emerged in recent years as an attractive vehicle to facilitate business relationships and transactions. The wording and architecture of the Act is somewhat complicated, but it is designed to achieve what is seemingly a simple concept—to permit persons or entities ("members") to join together in an environment of private ordering to form and operate the enterprise under an LLC agreement with tax benefits akin to a partnership and limited liability akin to the corporate form.

This is a purported derivative suit brought on behalf of a Delaware LLC calling into question whether: (1) the LLC, which did not itself execute the LLC agreement in this case ("the Agreement") defining its governance and operation, is nevertheless bound by the Agreement; and (2) contractual provisions directing that all disputes be resolved exclusively by arbitration or court proceedings in California are valid under the Act. Resolution of these issues requires us to examine the applicability and scope of certain provisions of the Act in light of the Agreement.

*   *   *

Facts

Plaintiff below-appellant Elf Atochem North America, Inc., a Pennsylvania Corporation ("Elf"), manufactures and distributes solvent-based maskants to the aerospace and aviation industries throughout the world. Defendant below-appellee Cyrus A. Jaffari is the president of Malek, Inc., a California Corporation. Jaffari had developed an innovative, environmentally-friendly alternative to the solvent-based maskants that presently dominate the market.

For decades, the aerospace and aviation industries have used solvent-based maskants in the chemical milling process.[3] Recently, however, the Environmental Protection Agency ("EPA") classified solvent-based maskants as hazardous chemicals and air contaminants. To avoid conflict with EPA regulations, Elf considered developing or distributing a maskant less harmful to the environment.

In the mid-nineties, Elf approached Jaffari and proposed investing in his product and assisting in its marketing. Jaffari found the proposal attractive since his company, Malek, Inc., possessed limited resources and little international

---

3. Manufactures of airplanes and missiles use maskants in the process of chemical milling in order to reduce the weight of their products. Chemical milling is a process where a caustic substance is placed on metal parts in order to dissolve the metal with which it comes into contact. Maskants are used to protect those areas of metal intended to be preserved.

sales expertise. Elf and Jaffari agreed to undertake a joint venture that was to be carried out using a limited liability company as the vehicle.

On October 29, 1996, Malek, Inc. caused to be filed a Certificate of Formation with the Delaware Secretary of State, thus forming Malek LLC, a Delaware limited liability company under the Act. The certificate of formation is a relatively brief and formal document that is the first statutory step in creating the LLC as a separate legal entity. The certificate does not contain a comprehensive agreement among the parties, and the statute contemplates that the certificate of formation is to be complemented by the terms of the Agreement.[5]

Next, Elf, Jaffari and Malek, Inc. entered into a series of agreements providing for the governance and operation of the joint venture. Of particular importance to this litigation, Elf, Malek, Inc., and Jaffari entered into the Agreement, a comprehensive and integrated document[6] of 38 single-spaced pages setting forth detailed provisions for the governance of Malek LLC, which is not itself a signatory to the Agreement. Elf and Malek LLC entered into an Exclusive Distributorship Agreement in which Elf would be the exclusive, worldwide distributor for Malek LLC. The Agreement provides that Jaffari will be the manager of Malek LLC. Jaffari and Malek LLC entered into an employment agreement providing for Jaffari's employment as chief executive officer of Malek LLC.

The Agreement is the operative document for purposes of this Opinion, however. Under the Agreement, Elf contributed $1 million in exchange for a 30 percent interest in Malek LLC. Malek, Inc. contributed its rights to the water-based maskant in exchange for a 70 percent interest in Malek LLC. The Agreement contains an arbitration clause covering all disputes. The clause, Section 13.8, provides that "any controversy or dispute arising out of this Agreement, the interpretation of any of the provisions hereof, or the action or inaction of any Member or Manager hereunder shall be submitted to arbitration in San Francisco, California...." Section 13.8 further provides: "No action...based upon any claim arising out of or related to this Agreement shall be instituted in any court by any Member except (a) an action to compel arbitration...or (b) an action to enforce an award obtained in an arbitration proceeding...." The Agreement also contains a forum selection clause, Section 13.7, providing that all members consent to: "exclusive jurisdiction of the state and federal courts sitting in California in any action on a claim arising out of, under or in connection with this Agreement or the transactions contemplated by this Agreement, provided such claim is not required to be arbitrated pursuant to Section 13.8"; and personal jurisdiction in California. The Distribution Agreement contains no forum selection or arbitration clause.

---

5. *See* 6 *Del. C.* § 18-201(d), which provides:

A limited liability company agreement may be entered into either before, after or at the time of the filing of a certificate of formation and, whether entered into before, after or at the time of such filing, may be made effective as of the formation of the limited liability company or at such other time or date as provided in the limited liability company agreement.

6. *See* the definition section of the statute, 6 *Del. C.* § 18-101(7), defining the term "limited liability company agreement" as "any agreement...of the...members as to the affairs of a limited liability company and the conduct of its business," and setting forth a nonexclusive list of what it may provide.

Elf's Suit in the Court of Chancery

On April 27, 1998, Elf sued Jaffari and Malek LLC, individually and derivatively on behalf of Malek LLC, in the Delaware Court of Chancery, seeking equitable remedies. Among other claims, Elf alleged that Jaffari breached his fiduciary duty to Malek LLC, pushed Malek LLC to the brink of insolvency by withdrawing funds for personal use, interfered with business opportunities, failed to make disclosures to Elf, and threatened to make poor quality maskant and to violate environmental regulations. Elf also alleged breach of contract, tortious interference with prospective business relations, and (solely as to Jaffari) fraud.

The Court of Chancery granted defendants' motion to dismiss based on lack of subject matter jurisdiction. The court held that Elf's claims arose under the Agreement, or the transactions contemplated by the agreement, and were directly related to Jaffari's actions as manager of Malek LLC. Therefore, the court found that the Agreement governed the question of jurisdiction and that only a court of law or arbitrator in California is empowered to decide these claims. Elf now appeals the order of the Court of Chancery dismissing the complaint.

Contentions of the Parties

Elf claims that the Court of Chancery erred in holding that the arbitration and forum selection clauses in the Agreement governed, and thus deprived that court of jurisdiction to adjudicate all of Elf's claims, including its derivative claims made on behalf of Malek LLC. Elf contends that, since Malek LLC is not a party to the Agreement, it is not bound by the forum selection provisions. Elf also argues that the court erred in failing to classify its claim as derivative on behalf of Malek LLC against Jaffari as manager. Therefore, Elf claims that the Court of Chancery should have adjudicated the dispute. Finally, Elf argues that the dispute resolution clauses of the Agreement are invalid under Section 109(d) of the Act, which, it alleges, prohibits the parties from vesting exclusive jurisdiction in a forum outside of Delaware.[10]

Defendants claim that Elf contracted with Malek, Inc. and Jaffari that all disputes that arise out of, under, or in connection with the Agreement must be resolved exclusively in California by arbitration or court proceedings. Defendants allege that the characterization of Elf's claim as direct or derivative is irrelevant, as the Agreement provides that the members would not institute "any" action at law or equity except one to compel arbitration, and that any such action must be brought in California. Defendants also argue that, in reality, Elf's claims are direct, not derivative, claims against its fellow LLC members, Malek, Inc. and Jaffari.

With regard to the validity of Section 13.7, defendants argue that Section 18-109(d) of the Act is a permissive statute and does not prohibit the parties from vesting exclusive jurisdiction outside of Delaware. Thus, defendants assert that

---

10. *See* 6 *Del. C.* § 18-109(d), which provides:
   In a written limited liability company agreement or other writing, a manager or member *may* consent to be subject to the nonexclusive jurisdiction of the courts of, or arbitration in, a specified jurisdiction, or the exclusive jurisdiction of the courts of the State of Delaware, or the exclusivity of arbitration in a specified jurisdiction or the State of Delaware....
(Emphasis added.)

the Court of Chancery correctly held that the dispute resolution provisions of the Agreement are valid and apply to bar Elf from seeking relief in Delaware.

General Summary of Background of the Act

The phenomenon of business arrangements using "alternative entities" has been developing rapidly over the past several years. Long gone are the days when business planners were confined to corporate or partnership structures.

Limited partnerships date back to the 19th Century. They became an important and popular vehicle with the adoption of the Uniform Limited Partnership Act in 1916. Sixty years later, in 1976, the National Conference of Commissioners on Uniform State Laws approved and recommended to the states a Revised Uniform Limited Partnership Act ("RULPA"), many provisions of which were modeled after the innovative 1973 Delaware Limited Partnership (LP) Act. Difficulties with the workability of the 1976 RULPA prompted the Commissioners to amend RULPA in 1985.

To date, 48 states and the District of Columbia have adopted the RULPA in either its 1976 or 1985 form. Delaware adopted the RULPA with innovations designed to improve upon the Commissioners' product. Since 1983, the General Assembly has amended the LP Act eleven times, with a view to continuing Delaware's status as an innovative leader in the field of limited partnerships.

The Delaware Act was adopted in October 1992. The Act is codified in Chapter 18 of Title 6 of the Delaware Code. To date, the Act has been amended six times with a view to modernization. The LLC is an attractive form of business entity because it combines corporate-type limited liability with partnership-type flexibility and tax advantages.[14] The Act can be characterized as a "flexible statute" because it generally permits members to engage in private ordering with substantial freedom of contract to govern their relationship, provided they do not contravene any mandatory provisions of the Act. Indeed, the LLC has been characterized as the "best of both worlds." The Delaware Act has been modeled on the popular Delaware LP Act. In fact, its architecture and much of its wording is almost identical to that of the Delaware LP Act. Under the Act, a member of an LLC is treated much like a limited partner under the LP Act. The policy of freedom of contract underlies both the Act and the LP Act.

In August 1994, nearly two years after the enactment of the Delaware LLC Act, the Uniform Law Commissioners promulgated the Uniform Limited Liability Company Act (ULLCA).[21] To coordinate with later developments in federal tax guidelines regarding manager-managed LLC's, the Commissioners adopted minor changes in 1995. The Commissioners further amended the ULLCA in

---

14. See 1 Larry E. Ribstein & Robert R. Keatinge, Ribstein and Keatinge on Limited Liability Companies, § 2.02, at 2 (1998); Martin I. Lubaroff & Paul M. Altman, Delaware Limited Liability Companies, in Delaware Law of Corporations & Business Organizations, §20.1 (R. Franklin Balotti & Jesse A. Finkelstein eds., 1998).

21. Jennifer J. Johnson, *Limited Liability for Lawyers: General Partners Need Not Apply*, 51 Bus. Law. 85, n. 69 (1995). In addition to the ULLCA, a Prototype Limited Liability Company Act ("Prototype Act") was drafted by the Subcommittee on Limited Liability Companies of the ABA Section of Business Law. The Prototype Act was released in the Fall of 1993 and has formed the basis for several LLC statutes enacted since that time. *See Id.*

1996. Despite its purpose to promote uniformity and consistency, the ULLCA has not been widely popular. In fact, only seven jurisdictions have adopted the ULLCA since its creation in 1994.[23] A notable commentator on LLC's has argued that legislatures should look to either the Delaware Act or the Prototype Act created by the ABA when drafting state statutes.[24]

Policy of the Delaware Act

The basic approach of the Delaware Act is to provide members with broad discretion in drafting the Agreement and to furnish default provisions when the members' agreement is silent. The Act is replete with fundamental provisions made subject to modification in the Agreement (e.g. "unless otherwise provided in a limited liability company agreement. . . .").[26]

Although business planners may find comfort in working with the Act in structuring transactions and relationships, it is a somewhat awkward document for this Court to construe and apply in this case. To understand the overall structure and thrust of the Act, one must wade through provisions that are prolix, sometimes oddly organized, and do not always flow evenly. Be that as it may as a problem in mastering the Act as a whole, one returns to the narrow and discrete issues presented in this case.

Freedom of Contract

Section 18-1101(b) of the Act, like the essentially identical Section 17-1101(c) of the LP Act, provides that "[i]t is the policy of [the Act] to give the maximum effect to the principle of freedom of contract and to the enforceability of limited liability company agreements." Accordingly, the following observation relating to limited partnerships applies as well to limited liability companies:

> The Act's basic approach is to permit partners to have the broadest possible discretion in drafting their partnership agreements and to furnish answers only in situations where the partners have not expressly made provisions in their partnership agreement. Truly, the partnership agreement is the cornerstone of a Delaware limited partnership, and effectively constitutes the entire agreement among the partners with respect to the admission of partners to, and the creation, operation and termination of, the limited partnership. Once partners exercise their contractual freedom in their

---

23. To date, the seven jurisdictions that have adopted the ULLCA are Alabama, South Dakota, the U.S. Virgin Islands, Hawaii, South Carolina, Vermont, and West Virginia. *See* Uniform Limited Liability Company Act (1995), Table of Jurisdictions Wherein Act Has Been Adopted and additional information provided by the Uniform Law Commissioners (Mar. 17, 1999).

24. *See* Larry E. Ribstein, *A Critique of the Uniform Limited Liability Company Act*, 25 Stetson L. Rev. 311, 329 (1995).

26. *See, e.g.*, 6 Del. C. §§ 18-107, 18-204(b), 18-209(b), 18-301(d), 18-302(d), 18-304(a) & (b), 18-402, 18-403, 18-404(d), 18-502(a) & (b), 18-503, 18-504, 18-605, 18-606, 18-702(a), (b) & (d), 18-704(b), 18-801(a)(4) & (b), 18-803(a), and 18-804(a)(2) & (3). For example, members are free to contract among themselves concerning management of the LLC, including who is to manage the LLC, the establishment of classes of members, voting, procedures for holding meetings of members, or considering matters without a meeting. *See* Lubaroff & Altman, *supra* note 14, at § 20.4.

partnership agreement, the partners have a great deal of certainty that their partnership agreement will be enforced in accordance with its terms.[27]

In general, the commentators observe that only where the agreement is inconsistent with mandatory statutory provisions will the members' agreement be invalidated. Such statutory provisions are likely to be those intended to protect third parties, not necessarily the contracting members. As a framework for decision, we apply that principle to the issues before us, without expressing any views more broadly.

The Arbitration and Forum Selection Clauses in the Agreement are a Bar to Jurisdiction in the Court of Chancery

In vesting the Court of Chancery with jurisdiction, the Act accomplished at least three purposes:

(1) it assured that the Court of Chancery has jurisdiction it might not otherwise have because it is a court of limited jurisdiction that requires traditional equitable relief or specific legislation to act;

(2) it established the Court of Chancery as the default forum in the event the members did not provide another choice of forum or dispute resolution mechanism; and

(3) it tends to center interpretive litigation in Delaware courts with the expectation of uniformity.

Nevertheless, the arbitration provision of the Agreement in this case fosters the Delaware policy favoring alternate dispute resolution mechanisms, including arbitration. Such mechanisms are an important goal of Delaware legislation, court rules, and jurisprudence.

Malek LLC's Failure to Sign the Agreement Does Not Affect the Members' Agreement Governing Dispute Resolution

Elf argues that because Malek LLC, on whose behalf Elf allegedly brings these claims, is not a party to the Agreement, the derivative claims it brought on behalf of Malek LLC are not governed by the arbitration and forum selection clauses of the Agreement.

Elf argues that Malek LLC came into existence on October 29, 1996, when the parties filed its Certificate of Formation with the Delaware Secretary of State. The parties did not sign the Agreement until November 4, 1996. Elf contends that Malek LLC existed as an LLC as of October 29, 1996, but never agreed to the Agreement because it did not sign it. Because Malek LLC never expressly assented to the arbitration and forum selection clauses within the Agreement, Elf argues it can sue derivatively on behalf of Malek LLC pursuant to 6 Del. C. § 18-1001.[35]

---

27. Martin I. Lubaroff & Paul Altman, *Delaware Limited Partnerships* § 1.2 (1999) (footnote omitted). In their article on Delaware limited liability companies, Lubaroff and Altman use virtually identical language in describing the basic approach of the LLC Act. Clearly, both the LP Act and the LLC Act are uniform in their commitment to "maximum flexibility." *See* Lubaroff & Altman, *supra* note 14, at § 20.4.

35. 6 Del. C. § 18-1001 provides: "Right to bring action. A member may…bring an action in the Court of Chancery in the right of a limited liability company to recover a judgment in its favor if managers or members with authority to do so have refused to bring the

We are not persuaded by this argument. Section 18-101(7) defines the limited liability company agreement as "any agreement, written or oral, *of the member or members* as to the affairs of a limited liability company and the conduct of its business."[36] Here, Malek, Inc. and Elf, the members of Malek LLC, executed the Agreement to carry out the affairs and business of Malek LLC and to provide for arbitration and forum selection.

Notwithstanding Malek LLC's failure to sign the Agreement, Elf's claims are subject to the arbitration and forum selection clauses of the Agreement. The Act is a statute designed to permit members maximum flexibility in entering into an agreement to govern their relationship. It is the members who are the real parties in interest. The LLC is simply their joint business vehicle. This is the contemplation of the statute in prescribing the outlines of a limited liability company agreement.

Classification by Elf of its Claims as Derivative is Irrelevant

Elf argues that the Court of Chancery erred in failing to classify its claims against Malek LLC as derivative. Elf contends that, had the court properly characterized its claims as derivative instead of direct, the arbitration and forum selection clauses would not have applied to bar adjudication in Delaware.

In the corporate context, "the derivative form of action permits an individual shareholder to bring 'suit to enforce a corporate cause of action against officers, directors and third parties.'"[39] The derivative suit is a corporate concept grafted onto the limited liability company form. The Act expressly allows for a derivative suit, providing that "a member...may bring an action in the Court of Chancery in the right of a limited liability company to recover a judgment in its favor if managers or members with authority to do so have refused to bring the action or if an effort to cause those managers or members to bring the action is not likely to succeed."[41] Notwithstanding the Agreement to the contrary, Elf argues that Section 18-1001 permits the assertion of derivative claims of Malek LLC against Malek LLC's manager, Jaffari.

Although Elf correctly points out that Delaware law allows for derivative suits against management of an LLC, Elf contracted away its right to bring such an action in Delaware and agreed instead to dispute resolution in California. That is, Section 13.8 of the Agreement specifically provides that the parties (*i.e.*, Elf) agree to institute "[n]o action at law or in equity based upon *any* claim arising out of or related to this Agreement" except an action to compel arbitration or to enforce an arbitration award.[42] Furthermore, under Section 13.7 of the

---

action or if an effort to cause those managers or members to bring the action is not likely to succeed."

36. 6 Del. C. § 18-101(7) (emphasis added).

39. *Kamen v. Kemper Fin. Serv.*, 500 U.S. 90, 95 (1991) (citation omitted). *See also Schleiff v. Baltimore & Ohio R.R. Co.*, Del. Ch., 130 A.2d 321, 327 (1955) (in derivative action, shareholder "stands in the shoes" of the corporation).

41. 6 Del. C. § 18-1001.

42. Agreement, § 13.8 (emphasis added). In its entirety, § 13.8 provides:
Disputed Matters.
Except as otherwise provided in this Agreement, any controversy or dispute arising out of this Agreement, the interpretation of any of the provisions hereof, or the action or inaction of any Member or Manager hereunder shall be submitted to arbitration in San Francisco, California before the American Arbitration Association under the commercial arbitration rules then obtaining of said Association. Any

Agreement, each member (*i.e.*, Elf) "consent[ed] to the exclusive jurisdiction of the state and federal courts sitting in California in *any* action on a claim arising out of, under or in connection with this Agreement or the transactions contemplated by this Agreement."[43] Sections 13.7 and 13.8 of the Agreement do not distinguish between direct and derivative claims. They simply state that the members may not initiate *any* claims outside of California. Elf initiated this action in the Court of Chancery in contravention of its own contractual agreement. As a result, the Court of Chancery correctly held that all claims, whether derivative or direct, arose under, out of or in connection with the Agreement, and thus are covered by the arbitration and forum selection clauses.

This prohibition is so broad that it is dispositive of Elf's claims (counts IV, V and VI of the amended complaint) that purport to be under the Distributorship Agreement that has no choice of forum provision. Notwithstanding the fact that the Distributorship Agreement is a separate document, in reality these counts are all subsumed under the rubric of the Agreement's forum selection clause for any claim "arising out of" and those that are "in connection with" the Agreement or transactions "contemplated by" or "related to" that Agreement under Sections 13.7 and 13.8. We agree with the Court of Chancery's decision that:

> plaintiff's claims arise under the LLC Agreement or the transactions contemplated by the Agreement, and are directly related to Jaffari's "action or inaction" in connection with his role as the manager of Malek. Plainly, all of plaintiff's claims revolve around Jaffari's conduct (or misconduct) as Malek's manager. Virtually all the remedies that plaintiff seeks bear directly on Jaffari's duties and obligations under the LLC Agreement. Plaintiff's complaint that "Jaffari...has totally disregarded his obligations under the *LLC Agreement* also lends support to my conclusion.[44]

The Court of Chancery was correct in holding that Elf's claims bear directly on Jaffari's duties and obligations under the Agreement. Thus, we decline to disturb its holding.

---

award or decision obtained from any such arbitration proceeding shall be final and binding on the parties, and judgment upon any award thus obtained may be entered in any court having jurisdiction thereof. No action at law or in equity based upon any claim arising out of or related to this Agreement shall be instituted in any court by any Member except (a) an action to compel arbitration pursuant to this Section 13.8 or (b) an action to enforce an award obtained in an arbitration proceeding in accordance with this Section 13.8.
Agreement, § 13.8.

43. Agreement, § 13.7 (emphasis added). In its entirety, § 13.7 provides:
Jurisdiction.
Each Member hereby consents to the exclusive jurisdiction of the state and federal courts sitting in California in any action on a claim arising out of, under or in connection with this Agreement or the transactions contemplated by this Agreement, provided such claim is not required to be arbitrated pursuant to Section 13.8. Each member further agrees that personal jurisdiction over him or her may be effected by service of process, and that when so made shall be as if served upon him or her personally within the State of California.
Agreement, § 13.7.

44. *Elf Atochem*, C.A. No. 16320, Letter Op. at 7 (emphasis in original).

The Argument that Chancery Has "Special" Jurisdiction for Derivative Claims Must Fail

Elf claims that 6 Del. C. §§ 18-110(a), 18-111 and 18-1001 vest the Court of Chancery with subject matter jurisdiction over this dispute. * * * In effect, Elf argues that the Act affords the Court of Chancery "special" jurisdiction to adjudicate its claims, notwithstanding a clear contractual agreement to the contrary.

Again, we are not persuaded by Elf's argument. * * *

* * *

Our conclusion is bolstered by the fact that Delaware recognizes a strong public policy in favor of arbitration. Normally, doubts on the issue of whether a particular issue is arbitrable will be resolved in favor of arbitration. In the case at bar, we do not believe there is any doubt of the parties' intention to agree to arbitrate *all* disputed matters in California. If we were to hold otherwise, arbitration clauses in existing LLC agreements could be rendered meaningless. By resorting to the alleged "special" jurisdiction of the Court of Chancery, future plaintiffs could avoid their own arbitration agreements simply by couching their claims as derivative. Such a result could adversely affect many arbitration agreements already in existence in Delaware.

Validity of Section 13.7 of the Agreement under 6 Del. C. § 18-109(d)

* * *

* * * ... Elf contends that Section 18-109(d)[A] prohibits vesting exclusive jurisdiction in a court outside of Delaware, which the parties have done in Section 13.7.

We decline to adopt such a strict reading of the statute. * * *

Conclusion

We affirm the judgment of the Court of Chancery dismissing Elf Atochem's amended complaint for lack of subject matter jurisdiction.

Notes

1. By holding that the LLC in the principal case was bound by an agreement it did not sign, what view of the LLC did the Delaware Supreme Court adopt? Is the statutory governance structure of the Delaware LLC Act mandatory or enabling?

2. Section 103(a) of the ULLCA provides

Except as otherwise provided in subsection (b), all the members of a limited liability company may enter into an operating agreement...to

---

A. [by editors] Section 18-109(d) provides:
  In a written limited liability company agreement or other writing, a manager or member *may* consent to be subject to the nonexclusive jurisdiction of the courts of, or arbitration in, a specified jurisdiction, or the exclusive jurisdiction of the courts of the State of Delaware, or the exclusivity of arbitration in a specified jurisdiction or the State of Delaware....
6 Del. C. § 18-109(d) (emphasis added).

regulate the affairs of the company and the conduct of its business, and to govern relations among the members, managers and company. To the extent the operating agreement does not otherwise provide, this [Act] governs relations among the members, managers and company.

ULLCA § 103(a). If the principal case had been decided under the ULLCA, would the result have been the same?

Chapter 2

Contractual Dealings by Agents

A. Firm's Liability in Contract for Acts of Its Agents

Problem 2.1

Equipment owner Kapperman was negotiating the possible sale of his broken road grader to Schladweiler for about $8500. Kapperman authorized Schladweiler only to obtain three bids to have the engine repair work done (so that Kapperman could then decide whether the repair was affordable). Instead, Schladweiler represented to Truck Repair that he had authority from Kapperman to obtain the repair on behalf of Kapperman, as long as the cost of the repair did not exceed $3500. Schladweiler did not get any other bids and ordered the work done by Truck Repair. Truck Repair did the work for $6400, released the road grader to Schladweiler, but has not been paid. Schladweiler is insolvent. Who is liable for the repair bill?

Kasselder v. Kapperman
316 N.W.2d 628 (S.D. 1982)

DUNN, Justice.

This is an appeal from an order and judgment entered in favor of appellees Alice and Gene Kasselder, doing business as A & G Diesel Truck Repair (Truck Repair), for repairs performed on a Galion road grader owned by appellee Jerome Kapperman (Kapperman).

Kapperman owns a Galion road grader that had a defective engine. Appellant James Schladweiler (Schladweiler) offered to purchase the grader for the sum of $8,500, if the grader was in running condition. Kapperman said he would pay up to $3,000 to have the engine repaired and Schladweiler said he could have it repaired for less than that sum at Truck Repair in Mitchell, South Dakota. Kapperman shipped the grader from Minnesota to Schladweiler's residence in Mitchell.

At the request of Schladweiler, Truck Repair's mechanics took the engine apart and discovered that it was not repairable. They suggested to Schladweiler that a new engine be purchased for $7,000. Schladweiler informed Kapperman of this information and Kapperman said he was not interested in spending that much money. Kapperman tried to locate a used engine that could be rebuilt, but was unsuccessful. The mechanics located a used engine in Omaha, Nebraska, and told Schladweiler the cost of repairs would be $1,000 to purchase the engine, $1,300 for labor, and the cost of oil and gaskets. Schladweiler informed Kapperman of this estimate and Kapperman approved the purchase of the engine but specified that he would not pay more than $3,000 in repair costs.

A short time later, the mechanics contacted their supplier in Sioux Falls, South Dakota and were informed that the supplier had repaired a similar engine for $5,000, which did not include repairing the cylinder head. The Omaha engine had a cracked cylinder head. Truck Repair relayed this estimate to Schladweiler. Schladweiler authorized the repairs, but did not inform Kapperman of this increased bid. The repairs to the engine took several months and Schladweiler periodically followed the progress of the repairs. At no time did Truck Repair discuss the cost of repairs with Kapperman. When the repairs were finally completed, the total cost was $6,441.06. Neither Kapperman nor Schladweiler would pay the bill.

The trial court found for Truck Repair and entered an order and judgment against Schladweiler in the amount of $3,441.06 plus interest and against Kapperman in the amount of $3,000 plus interest.

Schladweiler's only contention is that the evidence presented at trial was insufficient to support the trial court's finding that he was liable for $3,441.06, plus interest, of the Truck Repair bill. He alleges that his agency relationship with Kapperman should have precluded his liability.

An agency relationship is defined by SDCL 59-1-1 as "the representation of one called the principal by another called the agent in dealing with third persons." An agency relationship is either actual or ostensible. It is actual when the principal appoints the agent. It is ostensible when the principal by conduct or want of ordinary care causes a third person to believe another, who is not actually appointed, to be his agent.

To determine whether an agency relationship has in fact been created, we examine the relations of the parties as they exist under their agreement or acts. Agency

> is a legal concept which depends upon the existence of required factual elements: The manifestation by the principal that the agent shall act for him, the agent's acceptance of the undertaking, and the understanding of the parties that the principal is to be in control of the undertaking.

Watkins Co. v. Dutt, 84 S.D. 453, 457, 173 N.W.2d 41, 43 (1969).

The evidence indicates that this was not an ostensible agency. Kapperman made no representations or actions to cause Truck Repair to believe that was his agent. In fact, Kapperman did not deal with Truck Repair u Schladweiler ntil after he received the final bill from them. The only proof introduced at trial supporting an agency relationship in excess of $3,000 was the words and actions of Schladweiler. Ostensible agency for which a principal may be held liable must be traceable to the principal and cannot be established solely by the acts, declarations or conduct of an agent.

The evidence indicates that an actual agency relationship did exist between Kapperman and Schladweiler but only to the extent of $3,000. Kapperman allowed Schladweiler to act for him regarding repair of the grader but specified that he would not pay more than $3,000 for repair costs. Schladweiler agreed to represent Kapperman in the transaction with Truck Repair. However, Schladweiler exceeded the scope of his agency authority when he authorized repairs exceeding the scope of his agency authority when he authorized repairs exceeding $3,000 and failed to consult with Kapperman regarding the increased expenditures. Under SDCL 59-6-2,

> [w]hen an agent exceeds his authority, his principal is bound by his authorized acts so far only as they can be plainly separated from those which are unauthorized.

We hold that the trial court was correct in its determination that Schladweiler was liable for $3,441.06, plus interest, of the Truck Repair bill, because this sum represented the portion of the bill resulting from his unauthorized acts as agent.

We affirm the judgment and order of the trial court.

Notes

1. "Authority" is the agent's power to bind the principal "by acts done in accordance with the principal's manifestations of consent" to the agent. Restatement § 7. A principal is bound by the authorized acts of his or her agent in entering into contracts on the principal's behalf. Restatement §§ 140, 144, & 159. Under certain circumstances agents may have *power* to bind the principal by *unauthorized* acts, such as where the agent has *apparent authority* or *inherent agency power*, or where the principal is *estopped* from denying the agent's authority. Restatement §§ 8, 8A, & 8B. Chapter 3 discusses at greater length the creation and interpretation of authority, as well as an agent's power to bind the principal by unauthorized acts.

2. Where an agent enters into an unauthorized contract without having the power to bind the principal, the principal is not bound by the contract as actually made by the agent, or as it would have been made if the agent had acted within his or her authority. Restatement § 164(1). As indicated in *Kasselder v. Kapperman*:

> Where the only difference between the contract as authorized and the contract as made is a difference as to amount, or the inclusion or exclusion of a separable part, the principal is liable upon the contract as it was authorized to be made, provided that the other party seasonably manifests his willingness to accept the contract as authorized.

Restatement § 164(2).

3. At common law, a principal is *not* bound by the authorized contracts of his or her agent where the contract is under seal or is a *negotiable instrument*. Restatement §§ 151 & 152. Section 3-401 and Official Comment 1 of the *1990 Official Text* of the Uniform Commercial Code change this rule and hold the principal liable on negotiable instruments signed by an authorized agent, regardless of whether the principal's name appears on the instrument.

4. A principal must have the capacity to give a legal consent, as well as capacity to do the act that he or she is authorizing the agent to do. An infant, for instance, can employ an agent with authority to make fully enforceable contracts for necessities, but the contracts of the agent for other types of subject matter would be voidable at the election of the infant. *See* Restatement § 20.

5. Of course, business entities such as corporations, partnerships, ad limited liability companies can be principals. Indeed, because these entities must act

through human beings, the entities are the principals and their human representatives serve as their agents, servants, and independent contractors.

6. To be an agent, a person needs only the physical or mental capability to do the thing he or she has been appointed to do. Hence, almost anyone can serve as an agent. Even an infant or a mentally incompetent person might well have the capacity to bind a principal to a contract (or to cause tort liability for a master where they act as servants). *See* Restatement § 21.

B. Firm's Rights Under Contracts Entered Into by Its Agents

Third persons dealing with an agent may not know they are dealing with an agent. Where the third person has no notice that the agent is acting for a principal, the principal is said to be *"undisclosed."* Restatement § 4(3). Even where third persons know they are dealing with an agent, they may not have notice of the identity of the principal. In that situation the principal is said to be *"partially disclosed."* Restatement § 4(2). Where the third person has notice *both* that the agent is acting for a principal *and* of the principal's identity, the principal is said to *"disclosed."* Restatement § 4(1). To complicate matters further, even where the principal is disclosed in the sense that the third person has notice of the agency and of the principal's identity, the *written agreement* between the agent and third party may not fully disclose the principal.

To what extent does the degree of disclosure of the principal affect the principal's ability to enforce a contract entered into by the agent on the principal's behalf?

The Woodlawn Park Ltd. Partnership v. Doster Constr. Co., Inc.
623 So.2d 645 (La. 1993)

LEMMON, Justice

Plaintiff, the present owner of a shopping center, filed this action to recover damages related to alleged construction defects. Defendants are the contractor who constructed the shopping center and the testing engineers who tested the soil conditions. The primary issue presently before the court is whether an undisclosed principal has a right of action (a real and actual interest to bring the action) against the party who contracted with the undisclosed principal's agent.

Facts

James Maurin, Roger Ogden and Gerald Songy were in the business of developing shopping centers. Under the procedure used by these individuals, Maurin on April 28, 1981 signed an option to purchase the land on which the pertinent shopping center was to be developed, executing the option on behalf of a named partnership to be formed upon completion of the feasibility study. On May 7, 1982, the three individual partners and Maurin, as managing partner of the partnership, exercised the option to purchase the property.

During the development phase, the engineers prepared a proposal for engineering services for "Maurin & Ogden, Developers". On June 22, 1982, the director of construction of Maurin-Ogden, Inc. accepted the proposal.[2] On August 24, 1982, the partners formally executed the articles of partnership.[3] On November 11, 1982, the partnership purchased the property. In 1984 the partners first noticed the damage allegedly attributable to defendants' failures. Plaintiff then filed the instant action.

The engineers filed an exception of prescription in which they incidentally objected to Woodlawn Park's bringing the action because the partnership was not formally in existence on the date the engineers contracted with Maurin-Ogden, Inc. Plaintiff then amended the petition to allege that Maurin-Ogden, Inc. had acted as agents for the individuals, Maurin, Ogden and Songy, as well as for the partnership then contemplated and ultimately formed.

The engineers filed an exception of no right of action, which was maintained by the trial judge who granted plaintiff a specified period within which to amend the pleading to remove the objection.

Plaintiff again amended the petition to add Maurin, Ogden, Songy, and Maurin-Ogden, Inc. as plaintiffs. The engineers then filed motions to dismiss and exceptions of no right of action directed against all plaintiffs except Maurin-Ogden, Inc. The trial court maintained the exception and dismissed the action by the original plaintiff.

The court of appeal affirmed, reiterating its holding in *Teachers' Retirement System of La. v. Louisiana State Employees Retirement System,* 444 So.2d 193 (La.App. 1st Cir. 1983), *rev'd on other grounds,* 456 So.2d 594 (La. 1984), that an undisclosed principal has no right of action to bring suit in its own name against the party who contracted with the principal's agent. The court applied French law which distinguishes between mandate, in which the contracting party represents himself as acting for another, and commission or prête-nom, in which the contracting party makes no representation about acting for another. In the former situation, the court noted, the principal is liable to the other contracting party, but in the latter situation there is no liability on the principal, the prête-nom being the only party who can sue or be sued under the contract.

No Right of Action

An action may be brought only by a person having a real and actual interest which he asserts. The objection of no right of action is a peremptory exception which challenges the interest of the plaintiff in bringing the action.[5] The excep-

---

2. Maurin-Ogden, Inc. was the corporation used by the three individuals to perform the feasibility study and other preliminary work. The engineers rendered the soil testing report to Maurin-Ogden, Inc.

3. The name of the partnership was subsequently changed to Woodlawn Park Limited Partnership, which filed the present action.

5. It is important to distinguish between the exceptions of no right of action and lack of procedural capacity. The latter exception challenges the right of a party to proceed (although the party may be asserting a real and actual interest) because of some procedural incapacity such as minority.

tion focuses on the plaintiff before the court as a means of insuring that the cause of action against the defendant is brought by the party who has the actual interest in the claim which is asserted. One purpose of the exception of no right of action is to prevent the defendant from having to defend an action and possibly pay a claim which actually belongs to a party other than the plaintiff, thereby subjecting the defendant to the possibility of multiple lawsuits and multiple payments involving the same claim. By asserting the exception of no right of action, the defendant can insure that the party asserting the claim, rather than some other party, has the real and actual interest to do so.

Right of Action of Undisclosed Principal

At common law an agent has the power to make business contracts on behalf of the principal. This power derives from a relationship founded on consensual authority or apparent consensual authority and status, and the power may be exercised on behalf of an undisclosed principal. Athanassios N. Yiannopoulos, *Brokerage, Mandate, and Agency in Louisiana: Civilian Tradition and Modern Practice,* 19 La.L.Rev. 777 (1959). A person who contracts with the agent of an undisclosed principal, when the agent intended to contract on behalf of the principal within his power to bind the principal, is generally liable to the principal.[7] *Restatement (Second) of Agency* § 302 (1958).

In most jurisdictions a party who has contracted with the agent of an undisclosed principal has the right to sue the principal directly, once his identity is revealed. The converse is also true. An undisclosed principal, upon the revealing of his identity, has the right to bring suit to enforce the contract directly against the party who contracted with his agent.

Defendants urge this court not to follow the common law of agency, but to affirm the court of appeal by applying the French doctrine which holds that the agent for an undisclosed principal is a prête-nom and that only the agent may sue the third party for breach of contract. Citing Fred W. Jones, *Juridical Basis of Principal—Third Party Liability in Louisiana Undisclosed Agency Cases,* 8 La.L.Rev. 409 (1948), defendants argue that the question of the principal's right to sue or be sued by the third party is determined under French law according to whether the agent disclosed the agency relationship to the third party. Since the agency relationship was not disclosed in the present case, the court of appeal applied the doctrine of prête-nom and ruled that the undisclosed principal could not sue or be sued by the contracting third party.

La.Civ.Code art. 2985 defines mandate (as well as procuration or letter of attorney) as an act by which one person gives power to another to transact affairs for him and in his name. Under the literal terms of Article 2985 a mandatary always acts in a representative capacity and is therefore different from a common law agent, who may act for an undisclosed principal.[8] The Civil Code has never fully developed the concept of agency and representation with respect to the di-

---

7. The person is not liable to the principal when the contract is in the form of a sealed or negotiable instrument, when the contract excludes liability to an undisclosed principal or to the particular principal, or when the agent induces the contract by representing that he is not acting for a principal. *Restatement (Second) of Agency* §§ 303-04 (1958).

8. However, see *Sentell v. Richardson,* 211 La. 288, 29 So.2d 852 (1947) (the words "and in his name" are not essential to the definition of a procuration or power of attorney).

rect acquisition of rights and liabilities through the contractual action of a properly authorized intermediary who may or may not disclose his representative capacity. Yiannopoulos, *supra,* at 781 and 795. However, Louisiana courts, perhaps recognizing that agency as a field of commercial law should be uniform throughout the country, have adopted notions of common law agency. *Id.* at 790 and 795; *See also Ballister v. Hamilton,* 3 La.Ann. 401 (1848) (party who contracts with agent for undisclosed principal may recover balance due from principal upon discovery of his identity); *Williams v. Winchester,* 7 Mart. (N.S.) 22 (La. 1828) (when goods are sold to an agent of an unknown principal, the latter will be liable when discovered although the seller made no inquiry about representation); *Teche Concrete, Inc. v. Moity,* 168 So.2d 347, 353 (La.App. 3d Cir. 1964), *cert. denied,* 247 La. 251, 170 So.2d 509 (1965) (undisclosed principal liable individually for acts of corporation that acted as her prête-nom); Fred W. Jones, *supra* at 414.

We restate approval of the use of common law agency notions in commercial transactions. In matters of commercial law, Louisiana has frequently taken steps to make our law uniform with other states. Moreover, La.Civ.Code art. 3021 provides that a principal in Louisiana is bound by the authorized or ratified acts of his attorney in fact. There appears to be no valid reason for declining to apply this rule in commercial transactions when the principal is not disclosed. The issue simply becomes one of proof of the fact and the extent of the authority. Since the agent entered into the contract for the benefit of the undisclosed principal, there is no injustice in holding the principal liable under the contract. Nor is there any prejudice to the third party (absent special circumstances such as inducing consent to the contract by specific misrepresentation regarding the principal) in allowing the principal to enforce the contract, especially since the third party would be liable to the agent. But for Article 681, both the agent and the undisclosed principal could sue in separate actions. But when, as here, both the agent and the undisclosed principal are in the same action based on the same claim, the danger of multiple lawsuits and multiple payments (a danger which the exception of no right of action was designed to prevent) has been avoided.

Accordingly, the judgments of the lower courts are set aside, the exception of no right of action is overruled and referred to the merits, and the case is remanded to the district court for further proceedings.

Notes

1. Civil law jurisdictions often distinguish between "mandate" (agency) and "prête-nom" (literally, name-lending). What is the difference between these two concepts?

2. Restatement section 302 provides:

A person who makes a contract with an agent of an undisclosed principal, intended by the agent to be on account of his principal and within the power of such to bind his principal, is liable to the principal as if the principal himself had made the contract with him, unless he is excluded by the form or terms of the contract, unless his existence is fraudulently concealed or unless there is a set-off or similar defense against the agent.

As discussed in *The Woodlawn Park Limited Partnership v. Doster Construction Co., Inc.,* the civil-law's treatment of the undisclosed principal differs from that of the Restatement. Under the doctrine of *prête-nom,* undisclosed principals are not parties to contracts entered into by their *prête-noms.* Only the *prête-nom* may sue or be sued on such contracts; the principals may not sue or be sued in their own names. *See,* 2 MARCEL PLANIOL & GEORGE RIPERT, TREATISE ON THE CIVIL LAW, pt. 2, ¶2271 (Louisiana State Law Institute trans. 1959).

3. What risks are involved in the common law rule that undisclosed principals are parties to such contracts, and may sue or be sued on them? How can those risks be reduced?

4. Suppose that during negotiations, an agent fully discloses the principal's existence and identity. The agent then enters into a *written* contract in the agent's *own* name. The face of the contract does not disclose either the principal's identity or the fact that the agent is acting as an agent. May the principal enforce the contract in the principal's own name? The general answer is that the principal may do so, and may introduce parole evidence to prove the right to do so. Restatement § 190 & comment a. Even if the contract provides that it may not be assigned, the principal may nevertheless be able to enforce it. *See* Restatement section 303 comment c (an anti-assignment clause is not conclusive, but rather is only *evidence* of an intent to exclude an undisclosed principal). For example, in *Comind, Companhia de Seguros v. Sikorsky Aircraft Division of United Technologies Corp.,* 116 F.R.D. 397 (D. Conn. 1987), an undisclosed principal was allowed to enforce a written contract even though the contract *not only* failed to name the principal as a party, *not only* failed to expressly grant the principal any rights, *but also* contained a clause that the contract could not be assigned.

5. If you were representing a party to a written contract, how would you draft the contract to prevent it from being enforced by an undisclosed principal?

Problem 2.2

Acton was in business in Chicago as a retail dealer in costume jewelry. In addition, he frequently served as a purchasing agent for retailers of similar goods. In December, Pace, a retailer for whom Acton had occasionally acted in the past, wrote Acton authorizing him to purchase on Pace's behalf a specified quantity of costume jewelry from Tabb, a wholesaler. Pace added that because of certain transactions in the past, Tabb might refuse to deal with him and directed Acton not to disclose the buyer's identity. Acton, who occasionally dealt with Tabb on his own account, was indebted to Tabb for $3500 for various items purchased on credit earlier in the year under contracts that were reasonable and provident when made. Acton immediately contacted Tabb and arranged with him for the purchase of the costume jewelry. A written contract was entered into, delivery to be made February 1 at Acton's place of business, payment to be made ten days thereafter. Acton signed the contract in his own name, having made no mention of Pace, and Tabb assumed that Acton was the buyer. On February 1, Tabb failed to deliver under the contract, notifying Acton that he had learned for whom Acton was acting and that he would not fill the order. Informed of this, Pace promptly purchased similar costume jewelry in the open market. Pace suffered damages of $3500 with respect to the costume jewelry. Pace demanded that Tabb pay him $3500 damages. Tabb repeated his refusal to be bound by the contract, pointing out that had Tabb known the identity of Acton's principal, he would not have entered into the contract. Tabb also claimed that even if he were liable, he would be entitled to set off the $3500 owed him by Acton. What are Pace's rights, if any, against Tabb? Give reasons (Illinois Bar Examination, Feb. 1980).

Kelly Asphalt Block Co. v. Barber Asphalt Paving Co.
211 N.Y. 68, 105 N.E. 88 (1914)

CARDOZO, J.

The plaintiff sues to recover damages for breach of an implied warranty. The contract was made between the defendant and one Booth. The plaintiff says that Booth was in truth its agent, and it sues as undisclosed principal. The question is whether it has the right to do so.

The general rule is not disputed. A contract not under seal, made in the name of an agent as ostensible principal, may be sued on by the real principal at the latter's election. The defendant says that we should establish an exception to that rule, where the identity of the principal has been concealed because of the belief that, if it were disclosed, the contract would not be made. We are asked to say that the reality of the defendant's consent is thereby destroyed, and the contract vitiated for mistake.

The plaintiff and the defendant were competitors in business. The plaintiff's president suspected that the defendant might refuse to name him a price. The suspicion was not based upon any previous refusal, for there had been none; it had no other origin than their relation as competitors. Because of this doubt the plaintiff availed itself of the services of Booth, who, though interested to the defendant's knowledge of the plaintiff's business, was also engaged in a like business for another corporation. Booth asked the defendant for a price and received a quotation, and the asphalt blocks required for the plaintiff's pavement were ordered in his name. The order was accepted by the defendant, the blocks were delivered, and payment was made by Booth with money furnished by the plaintiff. The paving blocks were unmerchantable, and the defendant, retaining the price, contests its liability for damages on the ground that if it had known that the plaintiff was the principal it would have refused to make the sale.

We are satisfied that upon the facts before us the defense cannot prevail. A contract involves a meeting of the minds of the contracting parties. If 'one of the supposed parties is wanting,' there is an absence of 'one of the formal constituents of a legal transaction.' *Rodliff v. Dallinger,* 141 Mass. 1, 6, 4 N.E. 805, 807 (55 Am. Rep. 439). In such a situation there is no contract. A number of cases are reported where A has ordered merchandise of B, and C has surreptitiously filled the order. The question has been much discussed whether C, having thrust himself without consent into the position of a creditor, is entitled to recover the value of his wares. That question is not before us, and we express no opinion concerning it. We state it merely to accentuate the distinction between the cases which involve it and the case at hand. Neither of the supposed parties was wanting in this case. The apparent meeting of the minds between determinate contracting parties was not unreal or illusory. The defendant was contracting with the precise person with whom it intended to contract. It was contracting with Booth. It gained whatever benefit it may have contemplated from his character and substance. An agent who contracts in his own name for an undisclosed principal does not cease to be a party because of his agency. Indeed, such an agent, having made himself personally liable, may enforce the contract though the principal has renounced it. As between himself and the other party, he is liable as principal to the same extent as if he had not been acting for another. It is impossible in such circumstances to hold that the contract collapses for want of parties to sustain it. The contractual tie cannot exist where there are not persons to be bound; but here persons were bound, and those the very persons intended. If Booth had given the order in his own right and for his own benefit, but with the expectation of later assigning it to the plaintiff, that undisclosed expectation would not have nullified the contract. His undisclosed intention to act for a principal who was unknown to the defendant was equally ineffective to destroy the contract in its inception.

If therefore the contract did not fail for want of parties to sustain it, the unsuspected existence of an undisclosed principal can supply no ground for the avoidance of a contract unless fraud is proved. We must distinguish between mistake, such as we have been discussing, which renders the contract void *ab initio,* because the contractual tie has never been completely formed, and fraud which renders it voidable at the election of the defrauded party. *Rodliff v. Dallinger,* 141 Mass. 1, 6, 4 N.E. 805, 807 (55 Am. Rep. 439). In the language of Holmes, J., in the case cited:

> Fraud only becomes important, as such, when a sale or contract is complete in its formal elements, and therefore valid unless repudiated, but the right is claimed to rescind it.

If one who is in reality an agent denies his agency when questioned, and falsely asserts that his principal has no interest in the transaction, the contract, it may be said, becomes voidable, not because there is a want of parties, but because it has been fraudulently procured. When such a case arises, we shall have to consider whether a misrepresentation of that kind is always so material as to justify rescission after the contract has been executed. But no such situation is disclosed in the case at hand. Booth made no misrepresentation to the defendant. He was not asked anything, nor did he say anything, about the plaintiff's interest in the transaction. Indeed, neither he nor the plaintiff's officers knew whether the defendant would refuse to deal with the plaintiff directly. They suspected hostility, but none had been expressed. The validity of the contract turns thus, according to the defendant, not on any overt act of either the plaintiff or its agent, but on the presence or absence of a mental state. We are asked to hold that a contract complete in form becomes a nullity in fact because of a secret belief in the mind of the undisclosed principal that the disclosure of his name would be prejudicial to the completion of the bargain. We cannot go so far.

It is unnecessary, therefore, to consider whether, even if fraud were shown, the defendant, after the contract was executed, could be permitted to rescind without restoring the difference between the price received for the defective blocks and their reasonable value. It is also unnecessary to analyze the evidence for the purpose of showing that the defendant, after notice of the plaintiff's interest in the transaction, continued to make delivery, and thereby waived the objection that the contract was invalid.

The judgment should be affirmed, with costs.

Notes

1. Restatement section 302 provides that

[a] person who makes a contract with an agent of an undisclosed principal, intended by the agent to be on account of the undisclosed principal and within the power of such agent to bind his principal, is liable to the principal as if the principal himself had made the contract with him, unless he is excluded by the form or terms of the contract, unless his existence is fraudulently concealed or unless there is set-off or a similar defense against the agent.

Under Restatement section 304,

[a] person with whom an agent contracts on account of an undisclosed principal can rescind the contract if he was induced to enter into it by a representation that the agent was not acting for a principal and if, as the agent or principal has notice, he would not have dealt with the principal.

In *Kelly Asphalt Block Co. v. Barber Asphalt Paving Co.*, the Court reasons that neither the principal nor the agent *knew* that the third person would not deal with the principal. Did either the principal or the agent have *notice* of the third person's reluctance (under Restatement section 9(1), a person has *notice* of a fact if the person knows it, has reason to know it, should know it, has been given a notification of it)?

2. Would the court in *Kelly Asphalt Block Co. v. Barber Asphalt Paving Co.* have reached the same result if the third person were *suing to rescind* the contract, instead of trying to avoid responsibility for breach of warranty while retaining the sales proceeds?

3. If the contract entered into by the agent provides that the contract cannot be assigned, the principal is *not* excluded *per se*.

A clause in the contract against assignment does not of itself prevent the principal from bringing suit upon the contract. The existence of such a clause, however, may be considered as evidence that the parties intended to exclude the principal or that failure to reveal the existence of a principal is fraudulent within the rule stated in Section 304 *if there is other evidence to that effect.*

Restatement § 303 comment c (emphasis added). *Comind, Companhia de Seguros v. Sikorsky Aircraft Division of United Technologies Corp.* See *Cooper v. Epstein*, 308 A.2d 781 (D.C. Ct. App. 1973) (question of whether non-assignability clause excluded principal is a question of fact and summary judgment should not have been entered).

4. *Birmingham Matinee Club v. McCarty*, 152 Ala. 571, 44 So. 642 (1907), involved a suit by a principal for breach of a contract made by an agent in his own name for the sale of the principal's lands that called for the agent to convey unencumbered title *via* a warranty deed. The court invoked the rule preventing enforcement of the contract by an undisclosed principal where the contract involves elements of personal trust and confidence as a consideration moving from the undisclosed principal's agent to the other party to the contract:

The reason for this exception is manifest. If the party contracting without knowledge of the agency were bound to take the service or conveyance or property from the undisclosed principal, the well-recognized rule that one may determine for himself with whom he will deal or contract would be directly infracted; and the elements of the contract reasonably attributable to personal confidence and trust, including the financial responsibility of the agent with whom one deals as principal, would be stricken of force to which, under all principles of substantial justice and right, the relying party is entitled to the benefit.

Note that the undisclosed principal will *only* be denied the right to enforce the contract where the portion of the contract calling for personal trust and confidence remains *executory*; once that portion of the contract has been performed, the principal will be at liberty to enforce the contract. *See Strand v. Courier,* 434 N.W.2d 60 (S.D. 1988).

5. In *Hammon v. Paine,* 56 F.2d 19 (1st Cir. 1932), Hammon desired to engage in stock transactions but not in her own name. She turned over 5,000 shares of her stock to Cunniff to act on her behalf in trading. Cunniff employed the defendants, Paine, Webber & Co., as his brokers. Cunniff did not disclose the existence of Hammon. For a number of years, Cunniff had dealt with the defendants and had established accounts of his own numbered one to five. Hammon did not know this. Cunniff established account number six in order to deal with Hammon's stock. When Hammon requested return of her stock and the cash proceeds from the stock transactions, she was unable to receive a full return because Cunniff had a deficit in account five. Therefore, the defendants transferred part of the stock and cash from account six to cover the deficit in account five. Hammon sued to recover from the defendants and lost in the trial court. Hammon contended that she was the undisclosed principal of Cunniff and was therefore entitled to recover her stock and cash. The appellate court rejected her argument:

> One dealing with the agent of an undisclosed principal can do no other than treat the agent as the principal, and he cannot be deprived of any rights which have attached during such dealings when later the real party in interest claims the benefit of the transactions.

6. Restatement section 306 provides:

> (1) If the agent has been authorized to conceal the existence of the principal, the liability to an undisclosed principal of a person dealing with the agent within his power to bind the principal is diminished by any claim which such person may have against the agent at the time of making the contract and until the existence of the principal becomes known to him, if he could set off such claim in an action against the agent.

> (2) If the agent is authorized only to contract in the principal's name, the other party does not have set-off for a claim due him from the agent unless the agent has been entrusted with the possession of chattels which he disposes of as directed or unless the principal has otherwise misled the third person into extending credit to the agent.

Problem 2.3

Big Amusement, Inc., the operator of a world-famous amusement park in California, plans to open a major amusement park just outside a city in Florida. Big Amusement, Inc., hires Agent to purchase the necessary property, but directs Agent not to reveal Big Amusement's identity. Agent approaches Owner, who owns some suitably located agricultural land, and offers to buy the property at the market price for agricultural land. Owner believes Agent is acting on his or her own behalf, but does not ask Agent if that is the case. After the sale, Owner discovers that Big Amusement, Inc. is the true purchaser.

1. Has there even been a misrepresentation? *See* Restatement § 304 comments a and c.

2. Owner sues for rescission, claiming that Owner would have insisted on a higher price if Owner had known this. What result?

3. Would your answer change if Owner would have objected to the sale because he was going to retain his homestead on a corner of the property and did not want to live next door to a major amusement park?

4. How could the contract for the sale of the agricultural land have been drafted to protect the seller's concern? Should such language be included in the deed? Could such language be included in some other document that could be recorded?

C. Agent's Liability for Contractual Dealings

1. Agent's Duty to Fully Disclose Principal

Does an agent have a *duty* to disclose the identity of the principal, or a *right* to disclose the identity of the principal, or is some other description more accurate? Might there be occasions when the agent should not disclose the principal's identity?

Problem 2.4

Burbank was the representative and buyer for Ajax Sales Company. He had previously worked for various food and wholesale brokers and was known in the industry. Ajax wanted to buy one hundred bushels of Jonathan applies and instructed Burbank to obtain prices for them. Burbank contacted Apple Orchards, Inc. and inquired about the availability and price of the apples. He then informed Ajax and was directed to make the purchase. Burbank returned to Apple Orchards, Inc. and told them he wanted the one hundred bushels at the agreed price. He never advised the clerk of Apple Orchards about Ajax. Apple Orchards, Inc., prepared an invoice and delivered the apples to the address given by Burbank, which was the address of Ajax. When the apples arrived at Ajax's warehouse, Burbank called Apple Orchards and informed them the apples were for Ajax and should be billed to it. He was then informed that Ajax's credit was no good and that they wanted nothing to do with it. Apple Orchards, Inc. files its complaint against Burbank for the purchase price. What decision? Give reasons (Illinois Bar Examination, July 1983).

Clark v. Maddux
118 Ill. App. 3d 546, 454 N.E.2d 1179 (1983)

SEIDENFELD, Presiding Justice:

The plaintiff, a medical doctor, sued defendant, a lawyer, to recover a fee for review of medical information in connection with a medical malpractice case. The defendant appeals from the judgment of $4,350 and costs entered for the plaintiff, contending that he acted for a disclosed principal, his client, and therefore was not personally liable.

At trial plaintiff testified that he had a discussion with Shelley Gardner, who identified herself as an attorney from defendant's office. Gardner said the firm represented a case that she wished to discuss; he agreed to review the records involved in the case. He testified that there was "no real indication who was going to pay" his fee, but that it was his "assumption" that defendant's office would pay "since she agreed to the fee." He stated that at the time of conversation, there was no discussion of whether a suit had been filed; only that the firm represented the patient. He did testify, however, that "the malpractice case was directed against a doctor," naming him; that there was a "pending suit"; and that Gardner "indicated that they were suing a physician."

Gardner testified that she told Clark that Jenkins was a poor woman who was frequently unable to work. She testified that the firm's practice is to explain to the client that although costs may be advanced, the client is ultimately responsible. She testified that, in her conversation with plaintiff, she told him that she represented Arnetta Jenkins, who had a claim against the named doctor. She identified herself as an attorney working on behalf of Jenkins and informed Clark that a lawsuit had been filed. She never agreed to become personally liable for the plaintiff's services or to make the defendant personally liable. She had a conversation with Jenkins within two weeks after meeting with Clark; she gave Jenkins a status report, told her she had retained a physician, and, she was "sure" she told her what his charges were.

In his discovery deposition, some of which was read into evidence, defendant admitted that his firm had not asked Arnetta Jenkins to reimburse the firm for costs, as she would not be able to afford it.

Also in evidence was a letter sent by defendant in response to plaintiff's bill, over Gardner's signature. In substance the letter confirmed that an hourly charge of $300 had been agreed upon but protested the extensive literature research and medical report as allegedly not needed or authorized. The letter also stated that in the experience of the attorneys they had never been previously billed for secretarial copying services, and that the bill was "far in excess of the normal for initial interviews." An adjustment was requested.

The long settled rule in Illinois is that

> [w]here an agent in making a contract discloses his agency and the name of his principal[,] the agent is not liable on the contract unless he agrees to become personally liable.

The rule has been applied in various cases involving attorneys. In *Petrando v. Barry* (1955), 4 Ill. App. 2d 319, 124 N.E.2d 85, a printer sued an attorney for the cost of printing briefs, abstract, petition for rehearing, and petition for leave to appeal. The name of the attorney's client appeared on the cover pages of the printed materials and the plaintiff's business largely was of printing such materials. In holding for the attorney the court noted that the attorney-client relationship in some of its aspects is a relationship of agency, and that the printer was necessarily aware of the attorney's representative capacity. The fact that the plaintiff had billed the attorney or that the attorney rather than the client placed the printing order was held not critical, absent proof that the credit was given expressly or exclusively to the attorney with further proof that he intended to assume personal liability. In *International Service Corp. v. Ooms* (1969), 105 Ill. App. 2d 391, 245 N.E.2d 571, the plaintiff sued the defendant attorney for investigative work in a civil action, performed at the attorney's request. The court, noting the applicability of agent-principal rules to the attorney-client relationship, held that the defendant was not personally liable because he employed plaintiff while acting as an attorney for a client and the plaintiff was aware of this relationship. It made no difference that the plaintiff dealt directly with the defendant and not with the client. In *McCorkle v. Weinstein* (1977), 50 Ill. App. 3d 661, 662-64, 365 N.E.2d 953, the plaintiff, a court reporter, sued an attorney for the value of the court reporting services rendered in connection with a proceeding before the Pollution Control Board. The court affirmed a holding for the defendant even though the defendant was billed for the services and the defendant had initially requested the services. The court expressly rejected an argument also made by the plaintiff in this case that the promise of the attorney to pay be implied from the conduct of the parties, custom, and a consideration of the nature of the attorney's role in litigation and society generally. In *Association Claims Service v. Rinella & Rinella* (1979), 79 Ill. App. 3d 1023, 398 N.E.2d 1211, a law firm employed the plaintiff to serve subpoenas in a case. The plaintiff sued to recover for its services but the court held that the law firm was not liable because it employed plaintiff while acting as an agent for a client, a disclosed principal.

There is no doubt that Gardner told plaintiff that defendant was representing Arnetta Jenkins. Her name also was on the medical records given to plaintiff. Plaintiff admitted that Gardner told him that defendant's firm was representing Jenkins and, in fact, plaintiff conceded on cross-examination that he was told that a suit had been filed. Gardner testified that she told plaintiff that defendant represented Jenkins and that a suit had been filed. There was no showing, and no finding, that defendant had taken himself out of the disclosed principal rule by agreeing to be personally liable. Plaintiff testified only that he "assumed" that defendant would be liable. Gardner testified that she told plaintiff that Jenkins would ultimately pay. The letter from Gardner to Clark contests the reasonableness and propriety of the fee but it is not inconsistent with the position that, in accordance with the employment agreement, Jenkins was remaining liable although defendant was advancing costs. Defendant was thus not personally liable for the plaintiff's charges.

The judgment of the Circuit Court of DuPage County is reversed.

Copp v. Breskin
56 Wash. App. 229, 782 P.2d 1104 (1989)

WEBSTER, Judge.

Breskin & Robbins, a law firm, appeals a summary judgment in favor of Harley Copp, an expert witness hired by the firm on behalf of a client. Copp successfully claimed $14,789 for expert services.

Breskin & Robbins advised Copp before hiring him that fees "were being paid, and were to be paid" by the client. Copp says he would never accept employment if an attorney's obligation were dependent on reimbursement from a client. He made this policy known.

Breskin & Robbins concedes by way of deposition that, absent an agreement to the contrary, a provider of litigation services can expect an attorney in King County to pay the provider's bill whether or not the client reimburses the attorney. Copp, a California resident, is aware of a similar custom.

Copp sent Breskin & Robbins an initial bill which the firm paid with a "trust check" for $1,424. An accompanying letter assured Copp that any future charges would be paid within 30 days of his testimony. Breskin & Robbins claims it gave the assurance on behalf of the client and did not intend a guaranty. The client paid some of Copp's bills directly while he was in town for the trial. After trial, Copp sent Breskin & Robbins a final bill. He said he expected payment within 30 days, as previously agreed.

Breskin & Robbins replied that the client was willing to pay only 30 per cent of the bill. The firm offered to commence litigation on Copp's behalf, and eventually sued the client on its own behalf. It claimed $37,000 in litigation expenses allegedly incurred at the client's request, including amounts owing to Copp.

Subsequently, Copp filed this action against Breskin & Robbins. Breskin & Robbins admitted the amount owed, but averred as an affirmative defense that it hired Copp as agent of a disclosed principal, the client.

Breskin & Robbins relies on dictum to the effect that an attorney, as agent of a client, is not responsible for litigation costs, such as expert witness fees, unless the attorney personally agrees with the litigation service provider to pay them. *See Christensen, O'Connor, Garrison & Havelka v. Department of Rev.,* 97 Wash. 2d 764, 769-70, 649 P.2d 839 (1982). The *Christensen* dictum might be persuasive if it were not for a subsequent case which dealt with the same issue (whether reimbursements for costs advanced on behalf of a client are subject to business and occupation tax) but which disclaimed any ruling on the issue presented in this case. *See Walthew, Warner, Keefe, Arron, Costello & Thompson v. Department of Revenue,* 103 Wash. 2d 183, 190, 691 P.2d 559 (1984). *Walthew* held, as did *Christensen,* that reimbursements for litigation costs are exempt from B & O tax because the attorney receiving the reimbursement is not ultimately responsible for those costs. However, *Walthew* retracted the agency reasoning in *Christensen,* together with the suggestion that reimbursements might be taxable if an attorney agrees to pay them personally, holding instead that reimbursements for costs are per se exempt from B & O tax.

Walthew relied on the Code of Professional Responsibility, now the Rules of Professional Conduct, which forbid attorneys from advancing or otherwise paying the costs of litigation unless the client remains ultimately liable for them. *Walthew*, at 188, 691 P.2d 559 (discussing DR 5-103, now RPC 1.8(e)). Washington State Bar Association, Ethics Opinion 140 (1969), states:

> [W]hen the attorney has directly and personally ordered or arranged for services in circumstances under which the attorney did not make it clear (if such were [the] intent) to the person rendering the services that such person must look to the client alone for payment, the attorney has been derelict in preserving a good public image of the legal profession. *The primary responsibility of making it clear that the attorney acts in an agency capacity with no personal liability rests upon the attorney.* If [the attorney] has been derelict herein, others may reasonably be misled into believing that the attorney is agreeing to pay or to guarantee the payment of the obligation so created. In this circumstance it would be the ethical obligation of the attorney to pay such indebtedness and then look to [the] client for reimbursement and assume the risk of nonpayment.

(Emphasis added). The Rules of Professional Conduct prohibit attorneys from using the ignorance of litigation service providers to their financial advantage. Attorneys may not engage in conduct involving dishonesty, fraud, deceit, or misrepresentation. RPC 8.4(c). They must prevent or correct misunderstandings when the client's legitimate interests are not jeopardized. RPC 4.1, 4.3. They must avoid means that burden third persons without justification. RPC 4.4. The rules do not "undertake to define standards for civil liability of lawyers," RPC, Preliminary Statement, but that is often a necessary or logical consequence of upholding them.

Other jurisdictions are split as to whether an attorney is responsible to an expert or other service provider in the absence of a disclaimer. *See Annot., Attorney's Personal Liability for Expenses Incurred in Relation to Services for Client,* 66 A.L.R. 4th 256 (1988). Since 1955, three jurisdictions deciding the issue as a matter of first impression have reasoned that the attorney is an agent of a disclosed principal and, as such, is not liable unless the attorney expressly or impliedly agrees to be bound. *See Free v. Wilmar J. Helric Co.,* 70 Or. App. 40, 688 P.2d 117 (1984); *Hasbrouck v. Krsul,* 168 Mont. 270, 541 P.2d 1197 (1975); *see also Soro v. Bank of Miami,* 537 So. 2d 1135 (Fla. App. 1989) (agreement to be bound). During the same period, nine jurisdictions considering the issue anew or for the first time have held that formal agency reasoning does not accurately reflect the attorney's role as a strategist in litigation or the common understanding of litigation service providers. *See Gualtieri v. Burleson,* 84 N.C. App. 650, 353 S.E.2d 652 (1987); *Ingram v. Lupo,* 726 S.W.2d 791 (Mo. App. 1987) (rejecting earlier cases); *Gaines Reporting Serv. v. Mack,* 4 Ohio App. 3d 234, 447 N.E.2d 1317 (1982); *Theuerkauf v. Sutton,* 102 Wis. 2d 176, 306 N.W.2d 651 (1981); *Molezzo Reporters v. Patt,* 94 Nev. 540, 579 P.2d 1243 (1978); *C.C. Plumb Mixes, Inc. v. Stone,* 108 R.I. 75, 272 A.2d 152 (1971); *Roberts, Walsh & Co. v. Trugman,* 109 N.J. Super. 594, 264 A.2d 237 (1970); *Burt v. Gahan,* 351 Mass. 340, 220 N.E.2d 817, 15 A.L.R.3d 527 (1966); *see also In re Peters,* 332 N.W.2d 10, 17 (Minn. 1983) (disciplinary proceeding). The clear trend is to hold the attorney liable. One court, bound by prior cases siding with the attorney, nevertheless expressed the view that the attorney should be liable in the absence of a disclaimer, because the service provider deals with the attorney, not the client, and generally accepts employment based on the attorney's credit, not the client's. *See Rayvid v. Burgh,* 37 Misc. 2d 963, 234 N.Y.S.2d 868 (1962).

Justification for the disclosed agency rule is the probable intention of the parties, objectively manifested. Restatement (Second) of Agency § 320, Comments a-c; § 321, Comment a; § 328, Comment a (1958). When the circumstances indicate a probable intention that is contrary to the general rule, the reason for the rule is gone, and the rule should be modified to reflect this fact. Otherwise, the purpose of the rule—giving effect to the intentions of the parties—is lost. When a litigation service provider contracts with an attorney based on the attorney's credit, and the attorney is aware, or should be aware of this, it should not matter that the client's identity is known. The service provider reasonably expects that the attorney will be responsible, as surety or guarantor of the client's performance, RPC 1.8(e), and any contrary expectation of the attorney is unreasonable, if not fraudulent.

An agent may guarantee performance by the principal, and the existence of a guarantee "may be shown by proof of a custom to that effect." Restatement (Second) of Agency § 328, Comment b. Custom is determinative of the parties' intent where both parties are aware of it, and neither knows or should know that the other party has an intention contrary to it.

Here, Copp's testimony establishes that he relied upon a custom whereby experts look to attorneys for payment of their fees. Breskin & Robbins was aware of an identical custom locally. The statement that litigation costs were being paid and were to be paid by the client does not address the situation when the client is unwilling or unable to pay. Therefore, under the circumstances of this case, it was insufficient as a matter of law to apprise Copp of a change from customary practice. Copp accepted employment before meeting the client, and he sent bills to Breskin & Robbins, which the firm paid. This put the firm on notice that he was relying on its credit, not the client's, making an express disclaimer of responsibility essential to avoid liability. Breskin & Robbins assured Copp that any future charges would be paid within 30 days of his testimony. This assurance, on the firm's letterhead and signed "BRESKIN & ROBBINS /s/ Howard Breskin," did not disclose the agency character in which it was allegedly made. It is completely consistent with the customary practice of a firm pledging its credit to obtain expert services.

Breskin & Robbins advanced several thousand dollars by itself and through an associated attorney. This conflicts with the firm's assertion that the client alone was paying, and alone was expected to pay, the expenses of litigation. The advancements reveal the firm's personal interest in the litigation—established by a contingency fee agreement—evidencing an intent by the firm to become a party to the contract with Copp.

Breskin & Robbins offered to commence litigation against the client on Copp's behalf without any indication that there would be a charge for this service. The firm's offer reveals an understanding on its part that it was indebted to Copp. The lawsuit commenced by Breskin & Robbins on its own behalf against the client admits amounts owing to Copp as its damages. The firm would not have acted in this way if it believed it had adequately apprised Copp of an intention not to be liable for his services.

We hold that in these circumstances an attorney owes an expert or other litigation service provider an express disclaimer of responsibility if the attorney intends not to be bound by a contract for litigation services. This reflects the modern trend, which is to hold the attorney liable in the absence of an express disclaimer or other clear indication not to be bound. Putting the burden on the attorney promotes public trust and confidence in the legal profession, the supervision of which is the exclusive province and responsibility of the courts. Public trust in the profession and the courts would be "greatly endangered and jeopardized" by a technical defense of disclosed agency. Ethics Opinion 140.

The judgment is affirmed.

Note

The *Copp v. Breskin* court states that it is "rejecting" the agency rule that, unless otherwise agreed, an agent acting on behalf of a disclosed principal is not a party to the contract (and thus not liable on it). Is the reasoning in *Copp v. Breskin* inconsistent with that in *Clark v. Maddux*? *See* Restatement § 320.

Problem 2.5

1. The outcome in *Clark v.* Maddux (page 94) in favor of the law firm was an expensive victory. While an expensive *victory* is better than the expensive *loss* suffered by the law firm in *Copp. v. Breskin* (page 96), no law firm would knowingly expose itself to the risk of litigating the question of its liability to an expert or service provider. Draft the language of documents—both between it and its client, and between it and a third party (like the experts in the preceding cases)—that a law firm would use to avoid controversy over responsibility for fees for services of the third party, while complying with ethical standards.

2. What other suggestions do you have for a law firm that wishes to clarify and avoid liability for the provision of services by third parties for the benefit of the firm's clients? On what basis, if any, might the third-party object to your proposal?

Water, Waste & Land, Inc. v. Lanham
955 P.2d 997 (Colo. 1998) (*en banc*)

Justice SCOTT delivered the Opinion of the Court.

This case requires us to decide whether the members or managers of a limited liability company (LLC) are excused from personal liability on a contract where the other party to the contract did not have notice that the members or managers were negotiating on behalf of a limited liability company at the time the contract was made.[1] Because the county court found that the party dealing

---

1. The questions presented and framed by petitioner in the petition for certiorari were:

1. Whether the district court erred in holding that the individual defendant should be dismissed from the action, when the petitioner performed work for the respondent believing, because of representations made by respondent's agent, that the work was being performed for the benefit of the individual and knew nothing of the existence of a limited liability company.

2. Whether § 7-80-208, 2 C.R.S. (1997), should be interpreted such that an individual is able to claim protection from personal liability for amounts owing for services if that person has established a limited liability company, even though the

with the members or managers was unaware that they were acting as agents of a limited liability company when they negotiated the contract, and the evidence in the record supports the county court's findings, we see no legal basis to excuse the agents of the LLC from liability and therefore we reverse the judgment of the district court.

I.

Water, Waste, & Land, Inc., the petitioner, is a land development and engineering company doing business under the name "Westec." At the time of the events in this case, Donald Lanham and Larry Clark were managers and also members of Preferred Income Investors, L.L.C. (Company or P.I.I.). The Company is a limited liability company organized under the Colorado Limited Liability Company Act, §§ 7-80-101 to -1101, 2 C.R.S. (1997) (the LLC Act).

In March 1995, Clark contacted Westec about the possibility of hiring Westec to perform engineering work in connection with a development project which involved the construction of a fast-food restaurant known as Taco Cabana. In the course of preliminary discussions, Clark gave his business card to representatives of Westec. The business card included Lanham's address, which was also the address listed as the Company's principal office and place of business in its articles of organization filed with the secretary of state. While the Company's name was not on the business card, the letters "P.I.I." appeared above the address on the card. However, there was no indication as to what the acronym meant or that P.I.I. was a limited liability company.

After further negotiations, an oral agreement was reached concerning Westec's involvement with the Company's restaurant project. Clark instructed Westec to send a written proposal of its work to Lanham and the proposal was sent in April 1995. On August 2, 1995, Westec sent Lanham a form of contract, which Lanham was to execute and return to Westec.2 Although Westec never received a signed contract, in mid-August it did receive verbal authorization from Clark to begin work. Westec completed the engineering work and sent a bill for $9,183.40 to Lanham. No payments were made on the bill.

Westec filed a claim in county court against Clark and Lanham individually as well as against the Company. At trial, the Company admitted liability for the amount claimed by Westec. The county court entered judgment in favor of Westec. The county court found that:

(1) Clark had contacted Westec to do engineering work for Lanham;

(2) it was "unknown" to Westec that Lanham had organized the Company as a limited liability company; and

(3) the letters "P.I.I." on Clark's business card were insufficient to place Westec on notice that the Company was a limited liability company.

Based on its findings, the county court ruled that:

---

existence of the limited liability company is not disclosed at the time the services were requested or performed.

3. Whether the district court erred in determining that the county court should have found that respondent Clark was acting only as an agent for the limited liability company and not for the individual respondent Lanham, and that the contract therefore existed only between the petitioner and the limited liability company.

(1) Clark was an agent of both Lanham and the Company with "authority to obligate...Lanham and the Company";

(2) a valid and binding contract existed for the work;

(3) Westec "did not have knowledge of any business entity" and only dealt with Clark and Lanham "on a personal basis"; and

(4) Westec understood Clark to be Lanham's agent and therefore "Clark is not personally liable."

Accordingly, the county court dismissed Clark from the suit, concluding he could not be held personally liable, and entered judgment in the amount of $9,183 against Lanham and the Company. Lanham appealed, seeking review in the Larimer County District Court (district court).

The district court reversed, concluding that "[t]he issue which the court must address is whether the County Court erred in holding Lanham, a member and primary manager of the company, personally liable for a debt of the company." In addressing that issue, the district court found that Westec was placed on notice that it was dealing with a limited liability company based on two factors: (1) the business card containing the letters "P.I.I."; and (2) the notice provision of section 7-80-208, of the LLC Act. Principally in reliance upon the LLC Act's notice provision, section 7-80-208, which provides that the filing of the articles of organization serve as constructive notice of a company's status as a limited liability company, the district court held that "the County Court erred in finding that Westec had no notice that it was dealing with an L.L.C." Contrary to the trial court's findings, the district court held that "evidence presented at trial was uncontradicted that Westec knew it was dealing with a business entity (P.I.I.) and § 7-80-208 imputes notice that the entity was an 'L.L.C.' in addition to any common law presumption of a duty to inquire." In the district court's view, the notice provision, as well as Westec's failure to investigate or request a personal guarantee, relieved Lanham of personal liability for claims against the Company.

II.

Resolution of the controversy between Westec and Lanham requires us to analyze the relationship between the common law of agency and the reach of our statutes governing managers and members of a limited liability company. However, before doing so, it may prove helpful to first discuss the history and development of limited liability companies and their use in business enterprise.

The limited liability company is a relatively recent innovation in the law governing business entities. Wyoming adopted the first LLC statute in 1977, but the majority of states did not adopt LLC legislation until the 1990s, largely because the tax treatment of such companies was in doubt. *See* 1 Larry E. Ribstein and Robert R. Keatinge, Ribstein and Keatinge on Limited Liability Companies §§ 1.06 & 16.02 (1997). These doubts have been largely resolved, and the LLC has become a popular form of business organization because it offers members the limited liability protection of a corporation, together with the single-tier tax treatment of a partnership along with considerable flexibility in management and financing. The ability to avoid two levels of income taxation is an especially attractive feature of organization as a limited liability company. *See id.* §§ 1.03-1.06.

In 1990, our General Assembly adopted the LLC Act, a statute currently codified as amended at sections 7-80-101 through 7-80-1101, 2 C.R.S. (1997), making Colorado the third state, behind Wyoming and Florida, to do so.[3] Unlike a number of other states, where LLC statutes were based on a model act drafted by the National Conference of Commissioners on Uniform State Laws, Colorado's LLC Act combined features of the state's existing limited partnership and corporation statutes. In any case, the LLC Act includes the same basic features of limited liability, single-tier tax treatment, and planning flexibility shared by the Uniform Limited Liability Company Act and LLC legislation adopted by other states.

Colorado passed the LLC Act into law for several reasons, but the importance of the tax benefits derived from the use of the LLC should not be overlooked. "For . . . the drafters of [the] very early LLC statutes, securing the promised federal tax benefits was the paramount drafting concern." Dale A. Oesterle, *Subcurrents in LLC Statutes: Limiting the Discretion of State Courts to Restructure the Internal Affairs of Small Business,* 66 Univ. Colo. L.Rev. 881, 883. *See also* William J. Carney, *Limited Liability Companies: Origins and Antecedents,* 66 Univ. Colo. L.Rev. 855, 858 (IRS Revenue Ruling 88-76 (Rev. Rul. 88-76, 1988-2 C.B. 361)[(providing] that a Wyoming LLC could be classified as a partnership for tax purposes, "opened the floodgates and LLC statutes have now been adopted in nearly all the states"). Thus, it is clear that the "primary force of LLC statutes" has been to create a business entity that will meet the federal requirements for pass-through tax treatment. Robert B. Thompson, *The Taming of Limited Liability Companies,* 66 Univ. Colo. L Rev. 921, 930.

III.
A.

The district court interpreted the LLC Act's notice provision, *see* § 7-80-208, as putting Westec on constructive notice of Lanham's agency relationship with the Company. In essence, this course of analysis assumed that the LLC Act displaced certain common law agency doctrines, at least insofar as these doctrines otherwise would be applicable to suits by third parties seeking to hold the agents of a limited liability company liable for their personal actions as agents.

We hold, however, that the statutory notice provision applies only where a third party seeks to impose liability on an LLC's members or managers simply due to their status as members or managers of the LLC. When a third party sues a manager or member of an LLC under an agency theory, the principles of agency law apply notwithstanding the LLC Act's statutory notice rules.

B.

Under the common law of agency, an agent is liable on a contract entered on behalf of a principal if the principal is not fully disclosed. In other words, an agent who negotiates a contract with a third party can be sued for any breach of the contract unless the agent discloses both the fact that he or she is acting on behalf of a principal and the identity of the principal. As a leading treatise explains:

---

3. The LLC Act was amended in 1993, 1994, and 1997.

If both the existence and identity of the agent's principal are fully disclosed to the other party, the agent does not become a party to any contract which he negotiates.... But where the principal is partially disclosed (i.e. the existence of a principal is known but his identity is not), it is usually inferred that the agent is a party to the contract.

Harold Gill Reuschlein and William A. Gregory, The Law of Agency and Partnership § 118 (2d ed. 1990).

Other scholars agree that under the common law of agency, the duty to disclose the identity as well as the existence of the principal lies with the agent:

It is not sufficient that the third party has knowledge of facts and circumstances which would, if reasonably followed by inquiry, disclose the identity of the principal. The duty of disclosure clearly lies with the agent alone; the third party with whom the agent deals has no duty to discover the existence of an agency or ... the identity of the principal.

3A James Solheim and Kenneth Elkins, Fletcher Cyclopedia of the Law of Private Corporations § 1120 (1994 revised volume).

This somewhat counterintuitive proposition—that an agent is liable even when the third party knows that the agent is acting on behalf of an unidentified principal—has been recognized as sound by the courts of this state, and it is a well established rule under the common law. Thus, an agent is liable on contracts negotiated on behalf of a "partially disclosed" principal; that is, a principal whose existence—but not identity—is known to the other party.

C.

Whether a principal is partially or completely disclosed is a question of fact. On appeal from the county court, the district court had the power to find the facts independently by ordering a trial de novo. Instead, the district court exercised its authority to decide the case based on the record developed below; so it was bound to accept the facts as found by the county court and its review was limited to the sufficiency of the evidence.

These principles lead us to conclude that the district court erred in substituting its own factual determinations for the findings of the county court. If the district court had held a trial de novo, its conclusion that the initials "P.I.I." on Clark's business card sufficiently alerted Westec's representatives to the fact of Clark's agency relationship with the Company and to the Company's identity would be entitled to deference if supported by evidence in the record. However, we see the evidence as sufficient to support the county court's finding to the contrary. Indeed, neither the business card nor the unsigned contract documents, both of which are of obvious significance in evaluating whether Westec knew the identity of the entity represented by Clark and Lanham, are in the record before us. We are, therefore, bound to accept the county court's finding that Westec did not know Clark was acting as an agent for the Company or that the initials "P.I.I." stood for "Preferred Income Investors," a limited liability company registered under Colorado law. For the same reason, the district court erred in concluding that Clark was not acting as Lanham's agent. The trial record was sufficient to support the county court's finding that Clark was an agent for Lanham and this conclusion should not have been disturbed by the district court.

D.

In light of the partially disclosed principal doctrine, the county court's determination that Clark and Lanham failed to disclose the existence as well as the identity of the limited liability company they represented is dispositive under the common law of agency. Still, if the General Assembly has altered the common law rules applicable to this case by adopting the LLC Act, then these rules must yield in favor of the statute. We conclude, however, that the LLC Act's notice provision was not intended to alter the partially disclosed principal doctrine.

Section 7-80-208, C.R.S. (1997) states:

> The fact that the articles of organization are on file in the office of the secretary of state is notice that the limited liability company is a limited liability company and is notice of all other facts set forth therein which are required to be set forth in the articles of organization.

In order to relieve Lanham of liability, this provision would have to be read to establish a conclusive presumption that a third party who deals with the agent of a limited liability company always has constructive notice of the existence of the agent's principal. We are not persuaded that the statute can bear such an interpretation.

Such a construction exaggerates the plain meaning of the language in the statute. Section 7-80-208 could be read to state that third parties who deal with a limited liability company are always on constructive notice of the company's limited liability status, without regard to whether any part of the company's name or even the fact of its existence has been disclosed. However, an equally plausible interpretation of the words used in the statute is that once the limited liability company's name is known to the third party, constructive notice of the company's limited liability status has been given, as well as the fact that managers and members will not be liable simply due to their status as members.

Moreover, the broad interpretation urged by Lanham would be an invitation to fraud, because it would leave the agent of a limited liability company free to mislead third parties into the belief that the agent would bear personal financial responsibility under any contract, when in fact, recovery would be limited to the assets of a limited liability company not known to the third party at the time the contract was made. While Westec has not alleged that Clark or Lanham deliberately tried to conceal the Company's identity or status as a limited liability company, Lanham's construction would open the door to sharp practices and outright fraud. We may presume that in adopting section 7-80-208, the General Assembly did not intend to create a safe harbor for deceit. *See City of Westminster v. Dogan Constr. Co., Inc.*, 930 P.2d 585 (Colo. 1997) (statutory interpretation leading to absurd results is to be avoided). For this reason alone, a broad reading of the notice provision would be suspect.

In addition, statutes in derogation of the common law are to be strictly construed. For the reasons outlined above, the interpretation urged by Lanham would be a radical departure from the settled rules of agency under the common law. If the legislature had intended a departure of such magnitude, its desires would have to be expressed more clearly.

Other LLC Act provisions reinforce the conclusion that the legislature did not intend the notice language of section 7-80-208 to relieve the agent of a limited liability company of the duty to disclose its identity in order to avoid personal liability. For example, section 7-80-201(1), 2 C.R.S. (1997), requires limited liability companies to use the words "Limited Liability Company" or the initials "LLC" as part of their names, implying that the legislature intended to compel any entity seeking to claim the benefits of the LLC Act to identify itself clearly as a limited liability company. By way of further support for our conclusion, section 7-80-107, 2 C.R.S. (1997), provides two bases of individual liability for members: (1) for "alleged improper actions," and (2) "the failure of a limited liability company to observe the formalities or requirements relating to the management of its business and affairs when coupled with some other wrongful conduct."

As one commentator opined:

It would be an unwarranted stretch to say that these laws intend to extend the insulation of limited liability beyond that traditionally provided by the corporate form. That means that participants in closely held enterprises will continue to be liable for their acts taken in the entity's name that are wrongful or violate regulatory provisions either under agency law or by a court piercing the entity's veil.

Thompson, *supra* at 945.

Lanham received from Westec a form of contract demonstrating Westec's assumption that Lanham was the principal. At that point, he could have clarified his relationship to the Company. He did not do so. Hence, even if we were sympathetic to Lanham's plight, he had within his control the means to clearly state that he was acting only for the limited liability company. Moreover, we must avoid straying from long established principles of law and inserting uncertainty into accepted rules that govern business relationships.

In sum, then, section 7-80-208 places third parties on constructive notice that a fully identified company—that is, identified by a name such as "Preferred Income Investors, LLC," or the like—is a limited liability company provided that its articles of organization have been filed with the secretary of state. Section 7-80-208 is of little force, however, in determining whether a limited liability company's agent is personally liable on the theory that the agent has failed to disclose the identity of the company.

IV.

Under our interpretation, section 7-80-208 still offers significant protection to the members of a limited liability company. The notice provision protects the members from suit based on their status as members, as opposed to their acts as agents of the corporate entity.[4] If a third party such as Westec had tried to pierce

---

4. By our holding today, we by no means alter the import or reach of sections 7-80-208 and 7-80-705, 2 C.R.S. (1997). Both sections of our LLC Act provide protection to members and managers. Section 7-80-705 provides:

Liability of members and managers. Members and managers of limited liability companies are not liable under a judgment, decree, or order of a court, or in

the corporate veil to hold Clark and Lanham personally responsible for the Company's contractual debt based on the fact that they were members of the LLC, section 7-80-208 would protect them from liability. The distinction between the use of an agency theory and the doctrine of piercing the corporate or limited liability company[5] veil is significant. As one treatise explains:

> The undisclosed principal theory is a rule of law and applies regardless of a defendant's intent to engage in wrongful conduct; however, the doctrine of piercing the corporate veil is based in equity so that a failure to disclose must coexist with wrongful conduct or improper purpose or intent for the latter theory to apply and render personal liability.

3A James Solheim and Kenneth Elkins, Fletcher Cyclopedia of the Law of Private Corporations § 1120 (1994 revised edition).

V.

For these reasons, we conclude that where an agent fails to disclose either the fact that he is acting on behalf of a principal or the identity of the principal, the notice provision of our LLC Act, section 7-80-208, cannot relieve the agent of liability to a third party. When a third party deals with an agent acting on behalf of a limited liability company, the existence and identity of which has been disclosed, the third party is conclusively presumed to know that the entity is a limited liability company and not a partnership or some other type of business organization. Where the third party does not know the identity of the principal entity, however, the situation is fundamentally different because the third party is without notice and the law does not contemplate that he has any way of finding the relevant records.

If Clark or Lanham had told Westec's representatives that they were acting on behalf of an entity known as "Preferred Income Investors, LLC" the failure to disclose the fact that the entity was a limited liability company would be irrelevant by virtue of the statute, which provides that the articles of organization operate as constructive notice of the company's limited liability form. The county court, however, found that Lanham and Clark did not identify Preferred Income Investors, LLC, as the principal in the transaction. The "missing link" between the limited disclosure made by Clark and the protection of the notice statute was the failure to state that "P.I.I.," the Company, stood for "Preferred Income Investors, LLC."

Accordingly, the judgment of the district court is reversed and this case is remanded to that court with instructions that it reinstate the judgment of the county court.

---

any other manner, for a debt, obligation, or liability of the limited liability company.
Hence, we do not diminish the fact that assuming the articles of organization are filed, a member or manager "will not be liable simply due to their status" as member or manager. *See* Krendl & Krendl, *supra,* § 4.9.

5. Section 7-80-107 provides for resort to "the case law which interprets the conditions and circumstances under which the corporate veil of a corporation may be pierced under Colorado law."

Notes

1. What steps should "agents" Clark and Lanham (from the preceding case) have taken to protect against being sued and held liable to third parties with whom they dealt for the LLC? Could Clark and Lanham have entered into an indemnification provision to help protect themselves? If so, how should such a provision have been drafted? Would such an indemnification affect liability to third persons?

2. Under Restatement section 4, a principal is at least partially disclosed where the third person has *notice* the agent is acting for a principal, and (fully) disclosed where the third person also has *notice* of the identity of the principal. As discussed earlier, persons have "notice" of a fact when they know it, have *reason to know* it, or *should know* it. In *J. T. Doiron, Inc. v. Lundin*, 385 So. 2d 450 (La. Ct. App. 1980), an officer of a corporation employed an appraiser to appraise real property owned by the corporation. The appraiser met with the officer in the corporate offices and was introduced to its president. The property (or at least a portion of it) was carried in the name of the corporation on the tax rolls. The appraiser billed the corporation, but when the corporation failed to pay, the appraiser sued the officer. The court held that the officer had (fully) disclosed the principal, stating that even where there is no "straightforward disclosure,"

> an agent may still be able to escape individual liability by proving that sufficient indicia of the agency relationship were known by the third party to put him on notice of the principal/agent relationship. Express notice of the agent's status and the principal's identity is unnecessary if [the] facts and circumstances surrounding the transaction, combined with the general knowledge that persons in that type of business are usually acting as agents, demonstrate affirmatively that the third person should be charged with notice of the relationship.

3. In *Robert T. Reynolds Associates, Inc. v. Asbeck,* 23 Conn. App. 247, 580 A.2d 533 (1990), the disclosure by Mr. Reynolds that he was acting as president of "Acousticon Electronics"—a trade or assumed name used by a corporation, J.S. Sales Corporation International—was found to be insufficient to relieve Mr. Reynolds of liability on the contract:

> The defendant next argues that, because the plaintiff had notice that the defendant was acting in the capacity of an agent, he should not be personally liable. Here, the defendant argues that his consistent use of the words "its president" when dealing with the plaintiff and the fact that the name "Acousticon Electronics" appeared on all invoices and correspondence constituted notice that he was not making a personal promise and, therefore, should not be personally liable. The defendant relies on *Jacobs v. Williams*, 85 Conn. 215, 82 A. 202 (1912), for his assertion that the plaintiff had proper notice that he made a corporate obligation and not a personal obligation. That case is distinguishable from the present case. In *Jacobs*, the name of the alleged principal, the Glastonbury Power Company, appeared directly above the signatures of the two officers who also signed in their representative capacity. Further, the court in that case relied on the following rule:
>
>> [W]here the corporation appears as the primary signer, the almost universally accepted and reasonable rule of construction is

that where the signature is that of the corporation, and the name or names of one or more of its officers in their official capacity are appended as subscribing agents the corporation will be regarded as the signer and obligor, and the individuals will not be obligated, unless other language or the general tenor of the writing indicates a contrary intent.

In this case, the court found that AE was not a corporation. This finding is supported by the evidence. Thus, although the name of the business, "AE," may have been present in the correspondence between the parties, there was no evidence submitted to show that this business was a corporation. The only evidence indicating the possibility that this was a corporate obligation was that the correspondence was signed by the defendant as president. The proper name of the alleged corporation, however, was J.S. Sales Corporation International d/b/a Acousticon Electronics. The name of that corporation never appeared in any correspondence concerning this contract. Because this was not a corporate obligation, the mere fact that the defendant signed in a representative capacity will not permit him to avoid personal liability.

Last, the defendant argues that the plaintiff had notice of both the fact of his agency and the identity of his principal because the plaintiff knew that it was dealing with a certain principal and had previous dealings of the same nature through the agent's predecessor.

While it is true that

[a]n agent, by making a contract only on behalf of a competent disclosed principal whom he has the power to bind, does not thereby become liable for its nonperformance;

whether there was a nondisclosure of a competent principal so that the plaintiff might hold the defendant personally liable on the contract is a question of fact for the trial court.

The evidence showed that neither the defendant nor his alleged predecessors, Teal or Floyd, informed the plaintiff that a corporation existed.

4. Would the result in *Robert T. Reynolds Associates, Inc. v. Asbeck* have changed if the facts had shown that J.S. Sales Corporation International had filed an *assumed name certificate* in the appropriate place? Consider the arguments in *Metro Bulletins Corporation v. Soboleski*, 30 Conn. App. 493, 620 A.2d 1314 (1993): The majority concluded as follows:

The general rule is that "[t]he object or purpose of statutes which regulate the doing of business under a fictitious or assumed name is ... to protect the public *by giving notice* or information as to the person with whom they deal, and to afford protection against fraud and deceit." (Emphasis added.) 57 Am.Jur.2d, Names § 66. Our Supreme Court has recognized this rule as the purpose behind Connecticut's trade name statute by enunciating that "its object is to enable a person dealing with another trading under a name not his own, to know the man behind the name, that he may know or make inquiry as to his business character or financial responsibility...." *DiBiase v. Garnsey*, 103 Conn. 21, 27, 130 A. 81 (1925). The mandated disclosure is "intended for the protection of creditors...." *Wofsey v. New York & Stamford R. Co.,* 106 Conn. 254, 258, 138 A. 136 (1927).

In this respect, § 35-1 differs from the statutes governing trademarks and service marks, which are designed to give their owners protection from infringement or unauthorized use. If a trade or service mark owner elects not to register the mark, the only risk is exposure to use of the mark by a competitor. This contrasts sharply with the risks posed by the failure to file a certificate of trade name. Section 35-1 provides two substantial penalties for noncompliance. First, a failure to comply shall be deemed to constitute an unfair or deceptive practice under § 42-110b(a) of the Connecticut Unfair Trade Practices Act (CUTPA). As a result, a defendant faces the full range of civil penalties and liabilities applicable to a CUTPA violation. Second, the defendant may be criminally prosecuted and imprisoned for as long as one year and fined up to $500. From this we conclude that, even though as an incidental benefit § 35-1 may provide some protection to persons transacting business under a trade name, it is primarily intended to protect creditors by giving them constructive notice of the contents of the trade name certificate.

Section 35-1 contains several key provisions to achieve its purpose of notification. These include the mandate that each town clerk create and maintain a dual indexing system, thus enabling the public to find either the owner of a particular trade name or the trade name of a particular person or entity.

We are further persuaded that the statute was intended to provide constructive notice by its parallels with real property recording and indexing provisions. In requiring a filing and indexing system, § 35-1 is analogous to General Statutes § 7-25, which governs the recording and indexing of real property records. As is also true of real property records, a certified copy of a certificate of trade name is presumptive evidence in all courts in Connecticut of the facts stated in the certificate. See General Statutes § 7-23.

In light of the statute's specific mandates and substantial penalties, we cannot agree with the plaintiff's contention that § 35-1 is not a notice statute. The plaintiff's theory would mean that a business being conducted under a trade name could not use that trade name without providing an affirmative disclosure of the entity behind the business in every transaction with the public. Disclosure, however, is precisely the intended function of the statute. As a result, the plaintiff's theory would render the statute meaningless. We will not presume that the legislature intended to enact meaningless or useless legislation.

In the present case, because the certificate of trade name was filed before the parties entered into the contract, we hold that the plaintiff had constructive notice of the corporate principal's identity at the time of contracting. As stated by the Pennsylvania Supreme Court, construing a similar statute, the plaintiff "cannot plead ignorance of facts of which it is deemed to have constructive notice." *Ulick v. Vibration Specialty Co.,* 348 Pa. 241, 35 A.2d 332, 333 (1944). Accordingly, the judgment of the trial court must be reversed.

620 A.2d at 1317-19. The dissent responded as follows:

Notwithstanding our well established case law requiring an agent to disclose the principal to a third party, the result here enables the agent to escape personal liability after withholding critical information readily available to him but obtainable by the plaintiff only with considerable effort and inconvenience.

The majority concludes that the plaintiff had constructive notice that Bridgeside Pontiac was the principal behind the trade name thus placing on the plaintiff the burden of discovering the details of the trade name disclosure made under § 35-1. How, then, did the duty arise to search one or more trade name indices located, by the terms of § 35-1, wherever the "business is or is to be conducted or transacted"?

Section 35-1 is hardly a broad ranging statute fully protecting individuals doing business with persons or corporations using trade names. The plain and unambiguous terms of the statute, therefore, cannot fairly be read to include this additional provision.

The preferable result is to require the party having possession of the information about the principal's identity—in this case Soboleski—to disclose that information before the transaction is consummated.

In this case, Soboleski had within his control all of the information necessary to alert the plaintiff as to what entity Soboleski envisioned was to be bound by the legal consequences flowing from this contract. For whatever reasons, he failed to disclose any information and, in fact, completed the signature portion of the contract in an ambiguous manner. The simple fact is that only Soboleski is bound by this contract as he is the only individual or entity executing it with the plaintiff.

Our own Supreme Court indicated that the statute is for the benefit of others doing business with one operating behind a "name not his own." *Di Biase v. Garnsey,* [103 Conn. 21, 27, 130 A, 81 (1925)]. It seems inconsistent with that purpose when the statute is employed to avoid liability by the very person possessing the relevant information needed for a fair evaluation of the transaction.

The majority believes that the purpose behind the trade name statute would be undermined were the business using the trade name to be required to provide "an affirmative disclosure of the entity behind the business in *every transaction with the public.*" That concern would not be relevant in this case if this court were to hold that the disclosure of principal rule governs. The statute is not rendered meaningless if this court requires the party in control of the information to disclose it to the party with whom he is doing business. It does not seem too much to ask of an individual acting as an agent in a given transaction who wants to avoid personal liability on a particular contract specifically to disclose his principal to the other party. In all fairness, the failure to do so should prevent that individual from escaping personal liability.

620 A.2d 1319-20 (Schaller, J., dissenting).

5. *Unless otherwise agreed,* an agent acting for a *partially* disclosed principal is a party to a contract entered into on behalf of the principal. Restatement § 321. According to Comment a to section 321

The inference of an understanding that the agent is a party to the contract exists unless the agent gives such complete information concerning his principal's identity that he can be readily distinguished. If the party has no reasonable means of ascertaining the principal, the inference is almost irresistible and prevails in the absence of an agreement to the contrary.

Why should the inference that the agent is a party to the contract be "almost irresistible" when the third person knows the agent is acting for a principal?

2. Agent's Implied Warranty of Authority

When an agent discloses to a third party that the agent is acting on behalf of a principal, the agent might not expressly represent that the agent possesses the authority to so act. Does the agent at least impliedly warrant that the agent possesses the extent of authority s/he exercises on behalf of the principal?

Farm Credit Bank v. FCB Ltd. Partnership
825 F.Supp. 932 (D. Kan. 1993)

BELOT, District Judge.

This matter is before the court on the motion for summary judgment of defendants Paul Thomas Mann, Omega Development Corporation, and Omega Investments, Inc. Defendants claim that plaintiffs' cause of action is barred by the statute of limitations.

I. Background

This diversity action arises from a December 1986 agreement ("the Agreement") under which plaintiff Farm Credit Bank ("Farm Credit") agreed to loan funds to defendant FCB Limited Partnership ("FCB"). The purpose of the loan was to finance the purchase of real property ("the Project"). Pursuant to the loan agreement, Farm Credit and FCB also executed a lease agreement, whereby Farm Credit, as the tenant, obtained a leasehold estate in the Project from FCB, as the owner and landlord.

In late 1987, early 1988, Farm Credit and FCB entered into negotiations with a third-party interested in subleasing approximately 50,000 square feet of the Project. Defendants Omega Development Corporation and/or Omega Investments, Inc. (collectively "Omega") allegedly represented FCB and acted as its agent throughout the negotiations for this sublease. Plaintiffs also allege that P. Thomas Mann, President of Omega, participated in the sublease negotiations on behalf of Omega.

By letter dated January 4, 1988, Mann wrote to Farm Credit proposing certain terms relevant to the sublease negotiations. Mann explained the purpose of his proposed terms: "In order to make the transaction with the [third-party] more viable to [Farm Credit], it is necessary for [FCB] to make a concession to make the lease more attractive to [Farm Credit]." (Exh. "A" to Defendants' Brief in Support, Doc. 91). The "concession" that Mann proposed was an amendment to the "Borrower Escrow Fund" provision of the December 1986 Agreement.

Mann closed the letter by stating: "If the foregoing meets with your understanding and agreement, please indicate by signing below." The letter provides a space for the signature of Farm Credit, and was signed on January 13, 1988 by Dennis D. Nichols on behalf of Farm Credit.

Subsequent to the execution of the January 1988 letter agreement, Farm Credit learned that FCB had not authorized and would not ratify the agreement. Plaintiffs filed suit against FCB on September 12, 1990, and by amended complaint, filed suit against Mann and Omega on August 27, 1991.

II. Argument

Plaintiffs seek recovery against Mann and Omega for breach of their implied warranty of authority to contract on behalf of FCB. Such an action is recognized in Kansas:

> "A person who assumes to act as agent for another impliedly warrants that he has authority to do so; and if therefore he in fact lacks authority he renders himself personally liable on the warranty to one who deals with him in good faith in reliance thereon."

Hewey v. Miller, 132 Kan. 289, 290, 295 P. 723 (1931) (quoting 2 C.J. 803).[2] Plaintiffs also seek recovery against defendants for intentional or negligent misrepresentation of authority.

Defendants Mann and Omega move for summary judgment on the grounds that plaintiffs' claims are barred by the statute of limitations. According to defendants, plaintiffs' cause of action for breach of implied warranty of authority sounds in contract and accrued on January 4, 1988—the date on which Mann signed the letter agreement. Because plaintiff did not file suit within three years of this date, as required under K.S.A. s 60-512(1), defendants contend that this claim is barred.

The Restatement (Second) of Agency § 329 comment k (1958) states that a cause of action against an agent for breach of his implied warranty of authority "accrues when the third person learns that the agent does not have authority, or when he suffers damage or fails to gain the anticipated benefits, whichever occurs first". In Kansas, however, a discovery rule of accrual applies only to tort actions. If the cause of action sounds in contract, the date of the breach determines the time of accrual, and the plaintiff's knowledge of the breach or any injury caused thereby is irrelevant.

Plaintiffs contend that their action for breach of implied warranty of authority may sound in either tort or contract.

Kansas recognizes that an action for breach of implied warranty may sound in either tort or contract, and the plaintiff may proceed on either.

Plaintiffs' action for breach of implied warranty of authority may properly be characterized as sounding in tort. "A breach of contract may be said to be a

---

2. As the court construes plaintiffs' theory, plaintiffs do not seek recovery on the underlying contract itself, but on the breach of defendant's independent implied warranty that they possessed authority to bind their principal to the terms of the letter agreement. "The view generally followed is that the liability of the agent to a third person on a contract rests upon the theory or ground that he warrants his authority, and not that the contract is deemed his own." 3 Am.Jur.2d *Agency* § 304 (1986).

material failure of performance of a duty arising under or imposed by agreement. A tort, on the other hand, is a violation of a duty imposed by law, a wrong independent of contract." *Malone v. University of Kansas Med. Center,* 220 Kan. 371, 374, 552 P.2d 885 (1976) (citations omitted). Every person purporting to act for a principal has a duty toward third parties to refrain from making contracts the authority for which has not been granted by the principal. This duty does not depend on the existence of a contract; it may arise under the common law. *See Russell v. American Rock Crusher Co.,* 181 Kan. 891, 895, 317 P.2d 847 (1957) (agent's liability for the torts he commits does not derive from the contractual relationship between the principal and agent, but from the common law obligation of every person to act or use that which he controls so as not to injure another).

Thus, the court concludes that plaintiffs' claim for breach of implied warranty of authority may be considered to sound in tort. Accordingly, as to this theory of recovery, plaintiffs may rely on the discovery rule of the two year statute of limitations for tort actions.[3]

Accordingly, the court denies the motion for summary judgment.

IT IS SO ORDERED.

Notes

1. Suppose that an agent in good faith enters into a contract on behalf of his principal without knowing that the principal has died. As will be discussed in Chapter 17, the occurrence of certain events, such as the *death* of the principal, *automatically and without notice* terminate by operation of law the agent's power to bind the principal, so the agent has *not* bound the principal. Has the agent violated the implied *warranty* of authority? *See* Restatement § 329 comments b and d.

2. May an agent *disclaim* the Restatement section 329 implied warranty of authority?

3. In *Benner v. Farm Bureau Mutual Insurance Co.,* 96 Idaho 311, 528 P.2d 193 (1974), Bauman, an Idaho insurance agent, told the Benners that their Farm Bureau Mutual Insurance Co. insurance policy would be amended to cover personal property the Benners were moving to California. When the property was destroyed in a fire, Farm Bureau denied coverage, claiming that Bauman had no actual authority as to insurance policies covering risks outside of Idaho. The Benners sued both Farm Bureau and Bauman. Farm Bureau cross-claimed against Benner for exceeding his authority. The trial court held that:

---

3. Even if the court were to assume that plaintiffs' action could only sound in contract, it is unclear whether a contract action for breach of an agent's implied warranty of authority necessarily accrues on the date that the agent purports to contract on behalf of his principal. It has been stated that an agent's implied warranty of authority is of a continuing nature, and that the warranty continues to run at least until the third party learns of the agent's lack of authority. This view of the warranty also accounts for the Restatement rule that the action "accrues when the third person learns that the agent does not have authority, or when he suffers damage or fails to gain the anticipated benefits, whichever occurs first." Restatement (Second) of Agency § 329 comment k (1958). Thus, even applying the Kansas rule that an action for breach of contract accrues at the time of the breach, the time of the breach of this implied contract may coincide with plaintiff's discovery of Mann's lack of authority.

(i) Farm Bureau was liable to the Benners; although Bauman had no *actual* authority, he had *apparent* authority;

(ii) Bauman was liable to the Benners for breach of his implied warranty of authority; and

(iii) Bauman was liable to Farm Bureau for the losses resulting from his exceeding his authority.

Bauman appealed. The Idaho Supreme Court affirmed the lower court holding of liability to Farm Bureau. It reversed as to Bauman's liability for breach of the implied warranty of authority. The court reasoned that the implied warranty of authority "was not intended to apply" where the unauthorized act bound the principal under the doctrine of apparent authority. The court followed Restatement section 329, which reasons that:

if the principal becomes a party [to the transaction], the rights of the other party are not affect by the fact that the agent committed a wrong to his principal.

Restatement § 329 comment f.

Did the fact that Bauman acted outside the scope of his actual authority from Farm Bureau harm the Benners in any way? Why or why not?

3. Election of Remedies

Problem 2.6

Anderson sold goods to Brown in good faith, believing him to be a principal. Brown was in fact acting as Carey's agent and within the scope of his authority. The goods were charged to Brown, and on his refusal to pay, a proper action was brought by Anderson for the purchase price. While this action was pending, Anderson learned of Brown's relationship with Carey. Nevertheless, thirty days after learning of that relationship, Anderson secured a judgment against Brown and had an execution issued that was never satisfied. Three months after securing the judgment, Anderson brought an action against Carey for the purchase price of the goods. What decision? Give reasons [Illinois Bar Examination, Feb. 1980]. What should Anderson have done differently at the time of selling the goods to Brown? At the time of suing Brown? At the time of learning of Carey's involvement?

Orrock v. Crouse Realtors, Inc.

823 S.W.2d 40 (Mo. App. 1991)

CRANE, Judge.

Plaintiffs Alexander J. Orrock, Jr. and L. Charlene Orrock appeal from the order of the Circuit Court of Lincoln County sustaining the motion of defendant Crouse Realtors, Inc. for summary judgment in their action for breach of a residential sales contract and negligent and intentional misrepresentations in connection therewith. Defendant's motion alleged that the action, which sought to impose liability on defendant as a result of the acts of its agent, Michael Flynn, was barred because plaintiffs had previously obtained judgment against the agent for those acts.

Prior to the filing of this petition, plaintiff filed a petition in St. Louis County against defendant Crouse, another real estate agency, and Crouse's agent Michael Flynn. This petition alleged that defendant Crouse, acting through its agent Michael Flynn, breached a residential sales contract between the parties and made intentional and negligent misrepresentations with respect to the quality of the residence being purchased. On January 9, 1989, the plaintiffs took a default judgment against Flynn on the breach of contract count and the intentional misrepresentation count and dismissed all claims against Crouse and the other real estate company.

On November 21, 1990 plaintiffs filed this action in Lincoln County naming Crouse as the sole defendant. The Lincoln County petition again alleged that Crouse, acting through its agent Flynn, breached a residential sales contract between the parties and made intentional and negligent misrepresentations. Defendant Crouse moved for summary judgment on the grounds that the previous judgment against the agent constituted an election of remedies and thus barred the claim against Crouse as principal. Crouse did not allege in his motion that the judgment was satisfied and nothing else in the record indicates that the judgment was satisfied. Therefore, for the purposes of this motion, we assume the prior judgment is unsatisfied.

The prior judgment was based upon one count of intentional misrepresentation and one count of breach of contract. We first consider whether the entry of judgment against the agent on the intentional misrepresentation count constitutes an election of remedies which bars a subsequent action for intentional misrepresentation against the principal for misrepresentations made by that agent. The applicable rule is that if there is election to pursue one of two inconsistent theories, mere entry of judgment bars suit on the second theory. However, if there is an election between two consistent theories, only satisfaction of a judgment bars proceedings under the second theory.

This case does not involve an election of inconsistent remedies. The test of inconsistency is that one theory of recovery must allege what the other denies, or that the theory of one must be repugnant to the other. The plaintiffs obtained judgment against the agent and now bring suit against the principal under the same theories of law. Under these principles it is clear that "[A] person injured by the act of an agent for which the principal is liable can bring separate actions against either one." Seavey, *Agency* § 95, p. 170 (1964 Hornbook Edition).

Since the remedies against the principal and agent were consistent, only satisfaction of the claim against the agent would bar an action on the same claim against the principal.

> If the principal is liable solely because of the agent's conduct the satisfaction of judgment against one of them bars an action against the other.

Seavey, *supra*. Since the judgment against the agent on the intentional misrepresentation count was not satisfied, an action against the principal on this theory is not barred.

We next consider the breach of contract count. Defendant Crouse argues that the action against it was barred by the entry of judgment against its agent, citing *Stambaugh v. Wedlan,* 371 S.W.2d 361, 362-63 (Mo. App. 1963), for the rule that

> a person who has dealt with an agent of an undisclosed principal may elect to hold either the agent or principal [liable], he cannot hold both.

While this is a correct rule of law, it applies only where the principal is undisclosed. An undisclosed principal is discharged from liability upon a contract if the third party, knowing the identity of the principal, obtains a judgment for breach of contract against the agent who made the contract. Restatement (Second) of Agency § 210 (1957). This is because the liability of the agent and the undisclosed principal is an alternative and not a joint liability. It is clear from the pleadings that the St. Louis County action against Flynn was not premised on Crouse being an undisclosed principal.

Where the principal is disclosed, other rules govern the effect of the previous judgment. *See* Restatement (Second) of Agency § 184 comments a, b (1957). The application of these rules depends on the basis for the agent's contractual liability in the prior action. It is significant whether the agent was a party to the contract, and, if so, whether the agent was a joint contractor with the principal or if the third unsatisfied party had a separate contract with each. In either case, an unsatisfied judgment does not bar the third party from proceedings against the principal.

> Recovery of judgment against the agent of a disclosed or partially disclosed principal for failure of performance of a contract to which the agent is a party does not thereby discharge the principal.

Restatement (Second) of Agency § 184.

> If the agent is separately liable, the other party has two separate causes of action although based upon the same claim and only satisfaction of the judgment against the agent terminates the liability of the principal.

Restatement, *supra,* § 184, comment c. Because the principal was disclosed, the trial court erred in granting summary judgment.

The judgment of the trial court is reversed and the case is remanded.

Crown Controls, Inc. v. Smiley

110 Wash.2d 695, 756 P.2d 717 (1988)

DURHAM, Justice

The issue presented in this case is if the "election of remedies" doctrine should be applied when an agent fails to adequately disclose the identity of the principal on whose behalf he is contracting.

I. FACTS

Crown Controls, Inc. is a Washington corporation based in Lynnwood that acts as a sales representative for various suppliers of chemical control equipment. Its president and principal stockholder is Michael Slomer.

Jim Smiley operates a manufacturer's representative/distributorship business out of his residence in Bend, Oregon. Smiley used to own the trade name "Industrial Associates", but in January 1983 he transferred ownership of that name to an Oregon corporation called North American Drill Supply, Inc. (Drill Supply).

Pursuant to the laws of Oregon, Drill Supply registered its ownership of that name. On that registration form, Smiley is listed as the authorized representative of Drill Supply. Moreover, as of the time relevant to this case, Smiley was the president of Drill Supply and owned 75 percent of its stock, while his ex-wife owned the other 25 percent.

In June 1983, Smiley and Drill Supply had a customer in Guam who needed gas chlorination equipment for an irrigation project. Smiley telephoned Slomer of Crown Controls, identifying himself as an agent of Industrial Associates. After several telephone discussions regarding various items of equipment and their prices, Slomer agreed to supply and Smiley agreed to purchase gas chlorination equipment. It was subsequently delivered to and accepted by Smiley and Drill Supply's shipping agent in Portland, Oregon. Crown Controls billed Industrial Associates for $9,136.03.

Throughout the course of the negotiations between the parties, Smiley never disclosed to anyone at Crown Controls that he was acting on behalf of a corporate entity; he indicated only that he was an agent for "Industrial Associates". Crown Controls was not informed of Drill Supply's existence until litigation commenced.

At the same time as this transaction, Smiley and Drill Supply also ordered pump control valves from Crown Controls. The Guam customer eventually encountered problems with these valves and returned them to Crown Controls' supplier.

In December 1983, in response to repeated demands for payment for the gas chlorination equipment, Smiley tendered a check to Crown Controls in the amount of $5,547.92, an amount less than the $9,136.03 that was billed, on the "express condition that it is in full and complete satisfaction of all my obligations to you..." The lower amount represented an offset for damages attributable to the problems encountered with the rejected pump control valves. Crown Controls refused to accept payment on this condition and returned the check to Smiley.

Crown Controls filed a complaint against Smiley and Drill Supply in Snohomish County in order to collect the full amount billed for the chlorination equipment. Drill Supply responded by suing Crown Controls in an Oregon state court, seeking to recover damages attributable to the pump control valves. Smiley and Drill Supply also asserted these same damages as an affirmative defense in the Snohomish County action. The Oregon action was removed to federal court, where Drill Supply eventually received judgment in the amount of $3,363.11, plus interest.

In the Snohomish County action, Crown Controls moved for summary judgment. The trial court granted summary judgment against Drill Supply, doing business as Industrial Associates, but refused to grant summary judgment against Smiley, concluding that a material issue of fact existed concerning if Smiley had disclosed that he was acting on behalf of Drill Supply. Crown Controls tried to collect on the judgment against Drill Supply by garnishing its bank account in supplemental proceedings, but this proved unsuccessful because that account had already been closed.

Trial was held on March 14, 1985 on the issue of Smiley's liability. The court concluded that Smiley had breached his contract to pay for the chlorination equipment. The trial court further determined that Smiley had not sufficiently disclosed that he was acting on behalf of Drill Supply, causing Smiley to become personally liable for the debt. The court then held that Crown Controls had to elect whether it would pursue Smiley or Drill Supply in collecting on its judgment. Crown Controls elected to pursue Smiley, so the court vacated the earlier summary judgment Crown Controls had received against Drill Supply. Judgment was entered in the amount of $9,136.03, plus prejudgment and postjudgment interest.

Smiley appealed this judgment to the Court of Appeals. That court affirmed the trial court's holding that [Smiley] had failed to properly disclose the existence and identity of Drill Supply. However, the Court of Appeals rejected the election of remedies doctrine. Instead, the court imposed joint and several liability against Smiley and Drill Supply. *Crown Controls, Inc. v. Smiley*, 47 Wash.App. 832, 848, 737 P.2d 709 (1987).

Smiley filed a petition for review in this court, challenging the Court of Appeals decision with respect to each of the issues discussed in the preceding paragraph. This court accepted review.

II. ANALYSIS

Smiley argues that by obtaining a judgment against Drill Supply, and by attempting to collect on that judgment, Crown Controls elected to give up their rights against him. In support, Smiley points to this state's "election of remedies" doctrine. Under that doctrine, the liability of an agent and his undisclosed principal on a contract is only in the alternative. In other words, after learning all the relevant facts, a creditor must elect whether he will hold the agent or the principal liable for the debt. A creditor who elects to hold the previously undisclosed principal liable thereby discharges the agent, even if the creditor subsequently discovers that the principal is insolvent. Furthermore, the entry of a judgment against the principal amounts to an election to forego collecting from the agent.

As the Court of Appeals recognized, this doctrine has been a part of Washington case law since the turn of the century, and has been invoked many times, usually in dicta, although its rationale has never been set forth in any great detail.

Generally, opinions issued by this court are binding on the lower courts until they are overruled. In this case, the Court of Appeals rejected the "election of remedies" rule as being "illogical and contrary to the policy favoring full compensation of wronged parties." *Crown Controls*, 47 Wash.App. at 842, 737 P.2d 709. Accordingly, we accepted review to independently determine if a creditor should be forced to elect his remedies when suing an agent and an undisclosed principal.

Evaluation of the relative merits of the "election of remedies" doctrine in this context can be reduced to the following dilemma: legal commentators generally consider joint and several liability to be the better reasoned approach, but alternative liability has been the rule in this state for decades and it has long been the majority rule in other jurisdictions as well. For example, the Reporter for the American Law Institute stated that the Restatement adopted the theory of alternative liability because it felt bound by judicial precedent in the majority of jurisdictions, but felt the minority rule to be better reasoned. *See Grinder v. Bryans Rd. Bldg. & Supply Co.*, 290 Md. 687, 699-700, 432 A.2d 453 (1981) (citing Restatement of Agency s 435, explanatory notes (Temp. Draft No. 4, 1929)). Each of these considerations will be evaluated in greater detail, beginning with the relative merits of applying the doctrine in the context of undisclosed principals.

We have recognized in an earlier case the harsh nature of the "election of remedies" doctrine in general. *Barber v. Rochester*, 52 Wash.2d 691, 695, 328 P.2d 711 (1958). We have also indicated that:

> The doctrine of election of remedies is applicable only where there are available to the litigant at the time of the election, two or more coexistent remedies, which are repugnant and inconsistent. This rule is upon the theory that, of several inconsistent remedies, the pursuit of one necessarily involves or implies the negation of the others. The rule does not apply where the remedies are cumulative merely.

Willis T. Batcheller, Inc. v. Welden Constr. Co., 9 Wash.2d 392, 403-04, 115 P.2d 696 (1941), quoted in *Labor Hall Ass'n, Inc. v. Danielsen*, 24 Wash.2d 75, 84, 163 P.2d 167, 161 A.L.R. 1079 (1945). Accordingly, we must determine if it would be "repugnant and inconsistent" to allow creditors to have simultaneous remedies against an agent and his undisclosed principal.

The Court of Appeals relied heavily on the reasoning from a Maryland case that replaced the "election of remedies" rule in this context with a rule stating that judgments may simultaneously be entered against an agent and his undisclosed principal, although only one satisfaction may be obtained. *See Grinder v. Bryans Rd. Bldg. & Supply Co., supra.* This latter rule can be described more generally as joint and several liability, because it allows a creditor to collect from the agent, the principal, or both, until the judgment has been fully satisfied.

As *Grinder* points out, the "election of remedies" rule in the context of undisclosed principals was traditionally justified by three arguments. Two of these arguments, however, are clearly inadequate.[1] The remaining argument justifying the tradition of alternative liability is the "one contract—no windfall" rationale. According to this rationale, the plaintiff has only contracted for one cause of action and would receive an unjustified windfall if the creditor were allowed to sue the agent and the principal simultaneously. *See Grinder*, 290 Md. at 697, 432 A.2d 453.

However, opponents of alternative liability stress that a creditor has two distinct causes of action, both arising from the failure to perform the obligations of the contract. The undisclosed principal becomes liable because he initiates the contract and profits by it; the agent becomes liable because of his promise. These opponents maintain that the assertion of liability of either the agent or the principal is entirely in harmony with a claim against the other. *See, e.g.,* Merrill, *Election Between Agent and Undisclosed Principal: Shall We Follow the Restate-*

---

1. These arguments can be summarized as follows. First, alternative liability was intended to protect the principal from the vexation of having to defend two suits, one brought by the creditor and the other brought by the agent seeking indemnity for his own liability. This argument, however, does not adequately support the current theory of alternative liability, because modern pleading practice allows for impleading and consolidation of actions. Second, the theory was traditionally predicated on merger analysis, which stated that two rights of action brought against different parties, but based on the same set of facts, could not coexist when one action had been reduced to judgment. Merger analysis fails, however, in explaining why recovery of judgment against the agent before learning about the existence of an undisclosed principal does not bar a subsequent action against the principal. Grinder, 290 Md. at 696-97, 432 A.2d 453.

ment?, 12 Neb.L.Bull. 100, 122 (1933), cited in Grinder, 290 Md. at 703, 432 A.2d 453. This position has been maintained by most of the commentators, who "appear to be nearly unanimous in their support of the minority, *i.e.,* satisfaction, rule." *Grinder,* 290 Md. at 703-04, 432 A.2d 453 (citing J. Story, Agency § 295, at 378 (3d ed. 1846)); F. Wharton, Agency & Agents § 473 (1876); F. Mecham, Agency § 159 (1952); Ferson, Undisclosed Principals, 22 U.Cin.L.Rev. 131, 142-44 (1953).

Furthermore, there is no "windfall" to the creditor. Although he can seek to recover damages from more than one party, his aggregate recovery is limited by the amount of the judgment. Indeed, as the Court of Appeals pointed out, retention of the current law constitutes an unjustified windfall for the debtors who are able to use the doctrine to avoid debts that they are otherwise obligated to pay.

The opponents of alternative liability also point out the inequities created by that doctrine. As the *Grinder* court stated:

> In cases where election can become an issue, we are satisfied that adherence to [alternative liability] will create more unjust results and generate more mischief than would a change in the law to a rule that looks to one satisfaction. Under the [alternative liability] rule, if the problem arises out of separate actions, the second suit will likely have been brought because the judgment in the first action has not been satisfied. If judgment in the second action is denied solely because the law considers an election to have taken place, a just claim has necessarily been thwarted. If the creditor proceeds in an action in which both principal and agent are joined, an interlocutory judgment against one defendant, *e.g.,* by default or through summary judgment, can become a trap. It could leave the creditor with but one, possibly uncollectible, judgment, unless the election rule is further eroded, as some courts have done, by a requirement that an adversary call upon the plaintiff to elect before the first judgment is taken. The need to resort to this variation strongly suggests the dissatisfaction of courts with the basic election rule. If, in a joint action, the proceedings against each defendant are in tandem and the plaintiff is entitled, under the election rule, to a judgment against either, the decision requires knowledge of relative assets. This is not ordinarily a subject of pre-trial discovery and the choice involves the risk that the judgment opted for may prove to be uncollectible, while a solvent party may be discharged, because his liability is viewed as "alternative."

Grinder, 290 Md. at 707, 432 A.2d 453.

Other courts have also found the logic of the Maryland court to be persuasive. The Grinder rationale has been adopted in Minnesota and implicitly approved of by dictum in Oregon. *Engelstad v. Cargill, Inc.,* 336 N.W.2d 284 (Minn. 1983); *Carter v. Forstrom,* 80 Or.App. 213, 722 P.2d 23 (1986). Additionally, the drafters of the Restatement have stated that the "trend in development of the law" is to reject the theory that entry of judgment against a previously undisclosed principal releases the agent. Restatement (Second) of Judgments § 49, comment c (1982). We conclude that the *Grinder* rule of joint and several liability is the better reasoned approach, and that coexistent remedies against the agent and principal would be neither inconsistent nor repugnant.

Finally, we believe that a decision not to apply the "election of remedies" doctrine to these facts would not contravene the principles of *stare decisis.* When a certain legal principle has already been established in a jurisdiction, there is much to be said for its continued existence. The continuity of legal principles allows citizens to choose courses of action with a reasonable expectation of what the future legal consequences will be, even if those consequences might not arise for a considerable period of time. These interests, together with a desire to provide a society of laws and not of men, form the basis for the theory of stare decisis. However, the goal of obtaining stability in the law does not always justify the continued existence of clearly outdated rules. As we have stated several times:

> Stare decisis is a doctrine developed by courts to accomplish the requisite element of stability in court-made law, but is not an absolute impediment to change. Without the stabilizing effect of this doctrine, law could become subject to incautious action or the whims of current holders of judicial office. But we also recognize that stability should not be confused with perpetuity. If the law is to have a current relevance, courts must have and exert the capacity to change a rule of law when reason so requires. The true doctrine of stare decisis is compatible with this function of the courts. The doctrine requires a clear showing that an established rule is incorrect and harmful before it is abandoned.

[*In re Stranger Creek,* 77 Wash.2d 649, 653, 466 P.2d 508 (1970)], quoted in *In re Mercer,* 108 Wash.2d 714, 720-21, 741 P.2d 559 (1987) and *House v. Erwin,* 83 Wash.2d 898, 909, 524 P.2d 911 (1974).

In this regard, we find it unlikely that many citizens have relied on the "election of remedies" rule in ordering their legal affairs in this area. Moreover, we note that the Maryland court was apparently correct in its conclusion that "adherence to [alternative liability] will create more unjust results and generate more mischief than would a change in the law..." *Grinder,* 290 Md. at 707, 432 A.2d 453. In the almost 7 years since *Grinder* was filed, there have been no reported decisions in Maryland citing that case, indicating that the citizens of that state have had little difficulty in adapting to the new rule. For these reasons, as well as those given above concerning the inequitable nature of the "election of remedies" doctrine, we conclude that the doctrine in the context of undisclosed principals is incorrect and harmful.

In conclusion, we hold that the liability of an agent and his previously undisclosed principal is no longer alternative, but is joint and several. Accordingly, a creditor may recover judgments against both the principal and the agent, may attempt to collect its judgment against either party, and, to the extent that the judgment remains unsatisfied, may subsequently pursue collection from the other party.

We remand the case for the trial court to impose joint and several liability against Smiley and Drill Supply.

Notes

1. An agent acting for an undisclosed or partially disclosed principal generally is *not* relieved from liability on the contract short of a final judgment against the principal. This is true even though the third person may have indicated that he or she was going to hold the principal liable. The agent is only relieved from liability by conduct short of taking a final judgment against the principal

to the extent that he is prejudiced thereby if he changes his position in *justifiable reliance* upon a manifestation of the [third person] that he will look *solely* to the principal for performance.

Restatement § 336 (emphasis added).

2. In *Newark Parafinne Paper Co. v. Dugan*, 162 N.J. Super. 575, 394 A.2d 114 (1978), an agent had entered into a lease in the agent's own name, but on behalf of an undisclosed principal. After the principal had defaulted in the payment of rent, the landlord asserted a landlord's lien against $2,400 worth of the principal's property (as opposed to $66,000 due under the lease). The court held the agent was still liable reasoning that (i) the landlord's conduct was *not* a *definite* manifestation of an election to hold *only* the principal liable sufficient to permit the agent to rely on it, and (ii) in any event, there was no showing that the agent had in fact changed position in reliance on the manifestation.

3. The election of remedies doctrine can also apply to release an *undisclosed principal* from liability to the third person, but only so long as the third person *knows* of the identity of the principal. Restatement §§ 209 & 210.

4. The extract from *Bryans Road Building & Supply, Inc. v. Grinder* that is quoted in *Crown Controls, Inc. v. Smiley* raises the concern that, in actions against both the agent and the principal, an interlocutory judgment could "trap" the third party into an unwitting "election." The intermediate appellate opinion in *Grinder* addressed this concern when it held that, as a matter of *procedural law*, such interlocutory judgments are not *final*, so do not result in an election of remedies.

5. Which approach makes more sense, the election of remedies majority rule, or the "joint and several" ("one satisfaction") approach?

Problem 2.7

D is the owner of a very complete and rare stamp collection. He has been a competitor of P for many years. A year ago, D contracted to sell the collection to A. The terms of the contract were that A would pay $1000 down and $19,000 in twelve months. Delivery of the collection was to be made when the $19,000 was paid. A paid D the $10000 down payment. At the time of the original transaction, D told A that D did not want P to acquire the collection because of the way P had acted in the past. A said that he had no intention of selling to P, which was true. A few months later, A suddenly needed some capital and put all of his stamps up for sale with a dealer, advising the dealer that he had contracted to buy D's collection. The dealer sought bids from prospective purchasers, and P's bid was by far the highest bid received. Accordingly, A sold his collection to P. In connection with the sale, he executed an agreement with P whereby A sold and conveyed to P every right and title, both legal and equitable, that he had in D's collection, reciting that he had a contract to buy the collection. When the date for performance by A arose, P tendered to D $19,000 cash and asked for delivery of the collection. D refused and still refuses to deliver the collection. P has kept this tender open. P has instituted suit for specific performance to compel D to carry out the contract and to deliver the stamps to P. On the facts given, should P prevail? Discuss (Illinois Bar Examination, Feb. 1976).

Notes

1. In the preceding problem, if P had been unable to pay the $19,000, could D have enforced the contract against P?

2. If A had paid the $19,000 to D, could A have then sold the stamps to P?

3. In considering your answers to the questions in Notes 1 and 2, what difference would it make if the relations between A and P were characterized as an agency, an assignment from A to P or a sale from A to P? Are these three relationships mutually exclusive?

Chapter 3

Formation of Firms

A. Introduction

As you may recall from the introductory chapter, there are a number of different organizational forms available to those who wish to set up a business enterprise. The formalities required for formation differ depending on the type of firm which is chosen.

In addition, within a firm, a number of different relationships are not only possible, but probable. Some of the relationships will be created automatically upon the creation of the business. Other relationships are optional or variable. That is, regardless of the type of firm, it is possible to create additional agency relationships. The terms of these relationships are usually subject to the agreement of the involved parties. In addition, many of the relationships which are created by virtue of choosing to organize a business as one type of entity or another may be refined by further agreement of the parties.

This chapter focuses on the formation stage for these types of relationships. First, we will consider what it takes to set up an agency relationship in general and independent of the nature of the principal. Then, we will turn to a more focused consideration of the what it takes to organize the various kinds of business enterprises, and the types of relationships created by such choices.

B. Agency Relationships

Estate of Giannopoulos

89 Misc. 2d 961, 392 N.Y.S.2d 828 (Surrogate's Court 1977)

LOUIS D. LAURINO, Surrogate.

A firm of New York attorneys seeks to have the court entertain an application regarding the widow's alleged right of election to take against the decedent's Will. The widow, 'ARETI GIANNOPOULOS,' 'ARETI JANOPULLI' or 'ARETI GIANNOPULOS,' is a resident of Albania. The firm's authority to represent her is based upon a power of attorney allegedly executed by her in Albania. This "power of attorney' was filed for recording by the firm with a clerk of the court.

EPTL 13—2.3 provides that every power of attorney relating to an interest in an estate shall be in writing and acknowledged or proved in the manner prescribed by the laws of this state for the recording of a conveyance of real property and shall be recorded in the Surrogate's Court having jurisdiction. The statute also provides that the Surrogate may inquire into the validity of the power of attorney and prescribe rules consistent with the section.

In examining the power of attorney and the documents accompanying it in connection with the present application, the court finds that they do not comply with the various sections of the Real Property Law, the CPLR and the Uniform Rules [for All Surrogate's Courts in the Second Department] involved and that the instrument and accompanying papers should not have been accepted for filing.

Section 1830:33(b) of the Uniform Rules regarding the filing and recording of powers of attorney provides:

> The person offering the instrument for filing or recording shall furnish an affidavit of the attorney-in-fact, stating the circumstances under which the power of attorney was procured; the post office address of the grantor, the amount of his interest and relationship, if any, to decedent; the financial arrangement and exact terms of compensation of the attorney-in-fact or of any other person concerned with the matter; disbursements to be charged to the grantor; a copy of any agreement concerning compensation; name of any attorney representing the attorney-in-fact.

A member of the law firm to which the power allegedly runs has supplied an affirmation in connection with this rule. The only address given for the alleged grantor, 'Mrs. Giannopulos,' is 'Fier, Albania,' which is also the only address given for the grantor in the power itself. It might be argued that there are no house numbers in Fier, Albania, except that the application which the court is asked to entertain regarding the right of election contains the house numbers of a number of other persons residing in Fier.

The affirmation states the circumstances under which the power of attorney was received:

> We received this power of attorney in the normal course of business relationships with forwarders from Albania known as Shoqeria Komisionaria, who first apprised us of this estate and asked us to protect the interests of our client by letter dated October 20, 1975.

No attempt is given to explain who or what 'Shoqeria Komisionaria' is or what their interest is in the matter, financial or otherwise.

The affirmation goes on to state that the attorneys will receive no fees as attorney-in-fact and that as attorneys-at-law they will receive 20% of the net to their client, together with out-of-pocket expenses. There is nothing in the alleged power of attorney that reflects that such an arrangement has been agreed to by their alleged client, nor is a copy of any such agreement attached to the affirmation.

The translation accompanying the power of attorney is also defective. CPLR 2101 provides that when a paper served or filed is in a foreign language, it shall be accompanied by an English translation and an affidavit [under oath or an affirmation under pain of perjury] by the translator setting forth his qualifications and that the translation is accurate.

The translation of the main body of the power of attorney from Albanian to English was allegedly made by a lawyer residing in Albania, a country with which the United States does not maintain diplomatic relations. More importantly, the statement of the translator as to his qualifications and the accuracy of the translation is not given under oath or an affirmation under pain of perjury. There is a mere acknowledgement of his signature before a notary.

Section 312(2) of the Real Property Law sets forth the [required] contents of a certificate of authentication accompanying a certificate of acknowledgement made before a notary in a foreign country. The certificate of authentication accompanying the certificate of acknowledgement of the notary public before whom the widow allegedly appeared does not comply with this section. This failure to comply with the Real Property Law would in and of itself be sufficient reason to refuse to record the power of attorney. The signature of 'Mrs. Giannopoulos' and the acknowledgement before the 'notary' also raise grave questions as to whether the grantor knew what she was doing at the time of signing. The acknowledgement refers to the identity of the signer and states she is of full legal capacity and that she "executed the foregoing instrument and signed same in my presence as her free act and deed."

The Albanian text under which the signature of the alleged grantor appears is written in the Latin Alphabet. Yet the signature is written in the Greek Alphabet. As far as indicating any understanding of what was being signed, it is then the equivalent of the illiterate's 'X' In spite of this, there is no statement by the notary that the document was read to her or explained to her.

Based on all of the above, the court finds that this power of attorney was improperly accepted by the clerk for filing and recording.

As to the application made by the firm of attorneys to determine the validity of the widow's right of election and for other relief, without the power of attorney there is nothing to show under what authority these attorneys are acting.

Accordingly, the application is not entertained, as the firm is without legal authority to appear in this matter.

Notes

1. Agents are persons who are "authorized" to act for another, and by so acting, to bind that other person. *Actual* authority has been defined as "the power of the agent to affect the legal relations of the principal by acts done in accordance with the principal's manifestations of consent to him." Restatement (Second) of Agency § 7.

2. What is the source of the requirement that the power of attorney in *Estate of Giannopoulos* be given in a certain manner?

3. Suppose that a principal wishes to authorize an agent to take an action that itself requires formalities of action, such as a contract required to be in writing under the statute of frauds. Do those formalities of action apply to the principal's authorization of the agent? That is, must the form of authorization be of *equal dignity* to the underlying act?

At common law, equal dignity is only required for *contracts under seal*. Thus, a written contract signed by agent orally authorized to do so satisfies the statute of frauds. *E.g., Little v. Clark*, 592 S.W.2d 61 (Tex. Civ. App. 1979) (*contract* for sale of land). However, in most states, equal dignities in the authorization of an agent are required, at least for certain actions. Equal dignities are frequently required by statute as to such matters as *deeds*, contracts for the sale of land, or other contracts within the statute of frauds. The actions that require equal dignities vary from state to state.

4. Even where equal dignities are required, action on behalf of *corporate* principals raise special problems. Although a corporation is an entity—a legal person—it has no body. Of necessity, corporate action requires that *someone* act on behalf of the corporation. How, then, can the corporation meet the equal dignities requirement? This problem is handled by deeming that the acts of certain persons are *in themselves* the acts of the corporation. For example, under corporate law, the management of a corporation's business is entrusted to its *board of directors*. The board of directors is not, as such, an *agent* of the corporation, Restatement (Second) of Agency § 14C. Rather, it is that *part* of the corporation that acts on its behalf.

Second, under many state statutes, the authorized acts of certain *officers* are deemed to be the acts of the corporation, so that the authority of such officers to act need not be evidenced separately. For example, while Texas law requires that an agent's authority to sign a *deed* must be evidenced in recordable form (in writing, acknowledged, etc.), a corporate officer's deed is recordable if the officer acknowledges the deed as the act of the corporation. Such deeds are *prima facie* evidence of approval of the deed by the board of directors. TEX. REV. CIV. STAT. ANN. art. 1396-5.09 (Vernon's 1980).

Maricopa Partnerships, Inc. v. Petyak
790 P.2d 279 (Ariz. App. 1989)

HATHAWAY, Judge.

Edward and Jane Doe Petyak (appellants) appeal from a judgment in the amount of $29,800 entered in favor of The Maricopa Partnerships, Inc. (appellee), following a jury verdict. The sole issue on appeal is whether the trial court's instruction on the agency theory was an incorrect statement of the law constituting reversible error.

Appellant Edward Petyak, an American Airlines pilot, was also engaged in importing and reselling luxury cars. He met with appellee in the spring of 1985. Following a discussion of specifications, they orally agreed that appellant would locate and import a new Jaguar automobile for appellee. On June 4, 1985, appellee gave appellant a $2,500 check as a down payment. The vehicle was to be imported from Europe and delivered to appellee after completion of modifications to meet U.S. regulations.

There were delays in importing the Jaguar over a six-month period of time. Appellant advised appellee of the problems and indicated it might be another three to four months before the Jaguar would arrive, if at all.

Appellant apparently advised that he had seen newspaper ads in Dallas showing Jaguars available at similar prices. It is disputed whether appellee or appellant initially suggested pursuing the Dallas ads instead of waiting to import directly from Europe. It is undisputed that appellant agreed to look into the Dallas ads on behalf of appellee.

Appellant visited the Dallas dealership, Gerimco, and found a vehicle meeting appellee's specifications. He telephoned appellee from the dealership and negotiated the price and modifications between appellee and the dealer over the phone. It was agreed at that time that the purchase price would be $29,800, including modifications. Appellee and appellant agreed that Gerimco would ship the car to appellee in Phoenix. Appellant agreed to write his personal check for the purchase price and within several days appellee delivered a check to appellant for the purchase price, less the $2,500 deposit already paid. No profit to appellant was contemplated under these terms.

Appellant's cancelled check to Gerimco for $29,800 was admitted in evidence. Appellee's testimony both on direct and cross-examination was that the dealer, Gerimco, not appellant, was to deliver the car to Phoenix. The Jaguar never arrived in Phoenix. Upon inquiry, appellant learned that the dealer absconded with the money and the Texas bank which held the lien on the Jaguar repossessed it. Appellee demanded a refund of the purchase price which appellant refused to pay. Appellee then filed suit and following a three-day trial, the case went to the jury on two theories. Under the first theory, appellee alleged breach of a sales contract. Under the second, appellee alleged that appellant breached an agency agreement. The jury was instructed on both theories. On the agency issue, the court instructed:

> In deciding that issue, you must decide the extent of the agent's duties to the principal as determined by the terms of the agreement between the parties, interpreted in the light of the circumstances under which it was made. The plaintiff has the burden of proving the terms of the agency agreement.

> If the agent fails to accomplish what he agreed to achieve, there is a breach [of] contractual duty and the agent is liable to the principal for actual damages caused by the breach.

> You are to determine the terms of the agency agreement if you find the parties had a relationship of principal and agent.

During the settling of jury instructions, appellant's counsel objected to the refusal to give an instruction stating that before the jury could find breach of an agency agreement it would have to find that the agent failed to exercise reasonable care and skill in carrying out his duties. Following deliberation, the jury returned a general verdict in favor of appellee, finding damages of $29,800.

Appellants argue that the trial court erroneously instructed the jury on the law of agency. On review, we will consider as a whole the jury instructions given to determine whether the challenged instruction misled the jury as to the proper rule of law. They contend the instructions given resulted in strict liability if the jury found any breach, regardless of the circumstances. Under the instructions given, they reason that the jury would have to find against appellants on an agency theory if it found appellee did not receive the Jaguar (an already agreed fact) because it had no instructions regarding the reasonableness of the performance rendered.

Appellee responds that the trial court simply instructed the jury that appellee had the burden of establishing the existence of the agency contract, a breach by the appellant, and the resulting damages. Further, appellee contends the law does not require proof of the elements of a negligence claim in order to prove a breach of contract claim. Appellee cites Restatement (Second) of Agency, § 379, comment a, and § 400 (1958), as support.

In the absence of prior decisions to the contrary, we will follow the Restatement of the Law whenever applicable. Agency is both a consensual and a fiduciary relationship. Restatement (Second) of Agency, [§§ 376-431]. This creates a duty upon the agent to act in good faith and according to the terms of the agency agreement. The inherent nature of the agency relationship imposes a fiduciary duty upon the agent to act according to the terms of the agency agreement. We believe that Restatement (Second) of Agency, § 377 clarifies the law regarding the present issue before us. This section states that one who makes a contract with another to perform services as an agent for him is subject to a duty to act according to his promise. Comment a indicates the agent's liability and defenses for a breach of contract are according to those stated in the Restatement of Contracts and as set forth in the Restatement (Second) of Agency at §§ 399-431. Comment b [to § 377] explains that

> [u]nder ordinary circumstances, the promise to act as an agent is interpreted as being a promise only to make reasonable efforts to accomplish the directed results. If so interpreted, the promisor is not liable unless he fails to make such efforts as he reasonably can.

Therefore, a threshold finding would require the jury to consider whether the agent acted reasonably in executing the duties spelled out in the agency agreement.

Appellee argues that under Restatement (Second) of Agency, § 400 controls and appellant could have asserted any contract defenses excusing his performance, but failed to do so. Appellee contends the jury was properly instructed regarding liability for breach of the agency contract.

We believe that determining whether an agent has violated a duty owed to his principal does not depend upon that agent asserting a contract defense. We note that in the illustrations cited following § 400, each example finds liability only after the agent has negligently failed to perform. We read this to mean the agent has a duty to act with reasonable care and skill.

We find the instructions to the jury deficient in not informing the jury that the agent's liability was predicated upon a finding that the agent breached its duty to act with reasonable care and skill. We reverse and remand for further proceedings consistent with this opinion.

Note

Agency is both a contractual, as well as a fiduciary, relationship. Agency is contractual in the sense that it grows out of mutual consent to some undertaking:

> An agency relation exists only if there has been a manifestation by the principal to the agent that the agent may act on [the principal's] account, and consent by the agent so to act.

Restatement § 15. Unlike traditional contracts, creation of the agency relationship does not require a mutual exchange of consideration. Restatement § 16.

Because an agent is entrusted with the power to act on behalf of the principal, an agent is a fiduciary with respect to matters entrusted to the agent. *See* Restatement §§ 1, 13. Similarly, a servant is a fiduciary of the master and is subject to the same duties as an agent. Restatement § 429. Fiduciary relationships arise in a wide variety of other contexts. Attorneys, partners, corporate officers, and directors all act in fiduciary capacities and are subject to fiduciary duties. The nature and extent of the duties to which any particular fiduciary is subject are "determined by the terms of the agreement between the parties [and] interpreted in light of the circumstances." Restatement § 376.

The principal case centers on the interplay between the contractual and the fiduciary duties growing out of the agent's undertaking to act on the principal's behalf in locating and in purchasing a Jaguar. The principal argued that the contractual aspect of the relationship should control, and cited Section 400 of the Restatement, which provides that

> An agent who commits a breach of his contract with his principal is subject to liability to the principal in accordance with the principles of the Restatement of Contracts.

Restatement § 400. Comment a to Section 400 recognizes that "the application of the rules which apply to contracts in general is sometimes unique when applied to agency situations," but goes on to state that "there is no inconsistency between the rules of the two subjects." *Id.* comment a.

In the principal case, how does the court reconcile contractual and agency principles?

C. Partnerships

Section 6 of the Uniform Partnership Act (UPA) defines a partnership as "an association of two or more persons to carry on as co-owners a business for profit." Section 202(a) of the RUPA (the 1996 revision of the UPA) continues this definition in slightly altered form ("the association of two or more persons to carry on as co-owners a business for profit *forms* a partnership." RUPA § 202(a) (emphasis added). Unlike a corporation or a limited partnership, formalities are not necessary to create a partnership. While the informality of a partnership is one of the chief advantages of the partnership form of doing business, persons involved in a business relationship sometimes discover that they have become partners without realizing it. Becoming a partner has significant implications: partners are liable for partnership obligations; UPA § 15, RUPA § 306(a), and partners bear a share of partnership losses; UPA § 18(a), RUPA § 401(a)(2).

Dalton v. Austin

432 A.2d 774 (Me. 1981)

NICHOLS, Justice.

The Plaintiff, Emily Dalton, appeals from a judgment for the Defendant, Whitney W. Austin, Sr., entered by the Superior Court in Penobscot County after a jury-waived trial on her complaint for conversion of certain financial contributions she had made to a business in Bangor known as The Small Change Restaurant, of which Austin was originally the sole proprietor.

In March of 1974, the Plaintiff and Defendant reached an oral agreement concerning the business, the exact terms of which were the subject of conflicting testimony at trial. The Plaintiff, who had prior experience in the restaurant business, testified that she and the Defendant agreed to be equal partners in the restaurant and that, in consideration of certain financial contributions she was to make to the business, the Defendant agreed to incorporate the business, turn those business assets to which he had title over to the corporation, and distribute stock to the Plaintiff and himself. It appears, however, that the Plaintiff did not expect the business to be incorporated until after she became involved in its operation.

The Defendant testified that he and the Plaintiff agreed to become partners and that in consideration for being made a partner, the Plaintiff initially contributed her automobile to the business. The Defendant's understanding of the agreement differed from the Plaintiff's, however, in that he did not recall promising to turn assets over to the corporation, or to have stock issued and distributed. Rather, his testimony suggests that the agreement contemplated that the Plaintiff would ultimately purchase the restaurant, thus leaving him "free and clear" of the business, a circumstance the Defendant desired for reasons of health and overwork. In response to questions posed by opposing counsel as to whether the Defendant agreed to transfer assets in his name to the corporation and distribute stock to the Plaintiff, the Defendant testified that he did not remember or understand that arrangement but thought the heart of the agreement to be the Plaintiff's ultimate purchase of the entire business.

After the agreement was made, the Defendant no longer took an active part in management of the restaurant; the Plaintiff, on the other hand, operated the business on a day-to-day basis for several months. In the months that she managed the restaurant, the Plaintiff made major financial contributions to the business totaling $18,214.89. She made these contributions by directly paying the debts and operating expenses of the business. The Defendant testified that he had no knowledge of the nature or extent of her payments on behalf of the business and that he never personally received them.

Under the Plaintiff's management, business income declined dramatically. After operating the business for several months, the Plaintiff finally asked the Defendant to distribute the stock and transfer the assets. The record does not disclose whether the business was ever incorporated. Stock, however, was never distributed, and the Defendant's testimony suggests that ownership of business-related assets was never transferred to a corporation. Instead, a closing date for sale of the restaurant to the Plaintiff was set. On the advice of her attorneys, however, she ultimately refused to purchase the business from the Defendant and he eventually closed the business when its management totally failed. Thereafter, he made several attempts to lease profitably the business and finally sold it to a lessee. The proceeds from the sale, according to the Defendant's testimony, were used to pay mortgagees and creditors whose claims apparently exceeded the gain from the sale. The Defendant claims to have paid the balance out of personal funds.

At trial, after testimony by the two parties was heard, the presiding justice found for the Defendant. The justice specifically found that the parties were partners and that their original agreement created a partnership. From that finding, he concluded that neither party had a cause of action for restitution or conversion. In response to the request of the Plaintiff's counsel for a specific finding on whether an agreement existed between the parties in which the Defendant was obliged to transfer assets to the corporation and distribute stock, the court declined to rule on the specifics of any such agreement. Rather, the court limited its ruling to finding generally that a partnership agreement existed and that any controversy over the business arising out of the partnership was properly the subject of an action for an accounting between partners.

On appeal here, the Plaintiff contends the Superior Court erred in finding a partnership and in concluding that an action for conversion or money had and received was inappropriate.

We must uphold the Superior Court's conclusion that a partnership existed if competent evidence exists on the record to support that legal conclusion.

The Plaintiff argues that the Superior Court erred in concluding a partnership existed because no evidence of co-ownership or sharing of profits appears on the record.

Under the Uniform Partnership Act, which Maine adopted in 1973, as under the common law, the existence of a partnership is an inference of law based on established facts. Under the Act, a partnership is defined as "an association of 2 or more persons to carry on as co-owners a business for profit" [UPA § 6].

Evidence relevant to the existence of a partnership includes evidence of a voluntary contract between two persons to place their money, effects, labor, and skill, or some or all of them, in lawful commerce or business with the understanding that a community of profits will be shared. No one factor is alone determinative of the existence of a partnership, but the record before us supports the finding of the Superior Court.

While the specifics of the agreement were in dispute, evidence of an agreement between the parties existed. That agreement clearly related to operation of a business. Assets used in the business and capital contributions to the business were made by both parties. They consistently testified that both regarded themselves as partners. Finally, the Plaintiff actively managed the business for several months.

The Plaintiff contends, nevertheless, that there is no evidence of co-ownership or a sharing of profits. Under the Uniform Act, the concept of co-ownership does not necessarily mean joint title to all business assets. Rather, as the commentary to the Uniform Act suggests, the right to participate in control of the business is the essence of co-ownership. *See* Official Comment, UPA § 6.[1] Contrary to this Plaintiff's contention, then, the record sufficiently supports the existence of co-ownership inasmuch as it reveals that she actively managed the business for several months without the supervision of the Defendant. While the record is devoid of

---

1. The draftsman of the Model Act noted in the Comment following section 6:
    The definition asserts that the associates are "co-owners" of the business. This distinguishes a partnership from an agency — an association of principal and agent. A business is a series of acts directed toward an end. Ownership involves the power of ultimate control. To state that partners are co-owners of a business is to state that they each have the power of ultimate control.

evidence that the parties shared profits, sharing is not required if, as the evidence shows in this case, the agreement itself implies that the parties contemplated the sharing of profits. In the case before us evidence of actual sharing of profits was naturally absent, given the financial straits of the business.

We conclude that the Superior Court did not err in concluding that Austin and Dalton were engaged in a partnership.

The Plaintiff also argues that the Defendant is liable to her for conversion under theories of unjust enrichment or quasi-contract. The record before us indicates that the basis of Plaintiff's claim is intimately related to partnership affairs. Moreover, the record is replete with confusion and ambiguity concerning the winding up of the partnership as well as the manner in which the partnership property was ultimately liquidated. These circumstances both suggest the prudence of settling the dispute between these two litigants in one comprehensive proceeding for an account and provide adequate support for the finding below that an independent action was inappropriate.

We conclude that there was no error when the Superior Court entered judgment for the Defendant.

Notes

1. In *Dalton v. Austin,* the Court did not cite UPA section 7 in making its decision. What did the Court rely on instead? Why is UPA section 6 relevant to the question of whether the parties were partners?

2. A traditional principle of partnership law is that one partner may not sue the partnership or another partner on a matter arising out of partnership affairs until the partnership has been dissolved, its affairs wound up, and there has been an *accounting* of such affairs. This principle has several theoretical bases. First, to the extent a partnership is an aggregate, a partner's suit against the partnership is really a suit against the suing partner. Second, partnerships result in an interconnected web of financial relationships. Even though the "partnership" may be liable to a partner, that partner is responsible for a proportionate part of all partnership losses. UPA § 18(a). Moreover, the other partners may also have claims arising out of partnership affairs. The only way to tell if any particular partner is due anything is to close the partnership down and resolve all its affairs.

This rule is subject to numerous exceptions. Professors Bromberg and Ribstein list ten different contexts in which courts have allowed a suit between partners without a prior accounting. 2 A. BROMBERG & L. RIBSTEIN, BROMBERG & RIBSTEIN ON PARTNERSHIP 6:102-10 (1989). The primary exception is a suit arising out of a transaction sufficiently isolated from other partnership affairs that it can be resolved without a review of all partnership affairs. *Id.* at 6:107-08. In that connection, note that a minority of courts do not require a prior accounting in a suit between persons who are only joint venturers. *Compare Kaufmann v. Nolan,* 81 Or. App. 237, 724 P.2d 912, 913 (1986) (recognizing, but not applying, rule that accounting is not always required in a joint venture) *with Kartalis v. Commander Warehouse Joint Venture,* 773 S.W.2d 393 (Tex. App. 1989) (requiring prior accounting).

The rule that a partner may not sue another partner on a matter arising out of partnership affairs until there has been dissolution and an accounting has come under increasing criticism. At least one state's supreme court has already abolished it. *Sertich v. Moorman*, 783 P.2d 1199 (Ariz. 1989).

RUPA section 405 specifically permits both partnership and partner suits against partners. The Comment makes clear the intent to abolish the rule requiring a prior accounting.

Chariton Feed & Grain, Inc. v. Harder
369 N.W.2d 777 (Iowa 1985)

REYNOLDSON, Chief Justice.

We granted further review in this appeal to determine whether trial court erred in holding a landlord under the usual stock-share lease liable to a livestock feed supplier on the theories of partnership, agency and unjust enrichment. The court of appeals split three to three, hence the trial court's decision stood affirmed by operation of law.

Most of the facts developed at trial were undisputed. Defendant Isaac Harder, employed as an engineer in a Texas aircraft factory, purchased a 308-acre Marion County farm on contract in 1974. For reasons detailed later, it was unfortunate that he executed a routine fifty-fifty crop-share lease with defendant Carl Davidson,[2] to commence March 1, 1977. It was still more unfortunate that he executed a stock-share lease with Davidson for a term commencing March 1, 1978. As it turned out, the most Harder received for a $30,000 payment to Davidson for livestock was, according to Davidson, "maybe a few sheep."

There seems to be no dispute that the stock-share lease was prepared by Davidson, or by someone else at his direction. Although inartfully drawn in some respects, it appears to be the ordinary farm lease commonly employed in Iowa for situations in which the landlord and tenant share interests and expenses not only in the crops but also in the livestock. The instrument was entitled "Farm Lease," and consistently referred to the parties as "Landlord" and "Tenant." The tenant was to pay the landlord "1/2 of the receipts from all farm products sold." There is an itemization of the expenses to be shared, including feed. Other identified expenses were to be the separate obligations of the landlord and of the tenant. Especially relevant to the issues in this appeal are two paragraphs of the lease:

> 11. The Tenant shall have full management control, including but not limited to, when to sell the goods, where to sell the goods, to whom to sell the goods, what feed to buy, where to buy the feed, and how much feed to buy.

> 12. Tenant shall use the proper farming methods in the management of said farm.

No joint bank account was established. This left the problem of when and in what manner Harder was to pay his share of the joint expenses. Consistent with his contractual management role, Davidson bought feed from various firms. There is no evidence Harder ever exercised any control over where the feed was purchased, the amount, or the price. He did receive some of the bills

---

2. Davidson's wife and business entity also were named defendants. For simplicity, we shall refer to them as "Davidson."

and part of the time these accounts were placed in Harder's name. Sometimes Harder sent the feed expense money to Davidson, sometimes directly to the seller. Later, and long before any of the feed involved in this controversy was sold, Davidson—again exercising his contractual right to manage the operation—unilaterally started to purchase all feed in his own name and thereafter sought reimbursement from Harder for one-half. Davidson testified the parties understood that he was then going to take the responsibility for paying the feed bills.

The feed furnished by plaintiff Chariton Feed and Grain, Inc. (Chariton Feed), was fed to livestock in which Harder thought he had a one-half interest but which, in fact, Davidson brought to the farm through leases and other arrangements with third parties. On the occasions when Harder visited the farm he always was led to believe all the livestock he saw there was subject to the stock-share lease arrangement. There is no dispute that Davidson consistently lied to and misled Harder, and the stock-share lease agreement never functioned as contemplated by the written agreement. Harder lived in Texas and traveled about 750 to 800 miles to Iowa once or twice a year, when, of course, he would check on his substantial farm investment. At intervals Davidson sent him reports and accounts, usually showing expenses that exceeded the receipts. Davidson could not remember sending Harder any money.

The feed Davidson purchased from Chariton Feed was purchased in his own name during the period May 18, 1979 to June 21, 1980. The payments Davidson did make were on his personal checks, variously styled "Davidson's Holstein and Angus Farms" and "3-D Farms" (after his wife's name, Dorothy Darlene Davidson). Paul Umbenhower, manager and owner of Chariton Feed, testified Davidson led him to believe that he, Davidson, owned all the cattle on the Harder farm. The account was in Davidson's name alone. Umbenhower looked to Davidson alone for payment. There is no evidence Chariton Feed had any knowledge of an alleged interest of Harder in the livestock until all the feed had been purchased and Davidson was being pursued for payment.

In January 1981 Umbenhower placed a telephone call to Harder in Texas. The former testified at trial that, "I asked Mr. Harder if he was the one that was in partnership with Mr. Carl Davidson and he said, yes, he was." Harder denied he ever indicated to anyone he was a partner of Davidson in the farming operation. He testified concerning this conversation:

Q. All right. Just tell us as best you recall what he said to you and what you said to him.

A. He asked me if I owned half the cattle up in Iowa and at the time I thought I did and I did say, "Yes." Then he said that Carl had been charging feed to him and he owed a bill. Now, I don't remember whether he even told me the size and then he said that, you know, he never indicated I owed anything, didn't even ask me that. But he said he was going to take some action against Carl and I am sure I said, "Okay."

Trial court adopted Umbenhower's version of this conversation. The court further found that Harder in this telephone exchange "admitted liability for the feed purchased on account by Davidson from Chariton Feed & Grain, Inc." Even Chariton Feed does not contend there was any evidence to support the latter finding.

Both Davidson and Harder testified that in making their second agreement they intended to make a stock-share lease, not a partnership. There is a substantial question left by this record whether Davidson even intended to comply with a stock-share lease. Further evidence of Davidson's actual and fraudulent intent during his association with Harder was supplied through the testimony of John Jensen, county supervisor for the Farmers Home Administration (F.H.A.) in Marion County. Davidson sought an operating loan from F.H.A. in February 1979. He presented Jensen with a crop-share lease upon which Harder's name had been forged, and claimed to own all the livestock on the farm.

The record reflects that at least by the fall of 1980 Davidson was in deep financial trouble, and his creditors, including Chariton Feed, were closing in. He sold numerous cattle belonging to other people. Before or during January 1981, Davidson abandoned the farm and any agreement he had with Harder was terminated.

It was at this point that Harder, seeking to salvage something, authorized his brother-in-law, who lived in Knoxville, to pick up and sell some of the stock remaining on the farm. On January 19, 1981, several butcher hogs and small pigs were sold at public auction for $1768.69 in Harder's name. An attempt on January 20, 1981, to sell 50 stock cows in which Harder thought he owned an interest was aborted when a third party claimed them. By January 24, 1981, the sheriff was on the farm with F.H.A.'s Jensen, Harder and several third persons. When various owners finished claiming their livestock, thirteen dairy cows remained. These were sold and F.H.A. paid Harder one-half of the proceeds.

The court, proceeding for the most part from the above facts, concluded a partnership existed. In reaching this determination it may not have had the benefit of several Iowa decisions because, as the trial ended, the court advised counsel that, "rather than to have you submit any briefs—and I think it is a question of law—I think I will ask the same effort that would go into preparing briefs go into preparation of proposed Findings and Conclusions." The court also found Harder liable on the basis of agency, and on the ground of "unjust enrichment or quantum meruit."

Iowa decisions have treated these livestock-share leases as *sui generis*, and generally hold they are leases and not partnerships in the absence of stipulations or evidence clearly manifesting a contrary purpose. Our view that the lease in issue is the sort of ordinary farm lease commonly seen in Iowa is supported in this record by F.H.A.'s Jensen, who testified such stock-share leases are more common in Marion County than crop-share leases. Thus we reexamine our long-standing common law with a careful concern for the impact on the great number of Iowans who will be affected.

Narrowing our focus to the first issue before us, what constitutes a partnership and whether a written instrument creates a partnership is a question of law for the court. *Florence v. Fox*, 193 Iowa 1174, 1178, 188 N.W.966, 967 (1922) ("[T]he construction of the contract was a question of law for the court, and it was for the court to determine whether it constituted a partnership contract, and was so intended by the parties."). If the facts are undisputed, it is for the judge to decide whether a partnership exists. Thus our analysis of this question should address the following subsumed issues:

(1) Does the written agreement between Harder and Davidson establish the elements essential to the creation of a partnership? This is a question of law and trial court's determination is not binding on us.

(2) Did Harder and Davidson conduct themselves as though they considered themselves a partnership, thereby supplying the essential elements of a partnership? This is a question of fact only if there is a dispute whether certain events occurred or if different inferences may be drawn from acts the parties agree occurred. If there are disputed facts in this case, then the issue becomes whether the facts, as found by the trial court, constitute substantial evidence that the parties conducted themselves as partners.

In applying the above principles to these issues, however, due regard should be given to our historic treatment of these agricultural leases. We have held that it will not be presumed that the parties to such leases intended a partnership, in the absence of stipulations or evidence clearly manifesting such a purpose.

A leading Iowa decision is *Fox*. There the landlord provided the cows and was to receive one-half the milk and cream. Each party was to provide hogs, "share and share alike," and share in their increase. Each party was to own one-half the grain grown on the 120 acres leased. The parties were to share expenses of threshing and board of help, and both were to be informed of and have equal rights in the sale of stock and purchases of "stuff" for the farm. The court found the parties to stand in a tenant-landlord relationship, not a partnership. The court relied heavily upon the intention of the parties as expressed in the contract. The *Fox* court provided the public policy underlying its decision:

> If a partnership existed, it might be possible for the tenant, within the scope of the partnership, to purchase property and make the owner of the land responsible therefor in an amount largely in excess of the rent, and each might be responsible for the torts of the other committed within the scope of the agency. The courts hold quite generally that there are obvious reasons for holding that farm contracts or agricultural agreements, by which the owner of land contracts with another that such land shall be occupied and cultivated by the latter, each party furnishing a certain portion of the seed, implements, *and stock*, and that the products shall be divided at the end of a given term, or sold and the proceeds divided, shall not be construed as creating a partnership between the parties. Such agreements are common in this country, and are usually informal in their character, often resting in parol. In the *absence of stipulations or evidence clearly manifesting a contrary purpose, it will not be presumed that the parties to such an agreement intended to assume the important and intricate responsibility of partners, or to incur the inconveniences and dangers frequently incident to that relation.*

(Emphasis added.) *See Wilson v. Fleming*, 239 Iowa 718, 733, 31 N.W.2d 393, 401 (1948) (Agreement determined to be a stock-share lease, the court noting "[c]ourts are reluctant to construe an arrangement such as this between a farm owner and occupant as a partnership unless such relation is clearly shown.").

The only decision relating to leases from any jurisdiction found in trial court's decision is *Malvern Nat'l Bank v. Halliday*, 195 Iowa 734, 192 N.W. 843 (1923). In that case *both* the landlord and the tenant argued *in favor* of a finding of partnership. The written agreement referred frequently to "the firm." Of similar limited value here is the holding in *Miller v. Merritt*, 233 Iowa 230, 8 N.W.2d 726 (1943). The *Miller* agreement provided the business should be in the name of "Miller and Merritt Bros."; all receipts and disbursements should be made through a joint bank account in the name of Miller and Merritt; and both parties would cooperate fully in managing the "firm." The agreement contained copious references to "the firm," "partnership property" and "firm property." Quite predictably, the court found the arrangement to be a partnership, relying heavily on the intention of the parties.

Neither *Halliday* nor *Miller* modify our basic principle that a stock-share lease is not to be construed as a partnership in absence of clear evidence that the parties intended to create a partnership. It is noteworthy that in the Iowa decisions confronting the lease vis-a-vis partnership issue, this court has found the relationship between the parties to be a partnership only where the parties themselves expressly described their arrangement in those terms. The public policy articulated in *Fox*, quoted above, is supported in decisions from other jurisdictions including *Shrum v. Simpson*, 155 Ind. 160, 163, 57 N.E. 708, 709 (1900):

> There are obvious reasons for holding that farm contracts or agricultural agreements, by which the owner of land contracts with another that such lands shall be occupied and cultivated by the latter, each party furnishing a certain proportion of the seed, implements, and stock, and that the products shall be divided at the end of a given term, or sold and the proceeds divided, shall not be construed as creating a partnership between the parties. The parties to such agreements seldom contemplate anything more than a tenancy of the land, with provision for compensation to the landlord from the fidelity, labor, and skill of the tenant. There is no community of interest in the land, which is the principal thing in the agreement, and a division and several ownership of the crops and other products are usually provided for. While the custom of renting farm lands upon shares is general, the courts have seldom held that such agreements create partnerships between the owner of the land and the tenant.

As *Fox* and *Shrum* make clear, construing what essentially is a lease arrangement as a partnership exposes the parties to unwarranted and unexpected liability for conduct that he or she ordinarily is powerless to control or direct. The case before us is a vivid example. The $26,166.32 judgment charged against Harder could be only the beginning of successive judgments in favor of livestock owners and others Davidson defrauded, all without the knowledge of the unsuspecting Harder. Meanwhile, Davidson has insulated himself from liability by taking bankruptcy.

Against the backdrop of the above cases, we return to the two subsumed issues above identified.

Partnership Issue—The Written Agreement

The construction of a written contract, as already noted, is a question of law for the court. In construction of written contracts, the cardinal principle is that the intent of the parties must control; and except in cases of ambiguity, this is determined by what the contract itself says. An examination of the contract (exhibit two) in this case discloses that on its face it is the common stock-share lease. The elements of the landlord and tenant relationship are all patently present. Trial court makes no definitive finding that exhibit two, on its face, is a partnership and not a lease. Nonetheless, our review relating to this law issue requires examination of this "Farm Lease" to determine whether it exhibits the elements required to create a partnership. These are (1) an association, i.e., an intent by the parties to associate as partners; (2) a business; (3) earning of profits; and (4) co-ownership of profits, property and control.

A. *Intent to Associate.*

In Iowa, intention to associate is "the crucial test" of partnership. Exhibit two shows no intent by the parties to associate as partners. On the contrary, it recites an express intention to create the relationship of landlord-tenant. The words "partner," "partnership," "firm," or any other term usually deemed to show such an intent to form a partnership appear nowhere in the document. On the other hand, the agreement is entitled "Farm Lease." The word "Landlord" is used sixteen times; the word "Tenant" twenty times. The parties are identified in no other way. Such language, employed by the parties in their contract, is important in discerning their intent.

B. *A Business.*

It is clear from exhibit two that the parties had a business purpose, as opposed to a patriotic, civic, religious, sports, or similar non-business purpose.

C. *Earnings of Profits.*

For the purposes of this analysis, this element adds nothing other than to reinforce the "business" requirement mentioned in the last paragraph.

D. *Co-Ownership of Profits, Property and Control.*
1. *Profits*

Exhibit two contains no provision for the sharing of profits by Harder and Davidson. In paragraph two the lease requires that "[t]he Tenant shall pay to the Landlord ½ of the *receipts* from all farm products sold" (emphasis added). Paragraph four provides for the sharing of certain expenses. Reading these two provisions together, trial court inferred an agreement to share profits. This inference was the sole basis for the court's finding that the parties had a "community of interest" in profits.

Trial court's approach, of course, does not account for the requirement in the lease that each party individually assume certain expenses, which resulted in each showing a different level of profit or loss generated out of the farm operation. For example, Harder's 1979 tax return disclosed a substantial farm loss; Davidson's a profit of over $36,000.[3] Obviously, profit and loss under this agreement could not be determined until each party deducted from his share of the gross re-

---

3. No partnership [tax] returns were filed.

ceipts the expenses for which he individually was responsible. Thus, under exhibit two, Harder and Davidson did not "share profits."

Nor does exhibit two provide for the sharing of losses. Trial court inferred this, based upon the requirement that the parties share certain of the expenses, citing as authority 68 C.J.S. *Partnership* § 29(b)(2). The Iowa rule, however, is not the general rule stated in C.J.S. Our cases are in some disarray on this point, but stated most favorably to Chariton Feed, the Iowa rule is that an agreement to share losses may be inferred only where the partnership is established by other evidence.

Addressing the question of profits, trial court stated that "[i]n reaching its conclusion as to the existence of a partnership, the court notes [UPA Section 7(4)(b)] provides that the receipt by a person of a share of the profits of a business is prima facie evidence that he is a partner in the business." This conclusion does not take into account [UPA section 7(3)]:

> The sharing of gross returns does not of itself establish a partnership, whether or not the persons sharing them have a joint or common right or interest in any property from which the returns are derived.

Further, the statute referred to by trial court actually carries its own exception that further excludes this situation:

> The receipt by a person of a share of the profits of a business is prima-facie evidence that the person is a partner in the business, but no such inference shall be drawn if such profits were received in payment:

2. Property

Exhibit two contemplated co-ownership of only part of the property used in the livestock operation, being the livestock and feeding equipment. That of course does not, of itself, establish a partnership.

3. Control

Co-ownership of control, or a community of interest in the administration of the business, is a key element in determining the existence of a partnership.

Although obviously inartfully drawn, we find no ambiguity in the language of this "Farm Lease." Assuming trial court found it established a partnership we cannot agree with its conclusion of law. There remain for our review trial court's findings relating to the conduct of the parties, and its conclusion the parties created a partnership by their acts.

Partnership Issue — Conduct of the Parties
A. Intent to Associate.

We have noted that in Iowa the intent of the parties to associate as partners is "the crucial test." *Fox*, 193 Iowa at 1178. This is the most widely accepted test for determining whether a partnership exists.

At the outset we observe that if these parties had the intent to associate as partners, it was remarkable that no indication of that intent was included in the lease the parties signed to memorialize their agreement. A partnership can be formed only upon mutual consent of the parties and a meeting of the minds; the intention of one party alone cannot create the relation. It is clear that from the outset Davidson did not even intend to comply with the lease, let alone an unexpressed partnership understanding. The fact findings trial court adopted do not take into account Davidson's intent. A conclusion that Harder intended to associate as a partner is based upon two findings. The first was the court's selection of Umbenhower's version of the telephone call to Texas, rather than Harder's. In this version the latter, following all the relevant events, allegedly responded in the affirmative when asked if he was in partnership with Davidson. The second was Harder's efforts to sell livestock from the farm after Davidson had left the farm and their relationship had terminated. Trial court concluded "such control shows Harder believed himself to be more than a one-half owner of the livestock and a mere landlord."

Trial court's finding that Harder responded in the affirmative to the inquiry relating to a partnership is entitled to little weight on the scale of substantial evidence. Even in written instruments, the general rule is that "laymen misuse legal terms, and the fact they call each other partners is not conclusive if the essential elements of partnership are lacking in their relationship." When a party refers to himself or herself as a partner in the course of a conversation, courts are very reluctant to give the statement any weight at all.

Of similar inconsequential weight were Harder's desperate acts with respect to the livestock in which he thought he had an interest after Davidson departed the scene. No matter what arrangement Harder and Davidson had, the record affirmatively shows it had terminated at that point. Thus Harder's acts could neither be considered in furtherance of, nor in conformance with, a partnership association.

B. A Business.

There is no issue concerning this element, as it related to the acts of the parties.

C. Earnings of Profits.

Similarly, there is no issue relating to this element.

D. Co-Ownership of Profits, Property and Control.
  1. *Profits.*

Trial court's decision reveals no finding that the parties, by their behavior, indicated an intention to share profits. Certainly the distinction between a contemplated sharing of gross receipts and a sharing of profits is commonly drawn and recognized as valid. [UPA § 7(3)].

  2. *Property.*

Although the farm lease clearly provided for co-ownership of certain livestock and feeding equipment, Davidson's maneuvers largely avoided even this limited requirement. Trial testimony was undisputed that, as a result of Davidson's duplicity, Harder in fact never owned a one-half interest in livestock "other than a few sheep."

It is also important that the major assets utilized in this association—the real estate owned by Harder and the machinery owned by Davidson—were and remained the separate assets of the parties.

3. *Control.*

The main battleground at trial was the attempt to show that Harder, despite the lease provisions, exercised the requisite control of the business. Typically, testimony on this topic "concerns who gave instructions, hired and fired employees, had the say on how money was spent, or made important business decisions. If one participated to a significant degree in these functions, he had sufficient control. If he did not, the normal result is no partnership." Crane and Bromberg § 14(d). The search for objective evidence of joint control of the business usually focuses on acts such as holding licenses, assuming a firm name, keeping books that show a capital account for each party, or filing federal partnership tax returns. None of these indicia, of course, were present here. Significantly, Kevin Sharp, the farmhand who helped Davidson, testified that he was Davidson's employee and had never met Harder.

Trial court relied on the following findings in concluding Harder had the requisite control of the operations: feed accounts during an early period were put in Harder's name, thus enabling him to close the accounts had he become dissatisfied with the amount of feed or its cost; the parties corresponded or talked by telephone about once a month; Harder periodically visited the farm; Davidson furnished Harder a monthly accounting; and Harder sold hogs in his own name following Davidson's departure.

We already have discussed the feed account evidence. Had there been a joint bank account—one of the indicia of a partnership—other arrangements for Harder to pay the very substantial amounts Davidson was incurring in feeding other persons' livestock would have been unnecessary. As it happened, these bills, for a time, and some of Harder's bills for his separate expenses for building repair and improvement over a longer period of time, were sent directly to him. There was no modification of Davidson's right under the lease, to have sole control of "what feed to buy, where to buy the feed, and how much feed to buy," and there was undisputed evidence he consistently exercised that right. There is an inference Davidson thought Harder might be able to track his activities, thus causing Davidson to unilaterally terminate this procedure. Subsequently, Davidson purported to deduct Harder's share of the feed against milk and livestock sales, which Davidson of course received and controlled.

Regarding the telephone calls between Davidson and Harder, there again was no evidence Harder exercised or sought to exercise any control over the farming operations. When asked what was discussed during the telephone visits, Davidson testified:

A. Sometimes he just wanted to know how things was at the farm weather-wise, crop-wise; a lot of times my wife's health.

Q. Did he ever ask you anything about the livestock operation?

A. Sometimes he might ask me how they was doing when I had some ready to go.

Harder's testimony was this:

Q. And did you ever talk to him about it on the telephone like how do things look out on the farm or whatever?

A. In maybe general appearance. You know, like I would ask Carl the same thing, like how do things look.

Harder obviously had a considerable stake in the Iowa farm and its improve-ments, in addition to the $30,000 he spent for the illusory livestock. It is under-standable that he was interested in the progress of his investment, but there is nothing in the above evidence from which it could be concluded he was exercis-ing any control. This is also the rational explanation for the once-or-twice-per-year visits Harder made to Iowa, where he also had relatives.

We already have discussed Harder's conduct with respect to the livestock after the lease terminated. There remains the "monthly" accounting that David-son erratically sent Harder. Such accountings are not unusual in share lease arrangements, and do not signal an attempt to control the operation. Milk pro-ceeds were received every month. Obviously the parties concluded Harder would receive his rent monthly, in the form of receipts, less joint expenses. That this ap-parently generated no money to Harder is not controlling on the issue under con-sideration. Harder was obligated to itemize and show his share of receipts and expenses on his income tax return, and required the information supplied by the "accounting." Again, there is no indication in the record Harder exercised con-trol upon the basis of the information thus furnished.

None of the evidence, taken together, supplied substantial evidence for the court's conclusions that Harder exercised control of the farm operation or that the conduct of the parties disclosed their intent to associate as partners.

Finally, Chariton Feed concedes the weakness of its contentions when it states in its brief:

The trial court undertook to decide the issue of the existence of a partnership, as to the Plaintiff [Chariton Feed] and Defendant [Harder], and did not purport to find whether the Defendant and Davidson were partners as to each other, since that issue was not be-fore the trial court.

[UPA section 7(1)], however, expressly provides:

Except as provided by [UPA section 16], persons who are not partners as to each other are not partners as to third persons.

[UPA section 16], referred to in the statute just quoted, concerns the situation in which a person is made liable by estoppel. That statute, of course, has no applica-tion here because Chariton Feed concedes it did not even know of the stock-share lease, let alone an alleged partnership, when it extended credit to Davidson for feed.

In summary, we hold trial court erred in concluding, if in fact it did, the written agreement between Harder and Davidson created a partnership. Similarly, we hold trial court's conclusion that Harder's conduct is otherwise furnished the requisite proof of the existence of a partnership was not supported by substantial evidence.

We vacate the court of appeals disposition, reverse the district court judg-ment and remand for judgment for defendant Harder.

Notes

1. Under the common-law tests used in both *Dalton v. Austin* and *Chariton Feed & Grain Co. v. Harder,* as well as under UPA section 7(4) and RUPA sec-tion 202(c)(3), persons who share profits are presumed to be partners. In *Chari-ton Feed & Grain Co. v. Harder,* did the parties contemplate sharing profits? If

not, on what basis did the parties agree to share the returns from the sale of stock and crops? Why doesn't that basis imply that the parties were partners?

2. Persons who are *not* partners often share profits. Several of these kinds of non-partnership profit-sharing relationships are listed under UPA section 7(4). Courts evaluating a profit-sharing relationship to determine if there is a partnership often look to see if the parties are "acting like partners"—sharing control and losses.

Commentators frequently criticize this approach, arguing first that sharing of control and losses is a *consequence* of being partners, and not a condition of partner status. *See* UPA §§ 18(a), 18(e). Second, partners may delegate management, or allocate responsibility for losses, without ceasing to be partners.

What other factors could a court use in trying to decide if a share of profits was received as a partner, or in some other capacity?

P & M Cattle Co. v. Holler
559 P.2d 1019 (Wyo. 1977)

RAPER, Justice.

In the district court, the plaintiff-appellant, a partnership, sought and was denied recovery for losses incurred in 1974 under an alleged "oral joint venture agreement" to purchase, lease and sell livestock.

[T]he only real issue is whether the parties to this appeal were parties to a joint venture or partnership agreement to share losses as well as profits from a cattle purchase, feed and sell operation.

In 1971, the defendant was looking for someone to pasture cattle on the defendant's land at $3.00 per head per month. One of two partners in the plaintiff partnership expressed an interest and invited defendant to talk. As a result, the following written agreement was entered into:

2-23-1971

Contract—Rusty Holler (60 Bar Ranch) L. W. Maxfield and Bill Poage

Rusty to furnish grass for est 100 yr st and 21 heifers—

Maxfield & Poage to furnish money for cattle plus trucking & salt—and max of $300.00 per month for labor

Rusty to take cattle around May 1st and cattle to be sold at a time this fall agreed upon by all parties involved

Cost of cattle plus freight—salt and labor to be first cost

Net money from sale of cattle less first cost to be split 50-50 between Rusty (1/2) and Maxfield and Poage (1/2) (death loss to be part of first cost)

/s/ L. W. Maxfield

/s/ Bill Poage

LM

/s/ Rusty Holler

The 1971 agreement was orally renewed for the years 1972, 1973 and 1974. Plaintiff and defendant each realized substantial returns in the first three years but in 1974 there was not enough realized from the sale of cattle to pay first costs and a loss resulted. Plaintiff insists that the defendant is bound to pay it $44,500.00 representing one-half of the total cash loss in the sum of $89,000.00. The defendant personally expended first costs for expenses (salt) over and above the amount received from sale of cattle in sum of $3,967.76. Through an admitted error of defendant's counsel, along with a misunderstanding by defendant, only one-half of those expenses were claimed by defendant. When the error became apparent at or near the close of evidence, they elected not to amend the defendant's claim first made. The contract clearly states that plaintiff was to "furnish money for salt."

The parties never discussed nor is there any mention in the contract of what would happen if the cattle sold at a loss. Nor was any mention made of reimbursement or credit to the defendant for the value of his services and pasture or grass he contributed, in the event cattle sold at a loss.

A broad overview of the entire record suggests that this case involves only a contract in which plaintiff agreed to put up the money and defendant agreed to put up grazing land and grass, along with services, with a view to profit to both, each to bear their own losses. Before confirming that position, we must examine the law of joint ventures.

In Wyoming, a joint adventure partakes of the nature of a partnership and is governed substantially by the same rules of law, the principal distinction being that a joint adventure usually relates to a single transaction, though it may be continued over a period of years. Even though a joint adventure and a partnership are not identical, the relationship of co-adventurers is controlled largely by the law of partnership. A concise distinction between joint venture and partnership is drawn in 1 Cavitch, Business Organizations, s 13.05(2), pp. 677-678:

> It is apparent that the comparatively modern legal concept of joint adventure is intended to identify business ventures which, but for their limited scope and duration, would be partnerships. To date, however, there is no discernible legal difference between the two types of associations. As a result, the courts have held that the joint adventure is subject to the same rules of law which are applied to partnerships, especially when determining the rights of the parties *inter se.*

Since joint adventures, also frequently referred to as joint ventures, are a species of and governed by the law of partnerships, we must go to the Uniform Partnership Act. [UPA section 6] defines a partnership as follows: A partnership is an association of two or more persons to carry on as *co-owners* a business for profit.' (Emphasis added.) [UPA section 7] lays out the criteria for resolving the question as to whether a partnership obtains:

> In determining whether a partnership exists, these rules shall apply:
>
> (1) Except as provided by section 16 persons who are not partners as to each other are not partners as to third persons;
>
> (2) Joint tenancy, tenancy in common, tenancy by the entireties, joint property, common property, or part ownership does not of itself establish a partnership, whether such co-owners do or do not share any profits made by the use of the property;

(3) The sharing of gross returns does not of itself establish a partnership, whether or not the person sharing them have a joint or common right or interest in any property from which the returns are derived;

(4) The receipt by a person of a share of the profits of a business is prima facie evidence that he is a partner in the business, but no such inference shall be drawn if such profits were received in payment:

(a) As a debt by installments or otherwise,

(b) As wages of an employee *or rent to a landlord,*

(c) As an annuity to a widow or representative of a deceased partner,

(d) As an interest on a loan, though the amount of payment vary with the profits of the business,

(e) As the consideration for the sale of the good-will of a business or other property by installments or otherwise.

(Emphasis added.) As can be seen, an agreement to share profits is far from decisive that a partnership is intended.

As in any contractual relationship, the intent of the parties is controlling. The parties must intend to create the relationship of joint adventure or partnership. Superimposed upon the rule of intent, it is frequently held that where there is no express agreement to form a partnership, the question of whether such a relation exists must be gathered from the conduct, surrounding circumstances and the transactions between the parties. There is no automatic solution to the question of the existence of a partnership but it turns upon the facts and circumstances of association between the parties. No single fact may be stated as the complete and final test of a partnership. Even a written agreement, designating the parties as partners and providing for a sharing of the profits, is only evidential and not conclusive of the existence of a partnership.

In the case before us there was no express agreement to form a partnership. True, there was an agreement but nowhere in that document is there anywhere mentioned the term partnership. Nor is there anywhere mentioned any sharing of losses, which is normally concomitant with a sharing of profits in a partnership.[4] While [UPA section 7(4)] creates an inference, that inference is not conclusive.

We find in Wyoming two cases which reflect the usual holdings that division of profits has little significance by itself. In *Dunn v. Gilbert,* 1927, 36 Wyo. 249, 254 P. 121, it was held that the use of the expression fifty-fifty and an understanding to split the profits do not necessarily mean a joint adventure but such expression must be construed in the light of surrounding facts and circumstances.

---

4. [UPA section 18] sets out a rule allowing for contribution to pay losses:
   The rights and duties of the partners in relation to the partnership shall be determined, subject to any agreement between them, by the following rules:
   (a) Each partner shall be repaid his contributions, whether by way of capital or advances to the partnership property and share equally in the profits and [surplus] remaining after all liabilities, including those to partners, are satisfied; and must contribute towards the losses, whether of capital or otherwise, sustained by the partnership according to his share in the profits. (Emphasis added.)

In *State v. Bemis*, 1926, 34 Wyo. 218, 241, 242 P. 802, 809, the principal witness put up the money to buy and pay shipping costs of a carload of apples. The defendant was to share in the profits by arranging their sale. They sold at a loss and defendant kept all the money. In a prosecution for embezzlement, the defendant claimed a right to retain the funds by reason of a partnership. This court spoke approvingly of the principle that when a business is limited to a single venture, there must be pretty clear evidence of an intent to create a partnership relationship and an understanding for division of profits may only be considered in connection with the whole transaction.

Since we cannot look at the face of the instrument here and determine whether there is a partnership, it is necessary that we examine into the complete relationship between plaintiff and defendant. We can in such a circumstance go outside its four corners to test the claim of a would-be partner and look at what the parties did and how they treated the arrangement between them. The contemporary construction of a contract by acts of the parties is entitled to serious consideration by the court whose duty it becomes to determine its meaning. The reason for that view rests in the fact that the parties are less liable to have been mistaken as to the meaning of their contract while harmonious relations existed and during that period a practical and real construction would be in effect reflective of their true intentions and not interpretations ventured during the heat of litigation.

In the first place, the agreement is not labeled a "partnership agreement" nor is the term "partnership" anywhere mentioned within its terms. The plaintiff was itself a partnership made up of two ranchers well acquainted with that arrangement, one of whom drew the contract. From its inception, then, none of the parties ever identified it as such. The part was conceived in an atmosphere created by defendant's desire to sell grass. The division of losses was never discussed between the parties until the plaintiff delivered the bad news to the defendant following fall cattle sales in 1974. No partnership federal income tax return in any of the years 1971-74 was prepared and submitted to the Internal Revenue Service of the United States. On the income tax returns made by the plaintiff during the period in question, the part of profits paid to the defendant was carried as a business expense listed as "contract feeding." The defendant included such payments on his individual income tax return as a sale of "crops," nor were the cattle grazed on his place by the defendant carried on defendant's income tax return livestock inventory. The livestock were carried on plaintiffs' partnership income tax returns. On the check given by plaintiff to defendant in 1973, for defendant's share of profits at the end of the season, it was shown as being for "pasture."

Within the framework of the Uniform Partnership Act, we find rules available to the trial judge to determine that there was no partnership. The division of profits was only a measure—a standard of payment by plaintiff to defendant in discharge of a debt for services and grass under [UPA section 7(4)(a)] or in payment to defendant for wages of an employee in caring for the cattle while on his ranch and rent to him as landlord for his pasture under [UPA section 7(4)(b)] or sale of grass as personal property under [UPA section 7(4)(e)] or through a combination of those lettered subsections for wages and rent or sale of property. We need not determine precisely what it was as long as outside the pale of partnership. We are satisfied that no partnership was intended. The agreement was only an apparatus to pay defendant for his grass and services and we return to its terms after reconnoitering the outer regions.

Whether or not there is a joint venture is a question of fact and preeminently one for the finder of fact. The trial judge found for the defendant and we see substantial evidence to support that result.

Affirmed.

Notes

1. As indicated in *P & M Cattle Co. v. Holler*, a joint venture is similar to — "in the nature of" — a partnership, but is not, strictly speaking, a partnership. The formal difference is that a joint venture is formed for the purpose of carrying on a single transaction, rather than a series of transactions—a business. The modern joint venture is frequently a business venture between corporations. Until recently, there was some doubt as to whether corporations had the power to enter into partnerships, as opposed to joint ventures. *See* A. BROMBERG & L. RIBSTEIN, BROMBERG & RIBSTEIN ON PARTNERSHIP 2:23-26 (1988). As a result, may so-called joint ventures in fact operate over extended periods, and are indistinguishable from partnerships.

2. The common law test for a joint venture requires (1) a community of interest, (2) an agreement to share profits as principals, (3) an agreement to share losses, costs, and expenses, and (4) mutual rights of control. *See, e.g., Brown v. Cole*, 155 Tex. 624, 291 S.W.2d 704 (1956). Many courts are reluctant to find a joint venture unless *all* the elements are present. In *P & M Cattle Co. v. Holler*, the court indicated that where a "business" is limited to a single venture, a finding of "partnership" would require "pretty clear evidence of an intent to create a partnership relationship." Do such requirements make sense in the context of a joint venture? As to continuing partnerships?

3. Even though a joint venture is not a partnership, courts often apply partnership law, including the UPA, to joint ventures.

D. Firms with Limited Liability

1. Formalities of Formation

a. Limited Partnerships

The Revised Uniform Limited Partnership Act (RULPA) defines a limited partnership as "a partnership formed by two or more persons..., having one or more general partners and one or more limited partners." RULPA § 101(7). Subject to certain limitations, a "general partner" in a limited partnership "has the rights and powers and is subject to the restrictions and liabilities of a partner in a partnership without limited partners." RULPA § 404. Limited partners, on the other hand, have only limited rights and obligations. Limited partners generally are not liable for partnership obligations. RULPA § 303. Limited partners have no general right to participate in the management of the business, but only such voting rights as given under the limited partnership agreement. RULPA § 302. In fact, as discussed later in this chapter, limited partners who participate in the "control" of the limited partnership's business become liable as general partners for obligations of the limited partnership. RULPA § 303.

As discussed in the following extract from *Klein v. Weiss,* 284 Md. 36, 395 A.2d 126 (1978), the limited partnership form of business association began in the late 1700s and early 1800s:

Limited partnerships were unknown at common law; they are exclusively a creature of statute, their main purpose being to permit a form of business enterprise, other than a corporation, in which persons could invest money without becoming liable as general partners for all debts of the partnership. "The general purpose of [limited partnership] acts was not to assist creditors, but was to enable persons to invest their money in partnerships and share in the profits without being liable for more than the amount of money they had contributed. The reason for this was to encourage investing." *Gilman Paint & Varnish Co. v. Legum,* 197 Md. 665, 670, 80 A.2d 906, 908 (1951).

The first limited partnership statute in the United States was enacted by New York in 1822; Maryland adopted a similar statute [in] 1836. These early statutes required the recording of a partnership certificate giving notice to the public of the exact terms of the partnership, including the amount of the capital contributions of the limited partners, so that the public could deal with the partnership "advisedly." *Lineweaver v. Slagle,* 64 Md. 465, 2 A. 693 (1886). The fundamental difference between the liability of general and limited partners under these statutes was "that the former are responsible *in solido* for the debts and obligations of the firm, as in the case of ordinary partnerships, without regard to the amounts contributed by them to the social capital; whilst the latter is not personally liable if the statute has been complied with, because his cash contribution is substituted for a personal liability." *Safe Deposit Co. v. Cahn,* 102 Md. 530, 546, 62 A. 819 (1906). Strict compliance with all statutory provisions was deemed essential to create a limited partnership under these early statutes, since they were in derogation of the common law. As a consequence, even minor or trivial infractions of the statute were held by some courts to subject the limited partners to unlimited liability as general partners. Because the strict construction of these statutes inhibited the effective accomplishment of the purpose for which they were intended, the National Conference of Commissioners on Uniform State Laws proposed the adoption in 1916 of a Uniform Limited Partnership Act [(ULPA)]. Maryland enacted the [ULPA in] 1918, and the statute with minor modifications is now in effect in every state in the country except Louisiana. The Act's provisions are intended to govern the determination of essentially all questions arising out of the formation and operation of limited partnerships. The rule that statutes in derogation of the common law are to be strictly construed is expressly made inapplicable to the [ULPA].

Decisions interpreting the [ULPA] recognize that a limited partnership consists of general partners who conduct the business and who have unlimited liability to creditors for its obligations, and of limited partners who have no right to participate in the management of the business, and whose liability is limited to the amount of their capital contribution. As the Official Comment to section 1 of the [ULPA] makes clear, a limited partner, though so called by custom, is not "in any sense" either a partner or a principal in the business or transactions of the partnership; his liability, except for known false statements in the certificate of partnership, is to the partnership, and not to its creditors. Succinctly put, a limited partnership interest in a business is in the nature of an investment. Section 17(a) of the [ULPA] delineates the extent of the limited partner's investment in the business; it makes him liable to the partnership:

(1) For the difference between his contribution as actually made and that stated in the certificate as having been made; and

(2) For any unpaid contribution which he agreed in the certificate to make in the future at the time and on the conditions stated in the certificate.

The creation of a limited partnership is not a mere private, informal, voluntary agreement as in the case of a general partnership, but is a public and formal proceeding which must follow the statutory requirements of the [ULPA]. [Section 2(2) of the ULPA] prescribes that a limited partnership is formed "if there has been substantial compliance in good faith" with the requirements contained in section 2(1). That subsection mandates that a certificate of a partnership be signed by the parties, acknowledged, and recorded with the clerk of the court. It requires that the certificate set forth designated partnership details, including the name of the partnership, the character and location of the business, the identity of the general and limited partners, the term of the partnership, the cash contributions made by the limited partners, and such additional contributions, if any, which the limited partners have agreed to make in the future. The certificate is a statutory prerequisite to creation of a limited partnership and until it is filed, the partnership is not formed as a limited partnership. The principal function of the certificate is to give third persons notice of the essential features of the limited partnership. Of course, whether a limited partnership has been formed is of particular importance in determining whether a person has achieved the status of a limited partner with the attendant limitation of his liability to third persons dealing with the partnership.

The ULPA, first promulgated in 1916, was eventually adopted by virtually all of the fifty states. The ULPA has now largely been supplanted by the RULPA. The RULPA, adopted by the National Conference of Commissioners on Uniform State Laws in 1976 and substantially amended in 1985, has now been adopted in forty-six states.

For further information regarding the development of limited partnership law generally, and especially the 1985 RULPA, *see* Closen, *Limited Partnership Reform: A Commentary on the Proposed Illinois Statute and the 1976 and 1985 Versions of the Uniform Limited Partnership Act*, 6 N. ILL. L. REV. 205 (1986).

b. Limited Liability Companies

Limited liability companies (LLC's), like all other business forms that offer owners protection against personal liability for entity-level debts, can be formed only by compliance with specific, statutorily imposed procedures. These procedures involve the preparation of a document, often called articles of organization, which contain certain information as set out in the statute. This document must then be filed with the appropriate authority in order for the LLC to come into existence.

The need for a filed document exists primarily because of the fact that the owners of an LLC will not be liable for the debts of the business, at least not because of the fact that they are owners (often called "members") Rather, a creditor must proceed against the company itself. The filed document provides information relating to the correct name of the enterprise, the service agent and address at which process may be served. State statutes often require additional information as well (such as a dissolution date, or statement of purposes, or a statement about management of the enterprise), but *every* LLC statute includes the requirement that the organizational document include information necessary to bring suit against the business.

Notes and Problems

Review sections 18-101, 18-102, 18-104, 18-106, 18-201, 18-203 & 18-207 of the Delaware Limited Liability Company Act (Delaware LLC Act) and sections 101, and 105 to 211 of the Uniform Limited Liability Company Act (the ULLCA), all of which deal with formation of LLC's and all of which are included in the statutory supplement.

1. Suppose a new client, Lucy Lucky, comes to your law firm and proposes to form a new Delaware LLC with the following document. What advice should you give her? *See* ULLCA §§ 105 (dealing with name of LLC's), 108 (dealing with the designated office and agent for service of process), 203 (dealing with general contents of the Articles of Organization), and 205 (dealing with signing of records).

CERTIFICATE OF FORMATION
The undersigned authorized person forming this Limited Liability Company adopts the following Certificate of Formation:

First: The Name of the Limited Liability Company is: Lucky's Ltd.

Second: The address of the registered office of the Limited Liability Company which may be, but need not be, the place of business in the State of Delaware, shall be: P.O. Box 0001, Wilmington, DE.

Third: The name of the registered agent and the address of said agent shall be: Lucy Lucky, P.O. Box 0001, Wilmington, DE.

Fourth: The management of this Company may be vested in a manager or managers by inclusion of a provision to this effect in the written operating agreement of Lucky's, Ltd.

Fifth: This agreement shall be retroactively effective as of January 1, 1999.

Signed: _____

Name: _____
(Attorney)

It is important to strictly comply with statutory requirements in the certificate of formation. For example, although it is not an issue under the Delaware LLC Act because of careful statutory drafting, you should be aware that in some states the officials responsible for filing organizational documents will not accept documents which use the abbreviation "LLC" rather than "L.L.C." Certainly, using "Ltd." as an abbreviation for "limited liability company" will present problems, unless the relevant statute authorizes such an abbreviation.

Although you should always check with the statute when making sure that a document to be filed complies with relevant requirements, if you understand the reasons behind the statutory requirements, they may be easier to remember. For example, why do the Articles have to include a registered agent and address? Remember that if the LLC is sued, the plaintiff has to serve process on someone. The registered office and agent tells potential plaintiffs who to serve and where to serve them. This means that box office addresses will not be sufficient, and that a specific person (although not necessarily an individual) must be named as registered agent. Once you understand why the certificate must include this type of information, the specifics become much easier to remember.

There are in fact several problems with the proposed form. How many did you identify?

2. Suppose you used the same form as described in problem 1 to form an LLC under the ULLCA. Would the form work any better or differently under that statute? *See ULLCA* §§ 105 (dealing with name of LLC's), 108 (dealing with the designated office and agent for service of process), 203 (dealing with general contents of the Articles of Organization), and 205 (dealing with signing of records).

Note that this question illustrates a potential problem with using forms originally intended to comply with the statutes of a different jurisdiction. This form refers to the organizational document as the "Certificate of Formation." While this is the terminology employed in a number of state statutes (see, e.g., Del. Stat. § 18-201), the ULLCA uses "Articles of Organization." While it is possible that this document would be acceptable to the Secretary of State even with the nonconforming language, it is always better to use the same terminology as the applicable statute.

As for the document provided above, you should have noted that the document failed to include several items listed in § 203, and an attorney is not empowered to sign to Articles, although an attorney-in-fact would be.

c. Limited Liability Partnerships

In 1991, Texas became the first state to authorize the formation of limited liability partnerships (LLP's), by amending the Texas version of the Uniform Partnership Act. The Texas LLP Act permitted a general partnership to register as an LLP, provided the partnership met certain conditions. The partnership had to file a document with the state, and had to renew the registration annually. The partnership also had to pay an annual fee, and was further obligated to maintain certain financial reserves or minimum levels of insurance. The benefit of complying with these procedures was that general partners in a registered LLP would be shielded against unlimited personal liability for debts arising out of the misconduct of others associated with the partnership. Because the IRS had already announced that a business would not be taxed as a corporation solely because it offered owners limited liability, the LLP legislation provided a way for businesses to continue with a familiar form of business while avoiding some of the more egregious problems associated with personal liability for entity-level debts.

Other states quickly followed suit, although there were a number of variations that quickly appeared. Not all states required that an LLP maintain specified financial reserves or insurance; not all states required an annual renewal. Finally, some states (beginning with New York and Minnesota) authorized LLP's that not only protect partners against personal liability against debts arising out of the misconduct of others, but against personal liability for any and all entity-level obligations.

In 1994, the National Conference of Commissioners on Uniform State Laws (NCCUSL) had promulgated a revised Uniform Partnership Act (RUPA). It did not contain LLP language. Two years later, NCCUSL revised RUPA to add language authorizing general partnerships to register as LLP's. The name of this model legislation is technically the "Uniform Partnership Act (1996)," but most commentators continue to refer to it as "RUPA." RUPA, as revised in 1996, specifically authorizes the formation of LLP's. A single filing suffices; no annual renewals are required although the statute does require an annual report which requires that certain information be provided to the applicable state authority. There is no requirement that the LLP maintain any level of financial reserves or insurance. Finally, RUPA provides for full protection against personal liability, meaning that partners in an LLP formed under RUPA would have no personal liability for any entity-level debts. The only requirement is that a form be filed which contains certain information. The information must be updated annually, but a failure to make the required report can be remedied after the fact.

Because RUPA was enacted after most states had already promulgated their own LLP legislation, there continues to be significant variation from state to state. Therefore, the applicable state statutes should be consulted when there is any question about how to form an LLP, or whether an LLP in fact exists.

2. Limitations on Purpose or Business of Limited Liability Firms

Meyer v. Oklahoma Alcoholic Beverage Laws Enforcement Comm'n
890 P.2d 1361 (Okla. App. 1995)

STUBBLEFIELD, Judge.

This is an appeal from the district court's reversal of the declaratory ruling of the Oklahoma Alcoholic Beverage Laws Enforcement Commission (ABLE) that a newly created form of business entity, a limited liability company (LLC), is not entitled to receive and hold a retail package store license. Wanda L. Meyer, holder of a retail package store license, initiated these proceedings when she petitioned ABLE requesting a declaratory judgment that she could hold the license as an LLC, a business entity authorized by the Oklahoma Legislature in 1992 through the adoption of the Oklahoma Limited Liability Company Act (OLLC Act). ABLE denied the petition, thus holding that an LLC is not eligible to hold a retail package store license.

Meyer appealed the ABLE decision to the district court. That court focused on two provisions of the law:

(1) The Oklahoma constitutional provision, which only prohibits licensing of "corporations, business trusts, and secret partnerships," Okla. Const. art. 28, § 10: and,

(2) The provision in the LLC Act that authorized LLC's to "conduct business in any state *for any lawful purpose,* except the business of banking and insurance," 18 O.S.Supp. 1992 § 2002 (emphasis added) (footnote omitted).

Based upon those provisions, and a conclusion that the provisions of the Oklahoma Alcoholic Beverage Control Act "do not prohibit an LLC from holding a package store license," the trial court reversed the ABLE ruling and ordered it to "issue such license to petitioner as a limited liability company."

ABLE appeals, claiming that the order of the lower court is contrary to law in that an LLC is not authorized to hold a package store license. ABLE further claims that it could not be ordered to grant a license when no application by Meyer, as an LLC, was made.

The issue is one of first impression—whether an LLC, created pursuant to the OLLC Act, is eligible for issuance of a retail package store liquor license. Indeed, the issue could only have arisen after the 1992 legislative creation of the new form of business entity. LLCS were not a recognized business entity in this state at the time of adoption of our Constitution or at the time of adoption of the Oklahoma Alcoholic Beverage Control Act. However, both the Constitution and the Oklahoma Alcoholic Beverage Control Act do address qualifications of an applicant for a package store license.

The pertinent constitutional provisions are Okla. Const. art. 28, §§ 4 and 10. Section 4, in pertinent part, provides:

Not more than one retail package license shall be issued to any person or general or limited partnership.

Section 10, in pertinent part, provides:

No retail package store or wholesale distributor's license shall be issued to:

(a) A corporation, business trust or secret partnership.

(b) A person or partnership unless such person or all of the copartners including limited partners shall have been residents of the State of Oklahoma for at least ten (10) years immediately preceding the date of application for such license.

(c) A person or a general or limited partnership containing a partner who has been convicted of a violation of a prohibitory law relating to the sale, manufacture, or the transportation of alcoholic beverages which constituted a felony or misdemeanor.

(d) A person or a general or limited partnership containing a partner who has been convicted of a felony.

It is true, as noted by the trial court in its decision, that the specific constitutional prohibitions regarding license holders includes only corporations, business trusts, and secret partnerships. Of course, neither the framers nor amenders of the Constitution could have addressed the qualification or disqualification of LLC's as retail package store licensees, because the business entity did not exist in this state until 1992. Indeed, the testimony before ABLE indicated that the business form did not exist in this country until 1977. However, the Constitution did address all of the business formats as they existed at the time of adoption of the article on alcoholic beverage laws and enforcement and, significantly, section 4 names only individuals and partnerships as those entities to which a license may be issued.

Likewise, it is true that the Oklahoma Alcoholic Beverage Control Act does not prohibit an LLC from holding a license. However, what the Act does or does not prohibit is not dispositive because the Act does not purport to address the nature of the applicant—a matter controlled by the constitutional provisions. The Act does restate some of the disqualifications set forth in section 10 of the Constitution regarding residency, criminal conviction, etc., but does not purport to prohibit the licensing of corporations, business trusts and secret partnerships, which are specifically prohibited as licensees by the Constitution. It appears that qualification as a license holder, with regard to types of business entities, was left to the constitutional pronouncement.

When the legislature adopted the OLLC Act, it provided that:

[a] limited liability company may be organized under this act and may conduct business in any state for any lawful purpose, except the business of banking and insurance.

18 O.S.Supp. 1992 § 2002 (footnote omitted). Of course, such a legislative enactment could not countermand a constitutional prohibition, even if that had been the legislative intent. However, we do not believe the language of section 2002 indicates a legislative intent to extend the authority of LLC's in ways specifically prohibited elsewhere by statute, and particularly not to an act prohibited by the Oklahoma Constitution. Thus, we do not view section 2002 of the OLLC Act as sanction for the operation of a retail package store by an LLC.

If we interpreted section 2002 as argued by Meyer, then it could, in some respects, negate specific declarations of Okla. Const. art. 28, § 10. An LLC—neither a person, corporation nor partnership—is not specifically named in section 10 and, thus, if eligible as a licensee, its members would not be subject to the same restrictions regarding residence, violations of the liquor laws and status as a felon, which are imposed upon members of other permissible business entity licensees. Even the similar prohibitions in 37 O.S. 1991 § 527, are not drawn with this new business entity in mind and would not clearly apply to LLC members. Meyer apparently recognized this fundamental problem with the LLC business entity and by company rule restricted membership in keeping with the prohibitions of the Constitution and section 527. However, these restrictions are set out in fully amendable articles. Furthermore, the question is not whether the members of this particular LLC are eligible applicants because those members are not the applicants. The applicant is the LLC, and the question is whether the business entity is a permissible license holder.

Meyer argues that an LLC is essentially a partnership. However, the act creating the business form is in Title 18, which is entitled "Corporations." Furthermore, a provision in our Uniform Partnership Act states that "any association formed under any other statute of this state...is not a partnership under this act, unless such association would have been a partnership in this state prior to adoption of this act." 54 O.S. 1991 § 206(2).

Meyer claims that its expert witness, the only witness in all the proceedings, testified that an LLC was a partnership. However, contrary to Meyer's contention, the witness's testimony was not so unequivocal. The totality of the testimony was that an LLC is a hybrid that has attributes of both corporations and partnerships. The witness indicated an LLC is more like a partnership, but noted the primary difference is that all owners/members have limited liability in an LLC—something not found in partnerships. We conclude that the limitation of liability of all LLC members is a substantial difference especially relevant to the provisions of our liquor laws.

Our examination of the pertinent constitutional provisions leads us to conclude that their evident purpose was the assignment of personal responsibility for compliance with the liquor laws. Thus, business forms that did not insure such personal responsibility were excluded from eligibility for licensing.

The OLLC Act does exactly what its name indicates. It creates a form of business that has as its most important feature the limitation of liability of its members. This liability limitation is also a shield from the very responsibility and accountability that the constitutional provisions regarding alcoholic beverage laws and enforcement sought to impose.

The trial court reversed the ABLE decision as contrary to law. Based upon the foregoing analysis, we conclude that there was no such error and that the trial court erred in reversing the ABLE decision. Because of our ruling, we do not need to address ABLE's contention that the trial court erred in ordering it to grant a license when an application had not been made.

The judgment of the trial court is REVERSED.

Notes

1. Is the reasoning in *Meyer* consistent with that in *Swiezynski v. Civiello* (Chapter 1)?

2. The trial court concluded that the express provision of the Oklahoma LLC Act authorized LLC's to conduct *any* lawful business, and that there was nothing in the Oklahoma Constitution which required a different conclusion. Obviously, the Oklahoma Court of Appeals disagreed. If you were a justice on the Oklahoma Supreme Court deciding this case, which of these two approaches would you find the most persuasive? Why?

3. If Oklahoma adopts LLP legislation, under the reasoning of this opinion, would an Oklahoma LLP be able to obtain a retail package store license? Why or why not?

Opinion Number R-17
Comm. on Prof'l & Judicial Ethics
State Bar of Michigan
(Jan. 14, 1994)

SYLLABUS

It is permissible for a lawyer to form a professional limited liability company. The name of the company must contain the words "Professional Limited Liability Company" or the abbreviation "P.L.L.C." or "P.L.C."

A lawyer's selection of a limited liability company does not affect the liability of a lawyer rendering services to a client, a lawyer charged with supervisory responsibilities in reference to the rendition of services, or the firm.

TEXT

The issue under discussion is whether MRPC 1.8(h) prevents lawyers from using a limited liability company structure for their law firms and secondly, if not, what disclosures or explanations must be made to clients. MRPC 1.8(h) states:

A lawyer shall not:

(1) make an agreement prospectively limiting the lawyer's liability to a client for malpractice unless permitted by law and the client is independently represented in making the agreement; or

(2) settle a claim for such liability with an unrepresented client or former client without first advising that person in writing that independent representation is appropriate in connection therewith.

The Michigan Limited Liability Company Act specifically allows for the formation of professional limited liability companies including those formed for rendition of legal services. Therefore, in addition to professional corporations, partnerships and proprietorships, a group of lawyers forming a law firm in this state may also consider the limited liability company structure. MCL 450.4901(1) states:

A limited liability company may be formed under this Act for the purpose of rendering 1 or more professional services, as defined in Section 4902.

"Professional service" as defined in the Act includes attorney-at-law. MCL 450.905(2) and (3) state:

(2) This act shall not be construed to abolish, repeal, modify, restrict, or limit the law now in effect applicable to the professional relationship and liabilities between the person furnishing the professional services and the person receiving such professional services and to the standards for professional conduct. A member, manager, employee, or agent of a professional limited liability company shall remain personally and fully liable and accountable for any negligent or wrongful acts or misconduct committed by him or her, or by any person under his or her direct supervision and control, while rendering professional services on behalf of the company to the person for whom the professional services were being rendered.

(3) The limited liability company shall be liable up to the full value of its property for any negligent or wrongful acts or misconduct com-

mitted by any of its members, managers, employees or agents while they are engaged on behalf of the company in the rendering of professional services.

The statutory language of the Limited Liability Company Act Section 4905(2) and (3) closely parallels that of the Professional Services Corporation Act. Both acts make it clear that existing law regulating the professional relationship between the person furnishing the professional service and the person receiving the service continue to be governed by "standards of professional conduct". Explicitly, therefore, the Michigan Rules of Professional Conduct promulgated by the Supreme Court, specifically MRPC 1.8(h), still apply in the professional corporation or limited liability company structure.

A lawyer's selection of a limited liability company will not affect the liability of a lawyer rendering services to a client, a lawyer charged with supervisory responsibilities in reference to the rendition of services, or the firm. That selection will, however, eliminate vicarious liability of partners in certain circumstances.

Since ethics rules do not currently require disclosures or explanations to be made to a client regarding the business aspects of a professional corporation other than the fact that the professional corporation exists, lawyers belonging to a professional limited liability company do not have any ethical obligations to disclose the details of their business arrangement other than those legally required, *i.e.,* that the name of the limited liability company shall contain the words "Professional Limited Liability Company" or the abbreviation "P.L.L.C." or "P.L.C."

Notes

1. If the Michigan Limited Liability Company Act specifically allows for the formation of professional limited liability companies, including those formed for rendition of legal services, why was it necessary for lawyers to obtain permission from the State Bar of Michigan Standing Committee on Professional and Judicial Ethics? Consider the following extract from, *First Bank & Trust Co. v. Zagoria,* 250 Ga. 844, 302 S.E.2d 674, 675-76 (1983), in which the Georgia Supreme Court restricted the scope of limited liability of lawyers practicing as a professional corporation:

> We do not view this case as one in which we need to interpret the statute providing for the creation and operation of professional corporations. We rather view this case as one which calls for the exercise of this court's authority to regulate the practice of law. This court has the authority and in fact the duty to regulate the law practice.
>
> The diligence of this court has been directed toward the assurance that the law practice will be a professional service and not simply a commercial enterprise. The primary distinction is that a profession is a calling which demands adherence to the public interest as the foremost obligation of the practitioner.
>
> The professional corporation statute should be interpreted with this thought in mind. The legislature has the clear right to enact technical rules for the creation and operation of professional corporations, but it cannot constitutionally cross the gulf separating the branches of government by imposing regulations upon the practice of law.

By enacting the professional corporation statute the legislature performed a useful and constitutional act. A professional corporation has numerous legitimate business purposes. By conducting a law practice through the structure of a professional corporation, its shareholders realize the advantages of more orderly business operations, greater ease in acquiring, holding and transferring property, and more continuity of its existence. Additionally, a professional corporation affords to its shareholders insulation against liability for obligations which do not arise as a result of a breach of a lawyer's obligation to his client or an act of professional malpractice. The shareholders of a professional corporation have the same insulation from liability as shareholders of other corporations with respect to obligations of a purely business and nonprofessional nature. However, the influence of the statute upon the professional corporation cannot extend to the regulation of the law practice so as to impose a limitation of liability for acts of malpractice or obligations incurred because of a breach of a duty to a client.

The professional nature of the law practice and its obligations to the public interest require that each lawyer be civilly responsible for his professional acts. A lawyer's relationship to his client is a very special one. So also is the relationship between a lawyer and the other members of his or her firm a special one. When a client engages the services of a lawyer the client has the right to expect the fidelity of other members of the firm. It is inappropriate for the lawyer to be able to play hide-and-seek in the shadows and folds of the corporate veil and thus escape the responsibilities of professionalism.

We hold that when a lawyer holds himself out as a member of a law firm the lawyer will be liable not only for his own professional misdeeds but also for those of the other members of his firm. We make no distinction between partnerships and professional corporations in this respect. We cannot allow a corporate veil to hang from the cornices of professional corporations which engage in the law practice.

In *Zagoria,* the Georgia Supreme Court did not hold that it was unethical for lawyers to practice in a limited liability form. Instead, it held that lawyers would remain personally liable despite the form of the firm in which they practice. In *Hendersen v. HSI Financial Services, Inc.,* 266 Ga. 844, 471 S.E.2d 885 (1996), the Georgia Supreme Court revisited the issue:

Today we overrule *Zagoria* to the extent it states that this court, rather than the legislative enabling act, determines the ability of lawyers to insulate themselves from personal liability for the acts of other shareholders in their professional corporation. Although this court defines whether lawyers may practice their profession in a partnership, professional corporation, or other group structure, the relevant statutes govern whether a particular structural form provides its members with exemptions from personal liability.

Exercising our regulatory power, we hold that lawyers may practice their profession as shareholders in a professional corporation with the same rights and responsibilities as shareholders in other professional corporations. Allowing lawyers to organize their practice in this particular form will not undermine professional conduct or leave the public unprotected. Lawyers practicing in a professional corporation still owe a duty to clients and remain personally liable to them for acts of professional negligence. In addition, the professional corporation is liable for the malpractice of its members to the extent of its corporate assets.

Moreover, permitting lawyers to practice in a corporate entity is consistent with the legal profession's ethical standards. The ABA ruled in 1961 that an attorney may practice in a form of organization that limits liability to clients for legal malpractice without violating the Canons of Ethics so long as the lawyer rendering the legal services remains personally responsible to the client.[7] The ABA incorporated its ruling into the Model Code of Professional Responsibility that this court adopted as part of the state bar rules.[8] Many states have followed the ABA opinion by enabling attorneys to organize their practice in the form of professional corporations, limited liability companies, and limited liability partnerships.[9]

Id. at 845-46, 471 S.E.2d at 886-87.

2. The following extract from John T. Ballantine & Thomas E. Rutledge, *Kentucky Supreme Court Rejects Use of LLC's, LLP's and PSC's by Attorneys*, Bench & Bar, Vol. 60, No. 1, pg. 21 (Winter 1996), illustrates the problems that arise when professionals assume that they are authorized to practice in limited liability forms:

In a move surprising as well as disconcerting to law firms organized as limited liability companies (LLC's), registered limited liability partnerships (LLP's) and professional service corporations (PSC's), the Kentucky Supreme Court has rejected a proposed rule which would have expressly permitted the use of these forms of organizations by attorneys. In rejecting this proposed rule, the Supreme Court has undercut the primary reason for using one of these forms of business, namely limitation of vicarious liability for the wrongs of other attorneys.

Attorneys, like anyone seeking to form and run a business, must choose the corporation, general or limited partnership, the new limited liability company, and registered limited liability partnership, and any number of esoteric options such as the business trust. * * *

Despite these developments, the Kentucky Supreme Court has never adopted a rule expressly addressing the forms of organization that could be utilized by attorneys. Presented with a lack of direction, a proposed

---

7. ABA Comm. on Professional Ethics, Formal Op. 303 (1961) (attorneys practicing in corporate form).

8. *Rules and Regulations for the Organization and Government of the State Bar of Georgia,* 241 Ga. 643, 696 (1978).

9. *See, e.g., In the Matter of Florida Bar,* 133 So.2d 554 (Fla. 1961) (adopting rules that permit lawyers to practice law as a corporate entity under the Professional Services Corporation Act); N.C. State Bar R. subch. E, §.0100 (adopting regulations for professional corporations & professional limited liability companies practicing law); Va. Sup.Ct. R. Pt. 6, IV, Para. 14 (1996) (adopting Code of Ethics governing professional conduct of lawyers practicing through professional law corporations, professional limited liability companies, and registered limited liability partnerships).

rule on permissible forms of organization was drafted and presented to the Supreme Court for consideration. [The proposed rule] provided:

> A lawyer may practice with, in the form of, or as a partner, shareholder, member, manager, employee or agent of, a general partnership, a registered limited liability partnership, a professional service corporation or a limited liability company. In each case, the practice of law with or in the form of such entity shall be subject to these Rules and the statutes governing the formation and operation of such entity.

While the proposed rule was pending before the Supreme Court, a number of law firms adopted either the LLC or LLP form of organization. Of course, firms organized as PSC's have long been a fixture in Kentucky.

The Supreme Court rejected the proposed rule and wrote that:

> [T]he members of the Supreme Court of Kentucky do not agree that lawyers can so limit their liability.

If one concludes that the Supreme Court has rejected the use of limited liability structures by attorneys...[it may be improper] for lawyers to hold themselves out as practicing through a limited liability structure, implying that all attorneys "do not share fully in the responsibilities and liabilities of the other attorneys involved" when in fact that is exactly what the Supreme Court requires.

If this conclusion is correct, there remains the question of what should be done by those firms which have moved to the LLC/LLP/PSC forms of organization. Firms now organized as LLC's or LLP's may elect to return to the general partnership form. In doing so, those firms may reason that it is improper to adopt a business form affirmatively rejected by the Supreme Court. The conversion from LLC/LLP to general partnership will, in nearly all situations, be tax-free.

Another option would be to retain the LLC/LLP form, but abandon the aspect of the form criticized by the Supreme Court, namely limited liability. These firms would not assert the limited liability afforded by the LLC/LLP statutes against any malpractice claim. This course of conduct raises questions of whether and how attorneys should advise clients that the limited liability defense will not be raised against claims against the firm and its attorneys.

Still other firms may elect to not only retain the LLC or LLP form as well as the grant of limited liability.... Such a firm, when presented with a malpractice claim, would raise the statutory limited liability protection as a vehicle for a decision on the merits of vicarious liability among attorneys. this approach would require that the firm interpret the rejection of the proposed rule as something less than a determination on the merits of vicarious liability and something other than a determination that it is unethical to practice through an entity which purports to grant limited liability. In order to succeed, that firm would be required not only to persuade the Court that its interpretation is correct, but also to convince it that law firms, like all other businesses, should be able to make use of limited liability forms of business.

Firms organized outside of, but doing business in, Kentucky as a LLC or LLP will have to grapple with not only the rejection of the proposed rule but also conflicts of law principles. Briefly, the Kentucky LLC Act provides that a foreign LLC shall have no greater rights and privileges than does a domestic LLC. The same rule, even if unstated, should apply to LLP's. If, because of the action of the Supreme Court, an attorney cannot practice through a domestic LLC or LLP, it follows that that attorney would not be able to use a foreign LLC or LLP to achieve the same end. If a foreign attorney, a member of a foreign LLP, practices in Kentucky and commits malpractice, a court - Kentucky or foreign - could easily and properly ignore the purported limited liability of these structures and hold that under the law of Kentucky, where the tort occurred, all member/partners are vicariously liable.

Some Kentucky law firms are continuing to operate as LLC's, at least until the Kentucky Supreme Court clarifies its position. If you were practicing law in Kentucky, would you feel comfortable using an LLC?

Assume that the Kentucky Supreme Court's position is the same as that adopted in Zagoria: lawyers practicing in limited liability forms remain personally liable for professional obligations. How should lawyers signal to their clients that the normal attributes of their business entity do not apply to professional obligations? Is there a risk that clients will be misled?

3. Contracts Entered into before Formation of a Limited Liability Firm

Problem 3.1

Grace and Alice were starting their own record label, "White Rabbit Records." Grace's father, Lewis, agreed to invest in the business. The three of them agreed to organize the business as a limited liability company, in which Grace, Alice and Lewis were to be the only members.

Lewis gave Grace and Alice $100,000, which they deposited in a bank account under the name "White Rabbit Records." Grace started looking for a place to put the recording studio and offices. Alice started working on finding recording artists. On March 7, Alice signed a recording contract with Artist. The recording contract was in the name of "White Rabbit Records," and was signed as follows:

White Rabbit Records

By: /S/ Alice

Using forms she downloaded from the Internet, Grace prepared Articles of Organization for a limited liability company to be named "White Rabbit Records, LLC." On April 1, the three signed the Articles of Organization, and mailed them to Secretary of State of the State of Confusion for filing under the Confusion Limited Liability Company Act ("CLLCA").

Lewis invested in the business, but was not active in its operation. Grace and Alice both invested in, and were active in running the business. While Alice was off contacting bands and songwriters, Grace found a place to put their recording studio. On April 7, Grace signed a lease with Landlord. The lease showed "White Rabbit Records, LLC" as the lessee, and was signed as follows:

White Rabbit Records, LLC

By: /S/ Grace

Grace, member

On April 15, Grace received a letter from the Confusion Secretary of State, returning the Articles of Organization of White Rabbit Records, LLC, and advising that the Articles were being returned **without filing,** because the name "White Rabbit Records, LLC" was not available without a letter of consent from White Rabbit Magic, Inc. Grace, Alice and Lewis obtained the letter of consent, and mailed the consent, and the Articles of Organization for White Rabbit Records, LLC, to the Confusion Secretary of State. The Confusion Secretary of Sate accepted the Articles of Organization for filing, and issued a Certificate of Organization for White Rabbit Records, LLC , effective as of April 22.

1. Please advise each of Grace, Alice, Lewis and White Rabbit Records, LLC as to their respective responsibilities with respect to (a) the recording contract with Artist, and (b) the lease with Landlord. You may assume that, except as set forth above, the Lease has no provisions that would affect your answer.

2. Suppose that, instead of a limited liability company, the parties had formed a limited partnership, with Grace and Alice as general partners, and Lewis as a limited partner. Would that change the responsibilities of the parties on the Lease? Why or why not?

a. Traditional Approach

Goodman v. Darden, Doman & Stafford Assoc.

33 Wash.App. 278, 653 P.2d 1371 (Wash Ct. App. 1982)

DURHAM, Acting Chief Justice.

This is an appeal from an order that respondent John Goodman need not take part in arbitration proceedings arising out of a contract which he had signed as president of a corporation "in formation." Goodman had arranged with Darden, Doman & Stafford Associates (DDS), a general partnership, to renovate a Tacoma apartment building purchased by DDS. During the negotiations Goodman decided to incorporate and so informed DDS. The contract was ultimately executed between DDS and "BUILDING DESIGN AND DEVELOPMENT INC. (In formation), John A. Goodman, President." Work was to be completed by October 15, 1979; at that time it was not finished and was of allegedly poor quality. The corporate articles were filed on November 1, 1979, after the contract was in default.

Between August 17, 1979 and December 12, 1979, DDS made five progress payments on the contract. The first check was made out to "Building Design & Developement [sic] Inc. John Goodman." Goodman struck out his name as payee and endorsed the check "Bldg Design & Dev. Inc. John A. Goodman, Pres." He instructed DDS to make further payments to Building Design & Development, Inc., and DDS did so on the last four checks.

After ineffective attempts to remedy the problems, DDS served Goodman with a demand for arbitration under the American Arbitration Association Construction Industry Arbitration Rules in May 1980. Goodman moved in King County Superior Court for a stay of arbitration and an order dismissing him from arbitration. The trial court found that he was not a party individually to the contract and, thus, not a proper party to the arbitration proceedings.

The dispositive issue in this case involves the liability of promoters on pre-incorporation contracts. In general, a promoter is liable on a contract he makes for the benefit of a not-yet-formed corporation. The rule has been codified in RCW 23A.44.100:

> All persons who assume to act as a corporation without authority so to do shall be jointly and severally liable for all debts and liabilities incurred or arising as a result thereof.

Clearly, a corporation not yet in existence cannot authorize actions on behalf of itself.

Nevertheless, promoters are not personally liable for pre-incorporation contracts where the other party knows of the nonexistence of the corporation and agrees to look solely to the corporation. There is no dispute that DDS knew at the time of signing that the corporation was not yet in existence. The issue then is the specificity of the agreement to look solely to the corporation. Respondent argues that the agreement can be implied from conduct; appellant contends that the agreement must be express. This is a question of first impression in Washington.

As with any agreement, release of the promoter depends on the intent of the parties. Other jurisdictions present differing methods of determining intent. In Illinois, for example, the courts determine intent by looking to the contract and other contemporaneous documents. *Stap v. Chicago Aces Tennis Team, Inc.*, 63 Ill.App.3d 23, 20 Ill.Dec. 230, 379 N.E.2d 1298 (1978). *Stap* illustrates the problem with applying this approach in Washington. In *Stap*, the court found intent to release the promoter because the contract was signed between the plaintiff and the promoter acting on behalf of a corporation to be formed. We do not believe, however, that the mere signing of a contract with a corporation "to be formed" suffices to show agreement to look solely to the corporation. Washington law presumes that a promoter who signs "on behalf" of an unformed corporation remains liable. To say that contracting with a promoter in itself constitutes agreement to release him begs the question. The contract creates the presumed liability; something more is required to rebut the presumption and find release.[2]

Some jurisdictions require that the contract show clearly on its face that there is no intent to hold the promoter liable before he is released. The agreement must be "specific" or "express." In *RKO-Stanley Warner Theaters, Inc. v. Graziano*, 467 Pa. 220, 355 A.2d 830, 832 (1976), the contract stated:

---

2. The court in *Stap v. Chicago Aces Tennis Team, Inc.*, 63 Ill.App.3d 23, 20 Ill.Dec. 230, 379 N.E.2d 1298 (1978) also ignores the fact that when the contract was signed, the corporation was not yet in existence. In Washington there is "a strong inference that a person intends to make a present contract with an existing person." *White & Bollard, Inc. v. Goodenow*, 58 Wash.2d 180, 184, 361 P.2d 571 (1961), *quoting* Restatement (Second) of Agency § 326, Comment a (1958). The approach in *Stap* necessarily finds intent to contract with a nonexistent entity.

"It is understood by the parties hereto that it is the intention of the Purchaser to incorporate. Upon condition that such incorporation be completed by closing, all agreements, covenants, and warranties contained herein shall be construed to have been made between Seller and the resultant corporation and all documents shall reflect same."

The court held that "while [this paragraph] does make provision for recognition of the resultant corporation as to the closing documents, it makes no mention of any release of personal liability." Id. 355 A.2d at 833. Since the paragraph did not expressly provide for release on closing, the court found it ambiguous and construed it to hold the promoter liable until the corporation actually ratified the contract.

We do not go so far as the court in *RKO-Stanley Warner Theaters*. The agreement need not say in so many words "I agree to release" before intent to do so may be discerned. Certainly intent is the controlling requirement; this must be proven as for any contract, express or implied. The burden is on the promoter, as proponent of the agreement, to show by a preponderance all essential facts, including mutual intent. Where the promoter cannot show an express agreement, existence of the agreement may be shown by circumstantial evidence, but circumstances must be such as to make it clear by a preponderance of the evidence that the parties not only intended, but actually did make, the alleged agreement.

The record here reveals insufficient evidence of agreement or mutual intent that could support a finding that John Goodman was released from liability. There is no evidence of an express contract, either written or oral. Goodman indicated his wish to limit liability by forming a corporation, but the most the record shows is that DDS did not object to his incorporating; nothing indicates assent to limit liability. Even if the expression of desire constituted an offer to make release a term of the contract, silence is acceptance only when there is a duty to speak. DDS had no duty to correct, or even perceive, Goodman's mistaken interpretation of the promoter liability rules. The only other evidence of agreement lies in the progress payment checks which DDS made out to the corporation, at Goodman's request. This alone is insufficient to constitute intent to look solely to the corporation.

We, therefore, hold that where a promoter wishes to be released from liability for contracts he makes on behalf of a corporation not yet formed, he has the burden of proving the existence of an agreement to release him. The mere facts of contracting in the corporate name and payments made to the corporation are not sufficient to carry that burden. The trial court thus erred in finding that John Goodman was not a party to the renovation contract.

In light of this conclusion, we need not reach the issues of corporate disregard raised by appellant. The order excusing Goodman from arbitration proceedings is reversed and the case remanded for further proceedings.

SCHOFIELD and CALLOW, JJ., concur.

Notes

1. *Illinois Controls, Inc. v. Langham*, 70 Ohio St.3d 512, 639 N.E.2d 771 (Ohio 1994) involved a preincorporation agreement (which the Court referred to as the "PIA") among the persons who were to become shareholders of the corporation being formed. The PIA purported to make the as-yet-unformed corporation a party to the PIA. The Ohio Supreme Court held that the person who pur-

ported to sign on behalf of the corporation was party to the contract, even though all the parties knew that the corporation had not yet been organized. The Court explained its holding as follows:

> The legal relationship between a promoter and the corporate enterprise he seeks to advance is analogous to that between an agent and his principal. Thus, legal principles governing the relationship are derived from the law of agency. *See* 1 Restatement of the Law 2d, Agency (1958) 216, Section 84, Comment d; 2 Restatement of the Law 2d, Agency (1958) 78, Section 326, Comment b.

* * *

> It is axiomatic that the promoters of a corporation are at least initially liable on any contracts they execute in furtherance of the corporate entity prior to its formation. The promoters are released from liability only where the contract provides that performance is to be the obligation of the corporation; the corporation is ultimately formed; and the corporation then formally adopts the contract.

> It is generally recognized that where a pre-incorporation agreement merely indicates that it is undertaken on behalf of a corporation, the corporation will not be exclusively liable in the event of a breach. Under such circumstances the promoters of the corporation remain liable on the contract.

> Formation of the corporation following execution of the contract is a prerequisite to any release of the promoters from liability arising from the pre-incorporation agreement. Inasmuch as the promoter-corporation relationship is based on agency principles, a promoter will not be released from liability if the corporation is never formed, because one may not be an agent for a nonexistent principal. 2 Restatement of the Law 2d, Agency (1958), Section 326.

> Moreover, mere adoption of the contract by the corporation will not relieve promoters from liability in the absence of a subsequent novation. This view is founded upon "the well-settled principle of the law of contracts that a party to a contract cannot relieve himself from its obligations by the substitution of another person, without the consent of [the] other party." Ballantine, [Manual of Corporation Law & Practice (1930)], at 163. Consequently, the promoters of a corporation who execute a contract on its behalf are personally liable for the breach thereof irrespective of the later adoption of the contract by the corporation unless the contract provides that performance thereunder is solely the responsibility of the corporation.

> Applying these principles to the facts of the present case, we find that the promoters remain personally liable on the pre-incorporation agreement. While the corporation was subsequently formed as envisioned in the contract, the agreement does not state that the parties intended that the corporate entity was to be exclusively liable for any breach. Even if the agreement did so provide, there is no evidence that the corporation, once formed, formally adopted it.

639 N.E.2d at 780-81.

3. Restatement Section 326 is to the same effect as the principal case and *Illinois Controls, Inc. v. Langham:*

> Unless otherwise agreed, a person who, in dealing with another, purports to act as agent for a principal whom both know to be nonexistent or wholly incompetent, becomes a party to such a contract.

Comment b to Section 326 calls the promoter cases the "classic illustration" of dealings on behalf of a nonexistent person. Where the parties put the contract in only the name of the principal, the parties may have any one of a number of different intents as to the liability of the promoter:

> (1) They may understand that the other party is making a revocable offer to the nonexistent corporation which will result in a contract if the corporation is formed and accepts the offer prior to withdrawal. This is the normal understanding.
>
> (2) They may understand that the other party is making an irrevocable offer for a limited time. Consideration to support the promise to keep the offer open can be found in an express or limited promise by the promoter to organize the corporation and use his best efforts to cause it to accept the offer.
>
> (3) They may agree to a present contract by which the promoter is bound, but with an agreement that his liability terminates if the corporation is formed and manifests its willingness to become a party. There can be no ratification by the newly formed corporation, since it was not in existence when the agreement was made. See s 84, Comment c.
>
> (4) They may agree to a present contract on which, even though the corporation becomes a party, the promoter remains liable either primarily or as surety for the performance of the corporation's obligation.

Restatement § 326 comment b. Although the actual intent of the parties will be a question of fact (comment b),

> ... there is an inference that a person intends to make a present contract with an existing person. If, therefore, the other party knows that there is no principal capable of entering into such a contract, there is a rebuttable inference that, although the contract is nominally in the name of the nonexistent person, the parties intend that the person signing as agent should be a party, unless there is some indication to the contrary.

Restatement, § 326 comment a.

4. To what extent would the principles discussed in Chapter 2 apply in determining in the liability of an agent arising out dealings on behalf of a nonexistent principal?

5. In the corporation cases, the corporate principal is deemed not to exist until it has complied with the formalities required by state law for the formation of a corporation. Presumably, the same reasoning should apply to dealings on behalf of a limited partnership, limited liability partnership or a limited liability that is in the process of being formed.

6. As implied in the principal case, the "corporation" on whose behalf a promoter enters into a contract is not liable at the time the contract is made. The rationale is that the corporation does not yet exist, so it is incapable of being

bound. The cases also suggest that the corporation does not become liable upon incorporation for the contracts signed on its behalf (why not?). Instead, the corporation must either expressly or impliedly adopt the contract. An implied adoption is similar to an implied ratification. For example, in *Illinois Controls, Inc. v. Langham,* the corporation was found to have adopted the preincorporation agreement made on its behalf when the corporation accepted the benefits of the contract with knowledge of the agreement's terms. 639 N.E.2d at 780. See Chapter 9 for a discussion of ratification.

6. Where the promoter and the corporation are both liable on a preformation contracts, should the doctrine of election of remedies apply? In *Illinois Controls, Inc. v. Langham,* the court reasoned as follows:

> Inasmuch as both the promoters of Illinois Controls and the corporation itself are liable, the nature of this shared liability remains to be determined. While our research has failed to discover an Ohio decision which has addressed this specific issue, resort to agency principles is, again, instructive. The relationship between a promoter and a corporation to be formed can be compared to the relationship between an agent and an undisclosed principal. Where a contract is made in furtherance of the interests of an undisclosed principal, both the principal and the agent are liable for breach of its underlying obligations. Under such circumstances, the agent and the undisclosed principal are jointly and severally liable for breach of the agreement. *See Crown Controls, Inc. v. Smiley* (1988), 110 Wash.2d 695, 704, 756 P.2d 717, 721; *Engelstad v. Cargill, Inc.* (Minn. 1983), 336 N.W.2d 284, 286; *Grinder v. Bryans Rd. Bldg. & Supply Co., Inc.* (1981), 290 Md. 687, 706-707, 432 A.2d 453, 463-464; *Joseph Melnick Bldg. & Loan Assn. v. Melnick* (1949), 361 Pa. 328, 335, 64 A.2d 773, 777; *Williamson v. O'Dwyer & Ahern Co.* (1917), 127 Ark. 530, 192 S.W. 899; *Lull v. Anamosa Natl. Bank* (1900), 110 Iowa 537, 542, 81 N.W. 784, 786; *Cobb v. Knapp* (1877), 71 N.Y. 348, 353. *See, also, Maple v. Cincinnati, Hamilton & Dayton RR. Co.* (1883), 40 Ohio St. 313, 316-318 (joint and several liability between agent and disclosed principal for fraud committed by agent without knowledge of principal).
>
> These holdings are consistent with the shared liability for a contractual obligation undertaken by a promoter on behalf of a yet-to-be-formed corporation.
>
> We therefore conclude that where a corporation, with knowledge of the agreement's terms, benefits from a pre-incorporation agreement executed on its behalf by its promoters, the corporation and the promoters are jointly and severally liable for breach of the agreement unless the agreement provides that performance is solely the responsibility of the corporation or, subsequent to the formation of the corporate entity, a novation is executed whereby the corporation is substituted for the promoters as a party to the original agreement.

639 N.E.2d at 781-82.

Is the reasoning of the *Illinois Controls, Inc. v. Langham* court consistent with that in *Orrock v. Crouse Relators, Inc.,* page 114?

7. If no corporation exists at the time a preformation contract is signed, what is the nature of the business being conducted under the name of the corpo-

ration? If it turns out that the business cannot incorporate under the name used in signing the preformation contract, and the business incorporates under a different name, would that change the result?

Dwinell's Central Neon v. Cosmopolitan Chinook Hotel

21 Wash. App. 929, 587 P.2d 191 (1978)

McINTURFF, Judge.

Cosmopolitan Chinook Hotel (Cosmopolitan) appeals from a summary judgment, holding it liable as a general partnership and not as a limited partnership in connection with an action brought by Dwinell's Central Neon (Dwinell's) for breach of contract.

On October 25, 1972, Cosmopolitan and Dwinell's entered into three separate agreements for the lease-sale of neon signs. Dwinell's was represented by one of its salesmen and Cosmopolitan was represented by two of its partners. The contracts contained an acceleration clause in the event of Cosmopolitan's default and a provision for a reduction in the monthly payment should Dwinell's fail to properly maintain the signs.

In October, 1976, Cosmopolitan was behind on its payments and Dwinell's brought suit to accelerate the balance due under the contract. The complaint averred that Cosmopolitan was a general partnership due to its failure to comply with the statutory filing requirements of the [ULPA]. Cosmopolitan, on the other hand, claimed limited partnership status and stated that their status was known by Dwinell's at the time of contracting and was a matter of common knowledge in the community.

We are asked to consider whether summary judgment was proper in light of the following alleged factual issues left unresolved:

(1) Whether Dwinell's had actual knowledge of Cosmopolitan's limited partnership status at the time of contracting;

(2) Whether the court erred in concluding that Cosmopolitan was a general partnership;

At the time Dwinell's and Cosmopolitan entered into the lease-sale agreements, Cosmopolitan had taken no steps to comply with the filing requirements of [ULPA section 2]. It was not until February 1973, several months following execution of the contract with Dwinell's, that the certificate of limited partnership was filed. Cosmopolitan argues, however, that it was widely known in Yakima that a limited partnership had purchased the Chinook Hotel. Further, Cosmopolitan states that this fact was communicated to Dwinell's via its salesman. This information was allegedly communicated in the following manner — the word "partnership" was circled as identifying the "user" under the contract and the contract was signed, "Evan Bargman, V.P., R. Powers, President." According to Cosmopolitan, circling the word "partnership" best indicated its status as a limited partnership and the signatures clearly indicated that Bargman and Powers were not signing as general partners but as corporate officers of the general partnership.

The bare allegation in Cosmopolitan's affidavit "it was widely known and publicized in Yakima that it (the hotel) had been purchased by a limited partnership" is insufficient to raise a genuine issue of fact. It must furnish the factual evidence upon which it relies. Here, there is no factual evidence to support the allegation.

Secondly, a third party's knowledge regarding the status of a limited partnership is irrelevant when at the time of contracting, the partners have made no attempt to comply with the statutory information and filing requirements of the [ULPA].

Limited partnerships were unknown at common law and are purely creatures of statute. Parties seeking the protection of limited liability within the context of a partnership must follow the statutory requirements. To form a limited partnership, a certificate of limited partnership must be drafted and filed pursuant to [ULPA section 2]. While our courts no longer require literal compliance with the statute at one's peril, the statute does contemplate at least "substantial compliance with the requirements." [ULPA § 2(2)]. Here, there was no compliance with the statute at the time of contracting and the certificate of limited partnership was not filed until several months later. The object of statutory regulation of limited partnerships is to insure that limited partners do not find themselves exposed to the unlimited liability of a general partner.

The statute specifies the acts which must be performed by persons desiring to become limited partners. Cosmopolitan had not complied with any requirements of the statute at the time it entered into the contract with Dwinell's. Obviously, the purpose of the filing requirement was thwarted, that is, to acquaint third persons dealing with the partnership of the details of the partnership arrangement. A creditor has a right to rely upon there being substantial compliance with [ULPA section 2] before the protection of its provisions are afforded to any member of a partnership. Here there was no compliance.

Cosmopolitan, relying on the case of *Stowe v. Merrilees*, 6 Cal. App. 2d 217, 44 P.2d 368 (1935), contends that because [ULPA section 2] is silent as to when the certificate must be filed, a reasonable time is implied. Cosmopolitan submits that it substantially complied with the requirements of the statute by filing a certificate of limited partnership some 90 days *after* the contract went into effect. Reliance on *Stowe v. Merrilees* is misplaced. There, the partners executed a partnership agreement but failed to file the certificate until 49 days later. The court held that the firm became a limited partnership as to third parties who extended credit *subsequent* to the act of filing. Cosmopolitan wants the effect of filing the certificate of limited partnership to relate back to a contract previously entered into. To adopt this reasoning would render the statutory requirement of [ULPA section 2] meaningless and business relationships would be rendered unstable and unpredictable.

Thus, since there was no compliance with the [ULPA], the court was correct in holding as a matter of law that Cosmopolitan was liable as a general partnership on the contract with Dwinell's.

The judgment of the superior court is affirmed.

Notes

1. The principal case illustrates the pre-ULPA common-law approach to investors in what might be called a "defective limited partnership" — persons who

believe they are limited partners, but who are not because no limited partnership certificate was ever filed. Under this approach, limited liability was viewed as a statutory boon: only owners of properly formed limited-liability entities—then, shareholders in a corporation or limited partners in a limited partnership—were entitled to limited liability. Unless a corporation or a limited partnership had actually been formed, all persons involved in the business were liable as (general) partners. How does this basis of liability differ from the basis of liability in *Goodman v. Darden, Doman & Stafford Associates*?

2. In the principal case, the firm—Cosmopolitan Chinook Hotel—was treated as a (general) partnership. Did the limited partners intend to be (general) partners? Why didn't the court consider any of the factors discussed in the partnership formation cases discussed earlier in this Chapter?

3. In determining the liability of investors who thought they were becoming limited partners, should it make any difference that the creditor did not rely on the investors' being general partners?

b. Interaction of Statutes and Common Law

Problem 3.2

Investor invested money in Widgets, Ltd. At the time of the investment, Investor signed a Certificate and Agreement of Limited Partnership that specified that Investor would be a limited partner in Widgets, Ltd. Unknown to Investor, Widgets, Ltd. began doing business without filing the Certificate. After six months, Widgets, Ltd. distributed $1,000 in profits to Investor. After Investor received the profits distribution, Investor learned that Widgets, Ltd. was not a limited partnership.

Despite learning that Widgets, Ltd. was not a limited partnership, Investor took no action to procure the filing of the Certificate of Limited Partnership for Widgets, Ltd., nor did Investor withdraw from equity participation in the business. In fact, Investor continued to take distributions of profits after Investor learned the business was not a limited partnership.

Widgets, Ltd. is now insolvent, and two of its creditors have sued Investor, seeking to hold Investor personally liable for Widgets, Ltd.'s debts. Alan sold on open account goods worth $10,000 to Widgets, Ltd. after Investor had received the first distribution of profits, but before Investor learned there was no limited partnership. Betty loaned Widgets, Ltd. $25,000, after Investor had learned there was no limited partnership, and after Investor had received further distributions of profits.

Assume that neither Alan nor Betty knew of Investor's involvement with Widgets. Ltd. Under the ULPA, is Investor liable to either Alan or Betty? Under the RULPA?

Briargate Condominium Ass'n, Inc. v. Carpenter
976 F.2d 868 (4th Cir. 1992)

HAMILTON, Circuit Judge:

Judith Carpenter appeals the decision of the district court, entered after a trial to the bench, holding her liable as a general partner for debts of the Briargate Homes partnership (Briargate Homes or the Partnership) to Briargate Condominium Association, Incorporated (the Association). Carpenter asserts that the district court erred in concluding that she had not effectively withdrawn from the Partnership pursuant to [RULPA §] 304 and was, therefore, liable as a general partner for the partnership debts.

I.

This is a collection action. Briargate Homes was a North Carolina partnership which purchased several units in the Briargate Condominium complex in Richland County, South Carolina. By the terms of the master deed for the condominium property and the bylaws of the Association, the Association was entitled to levy assessments or "regime fees" against unit owners for maintenance, repair, and replacement of common areas in the complex and to sue for unpaid fees. The Partnership failed to pay assessed fees in the amount of $85,106.08 as of December 1, 1988, some of which accrued prior to February 1988 and some afterward. Five of Carpenter's six individual codefendants in this collection action settled with the Association for a total sum of $25,000, which was credited against the indebtedness. At the time of the district court's order of December 4, 1991, the total amount of fees and interest assessed against Carpenter individually and the Partnership was $104,146.75.

Briargate Homes was formed in the latter part of 1984 when William E. Goodall, Jr., Carpenter's accountant at that time, induced her and other of his clients to invest in the Partnership as a tax shelter. Goodall received funds from Carpenter and her then-husband Hicks to purchase units in the Briargate Condominium complex on behalf of the Partnership. While Carpenter contends that she believed she was investing in a limited partnership, Briargate Homes operated as a general partnership from its inception. No attempt was ever made to achieve actual or substantial compliance with the statutes governing the formation of a limited partnership. See [RULPA §] 201 (requiring filing of prescribed certificate for formation of limited partnership). Despite the deposition testimony of Hicks offered at trial and Carpenter's contentions, the district court concluded that Briargate Homes had never been represented as anything other than a general partnership.

At trial, there was extensive testimony concerning Carpenter's knowledge and belief about the status of the Partnership. Carpenter did not sign the Briargate Homes partnership agreement. She contends, and the district court so concluded, that she never personally saw copies of the K-1 partnership tax forms, which clearly identified her as a general partner in Briargate Homes. Carpenter claimed deductions respecting partnership losses and profits on her tax returns which were, apparently, only allowable to her if she was a general partner, not a limited partner.[3]

As early as April 1987, incident to her divorce, Carpenter or her attorneys had in their possession documents transferring her husband's share of Briargate Homes to her. The transfer documents explicitly state that Briargate Homes was

---

3. Following her renunciation of participation in Briargate Homes in February 1988, Carpenter repaid the Internal Revenue Service (IRS) for certain deductions taken with respect to Briargate Homes. The propriety or necessity of such repayment is not before the court on this appeal. See *infra* note 16.

a general partnership and that the interest transferred was a general partnership interest. Similarly, in June 1987, Carpenter attended a partnership meeting in which she was presented with documents which explicitly identified Briargate Homes as a general partnership. She did not sign these documents, but asserts that she took them to her lawyer for review. In December 1987, Carpenter attended another partnership meeting where she was again made aware that Briargate Homes was a general, not a limited, partnership.

On February 5, 1988, only days after a deposition in another case in which she was informed that she might be liable as a general partner, Carpenter notified the other partners and the Association by mail that she was withdrawing from any equity participation and renouncing any interest in the profits of Briargate Homes. Carpenter is an experienced businesswoman, serves on the board of directors of a bank, and has ready access to legal and other professional advice.

II.

The Association seeks to hold Carpenter liable for the balance of the fees owed by Briargate Homes on the basis that Carpenter was a general partner of Briargate Homes. Carpenter's defense is grounded in [RULPA §] 304[4] which provides:

(a) Except as provided in subsection (b), a person who makes a contribution to a business enterprise and erroneously but in good faith believes that he has become a limited partner in the enterprise is not a general partner in the enterprise and is not bound by its obligations by reason of making the contribution, receiving distributions from the enterprise, or exercising any rights of a limited partner, if, on ascertaining the mistake, he:

(1) Causes an appropriate certificate of limited partnership to be executed and filed; or

(2) Withdraws from future equity participation in the enterprise.

(b) A person who makes a contribution of the kind described in subsection (a) is liable as a general partner to any third party who transacts business with the enterprise (i) before the person withdraws from the enterprise, or (ii) before the person gives notice to the partnership of his withdrawal from future equity participation, but only if the third party actually believed in good faith that the person was a general partner at the time of the transaction.

---

4. This statute became effective October 1, 1986, when North Carolina adopted, with modifications not relevant to this case, the Revised Uniform Limited Partnership Act as proposed by the National Conference of Commissioners on Uniform Laws. [RULPA §§] 101, 1104. It replaced [ULPA §] 11 which stated:

A person who has contributed to the capital of a business conducted by a person or partnership erroneously believing that he has become a limited partner in a limited partnership, is not, by reason of his exercise of the rights of a limited partner, a general partner with the person or in the partnership carrying on the business, or bound by the obligations of such person or partnership; provided that on ascertaining the mistake he promptly renounces his interest in the profits of the business, or other compensation by way of income.

The North Carolina state appellate courts have not construed and applied this statute. In applying the statute to this case, therefore, this court must decide how the North Carolina Supreme Court would interpret and apply the statute if presented with the factual issues in this case.

Carpenter attacks the decision of the district court on two grounds. First, Carpenter argues that the district court erred in concluding that her notice of withdrawal from Briargate Homes was untimely and, therefore, ineffective to preclude liability as a general partner. Second, she asserts that the district court erred in applying an "objective" standard to determine if and when Carpenter met the good faith belief element of the statute. Each contention is addressed in turn.[6]

A.

In *Blow v. Shaughnessy*, 68 N.C.App. 1, 313 S.E.2d 868, 878-79, *cert. denied*, 311 N.C. 751, 321 S.E.2d 127 (1984), the North Carolina Court of Appeals recognized that old [ULPA §] 11 was "enacted in part to relax the strict rule of law that a general partnership existed in all cases where a purported limited partnership failed to comply with the applicable statute." *Id.* at 879 (citing *Giles v. Vette*, 263 U.S. 553, 563, 44 S.Ct. 157, 160, 68 L.Ed. 441 (1924)). Though there are significant differences in the language of the old statute and [RULPA §] 304, we believe that [RULPA §] 304 was adopted and would be applied with this same salutary purpose.

Given that purpose, we turn to the language of the statute. Subsection (a) specifies that a person who has contributed to a business enterprise "is not a general partner in the enterprise and is not bound by its obligations" [except under circumstances specified in subsection (b)] if two conditions are met.

First, at the time the person contributes to the business, the person must have a "good faith" belief "that he has become a limited partner" in the enterprise rather than a general partner. If there is no good faith basis for believing that a business is a limited partnership at the time of contribution, then there is no basis for obtaining relief under the statute. In such situation, assuming a general partnership was created, rules of law controlling liability to third parties by general partners would govern.

Second, the person must "on ascertaining the mistake" take one of two courses of action. He may correct the mistake in the form of the enterprise by fil-

---

6. At oral argument, counsel for the Association contended that [RULPA §] 304 might not be applicable to a case like this where the enterprise, Briargate Homes, was founded as and always existed as a general partnership. Counsel particularly noted that in *Vette v. Giles (In Re Marcuse & Co.)*, 281 F. 928 (7th Cir. 1922), *aff'd*, *Giles v. Vette*, 263 U.S. 553, 44 S.Ct. 157, 68 L.Ed. 441 (1924), the courts, in applying § 11 of the Uniform Limited Partnership Act of 1916 were dealing with a situation where the parties attempted to form a limited partnership, but did so in a defective manner. As the Seventh Circuit noted, however, application of § 11

is not limited to instances where there has been an attempted compliance with the provision of the new act. It includes in its terms any person who at any time contributed to a partnership, erroneously believing himself to be a limited partner.

Vette, 281 F. at 935. We conclude that North Carolina would apply [RULPA §] 304 broadly, as suggested by *Vette* with respect to § 11. *Cf. Blow*, 313 S.E.2d at 879 (applying predecessor statute, [ULPA] § 11 broadly in light of Supreme Court holding in *Giles v. Vette*).

ing an appropriate certificate of limited partnership. [RULPA §] 304(a)(1). *See also* [RULPA §] 201 (prescribing form of proper certificate). Under this option, the person may continue in the business with the limited liability he believed he possessed at the time of contribution. In the alternative, the person may give notice and withdraw completely from future equity participation in the business. [RULPA §] 304(a)(2). Unlike the predecessor statute, [RULPA §] 304 provides no specific time frame for pursuing either course of action.

If the two elements are met—a good faith belief at the time of contribution and either a proper certificate is filed or notice of withdrawal is given—then the person is liable *only* as a limited partner with respect to third parties dealing with the enterprise. Satisfaction of the two elements in subsection (a) effectively cuts off all personal liability as a general partner, unless subsection (b) applies.

Subsection (b) sets forth the *only* circumstances under which a person who meets the requirements of subsection (a) may incur liability like a general partner. Personal liability to third parties arises when the third party transacts business with the enterprise before the person files a proper certificate or withdraws. Imposition of liability is limited, however, by the requirement that at the time he transacts business, the third party "actually believed in good faith that the person was a general partner at the time of the transaction." [RULPA §] 304(b). Reliance on the part of the third party in the resources of the defendant as a general partner is absolutely essential before liability may be imposed for transactions occurring before withdrawal.

Unlike its predecessor statute, [ULPA §] 11, [RULPA §] 304 does not specify how quickly a proper certificate or notice of withdrawal must be filed after a person ascertains he is not a limited partner. The current statute deleted the word "promptly" contained in the prior statute. The present statute also added the language in subsection (b) regarding reliance by the third party as a prerequisite for imposing liability. This difference in the old and new statutes is significant. It reflects a shift in emphasis away from the speed with which withdrawal is effected to an emphasis on protection of reliance by third parties doing business with the enterprise. The key to liability is no longer, therefore, how quickly the first party corrects the error, but rather reliance by the third party on that person's apparent status as a general partner in transacting business with the enterprise.[9]

---

9. Because the application of the [RULPA] is not, by its terms, contingent on how soon a renunciation is filed, there exists the possibility that an individual could contribute with a good faith belief that a limited partnership existed, discover the mistake, and choose to sit on such knowledge. The individual could then bail out of the business when it appeared that some third party might believe he was a general partner and might look to that person's assets when transacting business with the enterprise. The fact that a person could act in such manner does not, however, necessarily harm the third party where there is in fact no reliance on the supposed status of the first party as a general partner. The possibility that an individual could reap profits or benefits from the enterprise prior to withdrawing was recognized in the cases applying old § 11 of the Uniform Act. There was debate as to whether the word "renounces" in the statute required disgorgement of all past benefits received from the enterprise. *See Giles,* 263 U.S. at 563, 44 S.Ct. at 160 (noting that individuals returned all dividends acquired, but reserving question of whether return necessary); *Gilman Paint & Varnish Co. v. Legum,* 197 Md. 665, 80 A.2d 906, 910-11 (1951) (holding no obligation to return past profits under facts of case). In adopting [RULPA §] 304, the legislature resolved this dilemma by eliminating the word "renounce" and choosing language specifically requir-

The change in the statute to delete the word "promptly" and add a reliance requirement distinguishes this case from *Vidricksen v. Grover*, 363 F.2d 372 (9th Cir. 1966) and *Direct Mail Specialist, Inc. v. Brown*, 673 F.Supp. 1540 (D.Mont. 1987), cases which the Association and the district court cite to assert that Carpenter's withdrawal was untimely. Both cases involved statutes patterned after § 11 of the old Uniform Limited Partnership Act with the requirement that withdrawal be effected "promptly." Both cases found the purported limited partner liable because withdrawal was not effected within some fixed period of time, not because some third party had relied mistakenly on the person being a general partner. [RULPA §] 304 specifically deleted the time limitation and substituted a reliance test; therefore, inserting a time limitation on withdrawal by implication would appear to contravene the statute.

This interpretation of [RULPA §] 304 is sensible. It comports with the remedial purpose of the statute to relieve persons from strict liability as general partners, as occurred under prior law, when they erroneously believe themselves limited partners. Furthermore, it provides adequate security to third parties who deal with the business entity by recognizing their right to recovery where valuable consideration has been extended to the enterprise in reliance on the ability to hold the first party liable as a general partner for the debt incurred.

Given this interpretation of the statute, we believe the judgment of the district court must be vacated, and the case remanded to the district court for additional findings.

First, the district court must determine whether or not Carpenter held a "good faith" belief that she was a limited partner at the time she initially joined and contributed to the Briargate Homes venture. Contrary to Carpenter's contention at oral argument, the district court's opinion does not resolve this issue. At pages four and five of its memorandum order entered October 2, 1991, the district court made several findings, particularly a finding that Briargate Homes was, from its inception, a general partnership and was never represented as anything else to anyone. The district court did not conclusively state, however, whether or not Carpenter had a "good faith" belief that she was becoming a limited partner at that time.[11] The district court did conclude that by at least mid-

---

ing withdrawal only from "future equity participation." The Reporter's comments on § 304 note this change:

> The provisions of subdivision (2) of Section 304(a) are intended to clarify an ambiguity in the prior law by providing that a person who chooses to withdraw from the enterprise in order to protect himself from liability is not required to renounce any of his then current interest in the enterprise so long as he has no further participation as an equity participant.

[RULPA] § 304, comment. Thus, where a person does not act promptly upon ascertaining the mistake, this provides no basis for recovery to a third party. While such conduct might appear inequitable, it is not inequitable as to third parties without reliance as set forth in [RULPA §] 304(b). *Cf. Giles*, 263 U.S. at 561, 44 S.Ct. at 160 (applying [ULPA] § 11 and holding that to allow recovery "would give creditors what they are not entitled to have" because they were in no worse position because of defendants' acts).

11. There was a direct factual dispute concerning whether or not Goodall had ever represented that Briargate Homes was a limited partnership. The district court apparently rejected the testimony of Hicks by deposition, and Carpenter, at trial, that Goodall represented that Briargate Homes was a limited partnership and accepted Goodall's testimony to the contrary.

1986 Carpenter could not have held a good faith belief she was a limited partner, but the key date, for purposes of the statute, is the date of the contribution to the enterprise. Should the district court conclude that Carpenter did not have a good faith belief that she was a limited partner at the time of the initial contribution, then the statute affords her no relief.

Second, assuming Carpenter demonstrates a good faith belief at the time she invested, then her notice of withdrawal effectively cut off liability for any fees accrued after such notice. To hold Carpenter liable for fees accrued prior to the notice, the district court must determine if and when the Association "actually believed in good faith that the person [Carpenter] was a general partner." [RULPA §] 304(b). Carpenter may be held liable only for those assessments made in reliance on the belief that the Association could look to the assets of Carpenter as a general partner to satisfy the debt. Absent such reliance, no personal liability as a general partner attaches to Carpenter for the debts of the Partnership to the Association.

Carpenter points to statements in the record indicating that agents of the Association apparently believed they were dealing with a limited partnership and were totally unaware of Carpenter's interest in the Partnership until the time of her notice withdrawing from any equity participation and renouncing any interest in the profits of Briargate Homes. To the extent the Association was unaware of Carpenter's participation and believed Briargate Homes was a limited partnership, it would appear impossible to conclude that the Association was misled to believe it could rely on Carpenter's assets in conducting business with Briargate Homes.[12] We decline, however, to rule on the issue in the first instance. It does not appear that this issue received much attention at trial. The district court should, on remand, review the record and may take additional evidence if necessary to aid its fact-finding on this issue.

B.

Carpenter also contends that the district court misapplied the "good faith" belief component of [RULPA §] 304 by adopting an objective, rather than a subjective, test for assessing good faith belief. Because the issue of good faith belief must be decided on remand, we address this issue below.

We believe that the North Carolina Supreme Court would adopt an objective standard when applying the good faith requirement in [RULPA §] 304. The statutory language itself suggests that a purely subjective approach to assessing what a person claiming the protection of [RULPA §] 304 believes is inappropriate. Protection is not afforded for just any subjective belief, no matter how unreasonable, but rather only for a "good faith" belief. Good faith encompasses "freedom from knowledge of circumstances which ought to put the holder on in-

---

12. The statute obviously creates something of a burden on a business to investigate other enterprises with whom it will conduct a transaction to determine who may be responsible for any debt incurred. In this case, if the Association had investigated the records and found no certificate of limited partnership, as required by statute, and had inquired of any of the partners concerning the members of the Partnership, there would presumably be a good faith basis for believing that Briargate Homes was a general partnership and Carpenter was a general partner. Such evidence, if it exists, may be presented to the district court on remand.

quiry.... [and] being faithful to one's duty or obligation." Black's Law Dictionary 623-24 (5th ed. 1979). Thus, while the inquiry necessarily entails determining what the individual person seeking to withdraw believed at the time he contributed to the enterprise, the inquiry must go further and ask whether such a belief was reasonable under the circumstances facing that particular individual.

Case law construing application of § 11 of the Uniform Limited Partnership Act provides some guidance on this issue. Though § 11 does not qualify the term "believing" with the term "good faith," courts applying § 11 assessed the alleged erroneous belief for objective indicia of good faith rather than accepting the mere protestations of the individual defendant. In *Giles*, the circuit court, in addressing "the good faith of the asserted erroneous belief" and the promptness with which the interest in the business was renounced, noted the reasonableness of the belief of Hecht and Finn, the withdrawing parties. The court observed:

> One can scarcely imagine circumstances under which error might have been more readily induced than those which this record presents. The new law had manifestly not then been published, and the three days which intervened between the time it became law and the time it became effective hardly gave opportunity for public discussion thereon. After the business started it does not appear that there was occasion for investigation as to its organization, nor that this was challenged, until about the time the concern got into difficulty. Even the New York Stock Exchange does not appear to have questioned its validity as a limited partnership. Consideration of the very exceptional circumstances shown induce quite inevitably the conclusion that, during all the time this business was carried on, it was in the honest, though erroneous, belief of all connected with it that it was a limited partnership....

Giles, 281 F. at 936. Similarly, in *Continental Waste System, Inc. v. Zoso Partners*, 727 F.Supp. 1143 (N.D.Ill. 1989), the district court, interpreting Illinois' statute patterned after [ULPA] § 11, applied an objective standard. In determining whether or not an issue of material fact existed precluding summary judgment for the person seeking to renounce, the court noted two events which indicated that the person "was or should have been aware" of his status as a general partner. *Id.* at 1147.

Carpenter asserts that other provisions of the North Carolina Revised Uniform Limited Partnership Act use language such as "knew or should have known," to indicate when an objective standard should be employed; therefore, the use of the phrase "in good faith believes" in [RULPA §] 304(a) must be subjective. *See* [RULPA §] 207(1). We are not persuaded, however. The term "good faith" necessarily qualifies the term "believes" to exclude a belief that is utterly foolish when evaluated in light of the circumstances facing a particular individual at the time they formed or held such belief. To adopt the position of Carpenter would drain the phrase "good faith" of all meaning and, in fact, redefine the term to protect a party's deliberate indifference to his or her personal and financial affairs.

Carpenter also argues that the district court erred in its discussion of certain tax law consequences of limited partnerships and capital calls in limited partnerships when assessing whether she met the good faith belief requirement. In making its findings on tax consequences and capital calls, the district court apparently relied on the testimony of Goodall. There is no record, however, of Goodall being qualified as an expert on these matters. He was apparently called only as a fact witness; therefore, the testimony was of dubious credibility. For example, Carpenter notes that while Goodall testified that capital calls never occur in limited partnerships, North Carolina law specifically provides rules governing such calls. [RULPA §] 502 (requiring that all promises to contribute by limited partners must be in writing to be enforceable).[15] On remand, the district court should carefully reevaluate the validity of Goodall's assertions on these matters and may, if it so desires, seek expert advice. We note, regardless of Goodall's testimony, that Carpenter apparently could not take the tax deductions she in fact originally took on her tax returns as a limited partner, which is evidenced by the amendment of her tax returns [as to deductions for Briargate Homes] following her notice of withdrawal.[16]

III.

In conclusion, we vacate the judgment of the district court and remand for further proceedings in accordance with this opinion. The district court should determine whether, at the time of contribution, Carpenter had a "good faith" belief that she had joined Briargate Homes as a limited partner. If she did not, [RULPA §] 304 has no application and affords Carpenter no relief. If she did, then her notice is effective to terminate all personal liability accrued after the notice was given. In addition, no personal liability attaches for assessments accrued before the notice unless the Association specifically believed in good faith that Carpenter was a general partner in Briargate Homes at the time it transacted business with the Partnership and the subject liabilities were incurred.

VACATED AND REMANDED.

Notes

1. Under ULPA section 11, investors in a defective limited partnership will not be treated as general partners so long as (i) they exercised only the rights of limited partners and (ii) they renounce all interest in the business "promptly" on learning that no limited partnership exists. The ULPA reasons that because persons in such a position never actively participated in the control of the business, they were not *co-owners* of the business, but rather only investors (why?). That is, they were not in any real sense "partners." *See, Voudouris v. Walter E. Heller & Co.,* 560 S.W.2d 202 (Tex. Civ. App. 1977); *cf., Klein v. Weiss,* page 150.

2. Given the UPA's basic approach, do you agree with the holding in *Gilman Paint & Varnish Co. v. Legum,* 80 A.2d 906 (Md. 1951) that investors could invoke section 11 and *retain* any profits received before they learned they were not limited partners? Why or why not?

Suppose that, instead of *renouncing* any interest in the profits, the investors procured the filing of the necessary limited partnership certificate showing them as limited partners. Would that be effective to protect the investors as *future*

---

15. The additional contributions made by Carpenter were not made pursuant to written agreement, but were apparently made voluntarily.

16. We need not address whether Carpenter was required to make these changes in order to receive [RULPA §] 304 protection.

(post-filing) liabilities? As to *past* (pre-filing) liabilities? Note that RULPA section 304 now directly addresses these questions.

Under the ULPA (and its counterpart, the UPA), what is the basis of individual liability for the obligations of a business? How does that approach differ from the pre-ULPA/UPA approach? To what extent is the earlier approach retained?

3. How does RULPA section 304's approach to the defective limited partnership differ from that of ULPA section 11? What does that say about the RULPA's concept of the basis of individual liability for the obligations of a business?

4. RULPA section 304(b) limits RULPA section 304(a) by allowing a third party who had transacted business with the "limited partnership" prior to the curative act (filing or withdrawal) to hold would-be limited partners liable as general partners if the third party "actually believed in good faith" that the persons were general partners. Is this consistent with UPA section 16, which only holds non-partners liable in estoppel, but only based on their own conduct or consent?

5. The question of whether "good faith" requires only *subjective* good faith or *objective* good faith is a perennial one. For example, the UCC defines good faith *generally* as requiring only "honesty in fact in the conduct or transaction in question." UCC § 1-201(19) (1990 Official Text). This is often referred to as the "pure heart, empty head" test. For purposes of UCC Article 3, Negotiable Instruments, good faith requires "the observance of reasonable commercial standards of fair dealing". UCC § 3-103(a)(4) (1990 Official Text). The Official Comment to UCC section 3-103 makes it clear that the fair dealing test does *not* require the exercise of ordinary care. UCC § 3-103 comment 4 (1990 Official Text). What does *Briargate Condominium Ass'n, Inc. v. Carpenter* require in the way of good faith?

6. For additional discussion, *see* Closen, *Limited Partnership Reform: A Commentary on the Proposed Illinois Statute and the 1976 and 1985 Versions of the Uniform Limited Partnership Act,* 6 N. ILL. L. REV. 205, 255- 58 (1986).

American Vending Services, Inc. v. Morse

881 P.2d 917 (Utah Ct. App. 1994)

Before BENCH, GREENWOOD and GARFF, JJ.

AMENDED OPINION

GREENWOOD, Judge:

Appellants, Wayne L. and Dianne L. Morse, individually and as Trustees of the Wayne L. Morse Irrevocable Family Trusts (Morses), appeal the trial court's ruling in their favor, asserting error in the court's legal conclusions regarding *de facto* corporations and corporations by estoppel as well as the court's decision regarding attorney fees. Appellee and Cross-appellant, American Vending Services, Inc. (AVSI) appeals the trial court's ruling against it, asserting that the trial court erred in finding that there was insufficient evidence to support AVSI's claims of fraudulent and negligent misrepresentation, breach of contract, and mutual mistake. We reverse in part and affirm in part.[3]

---

3. The concurring opinion of Judge Garff, concurred in by Judge Bench, represents the majority position regarding the scope of the corporation by estoppel doctrine in Utah. It does not, however, affect the result in this case. Furthermore, the lead opinion represents the majority opinion on the remaining issues.

BACKGROUND

The plethora of issues in this case arise from the relatively straightforward transaction of a car wash sale. Wayne L. and Dianne L. Morse built the car wash in 1984 and operated it for approximately eleven months. Thereafter, they entered into a contract with Douglas M. Durbano and Kevin S. Garn, both licensed attorneys acting as officers of AVSI, to purchase the car wash.[4] Mr. Durbano and Mr. Garn claim that they represented to the Morses that the corporate entity, AVSI, would purchase and operate the car wash. At the time the parties executed the contract on July 10, 1985, Mr. Durbano had not filed the Articles of Incorporation for AVSI, although he had received permission from the Utah Division of Corporations to use the name American Vending Services, Inc. Mr. Durbano claims that he had twice tried to file Articles of Incorporation for this corporate entity before the contract was executed. In both cases, however, the Articles of Incorporation were returned because of a name conflict.[5] The Articles of Incorporation for AVSI were finally executed on August 1, 1985 and subsequently filed on August 19, 1985. Mr. Durbano's explanation for not filing the Articles of Incorporation before the parties executed the contract on July 10, 1985 was that he was "moving offices and was too busy and distracted to file the articles." The Morses asserted personal liability of Mr. Durbano and Mr. Garn based on the fact that the corporation did not legally exist when the parties executed the contract. The trial court dismissed the Morses' claims against Mr. Durbano and Mr. Garn, finding that Mr. Durbano's efforts to twice file Articles of Incorporation "constitute[d] a bona fide attempt to organize the corporation."

AVSI operated the car wash for approximately three years.[6] It experienced financial difficulty, however, almost from the beginning and failed to make any payments to the Morses on the balance owing under the sales contract. Mr. Durbano and Mr. Garn claim that Mr. Morse provided them with projected income figures that were padded and false. Mr. Morse claims that the numbers were based on usage meters from the car wash which had been verified by another party. Mr. Morse also explains that the figures supplied to Mr. Durbano and Mr. Garn covered the best operating months of the year and thus were not tempered by the three or four slow months of operation. Finally, Mr. Morse claims that the car wash's financial troubles stemmed more from the inexperience of Mr. Durbano and Mr. Garn in operating a car wash than from incorrect income projections. Unable to profitably operate the car wash, AVSI eventually allowed the bank to foreclose on it.

---

4. The carwash sold for $65,000. The Morses transferred the $20,000 downpayment and the $45,000 promissory note from the sale of the carwash to the two family trusts shortly after the sale. About seven months after the transfer to the family trusts, the Morses filed for Chapter 7 bankruptcy.

5. The first two names that Mr. Durbano tried to use were American Food Services, Inc. and American Food and Vending Services, Inc. Mr. Durbano and Mr. Garn also operated a partnership during this time under the name American Food Services. This fact clouds the issue because it is not clear whether the corporate entity that Mr. Durbano initially tried to incorporate was intended to operate the carwash or to own or be related to the ongoing partnership business.

6. At trial, Mr. Garn's accountant, who prepared the books and tax returns for all of Mr. Garn's businesses, including AVSI, testified that the business income and expense from AVSI was reported by Mr. Garn and Mr. Durbano as if they were operating a partnership. The corporate tax returns for AVSI were filed, but with the notation written across the front of the returns that the corporation was inactive.

AVSI's sole allegation that Mr. Morse supplied it with incorrect and false income projections forms the basis of its argument that it should have been able to rescind the contract under either a) fraudulent misrepresentation, b) negligent misrepresentation, c) material breach of contract, or d) mutual mistake. The trial court found, however, that the evidence on these claims was "insufficient to permit AVSI the right to rescind the contract."

At the conclusion of trial, the court entered its Findings of Fact. Those relevant to the issues on appeal are summarized as follows:

(1) The Morses knew throughout the negotiations that Mr. Durbano and Mr. Garn intended to form a corporation to purchase the car wash;

(2) Mr. Durbano and Mr. Garn's efforts to file Articles of Incorporation and obtain preapproval for the name American Vending Services, Inc. constituted a bona fide attempt to organize the corporation;

(3) the Morses admitted AVSI's corporate existence in their initial answer to AVSI's complaint;

(4) the Morses intended to contract with AVSI rather than with Mr. Durbano and Mr. Garn individually; and

(5) AVSI's evidence concerning fraudulent and negligent misrepresentation, breach of contract, and mutual mistake was insufficient to allow AVSI the right to rescind the contract.

Based on these Findings of Fact, the trial court entered the following relevant Conclusions of Law:

(1) AVSI was a *de facto* corporation when it purchased the car wash;

(2) AVSI was a corporation by estoppel when it purchased the car wash;

(3) the Morses are estopped from denying the corporate existence of AVSI; and

(4) AVSI failed to establish the elements of its claims for fraud, misrepresentation, breach of contract, and mutual mistake.

The trial court awarded damages to the Morses against AVSI in the amount of $76,832.30, plus costs, interest, and reasonable attorney fees. The Morses now appeal the trial court's ruling because, although favorable to them in most respects, it was apparently a hollow victory; AVSI has no assets or income from which it can satisfy the judgment. Thus, the Morses appeal the trial court's ruling that Mr. Durbano and Mr. Garn are not personally liable on the contract. In response, Mr. Garn and Mr. Durbano filed a cross-appeal, arguing principally that the trial court erred in concluding that the evidence regarding AVSI's claims of fraudulent and negligent misrepresentation, breach of contract, and mutual mistake was insufficient to permit AVSI to rescind the contract.

ISSUES ON APPEAL

We address the following issues on appeal:

(1) Whether the trial court erroneously concluded that AVSI was a *de facto* corporation;

(2) Whether the trial court erred by concluding as a matter of law that AVSI was a corporation by estoppel, thereby precluding the Morses from denying its corporate existence;

(3) Whether the trial court (a) violated Rule 4-501 of the Utah Code of Judicial Administration by ruling on the Morses' request for attorney fees before they had an opportunity to submit a reply memorandum, (b) violated the standard announced in Dixie State Bank v. Bracken, 764 P.2d 985, 988 (Utah 1988), by reducing the Morses' requested attorney fees by ninety percent without supporting its decision with evidence from the record, and (c) whether the Morses are entitled to attorney fees on appeal; and

(4) Whether the trial court erred by finding that AVSI's claims for fraudulent and negligent misrepresentation, breach of contract, and mutual mistake were not supported by the evidence.

STANDARD OF REVIEW

The three issues raised by the Morses challenge the trial court's legal conclusions. We review those conclusions for correctness, according them no particular deference. The only issue raised by AVSI that we address involves a challenge to the legal sufficiency of the evidence. "When an appellant is essentially challenging the legal sufficiency of the evidence, a clearly erroneous standard of appellate review applies.... 'A finding attacked as lacking adequate evidentiary support is deemed "clearly erroneous" only if we conclude that the finding is against the clear weight of the evidence.' " *Reinbold v. Utah Fun Shares,* 850 P.2d 487, 489 (Utah App. 1993) (D 776 P.2d 896, 899-900 (Utah 1989)).

ANALYSIS
De facto Corporations in Utah

At common law, corporations could be either *de jure, de facto,* or by estoppel.

A *de jure* corporation is ordinarily thought of as one which has been created as the result of compliance with all of the constitutional or statutory requirements of a particular governmental entity. A *de facto* corporation, on the other hand, can be brought into being when it can be shown that a bona fide and colorable attempt has been made to create a corporation, even though the efforts at incorporation can be shown to be irregular, informal or even defective.

Corporations by estoppel come about when the parties thereto are estopped from denying a corporate existence. In other words, the parties may, by their agreements or conduct, estop themselves from denying the existence of the corporation.

Harris v. Stephens Wholesale Bldg. Supply Co., 54 Ala.App. 405, 309 So.2d 115, 117-18 (Ala.Civ.App. 1975) (citations omitted).

In Utah, corporate formation and all its attendant formalities are governed by the Business Corporation Act.[8] Two sections of that act are relevant to the is-

---

8. The Business Corporation Act, enacted by Utah in 1961, is found at Utah Code Ann. §§ 16-10-1 to -141 (1991). In 1992, the Utah Legislature enacted the Revised Business Corporation Act. Found at Utah Code Ann. §§ 16-10a-101 to -1704 (Supp. 1993), this revised act supersedes the original act as of its effective date, July 1, 1992. The Business Cor-

sues raised in this appeal. Section 16-10-51 indicates that a corporation's existence begins when the State issues the certificate of incorporation:

> Upon the issuance of the certificate of incorporation, the corporate existence shall begin, and the certificate of incorporation shall be conclusive evidence that all conditions precedent required of the incorporators have been complied with and that the corporation has been incorporated under this act, except as against this state in a proceeding to cancel or revoke the certificate of incorporation or for involuntary dissolution of the corporation.

Utah Code Ann. § 16-10-51 (1991). Additionally, section 16-10-139 provides:

> All persons who assume to act as a corporation without authority so to do shall be jointly and severally liable for all debts and liabilities incurred or arising as a result thereof.

Id. § 16-10-139.

At common law, the doctrine of *de facto* corporations was created to protect individuals from personal liability when they were legitimately conducting corporate business before the corporate formalities were complete. Under this doctrine, the corporation, rather than the individual incorporators, was held liable for preincorporation obligations if several factors were present:

> (1) A valid law existed under which such a corporation could be lawfully organized;

> (2) an attempt had been made to organize thereunder; and

> (3) the defective corporation was an actual user of the corporate franchise.

Robertson v. Levy, 197 A.2d 443, 445 (D.C.App. 1964) (*citing Tulare Irrigation Dist. v. Shepard,* 185 U.S. 1, 13, 22 S.Ct. 531, 536, 46 L.Ed. 773 (1902)). Often added to this list of requirements was a fourth one—"[g]ood faith in claiming to be and in doing business as a corporation." *Id.* Over time, the doctrine of *de facto* corporations has been "roundly criticized." *Id.*

This criticism provided partial impetus for the emergence of the Model Business Corporation Act (MBCA). The MBCA strove to codify a uniform set of laws regarding corporations and to provide some clarity and bright-line tests to previously clouded areas. Many states, including Utah, adopted the MBCA in whole or in part. Each of the MBCA's sections has comments indicating the purpose and intent of that section. MBCA sections 56 and 146 (corresponding to Utah's sections 51 and 139 respectively) contain an express intent to abolish the concept of *de facto* corporations. The comment to section 56 states:

> Under the Model Act, *de jure* incorporation is complete upon the issuance of the certificate of incorporation.... Under the unequivocal provisions of the Model Act, any steps short of securing a certificate of incorporation would not constitute apparent compliance. Therefore a *de facto* corporation cannot exist under the Model Act.

---

poration Act is controlling law in this case, however, as the facts arose prior to the revised act's passage. The Business Corporation Act was modeled after the Model Business Corporation Act, and Utah in fact adopted the Model Act without major changes.

Model Business Corporation Act Ann., § 56 cmt., at 205 (1971). Similarly, the comment to section 146 states:

> [S]ection [146] is designed to prohibit the application of any theory of *de facto* incorporation. The only authority to act as a corporation under the Model Act arises from completion of the procedures prescribed in section 53 to 55 inclusive. The consequences of those procedures are specified in section 56 as being the creation of a corporation. No other means being authorized, the effect of section 146 is to negate the possibility of a *de facto* corporation.
>
>   Abolition of the concept of *de facto* incorporation, which at best was fuzzy, is a sound result. No reason exists for its continuance under general corporate laws, where the process of acquiring *de jure* incorporation is both simple and clear. The vestigial appendage should be removed.

Id. § 146 cmt., at 908-09.

AVSI asserts on appeal that Utah continues to recognize the doctrine of *de facto* corporations notwithstanding Utah's 1961 adoption of the Business Corporation Act. To support its position, AVSI relies primarily on the case of *Vincent Drug Co. v. State Tax Commission,* 17 Utah 2d 202, 407 P.2d 683 (1965). *Vincent Drug,* decided four years after Utah enacted the Business Corporation Act, held that the plaintiff corporation in that case was a *de facto* corporation. In *Vincent Drug,* the incorporators filed Articles of Incorporation in January 1962 and paid the requisite filing and license fees of forty-five dollars. The corporation began conducting business shortly thereafter and elected a corporate fiscal year ending March 31. The Secretary of State subsequently returned the Articles of Incorporation to the corporation's counsel because the street addresses of the incorporators and directors had not been included. The State retained, however, the filing and license fees. The corporation supplied the omitted information and returned the Articles of Incorporation to the State, which then issued the certificate of incorporation on May 21, 1962. Two years later, the State Tax Commission assessed a tax deficiency against the corporation because the Commission deemed invalid the corporation's March 31 fiscal year end. Without any reference to the Utah Business Corporation Act, the Utah Supreme Court held for the plaintiff corporation and ruled that it was a *de facto* corporation as of the date it originally submitted the Articles of Incorporation, January 2, 1962.

Despite the holding in *Vincent Drug*,[10] we are convinced that more recent case law in Utah, supported by the comments to the MBCA, implicitly overrules *Vincent Drug* and supports our conclusion today that Utah's adoption of the Business Corporation Act extinguished the doctrine of *de facto* corporations. The 1977 Utah Supreme Court case of *Gillham Advertising Agency, Inc. v. Ipson,* 567 P.2d 163 (Utah 1977) impacts the present case in two important ways. First, *Gillham* is factually similar to the present case in that an individual signed an

---

10. Courts in two other jurisdictions have mentioned *Vincent Drug* in opinions discussing *de facto* corporations. Both courts similarly commented that the *Vincent Drug* court stated no rationale for its holding and is "unpersuasive." Timberline Equip. Co. v. Davenport, 267 Or. 64, 514 P.2d 1109, 1111 (1973); Thompson & Green Mach. v. Music City Lumber, 683 S.W.2d 340, 344 (Tenn.App. 1984).

agreement as president of a corporation that did not exist in Utah at the time of signing. The agreement imposed liability on the nonexistent corporation. The supreme court held that the individual was personally liable on the debt because there was no novation of the agreement by which the corporation agreed to pay the debt and the creditor did not release the individual who signed the agreement from liability. *Id.* at 164; *see also Sterling Press v. Pettit,* 580 P.2d 599, 600 (Utah 1978) (following, without citing, rationale of *Gillham* and holding individuals personally liable). Furthermore, the court also justified the imposition of personal liability on the individual because no corporation existed at the time the parties executed the agreement. *Gillham,* 567 P.2d at 164-65. Second, *Gillham* is important because it cited with approval the comments from section 146 of the MBCA demonstrating the MBCA's intent to extinguish *de facto* corporations. *Id.* at 166 (Maughan, J., dissenting)[11] (quoting Model Business Corporation Act Ann. § 146 cmt., at 908 (1971)); *see also Robertson v. Levy,* 197 A.2d 443, 446 (D.C.App. 1964) (noting that authorities on MBCA agree that it eliminated *de facto* corporations); *Timberline Equipment Co. v. Davenport,* 267 Or. 64, 514 P.2d 1109, 1110-11 (1973) (citing comment to section 146 in holding that *de facto* corporations no longer exist in Oregon).

Five years later, the Tenth Circuit quoted *Gillham* with approval. In *Loveridge v. Dreagoux,* 678 F.2d 870 (10th Cir. 1982), two individuals signed corporate debentures in their capacities as president and secretary of the corporation issuing the debentures. Two investors purchased the debentures one and five days, respectively, before the corporation was incorporated under the laws of Nevada. When the corporation failed to pay the debentures when they became due, the investors brought suit to recover their investments. *Id.* at 872-73. The Tenth Circuit determined that Utah law applied to the case under conflicts of law principles. Applying Utah law, the court held that the president and secretary of the corporation were personally liable on the debentures because at the time they had signed and sold them, no corporation existed. Citing *Gillham,* the Tenth Circuit noted that section 139 of Utah's Business Corporation Act imposes joint and several liability on persons who "presume to act for the nonexistent corporation." *Id.* at 878.

We find persuasive the reasoning of *Gillham, Sterling Press, Loveridge,* and the comments to sections 56 and 146 of the MBCA and rely on them for our holding that the doctrine of *de facto* corporations no longer exists in Utah. We believe that the Legislature intended to extinguish the doctrine of *de facto* corporations when it adopted the Business Corporation Act because the relevant portions of the Act, sections 51 and 139, were taken verbatim from the MBCA. The Legislature's word-for-word adoption of these sections can be reasonably construed as an implicit acceptance of the comments attached thereto which express the underlying intent of the MBCA generally and these sections specifically to abolish *de facto* corporations. In addition, we believe that the Utah Supreme Court has effectively overruled *Vincent Drug* by its subsequent holdings in *Gillham* and *Sterling Press.*[12]

---

11. Justice Maughan dissented on the basis that a valid Nevada corporation existed at the time in question, thereby shielding the individual from personal liability.

12. Even if *Vincent Drug* were still good law, however, it is factually distinguishable from the present case. The main distinction between *Vincent Drug* and the present case is that the State retained the filing fees in *Vincent Drug,* but in the instant case refused to ac-

Accordingly, the trial court erred when it concluded as a matter of law that AVSI was a *de facto* corporation when the car wash was purchased. It is undisputed that the State of Utah had not issued a certificate of incorporation to AVSI before the car wash was sold and transferred. Hence, pursuant to section 16-10-51, AVSI's corporate existence had not yet begun. Furthermore, section 16-10-139 imposes joint and several liability on Mr. Durbano and Mr. Garn for all the debts and liabilities that they incurred or that arose as a result of their actions before the corporation legally existed. In the present case, that liability is for the judgment amount entered against AVSI by the trial court.

Corporation by Estoppel in Utah

AVSI argues next that the Morses are estopped from arguing that it was not a corporation because the Morses knew all along that Mr. Durbano and Mr. Garn intended to have AVSI purchase and run the car wash. The question of whether the doctrine of corporation by estoppel remains viable in this State after adoption of the Business Corporation Act is an issue of first impression.[13]

The doctrine developed in the courts of equity to prevent unfairness. As one court has stated, "Corporation by estoppel is a difficult concept to grasp and courts and writers have 'gone all over the lot' in attempting to define and apply the doctrine." *Timberline Equipment Co. v. Davenport,* 267 Or. 64, 514 P.2d 1109, 1111 (1973). A treatise on corporations defines the doctrine as follows:

> The so-called estoppel that arises to deny corporate capacity does not depend on the presence of the technical elements of equitable estoppel, viz., misrepresentations and change of position in reliance thereon, but on the nature of the relations contemplated, that one who has recognized the organization as a corporation in business dealings should not be allowed to quibble or raise immaterial issues on matters which do not concern him in the slightest degree or affect his substantial rights.

Id. 514 P.2d at 1111-12 (*quoting* Ballantine, Manual of Corporation Law and Practice §§ 28-30 (1930)). Generally, courts apply this doctrine according to who is being charged with estoppel. Usually the courts are willing to apply corporation by estoppel when the case involves a defendant seeking to escape liability to a corporation by complaining that the corporation's existence is flawed. *Id.* at 1112. On the other hand, courts are typically more reluctant to apply the doctrine when individuals, usually incorporators, seek to escape liability by contend-

---

cept anything. By retaining the filing fees, while at the same time returning the Articles of Incorporation for the correction of only minor and immaterial omissions, the State arguably recognized, to a limited extent, that the corporation had "colorably" complied with the statute. In the present case, however, Mr. Durbano's two attempts to incorporate, using names that were not available and also wholly different from the ultimate name, i.e., AVSI, arguably fell short of any colorable compliance with the statute.

Additionally, the issue in *Vincent Drug* involved the liability of the corporation, not its incorporators. Therefore, the supreme court was presumably less concerned with distinguishing between *de facto* and *de jure* corporations.

13. The Utah Supreme Court has not specifically addressed whether the doctrine of corporation by estoppel still exists after adoption of the Business Corporation Act. *See In re Solar Energy Sales & Serv., Inc.,* 4 B.R. 364 (Bankr.D.Utah 1980) (declining to address whether Utah Supreme Court would recognize corporation by estoppel because of alternative ground for decision).

ing that the debtor is a corporation rather than the individuals who purported to act as a corporation. *Id.*

A review of jurisdictions that have addressed this issue reveals a divergence of views. For example, Oklahoma, and apparently Georgia, have adopted the position that the doctrine of corporation by estoppel cannot be invoked to deny corporate existence unless the corporation has at least a *de facto* existence. *Don Swann Sales Corp. v. Echols,* 160 Ga.App. 539, 287 S.E.2d 577, 579-80 (1981); *James v. Unknown Trustees,* 203 Okla. 312, 220 P.2d 831, 835 (1950). The District of Columbia and Tennessee have taken the position that the MBCA eliminated estoppel corporations altogether. *Robertson v. Levy,* 197 A.2d 443, 446 (D.C.App. 1964);[14] *Thompson & Green Mach. v. Music City Lumber Co.,* 683 S.W.2d 340, 344-45 (Tenn.App. 1984). Another view, taken by Alaska, allows corporations by estoppel even when the corporation has not achieved *de facto* existence. *Willis v. City of Valdez,* 546 P.2d 570, 574 (Alaska 1976). Still another jurisdiction, Arkansas, has stated that corporation by estoppel rests "wholly upon equitable principles...and should be applied only where there are equitable grounds for doing so." *Childs v. Philpot,* 253 Ark. 589, 487 S.W.2d 637, 641 (1972). Finally, Florida has adopted the position that the doctrine of corporation by estoppel cannot be invoked where the individual seeking to avoid liability had constructive or actual knowledge that the corporation did not exist. *Harry Rich Corp. v. Feinberg,* 518 So.2d 377, 381 (Fla.App. 1987).

I am unpersuaded by the argument that the adoption of the Utah Business Corporation Act extinguished the doctrine of corporation by estoppel in addition to *de facto* corporations.[15] While some jurisdictions have adopted this position, I find no basis in the comments to the MBCA for such a stance. Likewise, I find unconvincing those cases holding that a *de facto* corporation must exist before the theory of corporation by estoppel has viability. The theories of *de facto* and estoppel corporations are separate and distinct; the former is grounded in law while the latter is based on equity.

The fact that directors, officers, and shareholders in Utah generally enjoy limited liability is a benefit conferred by the Legislature and is the result of a public policy decision aimed at encouraging Utah's citizens to engage in private enterprise with all its attendant risks. To make this limited liability available with relative ease, the Business Corporation Act, and its successor, the Revised Business Corporation Act, make the act of incorporation fairly painless—both in

---

14. *Timberline Equipment Co. v. Davenport,* 267 Or. 64, 514 P.2d 1109, 1111 n. 1 (1973), noted that the same panel of judges in *Levy* that held that the MBCA revoked the doctrine of both *de facto* and estoppel corporations, later held, without mentioning *Levy,* that a party was estopped to deny the existence of a corporation in *Namerdy v. Generalcar,* 217 A.2d 109 (D.C.App. 1966).

In addition, the holding in Levy that the MBCA eliminated both *de facto* and estoppel corporations is unsupported by the comments to the MBCA. The comments to §§ 56 and 146 specifically address *de facto* corporations, but except for several annotations to cases discussing estoppel corporations, are silent as to whether the MBCA eliminated corporations by estoppel.

15. Judge Garff's concurring opinion, in which Judge Bench concurs, represents the majority view on this issue and holds that corporation by estoppel was eliminated by Utah's adoption of the Business Corporation Act. I would preserve a limited exception for the corporation by estoppel theory. We all agree, however, that Mr. Durbano and Mr. Garn may not, in this case, assert corporation by estoppel to avoid personal liability.

terms of the financial cost and effort required to incorporate. Given the ease of incorporating, I am hesitant to carve out exceptions to the general rule found in section 16-10-139 that individuals who assume to act as a corporation before that corporation exists are jointly and severally liable.

Notwithstanding my reluctance to make an exception, I am persuaded by the reasoning of the Florida Court of Appeals that the doctrine of corporation by estoppel should be viable in the narrow situation when those individuals acting on behalf of the corporation have no actual or constructive knowledge that the corporation does not exist. In *Harry Rich Corp.*, the appeals court focused on the language in Florida's statute that imposed joint and several liability on individuals who "assume to act" as a corporation.[16] 518 So.2d at 381. The court found significant that the statute does not impose liability on all those who "act," but only on those who "assume to act." Based on this distinction, the Florida court concluded that "the use of this language reflects an intent to limit the statute's application to those persons who knew or, because of their position, should have known" that the corporation did not exist. The court further noted that

> where corporation by estoppel (which allows recovery from the corporation) is retained alongside a statute imposing liability on an individual who assumes to act as a corporation, recovery from the individual should be permitted only where the individual acts with actual or constructive knowledge that no corporation exists. This slight windfall to the creditor can be justified on the ground that the individual has not been completely forthcoming to the creditor and should suffer the consequences.

Id.[17] I agree with this reasoning and would hold that the doctrine of corporation by estoppel, because it coexists with section 16-10-139, can be invoked only where both parties reasonably believe they are dealing with a corporation and neither party has actual or constructive knowledge that the corporation does not exist.

In the present case, the parties dispute whether both sides knew that a corporation was involved. Mr. Garn and Mr. Durbano claim that the Morses knew from the beginning that AVSI was to purchase the car wash. Conversely, the Morses claim that they only discovered the involvement of AVSI when they signed the papers at closing. Despite the parties' conflicting accounts, it is undisputed that at the time the Morses signed the contract, Mr. Durbano and Mr. Garn had actual or constructive knowledge that AVSI did not legally exist under the laws of Utah. Accordingly, neither Mr. Durbano nor Mr. Garn can invoke the doctrine of

---

16. Florida's statute, § 607.397, is derived from the 1969 version of the Model Business Corporation Act and does not differ materially from Utah's § 139.

17. Judge Garff, in his concurring opinion, takes issue with my reliance on Harry Rich because the Florida statute contains separate statutory language regarding corporate estoppel. I have two brief comments on this point. First, my reliance on Harry Rich focuses on the identical language found both in Florida's and Utah's statutes, which imposes joint and several liability on preincorporators, rather than on the additional estoppel language in Florida's statute. Second, Florida's specific statutory language on estoppel which differs from Utah's is inapposite to the present case. It prohibits individuals acting as a corporation from denying corporate, rather than personal, liability to third parties by raising lack of legal organization as a defense. In the present case, Mr. Durbano and Mr. Garn are seeking to avoid personal, rather than corporate, liability by seeking refuge under a corporate shield that is technically flawed.

corporation by estoppel to shield them from personal liability for the debts that they incurred while assuming to act on behalf of the nonexistent corporation.

Attorney Fees

*   *   *

The promissory note, trust deed, and purchase agreement signed by Durbano and Garn on behalf of American Vending all provide, in the event of default, for the payment of costs and attorney fees to the nonbreaching party. Accordingly, as the Morses brought the initial action to enforce the purchase agreement, promissory note, and trust deed, they are entitled to their attorney fees and costs incurred on appeal. Therefore, on remand the trial court should include these items in its award of attorney fees.

AVSI's Claims For Breach of Contract

*   *   *

CONCLUSION

We reverse the trial court's conclusions that AVSI was a *de facto* corporation and a corporation by estoppel at the time the car wash sale was consummated and hold that Mr. Durbano and Mr. Garn are personally liable, pursuant to Utah Code Ann. § 16-10-139 (1991), for the judgment entered by the trial court against AVSI. The doctrines of *de facto* corporation and corporation by estoppel were both eliminated with enactment of the Business Corporation Act. We also reverse and remand to the trial court on the issue of attorney fees.... Finally, we affirm the trial court's finding that the evidence underlying AVSI's contractual claims was insufficient.

REGNAL W. GARFF, Judge (concurring):

I concur with the reasoning of Judge Greenwood in all but that part of the opinion dealing with corporation by estoppel, wherein I concur in the result only.

I do not believe corporation by estoppel exists in Utah because Utah Code Ann. § 16-10-51 (1989) clearly states that corporate existence does not begin until the certificate of incorporation is issued. Because this wording is unambiguous, there is no justifiable reason to conclude that the legislative intent was otherwise.

The comment section to the Model Business Corporation Act that pertains to sections 51 and 139 of the Utah Act states, as noted by the majority, that "[u]nder the unequivocal provisions of the Model Act, any steps short of securing a certificate of incorporation would not constitute apparent compliance. Therefore a *de facto* corporation cannot exist under the Model Act." Although the comment is silent as to corporations by estoppel, there is no reason to assume that estoppel would not be included in the incontrovertible language of the statute. In other words, there is no compliance without the certificate. There is no authority to act unless the rather simple, straightforward procedures are followed.

I agree with the courts of appeal of the District of Columbia and Tennessee, whose statutes are substantially similar to those of Utah and the Model Act. Those courts rejected the concept of corporation by estoppel.

No longer must the courts inquire into the equities of a case to determine whether there has been "colorable compliance" with the statute.

The corporation comes into existence only when the certificate has been issued. Before the certificate issues, there is no corporation *de jure, de facto* or by estoppel.

* * *

It is immaterial whether the third person believed he was dealing with a corporation or whether he intended to deal with a corporation. The certificate of incorporation provides the cut off point; before it is issued, the individuals, and not the corporation, are liable.

Robertson v. Levy, 197 A.2d 443, 446-47 (D.C.App. 1964).

The General Assembly...saw fit to place statutory liability upon those who assume to act as a corporation without authority....No exceptions are contained in [the statute]. For this Court to hold that under the circumstances here Mr. Walker is not liable, it would be necessary that this Court rewrite the Tennessee General Corporations Act and hold that the Act does not mean what it says....

We are of the opinion that the doctrine of corporation by estoppel met its demise by the enactment of the [Act].

Thompson & Green Mach. v. Music City Lumber Co., 683 S.W.2d 340, 345 (Tenn.App. 1984).

Judge Greenwood relies on *Harry Rich Corp. v. Feinberg*, 518 So.2d 377 (Fla.App. 1987) to create corporation by estoppel in Utah in those limited situations where the individual seeking to avoid liability had no constructive or actual knowledge that the corporation did not exist. However, there is one significant difference between Florida and Utah: Florida has codified the doctrine of corporation by estoppel wherein private litigants are estopped from asserting the nonexistence of the corporation if they have, by conduct or words, affirmed or relied on its existence.

> Estoppel.—No body of persons acting as a corporation shall be permitted to set up the lack of legal organization as a defense to an action against them as a corporation, nor shall any person sued on a contract made with the corporation or sued for an injury to its property or a wrong done to its interests be permitted to set up the lack of such legal organization in his defense.
>
> In other words, the corporation may sue and be sued as if it existed if the parties to the contract behaved as if it existed.

Id. at 379 (quoting Fla.Stat. § 607.401). The Florida court went on to say,

in states such as Florida, where corporation by estoppel (which allows recovery from the corporation) is retained alongside a statute imposing liability on an individual who assumes to act as a corporation, recovery from the individual should be permitted only where the individual acts with actual or constructive knowledge that no corporation exists. *Id.* at 381 (emphasis added). Thus, Florida law recognizes corporate liability by estoppel, but conditions individual liability on knowledge.

Thus, I conclude that the Florida case is not applicable in Utah and should not be relied on to establish corporation by estoppel. I would rely on the clear, unambiguous language of the Utah statute.

I agree with the majority that Durbano and Garn are personally liable. However, I do so on the basis that the Business Corporation Act eliminated the doctrines of *de facto* corporations and corporations by estoppel.

BENCH, Judge, concurring.

I concur in the concurring opinion of Judge GARFF.

Notes

1. In *Cantor v. Sunshine Greenery, Inc.*, 165 N.J.Super. 411, 398 A.2d 571 (1979), articles of incorporation for Sunshine Greenery, Inc. had been signed, and sent for filing with the State. Two days before the Articles were deemed "filed," Brunetti and landlord (the plaintiff in the suit) signed a lease. The lease named the corporation as the tenant, as Brunetti signed as its President. The court held that Brunetti was not personally liable on the lease:

> In view of the late filing, Sunshine Greenery, Inc. was not a De jure corporation...when the lease was signed. Nevertheless, there is ample evidence of the fact that it was a De facto corporation in that there was a Bona fide attempt to organize the corporation some time before the consummation of the contract and there was an actual exercise of the corporate powers by the negotiations with plaintiffs and the execution of the contract involved in this litigation. When this is considered in the light of the concession that plaintiffs knew that they were dealing with that corporate entity and not with Brunetti individually, it becomes evident that the De facto status of the corporation suffices to absolve Brunetti from individual liability. Plaintiffs in effect are estopped from attacking the legal existence of the corporation collaterally because of the nonfiling in order to impose liability on the individual when they have admittedly contracted with a corporate entity which had De facto status. In fact, their prosecution of the claim against the corporation to default judgment is indicative of their recognition of the corporation as the true obligor and theoretically inconsistent with the assertion of the claim against the individual.

> * * * The act of executing the certificate of incorporation, the Bona fide effort to file it and the dealings with plaintiffs in the name of that corporation fully satisfy the requisite proof of the existence of a De facto corporation. To deny such existence because of a mere technicality caused by administrative delay in filing runs counter to the purpose of the De facto concept, and would accomplish an unjust and inequitable result in favor of plaintiffs contrary to their own contractual expectations.

Cantor v. Sunshine Greenery, Inc., 165 N.J.Super. 411, 398 A.2d 571, 573 (1979).

The reasoning of *Cantor* has an entire grab-bag of ideas, any one of which might be the critical factor in the opinion:

> a. In many states, even though it make take State officials a few days to process a filing, once the filing is processed, if the State finds that it complies with the statute and can filed, the State makes the incorporation effective as of *the date of receipt. See,* REV. MODEL BUS. CORP. ACT §§ 1.25 & 2.04 Official Comment (1984) (discussion of *Cantor* as illus-

trating the second class of fact patterns that give rise to claims of *de facto* corporation). In second of the paragraphs quoted above, the Court implies that it views "administrative delay in filing" to be the "cause" of Sunshine Greenery not being a *de jure* corporation at the time the lease was signed.

b. In the last sentence of the first paragraph quoted above, the court says that plaintiff's taking of a default judgment against Sunshine Greenery, Inc. was "theoretically inconsistent with" a claim against Brunetti. That sounds like an election of remedies argument. As discussed in Chapter 2, in a multi-party suit, a preliminary judgment against one party is not an election of remedies. See Note 4, page 122.

c. Last, the opinion seems to ground the *de facto* doctrine in estoppel. As discussed in the principal case, and in Note 2 below, although the rationale and the fact-patterns that give rise to estoppel are similar, estoppel is considered a distinct theory.

2. In *Timberline Equipment Co., Inc. v. Davenport*, 267 Or. 64, 514 P.2d 1109 (1973), the Oregon Supreme Court summarized the doctrine of "corporation by estoppel":

The defendant also contends that the plaintiff is estopped to deny that it contracted with a corporation.[1]

The doctrine of "corporation by estoppel" has been recognized by this court but never fully dissected. Corporation by estoppel is a difficult concept to grasp and courts and writers have "gone all over the lot" in attempting to define and apply the doctrine. One of the better explanations of the problem and the varied solutions is contained in Ballantine, Manual of Corporation Law and Practice §§ 28-30 (1930):

The so-called estoppel that arises to deny corporate capacity does not depend on the presence of the technical elements of equitable estoppel, viz., misrepresentations and change of position in reliance thereon, but on the nature of the relations contemplated, that one who has recognized the organization as a corporation in business dealings should not be allowed to quibble or raise immaterial issues on matters which do not concern him in the slightest degree or affect his substantial rights. Ballantine, *supra,* at 92.

As several writers have pointed out, in order to apply the doctrine correctly, the cases must be classified according to who is being charged with estoppel.

---

1. *Robertson v. Levy* (197 A.2d 443), held the adoption of the provisions of the Model Business Corporation Act eliminated the concept of corporations by estoppel as well as de facto corporations. However, the same court that decided *Robertson v. Levy,* with the same panel, held a party was estopped to deny the existence of the corporation. *Namerdy v. Generalcar,* 217 A.2d 109 (D.C.Ct. of App. 1966). *Robertson v. Levy* was not mentioned.

In view of our decision that the defense of estoppel was not established, we do not need to decide the effect of the new Business Corporation Act on the doctrine of estoppel. We observe, however, that '(a)lthough some cases tend to assimilate the doctrines of incorporation De facto and by estoppel, each is a distinct theory and they are not dependent on one another in their application.' *Cranson v. International Business Machine Corp.,* 234 Md. 477, 200 A.2d 33, 38 (1964).

When a defendant seeks to escape liability to a corporation plaintiff by contending that the plaintiff is not a lawful corporate entity, courts readily apply the doctrine of corporation by estoppel. *Thompson Optical Institute v. Thompson* (119 Or. 252, 237 P. 965), well illustrates the equity of the doctrine in this class of cases R. A. Thompson carried on an optical business for years. He then organized a corporation to buy his optical business and subscribed to most of the stock in this corporation. He chaired the first meeting at which the Board resolved to purchase the business from him. The corporation and Thompson entered into a contract for the sale of the business which included a covenant by Thompson not to compete. Thereafter, Thompson sold all of his stock to another individual. Some years later Thompson re-entered the optical business in violation of the covenant not to compete. The corporation brought suit to restrain Thompson from competing. Thompson defended upon the ground that the corporation had not been legally organized. We held, "The defendant cannot be heard to challenge the validity of the contract or the proper organization of the corporation."[2] 119 Or. at 260, 237 P. at 968.

The fairness of estopping a defendant such as Thompson from denying the corporate existence of his creation is apparent.

On the other hand, when individuals such as the defendants in this case seek to escape liability by contending that the debtor is a corporation,...rather than the individual who purported to act as a corporation, the courts are more reluctant to estop the plaintiff from attacking the legality of the alleged debtor corporation.

The most appealing explanation of why the plaintiff may be estopped is based upon the intention of the parties. The creditor plaintiff contracted believing it could look for payment only to the corporate entity. The associates, whatever their relationship to the supposed corporate entity, believed their only potential liability was the loss of their investment in the supposed corporate entity and that they were not personally liable.

From the plaintiff-creditor's viewpoint, such reasoning is somewhat tenuous. The creditor did nothing to create the appearance that the debtor was a legal corporate entity. The creditor formed its intention to contract with a debtor corporate entity because someone associated with the debtor represented, expressly or impliedly, that the debtor was a legal corporate entity.

Timberline Equipment Co., Inc., 514 P.2d at 1111-12.

The court in *Timberline Equipment Co., Inc.* did not decide whether the doctrine of corporation by estoppel survived the enactment of an MBCA-based statute. The trial court had found that the third parties dealing with the promoters did not believe that they were contracting with a corporate entity. Because there was evidence to support that finding—among other things, the contracts had been entered into contracts using the names "Kenneth L. Davenport, dba Aero-Fabb Co." or "Kenneth L. Davenport, dba Aero-Fabb Corp."—the Court

---

2. The court also based its decision upon a finding that the plaintiff was a de facto corporation.

did not disturb the trial court's findings. *Timberline Equipment Co., Inc.*, 514 P.2d at 1112-13.

3. Despite the adoption by many state business corporation acts of language similar to the language of MBCA section 146, courts have continued to use both the estoppel and the *de facto* corporation theories. In 1984, "a review of the underlying policies represented in earlier versions of the Model Act... [resulted in] the adoption of a slightly more flexible or relaxed standard," RMBCA 2.04 Official Comment (the 1984 revision renumbered the Act, and section 146 became section 2.04). RMBCA section 2.04 limits liability to "persons purporting to act as or on behalf of a corporation, *knowing* there was no incorporation." RMBCA § 2.04 (emphasis added).

4. The Official Comment to RMBCA section 2.04 notes that

> [a]nalogous protection has long been accorded under the uniform limited partnership acts to limited partners who contribute capital to a partnership in the erroneous belief that a limited partnership certificate has been filed. Uniform Limited Partnership Act § 12 (1916); Revised Uniform Limited Partnership Act § 3.04 (1976). Persons protected under § 3.04 of the latter are persons who "erroneously but in good faith" believe that a limited partnership certificate has been filed. The language of section 2.04 has essentially the same meaning.

RMBCA 2.04 Official Comment. How would the following persons be treated under each of RULPA 3.04 and RMBCA 2.04?

a. a promoter who contracts on behalf of the firm;

b. someone who is active in the firm's business, but who did not participate in the negotiation or execution of the contract being sued on; and

c. an investor who contributed capital to the firm, but who does not participate in the firm's business?

Is there a principled basis for distinguishing among these persons? As between each of these person and third parties, who is in the better position to guard against misunderstandings as to the persons to be bound on the contract? Why?

In *Timberline Equipment Co., Inc.*, the Court distinguished between passive investors and persons active in the business of the firm:

> In the first third of this century the liability of persons associated with defectively organized corporations was a controversial and well-documented legal issue. The orthodox view was that if an organization had not achieved de facto status and the plaintiff was not estopped to attack the validity of the corporate status of the corporation, all shareholders were liable as partners. This court, however, rejected the orthodox rule. In *Rutherford v. Hill*, 22 Or. 218, 29 P. 546, 29 Am.St.R. 596, 17 L.R.A. 549 (1892), we held that a person could not be held liable as a partner merely because he signed the articles of incorporation though the corporation was so defectively formed as to fall short of de facto status. The court stated that under this rule a mere passive stockholder would not be held liable as a partner. We went on to observe, however, that if the party actively participated in the business he might be held liable as a partner.

This controversy subsided 30 or 40 years ago probably because the procedure to achieve de jure corporate status was made simpler; so the problem did not arise.

*   *   *

We have found no decisions, comments to the Model Act, or literature attempting to explain the intent of [Model Act section 146 or the equivalent section of the Oregon Business Corporation Act].

We find the language ambiguous. Liability is imposed on "(a)ll persons who assume to act as a corporation." Such persons shall be liable 'for all debts and liabilities incurred or arising as a result thereof.'

We conclude that the category of "persons who assume to act as a corporation" does not include those whose only connection with the organization is as an investor. On the other hand, the restriction of liability to those who personally incurred the obligation sued upon cannot be based upon logic or the realities of business practice. When several people carry on the activities of a defectively organized corporation, chance frequently will dictate which of the several active principals directly incurs a certain obligation or whether an employee, rather than an active principal, personally incurs the obligation.

We are of the opinion that the phrase, "persons who assume to act as a corporation" should be interpreted to include those persons who have an investment in the organization and who actively participate in the policy and operational decisions of the organization. Liability should not necessarily be restricted to the person who personally incurred the obligation.

Timberline Equipment Co., Inc., 514 P.2d at 1113-14.

Is this a sensible way to draw the line between persons who are liable, and those who are not? Would the Court in *Timberline Equipment Co., Inc.* and the drafters of RMBCA section 2.04 draw the line in the same place?

5. On the issue of whether estoppel is available to protect persons otherwise liable under a statute similar to MBCA section 146 or RMBCA section 2.04, consider the following:

While no special provision is made in section 2.04, the section does not foreclose the possibility that persons who urge defendants to execute contracts in the corporate name knowing that no steps to incorporate have been taken may be estopped to impose liability on individual defendants. This estoppel may be based on the inequity perceived when persons, unwilling or reluctant to enter into a commitment under their own name, are persuaded to use the name of a nonexistent corporation, and then are sought to be held personally liable under section 2.04 by the party advocating that form of execution. By contrast, persons who knowingly participate in a business under a corporate name are jointly and severally liable on "corporate" obligations under section 2.04 and may not argue that plaintiffs are 'estopped" from holding them personally liable because all transactions were conducted on a corporate basis.

RMBCA § 2.04 Official Comment.

6. The estoppel and *de facto* corporation cases generally arise out of suits on contracts entered into on behalf of the corporation. Suppose that instead, the suit is by an "involuntary creditor" — a person harmed by tortious conduct of firm principals or firm employees. How would that change the calculus?

7. For a more complete discussion of estoppel and *de facto* corporation, see Norwood P. Beveridge, *Corporate Puzzles: Being a True and Complete Explanation of De Facto Corporations and Corporations by Estoppel, Their Historical Development, Attempted Abolition, and Eventual Rehabilitation*, 22 OKLA. CITY U. L. REV. 935 (1997).

Ruggio v. Vining
No. 2D99-1285, 2000 WL 377351
(Fla. Dist. Ct. App. April 14, 2000)

ALTENBERND, Acting Chief Judge.

R. Robert Ruggio appeals a summary final judgment in favor of Donald Q. Vining on a promissory note that Mr. Ruggio signed in his representative capacity as majority shareholder of Picture Archive Communications Services, a Florida limited liability company. The trial court determined that Mr. Ruggio was personally liable on the promissory note because the limited liability company had not yet been formed when he signed the note. We reverse and remand because the record does not resolve all material issues of fact regarding Mr. Vining's own knowledge and participation in the unformed limited liability company.

The record in this case is not extensive. Mr. Vining filed a complaint against Mr. Ruggio and Picture Archive Communications Services, L.L.C., to collect upon a $100,000 promissory note. A default judgment was entered against the limited liability company, and it is no longer an active participant in this lawsuit.

On the claim against Mr. Ruggio, the complaint alleged that Mr. Vining loaned money to the limited liability company on October 10, 1995. The complaint alleged that Mr. Ruggio signed the note on behalf of the company, representing that the limited liability company had already been formed. In fact, the limited liability company was registered with the Secretary of State of Florida on March 7, 1996. The complaint maintained that Mr. Vining did not know that the company had not been created. Thus, Mr. Vining alleged that Mr. Ruggio was personally liable for the loan.

Mr. Ruggio answered this complaint, admitting that the note existed and that the limited liability company was in default for failing to make interest payments. He affirmatively alleged, however, that Mr. Vining knew about the company's status when the note was delivered and that Mr. Vining had participated as an agent, officer, or representative of the unformed limited liability company in 1995 and 1996. Based upon these allegations, Mr. Ruggio raised three affirmative defenses, contending that Mr. Vining's claim was barred by laches, estoppel, and section 607.0204, Florida Statutes (1995).

The promissory note involved in this case is not a typical negotiable instrument. Mr. Vining loaned the money for a period of five years and required that the company make only annual interest payments. The provision for payment of principal upon this note is very unusual. The note stated, in part:

The holder of this note shall be entitled to issuance of 1% of all shares of stock authorized to be issued by the articles of incorporation filed in the State of Florida by the obligor of the note in lieu of payment at holder's election. Said election to be made in writing to the obligor, at the obligor's usual place of business at any time prior to the due date of this note. Such election and acceptance of shares issued shall constitute payment in full under the terms of this note.

When Mr. Vining first moved for summary judgment, he supported the motion with affidavits. On the issue of Mr. Vining's knowledge of and involvement with the company, his affidavit stated only: "At the time of the execution of the note, I was not aware that the limited liability company, Picture Archive Communications Services, had not yet been formed."

In opposition to summary judgment, Mr. Ruggio filed the affidavit of an attorney who had been involved in the creation of the company and the execution of the promissory note. The attorney claimed that he had extensive pre-incorporation dealings with Mr. Vining. During those dealings, they had discussed whether Mr. Vining should loan money to the new entity or whether he should make a contribution of equity. The attorney stated under oath:

On or about October 10, 1995, I discussed with Donald Q. Vining the fact that the corporation was not formed at the time he executed the promissory note and reminded him that he needed to determine how he wished to structure his equity position and method of repayment as to the money contributed.

The attorney further claimed that no funds changed hands when the note was executed. Finally, it was the attorney's position that the formal establishment of the company was delayed by Mr. Vining's indecision about whether he wanted to have an equity position, an issue which Mr. Vining told the attorney he had discussed with an accountant.

After the opposing affidavits were filed, Mr. Vining amended his motion for summary judgment. The amended motion essentially argued that sections 608.437 and 608.409(4), Florida Statutes (1995), applied in this case and that these statutes rendered the content of the opposing affidavits irrelevant. Section 608.437 provides:

All persons who assume to act as a limited liability company without authority to do so shall be jointly and severally liable for all debts and liabilities.

Section 608.409(4), Florida Statutes (1995), provides:

A limited liability company shall not transact business or incur indebtedness, except that which is incidental to its organization or to obtaining subscriptions for or payment of contributions, until the articles of organization have been filed by the Department of State.

It is clear from the summary judgment hearing that the trial court was persuaded by this argument and entered judgment accordingly. We disagree with the trial court's conclusion because the defenses and affidavits contained in the record raise material issues of fact, notwithstanding the provisions of section 608.437.

First, assuming that any person was acting "without authority" in the transactions surrounding the inception of this limited liability company, the affidavits in opposition to summary judgment and the unorthodox terms of the promissory note call into question whether Mr. Vining himself was assuming to act as the limited liability company when negotiating this loan for the unformed limited liability company. If so, Mr. Vining would be jointly and severally liable for the obligations incurred by the as-yet unformed company under section 608.437. The amount he might be entitled to collect on this company debt to himself, if any, would apparently be affected by principles of contribution.

Even if Mr. Vining was not acting on behalf of the unformed company, the defenses of waiver and estoppel create questions of fact in this case. This is true, even though those defenses are not specifically incorporated into section 608.437. Section 608.437, unlike section 607.0204, Florida Statutes (1995) (a similar provision applicable to corporations), does not make an exception for liabilities to persons who share knowledge of the company's nonexistence. Admittedly, the statute would have been better drafted if it had contained the language

> except for any liability to any person who also had actual knowledge that there was no organization of a limited liability company.

The legislature actually added this precise language to the statute in 1999. See Ch. 99-315, Laws of Fla.; § 608.4238, Fla. Stat. (1999). The new statutory language, however, does not apply to this 1995 promissory note. Nonetheless, the traditional defenses of waiver and estoppel remain available notwithstanding the silence of section 608.437 on this issue.

The purpose of statutes like section 608.437 is to protect innocent third parties who have dealings with an entity that does not exist and never becomes adequately capitalized. If Mr. Vining were permitted to obtain this judgment when he had actual knowledge of the circumstances, there would be a risk that Mr. Ruggio would not have the resources to pay truly innocent third parties who lacked such knowledge. Parties, by their own knowledge and conduct, can waive or be estopped to raise a wide array of constitutional, statutory, and common law rights that do not contain any express waiver or estoppel clause. Thus, there remains a genuine issue as to whether Mr. Vining is estopped or has waived his statutory claim under section 608.437.

Finally, section 608.437 should not be read in a vacuum. Section 608.409(4), Florida Statutes (1995), states that a limited liability company is not to transact business or incur indebtedness

> except that which is incidental for its organization or to obtaining subscriptions for or payment of contributions until the articles of organization have been filed by the Department of State.

As with traditional corporations, a promoter of a limited liability company must take steps to create a new company. The very nature of a legal entity created by a formal filing with the state requires that certain actions be taken prior to incorporation.

In this case, the record does not resolve whether the execution of this unusual promissory note was "incidental" for the limited liability company's organization or a "subscription" or "contribution." The attorney's affidavit alone created a question of fact as to whether Mr. Vining was making a loan or a "contribution" at the time the note was executed. See § 608.402(7), Fla. Stat. (1995). Thus, it is possible that section 608.409(4) authorized this note by Mr. Ruggio on behalf of the forming limited liability company and that section 608.437 is not dispositive. *Cf. Levine v. Levine,* 734 So.2d 1191, 1195-97 (Fla.2d DCA 1999) (limiting scope of business of dissolved corporation to acts of "wind[ing] up and liquidat[ing] its business and affairs"). Reversed and remanded for further proceedings consistent with this opinion.

CASANUEVA and GREEN, JJ., Concur.

Notes

1. How does section 608.437 of the Florida Limited Liability Company Act differ from RMBCA section 2.04? Does the difference in the two sections say anything about the propriety of applying either the *de facto* doctrine or estoppel?

2. How would the 1999 amendment affect the court's decision with regard to either the *de facto* doctrine or estoppel?

3. How does the position and knowledge of Vining in *Ruggio v. Vining* differ from that of the Morses in *American Vending Services, Inc. v. Morse*? Do the differences call for different results?

Chapter 4

Actual Authority of Agents, And Its Consequences

A. Introduction

Authority (often referred to as *actual* authority) is "the power of the agent to affect the legal relations of the principal by acts done in accordance with the principal's manifestations of consent to him." Restatement § 7.

B. Express Actual Authority

Because of the uncertainty and limitations of language, interpretation of written instruments is often a difficult matter. In hindsight, it may be discovered that the principal and agent did not have a mutual understanding of the extent of the authority. The instrument may be incomplete due to clerical error or faulty judgment of the principal in anticipating the circumstances that the agent might encounter. The principal may have supplemented the written grant of authority with amendments or limitations presented orally.

Problem 4.1

You are an associate in a law firm. Your supervising partner assigns you two client files.

a. Leslie Owner owns a small printing shop. Owner is married, and has two young children. Owner is also a member of the National Guard. Owner's unit has just been called into active duty, and is being assigned to Bosnia as a part of the United Nations peace-keeping forces. Owner wants to execute a general power-of-attorney giving her husband the power to run the printing shop while she is in Bosnia. She also wants her husband to manage her investments, which are her separate property.

b. Grandpa Jones is retired, and has substantial assets that greatly exceed the current exemptions for the imposition of estate taxes. Grandpa is 80 years old, and has just been diagnosed with Parkinson's disease. Grandpa is too preoccupied with his health to pay proper attention to his assets. He also knows that, with his advanced age, and his Parkinson's, it is likely that, in the next year or so, he will become unable to manage his affairs. To ensure that his property will be managed properly, Grandpa wishes to give his daughter a general power-of-attorney.

What should be your concerns in drafting the powers-of-attorney? Are the concerns in drafting Owner's power-of-attorney different from those in drafting Grandpa's? Would further information be helpful in drafting the powers-of-attorney? If you think it would, what information would you like, and why?

King v. Bankerd

303 Md. 98, 492 A.2d 608 (1985)

[margin note: POA has to expressly authorize the power to Gift the property –]

COLE, Judge.

[margin note: Issue]

The single issue presented in this case is whether a power of attorney authorizing the agent to "convey, grant, bargain and/or sell" the principal's property authorizes the agent to make a gratuitous transfer of that property.

[margin note: Bankerd's owned home, they separated and wife moved out. Bankerd moved a couple of years later and in wife moved in. Bankerd made no more payments on the home.]

The facts are uncomplicated. Howard R. Bankerd and his wife, Virginia, owned, as tenants by the entirety, a home in Montgomery County, Maryland. They resided there until 1966 when Mrs. Bankerd moved out as a result of marital problems. Bankerd continued to live at the property until July 1968, when he "left for the west." Mrs. Bankerd thereupon resumed residency of the property. For the ensuing twelve years, Bankerd lived at various locations in Nevada, Colorado, and Washington, and he made no payments on the mortgage, for taxes, or for the maintenance and upkeep of the home.

[margin note: Bankerd executed a POA to King. After a period of no communication, King requested that B sign a new POA, B signed it]

Before Bankerd's departure, he executed a power of attorney to Arthur V. King, an attorney with whom he was acquainted. From 1971 to 1974, Bankerd did not communicate or correspond with King in any manner. In 1975, however, King sent Bankerd a letter enclosing an updated power of attorney because the Washington Suburban Sanitary Commission was about to put a sewer adjacent to the subject property, and King believed the new power would be beneficial. This power of attorney, which is the center of the instant litigation, was executed by Bankerd and returned to King. Dated October 30, 1975, this power of attorney provides:

[margin note: 1975 POA]

> KNOW ALL MEN BY THESE PRESENTS, that I, Howard R. Bankerd, hereby make, constitute and appoint ARTHUR V. KING, my attorney for me, and in my name to convey, grant, bargain and/or sell the property designated in the Montgomery County land record as Lot 9 of an unrecorded subdivision as recorded in Liber 3027 at folio 293, situated at 14026 Travilah Road, Rockville, Maryland on such terms as to him may seem best, and in my name, to make, execute, acknowledge and deliver, good and sufficient deeds and conveyances for the same with or without covenants and warranties and generally to do and perform all things necessary pertaining to the future transfer of said property, and generally to do everything whatsoever necessary pertaining to the said property.

[margin note: No further communication until 1978]

After granting this power of attorney, Bankerd had no further communication with King until 1978.

[margin note: W requested in 1977 that King transfer the property to her since she had been upkeeping the property]

Mrs. Bankerd, who as noted above had been residing at and maintaining the subject property since 1968, requested King in September 1977 to exercise the

power of attorney and to transfer Bankerd's interest in the property to her. King
was aware that Mrs. Bankerd was nearing retirement and that she was "saddled"
with a property she could neither sell nor mortgage. Consequently, King attempted to locate Bankerd. King wrote to Bankerd on at least two occasions at a
Carson City, Nevada hotel where Bankerd had been living. Only one letter was
returned. King sent a third letter to Bankerd to another Carson City address, but
that letter was also returned. King also made several other efforts, albeit unsuccessful, to obtain Bankerd's address.

Mrs. Bankerd informed King that her husband had once attempted to give
the property away to a neighbor on the condition that the neighbor assume the
mortgage payments. Consequently, King asserted that he believed Bankerd "did-
n't give a damn" about the property, that Bankerd had abandoned his interest in
the property, and that given Bankerd's age (approximately sixty-nine years), King
believed that Bankerd might even be deceased. King therefore conveyed
Bankerd's interest in the property to Mrs. Bankerd by deed dated June 21, 1978.
Mrs. Bankerd paid no consideration for the transfer and King received no compensation for the conveyance on behalf of Bankerd. Mrs. Bankerd thereafter sold
the property to a third party for $62,500.

In 1981 Bankerd filed suit against King alleging breach of trust and breach of
fiduciary duty in King's conveyance of Bankerd's interest in the subject property
in violation of the power of attorney. After the completion of the discovery proceedings each party moved for summary judgment. [T]he trial court granted
summary judgment to Bankerd against King and awarded $13,555.05 in dam-
ages on the basis that King had negligently violated the fiduciary relationship
that existed between those two parties. The Court of Special Appeals affirmed,
holding that the broad language of the power of attorney did not authorize the
conveyance without consideration in favor of Bankerd.

King basically contends that the language contained in a document granting
a broad power of attorney be viewed in light of the surrounding circumstances to
determine whether the attorney in fact had authority to transfer the property
without consideration. Based on this contention, King concludes that the second
power of attorney did not as a matter of law preclude him from gratuitously
transferring Bankerd's property.

Similar to other jurisdictions, Maryland appellate courts have had relatively
few occasions to analyze powers of attorney. Because we last addressed the substantive law relating to powers of attorney over a half century ago, we shall review the relevant rules relating to powers of attorney.

Broadly defined, a power of attorney is a written document by which one
party, as principal, appoints another as agent (attorney in fact) and confers upon
the latter the authority to perform certain specified acts or kinds of acts on behalf
of the principal. This instrument creates a principal-agent relationship. *See* Restatement (Second) of Agency §§ 1, 34 (1958) (Restatement).

Various rules govern the interpretation of powers of attorney. [O]ne "well
settled" rule is that powers of attorney are "strictly construed as a general rule
and [are] held to grant only those powers which are clearly delineated[.]" [*Klein
v. Weiss*, 284 Md. 36, 61, 395 A.2d 126, 140 (1978).] Although our predecessors recognized this rule over a century ago in *Posner v. Bayless*, 59 Md. 56
(1882), they were careful to note that the rule of strict construction "cannot

override the general and cardinal rule" that the court determine the intention of the parties. To ascertain this intent, the *Posner* Court emphasized that the language used in the instrument and the object to be accomplished be viewed in light of the surrounding circumstances. Other courts of last resort have likewise embraced the rule of strict construction of powers of attorney. *See generally* Comment, Construction of Written Powers of Attorney, 18 Ohio St. L.J. 129, 130 (1957) (American courts follow the strict construction principle).

Another accepted rule of construction is to discount or disregard, as meaningless verbiage, all-embracing expressions found in powers of attorney. Restatement, § 34 comment h. Because powers of attorney are ordinarily very carefully drafted and scrutinized, courts give the terms used a technical rather than a popular meaning. Restatement, § 34 comment h. In addition, ambiguities in an instrument are resolved against the party who made it or caused it to be made, because that party had the better opportunity to understand and explain his meaning. *Id.* Finally, general words used in an instrument are restricted by the context in which they are used, and are construed accordingly.

In accordance with these principles, nearly every jurisdiction that has considered the issue has concluded that a general power of attorney authorizing an agent to sell and convey property, although it authorizes him to sell for such price and on such terms as to him shall seem proper, does not authorize the agent to make a gift of the property, or to convey or transfer it without a present consideration inuring to the principal. *See, e.g.,* Annot., 73 A.L.R. 884 (1931).

[W]e conclude that an agent holding a broad power of attorney lacks the power to make a gift of the principal's property, unless that power (1) is expressly conferred, (2) arises as a necessary implication from the conferred powers, or (3) is clearly intended by the parties, as evidenced by the surrounding facts and circumstances.

[T]he power to make a gift of the principal's property is a power that is potentially hazardous to the principal's interests. Consequently, this power will not be lightly inferred from broad, all-encompassing grants of power to the agent. [I]t is difficult to imagine how a gift of the principal's real property would be to the benefit of the principal when the power of attorney does not authorize such a gift or the principal does not intend to authorize such a gift.

The general power of attorney executed by Bankerd authorized King to "convey, grant, bargain and/or sell" the subject property "on such terms as to him may seem best." A strict construction of this broad language, however, makes clear that the instrument did not expressly authorize a gratuitous transfer of property. [W]e decline to interpret this broad, all-encompassing language as authority for the agent to make a gift of the principal's property.

The facts and surrounding circumstances presented in this case do not give rise to any fact or inference that King was authorized to make a gift of Bankerd's real property. In arguing that his conduct was reasonable under the circumstances, King points to his "beliefs" that Bankerd had abandoned the property, that Bankerd did not care about the property, and that Bankerd might be deceased. These arguments completely miss the mark. King's conduct could only be "reasonable" if Bankerd intended for King to give the property away. Although the facts and surrounding circumstances to which King points suggest reasons why he made the gift, they do not support an inference that Bankerd intended to authorize the gift.

In sum, there is no genuine dispute as to any material fact. [T]he facts are not susceptible of more than one permissible inference. [T]he trial court did not err in granting Bankerd's motion for summary judgment.

Notes

1. *King v. Bankerd* involved a suit by the principal against the agent for breach of duty in making a gift. Would the result change in a suit against the *donee*? Could and should attorney King have been held liable for punitive damages?

2. *De Bueno v. Castro*, 543 So. 2d 393 (Fla. App. 1989), upheld a transfer without consideration of real property owned by the principal, a foreign national, under a power of attorney granting the agent the authority, among other things,

> to represent me, claim for me and protect all my rights, interests and actions in everything concerning the business and interests that I have at present and that I might have in the future[, and,] in general, power of attorney to do, in respect and concerning my properties and rights, all and everything that I could do in my own benefit and without limitations.

The agent conveyed the property to a corporation owned by the principal's children from a former marriage. After the principal's death, his widow challenged the transfer. The trial court found that the principal not only had consented to the transfer, but had informally requested the agent to make the transfer as an estate-planning device. Is the result in *DeBueno v. Castro* consistent with the principles stated in *King v. Bankerd*?

3. A principal and agent should not rely on a court applying a broadly worded general power of attorney to unusual acts, such as a gift. For example, in *Von Wedel v. McGrath*, 180 F.2d 716 (3d Cir. 1950), the principal, a German national leaving the United States on the eve of World War II, made a general power of attorney authorizing his agent, among other things, "to do any and all acts which I could do if personally present." The power of attorney then set forth a "non-exclusive" list of specific powers that the court characterized as "ordinary business powers." After the outbreak of World War II, a statute was enacted under which the U.S. property of German nationals was forfeited to the government. Before that law was enacted, the agent attempted to transfer all of the principal's property to the principal's wife, a U.S. national. Despite the broad language of the power of attorney, and despite testimony that such a gift was among the purposes of the power of attorney, the court limited the power of attorney to the kinds of "ordinary business powers" as were specifically outlined in the power of attorney. Because gifts of the principal's property are not in the ordinary course of business, they were not within the scope of authority granted by the power of attorney.

4. Suppose that after a principal has authorized an agent to act on the principal's behalf in certain matters, the agent encounters unforeseen circumstances not covered by the principal's instructions. Suppose further that it is impracticable for the agent to communicate with the principal. Under Restatement section 47, the agent would be authorized to take such acts as the agent "reasonably believes

necessary to prevent substantial loss to the principal with respect to the interests committed to [the agent's] care." Could Restatement section 47 have been applied to uphold the gifts in *Von Wedel*?

5. In *Von Wedel*, would the agent have the authority to sue on behalf of the principal to divorce the principal's wife? Certainly, bringing a suit for divorce is something the principal "could do if personally present". But consider the following extract from *Murray ex rel. Murray v. Murray*, 426 S.E.2d 781 (S.C. 1993), that discusses the power of a *guardian* to sue for divorce on behalf of the guardian's ward:

Issue

> The issue of whether a guardian may sue for divorce on behalf of an incompetent person has never been directly addressed in this State. The majority rule is that, absent statutory authorization, a guardian cannot maintain an action on behalf of a mentally incompetent for the dissolution of the incompetent's marriage. Although there are statutes in practically every jurisdiction which give a guardian the general authority to maintain actions on behalf of an incompetent, it is generally held that these statutes do not apply to divorce actions unless the statute expressly so states. Annotation, *Power of Incompetent Spouse's Guardian, Committee, or Next Friend to Sue for Granting or Vacation of Divorce or Annulment of Marriage, or to Make a Compromise or Settlement in Such Suit*, 6 A.L.R.3d 681 (1966). The theory underlying the majority view is that a divorce action is so strictly personal and volitional that it cannot be maintained at the pleasure of a guardian, even if the result is to render the marriage indissoluble on behalf of the incompetent.

Holding

> We adopt the majority rule in the case of a spouse who is mentally incompetent as to his property and his person, and hold that he may not bring an action for divorce either on his own behalf or through a guardian. However, we decline to impose an absolute rule denying the right to seek a divorce if the spouse, although mentally incompetent with respect to the management of his estate, is capable of exercising reasonable judgment as to his personal decisions, is able to understand the nature of the action and is able to express unequivocally a desire to dissolve the marriage.

> It does not appear from the record that husband has ever been adjudicated incompetent or that the family court judge ever made any findings as to husband's competency. The record simply indicates that husband is "totally disabled and incapacitated." Respondent's brief describes husband as being "88 years old, sick, and confined to a nursing home." However, physical disability does not necessarily indicate that a person is mentally incompetent. In fact, respondent's brief states that "...this divorce action was instituted at the request of Fletcher Lee Murray to his Guardian ad Litem."

> [T]he case must be remanded to the family court for a determination of husband's competency. We further direct that if husband is found to be incompetent in that he can no longer manage his estate, but is able, as his son has alleged, to express a desire to obtain a divorce, husband may obtain a divorce through his Guardian ad Litem However, it is critical that the evidence of husband's desire to obtain a divorce be further devel-

oped. If husband is found to be mentally incompetent as to his property and his person, he may not bring an action for divorce either on his own behalf or through his Guardian ad Litem.

Is the reasoning of *Murray* ex rel *Murray v. Murray* consistent with that of *King v. Bankerd*?

6. What other actions could a principal not authorize an agent to undertake because, as the *Murray* court concluded, they are "so strictly personal and volitional"? What about military service, voting, marriage?

7. *Drake v. Superior Court,* 26 Cal. Rptr. 2d 829 (Ct. App. 1993) illustrates another limitation on the power of an agent holding a power of attorney. *Drake v. Superior Court* involved a "statutory form" power of attorney granting Drake the power to represent Posey in claims and litigation. The applicable statute gave the agent the power to "assert and prosecute before a court or administrative agency a claim, claim for relief, cause of action", and in that connection to perform "any lawful act" and "to appear for the principal". 26 Cal. Rptr. 2d at 830. Drake asserted the right to conduct litigation without the use of a lawyer. He argued that, as Posey's attorney-in-fact, he could exercise Posey's right to appear in court "*in propria persona*". The Court held that he could not, reasoning that the right to appear in *propria persona* was not delegable: "By definition, one cannot appear in '*propria*' persona for another person." *Id.* at 831. The court characterized the appearance in court on behalf of a principal and without a lawyer as the unauthorized practice of law. *Id.* at 831-33.

C. Implied Actual Authority

All forms of authority that are not express are necessarily implied. Actual authority might be implied-in-fact, and even implied-in-law (for instance, in the case of a business emergency confronting an agent who possesses some actual authority). Only actual authority can be expressly conferred upon an agent. The other kinds of authority—inherent and apparent/estoppel—necessarily arise by implication. Inherent authority is implied in law.

Problem 4.2

When its building needed painting, Church hired Bill to paint it. Church had hired Bill on various projects, including the last painting of the Church building. While working on those projects, Bill had often asked his brother, Sam, to help out as needed. In fact, Sam had helped Bill with painting portions of the building that were very high and difficult for one person to paint. When it came time to paint those portions of the building, Bill asked for permission to hire another worker. Although Church suggested that Bill might use Gary, who was hard to contact, Bill asked Sam to help out again. The morning that Bill and Sam came in to paint, Bill discovered that there wasn't enough paint, and sent Sam to the hardware store to purchase more paint. Does Sam have either express or implied authority to purchase the paint on behalf of the Church? How would you characterize such authority?

Mill Street Church of Christ v. Hogan

785 S.W.2d 263 (Ky. App. 1990)

HOWARD, Judge.

Mill Street Church of Christ and State Automobile Mutual Insurance Company petition for review of a decision of the New Workers' Compensation Board [hereinafter "New Board"] which had reversed an earlier decision by the Old Workers' Compensation Board [hereinafter "Old Board"]. The Old Board had ruled that Samuel J. Hogan was not an employee of the Mill Street Church of Christ and was not entitled to any workers' compensation benefits. The New Board reversed and ruled that Samuel Hogan was an employee of the church.

Samuel Hogan filed a claim for workers' compensation benefits for an injury he received while painting the interior of the Mill Street Church of Christ on December 15, 1986. In 1986, the Elders of the Mill Street Church of Christ decided to hire church member Bill Hogan to paint the church building. The Elders decided that another church member, Gary Petty, would be hired to assist if any assistance was needed. In the past, the church had hired Bill Hogan for similar jobs, and he had been allowed to hire his brother, Sam Hogan, the respondent, as a helper. Sam Hogan had earlier been a member of the church but was no longer a member. The church, at the time the painting project was undertaken, had switched to an Elder form of church government. At the time Bill Hogan was employed for other projects, the church operated under a congregational form of church government.

Dr. David Waggoner, an Elder of the church, soon contacted Bill Hogan, and he accepted the job and began work. Apparently Waggoner made no mention to Bill Hogan of hiring a helper at that time. Bill Hogan painted the church by himself until he reached the baptistery portion of the church. This was a very high, difficult portion of the church to paint, and he decided that he needed help. After Bill Hogan had reached this point in his work, he discussed the matter of a helper with Dr. Waggoner at his office. According to both Dr. Waggoner and Hogan, they discussed the possibility of hiring Gary Petty to help Hogan. None of the evidence indicates that Hogan was told that he had to hire Petty. In fact, Dr. Waggoner apparently told Hogan that Petty was difficult to reach. That was basically all the discussion that these two individuals had concerning hiring a helper. None of the other Elders discussed the matter with Bill Hogan.

On December 14, 1986, Bill Hogan approached his brother, Sam, about helping him complete the job. Bill Hogan told Sam the details of the job, including the pay, and Sam accepted the job. On December 15, 1986, Sam began working. A half hour after he began, he climbed the ladder to paint a ceiling corner, and a leg of the ladder broke. Sam fell to the floor and broke his left arm. Sam was taken to the Grayson County Hospital Emergency Room where he was treated. He later was under the care of Dr. James Klinert, a surgeon in Louisville. The church Elders did not know that Bill Hogan had approached Sam Hogan to work as a helper until after the accident occurred.

After the accident, Bill Hogan reported the accident and resulting injury to Charles Payne, a church Elder and treasurer. Payne stated in a deposition that he told Bill Hogan that the church had insurance. At this time, Bill Hogan told Payne the total number of hours worked which included a half hour that Sam

Hogan had worked prior to the accident. Payne issued Bill Hogan a check for all of these hours. Further, Bill Hogan did not have to use his own tools and materials in the project. The church supplied the tools, materials, and supplies necessary to complete the project. Bill purchased needed items from Dunn's Hardware Store and charged them to the church's account.

It is undisputed in this case that Mill Street Church of Christ is an insured employer under the Workers' Compensation Act. Sam Hogan filed a claim under the Workers' Compensation Act. The Old Board decided the case in favor of the Petitioners on June 20, 1988. The New Board reversed and entered its final order in favor of Sam Hogan on January 20, 1989. It remanded Samuel Hogan's claim to an administrative law judge for determination of compensation benefits to which Samuel Hogan may be entitled. The Petitioners now ask this Court to review and reverse the decision of the New Board.

Petitioners argue that the New Board also erred by applying the doctrine of implied authority as a basis for creation of an employment relationship between Sam Hogan and Mill Street Church of Christ.

[E]mployees covered [under the Kentucky Workers' Compensation Act] include:

every person, including a minor, whether lawfully or unlawfully employed, in the service of an employer under any contract of hire or apprenticeship, express or implied, and all helpers and assistants of employees whether paid by the employer or employee, if employed with the knowledge, actual or constructive of the employer.

Petitioners argue that the New Board erred by finding that a person hired under implied authority of an agent could be an employee for the purposes of this statute.

The statute specifically mentions that the contract of employment can be either express or implied. Additionally, the statute specifically applies to all helpers and assistants of employees whether paid by the employer or employee. Petitioners argue that the employee must be employed with the actual or constructive knowledge of the employer. They contend that the facts of this case cannot meet this test. We find that the Mill Street Church of Christ had knowledge that Bill Hogan would have to hire a helper as in the past. Since he had hired his brother in the past, and had not been instructed differently this time, the church should be imputed with the knowledge if it is found that its agent had the authority to hire a helper.

As part of their argument, petitioners argue the New Board also erred in finding that Bill Hogan possessed implied authority as an agent to hire Sam Hogan. Petitioners contend there was neither implied nor apparent authority in the case at bar.

It is important to distinguish implied and apparent authority before proceeding further. Implied authority is actual authority circumstantially proven which the principal actually intended the agent to possess and includes such powers as are practically necessary to carry out the duties actually delegated. Apparent authority on the other hand is not actual authority but is the authority the agent is held out by the principal as possessing. It is a matter of appearances on which third parties come to rely.

Petitioners attack the New Board's findings concerning implied authority. In examining whether implied authority exists, it is important to focus upon the agent's understanding of his authority. It must be determined whether the agent reasonably believes because of present or past conduct of the principal that the principal wishes him to act in a certain way or to have certain authority. The nature of the task or job may be another factor to consider. Implied authority may be necessary in order to implement the express authority. The existence of prior similar practices is one of the most important factors. Specific conduct by the principal in the past permitting the agent to exercise similar powers is crucial.

Burden is on person alleging agency to prove it exists

The person alleging agency and resulting authority has the burden of proving that it exists. Agency cannot be proven by a mere statement, but it can be established by circumstantial evidence including the acts and conduct of the parties such as the continuous course of conduct of the parties covering a number of successive transactions. Specifically one must look at what had gone on before to determine if the agent had certain authority. If considering past similar acts done in a similar manner, [and if] it is found that the present action was taken [within] the apparent scope of the agent's authority, the act is binding upon the principal.

① Prior similar practices

② Nature of the Task

In considering the above factors in the case at bar, Bill Hogan had implied authority to hire Sam Hogan as his helper. First, in the past the church had allowed Bill Hogan to hire his brother or other persons whenever he needed assistance on a project. Even though the Board of Elders discussed a different arrangement this time, no mention of this discussion was ever made to Bill or Sam Hogan. In fact, the discussion between Bill Hogan and Church Elder Dr. Waggoner indicated that Gary Petty would be difficult to reach and Bill Hogan could hire whomever he pleased. Further, Bill Hogan needed to hire an assistant to complete the job for which he had been hired. The interior of the church simply could not be painted by one person. Maintaining a safe and attractive place of worship clearly is part of the church's function, and one for which it would designate an agent to ensure that the building is properly painted and maintained.

[Affirmed.]

Notes

1. In *Mill Street Church of Christ v. Hogan,* what type of authority did Bill Hogan have to hire his brother — actual, implied, or apparent authority? Did the court really achieve its purpose to clarify this point?

2. Under the Restatement, "authority to appoint agents, subagents or subservants of the principal can be conferred in the same manner as authority to do other acts for the principal...." Restatement § 77.

3. As a general rule, an agent is generally authorized to delegate "the performance of incidental mechanical and ministerial acts," but may not delegate acts "which involve discretion or the agent's special skill." Restatement § 78. Restatement sections 79 and 80 list circumstances in which authority to appoint an agent (§ 79) or a subagent (§ 80) is inferred.

4. As opposed to agents, servants generally have no implied authority to delegate their responsibilities. Restatement § 81.

5. A subagent or subservant is not only the agent or servant of the principal, but also the agent or servant of the appointing agent or servant. Restatement § 5.

> An agent may be authorized to appoint another person to perform
> for the principal an act which the agent is authorized to perform or to

have performed. The agreement *may* be that upon the appointment of such a person the agent's function as agent is performed, and that thereafter the person so appointed is not to be the representative of the agent but is to act solely on account of the principal, in which case the one so appointed is an agent and not a subagent. On the other hand, the agreement *may* be that the appointing agent is to undertake the performance of the authorized act either by himself or by someone else and that the person so appointed while doing the act on account of the principal is also, in so doing, to be the agent of the appointing agent, who consequently will have the responsibility of a principal with respect to such person. If this is the agreement, the person so appointed is a subagent. *What the agreement is depends, as do other agreements, upon the manifestations of the parties as interpreted by the usages between them, the customs of business, and all other circumstances.*

Restatement § 5 comment a.

D. Agent's Duty of Loyalty

Problem 4.3

ABC Corporation sold mobile homes and developed mobile home parks. ABC employed Agent, a licensed real estate broker, to acquire land for development as mobile home parks, at a weekly salary of $125. Agent told ABC that Parkacre was available for purchase. ABC asked Agent to purchase the land as a "straw man," and then to convey the land to ABC. Agent told ABC that the land would cost $30,000, and ABC gave Agent that amount.

Unknown to ABC, Agent had an interest in Parkacre. Before he had been employed by ABC, Agent had paid $1,000 for an option to buy Parkacre for $15,000. When ABC gave Agent the $30,000 he asked for, Agent exercised his option to buy Parkacre. Agent then used $14,000 of the $30,000 to complete the purchase, and kept the remaining $16,000.

ABC has now sued Agent for breach of fiduciary duty, asking that Agent be required to give ABC the entire $15,000 profit on the transaction. Agent argues that ABC's sole remedy is to rescind the transaction — return Parkacre in exchange for the $30,000 purchase price. *See Desfosses v. Notis*, 333 A.2d 83 (Me. 1975).

Green v. H & R Block, Inc. (Part 2)
355 Md. 488, 735 A.2d 1039 (1999)

Read case and following notes, page 30.

Problem 4.4

B was County Clerk of County. As such, B advised County regarding the purchase and rental of voting machines. On B's recommendation, County dealt with Machine Corp. Unknown to County, Machine Corp. allegedly paid B almost $200,000 for the last three years, and an unknown amount for previous years. County sues B for a constructive trust over the funds B received from Machine Corp., as well as for an accounting of all amounts paid by it to B. B argues that a constructive trust is not a proper remedy, and that there was no showing that B's conduct harmed County. See *Cook County v. Barrett*, 36 Ill. App. 3d 623, 344 N.E.2d 540 (1975).

Problem 4.5

In 1980, elderly Mother, a widow, was hospitalized for medical problems. After she was released from the hospital, Mother asked Son to take her to an attorney so that she could settle her property and business affairs. On June 26, 1980, Son took Mother to see attorney Matthew Pyun, a friend of Son. At Mother's request, Pyun prepared a document, which Mother subsequently signed, giving Son a general power of attorney to manage Mother's affairs.

The June 26, 1980 power of attorney read in relevant part, as follows:

Mother hereby has made, constituted and appointed and by these presents do make, constitute and appoint Son my true and lawful attorney, for me in my name, place and stead, and for my use and benefit with full power and authority to do and perform every act, deed or thing that I might or could do if personally present, including without limitation, the following:

*   *   *

2. To bargain, contract, purchase, receive and take real property and/or any interests therein and to accept the seizin and possession thereof and the delivery of all deeds, leases, assignments, agreements, options and other conveyance documents thereto, and to rent, lease, sublease, bargain, sell, release, convey, mortgage, hypothecate, and in every manner deal with the real property I now own, and any real property I may hereafter acquire, upon such terms and conditions, and under such covenants as he shall think fit;

3. To bargain and agree for, buy, sell, mortgage, hypothecate and in any and every way and manner deal in and with goods and merchandise, choses in action and other property in possession or in action;

*   *   *

6. To sign, seal, execute, acknowledge and deliver for me and in my name, and as my act and deed, such deeds, options, grants, leases, assignments, covenants, indentures, agreements, mortgages, hypothecations, bills, checks, bonds, notes, receipts, evidences of debts, and such other instruments in writing of whatever kind and nature as may be necessary or proper in the premises.

Son did not use the June 26, 1980 power of attorney to transfer title to any of Mother's property until the summer of 1987. On June 20, 1987, Mother suffered a stroke and was hospitalized. Her treating physician discussed with Son and his four Sisters the possibility of Mother not being able to live beyond the next four days. The doctor also informed Defendant and Sisters that Mother, on the other hand, might have a prolonged recovery, in which case the cost of her care and treatment could consume all of her assets.

After the meeting with the doctor, Son decided to use the June 26, 1980 power of attorney to transfer all of Mother's assets to himself. Because Son initially could not locate the June 26, 1980 power of attorney, he requested that another attorney prepare another power of attorney and have Mother execute it at the hospital.

Upon arrival at Mother's hospital room on June 22, 1987, attorney found that Mother "was bedridden and unable to communicate verbally[.]" To determine whether Mother were mentally competent to execute this second power of attorney, attorney explained the contents of the power of attorney document to Mother and informed her that if she signed the document, she would be giving Son the ability to act on her behalf as to all property that she owned. Attorney asked Mother to squeeze his hand if she understood what he was explaining to her, and Mother responded by squeezing his hand. Attorney also asked Mother if it was her desire to convey her property to Son, and Mother again squeezed attorney's hand.

Because of her physical condition, Mother was unable on her own to sign her name on the power of attorney document. Son, therefore, assisted Mother by guiding her hand to the signature line of the document and holding her hand steady as she made an "X" mark. Attorney, who was also a notary public, then signed and sealed the notarial acknowledgment certificate on the document, thus certifying that Mother had appeared before him and had signed the document as her free act and deed. Attorney also required Mother to sign her "X" in his notarial record book, which contained documentation of all notarial acts performed by attorney. Attorney then had both Son and Son's wife sign the power of attorney document as witnesses. He also required wife and the following individuals, who were present in the hospital room and had witnessed Mother's signing of the power of attorney document, to sign his record book as witnesses to the transaction: two of the sisters and one of their daughters (two of Mother's daughters and one granddaughter).

Following Mother's execution of the second power of attorney, Son located the original June 26, 1980 power of attorney. Before Mother died on September 9, 1987, Son used the original power of attorney to transfer to himself Mother's interest in a lien-free home and other real property. In addition, Son put his name on the titles to Mother's bank accounts and car.

After Son made the foregoing transfers of title to Mother's property to himself, he informed Sisters of the transfers. He also assured them that they should not worry because "[i]t will all be equal.... When [M]other gets well, I will give everything back to [Mother]."

After Mother's death, however, Son changed his mind. Son then informed Sisters that Mother had expressed to him many times over the years of her intent to give him all of her property and that Mother had given him the power of attorney for that purpose. He also refused to commence a probate of Mother's will or to share Mother's property with Sisters in accordance with Mother's will or the statutes on intestacy. Under the will all of Mother's property was to be divided equally among her five children. The same division of property would result if Mother had died intestate., Defendant provided three affidavits in support of his assertion that

Mother had made several oral representations that she intended for Defendant to have all of her property. The affiants who signed the affidavits were as follows: Defendant; Defendant's wife, Maile Joshua; and Rose Kajioka Brash, Mother's niece.

1. Son was sued on behalf of the four sisters for breach of fiduciary duty. What result?

2. What might Son have done after Mother suffered her stroke in June of 1987 in order to accomplish his purpose?

3. Does a notary serve as an agent of a document signer who seeks a notarization from the notary? Should an attorney-notary draft a document for a client and serve as notary of the signatures of the client and witnesses on that document? *See* Michael L. Closen, Reform The Potential Attorney-Notary Conflict, NAT'L L.J., July 6, 1998, at A24.

4. In the actual case that is the above problem, the son was found liable for breach of fiduciary duty and assessed actual damages of about $35,000 and punitive damages of $95,000. *Kunewa v. Joshua,* 924 P.2d 559 (Hawaii App. 1996). How would you write the opinion?

Schock v. Nash
732 A.2d 217 (Del. 1999)

Before VEASEY, Chief Justice, WALSH, HOLLAND, HARTNETT and BERGER, Justices (constituting the Court *en Banc*).

HARTNETT, *Justice*

I. Facts and Procedural History

This action arises from a dispute as to the ownership of Anna M. Dever's property that, prior to her death, was transferred by her attorney-in-fact, Irma Schock, to herself and her family. If not so transferred, the property would have passed to Thomas Jefferson University under Dever's will.

Anna Dever and Irma Schock were neighbors and first became friends in the late 1980s when Andrew Schock, who was Irma's son and Ms. Dever's paperboy, invited Anna Dever to dinner. At the time of the introduction, Ms. Dever was a single elderly woman with no close family of her own. She subsequently, regularly attended Sunday meals at the Schock's home. The Schocks assisted Ms. Dever in various ways, such as making minor house repairs and shopping. On several occasions the Schock family aided Ms. Dever by getting her medical treatment when they found her in her home unconscious as a consequence of her diabetes. Irma Schock also assisted Ms. Dever with her financial affairs.

On September 17, 1994, Ms. Dever executed a Durable Power of Attorney ("the 1994 POA")[2] on a printed form prepared by Wilmington Trust Company.[3]

---

2. The execution of a durable power of attorney is authorized by the Delaware version of the Uniform Durable Power of Attorney Act. 12 *Del. C.* Ch. 49.

3. A second general power of attorney was also executed on April 24, 1995 with Irma as the attorney-in-fact. This power of attorney was not in issue in the proceedings below because Irma claimed she derived all her authority to make the disputed transactions from the 1994 POA. *See Nash v. Schock,* Del. Ch., C.A. No. 14721-NC (Dec. 3, 1997), *Mem. Op.* at 4 n. 2.

It was a general grant of authority and listed powers in six numbered paragraphs.[4] It also included an unnumbered paragraph.[A]

Irma Schock, the named attorney-in-fact, claims this paragraph gave her the power to gratuitously transfer substantially all of Ms. Dever's property to herself. At the time she executed the power of attorney, Ms. Dever also changed the name on her individual checking account in Wilmington Trust Company to "Anna Dever and Irma Schock as joint tenants with right of survivorship."[5] As will be discussed, before Ms. Dever's death, Irma Schock transferred most of the principal's property to herself or her family. This led to this suit being filed by the University and James V. Nash, the Administrator of the estate of Anna M. Dever (collectively "the Plaintiffs"). The suit challenges transfers made by Irma Schock to herself and her family.

Plaintiffs named as defendants Irma Schock, individually and as Guardian of the property of Anna M. Dever, Woldemar Schock, Amelia Schock and Angelina Minutola[6] (collectively "the Schocks") alleging that Irma Schock breached the fiduciary duties she owed to Dever as her attorney-in-fact because she improperly made gratuitous transfers to herself and her family. Plaintiffs asserted that all the Schocks had been unjustly enriched and therefore hold the proceeds of the inappropriate transfers in constructive trust for the University's benefit.

Anna Dever's Last Will and Testament, executed in 1971, named the University as the residual beneficiary of her estate. It had been her and her parents' long-time wish to establish a scholarship for needy medical students. The will named Ms. Dever's now deceased mother as primary beneficiary and the University as a contingent beneficiary if her mother did not survive her. Evidence was offered at trial that Ms. Dever had considered changing her Will to make Irma and Woldemar Schock the primary beneficiaries of her estate. At trial, Babe Giacoma, Ms. Dever's long-time friend, testified that Anna retitled her bank account to facilitate Irma Schock's ability to handle her finances and to make a gift of any funds left in the account after her death to Irma. Ms. Giacoma also testified that in 1994, Ms. Dever had considered drafting a new will with Irma and Woldemar Schock as the primary beneficiaries. At that time Ms. Giacoma was an employee of the New Castle County Register of Wills Office and advised Ms. Dever that she could use a power of attorney and joint accounts with right of survivorship to dispose of her estate. Ms. Dever never formally changed her will, but did execute the 1994 POA without any advice from an attorney.

On May 10, 1995, Anna Dever was admitted to the hospital. Attorney John Weaver testified by deposition that he visited Ms. Dever on May 18,

---

4. Paragraph one authorized the attorney-in-fact to "establish bank accounts and to make, draw, sign, issue and deliver Checks, Drafts, and other Orders, whether written or oral, by electronic or other means for the payment of money from any of my/our account(s) at Wilmington Trust Company including Checks or Orders to the order of cash or bearer or to the individual order of said Attorney." Paragraph five provided that the attorney-in-fact may "sell, transfer and do any other act concerning any stock, bonds, securities...or other property that I/we may have or possess...." *See Id*. at 11-12.

A. *[by the editors]* The text of the unnumbered paragraph appears in the text accompanying footnote 37.

5. The validity of the 1994 POA and the retitling of the bank account were not in issue at trial. Thus, there was no objection to Irma retaining the balance in the bank account at the time of the death of Ms. Dever.

6. Woldemar is Irma's husband, Amelia is her daughter and Angelina is Irma's mother.

1995 and she instructed him to draft a new will naming Irma and Woldemar Schock as the primary beneficiaries and the University as contingent beneficiary. On May 20, 1995, Ms. Dever slipped into a semi-conscious state and never formally changed her will. For purposes of this case, the parties agree that Ms. Dever lacked the legal capacity to manage her affairs after May 20, 1995.[7] Irma Schock was appointed guardian of Anna Dever's person and property by the Court of Chancery on August 11, 1995 after she discovered that Ms. Dever had two inconsistent "living wills." Anna M. Dever died on August 18, 1995.

The University was the sole beneficiary under Ms. Dever's unrevoked 1971 Will. Under the will, the University received Ms. Dever's home which was ultimately sold for approximately $108,000. The University alleges that the various transactions by Irma Schock reduced the assets in Ms. Dever's estate that it would have otherwise been entitled to receive as the sole beneficiary of her will. It is undisputed that after Ms. Dever became incapacitated, Irma liquidated all of Ms. Dever's stocks and a $5,000 Wilmington Savings Fund Society certificate of deposit and also transferred a $15,000 annuity from Great Northern Insured Annuity Corporation that named the University as beneficiary to a Penn Mutual annuity with Irma's daughter, Amelia, as the new beneficiary.

The proceeds from the stocks of Ms. Dever sold by Irma were approximately $144,722 and were placed into the Wilmington Trust joint bank account of Ms. Dever and Irma. Irma then wrote several checks and withdrew over $6,126.26 from this joint account to pay her personal and family expenses.[8] Between June 6 and June 27, 1995, Irma used approximately $140,000 from the joint account to purchase mutual funds in the joint names of herself and Anna M. Dever. On August 23, 1995, five days after Ms. Dever's death, Irma changed the title on the mutual fund accounts to show that they were jointly owned by her and her mother, Minutola. Irma testified at trial that she caused the mutual funds to be titled jointly with herself and her mother, without Minutola's knowledge, in order to take advantage of a lower taxable income base. At trial the Plaintiffs asserted that Irma liquidated approximately $20,000 in the mutual funds and gave the money to her husband, Woldemar, to be used in his business.[9]

Amelia Schock received approximately $13,796 from the Penn Mutual annuity upon Dever's death. Amelia loaned that money to Woldemar Schock, her father, under the name of his business. It was used by Woldemar to purchase a 1994 Ford Thunderbird that Amelia took with her to college. Irma testified that the automobile was purchased under the business name in order to receive a

---

7. Plaintiffs argued that Dever was incapacitated from May 20, 1995 until her death while Defendants assert that Dever had moments of lucidity. The trial court noted and the parties agreed that Dever's actual condition had no bearing on the disposition of this case.

8. Irma wrote a check in the amount of $4,366.36 to pay off a joint credit card in the names of Woldemar and Irma Schock, several checks totaling $859.40 for groceries and household goods, and withdrew cash in the amount of $400 in June and $500 in August 1995.

9. Later it was uncovered that Irma made additional loans to Woldemar for his businesses in the amount of $44,000. Woldemar asserts that the loans were made to two Delaware corporations: Kitchen and Bath Store, Inc. and Millwork Cabinet Shop, Inc. Neither corporation has issued any stock, however, Woldemar is the manager and treasurer/secretary and Irma is "listed" as the president for both corporations. *Id.* at 2-3.

lower insurance premium. Apparently no gift tax returns were ever filed concerning any of the property.

At trial the court reserved decision on plaintiff's motion in limine to preclude extrinsic evidence of Ms. Dever's intent when executing the 1994 POA but permitted plaintiffs to adduce the extrinsic evidence proffered for the record. In its Memorandum Opinion dated December 3, 1997, the Court of Chancery found that Irma Schock had breached her fiduciary duties because the power of attorney did not authorize her to make gratuitous transfers of Dever's property to herself and her family.[11]

The court adopted a "bright line test" for determining whether an attorney-in-fact had the power to self-deal or make gratuitous transfers. Because the court found that the power of attorney must expressly authorize such transfers, and the document in question did not, it found that it was unnecessary to decide the motion to exclude extrinsic evidence of Ms. Dever's intent It did state, however, that the result would not be changed by the extrinsic evidence.[14]

On June 11, 1998, the court entered a monetary *judgment* in favor of the plaintiffs, imposed a constructive trust on several items traceable as Ms. Dever's property, and ordered restitution.[15]

II. Claims of Appellants

The Schocks contend that the Court of Chancery erred in interpreting the power of attorney as not allowing Irma Schock to make gratuitous transfers to herself and her family and for failing to consider the extrinsic evidence of Anna M. Dever's intent. Woldemar, Amelia and Ms. Minutola also allege that the court erred as a matter of law in entering monetary judgments against each of them because it was inequitable and excessive. They also assert that if this court upholds the trial court's finding that Irma acted beyond her authority and that Angelina Minutola should not be dismissed from the case, the only appropriate remedy is an equitable lien against assets presently in the Schocks' possession that are traceable to Anna Dever. Additionally, Woldemar Schock asserts that the record does not support the finding that he aided and abetted Irma's breach of fiduciary duty and it was an error of law for the trial court to have directed him to make restitution because the funds he received were in the form of loans from Irma, that have already been partially repaid to her, and, therefore, he was not unjustly enriched.

* * *

IV. Fiduciary Duty Under a Power of Attorney

The creation of a power of attorney imposes the fiduciary duty of loyalty on the attorney-in-fact.[20] The issue raised in this appeal is whether the agent's fiduciary duty of loyalty was waived so as to have permitted her to self-deal or make gratuitous transfers to herself.

---

11. *Nash v. Schock*, Del. Ch., C.A. No. 14721-NC (Dec. 3, 1997) (Mem. Op.).
14. *Id.* at 10, 14-15, 23.
15. *Nash v.* Schock, Del. Ch., C.A. No. 14721-NC (June 11, 1998) (ORDER).
20. 3 Am. Jur. 2d *Agency* § 210 (1986); Uniform Durable Power of Attorney Act § 3 cmt. (1979).

Unlike corporate law[21] and limited partnership law[22] that provide statutory modifications to the common law of fiduciary duty, there is no statutory provision that alters the common law fiduciary duty of loyalty owed by an attorney-in-fact under a durable power of attorney.

The common law fiduciary relationship created by a durable power of attorney is like the relationship created by a trust.[24] The fiduciary duty principles of trust law must, therefore, be applied to the relationship between a principal and her attorney-in-fact. An attorney-in-fact, under the duty of loyalty, always has the obligation to act in the best interest of the principal unless the principal voluntarily consents to the attorney-in-fact engaging in an interested transaction after full disclosure.[25] At common law, transactions which violated the fiduciary duty of loyalty were void.[26] Under current Delaware law, these transactions are voidable at the behest of the beneficiary. Recently in *Stegemeier v. Magness*, we found that a transfer by the trustee to herself is voidable by the beneficiary unless the terms of the sale are approved by the court, the beneficiaries, or the grantor before the trustee took office.[28] If the transaction is challenged, the burden of

---

21. Although Delaware corporate law permits the waiver of liability for a breach of the common law duty of care that directors owe to a corporation and its stockholders by including a clear and unambiguous provision in the certificate of incorporation, it does not allow for a waiver of the directors' duty of loyalty. 8 *Del. C.* § 102(b)(7); *See Zirn v. VLI Corp.*, Del. Supr., 621 A.2d 773, 783 (1993). The statute does, however, provide corporate directors with a safe harbor from allegations of self-dealing if the transaction is approved by a majority of the informed and disinterested directors, or disclosed to and approved by the shareholders. 8 *Del. C.* § 144; *See, Stegemeier v. Magness*, Del. Supr., A.2d _, No. 143, 1998, Hartnett, J. (Apr. 30, 1999) at 12-13; *Oberly v. Kirby*, Del. Supr., 592 A.2d 445, 466-67 (1991). The corporate law does not eliminate claims for a breach of the fiduciary duty of loyalty, but under certain circumstances it shifts the burden of proof to the plaintiffs to prove the transaction was unfair. *See Cinerama, Inc. v. Technicolor, Inc.*, Del. Ch., 663 A.2d 1134 (1994), *aff'd*, Del. Supr., 663 A.2d 1156 (1995); *In re Wheelabrator Technologies, Inc. Shareholders Litig.*, Del. Ch., 663 A.2d 1194 (1995).

22. The duty of loyalty in a limited partnership can be modified by agreement because the statute which creates the limited partnership specifically provides for it. *See Sonet v. Timber Co.*, Del. Ch., 722 A.2d 319, 322-23 (1998) (discussing DRLPA expanding or restricting fiduciary duties in the partnership agreement); 6 *Del. C.* § 1101(d). Fiduciary duties are specifically incorporated into partnership law by the Delaware Uniform Partnership Law, 6 *Del. C.* § 1521(1), and apply to a general partner in an limited partnership. 6 *Del. C.* § 17-1105. *See also, In re Cencom Cable Income Partner, L.P. Litigation*, Del. Ch., C.A. No. 14634-NC (Feb. 15, 1996) (Mem. Op.).

24. 3 Am. Jur. 2d *Agency* § 210 (1986). "The fiduciary relationship existing between an agent and his principal has been compared to that which arises upon the creation of a trust, and the rule requiring an agent to act with the utmost good faith and loyalty toward his principal or employer applies regardless of whether the agency is one coupled with an interest, or the compensation given the agent is small or nominal or that it is a gratuitous agency." *Id.*; Restatement (Second) of Agency § 387 cmt. b (1958) ("The agent's duty is not only to act solely for the benefit of the principal in matters entrusted to him (see §§ 388-392), but also to take no unfair advantage of his position in the use of information or things acquired by him because of his position as agents or because of the opportunities which his position affords.... His duties of loyalty to the interests of his principal are the same as those of a trustee to his beneficiaries."); Restatement (Second) of Trusts § 170 (1959).

25. *Stegemeier v. Magness*, Del. Supr., A.2d _, No. 143, 1998, Hartnett, J. (Apr. 30, 1999) at 12-21; Restatement (Second) of Agency §§ 387, 389-391 (1958).

26. *Stegemeier v. Magness*, Del. Supr., A.2d _, No. 143, 1998, Hartnett, J. (Apr. 30, 1999) at 14.

28. *Id.* at [14-]15.

persuasion to justify upholding the transaction is on the fiduciary. Thus, Irma Schock and the other defendants had the burden to establish that Anna Dever consented to the gratuitous transfers to Irma and her family after full disclosure of all the facts. Anna Dever was incapacitated when the transactions occurred and is now deceased.

V. Strict Construction of a Power of Attorney

While a power of attorney is construed in accord with the rules for interpretation of other written instruments, it is "generally more strictly construed than ordinary contracts."[30] This is especially so where the authorized agent is given broad authority over all or much of the principal's property.[31] While a power of attorney is strictly construed, this Court, in a different context, has held that the accompanying circumstances including the relationship of the parties should be examined to determine the intent of the parties.[32]

VI. The Text of the Durable Power of Attorney

A careful reading of the power of attorney at issue shows that the alleged authority of Irma Schock to gratuitously convey trust property to herself and her family is not set forth. The trial court correctly found that the power of attorney "contains no language from which this Court could find a clear expression of Dever's intent to waive the fiduciary duty of loyalty implied by law, which would permit Schock to make gratuitous transfers."[33] We agree. The trial court applied a heightened scrutiny standard of review because the power of attorney in question was a pre-printed form, would require a liberal reading of the instrument to find the alleged authority, and such a reading would be inconsistent with the formal expressions of the principal's valid Last Will and Testament. While heightened scrutiny is unnecessary here, we agree that the use of a pre-printed form is a factor that may be considered by a trial court in determining the intent of the parties.[35]

The ultimate issue before us is whether the unnumbered paragraph in the power of attorney clearly expressed Ms. Dever's intent to allow Irma Schock to make gratuitous transfers to herself. The relevant language relied on by Irma Schock (in emphasis) reads:

> I/we do hereby expressly authorize and empower Wilmington Trust Company to permit my/our said Attorney to *deal with, control, transfer to the name of said Attorney, or to the name of others, appropriate to his or her own use or to the use of others, and dispose of,* any and all mon-

---

30. *Realty Growth Investors v. Council of Unit Owners*, Del. Supr., 453 A.2d 450, 454-55 (1982) (construing power of attorney to contain a narrow grant of authority for the determination of a specific interest in the common elements of a condominium); Restatement (Second) Agency § 34 cmt. h (1958).

31. Restatement (Second) Agency § 390 cmt. c (1958) quoted in footnote 54 herein.

32. *Realty Growth Investors v. Council of Unit Owners*, 453 A.2d at 455 ("The authorization of an agent is interpreted in light of the accompanying circumstances, including the relationship of the parties, general usage, and the method of doing business."); Restatement (Second) Agency § 34 cmt. h (1958).

33. *Nash v. Schock*, Mem. Op. at 11.

35. *See Realty Growth Investors v. Council of Unit Owners*, 453 A.2d 450; Restatement (Second) Agency § 34 cmt. h (1958).

eys, funds, accounts, Checks, Drafts, Notes, Bills of Exchange, other commercial paper, Certificates of Deposit or other Orders or instruments for the payment of money, bonds, stocks, and other securities, or any and all other property whatsoever, tangible or intangible, which may belong to me/us or in which I/we may have any interest, to the same full and unlimited extent and in the same manner as my/our said Attorney might or could do, if the same were his or her absolute property, hereby expressly authorizing my/our said Attorney to deposit my/our funds in his or her personal account, and I/we agree that Wilmington Trust Company shall not in any manner or for any cause be liable for any disposition which my/our said Attorney may make of the same or any part thereof.[37]

The trial court found that the language relied upon by Irma Schock did not give her unlimited power to dispose of Ms. Dever's property for Irma's own benefit but "merely authoriz[ed] Wilmington Trust Company to permit the attorney-in-fact to take administrative actions as if the accounts were hers alone even if those actions exceed[ed] her authority, without recourse to Wilmington Trust Company."[38] The trial court concluded "[t]he purpose of this unnumbered paragraph is to protect Wilmington Trust Company from claims by the principal that the bank improperly allowed the attorney-in-fact to make transactions beyond the scope of the powers granted in the first six paragraphs; it is not to protect the principal or the attorney-in fact."[39] We agree.

The power of attorney, if read literally, states that Wilmington Trust Company is authorized to permit Irma, the attorney-in-fact, to do an illegal act: to commit a breach of her fiduciary duty of loyalty by appropriating to her own use assets subject to the power. Because such a reading would implicate Wilmington Trust Company in the breach of a fiduciary duty, it is doubtful if that was the intent.[40]

Although the power of attorney may contain other ambiguities, we find, as a matter of law, that the instrument is clear and unambiguous in that it does not authorize the disputed transfers. Even assuming, arguendo, that Ms. Dever could waive the fiduciary duty of loyalty owed to her by Irma, the power of attorney, by its terms, is clearly not a consent by Ms. Dever for Irma to breach her fiduciary duty of loyalty or a waiver of Ms. Dever's right to void the transfer. Nor is there any creditable evidence that Irma Schock ever informed Ms. Dever of her intentions to convey Ms. Dever's property to herself during Ms. Dever's life time.

VII. Bright Line Rule

The Court of Chancery adopted a "bright line" rule as the rationale for its decision. [W]hile the use of the "bright line" rule in the present case would lead to the same result reached by us, its use in a future case might unduly restrict the

---

37. [*Nash v. Schock*, Mem. Op. at 12-13 (emphasis added.)] The language reflects that the bank, in preparing the durable power of attorney, was more interested in protecting itself than the assets of Ms. Dever.

38. *Id.* at 13.

39. *Id.* at 13-14.

40. *See Mills Acquisition Co. v. Macmillan, Inc.*, Del. Supr., 559 A.2d 1261, 1284 n. 33 (1989).

traditional ability of the Court of Chancery to consider all the facts and circumstances involved.

In adopting the "bright line" or "flat rule", the trial court relied on case law[44] from Hawaii,[45] South Carolina,[46] Iowa,[47] North Carolina,[48] Texas,[49] and Washington.[50] In *Kunewa v. Joshua*, the Intermediate Court of Appeals of Hawaii recognized that several other jurisdictions have adopted a similar rule, such as Alaska, New York, and Florida.[51] The court in *Kunewa v. Joshua* stated:

> [w]here a power of attorney does not expressly authorize the attorney-in-fact to make gifts to himself or herself, extrinsic evidence of the principal's intent to allow such gifts is not admissible. An attorney-in-fact may not make a gift to himself or herself unless there is clear intent in writing from the principal allowing the gift. Oral authorization is not acceptable.[52]

The "bright line" rule as it has been applied by most courts is not inconsistent with the traditional rule of trust law that a fiduciary's transfer to herself of trust property is voidable by the beneficiary unless the transfer is approved by the court, consented to by the settlor in advance, or consented to by the beneficiary affected after full disclosure. Here the settlor and beneficiary are the same. The power of attorney she exercised does not unambiguously authorize the transfers nor could it constitute a valid consent because a consent or waiver requires "the voluntary relinquishment of a known right."[54] "It implies knowledge of all mate-

---

44. *See Nash v. Schock*, Mem. Op. at 10 n. 9-11.

45. *Kunewa v. Joshua*, Haw. Ct. App., 924 P.2d 559, 565-66 (1996).

46. *Fender v. Fender*, S.C. Supr., 329 S.E.2d 430 (1985).

47. *In re Estate of Crabtree*, Iowa Supr., 550 N.W.2d 168, 170 (1996).

48. *Whitford v. Gaskill*, N.C. Supr., 480 S.E.2d 690, 692 (1997) *amended by* 489 S.E.2d 177 (1997).

49. *F.M. Stigler, Inc. v. H.N.C. Realty Co.*, Tex. Ct. App., 595 S.W.2d 158, 161 (1980), *rev'd by Land Title Co. of Dallas, Inc. v. F.M. Stigler, Inc.*, 609 S.W.2d 754 (1980).

50. *Bryant v. Bryant*, Wash. Supr., 882 P.2d 169, 172 (1994).

51. *Kunewa v. Joshua*, 924 P.2d at 565.

52. *Id.* The court *in Kunewa* cited the policy reasons articulated in *Estate of Casey v. Comm'r of Internal Revenue*, 4th Cir., 948 F.2d 895, 898 (1991):
[w]hen one considers the manifold opportunities and temptations for self-dealing that are opened up for persons holding general powers of attorney— of which outright transfers for less than value to the attorney-in-fact [himself] or herself are the most obvious—the justification for such a flat rule is apparent. And its justification is made even more apparent when one considers the ease with which such a rule can be accommodated by principals and their draftsman.
Kunewa v. Joshua, 924 P.2d at 565. It should be noted however, that the Fourth Circuit Court in *Casey* was speculating what rule the Virginia Supreme Court would adopt and later in another case it rejected the "bright line" rule noting that the Virginia Legislature had passed a statute which expressly rejected the flat rule and stating that the intent is found by examining the entire instrument and the surrounding circumstances. *See Estate of Ridenour v. Comm'r of IRS*, 4th Cir., 36 F.3d 332 (1994). Alabama also has a well criticized statute which "create[s] a presumption that gifts, even under the most general grants of power to the attorney-in-fact will be valid." *See also*, Hans A. Lapping, *License to Steal: Implied Gift-Giving Authority and Powers of Attorney*, 4 Elder L.J. 143, 167 (1996). Another court suggests a flat rule may be appropriate in the business setting but is not in a family relationship. *See Estate of Antone v. Staphos*, Conn. Super., No. CV93-05268411994, WL 669694, at 5, Corradino J. (Nov. 17, 1994).

54. *Klein v. American Luggage Works, Inc.*, Del. Supr., 158 A.2d 814, 818 (1960) ("[Waiver] implies knowledge of all material facts and of one's rights, together with a will-

rial facts and intent to waive."[55] There is nothing in the language of the power of attorney that indicates that Anna Dever ever knew of or consented to the specific transfers or waived her right to void them.

Additionally, when there is a close confidential relationship, as there was here, because Ms. Dever would naturally have relied on Irma Schock for advice, mere disclosure by Irma of her self-interest would not be enough. Irma had a duty to see that Ms. Dever received impartial advice based upon a carefully formed judgment.[56] Because this dispute involved the gratuitous transfer of essentially all of Ms. Dever's personal property, before her death, and the record is devoid of any advice by a competent and disinterested third person, it is clear that Irma Schock did not fulfill her fiduciary duty of loyalty to Ms. Dever.[57]

If the grantor's intent is the primary concern in interpreting a durable power of attorney, a bright line rule might not always serve the interest of justice, especially if a printed form of a durable power of attorney prepared by a bank is used. Where there are concerns of abuse by an attorney-in-fact because of self-dealing or taking advantage of the elderly, our current law is better able to protect those interests. A power of attorney is strictly construed and broad all-embracing expressions are discounted or discarded.[59] Any admissible extrinsic evidence must be carefully considered by the trial court so that it may determine that it was indeed the intent of the principal to make a gift or consent to a strictly enumerated act of self-dealing after receiving a full disclosure of all the facts.[60] The trial court can consider the witnesses' credibility and possible bias or self interest. Adopting a bright line rule might preclude a court from carefully considering all the surrounding circumstances to the detriment of the principal. Although a few states have adopted a "bright line" rule, we decline to do so. We are not convinced that it is superior to our existing law and it might result in an

---

ingness to refrain from enforcing those rights."); *Standard Accident Insurance Co. v. Ponsell's Drug Stores, Inc.*, Del. Supr., 202 A.2d 271, 274 (1964).

55. *Realty Growth Investors v. Council of Unit Owners*, 453 A.2d 456.

56. Restatement (Second) of Agency § 390 cmt. c (1958) ("The agent must not take advantage of his position to persuade the principal into making a hard or improvident bargain. If the agent is one upon whom the principal naturally would rely for advice, the fact that the agent discloses that he is acting as an adverse party does not relieve him from the duty of giving the principal impartial advice based upon a carefully formed judgment as to the principal's interests. If he cannot or does not wish to do so, he has a duty to see that the principal secures the advice of a competent and disinterested third person. An agent who is in a close confidential relation to the principal, such as a family attorney, has the burden of proving that a substantial gift to him was not the result of undue influence."); *In re Estate of Surian*, Del. Ch., C.A. NO. 9754-NC (July 12, 1990), Mem. Op. at 4-7; *Swain v. Moore*, Del. Ch., 71 A.2d 264, 267-68 (1950); *accord Robert O. v. Ecmel A.*, Del. Supr., 460 A.2d 1321 (1983).

57. Restatement (Second) of Agency § 390 cmt. c (1958); *In re Estate of Surian*, C.A. NO. 9754-NC, Mem. Op. at 4-7; *Swain v. Moore*, 71 A.2d. at 267-68.

59. Restatement (Second) Agency § 34 cmt. h (1958); *See also, King v. Bankerd*, Md Ct. App., 492 A.2d 608, 611-12 (1985) (holding that agent could not give away the principal's property unless that power was expressly given, arose as a necessary implication from conferred powers, or was clearly intended by the parties as evidenced by the surrounding facts and circumstances); *Kunewa v. Joshua*, Haw. Ct. App., 924 P.2d 559, 566 (1996) (holding that broad, all-encompassing grants of power to the agent must be discounted).

60. Another jurisdiction requires clear and convincing evidence as an alternative to adopting a bright line rule. *See Estate of Antone v. Staphos*, Conn. Super., No. CV93-0526844, 1994 WL 669694, Corradino, J. (Nov. 17,1994).

injustice, where, for example, the power of attorney on its face did not disclose that inadequate disclosures were made to the principal.

VIII. Admissibility of Extrinsic Evidence

The Schocks contend that the Court of Chancery improperly failed to consider extrinsic evidence because the document was ambiguous. We have held that the power of attorney is not ambiguous as to the issue of whether it granted Irma authority to make gratuitous transfers to herself. Even if it was ambiguous, this would not help the Schocks because the trial court noted that even if it considered the extrinsic evidence it would not change the result.[62] We agree.

Assuming, arguendo, that the power of attorney was ambiguous, several factors support the trial court's decision that the extrinsic evidence, if considered, would not have shown that Dever intended that the 1994 POA allow Irma Schock to make unlimited gratuitous transfers to herself and her family. First, the 1994 POA was on a pre-printed form prepared by Wilmington Trust Company and there is no evidence that Ms. Dever received any competent independent advice as to its meaning. Second, all of the transactions in question took place after Dever became incapacitated and she could therefore not have ratified them. Third, while Dever's conversation with Attorney Weaver may have shown that she intended to change her will to provide that after her death the bulk of her estate would go to Irma and Woldemar, if they survived her, this conversation occurred over a year after the 1994 POA was signed and does not establish her intent at the time she executed it. Nor does it show she intended to make a gift of substantially all her property to Irma Schock during her lifetime. Fourth, while Dever changed the title of her account with Wilmington Trust Company to show that it was to be held jointly with Irma Schock with right of survivorship, she took no action to change the title of her other property. Fifth, the conversation Ms. Dever had with Ms. Giacoma indicates that Giacoma's advice to Dever, to put her property in joint accounts with right of survivorship so as to dispose of her property outside of her will, was done primarily for Ms. Dever's convenience and for her concern that her bills were paid. Sixth, Dever did not destroy or revoke her 1971 will which left the bulk of her estate to the University. Seventh, there is no creditable evidence Irma Schock ever told Ms. Dever that she intended to transfer any of Ms. Dever's assets to herself. Eighth, there is no creditable evidence that Ms. Dever ever intended for the Schocks to receive any of her property before her death. Finally, and most persuasive, is the trial court's determination of Irma Schock's credibility: it is clear from the record that the trial court did not believe her testimony and criticized her for what it perceived as egregiously taking advantage of an elderly and dependent person. Even if we found the power of attorney was ambiguous, the Court of Chancery's findings are supported by the record, are based on live testimony of witnesses and determinations of credibility, and therefore, must be affirmed.

IX. Remedies

The trial court imposed a constructive trust on the following: $5,000 proceeds of a certificate of deposit; $4,366.36 paid from the joint account of Irma

---

62. *Nash v. Schock*, Mem. Op. at 14-15.

and Ms. Dever used to pay the personal debts of Woldemar and Irma Schock; $5,000 from the same joint account used to make a loan to Woldemar Schock's business; Mutual funds accounts held by Irma and Minutola; and a 1994 Ford Thunderbird in the possession of Amelia Schock. The total monetary judgment entered against Irma Schock was $174,644.12 and the court ordered her to submit an accounting to the court of all funds distributed by her as Ms. Dever's guardian. The trial court ordered restitution in the following amounts: Woldemar Schock-$73,366.36;[65] Amelia Schock-$13,796;[66] and Angelina Minutola-$154,194.[67] The trial court ordered that all the family members were jointly and severally liable with Irma Schock for the amounts assessed against them individually.

On June 18, 1998, Woldemar Schock, Irma's husband, moved, pursuant to Court of Chancery Rule 59(e), for a modification of the June 11, 1998 Order or in the alternative requesting reargument. In a letter opinion dated July 23, 1998, the trial court denied this motion. The court noted "the record appears quite clear that Woldemar knowingly aided and abetted his spouse's breach of fiduciary duty and became unjustly enriched as a result."[70]

*   *   *

The trial court correctly found that all the Schocks were unjustly enriched and ordered them to return any assets in their possession that were traceable to Irma Schock's breaches of fiduciary duty. The court later ordered that all the Schocks pay restitution in the amounts that they were individually unjustly enriched.

The Schocks assert that the trial court erred as a matter of law in imposing a constructive trust and ordering them to pay restitution to the University because it should have imposed only an equitable lien on the property. They also assert that absent a finding of wrongdoing, civil conspiracy or a breach of fiduciary obligation, the court incorrectly imposed a constructive trust on the automobile in the possession of Amelia Schock. Additionally, they challenge the monetary judgments entered against Angelina Minutola as an error of law, arguing that the court should have imposed an equitable lien instead.

*   *   *

XI. Restitution and Constructive Trusts

Angelina Minutola, the mother of Irma Schock, asserted that it was improper to hold her jointly liable with Irma, because the original transfer placing $140,398 in a joint brokerage account titled in the names of herself and Irma occurred without her knowledge of where the funds came from and the trial court specifically found that Minutola was not a wrongdoer. They assert that because

---

65. This amount included a $5,000 loan made by Irma Schock from the joint account, $20,000 for a loan made by Irma Schock from the brokerage account; $44,000 in other loans made by Irma Schock, and $4,366.36 for sums paid for joint liabilities of Irma and Woldemar. *Id.* at 2.

66. This amount was for the cost of the 1994 Ford Thunderbird purchased with the proceeds of an annuity held with Penn Mutual. *Id.* at 3.

67. This amount was for the $140,398 of the brokerage account which was jointly titled in Irma Schock and Minutola's names and $13,796 used to purchase the automobile for Amelia from a mutual fund held jointly with Irma. *Id.* at 3.

70. [*Nash v. Schock*, Del. Ch., C.A. No. 14721-NC (July 23, 1998) (Letter Op.)] at 2.

Ms. Minutola was not a "conscious wrongdoer", or an "innocent convertor", or a "gratuitous transferee" she can not be required to pay restitution. Additionally, Ms. Minutola asserts that because she has removed her name from the brokerage account and has not received any benefit from the account, she is innocent and should be dismissed from this action as requested in her motion to modify judgment which is pending in the court below. The issue of whether the judgment should be modified is not before us.

For a court to order restitution it must first find the defendant was unjustly enriched at the expense of the plaintiff. "Unjust enrichment is defined as 'the unjust retention of a benefit to the loss of another, or the retention of money or property of another against the fundamental principles of justice or equity and good conscience.'"[76] To obtain restitution, the plaintiffs were required to show that the defendants were unjustly enriched, that the defendants secured a benefit, and that it would be unconscionable to allow them to retain that benefit. Restitution is permitted even when the defendant retaining the benefit is not a wrongdoer. "Restitution serves to 'deprive the defendant of benefits that in equity and good conscience he ought not to keep, even though he may have received those benefits honestly in the first instance, and even though the plaintiff may have suffered no demonstrable losses.'"[79]

Although in February 1998, before the trial court issued its Final Order, Ms. Minutola transferred all her interest in the brokerage accounts to Irma, this is of no assistance to her. That transfer occurred after the trial court ruled that all the defendants were required to return all traceable assets. Ms. Minutola should have transferred her interest in the property to the estate or to the court, not to her daughter. Ms. Minutola received a property interest in the brokerage accounts when the accounts were titled jointly with Irma Schock. It is, therefore, not relevant that Minutola did not actually use any of the funds in the account.[81]

Because the judgment was joint and severable, the plaintiffs have the right to seek satisfaction from Ms. Minutola without first attempting to have the judgment satisfied from Irma Schock. Of course the plaintiffs are only entitled to recover the full amount of their judgment. If Minutola is forced to satisfy any part of the judgment she may be able to seek repayment from Irma Schock, but that issue is not before us.

Amelia Schock, the daughter of Irma, asserts that it was an error of law to award restitution against her because she was an "innocent converter" and that the appropriate remedy would have been to place an equitable lien on the 1994 Ford in her possession. For the same reasons addressed above regarding restitution and Minutola, these arguments are without merit and are rejected.

---

76. [*Fleer Corp. v. Topps Chewing Gum, Inc.*, Del. Supr., 539 A.2d 1060, 1062 (1988)] (quoting 66 Am. Jur. 2d *Restitution and Implied Contracts* § 3, p. 945 (1973)).

79. *Id.* [at 1063]

81. On July 24, 1998, Irma filed an accounting showing the majority of the withdrawals from the mutual fund accounts were for the benefit of her household, loans to Woldemar's businesses, payments to Irma's lawyer, payment of Amelia's tuition, and that no funds were used by Ms. Minutola. We note that while the interests of Ms. Minutola, the elderly mother of Irma, may be adverse to Irma's husband and daughter, she is represented by the same attorney representing them. If this is a legitimate concern, it can be addressed by the Court of Chancery when it considers Ms. Minutola's pending motion to modify judgment.

* * *

Amelia Schock also asserts that it was an error of law to impose a constructive trust on the 1994 Ford. Because the proceeds of the constructive trust placed on the annuity that was illegally cashed in by Irma Schock were used to purchase the automobile, this argument is without merit.

Woldemar Schock, the husband of Irma, asserts that the award of restitution against him was an error of law because the amounts in issue were loans made by Irma Schock to him for his businesses. He contends that the trial court contradicts itself in its July 23, 1998 opinion when it calls the loans a "charade" because it previously stated in its Memorandum Opinion dated December 3, 1997, that there was no wrongdoing in the secondary transactions. Woldemar argues that because this finding is not supported by the record and is not the product of an orderly and logical deductive reasoning process the monetary judgments against him should be reversed. He asserts that because the amount in question ($69,000) was in the form of loans to his business corporation and that he has already repaid about $45,000 to Irma, the award of restitution in the amount of $73,366.36 is unjustified and not supported by the record.

Woldemar's argument that the trial court's award of damages against him is inconsistent with its findings in its earlier memorandum opinion is without merit. In its later opinion, the trial court made it clear that it was implied in its earlier opinion that "Woldemar wrongfully enriched himself by knowingly aiding Irma's breach of fiduciary duty."[82] The court noted that it based its award of restitution on "Woldemar's actual notice, his cooperation, and his potential unjust gain from this wrongdoing."[83] Woldemar's arguments that the court should consider the fact that the exchanges of money was not a gift but loans that he has already partially repaid to Irma is without merit. Woldemar benefited from the complete amount he received and the funds should have been paid back to the Estate or to the Court instead of to his spouse, Irma.

The court made determinations of credibility and rejected Woldemar's explanations. Determinations of credibility will be given substantial deference. The trial court determined that Woldemar knew of the source of the funds and it rejected his testimony. The trial court's decision is the product of an orderly and logical deductive process and supported by the record; therefore, the trial court did not abuse its discretion and its award of damages is therefore affirmed.

The judgment of the Court of Chancery is therefore AFFIRMED and this matter is REMANDED to the Court of Chancery for consideration of the pending motion to amend the judgment.

Notes

1. Under what circumstances would the court in *Schock v. Nash* permit a principal to consent to conduct by an agent that otherwise would breach the agent's duty of loyalty? Would additional language in the power of attorney have avoided a breach of Irma Schock's duty as Ana Dever's agent? If you believe that it would have, what language would you suggest?

---

82. *Nash v. Schock*, Del. Ch., C.A. No. 14721-NC (Jul. 23, 1998), Letter Op. at 7.
83. *Id.* at 6.

A constru;tive

2. Is the opinion in *Schock v. Nash* consistent with section 390 of the Restatement, which provides as follows?

> § 390. Acting as an Adverse Party with Principal's Consent
>
> An agent who, to the knowledge of the principal, acts on [the agent's] own account in a transaction in which [the agent] is employed has a duty to deal fairly with the principal and to disclose to him all facts which the agent knows or should know would reasonably affect the principal's judgment, unless the principal has manifested to the agent that [the principal] knows such facts or that [the principal] does not care to know them.

3. Under what circumstances, if any, would the *Schock v. Nash* court or Restatement section 390 permit the agent to procure in advance a blanket waiver of the duty of loyalty?

4. Section 403 of the Restatement provides that, where "an agent receives anything as a result of his violation of a duty of loyalty to the principal, he is subject to a liability to deliver it, its value, or its proceeds, to the principal." Restatement § 403. The traditional equitable remedy against the agent is the constructive trust. See Restatement section 403 comment d.

5. In *Schock v. Nash,* on what basis does the court allow recovery against Irma Schock's mother, husband and daughter?

6. In *Cook County v. Barrett,* 36 Ill. App. 3d 623, 344 N.E.2d 540 (1975), the court commented on the utility of the constructive trust:

> The particular circumstances in which equity will impress a constructive trust are "as numberless as the modes by which property may be obtained through bad faith and unconscientious acts." The barriers to its effective operation are few. The form of the property claim determines nothing, since a constructive trust will extend to reach real and personal property, choses in action and funds of money. To make out a case a plaintiff must allege facts which disclose either actual or constructive fraud or an abuse of a confidential relationship. It is the latter situation with which this case is concerned.
>
> *　*　*
>
> * * * The obligations of a person who occupies that latter category are such that he must not place himself in a position which is adverse to that of his principal during the continuance of the agency.
>
> "[A]n agent should not unite his personal and his representative characters in the same transaction; and equity will not permit him to be exposed to the temptation, or brought into a situation where his own personal interests conflict with the interests of his principal and with the duties which he owes to his principal." 3 Pomeroy's Equity Jurisprudence (5th Ed.) sec. 959, p. 819.
>
> The remedy for breach of this duty is simple and salutary. Since a fiduciary is bound to act solely for the benefit of his principal, equity will intervene to prevent him from accruing any advantage-however innocently-from transactions conducted in behalf of the principal. So, when a fiduciary, who has acted for his beneficiary or principal, receives a gift, or bonus or commission from a party with whom he has transacted busi-

ness, that benefit may be recovered from him by the beneficiary of the fiduciary relationship. In *Janes v. First Fed. Sav. & Loan Ass'n*[, 57 Ill. 2d 398, 312 N.E.2d 605,] it was alleged that the defendant lending bank procured title insurance for its borrower on mortgaged property and charged the borrower the full price of that insurance, but subsequently received and retained a ten percent rebate from the title insurance company. The reviewing court ruled that under such facts the bank held the rebate upon a constructive trust for the borrower as beneficiary in the absence of the borrower's express contrary authorization. The court quoted approvingly from the American Law Institute restatements of the law of restitution and agency. The Restatement of Restitution, section 197, states:

Sec. 197. BONUS OR COMMISSION RECEIVED BY FIDUCIARY

Where a fiduciary in violation of his duty to the beneficiary receives or retains a bonus or commission or other profit, he holds what he receives upon a constructive trust for the beneficiary.

Comment a. Bribes and commissions. The rule stated in this Section is applicable not only where the fiduciary receives something in the nature of a bribe given him by a third person in order to induce him to violate his duty as fiduciary, but also where something is given to him and received by him in good faith, if it was received for an act done by him in connection with the performance of his duties as fiduciary. Thus, if a trustee, or corporate officer, or an agent entrusted with the management of property insures the property in a company of which he is an agent, and he receives from the company a commission for placing the insurance, he is accountable for the commission so received and holds it upon a constructive trust for his beneficiary.

[Comment] c. Where no harm to beneficiary. The rule stated in this Section is applicable although the profit received by the fiduciary is not at the expense of the beneficiary. Thus, where an agent to purchase property for his principal acts properly in making the purchase but subsequently receives a bonus from the seller, he holds the money received upon a constructive trust for his principal. The rule stated in this Section is not based on harm done to the beneficiary in the particular case, but rests upon a broad principle of preventing a conflict of opposing interests in the minds of fiduciaries, whose duty is to act solely for the benefit of their beneficiaries.

*   *   *

Despite the dearth of Illinois law on the subject, there is no logical reason why the remedy should not be extended to public officers in appropriate cases, the same as it would reach private trustees, employees and agents. Indeed, such application is no novelty. *United States v. Carter* (1910), 217 U.S. 286, 30 S. Ct. 515, 54 L. Ed. 769. The facts of *United States v. Carter* are especially illustrative. In that case the defendant, a captain in the Army Corps of Engineers, served as officer in charge of a vast public works project. His position carried with it large discretion, and numerous options were reserved to him as the government's agent in devising projects, drafting specifications, supervising and accepting work. It was alleged that he exercised this discretion uniformly to create profits for certain contractors at the expense of the United States and received in return secret cash payments exceeding $500,000. The Supreme Court decided that Carter had violated his fiduciary duty to the government and that he therefore held the secret payments in trust for the United States. Proof of the particular methods by which he had augmented the contractors' profits or the effectiveness of those methods was deemed immaterial to the government's case.

Barrett attempts to distinguish *Carter* as a suit in which the government paid inflated prices and traced the inflated sums into the hands of its employee, but this distinction is refuted by the court's own language:

> It is immaterial whether the complainant was able to show any specific abuse of discretion, or whether it was able to show that it had suffered any actual loss by fraud or otherwise. It would be a dangerous precedent to lay down as law that unless some affirmative fraud or loss can be shown, the agent may hold on to any secret benefit he may be able to make out of his agency. The larger interests of public justice will not tolerate, under any circumstances, that a public official shall retain any profit or advantage which he may realize through the acquirement of an interest in conflict with his fidelity as an agent.

A constructive trust is not an action for "recovery" or compensation under any theory of contract or tort. It is a strict equitable doctrine applied to cure a fiduciary's breach of his duty of loyalty by erasing the source of his conflict of interest, and transferring it to the innocent beneficiary. Bad faith is not an essential element of disloyalty and good faith is no defense to the charge. Courts are not interested in a fiduciary's particular motive for accepting a payment or gift, but rather with the general effect of such payments or gifts.

Problem 4.6

Both seller Xerxes and buyer Zamora retain the services of agent Yupon Properties (a real estate services mega-company) to represent them in a real estate transaction. Seller Xerxes uses Yupon to broker the deal; buyer Zamora uses Yupon to inspect the premises for possible defects. None of the three parties is aware of the dual representation. Some defects are identified by Yupon to Zamora, and remedied by Xerxes upon request by Zamora. At closing, the unknown dual representation is first discovered. The closing is nevertheless completed. Subsequently, the seller sues to recover the 6% broker's commission retained by Yupon. Should Xerxes prevail? Did Yupon violate any fiduciary duty?

Rogers v. Robson, Masters, Ryan, Brumund & Belom

81 Ill. 2d 201, 407 N.E.2d 47 (1980)

CHIEF JUSTICE GOLDENHERSH:

Plaintiff, James D. Rogers, M.D. appealed from the judgment of the circuit court of Will County entered in favor of defendants, Robson, Masters, Ryan, Brumund and Belom, upon allowance of their motion for summary judgment.

The appellate court reversed and remanded, and we allowed defendants' petition for leave to appeal.

In plaintiff's complaint, filed pro se, it is alleged that he had been named as a party defendant in an action alleging that a post-operative wound infection was due to the negligence and carelessness of the plaintiff and his codefendants; that discovery depositions taken by defendants, the attorneys employed by plaintiff's insurance company, showed that there was no negligence on the part of plaintiff; that despite that fact and contrary to plaintiff's wishes and instructions conveyed to the defendants, a settlement was negotiated in the malpractice action. The complaint alleged damages suffered by plaintiff.

Defendants' motion for summary judgment shows that at the time of the alleged negligent acts out of which the malpractice action arose plaintiff was insured by Employer's Fire Insurance Company, and that defendants negotiated a settlement with the plaintiff in the malpractice action and, upon execution of a covenant not to sue, paid $1,250 and effected dismissal of the action as to plaintiff. The policy under which plaintiff was insured provided that the written consent of a former insured was not required before the insurer made any settlement of any claim or suit "even if such claim or suit was made, preferred or alleged while such former insured was an insured under this policy."

In an affidavit filed in opposition to the motion for summary judgment plaintiff stated that during the pendency of the malpractice action he repeatedly informed one of the partners in the defendant law firm that he would not consent to the settlement of the action, that he was assured that the action would be defended, and that at no time was he advised that defendants intended to settle the malpractice suit.

The circuit court allowed defendants' motion for summary judgment and plaintiff appealed. In reversing, the appellate court held that under the terms of the policy plaintiff's insurer was authorized to settle the medical malpractice action without plaintiff's consent. It held, however, that when defendants became aware that a settlement was imminent and that plaintiff did not wish the case settled, a conflict arose which prevented their continuing to represent both plaintiff and the insurer without a full and frank disclosure of the circumstances. The appellate court held that defendants, having continued to represent both plaintiff and the insurer without the requisite disclosure, breached their duty to plaintiff and would be liable to him for any loss caused by the lack of disclosure.

Defendants contend that they did not breach an independent duty owed to plaintiff; that because the insurer was authorized to settle the malpractice litigation without plaintiff's consent, no conflict of interest arose between the parties to the insurance contract; and that the alleged conflict upon which the majority of the appellate court rests was not argued by plaintiff. They argue, too, that plaintiff suffered no damage as a proximate result of the alleged failure to advise him of the impending settlement. *Amici curiae,* the Illinois Defense Counsel and Illinois State Bar Association, argue that the appellate court erred in implying that proof of a violation of the canons or disciplinary rules of the American Bar Association Code of Professional Responsibility established a per se basis for imposing liability on an attorney in a malpractice action.

It is plaintiff's position that the appellate court correctly reversed the circuit court judgment for the reason that there is presented a genuine issue of material fact. He argues that it was the duty of defendants to inform him of the intent to settle and that his consent to the settlement was required.

Although defendants were employed by the insurer, plaintiff, as well as the insurer, was their client and was entitled to a full disclosure of the intent to settle the litigation without his consent and contrary to his express instructions. Defendants' duty to make such disclosure stemmed from their attorney-client relationship with plaintiff and was not affected by the extent of the insurer's authority to settle without plaintiff's consent. We need not and therefore do not consider the question whether plaintiff's insurance carrier was authorized to settle the malpractice action without his consent.

Further, since no disclosure was made and plaintiff was not given the opportunity to elect what course to pursue, we need not speculate what recourse, if any, plaintiff had under the terms of the insurance policy. Nor need we reach the question whether plaintiff can prove damages which are the proximate result of the breach of the duty to make a full disclosure of the conflict between defendants' two clients. It cannot be determined from this record what damages, if any, plaintiff can prove. We decide only that this record does not preclude the possibility that some damage to plaintiff may have flowed from defendants' alleged failure to make the requisite disclosure.

The record does not show that there is no genuine issue as to any material fact and the judgment of the appellate court is affirmed.

Notes

1. During the term of the agency, an agent may not, without the informed consent of the principal, act on behalf of persons whose interests conflict with those of the principal. The agent may not act on behalf of an adverse party in a transaction connected with the agency. Restatement § 391. In addition, the agent is prohibited from acting on behalf of any third person whose interests conflict with those of the principal, even if the third person is not engaging in a transaction with the principal. Restatement § 394. Of course, the corollary is that one may serve as a dual agent, provided that both principals are advised of the planned dual representation and agree to allow it.

2. In *Rogers v. Robson, Masters, Ryan, Brumund & Belom,* if the insurance company correctly interpreted the policy, how has the attorney damaged the client? What should the attorney in *Rogers v. Robson, Masters, Ryan, Brumund & Belom* have done when instructed by the insurance company to settle without the insured's consent? What damages might Doctor Rogers have suffered?

Chapter 5

Power of Agents to Bind the Firm by Unauthorized Acts

A. Introduction

An agent's power to bind the principal is the agent's *ability* to do so. *Authority* is the power to bind that results from the principal's "manifestations" to the agent of the principal's *consent* to be bound. *Compare* Restatement § 6 *with* Restatement § 7. Thus, an agent authorized to bind the principal has the power to do so.

But is the converse true? Does an agent have the *power* to bind the principal even though the agent was not *authorized* to do so? The use of agents to conduct business inevitably involves the risk that the agents will sometimes exceed their authority to bind the principal. Under what circumstances should the principal—or the third person dealing with the agent—bear the risk of unauthorized actions? Where the principal's manifestations are to the third party, regardless of whether the principal has also manifested to the agent an intention to create some amount of authority, should the third party be entitled to reasonably rely and to hold the principal bound for the agent's or the apparent agent's actions?

In trying to explain the circumstances in which an agent will have the power to bind the principal by unauthorized acts, courts and commentators have developed various doctrines. Bear in mind that doctrines are attempt to rationalize the law, to organize it into a logically consistent framework. While doctrines seek to explain the law, they are only approximations; as such, they inherently are incomplete.

Although the Restatement explains power to bind by unauthorized acts using the doctrines of apparent authority, estoppel to deny authority, and inherent agency power, many courts use only a single doctrine, "ostensible authority." Moreover, the Restatement categories themselves overlap in their application. Luckily, all four doctrines make similar inquiries. First, did the third party with whom the agent dealt believe that the principal had consented to the agent binding the principal? Second, was that belief reasonable under the circumstances? Third, to what extent was the principal responsible for that belief?

In studying opinions discussing the power to bind by unauthorized acts, keep in mind the tendency of courts to use the Restatement categories, as well as ostensible authority, interchangeably. Think of the Restatement categories as a set of tools you can use to organize your analysis. Regardless of how the *court* analyzes the facts, try each of the Restatement categories to see how the facts fit them.

B. Apparent Authority

Problem 5.1

Palmer was planning to establish a dealership to sell farm machinery. He hired Adams to organize and operate the business. Adams was expressly authorized to collect for machinery sold and to hire and discharge office help, mechanics, and sales people but was expressly forbidden to borrow any money on Palmer's credit. Palmer supplied the money to establish a bank account in the local bank. The account was in Palmer's name, but Adams had authority to write checks on the account. From time to time, the account was overdrawn by Adams, but Palmer had no knowledge or notice of the overdrafts. On each occasion, Adams made deposits to cover the overdraft. Subsequently, Palmer discharged Adams and learned for the first time that the account was overdrawn $2000. The bank brought an action to recover the amount of the overdraft from Palmer. May the bank recover? Give reasons. (Illinois Bar Examination, July 1976.)

Hamilton Hauling, Inc. v. GAF Corp.
719 S.W.2d 841 (Mo. App. 1986)

DIXON, Judge.

Plaintiff Hamilton Hauling, Inc., appeals from a jury verdict for defendant GAF Corporation in a contract action. The only claims of error relate to instructions. Fundamental to the instruction issue is whether John Bajt, an agent of GAF, had the authority to execute a contract on behalf of GAF. The contract in question required GAF, a manufacturer, to purchase a minimum of over $800,000 of raw materials annually from Hamilton Hauling for a period of ten years.

Bajt was a purchasing agent or buyer at GAF's Kansas City plant from 1973 until 1980. Duties of a purchasing agent generally included the acquisition and purchase of all raw materials and related supplies necessary to sustain plant production on a day-to-day basis.

In that capacity, Bajt conducted all negotiations and sales transactions with various vendors for the purchase of raw materials, particularly wood chips, for the Kansas City plant. In the last year of his employment, Bajt purchased approximately $6,000,000 worth of raw materials to be used in production at the plant. None of these purchases were by any document other than a purchase order pursuant to Bajt's actual authority.

The evidence showed that under GAF's internal policy, buyers at Bajt's level had authority to make purchase orders not exceeding $25,000 in amount or one year in duration. Any order or contract exceeding those limits had to be approved in advance by GAF's corporate headquarters. All purchase orders were eventually sent to corporate headquarters for review. Bajt acknowledged the

$25,000 limit on the purchase of items for maintenance, repair and operations, but denied that it applied to the acquisition of raw materials. No evidence was presented to show that buyers like Bajt customarily entered into long term contracts or contracts involving amounts over $25,000. In all his years with GAF, Bajt never entered into any long term contract except the one at issue in this case.

Hamilton Hauling, solely owned by Warren Hamilton, had supplied a variety of goods and services to GAF and its corporate predecessors at the plant since 1954. During his course of business with GAF, Hamilton had dealt with three different purchasing agents. Hamilton had never had a long term contract with GAF but dealt with it consistently on a purchase order basis. A purchase order could be cancelled by GAF at any time. Hamilton was aware that GAF had at one time entered into a contract with another wood chip vendor prior to the time the agreement here was executed. Bajt was also aware of that contract and knew that it had been signed at corporate headquarters.

A continuous, uninterrupted supply of wood chips was essential to meet the production demands of the plant. The harsh winter of 1978/1979 adversely affected GAF's ability to obtain an adequate supply of wood chips. Bajt negotiated with Hamilton for several months encouraging him to go into the wood chip business so that Bajt might obtain a dependable supplier of wood chips. Hamilton was wary about supplying wood chips to GAF on a purchase order basis because he previously had been cancelled twice by GAF on orders involving delivery of raw materials. Preparation by Hamilton to supply GAF with the needed wood chips would be costly, and Bajt was aware of that. On February 1, 1979, Bajt and Hamilton entered into a contract to purchase which required GAF to purchase approximately 26,000 tons of wood chips annually from Hamilton at a minimum cost of more than $800,000 per year for 10 years. The agreement was drawn up by Hamilton's attorney and signed by Bajt in Hamilton's office. Bajt left the original agreement with Hamilton. The agreement was subject to renegotiation of price increases at six-month intervals.

Bajt admitted that he never sent a copy of the contract to GAF's corporate headquarters. No one at GAF seemed to know about the agreement other than Bajt's secretary. Hamilton acknowledged that he never told his two associates in the wood chip business that he had a contract with GAF; in fact, he indicated to them that he only had a purchase order.

After the execution of the agreement, Bajt continued to issue standard purchase orders for all wood sold to GAF by Hamilton, and the purchase orders were routinely sent to GAF's corporate headquarters. The wood supplied by Hamilton pursuant to the purchase orders issued after the signing of the agreement was inconsistent with the tonnage requirements specified in the agreement. Bajt was terminated by GAF in September 1980 and in December 1980, GAF notified Hamilton Hauling that no further deliveries of wood chips would be accepted. Hamilton produced the contract. GAF disclaimed any knowledge of the contract and denied the authority of Bajt to have made such a contract on its behalf.

At trial Hamilton testified that Bajt had told him that he had authority to execute the contract and Hamilton believed him. There was substantial evidence, however, that Hamilton was aware of limitations on Bajt's authority to contract. Both of Hamilton's associates in the wood chip business testified that they had informed Hamilton of conversations with Bajt in which Bajt had indicated his limited authority to contract. These conversations took place prior to the execution of the agreement between Hamilton and Bajt.

Hamilton acknowledged that he had entered into contracts with two other corporations and in each instance the contract had been prepared and executed at the corporate headquarters of the respective company rather than by the local plant manager. It was Hamilton Hauling's theory throughout the trial that Bajt bound GAF because he acted with apparent authority.

On appeal, Hamilton Hauling complains that the instruction given by the trial court defining apparent authority was erroneous. [I]nstruction [9] reads as follows:

Acts are within an employee's apparent authority even though not specifically authorized if:

1. The defendant GAF Corporation knowingly permitted its employees to so act, and

2. Hamilton Hauling, Inc. knew that GAF Corporation knowingly permitted its employees to so act, and

3. Hamilton Hauling, Inc. acting reasonably and in good faith, actually believed that GAF employees had the authority to so act, and

4. Hamilton Hauling, Inc. relied on the authority of GAF Corporation's employees, and

5. Hamilton Hauling, Inc. will be damaged if said acts of GAF Corporation's employees are not binding on GAF Corporation.

Hamilton Hauling urges the instruction is erroneous because of the requirement that the jury find that Hamilton Hauling knew that GAF had knowingly permitted Bajt to contract. Hamilton Hauling says that this requirement is contrary to law and that Instruction A [offered by Hamilton] had no such requirement [and] should have been given. The tenor of the Hamilton Hauling argument is that Bajt's apparent authority arose from his position as a buyer and his actions in that position.

GAF contends that given the specific limitations on Bajt's authority there must be proof that GAF had acquiesced in Bajt's overstepping of his authority. GAF also contends the acquiescence must be known to Hamilton Hauling. The nub of the issue as to the instructional error turns on the positions of the parties as to the definition of apparent authority to be applied in the case.

Some review of the principles governing apparent agency will aid in the consideration of the issue. In the area of agency, Missouri courts have relied extensively on the RESTATEMENT (SECOND) OF AGENCY (1957).

It is generally held that when a principal "holds out" another as possessing certain authority, thereby inducing others reasonably to believe that authority exists, the agent has apparent authority to act even though as between himself and the principal, such authority has not been granted. Apparent authority differs from actual authority in that the principal communicates directly with a third person to create apparent authority; to create actual authority, the principal communicates directly with the agent. RESTATEMENT (SECOND) OF AGENCY § 8 comments a and e.

When a principal has by his voluntary act placed an agent in such a situation that a person of ordinary prudence, conversant with business usages and the nature of the particular business, is justified in presuming that such agent has authority to perform a particular act on behalf of his principal, the principal is estopped, as against such innocent third person, from denying the agent's authority to perform the act.

The "holding out" of the agent's authority by the principal party may be by action or inaction. The principal may directly communicate the authority to a third party or knowingly permit the agent to exercise such authority. *See Continental-St. Louis Corp. v. Ray Scharf Vending Co.,* 400 S.W.2d 467, 470 (Mo. App. 1966). The *Continental-St. Louis Corp.* court quotes 3 Am. Jur. 2d Agency § 74 (now § 79) as saying:

> [T]he rule is that if a principal acts or conducts his business, either intentionally or through negligence, or fails to disapprove of the agent's act or course of action so as to lead the public to believe that his agent possesses authority to act or contract in the name of the principal, such principal is bound by the acts of the agent within the scope of his apparent authority as to any person who, upon the faith of such holding out, believes, and has reasonable ground to believe, that the agent has such authority, and in good faith deals with him.

It must be emphasized that the third party must reasonably rely on the authority held out by the principal. The third party must know of facts demonstrating the principal's consent to the agent's actions.

Apparent authority exists only to the extent that it is reasonable for the third person dealing with the agent to believe that the agent is authorized.

RESTATEMENT (SECOND) OF AGENCY § 8 comment c. Further, the third party must actually believe the agent to be authorized. *Id.* Apparent authority is that which a reasonably prudent man, using diligence and discretion, in view of the principal's conduct would suppose the agent to possess.

> [T]he party who claims reliance [on an agent's apparent authority] must not have closed his eyes to warning or inconsistent circumstances. Authority is not "apparent" simply because the party claiming has acted upon his conclusions [nor] simply because it looked so to him. It is not a situation where one may read while he runs. It is only where a person of ordinary prudence, conversant with business usages and the nature of the particular business, acting in good faith, and giving heed not only to opposing inferences but also to all restrictions brought to his notice, would reasonably rely, that a case is presented within the operation of the rule.

Mechem on Agency (2nd Ed.), Vol. 1, Sec. 726, p. 513.

Where the agent has some present actual authority, apparent authority may arise in any of three ways. The basic requirement for the creation of apparent authority is that it is the principal who is responsible for the information received by the third party. RESTATEMENT (SECOND) OF AGENCY § 27 comment a. The principal must have intentionally caused the third party to believe that the agent is authorized to act for the principal or he should have realized his conduct would create such a belief on the part of the third party. *Id.* The information received by the third person may come directly from the principal by letter or word of mouth, from authorized statements of the agent, from documents or other indicia of authority given by the principal to the agent, or from third persons who have heard of the agent's authority through authorized or permitted channels of communication. Likewise, as in the case of authority, apparent authority can be created by appointing a person to a position, such as that of manager or treasurer, which carries with it generally recognized duties; to those who know of the appointment there is apparent authority to do the things ordinarily entrusted to one occupying such a position, regardless of unknown limitations which are imposed upon the particular agent. So, too, a person who permits another to do an act in such a way as to establish in a community a reputation of having authority to act, either by directing the agent so to represent, or by directing him to act and doing nothing to prevent the spread of such information by the agent or by others, creates apparent authority with respect to those who learn of the reputation. Third persons who are aware of what a continuously employed agent has done are normally entitled to believe that he will continue to have such authority for at least a limited period in the future, and this apparent authority continues until the third person has been notified or learns facts which should lead him to believe that the agent is no longer authorized. *Id.*

Establishment of apparent authority by direct, express statements is obvious. The other methods of creating apparent authority—by "position" and by "prior acts"—have both been recognized by Missouri courts.

Wynn v. McMahon Ford Co., 414 S.W.2d 330 (Mo. App. 1967), exemplifies the apparent authority that may be generated by an agent's position. In *Wynn*, defendant's agent, designated as used car sales manager, was placed by defendant in a managerial position. The court found that persons dealing with the agent could reasonably believe that he had authority to conclude sales transactions. According to the RESTATEMENT (SECOND) OF AGENCY § 49 comment c,

> [i]f a principal puts an agent into, or knowingly permits him to occupy, a position in which according to the ordinary habits of persons in the locality, trade or profession, it is usual for such an agent to have a particular kind of authority, anyone dealing with him is justified in inferring that he has such authority, in the absence of reason to know otherwise.

Another way apparent authority may be created is by acquiescence of the principal in prior acts of an agent.

> [W]herever a person has knowingly and without dissent permitted [an]other to act as his agent in such capacity, or where his habits and course of dealing have been such as to reasonably warrant the presumption that such other was his agent, authorized to act in that capacity, whether it be a single transaction or a series of transactions, his authority to act for him in that capacity will be conclusively presumed so far as it may be necessary to protect the rights of third persons who have relied thereon in good faith and in the exercise of reasonable prudence; and he will not be permitted to deny that such other was his agent, authorized to do the act he assumed to do, provided that such act is within the real or apparent scope of the presumed authority.

Bennett v. Potashnick, 214 Mo. App. 507, 514, 257 S.W. 836, 838 (1924). Apparent authority may result from a prior relation of agent and principal. The principal by allowing an agent to carry out prior similar transactions may create an appearance of authority of the agent to carry out such acts. As it is expressed by the RESTATEMENT,

> a person who permits another to do an act in such a way as to establish in a community a reputation for having authority to act, creates apparent authority with respect to those who learn of the reputation.

RESTATEMENT (SECOND) OF AGENCY § 27 comment a.

Hamilton Hauling argues that since Bajt was a purchasing agent, the authority to contract upon behalf of GAF is inferable from the position he held. Hamilton Hauling's theory of apparent authority was not supported by the evidence.

Apparent authority could only have resulted from some act or failure to act on the part of GAF. Hamilton testified that Bajt told him he had the authority to contract and Hamilton believed Bajt. Bajt's unauthorized representations are totally immaterial on the issue of apparent authority.

Hamilton Hauling claims Bajt's authority came from his position; however, there was no evidence of any sort in this case as to the usual authority of purchasing agents generally. There was nothing to support an inference that a vendor dealing with a purchasing agent expects that agent to have the power to make a contract like the long term agreement in evidence. There was evidence that Bajt had twice exceeded the company-imposed limits on his authority in making purchase orders. No purchase order represented a long-term contract and all purchase orders contained explicit limitations on the purchase including the right to cancel. There was no evidence that Bajt had ever entered into a long term contract on behalf of GAF; in fact, Bajt admitted that in all his years at GAF, he had not made any other such contract. Bajt was not clothed with apparent authority by virtue of his position.

Moreover, there was no evidence to support Hamilton's claim that he reasonably relied on Bajt's authority. Hamilton admitted that the contracts he had entered into with other corporations were signed at corporate headquarters, not locally. Apparent authority is not a "situation" where one can "read while he runs."

The judgment favoring GAF is affirmed.

Notes

1. Apparent authority is the basic doctrine used by the Restatement to allocate the risk of an unauthorized transaction entered into by an agent. Under Restatement sections 8 and 27 an agent's power to bind the principal by an unauthorized action is based on the *principal's manifestations*— written or spoken words or other conduct—to third persons. However, a *third person* dealing with an agent has a correlative *duty* to act reasonably in interpreting the principal's conduct; the third person must reasonably believe, based on the principal's conduct and in light of all accompanying circumstances, that the principal consents to being bound by the particular act in question. Restatement §§ 27, 34, 49.

One corollary of these principles is that apparent authority *cannot* be based solely on the *agent's* conduct. That is, a third person cannot reasonably believe the principal consents where the principal has not taken any action on which such a belief could be based. *E.g., Southwest Land Title v. Gemini Financial,* 752 S.W.2d 5 (Tex. App. 1988); *Barnes v. Treece,* 15 Wash. App. 437, 549 P.2d 1152 (1976).

Is the principle that third persons owe a *duty* to act reasonably in determining the scope of an agent's authority inconsistent with the principle from chapter 1 that third persons are the *beneficiaries* of an implied warranty of authority?

2. In *Hamilton Hauling, Inc. v. GAF Corp.,* when GAF appointed Bajt as its purchasing agent, what, if anything, was it "manifesting" to third persons about Bajt's authority to bind GAF? Could GAF have done anything to effectively prevent Bajt and other similarly situated agents from having eve the slightest appearance of authority to purchase more than $25,000 worth of materials per transaction or to enter into long term contracts—without jeopardizing GAF's business interests?

3. Traditionally, corporate officers—including a president—were viewed as having *neither* implied authority *nor* power to bind by an unauthorized act solely by virtue of holding corporate office. *See* H. HENN & J. ALEXANDER, LAWS OF CORPORATIONS 595-604 (3d ed. 1983). The *modern trend* is to give the president both implied and apparent authority to conduct ordinary business transactions. *Id.*

Under either the traditional or the modern view, a corporate officer, just as any other agent, may have *apparent authority* based on how the corporation in fact conducts its business, such as by customarily permitting its president to enter into ordinary business transactions.

Fennell v. TLB Kent Company
865 F.2d 498 (2d Cir. 1989)

MAHONEY, Circuit Judge:

This is an appeal from a final judgment of the United States District Court for the Southern District of New York, which dismissed plaintiff's action and approved a $10,000 settlement agreement. The attorneys for the parties negotiated a settlement and reported it to the court by telephone. [T]he district court dismissed the action and approved the settlement, finding that plaintiff's attorney had apparent authority to settle the case and plaintiff was accordingly bound by the settlement agreement.

Plaintiff-appellant Louis Fennell commenced this action against his employer, alleging wrongful discharge because of his race and age. Fennell was represented by C. Vernon Mason and several of his associates, including Fred K. Brewington.

On January 16, 1987, Brewington and Eugene Frink, defendants' attorney, agreed to settle the case for $10,000 during a telephone conversation. The settlement was reported to the court by both attorneys in a telephone conference call on January 20, 1987. The district court issued an order of dismissal on the same day.

Fennell [contends] that he had told Brewington on January 16, 1987 that he would not approve a $10,000 settlement, but he was willing to settle the case out of court "with the intentions of getting it out of the way and behind me." He also claimed that he had told Mason on January 20, 1987 that $10,000 was not a satisfactory settlement, and that he had tried several times in early February, 1987 to contact Mason's office by telephone about the case, but elicited no response. Fennell further stated that he had gone to Mason's office on February 20, 1987, at which time Mason informed him that the case had been settled for $10,000, whereupon Fennell reiterated his dissatisfaction with that settlement.

On February 27, 1987, Fennell wrote Mason expressing his dissatisfaction with the settlement agreement and indicating that he had "no further use of [Mason's] services." A copy of this letter was sent to the district court and received there on March 3, 1987. On March 20, 1987, Brewington wrote to the district court requesting that the "matter be restored to the calendar as the settlement which was authorized and accepted by our client is no longer acceptable to him," and that Mason and his associates be released by the court as counsel to Fennell.

[T]he district court held a hearing on June 16, 1987 to determine whether Fennell's case should be restored to the calendar. At the conclusion of the hearing, the district court dismissed the action and approved the settlement. This ruling was based upon a finding that Fennell's attorney had been clothed with "apparent authority" when he settled the case.

[T]wo circuits have ruled that where an action is based upon federal law, the authority of an attorney to settle that action is a federal question. In the absence of weighty countervailing considerations, we are inclined to follow our sister circuits in deeming federal law applicable to the question before us. In any event, to the extent that deference might be accorded to New York precedents concerning what is at root a fairly general question of agency law, the outcome would in our view be the same.

We begin with the undisputed proposition that the decision to settle is the client's to make, not the attorney's. On the other hand, if an attorney has apparent authority to settle a case, and the opposing counsel has no reason to doubt that authority, the settlement will be upheld.

The district court made the following findings concerning the issue of apparent authority: 1) that Mason and his associates represented Fennell "in dealing with the other side," 2) that they were authorized to appear at conferences for him, 3) that Fennell knew that settlement was being discussed, 4) that Fennell did not tell his counsel not to continue discussing settlement, 5) that Fennell would have accepted a higher settlement figure ($50,000-75,000), and 6) that Fennell did not tell defendants' counsel that the authority of plaintiff's counsel was limited in any way. The district court concluded that Fennell's counsel "had every appearance of being authorized to make a binding agreement with [defendants' counsel]."

Apparent authority is

the power to affect the legal relations of another person by transactions with third persons, professedly as agent for the other, arising from and in accordance with *the other's manifestations* to such third persons.

Restatement (Second) of Agency § 8 (1958) (emphasis added). Further, in order to create apparent authority, the *principal must manifest to the third party* that he "consents to have the act done on his behalf by the person purporting to act for him." *Id.* § 27. Second Circuit case law supports the view that apparent authority is created only by the representations of the principal to the third party, and explicitly rejects the notion that an agent can create apparent authority by his own actions or representations.

In this case, taking the facts as the district court found them, Fennell made no manifestations to defendants' counsel that Mason and his associates were authorized to settle the case. Fennell's attorneys accordingly had no apparent authority to settle the case for $10,000 without Fennell's consent. The district court's findings that Mason and his associates represented Fennell, and that they were authorized to appear at conferences for him, do not prove otherwise. A client does not create apparent authority for his attorney to settle a case merely by retaining the attorney.

Further, the court's findings that Fennell knew settlement was being discussed, did not ask his attorneys not to discuss settlement, would have accepted a higher settlement figure, and did not tell defendant's counsel that the authority of plaintiff's counsel was limited in any way, do not lead to a different outcome. These findings involve only discussions between Fennell and his attorneys or things that Fennell did not say to opposing counsel. None of these findings relates to positive actions or manifestations by Fennell to defendants' counsel that would reasonably lead that counsel to believe that Fennell's attorneys were clothed with apparent authority to agree to a definitive settlement of the litigation.

Finally, we note that the application of state law would not yield a contrary result. Defendants contend that *Hallock v. State,* 64 N.Y.2d 224, 474 N.E.2d 1178, 485 N.Y.S.2d 510 (1984), would call for a decision in their favor if New York law were considered applicable. We disagree.

Hallock held that a stipulation of settlement made by counsel in open court may bind his clients even where it exceeds his actual authority, provided that there is apparent authority. In that case, however, an applicable court rule required that attorneys attending pretrial conferences have authority to enter into binding court settlements on behalf of their clients, a co-plaintiff attended the conference from which Hallock was absent because of illness, and more than two months passed before plaintiffs made any objection to the settlement. We do not think the rule stated in *Hallock* would apply here.

We realize that the rule we announce here has the potential to burden, at least occasionally, district courts which must deal with constantly burgeoning calendars. A contrary rule, however, would have even more deleterious consequences. Clients should not be faced with a Hobson's choice of denying their counsel all authority to explore settlement or being bound by any settlement to which their counsel might agree, having resort only to an action against their counsel for malpractice. In any event, even if we were to consider such a rule advisable, the applicable precedents and settled principles of agency law would preclude its adoption.

Reversed and remanded for further proceedings not inconsistent herewith.

Notes

1. Why did the attorney in *Hallock* have apparent authority to settle, while the attorney in *Fennell v. TLB Kent Co.* did not? If some authority is presumed to accompany certain positions under appropriate circumstances (such as pursuant to community or industry custom), what authority apparently accompanies the appointment by a client of an attorney to represent her/him?

2. Note that some cases hold that where a party's attorney announces a settlement, in open court, the settlement will be presumed valid unless the party can prove the attorney had no authority to settle. *See, e.g., Kazale v. Flowers,* 541 N.E.2d 219 (Ill. App. 1989).

3. *Menard & Co. Masonry v. Marshall Building,* 539 A.2d 523 (R.I. 1988) involved a dispute growing out of the construction of a building. The general contractor on the project, Con-Sul, Inc. (Consul), contracted with Marshall Building Systems, Inc. (Marshall), to perform most of the work. Marshall entered into a contract "subcontracting" certain masonry work to Menard & Co. Masonry Building Contractors (Menard).

During construction, Con-Sul, the general contractor, called a meeting to discuss the completion of a wall needed to support equipment that was to be delivered in a few days. The meeting was attended by (i) Con-Sul's project manager (Pickett), (ii) Marshall's project manager (Stone) and Copithorne (who had represented Marshall in the negotiations with Menard and who had executed the contract with Menard), and (iii) Menard's project manager (Cillino). Con-Sul insisted that Menard work overtime if necessary to finish the wall. Menard's representative, Cillino, pointed out that the Menard-Marshall subcontract did not cover overtime expenses. At this point Copithorne assured Cillino that Menard would be paid for the overtime.

When Menard submitted invoices for the overtime work, Marshall refused to pay for them because the overtime had not been authorized by a written "change order," as required by the subcontract.

After the jury returned a verdict that Marshall was liable to Menard for the overtime, the trial court entered a directed verdict in favor of Marshall on the basis that there was no evidence from which the jury could conclude that Copithorne was authorized to agree to overtime. On appeal, the Rhode Island Supreme Court held that there was sufficient evidence of apparent authority to support the jury verdict:

> That Copithorne had authority to negotiate and execute the subcontract is undisputed by Marshall. Nor has Marshall shown that it communicated a subsequent limitation on Copithorne's authority to Marshall. He attended the meeting at which Menard was directed to perform overtime as Marshall's authorized representative. Thus, we conclude that Menard offered evidence upon which reasonable persons could differ, sufficient to defeat a motion for a directed verdict.

What is the basis of the holding in *Menard & Co. Masonry?* Does the fact that Copithorne had authority to enter into the original contract with Menard give him apparent authority to agree to a change? What other facts would you want to know in determining whether Copithorne had apparent authority? *See* Restatement § 51 comment c & Illustration 4.

C. Estoppel

Problem 5.2

Merchant is the business of selling, and of repairing used stereos. In the ordinary course of business, Buyer buys a stereo from Merchant. Buyer pays Merchant the purchase price, and takes delivery of the stereo. Merchant later discovers that the stereo sold to Buyer was not owned by Merchant, but rather was owned by Owner. Suppose that Merchant acquired possession of the stereo in one of two different manners:

a. Thief stole the stereo from Owner, and sold it to Merchant.

b. Owner left the stereo with Merchant to be repaired.

Did Merchant have power to transfer to Buyer Owner's title to the stereo? If you believe that Merchant did have that power, what was its source—express authority, implied authority, apparent authority or estoppel to deny agency power? Explain. *[handwritten: forgotten Paid for machine resold]*

Metalworking Machinery Co., Inc. v. Fabco, Inc.

17 Ohio App. 3d 91, 477 N.E.2d 634 (1984)

[handwritten: Argues it should be estopped from claiming ownership]

COLE, Judge.

This is an appeal taken from a decision of the Court of Common Pleas of Hancock County, wherein summary judgment was granted in favor of plaintiff, Metalworking Machinery Company (Metalworking), in the amount of $15,000, plus defendant, Yoder Machinery Company (Yoder).

The basic relevant facts in this case were stipulated to by the parties and are as follows.

[handwritten margin: M purchased from E, but did not pl^ machine. E sold same machine to Y who later sold to F]

On August 10, 1979, Metalworking purchased from East Coast Steel Company of Columbia, South Carolina (East Coast), a two wheel "Wheelabrator" metalworking machine[, for a] purchase price [of] $15,000. No certificate of title or bill of sale was involved.

On April 4, 1980, Yoder purchased the same metalworking machine from East Coast, said machine never having been picked up by Metalworking. Subsequently, in the usual course of its business, Yoder sold the same "Wheelabrator" to defendant/third party plaintiff, Fabco, Incorporated (Fabco), for a price of $31,500. Fabco also expended a substantial amount of money in rehabilitating and putting into service the machine.

It was also stipulated that East Coast was a manufacturing company and that the "Wheelabrator" machine was not sold by East Coast in the ordinary course of its business.

[handwritten margin: Tct: SJ in favor of M against F & SJ, in favor of F against Y]

Upon motions for summary judgment made by all of the parties, the trial court ordered that summary judgment be granted to the plaintiff, Metalworking, against Fabco, and further that summary judgment be granted to Fabco against Yoder. Both summary judgments granted were in the amount of $15,000.

[handwritten margin: Y argues that M is estopped from claiming ownership b/c]

The specific finding of the trial court to which Yoder now addresses its appeal is that there was no estoppel created by the fact situation upon which Yoder can rely as a defense.

It is appellant's argument that the plaintiff Metalworking should be estopped from asserting the fact of its own ownership of the machine because it, by leaving the machine in the possession of East Coast for some nine months, created an appearance of authority in East Coast to sell that machinery.

Metalworking became the owner of the "Wheelabrator" on August 10, 1979. R.C. 1302.44(A) provides:

A purchaser of goods acquires all title which his transferor had or had power to transfer.

Assuming as we must that the transferor East Coast had title, this passed to Metalworking and no title remained in East Coast. It is clear that Yoder in fact acquired no title, since on April 4, 1980, East Coast had no interest to transfer.

What East Coast did have was possession, the machine having been left with it. Was the act of Metalworking in leaving possession with East Coast a sufficient basis upon which to create an estoppel of Metalworking to assert its actual ownership?

In 42 Ohio Jurisprudence 3d, at 85, Section 54, it is stated:

It is only when the owner, by his own affirmative act, has conferred the apparent title and absolute ownership upon another, upon the faith of which the chose in action has been purchased for value, that he is precluded from asserting his real title.

Here we are concerned with personalty but the principle applies. There needs to be some affirmative act on which to base estoppel. There is no affirmative act by Metalworking. It simply left the machine in situs. It did nothing actively to clothe East Coast with any authority to sell. Appellant argues that Metalworking was negligent in letting the machine sit in Coast's possession for nine months. However, there is nothing in the factual situation as stipulated to show the appellant was aware of this length of possession or relied on it. Had the sale taken place on succeeding days the situation would be the same so far as the length of possession without title by East Coast is concerned. There is no causal relationship between the length of time and the ultimate purchase. The causal relation asserted concerns only the fact of possession by East Coast, not the duration of that possession.

Thus, the issue narrows to the question whether or not simply possession by East Coast with permission by Metalworking without more and without respect to the duration of possession is a sufficient basis for estopping Metalworking from asserting its title.

In 28 American Jurisprudence 2d (1966) 686, Estoppel and Waiver, Section 63, it is said:

Although mere possession and control of personal property are not ordinarily sufficient to estop the real owner from asserting his title against a person who has dealt with the one in possession on the faith of his apparent ownership, slight additional circumstances may turn the scale against the owner and estop him from asserting title against one who has purchased the property in good faith.

Here, however, there is nothing but possession involved. There are no indicia of ownership nor title documents entrusted to the possessor. The Ohio Uniform Commercial Code is quite clear that to create apparent authority to sell there must be more than simple possession. There must be a merchant of a specific type. R.C. 1302.44(B) states:

Any entrusting of possession of goods to a merchant who deals in goods of that kind gives him power to transfer all rights of the entruster to a buyer in ordinary course of business.

E was not a merchant in kind

Here the facts explicitly negate the application of this section as it is stipulated that East Coast was a manufacturing company and like machinery was not sold by it in the ordinary and usual course of its business.

There is evidence of no other act by Metalworking which could constitute this "slight additional circumstance."

[T]here is no evidence sufficient to warrant a finding of estoppel.

Judgment affirmed.

Notes

1. The Restatement distinguishes between apparent authority and estoppel. Under Restatement section 8B(1):

> A person who is not otherwise liable as a party to a transaction purported to be done on his account, is nevertheless subject to liability to persons who have changed their positions because of their belief that the transaction was entered into by or for him, if
>
> (a) he intentionally or carelessly caused such belief, or
>
> (b) knowing of such belief and that others might change their positions because of it, he did not take reasonable steps to notify them of the facts.

Estoppel differs from apparent authority in a couple of particulars. First, estoppel can be based on omissions, not just affirmative conduct. That includes situations in which the principal is aware that third parties might believe someone to have authority, and the principal fails to act reasonably to protect third parties. Second, while merely entering into a contract based on a reasonable belief of authority is sufficient to invoke apparent authority, it is *not* a change in position sufficient to invoke *estoppel*. Thus, in estoppel, while the conduct necessary to charge a principal is lower than in apparent authority, the third party must show something additional: a detrimental change in position.

The lines between apparent authority and estoppel are not all that clear. In fact, many opinions treat apparent authority and estoppel as a single doctrine (sometimes called *"ostensible* authority").

2. Why does possession of property not create apparent authority or estoppel as to the possessor's power to sell the property?

Problem 5.3

Principal is a small business that makes and sells Mission style wooden chairs, priced at $500 each. Agent was retained to sell the chairs on behalf of Principal. Agent contacted Buyer, a furniture store owner, and they agreed to the purchase of 6 chairs for $3000. Buyer paid Agent in cash, but Agent absconded with the money. So, Principal was not paid. Yet, Principal had clearly and unequivocally directed Buyer not to accept payment in cash. On the question of whether payment to the agent constituted payment to the principal, would it matter whether the agent was in possession of 6 chairs and delivered them to Buyer at the time of payment? Or, whether the payment was for an order for 6 chairs to be delivered in the future? What steps could Principal take to avoid similar problems in the future? What steps could Buyer take?

Goldstein v. Hanna
97 Nev. 559, 635 P.2d 290 (1981)

GUNDERSON, Chief Justice:

Appellants, Ronald and Mary Goldstein, sued respondent, Fuad Hanna, to compel specific performance of an option to purchase Hanna's condominium. The district court entered judgment in favor of Hanna.

On or about December 10, 1977, the parties entered into a lease relating to Hanna's condominium in Clark County, Nevada. The lease granted the Goldsteins an option to purchase the condominium, and declared

> the option may be exercised at any time after December 1, 1977 and shall expire at midnight December 9, 1978 unless exercised prior thereto.

Callahan Realty conducted all negotiations on behalf of respondent Hanna, and was designated in the agreement as his authorized agent. The Goldsteins dealt exclusively with Callahan Realty, both as tenants and prospective purchasers. They had no direct dealings with Hanna until after August 1978.

In the summer of 1978, the Goldsteins exercise[d] their option to purchase. They contemplated a purchase from Hanna, with a simultaneous sale from themselves to another purchaser. To effectuate this double sale, Callahan Realty established two escrows, both with closing dates of August 29, 1978. Shortly before the escrows were to close, however, the ultimate purchaser declined to perform.

Three days before their escrow with Hanna was due to close, the Goldsteins contacted Mr. Callahan. They advised Callahan [that] they would purchase the condominium themselves, rather than find another purchaser.[1] Callahan informed the Goldsteins that they need not consummate the purchase by August 29, because their option would continue to be valid under the terms of the lease until December 9, 1978. To insure that respondent Hanna shared this understanding of the option terms, Mr. Goldstein requested Callahan call Hanna, in his presence, and confirm the agent's representations.

Callahan called Hanna and advised him that the ultimate purchaser would not close escrow as planned. Callahan also told Hanna that the Goldsteins' option to purchase would still be in effect until expiration of the lease term. Although Hanna testified at trial that he never authorized Callahan Realty to extend the escrow, the record indicates he never asserted that the option would not remain viable following termination of the pending escrow. On this issue, it appears he remained silent, and thus permitted the Goldsteins to rely on Callahan's representations.

On August 31, Hanna notified the escrow holder to consider the escrow cancelled. On September 15, however, Hanna called the Goldsteins on at least two

---

1. The uncontroverted testimony of Ronald Goldstein reflects that he was prepared to fund the escrow himself when the ultimate purchaser declined to perform.

occasions and attempted to purchase their option rights in the property.[2] After the Goldsteins rejected Hanna's offer, they learned that Hanna purportedly had cancelled the escrow. Hanna then refused to participate in a second escrow initiated by the Goldsteins.

In our view, this case does not turn on whether Callahan correctly advised the Goldsteins concerning their contract with respondent Hanna. Nor need we decide whether Callahan had actual authority to alter the contract's terms. The doctrine of equitable estoppel clearly precludes Hanna from claiming that the Goldsteins' rights under the lease-option agreement expired on August 29, 1978.

According to § 8B(1) of the Restatement (Second) of Agency (1958), an equitable estoppel arises under the following circumstances:

> A person who is not otherwise liable as a party to a transaction purported to be done on his account, is nevertheless subject to liability to persons who have changed their positions because of their belief that the transaction was entered into by or for him, if
>
> > (a) he intentionally or carelessly caused such belief, or
> >
> > (b) knowing of such belief and that others might change their positions because of it, he did not take reasonable steps to notify them of the facts.

Where there is a duty to speak, silence can raise an estoppel quite as effectively as can words. A duty to speak arises when another is or may come under a misapprehension regarding the authority of the principal's agent. Under such circumstances, the principal is obligated to exercise due care, and to conduct himself as a reasonably prudent business person with normal regard for the interests of others. Restatement (Second) of Agency § 8B comment d. Thus,

> a person remaining silent when he ought, in the exercise of good faith, to have spoken, will not be allowed to speak when he ought, in the exercise of good faith, remain silent.

Gardner v. Pierce, 22 Nev. 146, 36 P. 782 (1894). Similarly, silence or failure to repudiate an agent's representations can give rise to an inference of affirmation. According to § 94, comment a, of the Restatement (Second) Agency (1958):

> Silence under such circumstances that, according to the ordinary experience and habits of men, one would naturally be expected to speak if he did not consent, is evidence from which assent can be inferred. Such inference may be made although the purported principal had no knowledge that the other party would rely upon the supposed authority of the agent; his knowledge of such fact, however, coupled with his silence, would ordinarily justify an inference of assent by him.

In the instant case, during his telephone conversation with Callahan, Hanna made no effort to assure that the Goldsteins were not misled or lulled by his agent's representations.[3] Hanna knew the Goldsteins might not hasten to complete

---

2. Appellants' uncontradicted testimony is as follows: "Mr. Hanna offered to buy our interest out. Maybe I am not using the right phrase. He offered us money to leave the property. He said that he wanted the place for himself."

3. The uncontroverted testimony of Mr. Goldstein indicates:

"A. I was concerned having, on Callahan's advice, used the last month's rent, in restoring this so as not to be in default of the agreement, and he called Mr.

the August escrow while assuming they still had several months to exercise the option. Consequently, Hanna's silence and acquiescence in his agent's representations manifestly caused the Goldsteins to do what they otherwise would not have done, *i.e.*, to permit, at least arguably, a lapse of their valuable option rights.[4]

> Persons ordinarily express dissent to acts done on their behalf which they have not authorized or of which they do not approve.

Restatement (Second) of Agency § 43 comment a. (1958). The doctrine of equitable estoppel is properly invoked whenever

> unconscionable injury would result from denying enforcement of the contract after one party has been induced by the other seriously to change his position in reliance on the contract.

Alpark Distributing Inc. v. Poole, 95 Nev. 605, 600 P.2d 229 (1979). In the case at bar, the detriment suffered by the Goldsteins involves the loss of the benefit of their bargain: the right to purchase the property for a specified sum.

Thus, we need not decide whether or not Callahan Realty would have had actual authority, acting alone, to extend the Goldsteins' right to exercise the option or to interpret the contract's meaning. In effect, Hanna imbued his agent, Callahan, with apparent authority to make the representations upon which the Goldsteins relied.

> Apparent authority (when in excess of actual authority) proceeds on the theory of equitable estoppel; it is in effect an estoppel against the owner to deny agency when by his conduct he has clothed the agent with apparent authority to act.

Ellis v. Nelson, 68 Nev. 410, 233 P.2d 1072 (1951).

We therefore conclude that the doctrine of equitable estoppel precludes Hanna from claiming a forfeiture of the Goldsteins' option rights. The cause is reversed and remanded for further proceedings consistent with this opinion.

MANOUKIAN, Justice, dissenting:

As we stated in *Tsouras v. Southwest Plumbing & Heating*, 94 Nev. 748, 751, 587 P.2d 1321, 1323 (1978):

> It is indispensable to keep in mind here that, as against the principal, there can be reliance only upon what the principal himself has said or done, or at least said or done through some authorized agent. The acts of the agent in question can not be relied upon as alone enough to support

---

Hanna at that time, at my insistence, in my presence he phoned him, and advised him of the problem, that there would be a delay in the closing of the escrow and that and he informed Mr. Hanna on the phone that evidently he asked if this invalidated it, and he told him it did not, it was good until the end of November."

"Q. What did Mr. Callahan indicate to you after the telephone conversation?"

"A. No problem. This is the basic phrase he used, no problem, we will go ahead and obtain a new buyer."

4. The record indicates that but for Hanna's silence the Goldsteins would have completed the escrow as scheduled. When Hanna informed the Goldsteins in mid-September 1978 that he did not intend to go through with an escrow with them, the Goldsteins promptly deposited with Western Title Company the necessary $82,000.00 to fulfill their part of the option agreement.

an estoppel. If his acts are relied upon there must also be evidence of the principal's knowledge and acquiescence in them.

Contrary to the majority view, appellants have failed to present any evidence of actions on the part of respondent which could be construed as clothing Callahan with the apparent authority to either extend the escrow or renew the option. Indeed, on cross-examination, Callahan testified that he had no authorization to extend the escrow, and that in the event appellants failed to timely comply, Hanna had instructed him to cancel the escrow.[5] Any representations that Callahan made regarding any extension of the escrow or regarding the option

> were merely hearsay, and, however much the (Goldsteins) may have been lured into relying upon them, they did not affect the rights of the (seller).

Tsouras v. Southwest Plumbing & Heating.

I would reject as unmeritorious the claim of equitable estoppel. Hanna failed to take any action, express or implied, that could be construed as clothing Callahan with the necessary authority. It necessarily follows that appellants' reliance was inappropriate, as application of the doctrine of estoppel would require that Hanna know about and acquiesce to any assertion on which the Goldsteins purportedly relied.

I would affirm the judgment of the trial court.

Notes

1. May an imposter cause liability for another on an agency theory? In *Hoddeson v. Koos Bros.*, 47 N.J. Super. 224, 135 A.2d 702 (1957), Mrs. Hoddeson, a customer of a large furniture store, alleged that when she entered the store, she was assisted by a distinguished looking gentleman in a light blue suit, that he took her order for certain furniture, that he accepted her payment in full in cash, and that the furniture was never delivered. The store claimed Mrs. Hoddeson was swindled by an imposter. The trial court dismissed the purchaser's complaint. On appeal, the complaint was reinstated:

> [T]here was evidence that the person whose identity is undisclosed approached Mrs. Hoddeson and her aunt in the store, publicly exhibiting the mannerisms of a salesman; inquired if he could be of service; upon being informed of the type of the articles in which Mrs. Hoddeson was interested, he was not only sufficiently acquainted with their description, but also where in the department they were respectively on display, guiding them without hesitation to the location of the mirror and then to that of the indicated bedroom furniture; he represented that those articles were not then available in stock, which significantly the store records disclosed to be true; his prophetic representation concerning their prospective arrival in stock proved to be prescient, unless he gleaned that information from the price tag; he accurately calculated their true sales prices and openly received the cash. Those activities precisely characteristic of the common experiences and practices in the trade were conspicuously pursued in market overt during a period of 30 to 40 minutes.

---

5. Callahan also testified that customarily brokers are without the authority to extend an escrow.

The point here debated is whether or not the evidence circumstantiates the presence of apparent authority.

Let us hypothesize for the purposes of our present comments that the acting salesman was not in fact an employee of the defendant, yet he behaved and deported himself during the stated period in the business establishment of the defendant in the manner described by the evidence adduced on behalf of the plaintiffs, would the defendant be immune as a matter of law from liability for the plaintiffs' loss? The tincture of estoppel that gives color to instances of apparent authority might in the law operate likewise to preclude a defendant's denial of liability. It matters little whether for immediate purposes we entitle or characterize the principle of law in such cases as 'agency by estoppel' or 'a tortious dereliction of duty owed to an invited customer.' That which we have in mind are the unique occurrences where solely through the lack of the proprietor's reasonable surveillance and supervision an impostor falsely impersonates in the place of business an agent or servant of his. Certainly the proprietor's duty of care and precaution for the safety and security of the customer encompasses more than the diligent observance and removal of banana peels from the aisles. Broadly stated, the duty of the proprietor also encircles the exercise of reasonable care and vigilance to protect the customer from loss occasioned by the deceptions of an apparent salesman. The rule that those who bargain without inquiry with an apparent agent do so at the risk and peril of an absence of the agent's authority has a patently impracticable application to the customers who patronize our modern department stores.

Our concept of the modern law is that where a proprietor of a place of business by his dereliction of duty enables one who is not his agent conspicuously to act as such and ostensibly to transact the proprietor's business with a patron in the establishment, the appearances being of such a character as to lead a person of ordinary prudence and circumspection to believe that the impostor was in truth the proprietor's agent, in such circumstances the law will not permit the proprietor defensively to avail himself of the impostor's lack of authority and thus escape liability for the consequential loss thereby sustained by the customer.

2. It would seem that an entity like a large department store would be virtually helpless to really prevent a skillful impostor from defrauding some customers unless at the turn of the 21st century there is anything different about business practice more than 40 years after the reported opinion. What steps should a store take to help prevent a repeat of what happened to the customer in this case?

D. Inherent Agency Power

Arguably, the principal should not be liable for actions of its agent that are not authorized, because when the agent exceeds his/her authority the agent does not really serve as agent as to those excessive activities. However, between the innocent third party and the innocent principal, the losses caused by the agent's misconduct must be borne. And, the law does not simply split the losses down the middle. How should this difficult decision be reached? Is it conceptually possible for an agent to possess a kind of authority (inherent authority) to do the unauthorized?

Among the difficult cases requiring assessment of damages between two innocent parties, the most difficult cases are those involving undisclosed principals.

Dupuis v. Federal Home Loan Mortgage Corporation

879 F.Supp. 139 (D. Me. 1995)

ORDER ON A STIPULATED RECORD

HORNBY, District Judge.

This case presents the always difficult question of which innocent party must bear the unavoidable consequences of a third party's wrongful acts. Fidelity Guarantee Mortgage Corporation ("Fidelity"), the original lender, caused much of the loss underlying this lawsuit. Fidelity, however, has been adjudged bankrupt and is judgment proof. The loss, therefore, must fall on one of the two innocent parties to this suit, the borrower Margaret Dupuis or the purchaser of her note and mortgage in the secondary market, Federal Home Loan Mortgage Corporation ("FHLMC").

The parties have stipulated the record for purposes of the liability issues in Dupuis's Complaint.

* * *

BACKGROUND

On July 30, 1990, Margaret Dupuis signed a promissory note to Fidelity for $156,000. She secured the note with a mortgage on her home. Dupuis intended to use the loan to repay creditors and finance a new addition to her home. At the closing or soon thereafter, Fidelity disbursed $115,152.44 of the loan to Dupuis or on her behalf. Fidelity and Dupuis agreed that Fidelity would hold $6,000 as a performance escrow and $1,601.88 for a tax and insurance escrow. Fidelity also held back $30,997.56, ostensibly for a home improvement escrow, only $6,000 of which was ever disbursed to Dupuis and $150 of which was disbursed to a private building inspector to inspect the Dupuis property. In fact, no written agreement ever established the escrow, and Fidelity's lawyer simply returned the money to Fidelity on October 10, 1990. Monthly payments were nevertheless calculated as if the entire loan had been paid to Dupuis. After intermittent periods of missed payments and makeups, Dupuis stopped making monthly payments in February, 1992.

On August 9, 1990, without notifying Dupuis, Fidelity assigned the note and mortgage to FHLMC as part of a bulk transfer of loans. FHLMC, in turn, contracted with Fidelity to service the note and mortgage pursuant to the terms of FHLMC's Sellers' and Servicers' Guide. Fidelity serviced the loan until the fall of 1992 when it filed for bankruptcy and ceased operations. Dupuis was unaware of the FHLMC assignment and servicing agreement until then.

Dupuis never received the remaining $24,847.56 home improvement "escrow" or the $6,000 performance escrow.

On occasion, Fidelity failed to pay Dupuis's homeowner's insurance premiums and real estate taxes from the tax and insurance escrow (sometimes but not always the escrow was insufficient) and consistently failed to pay Dupuis any interest on this escrow.

Fidelity persuaded Dupuis to pay a contractor $1,500 out of her own pocket to complete the roof on the addition and agreed to credit Dupuis's loan balance for that amount. Despite the agreement, Fidelity never credited Dupuis's account for the $1,500 she spent.

In July of 1991, vandals damaged Dupuis's swimming pool. In the fall of 1991, Dupuis received an insurance claim check of $5,458 for the damage. Dupuis signed the check over to Fidelity. Fidelity never credited Dupuis's loan for the amount of the check.

Fidelity's actions that Dupuis challenges were all unauthorized and improper under the Sellers' and Servicers' Guide.

On April 21 and May 11, 1993, FHLMC, through its new loan servicer, First Commercial Mortgage Company, notified Dupuis that her note was in default. FHLMC maintains that Dupuis must pay the full amount of the $156,000 note with interest and late charges, even though she never received over $30,000 of the loan and despite Fidelity's failure in servicing the loan to credit her with various items. As of September 22, 1994, the amount due under the note and mortgage, not considering any set-offs, was $223,542.95, with additional interest and late charges continuing to accrue.

BREACH OF CONTRACT (COUNT I)

The stipulated record contains five items that are clear breaches of contract: (1) Fidelity's failure to disburse the entire loan proceeds to Dupuis, (2) Fidelity's failure to pay Dupuis's homeowner's insurance premiums and real estate taxes from the fund escrowed for that purpose, (3) Fidelity's failure to pay interest on the escrowed funds, (4) Fidelity's failure to credit Dupuis's loan $5,458, the amount of the insurance claim check for the vandalized pool, and (5) Fidelity's failure to credit Dupuis's loan the amount she paid to close in the roof. FHLMC does not contend that these are not breaches. Instead, FHLMC argues that it has no responsibility or liability for Fidelity's wrongdoing.

Under both federal common law and Maine law, the Restatement (Second) of Agency provides the governing principles because both the federal courts and the Maine Law Court regularly rely on the Restatements where, as here, no applicable precedents exist.

(a) Agency Principles

The parties agree that Dupuis had no knowledge that FHLMC owned her note and mortgage until after Fidelity's bankruptcy. Thus, the typical arguments in agency cases about "apparent authority" are inapplicable. So far as Dupuis was concerned, Fidelity had no "apparent authority" to act on FHLMC's behalf; to Dupuis's knowledge, Fidelity was all there was. At first glance, that might seem to end the matter. If Dupuis had no knowledge that FHLMC held her note and mortgage, why should she now have any recourse against FHLMC? Why not limit her recourse to (bankrupt) Fidelity? The question cannot be answered as easily as it is asked because FHLMC, for its part, is striving to hold Dupuis liable for amounts far beyond what Fidelity could have collected. It is FHLMC that wants to avoid the defenses and claims Dupuis would have if Fidelity were trying to collect on the note and foreclose the mortgage.

The Restatement (Second) of Agency announces:

> A general agent for an undisclosed principal authorized to conduct transactions subject his principal to liability for acts done on his account, if usual or necessary in such transactions, although forbidden by the principal to do them.

Restatement (Second) of Agency § 194 (1957).[6] A general agent is "an agent authorized to conduct a series of transactions involving a continuity of service." *Id.* § 3(1).

FHLMC was certainly undisclosed so far as Dupuis was concerned. It is pretty obvious, then, that, if Fidelity was a general agent for FHLMC, FHLMC is liable, as an undisclosed principal, for Dupuis's contract claims. All that Restatement section 194 requires in addition is that Fidelity have been authorized to conduct transactions and that Fidelity's actions done on FHLMC's account be "usual or necessary in such transactions." Section 194 makes clear that whether FHLMC authorized or prohibited the specific acts in question is irrelevant. FHLMC hired Fidelity to service loans and mortgages in accordance with the Sellers' and Servicers' Guide, including those of Dupuis. Thus, Fidelity was "authorized to conduct transactions" involved in such servicing. Although FHLMC points to provisions of its Guide which, it argues, prohibited Fidelity from treating the Dupuis loan the way it did, Fidelity's acts—done on FHLMC's account—were "usual or necessary" acts in a servicing relationship. That is true for the withholding of loan proceeds until the servicer is satisfied that the improvements have been suitably completed; the collection and payment of real estate tax and insurance obligations; the payment of interest on escrowed funds; dealing with a casualty loss on the secured premises and allocation of insurance proceeds for the loss; and negotiating with the borrower to improve the premises in exchange for a further disbursement or a credit against the loan due.

FHLMC argues that Fidelity was an independent contractor rather than an agent and has pointed to language in the Guide that servicers are only independent contractors. But that position misperceives the applicable law of agency. A principal/independent contractor relationship is to be distinguished from a master/servant relationship, but an independent contractor can still be an agent. Restatement (Second) of Agency § 2(3). Lawyers appearing in court on behalf of a client are the classic example. Plainly, Fidelity serviced this note and mortgage on behalf of FHLMC and in that respect acted as agent.[7] The real issue is whether

---

6. Dupuis asserted at oral argument that this section only applies to torts and that section 186 applies to contracts. It appears, however, that section 186 applies to the creation of liability on the part of an undisclosed principal for acts done by an agent acting within his authority. Section 194, on the other hand, deals with the creation of liability for unauthorized acts. The stipulated record reveals that the acts in question here were unauthorized.

7. One bankruptcy court has found no agency relationship between FHLMC and a seller of notes like Fidelity. *In re Ellis*, 152 B.R. 211, 217-18 (Bankr.E.D.Tenn. 1993). Ellis did not deal with the servicing relationship, however, but only with the purchase and sale of notes, a subject on which I am in agreement with the bankruptcy court, as reflected in my earlier summary judgment decision. A second court, the Seventh Circuit, observed in *Mendrala v. Crown Mortgage Co.*, 955 F.2d 1132, 1141 (7th Cir. 1992), that a seller of loans to

Fidelity should be treated as a general agent. The Restatement gives two choices: "general agent," which I have already defined (and which produces liability for the undisclosed principal), and "special agent"—"an agent authorized to conduct a single transaction or a series of transactions not involving continuity of service," Restatement § 3(2) (and which results in no liability for the undisclosed principal). The commentary states that the distinction between these two categories is "one of degree." Comment a:

> [T]he number of acts to be performed in accomplishing an authorized result, the number of people to be dealt with, and the length of time needed to accomplish the result are the important considerations. Continuity of service rather than the extent of discretion or responsibility is the hall-mark of the general agent. The point at which one becomes a general agent can not be marked with exactitude. One who is an integral part of a business organization and does not require fresh authorization for each transaction is a general agent.

Applying these criteria, I conclude that Fidelity was a general agent for FHLMC with respect to servicing the loans it sold to FHLMC. A huge number of acts must be performed in servicing a loan and mortgage of many years duration. Although only one debtor needs to be dealt with, there are taxing authorities and insurance companies and, in a case like this, potential lienholders who are performing improvements to the property. The length of time is substantial for most home mortgages—here the mortgage term was thirty years. Although FHLMC has argued that its Sellers' and Servicers' Guide posed very severe limitations on what Fidelity could do, the Restatement commentary makes clear that "continuity of service" is the key, not the "extent of discretion or responsibility." As servicer, Fidelity became an integral part of FHLMC's administration of its secondary mortgage portfolio. Certainly, fresh authorization was not required for each element of the servicing relationship. Moreover, this was not a one-time event for Fidelity and FHLMC. Fidelity sold 221 loans to FHLMC from 1985 until its bankruptcy and was servicing some 109 loans for FHLMC when it was terminated on October 27, 1992.

I conclude, therefore, that under the Restatement (Second) of Agency, Fidelity must be considered a general agent and that FHLMC, as an undisclosed principal, is subject to liability on agency law principles for Fidelity's breaches of contract. I do not profess to understand all the policy reasons for why the Restatement drafters reached their liability conclusion for undisclosed principals from common law developments. The commentary unhelpfully states that the rule is an example of "inherent agency power." Restatement § 194 cmt. a. Restatement § 8 A defines "inherent agency power" as a term used to "indicate the power of an agent which is derived not from authority, apparent authority or Estoppel, but solely from the agency relation and exists for the protection of persons harmed by or dealing with a servant or other agent." Comment a to section 8 A states:

FHLMC "was an 'independent contractor' and 'not [FHLMC's] agent or assignee.'" This statement was made in the context of considering the *Merrill* doctrine that estoppel may not be used against the government. The dictum is broad; it appears, however, that the court did not give close attention to agency law principles and simply accepted the self-serving assertions in the FHLMC Sellers' and Servicers' Guide.

A principle which will explain [the] cases can be found if it is assumed that a power can exist purely as a product of the agency relation. Because such a power is derived solely from the agency relation and is not based upon principles of contracts or torts, the term inherent agency power is used to distinguish it from other powers of an agent which are sustained upon contract or tort theories.

Moreover,

[t]he common law has properly been responsive to the needs of commerce, permitting what older systems of law denied, namely a direct relation between the principal and a third person with whom the agent deals, even when the principal is undisclosed.... It would be unfair for an enterprise to have the benefit of the work of its agents without making it responsible to some extent for their excesses and failures to act carefully.

It seems to be this last factor that justifies the result the Restatement principles produce in this case. As a matter of agency law, it would be unfair for FHLMC to have the benefit of Fidelity's servicing of the note and mortgage without also making FHLMC responsible for Fidelity's excesses and failures. Dupuis always had reason to believe that whatever defaults had been committed by Fidelity could be used by her in defense against any action Fidelity might bring against her. The surprise was FHLMC's appearance, arguing that it was free of the Fidelity albatross.

(b) *Merrill* Doctrine

Despite FHLMC's liability at common law (federal or Maine), I conclude that the *Merrill* doctrine ultimately provides a complete defense to FHLMC on all of Dupuis's contract claims.

In *Federal Crop Ins. Corp. v. Merrill*, 332 U.S. 380, 68 S.Ct. 1, 92 L.Ed. 10 (1947), the United States Supreme Court held that, regardless of the harsh effect on an innocent citizen, an agent representing the Federal Crop Insurance Corporation could not bind the corporation beyond his actual authority. Here, it is undisputed that Fidelity's wrongful acts as an agent were explicitly contrary to and prohibited by FHLMC's Sellers' and Servicers' Guide. Thus, if FHLMC is entitled to *Merrill* protection like the Federal Crop Insurance Corporation in *Merrill*, FHLMC cannot be liable to Dupuis.

The Supreme Court has identified a very broad scope for the *Merrill* doctrine:

Government is not partly public or partly private, depending upon the governmental pedigree of the type of a particular activity or the manner in which the Government conducts it. The Government may carry on its operations through conventional executive agencies or through corporate forms especially created for defined ends. Whatever the form in which the Government functions, anyone entering into an arrangement with the Government takes the risk of having accurately ascertained that he who purports to act for the Government stays within the bounds of his authority.

332 U.S. at 383-84, 68 S.Ct. at 3 (*citation omitted*). FHLMC is one of the forms in which Congress has chosen to function. Congress established FHLMC in

1970 to implement an important government policy, creation of a secondary market for home mortgages. Although initially chartered with many governmental attributes, FHLMC was largely privatized in 1989. Thus, it continues to be a "corporate form [ ]" "especially created" by Congress "for defined ends." Although *Merrill* rejected estoppel principles arising out of apparent authority whereas I have concluded that the issue here is one of inherent (not apparent) authority, the primary factor that drove the conclusion in *Merrill* is equally applicable: Congress's ability to impose limits on what its creations may do. 332 U.S. at 385, 68 S.Ct. at 3-4. Congress established the FHLMC with specific powers, and the FHLMC has within those powers explicitly limited the authority of its agents. *Merrill* directs that a court must observe these limitations. Id.; accord *Mendrala v. Crown Mortgage Co.*, 955 F.2d 1132, 1140-41 (7th Cir. 1992). Although it is undoubtedly hard on Dupuis to subject her to this consequence—especially where she was unaware of FHLMC's involvement—that is the consequence of the *Merrill* principle. Accordingly, I conclude that Dupuis is unable to recover on any of her contract claims against FHLMC for Fidelity's actions.

Notes

1. Restatement section 8A indicates that inherent agency power is *distinct from* actual authority, apparent authority, and estoppel to deny authority, and derives solely from the general agency relationship itself. Consider Restatement Section 161, which states the circumstances in which an agent acting for a disclosed or partially disclosed principal will be liable for unauthorized acts of a general agent:

> 161. Unauthorized Acts of General Agent
>
> A general agent for a disclosed or partially disclosed principal subjects his principal to liability for acts done on his account which usually accompany or a incidental to transactions which the agent is authorized to conduct if, although they are forbidden by the principal, the other party reasonably believes that the agent is authorized to them and has no notice that is not so authorized.

As described above, is not inherent agency power analogous to

> a. the kind of *apparent authority*, discussed in *Hamilton Hauling, Inc. v. GAF Corp.*, that arises by appointing the agent to a position customarily carrying with it certain authority; and

> b. *implied authority*, as discussed in *Mill Street Church of Christ v. Hogan?*

2. A familiar proposition announced by many cases is that, when as between two innocent parties loss must fall upon one of them due to the misconduct of a third party (the agent), the loss should fall upon the one who created the enabling circumstances—the principal. Would you agree with the proposition that this principle is the basis for the outcomes in so many cases involving issues of apparent authority, agency by estoppel, and inherent authority?

3. Judge Learned Hand's opinion in *Kidd v. Thomas A. Edison, Inc.*, 239 f. 405 (S.D.N.Y. 1917), affirmed, 242 F. 923 (2d Cir. 1917) is widely cited as the origin of the doctrine of inherent agency power. In order to sell the Edison

phonograph, Edison conceived the idea of engaging some of the most popular singers to give recitals. The artist would sing, and the same song would be immediately reproduced by the phonograph, giving the audience an opportunity to compare the voice of the phonograph with the voice of the singer.

As a part of his duties as general supervisor of Edison's musical division, Fuller was given general responsibility for arranging the "tone-test" recitals, including authority to contract with the artists. Kidd claimed that Fuller had contracted for Edison to pay her $300 per week from October 15 to April 1, regardless of whether Edison Company booked any recitals. Edison argued Fuller was only authorized to agree to pay singers for those weeks during which she was booked for a recital.

Judge Hand characterized the question as one of apparent authority, but in the course of his opinion gave his views as to when a principal should be bound by an agent's unauthorized acts:

> If estoppel is the basis of all apparent authority, it existed here. Yet the argument involves a misunderstanding of the true significance of the doctrine. It is a fiction to say that the principal is estopped where he has not communicated with the third person and has thus misled him. There are, indeed, the cases of customary authority, which perhaps come within the range of a true estoppel; but in other cases the principal may properly say that the authority he delegated must be judged by his directions, taken together, and that it is unfair to charge him with misleading the public because his agent, in executing that authority, neither observed nor communicated an important part of his directions. Certainly it begs the question to assume that the principal has authorized his agent to communicate a part of his authority and not to disclose the rest.
>
> The considerations which have made the rule survive are apparent. If a man selects another to act for him with some discretion, he has by that fact vouched to some extent for his reliability. While it may not be fair to impose upon him the results of a total departure from the general subject of his confidence, the detailed execution of his mandate stands on a different footing. The very purpose of delegated authority is to avoid constant recourse by third persons to the principal, which would be a corollary of denying the agent any latitude beyond his exact instructions. Once a third person has assured himself widely of the character of the agent's mandate, the purpose of the relation demands the possibility of the principal's being bound through the agent's minor deviations.
>
> In the case at bar, there was no question of fact for the jury touching the scope of Fuller's authority. His general business covered the whole of the tone-test recitals; on him was charged the duty of doing everything necessary in the premises, without recourse to anyone else. It would certainly have been quite contrary to the expectations of the defendant if any of the prospective performers at the recitals had insisted on verifying directly with Maxwell the terms of his contract. It was precisely to delegate such negotiations to a competent substitute that they chose Fuller at all.

4. In *Kidd v. Thomas A. Edison, Inc.* (note 3 above), Judge Hand state that principal are accountable for "the agent's minor deviations." A major complication in deciding cases of possible inherent authority is that its analysis is engulfed

by the fog of the details about the degree of the agent's deviation. The more substantial the deviation, the more likely the misconduct was outside the boundaries of the agent's inherent authority.

5. Consider the following extract from *In re Hunt's Pier Associates,* 154 B.R. 436, 447-49 (U.S. Bankr., E.D. Pa. 1993), *aff'd,* 162 B.R. 442 (U.S. Dist. Ct., E.D. Pa. 1993):

> [I]f an agent discloses his principal and acts within his authority, suit can be brought only against the principal. If the agent does not disclose his principal and purports to be acting for himself, the third person, upon ascertaining the principal-agent relationship, has an alternative remedy, *i.e.,* he may elect to hold the agent personally liable, or he may sue the principal...

Moss v. Jones, 93 N.J.Super. 179, 183, 225 A.2d 369, 371 (App. Div. 1966).

We must observe that, in one respect, we find the legal analysis... to be wanting. It argues that *[the Agent]* was imbued with "apparent authority" to enter into contractual relations with the [Third Person]. However, in order to establish that apparent authority existed, the [Third Person] was obliged to prove that (1) the [Principal] made representations or exhibited conduct, (2) which was relied upon by the [Third Person], and that (3) such reliance was reasonable under the circumstances.

However, from the evidence before us, it is quite clear that the [Principal] did not exhibit conduct or make any representations that [the Agent] was its agent, or that [the Agent] was imbued with any type of authority. [The Third Person] never met, or even spoke, with [the Principal] during the performance of his duties. He firmly believed that [the Agent] was the owner, and he claimed to have never known of the [Principal]'s existence during the course of his business dealings with [the Agent]. Hence, the [Third Person]'s reliance on [the Agent's] authority to act for the [Principal] was not based upon the representations or conduct by the [Principal], but was derived from the acts, conduct, and representations of [the Agent], and from the agency relationship between the [Principal] and [the Agent] itself. Hence, "apparent authority" of [the Agent] to act for the [Principal] in his dealings with the [Third Person] was not present.

However, as the RESTATEMENT (SECOND) OF AGENCY, § 194, Comment *a,* at 430 (1958) ("the Restatement"), thusly makes clear, this factor is not decisive in favor of the [Principal]:

> *a.* Since apparent authority is the power which results from acts which appear to the third person to be authorized by the principal, if such person does not know of the existence of a principal there can be no apparent authority. Hence, the liability of the principal is not derived from the exercise of apparent authority by the agent. There may be, however, an apparent ownership, and from this there may be a power to affect the interests of the principal aside from any rule of agency. The rule stated in this Section is a companion to that stated in Section 161 (disclosed or

partially disclosed principals) and the Comments to that Section are applicable. Both rules are examples of inherent agency power.

The Restatement, at §§ 194, 195, thusly recites the rules of law, consistent with the New Jersey cases, which controls this dispute:

§ 194. Acts of General Agents

A general agent for an undisclosed principal authorized to conduct transactions subjects his principal to liability for acts done on his account, if usual or necessary in such transactions, although forbidden by the principal to do them.

§ 195. Acts of Manager Appearing to be Owner

An undisclosed principal who entrusts an agent with the management of his business is subject to liability to third persons with whom the agent enters into transactions usual in such businesses and on the principal's account, although contrary to the directions of the principal.

[The Agent] was placed to the position of a "manager appearing to be the owner" of [a business] by [the Principal]. The transactions of [the Agent] with the [Third Person] were "usual" for the [Principal] in the sense that they were necessary and foreseeable to effect [the Agent]'s expressly-authorized [transactions]. [The Agent's] deviations from the authority which he was given to manage the [business] were neither knowable nor foreseeable on the part of the [Third Person]. Therefore, they are insufficient to shield the [Principal] from liability for the [Third Person]'s services.[2]

Problem 5.4

Spears was employed by Zanac, Inc. as Assistant Manager of Seven Steers, a restaurant owned and operated by Zanac. As Assistant Manager, Spears was authorized, not only to take deliveries of supplies, and to hire and to fire waitresses, busboys and other employees, but also "to do other things that had to be done" at the restaurant.

When the restaurant's neon sign broke, the president of Zanac instructed Spears to "to price out the job" to obtain bids for the repair of the sign. When

---

2. We note the following Illustrations from the Restatement, at 431-32, which support the conclusions that the [Principal] is liable to the [Third Person]:

1. P employs A to manage his public house, directing A to represent that he is the owner, and to purchase no goods for the business except ales and bottled water, all other goods to be supplied by P. A purchases cigars from T for the business. P is subject to liability to T for the price of the cigars.

2. P employs A to manage his transfer business, permitting A to appear as the owner. He directs A to make no settlements with patrons of losses in excess of twenty dollars, until after consultation with him. T claims that he has suffered a loss by the negligence of one of the expressmen and A agrees, without consultation with P, to reimburse T by payment of $50. P is subject to liability upon the agreement.

Spears got Frazier's bid, he told Frazier that he'd have to get the approval of Zakas, Zanac's president. Three days later, Spears called Frazier, and told him, "Zakas said it was all right. Go ahead and repair the sign."

Frazier did the work, and submitted an invoice in the agreed amount. Zanac refused to pay. Zakas acknowledged gave Spears permission to get bids, but denied giving him permission "to spend my money" to contract for the work.

1. What would be the basis for. holding that Spears had agency power to bind Zanac to the contract to repair the neon signs? Does it arise from Spears' authority to solicit bids? Does it arise from Spears' position as "assistant manager"?

2. If on one hot July day Spears ordered the installation of central air conditioning in the restaurant, would Zanac be liable for it? What if Spears instead ordered ten fans at a cost of $495?

Note on Zanac Inc. v. Frazier Neon Signs Inc.

In *Zanac Inc. v. Frazier Neon Signs Inc.*, 134 Ga. App. 501, 215 S.E.2d 265 (1975), on which Problem 5.4 is based, the court found that Spears had inherent agency power to bind Zanac. The court reasoned that:

> We are not dealing with apparent authority in this case, since Zanac at no time manifested to Frazier that Spears was authorized to contract for the services rendered. *See* Restatement 2d, Agency, § 8 (1958). Nor may Spears' authority to contract be inferred from his authority to solicit bids for the job. *See* Restatement 2d, Agency, § 50 (1958). And it is questionable whether Spears' authority as an "assistant manager" included authority to "make contracts which are incidental to such business or are reasonably necessary in conducting it," or to make reasonable repairs, since Zanac's president stated that he specifically forbade such an expenditure unless it was an emergency. *See* Restatement 2d, Agency, § 73(a) & (b) (1958).

> Nevertheless, even without express, apparent or inferred authority, Spears, as the general agent for a partially disclosed principal, may bind the principal under his inherent agency powers. *See* Restatement (Second) of Agency, §§ 8A, 161. The latter section states:

>> A general agent for a disclosed or partially disclosed principal subjects his principal to liability for acts done on his account which usually accompany or are incidental to transactions which the agent is authorized to conduct if, although they are forbidden by the principal, the other party reasonably believes that the agent is authorized to do them and has no notice that he is not so authorized.

> Georgia courts have used the terms "apparent," "incidental," "implied" and "inferred" authority, interchangeably, without regard to their distinctions as noted in the Restatement (Second). Because of these vagaries, it is difficult to formulate a general rule governing authority of a general agent to make contracts, except to say that Georgia statute and

case law appear to be in accord with the Restatement, § 161, quoted above. In the present case we find there is sufficient evidence to support the trial court's conclusion that Spears had authority to enter into the contract and that same is binding on Zanac.

Additional Problems

5.5 In April 1975, the plaintiff, who was then a seventeen-year-old minor, saw a 1969 Chevrolet automobile on the defendant, Netzley's, used-car lot in which he became interested. He had three meetings with the defendant's salesman before consummating the purchase. The plaintiff's father, the third-party defendant, accompanied his son to the second meeting, test-drove the car, and discussed its price and condition with both his son and the salesman. The plaintiff returned alone for his third trip to the car lot a few days later and told the salesman that he had decided to buy and had money to do so. When the salesman requested that the plaintiff sign the contract to purchase, the plaintiff told him he did not believe he could do so because he was only seventeen years old and not of age, but when the salesman assured him that made no difference, the plaintiff signed the contract and paid the $1234.50 purchase price with a check received from his mother drawn on a joint account with his father. The plaintiff testified that this sum was a loan that he was to repay from the sale of a 1969 Volkswagen owned by him, though titled in his father's name. Although the sales contract and other supporting documents made out by defendant were directed to plaintiff alone as buyer, title to the car was subsequently taken in the names of both the father and son, and the father also obtained insurance on it in both their names. The father testified that the car belonged to his son; that he and his wife had loaned the money to him, as they had to other of their children, for that purpose; and that he insured it and caused hi name to be on the title only for convenience and security reasons. As sometimes happens, shortly after the sale a rod bearing gave out on the causing substantial damage to its engine. This occurred on the single occasion that the plaintiff's father had driven the car after its purchase. When the plaintiff sought to have the defendant repair the damages, he was told by the defendant that the car was purchased "as is" under the contract and carried no warranty for repair purposes. The plaintiff then elected to rescind the contract and tendered the automobile back to the defendant, demanding return of the purchase price. The defendant refused, and the plaintiff filed his complaint for rescission of contract based on his minority. The defendant counterclaimed against the plaintiff for recoupment of his loss or damages while the automobile was in the plaintiff's possession and also filed a third-party complaint against the plaintiff's father, seeking indemnification from him for any sums the defendant might have to pay to the plaintiff in the principal action. The third-party action appears to be based on alternative theories that the father and the son were engaged in a joint venture or that the son purchased the car as the father's agent. Did the son act as the father's agent under these circumstances? (*See Weisbrook v. Clyde C. Netzley, Inc.*, 58 Ill.App.3d 862, 374 N.E.2d 1102 (1978).)

5.6. Palmer was planning to establish a dealership to sell farm machinery. He hired Adams to organize and operate the business. Adams was expressly authorized to collect for machinery sold and to hire and discharge office help, mechanics, and sales people but was expressly forbidden to borrow any money on Palmer's credit. Palmer supplied the money to establish a bank account in the local bank. The account was in Palmer's name, but Adams had authority to write checks on the account. From time to time, the account was overdrawn by Adams, but Palmer had no knowledge or notice of the overdrafts. On each occasion, Adams made deposits to cover the overdraft. Subsequently, Palmer discharged Adams and learned for the first time that the account was overdrawn $2000. The bank brought an action to recover the amount of the overdraft from Palmer. May the bank recover? Give reasons. (Illinois Bar Examination, July 1976.)

5.7. Homer Hope, the owner of Red Acres, mailed a letter to Ralph Bookman, a real estate broker. Following is the material portion of the letter: "I have owned Red Acres for many years and I am thinking of selling this property. I have never met you, but a friend has advised that you are an industrious and honest real estate broker. I therefore employ you to find a purchaser for Red Acres at a price of $35,000." Ten days after receiving the letter, Bookman mailed the following letter to Hope: "Acting pursuant to your recent letter requesting me to find a purchaser for Red Acres, this is to advise that I have sold Red Acres to Joshua Redman for $35,500. I enclose your copy of the contract of sale signed by Redman. Your name was signed to the contract by me as your agent, and I also signed my name as agent for you. As you will note, the contract is very simple and merely provides that you agree to sell and Redman agrees to buy Red Acres for $35,000, the sale to be consummated within a reasonable time from this date." Hope believes he can obtain a much higher price for his property and consults you, showing you the two letters and inquiring whether he is obligated to convey Red Acres to Redman. What would you advise? Give reasons. (Illinois Bar Examination, July 1974.)

5.8. X Grocery Company, operator of a store, had employed Smith as manager of its retail outlet. Smith had been given authority from X Grocery Company to purchase supplies and good for resale and had conducted business for several years with Jones Company. Purchases by Smith from Jones Company had been limited to groceries. Smith then contacted Jones Company and had it deliver a television set to his home, advising Jones Company that the set was to be used in promotional advertising, the object of which was to increase X Grocery Company's business. The advertising did not develop. Smith disappeared from the area, taking the television set with him. Jones Company sued X Grocery Company for the purchase price of the set. What decision? Give reasons. (Illinois Bar Examination, Mar. 1967.)

5.9. Jess Higgins was authorized, under an agreement in writing with Tom Smith, to contract for the drilling of an oil well. In the agreement, the amount to be paid for the drilling was left blank. Higgins, without waiting for the insertion of the amount, went to Don Bittner, a well driller, showed his written authority to him, and contracted with him on behalf of Smith for the drilling of a well. When the drilling was completed, it proved to be a dry hole. Subsequently, Tom Smith refused to pay for the drilling of the well. As a result, Bittner brought an appropriate action against Smith to recover for the services performed. What mistakes did Smith make here? How could the document have been better drafted? Who will win the suit, and why? (Illinois Bar Examination, March 1960)

E. Special Topics

1. Introduction

Page 445

Up until now, we have focused on principals' liability *in contract* for authorized, and certain unauthorized, acts by their agents. This Section sets forth some closely related areas in which principals may be held liable, often *in tort*, for certain acts within their agents' actual or apparent authority.

2. Liability for Representations by Agents

Problem 5.10

Agent showed Purchasers a property that Sellers had listed with Agent for sale. The property had been damaged by fire. According to Purchasers, Agent told them it had been reconstructed and brought "totally up to code." Purchasers claim that Agent also told them there was a written appraisal on the property for $220,000. Following negotiations, Purchasers bought the property for $160,000 on January 18, 1980. Purchasers later discovered that the property did not comply with the building code, and that there was no written appraisal of $220,000. Purchasers returned the property to Sellers, who thereafter sold it to a third party. Are Sellers responsible for Agent's misrepresentations? If they are, may they recover from Agent? See *Dyer v. Johnson,* 757 P.2d 178 (Colo. App. 1988).

Cange v. Stotler & Co., Inc.
826 F.2d 581 (7th Cir. 1987)

CUMMINGS, Circuit Judge.

Plaintiff has sued defendant Stotler and Company, a futures commission merchant ("FCM"), to recover for "fraudulent and unauthorized trades for gold and silver futures contracts" charged to plaintiff's account with defendant. The complaint alleges misconduct of Dwight Wilson and Wilpadco, Inc., purportedly agents of defendant. Wilpadco was said to be wholly controlled by Wilson.

According to the complaint and plaintiff's affidavit filed in opposition to the motion to dismiss, plaintiff opened an account with defendant Stotler and Company through its agent Wilson and his company Wilpadco in early 1981 when a Stotler and Company Customer's Agreement was signed by one of defendant's partners and plaintiff. During four weeks in September 1982, nine unauthorized trades for the sale and purchase of gold and silver futures were charged to plaintiff's account with defendant, causing him losses of $59,150. These transactions were conducted by Wilson and Wilpadco, with commissions going to defendant. Plaintiff contends that he never traded in gold and silver futures. Wilson on his own initiative allegedly called plaintiff and told him of the first few trades and said they would be reversed since they were defendant Stotler and Company's mistakes. Plaintiff then discovered more unauthorized trades on his statement from defendant and in September and October 1982 notified Wilson who again told him that the trades were defendant's mistakes and would be reversed. The losses from the unauthorized trades remained on later statements but Wilson reassured him that defendant would refund the losses from those trades and later that the trades had in fact been reversed out but that plaintiff was misreading the statements.

When plaintiff's accountant discovered in August 1983 that the unauthorized trades still had not been reversed out, plaintiff wrote a letter to defendant requesting reimbursement and had that letter hand-delivered to Wilson. Allegedly, Wilson admitted that the trades were unauthorized and in late August 1983 he and Wilpadco apparently arranged for $15,483.21 to be transferred to plaintiff's account with defendant. Wilson also orally agreed to pay $5,000 a month into plaintiff's account with defendant to reimburse the remaining amount owed to plaintiff. When Wilson failed to make the September and October payments, plaintiff in November 1983 had Wilson sign an agreement to reimburse the rest of the charges plus interest in monthly payments of $1,000, with the first due on December 1, 1983. Wilson and Wilpadco are said to have acted with "express, implied or apparent authority" of defendant, and none of the three has made any subsequent payments to plaintiff.

The complaint charges violations of the [federal] Commodity Exchange Act, common law fraud, breach of fiduciary duty, violations of the Illinois Consumer Fraud and Deceptive Business Practices Act, and breach of the repayment agreement.

Prior to answering the complaint, defendant filed a motion to dismiss, relying on a one-year limitation clause in paragraph 14 of the Customer's Agreement with plaintiff.

The district court here erred in holding that defendant could not be estopped from asserting the limitation period due to defendant's lack of knowledge of or participation in its independent agent's conduct. Defendant admits that for purposes of this motion to dismiss or summary judgment motion Wilson must be assumed to be the agent of Stotler and Company, as the complaint alleges, and in fact there is much evidence to support the existence of an agency relationship: Wilson handled plaintiff's account with Stotler and Company; the Customer Agreement he gave plaintiff had Stotler and Company's name on it; the trades he executed on plaintiff's account were reflected on Stotler and Company confirmation slips and account statements; and Stotler and Company received commissions for executing the trades.

Plaintiff's first six counts are solely based on his losses from the alleged unauthorized trades made in violation of federal and state statutes and common law. The Commodity Exchange Act prohibits the cheating or defrauding of investors, and the knowing and deliberate execution of unauthorized trades, even if not done out of an evil motive or intent to injure the customer, violates that prohibition. The unauthorized trades were made through plaintiff's account with defendant by defendant's agent in charge of that account and presumably were acts within the scope of Wilson's agency with Stotler and Company. The fact that the agent's actions were illegal and fraudulent does not relieve the FCM, as the agent's principal, of civil liability under the vicarious liability principles [of the Commodity Exchange Act]. Nor does it matter that the FCM had no prior knowledge of the illegal acts and did not take commissions from the defrauded customer or otherwise benefit financially from the illegal acts.

The unauthorized trades by Wilson could be found to be within the scope of his agency with Stotler and Company and so too could his conduct that is alleged to have caused plaintiff not to file suit within the one-year limitations period. Wilson's acknowledgments that the trades were unauthorized and that plaintiff's correct account balance was different from that sworn on the account statements prepared by Stotler and Company could be found to be within the scope of his agency with Stotler and Company. For example, in a reparations case brought by a customer challenging unauthorized trades that an FCM's agent made, the Commodity Futures Trading Commission decided that the agent's admissions to the customer concerning the unauthorized nature of the trades, the consequent inaccuracies in the account statements issued by the FCM, and the amount owed, as reflected in a promissory note signed by the agent, were admissible against the FCM. The Commission reasoned that

> since the reporting of equity balances is a matter generally within the scope of an account executive's agency, his statements relating to the amount in complainant's accounts are admissible against [the FCM]

to prove the FCM's liability for the losses. *Stoller v. Siegel Trading Co.*, Comm. Fut. L. Rep. (CCH) & 22,224, at 29,204 (CFTC June 6, 1984).

Wilson's promises to plaintiff that the losses from the unauthorized trades would be refunded could also be found to be acts within the scope of his agency with defendant and, as such, would be admissible to estop defendant's assertion of a limitations defense. A customer has an "absolute right not to incur liability for any trade not authorized by him." The failure of the FCM's agent to inform the customer of this absolute right to a refund can defeat the FCM's otherwise valid defense, based on a customer's untimely request for a refund, that the customer ratified the trade. Because the FCM or its agent must ensure that the customer understands the right to a refund, it is expectable that when unauthorized trades occur, the FCM's agent handling the account will tell the customer that the losses from any unauthorized trades will be refunded and statements and promises to that effect could certainly be within the scope of the agency.

Here the trier of fact could find that Wilson's statements of the "correct" account balance and his promises of a refund for the unauthorized trades were acts within the scope of the inherent agency power of a person like Wilson handling a customer's account for an FCM. *See* Restatement (Second) of Agency §§ 8A, 161 (1958). Stotler and Company allowed Wilson to act as its agent in handling plaintiff's account, and absent proof that Stotler and Company informed plaintiff that Wilson would not have the customary power of a person in a similar agency relationship, the defendant is bound by the acts of its agent no matter its secret limitations to the contrary. This Court has before observed that

> [t]he powers of an agent are, prima facia, coextensive with the business intrusted to his care, and will not be narrowed by limitations not communicated to the person with whom he deals.

Lumbermen's Mut. Ins. Co. v. Slide Rule & Scale Eng'g Co., 177 F.2d 305, 309 (7th Cir. 1949). Judge Learned Hand articulated this concept of inherent agency power when he upheld a jury verdict for plaintiff based on a contract the jury found to be an unconditional engagement for a singing tour despite the principal's instructions to its agent to engage the singer only for such recitals as he could later persuade record dealers to book her for, instructions which were not told to plaintiff. *Kidd v. Thomas A. Edison, Inc.*, 239 F. 405 (S.D.N.Y. 1917), affirmed, 242 F. 923 (2d Cir. 1917). He reasoned that the scope of an agency must be measured

> not alone by the words in which it is created, but by the whole setting in which those words are used, including the customary powers of such agents

and thus the contract was enforceable because

> the customary implication would seem to have been that [the agent's] authority was without limitation of the kind here imposed.

The principal benefits from the existence of inherent authority because

> [t]he very purpose of delegated authority is to avoid constant recourse by third persons to the principal, which would be a corollary of denying the agent any latitude beyond his exact instructions.

The trier of fact could find that it is within the customary authority of an FCM's agent handling a customer's account to make statements of the account's correct balance and to promise refunds for losses from unauthorized trades. Thus the plaintiff's reliance on those statements and promises, notwithstanding contrary figures listed on the account statement issued by Stotler and Company, could be found to be reasonable. As such, the plaintiff's failure to bring suit within the one-year limitations period could be found to be attributable to Wilson's statements, and Stotler and Company would be estopped from asserting the bar of the limitations period. Here there were triable issues of fact regarding whether Wilson's acts dissuading plaintiff from timely bringing suit were within the scope of Wilson's agency with defendant and therefore summary judgment should have been denied on the first six counts.

Defendant argues that Wilson lacked the "apparent authority" for his actions to estop Stotler and Company from asserting the bar of the limitations period. First, defendant argues that plaintiff has failed to show "a single action on Stotler's part to create apparent authority" of Wilson but plaintiff need not prove any actions on Stotler and Company's part besides its allowing Wilson to act as its agent for handling plaintiff's account because the trier of fact could find Wilson's statements within his inherent authority. Representations of the principal to the third party are central for defining apparent authority, but in contrast, inherent authority originates from the customary authority of a person in the particular type of agency relationship and no representations beyond the fact of the existence of the agency need be shown. *See* Restatement (Second) of Agency § 161 comment b (1958). *Compare id.* at § 8 *with id.* at § 8A. *See generally id.* at §§ 194-195 (inherent agency power can subject undisclosed principal to liability for acts of his or her agent).[8] Plaintiff has provided evidence of the existence of the agency and it is a triable issue of fact whether the acts fall within such an agent's customary authority; therefore, this first argument is meritless.

---

8. Inherent authority not only can differ from apparent authority but also from actual authority. Unlike actual authority, inherent authority cannot be limited by secret instructions to an agent restricting his or her customary authority. Kidd v. Thomas A. Edison, Inc., 239 F. at 406; see Restatement (Second) of Agency 8A, 161 comment b (1958).

Notes

1. In Chapter 10, we will study *respondeat superior*, the liability of a master for torts committed by a servant in the scope of his or her employment. As we will see, *respondeat superior* is largely based on the master's right to control the servant's physical conduct in the performance of the work assigned to the servant. Is the principal's liability in *Dyer v. Johnson* based on *respondeat superior*? That is, is the principal liable because of the right to control the agent's physical conduct?

2. What is the relevance of the agent's *authority or apparent authority* to make the misrepresentation? Is the liability of the principal based on the principal's fault?

3. Consider the following extract from *Dyer v. Johnson,* 757 P.2d 178 (Colo. App. 1988), in which sellers of a house were held liable for misrepresentations by the selling agent:

> Generally, a principal may not be bound by the false representations of his agent made without his knowledge, consent, or authority. However, an exception to this rule exists if an agent has apparent authority to make a representation, the question whether such authority existed being one of fact. A principal may be held liable for the tortious conduct of an agent if the conduct was within the scope of employment. An agent is acting within the scope of employment if he is doing what is necessarily incidental to the work that has been assigned to him or which is customarily within the business in which the employee is engaged.

> In *Byrn v. Walker,* 275 S.C. 83, 267 S.E.2d 601 (S.C. 1980), the court reached a similar result, reasoning that:

>> If the representations are made by the agent as a part of the negotiation for the purpose of bringing about the sale, and by means of this it is brought about, the conveyance made, and the proceeds of the sale received, this brings the case within the general rule that a principal is responsible for such acts of his agent as are done within the scope of his authority, whether authorized or not, except by the general authority to do the principal act.

> The agent's misrepresentations at issue here, and the context in which they were made, were such that the trial court properly held Sellers liable for them.

> [We] agree with Sellers that the trial court erred in not requiring the agent and broker to indemnify them fully for the damages awarded to Purchasers. The damage award against Sellers was for $34,000. The basis of Sellers' liability was the acts of the agent and broker leading to application of the doctrine of respondeat superior; thus, we conclude the trial court erred in not entering judgment against the agent and broker for the full amount of the judgment against Sellers.

> The judgment in favor of Purchasers is affirmed. The judgment on the cross-claim is reversed and the cause is remanded with directions to award Sellers a judgment against the broker and agent for the full amount of the judgment entered against Sellers in favor of Purchasers.

4. Under Restatement section 383,

an agent is subject to a duty to the principal not to act in the principal's affairs except in accordance with the principal's manifestations of consent.

The acts which violate an agent's duty to act only as authorized include commission of a tort or crime—such as misrepresentation—for which the principal is held liable.

5. Under Restatement section 401, agents are liable to their principals for damages resulting from breaches of duties owed to the principal.

3. Agent Diversion of Funds

Problem 5.11

Lawyer is a trial lawyer employed by Firm, which, through its lawyers, is engaged in the practice of law, specializing in general civil litigation. Lawyer is senior enough that Lawyer has the authority to accept new cases on behalf of the Firm.

Client hired Lawyer to represent her in a suit against Defendant. Even though Firm policy required only a $1,500 retainer before accepting a new case, Lawyer asked for a $5,000 retainer. When Client asked how to fill out the check, Lawyer said that the Firm would stamp its name in as payee, so Client should leave the payee blank.

Unknown to Client, Lawyer was planning to leave the Firm, and didn't want Firm to know about Client's suit. Lawyer filled in the check by putting Lawyer's own name as the name of the payee. Lawyer then deposited the check in his personal bank account. Lawyer used the $5,000 to finalize the arrangements for Lawyer's new office by paying the first-month rent and security deposit. As Lawyer was driving home from signing the lease, Lawyer was killed in a car accident.

When Client inquired of the Firm about the status of the case, the Firm told her that it could not start work until Client had paid the $1,500 retainer. Client objected that Client had already paid a $5,000. May the Firm require Client to pay the $1,500 retainer that the Firm never received? If not, is the Firm also subject to liability to Client for the additional $3,500 demanded by Lawyer solely for Lawyer's own purposes?

Entente Mineral Co. v. Parker
956 F. 2d 524 (5th Cir. 1992)

THORNBERRY, Circuit Judge:

This is an appeal from a directed verdict. The defendant-appellee law firm was sued for vicarious liability. The district court directed a verdict in favor of the firm, concluding as a matter of law that the jury could not find vicarious liability. The plaintiff-appellant, Entente, appeals the district court's directed verdict.

In February 1987, H.B. Sneed ("Sneed"), a petroleum landman employed by Entente Mineral Company ("Entente"), negotiated with McKinley Young ("Young") to purchase one-half of Young's royalty interest in certain property. On February 23, Young and Sneed orally agreed that Entente would purchase one-half of Young's interest for $25,000. Sneed then presented a $25,000 draft and a royalty deed to Young. Young, who does not read well if at all, stated that he wanted his banker, Bruce Edwards ("Edwards")[,] to review the deed to ensure that it accurately reflected the terms of the oral agreement. Young and Sneed took the deed to Edwards, who suggested that Young's attorneys at the firm of Barrett, Barrett, Barrett, and Patton ("the firm") review the deed. Edwards telephoned Derek Parker, a partner in the firm, and arranged for Sneed and Young to meet with Parker.

That afternoon, Sneed and Young drove to the firm and met with Parker. Parker reviewed the deed and told Young that the deed reflected the terms and conditions of the oral agreement. He also advised Young that before signing the deed, he should have a title search performed to guarantee that he owned a one-sixteenth royalty, the one-half of one-sixteenth that he intended to sell to Entente and the one-half of one-sixteenth that he intended to retain. Young then asked Parker to perform the title search. Parker instructed Sneed and Young to return the next day at one o'clock p.m. to close the deal. Sneed left the royalty deed and the $25,000 draft with Parker.

After Sneed and Young left the firm, Parker telephoned his brother, who was an oil and gas lease and royalty speculator. Parker asked his brother whether he knew about a well being drilled on Young's property. After doing some research, Parker's brother informed him that the well looked promising and that he would provide financing to Parker if he attempted to purchase the royalty from Young. Parker's brother suggested offering Young $30,000 for the one-half royalty. Parker replied that he did not want to pay $30,000 and that he could probably buy it for $27,000. Later that day, Parker asked his partner Pat Barrett, Jr. whether he thought there was anything wrong with a lawyer's purchasing mineral interests from a client, and Barrett replied that he did not see anything wrong with it.

The following morning, Parker called Edwards and told him that he knew of someone who could make Young a better offer. He asked Edwards to have Young contact him. Young returned Parker's call and the two agreed to meet that afternoon at Edwards's bank. Once at the bank, Parker informed Young that he wanted to purchase the one-half royalty for $27,000. Young agreed, and they executed the same deed that Sneed had prepared except that Parker's name appeared in the Grantee blank.

When Sneed arrived at the firm, prepared to close the sale, he was informed that Young had received a better offer for the one-half royalty. Sneed asked who purchased the one-half royalty but was not given an answer. Eventually, Sneed discovered from the officially recorded deed that Parker had purchased the one-half royalty.

Entente sued Parker and the firm in federal district court based on diversity jurisdiction. Entente asserted that Parker's actions constituted tortious interference with business relations and contract in violation of Mississippi law, and that the firm was vicariously liable for Parker's tortious conduct. The court held a jury trial. At the close of Entente's evidence, the firm moved for a directed verdict on the ground that Parker's purchase of the royalty was not within the scope of

D⁴ Not w/in scope of employment.

[handwritten margin note: TCf: Agreed Not w/i scope or employment]

his employment, and hence, the firm could not be vicariously liable for any tort he may have committed in purchasing the royalty. The district court concluded that Parker had not been acting within the scope of his employment when he purchased the royalty and granted the firm's motion for directed verdict. Entente now appeals the district court's grant of the firm's motion for directed verdict.

Mississippi law applies in this diversity case. Accordingly, the law firm's vicarious liability for Parker's conduct is assessed under agency principles.

Section 219 of the Restatement (Second) of Agency discusses the circumstances in which a master is liable for the torts of his servant. Subsection (1) of § 219 provides that a master is vicariously liable for the torts of his servant that are committed within the scope of employment. Restatement (Second) of Agency § 219(1) (1958). Section 228 of the Restatement requires that, in order to be within the scope of employment, the [servant's] conduct must be actuated, at least in part, by a purpose to serve the master.

Subsection (2) of § 219 lists four situations in which conduct that fails to satisfy the "within the scope of employment" test found in § 228, may still provide a basis for imposing vicarious liability. Subsection (2) provides in part that

> A master is not subject to liability for the torts of his servants acting outside the scope of employment, unless:
>
> > (d) the servant purported to act or to speak on behalf of the principal and there was reliance upon apparent authority, or he was aided in accomplishing the tort by the existence of the agency relation.

[handwritten margin note: Master liable if it aided in accomplishing the tort.]

Thus, under the Restatement, a [master] is liable for the torts of his [servant] if the [servant] commits the tort while acting within the scope of his employment as defined by § 228, or if § 219(2) applies. The situations listed in § 219(2) are not necessarily exceptions to the scope of employment doctrine, but rather situations in which courts have decided to impose liability on the principal or employer even if the agent's conduct does not meet all of the traditional "within the scope of employment" criteria.

Section 261 is an extension of § 219(2)(d), and states that

[handwritten margin note: Master liable if enables agent.]

> A principal who puts a servant or other agent in a position which enables the agent, while apparently acting within his authority, to commit a fraud upon third persons is subject to liability to such third persons for the fraud.

Comment a to § 261 states that

> The principal is subject to liability under the rule stated in this section although he is entirely innocent, has received no benefit from the transaction, and as stated in Section 262, although the agent acted solely for his own purposes.

[handwritten margin note: even though innocent, no benefit, and though agent acted for own purpose]

Unlike § 228, § 261 assesses vicarious liability even though the agent[/servant's] conduct was not actuated by a purpose to serve the principal[/master]. Although Mississippi case law has not expressly differentiated between the two types of vicarious liability found in § 219(1) and § 219(2) of the Restatement, the distinction is implicit. Hence, cases imposing liability under the theory embraced by § 219(1) and defined in § 228, require the agent's conduct to be for the principal's purposes; while other cases, under the theory embodied in §§ 219(2)(d) and 261, allow liability even when an agent acts solely for his own purposes.

Recognizing the distinction between the types of liability, we first address whether Parker's purchase of the royalty was within the scope of his employment as defined by § 228, and second whether the firm can be held liable under the theory delineated in § 261.

1. *Was Parker's Conduct Within the Scope of His Employment?*

The district court concluded that Parker's purchase of the royalty from Young was an "abandonment of employment" and, therefore, not within the scope of his employment with the firm. Entente does not dispute that the firm is not in the business of buying minerals or that the firm received no gain from Parker's purchase of the royalty. Instead, Entente asserts that the district court improperly focused on the last event, the purchase itself, and that if the transaction is viewed in the proper context, Parker's conduct satisfies each element of § 228.

In essence, Entente contends that Parker purchased the royalty while acting as Young's attorney, and was motivated by the firm's purposes both when he agreed to meet with Young, a longstanding client, and when he agreed to perform the title search. Entente maintains that Parker's conduct, from the time he agreed to meet with Young to the time he purchased the royalty, is only one series of conduct that cannot be separated into distinct acts; in Entente's words, Parker's "legal engagement could not be turned on and off."

Entente would have us hold that once Parker began representing Young pursuant to the firm's purposes, no deviation from the firm's purpose could take him outside the scope of his employment. Such a holding would violate the well established rule that if an employee who is delegated to perform certain work for his employer steps or turns aside from his master's work or business to serve some purpose of his own, not connected with the employer's business, or, as it is often expressed, deviate -s or departs from his work to accomplish some purpose of his own not connected with his employment—goes on a "frolic of his own"—the relation of master and servant is thereby temporarily suspended, and the master is not liable for his acts during the period of such suspension. As the "abandonment of employment" doctrine is entrenched in the law of vicarious liability, we conclude, as the district court did, that the proper inquiry is whether, at the time of the purchase, Parker was acting within the scope of his employment.

There is no dispute that Parker purchased the royalty for himself and was acting in his own interest, not in the interest of the firm. There is also no dispute that the firm did not receive any benefit from Parker's purchase of the royalty. In fact, Young was never billed by Parker or the firm. In order to satisfy the § 228 definition of "within the scope of employment," Parker's conduct must have been motivated, at least in part, by a desire to serve the firm. It is undisputed that Parker was motivated only by a desire to serve himself when he purchased the royalty. Viewing the conduct from the proper perspective, as a matter of law, Parker could not have been acting within the scope of his employment when he purchased the royalty interest.

2. *Did the Agency Relationship Aid Parker in Committing Allegedly Tortious Acts, Within the Meaning of §§ 219(2)(d) and 261?*

Entente claims that two cases, *Billups Petroleum Co. v. Hardin's Bakeries Corp.*, 217 Miss. 24, 63 So. 2d 543 (1953), and *Napp v. Liberty National Life Insurance Co.*, 248 Miss. 320, 159 So. 2d 164 (1963), support its argument that conduct need not be motivated by any desire to serve a master in order to be within the scope of a servant's employment. As discussed above, Entente's argument conflates two theories of liability. We examine the *Billups* and *Napp* cases, however, to determine whether the type of liability anticipated by § 261 exists in this case. After a careful examination of the cases and the underlying theories of liability, we find that as a matter of law, the liability described in §§ 219(2)(d) and 261 does not exist in this case.

In *Billups*, a salesman for Hardin's Bakeries overcharged Billups for bread over a period of several months, and kept the excess for himself. The Mississippi Supreme Court held Hardin's Bakeries vicariously liable for its agent's fraud, stating that

> [t]he Principal is liable to third persons for injuries resulting from the fraud and deceit of his agent if such is within the scope of the agent's authority. Acts of fraud by the agent, committed in the course or scope of his employment, are binding on the principal, even though the principal did not know of or authorize the commission of the fraudulent acts, and although he derives no benefit from the success of the fraud, and the agent committed it for his own benefit.

Contrary to some of the language in the *Billups* case, the principal's liability is based on the theory embodied in §§ 219(2)(d) and 261 of the Restatement, rather than traditional "scope of employment" liability contained in § 219(1). The four cases the *Billups* court discusses in support of its holding evidence that the court imposed § 219(2)(d) liability. Each of the four cases involves fraud by an agent upon the principal's customer. Each case involved a situation in which the principal delegated to the agent the power to perform a certain task, such as collect monies for the principal. In each case, the agent acted for his own purposes, but the fraud transpired as part of the very duty that the principal authorized the agent to perform. Because the customers had a relationship with the principal that induced the customers to rely on the principal's agent, and the agent defrauded the customers in the performance of the duty entrusted to him by the principal, the agent was "aided in accomplishing the tort by the existence of the agency relation." Restatement (Second) of Agency, § 219(2)(d) (1958).

In *Napp*, the insurance company's agent defrauded a beneficiary by painstakingly convincing her that her husband's policy had lapsed before his death, but that the insurance company would pay half of the benefit she otherwise would have been due. In fact, the policy had not lapsed, and when the agent delivered a check for the full amount of the benefit to the beneficiary, he told her that the check had been made out for the incorrect amount, and that she would have to give half of it back to him to return to the company. He induced her to sign a receipt for the full amount and he kept one half of the money for himself. The court found that even though this conduct was not within the scope of the agent's employment contract, the company elected to have the agent deliver the check, and "could not delegate to one certain duties and then deny agency because the written contract between them limited his activities to other matters." Thus, as in *Billups*, the fraud in *Napp* transpired as part of the very duty that the agent was authorized to perform for the principal and customer.

Entente contends that, just as in *Billups* and *Napp*, Parker was aided in purchasing the royalty by the existence of his agency relationship with the firm. Entente advances that but for his employment at the firm, Parker never would have met Young and never would have had the opportunity to purchase the royalty; yet, but-for causation is irrelevant in this case. The proper inquiry for determining vicarious liability of a principal whose agent defrauds the principal's customer is the relationship between the principal and the customer. In *Billups*, the four cases it discusses, and *Napp*, the principal had a relationship with the customer and the customer was defrauded by the principal's agent. The courts reasoned that a principal who provides his agent with the tools or position necessary to perpetrate a fraud on the principal's customers should be held responsible to the innocent customers who relied on the agent. In this case, there was no relationship between the firm and Entente that could be imputed to the firm's agent. It is undisputed that neither Parker nor the firm represented Entente. The premise underlying § 219(2)(d) and § 261 liability, a relationship between the principal and an innocent third party, is absent in this case. Therefore, as a matter of law, the firm could not have been held vicariously liable for Parker's acts.

We AFFIRM the verdict directed by the district court.

Notes

1. The most frequent application of Restatement section 219(2)(d) is in situations to which Restatement section 261 applies. An agent acting within the scope of his or her apparent authority defrauds a third person (such as by receiving property) solely for personal reasons. Even though the agent acted *outside* the scope of his or her employment *as a servant*, the principal will be held liable because the principal put the agent in a position where third parties would rely on the agent's apparent authority.

2. See Chapter 14 for discussion of an agent's duties with respect to confidential information acquired from a principal or in the course of acting on behalf of the Principal.

4. Liability to Passengers

Pierson v. United States
527 F.2d 459 (9th Cir. 1975)

SNEED, Circuit Judge:

This case comes to us on an appeal from an order of the district court granting the motion of the United States for summary judgment against Mrs. Pierson in her suit under the Federal Tort Claims Act, 28 U.S.C. § 1346 (1970).

The facts are somewhat unusual. In brief, plaintiff's husband, Douglas Pierson, was killed in the crash of a United States Army aircraft on August 6, 1969 in the State of Washington. Mr. Pierson was then employed as a biologist by the State of Washington and was involved in radio-tracking elk on the Olympic Peninsula. We assume, without deciding, that this endeavor, although partially federally funded, was for all relevant purposes a state project.

In the early part of August 1969, Dr. Wendell Dodge, a United States Department of the Interior research biologist working for the Bureau of Sport Fisheries and Wildlife, made a request of Major Leo Schmitz, the standardization and training officer at Gray Army Air Field in Washington, for the use of a military aircraft. The aircraft was to be used in radio-tracking porcupines in the same general area where Pierson was radio-tracking elk. Major Schmitz obtained approval for this request from Dodge's supervisors, but not from his own, and authorized the use of a military aircraft in the project. It is undisputed that such authorization violated a number of Department of the Army and Department of Defense regulations. It will be assumed that Major Schmitz had no actual authority to authorize the flight, although apparently he did not realize this.

One porcupine tracking mission was flown on August 4, 1969. A second had been planned for August 8, but was changed to August 6 upon Pierson's request to Dodge to allow the plane to be used for the state elk tracking project. The rescheduling was apparently done without the knowledge of Major Schmitz. During the August 6 flight the aircraft crashed, killing all three occupants: the Army pilot, Pierson, and a telemetry expert who was employed by Mr. Dodge's agency. The flight request forms filled out by the pilot for the fatal flight misidentified the passengers as Department of the Army civilians ["D/A Civ."].

The Government in its brief offers three arguments to support an affirmance of the grant of summary judgment. The first argument turns on the apparent authority of Major Schmitz to authorize the use of military aircraft by employees of a state agency.

The Government argues that Major Schmitz had no apparent authority because he had no actual authority and because the United States had taken no action which could induce Pierson to believe that there was authority in Schmitz to allow a state employee to use the aircraft for an official state project not related to military affairs. The leading Washington case on apparent authority holds that the apparent authority of an agent can only be inferred from acts of the principal and not from acts of the agent. *Lamb v. General Associates, Inc.*, 60 Wash. 2d 623, 374 P.2d 677 (1962). *Lamb* goes on to state that:

> [t]he burden of establishing agency rests upon the one who asserts it. Facts and circumstances are sufficient to establish apparent authority only when a person exercising ordinary prudence, acting in good faith and conversant with business practices and customs, would be misled thereby, and such person has given due regard to such other circumstances as would cause a person of ordinary prudence to make further inquiry.
>
> A principal may be estopped to deny that his agent possesses the authority he assumes to exercise, where the principal knowingly causes or permits him so to act as to justify a third person of ordinary, careful, and

prudent business habits to believe that he possesses the authority exercised, and avails himself of the benefit of the agent's acts.

The question here, then, is whether under this state law standard the United States established that no issue of material fact as to apparent authority exists and no inference from the facts is possible which would establish apparent authority.

The actions of the principal upon which an inference of apparent authority can be based need not be explicit individual communications to the party alleging apparent authority. In *Walker v. Pacific Mobile Homes, Inc.*, 68 Wash. 2d 347, 413 P.2d 3 (1966) the question was the apparent authority of a mobile home salesman to take a consignment of the plaintiff's trailer on behalf of his employer in a situation in which it was clear that there was no actual authority. In finding apparent authority the Washington Supreme Court relied on the general appearance of authority which the dealer had given the salesman by placing him on a lot labeled with the dealer's name in circumstances where there was no reason for an ordinary man of prudence to believe that the salesman did not have full power to deal in trailers-—including the power to take consignments. There had been no specific representation made by the dealer with respect to consignments. In the case before us, Major Schmitz did have actual authority over the assignment and use of the aircraft which crashed when it was used for normal military training operations. Pierson knew that Schmitz had allowed Dodge to use an aircraft. According to the affidavit of Schmitz, his superiors knew of this use and did not prohibit it. The fact of the flight on August 4 and the failure to prohibit future flights is conduct by the principal (the U.S.) which would tend to establish that Schmitz had apparent authority to authorize *non-Department of Defense federal employees* to use military aircraft for a plainly non-military purpose. Hence, the issue narrows to the question of whether a reasonable and prudent man would have seen the difference between being a *non-Department of Defense federal employee* and a *state government employee* as important to the authority of Major Schmitz to allow the aircraft to be used. We cannot say that this distinction between Pierson and Dodge was enough to negate the apparent authority of Schmitz as a matter of law. The programs the two men were working on were very similar. The line between Defense Department employees and all other government employees seems to us to be, on its face, at least as significant as the federal/non-federal line. Pierson had good reason to believe the former line was not a restriction on Schmitz's power. He had no good reason to think that the latter distinction was a restriction on Schmitz.

Pierson apparently had no contact with Schmitz. He worked through Dodge who in turn contacted the Army for the rescheduling of the flight. If Pierson knew that Schmitz was not contacted, or had reason to believe that he was not, then the apparent authority of Schmitz is irrelevant. However, this is a factual question which cannot be resolved on the present record.

In short, we find none of the arguments put forth for summary judgment convincing. The Order is reversed and the cause remanded.

Note

One issue that frequently arises in respondeat superior cases involves the liability of the master to *passengers*. These cases often do not turn on questions as to scope of employment. For example, in *Pierson v. United States*, the pilot was clearly acting within the scope of his employment for the government. Instead, the question was whether the master owed any *duty* of care to the passenger. That turns on whether the passenger was a *trespasser* or an invitee/licensee. That status turns on whether the person inviting the passenger to ride in the vehicle had authority or apparent authority to do so. Restatement § 242.

F. Agent's Duty of Obedience

Problem 5.12

The state Notary Public Act requires a document signer to be in the physical presence of a notary at the time of the signing and notarization of a jurat on a document. A paralegal-notary working for a law firm was told by the senior partner to notarize a signature of a client on a document that had been signed at the partner's home the night before—out of the presence of the notary. The notary refused, and the partner immediately fired the notary. Would the notary have a cause of action against the law firm for retaliatory discharge? If the employee had been an attorney-notary under the same circumstances, would the attorney-notary have a cause for retaliatory firing?

Crawford v. DiMicco
216 So.2d 769 (Fla. Ct. App. 1968)

CROSS, Judge.

Appellants-defendants, H. Albert Crawford and Walter S. Buckingham, d/b/a Buckingham-Wheeler Agency, and Fidelity-Phoenix Insurance Corporation, appeal from a final judgment entered pursuant to a jury verdict in favor of the appellee-plaintiff, Charles R. DiMicco, in an action of negligence against Buckingham-Wheeler Agency for failure to obtain insurance coverage, and against Fidelity-Phenix Insurance Corporation on a binder of insurance.

The cross-plaintiff, Fidelity-Phenix Insurance Corporation, also appeals a final judgment pursuant to the jury's verdict in favor of the cross-defendant, Buckingham-Wheeler Agency, whereby the cross-plaintiff sought indemnity from the cross-defendant for any loss the cross-plaintiff sustained as a result of the plaintiff's recovery against cross-plaintiff. These cases have been consolidated on appeal.

On September 10, 1963, an employee of Buckingham-Wheeler Agency, met with the plaintiff at the plaintiff's home to discuss the placing of insurance on the plaintiff's boat, a 1950 20-foot Chris Craft Cruiser named 'Honey.' After the discussion the agency's employee advised the plaintiff that he was then and there binding a $5,000-all risks insurance coverage on the boat and that the plaintiff could consider such insurance coverage bound. It appears that the agency's employee bound such coverage, notwithstanding the fact that he had prior knowledge that the insurer, Fidelity-Phenix Insurance Corporation, would not insure a boat having a value of $5,000 or greater or a boat that was in excess of three years of age without a condition survey.

Some weeks after the meeting between the plaintiff and the agency's employee, the boat was damaged in a storm and finally sank. Plaintiff sought damages for this loss.

Fidelity-Phenix Insurance Corporation denied coverage had ever existed. Buckingham-Wheeler Agency admitted coverage had been bound, but contended the coverage had been cancelled prior to the loss by its employee telephoning the plaintiff and advising him that Fidelity-Phenix Insurance Corporation had declined to insure the risk. Plaintiff denies receiving this telephone call.

Plaintiff sued Buckingham-Wheeler Agency on the theory that Buckingham-Wheeler Agency, a general insurance agency, had been employed to place physical damage insurance on the boat but had negligently failed to do so; and sued Fidelity-Phenix Insurance Corporation on a binder of coverage of insurance on the boat.

Fidelity-Phenix Insurance Corporation answered and filed a cross-claim. The answer generally denied the material allegations of plaintiff's complaint, and further pleaded the affirmative defense that the plaintiff fraudulently concealed material and relevant facts when he applied for the insurance.

The Agency filed its answer, also generally denying the material allegations of the plaintiff's complaint and further pleaded the affirmative defense that although the Agency had placed the insurance coverage on the boat, as requested by the plaintiff, such insurance coverage had been cancelled before the loss occurred, and that the plaintiff fraudulently concealed material and relevant facts when he applied for the insurance.

The cross-claim of Fidelity-Phenix Insurance Corporation against Buckingham-Wheeler Agency was based on the theory of indemnity for loss arising out of a principal-agent relationship, since it was alleged that the agent negligently failed to follow the principal's instructions to cancel the insurance coverage, and that the agent exceeded its authority in binding the insurance coverage in the first instance.

The Agency filed its reply to the cross-claim, generally denying the material allegations and pleading the affirmative defenses that it had implied authority to bind the insurance coverage, and that it followed the principal's instructions to cancel the insurance coverage.

The case thereafter came on for trial before a jury. The jury returned two verdicts; one in favor of the plaintiff against both Buckingham-Wheeler Agency and the insurer, Fidelity-Phenix Insurance Corporation for $5,000, and another verdict in favor of the cross-defendant Buckingham-Wheeler Agency, and against the insurer-cross-plaintiff, Fidelity-Phenix Insurance Corporation.

Both Buckingham-Wheeler Agency and Fidelity-Phenix Insurance Corporation appeal the judgment entered in favor of the plaintiff, Charles R. DiMicco; and Fidelity-Phenix Insurance Corporation also appeals the judgment entered in favor of Buckingham-Wheeler Agency against it.

In the appeal by Buckingham-Wheeler Agency and Fidelity-Phenix Insurance Corporation against the plaintiff, DiMicco, they attack the entry of a judgment entered for DiMicco as erroneous on the basis that the judgment was entered upon an inconsistent verdict.

*   *   *

However, we glean from the record that there was no objection made by any of the parties to the various forms of the verdict that the jury might render. * * * The defendants had every opportunity to request the court to require a different verdict or to object to the form of the verdicts given. They did neither. Under these circumstances, they cannot now be heard to complain of the entry of the judgment upon the verdict.

Turning now to the action by the cross-plaintiff-insurer against the cross-defendant-agency, we are to determine if an insurance agent binds a contract of insurance which he is not authorized to do, is such agent liable to indemnify the company for its losses arising from the enforcement of the insurance contract so bound.

The facts as alluded to above are simple, and the law is equally so. It has long been well settled that an agent owes to his principal the obligation of high fidelity, and that he may not proceed without or beyond his authority, particularly where he has been forbidden to act and that so proceeding, his actions caused loss to his principal, the agent is fully accountable to the principal therefor. 2d Restatement of Agency, § 401. An elementary factor in the principal-agent relationship is control. As stated in 2d Restatement of Agency, § 14B(f), 'An agent acts for and on behalf of his principal and subject to his control. * * * The agent owes a duty of obedience to his principal.' *Ledbetter v. Farmers Bank & Trust Co.*, 4 Cir. 1944, 142 F.2d 147.

The record in this case reveals that the agency through its employee proceeded without and went beyond its authority as evidenced by the following testimony:

Q. Now, again, going back to this authority, Mr. Bishop, were you ever advised at any time by the Marine Office of America prior to this loss that surveys would be required on certain class vessels?

A. I believe so.

Q. Is it not true that you were advised that on all vessels having a value of $5,000.00 or over three years of age, that a survey would be required prior to its submission?

A. I was.

Q. Were you so advised of that?

A. Yes.

Q. And you received that advice many months prior to September 10, 1963, did you not?

A. Yes.

Q. What was the age of this vessel?

A. It was built in 1952.

Q. So, in 1963, it would have been ten or eleven years old?

A. Right.

Q. What value did you bind this vessel for?

A. $5,000.00.

Q. So, this vessel would have fallen within that express prohibition on two counts, both value and age?

A. Yes.

Q. But at the time, September 10, 1963, you were under definite instructions that any boat having a value of $5,000.00 or more or three years old or greater, there had to be a survey, is that correct?

A. This is true. I believe they would have issued port risk coverage or, with a discussion on the phone, would bind the coverage subject to the survey.

Q. But again, that would be up to them, after they were notified of this, this was not your written instructions, is that correct?

A. Yes. My written instructions have been reiterated to me, yes.

Q. Before binding this risk, did you require a survey?

A. No. I required a survey immediately after, though.

Q. Now, Mr. Bishop, turning for a moment to that, as I understand it you discussed this vessel with Mr. DiMicco and he asked for $5,000.00 value and you had never seen the boat when you told him it was bound. Is that generally correct?

A. Yes.

Q. As I understand your testimony, you did bind the boat after Mr. DiMicco told you it had been canceled and there had been a survey?

A. I bound it before that.

Q. Yes, but you left it bound?

A. Yes, sir.

The record further indicates that the agent's employee was informed on a prior occasion when dealing with insurance being placed on another vessel, that as a matter of course the insurer specifically instructed the agent's employee that a survey is required on vessels that are valued at $5,000 or over or are more than three years old, if the vessel was to be submitted to the insurer for insurance.

Under the facts of the instant case and the settled law applicable thereto, unless and until the principal with full knowledge of all the applicable facts waived the breach of its instructions, ratified or adopted the agent's act as its own, or facts otherwise raising an estoppel against the principal, the agent became and remained liable to the principal for the damages incurred in acting without authority to the disadvantage of its principal. The facts herein reveal no adoption, ratification or estoppel on the part of the principal-insurer.

The cross-defendant-agency through its employee, acted precipitatively, unreasonably and without authority. The testimony reveals vividly that the agency's employee admittedly and grievously breached his duty to the insurer by his initial unauthorized act in binding the vessel, and therefore the cross-defendant-agent cannot escape the loss or any part thereof and throw such loss upon the principal-insurer.

Accordingly, the judgment entered in favor of the plaintiff, Charles R. DiMicco, against the defendants, Buckingham-Wheeler Agency and Fidelity-Phenix Insurance Corporation is affirmed. The judgment entered on the cross-claim in favor of the cross-defendant, Buckingham-Wheeler Agency, against the cross-plaintiff, Fidelity-Phenix Insurance Corporation, is reversed, and the cause is remanded with directions to enter an appropriate judgment on the cross-claim in favor of the cross-plaintiff, Fidelity-Phenix Insurance Corporation, and against the cross-defendant, Buckingham-Wheeler Agency.

Notes

1. Under Restatement section 385, agents owe their principals a duty of obedience:

> (1) Unless otherwise agreed, an agent is subject to a duty to obey all reasonable directions in regard to the manner of performing a service that [the agent] has contracted to perform.

> (2) Unless [the agent] is privileged to protect [the agent's] own or another's interests, an agent is subject to a duty not to act in matters entrusted to [the agent] on account of the principal contrary to the directions of the principal....

2. What steps could the insurance company have taken to help its agents with their obedience of its instructions? What documents could have been prepared and delivered in the above case to avoid the agent's exceeding his authority and to avoid later disputes about the facts of the case?

Chapter 6

Management and Conduct
of Firm Business

A. Introduction

A primary consideration in organizing a business firm is choosing the firm's "governance structure"—allocating rights and responsibilities for managing the firm and for participating in its business. A key purpose of the law of business organizations is to provide a structure of inter-related rules that govern the firm. Each form of business entity—sole proprietorship, partnership, limited partnership, limited liability company, and corporation—has its own governance structure that derives from any underlying statute, as well as from the common law.

An important factor in choosing a business entity is identifying the governance structure that most suits the parties' needs. A key consideration is the extent to which a business entity allows *party autonomy*—gives parties the freedom to change or adapt the entity's native governance structure. Although most business entities allow some party autonomy, not all native governance structures are equally flexible. To the extent that an entity's governance structure gives the parties wide discretion, the structure is said to be *suppletory* or *enabling*. That is, the governance structure authorizes the parties' agreement, and supplements it by providing *default*—or back-up—rules that apply only where the parties have not agreed otherwise.

To the extent that an entity's governance structure constrains party discretion, the structure is said to be *regulatory* or *mandatory*. That is, the structure regulates party autonomy by preventing them from choosing a different governance structure. The governance structure is thus the framework within which the parties must work; it is the standard against which party choice is measured.

Of course, no native governance structure is wholly enabling or wholly mandatory. Even a structure that generally enables party autonomy has aspects that are mandatory. Even a structure that generally regulates party autonomy, often permits a measure of discretion in ordering governance.

In reading this Chapter, and later chapters, pay particular attention to whether the rules being discussed derive from the native governance structure of the business entity, or from the agreement of the parties. If the former, to what extent would the native governance structure allow the parties to adopt their own rules?

B. Partnerships

1. Introduction

Of all the organizational forms, the governance structure of partnerships is generally the most enabling. Consider Section 103 of the RUPA provides that

> Except as provided in subsection (b), relations among the partners and between the partners and the partnership are governed by the partnership agreement. To the extent that the partnership agreement does not otherwise provide, this [Act] governs the relations among the partners and between the partners and the partnership.

RUPA § 103(a) (brackets in original).

Nevertheless, Section 103(b) of the RUPA limits the discretion of the partners with respect to aspects of the statutory governance structure. As we shall see in a later chapter, many commentators strongly argue that parties should be permitted complete autonomy, at least as to "the relations among the partners and the between the partners and the partnership."

2. Partners as Agents

a. Apparent Authority

Problem 6.1

Randy, Gus and Susan are partners conducting business under the name "Randy's Grocery Store." Because Randy and Susan have strong moral objections to the sale of alcoholic beverages, the partners agreed that Randy's would not do so. For many years, Randy's never sold beer, wine or liquor.

Recently, Randy's sales have been down. One day, Gus was in the store, and noticed a lot of college T-shirts and sweat-shirts. Gus decided that Randy's could sell a lot of beer. Gus called up Spoetzel Brewing Co. and ordered several cases of "Shiner Bock" beer.

When the beer was delivered, Randy was on the loading dock, and refused to accept the delivery. Spoetzel Brewing sued Randy's and its partners for breach of contract. Randy's, Randy and Susan defend on two grounds. First, they argue that the partner's agreed that Randy's would not sell alcoholic beverages. Second, they argue that Randy's had never bought beer, wine or liquor. What result? Would either of the following make any difference in your analysis?

a. Spoetzel Brewing did not know that Gus was a partner in Randy's.

b. It is common (or uncommon) for groceries in the area to sell beer.

Why or why not?

Burns v. Gonzalez
439 S.W.2d 128 (Tex. Civ. App. 1969)

CADENA, Justice.

Plaintiff, William G. Burns, sued Arturo C. Gonzalez and Ramon D. Bosquez, individually and as sole partners in Inter-American Advertising Agency (herein called "the partnership"), to recover on a $40,000.00 promissory note executed by Bosquez in his own name and in the name of the partnership. After an interlocutory default judgment had been entered in favor of plaintiff against Bosquez, the trial court, sitting without a jury, entered the judgment appealed from, denying Burns any recovery against Gonzalez.

The sole business of the partnership was the sale, on a commission basis, of broadcast time on XERF, a radio station located in Ciudad Acuña, Mexico, and owned and operated by a Mexican corporation, Compania Radiodifusora de Coahuila, S.A. (herein called "Radiodifusora"). Bosquez and Gonzalez each owned 50% of the Radiodifusora stock, with Bosquez acting as president of the corporation.

The events culminating in this litigation began in 1957 when a written contract was entered into between Radiodifusora and the partnership, on the one hand, and Roloff Evangelistic Enterprises, Inc., and Burns, on the other. Under this contract Radiodifusora and the partnership, in consideration of the payment of $100,000.00 by Roloff and Burns, agreed to make available to them two 15-minute segments of broadcast time daily over XERF so long as the franchise of the radio station remained in force, beginning July 1, 1957. In accordance with the terms of the contract, Roloff and Burns paid the $100,000.00 in four equal installments on July 1, 1957, November 1, 1957, March 1, 1958, and July 1, 1958, with Burns retaining 15% of such payments as his commission, as he had a right to do under the terms of the contract.

Subsequently, Roloff assigned all of its rights under this contract to Burns, effective June 16, 1962. Both Radiodifusora and the partnership approved such assignment.

Because of labor disputes and other circumstances, the radio station was shut down at various times. With some exceptions, the broadcast periods described in the 1957 contract were not made available to Burns or to persons to whom he sold such broadcast periods, after June 16, 1962.

On November 28, 1962, Bosquez, purporting to act on his own behalf and on behalf of the partnership, executed the note in question, payable to Burns on November 28, 1964. According to a separate instrument signed by Bosquez on the same date, the radio station was in receivership and it was unlikely that the broadcast periods to which Burns was entitled under the 1957 contract would be made available to him for the two-year period ending November 28, 1964, the date on which the note was payable. This instrument recited that since Burns would derive an income of $20,000.00 a year from sale of such broadcast periods, the note in the amount of $40,000.00 had been executed and delivered to Burns to compensate him for the income which he would have derived during the two-year period ending November 28, 1964. Bosquez testified, and Burns does not deny, that "one of the reasons" why he executed the note was the promise by Burns not to sue Radiodifusora.

The next relevant instrument is dated May 24, 1963. It is a contract between Burns and Bosquez, who purported to act on behalf of Radiodifusora and the partnership. The preamble to this agreement refers to the 1957 contract, the assignment of Roloff's rights thereunder to Burns, the approval of such assignment by Radiodifusora and the partnership, and the breach of such contract. No mention is made of the 1962 note. After this reference to the prior course of dealings between the parties, the agreement recognizes the rights of Burns under the 1957 contract, and Radiodifusora agrees to make the broadcast periods described in that contract available to Burns beginning September 1, 1963. As consideration for this promise by Radiodifusora, Burns agreed to pay Radiodifusora one-half of the amounts realized by him from sale of such time, and agreed not to file suit against Radiodifusora. The contract concludes with the recital that all understandings between the parties had been reduced to writing and were embodied therein.

Although Gonzalez denied under oath the authority of Bosquez to execute the 1962 note, the trial court held that the note was an obligation of the partnership. The judgment in favor of Gonzalez was based on the theory that he had been relieved of liability on the note as a result of the 1963 agreement.

Under Sec. 9(1), UPA,

"Every partner is an agent of the partnership for the purpose of its business, and the act of every partner, including the execution in the partnership name of any instrument, *for apparently carrying on in the usual way the business of the partnership* of which he is a member, binds the partnership, unless the partner so acting has in fact no authority to act for the partnership in the particular matter, and the person with whom he is dealing has knowledge of the fact that he has no such authority."

(Emphasis added.) In this case, in fact, Bosquez had no authority to bind the partnership by executing a negotiable instrument. But, since this express limitation on the authority of Bosquez to bind the partnership by executing a negotiable instrument was unknown to Burns, then, under the language of Sec. 9(1), his act in executing the note would bind the partnership if such act can be classified as an act "for apparently carrying on in the usual way the business of the partnership."

As we interpret Sec. 9(1), the act of a partner binds the firm, absent an express limitation of authority known to the party dealing with such partner, if such act is for the purpose of "apparently carrying on" the business of the partnership in the way in which other firms engaged in the same business in the locality usually transact business, or in the way in which the particular partnership usually transacts its business. In this case, there is no evidence relating to the manner in which firms engaged in the sale of advertising time on radio stations usually transact business. Specifically, there is no evidence as to whether or not the borrowing of money, or the execution of negotiable instruments, was incidental to the transaction of business, "in the usual way," by other advertising agencies or by this partnership, Inter-American Advertising Agency. It becomes important, therefore, to determine the location of the burden of proof concerning the "usual way" of transacting business by advertising agencies.

Sec. 9(1) states that the act of a partner "for apparently carrying on in the usual way the business of the partnership" binds the firm. This language does not place the burden of proof on the nonparticipating partner to establish the nonexistence of the facts which operate to impose liability on the firm. If the Legislature had intended to place the burden of proof on the non-participating partner, it could have done so easily. The statute could have been drafted to declare that the act of a partner binds the firm "unless it is shown that such act was not for apparently carrying on in the usual way the business of the partnership." Actually, the liability-imposing language of Sec. 9(1) indicates that the burden of proof is on the person seeking to hold the non-participating partner accountable. It is not couched in terms appropriate for the establishment of a presumption, "administrative" or otherwise. The language relating to carrying on in the usual way the business of the partnership is no more than a statement of the rule concerning vicarious liability based on "apparent" authority.

We conclude that, under a reasonable interpretation of the language of Sec. 9(1), the burden of proving the "usual way" in which advertising agencies transact business was upon Burns.

Our conclusion is supported by the fact that the liability of partners with respect to third persons is largely determined by reference to the principles of law of agency. UPA, Sec. 4(3). One who asserts that the particular act of an agent is within the scope of the agent's authority has the burden of proving the extent of such authority. We recognize, of course, that there are aspects in which the partner-agent differs from the "ordinary" agent. But we know of no distinction which compels application of different rules concerning the burden of proof in connection with establishment of the extent of the agent's power. The principle for imposing liability on the non-acting party, be he partner or ordinary principal, is that he has "held out" the actor as being empowered to perform acts of the nature of the act in question. If A seeks to impose liability on B for the act of C on the theory that B held C out as having power to do such act, clearly the burden of establishing the facts which constitute such holding out is on A.

In the case of an ordinary agent, "holding out" is established by showing that the principal placed the agent in a position which ordinarily carries with it generally recognized powers. The agent will then have, as far as third parties are concerned, the power to do the things ordinarily done by one occupying such a position, unless the third party has knowledge of limitations on the powers of the agents. In *Collins v. Cooper*, 65 Tex. 460, 464 (1886), the Supreme Court said that in determining the extent of an agent's power, it "becomes necessary, to consider the character of the business, the manner in which it is usual to carry on such a business, and where the agency has continued for a long time, the manner in which the particular business was carried." This is the same principle which is made applicable to problems concerning the power of partners by Sec. 9(1).

There are many statements to the effect that members of a "trading" partnership have implied authority to bind the partnership by issuing commercial paper, while members of a "non-trading" partnership have no such implied authority. But we do not base our holding on the ground that the partnership here was the non-trading type. It is apparent that the attempted distinction between the two types of partnership is nothing more than a shorthand rendition of the notion that B is liable for the act of C if B has "held out" to other persons that C is empowered to perform acts of that particular nature. The nature of the distinction is revealed by the language of Chief Justice Stayton in *Randall v. Meredith*, 76 Tex. 669, 13 S.W. 576, 582-583 (1890):

> If the partnership contemplates the periodical or continuous or frequent purchasing, not as incidental to an occupation, but for the purpose of selling again the thing purchased, either in its original or manufactured state, it is a trading partnership; otherwise, it is not. There is no doubt that all partnerships which fall within this definition are trading partnerships, and it may be that it is broad enough to cover all that should be so classed. If these were not embraced within this definition, in which each partner is clothed with power to borrow money, they may be recognized by the character of the business pursued, which makes frequent resort to borrowing a necessity, not existing by reason of embarrassments, or on account of some fortuitous event, but for the advantageous prosecution of even a prosperous business.
>
> An act may be necessary for the carrying on of the business of a partnership, but when done by one partner the firm cannot be bound by it, unless he has express or implied power to do the act. Whether he has the implied power depends on whether the act be "necessary to carry on the business in the ordinary way. A partner's power is to do only what is usual, and not what is unusual because necessary."
>
> Whether the work was done in the usual course of business, or was necessary, was not the inquiry to which the mind of the jury should have been directed. The work may have been done in the usual course of business, or necessary, but this would not confer on the partner power to borrow money to pay for it, unless the exercise of that power was usual in the ordinary conduct of such a business.

It appears that the tests announced in *Randall* for determining whether a partnership is to be classed as trading or non-trading is exactly the same test for imposition of liability embodied in Sec. 9(1). This explains the fact that the UPA makes no mention of the distinction between trading and non-trading firms.

We are aware of the language in *Crozier, Rhea & Co. v. Kirker*, 4 Tex. 252, 258-259 (1849), to the effect that every partner has implied power to bind his co-partners by executing notes for commercial purposes consistent with the object of the partnership. Similar language is found in *Brewer v. Big Lake State Bank*, 378 S.W. 2d. 948, 951 (Tex. Civ. App.—El Paso 1964), and *Ft. Dearborn Nat. Bank v. Berrott*, 23 Tex. Civ. App. 662, 57 S.W. 340, 341 (San Antonio, 1900). But in each of these cases the partnership business contemplated "the periodical or continuous or frequent purchasing, not as incidental to an occupation, but for the purpose of selling again the thing purchased." Where the partnership business is of that nature, it is usual and customary to purchase on credit and to execute paper evidencing the existence of the partnership debt. That is, to use the language of Sec. 9(1), in such partnership, "carrying on in the usual way the business of the partnership" involves borrowing and the issuance of commercial paper. Or, to use the language of *Randall*, the nature of such a partnership "makes frequent resort to borrowing a necessity, not existing by reason of embarrassments, or on account of some fortuitous event, but for the advantageous prosecution of even a prosperous business." The statements in *Crozier*, *Brewer* and *Berrott* relating to implied authority of a partner to issue negotiable paper must be construed as being applicable to the types of partnerships there involved. If not so limited, then the assertions that every partner has implied authority to bind the firm by executing negotiable instruments must be disregarded as incorrect, irreconcilable with the analysis of the problem in *Randall*, and inconsistent with the plain language of Sec. 9(1). The power of a partner to issue commercial paper arises not from the existence of the partnership, but from the nature of the partnership business and the manner in which such business is usually conducted. This is the plain meaning of Sec. 9(1).

The only thing we know of the nature of the partnership here is that it was restricted to sale of broadcast time over XERF on a commission basis. There is nothing to show that the transaction of such business required "periodical or continuous or frequent purchasing" or made "frequent resort to borrowing a necessity, not existing by reason of embarrassments, or on account of some fortuitous event, but for the advantageous prosecution of even a prosperous business." The assets of the partnership consisted of a few desks, chairs, typewriters and office supplies.

We disagree with the contention put forward by Burns to the effect that Bosquez was the managing partner. At best, the record reflects that both Bosquez and Gonzalez were active in the management of the business. As a matter of fact, with the exception of the transactions involving the 1962 note and the 1963 agreement, the record discloses that all instruments significantly affecting the relations between the partners and Burns were signed by both Bosquez and Gonzalez.

Since the evidence does not disclose that Bosquez, in executing the 1962 note, was performing an act "for apparently carrying on in the usual way the business of the partnership," there is no basis for holding that the note sued on was a partnership obligation.

Since Burns filed no pleadings alleging that Gonzalez had ratified the act of Bosquez, or that Gonzalez had been guilty of any acts giving rise to an estoppel, it is not possible to hold Gonzalez liable on any theory of ratification or estoppel.

The judgment of the trial court is affirmed.

Notes

1. Under RUPA section 301(1), where a partner is "apparently carrying on in the usual way" *either* the partnership business (as actually conducted by the partnership) *or* business of the kind carried on by the partnership unless the party dealing with the partner "knew or had received a notification that the partner lacked authority."

2. Do you agree with the principal case's reasoning that a partner's power to bind the partnership under UPA section 9(1) and RUPA section 301(1) is based on apparent authority? Suppose that the third person dealing with the partner did not know that the partner was a partner in the business?

3. Besides apparent authority, what other agency principles discussed in Chapter 4 and Chapter 5 might account for the power of a partner to bind the partnership and the other partners?

4. Should partners be allowed to change the rules provided in UPA section 9(1) and RUPA section 301(1). See RUPA section 103(b)(10).

Problem 6.2

Brundidge, Fountain, Elliott & Churchill is a partnership engaged in the practice of law in Dallas, Texas. Lyon, a partner of the law firm, represented Cook in a divorce proceeding, and also prepared a will for her. The law firm billed for Lyon's services, and Cook paid the law firm.

Cook and some relatives had just received $60,000 from the sale of some property in Illinois. Cook asked Lyon to help them find someone to consult with about investing the money. Lyon told her he was a silent partner in a real estate firm and might be able to help her. He said that he had invested in a California fast-food franchise called "Yummers," at a substantial profit, and had obtained a franchise for a corporation hew was forming, Texas Yummers Corporation, to open a "Yummers" in Texas.

Cook decided to invest in Yummers. At Cook's request, her Illinois attorney sent Lyon the proceeds of the sale of the land in Illinois. The attorney sent Lyon a $60,000 check payable to "Warren Lyon as Attorney for Cook." The check was mailed to and received by Lyon at the office of the law firm but the funds were never deposited in or handled by or through any account of the law firm. Instead, the funds were deposited in an account in the name of Texas Yummers.

On July 9, 1969 Cook and Texas Yummers Corporation signed a contract under which Cook agreed to loan Texas Yummers a minimum of $50,000 to be used in the construction of a Yummers store in Dallas. Lyon signed the contract as president of Texas Yummers. Cook claims that Lyon made several representations at the time of signing:

(a) that he had prepared the contract, that it was a good and valid mortgage contract and that as their attorney he could assure them that their interests were well-protected;

(b) that the money would be placed in a trust account until it could be invested in the new store:

(c) that the money was going to be held until actually the property was bought and the building begun and the pay back started, which was September 15.

(d) that the money was to be repaid at one thousand dollars a month for fifteen years.

The payment due in September 15, 1969, under the July 9 contract was not made. During October and November of 1969, Lyon persuaded Cook to exchange her rights under the July 9 contract for stock in Texas Yummers. Cook agreed to take 36,000 shares, at $1.00 per share, plus a $19,000 note from Texas Yummers. On December 4, Texas Yummers, through Lyon as its president, signed the Note and gave it to Cook. In February of 1970, Cook received what purported to be stock certificates for Texas Yummers.

On July 21, 1972, a Petition for Involuntary Bankruptcy of Texas Yummers was filed; on August 11, the corporation was adjudged bankrupt.

Cook sued Lyon, claiming that, in obtaining the funds she invested in Texas Yummers, Cook had misrepresented material facts about the investment Cook also sued the law firm, Brundidge, Fountain, Elliott & Churchill, seeking to hold the firm liable for Cook's fraud.

1. Assuming that Lyon did in fact make material misrepresentations is the law firm subject to liability to Cook on account of those misrepresentations? On what basis?

2. Even if the law firm is not responsible for Lyon's misrepresentations, is the law firm otherwise obligated to return the funds sent to Lyon as her attorney at the law firm's address? On what basis?

Kansallis Finance Ltd. v. Fern
421 Mass. 659, 659 N.E.2d 731 (1996)

Before LIACOS, C.J., and ABRAMS, LYNCH, GREANEY and FRIED, JJ.

FRIED, Justice.

The United States Court of Appeals for the First Circuit has certified to this court, pursuant to S.J.C. Rule 1:03, as appearing in 382 Mass. 700 (1981), the following two questions of State law:

"1. Under Massachusetts law, to find that a certain act is within the scope of a partnership for the purpose of applying the doctrine of vicarious liability, must a plaintiff show, inter alia, that the act was taken at least in part with the intent to serve or benefit the partnership?

"2. May defendants be found vicariously liable for authorized conduct by their partner that violated Mass.Gen.L. ch. 93A, even if they were entirely unaware of and uninvolved with that conduct?"

Kansallis Fin. Ltd. v. Fern, 40 F.3d 476, 481-482 (1st Cir. 1994).

In order that we may give the guidance that the Court of Appeals seeks, we offer the more extensive "discussion of relevant Massachusetts law" that the Court of Appeals invites in its certification order.

The questions arise out of an appeal by Kansallis Finance Ltd. (plaintiff) from a trial in the United States District Court for the District of Massachusetts. The Court of Appeals stated that the first question concerns an issue on which an apparent conflict exists in Massachusetts precedent, and that the second question concerns a separate issue on which there is no controlling Massachusetts precedent.

I.

We summarize the facts relevant to the questions certified. Stephen Jones and the four defendants were law partners in Massachusetts when, in connection with a loan and lease financing transaction, the plaintiff sought and obtained an opinion letter from Jones. In the order of certification, the Court of Appeals states that the letter, executed in Massachusetts and issued on "Fern, Anderson, Donahue, Jones & Sabatt, P.A." letterhead, "contained several intentional misrepresentations concerning the transaction and was part of a conspiracy by Jones and others (though not any of the defendants here) to defraud Kansallis." Although Jones did not personally sign the letter, he arranged for a third party to do so, and both the District Court judge and the jury found that Jones adopted or ratified the issuance of the letter. Jones was later convicted on criminal charges for his part in the fraud, but the plaintiff was unable to collect its $880,000 loss from Jones or his coconspirators.

In an effort to recover its loss, the plaintiff brought suit in the United States District Court for the District of Massachusetts seeking compensation from Jones's law partners on the theory that the partners were liable for the damage caused by the fraudulent letter. Advancing the claim on essentially three grounds, the plaintiff asserted that defendants are liable for the letter because: (1) the defendants gave Jones apparent authority to issue the letter; (2) Jones acted within the scope of the partnership in issuing the letter; and (3) the issuance of the letter violated G.L. c. 93A [a consumer protection statute], under which the partners are vicariously liable. The District Court submitted the first two common law claims to the jury and reserved the c. 93A count to itself. Both the judge and jury, for different reasons, decided that defendants were not liable for Jones's conduct. The Court of Appeals affirmed both the judge's and the jury's factual findings and certified two questions to this court in order to resolve the legal issues.

On plaintiff's common law claims, the jury based their verdict on their findings that

(1) Jones did not have apparent authority to issue the opinion letter[2] and

(2) that his action in issuing the opinion letter was outside the scope of the partnership.

On appeal to the Court of Appeals, the plaintiff contended that the jury based their second finding on an erroneous instruction directing that, to find Jones's actions within the scope of the partnership, the issuance of the letter must satisfy a three-prong test. It must have:

(1) been "the kind of thing a law partner would do";

(2) "occurred substantially within the authorized time and geographic limits of the partnership; and"

(3) been "motivated at least in part by a purpose to serve the partnership."

Although the jury did not indicate which prong the plaintiff failed to satisfy, the plaintiff objected to the addition of the third prong, and it is on the correctness of including this third prong in the test that the Court of Appeals now seeks guidance. The Court of Appeals found our law on this issue unclear because it found that two decisions, *Wang Labs., Inc. v. Business Incentives, Inc.*, 398 Mass. 854, 859, 501 N.E.2d 1163 (1986), and *New England Acceptance Corp. v. American Mfrs. Mut. Ins. Co.*, 373 Mass. 594, 597, 368 N.E.2d 1385 (1977), appeared to pull in opposite directions. The Court of Appeals therefore certified this first question to us.

---

2. The judge instructed the jury that "[t]here is no contention here that Jones had actual authority from the defendants to issue this Opinion Letter."

*   *   *

II.
A.

The parties have cited to us cases from this and other jurisdictions, as well as general principles set out in the Restatement (Second) of Agency and in the Uniform Partnership Act, codified at G.L. c. 108A. Whatever difficulties this array of authorities presents may in part be attributed to the fact that the issue of vicarious liability has engendered somewhat divergent formulations in the several different contexts in which it has arisen. The genus here is agency, and two of its species, for which there are special rules for determining vicarious liability, are partnership and master-servant.

In the context of a partnership, the person acting and the persons who might be held liable for his actions usually stand on an equal footing and may be thought of as equally implicated in a joint enterprise. By contrast, the law of the vicarious liability of a master for the acts of his servant grew up in circumstances where the actor was often in a subordinate position and had a limited interest in the enterprise which he assists. Yet both servants and partners are categorized as agents of their principals. In the partnership context, while each partner is the agent of the partnership, he also stands in the role of a principal—a reciprocity that is lacking in the master-servant relation. Finally, there is an important practical distinction between determining vicarious liability for harms that come about through the victim's voluntary interactions with the purported agent—as in the case of contracts, of fraud and of misrepresentation—and those that are inflicted on a victim who has made no choice to deal with the agent, as in the case of an accident, an assault or a trespass. Only in the former instance is the inquiry into apparent authority particularly apt, since where the victim transacts business with the agent, the victim's ability to assess the agent's authority will bear on whether and in what ways he chooses to deal with him. By contrast, where the victim has not chosen to deal with the agent by whose act he suffers harm—as in an automobile accident—the scope of employment seems the natural determinant of vicarious liability, and that is where the concept has had its most usual application.

Standing behind these diverse concepts of vicarious liability is a principle that helps to rationalize them. This is the principle that as between two innocent parties—the principal-master and the third party—the principal-master who for his own purposes places another in a position to do harm to a third party should bear the loss. A principal who requires an agent to transact his business, and can only get that business done if third parties deal with the agent as if with the principal, cannot complain if the innocent third party suffers loss by reason of the agent's act. Similarly, the master who must put an instrument into his servant's hands in order to get his business done, must also bear the loss if the servant causes harm to a stranger in the use of that instrument as the business is transacted.

This overarching principle measures the imposition of vicarious liability in particular contexts and suggests its own limitations. Where there is actual authority to transact the very business or to do the very act that causes the harm, the agent acts as the extension of the will of his principal and the case for vicarious liability is clear. Where the authority is only apparent, vicarious liability recognizes that it is the principal who for his own purposes found it useful to create the impression that the agent acts with his authority, and therefore it is the principal who must bear the burden of the misuse to which that appearance has been put.[5] But there is little fairness in saddling the principal with liability for acts that a reasonable third party would not have supposed were taken on the principal's behalf. Similarly, where the servant acts beyond the scope of his employment he is more like a thief who causes harm with an instrumentality he had no right to use.

Where the wrongdoer transacts business with the victim, the authority—actual or apparent—of the agent to act on the principal's behalf may be conceptualized as the dangerous instrumentality the principal has put in the agent's hands, enabling him to do harm with it. And this creates the temptation to use the concepts of apparent authority and scope of employment interchangeably. But they are not equivalent concepts. A servant or agent may sometimes act within the scope of his master's employment and yet lack apparent authority. The clearest instances are in accident cases where the victim neither knew nor cared what the wrongdoer's relation to his employer might be. Another rarer divergence may be illustrated by the present case. The scope of employment test asks the question: is this the kind of thing that in a general way employees of this kind do in employment of this kind. It does not ask the different question: whether a reasonable person in the victim's circumstances in the particular case would have taken the agent to be acting with the principal's authority. And so there arises the possibility of vicarious liability where the victim transacted business or otherwise dealt with an agent who lacked even apparent authority in the particular matter.

In the case before us here, the jury instructions required the jury to consider both routes to vicarious liability. The jury found that Jones acted without actual or apparent authority, presumably because the form and circumstances of the letter were such that they concluded that no reasonable person in the plaintiff's position would have believed that the letter was issued with the partnership's authority. But then they were asked in the alternative whether Jones "acted in the scope of the partnership." *See Bachand v. Vidal,* 328 Mass. 97, 100, 101 N.E.2d 884 (1951) (partners liable for tortious acts done by another partner "within the scope of the business of the firm"); *Bunnell v. Vrooman,* 250 Mass. 103, 106, 145 N.E. 58 (1924) (refusing to impose liability on copartners for one partner's tortious use of partnership property for strictly personal pleasure). This further question was taken to ask whether writing this opinion letter was the kind of thing that the partnership did—even if there was no apparent authority for this particular letter. This is the alternative theory, which the District Court labeled "vicarious liability," and under this alternative the defendants might yet be liable if the jury found all three of the conditions set out above in its charge on that issue. The rationale for this possibly more extended liability recognizes an authority in each partner to take the initiative to enlarge the partnership enterprise even without the authority—actual or apparent—of his partners, so long as what he does is within the generic description of the type of partnership involved. Whatever the harshness may be of such a rule extending vicarious liability past

---

5. While the appearance in apparent authority is measured by the standard of reasonableness, it is only those things that the principal has done to create the appearance that are so measured.

apparent authority, it is mitigated by the third factor, requiring that the unauthorized but law partner-like act be intended at least in part to serve the partnership. Since there is then some possibility that the partnership will benefit from the errant partner's act, then as between two innocent parties it is not unfair that the one whom the wrongful act may have and was meant to benefit must bear the burden of the harm.

B.

Our cases and statutes can readily be rationalized against the background of these principles. The Uniform Partnership Act provides as general principles that:

[1] the law of agency shall apply under that chapter, [UPA] § 4(3);

[2] the act of every partner apparently carrying on in the usual way the business of the partnership binds it, [UPA] § 9(2); and

[3] an act of the partner which is not apparently for the carrying on of the business of the partnership in the usual way does not bind it unless authorized, [UPA] § 9(2).

Where, however, by any wrongful act of a partner acting in the ordinary course of the business of the partnership, or with the authority of the copartners, loss or injury is caused to a third person, or a penalty is incurred, the partnership is liable therefore, [UPA] § 13.

Because the Uniform Partnership Act at § 4(3) specifically provides that the law of agency applies, it is appropriate to refer, as did the District Court in formulating its jury instructions, to the Restatement (Second) of Agency (1957). The District Court derived the second theory of liability, which it labeled vicarious liability and on which it instructed the jury regarding the scope of the partnership business, from § 228(1) of the Restatement (Second) of Agency. Section 228(1) provides in relevant part that conduct of a servant is within the scope of his employment, if but only if the conduct is (a) of the kind he is employed to perform, (b) within the partnership's authorized time and space limits, and (c) actuated, at least in part, by a purpose to serve the master. Subsection (2) states the complementary proposition that conduct is not within the scope of employment if it is different in kind from that authorized or too little actuated by a purpose to serve the master.

Section 261 states the alternative ground of vicarious liability based on apparent authority: that a principal who puts an agent in a position which enables the agent, while apparently acting within his authority, to commit a fraud on a third party is subject to liability to the third party. And § 262 states the complementary proposition that a person who otherwise would be liable to another for the misrepresentations of one acting for him is not relieved from liability by the fact that the agent acts entirely for his own purposes, unless the other has notice of that. Thus, under § 262, if an agent has actual or apparent authority, the principal is not relieved of liability for that agent's misrepresentation even though the requirements of § 228(1)(c) have not been met.

The two cases which concerned the Court of Appeals may be understood in this light. *Wang Labs., Inc. v. Business Incentives, Inc.*, 398 Mass. 854, 501 N.E.2d 1163 (1986), a G.L. c. 93A case, did indeed require and find an intention to benefit the corporate principal as a condition of vicarious liability, but in that case we did not address and so did not negate the possibility of vicarious liability by the route of apparent authority. Moreover, the harm complained of in Wang, which was akin to the tort of intentional interference with contractual relations, did not require for its accomplishment that the victim rely on the agent's authority, and so an analysis in terms of apparent authority would have been beside the point—every bit as much as it would be in an automobile accident or an assault. By contrast, in *New England Acceptance Corp. v. American Mfrs. Mut. Ins. Corp.*, 373 Mass. 594, 368 N.E.2d 1385 (1977), a contract or tort case, the fraud that was worked on the plaintiff depended for its accomplishment on the plaintiff's believing that the agent was acting with his principal's authority. It is for that reason that we adopted our Appeals Court's conclusion in that case that there could be vicarious liability even though "the agents were acting entirely for their own purposes." Indeed, as we have pointed out, that will usually be the case where a dishonest agent misuses his apparent authority to work a fraud upon both his principal and a third party.[9]

C.

Accordingly, if we take the first certified question to ask whether a partner must necessarily at least in part act for the benefit of the partnership if the partnership is to be liable for his actions, the answer is "no". But the answer is "no" only because under our law—and the law of partnership and agency generally—there are two routes by which vicarious liability may be found. If the partner has apparent authority to do the act, that will be sufficient to ground vicarious liability, whether or not he acted to benefit the partnership. It is only where there is no apparent authority, which is what the jury found on the common law counts here, that there may yet be vicarious liability on the alternative ground requiring such an intent to benefit the partnership. Since there is no evidence that Jones was acting to benefit the partnership, the District Court's judgment for the defendants on the common law counts accords with our statutes and precedents. The jury instructions on the common law claims were correct.

III.

The second question asks whether there must be a finding that the partners were at all aware of or involved in Jones's misconduct before they may be held liable to Jones's victim under G.L. c. 93A. This question raises a difficulty of a different order, because it arises under a statute, c. 93A, which was designed to

---

9. The approach set out here is consistent with our decision in *DeVaux v. American Home Assurance Co.*, 387 Mass. 814, 444 N.E.2d 355 (1983). The plaintiff had written and called the defendant's law office requesting legal assistance in regard to a possible tort claim. The letter and calls were received by a secretary who did not bring them to the defendant attorney's attention until after the statute of limitations on the plaintiff's claim had run. The plaintiff sued the attorney for malpractice on alternative theories that the secretary's actions bound her employer: (a) because the secretary was acting within the scope of her employment, and (b) because she had apparent authority to establish an attorney-client relationship. We held that, "[u]nder either theory, the question whether there was an attorney-client relationship depends on the reasonableness of the plaintiff's reliance." Id. at 819, 444 N.E.2d 355. This emphasis on the plaintiff's reliance interest is entirely appropriate in most cases. It is only in the rare event that the reliance, while present is not reasonable, and yet when the agent acts in part to benefit the principal, an additional reason to cast responsibility on the principal may be found. To the same effect is the decision of the First Circuit Court of Appeals in *Sheinkopf v. Stone*, 927 F.2d 1259 (1st Cir. 1991).

offer broader and more comprehensive relief to victims of dishonesty than may be available at common law. * * *

* * *

Accordingly, the simple answer to the second question—whether a defendant may be vicariously liable under c. 93A for conduct of which it was entirely unaware and with which it was entirely uninvolved—is "yes."

The statute does, however, by its terms make a distinction between cases where simple compensatory damages are paid to the plaintiff and where there are double or treble—that is, punitive—damages. * * * The Court of Appeals's query concerning awareness and involvement aptly identifies one factor bearing on the higher degree of culpability necessary for punitive damages in the context of vicarious liability.

* * *

IV.

To summarize, we hold that under the law of the Commonwealth a partnership may be liable by one of two routes for the unauthorized acts of a partner: if there is apparent authority, or if the partner acts within the scope of the partnership at least in part to benefit the partnership. Where there is neither apparent authority nor action intended at least in part to benefit the partnership, there cannot be vicarious liability. Accordingly, we answer the first question "no," but only because even if a partner acts with no purpose to benefit the partnership, vicarious liability may yet be appropriate, if he is clothed with apparent authority. In this case, however, the jury found that there was no apparent authority. We answer the second question "yes," but add that, while c. 93A permits a finding that an innocent and uninvolved partner may be vicariously liable for the acts of his partner, some further showing of culpability or involvement must be made to justify multiple damages.

Notes

1. Is the reasoning in the principal case consistent with the reasoning in *Burns v. Gonzalez*, page 287?

2. In the principal case, how would you instruct the jury on the questions of Jones' apparent authority?

3. Whether a law firm (or other professional firm) is liable when one of its partners receives, and then misappropriates, funds is a perennial question. As discussed in the principal case, UPA section 13 provides that

§ 13. Partnership Bound by Partner's Wrongful Act

Where, by any wrongful act or omission of any partner acting in the ordinary course of the business of the partnership or with the authority of his co-partners, loss or injury is caused to any person, not being a partner in the partnership, or any penalty is incurred, the partnership is liable therefor to the same extent as the partner so acting or omitting to act.

UPA section 14 provides that

§ 14. Partnership Bound by Partner's Breach of Trust

The partnership is bound to make good the loss:

(a) Where one partner acting within the scope of his apparent authority receives money or property of a third person and misapplies it; and

(b) Where the partnership in the course of its business receives money or property of a third person and the money or property so received is misapplied by any partner while it is in the custody of the partnership.

RUPA section 305 combines UPA sections 13 and 14:

Section 305. Partnership Liable for Partner's Actionable Conduct.

(a) A partnership is liable for loss or injury caused to a person, or for a penalty incurred, as a result of a wrongful act or omission, or other actionable conduct, of a partner acting in the ordinary course of business of the partnership *or with authority of the partnership*.

(b) If, in the course of the partnership's business or *while acting with authority of the partnership*, a partner receives or causes the partnership to receive money or property of a person not a partner and the money or property is misapplied by a partner, the partnership is liable for the loss.

(Emphasis added). The commentary to RUPA section 305 indicates that the language "with the authority of the partnership", as used in subsection 305(a),

is intended to include a partner's actual, as well as, apparent authority.

On the other hand, the same comment indicates that the partnership is liable for misapplication of funds

received by a partner in the course of the partnership's business or otherwise within the scope of the partner's *actual* authority.

(Emphasis added.) Is RUPA section 305(b) consistent with the principal case?

4. In *Cook v. Brundidge, Fountain, Elliott & Churchill*, 533 S.W.2d 751 (Tex. 1976), the case from which Problem 6.2 is drawn, the Supreme Court of Texas reasoned that the courts below committed error in granting and affirming summary judgment in favor of the law firm:

The question of the liability of a professional partnership of attorneys for the acts of a partner not strictly legal in nature, but which occur during the existence of the attorney-client relationship in recognized legal matters, is of first impression in our jurisdiction. Other jurisdictions have dealt with the problem of determining the scope of business of a professional partnership in various ways. In *Rouse v. Pollard*, 130 N.J.Eq. 204, 21 A.2d 801 (Ct.Err. & App. 1941), the partner of a law firm persuaded a client whom he was representing in a divorce to entrust him with some of her money for investment with 'the firm.' The client sued the partner and the partnership to recover her funds, and the trial court dismissed the suit as to the partnership on the ground that the partner's actions were not within the normal scope of business of a law practice. Affirming the trial court's dismissal, the New Jersey Court of Errors and Appeals relied on a distinction developed in England:

The English cases sustain the principle that where money is received by one member of a law partnership for the expressed purpose of a special investment,...there may be liability by one partner for the misconduct of another in the misapplication of the fund, but that if one of the partners receives money indefinitely, to lay out when a proper security may be found, he is not acting within the character of an attorney and does not thereby make his partner liable. 21 A.2d at 804.

* * *

In *Croisant v. Watrud*, 248 Or. 234, 432 P.2d 799 (1967), plaintiff had engaged an accounting firm to advise her on tax matters and to prepare tax returns for her business enterprises. After selling one of her businesses, she made arrangements with a member of the accounting firm, who had handled the business of plaintiff for the firm previously, to collect payments under the contract of sale, as well as some collection of rents from other property, and to make various disbursements of the money. The funds collected were deposited in an account of plaintiff, from which the accountant had authority to make withdrawals. The accountant misapplied some of the funds, and plaintiff sued the accountant's partnership to recover the loss. The Oregon Supreme Court, reversing a judgment in favor of the partnership, held that the partnership was liable for plaintiff's loss, even though the accountant's services to plaintiff were not services ordinarily performed by accounting firms:

> If a third person reasonably believes that the services he has requested of a member of an accounting partnership is (sic) undertaken as a part of the partnership business, the partnership should be bound for a breach of trust incident to that employment even though those engaged in the practice of accountancy would regard as unusual the performance of such service by an accounting firm.

> The reasonableness of a third person's belief that a partner is acting within the scope of the partnership should not be tested by the profession's own description of the function of its members. Those who seek accounting services may not understand the refinements made by accountants in defining the services they offer to the public. Whether a third person's belief is reasonable in assuming that the service he seeks is within the domain of the profession is a question which must be answered upon the basis of the facts in the particular case. 432 P.2d at 803.

It is doubtful if the treatment of the problem by these various jurisdictions, and the rationale applied for solutions, can be harmonized; or that an accepted rule can be said to appear. A stricter view against the liability of a professional partnership for the misdeeds of a partner with a client is indicated in Rouse...; a more liberal view is indicated in... Croisant. Surprisingly, also, only two of the jurisdictions,..., considered the problem in the light of their respective uniform partnership acts which, in our view are particularly relevant, if not controlling. Indeed, the conclusions we reach, later stated, rest in great measure upon the provisions of the Texas Uniform Partnership Act

*   *   *

There are, admittedly, compelling and unique considerations with respect to partners engaged in the practice of law. The fiducial obligations of a law partnership set it apart from commercial partnerships. * * * These characteristics and obligations inherent in the practice of law are universally understood and acknowledged by the legal profession. Nevertheless, the provisions of [the UPA] are expressly applicable to a professional partnership such as one of law. Section 6 of the Act defines a partnership as 'an association of two or more persons to carry on as co-owners a business for profit.' Section 2 defines 'business' as including 'every trade, occupation, or profession.' Governing the issue at hand, *i.e.,* the conditions to liability of a partnership for the acts of a partner, Sections 9, 13 and 14 of the Act provide:

*   *   *

We have recently spoken of apparent authority in terms of estoppel, and have said that one seeking to charge a principal through apparent authority of an agent must prove such conduct on the part of the principal as would lead a reasonable prudent person to suppose that the agent had the authority he purports to exercise. The extent of authority of a partner is determined essentially by the same principles as those measuring the scope of the authority of an agent. * * *

*   *   *

As stated before, it is not claimed either that Lyon was authorized by the partnership to act as he did in the Yummers matter or that Betty L. Cook, et al, had notice or knowledge that Lyon had no authority to act for the partnership in what he did. Assuming misapplication of the funds, the crucial consideration in determining whether the law firm is bound by the acts of Lyon by force of the statutory provisions is whether in receiving the funds of Betty L. Cook, et al, in the sum of $60,343.25, Lyon was 'apparently carrying on in the usual way the business of the partnership' (Sec. 9); or, as also expressed, whether he was 'acting in the ordinary course of the business of the partnership' (Sec. 13). If so, it would follow that Lyon was 'acting within the scope of his apparent authority' when he received the money and property of Betty L. Cook, et al; and that the law firm is 'bound to make good the loss' from his misapplication of the funds (Sec. 14).

It was the burden of the law firm as the defendant-movant for summary judgment to establish as a matter of law that no fact issue stands in the way of judgment in its favor. The summary judgment burden was that of establishing the negative of the statutory issues, namely, that Lyon was not apparently carrying on in the usual way the business of the law firm, *i.e.,* was not acting in the ordinary course of its business and hence was not acting within the scope of apparent authority by force of statute. * * *

As noted earlier, the thrust of the affidavits... in support of the motion for summary judgment was that the law firm is engaged exclusively in the practice of law, and that Lyon was not acting for the partnership in performing the services in question. But at the least, the acceptance by Lyon of the check of $60,343.25 payable to 'Warren Lyon as Attorney for' Betty L. Cook, et al, together with the deposition testimony of Betty L. Cook upon which the motion of the law firm for summary judgment also relied for support, and, further, the affidavit of Betty L. Cook and that of the Illinois attorney, demonstrate the existence of fact issues with respect to the statutory conditions to liability of the partnership. This being so, the record does not establish conclusively that the law firm is not accountable to Betty L. Cook, et al, for the acts of Lyon.

b. Estoppel

Problem 6.3

Ole consents to Lena telling Finn that Ole and Lena are partners in the practice of law (which they are not). Believing that he is dealing with Lena and Ole as partners, Finn lends money to Lena to buy a law library.

1. Is Ole subject to liability to Finn for the loan to Lena?

2. Would it make any difference in you answer if Lena instead borrowed money for the purpose of buying a sports car? Office supplies?

Problem 6.4

Odo and Worf are partners in the investment banking business. Odo and Worf both consent to Basheer holding himself out as their partner to Dax. Apparently acting for partnership purposes, Basheer borrows money from Dax, who thinks she is lending to the partnership.

1. Who is liable on the loan?

2. Would it make any difference to your answer if Odo, but not Worf, consented to being held out?

3. Would it make any difference in your answer if Worf had consented to Basheer holding himself as a partner to Quark, but had never consented to any holding out to Dax?

Cheesecake Factory, Inc. v. Baines
1998 NMCA 120, 964 P.2d 183 (N.M. App. 1998)

HARTZ, Chief Judge.

(1) John R. Baines appeals a judgment entered against him in favor of Cheesecake Factory, Inc. The claim against Baines arose out of deliveries of goods to Triples American Grill, an Albuquerque sports bar and restaurant owned by Triple Threat, Inc. Cheesecake Factory contended that it did not know that the business was owned by a corporation and that it extended credit because it believed that the business was owned by a partnership that included Baines as a member. Applying the New Mexico statute on partnership by estoppel, the district court entered judgment against Baines. Baines paid the judgment and appealed. We affirm.

I. WAIVER OF RIGHT TO APPEAL

[In Paragraphs (2) through (8), the Court ruled that, by paying the judgment, Baines did not waive his right to appeal.]

II. PARTNERSHIP BY ESTOPPEL

(9) Triples American Grill was owned by a corporation, Triple Threat, Inc. Cheesecake Factory, however, contended that it did not know that the entity to which it was advancing credit was a corporation. It claimed that representations by Frank Kolk, the manager of the business, caused it to believe that the sports bar was owned by a partnership. Its theory of liability in the district court was that Baines was a partner by estoppel and therefore liable for the debt incurred by the sports bar. The district court agreed. We affirm because the evidence at trial, viewed in the light most favorable to the judgment, could persuade a rational trier of fact that Baines was a partner by estoppel.

(10) The New Mexico Uniform Partnership Act contains the following provision:

Partner by estoppel.

A. When a person, by words spoken or written or by conduct, represents himself, or consents to another representing him or anyone, as a partner in an existing partnership or with one or more persons not actual partners, he is liable to any such person to whom such representation has been made, who has, on the faith of such representation, given credit to the actual or apparent partnership, and if he has made such representation or consented to its being made in a public manner he is liable to such person, whether the representation has or has not been made or communicated to such person so giving credit by or with the knowledge of the apparent partner making representation or consenting to its being made.

(1) When a partnership liability results, he is liable as though he were an actual member of the partnership.

(2) When no partnership liability results, he is liable jointly with the other persons, if any, so consenting to the contract or representation as to incur liability, otherwise separately.

B. When a person has been thus represented to be a partner in an existing partnership, or with one or more persons not actual partners, he is an agent of the persons consenting to such representation to bind them to the same extent and in the same manner as though he were a partner in fact, with respect to persons who rely upon the representation. Where all the members of the existing partnership consent to the representation, a partnership act or obligation results; but in all other cases it is the joint act or obligation of the person acting and the persons consenting to the representation.

NMSA 1978, Section 54-1-16 (1947) (repealed 1997). The language is essentially identical to Section 16 of the Uniform Partnership Act (1914). (We should note that the Uniform Partnership Act was superseded in New Mexico after the trial in this case. The Uniform Partnership Act (1994), which is codified at NMSA 1978, §§ 54-1A-101 to -1005 (1996), became effective July 1, 1997.)

(11) Under this section even though an enterprise is a corporation, a person can be treated as a partner, and consequently exposed to personal liability for the corporation's debts, when representations are made that the enterprise is a partnership and the person is a partner. The representations must be made by the purported partner or with the purported partner's consent. The section distinguishes between representations made in a "public manner" and other representations (which we will refer to as "private" representations).

> If the representation is privately made, it may be taken advantage of only by persons to whom it was made; if it was publicly made, anyone (roughly speaking) can make use of it.

Alan R. Bromberg, Crane and Bromberg on Partnership 197 (1968) (footnotes omitted).

(12) One issue on appeal is whether Cheesecake Factory can recover regardless of whether it relied on representations of Baines' partnership status. When a representation is private, the statute explicitly requires the claimant to establish that it "has on the faith of such representation, given credit to the actual partnership." Section 54-1-16(A). Cheesecake Factory argues that no such reliance is necessary if the representations are made "in a public manner." Id. Accordingly, it asserts that it need prove only that Baines made or consented to public representations of his partnership status. As an alternative basis for affirmance, Cheesecake Factory argues that it in fact relied on private representations of Baines' partnership status.

(13) We begin by discussing whether the statute requires reliance on representations made in a public manner. We determine that the prudent course on this appeal is to assume that reliance is required. We then proceed to review whether the evidence will support findings that (1) Baines consented to representations to Cheesecake Factory of his partnership status and (2) Cheesecake Factory relied on such representations.

A. Representations Made in a Public Manner

(14) Cheesecake Factory contends that if Baines' partnership interest was represented "in a public manner," Baines is liable to Cheesecake Factory regardless of whether it relied on such representations. We are not persuaded.

(15) At the outset of our discussion, we must acknowledge that strong support for Cheesecake Factory's contention can be found in our Supreme Court's decision in Gilbert v. Howard, 64 N.M. 200, 326 P.2d 1085 (1958). The Court paraphrased the statutory provision as follows:

> The statutory test for partnership by estoppel requires that (1) credit must have been extended on the basis of partnership representations or (2) that the alleged partner must have made or consented to representations being made in a public manner whether or not such representations were actually communicated to the person extending credit.

Id. at 202, 326 P.2d at 1086. The Court found that the first test had not been met in that case:

> Since plaintiffs did not even know Moore existed at the time of the leasing there could have been no reliance upon his credit and defendant Moore is not liable under the first part of [Section 54-1-16], which is the

same as the common-law test for liability in New Mexico before the adoption of the Uniform Partnership Act in 1947.

Id. at 202-203, 326 P.2d at 1086. The opinion then contains the passage chiefly relied upon by Cheesecake Factory:

However, the last part of [Section 54-1-16] reads as follows:

'...and if he has made such representation or consented to its being made in a public manner he is liable to such person, whether the representation has or has not been made or communicated to such person so giving credit by or with the knowledge of the apparent partner making representation or consenting to its being made.'

This section extends liability beyond the common-law test of reliance so that when one has by his acts or his consent to the acts of others allowed or caused the general community to believe that he is a partner then he is such by estoppel even though this particular creditor may not have heard the representation. This relieves the creditor of the task of proving that he actually knew of such representation and makes the representation itself an offense without the added factor of reliance.

Id. at 203, 326 P.2d at 1087 (ellipses in original). In that appeal, however, the Court ruled that the representations had not been made in a "public manner," so the defendant was not liable under the statute. *Id.* at 203-04, 326 P.2d. at 1087-88.

(16) *Gilbert* was followed a dozen years later. In *Anderson Hay & Grain Co. v. Dunn*, 81 N.M. 339, 467 P.2d 5 (1970) our Supreme Court repeated *Gilbert* 's paraphrase of the statutory test for partnership by estoppel, *Id.* at 341, 467 P.2d at 7, although it ruled that there was reliance in that case.

(17) Despite this weighty authority, we are reluctant to adopt the proposition that reliance need not be shown when representations of partnership are made publicly. If the issue were squarely put to our Supreme Court, we believe that it would always require reliance to establish a partner by estoppel under Section 54-1-16. The following considerations lead us to this conclusion.

(18) First, as partially acknowledged in *Gilbert*, recognizing estoppel without reliance would be a sharp departure from firmly grounded common-law principles. The foundation of estoppel is that one is bound by saying or doing something upon which another relies to his or her detriment. Why should that principle not be followed in this context? Why should a person who did not rely on the existence of the partnership be permitted to claim an estoppel?

(19) Of course, statutes often change the common law, and judges would be abusing their power if they insisted on following the common law despite contrary statutory enactments. The point here is only that a court is well-advised to take a second look at statutory language if an initial reading suggests a meaning that constitutes a sharp break with long-standing principles for no apparent reason.

(20) A second [l]ook at the language of Section 54-1-16 suggests that the portion of Subsection A relating to public representations does not remove the requirement of reliance. Consider the language of Subsection B:

When a person has been *thus represented* to be a partner in an existing partnership, or with one or more persons not actual partners, he is an agent of the persons consenting to such representation to bind them to the same extent and in the same manner as though he were a partner in fact, with respect to persons who rely upon the representation.

(Emphasis added). The word "thus" is a reference back to Subsection A. Accordingly, under Subsection B even when the representation has been made "in a public manner," the purported partners are bound only "to persons who rely upon the representation." It would be remarkable to require reliance under Subsection B but not under Subsection A.

(21) Most important of all, the best reading of Subsection A is that the fact of public representation does not eliminate the requirement of reliance. The language regarding public representations states: "if he has made such representation or consented to its being made in a public manner he is liable to *such person....*" (Emphasis added). Who is "such person"? The obvious candidate is the person described earlier in the sentence: a person "to whom such representation has been made, who has, on the faith of such representation, given credit to the actual or apparent partnership." In other words, "such person" is one who has relied on the representation. The purported partner is liable only to one who has relied.

(22) What, then, is the purpose of the language relating to public representations? What follows from a public representation that does not result from a private one? Only that one can be a partner by estoppel, and therefore liable to one who has relied on a representation, even though the partner by estoppel did not know of or consent to the representation being made to the person who relied. Ordinarily, a purported partner cannot be held liable as a partner by estoppel to someone to whom the representation was made unless the purported partner made the representation to the person who relied or consented to the representation being made to that person. But if the representation of partnership is made "in a public manner," the person claiming partnership by estoppel need not prove that the purported partner authorized the representation to that particular person. Not only is this a reasonable reading of the statutory language, it makes sense as a proposition of law. One who consents to a public announcement that he or she is a partner can expect unknown others to hear and rely on the announcement; and holding the purported partner to the consequences is a fair result under familiar equitable concepts.

(23) Outside of New Mexico case law, the authorities support this interpretation. Referring to the language regarding public representations, Professor Painter wrote:

This awkward clause is apparently little more than an attempt to codify what may have been the law in America and what in England was the law by statute; namely that, if there is a hold out "in a public manner" either by the defendant or by another with the defendant's consent, then the defendant need not consent specifically to the particular form of holding out upon which the plaintiff has relied. Why this relatively simple concept required such complex terminology is an enigma.

William H. Painter, *Partnership by Estoppel,* 16 Vand.L.Rev. 327, 338 (1963) (hereinafter Painter). Likewise, 1 Bromberg and Ribstein on Partnership at 2:161-162 (1998 Supp.) states:

> It has been held that the portion of [Section 16 of the Uniform Partnership Act] dealing with representations "made in a public manner" removes the reliance requirement with respect to public representations. But this provision appears to relate only to the purported partner's consent to the representation to a particular plaintiff... rather than to the reliance requirement, so that a public representation would not create an estoppel as to one who does not become aware of it.

(Footnotes omitted). We note that Section 308 of the Revised Uniform Partnership Act (adopted in New Mexico effective July 1, 1997, under the title "Uniform Partnership Act (1994)," Section 54-1A-1202) uses much clearer language:

> If the representation, either by the purported partner or by a person with the purported partner's consent, is made in a public manner, the purported partner is liable to a person who relies upon the purported partnership even if the purported partner is not aware of being held out as a partner to the claimant.

Section 54-1A-308(a) (1997). As explained by one commentator:

> [The Revised Uniform Partnership Act] has resolved any doubts that may exist about the necessity of a creditor to prove reliance in a public holding out case, a problem that was created by some abstruse language in [Section 16 of the Uniform Partnership Act] that, carelessly read, seemed to obviate the requirement of reliance in a public holding out.

J. Dennis Hynes, *Agency, Partnership, and the LLC—In a Nutshell* at 114 (1997). Thus, we will assume for purposes of this appeal that Cheesecake Factory had to establish reliance.

B. Consent to Being Represented as a Partner

(24) We now turn to the two elements of Cheesecake Factory's cause of action that Baines contends are missing. First, we address whether Baines consented to Kolk's representation to Cheesecake Factory that he and Baines were partners in Triples American Grill. Then we address the question of reliance. We hold that the evidence was sufficient to prove both elements.

(25) Steve Mager, the president of Cheesecake Factory, testified that before Cheesecake Factory advanced credit to the sports bar, Kolk told him that Kolk and Baines were in a partnership of three persons that owned the bar. Although there was no direct evidence that Baines authorized Kolk to tell Cheesecake Factory that Baines was a partner in the business, there was ample evidence to support an inference that Baines consented to Kolk's making such a representation. Among that evidence was the following: Cheesecake Factory first extended credit to the business on February 10, 1993. On February 23, 1993, an account was opened at Western Bank of Albuquerque in the name of "Baines: Bob DBA Triples American Grill." (Baines was generally known in the community as "Bob" Baines.) The signature card contains two signatures, those of "Bob Baines, owner" and "Frank Kolk, owner." On March 3, 1993, a payroll account was opened at Western Bank in the same name. The signatures on the signature

card were "Bob Baines" and "Frank Kolk." Baines was frequently present at the sports bar and freely entered the business office. As a result, employees believed that Baines was a partner. In addition, there was testimony that Baines himself had told others that "he had a sports bar" and "was a partner" in the business. Although these statements by Baines may have been as much as nine months after Kolk first told Mager that Baines was a partner, they are probative of a consistent pattern of behavior over the course of several months indicating Baines' consent, indeed desire, to be perceived as a partner in the business. Viewing the evidence in the light most favorable to the judgment, see *id.*, we believe that the district court could reasonably infer that Baines consented to Kolk's representing Baines' partnership status to Cheesecake Factory.

C. Reliance

(26) Finally, we address the claim that Cheesecake Factory did not prove that it relied on the purported partnership. In one respect the evidence of reliance by Cheesecake Factory is clearly supported by the evidence. Mager and his sales manager, Don Grosso, testified that Cheesecake Factory was willing to extend credit to the new business only because it was a partnership. In particular, they testified that credit would not have been extended to a new restaurant organized as a corporation because the restaurant business is risky and it may be impossible to collect a debt from a failed corporation. Mager testified that he had "never gotten burnt" by a partnership and "I'm more likely to go in looking at it from the bright side because there are partners involved and liability runs to the individual partners."

(27) Cheesecake Factory contends that reliance on the existence of a partnership sufficed for creation of a partner by estoppel. It relies on *Hunter v. Croysdill*, 169 Cal.App.2d 307, 337 P.2d 174 (1959). Considering language in the California Corporations Code identical to that in Section 54-1-16(A), *Hunter* said:

> Defendant takes the position that as plaintiffs did not make exhaustive inquiries into his financial status, they could not have relied thereon. There is no requirement that credit be given in reliance upon the financial status of the apparent partner, but only that the party claiming the benefit of [the California counterpart to Section 54-1-16] relied on the existence of the partnership.

337 P.2d at 179.

(28) The rule in Hunter is an attractive one for Cheesecake Factory, because the evidence of reliance on Baines' credit is slim. Cheesecake Factory sought no financial statement from Baines and made no credit inquiry or, apparently, any inquiry whatsoever about Baines. Mager said simply that he was familiar with the name Baines and associated it with the construction or automobile business. Also, Mager said that he was told by Kolk that the partners owned the extensive sports memorabilia on display, that one of the partners was going to arrange for display of a pace car, and that Baines was helping to remodel the restaurant.

(29) Mager's failure to obtain a credit check on Baines limits the extent to which Cheesecake Factory could reasonably rely on Baines to cover debts incurred by the sports bar. But that does not mean that Cheesecake Factory could

not reasonably rely at all on the fact that Baines was a partner. As indicated by Mager's testimony, the very fact of a person's being a partner provides some comfort for creditors. One whose personal assets are at risk in a business venture can be expected to take a particular interest in having the enterprise run properly and paying its bills out of business revenue. Moreover, the evidence at trial, although marginal, would support the inference that Mager reasonably believed Baines to be the proprietor of an established business. At least two rational inferences can be drawn from that fact. First, as proprietor of an established business, Baines would have expertise that could be helpful in the financial affairs of the sports bar. Second, even if Mager could not be confident that Baines could pay very large debts, he could expect Baines to be financially responsible. Cheesecake Factory's dealings with the sports bar would not be likely to lead to huge debts. We note that the principal amount owed on open account in this case was slightly more than $20,000. Although this is not an insignificant amount, even one without great wealth—and probably most owners of established businesses— could be expected to pay off a substantial portion of the sum. Thus, the evidence at trial would support a rational inference that Cheesecake Factory reasonably relied on Baines' being a partner.

(30) One possible reaction to this analysis is that it proves too much. By the above reasoning the trier of fact could almost always find reasonable reliance. That may be true. But that is not necessarily contrary to the rationale of the statute. The nature of the reliance required to establish partnership by estoppel has been little explored by courts or commentators. See Painter, *supra,* at 334. As previously noted, California has ruled that the creditor need rely only on the existence of the partnership. See Hunter, 337 P.2d at 179. Perhaps this ruling reflects the realization that once the creditor relies on the existence of the partnership, the creditor will be relying to some extent on each of the partners. On that basis we might be inclined to adopt the California rule. In our view, however, faithfulness to the statutory language requires us to leave open the possibility in any particular case that there was no reliance on a particular person's being a member of the partnership. We find the words of Professor Painter to be persuasive. In discussing whether a plaintiff should be required to prove that it would not have extended credit but for the representation of partnership, he wrote as follows:

> [W]here the plaintiff has not previously dealt with the firm, it seems unduly burdensome to impose upon him the rigors of a "but-for" test, since this complicates the problems of proof to the point that recovery is unusually difficult. This seems to be a reasonable view; in most instances where the plaintiff is aware of the holding out and, being so aware, extends credit to what he supposes is a partnership, he will be motivated at least in part by an assumption, albeit a vague one, that the defendant is financially responsible and that his credit stands back of that of the firm. Hence there should be at least a presumption of reliance on the defendant's financial responsibility, subject to possible rebuttal by a showing of complete indifference on the part of the plaintiff to the representation.

Painter, *supra,* at 335 (footnotes omitted) (emphasis added). See Allen Dewey, *Partnerships—Partnership by Estoppel—Proof of Reliance by Creditor Dealing with Persons in Belief of Partnership,* 56 Mich.L.Rev. 139 (1957).

(31) In sum, the test for reliance is not whether it would have been good business practice to advance credit relying solely on Baines' being a partner. Many factors may go into the decision whether to advance credit. The only question is whether it was reasonable for one of the factors to be that Baines was a partner. Although it may be tempting to rule against a creditor who apparently has not engaged in the wisest business practices, it must be realized that the partner by estoppel is the "victim" only of misrepresentations that he himself authorized. This is a close case, but we hold that the evidence of reliance is sufficient to sustain the judgment.

III. CONCLUSION

(32) For the above reasons, we affirm the judgment below. We award Cheesecake Factory attorney fees of $3,000.00 and its costs on appeal.

(33) IT IS SO ORDERED.

Notes

1. Under UPA section 16, a holding out of a person as a partner may occur in two different contexts. First, as in Problem 6.3, there may not be any existing partnership. Second, as in Problem 6.4, a person may be held out as a partner in an existing partnership. How does UPA section 16(2) handle Problems 6.3 and 6.4?

2. RUPA section 308 generally parallels UPA section 16, except that it calls persons liable under that section "purported partners," rather than "partners by estoppel".

Problem 6.5

With the consent of Dick, Jane holds herself out to Emily as being a partner of Dick's. Emily signs a contract to sell widgets to what she believes is the Dick and Jane partnership on open account. Before Jane delivers the widgets, Dick tells her that there is no partnership and tells her that he will not be liable for the contract. Assuming the transaction is one that would have bound the partnership if made by a partner.

   1. Under UPA section 16 may Emily bring an action for breach of contract against Dick?

   2. Could Emily do so under RUPA section 308?

3. Partners as Managers

a. Generally

Problem 6.6

Matthew, Emily and Paul are partners in a newly opened grocery business, MEP Grocers. Except for an agreement to be partners, and to divide profits equally, the partners have no other written or oral agreement as to partnership business or affairs.

1. Without first discussing the matter with his partners, Matthew contacted Arrow Bread Company, and contracted for Arrow to sell bread to MEP Grocers for a week. At the same time, and also without discussing the matter with his partners, Paul contracted with Wholesome Bakers, Inc. for the purchase of bread by MEP Grocers for a month. Assume that the partners have no existing practice

a. Is the partnership subject to liability to either Arrow or Wholesome?

b. As among the partners, are either Matthew or Paul liable to Emily or to MEP Grocers for contracting for the purchase of bread without first consulting the other partners?

2. The partners meet to discuss the matter. Matthew likes the quality and flavor of Arrow's bread, while Emily and Paul prefer Wholesome's wider variety. Over Matthew's objections, Emily and Paul decide to buy bread from Wholesome, rather than from Arrow. Matthew writes Wholesome a letter in which he denies the authority of Emily and Paul to bind MEP Grocers. He also disclaims any liability on any new purchases from Wholesome. Thereafter, Emily and Paul contract for additional purchases of bread from Wholesome.

a. Are either MEP Grocers or Matthew subject to liability to Wholesome on the contract?

b. What action, if any, could Matthew have taken to avoid liability on purchases from Wholesome?

3. After losing the vote, Matthew again contracts to buy bread for another week from Arrow. Assume that Arrow does not know of the partners' vote.

a. Are either MEP Grocers, Emily or Paul subject to liability to Wholesome on account of the contract?

b. As among the partners, is Matthew liable to MEP Grocers or to

4. Suppose that after Matthew learned that Paul wants to buy bread from Wholesome, and not from Arrow, but before either of them had talked to Emily, Matthew contracts to buy bread from Arrow for another week.

a. Is the partnership subject to liability to either Arrow or Wholesome?

b. As among the partners, is Matthew liable to Emily or to MEP Grocers for contracting for the purchase of bread without first consulting the other partners? Emily and Paul for contracting with Arrow after the partners' vote?

National Biscuit Co., Inc. v. Stroud
259 N.C. 467, 106 S.E.2d 692 (1959)

The case was heard in the Superior Court upon the following agreed statement of facts:

On 13 September 1956 the National Biscuit Company had a Justice of the Peace to issue summons against C. N. Stroud and Earl Freeman, a partnership trading as Stroud's Food Center, for the nonpayment of $171.04 for goods sold and delivered. After a hearing the Justice of the Peace rendered judgment for plaintiff against both defendants for $171.04 with interest and costs. Stroud appealed to the Superior Court: Freeman did not.

In March 1953 C. N. Stroud and Earl Freeman entered into a general partnership to sell groceries under the name of Stroud's Food Center. Thereafter plaintiff sold bread regularly to the partnership. Several months prior to February 1956 the defendant Stroud advised an agent of plaintiff that he personally would not be responsible for any additional bread sold by plaintiff to Stroud's Food Center. From 6 February 1956 to 25 February 1956 plaintiff through this same agent, at the request of the defendant Freeman, sold and delivered bread in the amount of $171.04 to Stroud's Food Center. Stroud and Freeman by agreement dissolved the partnership at the close of business on 25 February 1956, and notice of such dissolution was published in a newspaper in Carteret County 6-27 March 1956.

The relevant parts of the dissolution agreement are these: All partnership assets, except an automobile truck, an electric adding machine, a rotisserie, which were assigned to defendant Freeman, and except funds necessary to pay the employees for their work the week before the dissolution and necessary to pay for certain supplies purchased the week of dissolution, were assigned to Stroud. Freeman assumed the outstanding liens against the truck. Paragraph five of the dissolution agreement is as follows: "From and after the aforesaid February 25, 1956, Stroud will be responsible for the liquidation of the partnership assets and the discharge of partnership liabilities without demand upon Freeman for any contribution in the discharge of said obligations." The dissolution agreement was made in reliance on Freeman's representations that the indebtedness of the partnership was about $7,800 and its accounts receivable were about $8,000. The accounts receivable at the close of business actually amounted to $4,897.41.

Stroud has paid all of the partnership obligations amounting to $12,014.45, except the amount of $171.04 claimed by plaintiff. To pay such obligations Stroud exhausted all the partnership assets he could reduce to money amounting to $4,307.08, of which $2,028 was derived from accounts receivable and $2,278.44 from a sale of merchandise and fixtures and used over $7,700 of his personal money. Stroud has left of the partnership assets only uncollected accounts in the sum of $2,868.77, practically all of which are considered uncollectible.

Stroud has not attempted to rescind the dissolution agreement, and has tendered plaintiff, and still tenders it, one-half of the $171.04 claimed by it.

From a judgment that plaintiff recover from the defendants $171.04 with interest and costs, Stroud appeals to the Supreme Court.

PARKER, Justice.

C. N. Stroud and Earl Freeman entered into a general partnership to sell groceries under the firm name of Stroud's Food Center. There is nothing in the agreed statement of facts to indicate or suggest that Freeman's power and authority as a general partner were in any way restricted or limited by the articles of partnership in respect to the ordinary and legitimate business of the partnership. Certainly, the purchase and sale of bread were ordinary and legitimate business of Stroud's Food Center during its continuance as a going concern.

Several months prior to February 1956 Stroud advised plaintiff that he personally would not be responsible for any additional bread sold by plaintiff to

Stroud's Food Center. After such notice to plaintiff, it from 6 February 1956 to 25 February 1956, at the request of Freeman, sold and delivered bread in the amount of $171.04 to Stroud's Food Center.

In *Johnson v. Bernheim*, 76 N.C. 139, this Court said:

A and B are general partners to do some given business; the partnership is, by operation of law, a power to each to bind the partnership in any manner legitimate to the business. If one partner go to a third person to buy an article on time for the partnership, the other partner cannot prevent it by writing to the third person not to sell to him on time; or, if one party attempt to buy for cash, the other has no right to require that it shall be on time. And what is true in regard to buying is true in regard to selling. What either partner does with a third person is binding on the partnership. It is otherwise where the partnership is not general, but is upon special terms, as that purchases and sales must be with and for cash. There the power for each is special, in regard to all dealings with third persons at least who have notice of the terms.

There is contrary authority. 68 C.J.S. Partnership 143, pp. 578-579. However, this text of C.J.S. does not mention the effect of the provisions of the [UPA].

[UPA section 9] is entitled "Partner Agent of Partnership as to Partnership Business," and subsection (1) reads:

Every partner is an agent of the partnership for the purpose of its business, and the act of every partner, including the execution in the partnership name of any instrument, for apparently carrying on in the usual way the business of the partnership of which he is a member binds the partnership, unless the partner so acting has in fact no authority to act for the partnership in the particular matter, and the person with whom he is dealing has knowledge of the fact that he has no such authority.

[UPA section 9(4)] states:

No act of a partner in contravention of a restriction on authority shall bind the partnership to persons having knowledge of the restriction.

[UPA section 15] provides that "all partners are jointly and severally liable for the acts and obligations of the partnership."

[UPA section 18] is captioned "Rules Determining Rights and Duties of Partners." Subsection (e) thereof reads:

All partners have equal rights in the management and conduct of the partnership business.

Subsection (h) hereof is as follows:

Any difference arising as to ordinary matters connected with the partnership business may be decided by a majority of the partners; but no act in contravention of any agreement between the partners may be done rightfully without the consent of all the partners.

Freeman as a general partner with Stroud, with no restrictions on his authority to act within the scope of the partnership so far as the agreed statement of facts shows, had under the Uniform Partnership Act "equal rights in the management and conduct of the partnership business." Under [UPA section 18(h)] Stroud, his co-partner, could not restrict the power and authority of Freeman to buy bread for the partnership as a going concern, for such a purchase was an "ordinary matter connected with the partnership business," for the purpose of its business and within its scope, because in the very nature of things Stroud was not, and could not be, a majority of the partners. Therefore, Freeman's purchases of bread from plaintiff for Stroud's Food Center as a going concern bound the partnership and his co-partner Stroud. The quoted provisions of our Uniform Partnership Act, in respect to the particular facts here, are in accord with the principle of law stated in *Johnson v. Bernheim, supra.*

In Crane on Partnership, 2d Ed., p. 277, it is said:

> In cases of an even division of the partners as to whether or not an act within the scope of the business should be done, or which disagreement a third person has knowledge, it seems that logically no restriction can be placed upon the power to act. The partnership being a going concern, activities within the scope of the business should not be limited, save by the expressed will of the majority deciding a disputed question; half of the members are not a majority.

At the close of business on 25 February 1956 Stroud and Freeman by agreement dissolved the partnership. By their dissolution agreement all of the partnership assets, including cash on hand, bank deposits and all accounts receivable, with a few exceptions, were assigned to Stroud, who bound himself by such written dissolution agreement to liquidate the firm's assets and discharge its liabilities. It would seem a fair inference from the agreed statement of facts that the partnership got the benefit of the bread sold and delivered by plaintiff to Stroud's Food Center, at Freeman's request, from 6 February 1956 to 25 February 1956. But whether it did not, Freeman's acts, as stated above, bound the partnership and Stroud.

Affirmed.

Covalt v. High
100 N.M. 700, 675 P.2d 999 (App. 1983)

DONNELLY, Judge.

Can a partner recover damages against his co-partner for the co-partner's failure or refusal to negotiate and obtain an increase in the amount of rental of partnership property?

The plaintiff, Louis E. Covalt, filed suit against defendant, William L. High, seeking (1) the sale of real property in lieu of partition, (2) an accounting as to former partnership property, and (3) seeking both actual and punitive damages. Covalt alleged High had breached his fiduciary duty as a partner resulting in a loss of increased rentals. Covalt also filed a separate action against Concrete Systems, Inc. (CSI), Mildred L. High and Mark High (wife and son of William High), as corporate shareholders, seeking dissolution of the corporation, damages for alleged misuse of corporate funds, and seeking a dissolution and accounting of partnership assets. By order of the district court the two cases were consolidated for trial.

The answers of defendants denied any wrongdoing and contained a counter-claim asserting, *inter alia*, that Covalt as former employee of CSI had wrongfully converted corporate assets and wrongfully interfered with contractual relations between the corporation and others.

The trial court ordered that Covalt's claim for loss of rental income, allegedly owed by defendant to the former partnership, be bifurcated from the remaining issues and tried separately to the court. Following trial thereon, Covalt was awarded judgment against William L. High, individually, in the sum of $9,500, plus prejudgment interest in the sum of $2,269.

High appeals the partial judgment entered solely against him. The single issue presented on appeal is whether the trial court erred by ruling that High breached a fiduciary duty of fairness to his former partner Covalt by failing to negotiate and obtain an increase in the amount of rental for the partnership realty.

Covalt and High were corporate officers and shareholders in CSI. Covalt owned 25% of the stock and High owned the remaining 75% of the stock. Both men received remuneration from the corporation in the form of salaries and bonuses. In late 1971, after both High and Covalt had become corporate officers, they orally agreed to the formation of a partnership. The partnership bought real estate and constructed an office and warehouse building on the land. In February, 1973, CSI leased the building from the partnership for a five-year term. Following the expiration of the initial term of the lease, CSI remained a tenant of the building; the corporation and the partnership orally agreed to certain rental increases. The corporation made substantial improvements to the leasehold. Under the original lease any improvements to the premises were to accrue to the partnership upon termination of the lease.

In December, 1978, Covalt resigned his corporate position and was employed by a competitor of CSI. Covalt, however, remained a partner with High in the ownership of the land and the building rented to CSI. On January 9, 1979, Covalt wrote to High demanding that the monthly rent for the partnership real estate leased to CSI be increased from $1,850 to $2,850 per month. Upon receipt of the letter, High informed Covalt he would determine if the rent could be increased. Thereafter, however, High did not agree to the increased rent and took no action to renegotiate the amount of the monthly rent payable.

At the trial, High testified that he felt CSI could not afford a higher rent and that the corporation had a poor financial status. The trial court, however, adopted findings that CSI could afford the requested rental increase and that High's failure to assent to his partner's demand was a breach of his fiduciary duty. The trial court also found that at the time of Covalt's demand, a reasonable monthly rental would have been $2,850 per month or more.

The trial court adopted findings of fact, that:

18. At all material times, William High was the managing partner of the partnership and had a duty of utmost fairness to his partner, Mr. Covalt, which required him to obtain a reasonable rental on the property.

55. William High refused to see that the rental on the Richmond property was raised to $2,850 a month, and said refusal was a breach of his fiduciary duty of utmost fairness to his partner, Louis Covalt.

The court also found that the partnership between High and Covalt was dissolved by written agreement dated August 27, 1980. Under the terms of the dissolution, High paid Covalt $170,000, in cash, plus installment payments for his one-half interest as a partner, and for other property in which the two parties held joint interests.

The court further found that the rental rate in effect when the written lease expired on January 31, 1978, was $1,850 per month, no other written lease was ever executed by the partnership and CSI, and that the partners never had any specific agreement as to how the partnership would set the rent to be charged CSI. As between the partners, that calculation was left up to High. The court adopted a finding that High, as Covalt's partner, did not agree with Covalt's demand to raise the monthly rental payable by CSI.

The trial court also found:

> 34. On January 9, 1979, when Covalt made his demand on [CSI] for a rental increase, High, as President of [CSI] owed a duty to the Corporation and all shareholders, including Covalt, to exercise his best judgment to operate the Corporation as profitably as possible.

> 35. That High, in failing or refusing to accede to the demand by Covalt to raise the rent, was fulfilling this duty owed to the Corporation and its shareholders, including Covalt.

Based on the foregoing findings, the trial court concluded that High breached his fiduciary duty to Covalt, resulting in damage to Covalt in the sum of $9,500 as lost rentals, plus prejudgment interest through April 30, 1982, in the amount of $2,269.66.

Fiduciary Duty as a Partner

Did High breach a fiduciary partnership duty to Covalt warranting an award of damages?

The status resulting from the formation of a partnership creates a fiduciary relationship between partners. The status of partnership requires of each member an obligation of good faith and fairness in their dealings with one another, and a duty to act in furtherance of the common benefit of all partners in transactions conducted within the ambit of partnership affairs.

The problems which have arisen between the parties herein emphasize the importance of formulating written partnership agreements detailing the rights and obligations of the partners. Here, at the time of Covalt's demand for an increase in rents, both he and High simultaneously occupied the positions of corporate shareholders in CSI and as partners engaged in the ownership and rental of real property to the same corporation. Prior to Covalt's resignation as a corporate officer, he also served as vice president of CSI. The trial court found that High occupied the position of managing partner of the partnership.

Except where the partners expressly agree to the contrary, it is a fundamental principle of the law of partnership that all partners have equal rights in the management and conduct of the business of the partnership. [UPA § 18(e).] As specified in the Uniform Partnership Act..., where there is a difference of opinion between the partners as to the management or conduct of the partnership business, the decision of the majority must govern. [UPA § 18(h).]

Under [UPA section 18(e)], Covalt was legally invested with an equal voice in the management of the partnership affairs. Assuming, but not deciding, that High's status as a managing partner is not to be considered, neither partner had the right to impose his will or decision concerning the operation of the partnership business upon the other. The fact that a proposal may in fact benefit the partnership does not mandate acceptance by all the partners. As specified in [UPA section 18(h)], "any difference arising as to ordinary matters connected with the partnership business may be decided by a majority of the partners; but no act in contravention of any agreement between the partners may be done rightfully without the consent of all the partners."

As stated in *Lindley on the Law of Partnership*, at 354 (E. Scamell 12th ed. 1962) (hereinafter referred to as *Lindley*), as to differences arising in the ordinary scope of the partnership business:

> [I]f the partners are equally divided, those who forbid a change must have their way. [O]ne partner cannot either engage a new or dismiss an old servant against the will of his co-partner; nor, if the lease of the partnership place of business expires, insist on renewing the lease and continuing the business at the old place.

In *Summers v. Dooley*, 94 Idaho 87, 481 P.2d 318 (1971), the Supreme Court of Idaho was confronted with a similar problem arising out of a partnership of two individuals. There, the partners were engaged in a trash collection business and each contributed to the necessary labor. Over the objection of one partner, the other hired an additional employee. The disagreement over the hiring and compensation of the new employee resulted in a suit between the partners. The one partner sought to compel his co-partner to contribute to the expenses for hiring the additional man. The court held that, based upon the Idaho statute, mirroring the Uniform Partnership Act and identical to that adopted by New Mexico, the statutory language that any differences between partners as to the ordinary course of partnership business "may be decided by a majority of the partners" is mandatory rather than permissive in nature.

In keeping with *Lindley* and *Summers*, as between the partners themselves, in the absence of an agreement of a majority of the partners—an act involving the partnership business may not be compelled by the co-partner. If the parties are evenly divided as to a business decision affecting the partnership, and in the absences of a written provision in the partnership agreement providing for such contingency, then, as between the partners, the power to exercise discretion on behalf of the partners is suspended so long as the division continues. The rule is different, however, as to transactions between partners and third parties. *See Dotson v. Grice*, 98 N.M. 207, 647 P.2d 409 (1982) (holding that in dealing with third parties a partner has the authority to act on behalf of the partnership in the usual way, even without the consent of the other partner).

Similarly, it is observed in 1 J. Barrett & E. Seago, *Partners and Partnerships Law and Taxation*, at 484 (1956):

> Where the partnership consists of only two partners there is ordinarily no question of one partner controlling the other and there is no majority. The rights of each of the two partners are equal. If the partners are unable to agree and if the partnership agreement does not provide an

acceptable means for settlement of this disagreement, the only course of action is to dissolve the partnership.

At the time of the formation of the partnership, both Covalt and High were officers and shareholders of CSI. Each was aware of the potential for conflict between their duties as corporate officers to further the business of the corporation, and that of their role as partners in leasing realty to the corporation for the benefit of the partnership business. In the posture of being both a landlord and representatives of the tenant they had conflicting loyalties and fiduciary duties. After Covalt's resignation as an officer of the corporation he continued to remain a shareholder of the corporation. Each party's conflict of interest was known to the other and was acquiesced in when the partnership was formed.

Under the facts herein, in the absence of a mutual agreement between the partners to increase the rent of the partnership realty, we hold that one partner may not recover damages for the failure of the co-partner to acquiesce in a demand by the plaintiff that High negotiate and execute an increase in the monthly rentals of partnership property with CSI. Thus, there was no breach of a fiduciary duty. In the absence of a mutual agreement, or a written instrument detailing the rights of the parties, the remedy for such an impasse is a dissolution of the partnership.

[T]he judgment awarding damages is reversed.

Notes

1. What is the difference between *National Biscuit Co., Inc. v. Stroud* and *Covalt v. High*, on the one hand, and *Burns v. Gonzalez*, page 287, on the other?

2. Under the opinions in *National Biscuit Co., Inc. v. Stroud* and *Covalt v. High*, when does a partner act *rightfully* (as against the other partners) in the partnership business? What is the *source* of a partner's *right* to act in the partnership business? Is it possible to reconcile the *results* of *National Biscuit Co., Inc. v. Stroud* and *Covalt v. High*?

3. The provisions of UPA section 18(h) may be varied by agreement among the partners. For example, partners often agree to vote according to their *interests*, rather than *per capita*. Any agreement intended to apply to matters that would require partner *unanimity* under the UPA should do so expressly and unambiguously. Several cases have limited the provisions of partnership voting agreements to voting on *ordinary* matters, reasoning that voting rights as to "extraordinary" matters are so "fundamental and vital" that any ambiguity as to the application of the agreement should be resolved *against* surrender of such rights. *E.g.*, *Wilzig v. Sisselman*, 182 N.J. Super. 519, 535, 442 A.2d 1021, 1030 (1982). *See generally*, A. BROMBERG & L. RIBSTEIN, BROMBERG & RIBSTEIN ON PARTNERSHIP 6:40-41, 6:436-49 (1988).

4. RUPA sections 401(f) and 401(j) are the RUPA equivalents of UPA sections 18(e) and 18(h).

5. What does UPA section 18(e) (equal rights to participate in management) have to do with whether the defendant in *Covalt v. High* violated defendant's duty of loyalty? Is the holding in *Covalt v. High* consistent with *Schock v. Nash*, page 216? For additional discussion of the parties' ability to contract as to fidu-

ciary duties, see *Labowitz v. Dolan*, page 367, and *Sonet v. [Plum Creek] Timber Company*, page 378, and the following notes in Chapter 7.

b. Transactions out of the Usual and Regular Course of Business

Vinson v. Marton & Associates
159 Ariz. 1, 764 P.2d 736 (App. 1988)

KLEINSCHMIDT, Judge.

This is an appeal from summary judgment in favor of defendants in a lawsuit for specific performance of a real estate contract. We must determine whether the unanimous consent of the partners was required to convey the partnership's sole asset.

Marton & Associates was a partnership formed in 1960 for the purpose of buying, selling and exchanging real property. The partnership's sole asset was a 238 acre parcel of land near Buckeye, Arizona. The original partners were Larry Marton, Larry Melcher, Dr. A.J. Silva, Richard Stephenson, Dr. Franklin Laneback, Robert Creighton, Charles Johnston and Powell Gillenwater. After Dr. Silva's death, his interest in the property passed by inheritance to Mary Silva, John Silva and the Celeste Silva-Brock Trust; after Dr. Laneback's death, his interest passed to his widow Phyllis Laneback; and after Powell Gillenwater's death, his interest passed to Danielle Gillenwater-Civer. Robert Creighton's interest was transferred to the Robert and Catherine Creighton Trust. The record does not disclose what happened to the interests of Richard Stephenson and Charles Johnston.

In November 1985, John Vinson entered into a contract to purchase the parcel of land owned by Marton & Associates. The purchase agreement was signed by Larry Melcher and John Silva for the sellers. Vinson alleged that Melcher, Silva and their realtor, C.B. Stauffer, represented that they were authorized to sign on behalf of the partnership. At the time Melcher signed the contract he held powers of attorney executed in 1979 from Larry Marton, the Creighton Trust and Phyllis Laneback. Stauffer informed Vinson that the land had been listed for sale by the partnership for several years.

Escrow instructions were issued on December 2, 1985, and were signed by Larry Marton, Larry Melcher, Mary Silva, Celeste Silva-Brock, John Silva, Phyllis Laneback, Robert Creighton and Catherine Creighton. Danielle Gillenwater-Civer was the only person with an interest in the property who did not sign the escrow instructions. After the escrow instructions were signed, Stauffer presented the partnership with another offer to purchase the property at a higher price. Subsequently, the partnership and the individual partners refused to convey the property to Vinson.

Vinson filed suit alleging two counts for breach of contract against the partnership and the individual partners and seeking specific performance of the contract. Alternatively, Vinson sought damages in a third count against John Silva and Larry Melcher for damages resulting from their having entered into a contract without authority to do so. In count four, the plaintiffs sought damages against Melcher, Silva, Stauffer, and P.R. Powell and Associates, Stauffer's employer, for false representation.

All parties filed motions and cross motions for summary judgment, and the trial court granted judgment in favor of defendants on the first two counts of the complaint.

After the appeal relating to counts one and two of the complaint was filed, Vinson, Melcher, Powell and Stauffer entered into a settlement agreement respecting counts three and four. The settlement agreement specifically permitted Vinson to proceed with his appeal on counts one and two. Vinson agreed to release Melcher, Stauffer and Powell from any liabilities arising from the sale of the property at issue and not to sue Melcher individually or as a partner in Marton & Associates under counts one and two of the complaint. It permits Vinson to do whatever is necessary to preserve his rights to proceed against the other defendants under counts one and two of the complaint. Silva and his wife refused to enter into the settlement agreement.

The Sale Was Controlled by the Partnership Agreement

The trial court's minute entry granting summary judgment provides in part:

The plaintiffs entered into a contract for the sale of the sole partnership asset with some but not all of the partners. The plaintiffs contend that Article VII of the Partnership Agreement allows a majority of the partners to conduct all business of the partnership. *Because a number of original partners are now deceased, this provision is not controlling upon the successor partners.* (All apparently agree that a partnership of some sort does exist.)

With no controlling language in the agreement, the provision of [UPA section 9] controls. In a recent decision the Court of Appeals has held that the concurrence of all of the partners is necessary to conclude a sale such as the one proposed in this case. (Emphasis added.)

In referring to [UPA section 9] as controlling, the trial court was apparently relying on subsection [(3)(c)], which requires unanimous consent of the partners to do any act that would make it impossible to carry on the ordinary business of the partnership. We disagree with the trial court's conclusion that the death of some of the partners rendered the partnership agreement inapplicable to this transaction. Article IX of the agreement provides:

It is further agreed that *the death or insanity of one or more of the partners of this partnership shall not dissolve the partnership*, but the same shall be continued by the remaining partners, and in the event of the death of any partner his personal representative shall immediately offer the partnership interest of the deceased partner for sale, first to the partnership and upon its refusal, then to as many of the partners individually as wish to participate, at its actual value to be determined by three arbitrators. (Emphasis added.)

Accordingly, the partnership agreement pursuant to its own terms continued in force after the death of any partner.

[UPA section 18] provides in part that "[t]he rights and duties of the partners in relation to the partnership shall be determined, *subject to any agreement between them*, by the following rules." (Emphasis added.) Other jurisdictions that, like Arizona, have adopted the Uniform Partnership Act recognize that partners may agree to terms different from the Uniform Partnership Act and be bound by those terms.

The rule that a partnership agreement controls over the Uniform Partnership Act has been acknowledged specifically with respect to death provisions in such an agreement. Accordingly, we find that the partnership agreement remained effective and there was no dissolution of Marton & Associates because of the death of some of the original partners.

Unanimous Consent of All Partners Was Not Required for the Sale of the Property at Issue

Article VII of the partnership agreement provides in part:

> *All business* of this partnership shall be carried on by, and only by, the majority vote of the partners, however, it is agreed that this partnership shall never allow the annual payments on its investment to exceed $500 per unit without the unanimous written consent of the partners. (Emphasis added.)

Marton & Associates argues that Article VII does not govern the sale of the sole partnership asset because it is not a sale in the ordinary course of business. Rather, it argues that the sale is controlled by the provisions of [UPA section 9], which requires a unanimous vote of the partners.

Vinson contends that [UPA section 9] is inapplicable because the partnership agreement expressly permits an act with less than a unanimous vote. He argues that "all business" includes a sale of the partnership's sole asset. He also argues that, even assuming arguendo that "all business" means the "ordinary business" of the partnership, this sale was in the ordinary course of business under [UPA section 9].

[UPA section 9(1)] provides:

> Every partner is an agent of the partnership for the purpose of its business, and the act of every partner, including the execution in the partnership name of any instrument, for apparently *carrying on in the usual way the business of the partnership* of which he is a member binds the partnership, unless the partner so acting has in fact no authority to act for the partnership in the particular matter, and the person with whom he is dealing has knowledge of the fact that he has no authority [(emphasis added)].

[UPA section 9(3)] provides that the authorization of all partners is required to do certain acts, including:

> [(b)] Dispose of the good-will of the business.

> [(c)] Do any other act which would make it impossible to carry on the ordinary business of a partnership.

Marton & Associates cites cases standing for the general proposition that unanimous consent of all partners must be obtained in order to sell the capital assets of the partnership.

However, numerous cases interpreting 9 of the Uniform Partnership Act hold that where the business of the partnership is to sell real estate, the sale of real estate, including real estate that is the sole asset, is a sale in the usual course of business.

Marton & Associates cites *Jolly v. Kent Realty, Inc.*, 151 Ariz. 506, 729 P.2d 310 (App. 1986), for the proposition that the sale of a sole partnership asset requires unanimous approval of all partners under [UPA section 9]. This misstates the holding of that case. In *Jolly* this court found that the sale of the partnership's capital asset was not "carrying on in the usual way of business" under [UPA section 9(1)]. In concluding that one partner could not bind the partnership to the sale of an apartment complex, the court found no evidence to establish that the partnership's "usual business" was the "selling or exchanging of apartment investments." It treated the partnership as one whose "usual business" was *operating* the apartment complex. Thus the court held that one partner could not bind the partnership to a sale of the complex because the agreement provided that 51% of the partners approve "decisions affecting the future worth of the investment."

In contrast to *Jolly* the record in this case reflects that the partnership was established to buy and sell property. It held the undeveloped land as an investment to sell for profit. This was its only business—its "stock in trade."

[*Kristerin Dev. Co. v. Granson Inv.*, 394 N.W.2d 325 (Iowa 1986)] involved circumstances very similar to the instant case. In 1976, the partnership bought an apartment building. In 1980, the building was listed for sale with a realtor. Two of the three partners executed the purchase contract and assured the buyer that two signatures were sufficient to bind the partnership. The partnership ultimately refused to go through with the sale, and the buyer sued for breach of contract. The trial court directed a verdict in favor of the partnership on grounds that the partnership could only be bound by a contract signed by all partners. In reversing the trial court the Iowa Supreme Court stated:

> [A] contract executed by one partner alone to sell partnership real estate is binding on the other partners provided the partnership is in the business of buying or selling real estate.

The Iowa Supreme Court considered [UPA section 9(1)] and found that the "apparent scope of the partnership business depends primarily on the conduct of the partnership and its partners and what they cause third persons to believe about [their] authority." Further, the court rejected the partnership's contention that the fact that the partnership owned only one asset took the sale out of the "usual course of business."

Vinson argues that, since Marton & Associates was in the business of investing in land, the fact that it sold its sole asset did not prevent it from continuing business. It could have chosen to reinvest in other property. A partnership in the business of buying and selling property does not necessarily cease to do business if it sells all its real property. Thus, he argues that [UPA section 9(3)] is not applicable to this transaction. We agree.

In addition, we find that the partnership agreement itself authorizes "all business" to be transacted by a majority vote with one stated exception—the authorization of investment expenditures to exceed $500 per unit. The expression in a contract of one or more things in a class implies the exclusion of all other things. Thus, by identifying expenditures as requiring unanimous approval, the contract impliedly excludes other decisions. We find that under the partnership agreement and [UPA section 9], a majority of the partners of Marton & Associates had authority to sell the real property at issue.

Summary judgment in favor of defendants is reversed, and this matter is remanded to the trial court for proceedings in accordance with this opinion.

C. Corporations

In many ways, the governance structure of a corporation is the polar opposite of that of a partnership. Unlike partners, shareholders have no right , merely by virtue of being shareholders, to participate in the management and conduct of partnership business. Management of the business and affairs of a corporation is vested in its *board of directors*. The board of directors generally delegates the authority to run business of the corporation on a day-to-day basis to *officers* elected by the board of directors.

Shareholders are not agents of the corporation, and have no right to participate in the conduct of the corporation's business. Shareholders—even *all* the shareholders—have no right to instruct the board of directors or to interfere in its management of the corporation's business and affairs. The shareholders can affect corporate management in only two respects. First, shareholders elect the persons who will constitute the board of directors. Second, the board of directors cannot take certain extraordinary actions—amending the articles of incorporation, merging the corporation, selling all or substantially all of the corporation's assets—without first getting shareholder approval.

Moreover, whenever shareholder or board of director action is required, that action may not be taken informally, but must be taken only by a majority vote at a meeting. Meetings may be held only after proper notice, and require the presence of a minimum number of the shareholders, or directors, as the case may be (this minimum number is called a quorum).

Historically, shareholders have little discretion to vary this governance structure. They may work within the structure by changing quorum or voting requirements, or by issuing different classes of stock, but only in the manner permitted by statute. For example, the vote required to approve matters coming before the board of directors may be increased, but only by amending the bylaws or the articles of incorporation; it may not be changed by shareholder agreement. In any event, the shareholders generally may not abolish the board of directors and assume direct management of the corporation.

The last 25 years have seen increased flexibility in the corporate form. First, courts began to allow all the shareholders of a small corporation (so-called "close corporations") some ability to interfere in the discretion of the board of directors, such as specifying the identity of officers or the terms of their employment with the corporation. However, the outer limits of that flexibility were never clear (some courts indicated that the shareholders could not deprive the board of *all* authority to run the corporation).

Second, many states passed "close corporation supplements" to their business corporation acts. The close corporation supplements created a special statutory structure that generally applied only to close corporations. These supplements authorized all the shareholders to enter into unanimous shareholder agreements with regard to the business and affairs of the corporation, and to do so without regard to the traditional role of the board of directors. In fact, shareholders were permitted to abolish the board of directors and assume direct management of the corporation, or to appoint a manager. For reasons the close corporation supplements were not widely used.

Third, in 1990, the Committee on Corporate Laws of the ABA Section on Business Law of added Section 7.32 to the Model Business Corporation Act (1984).[A] Under Section 7.32, unless shares of a corporation are publicly traded, its shareholders may, by unanimous shareholder agreement, elect out of the board-dominant governance structure and substitute their own governance structure.[B] As of January 1, 1998, seventeen states had adopted provisions identical to, or based upon, Section 7.32.[C]

D. Limited Partnerships

1. Introduction

The governance structure of the limited partnership lies between that of the partnership and the corporation. So far as general partners are concerned, they generally have the same rights, and are subject to the same obligations, as are partners in a regular partnerships.[D] Limited partners have no rights by virtue of being limited partners, to participate in management or conduct of the partnership business.

2. Voting Rights of Limited Partners

Wasserman v. Wasserman
7 Mass. App. 167, 386 N.E.2d 783 (1979)

GRANT, Justice.

This is an action brought in the Superior Court by Peter Wasserman (Peter) against Max Wasserman (Max) and Jeanne L. Wasserman (Jeanne) by which Peter seeks to establish his position as the sole general partner of a limited partnership known as Sherman Associates, an order that Max and Jeanne turn over to him the books and records of the partnership, an injunction against their interfering with his management of the affairs of the partnership, and an accounting with respect to certain fees which the partnership has paid Jeanne for her services in managing the real estate owned by the partnership. The action was heard and determined on cross motions for summary judgment. Peter's motion was denied, the defendants' motion was allowed, and Peter has appealed from the ensuing final judgment of dismissal.

A. 2 MODEL BUS. CORP. ACT ANN. § 7.32 History (1997 Supp. 1998).

B. *Id.* at § 7.32(a) & (d).

C. *Id.* at § 7.32 Statutes (Alabama, Alaska, Arizona, Connecticut, Florida, Georgia, Idaho, Mississippi, Montana, Nebraska, New Hampshire, Oregon, Texas, Utah, Virginia, .Washington, and Wyoming).

D. ULPA § 9; RULPA § 403.

On January 4, 1971, Max and Jeanne entered into a written agreement of limited partnership for the purpose of acquiring, constructing and operating a project of low and moderate income housing in Cambridge. By the terms of that agreement Max was constituted the sole general partner of the partnership, and Max and Jeanne became the only Class B limited partners. The agreement expressly provided, among other things, that it had been made and entered into pursuant to the provisions of the [ULPA] and that the general partner (Max) should have "no authority to admit a person as a general partner." [ULPA § 9(f).] The certificate required by [the ULPA] was executed by Max and Jeanne in the capacities already indicated, was sworn to by them, and was filed on February 9, 1971.

On or about July 15, 1971, Max and Jeanne entered into an agreement in writing which superseded and recast the provisions of the agreement of the previous January. Max continued as the sole general partner, and Max and Jeanne continued as the only Class B limited partners. Section 10.2 of the amended agreement reads in material part as follows:

> At any time the then General Partners or Partner by unanimous consent or in the event there shall be no General Partners, Wasserman Development Corporation, may designate any one or more of the following individuals to become a General Partner without approval of any Limited Partner: (1) Any officer or director of Wasserman Development Corporation or Jacet Construction Corporation. (2) Any fiduciary under the will or a trust instrument of Max Wasserman. (3) Any other Person whose designation shall receive the consent of the Limited Partners.[i] This agreement shall constitute the written consent of every Limited Partner to admit as a General Partner any Person designated in the manner above provided.

The agreement was signed by Max in his capacities as the general partner and a Class B limited partner and by Jeanne in her capacity as a Class B limited partner. Acting in those same capacities, Max and Jeanne executed, swore to, and, on October 14, 1971, filed an amendment of the certificate of limited partnership.

Following the execution of the foregoing amendment of the partnership agreement, fourteen persons were admitted as Class A limited partners of Sherman Associates. Each of the fourteen signed a counterpart of the amended agreement. On March 3, 1972, there was filed with the Secretary of the Commonwealth a second amendment of the certificate of limited partnership which reflected the admission of the Class A limited partners and which was signed and sworn to by Max as the general partner and as a Class B limited partner and by Max as "attorney in fact" for Jeanne and all the Class A limited partners.

At some point (the actual sequence of events is not clear from the record) Max, as the general partner, entered into an agreement with Jeanne, as the principal of a concern known as Sandell Management Company, under which the partnership agreed to pay Jeanne six percent of the gross collections from the operation of the project for her services in managing the project. The agreement

---

i. The words "Consent of the Limited Partners" are defined in the amended agreement as "the written consent or approval of Class A Limited Partners whose aggregate Capital Contributions represent at least sixty percent (60%) of the Class A Class Contribution."

with Jeanne was to last through May 31, 1977, and has yielded her a gross of approximately $42,000 annually.

On January 21, 1975, Max, utilizing the letterhead of Wasserman Development Corporation, wrote each of the limited partners, advising them that the project had been fully rented and was showing a positive cash flow, that he desired to retire, and that he intended to name Peter as the general partner of Sherman Associates pursuant to the provisions of the above quoted [section] 10.2 of the amended partnership agreement. On February 3, 1975, Max, purporting to act under [section] 10.2, executed a formal written designation of "Peter W. Wasserman, Vice President of Wasserman Development Corporation to be a new general partner of the Partnership," subject to the performance of certain conditions which were later fulfilled.[ii] On March 1, 1975, Max executed a written assignment to Peter of Max's entire interest as general partner of the partnership. On March 10, 1975, Peter executed a written acceptance of his designation as general partner, in which he agreed to be bound by the terms and provisions of the amended partnership agreement.

On March 18, 1975, there was filed a third amendment of the certificate of limited partnership which recited on its face that it was being filed "(i)n order to reflect the admission of Peter Wasserman as an additional general partner and the subsequent retirement of Max Wasserman as general partner." This amendment was signed and sworn to by Max as "former General Partner and Class B Limited Partner," by Peter as "General Partner," and by Peter as "attorney-in-fact" for Jeanne and all the Class A limited partners.

Between March 1, 1975, and May 31, 1977, Peter performed various functions which would normally be expected of the general partner, such as the execution and filing of the partnership's Federal income tax returns for the years 1975 and 1976 and the execution and delivery of various financial reports required by the United States Department of Housing and Urban Development. On the latter date Peter notified Jeanne that the partnership would not renew the aforementioned management agreement which Max had entered into with her and which was due to expire on May 31, 1977. Max and Jeanne immediately took the position that Max was still the sole general partner of Sherman Associates, and on May 19, 1977, Max purported to extend the life of the agreement with Jeanne until May 31, 1979. Those actions, and Max's refusal to deliver the partnership books and records to Peter, led to the commencement of the present action.

The principal controversy between the partners is as to the effect which should be given to the provisions of [ULPA section 9(1)(e)], which reads:

> A general partner shall have all the rights and powers and be subject to all the restrictions and liabilities of a partner in a partnership without limited partners, except that without the written consent or ratification of the specific act by all the limited partners, a general partner or all of the general partners have no authority to (A)DMIT A PERSON AS A GENERAL PARTNER.

Peter contends (1) that Max and Jeanne gave the only consent required by [ULPA § 9(1)(e)] when, as limited partners, they signed the amended partnership

---

ii. It is agreed that Peter was an officer of Wasserman Development Corporation on February 3, 1975.

agreement of July 15, 1971, and (2) that, in any event, they have, by their subsequent actions, consented to or ratified Max's actions in substituting Peter as the sole general partner. Max and Jeanne dispute both propositions and rely on affidavits submitted by Jeanne and by two of the Class A limited partners to the effect that none of them has, as matter of fact, consented to or ratified any such substitution.

It is clear to us, as matter of construction, that the purpose and intent of § 10.2 of the amended agreement of partnership were to express and supply in advance, and without prior consultation with them, whatever consent might be required of the other limited partners to Max's designation as a general partner of "(1) Any officer or director of Wasserman Development Corporation or Jacet Construction Corporation (or) (2) Any fiduciary under the will or a trust instrument of Max Wasserman" and that Max was to be required to consult and obtain the consent of the other limited partners only in the event he should wish to designate "(3) Any person" not embraced within (1) or (2). Given (a) the fact that (1) was preceded by the words "without approval of any Limited Partner" and (b) the concluding sentence ("This agreement shall constitute the written consent of every Limited Partner to admit as a General Partner any Person designated in the manner above provided"), we see no other sensible construction of § 10.2.

The question remains whether an agreement such as the foregoing can constitute the "written consent" contemplated by [ULPA section 9(1)]. The question was left unanswered in *Lehrberg v. Felopulos*, 356 Mass. 148, 155, 248 N.E.2d 648 (1969). However, the cases from other jurisdictions which have considered the question have either held or assumed that the required consent can be found in the express provisions of a partnership agreement. The rationale appears to have been that in the absence of an express prohibition, the Act leaves the members of a limited partnership free to determine their rights with respect to each other by any contractual agreement which does not contravene public policy or run afoul of the common law.

Jeanne points to [RULPA section 401], and particularly to the Commissioners' Comment thereon. [RULPA section 401 reads] as follows: "After the filing of a limited partnership's original certificate of limited partnership, additional general partners may be admitted only with the specific written consent of each partner." The comment reads: "Section 401 is derived from Section 9(1)(e) of the prior law and carries over the unwaivable requirement that all limited partners must consent to the admission of an additional general partner and that such consent must specifically identify the general partner involved." We see nothing in the proposed new section, or in the comment, which precludes a conclusion that the written consent contemplated by § 9(1)(e) can be found in the provisions of a partnership agreement. The purpose of that section, as well as of the proposed new section, is to give each limited partner, who has no voice in the operation of the partnership business, the opportunity to prevent his investment from falling into the hands of an unknown or unwanted general partner. We think that purpose was served by the express provisions of § 10.2(1) of the amended partnership agreement in the present case. Nor do we perceive any difficulty with the Commissioners' concern for specificity; Jeanne, who is Max's wife and Peter's mother, is hardly in a position to say she did not know who controlled Wasserman Development Corporation or that Peter was a stranger to her or the corporation.

We hold that Jeanne gave her consent to the designation of Peter as a general partner when she signed the amended partnership agreement of July 15, 1971. Accordingly, it becomes unnecessary to consider whether Jeanne may also have consented to or ratified that designation in 1975 or at any subsequent time.

The order allowing the defendants' motion for summary judgment and the judgment are reversed.

Notes

1. Section 9 of the ULPA qualifies the powers of a general partner to take certain actions with respect to the limited partnership or its business, without first getting approval from the limited partners:

> [W]ithout the written consent or ratification of the *specific act* by *all* the limited partners, a general partner or all the general partners have no authority to
>
> > (a) Do any act in contravention of the certificate,
> >
> > (b) Do any act which would make it impossible to carry on the ordinary business of the partnership,
> >
> > (c) Confess a judgment against the partnership,
> >
> > (d) Possess partnership property, or assign their rights in specific partnership property, for other than a partnership purpose,
> >
> > (e) Admit a person as a general partner,
> >
> > (f) Admit a person as a limited partner, *unless the right so to do is given in the certificate,*
> >
> > (g) Continue the business with partnership property on the death, retirement or insanity of a general partner, *unless the right so to do is given in the certificate.*

ULPA § 9. If you were asking for a reconsideration of the opinion in the principal case, what argument could you make based on the language of ULPA Section 9?

2. Would the argument in the principal case have satisfied the court in *Schock v. Nash*, page 216? Why or why not? On what basis could *Schock* be distinguished?

3. The RULPA gives limited partners only narrow approval rights. In the absence of contrary provisions in the partnership agreement — or at least in a *written* partnership agreement — the RULPA requires written consent of *all* partners is required for the following actions:

> a. the admission of additional *general* partners, RULPA § 401;
>
> b. the admission of additional *limited* partners, RULPA § 301(b);
>
> c. the continuation of business after the withdrawal of a general partner, RULPA § 801(4).

Under RULPA section 302, the partnership agreement may give all or specified portions of the limited partners the right to vote on any matter, and may provide that the limited partners vote on a per capita, or some other, basis.

Fox v. I-10, Ltd.

957 P.2d 1018, 98 CJ C.A.R. 1308 (Colo. 1998)

Justice KOURLIS delivered the Opinion of the Court.

William Fox, individually, and as trustee for a pension plan and a profit sharing plan, (Fox) is a limited partner in I-10 Ltd. (the Partnership or I-10). Fox appeals a judgment of the court of appeals holding that the amendment provisions in the partnership agreement and applicable statutes allowed the limited partners to increase their capital contribution obligation by majority vote. We granted certiorari to consider the propriety of this ruling,[1] and now conclude that the majority vote provision plainly allows amendment of the limited partners' capital contributions; and this provision is not contrary to statutory provisions requiring capital contributions to be set forth in a certificate of limited partnership.

I.

In 1982, Fox purchased approximately 20% of the available limited partnership units in a Colorado limited partnership known as I-10 Ltd. Fox and several other limited partners (LPs) executed a limited partnership agreement with the general partner, MSP Investment Co., (MSP) dated November 1, 1982 (the Agreement). The purpose of the Partnership was to acquire, develop and hold for resale 305 acres of land in Pima County, Arizona.

Article 4.09 of the Agreement provided:

> Additional Assessments. If at any time after the formation of the Partnership the General Partner determines that additional contributions to the capital of the Partnership are necessary or desirable for any purpose, the General Partner shall mail a notice to each Limited Partner specifying the aggregate amount of additional capital to be contributed to the Partnership, such Limited Partner's pro rata share of the additional capital required, the purpose for the assessment, the intended use of the proceeds thereof, and the penalty to be imposed for failure to meet the assessment.... The total additional capital contribution required to be made by each Limited Partner hereunder shall not exceed an amount equal to four hundred percent (400%) of the initial capital contribution to the Partnership of each Limited Partner.

Article 7.00 dealing with amendments set forth two methods of amending the agreement depending upon the nature of the proposed change. Article 7.01 allowed the general partner, in its sole discretion, and as attorney in fact for the limited partners, to make certain "routine amendments" without the need for any partnership vote. These types of amendments related mainly to administrative matters such as preservation of proper status for federal income tax purposes.

Article 7.02 encompassed all other, non-routine amendments, and provided that, except for amendments affecting MSP's rights, all other amendments to the agreement would be made by majority vote:

---

1. Our order granting certiorari sets forth the following issue:

Whether the court of appeals erred in concluding that limited partners in a Colorado limited partnership who contributed sums certain to the partnership as set forth in the partnership agreement and certificates can become obligated to contribute additional capital to the partnership without their consent following a majority vote of the partners.

Other Amendments. All amendments, other than those set forth in paragraph 7.01 hereof, shall be proposed in writing by the General Partner or by Limited Partners owning not less than twenty-five percent (25%) of the Limited Partners' aggregate Interest in the Partnership for voting purposes. Any proposed amendment shall not become effective until it has been considered at a meeting of the Limited Partners duly held for that purpose and has received the affirmative vote of a majority of the Limited Partners' aggregate Interest in the Partnership and the approval of the General Partner. Notwithstanding the foregoing provisions of this paragraph to the contrary, no amendment shall be made to this Agreement which would deprive the General Partner of its Interest in the Partnership, or of any compensation or reimbursement of expenses due to the General Partner as provided herein.

In May of 1983, the Partnership filed a certificate of limited partnership in accordance with then-existing requirements under The Colorado Uniform Limited Partnership Act (CULPA). This previous version of the statute required a limited partnership to specify in the certificate the amount each partner had contributed and had agreed to contribute in the future. See § 7-62-201(e), 3 C.R.S. (1973) (repealed 1986) (hereafter Section 201(e)). In addition, the certificate was to include a description of the "times at which or events on the happening of which any additional contributions agreed to made by each partner are to be made." § 7-62-201(f), 3 C.R.S. (1973) (repealed 1986) (hereafter Section 201(f)). CULPA was amended in 1986, and these items are no longer required in the certificate.

In accordance with these statutory provisions, the original certificate reflected that Fox had contributed a total of $85,000 to the Partnership and had agreed to potential future assessments not exceeding $340,000 (400% of $85,000). The certificate also stated that article 4.09 of the Agreement governed the times at which, or events upon the happening of which, the partners had agreed to make additional contributions. The Partnership attached a copy of article 4.09 as an exhibit to the certificate.

Over the next few years, the Partnership found it necessary for various reasons to amend the Agreement several times. In February 1986, MSP sent a letter and a proxy to the limited partners proposing certain amendments to the Agreement. Efforts to sell the property had failed, and MSP sought amendments that would, among other things, change the purpose of the Partnership to include a possible land exchange with the State of Arizona, and amend article 4.09 to increase potential assessments from 400% to 600% of the original investment.

In its letter, MSP focused on the proposed change in purpose and noted that such a change could only be accomplished if each partner agreed. This was true because article 2.04 of the Agreement required 100% of all outstanding interests in the Partnership to consent to any action of the general partner that was inconsistent with the existing "principal business and purpose of the Partnership." Because the Agreement did not contemplate a land exchange, MSP recognized that it had to obtain consent of all the partners to make this change.

In the proxy accompanying the letter, MSP set out all the proposed amendments to the Agreement, including, among others, the capital contribution increase, and specified that amendment would be accomplished by majority vote as required in article 7.02 of the Agreement.[2]

At a meeting in March of 1986, MSP and all of the limited partners, including Fox, voted to amend paragraph 4.09 and increase the contribution cap to 600%. The Partnership filed an amended certificate reflecting the new cap and adjusting the total potential contributions accordingly. As with the original certificate, the amended certificate also stated that article 4.09 governed the times and events that could trigger obligations under the new cap.

The Partnership thereafter was unable to secure a suitable exchange or sale of its land, and by 1993 needed additional cash to finish paying its mortgage. MSP again proposed to amend article 4.09 of the Agreement by increasing the contribution cap to 800%. At a meeting in December of 1993, a majority of the partners (all partners except Fox) voted to amend article 4.09 and increase the cap to 800%. Fox voted against the amendment. Shortly after the majority vote, MSP sent Fox a notice of additional assessment for amounts in excess of the previous 600% cap. Fox paid the assessment up to 600% of his initial contribution, but refused to make further contributions. Fox then filed an action in the district court seeking a declaratory judgment that he had no obligation beyond the 600% cap, and seeking an injunction preventing the Partnership from declaring him in default under the terms of the Agreement.

The district court granted summary judgment for Fox and entered an order declaring that the Agreement did not permit an increase in the limited partners' capital contribution by majority vote. The district court also found that even if the Agreement were to permit such an amendment, it would be contrary to the provisions of CULPA. The court of appeals reversed, holding that the language of the Agreement did, in fact, allow this amendment by majority vote, and that the statutes did not prohibit it. We agree.

II.

We begin our analysis with a review of well-settled principles of contract law. Our courts have repeatedly recognized the sanctity of contracts and the court's role in enforcing them. Quoting the United States Supreme Court, we have held that:

> the right of private contract is no small part of the liberty of the citizen, and...the usual and most important function of courts of justice is rather to maintain and enforce contracts, than to enable parties thereto to escape from their obligation....

Francam Bldg. Corp. v. Fail, 646 P.2d 345, 349 (Colo. 1982) (*quoting Baltimore & Ohio Southwestern Ry. v. Voigt*, 176 U.S. 498, 505, 20 S.Ct. 385, 387, 44 L.Ed. 560 (1900)). Where a party enters into a contract absent fraud, duress or

---

2. I-10 contends that the 1986 amendment proceedings provide evidence of the parties' intent that article 4.09 could be amended by the procedures in article 7.02. Fox points out that the letter refers to unanimous consent and the proxy indicates that majority vote, even for the change in purpose, is appropriate. Accordingly, Fox argues, the parties' intentions are unclear and the court can glean no reliable evidence of intent from the 1986 amendment proceedings. We need not resolve this issue. Because, as discussed herein, we conclude that the Agreement is clear and unambiguous, we do not resort to extrinsic evidence of the parties' intent.

incapacity, the courts will not relieve that party of the consequences of the bargain simply because it may have been improvident.

The court's duty is to interpret and enforce contracts as written between the parties, not to rewrite or restructure them. The court will not interfere with the valid bargain of the parties:

> The impossibility of courts attempting to act as business clearing houses for the readjustment of legitimate profits and losses occurring in the marts of trade and commerce is obvious at a glance. To attempt it... would be an unwarranted interference with the freedom of action of business men in their private affairs.

Nelson v. Van Schaack & Co., 87 Colo. 199, 203, 286 P. 865, 867 (1930).

Parties to a contract, therefore, may agree on whatever terms they see fit so long as such terms do not violate statutory prohibitions or public policy. *See e.g.,...; Westminster Properties, Inc. v. Atlanta Assocs.,* 250 Ga. 841, 301 S.E.2d 636, 638 (1983) ("Partners generally, be they general or limited, may make any agreement between themselves that they deem desirable so long as said agreement is not in violation of prohibitory statutory provisions, the common law, or relevant considerations of public policy."). Additionally, where a contract is clear and unambiguous, courts must give effect to the plain and ordinary meaning of its terms.

III.

Hence, we look first to the terms of the Agreement itself to determine whether Fox can be required, by majority vote, to increase his capital contribution. Fox asserts that there is tension between article 4.09, placing a definitive cap on contributions, and article 7.02, allowing amendment of the Agreement by majority vote, thereby creating an ambiguity with respect to the parties' intent. We do not agree.

Article 7.02 plainly states that "[a]ll amendments, other than those [routine amendments] set forth in paragraph 7.01" may be accomplished by majority vote. Article 7.02 goes on to specify that certain items are excluded from amendment by the majority vote procedure set out therein. Increase in capital contributions is not among the exclusions of article 7.02. Furthermore, article 2.04 specifically requires unanimous consent of the limited partners prior to allowing the general partner to take certain actions. Hence the parties clearly excluded certain items from amendment by majority vote, but did not exclude a change in capital contributions from this method of amendment. Neither the language in article 4.09, nor any other language in the Agreement, creates doubt about whether article 7.02 provides the proper procedure for amending article 4.09.

Fox argues that the ceiling on a limited partner's capital contribution is such a fundamental aspect of a limited partnership that, as a matter of law, it may not be amended by majority vote regardless of what the Agreement might state. In other words, an LP's liability is "limited" by virtue of the very nature of limited partnerships and this fundamental precept cannot be altered without consent of the limited partner. We agree that the limit on an LP's liability represents a defining characteristic of a limited partnership interest. An LP's liability is limited by operation of law with respect to creditors of the partnership. An LP's liability to the partnership is also limited, but this limitation is defined, not by operation of law, but by the partnership agreement as the amount of capital which an LP agrees to contribute. While LPs may not, for example, agree among themselves to treat each other internally as general partners and still preserve their limited liability status with respect to creditors, there is no fundamental tenet of limited partnership law that prevents LPs from voluntarily agreeing, by majority vote or otherwise, to increase their capital contribution to the partnership.

The Washington Court of Appeals faced a remarkably similar situation in *Diamond Parking Inc. v. Frontier Bldg. Ltd. Partnership,* 72 Wash.App. 314, 864 P.2d 954 (1993). In that case the partnership agreement allowed for amendment by a 70% vote. *See id.* at 957. The holders of seventy-four percent of the partnership interests voted to restructure the partnership so as to increase the interests of those LPs who contributed additional capital. *See id.* The court enforced this amendment provision in the agreement noting that the "partnership agreement is the law of the partnership." *See id.* We find the Washington court's words particularly apposite to the instant case that a party "[h]aving elected to join the partnership with this type of majority voting provision...cannot now complain merely because the partnership adopted an amendment of which he did not approve." *Id.*

We thus conclude that the plain language of the Agreement allows a majority of the partners to vote to amend the capital contribution amount, and no "fundamental right" invalidates that contractual term. Rather, if any fundamental right is implicated, it is the fundamental right to enter into a contract and expect its terms to be enforced.

IV.

We now turn to the provisions of CULPA and consider whether it imposes other obligations on the parties, or supersedes the Agreement.

A.

CULPA requires limited partnerships to file a certificate of limited partnership with the secretary of state. Fox contends that the provisions in CULPA requiring identification of the limited partners' capital contributions on the certificate prohibit I-10, as a matter of law, from imposing additional capital contributions without Fox's consent. The prior version of CULPA required that the certificate of limited partnership specify in pertinent part:

(e) The amount of cash and a description and statement of the agreed value of the other property or services contributed by each partner and which each partner has agreed to contribute in the future; [and]

(f) The times at which or events on the happening of which any additional contributions agreed to be made by each partner are to be made;

§ 7-62-201, 3 C.R.S. (1973) (repealed 1986).

The 1986 amendments to CULPA eliminated these requirements in the certificate, and added a provision in another section that "[n]o promise by a limited partner to contribute to the limited partnership is enforceable unless set out in a writing signed by the limited partner." § 7-6-502(3), 2 C.R.S. (1997). Fox asserts that this later provision was enacted to provide essentially the same protections as those in the old Sections 201(e)and (f). Accordingly, Fox maintains that amendment of capital contribution without consent of all affected partners violates both the old and new versions of CULPA.

The old statute required the filing of a certificate that identified the capital contributions of the partners and that was signed by the LP. The new statute provides that capital contributions are not enforceable unless set out in a writing signed by the LP. The thrust of Fox's argument is that both provisions are intended to protect LPs from any changes in their capital contributions to the partnership, and thus embody a statutory requirement that capital contributions cannot be changed without consent of the affected LP. We are not persuaded.

Certificates of limited partnership serve the goal of giving third parties, specifically potential creditors, notice concerning matters of importance to them in dealing with the partnership. The certificate is not designed to protect or govern the rights of the partners as among themselves, and it cannot trump a valid contractual term.

The recent legislative history surrounding elimination of the certificate requirements, both in the uniform law and in Colorado's version, supports the conclusion that the requirements were never intended to protect limited partners, much less hold sway over contractual obligations among the partners. The National Conference of Commissioners on Uniform State Laws adopted amendments to The Uniform Limited Partnership Act (ULPA) in 1985. Section 201 governs the requirements in the certificate. See Unif. Limited Partnership Act § 201, (amended 1985) 6A U.L.A. 95 (1995). The comment to section 201 of ULPA states that the elimination of many items in the certificate is:

> in recognition of the fact that the partnership agreement, not the certificate of limited partnership, has become the authoritative and comprehensive document for most limited partnerships, and that creditors and potential creditors of the partnership do and should refer to the partnership agreement and to other information furnished to them directly by the partnership and by others, not to the certificate of limited partnership, to obtain facts concerning the capital and finances of the partnership and other matters of concern.

Unif. Limited Partnership Act § 201, cmt. (amended 1985) 6A U.L.A. 96 (1995). The requirements in the certificate focus on what creditors need to know. The change clarifies that the partnership agreement controls the rights and obligations of the partners among themselves, and creditors, in the interest of obtaining accurate information, should refer to this document rather than the certificate. The previous comment to section 201 of ULPA stated that:

> the certificate is intended to serve two functions: first, to place creditors on notice of the facts concerning the capital and finances of the partnership and the rules regarding additional contributions to and withdrawals from the partnership; second, to clearly delineate the time at which persons become general partners and limited partners.

Unif. Limited Partnership Act § 201, cmt. (amended 1985) 6A U.L.A. 96 (1995). Again, the focus is on providing creditors with the information they need, i.e., capital structure and liability to outside parties.

In 1986, Colorado amended CULPA to conform to the 1985 amendments to ULPA. Colorado's legislative history is consistent with the comments to the changes in ULPA. In testimony before the Senate Judiciary Committee, a representative from the secretary of state's office discussed the elimination of certain items in the certificate. *See* Hearing on H.B. 1182 Before the Senate Judiciary Committee, 55th Gen. Assembly, 2d Sess., Mar. 12, 1986 (statements by Don Thompson, Division of Commercial Recording, Secretary of State). He explained that the requirements were being pared down as a matter of efficiency. The new requirements would alert the public as to the existence of a limited partnership. Any specific information would come from the partnership agreement itself. The process of filing a certificate thereby becomes much faster and the secretary of state's staff does not need to check certificates for a laundry list of unnecessary items. A document submitted to the committee along with the proposed amendments states:

> Much of the information required by current law to be set forth in the certificate is being eliminated because it deals with information relative to the rights and duties between the partners and not affecting the partnership's duties to persons outside the partnership. Such information already is contained in the partnership agreement. Thus, the requirement of current law to set forth this information in the certificate adds no material benefit and may harm the parties by creating traps for the unwary or creating inconsistencies or ambiguities.

Hearing on H.B. 1182 Before the Senate Judiciary Committee, 55th Gen. Assembly, 2d Sess., Mar. 12, 1986 (Summary of Changes to Limited Partnership Statutes) (emphasis added). The drafters apparently were troubled by the possibility of an inconsistency between the agreement and the certificate creating unnecessary confusion and contention. The case now before us represents just such a circumstance.

It is clear from the precedent, treatises and legislative history that the law does not intend the certificate of limited partnership to control the rights and obligations of partners among themselves. The requirements of Sections 201(e) and (f) do not create a statutory mandate prohibiting limited partners from contractually agreeing to allow an increase in capital contributions by majority vote.

B.

Fox also argues that the certificates filed by I-10 did not meet the requirements for stating the LPs' capital contribution obligations under the previous version of the statute.[3] Section 201(f) requires the certificate to specify the events that can trigger additional capital contributions. Fox asserts that if majority vote of the partners constituted such an event, the statute mandated that it be so identified on the certificate. I-10's original and amended certificates state that article 4.09 governed the times or events upon which partners had agreed to make future contributions. Hence, Fox argues that majority vote cannot be an event trig-

---

3. The court of appeals applied the previous version of the statute because the parties assumed in their briefs to that court that the previous version of the statute applied. In this court, the parties have indirectly raised this issue. We apply the stricter certificate requirements in order to give Fox the benefit of the most protective provisions since section 7-62-1102, 2 C.R.S. (1997) prevents application of the 1986 amendments in such a manner as to impair any contract or affect any right accrued prior to July 1, 1986. *See* § 7-62-1102, 2 C.R.S. (1997).

gering capital contributions because the certificate and amended certificates do not so state.

First, we do not believe that the statutory language requires identification of the process by which partners may amend their agreement. Second, even if this were the case, such an error in the certificate would not relieve the partners of their contractual obligations to one another. Section 201(f) requires the certificate to include those events already contractually agreed to by the parties as triggering additional capital obligations. Third parties want to know what contribution they can rely upon from each partner. Here, article 4.09, attached to the certificate, accurately reflects that partners could be required, at the discretion of MSP, to contribute up to 400% (and later 600%) of their initial contributions.

The pre-1986 version of section 7-62-202, dealing with amendments to the certificate, also sheds light on the intended application of Section 201(f). In interpreting statutes, courts must read and consider the statute as a whole and give consistent, harmonious and sensible effect to all of its provisions.

Section 7-62-202(2)(a) required amendments to reflect "*a change in the amount* or character of the contribution of any partner or in any partner's obligation to make a contribution." § 7-62-202(2)(a), 3 C.R.S. (1973) (repealed 1986) (emphasis added). If the General Assembly had intended Section 201(f) to include more than just the current agreement with respect to what additional contributions could be required, there would have been no need for section 7-62-202(2)(a) to refer to a change in any partner's obligation to contribute. The first part of Section 202(2)(a) refers to "a change in the amount" of the capital contribution. This covers the situation in which a triggering event or time has occurred and partners have actually been called upon to increase their contributions. The second part of Section 202(2)(a) contemplates the possibility that a partner's obligation to contribute, rather than just the amount of the contribution, might change. This would refer to a change in the times or triggering events for additional capital contributions.

If Section 201(f) required a partnership to specify any and all potential changes in a partner's obligation to contribute, such as by majority vote amendment, then section 202(2)(a) would only need to record a change in the amount resulting from such vote. The language contemplating a change in the partner's obligation to contribute would be superfluous.

We conclude that Section 201(f) required the partners to record those contributions the parties had already agreed to, i.e., 400% of the initial contribution, and Section 202(2)(a) required the partners to record any change in the obligation accomplished by amendment, i.e., 600%, and then 800% of the initial contribution.

Finally, as the cases and authorities discussed in section IV.A. above make clear, even if we were to conclude that I-10's certificates contained an error of this type, such an error would not supersede the partners' contractual obligations. Fox is not a creditor of I-10 seeking to prove that he was harmed by an error in the certificate, but rather a party to a contract seeking to elevate the certificate over contractual obligations.

V.

The Agreement, by its plain language, allows the parties to amend article 4.09 by majority vote. Neither a "fundamental right" of limited partnership nor CULPA precludes parties from agreeing to such an amendment procedure. Additionally, I-10 did not violate the certificate requirements of Sections 201(e) and (f), and in any event, the partners' rights and obligations inter se are governed by the partnership agreement, not by the certificate. Accordingly, we hereby affirm the court of appeals' decision reversing the district court's judgment, and remand for further proceedings consistent with the views expressed in this opinion.

Notes

1. In the principal case, on what basis did Fox argue that a limited partners' maximum agreed capital contribution could only by changed by agreement of that partner? Would your evaluation of Fox's argument change according to the consequences of a call for additional capital contributions? For example, consider the following alternate approaches for breach of the obligation to make additional capital contributions:

a. The obligation was fully enforceable, and the limited partnership could sue Fox to collect any unpaid contribution.

b. The limited partnership could not sue Fox to collect any unpaid contribution. The limited partnership's sole remedy was the right to proportionately reduce Fox's profit-sharing ratio.

2. What is the purpose of the required certificate of limited partnership? Do you agree with the construction of the court in the principal case?

3. Limitations on Contractual Expansion of Limited Partner Rights

Gast v. Petsinger

228 Pa. Super. 394, 323 A.2d 371 (1974)

HOFFMAN, Judge:

This appeal is from a summary judgment involving a contract dispute. Appellant charges in his Complaint that he was employed by LNG Services as a project engineer in 1968. For over a year, he was paid his agreed salary of $15,000.00 per year. From October of 1969 until March of 1971, when he severed his employment from the business, he continued in his capacity without pay. Upon tendering notice of termination of employment, appellant submitted a claim for back pay and expenses. This amount was never paid and a suit in assumpsit was thereupon instituted. The Complaint states that the business known as LNG Services is formally a limited partnership. The only named general partner is the defendant, Robert E. Petsinger. Nevertheless, appellant claims that the other named individual defendants, while ostensibly limited partners, were, by virtue of their participation in the enterprise, acting as general partners, and should therefore be liable for the monies due him.

[T]he Court entered an Order granting defendants' Motion of Summary Judgment. The plaintiff-appellant has appealed to this Court asserting that the [record] establish[es] certain involvement in the partnership by the named defendants that presents a factual dispute on the question of control which should be submitted to a jury.

We have examined the record in this case and find the following to be degree and kind of participation of the Limited Partners in LNG Services:

1. All Limited Partners have the following rights and powers as described in the Limited Partnership Agreement:

(a) the right to receive distributions from time-to-time and upon dissolution;

(b) the right to prevent the transfer of assets and other acts 'outside the ordinary business of the partnership' unless an aggregate of 50% in interest give written consent to the transfers of acts;

(c) the right to examine the books and records of the partnership at the principal office of the partnership;

(d) the right to attend meetings 'for the purpose of receiving the report of the General Partner and for taking any action referred to' in clause (b), *supra*;

(e) the right to transfer, sell or assign their interests to third parties;

(f) and, upon the death of a Limited Partner, to have his or her share of the profits and distributions inure to his or her Estate.

2. According to the Limited Partnership Agreement, 'the management and control of the Partnership's day-to-day operation and maintenance of the property of the Partnership shall rest exclusively with the General Partner.' Consistent with statutes regulating limited partnerships, the Agreement places the 'control' of the business in the hands of the General Partner. The Limited Partners, by virtue of their capital contributions, have the powers mentioned above, and prohibited from taking any 'part in the conduct or control of the Partnership and its business and shall have no right or authority to act for, or bind, the Partnership.'

3. The organization of LNG Services is in conformance with the [ULPA]. The certificate is in good order, and the Agreement delineates the powers, rights and liabilities of the General and Limited Partners in express terms. None of the powers mentioned therein exceed the degree of 'control' which converts the status of a limited partner to that of general partner. In two sections of the ULPA, the statute clearly limits the liability of the limited partner: "A limited partner shall not become liable as a general partner unless, in addition to the exercise of his rights and powers as a limited partner, he takes part in the control of the business." [ULPA § 7.]

In [*Freedman v. Philadelphia Tax Review Board*, 212 Pa. Super. 442, 446, 243 A.2d 130, 133 (1968)], we defined the limited partnership as

an entity in which one or more persons, with unlimited liability, manage the partnership, while one or more other persons only contribute capital; these latter partners have no right to participate in the management and operation of the business and assume no liability beyond the capital contributed.

We concluded that: "By adhering to this arrangement, the limited partner is exempted from general liability and places his capital alone at the peril of the business."

Each of the limited partners in the instant case contributed capital to the partnership and enjoyed certain powers and rights which have been recognized as consistent with the concept of a 'limited partner.' Each received reports and materials periodically concerning the Partnership sent by the General Partner. The record discloses that [certain] limited partners also on occasion attended meetings of the partnership called by the General Partner between March and July 1969 for the purpose of reporting on the business of the partnership and amending the Agreement. In addition, [certain limited] partners attended personal meetings between the General Partner and certain employees for the purpose of raising additional capital. [Other limited] partners did no more than receive the aforementioned reports of the partnership.

Only Dr. Garwin and Jerome Apt, Jr., appear to have acted in capacities which require some discussion and evaluation. In addition to receiving reports and attending meetings wherein status reports and additional capital investments were discussed, Dr. Garwin was employed by the Partnership as an independent engineering consultant with respect to certain projects undertaken by LNG Services for which service he was retained by the General Partner and in which, he and the General Partner assert, he remained subject to the supervision and control of Petsinger, the General Partner. Apt was also engaged from time to time as an independent consultant on certain projects. These individuals were described as 'Project Managers' on several booklets which were attached to appellant's deposition as exhibits.

Accepting all the facts as asserted by the plaintiff as true, we do not believe that, at least with respect to several of the appellees, this case so clearly was devoid of a single factual issue as to remove the matter from the deliberation of a jury.

The key issue before the lower court was whether the appellant had presented an arguable case demonstrating that some or all of the appellees had 'The take(n) part in the control of the business.' The question of 'control' has not been squarely met in Pennsylvania. We are, however, guided by decisions in a number of jurisdictions following the ULPA which have construed the term in various factual contexts. One excellent Harvard Law Review article examining this problem identifies the problem and the important factors to consider. "Investing Partners want to limit their liability in connection with the enterprise. They will not participate in managing the partnership's ordinary investment activities (h)owever, as a practical matter, it is unlikely that major commitments of capital would be made without informing and perhaps consulting with Investing Partners." Feld, *The 'Control' Test for Limited Partnerships*, 82 Harv. L. Rev. 1471, 1474.

State and federal courts have taken a similar view. The courts have held, without satisfactorily describing the standards by which to judge a limited partner's activities, that the following did not constitute taking part in the 'control' of the business: acting as a foreman in the employ of the partnership, with the power to purchase parts as necessary without consulting the general partner, but without the power to extend credit without prior approval from the general partner or deal with the partnership account, acting as a member of the board of directors of the partnership (although the Court noted that he never did actually serve as such), acting as sales manager in a new car sales department of the partnership without power to hire or fire, and, with power to order cars only with the general partner's approval, and, participating in the choice of key employees and giving a certain degree of 'advice.'

An analysis of the cases reveals that they were decided on their own facts and are of little use in forming rules or standards. In each case, it was not the position of the limited partner that was stated as permissible, but the actual role and degree of participation that each had in relation to the general partner. A reading of those cases reinforces the belief of this Court that the determination must be made on an *ad hoc* basis, and while employment may not be conflicting with the status of a limited partner, the 'control' that partner has in the day-to-day functions and operations of the business is the key question. Does the limited partner have decision-making authority that may not be checked or nullified by the general partner? As Alan Feld notes in his article:

> [While] some cases would permit the limited partner to 'advise' the general partners, it is not at all clear that Investing Partners may do so without fear of liability in view of the weight their advice is likely to carry, both because of the size of their investment and because they are 'carrying' Managing Partners' interests. The determination of control is a factual one and this relationship may, as a practical matter, give any 'advice' the color of a command in the partnership.

Here, the appellant testified that partners Apt and Garwin acted in the partnership as 'Project Managers.' He stated in his deposition that the appearance of their names on brochures and reports, the obvious weight their 'advice' carried in their recommendations and report on key projects, and their managerial responsibilities, all contributed to a belief that they exercised 'control.' The defendant Petsinger, the General Partner, confirms the fact that these two individuals acted as independent 'consultants' on various 'projects.' He denies their authority or right to control the business decisions. His statement as defendant is conclusionary, and since we are reviewing this appeal on a summary judgment, the inference most favorable to the plaintiff must be made.

It may be true that once all the facts are in the appellees, Apt and Garwin, will have been found not to have exercised the degree of 'control' necessary to impose general liability upon them. We agree that the nature of the business of LNG Services, described as having as its purposes 'the management of the development, engineering, and technical advice relating to the development or uses for liquefied natural gas, etc.,' required the utilization of expert opinion of technical minds. It is not apparent from the face of the record that the technical skills and training of Apt and Garwin did not by virtue of their retention as 'Project Managers' place them in a position where their 'advice' did influence and, perhaps, control the decisions of the General Partner, whose particular expertise is unknown.

With respect to the [other limited partners], we affirm the order of the court below granting defendants' motion for summary judgment. None of [those limited] partners is shown to have engaged in any activity or participated beyond those lawfully and expressly stated in the Limited Partnership Agreement. With respect to the appellees, Jerome Apt, Jr., and Dr. Leo Garwin, we reverse the order and judgment of the court below, and remand the case for further proceedings consistent with this opinion.

Notes

1. Before the adoption of the ULPA, a limited partner could be held liable for partnership obligations if the limited partner participated in the *conduct* of partnership business. ULPA § 1 Comment. ULPA section 7 was intended to liberalize the law: a limited partner would not become liable as a general partner unless the limited partner participated in the *control* of the business (as opposed to merely participating generally).

2. Under ULPA Section 7, what is the basis for holding the limited partner liable as a general partner? Is creditor reliance or lack of reliance on the limited partner's conduct relevant under ULPA Section 7?

Frigidaire Sales Corp. v. Union Properties, Inc.
14 Wash. App. 634, 544 P.2d 781 (1976),
aff'd 88 Wash.2d 400, 562 P.2d 244 (1977)

CALLOW, Judge.

The plaintiff, Frigidaire Sales Corporation, appeals from a superior court judgment dismissing its claim against defendants Leonard Mannon and Raleigh Baxter. The sole issue presented on appeal is whether individuals who are limited partners become liable as general partners when they also serve as active officers or directors, or are shareholders of a corporation which is the managing general partner of the limited partnership.

The parties agreed on the facts. On January 15, 1969, Frigidaire Sales Corporation entered into a contract with Commercial Investors, a limited partnership, for the sale of appliances to Commercial. The contract was signed on behalf of Commercial Investors by defendants Mannon and Baxter in their respective capacities as president and secretary-treasurer of Union Properties, Inc., the corporate general partner of Commercial Investors. Mannon and Baxter were also directors of Union Properties, Inc., and each owned 50 percent of the outstanding shares of Union Properties, Inc. In their capacities as directors and officers of Union Properties, Inc., the defendants exercised the day-to-day management and control of Union Properties, Inc. Both defendants also held one limited partnership unit out of a total of 52 outstanding partnership investment units in Commercial Investors.

Frigidaire Sales Corporation, as the creditor, instituted this action against the general partner Union Properties, Inc. and the defendants Mannon and Baxter individually when Commercial Investors, as the debtor and as the purchaser of the appliances, failed to pay the November 1970 installment and all subsequent installments due on the contract. The trial court entered judgment for the plaintiff against Union Properties, Inc., but dismissed the plaintiff's claim against Mannon and Baxter. The plaintiff appeals the dismissal of the individual defendants.

Is the Dominant Consideration Creditor Reliance or Prohibited Control?

The plaintiff contends that the defendants, as limited partners, controlled the business because they were (1) sole shareholders of Union Properties, Inc., the general partner; (2) on the board of directors of Union Properties, Inc.; (3) president and secretary of Union Properties, Inc.; and (4) exercised the day-to-day management of Union Properties, Inc. The defendants contend, on the other hand, that the limited partnership was controlled by its general partner Union Properties, Inc., a distinct and separate legal entity, and not by the defendants in their individual capacities.

The precise issue has not been previously raised in Washington, and the term "control" as used in [ULPA section 7] has not been defined with the present problem in mind.

The issue recently received attention in Texas. In *Delaney v. Fidelity Lease, Ltd.*, 526 S.W.2d 543 (Tex. 1975), the limited partners controlled the business of the limited partnership as officers, directors and stockholders of the corporate general partner. The Texas Supreme Court held at 545:

> [T]hat the personal liability, which attaches to a limited partner when "he takes part in the control and management of the business," cannot be evaded merely by acting through a corporation.

The opinion overrules the decision of the Texas Court of Civil Appeals, in which it had been stated:

> The logical reason to hold a limited partner to general liability under the control prohibition of the Statute is to prevent third parties from mistakenly assuming that the limited partner is a general partner and to rely on his general liability. However, it is hard to believe that a creditor would be deceived where he knowingly deals with a general partner which is a corporation. That in itself is a creature specifically devised to limit liability. The fact that certain limited partners are stockholders, directors or officers of the corporation is beside the point where the creditor is not deceived.

Delaney v. Fidelity Lease, Ltd., 517 S.W.2d 420, 425 (Tex. Civ. App. 1974).

The Supreme Court opinion in *Delaney* was concerned that the statutory requirements of at least one general partner with general liability in a limited partnership could be circumvented by limited partners operating the partnership through the corporation with minimum capitalization and, therefore, with limited liability. The fear is, however, not peculiar to a limited partnership with a corporate general partner. An individual may form a corporation with limited capitalization and thereby attempt to avoid personal liability. When one acts in such fashion, however, the inadequate capitalization is a factor in determining whether to disregard the corporate entity. If a corporate general partner in a limited partnership is organized without sufficient capitalization so that it was foreseeable that it would not have sufficient assets to meet its obligations, the corporate entity could be disregarded to avoid injustice. We find no substantive difference between the creditor who does business with a corporation that is the general partner in a limited partnership and a creditor who simply does business with a corporation. In the absence of fraud or other inequitable conduct, the corporate entity should be respected.

We note that the decision of the Supreme Court of Texas in *Delaney* relies upon the reasoning of the dissent filed in the Texas Court of Civil Appeals. We believe that the dissent, however, is based in part upon the incorrect premise that a corporation may not be a general partner under the Uniform Limited Partnership Act. We have shown that this is not so under the Washington Act. Moreover, the dissent based its reasoning upon the assumption that, because the limited partners acted as officers of the corporate general partner, they "were obligated to their other partners to so operate the corporation as to benefit the partnership." We find no inherent wrong in this. Persons in the position of the individual defendants in this case would be bound to act in the best interests of both the corporate general partner and the limited partners under the guidelines of [ULPA section 12]. The dual capacities are not inimical as asserted.

Apparently prior to the filing of the Texas Supreme Court decision in *Delaney*, a law review article discussing the Texas Court of Civil Appeals decision in *Delaney v. Fidelity Lease, Ltd.*, 517 S.W.2d 420 (Tex. Civ. App. 1974), appeared in 6 Texas Tech. L. Rev. 1171 (1974). Therein the author observed:

> In *Delaney* the court was confronted squarely with the choice of adopting a creditor reliance test or imposing personal liability because of the statutory control prohibition, even though the plaintiff originally did not require the defendant's personal guaranty in the execution of the lease. By adopting the creditor reliance test the court has expanded the permissible forms of business organizations. Texas businessmen now can combine the advantages of both the partnership and the corporation. The desirability of the court's decision is demonstrated by the fact that under such an arrangement the limited partners may enjoy the conduit theory of income taxation as well as complete protection from personal liability. The additional benefit flowing from the *Delaney* decision is that the businessman now can take advantage of these previously existing benefits without forfeiting managerial control of the organization.

Moreover, a literal reading of [ULPA section 7] that disregards the existence of the corporate entity as a general partner is not justified. The consideration of the issue must inquire not only whether a limited partner has participated in a forbidden control, but also whether the corporate entity should be regarded or disregarded. In Horowitz, *Disregarding the Entity of Private Corporations*, 15 Wash. L. Rev. 1, 11 (1940), certain principles are suggested for testing whether corporate entities should be acknowledged or disregarded. The principles, pertinent to our inquiry, were stated to be:

> (a) If there is an overt intention to regard or disregard the corporate entity, effect will be given thereto unless so to do will violate a duty owing.

> (b) The overt intention is that of the corporation whose entity is sought to be disregarded or of the person or persons owning its stock and sought to be visited with the consequence of regard or disregard of the corporate entity.

> (c) The duty owing must be owing to the person seeking to invoke the doctrine, and such duty may arise from common law and equity, contract or statute.

Here, there was an overt intention to regard the corporate entity and no showing of the violation of any duty owing to the creditor. The creditor dealt with the corporate general partner in full awareness of the corporate status of the general partner. There is no showing of any fraud, wrong or injustice perpetrated upon the creditor, merely that [ULPA section 7] provides that a limited partner becomes liable as a general partner if he takes part in the control of the business. When these are the circumstances, we hold that the corporate entity should be upheld rather than the statute applied blindly with no inquiry as to the purpose it seeks to achieve. As observed in the comment to section 1 of the ULPA :

> No public policy requires a person who contributes to the capital of business, acquires an interest in the profits, and some degree of control over the conduct of the business, to become bound for the obligations of the business; provided creditors have no reason to believe at the times their credits were extended that such person was so bound.

A limited partner is made liable as a general partner when he participates in the "control" of the business in order to protect third parties from dealing with the partnership under the mistaken assumption that the limited partner is a general partner with general liability. If a limited partnership certificate pursuant to [ULPA section 2(1)] is properly prepared and filed and the limited partner does not participate in the control of the business, it is unlikely that third parties will be misled as to the limited liability of the limited partners. The underlying purpose of the control prohibition of [ULPA section 7] is not furthered, however, by prohibiting limited partners from forming a corporation to act as the sole general partner in a limited partnership. A third party dealing with a corporation must reasonably rely on the solvency of the corporate entity. It makes little difference if the corporation is or is not the general partner in a limited partnership. In either instance, the third party cannot justifiably rely on the solvency of the individuals who own the corporation.

We hold that limited partners are not liable as general partners simply because they are active officers or directors, or are stockholders of a corporate general partner in a limited partnership.

Affirmed.

Notes

1. *Frigidaire Sales Corp. v. Union Properties, Inc.* and *Delaney v. Fidelity Lease, Ltd.* (discussed in *Frigidaire Sales Corp.*) stand on opposite sides of a *second*, modern, development with respect to limited partner participation. *Frigidaire Sales Corp.*, and similar cases, impose an additional *creditor reliance* test to limited partner liability: it is not enough that the limited partner have participated in control, that participation must also have *misled* creditors as to the limited partner's status. The *Delaney* case quite rightly points out that ULPA section 7 says nothing about reliance (why not?). However, *Delaney* is on the wrong side of historical forces: RULPA section 303 adopted *Frigidaire Sales Corp.*'s requirement of creditor reliance.

> [The creditor reliance test] was adopted partly because of the difficulty of determining when the "control" line has been overstepped, but also (and more importantly) because of a determination that it is not sound public policy to hold a limited partner who is not also a general partner liable for the obligations of the partnership except to persons who have done business with the limited partnership reasonably believing, based on the limited partner's conduct, that he is a general partner.

RULPA § 303, Official Comment.

2. RULPA section 303(b) also added a non-exclusive "laundry list" of activities that are not participation in control. The list of permitted limited partner activities is wide ranging, running from acting as a shareholder, director, or officer of a corporate general partner (thus adopting the *Frigidaire Sales Corp.* holding) to consulting with and advising a general partner, to voting on any matter with respect to which a limited partner vote is required by the RULPA *or by the limited partnership agreement.*

Paragraph (b) is intended to provide a "safe harbor" by enumerating certain activities which a limited partner may carry on for the partnership without being deemed to have taken part in control of the business. This "safe harbor" list has been expanded beyond that set out in the 1976 Act to reflect case law and statutory developments and more clearly to assure that limited partners are not subjected to general liability where such liability is inappropriate.

RULPA § 303, Official Comment.

For additional discussion of ULPA section 7 and RULPA section 303, *see* Closen, *Limited Partnership Reform: A Commentary on the Proposed Illinois Statute and the 1976 and 1985 Versions of the Uniform Limited Partnership Act,* 6 N. ILL. L. REV. 205, 250-55 (1986).

Note on "Re-RULPA" Section 303

The National Conference of Commissioners on Uniform State Laws has appointed a Drafting Committee to revise the RULPA [Uniform Limited Partnership Act (1976) with 1985 Amendments]. The July 1999 draft of the Revision (which is being called "Re-RULPA") would give limited partners limited liability equivalent to that of shareholders in a corporation:

SECTION 303. NO LIABILITY AS LIMITED PARTNER TO THIRD PARTIES. A limited partner is not liable for a debt, obligation, or other liability of the limited partnership solely by reason of being a limited partner, even if the limited partner participates in the management and control of the limited partnership

With the advent of the LLC and the LLP as business forms, is any purpose served by continuing the rule that limited partners who participate in control become liable as general partners? Could the same arguments have been made in 1916 and 1976 at the times of the adoption of earlier versions of the Uniform Limited Partnership Acts?

E. Limited Liability Companies

1. Introduction

Limited liability companies do not have a standard governance structure. The ULLCA was promulgated well into the development of the limited liability company as a business form, so it is not as widely adopted as are (or were) the various uniform partnership and limited partnership acts.

The most common governance structure of LLC acts is "member management". Not coincidentally, in a member-managed LLC, members generally have the rights and powers of partners in a partnership to participate in the management and conduct of LLC business. *E.g.*, ULLCA §§ 301(a), 404(a). Indeed, the LLC business form was developed for the purpose of combining the limited liability of shareholders with the governance structure of partnerships.

The alternate governance structure of LLC acts is "manager-management". In a manager-managed LLC, management of the business and affairs of the LLC is vested in the manager, who generally have the rights and powers of partners in a partnership. Members generally have no right as such to participate in the management or conduct of LLC business, *e.g.*, ULLCA §§ 301(b), 404(b), but may have the right to select the manager, ULLCA § 404(3)

Under the ULLCA, an LLC's articles of organization must specify whether the LLC is to be manager-managed. ULLCA § 203(a)(6).

Under ULLCA 404, except with respect to matters requiring the consent of all members under 404(c), either the members or the managers may by majority vote determine "any matter relating to the business of the company". By way of contrast, in a member-managed Delaware LLC, members vote according to the profits interests of the members, rather than per capita.

Under ULLCA section 404(c), the matters that require the consent of all members are:

(1) amendment of the operating agreement;

(2) authorization or ratification of acts or transactions which would otherwise violate the duty of loyalty;

(3) amendment to the articles of organization;

(4) compromising an obligation to make a contribution to the LLC;

(5) compromising, as among members, the obligation of a member to make a contribution or return money or other property paid or distributed in violation of the ULLCA

(6) making interim distributions;

(7) admitting a new member;

(8) using the company's property to redeem an interest subject to a charging order;

(9) dissolving the company

(10) A waiver of the right to have the company's business wound up and the company terminated under Section 802(b);

(11) The consent of members to merge with another entity under Section 904(c)(1); and

(12) The sale, lease, exchange, or other disposal of all, or substantially all, of company's property with or without goodwill.

Regardless of whether an LLC is member-managed or manager-managed, action by the members or managers does not require a meeting. ULLCA § 404(d).

Problem 6.7

Lucy is a member of Belle's Ice Cream Shop, LLC, a member-managed limited liability company organized under the ULLCA. The LLC has two other members, Mary and Paula.

The LLC holds title in its name to a building just off the town square in Sealy, which it has been using to operate a small ice cream shop under the name "Belle's". Business had turned down in Sealy. Believing that Belle's would do better in nearby Brenham, Lucy asked the Neighbor, who owned the store next door, if he was interested in buying the building and lot. Lucy and Neighbor agreed to a price of $250,000. Neighbor paid Lucy the $250,000, and Lucy signed, acknowledged and delivered a Deed transferring the LLC's interest in the building and lot.

Lucy had never discussed a possible sale with Mary or Paula, and did not have their consent to a sale of the property. Mary and Paula have asked you if they may recover the property.

1. Assuming that the articles of organization of the LLC have no provisions that might affect your answer, please advise Mary and Paula, giving reasons to support your answer. See ULLCA §§ 301, 404(c).

2. Would your answer change if Lucy, Mary and Paula had been operating Belle's Ice Cream Shop as a partnership under the UPA? See UPA §§ 9, 10, 18. As a partnership under the RUPA? See RUPA §§ 301, 302, 401.

2. LLC Operating Agreements

Elf Atochem North America, Inc. v. Jaffari
727 A.2d 286 (Del. 1999)
Read case and following notes, page 70.

Chapter 7

Managerial Discretion and Fiduciary Duties

A. Business Judgment Rule

Problem 7.1

Wood was recently divorced from her husband. Pugh represented Wood in the divorce proceedings and in the property settlement. Wood's husband owned some unvested stock options. At the time of the property settlement, the state's highest court had not yet been decided on the proper treatment in a marital property settlement of either unvested stock options or taxes on unrealized capital gains.

Pugh advised Wood to settle at a value that excluded the unvested stock options and other items. Wood claims that Pugh told her the settlement amounted to 40 percent of the marital estate. When Wood asked if that was appropriate amount, she said Pugh told her a judge might award her anywhere from 35 to 50 percent. Wood claims that Pugh never discussed the different terms of the settlement, never mentioned any alternatives to settling, never provided any reasons to reject the settlement, and never discussed the potential outcome of a trial. She stated that she would not have signed the agreement if Pugh had told her that a trial court might include the unvested stock options as part of the marital estate and that a trial court might prohibit the deduction of potential capital gains tax when valuing the stock, contrary to what the settlement proposed.

Are Pugh and his firm liable to Wood for malpractice or breach of fiduciary duty? *See Wood v. McGrath, North, Mullin & Kratz, P.C.*, 256 Neb. 109, 589 N.W.2d 103 (1999).

Myers v. Maxey
915 P.2d 940 (Okla. App. 1995)

MEMORANDUM OPINION

Appellants, the widow, daughter and stepdaughter of deceased, sued attorneys and their law firm for legal malpractice, alleging the attorneys failed to have a will made by deceased (who had been placed under guardianship) subscribed and acknowledged before a district judge as required by 84 O.S. 1991 § 41(B).

The trial court granted a motion for a directed verdict by one of the attorneys, and entered judgment on a jury verdict in favor of the other attorney and the law firm. * * *

In February 1989, after a stroke left Escal Myers in a wheelchair, his facial muscles partially paralyzed, and his left arm and leg useless, his wife Beatriz [Betty] was appointed guardian of Escal's person and limited guardian of his property. Later that year, Betty and a friend met with Preston and Maxey and asked them to prepare an estate plan for her and Escal, and to handle certain other matters. A primary concern of Escal and the Appellants was avoidance of a will contest by Escal's daughter by his former marriage, Janet Hardiman. Attorneys agreed to represent Escal, and later confirmed their representation by letter to him. Maxey prepared a revocable "living" trust for Escal, and a will with "pour-over" provisions to transfer any of Escal's undisposed assets into the trust when he died. Following Escal's wishes, the new will provided that Hardiman would receive only $5,000 from his estate. The new will and the living trust were signed at Escal's home on December 29, 1989.

At the time Maxey prepared the will, 84 O.S.Supp. 1982 §41(B) provided that:

> [A]ppointment of a guardian or conservator does not prohibit a person from disposing of his estate, real and personal, by will; provided, that when any person subject to a guardianship or conservatorship shall dispose of such estate by will, such will must be subscribed and acknowledged in the presence of a judge of the district court. Subscribing and acknowledging such will before a judge shall not render such will valid if it would otherwise be invalid.

Maxey never recommended to Escal that he sign his new will before a judge, and did not advise him that §41(B) might have required him to do so. She did, however, recommend by letter to Escal

> that the court approve the [living] Trust and reaffirm your ability to determine how you want your property to be distributed upon your death.

She acted ostensibly in reliance on her reading of the recently enacted Oklahoma Guardianship Act, 30 O.S.Supp. 1988 §§1-101 et seq. [Guardianship Act], and the court order by which Escal had been made his wife's ward. In the guardianship court's dispositional order, the court had placed Escal under guardianship of his person—which meant he could not vote, serve as a juror, drive a car, or make personal medical decisions—and under limited guardianship of his property. And, as then required by the Guardianship Act, the guardianship court had made a specific finding that Escal possessed and retained "sufficient mental capacity in addition to cooperation with the guardian [Betty] in management of his financial resources and affairs to make a will or execute any other document directing the disposition of [his] property upon [his death]."

Escal died in February 1991, but when his 1989 will was offered for probate, the probate court refused to admit it. From the limited portion of the probate record before us, it appears that the court denied admission of the 1989 will because it had not been subscribed and acknowledged before a district judge in compliance with §41(B), and despite argument (and testimonial opinion from Maxey) that, since the guardianship court's dispositional order did not expressly limit Escal's testamentary capacity, he did not have to comply with § 41(B). As a result of the probate court's refusal to admit the will, and also because Escal had not transferred all of his assets to the trust before he died, there remained a substantial estate to pass under the law of intestate succession. The parties here have stipulated that by successfully contesting the will Janet Hardiman received almost $150,000 more from Escal's estate than she would have otherwise received had she been limited to the $5,000 bequest in his 1989 will.

Maxey, a recent law school graduate at the time she prepared Escal's 1989 will, testified that she discussed the requirements of § 41(B) with another lawyer at her law firm:

> A. [By Ms. Maxey] We did not believe it was necessary to have the will signed in front of a judge. The import and emphasis to us was to avoid a probate at all costs, set up a trust, or to transfer the property into joint tenancy.... [W]hen I discussed this with [the other lawyer], relying on the guardianship order, we did not feel it was necessary to have this executed in front of a judge.

> Q. [By Ms. Irish] Did it ever occur to you to err on the side of caution and get this will signed in front of a judge?

> A. In my opinion under the new guardianship act there was absolutely no requirement when a court has already determined that the ward had no restriction as to a will.

Yet, Maxey conceded elsewhere in her testimony that there was a valid distinction to be made between making a will and executing one — between deciding how property should pass after death and signing the document itself — and that statutory restrictions upon executing a will would seem to impinge upon the freedom to make a will.

With this factual background, we proceed to consider the parties' arguments for and against reversal. * * *

[W]e pause to discuss what, clearly, is the legal crux of this case: the fundamental disagreement about the proper interpretation of § 41(B) in light of the subsequent enactment of the Guardianship Act. At trial, each side presented expert testimony on this point. For Appellants, Robert Huff, author of the seminal treatise on Oklahoma probate law testified,

> There's no doubt in my mind that it [the will of someone under guardianship] must be executed in front — in the presence of a district judge.

For Appellees, Theresa Collett, a member of the legislative task force which drafted the Guardianship Act, opined that the subscription and acknowledgment requirement of § 41(B) did not apply to someone such as Escal Myers, who had been expressly declared by a guardianship dispositional order, made in conformity with the existing Guardianship Act, to be able to

> make a will or execute any other document directing the disposition of the ward's property upon [his] death...

Ms. Collett placed particular emphasis on the Guardianship Act's declaration that a person placed under guardianship

> shall retain all legal rights and abilities other than those expressly limited or curtailed in [the dispositional or subsequent guardianship] orders

* * *

A lawyer is not expected to be perfect in giving advice to her clients. One who alleges negligence by an attorney must plead and prove the attorney-client relation, a breach of duty arising from the relation, and injury proximately caused by the breach.

In *Collins v. Wanner*, 382 P.2d 105 (Okla. 1963), the Supreme Court of Oklahoma first recognized the "good faith" rule:

> [W]here, as here, negligence is predicated upon the attorney's alleged ignorance of the law, the rule has been followed in many jurisdictions that an attorney is not liable for reaching a conclusion as to a controversial point of law which by subsequent authoritative decision is proved to be erroneous. [citations] In [*Hodges v. Carter*, 239 N.C. 517, 80 S.E.2d 144, 45 A.L.R.2d 1 (1954)] this was said in the body of the opinion:
>
> > An attorney who acts in good faith and in an honest belief that his advice and acts are well founded and in the best interest of his client is not answerable for a mere error of judgment or for a mistake in a point of law which has not been settled by the court of last resort in his State and on which reasonable doubt may be entertained by well-informed lawyers. [citations]
>
> * * * [S]ince the point of law upon which defendants reached an erroneous conclusion was unsettled at the time the conclusion was reached and was one upon which, as reflected by the opinion rendered therein and evidence that defendants caused to be introduced here, qualified and experienced lawyers differed, defendants cannot be said to have been negligent in reaching the conclusion thereon that they reached.

Collins, 382 P.2d at 109.... * * *

In other jurisdictions it is not enough that an attorney acts under a subjective belief that she is acting in good faith; the attorney's good faith is in those cases measured by an objective standard. * * * An objective approach to the question of good faith seems commendable in our view, lest an attorney's own protestations of good faith insulate him from a charge of negligence. An objective approach to the good faith defense also dovetails nicely with the general standard of reasonableness which is the essential inquiry in a negligence case.

Appellants contend there could be no mere error of judgment or mistake on an unsettled point of law in this instance because the reading of § 41(B) is not a matter upon which reasonable doubt could have been entertained by well-informed lawyers. * * * Appellees, on the other hand, point out that seemingly well-informed lawyers did in fact express quite different views at trial about how § 41(B) should be read in light of the Guardianship Act. And, obviously, the Supreme Court of Oklahoma has not spoken on this issue yet. * * *

When a court interprets a statute, it must adhere to the plain and ordinary meaning of the terms employed by the legislature, unless a contrary intent appears from consideration of the statute as a whole. * * * In this case we are presented one statute which, while recognizing that someone under guardianship is not thereby precluded from making a will, clearly requires that any will made by a person under guardianship must be subscribed and acknowledged before a district judge; and another statute which was enacted so that a ward could, as fully as possible, participate in decisions which affect him, and which provides that a person placed under guardianship is not thereby deprived of his testamentary powers unless specifically limited by dispositional or subsequent court order.

We do not discern any outward inconsistency between § 41(B) and the Guardianship Act. But we are not here to decide an original issue of statutory interpretation. Rather, we consider only a threshold issue: whether either of the two interpretations expressed by the experts in this case is so implausible as to make it unreasonable, as a matter of law, for an attorney to use it as the basis for acting in her client's best interests. In considering that issue we must accept the unquestioned credentials of the two expert witnesses who testified before the jury; and, under the circumstances of this case, the fact of their divergent opinions about how these two statutes should be read each with the other. It ultimately does not matter whether we would adopt one or the other interpretation as our own, but only whether a well informed lawyer could reasonably entertain one or the other interpretation in the course of representing her client.

* * * Under the circumstances presented in this case, we are constrained to hold that the trial court did not err by denying Appellants' motion for directed verdict.

Notes

1. The general duty of care of a *paid agent* is easy to state:

> Unless otherwise agreed, a paid agent is subject to a duty to the principal to act with standard care and with the skill which is standard in the locality for the kind of work which [the agent] is employed to perform and, in addition, to exercise any special skill that [the agent] has.

Restatement § 479(1). The problem, of course, is in *applying* this standard as to an agent's duty of care.

2. One perennially controversial subject is the standard by which to measure the conduct of a fiduciary entrusted with complex matters involving discretion and judgment. What happens when the fiduciary's exercise of judgment leads to a loss? On the one hand, no fiduciary has perfect foresight and perfect knowledge; even an ordinarily skillful, competent, and careful fiduciary will make decisions that will *seem* improper in the harsh glare of hindsight. No fiduciary should be made into a *guarantor* or *insurer* of a favorable result. *See* Restatement (Second) of Agency § 379 comment c. On the other hand, if a duty of care is to have any meaningful substantive content, a fiduciary *should* be held accountable for a failure to act with ordinary skill, competence, and care.

3. In *Cosgrove v. Grimes,* 774 S.W.2d 662 (Tex. 1989), the Texas Supreme Court considered and rejected the argument that subjective good faith should be a defense in a suit against a lawyer:

> Some courts have held that if an attorney makes an error in judgment, but acted in good faith and in what the attorney believed was the client's best interest, the attorney is not liable for malpractice. In the instant case the jury found that Grimes had acted in good faith in relying on the information Cosgrove allegedly furnished to Grimes, and the trial court rendered judgment for Grimes.

There is no subjective good faith excuse for attorney negligence. A lawyer in Texas is held to the standard of care which would be exercised by a reasonably prudent attorney. The jury must evaluate his conduct based on the information the attorney has at the time of the alleged act of negligence. In some instances an attorney is required to make *tactical or strategic* decisions. Ostensibly, the good faith exception was created to protect this unique attorney work product. However, allowing the attorney to assert his subjective good faith, when the acts he pursues are unreasonable as measured by the reasonably competent practioner standard, creates too great a burden for wronged clients to overcome. The instruction to the jury should clearly set out the standard for negligence in terms which encompass the attorney's reasonableness in choosing one course of action over another.

If an attorney makes a decision which a reasonably prudent attorney could make in the same or similar circumstance, it is not an act of negligence even if the result is undesirable. Attorneys cannot be held strictly liable for all of their clients' unfulfilled expectations. An attorney who makes a *reasonable* decision in the *handling* of a case may not be held liable if the decision later proves to be imperfect. The standard is an objective exercise of professional judgment, not the subjective belief that his acts are in good faith.

774 S.W.2d at 664-65 (emphasis added).

4. In *Wood v. McGrath, North, Mullin & Kratz, P.C.*, 256 Neb. 109, 589 N.W.2d 103 (1999), Wood sued her lawyer (Pugh) for malpractice in advising here as to a property settlement in her divorce. Wood invoked "judgmental immunity", claiming that he should not be responsible for a subsequent resolution of an unsettled question. The Nebraska Supreme Court held that Pugh should have advised Wood as to the unsettled state of the law and as to the effect of the law on her rights:

The decision to settle a controversy is the client's. If a client is to meaningfully make that decision, he or she needs to have the information necessary to assess the risks and benefits of either settling or proceeding to trial. "A lawyer should exert his or her best efforts to ensure that decisions of a client are made only after the client has been informed of relevant considerations." The desire is that a client's decision to settle is an informed one.

The attorney's research efforts may not resolve doubts or may lead to the conclusion that only hindsight or future judicial decisions will provide accurate answers. The attorney's responsibilities to the client may not be satisfied concerning a material issue simply by determining that a proposition is doubtful or by unilaterally deciding the issue. Where there are reasonable alternatives, the attorney should inform the client that the issue is uncertain, unsettled or debatable and allow the client to make the decision.

* * *

We conclude that the doctrine of judgmental immunity does not apply to an attorney's failure to inform a client of unsettled legal issues relevant to a settlement. Our conclusion makes no judgment as to whether Pugh was negligent. It imposes no additional duty as a matter of law to research or inform a client on unsettled legal matters. Rather, it simply directs that...whether an attorney is negligent for such a failure is determined by whether the attorney exercised the same skill, knowledge, and diligence as attorneys of ordinary skill and capacity commonly possess and exercise in the performance of all other legal tasks. At the same time, an attorney's ultimate recommendation in an area of unsettled law is immune from suit. * * * Such a result gives the client the benefit of both professional advice and the information necessary to make an informed decision whether to settle a dispute.

Problem 7.2

Mt. Hood Meadows, Oreg., Ltd. is a limited partnership established to carry on the business of constructing and operating a winter sports development. Under the limited partnership agreement, management of the business and affairs of Mt. Hood Meadows is the responsibility of its general partner, Mt. Hood Meadows Development Corp. That agreement also provides that the limited partners have no right to take part in the control of the business. For the years in which profits were earned after 1974, the general partner elected to distribute only 50 percent of the limited partners' taxable profits. The remaining profits were retained and reinvested in the business. Three of the limited partners have sued to force the general partner to distribute the retained profits.

Assume that the limited partnership agreement does not require the distributions, and that they are not required under the applicable statute. On what basis, if any, should a court interfere in the general partner's decision as to the distribution of profits?

Kamin v. American Express Company
86 Misc.2d 809, 383 N.Y.S.2d 807 (Sup. Ct. 1976)

OPINION OF THE COURT

Edward J. Greenfield, J.

In this stockholders' derivative action, the individual defendants, who are the directors of the American Express Company, move for an order dismissing the complaint for failure to state a cause of action pursuant to CPLR 3211 (subd [a], par 7), and alternatively, for summary judgment pursuant to CPLR 3211 (subd [c]).

The complaint is brought derivatively by two minority stockholders of the American Express Company, asking for a declaration that a certain dividend in kind is a waste of corporate assets, directing the defendants not to proceed with the distribution, or, in the alternative, for monetary damages. The motion to dismiss the complaint requires the court to presuppose the truth of the allegations. It is the defendants' contention that, conceding everything in the complaint, no viable cause of action is made out.

After establishing the identity of the parties, the complaint alleges that in 1972 American Express acquired for investment 1,954,418 shares of common stock of Donaldson, Lufken and Jenrette, Inc. (hereafter DLJ), a publicly traded corporation, at a cost of $29,900,000. It is further alleged that the current market value of those shares is approximately $4,000,000. On July 28, 1975, it is alleged, the board of directors of American Express declared a special dividend to all stockholders of record pursuant to which the shares of DLJ would be distributed in kind. Plaintiffs contend further that if American Express were to sell the DLJ shares on the market, it would sustain a capital loss of $25,000,000 which could be offset against taxable capital gains on other investments. Such a sale, they allege, would result in tax savings to the company of approximately $8,000,000, which would not be available in the case of the distribution of DLJ shares to stockholders. It is alleged that on October 8, 1975 and October 16, 1975, plaintiffs demanded that the directors rescind the previously declared dividend in DLJ shares and take steps to preserve the capital loss which would result from selling the shares. This demand was rejected by the board of directors on October 17, 1975.

It is apparent that all the previously-mentioned allegations of the complaint go to the question of the exercise by the board of directors of business judgment in deciding how to deal with the DLJ shares. The crucial allegation which must be scrutinized to determine the legal sufficiency of the complaint is paragraph 19, which alleges:

> 19. All of the defendant Directors engaged in or acquiesced in or negligently permitted the declaration and payment of the Dividend in violation of the fiduciary duty owed by them to Amex to care for and preserve Amex's assets in the same manner as a man of average prudence would care for his own property.

Plaintiffs never moved for temporary injunctive relief, and did nothing to bar the actual distribution of the DLJ shares. The dividend was in fact paid on October 31, 1975. Accordingly, that portion of the complaint seeking a direction not to distribute the shares is deemed to be moot, and the court will deal only with the request for declaratory judgment or for damages.

Examination of the complaint reveals that there is no claim of fraud or self-dealing, and no contention that there was any bad faith or oppressive conduct. The law is quite clear as to what is necessary to ground a claim for actionable wrongdoing.

> In actions by stockholders, which assail the acts of their directors or trustees, courts will not interfere unless the powers have been illegally or unconscientiously executed, or unless it be made to appear that the acts were fraudulent or collusive and destructive of the rights of the stockholders. Mere errors of judgment are not sufficient as grounds for equity interference; for the powers of those entrusted with corporate management are largely discretionary.

(*Leslie v Lorillard*, 110 NY 519, 532)

More specifically, the question of whether or not a dividend is to be declared or a distribution of some kind should be made is exclusively a matter of business judgment for the board of directors.

> Courts will not interfere with such discretion unless it be first made to appear that the directors have acted or are about to act in bad faith and

for a dishonest purpose. It is for the directors to say, acting in good faith of course, when and to what extent dividends shall be declared...The statute confers upon the directors this power, and the minority stockholders are not in a position to question this right, so long as the directors are acting in good faith.

(*Liebman v Auto Strop Co.,* 241 NY 427, 433-434).

Thus, a complaint must be dismissed if all that is presented is a decision to pay dividends rather than pursuing some other course of conduct. A complaint which alleges merely that some course of action other than that pursued by the board of directors would have been more advantageous gives rise to no cognizable cause of action. Courts have more than enough to do in adjudicating legal rights and devising remedies for wrongs. The directors' room rather than the courtroom is the appropriate forum for thrashing out purely business questions which will have an impact on profits, market prices, competitive situations, or tax advantages. As stated by Cardozo, J., when sitting at Special Term, the substitution of someone else's business judgment for that of the directors "'is no business for any court to follow.'" (*Holmes v Saint Joseph Lead Co.,* 84 Misc 278, 283, *quoting from Gamble v Queens County Water Co.,* 123 NY 91, 99.)

It is not enough to allege, as plaintiffs do here, that the directors made an imprudent decision, which did not capitalize on the possibility of using a potential capital loss to offset capital gains. More than imprudence or mistaken judgment must be shown.

> Questions of policy of management, expediency of contracts or action, adequacy of consideration, lawful appropriation of corporate funds to advance corporate interests, are left solely to their honest and unselfish decision, for their powers therein are without limitation and free from restraint, and the exercise of them for the common and general interests of the corporation may not be questioned, although the results show that what they did was unwise or inexpedient.

(*Pollitz v Wabash R.R. Co.,* 207 NY 113, 124.)

Section 720 (subd [a], par [1], cl [A]) of the Business Corporation Law permits an action against directors for

> [t]he neglect of, or failure to perform, or other violation of his duties in the management and disposition of corporate assets committed to his charge

This does not mean that a director is chargeable with ordinary negligence for having made an improper decision, or having acted imprudently. The "neglect" referred to in the statute is neglect of duties (i.e., malfeasance or nonfeasance) and not misjudgment. To allege that a director "negligently permitted the declaration and payment" of a dividend without alleging fraud, dishonesty or nonfeasance, is to state merely that a decision was taken with which one disagrees.

Nor does this appear to be a case in which a potentially valid cause of action is inartfully stated. The defendants have moved alternatively for summary judgment and have submitted affidavits under CPLR 3211 (subd [c]), and plaintiffs likewise have submitted papers enlarging upon the allegations of the complaint. The affidavits of the defendants and the exhibits annexed thereto demonstrate that the objections raised by the plaintiffs to the proposed dividend action were carefully considered and unanimously rejected by the board at a special meeting called precisely for that purpose at the plaintiffs' request. The minutes of the special meeting indicate that the defendants were fully aware that a sale rather than a distribution of the DLJ shares might result in the realization of a substantial income tax saving. Nevertheless, they concluded that there were countervailing considerations primarily with respect to the adverse effect such a sale, realizing a loss of $25,000,000, would have on the net income figures in the American Express financial statement. Such a reduction of net income would have a serious effect on the market value of the publicly traded American Express stock. This was not a situation in which the defendant directors totally overlooked facts called to their attention. They gave them consideration, and attempted to view the total picture in arriving at their decision. While plaintiffs contend that according to their accounting consultants the loss on the DLJ stock would still have to be charged against current earnings even if the stock were distributed, the defendants' accounting experts assert that the loss would be a charge against earnings only in the event of a sale, whereas in the event of distribution of the stock as a dividend, the proper accounting treatment would be to charge the loss only against surplus. While the chief accountant for the SEC raised some question as to the appropriate accounting treatment of this transaction, there was no basis for any action to be taken by the SEC with respect to the American Express financial statement.

The only hint of self-interest which is raised, not in the complaint but in the papers on the motion, is that 4 of the 20 directors were officers and employees of American Express and members of its executive incentive compensation plan. Hence, it is suggested, by virtue of the action taken earnings may have been overstated and their compensation affected thereby. Such a claim is highly speculative and standing alone can hardly be regarded as sufficient to support an inference of self-dealing. There is no claim or showing that the four company directors dominated and controlled the 16 outside members of the board. Certainly, every action taken by the board has some impact on earnings and may therefore affect the compensation of those whose earnings are keyed to profits. That does not disqualify the inside directors, nor does it put every policy adopted by the board in question. All directors have an obligation, using sound business judgment, to maximize income for the benefit of all persons having a stake in the welfare of the corporate entity. What we have here as revealed both by the complaint and by the affidavits and exhibits, is that a disagreement exists between two minority stockholders and a unanimous board of directors as to the best way to handle a loss already incurred on an investment. The directors are entitled to exercise their honest business judgment on the information before them, and to act within their corporate powers. That they may be mistaken, that other courses of action might have differing consequences, or that their action might benefit some shareholders more than others present no basis for the superimposition of judicial judgment, so long as it appears that the directors have been acting in good faith. The question of to what extent a dividend shall be declared and the manner in which it shall be paid is ordinarily subject only to the qualification that the dividend be paid out of surplus (Business Corporation Law, § 510, subd [b]). The court will not interfere unless a clear case is made out of fraud, oppression, arbitrary action, or breach of trust.

* * *

In this case it clearly appears that the plaintiffs have failed as a matter of law to make out an actionable claim. Accordingly, the motion by the defendants for summary judgment and dismissal of the complaint is granted.

Notes

1. In *Brehm v. Eisner*, 746 A.2d 244 (Del. 2000), a shareholder of the Walt Disney Company claimed that Disney's directors had breached their fiduciary duties in making decisions about the employment, and subsequent termination, of Disney's president. In the dismissing the derivative suit brought by the shareholder, Chief Justice Veasey discussed the so-called '*business judgment rule*" and the difference between "ideal corporate governance practices" and "standards of liability":

> This is a case about whether there should be personal liability of the directors of a Delaware corporation... for lack of due care in the decision-making process and for waste of corporate assets. This case is not about the failure of the directors to establish and carry out ideal corporate governance practices.

> All good corporate governance practices include compliance with statutory law and case law establishing fiduciary duties. But the law of corporate fiduciary duties and remedies for violation of those duties are distinct from the aspirational goals of ideal corporate governance practices. Aspirational ideals of good corporate governance practices for boards of directors that go beyond the minimal legal requirements of the corporation law are highly desirable, often tend to benefit stockholders, sometimes reduce litigation and can usually help directors avoid liability. But they are not required by the corporation law and do not define standards of liability.

> The inquiry here is not whether we would disdain the composition, behavior and decisions of Disney's [board of directors] if we were Disney stockholders. In the absence of a legislative mandate, that determination is not for the courts. That decision is for the stockholders to make in voting for directors, urging other stockholders to reform or oust the board, or in making individual buy-sell decisions involving Disney securities. * * *

Brehm v. Eisner, 746 A.2d at 255-56.

2. As applied in evaluating the decisions of a corporate officers or directors, the business judgment rule protects them from liability on account of business judgments made in good faith:

> A director or officer who makes a business judgment in good faith fulfills his duty [of care] if:

> (1) he is not interested in the subject of his business judgment;

> (2) he is informed with respect to the subject of his business judgment to the extent he reasonably believes necessary; and

> (3) he rationally believes that his business judgment is in the best interests of the corporation.

AMERICAN LAW INSTITUTE, PRINCIPLES OF CORPORATE GOVERNANCE § 4.01(c) (1991).

3. *Ferguson v. Williams*, 670 S.W.2d 327 (Tex. Ct. App. 1984) grew out of the failure of a real-estate joint venture. Williams, a passive investor, claimed that the managing joint-venturers were negligent in operating the joint venture. The trial court agreed, but the appellate court did not, saying:

> As to the findings by the trial court that appellants Ferguson and Welborn were guilty of negligence in the management of the affairs of the business and that such negligence was the proximate cause of Williams' loss of his invested funds, we hold *as a matter of law* that negligence in the management of the affairs of a general partnership or joint venture does not create any right of action against that partner by other members of the partnership. It is only when there is a breach of trust, such as when one partner or joint venturer holds property or assets belonging to the partnership or venture, and converts such to his own use, would such action lie. In the ordinary management and operation of a general partnership or joint venture there is no liability to the other partners or joint venturers for the negligence in the management or operation of the affairs of the enterprise. Appellee cites us no authority, and we have found none, to support his theory of this case. None of the "negligence" findings involve any breach of trust or fiduciary duty of Ferguson and Welborn to Williams.

Id. at 331 (emphasis added).

4. In *Brooke v. Mt. Hood Meadows Oreg., Ltd.*, 81 Or.App. 387, 725 P.2d 925 (1986), the general partner of Mt. Hood Meadows, Oreg., Ltd. distributed only a portion of the partnership's profits. The remainder were retained and reinvested in the business. One of the limited partners sued to force the distribution of the retained profits. After rejecting the argument that the partners were entitled to distributions, the court refused to interfere with the general partner's policy as to distributions:

> [Article X[B] of the limited partnership agreement provides] that all management decisions of the partnership be the responsibility of the general partner and that the limited partners have no right to take part in the control of the business. * * * Management of the business necessarily includes decisions regarding the management of profits, unless the parties have specified otherwise in the limited partnership agreement.

B. [Note by editors] Article X of the limited partnership agreement provides:
POWERS AND RESPONSIBILITIES, COMPENSATION

Management and control of the partnership business shall be vested exclusively in the general partner, who, except as otherwise herein provided, shall have all the rights and powers and be subject to all the restrictions and liabilities of a general partner. * * *

None of the limited partners shall have any voice or take any part in the control or management of the business of the partnership nor shall any limited partner have any power or authority to act for or on behalf of the partnership in any respect whatever....

*   *   *

* * *. We conclude that the agreement contains no provision expressly directing the general partner to distribute profits to the limited partners.

Plaintiffs argue that the authority to retain profits is one that must be granted expressly to the general partner and that, in the absence of a grant, is presumed to have been withheld. That proposition is too broad. With certain exceptions and unless otherwise agreed, a broad grant of authority to manage a business, such as that applicable here, includes the authority to conduct all affairs reasonably necessary or incidental to the expressly authorized business. Decisions regarding the management, including the distribution, of profits fall within that broad authority.

*   *   *

The availability of cash for distribution, however, depends strictly on management's operation of the business. The business' future cash needs are also determined by management. That is why the decision as to how much, if any, of a limited partner's share of the profits is to be distributed is a management decision. * * *

A limited partner's position is analogous to that of a corporate shareholder, whose role is that of an investor with limited liability, and with no voice in the operation of the enterprise. * * * A general partner's relationship to the limited partners is analogous to the relationship of a corporate board of directors to the corporate shareholders; the general partner functions as a fiduciary with a duty of good faith and fair dealing. Like the corporate director's fiduciary responsibility to the shareholders for the declaration of dividends, the general partner's duty to the limited partners in the distribution of profit is discharged by decisions made in good faith that reflect legitimate business concerns. There is no contention here that the general partner acted in bad faith in failing to distribute all of the profits.

5. Under the RUPA section 404(e):

A partner owes a duty of care to the partnership and the other partners to act in the conduct of the business of the partnership in a manner that does not constitute *gross negligence* or *willful misconduct. An error in judgment or a failure to use ordinary care is not gross negligence.*

RUPA § 4.04(e) (emphasis added).

6. How would the reasoning of *Myers v. Maxey,* page 349, apply to decisions of managers of a business? Do *Kamin v. American Express, Ferguson v. Williams* (Note 3) and *Brooke v. Mt. Hood Meadows Oreg., Ltd.* (Note 4) go too far in protecting business managers?

7. In *Brehm v. Eisner* (Note 1), Chief Justice Veasey suggests that shareholders of a public corporation who disagree with a board of directors' management have two remedies: they can elect a different directors, or they can sell their shares? Are those options likely to be open to a limited partner or a member of an LLC?

B. Duty of Loyalty

Problem 7.3

Read Problem 4.5, page 214.

Schock v. Nash

Read case and following notes, page 216.

Starr v. International Realty, Ltd.

271 Or. 396, 533 P.2d 165 (1975)

TONGUE, Justice.

This is a suit by the partners in a real estate venture to require the Realtor and promoter of the venture, who was also a partner, to account to the partnership for the commission received by him as the Realtor without consent of the remaining partners and to hold in trust for the partnership the vendor's interest in the real estate purchased, which he also acquired without their consent. Defendants appeal from an adverse decree and plaintiffs cross-appeal from other portions of that decree.

The case involves a group of prominent Portland doctors and others in high income tax "brackets" and in need of "tax shelters." They were persuaded by one Stanley G. Harris, a Portland "expert" in real property investments, that by investing $285,000 and joining with him in a partnership for the purchase of an apartment house then under construction, the entire down payment of $265,000 could be treated for federal income tax purposes as "prepaid interest," thereby saving large amounts otherwise payable in income taxes.

It would serve no useful purpose to summarize the entire transaction for the purchase of this property for the sum of $2,010,000 in all of its details, as "put together" by Harris. Suffice to say that we have reviewed the lengthy transcript of the testimony of some 21 witnesses, together with 94 exhibits, and agree with the trial court in its findings that Harris did not reveal to his partners that the property could have been purchased for $907,500 "net" to the seller (including $207,500 to the seller to "cash [him] out of the transaction" and the assumption of a $700,000 mortgage), and that a commission of $100,000, together with an escrow fee of $2,500, was to be paid to International Realty Ltd., of which Harris was president, or that Harris had made an agreement with the seller of the property under which International or Harris would acquire the vendor's interest to the contract under which the property was being purchased by the partnership.

1. *Defendants' failure to disclose the receipt of the broker's commission.*

In *Liggett v. Lester*, 237 Or. 52, 58, 390 P.2d 351 (1964), although under different facts, we stated that:

> The rule which requires an accounting for secret profits applies to commissions and discounts *secretly obtained* by a partner on purchases made by him for the firm. It was Lester's duty to obtain petroleum products for the partnership at the best price possible.

The case at bar involves purchases for the partnership resulting in *secret commissions* or discounts. Where a secret discount is withheld by one partner on purchases which he has made on behalf of the partnership, the entire amount of the discount must be accounted for. (Emphasis added.)

To the same effect, see Crane and Bromberg on Partnership 389-90, 68 (1968). The question to be decided in this case, however, is whether the $100,000 commission paid to International of which Harris was the president, was a "secret" commission.

Defendants contend that the broker's commission paid to International was not "secret" or "concealed"; that "explicit consent" is not required; and that "sufficient disclosure" was made "through documents, through the plaintiffs' general knowledge of the general manner in which real estate transactions are conducted, and through specific conversations." Defendants "do not contend that plaintiffs explicitly and expressly consented to the commission."

It appears from the testimony that most of the plaintiffs knew or should have known that Harris and International were in the real estate business and that a Realtor's commission in some amount would normally be paid to some Realtor on this transaction. Apparently, because their interest in the income tax advantages of the transaction was so dominant and overriding, the doctors did not inquire whether such a commission would be paid to Harris or to International, or in what amount, and Harris did not tell them. It is contended by the doctors, however, that in this case they are entitled to the benefit of the equivalent of a role more familiar to them in the practice of medicine—that of "informed consent."

In *Liggett v. Lester, supra,* we also said:

Although Liggett was aware of Lester's bulkplant operation, it is clear that Lester failed to disclose the additional discounts he was receiving on the sales to the partnership. Lester not only failed to offer his partner an opportunity to share in the discount, but he tried to keep Liggett from learning of it. Liggett discovered this state of affairs by chance. Lester cannot rely upon the foregoing right to engage in other business since Liggett's consent was not truly obtained.

It is contended by defendants that *Liggett* is not controlling because the defendant in that case "actively attempted to keep his partner from learning of the discount." In our view, however, the rule as stated by this court in *Liggett* is not limited to cases involving "active attempts" to conceal.

[UPA section 21(1)] provides:

Every partner must account to the partnership for *any benefit*, and hold as trustee for it any profits derived by him *without the consent* of the other partners from any transaction connected with the formation, conduct, or liquidation of the partnership or from any use by him of its property. (Emphasis added.)

In *Fouchek et al. v. Janicek,* 190 Or. 251, 262, 225 P.2d 7 83 (1950), we said that this section from the [UPA] states "the essence of the fiduciary [duty] of a partner," as stated by Justice Cardozo in *Meinhard v. Salmon,* 249 N.Y. 458, 463, 164 N.E. 545 (1929), as follows:

Joint adventurers, [and] copartners, owe to one another, while the enterprise continues, the duty of the finest loyalty. Many forms of conduct permissible in a workaday world for those acting at arm's length are forbidden to those bound by fiduciary ties. A trustee is held to something stricter than morals of the market place. Not honesty alone, but the punctilio of an honor the most sensitive, is then the standard of behavior. As to this there has developed a tradition that is unbending and inveterate. Uncompromising rigidity has been the attitude of courts of equity when petitioned to undermine the rule of undivided loyalty by the 'disintegrating erosion' of particular exceptions. Only thus has the level of conduct for fiduciaries been kept at a level higher than that trodden by the crowd. It will not consciously be lowered by any judgment of this court.

Real estate brokers are subject to potential conflicting interest in many transactions. Even when a real estate broker does not become a partner in a venture involving the purchase of property this court has held that he owes a fiduciary duty to protect his client's interests and also "to make a full, fair and understandable explanation to his client before having him sign any contract."

When, as in this case, a real estate broker undertakes to join as a member of partnership or joint venture in the purchase of real property on which he holds a listing, he is also subject to the fiduciary duties of undivided loyalty and complete disclosure owed by one partner to another. Indeed, one of the fundamental duties of any partner who deals on his own account in matters within the scope of his fiduciary relationship is the affirmative duty to make a full disclosure to his partners not only of the fact that he is dealing on his own account, but all of the facts which are material to the transaction. As held in *Duniway v. Barton*, 193 Or. 69, 78, 237 P.2d 930 (1951), although not involving a partnership, a fiduciary has a duty "not only not to misrepresent," but to "disclose fully all the material facts within his knowledge."

It follows that the "consent of the other partners" required by [UPA section 21(1)] before any partner may retain "any benefit" from "any transaction connected with the formation [or] conduct" of a partnership must necessarily be an "informed consent" with knowledge of the facts necessary to the giving of an intelligent consent.

In this case, Harris did not inform plaintiffs or disclose to them the fact that this property could have been purchased for $907,500 "net" to the seller or that upon its purchase for $1,010,000 Harris or International (of which Harris was the president) would be paid a commission in the amount of $100,000. In the absence of such a disclosure there could be no effective "consent" by plaintiffs to the payment or retention by Harris of any such "benefit" from that transaction, for the purposes of [UPA section 21(1)].

For these reasons we must reject defendants' contention that the broker's commission paid to International was "neither secret nor concealed." For the same reasons, the trial court did not err in requiring defendants to account to the partnership for that commission.

2. Defendants' failure to disclose the agreement to receive an assignment of the vendor's interest in the sales contract.

Defendants make no contention that they originally informed plaintiffs of the agreement by which the vendor's interest in the contract under which this property was being purchased by the partnership would be assigned to International. Defendants contend, however, that in 1970 Harris "spoke with each of the partners except [one] about possible acquisition of the vendor's interest" and that "none of the partners expressed any desire to purchase the interest, even though Harris apparently offered it at a substantial discount." Defendants also cite cases from other states in support of the contention that "a partner may purchase the fee to the property which the partnership has leased, provided he practices no deception or fraud upon his co-partners."

Again, we consider the better rule, and the established rule in Oregon to be that the absence of "deception or fraud" is not sufficient to justify a partner in acquiring such an interest in property being purchased under contract by the partnership. On the contrary, we hold that the acquisition by International (and subsequently by Harris and his wife) of the vendor's interest in the property being purchased under contract by the partnership of which Harris was a member was a "benefit" that was connected with the formation [and] conduct" of the partnership and was subject to [UPA Section 21], so as to require "consent" by the other parties and so as also to be subject to the duty of full disclosure to the same extent as the receipt of the commission on the sale, as previously discussed.

The same result also follows under established rules of agency. Thus, as stated in Restatement 2d of Agency 208-09, § 390, comment *a*:

> One employed as agent violates no duty to the principal by action for his own benefit *if he makes a full disclosure of the facts* to an acquiescent principal and takes no unfair advantage of him. Before dealing with the principal on his own account, however, *an agent has a duty, not only to make no misstatements of fact, but also to disclose to the principal all relevant facts fully and completely*. A fact is relevant if it is one which the agent should realize would be likely to affect the judgment of the principal in giving his consent to the agent to enter into the particular transaction on the specified terms. Hence, the disclosure must include not only the fact that the agent is acting on his own account, but also all other facts which he should realize have or are likely to have a bearing upon the desirability of the transaction from the viewpoint of the principal. (Emphasis added.)

It follows that the trial court did not err in holding that Harris holds the vendor's interest in this contract in trust for the benefit of the partnership.

4. Plaintiffs are entitled to the full amount of the sums misappropriated without deduction of amounts paid to employees.

Plaintiffs' remaining contention on cross-appeal is that the trial court erred in allowing defendants a set-off of some $34,656.10, representing that portion of the $82,500 found to have been misappropriated by the defendants which was paid to salesmen who secured the original listing and who secured the various "clients" who became partners in the venture. Plaintiffs again cite *Liggett v. Lester*, in which we distinguished cases involving "dealings with third parties" and held, under the facts of that case, that a partner who had withheld a "secret discount" must account for that "entire amount."

To the same effect, the following rule is stated in 1 Rowley on Partnership 532, § 21.1 (2d ed. 1960):

> The partner receiving secret commissions on the partnership transac-

tions must account for the whole amount of the commissions so received even though he may have been assisted in the deal by a third person, to whom he paid a part of such commissions.

Defendants contend, on the contrary, that "[t]he power of a court of equity to fashion justice should not be limited" and that "[r]emedies should be shaped to meet the needs of justice required by the facts of each case."

After a review of this record, however, we believe that the facts of this case are sufficiently aggravated that the defendants should be held liable to account for payment to the partnership of the full amount misappropriated by defendants, without deductions or set-off of payments made to employees.

The fact that in this case the commission received by International and by Harris was shared with salesmen employed by them does not, in our opinion, require a different result under the facts of this case.

Except as modified by the disallowance of the set-offs claimed by defendants, the decree of the trial court is affirmed and the case is remanded for the purpose of computing the amount to be awarded by the final judgment.

Notes

1. RUPA Section 404(b) describes a partner's duty of loyalty as follows:

A partner's duty of loyalty to the partnership and the other partners is limited to the following:

(1) to account to the partnership and hold as trustee for it any property, profit, or benefit derived by the partner in the conduct and winding up of the partnership business or derived from a use by the partner of partnership property, including the appropriation of a partnership opportunity;

(2) to refrain from dealing with the partnership in the conduct or winding up of the partnership business as or on behalf of a party having an interest adverse to the partnership; and

(3) to refrain from competing with the partnership in the conduct of the partnership business before the dissolution of the partnership.

RUPA § 404(b).

2. In *Covalt v. High,* page 315, Covalt and High, as partners, owned and leased property to a corporation owned by them. High owned 75% of the outstanding stock of the corporation, and Covalt owned 25%. The partnership agreement made High managing partner and gave him authority to set the rent to be charged the corporation. After Covalt left the employ of the corporation, Covalt sued High for breach of fiduciary duty in failing to charge the corporation a reasonable rental value. Despite findings by the trial court that High was not charging a reasonable rent, the appellate court found no breach of duty. The appellate court treated the case as involving only a dispute among partners. The court reasoned that, because the two were equal partners, there was no basis on which Covalt could insist on a higher rent.

a. Is the opinion in *Covalt v. High* consistent with the opinion in *Starr v. International Realty?*

b. In determining whether High breached his duty of loyalty, would it make any difference if, at the time the partners invested in the land and agreed to rent it to the corporation, the rental agreed to by the partners was less than the fair rental value of the property? How would *Schock v. Nash*, page 216, bear on this question? For additional discussion of the parties' ability to contract as to fiduciary duties, see *Sonet v. [Plum Creek] Timber Company*, page 378, and the following notes later in this Chapter.

Problem 7.4

Covalt and High were corporate officers and shareholders in Concrete Systems, Inc. (CSI). Covalt owned 25% of the stock and High owned the remaining 75% of the stock. Both men received remuneration from CSI in the form of salaries and bonuses.

In late 1971, after both High and Covalt had become corporate officers of CSI, they formed a partnership. The partnership bought land and built an office and warehouse building. In February, 1973, CSI leased the building from the partnership for a five-year term. Following the expiration of the initial term of the lease, CSI remained a tenant of the building; the corporation and the partnership orally agreed to certain rental increases. The corporation made substantial improvements to the leasehold. Under the original lease any improvements to the premises were to accrue to the partnership upon termination of the lease.

In December, 1978, Covalt resigned his position as an officer of CSI and went to work for one of its competitors. Covalt, however, remained a partner with High in the ownership of the land and the building rented to CSI. On January 9, 1979, Covalt wrote to High demanding that the monthly rent for the partnership real estate leased to CSI be increased from $1,850 to $2,850 per month. High refused to increase the rent and took no action to renegotiate the amount of the monthly rent payable.

Assuming that $2,850 was the fair rental value of the land and building, has High had breached his fiduciary duty as a partner? *See Covalt v. High*, 100 N.M. 700, 675 P.2d 999 (App. 1983).

Labovitz v. Dolan
189 Ill.App.3d 403, 545 N.E.2d 304, 136 Ill.Dec. 780 (1989)

Justice SCARIANO delivered the opinion of the court:

We have for decision in this case the issue, as posited by the plaintiffs, of whether management discretion granted solely and exclusively to a general partner in a limited partnership agreement authorizes the general partner to use economic coercion to cause his limited partner investors to sell their interests to him at a bargain price.

Plaintiffs as limited partners invested over $12 million dollars in a cablevision programming limited partnership sponsored and syndicated by defendant general partner Dolan. In 1985 the partnership reported earnings of over $34 million dollars, and in 1986 it had earnings of just under $18 million dollars, as a result of which each of the limited partners was required to report his prorata share on his personal income tax returns for those years. Plaintiffs claim that although the partnership had cash available to fund the limited partners' tax obligations, Dolan elected to make only a nominal distribution of cash to cover such liability; accordingly, in 1985 and in 1986 the limited partners were required to pay taxes almost entirely from their own funds on income retained by the partnership. In late November of 1986 an affiliate owned and controlled by Dolan offered to buy out the interests of the limited partners for approximately two-thirds of their book value. Over 90% of the limited partners accepted the offer, but simultaneously filed suit claiming Dolan's tactics to be a breach of his fiduciary duty to them. The circuit court dismissed plaintiffs' complaint with prejudice, holding that Dolan's acts were within the broad discretion granted him under the terms of the partnership agreement. Plaintiffs appeal from that ruling.

The limited partnership in this case, Cablevision Programming Investments (CPI) was organized for the purpose of investing in entities that produce and acquire programming for marketing and distribution to cable and other pay television services. Dolan and the Dolan-owned and controlled Communications Management Corporation of Delaware (CMC) were the general partners in this venture. In 1980, CPI sold 85 limited partnership units at a per unit price of $200,000; plaintiffs purchased 62.4595 of those units for a collective price of $12,491,900 and constituted 73% of all investors. The 263 page Private Placement Memorandum (PPM) explained that the proceeds of the CPI offering would be used to purchase 100% of the Class A limited partnership interests in another entity (Rainbow) that was organized for the same purpose as CPI; that Rainbow would fund subsidiary partnerships that would produce a variety of programming for distribution to cable TV systems and would have the same general partners as CPI; and that Rainbow would fund another Dolan-controlled entity, Rainbow Programming Services Company, which would distribute "affiliated and unaffiliated cable programming."

The PPM also advised investors that their rights and obligations "are governed by the Articles of Limited Partnership" (the Articles), which were bound as an exhibit to the PPM, and added, in a section entitled "Projected Results of Operations of Cablevision Programming Investments," that:

> The Partnership, Cablevision and its affiliates' intended policy is to make cash distributions to partners each year in an amount approximating the amount of taxable income reflected each year, after providing for adequate working capital requirements deemed necessary by the General Partners. Although the projections assume that this policy can be followed in the future, there are significant contingencies relating to many factors which, from time to time, may prohibit any distributions, including, but not limited to cash, cash availability, general working capital requirements, lending restrictions and revised costs and capital requirements.

The Articles provided that Dolan will have

> full responsibility and exclusive and complete discretion in the management and control of the business and affairs of the partnership;

that "Dolan in his sole discretion shall determine the availability of Cash Flow for distribution to partners"; that they contain the entire understanding among the partners and supersede any prior understanding and/or written or oral agreements among them;

and that Dolan would be liable to the limited partners for his willful misconduct but not for

errors in judgment or for any acts or omissions that do not constitute willful misconduct.

CPI limited partnership interests were offered and sold only to "wealthy and sophisticated investors." To qualify for exemption from registration under securities laws, the partnership interests were stated in the PPM to be

suitable only for investors with a net worth in excess of $750,000 (excluding home, furnishings, and automobiles) per unit purchased, and having an anticipated taxable income in 1980, 1981 and 1982 of which a substantial portion would have been taxable in each year for Federal income tax purposes at a rate of 50% or more.

Prospective investors were apprised in the PPM, that the "offering and the operations of the entities summarized [therein] are complex," and that a "thorough understanding of such matters is essential in order for prospective investors to evaluate the merits and risks of the offering". In addition, investors were required to represent that they or their representatives were "capable of evaluating the merits and risks of the investment." The offering of 85 units was fully subscribed.

The articles provided also that net profits, net losses and cash flow were to be allocated as follows: Dolan .5%, CMC .5%, and limited partners 99%. In 1985, the partnership earned $34,101,000; in 1986 it earned $17,842,000. As noted above, the limited partners were required to pay taxes on these earnings, but Dolan did not distribute cash in an amount sufficient to cover their tax liability. Dolan did, however, lend CPI money to other companies he controlled.

An examination of a limited partner's "K-1" tax form reveals that from 1980 through 1984 CPI provided no cash to the limited partners but did afford them some tax benefits. In 1985, each partner was required to report a taxable income of $415,331 per unit, while Dolan distributed only $12,000 per unit; and in 1986 the partners were required to report a taxable income of $216,750 per unit, while again receiving a distribution of only $12,000 per unit.

On November 25, 1986 Cablevision Systems Corporation (CSC), owned and controlled by Dolan, made an offer to purchase all of the CPI limited partnership interests for $271,870 per unit, payable $90,623 in cash and the remainder was to be paid either in 9% notes due on June 30, 1988, and June 30, 1989, or in CSC Class A common stock. The offer disclosed that "Dolan and his affiliates would derive substantial benefits in connection with the offer" and that

although the partnership was potentially very valuable... it was extremely difficult to determine its true value since it was likely that current assumptions would not materialize and that unanticipated events and circumstances would occur.

The offer further disclosed that although the partnership had incurred an operating loss of $96,000 per unit in 1986, proceeds from extraordinary and nonrecurring sales of assets would result in sizable taxable income to those limited partners who retained their interests. However, the offer continued, by selling their interests, limited partners would realize not only an added $71,870 per unit in cash profits on their initial investment in addition to the $24,000 previously distributed, but they could also convert their position in 1986 from that of having large taxable income to that of showing a sizable tax loss. This was because, as the offer explained, each limited partner's capital account had been inflated for tax purposes by proceeds from extraordinary and non-recurring sales to the extent that the book value of a limited partnership interest was shown at $405,000. The "business reasons" given for making the offer were that

> the buyout would avoid conflicts since both the operating and the programming entities would be under the same ownership, and would provide a needed source of funds for the development of the programming companies.

The articles provided that a limited partner could not sell or otherwise transfer his interest in the partnership without the prior written consent of the general partners. More than 90% of the limited partners elected to accept CSC's offer and sold their interests in CPI to CSC.

On December 1, 1986, plaintiff Joel Labovitz, who had owned three units, filed a class action complaint, but after other former owners joined in his suit as individual plaintiffs, that complaint was withdrawn and this action was substituted.

On April 5, 1988, defendants moved to dismiss plaintiffs' complaint, and on June 21, 1988, as noted above, the circuit court dismissed the complaint with prejudice. Both parties place heavy reliance upon the documents considered by the trial court and discussed herein, namely, the PPM, the Articles, and defendant's offer to buy the interests of the limited partners. In fact, since plaintiffs omitted attaching copies of these documents to their complaint, which made reference thereto, defendants supplied them in support of their motion to dismiss. In their complaint plaintiffs sought the imposition of

> a constructive trust upon the funds held by Dolan, the Partnership and Rainbow which were not required to meet current obligations, to maintain a sound financial position or establish reasonable reserves, and distribute these funds to plaintiffs,

and for damages for breach of fiduciary duty. Plaintiffs appeal the order of dismissal, contending that since "'discretion' can never be exercised in breach of a fiduciary duty," the trial court erred in holding that the PPM and the Articles granted Dolan the discretion to treat his limited partners as he did, without permitting a trial that would inquire into his intent regarding the fairness of the transactions at issue.

In what has become the most celebrated pronouncement characterizing the fiduciary relationship that exists among partners, Chief Judge Benjamin N. Cardozo stated for the court in the case of *Meinhard v. Salmon* (1928), 249 N.Y. 458, 463-64, 164 N.E. 545, 546 that:

> ...copartners, owe to one another...the duty of the finest loyalty. Many forms of conduct permissible in a workaday world for those acting at arm's length, are forbidden to those bound by fiduciary ties. A trustee is

held to something stricter than the morals of the market place. Not honesty alone but the punctilio of an honor the most sensitive, is then the standard of behavior. As to this there has developed a tradition that is unbending and inveterate. Uncompromising rigidity has been the attitude of courts of equity when petitioned to undermine the rule of undivided loyalty by the 'disintegrating erosion' of particular exceptions. [Citation] Only thus has the level of conduct for fiduciaries been kept at a level higher than that trodden by the crowd. It will not consciously be lowered by any judgment of this court.

Judge Cardozo's standard has been adopted by the courts of virtually every American jurisdiction, including our own. Indeed, defendants do not argue otherwise. As between partners, Judge Cardozo went on to hold, "the heavier weight of duty" rests upon him who manages the affairs of the partnership. Accordingly, plaintiffs argue, Dolan, as general partner, owed the limited partners a duty of good faith and loyalty. More specifically, they add, partners owe each other the duty to exercise the highest degree of honesty, fairness and good faith in their dealings with one another and in the handling of partnership assets. Plaintiffs complain that the circuit court did not appear to apprehend this duty, but instead, treated Dolan and his limited partners as arm's length strangers.

Dolan's discretion to withhold cash, plaintiffs assert, was not absolute; it was limited by an implied covenant of good faith and fair dealing implicit in every Illinois contract and by his fiduciary duty to his partners. In Illinois, they aver, such a covenant is implied in every contract absent an express disavowal, and that it

has its most natural and common application to the situation where one party exercises discretionary authority in a manner that affects the rights and duties of the other party.

Rao v. Rao (7th Cir. 1983), 718 F.2d 219, *citing Foster Enterprises v. Germania Federal Savings & Loan Assoc.* (1981), 97 Ill.App.3d 22, 30, 52 Ill.Dec. 303, 421 N.E.2d 1375.)

Good faith between contracting parties requires that a party vested with contractual discretion must exercise his discretion reasonably and may not do so arbitrarily or capriciously.

Foster Enterprises, 97 Ill.App.3d at 22, 52 Ill.Dec. 303, 421 N.E.2d 1375.

Plaintiffs accordingly urge that the manner in which Dolan exercised his discretion must be measured against this "good faith" standard implicit in every Illinois contract. The circuit court, according to plaintiffs, instead of employing this standard, treated the partners not as parties to a contract, but as strangers with no relationship, focusing its holding on a narrow reading of *Nelson v. Warnke*, 122 Ill.App.3d 381, 77 Ill.Dec. 900, 461 N.E.2d 523. In *Nelson*, the plaintiff claimed that the general partner breached his fiduciary duty by allowing funds held for distribution to the limited partners to remain in non-interest bearing accounts. The court held the money to be partnership funds and dismissed Nelson's action because the partnership agreement expressly permitted the general partner to so invest such funds. Plaintiffs reason that in *Nelson*, since the general partner did not personally benefit from his failure to invest funds in interest-bearing accounts, for example, by lending money to himself, his family or friends at no interest, the court would have reached a different result.

Plaintiffs point out that the PPM provides that:

Distributions of Cash Flow of the Partnership and Cablevision will be made at such times and in such amounts as Charles F. Dolan, as the individual General Partner of both partnerships, in his sole discretion shall determine, subject to any restrictions on distributions to partners contained in loan agreements which may be entered into by Cablevision as a condition to its borrowings and which restrictions are not ascertainable at this time.

*   *   *

The Partnership, Cablevision and its affiliates' intended policy is to make cash distributions to partners each year in an amount approximating the amount of taxable income reflected each year, after providing for adequate working capital requirements deemed necessary by the General Partners.

Thus, plaintiffs argue, Dolan made it clear in the PPM that he intended to distribute cash flow annually when not required to meet current obligations; accordingly his "discretion" to distribute cash flow was limited by his fiduciary duties to his partners.

Defendants respond that the Articles "unambiguously" support the trial court's conclusion that Dolan had the sole discretion to determine the availability of cash for distribution to the limited partners, pointing to section 7.3 of the Articles which provides that: "Dolan in his sole discretion shall determine the availability of cash flow for distribution to partners."

Defendants maintain with great insistence that plaintiffs do not and cannot point to any provision in the Articles which expressly or impliedly limited Dolan's discretion to determine whether partnership funds were needed for partnership purposes or could be distributed as cash to the limited partners; instead, defendants interpret plaintiffs' argument as being that certain statements contained in the PPM dilute that discretion. However, defendants assert, this argument is seriously impaired by the fact that the Articles, and not the PPM defined the partners' rights and obligations, pointing to Section 15.10 of the Articles which provides in pertinent part:

These Articles contain the entire understanding among the partners and supersedes [sic] any prior understandings and/or written or oral agreements among them respecting the within subject matter.

Defendants claim that although the "rights and obligations of the Investors are governed by the Articles," the PPM was merely "intended to furnish information to the proposed investors with respect to the investment described." Thus, defendants contend, the PPM is entirely consistent with the Articles' grant of sole discretion to Dolan to determine how partnership proceeds should be allocated.

Defendants point out that the trial judge, having both the PPM and the Articles before him, held that these documents conferred upon Dolan, as general partner,

the discretion and the decision-making power to decide whether there was adequate working capital required for the operation by this general partner, of this limited partnership, and that he had the right to make revisions of policy and that it was made clear in that document that contingencies could prohibit distribution.

In support of his holding the judge specifically relied upon Section 7.3 of the Articles, conferring "sole discretion" on Dolan to determine the availability of cash flow for distribution to partners, as well as on Section 8.6, providing that the general partner shall not be liable for errors in judgment, and that Dolan's liability is to be limited to acts or omissions which amount to willful misconduct. Defendants aver that any fair reading of the PPM must lead to the conclusion, as it did in the trial court, that Dolan neither made a representation nor a binding commitment to distribute cash flow.

Defendants' further response to plaintiffs is that the general partner's specific authority to determine how partnership proceeds should be allocated was not inconsistent with any fiduciary duty owed by Dolan to the plaintiffs, insisting that partners have the right to establish among themselves, by a partnership agreement, their rights, duties and obligations. Defendants add that a limited partner who endows a general partner with certain powers to operate the partnership may not later complain that the general partner, by exercising those powers, has breached some fiduciary duty, citing *Nelson v. Warnke*, 122 Ill.App.3d 381, 77 Ill.Dec. 900, 461 N.E.2d 523.

In construing a partnership agreement, defendants urge, a court should consider the object, purpose and nature of the agreement, and that the constraints plaintiffs now seek to place on Dolan's sole discretion are antithetical to the nature and purpose of the limited partnership formed in this case, which was designed, they argue,

> to offer wealthy and sophisticated investors a unique investment opportunity—access to a family of related entities in an emerging industry, guided by a pioneering and immensely successful talent.

Dolan was given, they continue,

> the sole discretion to determine whether partnership proceeds were needed to fund related entities or could be distributed as cash to the limited partners so that he would have the flexibility needed to meet and anticipate the ever-changing business conditions in the industry,

and in deciding how to allocate partnership proceeds,

> Dolan was called upon to exercise his business judgment in anticipating future needs, expanding profitable areas and exploring promising new fields.

Plaintiffs now attempt, defendants claim,

> to second-guess Dolan's business judgment with respect to whether proceeds withheld from distribution were needed for the sound operation of CPI's business affairs and to have the court do likewise.

OPINION

It is abundantly clear, as defendants point out, that Dolan was granted rather wide latitude in deciding whether or not to distribute cash to the limited partners; the Articles grant him "sole discretion" in the matter, and do not mention any distribution for the purpose of meeting the limited partners' tax obligations.

Even in the PPM, where distributions of cash approximating the amount of taxable income each year are projected in tabulated form, the language is far from precise and gives the general partner rather liberal discretionary powers as to such distribution.

It is also clear, however, that despite having such broad discretion, Dolan still owed his limited partners a fiduciary duty, which necessarily encompasses the duty of exercising good faith, honesty, and fairness in his dealings with them and the funds of the partnership. It is no answer to the claim that plaintiffs make in this case that partners have the right to establish among themselves their rights, duties and obligations, as though the exercise of that right releases, waives or delimits somehow, the high fiduciary duty owed to them by the general partner—a gloss we do not find anywhere in our law. On the contrary, the fiduciary duty exists concurrently with the obligations set forth in the partnership agreement whether or not expressed therein. Indeed, at least one of the authorities relied upon by defendants is clear that although "partners are free to vary many aspects of their relationship inter se, . . . they are not free to destroy its fiduciary character." Saballus, 122 Ill.App.3d at 116, 77 Ill.Dec. 451, 460 N.E.2d 755.

Thus, the language in the Articles standing alone does not deprive plaintiffs of the trial they seek against Dolan for breach of fiduciary duty. We therefore agree with plaintiffs that the trial court did not give due consideration to Dolan's duty as general partner to exercise the highest degree of honesty and good faith in his handling of partnership assets, and instead treated the parties as arm's length strangers, holding that no inquiry could be made into the fairness of the transactions at issue because of the language in the Articles regarding Dolan's discretion. Yet

in any fiduciary relationship, the burden of proof shifts to the fiduciary to show by clear and convincing evidence that a transaction is equitable and just.

(Bandringa v. Bandringa (1960), 20 Ill.2d 167, 170 N.E.2d 116) Indeed, cases cited and relied upon by defendants hold that

where there is a question of breach of a fiduciary duty of a managing partner, all doubts will be resolved against him, and the managing partner has the burden of proving his innocence.

Saballus, 122 Ill.App.3d at 117-18, 77 Ill.Dec. 451, 460 N.E.2d 755 (Emphasis supplied.)

Defendants, however, charge that in an attempt to sustain this appeal, plaintiffs advance for the first time a new theory not presented in their pleadings, nor argued below and never ruled upon by the trial court: that in exercising his sole discretion to determine whether partnership income was needed for partnership purposes or was available for cash distributions to the limited partners, Dolan did not act in "good faith" because he was motivated by the specific intent of forcing the limited partners to sell their interests.

Defendants err. Plaintiffs' complaint in essence charges that Dolan, as general partner, owed plaintiffs, his limited partners, a fiduciary duty "to distribute available cash flow to his partners in 1983 through 1986," which duty he breached because "he never intended to pay cash flow to the limited partners," thus "forcing or squeezing his limited partners into accepting his below book value offer" to buy out their interests, to their financial damage. The complaint goes on to allege that by Dolan's selling of the 85 limited partnership units at $200,000 per unit, $17,000,000 was realized as capital for the partnership. After deducting $2,000,000 to pay fees to Dolan and to reimburse him for attorney and accounting fees and other costs incurred in the preparation of the PPM, the sum of $15,000,000 remained as the partnership's capital. In addition to the cash flow generated by operations, the partnership and its related entities realized cash as follows: $20,000,000 in 1983 by selling interests in two related entities to a subsidiary of The Washington Post. In 1985 there was a $31,600,000 gain upon the sale of an interest in a related entity to a subsidiary of CBS, Inc., plus $50,000,000 when a lawsuit against Ted Turner and MGM was settled. In 1986 approximately $20,000,000 was paid to the partnership by MGM/UA Home Entertainment Group in exchange for a license option agreement, and $3,500,000 in exchange for the termination of a distribution agreement.

In 1985 the partnership showed income of $2,778,000 exclusive of the gain on the sale of assets, and after allowing for depreciation of $1,289,000. During 1986 the balance in the partnership cash account increased $11,000,000; receivables from parties "related" to Dolan and the partnership increased $3,600,000; and long term notes receivable increased $9,000,000. For the year ending December 31, 1986, partnership net income was $17,658,000 and working capital increased by $10,220,000. A footnote to the financial statement for the year ended December 31, 1985, discloses that Dolan retained significant amounts of money within the partnership which were loaned to "related parties"; more specifically, that Rainbow had advanced funds to Rainbow Programming Services Company "which, at December 31, 1985 & 1984, amounted to approximately $13,417,000 and $19,139,000 respectively," besides Rainbow's having made a capital contribution of $8,800,000 to RPSC.

We can think of no reason as to why these allegations should not be found to be sufficient to encompass the claim raised on this appeal, and sufficient also to apprise defendants thereof. Plaintiff's allegation that Dolan, by breaching his fiduciary duty, "squeezed" plaintiffs out, despite its employment of a breezier, more colorful syntax than a simple charge of "willful misconduct," in the precise words of the articles, does not fail, in its context, to comply with the requirement of our Code of Civil Procedure relating to the proper pleading of a cause of action. We further note that the trial judge made it quite clear in his remarks at the hearing on defendants' motion to dismiss that he had no difficulty in apprehending the allegations contained in plaintiffs' complaint or their claim advanced in oral argument that Dolan had breached his fiduciary duty by "failing to distribute cash" and "by using undue influence to have an affiliate offer to buy out those limited partners at a price."

In the alternative, defendants urge that should this court undertake to consider plaintiffs' "new" theory, it still should not inquire into the motivation behind Dolan's exercise of his discretion in allocating partnership funds because plaintiffs do not allege that Dolan acted other than in the manner contemplated by the partnership documents and in furtherance of the partnership's declared purpose, contending that general partners who exercise powers given to them under a partnership agreement do not thereby breach any fiduciary duty, regardless of their motivation, citing *Murphy v. Gutfreund* (S.D.N.Y. 1984), 583

F.Supp. 957, 971. However, we regard this argument as having a timbre no different in resonance from the one we have disposed of above, namely, that partners have the right to establish among themselves their rights and responsibilities. We need not, therefore, give it any further or any different consideration here.

Defendants next assert that the good faith doctrine protects only the reasonable expectations of the contracting parties, and that a party's legitimate expectations are not violated where there is good cause for a party's exercise of its contractual discretion, regardless of what other motives the acting party may have. In *Dayan [v. McDonald's Corp.* (1984), 125 Ill.App.3d 972, 989-90, 81 Ill.Dec. 156, 466 N.E.2d 958], plaintiff's franchise agreement had been terminated after he violated its terms. Plaintiff contended that the franchisor had terminated him not because he had violated the franchise agreement, but because the franchisor desired to recapture the franchisee's lucrative market for himself. The court ruled that since there was good cause to support the franchisor's exercise of his discretion to terminate the franchise agreement, it would make no further inquiry into the franchisor's motivation.

Defendants here make the same contention: that no inquiry into Dolan's motivation is necessary to protect the reasonable expectations of the limited partners, and more particularly, that plaintiffs could have no reasonable expectation that Dolan would distribute partnership funds to them instead of utilizing such funds to meet partnership needs, pointing out that partnership documents warned prospective investors that they could lose their entire investment, and that no representation as to the availability of future cash for distribution to the limited partners could be made. Defendants add that the allegation that Dolan breached his fiduciary duty to the limited partners by forcing them to choose between selling their interests at an unfairly low price, or remaining a powerless limited partner depends on whether or not Dolan promised to distribute cash in the manner in which plaintiffs allege, and since he did not make any such commitment, the allegations of the complaint are undercut and must be dismissed — the very basis upon which the trial court granted defendants' motion to dismiss.

As Professor Daniel S. Reynolds of the Northern Illinois University School of Law states in his article, "Loyalty and Limited Partnership," 34 Kansas Law Review 1, (1985),

> Self-dealing and conflicts of interest are endemic to the limited partnership. Limited partnerships 'are born in conflicts of interest, live in conflicts of interest, and sometimes poof out of existence in conflicts of interest.' [Quoting from 16 Sec.Reg. & L.Rep. BNA 1559 (1984).] The general partners are typically the organizing entrepreneurs or promoters. They may be affiliated with the sellers of the enterprise's assets, and are frequently involved in multiple, potentially competing related enterprises. This may be good, bad, or indifferent. Categorical prohibitions of conflicting interests might be a coherent response to all this, but a potentially fatal one as well for whatever assumed benefits of flexibility in capital formation the form provides. Categorical permission for conflicting interests might also be a coherent response, but one running all the risks that 'fiduciary ideology' is supposed to prevent. What is desired is a scheme for containing conflicts, a fairness-promoting regime that ensures, to the extent possible, that investors in the limited partnership are not being exploited, overreached, or taken advantage of by the managers of their money.

Defendants prevailed in the trial court on the ground that the claim is defeated by affirmative matter, namely, Dolan's sole discretion in the matter of distributing cash flow. As to such affirmative defense, defendants choose to remain completely oblivious to the fact that although the Articles clearly gave the general partner the sole discretion to distribute cash as he deemed appropriate, that discretion was encumbered by a supreme fiduciary duty of fairness, honesty, good faith and loyalty to his partners. Language in an agreement such as "sole discretion" does not metamorphose the document into an unrestricted license to engage in self-dealing at the expense of those to whom the managing partner owes such a duty. Defendants cite no authority, and we find none, for the proposition that there can be an a priori waiver of fiduciary duties in a partnership — be it general or limited. Nor is the practice of imposing purported advance waivers of fiduciary duties in limited partnership enterprises to be given judicial recognition on the basis of the facts developed in this case. Defendants' argument that the good faith doctrine protects only the reasonable expectations of the contracting parties is, we think, aptly answered by plaintiffs' statement to the trial judge:

> ...the risk we took was that the business would not succeed. We did not take the risk that the business would succeed so well that the general partner would squeeze us out and take the investment for himself;

an argument, by the way, that sets forth a precise formulation of the exact issue in this case.

Our courts are not bound to endow it as doctrine that where the general partner obtains an agreement from his limited partner investors that he is to be the sole arbiter with respect to the flow that the cash of the enterprise takes, and thereby creates conditions favorable to his decision that the business is too good for them and contrives to appropriate it to himself, the articles of partnership constitute an impervious armor against any attack on the transaction short of actual fraud. That is not and cannot be the law. And that is precisely the gravamen of plaintiffs' complaint: that the general partner refused unreasonably to distribute cash and thereby forced plaintiffs to continually dip into their own resources in order to pay heavy taxes on large earnings in a calculated effort to force them to sell their interests to an entity which Dolan owned and controlled at a price well below at least the book value of those interests. Such a claim plainly presents an issue for the finder of fact, namely, whether or not Dolan was serving his own interests or those of the partnership. Although defendants state in their brief that Dolan allocated the partnership's funds to meet its needs and to serve its purposes, and although in oral argument defendants represented that the partnership was continually short of cash, the record at this stage is totally devoid of any such evidence. To be sure, all of the allegations made by plaintiffs in their complaint and noted above stand, according to the record made in this case, as unrebutted, undenied, unexplained and uncontroverted.

Plaintiffs therefore correctly maintain that they "were entitled to a trial in which Dolan must prove he acted fairly and not as his limited partners' business adversary." Accordingly, we hold that plaintiffs were entitled to a trial on the issues formulated in this case.

REVERSED AND REMANDED.

Notes

1. *Brooke v. Mt. Hood Meadows Oreg., Ltd.*, page 642, states that

the general partner's duty to the limited partners in the distribution of profit is discharged by decisions made in good faith that reflect legitimate business concerns.

In *Labowitz v. Dolan*, the general partner argues that a partners obligations under a partnership are limited to the *covenant* of good faith and fair dealing that arises (in most states) *out of a contract.* The covenant of good faith and fair dealing prevents a party to an agreement from denying the other party's "reasonable expectations" to receive the benefits of the contract. The general partner then argued that, because the partnership agreement gave him the exclusive power to manage the partnership in his sole discretion, he owed no fiduciary duties in the use of that power. That is, the general partner argued that the limited partners could have no reasonable expectations to distributions. How did the court respond to that argument?

2. Is the general partner's argument in *Labowitz v. Dolan* consistent with Restatement section 13, under which agents are fiduciaries of their principals? Comment a to that section explains:

The agreement to act on behalf of a principal *causes* the agent to be a fiduciary, that is, a person having a duty, created by his undertaking, to act primarily for the benefit of another in matters connected with his undertaking.

Restatement § 13 Comment (emphasis added). By the same reasoning, doesn't a general partner's agreement to act as a general partner, with power to manage the business and affairs of the partnership, make the general partner a fiduciary?

3. In *Labowitz v. Dolan*, the Articles of Limited Partnership gave the general partner "in his sole discretion shall determine the availability of Cash Flow for distribution to partners." The general partner argued that this language amounted to a *waiver* of the general partner's duty of loyalty in administering distributions. Would this language have satisfied the court in *Schock v. Nash*, page 216?

Sonet v. [Plum Creek] Timber Company, L.P.
722 A.2d 319 (Del. Ch. 1998)

MEMORANDUM OPINION

CHANDLER, Chancellor.

This dispute arises out of a transaction in which a limited partnership organized under Delaware law seeks to convert itself into a real estate investment trust ("REIT"). The issue presented is this: Where a limited partnership agreement unambiguously provides that the general partner has sole discretion over setting and approving the terms of a transaction, and where unitholders of the limited partnership have the power to veto the transaction as a function of a supermajority vote requirement, are there any other fiduciary duty principles that must apply to the proposed transaction as a matter of law? Stated differently, what controls the governance process in the context of limited partnerships—the partnership agreement or common law fiduciary duty doctrines? For the reasons stated below, I dismiss Plaintiff's amended complaint, concluding as a matter of law that the unambiguous terms of the partnership agreement have the effect of limiting the Court's review of the transaction presently in dispute.[1]

I. BACKGROUND

Jerrold M. Sonet ("Plaintiff") is a holder of depository units ("Units") representing limited partnership interests in Plum Creek Timber Company, L.P., a Delaware limited partnership (the "Partnership"). The Partnership is registered with the Securities and Exchange Commission and the Units are publicly traded on the New York Stock Exchange. The Partnership and its corporate subsidiaries own, manage and operate approximately 2.4 million acres of timberland and twelve wood products conversion facilities in the Northwest and Southeast United States.

Defendant Plum Creek Management Company, L.P., a Delaware limited partnership, is the general partner of the Partnership ("Management" or the "General Partner"). Defendant PC Advisory Corp. I, a Delaware corporation ("PC Advisory") (with the Partnership and Management, hereinafter referred to as "Defendants"), is the ultimate general partner of Management and, thus, might be considered the indirect general partner of the Partnership.

Management has a 2% general partner interest in the income and cash distributions of the Partnership, subject to certain adjustments. Specifically, pursuant to the limited partnership agreement (the "Partnership Agreement" or the "Agreement"), Management is required to make quarterly cash distributions of all "Available Cash," 98% of which goes to unitholders and 2% of which goes to Management. When the distribution of cash exceeds certain quarterly target levels, Management is entitled to receive an additional "incentive distribution" equal to a percentage of such excess, on a sliding scale which increases up to a maximum of 35% of distributions above the highest target level.

In June of 1998 the Partnership announced a plan to convert itself into a REIT by way of a merger with an entity specifically created for the purpose of conversion. Under the terms of that conversion Units would be converted into shares in the new REIT on a one-to-one basis. In addition, under the terms of the proposed conversion, in lieu of its 2% interest and its incentive distribution rights, Management would receive REIT shares equal to 27% of the total shares outstanding. The essence of Plaintiff's case is that the proposed allocation to Management of the new REIT is unfair and is the result of, among other things:

1) a self-dealing transaction between the General Partner and the Partnership;

2) improper manipulations of past distributions;

---

1. As a preliminary manner, I pause to thank the attorneys who argued this case before me for their clear presentation of the issues. Mr. Silverman of Silverman, Harnes, Harnes, Prussin & Keller, Mr. Finkelstein, of Richards, Layton & Finger, and Mr. Welch, of Skadden, Arps, Slate, Meagher & Flom LLP also provided the Court with concise and instructive post-argument memoranda that I relied on heavily in my analysis of the limited partnership agreement.

3) an attempt by PC Advisory to limit its exposure to upcoming losses;

4) unlawful entrenchment of PC Advisory and its principals, who will effectively control the new entity; and

5) manipulative timing of the transaction, which will shield unitholders from knowing of imminent losses caused by fundamental economic downturns.

In addition to the foregoing, Plaintiff claims that the Defendants understood that they had a duty to treat the unitholders fairly, and by taking voluntary precautions to meet that duty, Defendants were bound by operation of law to assume the fulfillment of traditional fiduciary duties.

II. ARGUMENTS

In essence, Plaintiff's claims can be characterized broadly as duty of loyalty claims.[2] Plaintiff takes the position that, under the Agreement, nothing modifies the default fiduciary duties that underlie the Delaware Revised Uniform Limited Partnership Act.[3] Thus, Plaintiff claims, it is entirely proper for this Court to review Management's and PC Advisory's self-interested actions vis-a-vis the unitholders and the potential harms that the unitholders might suffer under the proposed conversion, in light of established fiduciary principles.

Defendants claim that, under Delaware limited partnership law, this Court should not reach that far. Stated simply, Defendants argue that Delaware limited partnership law recognizes that by virtue of a clearly written partnership agreement limited partnerships are explicitly authorized by statute to modify the default rules which might otherwise govern the relationship between general partners and limited partners, and between limited partners themselves. Thus, in this case Defendants argue that I should look to the Partnership Agreement to resolve this dispute. Since the Partnership Agreement defines the role of the general partner and the limited partners in the governance of the partnership, according to the Defendants, no need exists to go outside of that document to assess the propriety of the Defendants' actions in this case.

III. ANALYSIS

Delaware's limited partnership jurisprudence begins with the basic premise that, *unless limited by the partnership agreement,* the general partner has the

---

2. In his brief, Plaintiff argues that the Court should view this transaction as a "controlled" transaction or, in other words, a situation where a control group dictates the terms of the transaction to the detriment of other equity holders. Thus, Plaintiff's claim amounts to an allegation of self-dealing. Plaintiff goes on to argue that because the General Partner is allowed to dictate the terms of the transactions (a fact conceded by the Defendants) this Court should assert its equity powers to protect the unitholders just as it would protect minority shareholders in an improper self-dealing transaction. It is true that in certain situations, for instance a parent-subsidiary merger where minority shareholders are frozen out, Delaware courts have held that the parent company owes fiduciary duties to minority shareholders. *See Sinclair Oil Corp. v. Levien,* Del.Supr., 280 A.2d 717, 720 (1971). As I explain later, however, I refuse in these circumstances to import protections developed in the corporate context into our limited partnership jurisprudence.

3. 6 Del. C. § 17-101, et seq.

fiduciary duty to manage the partnership in its interest and in the interests of the limited partners.[4] That qualified statement necessarily marries common law fiduciary duties to contract theory when it comes to considering actions undertaken in the limited partnership context. Thus, I think it a correct statement of law that principles of contract preempt fiduciary principles where the parties to a limited partnership have made their intentions to do so plain.

For instance, in *Kahn v. Icahn,*[5] this Court held that where a limited partnership agreement explicitly provided that the general partner and its affiliates were authorized to compete with the partnership, the limited partners could not then properly maintain a usurpation of partnership opportunity claim when the general partner and its affiliate began to actually compete with the partnership as anticipated by the agreement. That holding was premised on the legal determination that

> as a matter of statutory law, the traditional fiduciary duties among and between partners are defaults that may be modified by partnership agreements. This flexibility is precisely the reason why many choose he limited partnership form in Delaware.[6]

Delaware cases routinely uphold this view of limited partnership law.[7] Those commentators who have addressed the subject at the deepest levels agree that the partnership form is particularly useful due to its contract theory-based structure.[8]

---

4. *See Boxer v. Husky Oil Co.,* Del. Ch., 429 A.2d 995, 997 (1981).

5. Del. Ch., C.A. No. 15916, at 5-7, Chandler, C., 1998 WL 832629 (Nov. 12, 1998).

6. *Id.* at 6. Section 17-1101(d) of the Delaware Revised Limited Partnership Act sets out the relevant policy consideration:
   > To the extent that, at law or in equity, a partner or other person has duties (including fiduciary duties) and liabilities relating thereto to a limited partnership or to another partner...(2) the partner's or other person's duties and liabilities may be expanded or restricted by the provisions in a partnership agreement.

7. *See, e.g., In re Cencom Cable Income Partners, L.P. Litig.,* Del. Ch., C.A. No. 14634, at 10, Steele, V.C., 1996 WL 74726 (Feb. 15, 1996) (limited partnership agreements may authorize actions and modify fiduciary duties creating "safe harbors"). *See also Wilmington Leasing, Inc. v. Parrish Leasing Company, L.P.,* Del. Ch., C.A. No. 15202, at 30, Jacobs, V.C., 1996 WL 752364 (Dec. 23, 1996) ("Where, as here, a [p]artnership [a]greement specifically addresses the rights and duties of the partners, any fiduciary duty that might be owed by the... [p]artners is satisfied by compliance with the applicable provisions of the partnership agreement."); *In re Marriott Hotel Properties II L.P. Unitholders Litig.,* Del. Ch., C.A. No. 14961, at 11, 14-15, Allen, C., 1996 WL 342040 (June 12, 1996); *US West, Inc. v. Time Warner, Inc.,* Del. Ch., C.A. No. 14555, Allen, C., 1996 WL 307445 (June 6, 1996); *Litman v. Prudential-Bache Properties, Inc.,* Del. Ch., C.A. No. 12137, at 10, Chandler, V.C., 1993 WL 5922 (Jan. 4, 1993) (where partnership agreement expressly acknowledged potential conflicts of interest the court barred derivative claims), *remanded on other grounds,* Del.Supr., C.A. No. 61, Moore, J., 1993 WL 603303 (Nov. 18, 1993), *aff'd,* Del.Supr., 642 A.2d 837 (1994).

8. *See generally* Frank H. Easterbrook & Daniel R. Fischel, The Economic Structure of Corporate Law 1-39 (1991); Henry N. Butler & Larry E. Ribstein, *Opting Out of Fiduciary Duties: A Response to the Anti-Contractarians,* 65 Wash. L.Rev. 1 (1990); Frank H. Easterbrook & Daniel R. Fischel, *Contract and Fiduciary Duty,* 36 J.L. & Econ. 425 (1993); Richard A. Epstein, *Contract and Trust in Corporate Law: The Case of Corporate Opportunity,* 21 Del. J. Corp. L. 1 (1996). For a contrary view, see Deborah A. DeMott, *Beyond Metaphor: An Analysis of Fiduciary Obligation,* 1988 Duke L.J. 879; Melvin Aron Eisenberg, *The Limits of Cognition and the Limits of Contract,* 47 Stan. L.Rev. 211 (1995); Lawrence E. Mitchell, *The Death of Fiduciary Duty in Close Corporations,* 138 U. Pa. L.Rev. 1675 (1990).

A. Limited Partnerships Generally

Limited partnerships have become the limited liability entity of choice for certain closely-held business ventures and are especially prevalent in enterprises where a general partner (or a corporate subsidiary) is actively engaged in investing the limited partners' passive investments. While originally used as a way of achieving preferential tax treatment, because of recent modifications to federal tax law, it is unclear that the limited partnership form provides significant tax benefits compared to other limited liability and so-called pass-through entities.[9] Clearly some other relevant characteristic of the limited partnership must contribute to its increasing popularity. One might reasonably conclude that the statutory authority granted to limited partnerships to contract around—or to enhance—fiduciary duties goes a long way in explaining this popularity.

Although particularly well suited for closely-held businesses, limited partnerships have grown in popularity over the last forty years as publicly-traded entities (known as master limited partnerships) and are often designed to roll-up, or consolidate, a number of smaller limited partnerships.[10] If embodied in a security (*e.g.,* the Units in this case) which represents a transferable interest in the entity, limited partnership interests can become more liquid as a result of exchange listing, security registration, and more widely-known public information about a limited partnership. Such investment vehicles can greatly facilitate the accretion of capital for further expansion of a partnership's objectives.

One might reasonably doubt whether the limited partnership structure is the most efficient means of attracting capital for business ventures (especially in the context of widely held equity participation). One reason for this doubt is that there is uncertainty about the legal protections afforded to limited partners in any particular limited partnership. Considering § 17-1101(d) of the Delaware Revised Uniform Limited Partnership Act's apparently broad license to enhance, reform, or even eliminate fiduciary duty protections, it is unclear how the market goes about pricing the value of protections afforded to limited partners in any particular flavor of limited partnership.[11]

The desirability, from an efficient-pricing perspective, of the potentially infinite variations on modified fiduciary duties in the context of widely-held limited partnerships is not a matter for adjudication in cases involving the limited partnership form. It is evident, however, that the Delaware Legislature has seen fit to

---

9. *See generally* George K. Yin, *The Taxation of Private Business Enterprises: Some Policy Questions Stimulated by the "Check-the-Box" Regulations,* 51 SMU L.Rev. 125 (1997) (Professor Yin of the University of Virginia and Professor David Shakow of the University of Pennsylvania are credited for their expert stewardship as co-reporters to the American Law Institute's Federal Income Tax Project on the Taxation of Pass-Through Entities). Although not relevant to my decision in this matter, it is interesting to note that 3984, 4038 and 5800 Delaware limited partnerships were formed in each of the last three years, respectively. And, according to Laura Y. Marvel, Corporations Administrator for the Division of Corporations, the Division estimates that almost 6000 domestic limited partnerships were formed for fiscal year 1998. Obviously, the market for this alternative entity remains vibrant.

10. *See* Donna D. Adler, *Master Limited Partnerships,* 40 U. Fla. L.Rev. 755, 756-57 (1988).

11. Such market pricing difficulties are less relevant in the context of Delaware corporations that, as an empirical matter, often have very similar corporate charters and where the legal protections routinely afforded to corporations' shareholders flow from an established and predictable jurisprudence.

enact the Delaware Revised Uniform Limited Partnership Act and promoters and organizers have increasingly adopted that organizational form for their ventures. Once authorized by law, the decision to adopt and operate under a particular limited liability structure is the sort of fundamental business decision that courts routinely protect. As a general matter, courts should be, and are, reluctant to import jurisprudence from one area of the law—which is loaded with notions of efficiency and fairness that are well developed for that particular context—into a separate area of the law—where many procedural and substantive aspects present in other legal regimes are only optional defaults. Mindful of that caution, I decline to rely unnecessarily on this Court's traditional analyses involving fiduciary duties in the corporate context. When a particular limited partnership has plainly opted out of the statutory default scheme, judicial review, in my opinion, must look to the limited partnership's distinct doctrinal foundation in contract theory. There is no reason, at least in the case before me, to depart from that source to further some highly generalized interest of equity.

In short, I think that under Delaware limited partnership law a claim of breach of fiduciary duty must first be analyzed in terms of the operative governing instrument—the partnership agreement—and only where that document is silent or ambiguous, or where principles of equity are implicated, will a Court begin to look for guidance from the statutory default rules, traditional notions of fiduciary duties, or other extrinsic evidence. In this case, my task is easy as I find that the partnership agreement in issue is clear on the threshold question of how the transaction in dispute should be governed.

B. The Partnership Agreement

The Agreement provides the General Partner with the discretion and power to manage virtually all of the affairs of the Partnership. To counterbalance the significant powers of the General Partner, the Agreement establishes an integrated framework of checks on that power. With respect to many of the day-to-day affairs of the Partnership, which are not subject to unitholder ratification, the General Partner's discretion is counterbalanced by the requirement that all of the General Partner's actions be fair and reasonable to the Partnership.[12] With respect to certain extraordinary acts or transactions, such as mergers, the General Partner is given much broader latitude, namely "sole discretion." In the case of a merger in particular, however, the General Partner's sole discretion is checked by the Agreement's requirement that *a supermajority of unitholders (66 2/3 %) must approve the transaction.*

Plaintiff argues that under § 6.1 of the Agreement[13] any merger proposed by the General Partner (*e.g.,* the merger used to effectuate the conversion to a REIT)

---

12. In some sense the provisions that provide for this aspect of the relationship are an explicit acceptance of the default duty of loyalty and fair dealing rules.

13. Section 6.1 provides in relevant part:

   In addition to the powers now or hereafter granted a general partner of a limited partnership under applicable law or which are granted to the General Partners under any other provision of this Agreement, the General Partner...shall have full power and authority to do all things deemed necessary and desirable by it to conduct the business of the Partnership...including, without limitation,...(iii) the acquisition, disposition, mortgage, pledge, encumbrance, hypothecation or exchange of any assets of the Partnership or the merger or other combination of the Partner-

must be fair and reasonable to the Partnership. I understand Plaintiff to contend that since there is no language in § 6.1 that limits or expands the General Partner's discretion in the event of a merger, the fiduciary default rule that the terms of any transaction must be fair, reasonable, and aimed at furthering the interests of the partnership (and the limited partners) must apply. The problem with Plaintiff's argument is that it ignores the remainder of the Agreement. It also fails to recognize the rather practical problem of the impossibility of writing contract provisions that incorporate every bell and whistle all at once. As the following analysis shows, this Agreement is sufficient in communicating the intended governance structure. To understand that structure one needs to read the Agreement as a whole, and not just concentrate on one provision that mentions one of the "magic words."[14]

The Agreement contemplates two fundamentally different types of managerial actions that may be taken: those that do not require unitholder approval and those that do. The requirement that the General Partner's action be "fair and reasonable" has no application where unitholder approval is required, such as with the proposed merger. Under the terms of § 6.9(a) of the Agreement, where unitholder approval is not required, e.g., day-to-day management decisions of the Partnership, a requirement that the transaction be "fair and reasonable" is used as a surrogate check, in lieu of unitholder approval, on the General Partner's power.[15] In these situations, when a transaction is objectively "fair and rea-

---

ship with or into another entity (all of the foregoing subject to any prior approval which may be required by [66 2/3% of the outstanding Units, as provided by other sections in the agreement]).
Obviously, § 6.1 is simply a broad enabling provision that confers upon the General Partner the power and authority to manage the affairs of the Partnership.

14. Because I find that the Partnership Agreement is clear and unambiguous on its face, I do not reach Plaintiff's argument that other extrinsic evidence (e.g., the Partnership's 1989 Offering Prospectus or the Unanimous Consent Resolution of March 4, 1998) might justify the imposition of common law fiduciary duties. See SBC Interactive, Inc. v. Corporate Media Partners, Del.Supr., 714 A.2d 758, 761 (Aug. 10, 1998) ("We also agree with the Court of Chancery's ruling that the [partnership] Agreement is unambiguous, and its refusal to consider evidence extrinsic to the partnership agreement is correct.").

15. Section 6.9 of the Agreement illuminates this dynamic, specifically providing:
6.9 (with emphasis added): Resolution of Conflicts of Interest.
(a) Unless otherwise expressly provided in this Agreement, whenever a potential conflict of interest exists or arises between the General Partner or any of its Affiliates, on the one hand, and the Partnership or any Partner, on the other hand, any resolution or course of action in respect of such conflict of interests shall be permitted and deemed approved by all Partners, and shall not constitute a breach of this Agreement, of any agreement contemplated herein, or any duty stated or implied by law or equity, if the resolution or course of action is, or, by operation of this Agreement, is deemed to be fair and reasonable to the Partnership. Any such resolution or course of action in respect of any conflict of interest shall not constitute a breach of this Agreement, or of any other agreement contemplated herein, or of any duty stated or implied by law or equity, if such resolution or course of action is fair and reasonable to the Partnership. The General Partner shall be authorized in connection with its resolution of any conflict of interest to consider (i) the relative interest of any party to such conflict, agreement, transaction, or situation and the benefits and burdens relating to such interests; (ii) any customary or accepted industry practices; (iii) any applicable generally accepted accounting practices or principles; and (iv) such additional factors as the General Partner determines in its sole discretion to be relevant, reasonable or appropriate under the

sonable," it is "deemed approved" by the unitholders. In any event, pursuant to § 6(b) of the agreement, in situations where the General Partner is authorized to act according to its own discretion, there is no requirement that the General Partner consider the interests of the limited partners in resolution of a conflict of interest.

Section 6.9(a), when it refers to a "fair and reasonable resolution," refers to situations where the General Partner makes unilateral decisions and where the unitholders will not explicitly approve the terms of the decision. Section 6.9 does not apply to the present case because it applies when the General Partner engages in unilateral action. In the case of the merger (and concomitant conversion) contemplated in this case, the General Partner's actions are not unilateral because of the required unitholder vote. It makes no sense, therefore, for the decision to merge to be "deemed" approved because, pursuant to Article XVI of the agreement, it must actually be approved by 66 2/3% of the outstanding units.[16] Thus, § 6.9(a) is inapplicable to the present case. In addition, § 6.9(a) applies only "[u]nless otherwise expressly provided in [the] [A]greement." As further analysis shows, §§ 16.2 and 16.3 are clearly the operative sections that govern the disputed merger.

The procedures pursuant to which a merger may be effectuated are set forth under Article XVI of the Agreement, which is titled "Merger." Sections 16.2 and 16.3 provide the blueprint for proceeding with a merger transaction.[17] First, the

---

circumstances. Nothing contained in this Agreement, however, is intended to nor shall it be construed to require the General Partner to consider the interests of any Person other than the Partnership. In the absence of bad faith by the General Partner, the resolution, action or terms so made, taken or provided by the General Partner with respect to such matter shall not constitute a breach of this Agreement or any other agreement contemplated herein or a breach of any standard of care or duty imposed herein or therein under the Delaware Act or any other law, rule or regulation.

(b) Whenever this Agreement or any other agreement contemplated hereby provides that the General Partner or any of its Affiliates is permitted or required to make a decision (i) in its "discretion" or under a grant of similar authority or latitude, the General Partner or such Affiliate shall be entitled to consider only such interests and factors as it desires and shall have no duty or obligation to give any consideration to any interest of, or factors affecting, the Partnership or any Limited Partner, or (ii) in "good faith" or under another express standard, the General Partner or such Affiliate shall act under such express standard and shall not be subject to any other or different standards imposed by this Agreement or any other agreement contemplated hereby.

(c) Whenever a particular transaction, arrangement or resolution of a conflict of interest is required under this Agreement to be "fair and reasonable" to any Person, the fair and reasonable nature of such transaction, arrangement or resolution shall be considered in the context of all similar or related transactions.

16. Unitholders have the unfettered discretion to veto such a transaction by declining to grant it supermajority approval, even if the proposed merger were more than fair and reasonable by any objective measure. In other words, the unitholders have the right to reject a proposed merger for any reason whatsoever, whether rational or irrational, or conversely, to approve it on a basis other than an objective fairness test. In addition, at oral argument counsel for the Defendants represented to the Court that the General Partner and PC Advisory control no more than 4% of the limited partnership Units. Thus, there is no threat that the General Partner could "control" the outcome of a vote.

17. Sections 16.2 and 16.3 provide, in relevant part (with emphasis added):

16.2 Procedure for Merger or Consolidation. Merger or consolidation of the Partnership pursuant to this Article requires prior approval of the General Partner.

General Partner is permitted to enter into a merger in its sole discretion (*i.e.*, on the terms that the General Partner sees fit without required reference to the limited partners' interests). Second, the merger agreement is presented for a vote. Third, the merger agreement is approved upon receiving the endorsement of at least 66 2/3% of the outstanding Units. This careful framework established by the Agreement confirms that to the extent that unitholders are unhappy with the proposed terms of the merger (and in this case the resultant conversion) their remedy is the ballot box, not the courthouse.

C. Assumption of Fiduciary Duties

Plaintiff puts forth the alternative argument that, even if the General Partner did not originally owe common law fiduciary duties as a matter of law or by virtue of the Agreement, when the General Partner appointed a special committee to oversee the transaction, it undertook to conduct the process in a fair, diligent and independent manner. Plaintiff contends that the Defendants structured the transaction to create an atmosphere of fair dealing that, allegedly, would help them obtain the support of the unitholders. Thus, Plaintiff concludes that Defendants voluntarily assumed fiduciary duties that they may not have otherwise owed.

In support of this reasoning, Plaintiff relies heavily on *Cencom Cable Income Partners, L.P., Litigation.*[18] In *Cencom*, Vice Chancellor Steele refused to dismiss claims that the general partner had breached a "voluntarily assumed" fiduciary duty that was not originally imposed by the partnership agreement. The Vice Chancellor found that the general partner voluntarily undertook the responsibility of retaining a law firm to act as "independent" counsel for the limited partners to assure the integrity of the transaction and to attest to the fact that terms of the partnership agreement were followed. Vice Chancellor Steele determined that there were issues of fact to be resolved as to whether the "independent" counsel actually performed "as advertised." Central to the holding in *Cencom* is

---

If the General Partner shall determine, *in the exercise of its sole discretion,* to consent to the merger or consolidation, the General Partner shall approve the Merger Agreement, which shall set forth:

(a) The names and jurisdictions of formation or organization of each of the business entities proposing to merge or consolidate;

(b) The name and jurisdictions of formation or organization of the business entity that is to survive the proposed merger or consolidation (hereafter designated the "Surviving Business Entity");

(c) The terms and conditions of the proposed merger or consolidation....

16.3 Approval by Limited Partners of Mergers or Consolidation.

(a) The General Partner of the Partnership, upon its approval of the Merger Agreement, shall direct that the Merger Agreement be submitted to a vote of the Limited Partners whether by a meeting or by written consent....

(b) The Merger Agreement shall be approved upon receiving the affirmative vote or consent of the holders of at least 66⅔% of the outstanding Units of each class unless the Merger Agreement contains any provision, which if contained in an amendment to the Agreement, the provisions of this Agreement or the Delaware Act would require the vote or consent of a greater percentage of the Percentage Interests of the Limited Partners or of any class of Limited Partners, in which case such greater percentage vote or consent shall be required for the approval of the Merger Agreement.

18. Del. Ch., C.A. No. 14634, Steele, V.C., 1997 WL 666970 (Oct. 15, 1997).

the fact that the general partner circulated a disclosure statement that described what the independent counsel was supposed to do. Because of this affirmative disclosure, Vice Chancellor Steele held that

> the General Partner voluntarily assumed a duty to ensure that [the independent counsel] would fulfill [its] obligations and that the Limited Partners could rely on the General Partner's representations that the [independent counsel] would do so.[19]

Cencom can be distinguished easily from the present case. Here, the proxy statement has not yet been distributed. In fact, the Defendants in this case have not yet sought unitholder action. There is no element of reliance on misleading voluntary disclosure intended to induce the unitholders' acquiescence to the proposed conversion. Nor has Plaintiff complained about the adequacy of disclosures about the transaction.

Plaintiff asks me to conclude, as a matter of law, that merely because the General Partner appointed a special committee to oversee the transaction, the General Partner thereby imported common law fiduciary duties into its relationship with the unitholders. I cannot agree with this view. Even if the General Partner's aim was to conduct a process in a manner designed to help obtain the support of the unitholders, without misleading affirmative disclosures professing the fairness and independence of the special committee, it would unreasonably distort the Agreement to hold this General Partner to common law fiduciary standards. Plaintiff's asserted theory of voluntary assumption of common law fiduciary duties is actually a *potential* disclosure claim. As such, it is not ripe and must be dismissed.

IV. CONCLUSION

The Partnership Agreement is clear and unambiguous. It provides that the General Partner can propose a merger on *any* terms, and that if the unitholders are displeased with those terms they are free to reject it. Since Plaintiff alleges only the mere potential for misleading disclosure, or only a possibility of disclosure that omits material information (*e.g.*, a change in the Partnership's underlying economic condition), I cannot entertain the claim that the proposed conversion is unfair or that its timing is manipulative. As Plaintiff has failed to state a claim upon which relief can be granted, the amended complaint is dismissed.

IT IS SO ORDERED.

Notes

1. Do the Illinois court in *Labowitz v. Dolan*, page 367, and the Delaware Chancellor in *Sonet v. [Plum Creek] Timber Company* share the same view of the source and nature of fiduciary duties? Would the result in those case have changed if they had been decided in the other court?

---

19. *Id.* at 16. The Opinion goes on to say: "This conclusion turns not on what the General Partner may or may not have understood its fiduciary obligations to entail (a meaningless, subjective inquiry), but on the fact that it actively undertook this role ostensibly (1) to actually confer a benefit on the Limited Partners or (2) to convince them the self-interested transaction would conform to the terms of the Partnership agreement in order to induce their approval." *Id.*

2. The extent to which fiduciaries should be allowed to contract around fiduciary duties is a matter of continuing debate. Those who view themselves as "traditionalists" argue that fiduciary duties are *mandatory:*

> [T]he fiduciary duties of partners under the UPA and the common law are matters essentially of status and not of agreement, of tort and not of contract. Simply by virtue of being a partner, one owes the other partners and the partnership certain duties. And, except for narrow and specific waivers following full disclosure, those status-based fiduciary duties are not amendable by the parties.

Allan W. Vestal, *"Assume A Rather Large Boat...": The Mess We Have Made Of Partnership Law,* 54 WASH. & LEE L. REV. 487, 530 (1997). This is the approach taken in *Schock v. Nash,* page 216, in Chapter 4.

The alternative view is that business relationships and entities are contractual:

> Fiduciary duties can be characterized as a hypothetical bargain—that is, contract terms the parties themselves would have agreed to in the absence of transaction costs. * * * Anticipating the parties' own deal makes sense as a way of economizing on contracting costs only if the parties could make their own alternative deal. Otherwise, the court might as well supply its own idea of the "right" contract terms regardless of whether the parties would have wanted them. Thus, the application of hypothetical bargain reasoning to fiduciary duties suggests that these duties are waivable.

Larry E. Ribstein, *Fiduciary Duty Contracts In Unincorporated Firms,* 54 WASH. & LEE L. REV. 537, 541-42 (1997) (citations omitted). The "hypothetical bargain" approach emphasizes party autonomy. Under this view, entity law should be suppletory; it should supply default rules that apply only if the parties have not contracted as to fiduciary duties.

For additional discussion, see Claire Moore Dickerson, *Cycles and Pendulums: Good Faith, Norms, and the Commons,* 54 WASH. & LEE L. REV. 399 (1997); J. Dennis Hynes, *Freedom of Contract, Fiduciary Duties, and Partnerships: The Bargain Principle and the Law of Agency,* 54 WASH. & LEE L. REV. 439 (1997); Lawrence E. Mitchell, *The Naked Emperor: A Corporate Lawyer Looks At RUPA's Fiduciary Provisions,* 54 WASH. & LEE L. REV. 465 (1997); Donald J. Weidner, *Foreword to Freedom of Contract and Fiduciary Duty: Organizing the Internal Relations of the Unincorporated Firm,* 54 WASH. & LEE L. REV. 389 (1997).

3. The Delaware Uniform Limited Partnership Act generally defers to party autonomy:

> It is the policy of this chapter to give maximum effect to the principle of freedom of contract and to the enforceability of partnership agreements.

6 DEL. CODE § 17-1101(c) (1999). It also specifically authorizes parties to contract with respect to fiduciary duties:

> To the extent that, at law or in equity, a partner or other person has duties (including fiduciary duties) and liabilities relating thereto to a limited partnership or to another partner,
>
> > (1) any such partner or other person acting under a partnership agreement shall not be liable to the limited partnership or to

any such other partner for the partner's or other person's good faith reliance on the provisions of such partnership agreement, and

(2) the partner's or other person's duties and liabilities may be expanded or restricted by provisions in a partnership agreement.

6 DEL. CODE § 17-1101(d) (1999).

4. In *Sonet v. Plum Creek Timber Company, L.P.*, No. 16931, 1999 WL 160174 (Del. Ch. Ct. March 18, 1999) (*Sonet II*), Vice Chancellor Jacobs found that the proxy materials used by Plum Creek Management, L.P., were materially misleading, and entered an preliminary injunction requiring curative disclosure. Judge Jacobs reasoned as follows:

> The relevant merits analysis is governed by well established principles. When controlling persons seek shareholder approval of a transaction, they have a fiduciary duty to honestly provide full and fair disclosure of all material facts relating to that transaction.[33] That proposition is equally applicable to fiduciaries of limited partnerships. The burden is on the fiduciary to demonstrate that all material facts were disclosed.[34] Where, as here, the lone source of the disclosure is a fiduciary having a conflicting interest, "a more compelling case for the application of the recognized disclosure standards" is presented.[35] In that context, the materiality standard remains unchanged, but the scrutiny of the disclosures made in that context is more exacting. Where a party is found to have disseminated materially misleading information to stockholders (or in this case, Unitholders), preliminary injunctive relief requiring curative disclosure may be awarded.[6]

*   *   *

> This Court takes no pleasure in holding up a transaction to require further disclosure, especially where a finely crafted Proxy Statement otherwise sets forth at great length many facts that are material to the REIT Conversion. This result is, however, a logical consequence of the ruling in *Sonet I* and the defendants' litigating position which prompted that ruling. The result is also compelled by sound policy.

---

33. Malone v. Brincat, *Del.Supr., 722 A.2d 5 (1998) (holding that "when directors communicate publicly or directly with shareholders about corporate matters the sine qua non of directors' fiduciary duty to shareholders is honesty.");* Stroud v..Grace, *Del.Supr.,* 606 A.2d 75 (1992); Weinberger v. U.O.P., Inc., *Del.Supr.,* 457 A.2d 701 (1983).

34. *Rosenblatt v. Getty Oil Co.,* Del.Supr., 493 A.2d 929, 937 (1985).

35. *Wacht v. Continental Hosts, Ltd.,* Del. Ch., C.A. No. 7954, mem. op. at 7, Berger, V.C. (Apr. 11, 1986) (involving a cash-out merger); see also In re Radiology Assoc., Inc. Litig, Del. Ch., C.A. No. 9001, Chandler, V.C. (May 16, 1990) (involving cash-out merger); Blanchette v. Providence & Worcester Co., D.Del., 428 F .Supp. 347, 354-356 (1997) (Exchange offer); Barkan v. Amsted Indus., Inc., Del. Ch., 567 A.2d 1279 (1989) (Management buyout); Eisenberg v. Chicago Milwaukee Corp., Del. Ch., 537 A.2d 1051, 1057 (1987) (Self-tender offer).

6. See Eisenberg, 537 A.2d at 1062 ("An injunction is the remedy most likely to achieve disclosure of the information necessary to achieve an informed decision..."); Sealy Mattress Co. of N.J. v. Sealy, Inc., Del. Ch., 532 A.2d 1324, 1340-41 (1987) ("[P]laintiffs have not received sufficient information to make an informed decision among the available alternatives....In this case the inability to make that choice constitutes irreparable harm.").

In *Sonet I,* the Chancellor held that in this specific partnership agreement, the Unitholders had contracted away their right to seek judicial review of the REIT Conversion based upon substantive fiduciary duty principles. In its place, the parties' contract substituted the protection of a required two-thirds supermajority Unitholder approval of the transaction. The result was to shift the fiduciary duty focus from the domain of substantive fairness to the realm of full, honest, and complete disclosure.

In these circumstances, and given the nature of this transaction, those disclosure duties are and should be exacting. As was the case in *Blanchette* and *Eisenberg,*[5] the REIT Conversion is a transaction where the fiduciaries responsible for the disclosures have an economic interest that is adverse to the interests of their beneficiary investors, the Unitholders. The GP and Management, who conceived and initiated the transaction and controlled the process by which it came to be recommended to the Unitholders, have an interest in maximizing their percentage ownership of the new REIT entity. That can only occur at the expense of the Unitholders, whose interest is in minimizing the percentage ownership of the GP. Because (under *Sonet I*) the Unitholders have no judicial review remedy, their sole protection is their right to vote the proposal up or down. And because the only source of the facts that will inform that vote are conflicted fiduciaries (the GP), only a most stringent disclosure standard, enforced by careful judicial scrutiny, can assure that the Unitholders' right to vote will have meaning. In this case the disclosures fell short of that standard and, as a consequence, the Unitholders are entitled to injunctive relief that will cure the informational gap.

Is the Chancellor's opinion in *Sonet II* consistent with the holding and reasoning of *Sonet I* that, where the supermajority voting requirement applied, the Plum Creek Timber Company Partnership Agreement displaced fiduciary duties?

5. Although the RUPA generally defers to the agreement of the parties, RUPA § 103(a), it limits the ability of parities to contract with respect to their duties as partners:

> (b) A partnership agreement may not:
>
> *   *   *
>
> (3) *eliminate* the duty of loyalty under Section 404(b) or 603(b)(3); but:
>
>> (i) the partnership agreement may identify specific types or categories of activities that do not violate the duty of loyalty, *if not manifestly unreasonable;*
>>
>> (ii) all of the partners or a number or percentage specified in the partnership agreement may authorize or ratify, *after full disclosure* of all *material* facts, *a specific act or transaction* that otherwise would violate the duty of loyalty;
>
> (4) *unreasonably reduce* the duty of care under Section 404(c) or 603(b) (3);

---

5. *See supra* note 35.

(5) *eliminate* the obligation of good faith and fair dealing under Section 404(d), but the partnership agreement may *prescribe the standards* by which the performance of the obligation is to be measured, *if the standards are not manifestly unreasonable;*

RUPA § 103(b) (emphasis added).

6. As might be expected, the Delaware version of RUPA section 103 allows the parties greater freedom to contract with respect to their duties as partners:

§ 15-103 Effect of partnership agreement; nonwaivable provisions.

*　　*　　*

(b) The partnership agreement may not:

*　　*　　*

(3) *eliminate* the obligation of good faith and fair dealing under Section 15-404(d), but the partnership agreement may *restrict* the obligation or *prescribe the standards* by which the performance of the obligation is to be measured;

*　　*　　*

(c) It is the policy of this chapter to give maximum effect to the principle of freedom of contract and to the enforceability of partnership agreements.

(d) A partner or another person shall not be liable to the partnership or the other partners or another person for the partner's or other person's good faith reliance on the provisions of the partnership agreement.

6 DEL. CODE § 15-103 (1999) (emphasis added). Is the Chancellor's opinion in *Sonet II* (see Note 3 above) consistent with the Delaware version of RUPA section 103?

7. Under the facts of Problem 7.4, the trial court found a breach of fiduciary duty on the part of High. The appellate court reversed, reasoning:

At the time of the formation of the partnership, both Covalt and High were officers and shareholders of CSI. Each was aware of the potential for conflict between their duties as corporate officers to further the business of the corporation, and that of their role as partners in leasing realty to the corporation for the benefit of the partnership business. In the posture of being both a landlord and representatives of the tenant they had conflicting loyalties and fiduciary duties. After Covalt's resignation as an officer of the corporation he continued to remain a shareholder of the corporation. Each party's conflict of interest was known to the other and was acquiesced in when the partnership was formed.

Covalt v. High, 100 N.M. 700, 675 P.2d 999 (App. 1983). How would the *Labowitz v. Dolan,* page 367, court have ruled? The chancellor in *Sonet v. [Plum Creek] Timber Company?*

Chapter 8

Firm's Accountability for Notification to and Knowledge of the Agent

A. General Rules

1. Knowledge

E. Udolf, Inc. v. Aetna Casualty & Surety Company
214 Conn. 741, 573 A.2d 1211 (1990)

HULL, Associate Justice.

The sole issue in this appeal is whether the plaintiff, E. Udolf, Inc., was entitled to coverage under certain employee dishonesty insurance policies issued by the defendants, Aetna Casualty and Surety Company (Aetna) and Fire and Casualty Insurance Company of Connecticut (Fire and Casualty), for the misappropriation of monies by an employee of the plaintiff. The plaintiff notified the defendants of losses it had incurred as a result of an employee's dishonesty and sought from the defendants indemnification, plus interest, for those losses. Upon the defendants' refusals to pay its claim, the plaintiff instituted the present action. The matter was thereafter tried to the court and judgment was rendered in favor of the defendants. From this judgment the plaintiff appeals.

The underlying facts as found by the trial court are as follows. The plaintiff is a small corporation that operates a retail men's clothing store in the city of Hartford. During the relevant period, 1980 through 1983, the plaintiff employed between eight and ten employees. The only officer, director and shareholder of the plaintiff was Leonard Udolf, who was present in the store approximately 10 to 20 percent of the time. In his absence the store was run by Kenneth Auer, the store manager. Auer was the overseer of the store and was principally in charge of its operations in the absence of Leonard Udolf. He was expected, however, to report all relevant activities to Leonard Udolf.

During the years 1980 and 1981, Lynn Bjork, an employee of the plaintiff, misappropriated $6000 from the plaintiff. To effect the misappropriations, she substituted her personal checks for money generated by the plaintiff's sales, and then simply put these checks in her desk rather than depositing them into the

393

plaintiff's account. In the spring of 1981, during one of Leonard Udolf's frequent absences from the store, Anna Shukis, the plaintiff's bookkeeper, discovered the misappropriations and immediately informed Auer of them. Auer and Shukis were expected to inform Leonard Udolf of activities such as Bjork's misappropriations. They, however, did not consult with Leonard Udolf, but rather agreed with one another to allow Bjork to repay the $6000 and remain employed by the plaintiff. Thereafter, Bjork repaid the $6000.

Beginning in late 1981, and continuing until February, 1983, Bjork again misappropriated monies from the plaintiff, totaling $48,715.08. These misappropriations were discovered in February, 1983, and Bjork was immediately fired by Auer on the direct order of Leonard Udolf.

Pursuant to employee dishonesty insurance policies that the plaintiff had purchased from Aetna and from Fire and Casualty, the plaintiff notified the two companies of the losses incurred as a result of Bjork's misappropriations. Both Aetna and Fire and Casualty refused to indemnify the plaintiff for those losses, claiming that the language of the policies excluded coverage for Bjork's actions. Aetna's refusal to pay was based on the following provision contained in section 7 of its policy:

> The coverage of Insuring Agreement I shall not apply to any Employee from and after the time that the Insured or any partner or officer thereof not in collusion with such Employee shall have knowledge or information that such Employee has committed any fraudulent or dishonest act in the service of the Insured or otherwise, whether such act be committed before or after the date of employment by the Insured.

Fire and Casualty's refusal was based on similar language contained in section 1(3) of its policy:

> Insurance hereunder shall be deemed cancelled as to any Employee immediately upon discovery by the Insured, or any partner or officer, of any fraudulent or dishonest act of such Employee.

The trial court concluded that, under the terms of the policies, the plaintiff was not entitled to recovery of the losses it had incurred as a result of Bjork's actions. The basis of the court's conclusion was its determination that the knowledge of Auer and Shukis concerning misappropriations committed by the plaintiff's employees was imputed to the plaintiff. The court thus reasoned that because the 1980-81 misappropriations by Bjork constituted "fraudulent or dishonest act[s]" within the scope of [the insurance policies], and because the plaintiff, by imputation of Auer's and Shukis' knowledge, became aware of those misappropriations no later than the summer of 1981, any subsequent losses caused by a "fraudulent or dishonest act" on the part of Bjork were excluded from coverage under the policies. In so concluding, the court rejected the plaintiff's claim that, because Auer and Shukis did not inform Leonard Udolf of Bjork's 1980-81 misappropriations, they were in collusion with Bjork. The court stated that while the failure of Auer and Shukis to notify Leonard Udolf may have been an act of poor judgment, it was not a fraudulent act and therefore was not collusive.

The plaintiff concedes that generally

> notice to, or knowledge of, an agent while acting within the scope of his authority and in reference to a matter over which his authority extends, is notice to, or knowledge of, the principal.

West Haven v. United States Fidelity & Guaranty Co., 174 Conn. 392, 395, 389 A.2d 741 (1978). As stated in the Restatement (Second) of Agency § 272

> a principal is affected by the knowledge of an agent concerning a matter as to which he acts within his power to bind the principal or upon which it is his duty to give the principal information.

The plaintiff argues, however, that this agency principle should not apply in the context of employee dishonesty insurance . . .

The trial court was unpersuaded by the plaintiff's argument and the cases on which it was based, and relied instead primarily on *Ritchie Grocer Co. v. Aetna Casualty & Surety Co.*, 426 F.2d 499 (8th Cir. 1970), in concluding that the knowledge of Auer and Shukis concerning Bjork's 1980-81 activities should be imputed to the plaintiff. The similarities between *Ritchie* and the instant case are striking. At issue in *Ritchie* was the same policy exclusion as in the present case.

The underlying facts involved in *Ritchie Grocer Co.* were as follows. Joseph Polk, the manager of a branch office of the plaintiff's wholesale grocery business, received an application for employment from Wayne Kemp. Prior to hiring Kemp, Polk inquired into Kemp's reputation for trustworthiness and discovered that several months earlier Kemp and two other boys had broken into a gas station and had stolen some tires and money. Notwithstanding that information, Polk hired Kemp as a truck driver for the plaintiff. During the eighteen months that Kemp was employed by the plaintiff, he misappropriated $17,486.20, for which the plaintiff made a claim under its fidelity policy. The insurance company defended on the grounds that Polk's knowledge of Kemp's prior "fraudulent or dishonest" act made him a known risk and excluded him from coverage under the policy's terms. The District Court held in favor of the insurance company on this ground and the Eighth Circuit Court of Appeals affirmed, reciting the general agency principle that knowledge of an agent acquired in the ordinary discharge of his duties for the corporation is generally to be imputed to the principal.

The cases relied upon by the trial court and the cases cited by both the plaintiff and the defendants lack any meaningful analysis of the reasons that imputation was either appropriate or inappropriate under the facts of the particular cases. We conclude, however, that a proper analysis flows logically from the tension between the conflicting views presented by the plaintiff and the defendants. The plaintiff argues that the general rule imputing knowledge of an agent to a principal presumes the agent's loyalty in the performance of his duties. The corporation purchases fidelity insurance to protect itself from the risk that the employee will be disloyal. The plaintiff claims that it, therefore, would be "absurd" to hold that each employee so insured was an agent of the plaintiff whose duty it was to discover and report acts of dishonesty by other employees. Moreover, the plaintiff argues, if the neglect or reluctance of the insured's employees to report on one another relieved the insurance carrier of its liability, the corporation would be denied a remedy. The defendants' counterpoint is that, taken to its extreme, the plaintiff's contention would render "prior employee dishonesty" exclusions useless. Without employee imputation, the defendants argue, it would be impossible to charge an insured corporation with knowledge of an employee's prior wrongful actions.

The answer to this conundrum can be found in the cases relied upon by the trial court, although not explicitly articulated therein. We conclude that the knowledge of an employee may be imputed to an employer under an employee dishonesty insurance policy if the employee holds a position of management or control in the exercise of which a duty to report known dishonesty of a fellow employee can be found to exist either explicitly or by fair inference from a course of conduct.

On appeal, the plaintiff argues that the evidence presented at trial indicated various limitations on the responsibilities of Auer and Shukis that made imputation inappropriate. The trial court, however, concluded that Auer was principally in charge of operations during Leonard Udolf's absences from the store and that one of his responsibilities in that capacity was to report matters such as misappropriations to Leonard Udolf. The court further determined that Anna Shukis, the plaintiff's bookkeeper, was responsible for running the bookkeeping operation and that she likewise had a responsibility to report to Leonard Udolf any misappropriations that occurred in that department. The nature and extent of an agent's authority is a question of fact for the trier.

Bjork testified at trial that in 1980-81, Auer's position was that of "store manager." Although Auer testified at trial that he was only the "sales manager," this testimony was inconsistent with his prior deposition testimony in which Auer had claimed that he was in fact the "store manager." Further, while Auer stated that he did not have the authority to hire and fire employees in 1980-81, he did arrange with Bjork, without first consulting with Leonard Udolf, for repayment of the $6000 and then fired Bjork upon learning of the 1983 misappropriations. Auer's testimony also revealed that he was expected to report to Leonard Udolf everything that happened in the store. Finally, Leonard Udolf was present in the store only 10 to 20 percent of the time. Although Leonard Udolf claimed at trial that he was always in charge of the store, even while absent, this claim conflicted with his deposition testimony in which, in response to the question of "who was in charge of the operations in your absence," he answered: "Well I felt I had them in capable hands with Ken Auer on the floor and in the office with Ann Shukis and the other girls."

We conclude that the trial court's factual findings concerning the responsibilities and consequent duties of Auer and Shukis were supported by the evidence. Therefore, since the court found that the positions held by Auer and Shukis gave rise to a duty to report misappropriations to Leonard Udolf, the court's imputation to the plaintiff of Auer's and Shukis' knowledge concerning Bjork's 1980-81 actions was not error.

Notes

1. Restatement section 272 provides that the principal will be affected by the knowledge of an agent either

(i) when the knowledge concerns a matter within the scope of the agent's power to bind the principal *or*

(ii) when the agent has a duty to give the principal that information.

A principal will not be affected by an agent's knowledge concerning a matter outside the scope of the agent's actual authority, but within the agent's apparent authority, unless a third person has relied on the agent's apparent authority. Restatement § 273.

2. An agent has a duty to inform the principal of information learned by the agent that relates to the matters entrusted to the agent by the principal:

> An agent may have a duty to act upon, or to communicate to his principal information which [the agent] has received, although not specifically instructed to do so. The duty exists if [the agent] has notice of facts which, in view of [the agent's] relations with the principal, [the agent] should know may affect the desires of [the agent's] principal as to [the agent's] own conduct or the conduct of the principal or of another agent. [This] duty is inferred from [the agent's] position, just as authority is inferred. The extent of the duty depends upon the kind of work entrusted to [the agent], [the agent's] previous relations with the principal, and all the facts of the situation.

Restatement § 381 comment a.

3. As used in the Restatement, *knowledge* of a fact is limited to actual conscious awareness of it. See Restatement § 9 comment c. Persons have *notice* of a fact when they know it, have reason to know it, should know it, or have been notified of it. Restatement § 9(1). The rules regarding attributing to the principal an agent's knowledge also apply to the attribution of notice. Restatement §§ 9(3), 272 comment b. So, what is the difference between knowledge and notice?

4. A principal will not necessarily be held responsible for an agent's knowledge for all purposes. For example, in *Sisk v. McPartland,* 267 Ore. 116, 515 P.2d 179 (1973), the trial court entered a default judgment against the defendant, Zelle, after striking Zelle's answer on account of her failure to appear at a deposition. Plaintiff had served Zelle's attorney, Griffith, with formal notice of the deposition, but Griffith was unable to inform Zelle of the deposition. The appellate court reversed the default judgment on the ground that a *willful* failure to appear was necessary to strike an answer:

> Even if we assume that defendant Zelle received proper notice of the deposition through service on her attorney, we do not believe that her failure to appear can properly be characterized as "willful." [A willful act is generally defined as one which "(proceeds) from a conscious motion of the will; voluntary" or is "designed; intentional; not accidental or involuntary." Black's Law Dictionary 1773 (rev. 4th ed. 1968).]
>
> The record suggests that defendant Zelle might have had actual knowledge of the lawsuit but nothing in the record suggests that she had actual knowledge of the deposition. According to an established principle of agency law, notice given an agent is attributable to the principal. [Restatement (Second) of Agency § 268.] Nevertheless, courts recognize the distinction between vicarious notice and notice based on actual knowledge when construing a statute or contract which imposes liability on the basis of actual knowledge only.
>
>> If the state of mind of a principal in a transaction is a factor, a notification by a third person giving information to an agent who does not communicate it to the principal does not operate with like effect as a similar notification given to the principal.

Restatement (Second) of Agency § 268, Comment d.

In many situations, in order for one to be responsible, it is necessary that the act should be done with knowledge in a subjective sense, and it is not sufficient that one has means of information. *Id.* § 275, Comment b.

We believe that the requirement that the failure to attend the deposition be willful, indicates that the party must have actual notice of the deposition and not notice imputed from the knowledge of an agent attorney. The legislative aim is to discourage the deliberate obstruction of established discovery procedures. Only when the party has actual notice of the pending deposition can the subsequent failure to appear be accurately described in words such as "willful," "conscious," "designed," or "intentional." A failure to attend due to ignorance of the hearing is simply not a willful act. Since defendant Zelle's failure to attend the deposition was not willful, the trial court erred in striking her answer and placing her in default.

Problem 8.1

Tom and Paul are partners in Law Firm. Tom and Paul agree that Tom will act as managing partner. As such, Tom handles all administrative and personnel matters.

On repeated occasion, Paul sees Associate, during the normal course of a working day, become unreasonably angry with secretaries and paralegals. Paul always admonished Associate to act in a more appropriate manner, but did not report Associate's conduct to Tom. Several months later, Associate becomes angry, and hits Clerk.

Clerk has now sued Law Firm, claiming that Law Firm knew of Associate's explosive tendencies and negligently failed to either fire or control Associate. In Clerk's suit, will Law Firm be responsible for Paul's knowledge? See UPA § 12, RUPA § 102(f). Compare, ULLCA § 102.

2. Notification

Dvoracek v. Gillies

363 N.W.2d 99 (Minn. App. 1985)

LANSING, Judge.

The tenant in this unlawful detainer action appeals from a judgment determining that the landlord is entitled to restitution of the premises because the lease term had expired. The trial court directed a verdict for the landlord at the close of evidence, finding as a matter of law that the tenant had given inadequate notice to renew the lease.

Stephen Gillies rented commercial space from Cleo Dvoracek at 3014 South Lyndale Avenue. Gillies does business as Gemini Service Center, an automobile and marine repair service. Dvoracek owns the adjoining premises and business, called Art Materials, Inc., at 3018 South Lyndale Avenue. She works there full-time and employs about 18 people.

The parties executed a lease that provided for a one-year term expiring May 31, 1984, with an option to renew for a two-year period and a right of first refusal for an additional two-year period. Paragraph 2.2 of the lease required the tenant to give the landlord a written renewal notice at least 60 days before the lease expired. In addition, paragraph 25 provided:

Any notice required under this Lease shall be in writing, and shall be deemed to have been given if deposited in the United States mail, postage prepaid, certified or registered mail, return receipt requested, and addressed as follows:

> Landlord: Cleo Dvoracek
> 3018 Lyndale Avenue South
> Minneapolis, MN 55408
>
> Tenant: Stephen Gillies
> 2645 Lyndale Avenue South
> Minneapolis, MN 55408

Gillies testified that he hand-delivered all his rent checks to Dvoracek at Art Materials because it was right next door. If Dvoracek was not available, he left the checks with employees at the city desk there. Dvoracek admitted that Gillies had left rent checks with employees at the city desk in the past and that she had hand-delivered notices to him in the past.

Gillies testified that on the morning of March 16, 1984, he dictated a letter giving notice of his intent to renew the lease for two years. His secretary typed and notarized the letter at Gillies' office in his home at 2645 South Lyndale. They drove together to the common driveway between Art Materials and the Gemini Service Center. Gillies went into a nearby store to copy the letter, while his secretary waited in the car. When he returned he handed the copy to his secretary, put the original into an envelope, and went into Art Materials sometime around noon. He said he asked for Dvoracek and was told she was not available. He left the letter with an employee at the city desk and said, "Please see that Cleo gets this." He said the employee responded, "I certainly will," but he doesn't remember if the employee was a man or woman. The secretary, who had worked for Gillies for 15 years, testified to the same sequence of events.

Dvoracek and her employees who testified denied receiving the letter, although some employees who had worked that day did not testify. According to the employees' testimony, anyone working in the store that day could have attended the city desk over the lunch hour.

Dvoracek received a letter from Gillies on about May 1 asking her to repair the air conditioning before the summer. She responded with a letter from her attorney dated May 14, advising Gillies that she had received no notice of his intent to renew the lease and that the lease was to terminate on May 31. Gillies attempted to pay the June rent, but Dvoracek refused to accept it.

This unlawful detainer action was brought in June 1984. The trial court directed a verdict for the landlord at the close of evidence on the ground that, even assuming Gillies delivered the notice as he had testified, Dvoracek's employees were not her agents for purposes of receiving the renewal notice.

Gillies argues that the landlord's employees had either actual or apparent authority to accept the renewal notice and that the evidence presented at minimum a question for the jury. A notification given to an agent is notice to the principal if it is given to "an agent authorized to receive it" or to "an agent apparently authorized to receive it." *Distillers Distributing Co. v. Young*, 261 Minn. 549, 552, 113 N.W.2d 175, 177 (1962) (quoting Restatement (Second) of Agency § 268 (1957)). The existence of an agency relationship is a fact question for the jury.

The trial court relied on *Prendergast v. Searle,* 81 Minn. 291, 294, 84 N.W. 107, 109 (1900), in directing a verdict for the landlord. In *Prendergast* the court held that evidence should have been admitted tending to show that the tenant had mailed a notice to an agent of the landlord, because the agent had "the charge and management of his principal's business with reference to such tenancy."

The trial court determined that, even assuming Gillies delivered the letter to an Art Materials employee, the notice was inadequate because Dvoracek's employees were not agents "having the charge and management" of her rental property business. In *Prendergast* the agent did have the charge and management of the principal's rental business, but the case does not establish a rule of law that such agents are the only ones who may receive notices. Agency is a fact question. The question here is whether Dvoracek's employees became her agents for the purpose of receiving Gillies' renewal notice.

The record shows that Gillies always hand-delivered his rent checks to either Dvoracek or her employees at Art Materials. Although Dvoracek testified that she had not expressly authorized her employees to accept hand-delivered correspondence from Gillies, she allowed the practice to continue. She never told Gillies not to leave correspondence at the city desk, and she never told the employees at the city desk not to accept deliveries for her. Furthermore, mail sent to Dvoracek at 3018 South Lyndale is delivered to the city desk.

Viewing the evidence in the light most favorable to Gillies, a jury could reasonably have concluded that Dvoracek had either impliedly authorized her employees to accept the notice or had consented to Gillies' practice of hand-delivering correspondence to them, so that he was justified in relying on them as her agents. We reverse and remand for another trial on this issue.

Notes

1. Be careful to distinguish *knowledge and notice*, on the one hand, and *notification*, on the other hand. As indicated in the notes following *E. Udolf, Inc. v. Aetna Casualty & Surety Company,* knowledge and notice involve responsibility for *awareness* of information. Notification is a formal act intended in itself to determine the rights of the parties, regardless of the degree of knowledge of the recipient. Restatement § 9(3) & comment f. In *Dvoracek,* for example, Gillies delivered his letter to Dvoracek's "city desk" for the purpose of exercising his option to renew the lease. Unfortunately, the word "notice" can be used in two different contexts. Notice often refers to a person's responsibility for information because they know it or have *constructive knowledge of it* (reason to know it, should know it or receipt of a notification of it). *See* Restatement § 9(1). Notice is also used in the context of *notification*. In *Dvoracek,* for example, Gillies sent a "notice" of his intent to renew the lease. Similarly, in *Sisk v. McPartland,* the plaintiff gave the defendant's attorney "notice" of the deposition of the defendant. In reading cases dealing with notification and knowledge, students should

be alert to whether the court is using the word "notice" in a notification or constructive knowledge sense.

2. *Dvoracek* did not involve the question of whether the notification resulted in constructive knowledge. Instead, the issue was whether the notification was *legally effective* to renew the lease. The question of the effectiveness of a notification to an agent is similar to the questions studied in chapter 2: did the notification *bind* the principal? As a result, the rules regarding notification are somewhat different from those regarding the attribution of knowledge and notice. For example, notification to an agent is notification to the principal if the agent was actually *or apparently* authorized to receive the notification. Restatement § 268. *Knowledge* that is only within an agent's apparent authority will not be *attributed* to the principal unless a third party relied on the appearance of authority. Restatement § 273.

3. The question of the effect of notification, knowledge, and notice is not limited to principals and agents. A *master* will be affected by notification to, or knowledge or notice of, a *servant* so long as the servant had a duty to act on or communicate the information or notification as a part of the servant's employment or apparent employment. Restatement § 283.

3. Prior or Causally Obtained Knowledge or Notification

Problem 8.2

Thomas allegedly assaulted and raped R.B. in an apartment rented to R.B. by Apartments. At the time of the assault, Thomas was living with Carol, the property manager of Apartments. Thomas was Carol's ex-husband, and she knew that, prior to their marriage, Thomas had been convicted of rape. Assume that Apartments would *not* owe R.B. a duty to take reasonable precautions against Thomas' rape, *unless* Apartments knew of Thomas' prior convictions. If Carol never told anyone at Apartments about Thomas' prior conviction, did Apartments owe a duty to R.B.? See *R.B.Z. v. Warwick Development Co.,* 725 So.2d 261 (Ala. 1998).

Davenport v. Correct Manufacturing Corp.
24 Ohio St. 3d 131, 493 N.E.2d 1331 (1986)

FACTS*

This case involves the appeal by Davenport from a summary judgment in favor of E.H.J. Skyworker Services, Inc. (Skyworker). Davenport alleged that he was injured when a "cherry picker" owned by his employer, Fisher, collapsed due to the failure of a defectively designed "rod end assembly." Davenport alleged, among other things, that before the accident Skyworker had repaired the cherry picker and had failed to warn Fisher that the rod end assembly was defective. Skyworker responded that it did not know of the defect and had no duty to dis-

---

* [Footnote by the editors.] The following description of the facts and procedural history was prepared by the editors and not by the court.

cover it. The summary judgment record included a disputed statement that a representative of manufacturer of the cherry picker had told Herbert A. Van Dyke, an agent of Skyworker at the time of the repair, of the need to replace the defective part with a new one. Skyworker claimed it was not responsible for Van Dyke's knowledge because the alleged conversation with the manufacturer's representative had occurred *before* Van Dyke had become an agent of Skyworker.

The trial court granted summary judgment in favor of Skyworker. On appeal, the court of appeals reversed the summary judgment, but ruled that Skyworker could not be held accountable for the knowledge of an agent acquired prior to the time the agent became an agent. On appeal, the Ohio Supreme Court rendered the following opinion.

PER CURIAM

Because a number of disputed questions of material fact remain, we hold that the trial court improperly granted Skyworker's motion for summary judgment. These factual questions include: whether [Van Dyke] in fact knew of the danger; and whether any such knowledge was obtained after Skyworker [employed Van Dyke] and could therefore be imputed to the corporation.

We affirm the judgment of the court of appeals and remand the cause for further proceedings in the trial court.

WRIGHT, Justice [with Sweeney and Brown, JJ.], concurring in part and dissenting in part.

I agree with the majority that sufficient questions of material fact exist for Davenport to withstand a motion for summary judgment. I believe, however, that this court should go one step further and lay to rest the Ohio rule that prohibits courts from imputing to a corporation the knowledge of a corporate agent which was acquired before that agent was employed by the corporation.

The general rule is that relevant knowledge is imputed to the corporation or principal in such a situation. See Restatement of the Law 2d, Agency (1958), Section 276. The time when the knowledge is acquired should be relevant only to draw the appropriate inference as to the existence of knowledge. If the knowledge was acquired either before the agency relationship existed or while the agent was not acting for the purposes of the principal and the agent has forgotten the knowledge, the principal would not be held liable because the agent had no duty to the principal to remember it. *Id.*, Comment b. Likewise, the knowledge would not be imputed to the principal if the agent acquired it while acting in a position of confidentiality. Knowledge would be imputed only if it can reasonably be said to be present in the agent's mind while he was acting for the principal or if it was acquired so recently as to raise the presumption that he still retained it in his mind.

This general rule makes much more sense than the so-called Ohio rule. Herbert A. Van Dyke's post-[employment] actions in servicing Fisher's skyworker [cherry picker] would permit an inference that he was acting with previously acquired knowledge about such units.

A person often is employed by a corporation because of his specialized knowledge, obtained through either educational training or job experience. It is illogical to hold that the person does not have this knowledge for purposes of corporate liability. This court should overrule the court of appeals to the extent that it held that any knowledge acquired by Van Dyke before [employment by] Skyworker could not be imputed to the corporation for purposes of this case. On remand, Davenport should be required to establish that it would be reasonable to infer that Van Dyke knew of the dangerous condition of the rod-end assembly in the Fisher skyworker.

Notes

1. The dispute regarding whether the principal should be affected by the knowledge or notice of an agent where that knowledge or notice was acquired *casually* (outside of the agent's "employment") turns on the question of whether the agent should be expected to recall "extraneous" information. Certainly, an agent may no longer have knowledge—actual conscious awareness of the information—and should not automatically be expected to recall it (should not automatically have reason to know). On the other hand, if the agent does recall it, or reasonably should have recalled it, while acting with authority or with a duty to inform, the principal should be accountable for that information unless the information was confidential information the agent was not privileged to disclose.

2. This is another context in which the rules regarding notification differ from those regarding knowledge and notice. Recall that the issue in notification is whether the agent had power to bind the principal. Thus, a notification is effective only if the agent had such power at the time the notification was received. Restatement § 269.

B. Time From Which Notification or Knowledge Affects Principal

Problem 8.3

Owner owns and operates Mall. Alan and Betty are leasing agents for the Mall and share an office suite in the Mall..As such, each is authorized to negotiate and to sign, on Owner's behalf, leases covering space in the Mall. On Friday, Betty leased space to Laser, who planned to open a laser-tag game in the Mall.

Unknown to Betty, on Monday, Alan had leased space in the Mall to Arcade, who planned to open a video arcade in the Mall. As a condition for signing the lease, Arcade insisted on the inclusion of an "exclusivity provision" under which Owner agree not to lease space in the Mall to any other arcade or amusement center. Alan forgot to tell either Owner or Betty about the exclusivity provision included in Arcade's lease.

Assume that Alan had authority to agree to the inclusion of the exclusivity provision, and that Owner will be liable to Arcade for breach of contract. Assume further that Owner will also be liable for special damages if it knowingly breached the lease with Arcade. Will Owner be responsible for special damages?

Biggs v. Terminal Railroad Association
110 Ill. App. 3d 709, 442 N.E.2d 1353 (1982)

KARNS, Presiding Justice:

Rodney Steven Biggs brought this action under the Federal Employers' Liability Act to recover damages for personal injuries sustained while employed as a track laborer for defendant, Terminal Railroad Association of St. Louis. Defendant appeals from the judgment entered in the circuit court of Madison County on a jury verdict in plaintiff's favor.

The testimony established that plaintiff and co-employee, Robert Parr, were track laborers and had been working for defendant 15 days on April 17, 1979. On that morning, plaintiff, Parr and 10 to 12 other employees reported for work at a shanty at the railroad yards. While in the shanty, plaintiff related to the men a dream he had the night before about Parr pouring "Cheerios" in the heating and air conditioning ducts of plaintiff's trailer. Plaintiff testified that some of the men laughed but that there was no other reaction to the story. At that time, Ron Gartner, the track foreman, told the men to get their tools and get to work. Plaintiff and Parr then walked to the tool shed. Plaintiff repeated the dream in the tool shed to Gartner at which time Parr asked Gartner if he (Parr) could beat-up plaintiff. Plaintiff further testified that Gartner responded by saying that he wanted to get out of the shed first. Gartner testified he responded by telling Parr and plaintiff to get to work. Gartner then left the shed. Plaintiff then testified that Parr hit him on the jaw. Subsequently, plaintiff went outside and began pulling spikes at the track. When Parr came out plaintiff said, in Gartner's presence, "[H]ow come you hit me?" Parr then began grabbing at plaintiff and plaintiff reacted by striking Parr with a railroad spike he had in his hand. The spike cut Parr's lip. Parr picked up a pick axe and threatened plaintiff but threw the axe down without striking plaintiff. Plaintiff testified he turned away, believing Parr was now in control of himself. At that point, plaintiff was struck on the head with a railroad spike by Parr.

Gartner testified that he saw nothing occur between plaintiff and Parr in the tool shed and that he was turned away from plaintiff and Parr outside at the track until after Parr's lip was cut. When Parr picked up the axe, Gartner told him to drop it and get to work. When Parr did so, Gartner testified that he then turned back to his work having no reason to suspect further trouble.

The principles of law in these cases are well established. A railroad, as any employer, may be held liable under the Act where the assault by the fellow employee may be said to be within the scope of his employment, but the employee acts negligently. Liability may also be predicated upon the direct negligence of the railroad in knowingly employing, or retaining in its employ, a person with a quarrelsome disposition and vicious propensities who might reasonably be said to be a threat to other employees while performing their jobs within the scope of their employment. (Restatement (Second) of Agency § 213 (1957).)

Initially, we note that plaintiff makes no claim that defendant is vicariously liable under the principles of respondeat superior, that is, negligent because Parr acted negligently while acting within the scope of his employment. Instead, plaintiff's claim is one of direct negligence.

Plaintiff alleged three separate acts of negligence: failure to protect plaintiff from Parr, failure to provide plaintiff with a reasonably safe place to work and retention of Parr in its employ although it knew or should have known Parr was an ill-tempered and vicious person.

The reported cases establish that before the railroad may be found negligent, it must have had prior notice of the assailant-employee's violent propensities. Without any notice, defendant could not be negligent by retaining Parr in its employ. And, it could not be negligent by failing to protect plaintiff or by failing to provide plaintiff with a safe place to work if it did not know of Parr's violent nature and thus could not foresee any harm to plaintiff.

It was not alleged, nor was there any evidence, that defendant was negligent in employing an employee with known vicious propensities. There was no evidence that Parr had ever been quarrelsome or a person of violent disposition. The only evidence of this kind was the attack on plaintiff and if defendant was negligent in retaining Parr in its employ, the only evidence of prior notice of Parr's vicious disposition was that brought to the attention of Gartner, the track foreman, on the morning of the incident.

A corporate defendant acts only through its officers and employees. We do not believe that this brief notice of Parr's violent manner, brought only to the attention of the track foreman, could be considered to be notice of the corporate defendant under these facts. The Restatement (Second) of Agency, § 213, comment d, states that an employee must have some antecedent reason to believe that the employee presents an undue risk of harm to others because of his vicious nature.

Both plaintiff and Gartner testified that Parr had not caused any previous trouble nor had Parr and plaintiff had any other conflicts. The incident on April 17 was an isolated, brief occurrence. It was uncontradicted that Gartner did not see Parr hit plaintiff in the tool shed. Thus, any notice defendant had of Parr's violent nature occurred as the events at the track took place. Although the witnesses did not give a specific timetable, the events at the track were characterized as occurring very quickly.

In addition to the briefness of the events, it was uncontradicted that Gartner did not see much of what occurred. He did not see Parr strike plaintiff in the tool shed. At the track he was turned away from plaintiff and Parr as he did his work. He did not see Parr grabbing and coming at plaintiff nor did he see plaintiff graze Parr's lip with the spike. Not until Parr raised the axe did Gartner see any trouble and Parr quickly dropped the axe at Gartner's request.

Although plaintiff claims Gartner did nothing to defuse the trouble between plaintiff and Parr, we are at a loss as to what Gartner could have done bearing in mind Gartner saw very little of a very brief occurrence. The one case that has considered the question of the duty of a supervisory employee in this situation has denied that a supervisory employee has a duty to anticipate and prevent the conduct of an employee, such as Parr, in this situation. *Atlantic Coast Line R. Co. v. Southwell* (1927), 275 U.S. 64, 48 S. Ct. 25, 72 L. Ed. 157.

Plaintiff relies on the decision in *Harrison v. Missouri Pacific R.R. Co.* (1963), 372 U.S. 248, 83 S. Ct. 690, 9 L. Ed. 2d 711. In that case plaintiff was assaulted by a fellow employee whom he accused of stealing a ballast fork. A jury awarded damages to plaintiff but the Illinois circuit court granted the railroad's motion for judgment notwithstanding the verdict. The appellate court affirmed, holding there was insufficient evidence that the railroad knew or should have known of the assailant's violent nature prior to the assault. (*Harrison v. Missouri Pac. R.R. Co.* (4th Dist. 1962), 35 Ill. App. 2d 66, 181 N.E.2d 737.) In a per curiam opinion, the United States Supreme Court found the evidence sufficient to sustain the jury verdict and reversed. The testimony established that when the assailant was assigned to plaintiff's crew, the roadmaster warned plaintiff about assailant, calling him a bad actor and a troublemaker. Plaintiff testified that he complained to the roadmaster several times about his assailant's misconduct prior to the assault. After plaintiff reported the assault, the roadmaster again said "I told you to watch out for him." The Supreme Court noted that the testimony was contradicted but that if believed by the jury it was sufficient evidence to support the railroad's notice of assailant's violent propensities.

We find the evidence of notice in *Harrison* quite different from the facts here. In *Harrison* the railroad's notice arose because plaintiff complained about the assailant several times and because the roadmaster knew of the assailant's vicious nature. Neither of those factors were present here.

Finding no negligence on the part of the defendant railroad, the trial court erred in denying defendant's motions for directed verdict and judgment notwithstanding the verdict. Accordingly, the judgment of the circuit court of Madison County is reversed.

Notes

1. "Knowledge is important only if, because of it, one can intelligently choose [one's] course of action." Restatement § 278 comment a. Thus, before a principal may be charged with an agent's knowledge or notice, the agent must have had *both* a reasonable time to communicate the information to the principal, Restatement § 278, and the principal must have had a reasonable opportunity to act on it. *Id.* comment a.

2. In the case of organizations with many agents or servants, a reasonable opportunity to communicate and act on information means that there must be sufficient time for information to filter through the organization and into the hands of the agents or servants acting on behalf of the principal (master). This rule is embodied in the Uniform Commercial Code's rules regarding the attribution of notice and knowledge:

> Notice, knowledge or a notice or notification received by an organization is effective for a particular transaction from the time when it is brought to the attention of the individual conducting the transaction, *and in any event from the time when it would have been brought to his attention if the organization had exercised due diligence.* An organization exercises due diligence if it maintains reasonable routines for communicating significant information to the person conducting the transaction *and* there is reasonable compliance with the routines. Due diligence does not require an individual acting for the organization to communicate the information unless such communication is part of his regular duties or unless he has reason to know of the transaction and that the transaction would be materially affected by the information.

U.C.C. § 1-201(27) (Official Text 1990) (emphasis added).

3. This is another context in which the rules regarding notification vary from those regarding knowledge and notice. Because notification is a legal act intended to be effective in and of itself, notification to an authorized or apparently authorized agent is effective *immediately*. As to the informational aspects of a notification (recall that receipt of a notification is also *notice*), notice is also effective immediately. Restatement § 270. However, where the principal is *required to act* on account of the notification, the principal is allowed reasonable time for the agent to *communicate* the fact of notification, as well as reasonable time to *act* on the notification. *Id.* comment a.

C. Adverse Agents

Federal Deposit Insurance Corporation v. Smith
328 Or. 420, 980 P.2d 141 (1999)

Before Carson, Chief Justice, and Gillette, Van Hoomissen, and Durham, Justices.

GILLETTE, J.

The questions presented in this case have been certified to us by the United States Court of Appeals for the Ninth Circuit under the Uniform Certification of Questions of Law Act, ORS 28.200 *et seq.*, and ORAP 12.20. The certified questions involve whether Oregon applies the doctrine of "adverse domination" in the context of a corporation suing its directors and officers and, if it does, what version of that doctrine applies. For the reasons that follow, we conclude that Oregon does apply the doctrine and that the "disinterested majority" version of the doctrine applies in this case.

We take the facts from the Ninth Circuit certification order:

> Family Federal Savings & Loan Association (Family Federal) was a federally insured thrift headquartered at Dallas, Oregon. On January 10, 1990, the Office of Thrift Supervision determined that Family Federal was insolvent. The Office, therefore, appointed the Resolution Trust Corporation [(RTC)] as receiver for Family Federal, and on that date, RTC purchased all of Family Federal's claims against its directors and officers. Over three years later, on September 8, 1993, RTC, as successor in interest to Family Federal, filed this action against Kenneth Smith, Richard Hoffman, Robert Bateman, William Dalton, Jack Darley, Stanley Hammer, and Robert Lorence. It alleged causes of action for negligence, breach of fiduciary duty, and breach of contract.
>
> In January of 1984, Smith, Dalton, Darley, Hammer and Lorence were members of the board of directors of Family Federal. Bateman became a member in 1984, after the death of another member. At all relevant times, they constituted the majority of the board of directors of Family Federal. Hoffman was * * * Family Federal's Loan Manager at all relevant times.
>
> In January of 1984, the Board of Directors approved the purchase of a $2,000,000 participation in a $31,000,000 loan to finance construc-

tion of a hotel, and by May of that year the directors and officers were aware of difficulties which had come to light; it then appeared that the loan had been ill advised.

In May of 1985, the directors agreed to fund $2,900,000 of time share loan paper, which involved time share units located at Indian Wells Resort. That also turned out to be a poor investment, which was criticized by federal examiners as early as April of 1986.

Stephen Way, who did not participate in those transactions, became a director in August of 1987. Before that, he had been an officer and had attended board meetings from at least November 1983 forward. Other officers also attended board meetings throughout that time.

F.D.I.C. v. Smith, 83 F.3d 1051, 1052 (9th Cir. 1996).

RTC's claims are based on defendants' approval of the multi-million dollar investments described above. RTC's complaint alleges negligence, breach of fiduciary duty, and breach of contract, but does not accuse defendants of acting in their own interests or allege fraud or intentional misconduct.

RTC is a federal entity that is asserting a claim against the officers and directors of Family Federal. It received the claim by assignment upon being appointed as receiver for Family Federal. When a federal entity attempts to assert a claim under such circumstances, the court must conduct a two-step analysis to determine what statute of limitations applies. First, the court must determine whether the applicable state limitations period expired before the assignment. If it expired, there is no claim to be assigned, and the action is barred as a matter of law. If a viable claim existed at the time of assignment, however, then the court must determine whether the applicable federal statute of limitations has expired.[2] The question of adverse domination is relevant to the first prong of the foregoing analysis, *viz.*, determining whether the state statute of limitations already had expired before the federal entity stepped in.

After RTC filed its action, defendants moved for summary judgment on the ground that RTC's claims were barred by Oregon's two-year statute of limitations contained in ORS 12.110(1).[3]

The district court denied defendants' motion, concluding that, in this case, Oregon would recognize the doctrine of "adverse domination" and would hold that, under that doctrine, accrual of the claims was delayed until RTC took control of Family Federal in 1990, making RTC's complaint timely under an applicable three-year federal statute of limitations. *Resolution Trust Corp. v. Smith*, 872 F.Supp. 805, 813-15, *amended* 879 F.Supp. 1059 (D.Or. 1995). The district court granted defendants' motion for an interlocutory appeal of that ruling.

---

2. When a federal entity becomes conservator of a financial institution, acquiring the assets of that institution, 12 USC § 1821(d)(14) of the Financial Institutions Reform, Recovery and Enforcement Act of 1989 provides that the entity will have three additional years from the date of conservatorship or accrual, whichever is later, in which to file suit on a tort claim and six additional years in which to file suit on a contract claim.

3. ORS 12.110(1) provides, in part: "An action * * * for any injury to the * * * rights of another, not arising on contract, and not especially enumerated in this chapter, shall be commenced within two years; provided that in an action at law based upon fraud or deceit, the limitation shall be deemed to commence only from the discovery of the fraud or deceit."

Because Oregon appellate courts have not previously decided the issue whether Oregon recognizes the doctrine of adverse domination, the Ninth Circuit certified the following two questions to this court:

(1) Under Oregon law[,] does the doctrine of adverse domination delay the running of the statute of limitations for causes of action based upon negligence? Does it do so for causes of action based upon breach of fiduciary duty? Does it do so for causes of action based upon breach of contract?

(2) If the doctrine of adverse domination does apply to any or all of the mentioned causes of action, what version is applied, the disinterested majority version or the single disinterested director version?

Smith, 83 F.3d at 1053.

Before turning to an analysis of Oregon law, some background information is helpful. The doctrine of adverse domination has gained currency in recent years in the context of litigation against directors and officers of insolvent financial institutions. The doctrine serves either to delay the accrual of a claim by a corporation against its directors and officers, or, in the alternative, to toll the running of the applicable statute of limitations. The doctrine is premised on the theory that it is impossible for the corporation to bring the action while it is controlled, or "dominated," by culpable officers and directors. Courts applying the doctrine of adverse domination have reasoned that corporations act only through their officers and directors, and those officers and directors cannot be expected to sue themselves or to initiate any action contrary to their own interests.[4] *See, e.g., Hecht v. Resolution Trust,* 333 Md. 324, 340, 635 A.2d 394, 402 (Md 1994) (explaining the rationale behind the doctrine); *Federal Sav. and Loan Ins. Corp. v. Williams,* 599 F.Supp. 1184, 1194 (D.Md. 1984) (same); *Federal Deposit Ins. Corp. v. Bird,* 516 F.Supp. 647, 651 (D.P.R. 1981) (same). Similarly, culpable corporate officers and directors cannot be expected to disclose their wrongful conduct to the corporation.

Courts that apply the doctrine of adverse domination have developed two versions of the doctrine, the "disinterested majority" version and the "single disinterested director" version. The versions differ with respect to the degree of control or domination considered necessary to delay accrual of a claim or to toll the otherwise applicable statute of limitations. Under the disinterested majority version, a plaintiff benefits from a presumption that the cause of action does not accrue or the statute of limitations does not run so long as the culpable directors remain in the majority, *i.e.,* until the corporation has a disinterested majority of nonculpable directors. *See, e.g., Resolution Trust Corp. v. Scaletty,* 257 Kan. 348, 351-52, 891 P.2d 1110, 1113 (Kan 1995) (explaining the two versions of

---

4. A minority of courts that have considered this issue have declined to recognize the doctrine of adverse domination, concluding that the doctrine is inconsistent with applicable state law tolling doctrines and policies of strictly construing statutes of limitations. *See, e.g., Resolution Trust Corp. v. Armbruster,* 52 F.3d 748, 752 (8th Cir. 1995) (concluding that Arkansas courts do not recognize the doctrine of adverse domination); *Resolution Trust Corp. v. Artley,* 28 F.3d 1099, 1102 (11th Cir. 1994) (finding the doctrine inapplicable under Georgia law); *F.D.I.C. v. Cocke,* 7 F.3d 396, 402-03 (4th Cir. 1993) (declining, under Virginia law, to apply the doctrine to the case at issue but noting that Virginia recognizes the tolling doctrine of equitable estoppel in cases involving intentional concealment).

the doctrine); *Williams, 599 F.Supp.* at 1193-94 (describing the "disinterested majority" version). Defendants can rebut that presumption with evidence that someone other than the wrongdoing directors had knowledge of the basis for the cause of action, combined with the ability and the motivation to bring an action. *Resolution Trust Corp. v. Grant,* 901 P.2d 807, 816 (Okl. 1995).

In contrast, under the single disinterested director version of the doctrine, statutes of limitations are tolled only so long as there is no director with knowledge of facts giving rise to possible liability who could have induced the corporation to bring an action. Under that version, a plaintiff has the burden of showing that the culpable directors had full, complete, and exclusive control of the corporation, and must negate the possibility that an informed director could have induced the corporation to sue. *Scaletty,* 257 Kan. at 352, 891 P.2d at 1113; *see also Farmers & Merchants Nat. Bank v. Bryan,* 257 Kan at 352, 902 F.2d 1520, 1523 (10th Cir1990) (" '[O]nce the facts giving rise to possible liability are known, the plaintiff must effectively negate the possibility that an informed director could have induced the corporation to sue.' ") (*quoting International Rys. of Cent. Am. v. United Fruit Co.,* 373 F.2d 408, 414 (2d Cir. 1967)).

With that background in mind, we turn now to the first certified question, which we repeat here for convenience:

> Under Oregon law does the doctrine of adverse domination delay the running of the statute of limitations for causes of action based upon negligence? Does it do so for causes of action based upon breach of fiduciary duty? Does it do so for causes of action based upon breach of contract?

We begin our analysis with the primary issue, *viz.,* whether Oregon recognizes the doctrine of adverse domination. In considering that question, the federal district court treated adverse domination as a corollary to Oregon's "discovery" rule, a rule of interpretation of statutes of limitation that has the effect of tolling the commencement of such statutes under certain circumstances.[5] The district court concluded that Oregon would adopt the adverse domination doctrine and applied the doctrine in the context of RTC's

Like the district court, we also use the discovery rule as a starting point in our analysis. In general terms, a cause of action does not accrue under the discovery rule until the claim has been discovered or, in the exercise of reasonable care, should have been discovered. *Gaston v. Parsons,* 318 Or. 247, 256, 864 P.2d 1319 (1994). This court explained in *Gaston,* in the context of a medical negligence claim, that, under the discovery rule, a plaintiff must have a reasonable opportunity to become aware of the following three elements before the statute of limitations will begin to run: (1) harm; (2) causation; and (3) tortious conduct. 318 Or. at 255-56, 864 P.2d 1319. *See also Doe v. American Red Cross,* 322 Or. 502, 513, 910 P.2d 364 (1996) (identifying tortious conduct as the third element of the discovery rule in the context of ORS 12.110(1)). The *Gaston* court explained that

---

5. Other courts that have considered this issue have treated the matter similarly. *See, e.g., Resolution Trust Corp. v. Chapman,* 895 F.Supp. 1072, 1078 (C.D.Ill. 1995) ("In sum, the adverse domination doctrine is simply a common sense application of the discovery rule to a corporate plaintiff.").

the statute of limitations begins to run when the plaintiff knows or in the exercise of reasonable care should have known facts which would make a reasonable person aware of a substantial possibility that each of the three elements * * * exists.

318 Or. at 256.

Gaston and *Doe* concern an *individual's* knowledge or discovery that he or she may have a claim. If the principles discussed in those cases also pertain to the corporate context, they do so by analogy. To complete the analogy, then, we must determine when, under Oregon law, a corporation can be deemed to "know" that it has a claim.

A potential corporate plaintiff is not a sentient being and, therefore, cannot "know," be aware of, or discover anything, except through the agency of its officers, directors, and employees. A corporation generally is charged with knowledge of facts that its agents learn within the scope of their employment. However, while it is appropriate to impute knowledge of an agent to its principal in order to protect innocent third parties, that rule should not be used to shield agents whose wrongful conduct harms their own principal, where the action is one brought by the principal against the agent.

Oregon courts long have recognized such an "adverse interest" exception. As the court stated in *Saratoga Inv. Co. v. Kern,* 76 Or. 243, 254, 148 P. 1125 (1915), a corporation is charged with knowledge of what its agent knows, unless "the agent's *relations to the subject matter are so adverse as to practically destroy the relationship,* as when the agent is acting in his own interest and adversely to that of his principal, or is secretly engaged in attempting to accomplish a fraud which would be defeated by a disclosure to his principal." (Emphasis added.) *See also* Restatement, Agency, § 279 (1958) ("The principal is not affected by the knowledge of an agent as to matters involved in a transaction in which the agent deals with the principal * * * as * * * an adverse party.").

Defendants argue that a director's good faith actions in approving a loan, with the belief that he or she is acting in the best interests of the bank, cannot reasonably be characterized as being "so adverse as to practically destroy the relationship." Rather, according to defendants, a director's acts must constitute intentional misconduct, self-dealing, or fraud in order to rise to that level. We do not believe that the principle variously described in *Saratoga* and the *Restatement* is (or should be) so limited.

The "subject matter" to be considered when evaluating the degree of the director's adverse interest is the decision whether to make a claim, not the underlying acts that gave rise to that claim. The culpable directors' interest in bringing a claim against themselves certainly is adverse to that of the corporation. In *Saratoga* terms, at least as to that issue, the agent/principal relationship is nonexistent. Of course, in a corporate mismanagement case, the wrongdoers, who are running the corporation, necessarily possess personal knowledge of the facts that would support a claim against them. Realistically, however, the corporation has neither meaningful knowledge nor the ability to act on such knowledge, until the wrongdoing directors and officers no longer control it. We conclude that knowledge of the wrongdoing directors or officers of facts that would give rise to legal liability to the corporation on the part of those directors or officers will not be imputed to the corporation so long as those directors or officers control the corporation.[6]

Based on the foregoing, we hold that Oregon recognizes the adverse domination doctrine, which is analogous to Oregon's discovery rule in the context of a claim by a corporation against its former directors and officers for their alleged mismanagement of corporate affairs. The question remains whether this court would apply that doctrine to claims of the kind asserted here, *viz.*, negligence, breach of fiduciary duty, and breach of contract.

This court has applied the discovery rule to negligence actions subject to the statutes of limitations expressed at ORS 12.110(1) and ORS 12.010. By extension, the doctrine of adverse domination also would apply to claims governed by those statutes, *i.e.*, negligence actions. Actions for breach of fiduciary duty are governed, for limitations purposes, by the same limitations provision that applies to negligence actions, *viz.*, ORS 12.110(1). Although this court has not applied the discovery rule specifically in that context, we see no reason to treat the matter differently, especially given the close relationships ordinarily involved and the degree of trust extended to the fiduciary. Accordingly, we also accept the doctrine of adverse domination in that context.

With respect to whether the doctrine of adverse domination applies in the context of a breach of contract action, it does not appear from the facts reported in the Ninth Circuit's certification order, quoted [above], that the issue is presented by this case. RTC succeeded to First Family's assets within six years of the date of the earliest loan that RTC now claims was inappropriate. Oregon's statute of limitations for contract actions is six years. ORS 12.080(1). Thus, the statute had not run on any of RTC's contract claims and RTC had six more years under 12 USC § 1821(d)(14) to bring its contract claims. It has done so. Because the issue proffered by the Ninth Circuit is not presented as to RTC's breach of contract claims, we do not answer it.

We turn to the second certified question:

If the doctrine of adverse domination does apply to any or all of the mentioned causes of action, what version is applied, the disinterested majority version or the single disinterested director version?

As noted, the "disinterested majority" version of the adverse domination doctrine creates a rebuttable presumption that a corporation does not have a full and fair opportunity to bring claims against its directors during the time that culpable directors constitute a majority of the board. Defendants may overcome that presumption by showing that some person or group had both sufficient knowledge and power to bring an action against the majority of the board. The single disinterested director version, by contrast, places the burden on the corporate plaintiff to show that no one was in a position to bring an action on behalf of the corporation.

We conclude that the "disinterested majority" version of the doctrine more closely mirrors human nature. Because a board composed of a majority of culpable directors will rarely, if ever, facilitate the assertion of claims against its mem-

---

6. We address the issue of when a corporation is deemed to be "controlled" by those individuals in connection with our response to the Ninth Circuit's second question.

bers, it is appropriate that those directors bear the burden of proving otherwise. Other courts reaching this conclusion have reasoned similarly:

> As long as the majority of the board of directors are culpable they may continue to operate the association and control it in an effort to prevent action from being taken against them. While they retain control they can dominate the non-culpable directors and control the most likely sources of information and funding necessary to pursue the rights of the association. As a result, it may be extremely difficult, if not impossible, for the corporation to discover and pursue its rights while the wrongdoers retain control.

Federal Sav. and Loan Ins. Corp. v. Williams, 599 F.Supp. 1184, 1193-94 n. 12 (D.Md. 1984). *See also, e.g., Resolution Trust Corp. v. Grant,* 901 P.2d 807, 818 (Okl. 1995); *Hecht v. Resolution Trust,* 333 Md. 324, 349-51, 635 A.2d 394, 407-08 (Md 1994) (both to the same effect).

Defendants argue that the foregoing approach does not comport with the currently accepted approach to the discovery rule. According to defendants, because

> Oregon places the burden on the plaintiff to submit facts showing why initiation of the action was delayed based on the discovery rule[,] * * * it follows that a plaintiff trying to delay the statute of limitations on adverse domination grounds should likewise bear the burden to plead and prove the reason for delay.

Defendants conclude that only the single disinterested director version of the adverse domination doctrine follows that principle. That conclusion, however, is not compelled by defendants' premise: A plaintiff still would be required to plead and prove facts showing that it was adversely dominated, *i.e.,* that the board was composed of a majority of culpable directors, under the disinterested majority version of the adverse domination doctrine.

We conclude that Oregon applies the doctrine of adverse domination to causes of action based on negligence and breach of fiduciary duty. We decline to address whether the doctrine of adverse domination applies to causes of action based on breach of contract. We further conclude that Oregon applies the disinterested majority version of the doctrine in contexts in which it is applicable.

Certified questions answered.

Notes

1. In corporations, authority to manage the corporation is vested in the board of directors as a body; individual directors have no authority to act on behalf of the corporation. In partnerships, each partner has equal rights in the management or conduct of partnership business. UPA §§ 18(e), (f); RUPA §§ 401(f), (j). Should the adverse domination doctrine apply to partnerships? If it does apply, should the disinterested majority or the single disinterested partner version apply?

2. The principal case states that the presumption raised by the adverse domination doctrine can be overcome by showing that "some person or group had both sufficient knowledge and power to bring an action against the majority of the board." Suppose that a shareholder learns of the directors' misconduct.

Whether that is sufficient to overcome the presumption depends on whether a shareholder has power to bring a "derivative suit" in the right of the corporation.

As a general rule, shareholders must defer to the power of the board of directors to bring a derivative suit, by demanding that the board bring suit on the corporation's behalf. *Aronson v. Lewis*, 473 A.2d 805 (Del. 1984). Derivative suits are permitted only where the board of directors is incapable of discharging its responsibility to manage the suit. Under Delaware law, where a majority of the board is personally interested in the law suit, a shareholder may bring a derivative suit without first demanding that the board do so. *Aronson v. Lewis*, 473 A.2d at 805.

Under the Revised Model Business Corporation Act, unless the corporation is threatened with irreparable harm, shareholders must demand that the board act, and wait ninety days before bringing a derivative suit. RMBCA § 7.42. Whether the shareholder may thereafter bring suit depends on whether an independent, disinterested, body—either a majority of the board, a committee, or a court-appointed panel—decided, after a reasonable investigation, that a suit was not in the best interests of the corporation. RMBCA § 7.44.

3. The adverse agent is another context in which the rules regarding notification differ from those regarding knowledge and notice. Notification by a third person given to an agent acting adversely to the principal is effective unless the third person has notice the agent is acting adversely. Restatement § 271. Presumably, the basis for the difference in treatment is that, in the case of notification, the third person is reasonably relying on the authority or apparent authority of the agent to act for the principal in receiving the notification.

Lanchile Airlines v. Connecticut General Life Ins.

759 F. Supp. 811 (S.D. Fla. 1991)

MORENO, District Judge.

THIS MATTER is before the Court on defendant's, Connecticut General Life Insurance Company of North America ("CIGNA"), Motion for Summary Judgment.

In its most simplistic form, this case centers on the conduct of the two principals and their agents in the negotiation and performance of a contract for insurance. Plaintiff LanChile was represented by its agent, defendant Santiago Rodriguez. Defendant CIGNA was represented by its agent, defendant Michael Molina. Unbeknownst to the principals, Rodriguez and Molina were partners in defendants S & M Insurance Consultants, Inc.

Together, defendants Rodriguez and Molina arranged for CIGNA to provide group health insurance benefits to LanChile. LanChile paid for, and received, the insurance that it sought, at the price that it agreed upon, for over four years. LanChile made these payments to S & M, rather than directly to CIGNA.

The crux of this action concerns certain administrative/consulting fees received by S & M. LanChile asserts that the fee arrangement was undisclosed and that it was not until March 1989, over four years after the inception of the contract, that plaintiff allegedly discovered that the premiums it paid for health insurance included a service fee for S & M. CIGNA counters that LanChile was well aware, or at least should have been, of the fee arrangement at the time of the contract formation. The total amount paid as a fee to S & M over the four year period is approximately $279,000.

Beginning in March 1983, LanChile's insurance broker or agent-of-record for group health insurance was Santiago Rodriguez. As LanChile's agent, Rodriguez was charged with finding health insurance coverage for LanChile's employees, at a level of benefits and premium costs acceptable to LanChile.

In late 1983, LanChile, which was then insured by CIGNA, was informed that its insurance premiums would increase by approximately 46 percent for 1984. Juan Matus, LanChile's Head of Administration and Finance for North America, was responsible for obtaining group health insurance for LanChile's employees. Guillermo Goldberg, then General Manager for North America, was responsible for overseeing Mr. Matus, including the administration of LanChile's employee group health insurance. Goldberg and Matus instructed Rodriguez to procure comparable insurance coverage for LanChile's employees at a lower cost to LanChile than the projected 46 percent increase.

In 1983, Michael Molina became CIGNA's group insurance representative for LanChile. Molina, CIGNA's agent, and Rodriguez, LanChile's agent, were also principals and owners of S & M Insurance Consultants, Inc. In late 1983, Molina and Rodriguez proposed to LanChile an insurance plan that not only avoided the scheduled 46% increase in CIGNA's insurance premiums for 1984, but provided approximately a 5% decrease in LanChile's overall cost of insurance.

The plan provided for basic hospitalization coverage to be provided by Empire Blue Cross and Blue Shield of New York with a wraparound major medical plan underwritten by CIGNA. From January 1984 through March 1988, LanChile timely made all premium payments and enjoyed the insurance coverage they were entitled to pursuant to the Blue Cross and CIGNA insurance policies.

The definitive question in this lawsuit is which party must bear the financial responsibility for the fraudulent acts of an agent. While the general issue has been visited by numerous courts over the years, the Court has found little guidance for the case at bar which contains equally culpable agents representing both principals. CIGNA asks this Court to determine that, as a matter of law, it is less responsible for the acts of its agent than is LanChile for the same acts of its agent. The Court finds that this ultimate conclusion can only be reached upon resolution of numerous factual issues which are hotly contested. Such issues are, therefore, questions for the jury.

The [issue] for determination by the Court [is] whether the knowledge of defendant Rodriguez, as the agent for plaintiff LanChile, can be attributed to LanChile.

CIGNA asserts that each of LanChile's claims for relief necessarily relies on LanChile's contention that it was not informed of the administrative/consulting fees being charged by S & M. CIGNA alleges that LanChile's claims fail because it had actual, constructive and imputed knowledge of the fees it was paying to S & M for its services.

LanChile correctly notes that a court must not decide any factual issues it finds in the record. It is well-settled that under Florida law, a question of agency is reserved to the trier of fact when resolution of the issue depends on the inferences to be drawn from the facts adduced.

It is the most elementary hornbook law that this Court cannot resolve a factual dispute upon a motion for summary judgment as to whether LanChile had actual or constructive knowledge that it was paying S & M a fee for procuring insurance. Actual or constructive knowledge is a factual question; the existence or non-existence of this knowledge is the pivotal fact around which this case turns. Not so clear, however, is the issue of whether Rodriguez' knowledge may be imputed to LanChile.

Circumstances where knowledge may be imputed typically involve questions of law rather than fact. The general rule is that whatever knowledge an agent acquires within the scope of his authority is imputed to his principal.

However, knowledge and misconduct of an agent will not be imputed to a principal if an agent is "secretly acting adversely to the principal and entirely for his own or another's purposes." Restatement (Second) of Agency, § 282 (1958). The law does not then presume that the wrongdoer would perform his usual duty of disclosing all material facts regarding his action if such disclosure would reveal his fraud. Restatement, § 282(1).

The Restatement also provides that a principal will be held to the knowledge of an agent who acts adversely to the principal if: the agent enters into negotiations within the scope of his powers and the person with whom he deals reasonably believes him to be authorized to conduct the transaction; or, before he has changed his position, the principal knowingly retains a benefit through the act of the agent which otherwise he would not have received. Restatement, § 282(2)(b) and (c).

The threshold determination, then, is whether the agent was "acting adversely." The Restatement counsels that the mere fact that the agent's primary interests are not coincident with those of the principal does not prevent the latter from being affected by the knowledge of the agent if the agent is acting for the principal's interests. Restatement, § 282, comment c. This comment however does not offer sufficient guidance for the Court to make a legal determination as to whether Rodriguez was secretly acting adversely to LanChile and entirely for his own or S & M's purposes.

The Court is unable to determine as a matter of law, that Rodriguez' conduct in charging LanChile an amount that it had agreed to pay for insurance, but was in excess of the actual cost of the insurance, is adverse to LanChile. Similarly, the Court is not convinced that Rodriguez was acting entirely for his own or S & M's purposes. While Rodriguez retained a portion of the premiums paid by LanChile as an undisclosed fee, he did arrange the health insurance desired and received by LanChile. The Court concludes that these issues are factual determinations that can only be made by the jury.

In accordance with the foregoing, CIGNA's Motion for Summary Judgment is DENIED.

Notes

1. *Center v. Hampton Affiliates, Inc.,* 66 N.Y.2d 782, 497 N.Y.S.2d 898, 488 N.E.2d 828 (1985), involved the question of whether a corporation that had purchased certain shares of stock should be charged with the knowledge of its purchasing agent that the transfer to the corporation violated the rights of a third person:

[The adverse agent] exception provides that when an agent is engaged in a scheme to defraud his principal, either for his own benefit or that of a third person, the presumption that knowledge held by the agent was disclosed to the principal fails because he cannot be presumed to have disclosed that which would expose and defeat his fraudulent purpose (Restatement [Second] of Agency § 282 [1]). To come within the exception, the agent must have totally abandoned his principal's interests and be acting entirely for his own or another's purposes. It cannot be invoked merely because he has a conflict of interest or because he is not acting primarily for his principal (*see* Restatement [Second] of Agency § 282[1] comment c). Defendants' moving papers contain only conclusory allegations that [the agent] was seriously conflicted throughout these transactions and tried to defraud the corporation. These allegations do not establish sufficient adversity as a matter of law to negate imputed knowledge to the corporation at the time it took delivery of the shares.

2. Often an agent will act on behalf of more than one principal at the same time. For example, in *Manley v. Ticor Title Insurance Co.*, 168 Ariz. 568, 816 P.2d 225 (1991), an escrow agent in a real estate transaction knew that a lien on the property had not been discharged. The court held that even though the escrow agent was a "dual agent" acting on behalf of both the buyer and the seller, the escrow agent was not an "adverse agent," and attributed the escrow agent's knowledge to the buyers.

3. One of the common exceptions to the adverse agent exception is the "sole actor doctrine." Restatement sections 282(2)(b) & (c), referred to in *LanChile Airlines v. Connecticut General Life Ins.*, are the Restatement's formulation of the sole actor doctrine:

> The principal is affected by the knowledge of an agent who acts adversely to the principal:
>
> *   *   *
>
> (b) if the agent enters into negotiations within the scope of [the agent's] powers and the person with whom he reasonably believes [the agent] to be authorized to conduct the transaction; or
>
> (c) if, before [the principal] has changed position, the principal knowingly retains a benefit through the act of the agent which otherwise [the principal] would not have received.

The basis of the sole actor doctrine, or at least that part embodied in Restatement section 282(2)(c), is estoppel. The insureds in *LanChile Airlines* should not be permitted to keep (retain) the benefit of Rodriguez's conduct (coverage under the insurance policy) while at the same time avoiding responsibility for Rodriguez's knowledge at the time the insurance policy was procured. *See* Restatement § 282 comment h; *Mantanuska Valley Bank v. Arnold*, 116 F. Supp. 32 (D. Alaska 1953). In this respect, the sole actor doctrine is only a variant of the rule against partial ratifications (to be discussed in chapter 4).

Restatement section 282(2)(b), which charges the principal with the knowledge of a (sole) agent arising out of a transaction in which the agent deals with an innocent third party within the scope of the agent's powers to bind the princi-

418 AGENCY, PARTNERSHIPS AND LIMITED LIABILITY COMPANIES

pal, involves a somewhat different proposition. Consider, for example, illustration 7 to Restatement section 282:

> A is authorized by P to sell P's horse and to represent it as it is. A, intending to keep the proceeds from the sale and intending also to defraud the purchaser, sells the horse to T, representing the horse to be sound, although knowing the horse to be unsound. A absconds with the proceeds. P is bound by A's knowledge that the horse is unsound.

Clearly P has not retained the benefits of A's misrepresentation. If P is to be liable for the misrepresentation, it must be on the basis that A had *power to bind* P to the misrepresentation, either on the basis of apparent authority or because T reasonably believed the agent had authority to make the representation. *See* Restatement § 282 comment f.

State Farm Fire & Casualty Co. v. Sevier
272 Or. 278, 537 P.2d 88 (1975)

TONGUE, Justice.

This is an action by an insurance company for a declaratory judgment that it had "validly rescinded" a policy of automobile liability insurance because of misrepresentations by the insured in his application for the policy. The named defendants included not only the insured, but also the personal representative of a person killed in a subsequent accident with the insured before the policy was rescinded. The case was tried before the court, without a jury. Plaintiff appeals from an adverse judgment.

From 1961 to 1970 Kenneth Sevier had been at the Veterans Administration "Domiciliary" hospital in White City, near Medford, except for several months in California and occasional furloughs to his original home in Arkansas. During that entire period he had no Oregon driver's license, but he did have a California driver's license. In 1969 he was arrested and convicted in Oregon for driving under the influence of intoxicating liquor.

In December 1969 he returned to his "home town" in Arkansas. On May 29, 1970, having purchased an automobile, he went to see Jack Henderson, one of plaintiff's insurance agents. Henderson filled out an application for a policy of automobile insurance which included a question asking whether, during the past five years, the applicant had been convicted for traffic violations and a question asking whether his license to drive was ever suspended, revoked or refused.

Sevier testified that Henderson did not ask him those two questions. He also testified that he had known Henderson "for a long time" and that he told Henderson that he had been picked up and convicted for drunken driving in Oregon. He also testified that Henderson said "to Hell with it, maybe they'll never find it out"; that he did not know that Henderson put a "no" answer in the "box" for that question; and that he signed the application as filled out by Henderson.

Henderson testified that he asked both questions. He also admitted that Sevier told him that he had been stopped by the police for drinking and driving and given a "balloon" or "breathalyzer" test, but said that he had not been convicted for DUIL.

That application for insurance was then sent to plaintiff's office in Monroe, Louisiana, for consideration by its underwriting department. The application showed "no" answers to both questions and made no reference to the 1969 DUIL arrest and conviction in Oregon.

Plaintiff's underwriting department then had a "routine, general" investigation of Sevier made by the Retail Credit Company. That investigation included contacts at White City, apparently because his application indicated "physical or mental defects" or limitations and because of further information from Henderson that Sevier had been at the Veterans "Domiciliary" in White City for nine years. No request was made, however, for a "motor vehicle record check," as would have been done by Retail Credit as part of its investigation upon request.

Plaintiff's witness testified that if plaintiff had been informed by its agent Henderson that Sevier had been stopped for drinking and driving and had been required to take a test (as admitted by Henderson), "there is a good chance" that a motor vehicle check would have been requested. The same witness testified that if plaintiff had been informed by Henderson that Sevier had been convicted of DUIL it would not have issued the policy to Sevier.

In any event plaintiff issued a policy of automobile liability insurance to Sevier in Arkansas for a period of six months, effective July 7, 1970.

In September 1970 Sevier returned to White City. He was told by Henderson to re-apply for a policy in Oregon. According to plaintiff's witnesses, when a policyholder moves from another state to Oregon, a new application is then filled out and submitted to plaintiff's underwriting department, which then also has and reviews a file from the other state including the original application.

In November 1970, Sevier went to the office of one of plaintiff's agents in Medford, who filled out a new application. That agent considered his Arkansas policy to be "a policy that was in force" and that "all I was doing was taking a transfer on the policy that was already in force."

That application was then signed by Sevier and sent to plaintiff's Oregon underwriting department and a new policy was issued for an additional six months, effective January 7, 1971. According to plaintiff's witnesses, that policy was issued based on the new application and on the information in the "Arkansas file" with no additional investigation. Plaintiff's witnesses also testified, however, that if Henderson, the original agent, had made a notation on the file that Sevier had been stopped in Oregon for drinking they would have made a further investigation and that if it had appeared that Sevier had been convicted of DUIL the new policy would not have been issued and the original policy would have been rescinded.

On March 15, 1971, Sevier was involved in the accident in which Mr. Sutton was killed and his wife injured. Within approximately two weeks after the accident, plaintiff's Oregon underwriting department superintendent learned from its claims department that there was a "total loss," with "drinking involved," and of the previous DUIL conviction. On May 7, 1971, plaintiff called the Oregon Department of Motor Vehicles by telephone to confirm that conviction.

On July 7, 1971, more than three months after learning in late March from its claims department of Sevier's DUIL conviction of 1969 and more than one year after its agent Henderson was informed of that fact by Sevier, plaintiff sent a letter to Sevier enclosing a check for the amount of all premiums paid by him in both Arkansas and Oregon and rescinding the policy. The tender of that check was refused by Sevier.

On August 10, 1971, plaintiff filed a complaint in this action, alleging that the policy was issued in reliance upon misrepresentations by Sevier and seeking a declaratory judgment that it had "validly rescinded" the policy and that plaintiff had no liability under it for the death of Mr. Sutton or the injury to his wife. Defendants' answer to that complaint alleges, as an affirmative defense, that "plaintiff was negligent in failing to investigate the insured and therefore is estopped to rescind the policy because of alleged misrepresentations."

The trial court found that at the time of his original application the insured told plaintiff's agent in Arkansas that "he had lived in Oregon the previous nine years"; that "he had been charged for driving and drinking and had taken some type of test"; and that he had a "drinking conviction." The court found further that the plaintiff was negligent in that its agent "failed to note the information given to him by Sevier on the application concerning Sevier's being stopped for a drinking and driving charge"; in that it failed "to request a motor vehicle check in Oregon at the time of the Arkansas application, which would have disclosed that Sevier had been convicted" of DUIL; and in that it renewed "the policy in Oregon, relying upon its Arkansas application where there had been no motor vehicle check."

Based upon these findings the trial court concluded that "plaintiff had a duty to the public to make a reasonable investigation of the insurability of Sevier within a reasonable time after the issuance of the policy," and that its failure "to make such reasonable investigation" prohibits it "from rescinding the Sevier policy as to the claims of" the other defendants. As authority for that holding the trial court cited the decision by the California Supreme Court in *Barrera v. State Farm Mutual Automobile Ins. Co.,* 71 Cal. 2d 659, 456 P.2d 674 (1969). In *Barrera* it was held, under somewhat similar facts, that an automobile insurance company has a duty to the public to make a reasonable investigation within a reasonable time after the issuance of a policy and that it cannot thereafter rescind a policy so as to deny its coverage to the claim of an injured person.

Plaintiff's primary contention on this appeal is that in Oregon the rights of an injured person are no greater than the rights of the insured, with the result that the failure of an insurance company to make a motor vehicle check or other investigation of the insured does not take away its right to rescind a policy for false representations by an insured "as to the claims" of an injured person, despite the holding to the contrary by the California court in *Barrera.*

Plaintiff also contends, in response to a request by this court for supplemental briefs, that the decision of the trial court in this case cannot properly be affirmed by application of the usual rule of contract law that a party to a contract who has knowledge of facts constituting grounds for rescission must do so promptly or lose the right to rescind. The reason why that rule does not apply in this case, according to the plaintiff, is that the knowledge of its agent that Sevier had been convicted of DUIL was not imputed to it by reason of collusion between Sevier and his agent, in that Sevier knew that the answers contained in the application for the policy were false and participated in the fraud.

The general rules of contract and agency law are well established to the effect that notice to an agent is notice to his principal; that a party who has notice of grounds for the rescission of a contract and who elects to rescind it must do so promptly or lose his right to rescind.

Consistent with these established rules, it has been held by other courts that an insurance company which has knowledge through one of its agents of the falsity of facts stated in an application for insurance and which nevertheless issues an insurance policy is either "estopped" from rescinding the policy based upon the alleged misrepresentation of such facts or cannot then establish that it acted in reliance upon such misrepresentations, as necessary for the rescission of a contract for misrepresentation.

In this case plaintiff, through its agent Henderson, acquired knowledge of the fact that Sevier had at least been stopped by the police for drinking and driving and had been given a "balloon" or "breathalyzer" test. Indeed, the trial court found that plaintiff's agent had knowledge of the fact that Sevier had been convicted for DUIL. As a corporation, plaintiff could act only through its agents and employees and once it acquired knowledge of that fact through one of its agents or employees plaintiff was chargeable with continued knowledge of that fact, regardless of whether or not its agent Henderson failed to make a written record of that fact or to convey that information to other agents or employees of the plaintiff.

It follows, in our opinion, that at the time that both the Arkansas policy and the Oregon "renewal" policy was issued plaintiff had knowledge of facts which constituted sufficient grounds for the rescission of both policies. It also follows, in our opinion, that if plaintiff desired to elect to rescind the Oregon policy it was required to do so promptly, and that in this case plaintiff did not undertake to rescind promptly, but did not do so until July 7, 1971, the date on which the Oregon policy expired by its terms. We hold that it was then too late to do so.

Because we decide this case upon these grounds we need not consider and decide the questions whether plaintiff, as an automobile liability insurance company, had a duty to the public, under the facts and circumstances of this case, to make a reasonable investigation of Sevier before it issued to him a policy of automobile liability insurance and whether the plaintiff was negligent, under the facts and circumstances of this case, in that it failed to make such an investigation.

For the same reasons, we need not decide whether to adopt the rule adopted by the California Supreme Court in *Barrera* as apparently adopted by the trial court as the basis for its decision and as strongly urged by the defendants on this appeal.

Plaintiff vigorously contends that the knowledge of its agent of Sevier's DUIL conviction was not imputed to it because of alleged collusion between its agent and Sevier to withhold knowledge of that fact from it.

Plaintiff's claim of collusion is based upon testimony that Sevier was given an opportunity to read the application before signing it and knew that the answers in the application as filled in by plaintiff's agent were false and upon the further testimony that, according to Sevier, when he told plaintiff's agent of his DUIL conviction the agent said "to Hell with it, maybe they'll never find it out."

The evidence was conflicting on both of these points. Plaintiff's agent denied that he said "to Hell with it, maybe they'll never find out." He also testified that he was not sure whether or not Sevier read the application before signing it. At the time of his deposition Sevier said that he knew that the agent wrote down false answers in the application before he signed it, but on trial he testified that he did not know what answers the agent wrote down.

[W]e hold that for the purposes of this case the knowledge of plaintiff's agent that Sevier had been convicted of DUIL was imputed to the plaintiff.

There may be good reasons why, in litigation between an insurance company and an insured who has acted in collusion with an agent of the company in concealing facts from it, there should be an exception to the general rule that knowledge to the agent of the company is to be imputed to it. The reason for that result in such cases is not so much that the knowledge of the agent was not imputed to the principal, but that a participant in a fraud should not be permitted to profit from his own fraud. Such reasons, however, have no proper application in litigation between an automobile insurance company and an innocent person who was injured by the negligence of the insured. The cases cited by plaintiff, all from other jurisdictions, either involve litigation between the insurer and insured or do not discuss the question whether a different rule should apply in cases involving innocent third parties.

The rule that knowledge of an agent is to be imputed to his principal, regardless of actual knowledge by the principal, is a rule based upon considerations of public policy to the effect that one who selects an agent and delegates authority to him should incur the risks of the agent's infidelity or want of diligence rather than innocent third persons. Those reasons of public policy are not present in cases involving litigation between a principal and a third party who has acted in collusion with the agent. When, however, as in this case, the injured party is one who did not act in collusion with the agent, those same reasons of public policy are present.

A rule in automobile insurance cases under which knowledge of an agent is imputed to his principal in cases involving third persons injured in automobile accidents, despite possible collusion between the insured and the insurance agent, would not encourage fraud, as suggested by the plaintiff. On the contrary, it provides no inducement for the insured to enter into a fraudulent scheme with the agent of the insurance company for the reason that if collusion is proven the insurer, after satisfying the injured person's claim, may prosecute a cause of action against the insured for fraud or, in an action brought by the insured, defend on the ground of collusion. Instead, this rule should encourage the insurer to select and to supervise its agents with greater care.

For these reasons we hold that when Sevier told plaintiff's agent of his DUIL conviction, knowledge of that fact was imputed to the plaintiff insurance company for the purposes of this case.

For all of the reasons stated above, and finding no error, we affirm the judgment of the trial court.

O'CONNELL, Chief Justice ([with Denecke and Holman, JJ.], dissenting).

The majority holds that an injured third party may recover on a policy of insurance even though the insured would not be allowed to enforce the policy. In so doing, it introduces much confusion into the law of agency and, although purporting to avoid the question, effectively adopts the reasoning and effect in *Bar-*

rera which rejects the fundamental principles of the law of contract. The opinion of the majority is not supported either by logic or any of our prior cases on the subject.

The point the majority fails to note is that the rights of one injured through the negligence of the insured are derivative of the rights of the insured. The third party, however innocent, has no right to recover from the insurer unless there is a duty to pay the losses of the insured growing out of a valid contract of insurance or a duty to the public "at large." Since the majority does not deem it necessary to follow *Barrera* in recognizing such a duty to the public, it must explain how the third party may recover on a contract of insurance to which it is not a party or an intended beneficiary and which is rendered voidable as to the insured through his misrepresentations of a material fact. This the majority does not do.

It is clear that plaintiff is entitled to rescind the contract as to Sevier, its insured. Defendants contend that Henderson's knowledge, which was admittedly not transmitted to plaintiff's underwriters, should be imputed to plaintiff. The general rule of imputation of knowledge or notice is well settled:

> The corporation is affected or charged with knowledge of all material facts of which its officer or agent receives notice or acquires knowledge while acting in the course of his employment and within the scope of his authority, even though the officer or agent does not in fact communicate his knowledge to the corporation through its other officers or agents.

This general rule is subject to an exception, however, which is applicable to the facts of this case. The knowledge or notice of the agent is not imputed to the principal when the person knows the agent is acting adversely to the interests of the principal. In the present case, Sevier testified that when he told Henderson of his arrest for DUIL, Henderson stated, "to Hell with it, maybe they'll never find out." Thus, even by his own testimony, there can be no reasonable room for doubt that Sevier knew that Henderson was not going to convey the information to plaintiff. Therefore, Henderson's knowledge cannot be imputed to plaintiff.

It is, perhaps, the majority's position that the policy that "one who selects an agent and delegates authority to him should incur the risks of the agent's infidelity or want of diligence rather than innocent third persons," should be extended to protect one in the position of defendant Sutton. The problems with such approach, if intended by the majority, are insurmountable. Defendant Sutton's damages were not caused, in any reasonable sense, by the misfeasance of plaintiff's agent. She cannot have relied upon the presence of insurance in sharing the road with Sevier, since insurance is not a pre-condition for driving in Oregon. Moreover, even if a theory of causation could be constructed, there is no finding that plaintiff was negligent in hiring or retaining the services of Henderson, nor is there any basis apparent in the record for such a finding. Nor does the majority purport to make a principal strictly liable for the breaches of fiduciary duty of an agent.

I am forced to conclude, therefore, that the majority's position is supportable only on the basis of the imposition of a newly created duty on insurers to investigate the representations of applicants for automobile liability insurance based upon some theory of strict liability, even though the majority [sic] purports to avoid consideration of this question. Therefore, I would hold that plaintiff was entitled to rescind the policy and is not liable to either defendant.

Notes

1. Was Henderson acting as an adverse agent? Had Henderson completely abandoned State Farm's interests so as to act entirely for Sevier's purposes? Would your answer change if Henderson had authority or apparent authority to determine what information was required to be reported on the application?

2. Is the underlying issue in *State Farm Fire & Casualty Co. v. Sevier* the effectiveness of Sevier's *notification* to the agent, or is it the effect of the agent's (Henderson's) *knowledge*? Should that make any difference in how the case should be analyzed?

3. The *Sevier* trial court ruled that State Farm owed a duty to persons who might be injured by one of its insured drivers. Under Restatement section 282(2)(a), the existence of such a duty would make the adverse agent rule inapplicable:

> The principal is affected by the knowledge of an agent who acts adversely to the principal if the failure of the agent to act upon or to reveal the information results in a violation of a contractual or relational duty of the principal to a person harmed thereby[.]

4. On appeal, the *Sevier* majority claimed it could resolve the case without relying on any duty on the part of State Farm owed to the victim. Wholly apart from the soundness of the majority's reasoning on the agency law issue, note that the trial court's formulation of State Farm's duty was quite broad. State Farm's duty was not limited to a duty to act on any information obtained in the application process. Instead, the trial court imposed a *general* duty to *investigate* the driving record of applicants for insurance. The majority clearly was reluctant to reach the question of whether State Farm owed any duty *at all*, much less grapple with the question of the *scope* of any such duty.

5. The *Sevier* dissent argues that in the absence of any duty owed by State Farm, the victim's rights *under the policy* are *derivative* of those of the insured. Regardless of whether we are talking about knowledge or notification, *Sevier* has no rights against State Farm (why?). If the victim has no contractual rights against State Farm, and if State Farm (and the agent, Henderson) were not *negligent* because neither owed any duty to the victim, why does equity require that the victim recover from State Farm?

The *Sevier* majority relied solely on the principle that, as between the principal and an innocent third party (the victim), the principal should bear the risk of the agent's misconduct. Based on the materials in chapter 2, do you agree with the proposition that the principal is *per se* responsible for all actions of an agent? For example, is a principal always bound by an agent's unauthorized actions? If not, what is the basis for holding the principal liable?

Consider again the differences in the Restatement's treatment of an agent's *knowledge* and a *notification* given to an agent. Notification to an agent *apparently* (but not actually) authorized to receive it is effective against the principal. Restatement § 268(1)(a), (b). On the other hand, an agent's *knowledge* concerning matters within the agent's apparent (but not actual) authority *only* affects the principal where a third party has *relied* on the appearance of authority. Restatement § 273. Similarly, while the adverse agent rule applies to the adverse agent's knowledge, it applies to a *notification only* where the third party had *notice* the agent was acting adversely to the principal. *Compare* Restatement § 282(1) (knowledge) *with* Restatement § 271 (notification).

Given that the only time the question of knowledge or notification will come up is when there is a (presumably) innocent third person, what does the *Sevier* majority's reasoning do to the adverse agent rule?

Chapter 9

Ratification of Unauthorized Transactions

Like the doctrines of apparent authority, estoppel to deny agency power and inherent agency power, the doctrine of ratification arises out of the risk of unintended dealings inherent in the use of agents in the marketplace. Even where an agent dealing with a third party has acted outside the scope of the agent's power to bind the principal, the principal may nevertheless be bound if the principal ratifies the agent's act.

A. Affirmance

Botticello v. Stefanovicz
177 Conn. 22, 411 A.2d 16 (1979)

PETERS, Associate Justice.

The defendants, Mary and Walter Stefanovicz (hereinafter "Mary" and "Walter") in 1943 acquired as tenants in common a farm situated in the towns of Colchester and Lebanon. In the fall of 1965, the plaintiff, Anthony Botticello, became interested in the property. When he first visited the farm, Walter advised him that the asking price was $100,000. The following January, the plaintiff again visited the farm and made a counteroffer of $75,000. At that time, Mary stated that there was "no way" she could sell it for that amount. Ultimately the plaintiff and Walter agreed upon a price of $85,000 for a lease with an option to purchase; during these negotiations, Mary stated that she would not sell the property for less than that amount.

The informal agreement was finalized with the assistance of counsel for both Walter and the plaintiff. The agreement was drawn up by Walter's attorney after consultation with Walter and the plaintiff; it was then sent to, and modified by, the plaintiff's attorney. The agreement was signed by Walter and by the plaintiff. Neither the plaintiff nor his attorney, nor Walter's attorney, was then aware of the fact that Walter did not own the property outright. The plaintiff, although a successful businessman with considerable experience in real estate never requested his attorney to do a title search of any kind, and consequently no title search was done. Walter never represented to the plaintiff or the plaintiff's attorney, or to his own attorney, that he was acting for his wife, as her agent. Mary's

427

part ownership came to light in 1968, when a third party sought an easement over the land in question.

Shortly after the execution of the lease and option-to-purchase agreement, the plaintiff took possession of the property. He made substantial improvements on the property and, in 1971, properly exercised his option to purchase. When the defendants refused to honor the option agreement, the plaintiff commenced the present action against both Mary and Walter, seeking specific performance, possession of the premises, and damages.

The trial court found the issues for the plaintiff and ordered a specific performance of the option-to-purchase agreement. In their appeal, the defendants [claim] that Mary was never a party to the agreement, and its terms may therefore not be enforced [as] to her.

The plaintiff alleged, and the trial court agreed, that although Mary was not a party to the lease and option-to-purchase agreement, its terms were nonetheless binding upon her because Walter acted as her authorized agent in the negotiations, discussions, and execution of the written agreement. The defendants have attacked several findings of fact and conclusions of law, claiming that the underlying facts and applicable law do not support the court's conclusion of agency.

Marital status cannot in and of itself prove the agency relationship. Nor does the fact that the defendants owned the land jointly make one the agent for the other. Moreover, the fact that one spouse tends more to business matters than the other does not, absent other evidence of agreement or authorization, constitute the delegation of power as to an agent. [I]t is clear that the facts found by the court fail to support its conclusion that Walter acted as Mary's authorized agent, and the conclusion therefore cannot stand.

The plaintiff argues, alternatively, that even if no agency relationship existed at the time the agreement was signed, Mary was bound by the contract executed by her husband because she ratified its terms by her subsequent conduct. The trial court accepted this alternative argument as well, concluding that Mary had ratified the agreement by receiving and accepting payments from the plaintiff, and by acquiescing in his substantial improvements to the farm.

Ratification is defined as "the affirmance by a person of a prior act which did not bind him but which was done or professedly done on his account." Restatement (Second), Agency § 82 (1958). Ratification requires "acceptance of the results of the act with an *intent* to ratify, and with *full knowledge of all the material circumstances*." *Ansonia v. Cooper*, 64 Conn. 536, 544, 30 A. 760, 762 (1894) (emphasis added).

The [trial court] finding neither indicates an intent by Mary to ratify the agreement, nor establishes her knowledge of all the material circumstances surrounding the deal. At most, Mary observed the plaintiff occupying and improving the land, received rental payments from the plaintiff from time to time, knew that he had an interest in the property, and knew that the use, occupancy, and rentals were pursuant to a written agreement she had not signed. None of these facts is sufficient to support the conclusion that Mary ratified the agreement and thus bound herself to its terms. It is undisputed that Walter had the power to lease his own undivided one-half interest in the property; and the facts found by the trial court could be referable to that fact alone. Moreover, the fact that the rental payments were used for "family" purposes indicates nothing more than one spouse providing for the other.

The plaintiff makes the further argument that Mary ratified the agreement simply by receiving its benefits and by failing to repudiate it. *See* Restatement (Second), Agency § 98 (1958). The plaintiff fails to recognize that before the receipt of benefits may constitute ratification, the other requisites for ratification must first be present. "Thus if the original transaction was not purported to be done on account of the principal, the fact that the principal receives its proceeds does not make him a party to it." Restatement (Second), Agency § 98, comment f (1958). Since Walter at no time purported to be acting on his wife's behalf, as is essential to effective subsequent ratification, Mary is not bound by the terms of the agreement, and specific performance cannot be ordered as to her.

Our conclusion that there can be no recovery against Mary is not dispositive of the rights that the plaintiff may have against Walter. A person who contracts to convey full title to real property is not himself excused from performance, or immune from liability for breach, because of his inability to convey more than an undivided half interest in the property.

We turn now to the question of relief. In view of our holding that Mary never authorized her husband to act as her agent for any purpose connected with the lease and option-to-purchase agreement, recovery against her is precluded. As to Walter, the fact that his ownership was restricted to an undivided one-half interest in no way limited his capacity to contract. He contracted to convey full title and for breach of that contract he may be held liable. The facts of the case are sufficient to furnish a basis for relief to the plaintiff by specific performance or by damages.

Since no third parties are here involved, the form of relief to be accorded must take into account the plaintiff's preference as well as the court's own discretion, "depending upon the equities of the case and based on reason and sound judgment."

There is error as to the judgment against the defendant Mary Stefanovicz; the judgment as to her is set aside and the case remanded with direction to render judgment in her favor. As to the defendant Walter Stefanovicz, there is error only as to the remedy ordered. The judgment as to him is set aside and the case remanded for a new trial limited to the form of relief.

Notes

1. May an undisclosed or partially disclosed principal ratify an unauthorized act? Under the Restatement, a person (the "ratifier") only has the right to ratify the act of another (the "actor") where (i) the actor purported to act as an agent, section 85, and (ii) the actor either identified the ratifier as the principal or intended to act on account of the ratifier, sections 85 comment c & 87. Note that this prevents a stranger from intervening to take advantage of a good deal. Despite these limitations on the power to ratify an unauthorized transaction, nothing prevents the would-be ratifier from entering into a *separate, new contract* with the third party. *See* Restatement § 104.

2. Under the Restatement, a principal may "affirm" a transaction either by *electing* to be bound or by *conduct*. § 83. As indicated in *Botticello*, one type of conduct constituting an affirmance is the knowing *acceptance* by the principal of

benefits from the transaction. Note, however, that for an implied affirmance by conduct, the conduct must be such that it can only be justified if the principal is electing to affirm the transaction (why?). Restatement § 83. For acceptance of benefits to constitute affirmance, the principal must have no claim to the accepted benefits other than through or under the transaction in question. Restatement § 98. How did the *Botticello* court apply this principle?

3. A ratifier may elect to avoid an affirmance if at the time of the affirmance the ratifier was ignorant of any material fact involved in the affirmed transaction. *See* Restatement § 91. Material facts are those which

> substantially affect the existence or extent of the obligations involved in the transaction, as distinguished from those which affect the values or inducements involved in the transaction.

If the ratifier does not have *actual knowledge* of material facts, but only *reason to know* them, then the ratifier may avoid the affirmance. Restatement § 91 comment c.

4. In order to ratify, a principal must have been able to undertake the transaction both at the earlier time when the agent acted and at the later time of the act of ratification. Thus, for example, a principal cannot ratify a transaction which the principal could not have entered into *at the time the agent acted*. *See, e.g., Zottman v. City and County of San Francisco,* 20 Cal. 96 (1862) (transaction could not legally have been entered into). In addition, a principal cannot ratify a transaction which the principal does not have the authority to enter *at the time of the attempted ratification. See, e.g., Taslich v. Industrial Commission,* 71 Utah 33, 262 P. 281 (1927) (statutory period for action by principal had elapsed before ratification of timely but unauthorized action by the agent).

5. Note that ratification of prior unauthorized acts can form the basis for a claim of *apparent authority.* Suppose an agent enters into an unauthorized transaction which the principal ratifies without indicating to the third party that the agent had acted without authority. Suppose further that the same third party again deals with the agent, and the agent again exceeds authority in a similar fashion. The principal may be bound to the second contract on the basis of the apparent authority created by the manifestation to the third party that the agent had authority to deal. *See, e.g., Lewis v. Cable,* 107 F. Supp. 196 (W.D. Pa. 1952). Would it make a difference in the outcome if at the time of ratifying the first transaction the principal advised the third party of the lack of authority of the agent regarding the first transaction?

Problem 9.1

Allen, purporting to represent Paula but without authority or power to bind, leases Paula's farm to Terry for a term of five years. Allen tells Paula what he has done, but does not tell her the term of the lease. Without inquiring as to the lease term, Paula demands, and accepts from Terry, the security deposit and first month's rent. In view of Paula's willful ignorance of the lease term, may Paula avoid the lease after she learns the term is five years? Did Paula know enough facts that she should have investigated before affirming instead of blundering ahead heedless of her ignorance? Under Restatement 91 & comment e, Paula may be found to have *assumed the risk* of proceeding with only generalized knowledge of the circumstances. Would it make any difference if the terms of similar farm leases customarily range between three and five years? One to two years? *See* Restatement § 91 comment e, illustration 15.

Rakestraw v. Rodrigues
104 Cal. Rptr. 57, 500 P.2d 1401 (Cal. 1972)

WRIGHT, Chief Justice.

Sherwood T. Rodrigues (Rodrigues) appeals from a judgment upon a jury verdict for $30,000 in favor of Joyce Rakestraw (Joyce). His claimed liability arises out of involvement in a transaction whereby Joyce's name was forged on a promissory note and a deed of trust in order to obtain funds for a business venture of her then husband William Rakestraw (William), who was also a cross-defendant.

The action was initiated by Acme Financial Corporation (Acme) and Security Title Insurance Company (Security) to enforce payment of a $75,000 promissory note bearing Joyce's purported signature which in fact had been forged and which was secured by a deed of trust (also forged) covering property owned by her. Joyce, Robert Ellinghouse (Ellinghouse), who affixed the notarial acknowledgment on the deed of trust and Agricultural Insurance Company (Agricultural) as surety on Ellinghouse's bond as a notary public, were named defendants. Joyce asserted the forgeries as a defense to the action and cross-complained against Rodrigues and William.

Joyce entered into a stipulated judgment with Acme and Security by which she agreed to be bound by the note and deed of trust. Joyce's cross-complaint against Rodrigues and William proceeded to trial and resulted in a jury verdict in her favor. Rodrigues' motion for judgment notwithstanding the verdict was denied, as were motions for a new trial. Rodrigues and William appealed from the judgment.

In late 1964 Joyce discussed with William the possibility of using her separate improved real property in Woodside as collateral for a loan to provide capital for the operation of a supermarket. On January 28, 1965, Joyce executed but did not deliver a promissory note in the amount of $40,000 and, as security for the obligation, a deed of trust on her Woodside property. Although at that time she expected to obtain a loan, the transaction was never completed. Joyce thereafter withdrew her consent to the use of her Woodside property as collateral. William, however, signed Joyce's name to both a promissory note for $75,000 in favor of Acme and a deed of trust on her Woodside property securing the loan. The signature on the deed of trust was notarized by Ellinghouse on February 18, 1965. Although Rodrigues, an auditor and a close friend and business associate of William, denied any participation in the execution and notarization of the deed of trust, the evidence supports implied findings that he told Ellinghouse he had seen Joyce sign the document and requested Ellinghouse to attest that she had acknowledged the execution of the instrument.

William took the forged documents to Acme and arranged for the loan. A check was drawn by Acme payable to William and Joyce which she endorsed without realizing that she was purportedly liable on the note or that her property had purportedly been encumbered. The major portion of the proceeds of the loan was used to satisfy obligations incurred in connection with a supermarket which was owned and operated by the William Rakestraw Co., Inc. (the corporation).

Joyce concedes that within a few days after she endorsed the check she learned of the forgeries. Later in conversations with her husband and others she claimed that she was the owner of the supermarket since her property had been used as security to finance it. She also demanded that stock in the corporation be issued to her. William, however, refused to issue or transfer any stock to her and initially refused to permit her to take any active role in the operation of the business.

Shortly after the discovery of the forgeries Joyce consulted an attorney who advised her to report the matter to the trustee designated in the deed of trust. Joyce, however, did not follow this advice and sought no remedy until three years later when both the business and her marriage had failed and the complaint had been filed by Acme and Security. Notwithstanding the position first taken by William he later permitted Joyce to take an active role in the affairs of the corporation during a period of time before its ultimate failure. Although she denied at trial that she managed the business she did testify that she went to the market "every single day" and she further testified that one of the primary reasons why she did not take more timely action to challenge the forgeries was her belief that she had an equitable interest in the corporation.

Joyce benefited financially through corporate operations made possible by the loan. Approximately $1,000 from an account of the corporation was applied toward a loan previously obtained by Joyce which was also secured by a deed of trust covering her Woodside property, and the corporation paid $3,612.50 in taxes on the parcel. In addition, William's paychecks from the corporation were deposited in a joint account standing in the names of William and Joyce and all payments applied on the Acme loan (totaling $36,250) were made by the corporation. Pursuant to the stipulated judgment, Joyce paid Acme the balance of $38,750. The jury impliedly found that she received benefits made possible by the loan in the sum of $8,750 and, accordingly, awarded her $30,000 compensatory damages on her cross-complaint. Rodrigues asserts that because Joyce ratified the forgeries he is relieved from any liability in damages to her.

The issues we deal with involve the application of traditional principles of agency law. Two basic rules are involved: (1) ratification by a person of an act purportedly done on his behalf not only creates the relationship of principal and agent but also constitutes approval by the ratifier of the purported agent's act, relieving such agent of liability to the ratifier for the act; and (2) forgeries can be ratified thereby relieving the wrongdoer agent of liability to the principal.

The first rule is embodied in Civil Code section 2307 which provides: "An agency may be created, and an authority may be conferred, by a precedent authorization *or a subsequent ratification.*" (Italics added.) Ratification is the voluntary election by a person to adopt in some manner as his own an act which was purportedly done on his behalf by another person, the effect of which, as to some or all persons, is to treat the act as if originally authorized by him. A purported agent's act may be adopted expressly or it may be adopted by implication based on conduct of the purported principal from which an intention to consent to or adopt the act may be fairly inferred, including conduct which is "inconsistent with any reasonable intention on his part, other than that he intended approving and adopting it." It is essential, however, that the act of adoption be truly voluntary in character. Moreover, there can be no adoption if the act, although voluntary, is done only because the purported principal is obligated to minimize his losses caused by the agent's wrongful act or because of duress or misrepresentation by the agent.

Generally, the effect of a ratification is that the authority which is given to the purported agent relates back to the time when he performed the act. Since he is considered to be an agent with authority at the time he performed the act, he does not incur liability for acts done within the scope of that authority.

As to the second rule here involved, it is well settled in California "that a principal may ratify the forgery of his signature by his agent." We conclude that the ratification of an act of forgery by one held out to be a principal creates an agency relationship between such person and the purported agent and relieves the agent of civil liability to the principal which otherwise would result from the fact that he acted independently and without authority.

We now turn to the facts of this case. Joyce concedes that she became aware of the forgeries within a few days after she had endorsed the check from Acme and thereafter consulted an attorney in connection therewith. Accordingly, the requirement of knowledge of the material facts essential to voluntary ratification is satisfied. The doctrine of exoneration by ratification, however, "is limited, so far as the agent is concerned, to those cases where there remains with the principal, after his first complete knowledge of the transaction, the power to rescind, and failing so to do he is properly charged with full acceptance of all the responsibilities of the contract, even to the exoneration of his agent, because, with the ability to rescind, if he rescinded, the transaction would be at an end and nobody would be injured." Here it is clear that Joyce elected not to rescind at a time when she was fully informed and had power to do so and had been advised of her rights.

It was not until three years after discovery of the forgeries, and then only when a complaint was filed against her, that Joyce sought relief. Her conduct during the interim period has been previously set forth and is revealing. When both her marriage and the business failed she formally asserted for the first time a claim for wrongdoing against her former husband and Rodrigues. It thus appears as a matter of law that Joyce affirmatively endorsed the fraudulent acts of William and Rodrigues in anticipation of benefits to be gained, and sought to negate her endorsement thereof only when benefits failed to materialize as anticipated.

Joyce contends that her approval of the transaction and acceptance of benefits was involuntary because at the time she discovered the forgeries she could not rescind the transaction by returning the proceeds of the loan as they had already been expended. There is no merit in this contention. Whether or not she was in a position to return the proceeds of the loan, she could have disavowed the transaction and relieved herself of potential liability by informing Acme and Security of the forgeries. At the time of discovery she had done nothing to preclude her from asserting that the signatures were not hers. Had she then repudiated the forgeries, her failure to take action to force the corporation to make restitution of the proceeds of the loan would not have validated the forged signatures.

Joyce also contends that there can be no ratification of Rodrigues' acts since such ratification had to be in writing. Civil Code section 2310, a codification of the "equal dignities" doctrine, provides: "A ratification can be made only in the manner that would have been necessary to confer an original authority for the act ratified, or where an oral authorization would suffice, by accepting or retaining the benefit of the act, with notice thereof." Since authorization to bind a principal to a deed of trust must be in writing (Civ. Code, § 2309) and because her consent to or adoption of the fraudulent acts was not in writing, Joyce argues that there has been no valid ratification.

Joyce's liability, however, arises from the promissory note; the deed of trust only secured the note. An agent's authority to execute a promissory note need not be in writing and, accordingly, Joyce's ratification of the note likewise need not have been in writing. Her ratification of the transaction in part, moreover, constituted a ratification of the entire transaction including acts by Rodrigues.

Finally, Civil Code section 2310 was not intended to apply to a ratification as between a principal and agent. In [*Sunset-Sternau Food Co. v. Bonzi*, (1964) 60 Cal. 2d 834, 36 Cal. Rptr. 741, 389 P.2d 133] we held that Civil Code section 2309, requiring that authorization for a contract required in law to be in writing must also be in writing, was not intended to apply [in disputes] between an agent and principal. The decision's rationale applies with equal force to Civil Code section 2310. That section, therefore, is inapplicable as between the principal and the agent, and thus inapplicable in the present case.

As Joyce's ratification of the fraudulent transaction relieved Rodrigues of liability to her as a matter of law, the trial judge improperly denied his motion for judgment notwithstanding the verdict. The judgment insofar as it relates to Rodrigues is therefore reversed and the cause remanded with directions to enter judgment in his favor.

Notes

1. Joyce endorsed the check representing the proceeds of the challenged loan. That would seem to be an affirmance in and of itself. If that is the case, why is the remainder of the opinion necessary? In any event, note that a ratifier may also impliedly affirm a transaction by *retaining* (as opposed to *accepting*) benefits arising out of the transaction. Restatement § 99.

2. In order for the principal to be held to have ratified due to knowingly accepting or retaining benefits of an unauthorized transaction, must the benefit be actual? Would only a potential for gain be sufficient?

3. The holdings of *Rakestraw v. Rodriguez* and *Sunset-Sternau Food Co. v. Bonzi* (cited in *Rakestraw*) regarding the application of the equal dignities doctrine are limited to disputes between the principal and the agent. As between the principal and *third persons*, the California statute requires equal dignities in the appointment of the agent. In any event, note that where the agent's *authorization* requires certain formalities, the *ratification* must use the same formalities. Restatement § 93(2) & comment.

3 A's Towing Co. v. P & A Well Service, Inc.
642 F.2d 756 (5th Cir. 1981)

TATE, Circuit Judge:

Chevron appeals from a judgment holding it liable in damages for its cancellation of a service contract.

In December of 1975, Chevron U.S.A., Inc. (Chevron) hired P & A Well Service, Inc. (P & A) to plug and abandon a Chevron well located in the Louisiana coastal waters of Breton Sound. The contract provided that P & A would complete the work within sixty days and would receive $28,900 and the rights to the tubing recovered from the well.

Work commenced in early March of 1976. In late March, equipment problems led the parties to agree to a different method of plugging the well. During the ensuing delay period, rough weather damaged a P & A barge, forcing P & A to withdraw from the well site on April 5, 1976, to obtain repairs.

On April 9, 1976, P & A's president, Edward Estis, telephoned Chevron's Algiers office and was told by an unidentified individual that the Breton Sound contract was cancelled, and that P & A should not return to complete its work at that site. In reliance upon that order, P & A did not return to the Breton Sound well. On June 26, 1976, Chevron sent a letter to P & A cancelling the Breton Sound contract, and in August of 1976, Chevron itself plugged and abandoned that well.

On August 10, 1976, P & A sent an invoice billing Chevron for costs incurred in its attempt to complete the Breton Sound contract, including the salvage value of the unrecovered tubing. This litigation was precipitated when 3 A's Towing Company brought suit against P & A to recover sums due under certain towing contracts. P & A filed a third party demand against Chevron to recover the towing charges incurred in connection with the Breton Sound contract and in addition the lost profit resulting from Chevron's cancellation.

Following a bench trial, the district court concluded that since P & A had not forfeited its right to perform as of June 25, 1976, Chevron's letter cancellation of that date without first putting P & A in default constituted a violation of the contract, and that in any event, Chevron had attempted to cancel the contract during the telephone conversation on April 9, 1976. Accordingly, the district court held that P & A was entitled to recover the profit it would have made had it been permitted to complete its performance, and entered judgment in favor of P & A in the amount of $77,980, with interest and costs.

Chevron does not dispute on this appeal that the April 9 telephone conversation did in fact occur. Chevron argues, rather, that since the unidentified individual who purported to cancel the contract was without authority—express, implied, or apparent—to act for Chevron in that regard, the cancellation cannot legally be imputed to Chevron.

The law and jurisprudence of Louisiana clearly establish that the unauthorized act of one purporting to bind a corporation may be implicitly ratified by the corporate principal through the knowing acquiescence of those having the authority, so long as the unauthorized act is not violative of the corporate charter, state law, or public policy. Such ratification has retroactive effect and is equivalent to prior authority. A ratification may be held to have occurred when corporate personnel with the authority to bind the corporation acquire, or are charged with, knowledge of the unauthorized act and fail to repudiate it within a reasonable period of time. Although the acceptance of benefits by a corporation may evidence ratification, the cited decisions do not hold such to be a requirement for ratification of an act by a corporate employee repudiating a corporate obligation.[1]

We find sufficient evidence in this record to support a conclusion that Chevron acquiesced in the April 9 telephone cancellation of the Breton Sound contract, thereby implicitly ratifying it and adopting it as an act of the corporation.

The Breton Sound contract was negotiated for Chevron by E.J. Morgan, a staff engineer in Chevron's Algiers office. The contract was signed in Morgan's office. All subsequent discussions of the contract were with Morgan, or with his replacements, C.R. Block and Richard Gist. Virtually all of P & A's dealings with Chevron in connection with the Breton Sound well were conducted over Morgan's telephone. It was Morgan who represented Chevron in altering the procedure to be used in plugging the well and who agreed on Chevron's behalf to supply the mud for the new procedure.

On April 8, 1976, a call was placed to the home of P & A's president, Edward Estis, and a message was left requesting Estis to return the call. The number given was later determined to be that of James Isonhood, E.J. Morgan's immediate inferior, in Chevron's Algiers office. On April 9, 1976, Estis returned the call to the designated number and received no answer. He then called E.J. Morgan's number and spoke to the now-unknown individual who purported to cancel the Breton Sound contract.

Francis R. Daigle, the person who was second in rank at the Algiers office and E.J. Morgan's immediate supervisor, testified that he was aware of the fact and the substance of the April 9 telephone conversation. That testimony was at least suggestive of a more general awareness throughout the Algiers office.

---

1. Chevron incidentally suggests that a corporation cannot be held to have ratified the unauthorized act of its agent under circumstances such as these unless it had full knowledge of the act and received and accepted the benefits incurring to it from the act. Chevron thus appears to argue that since no benefits accrued to it from the cancellation of the contract on April 9, it cannot be held to have tacitly ratified it.

We disagree.

[T]he general rule that a ratification occurs when personnel with the authority to bind the corporation acquire knowledge of the unauthorized act and thereafter fail to repudiate it within a reasonable period of time is particularly applicable where the delay in repudiating is a long one, where the failure to repudiate is accompanied by acts indicating approval of the unauthorized act—such as receiving and retaining the benefits accruing from it—or where the circumstances call for a quick repudiation. There is no *requirement* that some measurable benefit inure to the corporate principal from the unauthorized act.

To be sure, where the unauthorized act consists of the making of a contract that purports to bind a corporate principal, there is no more telling indication of the principal's ratification or approval of that act than its receipt and retention of the contracted-for benefits. But not all unauthorized acts involve the potential flow of some measurable benefit or consideration from a third party to the principal. In such cases, the principal's ratification or approval of the repudiation must obviously be manifested in terms other than the receipt of contracted-for benefits.

Despite that awareness, and despite numerous subsequent contacts between Chevron personnel and P & A personnel, neither Daigle nor any other Chevron employee ever repudiated that conversation, requested P & A to resume its operations on the Breton Sound well, or even inquired into P & A's continued absence from the well site. Chevron took no action in the ensuing weeks that was in any way inconsistent with a cancellation by telephone on April 9. The record shows that telephone cancellation with a follow-up letter of cancellation was an accepted practice in contracts of this sort; and indeed, on June 25, 1976, Chevron notified P & A by letter that it considered the contract cancelled, and thereafter rendered performance by P & A impossible by plugging and abandoning the Breton Sound well with its own resources in August of that year.

Under these facts, we find ample support for a conclusion that Chevron ratified the telephone cancellation by acquiescing in it, and therefore find it unnecessary to determine whether Chevron could likewise be bound by the cancellation under theories of actual or apparent authority. Chevron personnel with the authority to bind the corporation had knowledge of the telephone cancellation and failed to repudiate it within a reasonable period of time. We therefore find no error in the district court's conclusion that *Chevron* had attempted to cancel the Breton Sound contract by telephone on April 9, 1976.

AFFIRMED.

Note

Under the Restatement, silence or a failure to act indicates affirmance "under such circumstances that, according to the ordinary experience and habits of men, one would naturally be expected to speak [or act] if he did not consent." Section 94 comment a. In determining whether the circumstances are such as to imply an affirmance, recall that under Restatement section 83, implied affirmance requires that the affirming conduct must be justifiable only if the ratifier was electing to affirm the transaction.

Should it make any difference if the claimed affirmance relates to an act of a stranger, as opposed to an *actual* agent exceeding the scope of his or her power to bind?

B. Knowledge of Agents

Estate of Sawyer v. Crowell

559 A.2d 687 (Vt. 1989)

GIBSON, Justice.

Defendant, Charles E. Crowell, appeals a decision of the Chittenden Superior Court ordering him to pay the sum of $50,000 to the plaintiff, the Estate of Thomas C. Sawyer (Estate), an estate administered under the jurisdiction of the Chittenden Probate Court. Attorney John Durrance served as administrator of the Estate from the death of Thomas Sawyer in 1980 until March of 1982. The superior court determined that defendant materially breached an agreement between the parties and was liable as a result.

In 1980, defendant co-founded the Vermont Real Estate Investment Trust (VREIT). The stated purpose of VREIT was to provide a vehicle for investments in Vermont real estate ventures. Defendant ran VREIT single-handedly as its president from its creation until January of 1982. This case arises out of the alleged misuse of money entrusted by the Estate to the defendant for investment during 1981.

In February of 1981, attorney Durrance contacted defendant to discuss investing $50,000 of the Estate's funds in high-grade commercial paper. On February 11, 1981, the two met and agreed that defendant would invest the $50,000 in six-month commercial paper through Crowell, England & Co., of which defendant was the sole principal. Mr. Durrance stressed that the money was to be invested conservatively in a national corporation and ruled out VREIT as an investment. On March 5, 1981, defendant purchased commercial paper issued by the Ford Motor Credit Corporation with a maturity date of August 12, 1981.

On August 12, 1981, defendant and Mr. Durrance met on the street and discussed the reinvestment of the Estate's funds. Mr. Durrance told defendant that he wanted to reinvest the money, including interest, for a shorter period of time in order to ensure that the proceeds would be available at the end of the year—the anticipated date of the closing of the Estate. Mr. Durrance asked defendant to reinvest the funds in high-grade commercial paper for thirty days with a continuous rollover. He did not, however, specify a particular investment. Defendant subsequently invested the funds in VREIT.

In mid-October, Mr. Durrance asked his secretary to inquire about the requirements for withdrawing the Estate's money from its investment with defendant. By letter dated October 14, 1981, the secretary asked defendant how to continue the investment and the procedure for withdrawal of funds. Defendant responded by letter dated October 15, 1981, addressed only to the secretary, that three days' written notice was required for withdrawal of the funds. Defendant also included in the letter the information that the funds were invested in VREIT commercial paper.

Upon receipt of this response, the secretary informed Mr. Durrance of the notice requirement for fund withdrawal, but did not discuss with him the fact that defendant had invested the money in VREIT. Instead, she placed the letter in the file.

On December 31, 1981, after learning that funds belonging to another client had been invested in VREIT and that VREIT was having difficulty returning them, Mr. Durrance consulted the Estate file and found the October 15th letter. He immediately contacted defendant and demanded the return of the Estate's funds. Shortly thereafter, but before any money was returned to the Estate, VREIT filed a petition in bankruptcy.

The superior court concluded that the deposit of the Estate's funds in VREIT constituted a material breach of the agreement under which defendant had undertaken to invest the Estate's money. The court ordered that the Estate recover the $50,000 from defendant, less any amount recovered in bankruptcy, plus interest at 15% from August 12, 1981 (the date of the breach).

[Defendant] argues that the October 15th letter from defendant to Mr. Durrance's secretary constituted notice to Mr. Durrance of the funds' investment in

VREIT, and that by not acting at such time to disaffirm the investment, Mr. Durrance ratified it.

Defendant argues that he is not liable for any breach, contending that where financial investments are concerned, a customer is deemed to have ratified a wrongful investment upon his failure to repudiate it promptly after he becomes chargeable with knowledge thereof. In support, he urges us to accept his conclusion that Mr. Durrance was chargeable with knowing the funds were invested in VREIT when his secretary received the October 15th letter. Because Mr. Durrance was then chargeable with the knowledge, the argument proceeds, his failure to repudiate the VREIT investment at that time constituted ratification of it.

As a general rule, the knowledge of an agent acting within the scope of his or her authority is chargeable to the principal, regardless of whether that knowledge is actually communicated.[2] Thus, in order for Mr. Durrance to be chargeable with knowledge of the VREIT investment on October 15th, it was necessary for defendant to establish that it was within the scope of the secretary's authority to obtain that information. This, defendant, failed to do.

Although the trial court did not directly address the issue in terms of "scope of authority," it clearly found that with respect to the correspondence of October 14-15, the secretary's authority did not extend to inquiring where the Estate's funds were invested:

> No confirmation [of the reinvestment] was sent by Crowell to Durrance, and Durrance did not ask for any. [Durrance] had asked his secretary simply to obtain specific information, and she had done so to the extent of his inquiry.

Finding of fact No. 14. The court then concluded:

> Durrance did not ask his secretary to inquire where the funds had been invested. His only inquiry was how to continue the investment and how long it would take to withdraw the funds. Durrance had neither actual notice of the VREIT investment nor constructive notice of the breach.

The existence and extent of an agent's authority is a question of fact. There is no evidence in the record that the secretary knew the money should not have been invested in VREIT, or that there was any restriction on its investment. Without such knowledge, she had no reason to bring that information to Mr. Durrance's attention. As defendant has made no showing that the secretary had any authority extending beyond the inquiry contained in her letter, the court's finding is not clearly erroneous, and we will not disturb it here. Since the secretary's knowledge of the VREIT investment did not arise within the scope of her authority, Mr. Durrance cannot be charged with such knowledge.

---

2. Defendant bases part of his argument on the contention that the secretary's authority was "apparent" if not truly "actual." His reliance on this distinction is misplaced, however. Actual authority is that conveyed by the principal directly to the agent, while apparent authority is the scope of an agent's authority manifested by the principal to a third party, not the agent. Restatement (Second) of Agency §§ 7 and 8 (1958). Thus, although the secretary's actions in writing the letter and requesting information might "reasonably appear" to defendant to be actions done within her scope of authority, he offered no evidence to prove that her authority to do more than inquire as to how to continue the investment and withdraw funds was communicated to him by Mr. Durrance, the principal.

By doing nothing from time letter sent Ratified

Defendant next argues that by doing nothing from October 15 until December 31, Mr. Durrance ratified the contents of the October 15th letter to the secretary. This argument is premised on the doctrine of ratification, under which a principal may affirm a prior action by an agent which did not bind the principal but was purportedly done on his or her account, with the ratification "relating back" to the time of the actual act. *See* Restatement (Second) of Agency § 82. It is clear that if Mr. Durrance ratified his secretary's actions in obtaining the additional information, he would be chargeable with that knowledge as of October 15.

Silence is capable of constituting ratification but not here

Affirmance alone will not bind the Principal. The "P" must have actual knowledge of material facts being adopted. If no knowledge Affirmance may be avoided

Defendant argues, in essence, that Mr. Durrance's silence after the October 15th letter was received in his office amounted to a ratification of its contents. While we accept the proposition that in certain circumstances it is possible for silence to be construed as an affirmance resulting in ratification, see Restatement (Second) of Agency § 94 comment a, we do not reach that conclusion here. Affirmance alone will not necessarily bind a principal who acts upon incomplete or inaccurate information. The law is clear that for ratification of an unauthorized act to occur so as to bind the principal, he or she must have *actual knowledge* of the material facts being adopted at the time affirmance occurs. Absent such knowledge, an affirmance may be avoided upon the principal's learning the material facts. Restatement (Second) of Agency § 91.

In this case, the court concluded that Mr. Durrance had neither actual nor constructive knowledge of the VREIT investment at the time his secretary received the October 15th letter. As defendant has not met his burden of showing that this conclusion was not supported by the findings of fact, there is no error. Since Mr. Durrance moved promptly to disaffirm the wrongful investment as soon as he received actual notice of it on December 31 (a fact not disputed by defendant), we conclude that he thereby avoided whatever affirmance of the breach which could have arisen from his earlier silence.

Affirmed.

π promptly moved to disaffirm upon actual knowledge

Note

Earlier in this chapter we discussed the right of a ratifier who did not know all the material facts to avoid the affirmance. Suppose that the ratifier's *agent* did know all such facts. May the ratifier still avoid the affirmance? As indicated in *3 A's Towing Co. v. P & A Well Service, Inc.*, page 435, and *Estate of Sawyer v. Crowell*, the general rules holding a principal accountable for the knowledge of an agent apply in a ratification context to prevent the ratifier from avoiding the affirmance. Note, however, that the principal will *not* be charged with an agent's knowledge of facts relating to the agent's *own unauthorized acts*. Restatement §§ 91 comment c, 280.

C. Partial Ratifications

Many transactions entered into by agents or purported agents on behalf of principals will be of some degree of complexity. There may be multiple provisions of written agreements, or there may be multiple segments of transactions (such as the negotiation, execution, performance, and enforcement components of contracts). Even these components may be further subdivided. Should a principal be allowed to select among the parts of a transaction, to ratify certain portions, and to disaffirm others?

Problem 9.2

Thief steals a truckload of bricks from Brick Company, then purports to act as its agent in selling the stolen bricks to Third Party. Suppose further that Thief, purporting to act as Brick Company's servant in delivering the bricks, runs over and injures Pedestrian while delivering the bricks. Assuming Brick Company knows all the facts and sues Third Party to collect payment for the bricks, would it also be ratifying the tort under the "no partial ratifications" doctrine? Is the delivery independent from the ratified sale? Is the tort independent from the delivery? *See* Chapter 10 for a fuller discussion of the topic of ratification of torts.

Navrides v. Zurich Insurance Co.
5 Cal. 3d 698, 488 P.2d 637 (1971)

SULLIVAN, Justice.

In this action against defendant insurance company arising out of the compromise of a personal injury claim made with the company by plaintiff's attorney without her consent, we must decide whether defendant was discharged from liability where its settlement draft after delivery to the attorney was cashed on plaintiff's forged endorsement and the proceeds of the draft appropriated.

On February 19, 1962, plaintiff Audrey Navrides was injured on the premises of one Crancer who was insured by defendant Zurich Insurance Company (Zurich). She employed an attorney, Robert S. Forsyth, who filed an action for damages on her behalf. Forsyth negotiated with Zurich a compromise settlement of plaintiff's claim for $9,000. Plaintiff rejected the compromise but Forsyth represented to Zurich that she had approved. Zurich then delivered to Forsyth for signature a release of all claims, a request for the dismissal of the pending action and a draft dated September 22, 1964 in the sum of $9,000 payable to "Audrey R. Navrides and Robert S. Forsyth, her attorney." Forsyth retained the draft and returned to Zurich the release purportedly signed by plaintiff, together with the request for dismissal. The latter document was thereupon filed and the action dismissed.

On September 25, 1964, the settlement draft, bearing the purported endorsements of plaintiff and Forsyth, was cashed at the Bank of America and eventually charged to Zurich's account with the Continental Bank. Plaintiff's signature on the release and her endorsement on the draft were forgeries. She received no money from the settlement. About a year later, plaintiff discovered that her personal injury action had been dismissed and that the above settlement draft had been delivered to her attorney. She was unable to effect any recovery from the latter.

On December 14, 1965 plaintiff commenced this action against Zurich and the Bank of America.[3]

---

3. Apparently plaintiff made no attempt to set aside the unauthorized dismissal of her personal injury action. We need not speculate as to the probable success of any such pro-

Plaintiff's first stated cause of action against Zurich alleged in substance that the latter for a valuable consideration drew, executed and delivered the draft to plaintiff, that the draft was wrongfully paid by the Bank of America on a forged endorsement, that Zurich "has not paid said check, nor any part thereof to plaintiff, and by reason of said fact, there has been a failure of consideration" and that defendant owed plaintiff the sum of $9,000. The trial court essentially found that all of the material allegations of the first cause of action were true, that plaintiff did not affix, or authorize anyone to affix, her signature to the draft, and that she was not estopped from asserting that she neither signed nor authorized an endorsement of the draft. From these facts the court concluded simply that (1) plaintiff's signature was a forgery and (2) that Zurich owed plaintiff $9,000 plus interest. Judgment was entered accordingly.

The trial court's conclusion that plaintiff's signature on the draft was a forgery is amply supported by the findings and the evidence. Unfortunately, however, the court nowhere indicates any legal theory explaining its leap from its findings and first conclusion of law to its second conclusion that Zurich owed plaintiff $9,000 plus interest. It is a fair assumption that the trial judge concluded that the forged endorsement was wholly inoperative and that as a consequence Zurich still owed plaintiff $9,000.

Although Forsyth clearly had no authority, express or implied, to compromise plaintiff's claim, the record before us establishes as a matter of law that plaintiff, by bringing the instant action against Zurich for the $9,000, ratified the settlement. As we shall explain, by so doing she necessarily approved Zurich's delivery of the draft to Forsyth and the latter's delivery to Zurich of the release (on which her signature had been forged) and the request for the dismissal of her action.

It is well settled that a client may ratify the unauthorized actions of his attorney, that a principal may ratify the forgery of his signature by his agent, and that a principal may ratify the unauthorized act of an agent by bringing suit based thereon.

By virtue of such ratification, there then existed between plaintiff and Zurich a *valid* compromise agreement which was fully performed on the part of plaintiff by Forsyth's delivery of the release and dismissal to Zurich. The true and indeed only tenable theory of plaintiff's action thus emerges: that Zurich owes her $9,000 under the settlement agreement and that she had not been paid. Indeed at oral argument plaintiff's present counsel conceded that by bringing suit against Zurich she had ratified the settlement and was seeking to enforce it. However, inherent in the ratification of the settlement is ratification of Forsyth's authority to settle the claim, which necessarily includes authority to receive and collect the payment of the settlement on behalf of plaintiff.

Unfortunately for plaintiff, she cannot stop at this point. She must reckon with the elementary rule of agency law that a principal is not allowed to ratify

---

ceedings had they been undertaken. Nevertheless we observe that the law is well settled that an attorney must be specifically authorized to settle and compromise a claim, that merely on the basis of his employment he has no implied or ostensible authority to bind his client to a compromise settlement of pending litigation and that clearly he has no authority pursuant to an unauthorized settlement to enter a dismissal with prejudice.

the unauthorized acts of an agent to the extent that they are beneficial, and disavow them to the extent that they are damaging. If a principal ratifies part of a transaction, he is deemed to ratify the whole of it. Rest. 2d Agency, § 96. The reason for the rule is obvious. Ratification is approval of a transaction that has already taken place. Accordingly the principal has the power to approve the transaction only as it in fact occurred, not to reconstruct it to suit his present needs. As the court said in *Gift v. Ahrnke* (1951), 107 Cal. App. 2d 614, 623, 237 P.2d 706, 710, "A principal "cannot split the agency transaction into separate parts, and take the benefits without the burden.' " In the instant case plaintiff, by ratifying Forsyth's settlement of her pending action for damages for personal injuries, necessarily ratified the entire transaction between Forsyth and Zurich, including Forsyth's receipt of the settlement draft.

We, therefore, turn to consider whether Zurich's delivery of the draft to Forsyth discharged the insurance company from all liability to plaintiff, notwithstanding the fact that the draft was subsequently cashed on plaintiff's forged endorsement and its proceeds converted. We begin by adverting to established principles of agency dealing with the authority of agents to receive payment.

An attorney has authority "To receive money claimed by his client in an action or proceeding during the pendency thereof and upon payment thereof, and not otherwise, to discharge the claim." (Code Civ. Proc. § 283, subd. 2.) This statute, enacted in 1872, codifies the well-established proposition of law that an attorney who has authority to settle or collect a claim also has authority to receive payment in money and that such payment to the attorney discharges the claim, even if the attorney absconds with the money.

However, the mere giving of a check payable to the agent does not constitute payment. "A check is never a payment of the debt for which it is given until the check itself is paid or otherwise discharged, unless expressly agreed to be taken in payment." But once the check is paid, the payment of the underlying debt which was theretofore conditional becomes absolute and relates back to the date of the delivery of the check.

The foregoing authorities support the now-settled rule that where an agent authorized to collect a debt owing to his principal accepts in lieu of cash a valid check *payable to the agent*, the debtor is discharged upon payment of the check, although the agent absconds with the proceeds, since payment to the agent is equivalent to payment to the principal.

Section 178(2) [of the Restatement of Agency 2d] provides: "If an agent who is authorized to receive a check payable to the principal as conditional payment forges the principal's endorsement to such a check, the maker is relieved of liability to the principal if the drawee bank pays the check and charges the amount to the maker."

Upon application of the foregoing rule of agency we conclude that there is no basis in the record before us upon which to sustain the judgment.

The judgment is reversed.

Notes

1. The general rule against partial ratification does not apply to situations involving distinct transactions or separate acts. Restatement 96 comment b. For ex-

ample, in *Navrides v. Zurich Insurance Co.*, although the attorney had *power to bind* Navrides by his forgery of Navrides's signature, that forgery was a separate act *and was not* ratified by Navrides's ratification of the settlement. *See* Restatement 96 comment b, illustration 6. Whether Navrides has ratified the forgery is important in light of the "relation back" doctrine and the rule discussed in *Rakestraw v. Rodrigues*, page 431, that a principal's ratification of an agent's unauthorized act "exonerates" the agent as against the principal.

Chapter 10

Liability for Wrongful Acts of Servants

A. Introduction

Up until now, we have focused largely on contractual issues, on the *agent's* ability to *bind* the *principal* by acts within his or her actual or apparent authority. We now turn our attention to the liability of the principal for the incidental torts committed by the agent in course of carrying out the agency. As a general rule, a person is *not* liable for the incidental torts of an agent *unless* (i) the agent was also a *servant* and (ii) the tortious acts were committed in the servant's *scope of employment*. Restatement § 219(1).

> A servant is defined as a person employed to perform personal service for another in his affairs, and who, in respect to his physical movements in the performance of the service is subject to the other's control or right to control, while an agent is defined as a person who represents another in contractual negotiations or transactions akin thereto. The reason assigned for the importance of making the distinction is that an agent who is not at the same time acting as servant cannot ordinarily make his principal liable for incidental negligence in connection with the means incidentally employed to accomplish the work intrusted to his care.

Stockwell v. Morris, 46 Wyo. 1, 22 P.2d 189, 191 (1933). A principal who has employed a servant is called a *"master."* Restatement § 2(1).

Where the principal has not reserved the right to control the agent's physical conduct, the agent is *not* a servant, but only an *independent contractor*, and the principal generally will not be liable for the agent's incidental torts. This chapter focuses on the liability of the master, and of the servant, for the servant's torts. Chapter 11 deals with independent contractors.

B. Duties in Selecting and Supervising Servants

Evans v. Morsell
284 Md. 160, 395 A.2d 480 (1978)

ELDRIDGE, Judge.

We issued a writ of certiorari in this case in order to consider the principles applicable to an action against an employer based upon the alleged negligent hiring or retention of an employee.

The plaintiff Joseph Evans brought this action for compensatory and punitive damages for personal injuries which he sustained as a result of being shot by a bartender in a tavern owned by the defendant. The plaintiff alleged in his declaration that he entered the defendant's establishment "as a customer and invitee," that he was acting in a peaceful manner when he was "maliciously shot with a twelve gauge shotgun" by the bartender, Jessie Hopkins, and that the defendant "knew or should have known of the vicious propensities" of his employee Hopkins because of the latter's "past record of criminal assaults." The plaintiff went on to assert that the defendant tavern owner breached his duty to the plaintiff, a customer, "by employing a person of the character of Jessie Hopkins, in a sensitive position as that of bartender, and permitting him access to a dangerous weapon." The case was tried before a jury in the Superior Court of Baltimore City, and, at the close of all of the evidence, the trial judge granted the defendant's motion for a directed verdict.

The plaintiff testified that on the evening of April 27, 1973, he entered the defendant's tavern, went to the bar, and asked the bartender Hopkins for some beer. According to plaintiff, he was refused service by the bartender, and later by the defendant owner, on the ground that previously he had allegedly brought beer into the bar from someplace else. After being denied service, the plaintiff talked a while with some other customers and then left the tavern. Later that evening, the plaintiff came back to the tavern and, as he testified:

> I was snapping my fingers to the music. When I look up the bartender is aiming a shotgun at me. So I just stood there. Then he got a wild look in his face so I threw my arm across my head and started spinning and I got hit in my arm and got hit in my stomach, and I ran to the door. When I reached for the door that's when he shot me in my upper thighs and leg.

The bartender Hopkins was later convicted of assault and sentenced to twelve years' imprisonment.

The plaintiff testified that he did nothing to provoke the bartender and that he never had any arguments with him, although Hopkins "had a few words with me the day before." The plaintiff also testified that he was a regular patron of the defendant's tavern and that he had seen Hopkins "drunk and arguing with other customers" on several occasions before this. However, he did not testify to any facts indicating that the owner was present on such occasions or had any knowledge of his employee's arguing with other customers.

The evidence further showed that the defendant had purchased the tavern in November 1972, and had hired Hopkins as a bartender in December 1972. At that time, Hopkins had a significant criminal record, with several convictions for assault—all in the 1950's and 1960's. The defendant was not aware of this, and made no inquiry of Hopkins concerning a possible criminal record.

Hopkins had worked for the prior owner of the tavern for eighteen months as a bartender. The prior owner testified that Hopkins, although he would occasionally "go on a drunk," never got drunk in the tavern, was a "good worker," was "honest" and had never assaulted anyone or had fights with anyone in the tavern. The former owner of the tavern also testified that when he sold the business to the defendant, the defendant inquired about previous employees, and the witness recommended Hopkins as a good worker and a person whom the defendant should employ. Additionally, the former owner testified that he had been in the tavern business for about ten years, that he had known other tavern owners in the area, and that there was no practice among the owners to inquire concerning the possible criminal records of persons who were applying for positions of bartenders.

The defendant testified that he had been a Baltimore City police officer for seventeen years before leaving the police force and purchasing the tavern in November 1972. While he was a police officer, he had known Mr. Hopkins and never had any difficulty with him. The defendant confirmed that before employing Hopkins, he had inquired of the former owner of the tavern, and the former owner told him that Hopkins was a "good worker." Additionally, the defendant testified that between the time that he had hired Hopkins and the shooting on April 27, 1973, he was aware of no fights with customers or any other actions by the bartender that would lead him to believe that such a shooting might take place. The defendant kept the shotgun in a back room directly behind the bar because he kept a large amount of cash on hand for check cashing purposes.

Finally, the records supervisor in the Central Records Division of the Baltimore City Police Department testified that in 1972, if an employer wanted the criminal record of an employee or prospective employee, the employer could not get it himself, but he could require the employee or prospective employee to obtain it. If he did, the Police Department would furnish the employee or prospective employee with a certified copy of his criminal record or a letter stating that he did not have a criminal record.

The plaintiff argues here, as he did below, that under circumstances such as existed in this case, the defendant breached a duty to the plaintiff by not inquiring about Hopkin's criminal record before hiring the bartender.[2]

Long ago this Court recognized, prior to the enactment of the Worker's Compensation Act and in the somewhat different context of an employee injured by the alleged negligence of a drunken co-worker, that in hiring and retaining someone, an employer owes a duty to his other employees and to the general public to use reasonable care. Judge McSherry thus stated for the Court in *Norfolk and Western Railroad Co. v. Hoover*, 79 Md. 253, 262, 29 A. 994 (1894):

---

2. Both in the trial court and in this Court, the plaintiff's contention has been that the defendant himself was negligent in hiring and retaining the bartender. At no time has the plaintiff suggested that the defendant might be vicariously liable under the doctrine of respondeat superior. Consequently, we do not consider such possibility, and cases dealing with the respondeat superior liability of an employer for the intentional torts of his employee committed in the scope of employment are not here applicable.

But he owes to each of his servants the duty of using reasonable care and caution in the selection of competent fellow-servants, and in the retention in his service of none but those who are. If he does not perform this duty, and an injury is occasioned by the negligence of an incompetent or careless servant, the master is responsible to the injured employee, not for the mere negligent act or omission of the incompetent or careless servant, but for his own negligence in not discharging his own duty towards the injured servant. As this negligence of the master must be proved, it may be proved like any other fact, either by direct evidence or by the proof of circumstances from which its existence may, as a conclusion of fact, be fairly and reasonably inferred. That drunkenness on the part of a railroad employee renders him an incompetent servant will scarcely be disputed; nor can it be questioned *that a master who knowingly employs such a servant, or who, knowing his habits, retains him in his service, would be guilty of a reckless and wanton breach of duty, not only to the public, but to every employee in his service.*

(Emphasis supplied). The Court went on to point out that there is a rebuttable presumption that an employer uses due care in hiring an employee, and that this presumption may of course be overcome by direct or circumstantial evidence. The Court also indicated that the employer's failure to make a proper inquiry may under some circumstances constitute negligence itself.

Similar principles have been applied by the court in cases like the one at bar, involving intentional torts committed by employees or other agents upon members of the public. A critical standard here is whether the employer knew or should have known that the individual was potentially dangerous. As stated by the Supreme Court of New York, Appellate Division, in *Vanderhule v. Berinstein*, 285 App. Div. 290, 136 N.Y.S.2d 95, 100 (1954):

The ultimate duty of the defendants, for a breach of which the defendants could be held liable, was the duty to refrain from hiring or retaining anyone whom they knew or, in the exercise of reasonable care, they should have known was potentially dangerous.

And as pointed out by the court in *Fleming v. Bronfin*, 80 A.2d 915, 917 (D.C. Mun. App. 1951):

One dealing with the public is bound to use reasonable care to select employees competent and fit for the work assigned to them and to refrain from retaining the services of an unfit employee. When an employer neglects this duty and as a result injury is occasioned to a third person, the employer may be liable even though the injury was brought about by the willful act of the employee beyond the scope of his employment. This principle has been applied in a variety of cases dealing with innkeepers, carriers, stores, apartment houses, and other business.

See also Restatement of Agency 2d, § 213, Comment d.[3]

---

3. Although most cases dealing with negligent hiring or retention involved employees, the applicable principles appear to be the same regardless of whether the employer hires an employee or an independent contractor to deal with his customers. *Bennett v. T & F Distributing Co.*, 117 N.J. Super. 439, 285 A.2d 59 (1971).

Where an employee is expected to come into contact with the public, which is obviously the situation concerning a bartender, it has been held that the employer must make some reasonable inquiry before hiring or retaining the employee to ascertain his fitness, or the employer must otherwise have some basis for believing that he can rely on the employee. The nature and extent of the inquiry that is needed will naturally vary with the circumstances.

However, the majority of courts flatly reject the contention of the plaintiff in the present case, namely that where an employee is to regularly deal with the public, an inquiry into a possible criminal record is required. On the contrary, the cases hold if the employer makes adequate inquiry or otherwise has a sufficient basis to rely on the employee, there is no need to inquire about a possible criminal record.[4]

We agree with the cases holding that an employer ordinarily has no duty to inquire concerning the possible criminal record of a prospective employee. It may today be quite difficult to obtain criminal records. In addition, when one has completed a criminal sentence or has been paroled, the employer to some extent is entitled to rely upon the determination of the government's criminal justice system that the individual is ready to again become an active member of society.[5] Furthermore, it would impose a significant burden upon employers, as well as upon unemployed prospective employees, if an employer had to regularly investigate the possible criminal background of applicants for employment.

Applying the foregoing principles to the instant case, we agree with the defendant that the motion for a directed verdict was properly granted. There was no evidence whatever that the defendant knew or should have known that the bartender Hopkins was potentially dangerous. The defendant did inquire about Hopkins before employing him, asking the former owner of the tavern who had been Hopkins' employer for eighteen months. The former owner recommended Hopkins to the defendant, telling him that he was a "good worker" and that he would employ him. Moreover, the defendant himself in his prior capacity as a police officer knew Hopkins as a bartender and had no difficulty with him. The only basis for a jury issue advocated by the plaintiff, both in the trial court and this Court, is the plaintiff's contention that in every case like the instant one, the employer must inquire concerning the possible criminal record of a prospective employee. However, as previously discussed, we cannot accept such a proposition.

JUDGMENT OF THE SUPERIOR COURT OF BALTIMORE CITY AFFIRMED.

---

4. Furthermore, even where the employer knows of a criminal record and still hires the employee, this does not automatically make out a prima facie case of negligent hiring. Instead, it depends upon the nature of the criminal record and the surrounding circumstances. *Argonne Apartment House Co. v. Garrison*, 59 App. D.C. 370, 42 F.2d 605, 608 (1930) (prior conviction for intoxication did not put employer on notice that the employee might be dishonest); *Strawder v. Harrall*, 251 So. 2d 514, 518 (La. App. 1971) (employer's knowledge that employee was on parole from the penitentiary was not sufficient to render it negligent to hire employee as a service station attendant); *Bradley v. Stevens*, 329 Mich. 556, 46 N.W.2d 382, 385 (1951) (knowledge by service station owner that employee was convicted of nonsupport was insufficient to put employer on notice that employee might attack female customer).

5. There are limits to this idea, however, depending upon the sensitivity of the position, the nature of the past criminal conduct, and the surrounding circumstances.

Notes

1. Suppose that in *Evans v. Morsell* the owner of the bar (Morsell) had known that Hopkins had a criminal record of violent assaults. Would Morsell then have been negligent in hiring Hopkins as a bartender?

2. Assume Morsell *was* negligent in hiring Hopkins, and thus liable to Evans for Hopkins' assault. Would Morsell be liable *solely* because of Hopkins' act? Would Morsell's negligence be the *proximate cause* of Evans' injuries, given Hopkins' intentional tort?

3. In addition to exercising care in the selection of servants, the master must also exercise care in instructing, supervising, and controlling the agent. Under Restatement section 213

> A person conducting an activity through servants or other agents is subject to liability for harm resulting from his conduct if he is negligent or reckless:
>
> > (a) in giving improper or ambiguous orders of in failing to make proper regulations; or
>
> > (b) in the employment of improper persons or instrumentalities in work involving risk of harm to others:
>
> > (c) in the supervision of the activity; or
>
> > (d) in permitting, or failing to prevent, negligent or other tortious conduct by persons, whether or not his servants or agents, upon premises or with instrumentalities under his control.

Restatement § 213.

4. As noted in *Norfolk & Western RR Co. v. Hoover* (discussed in *Evans v. Morsell*), a master negligent in employing (or retaining), supervising, or controlling an intoxicated servant may be liable for the servant's negligence or reckless conduct in the scope of the servant's employment. May the master be liable for the operation by the servant of a motor vehicle while intoxicated where the servant is *not* acting in the scope of employment? Consider the facts in the controversial case of *Clark v. Otis Engineering Corp.*, 633 S.W.2d 538 (Tex. App. 1982), *aff'd* 668 S.W.2d 307 (Tex. 1983). During the evening shift at the Otis plant, Matheson, one of Otis' workers, became too intoxicated to operate the machinery. Instead of sending Matheson to the company nursing station to sober up, Matheson's supervisor not only told Matheson to go home, he escorted Matheson to the company parking lot and poured him into his car (he did ask if Matheson could make it home). On the way home, Matheson had an accident in which Matheson and three other persons were killed. The autopsy revealed that Matheson's blood alcohol level was 0.268%. A wrongful death action was brought against Otis, alleging that it was negligent in its handling of the situation.

Similarly, the plaintiff has not relied upon the doctrine of negligent entrustment with respect to the shotgun, although plaintiff does point to the presence of the shotgun as one of the circumstances which allegedly imposed the duty on the defendant to inquire about the bartender's criminal record.

The trial court entered summary judgment in favor of Otis, and the Texas Court of Appeals reversed:

In ordinary circumstances, a person has no duty to use care to control the conduct of a third person in order to prevent that person from causing harm to others unless there exists between the actor and the third person some special relation which imposes such a duty. Restatement (Second) of Torts § 315 (1965). The bare relation of employer-employee is not one which in itself imposes such a duty unless the employee is upon the employer's premises or using his chattel, and the employer has the required knowledge of ability and necessity for controlling the employee. Restatement (Second) of Torts § 317 (1965). Nevertheless, such a relation may arise when a person takes charge of a third person whom he knows or should know is likely to cause harm to others if not controlled. Restatement (Second) of Torts § 319 (1965).

One of the earliest cases to apply this principle is *Missouri, K. & T. Ry. Co. of Texas v. Wood,* [95 Tex. 223, 66 S.W. 449 (1901),] where our Supreme Court held that a railroad company which negligently allowed an employee suffering from smallpox to escape from quarantine was liable to others who were exposed to the disease by coming into contact with him after his escape. Other cases have applied the general rule to an infirmary which negligently allowed a crazed and drunken inmate to escape from his room and injure another inmate, *University of Louisville v. Hammock,* [127 Ky. 564, 106 S.W. 219 (1907),] and where the superintendent of a state insane asylum negligently paroled an inmate who later destroyed the plaintiff's property by burning it, *Austin W. Jones Co. v. State,* [122 Me. 214, 119 A. 577 (1923)].

Otis argues that there is no evidence raising a fact issue as to whether it took or attempted to take control of Matheson on the occasion in question. Matheson was so intoxicated that he was practically helpless. His supervisor found it necessary to take him off duty before his work shift ended in order to protect him from his machine on which he was working. He was ordered to go home prior to the end of his shift, and the supervisor accompanied him to the parking lot to begin his ill-fated attempt to reach home by driving on the heavily traveled highway. Viewing these facts and the other summary judgment evidence most favorably to the appellants, we find them sufficient to raise a genuine issue of fact on the question of whether Otis, through its agents and employees, took charge or attempted to take charge of Matheson at the time of these events.

There is also sufficient summary judgment evidence raising fact issues as to negligence and proximate cause. Matheson's extreme intoxication on the occasion was well known to his supervisor and his fellow workers. They knew that he was not in a condition to drive safely. They had a nurse's station available where ill or disabled employees could be taken and cared for, yet they accompanied him to the parking lot and, it may be inferred, sent him out on the highway. Mr. Roy testified that he feared Matheson might have a collision, and when he heard of the wreck he immediately suspected that Matheson was involved. There is no summary judgment evidence that Matheson's intoxication actually caused the collision, but Otis did not attempt to negate that fact in its summary judgment motion, so if fact issues were raised on the other essential elements of the Clarks' cause of action, Otis failed to carry its burden to sustain a summary judgment.

Cases relied upon by Otis, such as *Pilgrim v. Fortune Drilling Co., Inc.*[, 653 F.2d 982 (5th Cir. 1981),] are clearly distinguishable. In *Pilgrim*, for example, where the claim of negligence was based on the employer's failure to prevent exhausted employees from driving long distances to their homes, there was no evidence of an assumption of any degree of control over the employee by the employer, there was no evidence that the employee was obviously incapacitated, the employee's work shift had terminated, and he had voluntarily left the premises.

We are not to be understood as holding that in ordinary circumstances an employer is responsible for the acts of his employees while they are off duty, off premises, and not using company facilities. The contrary is the case, even if the employer knows of a dangerous condition involving the employee. But where the employer-employee relationship exists and there is action on the part of the employer amounting to an assumption of some control over the employee who is likely to be dangerous to others, that special relation recognized by the Restatement in § 319 arises, which may in a proper case impose a duty of reasonable care and the resulting liability if that duty is breached.

The decisions have thus far applied the rule of control only where there has been a type of institutional custody of the dangerous person, but we do not believe the rule should necessarily be restricted to that type of case. Rather, we think its application should depend upon the facts of each case, evaluated upon a consideration of the defendant's ability, opportunity and duty to act, and the reasonable foreseeability of the consequences of a failure to act.

The issue is not Otis' failure to control Matheson's conduct on the highway; it is the failure to control him before he got on the highway. In fact, it may be said that appellants' case here is not merely that of a failure to exercise reasonable care to restrain Matheson; the evidence can be construed to show an element of affirmative action in Otis' sending from its premises onto a crowded highway a person so dangerous to himself and others. It has been held that when such affirmative action is involved, liability may be imposed even though there is no relationship between the defendant and the dangerous person.

Obviously, we are not holding that the evidence establishes the Clarks' cause of action. It may or may not do so in a trial of the case. We simply conclude that, viewed most favorably to their position, material issues of fact have been raised which preclude summary judgment.

The Texas Supreme Court affirmed the holding of the Court of Appeals:

[W]hen, because of an employee's incapacity, an employer exercises control over the employee, the employer has the duty to take such action as a reasonably prudent employer under the same or similar circumstances would take to prevent the employee from causing an unreasonable risk of harm to others. Such a duty may be analogized to cases in which a defendant can exercise some measure of control over a dangerous person when there is a recognizable great danger of harm to third persons. *See, e.g., Restatement (Second) of Torts, § 319.* Additionally, we adopt the rule from cases in this Restatement area that the duty of the employer is not an absolute duty to insure safety, but requires only reasonable care.

5. As noted by the *Evans v. Morsell* court (in footnote 3), the employer of an independent contractor must also exercise care in selecting, instructing, and supervising the independent contractor. *See Redinger v. Living, Inc.* in Chapter 11, "Independent Contractors."

C. Liability Without Fault (Respondeat superior)

1. Scope of Employment

Why should a master be held responsible for torts of a servant when the master was not himself or herself negligent in selecting, supervising, or controlling the servant? Consider the following extract from *Fruit v. Schreiner*, 502 P.2d 133, 139-40 (Alaska 1972):

> The origins of the principle whereby an employer may be held vicariously liable for the injuries wrought by his employee are in dispute. Justice Holmes traces the concept to Roman law while Wigmore finds it to be of Germanic origin. The doctrine emerged in English law in the 17th Century. Initially a master was held liable for those acts which he commanded or to which he expressly assented. This was expanded to include acts by implied command or authority and eventually to acts within the scope of employment. The modern theory evolved with the growth of England's industry and commerce.
>
> A truly imaginative variety of rationale have been advanced by courts and glossators in justification of this imposition of liability on employers. Among the suggestions are the employer's duty to hire and maintain a responsible staff of employees, to "control" the activities of his employees and thus to insist upon appropriate safety measures; the belief that the employer should pay for the inherent risks which result from hiring others to carry on his business; the observation that the employer most often has easier access to evidence of the facts surrounding the injury; and the metaphysical identification of the employer and employee as a single "persona" jointly liable for the injury which occurred in the context of the business.
>
> Baty more cynically states: "In hard fact, the reason for the employers' liability is the damages are taken from a deep pocket."
>
> The two theories which carry the greatest weight in contemporary legal thought are respectively, the "control" theory which finds liability whenever the act of the employee was committed with the implied authority, acquiescence or subsequent ratification of the employer, and the "enterprise" theory which finds liability whenever the enterprise of the employer would have benefited by the context of the act of the employee but for the unfortunate injury.

Since we are dealing with vicarious liability, justification may not be found[ed] on theories involving the employer's personal fault such as his failure to exercise proper control over the activities of his employees or his failure to take proper precautions in firing or hiring them. Lack of care on the employer's part would subject him to direct liability without the necessity of involving respondeat superior.

ER's lack of care = direct liability

Regardless of the *rationale* for imposing liability on the master for *some* torts of the servant, the law must identify those risks properly allocable to the master. The *scope of employment* doctrine is the primary test used to allocate the risks of servant misconduct.

Problem 10.1

Sadler was a servant employed by Restaurant as its janitor. One of Sadler's duties was to dispose of trash. In the past, Sadler had burned the trash. After one fire had gotten out of control and had set nearby grass on fire, Restaurant instructed Sadler that he was not to burn the trash. Instead, he was to place it in a metal container at the rear of the Restaurant's property. Despite Restaurant's instructions, Sadler decided to burn some of the Restaurant's trash. The fire got out of control, and spread to the grass, and then to a house owned by Lewis. Is Restaurant subject to liability for the fire? *See Ohio Farmers Ins. Co. v. Norman,* 122 Ariz. 330, 594 P.2d 1026 (1979).

Thompson v. United States

504 F. Supp. 1087 (D.S.D. 1980)

DONALD J. PORTER, District Judge.

The facts of this case are dismayingly simple. On July 12, 1975, Benjamin Kitteaux was a CETA trainee employed by the Crow Creek Sioux Tribe as a police officer. On that day, while Kitteaux was on duty, he entered the police station of the Bureau of Indian Affairs (BIA), United States Department of the Interior, where the tribal police were headquartered, drew his gun, and pointed it at Tommy Thompson. Kitteaux then put the gun down alongside his holster, and in a simulation of a "fast draw," pulled the gun up again. This appears to have been a frequent practice of his. This time, however, the gun fired, the bullet struck Thompson in the chest, and Thompson died.

Slightly more than one month later, on August 25, 1975, Kitteaux came before this Court, and on his plea of guilty, was convicted of involuntary manslaughter.

An administrative claim for damages resulting from Thompson's death was filed with the Department of the Interior, and was denied. Thereafter, suit was filed against the United States under the Federal Tort Claims Act.

It is not enough to show that a particular individual was an employee of the United States at the time an accident occurred; a plaintiff must also show that at the time of the injury, the employee was "acting within the scope of his office or employment." This must be determined by the law of the state where the act occurred.

The law of South Dakota on this point is reasonably clear. The employer-master is liable for the acts of the servant, within the general scope of his employment, while engaged in his master's business, and *done with [sic] a view to the furtherance of that business and the master's interest even though the acts be done wantonly and wilfully.*

Skow v. Steele, 49 N.W.2d 24 (S.D. 1951).

In *Skow*, for example, the facts were that defendant had sent his brother onto the farm defendant rented to plaintiff to supervise the shelling of corn. Plaintiff protested, and defendant's brother assaulted plaintiff. Upholding the jury verdict against the defendant employer, the court stated that whether the assault occurred in the scope of the employee's office was an issue for the finder of fact:

> This is so because the servant's motive is usually a material issue. Thus in this case the real question presented is whether [the servant] committed the assault as a result of his desire to [carry out the master's business], or whether he assaulted plaintiff simply to effect some purpose of his own.

Can it be said that Kitteaux was acting within the scope of his employment when Thompson was killed? Kitteaux was on duty at the time, within the confines of the BIA police station, armed with his BIA-issued gun. This leaves the question of his *motive* in leveling his gun at Thompson, which *Skow* indicates is particularly one for the finder of fact. To reach a determination of this matter, one must consider the context in which the act took place.

Kitteaux was a recently hired police trainee. As a part of his training as a policeman, he was given firearms training by a Special Agent of the FBI, David Powers. This training includes, as Powers testified, extensive instruction of "quick draw." Given this background, and the circumstances with which Kitteaux was surrounded on the day the shooting occurred, the Court must draw the inference that, though tragically misguided, Kitteaux's motive in pulling his gun up and pointing it at Thompson was to practice and perfect his police firearms techniques. In this unfortunate way, Kitteaux evidently intended to improve himself as a policeman, and to thereby carry out his employer's business. It could not be contended that if a similar accident had occurred on a firearms range, in the course of firearms practice by a government employee, the United States would not be liable. Simply because the situs of the practice is moved from a range to the interior of a BIA police station, the result is not changed.

Defendant complains that such behavior was strictly forbidden. Whether it was forbidden or not does not allow defendant to escape liability, for the law is plain that an "act may be within the scope of employment even though forbidden or done in a forbidden manner." As Prosser said, if a master could escape liability by ordering his servant to act carefully, few employers could ever be held liable.

> If the other factors involved indicate that the forbidden conduct is merely the servant's own way of accomplishing an authorized purpose, the master cannot escape responsibility no matter how specific, detailed and emphatic his orders may have been to the contrary.

Prosser, Torts, 461 (4th ed. 1971). As made clear before, Kitteaux's "practice" on Thompson was Kitteaux's way of perfecting his mastery of his gun, a goal which Power's testimony shows was highly desired, even if Kitteaux's way of doing it may have been forbidden. It is thus the ruling of this Court that the shooting which took Tommy Thompson's life occurred in the scope of Benjamin Kitteaux's office as a federal employee.

[This Court therefore holds that defendant is liable in the amount of $35,000 for pecuniary damages resulting from this death.]

Notes

1. Restatement section 228 sets forth the general test for determining whether a servant's act is within the scope of employment:

(1) Conduct of a servant is within the scope of employment if, *but only if*:

(a) it is of the kind he is employed to perform;

(b) it occurs substantially within the authorized time and space limits;

(c) it is actuated, *at least in part*, by a purpose to serve the master; and

(d) if force is used by the servant against another, the use of force is *not un*expectable by the master.

(2) Conduct of a servant is not within the scope of employment if it is different in kind from that authorized, far beyond the authorized time or space limits, or *too little actuated* by a purpose to serve the master.

(emphasis added). Restatement section 229 elaborates on the general test as follows:

(1) To be within the scope of the employment, conduct must be of the same general nature as that authorized, or incidental to the conduct authorized.

(2) In determining whether or not the conduct, *although not authorized,* is nevertheless so similar to or incidental to the conduct authorized as to be within the scope of employment, the following matters of fact are to be considered:

(a) whether or not the act is one commonly done by such servants;

(b) the time, place and purpose of the act;

(c) the previous relations between the master and the servant;

(d) the extent to which the business of the master is apportioned between different servants;

(e) whether or not the act is outside the enterprise of the master or, if within the enterprise, has not been entrusted to the servant;...

(i) the extent of departure from the normal method of accomplishing an authorized result; and

(j) whether or not the act is seriously criminal.

(emphasis added).

2. In *Thompson v. United States,* Kitteaux was not motivated *solely* by a desire to serve the master. Why did that not make any difference in the result? Should it have?

3. Servants have considerable leeway before their acts will be considered outside the scope of employment. Some of the cases refer to those deviations from the "straight and narrow" that do *not* take the servant outside the scope of employment as "mere *detours.*" Similarly, where the servant's conduct is "different in kind from that authorized, far beyond the authorized time and place limits, or too little actuated by a purpose to serve the master," Restatement § 228(2), and thus *outside* the scope of employment, the courts characterize the conduct as involving a "frolic." Students should be careful to note that "detour" and "frolic" are only *labels* attached to *conclusions* that the servant's conduct is, or is not, within the scope of employment; they are *not substitutes* for analysis.

4. In *Thompson v. United States,* the government was held liable *despite* the fact that Kitteaux violated an *express policy* prohibiting police officers from drawing their weapons in the station house. *Accord* Restatement § 230 ("An act, although forbidden, or done in a forbidden manner, may be within the scope of employment."). If masters cannot limit their *respondeat superior* exposure by exercising care in instructing and supervising their servants, is there *any* way they can limit their liability in respondeat superior?

5. Under Restatement section 239

> [a] master is not liable for injuries caused by the negligence of a servant in the use of an instrumentality which [is] of a substantially different kind from that authorized as a means of performing the master's service, or over the use of which the master is to have no right of control.

Is Restatement section 239 consistent with the principles embodied in Restatement sections 228 and 229? On what basis should the master avoid liability under the circumstances described in Restatement section 239?

Problem 10.2

The tragic vehicular accident underlying this action occurred when a sixteen-year-old employee, Robert Bruno, at a gasoline station from which an Avis car rental agency was being operated, drove in a rental car to pick up lunch, tarried briefly with his girlfriend passenger, and collided with another automobile during his return, killing two of its occupants and seriously injuring two others. In 1965, House began operating an Avis rental franchise from his gasoline station in Mount Kisco, New York. House employed boys ranging from fourteen to sixteen years in age as part-time employees. The duties of these youngsters, some of whom, like Bruno, were not licensed to drive, included selling gasoline, renting vehicles, running the computer, refueling Avis cars, and moving the cars about on the premises when necessary. During periodic inspections of House's premises, Avis representatives saw these young employees driving company vehicles at the station. On Sunday afternoon, and from 5:30 P.M. to 9:00 P.M. on other nights, House would depart, leaving a boy or boys in full charge of his operations and with keys to all the cars. On March 17, 1974, Sunday sales of gasoline were still banned due to the Arab oil embargo, and the House station was open solely to rent Avis cars. House arrived at 10:00 A.M., stayed for about an hour, and left Bruno alone and in charge for the rest of the day. At about 1:30 P.M. Greg Adams, another young House employee, appeared at the station to work on his own car and agreed to watch the station while Bruno and his girlfriend went to pick up a pizza for lunch for Adams and Bruno. Bruno took a key off a rack and drove away in an Avis car. After the pizza was purchased at Leonardi's, Bruno drove to a nursery in Armonk where he and his girlfriend talked for about twenty minutes. When they left the nursery, Bruno intended to drive the girl home and return to work, but about a mile from her house and a mile from the House station, the car went out of control, entered the opposing lane of traffic, and crashed head on with a car driven by Adele O'Boyle. O'Boyle and her infant daughter perished, and her husband and mother suffered serious injuries. Four weeks earlier, another young employee had pocketed a set of keys and had taken off with an Avis car. He was arrested for speeding in Connecticut and was discharged from his employment as a result. On what theories will the plaintiffs sue? Who will be the defendants? Who will prevail? (See *O'Boyle v. Avis Rent-A-Car System, Inc.*, 78 A.D.2d 431, 435 N.Y.S.2d 296 (1981).)

Henderson v. AT&T Information Systems

552 A.2d 935 (Md. App. 1989)

KARWACKI, Judge.

On October 17, 1986, appellant Michael E. Henderson filed a complaint against Daniel Zuckerman seeking damages for injuries arising out of a January 11, 1986 motor vehicle accident. His original complaint was amended on December 18, 1986 to assert that Zuckerman's employer, AT&T Information Systems, Inc. (AT&T), the appellee, was vicariously liable for Zuckerman's negligence. Carmen Crews, a passenger in Henderson's vehicle at the time of the accident, intervened in the action as a co-plaintiff on June 22, 1987 and joins Henderson as an appellant in the case before this Court.

At the hearing on the summary judgment motion, Judge Ward ruled, as a matter of law, that AT&T's employee, Zuckerman, was not acting within the scope of his employment at the time of the motor vehicle accident and, therefore, that AT&T was not vicariously liable.

Since this is an appeal from an order granting appellee summary judgment, we shall review the evidence before the hearing judge in a light most favorable to the appellants and resolve all inferences from that evidence in their favor.

In the early afternoon of January 11, 1986, the appellants were traveling in a southbound direction on Interstate Route 95 (JFK Highway). Due to the abrupt loss of a wheel the 1979 Dodge van in which they were traveling came to a complete stop in the center southbound lane of the highway. Henderson exited the vehicle to search for the wheel, while Crews remained in the van. While Henderson was looking in the rear of the vehicle for emergency flares to display, he and the disabled van were struck from behind by an automobile which Zuckerman was driving in a southbound direction on I-95. As a result of the accident Henderson sustained severe injuries including the loss of both legs.

Mr. Zuckerman was en route from New Jersey to Virginia at the time of the accident. He owned the 1976 AMC Hornet he was operating.

Zuckerman became employed by AT&T in March of 1985. Under the terms of his employment, Zuckerman was to work at appellee's Homdel, New Jersey location, as a software engineer, until the fall of 1985 when he was to participate in AT&T's Graduate Study Program, One Year on Campus (OYOC). As a participant in the OYOC program, Zuckerman would become a full time resident student at an approved graduate institution for one year. Zuckerman was given a list of AT&T approved colleges from which to choose in applying for graduate school. Zuckerman ultimately decided to attend the University of Virginia. Mr. Ritacco, Zuckerman's supervisor at AT&T, approved Zuckerman's selection and agreed that Zuckerman would begin his studies in January of 1986.

AT&T, pursuant to the OYOC program, advanced 100% of all tuition and fees for Zuckerman's course of study at the University of Virginia. Zuckerman was compensated at 60% of his regular salary while attending school. In the event Zuckerman did not complete his course of study he was subject to termination of employment by AT&T. If he successfully completed his course of study at the University of Virginia, Zuckerman would receive a salary increase from AT&T when he returned to work, reflecting his additional education.

Zuckerman worked at AT&T's Homdel location through Friday, January 10, 1986. He left New Jersey to drive to Charlottesville, Virginia on Saturday, January 11, 1986. Classes began on Tuesday, January 14, 1986. Zuckerman elected to drive his own vehicle and was being reimbursed 21 cents per mile by AT&T. Zuckerman had the option of flying, or taking any mode of transportation he chose, to get to the University of Virginia. Zuckerman's household belongings were relocated at AT&T's expense.

In AT&T's OYOC Relocation Policy Manual specific rules were set out for the reimbursement of travel expenses. The maximum reimbursable mileage from Homdel to Charlottesville was estimated at 320 miles and Zuckerman was allowed one day to make the trip. AT&T would pay for three meals and one night's lodging for this trip. If Zuckerman chose to deviate from this guideline, he would not be reimbursed for any additional expenses. Zuckerman was required to fill out an en route trip expense log for submission to AT&T.

Under the doctrine of respondeat superior, an employer is vicariously liable for the negligent acts of its employee if those acts are committed within the scope of employment. To be within the scope of employment the conduct of the employee must be

> of a kind the actor is employed to perform, occur during a period not unreasonably disconnected from the authorized period of employment, in a locality not unreasonably distant from the authorized area, and actuated at least in part by a purpose to serve the master.

A. & P. Co. v. Noppenberger, 171 Md. 378, 390, 189 A. 434 (1937), quoting the Restatement (Second) of Agency § 229 (1958). In short, the test for determining if an employee is acting within the scope of employment is "whether the servant was advancing his master's interests in doing what he did at the time he did it." *Rusnack v. Giant Food, Inc.*, 26 Md. App. 250, 261-65, 337 A.2d 445 (1975), *cert. denied*, 275 Md. 755 (1975).

In *Henkelmann v. Metropolitan Life Insurance Co.*, 180 Md. 591, 599, 26 A.2d 418 (1942), the Court of Appeals discussed respondeat superior liability with respect to the use of automobiles. The Court stated:

> In recent years, on account of the extensive use of the motor vehicle with its accompanying dangers, the courts have realized that a strict application of the doctrine of respondeat superior in the modern commercial world would result in great injustice. It is now held by the great weight of authority that a master will not be held responsible for negligent operation of a servant's automobile, even though engaged at the time in furthering the master's business unless the master expressly or impliedly consents to the use of the automobile, and had the right to control the servant in its operation, or else the use of the automobile was of such vital importance in furthering the master's business that his control over it might reasonably be inferred.

In *Henkelmann*, the employee was an insurance salesman who was involved in an automobile accident on his way, in his own vehicle, to his assigned "territory." A car was not necessary to the performance of his duties and the employer had never consented to or authorized the use of a personal vehicle either to travel to or from the assigned area or while working within it. The Court of Appeals held that the insurance company was not vicariously liable for the negligence of its salesman under these circumstances.

The general rule is that, absent special circumstances, an employer will not be vicariously liable for the negligent conduct of his employee occurring while the employee is traveling to or from work. It is essentially the employee's own responsibility to get to and from work. Restatement (Second) of Agency § 229, comment d (1958). Appellants recognize this general rule but argue that it is not applicable to the instant case. Zuckerman, they contend, was not merely traveling to work on January 11, 1986; he was relocating at the specific direction of AT&T. Appellants argue that there was sufficient evidence of AT&T's consent to the use of Zuckerman's personal automobile and AT&T's control of the operation of the automobile to create vicarious liability for its employee's negligent operation of said automobile. The hearing judge disagreed and held that *Dhanraj v. Potomac Electric Power Co.*, [305 Md. 623, 506 A.2d 224 (1986)] was dispositive.

In *Dhanraj*, a PEPCO employee, while driving his own vehicle, was involved in an automobile accident while traveling to an employer endorsed six-week training located some distance from both his home and from his ordinary work place. The employee was given a travel allowance in order to attend these classes, but was not told what means of transportation to utilize. Further, the employee was not compensated for his travel time. His work day began when he reached the training facility and ended when he departed. The plaintiff sued PEPCO, alleging respondeat superior liability. The hearing judge entered summary judgment in favor of PEPCO; we affirmed, as did the Court of Appeals. In upholding the summary judgment, the Court of Appeals concluded that:

> [I]f Sandy [PEPCO's employee] was negligent as alleged, PEPCO was not vicariously liable for his tortious conduct under the doctrine of respondeat superior. PEPCO did not expressly or impliedly consent to the use of the automobile; it had no right to control Sandy in its operation, and the use of the automobile was not of such vital importance in

furthering PEPCO's business that the control over it might reasonably be inferred.

Appellants attempt to distinguish *Dhanraj* from the instant case, asserting that:

1. AT&T required Zuckerman to drive his personal vehicle to the University of Virginia.

2. AT&T consented to Zuckerman's use of his personal vehicle as the means of transportation to the University of Virginia.

3. AT&T specifically controlled the use of Zuckerman's vehicle during his trip to the University of Virginia.

4. AT&T considered and recognized Zuckerman's injuries as having been incurred on a company related business trip and paid Zuckerman full benefits and salary during the time he was recuperating.

We are not persuaded.

Appellants contend that AT&T required Zuckerman to drive his own vehicle to graduate school. They suggest that since the OYOC Policy Manual stated that AT&T would not pay for the relocation of Zuckerman's automobile, he was required to drive it to Virginia. We do not agree. In several letters addressed to Mr. Zuckerman and in various provisions of the OYOC policy Manual, it is clearly stated that Zuckerman was entitled to choose his manner of transportation to Virginia. He would be reimbursed for "air or surface transportation" whichever he chose. When Zuckerman visited the University of Virginia in November of 1985, for an "exploratory trip," he flew to Charlottesville at AT&T's expense.

Whereas it seems that Zuckerman reviewed the OYOC Manual and discussed his travel plans with his supervisor, Mr. Ritacco, the final decision to drive to Virginia was his. While it did not matter to AT&T if Zuckerman had the use of his car at school, it obviously benefitted Zuckerman to have his own vehicle for transportation while living away from home for a year.

Appellants next attempt to distinguish *Dhanraj* from the instant case on the basis of consent. In *Dhanraj* the employee was given a travel allowance to use however he chose to do so. Here, since Zuckerman was given a specific amount of money per mile, appellants argue that AT&T knew he was driving and consented to the use of his personal automobile. Appellants cite *Regal Laundry Co. v. Abell Co.*, 163 Md. 525, 163 A. 845 (1933) as dispositive of this issue.

The tort-feasor in *Regal* was a newspaper reporter who was assigned to cover a political campaign. The accident in question occurred while the reporter was en route, in his own vehicle, from a political event in Salisbury, which he covered for the newspaper, to his office in Baltimore, where he was to receive further assignments. The Court of Appeals reversed a judgment, entered upon a directed verdict in favor of the newspaper, on the ground that the employer knew the reporter was using his own automobile in carrying out assignments and agreed to reimburse him for that expense. *Regal* was distinguished, by this Court, from the facts in *Dhanraj* because the newspaper employee was "on the job" at the time of the accident. It was his regular job to travel from place to place to cover newsworthy events. Such was not the situation in *Dhanraj* and is not in the instant case.

In *L.M.T. Steel Products v. Peirson*, 47 Md. App. 633, 425 A.2d 242 (1981), cert. denied, 290 Md. 717 (1981), an employee was driving his vehicle, during working hours, from a job site to a telephone booth to make a job related telephone call when the accident occurred. The jury's verdict against the employer was upheld. This Court agreed that the evidence was legally sufficient to show the employer's implied consent to the use of the automobile in furtherance of its interests. Later, in distinguishing *L.M.T. Steel Products v. Peirson*, we stated that

> unlike the incident in the case sub judice, the happening in L.M.T. occurred while the employee was en route on a clear business purpose during working hours.

Zuckerman was not "on the job" at the time of the accident. Further, he was not hired by AT&T for a position that required any amount of driving. This was a one time journey which Zuckerman agreed to make at his convenience, on a Saturday morning. Unlike the PEPCO employee in *Dhanraj*, Zuckerman was a salaried employee. That does not mean, however, that Zuckerman was being compensated for his time traveling to Virginia. While at graduate school Zuckerman was to be paid to pursue a course of study which hopefully would benefit AT&T in the future. That was the business purpose Zuckerman was executing, not driving his car for the benefit of AT&T.

Assuming arguendo that AT&T impliedly or expressly consented to the use by Zuckerman of his personal automobile, Henderson's argument fails the *Henkelmann* and *Dhanraj* tests on the basis of control. As stated supra, for an employer to be liable for its employee's negligence in an automobile accident, the employer must have had

> the right to control the servant in its [the vehicle's] operation, or else the use of the automobile was of such vital importance in furthering the master's business that his control over it might reasonably be inferred.

Appellants argue that AT&T specifically controlled Zuckerman's use of his car by requiring him to follow the most direct route from New Jersey to Virginia. This contention is not borne out by Zuckerman's deposition testimony upon which appellants rely. When questioned about his route to Virginia, Zuckerman replied,

> the mileage had been established for me and I was following a route which most people by looking at a map would follow. If you draw a line, that's roughly how you go.

The fact that Zuckerman was given a specified amount for reimbursable mileage does not mean that AT&T required him to travel a certain route. Zuckerman could have taken any route he chose and would have been reimbursed the same amount by AT&T.

Last, appellants contend that AT&T should be held vicariously liable since it considered Zuckerman's accident an "on the job" injury and paid him salary and benefits while he was recuperating. Here, appellants confuse questions of scope of employment for purposes of workers' compensation with those pertaining to third party negligence actions. In *Dhanraj v. Potomac Elec. Power Co.*, the Court of Appeals refused to resort to cases construing the Workers' Compensation Act to determine the applicability of the doctrine of respondeat superior to the facts in that case. Likewise in other jurisdictions it has been held that the analysis of scope of employment for workers' compensation purposes is not apposite to the analysis of scope of employment for establishing liability under respondeat superior.

In *Dinkins* [*v. Farley*, 434 N.Y.S.2d 325, 329, 106 Misc. 2d 593 (1980)], an employee of Xerox Corporation was driving a borrowed car to night school graduate courses when he was involved in an accident. The employee was attending night school pursuant to a tuition aid program provided by Xerox. The plaintiff sued the driver of the automobile (the student-employee), the vehicle owner and Xerox. In granting Xerox summary judgment, the court stated:

> If Xerox could be held liable in this case under respondeat superior, other circumstances come to mind which would also appear to impose liability upon it. For example, if Victor Farley [employee] carelessly handled volatile materials in a chemistry class and another student were injured or property were destroyed, Xerox could be held responsible. If Xerox is responsible for what an employee does on his way to class, why would it not be equally responsible for what an employee does in class? Or, if educational sabbaticals funded by scholarship grants under the same aid program were encouraged by Xerox, it could be responsible for injuries caused by one of its employees during such a sabbatical driving to or from class at a university hundreds of miles away from the plant.

Further, in discussing whether a workers' compensation analysis should be applied the court held:

> To obtain compensation benefits all that an employee need do is establish that his injury was caused by an activity related to his job. However, respondeat superior mandates that the employee be either under the control of the employer at the time of the injury or that he could have been. Whereas qualifying for workers' compensation benefits requires only that the injury occur out of and in the course of employment, recovery under the doctrine of respondeat superior necessitates that the employee be acting in the scope of his employment, a much narrower test.

We hold that whether Zuckerman was paid workers' compensation benefits for the injuries he suffered in the accident is immaterial to the issue of AT&T's vicarious liability for his negligence.

JUDGMENT AFFIRMED.

Notes

1. One exception to the rule of master non-liability for the torts of servants traveling to and from work is the so-called *"special errand"* rule. Where the servant performs a "special errand" on behalf of the master that would otherwise have required a separate trip by another servant, the servant will be deemed to be acting within the scope of employment (why?). *E.g., Faul v. Jelco*, 122 Ariz. 490, 595 P.2d 1035 (1979) (facts not sufficient to invoke special errand exception).

2. In *Henderson v. AT&T Information Systems*, the court distinguished between the respondeat superior concept of *scope* of employment and the *workers' compensation* concept of *course* of employment, and refused to apply workers' compensation cases in a respondeat superior context. Why?

3. Where the servant is employed at a job site *remote* from his or her regular residence, the question of the master's responsibility for the servant's negligent torts while traveling to and from work becomes especially acute. The majority of courts that have considered this issue have applied the basic "coming & going" rationale as articulated in *Henderson v. AT&T Information Systems*: (i) the servant is furthering his or her own interests (the servant's personal arrangements do not concern the master); and (ii) the master still has no express or implied control over the servant's conduct. *E.g., Faul v. Jelco, Inc.*, 122 Ariz. 490, 595 P.2d 1035 (1979); *Pilgrim v. Fortune Drilling*, 653 F.2d 982 (5th Cir. 1981).

In *Hinman v. Westinghouse Electric Co.*, 2 Cal. 3d 956, 88 Cal. Rptr. 188, 471 P.2d 988 (1970), the California Supreme Court held the master liable where the master had not only compensated the employee for travel expenses, but also for travel *time*. Although the fact that the master is paying for the servant for his or her time while commuting may imply that the master has the right to *control* the servant's conduct while commuting, *see Luth v. Rogers & Babler Construction Co.*, 507 P.2d 761 (Alaska 1973), the California Supreme Court did not primarily rely on that. Instead, the court reasoned that the master, by *benefiting* from distant labor markets, had *increased the risk* to the public, so should bear the cost of resulting injuries. In so doing, the court changed the California justification for respondeat superior from a *control* theory to an *enterprise liability* theory.

Problem 10.3

Brian was sixteen years old. He lived on Cattle Ranch, where his father was employed as a foreman. Although he was not paid by Cattle Ranch, Brian often helped his father out. He often rode in roundups and did "repairs and that sort of thing." Squirrels often dig near the ranch's corrals. They undermine the fence postholes, and the fences collapse. To keep the squirrel problem in control, Brian often shot them. Brian had been shooting squirrels at a corral. Brian's gun was in its holster as Maxwell approached. An argument ensued, and Brian drew the gun and pointed it at Maxwell. Though Brian did not intend to fire the gun, it accidentally went off, hitting at Maxwell. Assuming that Brian was a its servant, is Cattle Ranch subject to liability for the injuries to Maxwell? *See Maxwell v. Bell*, 121 Ariz. 475, 591 P.2d 567 (1979).

Sage Club v. Hunt
638 P.2d 161 (Wyo. 1981)

BROWN, Justice.

Appellant, The Sage Club, appeals a judgment entered against it in a lawsuit arising out of an altercation between a bartender employed at the club, Mr. Thyfault, and a customer, appellee David Leland Hunt. The trial court entered a default judgment against Mr. Thyfault and held The Sage Club liable under the theories of respondeat superior and negligence in continuing to employ Mr. Thyfault. Appellant asserts that it cannot be held liable for the intentional tort of its employee because the tort was personal to Mr. Thyfault and was not within the scope of employment.

A dispute took place over money which appellee had left on the bar. Appellee thought that someone, supposedly Thyfault, had taken more money than he was entitled to take for his drinks. Mr. Thyfault undoubtedly resented the insinuation, so he jumped over the bar and attacked appellee. Thyfault hit appellee in the face, breaking his nose and inflicting other bruises, and then threw appellee down the stairs, reinjuring his back.

This court has held that an employer may be held liable for the negligent acts of an employee acting within the scope of employment. We have not, however, had occasion to rule on whether an employer may be held responsible for the intentional tort of an employee. The majority rule, in fact the universally accepted rule, holds employers liable for the intentional torts of employees committed within the scope of employment. Prosser, Law of Torts, § 70, p. 464 (4th ed., 1971). The rule is a matter of economic and social policy, based both on the fact that the employer has the right to control the employee's actions and that the employer can best bear the loss as a cost of doing business. The Restatement (Second), Agency 2d § 245 (1958), phrases the rule as:

> A master is subject to liability for the intended tortious harm by a servant to the person or things of another by an act done in connection with the servant's employment, although the act was unauthorized, if the act was not unexpectable in view of the duties of the servant.

We agree with the accepted rule and hold that an employer may be held liable for the intentional tort of an employee if the employee is acting within the scope of employment.

Appellant here contends that Mr. Thyfault was not acting within the scope of employment because the altercation which took place was a personal one between Thyfault and appellee. The question of whether an employee is acting within the scope of employment is one for the trier of fact, in this case the trial court, and becomes a question of law when only one reasonable inference can be drawn about the question from the evidence. We think the evidence here was sufficient to show that Thyfault was acting within the scope of employment when he attacked appellee. We said in *Combined Insurance Co. of America v. Sinclair*, [584 P.2d 1034, 1041 (Wyo. 1978),] that in general the servant's conduct is within the scope of his employment,

> if it is of the kind which he was employed to perform, occurs substantially within the authorized limit of time and space, and is actuated, at least in part, by a purpose to serve the master,

citing Prosser, Law of Torts, p. 461 (4th ed.). Here, Mr. Thyfault's duties included collecting money for drinks, and he lost his temper over that matter. His duties also included keeping order in the bar and removing disruptive customers, which Thyfault apparently tried to do by pushing appellee down the stairs.

Appellant relies on *Lombardy v. Stees*, 132 Colo. 570, 290 P.2d 1110 (1956), for the proposition that since the assault was purely personal, it was not within the scope of employment. In that case, however, the evidence showed that the only express instruction to the bartender was that if anyone got too much to drink he was not to be served further. The bartender there had no authority to act as a bouncer; Thyfault did, and his employment was of such a nature as to contemplate the use of force. Indeed, the owner of The Sage Club testified that Thyfault sometimes had to remove people from the club on a daily basis.

In addition to the facts set out in *Combined Insurance Co. of America v. Sinclair*, an important factor in deciding a principal's liability for his agent's intentional torts is whether "the use of force is not unexpectable by the master." Restatement (Second), Agency 2d § 228(1)(d) (1958). Where the nature of the employment is such that the master must contemplate the use of force by the servant, the master will be held liable for the willful act of the servant even though he had no knowledge that the act would take place. The employer need not have foreseen the precise act or exact manner of injury as long as the general type of conduct may have been reasonably expected. Some who frequent grogshops are not the most docile members of society. Where an employee is serving in this type of environment as a bartender, the master is usually responsible if the employee loses his temper and willfully injures a patron because the result is foreseeable in view of the servant's job.

This court will therefore not indulge in nice distinctions to determine whether the excessive force was motivated by personal reasons. It is appellant's misfortune to have hired a quarrelsome and violent bartender who in turn attacked a plaintiff experienced at collecting on injury claims. Appellant evidently allowed Thyfault to use force at his discretion, and he was performing work of the kind he was employed to perform. The assault occurred within the authorized limits of time and space and was motivated, at least partially, by a desire to serve the Sage Club. Appellant is consequently vicariously liable to Mr. Hunt under the doctrine of respondeat superior.

Affirmed.

Notes

1. Under Restatement section 245, intentional torts are not *per se* outside the scope of employment, so long as the tort was "not unexpectable" in view of the servant's duties. Is that the same as saying the tort must have been expectable, that is, *foreseeable*?

2. The case of *Manning v. Grimsley*, 643 F.2d 20 (1st Cir. 1981), involved an intentional tort committed during a professional baseball game at Fenway Park in Boston between the Baltimore Orioles and the Boston Red Sox. Ross Grimsley, a Baltimore pitcher, was warming up in the right field bullpen. Some spectators, including the plaintiff, were seated behind a wire mesh fence in bleachers next to the bullpen. The spectators continuously heckled Grimsley. Several times Grimsley looked directly at the hecklers. Later, Grimsley's catcher left his catching position and was walking over to the bench. Grimsley faced the bleachers and wound up or stretched as though to pitch in the direction of the bullpen plate, but threw the ball at more than 80 miles an hour directly toward the hecklers in the bleachers. The ball passed through the wire mesh fence and hit the plaintiff.

The trial court's directed verdict in favor of Baltimore was reversed on appeal. The appellate court held that Grimsley's intentional tort was within the scope of his employment:

> [W]here a plaintiff seeks to recover damages from an employer for injuries resulting from an employee's assault [w]hat must be shown is that the employee's assault was in response to the plaintiff's *conduct* which was *presently interfering with the employee's ability to perform his duties successfully*. This interfer-

ence may be in the form of an *affirmative attempt to prevent an employee from carrying out his assignments.*

Miller v. Federated Department Stores, Inc., 364 Mass. 340, 349-350, 304 N.E.2d 573 (1973). (Emphasis added.)

The Baltimore [Orioles contend] that the heckling from the bleachers constituted words which annoyed or insulted Grimsley and did not constitute "conduct" and that those words did not "presently" interfere with his ability to perform his duties successfully so as to make his employer liable for his assault in response thereto.

Our analysis of the *Miller* case leads us to reject the contention. There a porter, whose duties consisted of cleaning the floors and emptying the trash cars in Filene's basement store, slapped a customer who had annoyed or insulted him by a remark that "If you would say "excuse me,' people could get out of your way." The Massachusetts Supreme Judicial Court held that while the employee "may have been annoyed or insulted by" the customer's remark, "that circumstance alone does not justify imposition of liability on" the employer.

Miller's holding that a critical comment by a customer to an employee did not in the circumstances constitute "conduct" interfering with the employee's performance of his work is obviously distinguishable from the case at bar. Constant heckling by fans at a baseball park would be, within the meaning of *Miller,* conduct. The jury could reasonably have found that such conduct had either the affirmative purpose to rattle or the effect of rattling the employee so that he could not perform his duties successfully. Moreover, the jury could reasonably have found that Grimsley's assault was not a mere retaliation for past annoyance, but a response to continuing conduct which was "presently interfering" with his ability to pitch in the game if called upon to play. Therefore, the battery count against the Baltimore Club should have been submitted to the jury.

Is *Manning v. Grimsley* consistent with *The Sage Club v. Hunt*? Was Grimsley's assault motivated at least in part by a purpose to serve the master?

3. *Noah v. Ziehl,* 759 S.W.2d 905 (Mo. App. 1988), involved an intentional tort committed by Overton, a "doorman" and bouncer at a nightclub. Noah had spent almost three hours at the club, during which time he and a friend had consumed at least two pitchers of beer. There was disputed testimony that earlier in the evening, the club manager had broken up a fight between Overton and Noah in which Overton had come out much the worse and swearing that he would "get back" at Noah. As Noah was leaving the club, he "patted [a woman] on her behind end to get her going." As it turned out, the woman was Overton's girlfriend. Overton became enraged. Although the facts were disputed, apparently Overton grabbed Noah by the hair, and they struggled out of the club and into the parking lot. At one point, Overton stuck his fingers "up to his knuckles" into Noah's eye sockets, and may have beat Noah's head against a wall several times. Noah ended up on the ground, with Overton on top of him and beating at his head. Eventually, Overton pulled a "buck knife," and stabbed Noah several times.

The jury's verdict against the owner of the club was reversed on appeal:

Whether or not an employee's use of force is within the scope of his employment is dependent on many factors. Of primary importance are the nature of the principal's business, whether or not the employment will bring the employee into contact with the public and the likelihood that the employment will involve the use of force and whether or not the employee acts from a personal motive. In *Wellman v. Pacer Oil Co.,* [504 S.W.2d 55 (Mo. 1973),] our Supreme Court held that an employer was not responsible for the personal act of a gas station attendant who shot a customer. The Supreme Court concluded that the actions of the employee were so outrageous and criminal—so excessively violent as to be totally without reason or responsibility—and hence "must be said, as a matter of law, not to be within the scope of employment." [*Id.*] at 58.

Similarly, in *Henderson v. Laclede Radio, Inc.,* [506 S.W.2d 434 (Mo. 1974)], the Supreme Court held that a salesman for a radio station committed an outrageous and unforeseeable act when he made an unprovoked attack on plaintiff and kicked plaintiff's leg with sufficient force to fracture a bone, when trying to collect a bill.

The doctrines in *Wellman* and *Henderson*, although framed in terms of outrageous conduct or unexpected results, are part and parcel of the principle that when conduct of an employee exceeds the scope of employment and are done, not in furtherance of the employer's business, but to gratify the employee's feelings of resentment or revenge, the conduct is outside the scope of his employment.

The fact that we deal here with a liquor establishment and Overton was a "doorman" or "bouncer" does not, under the facts here, affect our conclusion. It is true that the nature of the duties of a "bouncer" often affect the vicarious liability of the employer. By the nature of the business and the nature of the employment an employer cannot object if [a bouncer] vigorously acts in furtherance of his employer's business. It is a job calling more for force than finesse; if a jury finds that more force was used than the situation quite warranted, it seems neither unlikely nor unreasonable that such a happening will be considered one of the risks of the saloon business and that the tort will be treated as committed in the [scope] of employment.

But, under the facts here, we believe that Overton's conduct in assaulting Noah exceeded the scope of employment. The conduct of Overton outside the tavern exceeded reasonable bounds and was excessively violent and not to be expected by his employer. Neither was such conduct at the time in furtherance of the employer's business. Overton admitted he sought "revenge," that he "lost complete control" and that he did some "pretty crude things" to Noah.

We hold that the conduct of Overton exceeded the scope of his employment, in that his conduct was not, at the time, in furtherance of his employer's business.

We reverse the judgment with directions to enter judgment in favor of [the owner of the nightclub].

Compare the holding in *Noah v. Ziehl* with Restatement section 245 comment f:

Servant actuated by personal motives. The liability of a master for the use of force by a servant is not prevented by the fact that a servant acts in part because of a personal motive, such as revenge. The master, however, is relieved from liability under the rule stated in this Section if the servant has not intent to act on his master's behalf, although the events from which the tortious act follows arise while the servant is acting in the employment and the servant becomes angry because of them. The fact that the servant acts in an outrageous manner or inflicts punishment out of all proportion to the necessities of his master's business is evidence indicating that the servant has departed from the scope of employment in performing the act.

Do you agree with the holding in *Noah v. Ziehl* that Overton's act was outside the scope of employment *as a matter of law*?

If you had represented the owner of the nightclub, would you have been satisfied with a jury instruction outlining the *general principles* used to determine whether an act is within the scope of employment?

4. Once a servant has departed from the scope of employment, has he or she abandoned it forever or can he or she reenter the employment? The seminal case on the reentry doctrine—the resumption of employment—is *Fiocco v. Carver*, 234 N.Y. 219, 137 N.E. 309 (1922). The defendants sent a truckload of merchandise from Manhattan to Staten Island. After making the delivery, their driver was to bring the truck back to their garage on the west side of the city. Instead, he went to the east side to visit his mother. A neighborhood carnival was in progress in the street, and a crowd of boys dressed in fantastic costumes asked the driver for a ride on his truck. He agreed and made a tour of the district with them on board. When the driver stopped the truck in front of a poolroom and left it momentarily, the plaintiff child climbed on board the truck. The driver told the boys to get off the truck, but before the plaintiff could reach the ground, the driver started the truck, and plaintiff's foot was drawn into the wheel. Even though the driver said that his purpose then was to go back to the garage, the court held he had not reentered the scope of employment:

> At the time of the accident, the truck was crowded with boys, whom the driver was taking on a frolic. They filled not only its body but the roof and side and box. All we can find from the driver's testimony is a suggestion that the servant had at last made up his mind to put an end to his wanderings and return to the garage. He was still far away from the point at which he had first strayed from the path of duty, but his thoughts were homeward bound. Is this enough, in view of all the circumstances, to put him back in the sphere of service?
>
> We have refused to limit ourselves by tests that are merely mechanical or formal. Location in time and space are circumstances that may guide the judgment but will not be sufficient to control it, divorced from other circumstances that may characterize the intent of the transaction. The dominant purpose must be proved to be the performance of the master's business. Until then, there can be no resumption of a relation that has been broken and suspended. The field of duty, once forsaken, is not to be reentered by acts evincing a divided loyalty and thus continuing the offense. Many of the illicit incidents of the tour about the neighborhood persisted. The company of merrymakers was still swarming about the truck. Add to this that the truck was still far away from the

route that it would have traveled if the servant had followed the line of duty from the beginning. Division more substantial must be shown before a relation, once ignored and abandoned, will be renewed and reestablished.

Problem 10.4

The plaintiff had purchased from a third party a television on which the defendant held an unrecorded chattel mortgage. An oral arrangement was worked out between the parties whereby the plaintiff agreed to pay the defendant the sum of $100 at the rate of $15 per week. On the day in question, the plaintiff had failed to make any payments as agreed, and the defendant dispatched its agent to the plaintiff's home to adjust the account or to seize the television. The plaintiff's children told the agent that their father had taken their mother to see a doctor and requested that he return later. The agent returned to the plaintiff's home that night, accompanied by two men described as detectives. The agent stated that he had come for the television, emphasizing the purpose of his mission with profanity. The plaintiff requested the agent not to enter his home because his wife was sick and nervous. Despite this admonition, the agent entered the plaintiff's home and removed a small radio and lamp that were on top of the television, throwing them to the floor and breaking them. He then picked up the television and table on which it was placed, carried them out of the home to his automobile, and delivered them to the defendant. On his way out of the plaintiff's home, the agent slammed and broke the glass installed in the front door. The defendant accepted the television. Will the defendant be accountable for the trespass of the agent? (*See Lockhart v. Friendly Fin. Co.,* 110 So. 2d 478 (Fla. Dist. Ct. App. 1959).)

Note on Ratification of Torts and Crimes

Although it may seem incredible, a master may ratify a tort committed by a non-servant or a servant acting outside the scope of employment. Restatement § 218. For the most part, the principles developed in chapter 4, including the partial ratification rule, also apply to the ratification of torts.

For example, in *Dempsey v. Chambers,* 154 Mass. 330, 28 N.E. 279 (1891), Patrick Dempsey sued James Chambers for McCullock's negligence in unloading coal ordered by the plaintiff from the defendant. McCullock, who was not Chambers' servant, undertook to deliver the coal without his knowledge. While he was delivering the coal, McCullock broke a pane of glass in the window of the plaintiff's building. Afterward, with full knowledge of the accident and of McCullock's delivery of the coal, Chambers billed Dempsey for the coal.

The earliest instance of liability by ratification in the English law was where a man retained property acquired through the wrongful act of another. If we assume that an alleged principal, by adopting an act that was unlawful when done, can make the act lawful, it follows that he adopts at his peril and is liable if it should turn out that his previous command would not have justified the act. It has never been doubted that a person's subsequent agreement to a trespass done in his name and for his benefit amounts to a command so far as to make him answerable.

Doubts have been expressed about whether this doctrine applied to a case of a bare personal tort. If a man assaulted another in the street out of his own head, it would seem rather strong to say that if he merely called himself my servant and I afterward assented, our mere words, without more, would make me a party to the assault. Perhaps the application of the doctrine would be avoided on the ground that the facts did not show an act done for the defendant's benefit.

But the language generally used by judges and text writers and the decisions we have been able to find are broad enough to cover a case like the present one where the ratification is established. The ratification was not directed specifically to McCullock's trespass, and that act was not for the defendant's benefit if taken by itself, but it was so connected with McCullock's employment that the defendant would have been liable as master if McCullock really had been his servant when delivering the coal. The defendant's ratification of the employment established the relation of master and servant from the beginning, with all its incidents, including the anomalous liability for his negligent acts. The ratification goes to the relation and establishes it ab initio. The relation existing, the master is answerable for torts he has not ratified specifically, just as he is for those he has not committed, and as he may be for those he has expressly forbidden.

Even where a servant acts *within* the scope of employment, ratification may be important in determining whether the master should be liable for *punitive damages*. Under Restatement section 217C, punitive damages (assuming that they are otherwise appropriate) may be imposed on a master or principal on account of a servant's or agent's wrongful act,

> if, but *only* if:
>
> (a) the principal authorized the doing and the manner of the act, or
>
> (b) the agent was unfit and the principal was reckless in employing him, or
>
> (c) the agent was employed in a managerial capacity and was acting in the scope of employment, or
>
> (d) the principal or a managerial agent of the principal *ratified* or approved the act.

(emphasis added).

2. Abuse of Position

Suppose a servant acts for purely personal reasons and without any purpose to serve the master. Under traditional analysis, such acts will be *outside* the scope of the servant's employment. Suppose further that the servant's employment *facilitated* the misconduct, but that the master was not negligent in selecting, retaining, supervising, or controlling the servant. How should the law allocate the risk of such misconduct? May the master nevertheless be liable without fault under respondeat superior?

Entente Mineral Co. v. Parker

Read case and following notes, page 271.

Problem 10.5

Jones was a supervisor formerly employed by Acme Vacuum Company. Smith had been hired by Jones to sell vacuum cleaners door-to-door. Smith had completed her first week of training, observing others in the field and attending meetings. On Saturday, Jones called Smith at home, and told that that if she wanted to make some money, she should come by the office and sign some contracts. Because Acme employees are paid only through commissions, Jones expected Smith to come to the office. When she arrived, Jones was alone. As Smith signed the papers, she felt Jones breathing down the back of her neck. As she turned to leave, Jones ordered her to remove her clothes. Smith testified that she was terrified and that after she removed her clothes, Jones ordered her to have at least four separate acts of intercourse. Following the episode, Jones told Smith that if she "stuck with" Jones, she'd "have no worries." Smith has sued Acme for sexual harassment under state and federal employment discrimination laws. What result? *See, McCalla v. Ellis,* 180 Mich. App. 372, 446 N.W.2d 904 (1989).

Burlington Industries, Inc. v. Ellerth

524 U.S. 742, 141 L.Ed.2d 633, 118 S.Ct. 2257

KENNEDY, Justice, with whom

We decide whether, under Title VII of the Civil Rights Act of 1964, 78 Stat. 253, as amended, 42 U.S.C. § 2000e et seq., an employee who refuses the unwelcome and threatening sexual advances of a supervisor, yet suffers no adverse, tangible job consequences, can recover against the employer without showing the employer is negligent or otherwise at fault for the supervisor's actions.

I

Summary judgment was granted for the employer, so we must take the facts alleged by the employee to be true. The employer is Burlington Industries, the petitioner. The employee is Kimberly Ellerth, the respondent. From March 1993 until May 1994, Ellerth worked as a salesperson in one of Burlington's divisions in Chicago, Illinois. During her employment, she alleges, she was subjected to constant sexual harassment by her supervisor, one Ted Slowik.

In the hierarchy of Burlington's management structure, Slowik was a mid-level manager. Burlington has eight divisions, employing more than 22,000 people in some 50 plants around the United States. Slowik was a vice president in one of five business units within one of the divisions. He had authority to make hiring and promotion decisions subject to the approval of his supervisor, who signed the paperwork. According to Slowik's supervisor, his position was "not considered an upper-level management position," and he was "not amongst the decision-making or policy-making hierarchy." Ibid. Slowik was not Ellerth's immediate supervisor. Ellerth worked in a two-person office in Chicago, and she answered to her office colleague, who in turn answered to Slowik in New York.

Against a background of repeated boorish and offensive remarks and gestures which Slowik allegedly made, Ellerth places particular emphasis on three alleged incidents where Slowik's comments could be construed as threats to deny her tangible job benefits. In the summer of 1993, while on a business trip, Slowik invited Ellerth to the hotel lounge, an invitation Ellerth felt compelled to accept because Slowik was her boss. When Ellerth gave no encouragement to remarks Slowik made about her breasts, he told her to "loosen up" and warned, "[y]ou know, Kim, I could make your life very hard or very easy at Burlington."

In March 1994, when Ellerth was being considered for a promotion, Slowik expressed reservations during the promotion interview because she was not "loose enough." The comment was followed by his reaching over and rubbing her knee. Ellerth did receive the promotion; but when Slowik called to announce it, he told Ellerth, "you're gonna be out there with men who work in factories, and they certainly like women with pretty butts/legs."

In May 1994, Ellerth called Slowik, asking permission to insert a customer's logo into a fabric sample. Slowik responded, "I don't have time for you right now, Kim—unless you want to tell me what you're wearing." Ellerth told Slowik she had to go and ended the call. A day or two later, Ellerth called Slowik to ask permission again. This time he denied her request, but added something along the lines of, "are you wearing shorter skirts yet, Kim, because it would make your job a whole heck of a lot easier."

A short time later, Ellerth's immediate supervisor cautioned her about returning telephone calls to customers in a prompt fashion. In response, Ellerth quit. She faxed a letter giving reasons unrelated to the alleged sexual harassment we have described. About three weeks later, however, she sent a letter explaining she quit because of Slowik's behavior.

During her tenure at Burlington, Ellerth did not inform anyone in authority about Slowik's conduct, despite knowing Burlington had a policy against sexual harassment. In fact, she chose not to inform her immediate supervisor (not Slowik) because "'it would be his duty as my supervisor to report any incidents of sexual harassment.'" On one occasion, she told Slowik a comment he made was inappropriate.

In October 1994, after receiving a right-to-sue letter from the Equal Employment Opportunity Commission (EEOC), Ellerth filed suit in the United States District Court for the Northern District of Illinois, alleging Burlington engaged in sexual harassment and forced her constructive discharge, in violation of Title VII. The District Court granted summary judgment to Burlington. The Court found Slowik's behavior, as described by Ellerth, severe and pervasive enough to create a hostile work environment, but found Burlington neither knew nor should have known about the conduct. There was no triable issue of fact on the latter point, and the Court noted Ellerth had not used Burlington's internal complaint procedures. Although Ellerth's claim was framed as a hostile work environment complaint, the District Court observed there was a *quid pro quo* "component" to the hostile environment. Proceeding from the premise that an employer faces vicarious liability for *quid pro quo* harassment, the District Court thought it necessary to apply a negligence standard because the *quid pro quo* merely contributed to the hostile work environment. The District Court also dismissed Ellerth's constructive discharge claim.

The Court of Appeals en banc reversed in a decision which produced eight separate opinions and no consensus for a controlling rationale. The judges were able to agree on the problem they confronted: Vicarious liability, not failure to comply with a duty of care, was the essence of Ellerth's case against Burlington on appeal. The judges seemed to agree Ellerth could recover if Slowik's unfulfilled threats to deny her tangible job benefits was sufficient to impose vicarious liability on Burlington. *Jansen v. Packaging Corp. of America,* 123 F.3d 490, 494 (C.A.7 1997) (*per curiam*). With the exception of Judges Coffey and Easterbrook, the judges also agreed Ellerth's claim could be categorized as one of *quid pro quo* harassment, even though she had received the promotion and had suffered no other tangible retaliation.

The consensus disintegrated on the standard for an employer's liability for such a claim. Six judges, Judges Flaum, Cummings, Bauer, Evans, Rovner, and Diane P. Wood, agreed the proper standard was vicarious liability, and so Ellerth could recover even though Burlington was not negligent. They had different reasons for the conclusion. According to Judges Flaum, Cummings, Bauer, and Evans, whether a claim involves a *quid pro quo* determines whether vicarious liability applies; and they in turn defined *quid pro quo* to include a supervisor's threat to inflict a tangible job injury whether or not it was completed. Judges Wood and Rovner interpreted agency principles to impose vicarious liability on employers for most claims of supervisor sexual harassment, even absent a *quid pro quo*.

Although Judge Easterbrook did not think Ellerth had stated a *quid pro quo* claim, he would have followed the law of the controlling State to determine the employer's liability, and by this standard, the employer would be liable here. In contrast, Judge Kanne said Ellerth had stated a *quid pro quo* claim, but negligence was the appropriate standard of liability when the *quid pro quo* involved threats only.

Chief Judge Posner, joined by Judge Manion, disagreed. He asserted Ellerth could not recover against Burlington despite having stated a *quid pro quo* claim. According to Chief Judge Posner, an employer is subject to vicarious liability for "act[s] that significantly alter the terms or conditions of employment," or "company act[s]." *Id.,* at 515. In the emergent terminology, an unfulfilled *quid pro quo* is a mere threat to do a company act rather than the act itself, and in these circumstances, an employer can be found liable for its negligence only. Chief Judge Posner also found Ellerth failed to create a triable issue of fact as to Burlington's negligence. *Id.,* at 517.

Judge Coffey rejected all of the above approaches because he favored a uniform standard of negligence in almost all sexual harassment cases. *Id.,* at 518.

The disagreement revealed in the careful opinions of the judges of the Court of Appeals reflects the fact that Congress has left it to the courts to determine controlling agency law principles in a new and difficult area of federal law. We granted certiorari to assist in defining the relevant standards of employer liability.

II

At the outset, we assume an important proposition yet to be established before a trier of fact. It is a premise assumed as well, in explicit or implicit terms, in the various opinions by the judges of the Court of Appeals. The premise is: a trier of fact could find in Slowik's remarks numerous threats to retaliate against Ellerth if she denied some sexual liberties. The threats, however, were not carried out or fulfilled. Cases based on threats which are carried out are referred to often as *quid pro quo* cases, as distinct from bothersome attentions or sexual remarks that are sufficiently severe or pervasive to create a hostile work environment. The terms *quid pro quo* and hostile work environment are helpful, perhaps, in making a rough demarcation between cases in which threats are carried out and those where they are not or are absent altogether, but beyond this are of limited utility.

Section 703(a) of Title VII forbids

an employer-

(1) to fail or refuse to hire or to discharge any individual, or otherwise to discriminate against any individual with respect to his compensation, terms, conditions or privileges of employment, because of such individual's...sex. 42 U.S.C. § 2000e-2(a)(1).

"*Quid pro quo*" and "hostile work environment" do not appear in the statutory text. The terms appeared first in the academic literature, *see* C. MacKinnon, Sexual Harassment of Working Women (1979); found their way into decisions of the Courts of Appeals, *see, e.g., Henson v. Dundee,* 682 F.2d 897, 909 (C.A.11 1982); and were mentioned in this Court's decision in *Meritor Savings Bank, FSB v. Vinson,* 477 U.S. 57, 106 S.Ct. 2399, 91 L.Ed.2d 49 (1986). *See generally* E. Scalia, The Strange Career of *Quid pro quo* Sexual Harassment, 21 Harv. J.L. & Pub. Policy 307 (1998).

In *Meritor,* the terms served a specific and limited purpose. There we considered whether the conduct in question constituted discrimination in the terms or conditions of employment in violation of Title VII. We assumed, and with adequate reason, that if an employer demanded sexual favors from an employee in return for a job benefit, discrimination with respect to terms or conditions of employment was explicit. Less obvious was whether an employer's sexually demeaning behavior altered terms or conditions of employment in violation of Title VII. We distinguished between *quid pro quo* claims and hostile environment claims, and said both were cognizable under Title VII, though the latter requires harassment that is severe or pervasive. The principal significance of the distinction is to instruct that Title VII is violated by either explicit or constructive alterations in the terms or conditions of employment and to explain the latter must be severe or pervasive. The distinction was not discussed for its bearing upon an employer's liability for an employee's discrimination. On this question *Meritor* held, with no further specifics, that agency principles controlled.

Nevertheless, as use of the terms grew in the wake of *Meritor,* they acquired their own significance. The standard of employer responsibility turned on which type of harassment occurred. If the plaintiff established a *quid pro quo* claim, the Courts of Appeals held, the employer was subject to vicarious liability. The rule encouraged Title VII plaintiffs to state their claims as *quid pro quo* claims, which in turn put expansive pressure on the definition. The equivalence of the *quid pro quo* label and vicarious liability is illustrated by this case. The question presented on certiorari is whether Ellerth can state a claim of *quid pro quo* harassment, but the issue of real concern to the parties is whether Burlington has vicarious liability for Slowik's alleged misconduct, rather than liability limited to its own negligence. The question presented for certiorari asks:

> Whether a claim of *quid pro quo* sexual harassment may be stated under Title VII. . . . where the plaintiff employee has neither submitted to the sexual advances of the alleged harasser nor suffered any tangible effects on the compensation, terms, conditions or privileges of employment as a consequence of a refusal to submit to those advances? Pet. for Cert. i.

We do not suggest the terms *quid pro quo* and hostile work environment are irrelevant to Title VII litigation. To the extent they illustrate the distinction between cases involving a threat which is carried out and offensive conduct in general, the terms are relevant when there is a threshold question whether a plaintiff can prove discrimination in violation of Title VII. When a plaintiff proves that a tangible employment action resulted from a refusal to submit to a supervisor's sexual demands, he or she establishes that the employment decision itself constitutes a change in the terms and conditions of employment that is actionable under Title VII. For any sexual harassment preceding the employment decision to be actionable, however, the conduct must be severe or pervasive. Because Ellerth's claim involves only unfulfilled threats, it should be categorized as a hostile work environment claim which requires a showing of severe or pervasive conduct. For purposes of this case, we accept the District Court's finding that the alleged conduct was severe or pervasive. The case before us involves numerous alleged threats, and we express no opinion as to whether a single unfulfilled threat is sufficient to constitute discrimination in the terms or conditions of employment.

When we assume discrimination can be proved, however, the factors we discuss below, and not the categories *quid pro quo* and hostile work environment, will be controlling on the issue of vicarious liability. That is the question we must resolve.

III

We must decide, then, whether an employer has vicarious liability when a supervisor creates a hostile work environment by making explicit threats to alter a subordinate's terms or conditions of employment, based on sex, but does not fulfill the threat. We turn to principles of agency law, for the term "employer" is defined under Title VII to include "agents." In express terms, Congress has directed federal courts to interpret Title VII based on agency principles. Given such an explicit instruction, we conclude a uniform and predictable standard must be established as a matter of federal law. We rely "on the general common law of agency, rather than on the law of any particular State, to give meaning to these terms." *Community for Creative Non-Violence v. Reid,* 490 U.S. 730, 740, 109 S.Ct. 2166, 2173, 104 L.Ed.2d 811 (1989). The resulting federal rule, based on a body of case law developed over time, is statutory interpretation pursuant to congressional direction. This is not federal common law in "the strictest sense, i.e., a rule of decision that amounts, not simply to an interpretation of a federal statute . . . , but, rather, to the judicial 'creation' of a special federal rule of decision." *Atherton v. FDIC,* 519 U.S. 213, 218, 117 S.Ct. 666, 670, 136 L.Ed.2d 656 (1997). State court decisions, applying state employment discrimination law, may be instructive in applying general agency principles, but, it is interesting to note, in many cases their determinations of employer liability under state law rely in large part on federal court decisions under Title VII.

As *Meritor* acknowledged, the Restatement (Second) of Agency (1957) (hereinafter Restatement), is a useful beginning point for a discussion of general agency principles. Since our decision in *Meritor,* federal courts have explored agency principles, and we find useful instruction in their decisions, noting that "common-law principles may not be transferable in all their particulars to Title VII." The EEOC has issued Guidelines governing sexual harassment claims under Title VII, but they provide little guidance on the issue of employer liability for supervisor harassment. *See* 29 CFR § 1604.11(c) (1997) (vicarious liability for supervisor harassment turns on "the particular employment relationship and the job functions performed by the individual").

A

Section 219(1) of the Restatement sets out a central principle of agency law:

A master is subject to liability for the torts of his servants committed while acting in the scope of their employment.

An employer may be liable for both negligent and intentional torts committed by an employee within the scope of his or her employment. Sexual harassment under Title VII presupposes intentional conduct. While early decisions absolved employers of liability for the intentional torts of their employees, the law now imposes liability where the employee's "purpose, however misguided, is wholly or in part to further the master's business." W. Keeton, D. Dobbs, R. Keeton, & D. Owen, Prosser and Keeton on Law of Torts § 70, p. 505 (5th ed. 1984) (hereinafter Prosser and Keeton on Torts). In applying scope of employment principles to intentional torts, however, it is accepted that "it is less likely that a willful tort will properly be held to be in the course of employment and that the liability of the master for such torts will naturally be more limited." F. Mechem, Outlines of the Law of Agency § 394, p. 266 (P. Mechem 4th ed., 1952). The Restatement defines conduct, including an intentional tort, to be within the scope of employment when "actuated, at least in part, by a purpose to serve the [employer]," even if it is forbidden by the employer. Restatement §§ 228(1)(c), 230. For example, when a salesperson lies to a customer to make a sale, the tortious conduct is within the scope of employment because it benefits the employer by increasing sales, even though it may violate the employer's policies.

As Courts of Appeals have recognized, a supervisor acting out of gender-based animus or a desire to fulfill sexual urges may not be actuated by a purpose to serve the employer. The harassing supervisor often acts for personal motives, motives unrelated and even antithetical to the objectives of the employer. *Cf.* Mechem, *supra,* § 368 ("for the time being [the supervisor] is conspicuously and unmistakably seeking a personal end"); see also Restatement § 235, Illustration 2 (tort committed while "[a]cting purely from personal ill will" not within the scope of employment); § 235, Illustration 3 (tort committed in retaliation for failing to pay the employee a bribe not within the scope of employment). There are instances, of course, where a supervisor engages in unlawful discrimination with the purpose, mistaken or otherwise, to serve the employer. *E.g., Sims v. Montgomery County Comm'n,* 766 F.Supp. 1052, 1075 (M.D.Ala. 1990) (supervisor acting in scope of employment where employer has a policy of discouraging women from seeking advancement and "sexual harassment was simply a way of furthering that policy").

The concept of scope of employment has not always been construed to require a motive to serve the employer. Federal courts have nonetheless found similar limitations on employer liability when applying the agency laws of the States under the Federal Tort Claims Act, which makes the Federal Government liable for torts committed by employees within the scope of employment. 28 U.S.C. § 1346(b); *see, e.g., Jamison v. Wiley,* 14 F.3d 222, 237 (C.A.4 1994) (supervisor's unfair criticism of subordinate's work in retaliation for rejecting his sexual advances not within scope of employment); *Wood v. United States,* 995 F.2d 1122, 1123 (C.A.1 1993) (BREYER, C.J.) (sexual harassment amounting to assault and battery "clearly outside the scope of employment"); *see also* 2 L. Jayson & R. Longstreth, Handling Federal Tort Claims § 9.07[4], p. 9-211 (1998).

The general rule is that sexual harassment by a supervisor is not conduct within the scope of employment.

B

Scope of employment does not define the only basis for employer liability under agency principles. In limited circumstances, agency principles impose liability on employers even where employees commit torts outside the scope of employment. The principles are set forth in the much-cited § 219(2) of the Restatement:

> (2) A master is not subject to liability for the torts of his servants acting outside the scope of their employment, unless:
>
> > (a) the master intended the conduct or the consequences, or
> >
> > (b) the master was negligent or reckless, or
> >
> > (c) the conduct violated a non-delegable duty of the master, or
> >
> > (d) the servant purported to act or to speak on behalf of the principal and there was reliance upon apparent authority, or he was aided in accomplishing the tort by the existence of the agency relation.

See also § 219, Comment e (Section 219(2) "enumerates the situations in which a master may be liable for torts of servants acting solely for their own purposes and hence not in the scope of employment").

Subsection (a) addresses direct liability, where the employer acts with tortious intent, and indirect liability, where the agent's high rank in the company makes him or her the employer's alter ego. None of the parties contend Slowik's rank imputes liability under this principle. There is no contention, furthermore, that a nondelegable duty is involved. So, for our purposes here, subsections (a) and (c) can be put aside.

Subsections (b) and (d) are possible grounds for imposing employer liability on account of a supervisor's acts and must be considered. Under subsection (b), an employer is liable when the tort is attributable to the employer's own negligence. Thus, although a supervisor's sexual harassment is outside the scope of employment because the conduct was for personal motives, an employer can be liable, nonetheless, where its own negligence is a cause of the harassment. An employer is negligent with respect to sexual harassment if it knew or should have known about the conduct and failed to stop it. Negligence sets a minimum standard for employer liability under Title VII; but Ellerth seeks to invoke the more stringent standard of vicarious liability.

Subsection 219(2)(d) concerns vicarious liability for intentional torts committed by an employee when the employee uses apparent authority (the apparent authority standard), or when the employee "was aided in accomplishing the tort by the existence of the agency relation" (the aided in the agency relation standard). Ibid. As other federal decisions have done in discussing vicarious liability for supervisor harassment, we begin with § 219(2)(d).

C

As a general rule, apparent authority is relevant where the agent purports to exercise a power which he or she does not have, as distinct from where the agent threatens to misuse actual power. *Compare* Restatement § 6 (defining "power") *with* § 8 (defining "apparent authority"). In the usual case, a supervisor's harassment involves misuse of actual power, not the false impression of its existence. Apparent authority analysis therefore is inappropriate in this context. If, in the unusual case, it is alleged there is a false impression that the actor was a supervisor, when he in fact was not, the victim's mistaken conclusion must be a reasonable one. Restatement § 8, Comment c ("Apparent authority exists only to the extent it is reasonable for the third person dealing with the agent to believe that the agent is authorized"). When a party seeks to impose vicarious liability based on an agent's misuse of delegated authority, the Restatement's aided in the agency relation rule, rather than the apparent authority rule, appears to be the appropriate form of analysis.

D

We turn to the aided in the agency relation standard. In a sense, most workplace tortfeasors are aided in accomplishing their tortious objective by the existence of the agency relation: Proximity and regular contact may afford a captive pool of potential victims. Were this to satisfy the aided in the agency relation standard, an employer would be subject to vicarious liability not only for all supervisor harassment, but also for all co-worker harassment, a result enforced by neither the EEOC nor any court of appeals to have considered the issue. The aided in the agency relation standard, therefore, requires the existence of something more than the employment relation itself.

At the outset, we can identify a class of cases where, beyond question, more than the mere existence of the employment relation aids in commission of the harassment: when a supervisor takes a tangible employment action against the subordinate. Every Federal Court of Appeals to have considered the question has found vicarious liability when a discriminatory act results in a tangible employment action. In *Meritor*, we acknowledged this consensus. *See* 477 U.S., at 70-71, 106 S.Ct., at 2407-2408 ("[T]he courts have consistently held employers liable for the discriminatory discharges of employees by supervisory personnel, whether or not the employer knew, or should have known, or approved of the supervisor's actions"). Although few courts have elaborated how agency principles support this rule, we think it reflects a correct application of the aided in the agency relation standard.

In the context of this case, a tangible employment action would have taken the form of a denial of a raise or a promotion. The concept of a tangible employment action appears in numerous cases in the Courts of Appeals discussing claims involving race, age, and national origin discrimination, as well as sex discrimination. Without endorsing the specific results of those decisions, we think it prudent to import the concept of a tangible employment action for resolution of the vicarious liability issue we consider here. A tangible employment action constitutes a significant change in employment status, such as hiring, firing, failing to promote, reassignment with significantly different responsibilities, or a decision causing a significant change in benefits.

When a supervisor makes a tangible employment decision, there is assurance the injury could not have been inflicted absent the agency relation. A tangible employment action in most cases inflicts direct economic harm. As a general proposition, only a supervisor, or other person acting with the authority of the company, can cause this sort of injury. A co-worker can break a co-worker's arm as easily as a supervisor, and anyone who has regular contact with an employee can inflict psychological injuries by his or her offensive conduct. But one co-worker (absent some elaborate scheme) cannot dock another's pay, nor can one co-worker demote another. Tangible employment actions fall within the special province of the supervisor. The supervisor has been empowered by the company as a distinct class of agent to make economic decisions affecting other employees under his or her control.

Tangible employment actions are the means by which the supervisor brings the official power of the enterprise to bear on subordinates. A tangible employment decision requires an official act of the enterprise, a company act. The decision in most cases is documented in official company records, and may be subject to review by higher level supervisors. The supervisor often must obtain the imprimatur of the enterprise and use its internal processes.

For these reasons, a tangible employment action taken by the supervisor becomes for Title VII purposes the act of the employer. Whatever the exact contours of the aided in the agency relation standard, its requirements will always be met when a supervisor takes a tangible employment action against a subordinate. In that instance, it would be implausible to interpret agency principles to allow an employer to escape liability, as *Meritor* itself appeared to acknowledge.

Whether the agency relation aids in commission of supervisor harassment which does not culminate in a tangible employment action is less obvious. Application of the standard is made difficult by its malleable terminology, which can be read to either expand or limit liability in the context of supervisor harassment. On the one hand, a supervisor's power and authority invests his or her harassing conduct with a particular threatening character, and in this sense, a supervisor always is aided by the agency relation. See *Meritor*, 477 U.S., at 77, 106 S.Ct., at 2410-2411 (Marshall, J., concurring in judgment) ("[I]t is precisely because the supervisor is understood to be clothed with the employer's authority that he is able to impose unwelcome sexual conduct on subordinates"). On the other hand, there are acts of harassment a supervisor might commit which might be the same acts a co-employee would commit, and there may be some circumstances where the supervisor's status makes little difference.

It is this tension which, we think, has caused so much confusion among the Courts of Appeals which have sought to apply the aided in the agency relation standard to Title VII cases. The aided in the agency relation standard, however, is a developing feature of agency law, and we hesitate to render a definitive explanation of our understanding of the standard in an area where other important considerations must affect our judgment. In particular, we are bound by our holding in *Meritor* that agency principles constrain the imposition of vicarious liability in cases of supervisory harassment. Congress has not altered *Meritor's* rule even though it has made significant amendments to Title VII in the interim.

Although *Meritor* suggested the limitation on employer liability stemmed from agency principles, the Court acknowledged other considerations might be relevant as well. For example, Title VII is designed to encourage the creation of antiharassment policies and effective grievance mechanisms. Were employer liability to depend in part on an employer's effort to create such procedures, it would effect Congress' intention to promote conciliation rather than litigation in the Title VII context, and the EEOC's policy of encouraging the development of grievance procedures. To the extent limiting employer liability could encourage employees to report harassing conduct before it becomes severe or pervasive, it would also serve Title VII's deterrent purpose. As we have observed, Title VII borrows from tort law the avoidable consequences doctrine, and the considerations which animate that doctrine would also support the limitation of employer liability in certain circumstances.

In order to accommodate the agency principles of vicarious liability for harm caused by misuse of supervisory authority, as well as Title VII's equally basic policies of encouraging forethought by employers and saving action by objecting employees, we adopt the following holding in this case and in *Faragher v. Boca Raton,* 524 U.S. 775, 118 S.Ct. 2275, 141 L.Ed.2d 662 (1998), also decided today. An employer is subject to vicarious liability to a victimized employee for an actionable hostile environment created by a supervisor with immediate (or successively higher) authority over the employee. When no tangible employment action is taken, a defending employer may raise an affirmative defense to liability or damages, subject to proof by a preponderance of the evidence. The defense comprises two necessary elements:

(a) that the employer exercised reasonable care to prevent and correct promptly any sexually harassing behavior, and

(b) that the plaintiff employee unreasonably failed to take advantage of any preventive or corrective opportunities provided by the employer or to avoid harm otherwise.

While proof that an employer had promulgated an anti-harassment policy with complaint procedure is not necessary in every instance as a matter of law, the need for a stated policy suitable to the employment circumstances may appropriately be addressed in any case when litigating the first element of the defense. And while proof that an employee failed to fulfill the corresponding obligation of reasonable care to avoid harm is not limited to showing any unreasonable failure to use any complaint procedure provided by the employer, a demonstration of such failure will normally suffice to satisfy the employer's burden under the second element of the defense. No affirmative defense is available, however, when the supervisor's harassment culminates in a tangible employment action, such as discharge, demotion, or undesirable reassignment.

IV

Relying on existing case law which held out the promise of vicarious liability for all *quid pro quo* claims, Ellerth focused all her attention in the Court of Appeals on proving her claim fit within that category. Given our explanation that the labels *quid pro quo* and hostile work environment are not controlling for purposes of establishing employer liability, Ellerth should have an adequate opportunity to prove she has a claim for which Burlington is liable.

Although Ellerth has not alleged she suffered a tangible employment action at the hands of Slowik, which would deprive Burlington of the availability of the affirmative defense, this is not dispositive. In light of our decision, Burlington is still subject to vicarious liability for Slowik's activity, but Burlington should have an opportunity to assert and prove the affirmative defense to liability.

For these reasons, we will affirm the judgment of the Court of Appeals, reversing the grant of summary judgment against Ellerth. On remand, the District Court will have the opportunity to decide whether it would be appropriate to allow Ellerth to amend her pleading or supplement her discovery.

The judgment of the Court of Appeals is affirmed.

It is so ordered.

Justice THOMAS, with whom Justice SCALIA joins, dissenting.

The Court today manufactures a rule that employers are vicariously liable if supervisors create a sexually hostile work environment, subject to an affirmative defense that the Court barely attempts to define. This rule applies even if the employer has a policy against sexual harassment, the employee knows about that policy, and the employee never informs anyone in a position of authority about the supervisor's conduct. As a result, employer liability under Title VII is judged by different standards depending upon whether a sexually or racially hostile work environment is alleged. The standard of employer liability should be the same in both instances: An employer should be liable if, and only if, the plaintiff proves that the employer was negligent in permitting the supervisor's conduct to occur.

*   *   *

Rejecting a negligence standard, the Court instead imposes a rule of vicarious employer liability, subject to a vague affirmative defense, for the acts of supervisors who wield no delegated authority in creating a hostile work environment. This rule is a whole-cloth creation that draws no support from the legal principles on which the Court claims it is based. Compounding its error, the Court fails to explain how employers can rely upon the affirmative defense, thus ensuring a continuing reign of confusion in this important area of the law.

In justifying its holding, the Court refers to our comment in *Meritor Savings Bank, FSB v. Vinson* that the lower courts should look to "agency principles" for guidance in determining the scope of employer liability. The Court then interprets the term "agency principles" to mean the Restatement (Second) of Agency (1957). The Court finds two portions of the Restatement to be relevant: § 219(2)(b), which provides that a master is liable for his servant's torts if the master is reckless or negligent, and § 219(2)(d), which states that a master is liable for his servant's torts when the servant is "aided in accomplishing the tort by the existence of the agency relation." The Court appears to reason that a supervisor is "aided . . . by . . . the agency relation" in creating a hostile work environment because the supervisor's "power and authority invests his or her harassing conduct with a particular threatening character."

Section 219(2)(d) of the Restatement provides no basis whatsoever for imposing vicarious liability for a supervisor's creation of a hostile work environment. Contrary to the Court's suggestions, the principle embodied in § 219(2)(d) has nothing to do with a servant's "power and authority," nor with whether his actions appear "threatening." Rather, as demonstrated by the Restatement's illustrations, liability under § 219(2)(d) depends upon the plaintiff's belief that the agent acted in the ordinary course of business or within the scope of his apparent authority.[4] In this day and age, no sexually harassed employee can reasonably believe that a harassing supervisor is conducting the official business of the company or acting on its behalf. Indeed, the Court admits as much in demonstrating why sexual harassment is not committed within the scope of a supervisor's employment and is not part of his apparent authority.

Thus although the Court implies that it has found guidance in both precedent and statute[,] its holding is a product of willful policymaking, pure and simple. The only agency principle that justifies imposing employer liability in this context is the principle that a master will be liable for a servant's torts if the master was negligent or reckless in permitting them to occur; and as noted, under a negligence standard, Burlington cannot be held liable.

The Court's decision is also in considerable tension with our holding in *Meritor* that employers are not strictly liable for a supervisor's sexual harassment. Although the Court recognizes an affirmative defense[,] it provides shockingly little guidance about how employers can actually avoid vicarious liability. Instead, it issues only Delphic pronouncements and leaves the dirty work to the lower courts....

*   *   *

The Court's holding does guarantee one result: There will be more and more litigation to clarify applicable legal rules in an area in which both practitioners and the courts have long been begging for guidance. *   *   *

*   *   *

Popular misconceptions notwithstanding, sexual harassment is not a freestanding federal tort, but a form of employment discrimination. As such, it should be treated no differently (and certainly no better) than the other forms of harassment that are illegal under Title VII. I would restore parallel treatment of employer liability for racial and sexual harassment and hold an employer liable for a hostile work environment only if the employer is truly at fault. I therefore respectfully dissent.

Notes

1. On what basis does the court in *Ellerth* give the employer an affirmative defense? Is the affirmative defense a satisfactory way to balance the policy concerns involved? Is this an appropriate role for a court interpreting a statute?

---

4. *See* Restatement § 219, Comment e; § 261, Comment a (principal liable for an agent's fraud if "the agent's position facilitates the consummation of the fraud, in that from the point of view of the third person the transaction seems regular on its face and the agent appears to be acting in the ordinary course of business confided to him"); § 247, Illustrations (newspaper liable for a defamatory editorial published by editor for his own purposes).

2. In *McCalla v. Ellis,* 180 Mich. App. 372, 446 N.W.2d 904 (1989), a supervisor implied to an employee that favorable job treatment depended on the employee granting him sexual favors. The employee submitted, and resigned before returning to work. Relying on Restatement section 219(2)(d), the court found a state civil rights act violation

[H]arassment may be express or implied. It may be evidenced by a single incident. The classical example of *quid pro quo* harassment is the situation in which the plaintiff is fired because of a refusal to succumb to sexual demands. Where an employee involuntarily resigns in order to escape an employment situation made intolerable because of sexual harassment, the termination of employment is considered a constructive discharge or firing.

As to the respondeat superior element, defendant argues that it could not be liable because it did not authorize Ellis to rape the plaintiff and because it had no notice of Ellis' sexual proclivity prior to the incident.

* * * Defendant does not contest that Ellis was an agent at least to the extent that he was in its employ as a supervisor with authority to make employment decisions.

Under the Restatement (Second) of Agency, § 219(2)(d), an employer may be liable for its employee's actions where the employee "was aided in accomplishing the tort by the existence of the agency relation[ship]." Even if the act is not within the scope of his employment and the employee is acting entirely for his own benefit, the employer may be liable where the employee exercises the authority actually delegated to him by his employer in acting so as to affect the employment status of subordinates. Where it is the employer's delegation of authority that empowered the supervisor to act, the employer can be found liable. * * *

* * * [I]n the *quid pro quo* claim, the federal courts have imposed strict liability on the employer even absent proof that higher management knew or should have known of the sexual harassment. The reason for imposing strict liability in a *quid pro quo* case [is]:

In such a case, the supervisor relies upon his apparent or actual authority to extort sexual consideration from an employee. Therein lies the *quid pro quo*. In that case the supervisor uses the means furnished to him by the employer to accomplish the prohibited purpose. He acts within the scope of his actual or apparent authority to "hire, fire, discipline or promote." Because the supervisor is acting within at least the apparent scope of the authority entrusted to him by the employer when he makes employment decisions, his conduct can fairly be imputed to the source of his authority.

Therefore, in this case, plaintiff must show that she left her employment because the sexual conduct of her supervisor, acting within at least the apparent scope of his authority, either expressly or impliedly affected her employment status or benefits to the extent that unwelcome sexual harassment can be shown to exist.

3. How would the court in *Burlington Industries, Inc. v. Ellerth* apply Title VII in *McCalla v. Ellis*? Was any "tangible employment decision" taken? If not, is the injury one which "could not have been inflicted absent the agency relation"?

Problem 10.6

Bremen State Bank was moving from one location to another. On the day before the move, Bank instructed its tellers not to follow their usual practice of putting their money at the end of the day in metal lockers inside the vault. Instead, they were to leave their money in canvas bags on the floor of the vault. One teller, did not receive these instructions and thus put her cash-drawer money, $10,342.03, in her metal locker instead of on the vault floor. Arrangements had been made for the police to move the bank's money and for Bekins to move the office equipment, including the metal lockers inside the vault. After the police, under guard, had moved the money from the vault floor to the new location, Bekin's employees entered the bank and began their job. While removing some of the metal lockers from the vault, one of Bekins' employees, Francis, noticed that something was inside one of the lockers. After placing the locker in a van, Francis opened it, and discovered the money. Instead of turning the money in, Francis stuck it in the pocket of his overalls, and stole it. Is Bekins subject to liability for the amount stolen by Francis? *See Bremen State Bank v. Hartford Accident & Indem. Co.*, 427 F.2d 425 (7th Cir. 1970).

Stropes v. Heritage House Children's Ctr.
547 N.E.2d 244 (Ind. 1989)

DeBRULER, Justice.

Fourteen-year-old David Stropes was the victim of cerebral palsy and severe mental retardation. He had the mental capacity of a five-month-old infant and was without the verbal and motor skills necessary to perform or assist in even the simplest tasks associated with his own sustenance or sanitation. David had been placed at the Heritage House Children's Center of Shelbyville, Inc. (Heritage), as a ward of the Marion County Welfare Department to assure his maintenance, security, and well-being.

Robert Griffin, a nurse's aide employed by Heritage, was expected to feed, bathe, and change the bedding and clothing of residents, including David Stropes, as well as to monitor their comfort and safety. To fulfill these duties, Griffin was required to minister to residents in their beds, remove their clothing, and touch and handle their bodies. During his 11:00 p.m. to 7:00 a.m. shift on February 28, 1986, Griffin entered David's room to change the boy's bedding and clothes for the day. After Griffin stripped off the sheets, he [sexually assaulted him]. Griffin stopped the assault when David made a sound indicating that he was in pain, then finished changing the boy's clothes. This incident was seen and reported by another Heritage employee, and Griffin ultimately was charged with and pleaded guilty to criminal deviate conduct, a Class B felony, and child molesting, a Class C felony.

David Stropes, by his next friend, Pamela Taylor, filed a complaint against Heritage and Griffin which asked for compensation and punitive damages and which was based in part on a claim that Heritage was responsible for acts committed by Griffin while on duty. Heritage moved for summary judgment on that claim, arguing that this sexual assault was outside the scope of Griffin's employment and that, therefore, Heritage could not be held liable under the doctrine of respondeat superior. The trial court granted that motion with no accompanying findings of fact or conclusions of law on May 29, 1987. On July 20, 1987, the trial court modified its initial order by adding the following conclusion of law:

> That the act of committing a sexual assault was[,] as a matter of law, outside the scope of Robert Griffin's employment and, as a result, plaintiff cannot recover against The Heritage House, Inc. based upon a theory of respondeat superior.

[T]he Court of Appeals affirmed the decision of the trial court in an unpublished opinion.

The question presented for our review is whether, as a matter of law, Heritage may be subject to liability for its employee's wrongful acts under the doctrine of respondeat superior as traditionally applied.

Respondeat superior imposes liability, where none would otherwise exist, on an employer for the wrongful acts of his employee which are committed within the scope of employment. The Court of Appeals has stated, "In order to be within the scope of employment the employee must be in the 'service of the employer.'" *Shelby v. Truck & Bus Group Div. of GMC* (1989), Ind. App., 533 N.E.2d 1296, 1298. Acts for which the employer is not responsible are those done "on the employee's own initiative," "with no intention to perform it as part of or incident to the service for which he is employed." However, an employee's wrongful act may still fall within the scope of his employment if his purpose was, to an appreciable extent, to further his employer's business, even if the act was predominantly motivated by an intention to benefit the employee himself. Two cases decided under Indiana law have held employers liable for criminal acts of their employees, despite the fact that the crimes were committed to benefit the employee, because the criminal acts originated in activities so closely associated with the employment relationship as to fall within its scope.

In *Gomez v. Adams*, 462 N.E.2d 212, a security officer employed by a private security agency arrested Adams and confiscated his personal identification. The agency's officers were authorized "to request, receive and retain personal identification while investigating disturbances or in effecting arrests," and to retain confiscated items until turning them over to the agency office, which was to be done as soon as practicable. Officers were not authorized to retain items for their personal use. This officer kept Adams confiscated identification past the end of his shift and later used it to cash a check to which he had forged Adams' name. Adams sued the security agency under the doctrine of respondeat superior for damages arising from the conversion of his identification and the forgery of his signature. The jury found for Adams and awarded him $80,000 in compensatory and punitive damages.

Although the Court of Appeals reversed the judgment, the security agency was not totally freed from liability. The Court found that the forgery was, as a matter of law, outside the scope of the officer's employment because it was "divorced in time, place, and purpose from [the officer's] employment duties" and because the only connection between the forgery and the employer was that the officer "was enabled to commit the act by virtue of his confiscation of Adams' papers while performing his duties as a security officer." The security agency did not escape liability for the conversion, however, because "[t]here was sufficient evidence for the jury to reasonably conclude that [the officer] was within the scope of his employment when he converted the check-cashing card to his own use." In reaching its decision, the Court of Appeals distinguished *Eagle Machine Co., Inc. v. American Dist. Telegraph Co.* (1957), 127 Ind. App. 403, 140 N.E.2d 756, where a business which sold and provided maintenance service for alarm systems was held not to be liable under respondeat superior for thefts committed by its employees against one of its customers. The Court stated:

> In *Eagle Machine*, the duties of the employees did not include confiscation or retention of property, nor were the employees authorized to handle business property or inventory with the exception of the alarm system. Furthermore, the nature of their acts were [sic] entirely different than the service for which they were employed, and were motivated entirely by personal interests rather than the employer's interest. *Eagle Machine* is inapplicable to the instant case because [the officer's] actions were, at least for a time, authorized by his employer, related to the service for which he was employed, and motivated to an extent by [the agency's] interests.

The Seventh Circuit Court of Appeals, sitting in diversity, relied on *Gomez* to decide a respondeat superior claim in *Tippecanoe Beverages v. S.A. El Aguila Brewing* Co., 833 F.2d 633 (7th Cir. 1987) (Posner, J.). The Seventh Circuit affirmed a judgment against El Aguila based on the conversion by one of its employees of a cashier's check given by Tippecanoe Beverages in payment for a shipment of beer. The Court found that a reasonable jury could find that the employee had acted to further, "to an appreciable extent, his master's business," analogizing the facts at hand to those in *Gomez*:

> [S]ince it was [the officer's] job to take Adams' personal effects for safekeeping during the scuffle and subsequent arrest, "the confiscation was undertaken in furtherance of [his employer's] business." Likewise here, whatever [El Aguila's employee] had in mind when he received payment from [Tippecanoe Beverages] for the beer, the transaction was within the scope of [his] authority.

It is significant that neither of these cases was dismissed on summary judgment. Both factual episodes involved authorized acts unquestionably within the scope of employment, the confiscation of identification pursuant to arrest and the acceptance of money given in payment for goods, and unauthorized acts unquestionably outside the scope of employment, the criminal conversion of items rightfully received, yet the employers were not automatically shielded from liability. The plaintiffs sought to impose liability under respondeat superior for crimes clearly committed ultimately to benefit the employee rather than the employer, yet the doctrine did not insulate the employer from subjection to trial. Instead, both cases went to the jury for a determination of whether the employees acted to further, "to an appreciable extent, his master's business."

The question of employer liability under respondeat superior here should have gone [to] trial as it did in *Gomez* and *El Aguila*. Like the employees in those cases, Heritage's employee committed some acts unquestionably within the scope of his employment. Griffin began the episode by performing a fully authorized act, stripping the sheets from David's bed prior to changing the bedding. He was also authorized to undress David Stropes and to touch his genitals and other parts of his body when bathing him and changing his clothes. Had David been distressed or frightened, the nurse's aide could have appropriately offered comfort and assurance by a pat or a caress; had he been violent or resistant, Griffin could have used appropriate physical force to restrain him. Griffin also ended the episode with a fully authorized act, dressing David for the day. Like the conversions committed by the *Gomez* and *El Aguila* employees, it is beyond question that the abuse David suffered at Griffin's hands was unauthorized by Heritage and committed for Griffin's own gratification.

The fact that this was a sexual assault is not per se determinative of the scope of employment question. A blanket rule holding all sexual attacks outside the scope of employment as a matter of law because they satisfy the perpetrators' personal desires would draw an unprincipled distinction between such assaults and other types of crimes which employees may commit in response to other personal motivations, such as anger or financial pressures. Rather, the nature of the wrongful act should be a consideration in the assessment of whether and to what extent Griffin's acts fell within the scope of his employment such that Heritage should be held accountable.

Rape and sexual abuse constitute arguably the most egregious instances of wrongful acts which an employee could commit on the job and lend themselves to arguably the most instinctive conclusion that such acts could never be within the scope of one's employment, yet other courts have recognized that the resolution of the question does not turn on the type of act committed or on the perpetrator's emotional baggage accompanying the attack. Rather, these courts indicate that the focus must be on how the employment relates to the context in which the commission of the wrongful act arose. The Minnesota Supreme Court has gone so far as to say that "the employee's motivation should not be a consideration" at all in determining the imposition of liability. *Marston v. Minneapolis Clinic of Psychiatry* (1982), Minn., 329 N.W.2d 306, 311. There, a mental health facility was held liable under respondeat superior for sexual improprieties committed by one of its doctors who exploited the physical or emotional access to two patients afforded by their association through the clinic. The Court stated,

> [I]t is both unrealistic and artificial to determine at which point the [acts] leave the sphere of the employer's business and become motivated by personal animosity—or an improper, personal benefit.

In *Lyon v. Carey*, 533 F.2d 649 (D.C. Cir. 1976), a customer was raped by a delivery man following an argument over the terms of the delivery. The scope of employment question was found to be

> a question of fact for the trier of fact, rather than a question of law for the court, whether the assault stemmed from purely and solely personal sources or arose out of the conduct of the employer's business.

The Court stated that cases of this sort

> are decided on the basis that a master is liable for an assault *arising out of*, and committed *in the course of* the employment, even though it is accompanied by or motivated in part by emotions of passion, savagery or personal revenge,

(emphasis in original), and found that it was the jury's job to determine whether the assault was "the result of only propinquity and lust" or whether it "stemmed from job-related sources."

A jury presented with the facts of this case might find that Robert Griffin acted to an appreciable extent to further his master's business, that his actions were, "at least for a time, authorized by his employer, related to the service for which he was employed, and motivated to an extent by [his employer's] interests," and that, therefore, his wrongful acts fell within the scope of his employment and Heritage should be accountable. Conversely, a jury might find that Griffin's acts were so "divorced in time, place and purpose" from his employment duties as to preclude the imposition of liability on his employer. The nature of the acts were, at the very least, sufficiently associated with Griffin's authorized duties to escape dismissal on summary judgment. The trial court's entry of judgment for Heritage on that motion is therefore reversed.

The opinion of the Court of Appeals is vacated, the trial court is reversed, and this cause is remanded with instructions to grant David's motion to proceed to trial on all claims in a manner not inconsistent with this opinion.

Notes

1. In *Stropes v. Heritage House Children's Ctr.*, the court, in holding there was a question of fact as to whether the sexual assault was within the scope of employment, relied in part on language from *Marston v. Minneapolis Clinic of Psychiatry* to the effect that the traditional focus on a servant's motives or purpose was "both unrealistic and artificial." The court also relied on *Gomez v. Adams* and *Tippecanoe Beverages v. S.A. El Aguila Brewing Co.*, both of which involved employee conversion of property they were authorized to receive on behalf of their employer. In *Entente Mineral Co. v. Parker*, page 271, Judge Thornberry pointed out that the Restatement section 219(2)(d) liability is often "conflated" with Restatement section 219(1) scope of employment liability. Does the *Stropes v. Heritage House Children's Ctr.* opinion make the same error?

2. *Mary M. v. City of Los Angeles*, 54 Cal. 3d 202, 285 Cal. Rptr. 99, 814 P.2d 1341 (1991), involved the responsibility of the City of Los Angeles for a police officer's criminal rape of a woman the officer had detained. About 2:30 a.m., Sergeant Schroyer of the Los Angeles Police Department stopped Mary M. for erratic driving. Schroyer was in uniform, wore a badge and a gun, and was driving a marked black-and-white police car. When Mary M. did not do well on a field sobriety test, she began to cry, and pleaded with Schroyer not to arrest her. Schroyer ordered her to get in the police car, and drove her home. When they arrived, Schroyer told her that he expected "payment" for taking her home instead of to jail. She tried to run away, but Schroyer threw her on the couch. She screamed, but Schroyer put his hand over her mouth and threatened to take her to jail. At that point, she stopped struggling, and Schroyer raped her.

At trial, the jury found that Sergeant Schroyer was acting within the scope of his employment. On appeal, the court of appeals reversed, holding that Schroyer's conduct was, as a matter of law, outside the scope of his employment:

> [Schroyer's rape of Mary M. was] an independent, self-serving pursuit wholly personally motivated and unrelated to his law enforcement duties.

Mary M. v. City of Los Angeles, 246 Cal. Rptr. 487 (App. 1988). The California Supreme Court reversed the court of appeals. Although the court couched its analysis in terms of scope of employment, and did not even cite Restatement section 219(2)(d), its ruling focused on the officer's abuse of his authority as a police officer:

[S]ociety has granted police officers extraordinary power and authority over its citizenry. An officer who detains an individual is acting as the official representative of the state, with all of its coercive power. As visible symbols of that power, an officer is given a distinctively marked car, a uniform, a badge, and a gun. As one court commented,

> police officers [exercise] the most awesome and dangerous power that a democratic state possesses with respect to its residents—the power to use lawful force to arrest and detain them.

(*Policeman's Benev. Ass'n of N.J. v. Washington Tp.* (3rd Cir. 1988) 850 F.2d 133, 141.) Inherent in this formidable power is the potential for abuse. The cost resulting from misuse of that power should be borne by the community, because of the substantial benefits that the community derives from the lawful exercise of police power.

The City nevertheless maintains that a police officer who commits rape while on duty can never be acting within the scope of his employment because the conduct is so unusual that to impose liability on the officer's employer in that instance would be unfair.

As noted previously, society has granted police officers great power and control over criminal suspects. Officers may detain such persons at gunpoint, place them in handcuffs, remove them from their residences, order them into police cars and, in some circumstances, may even use deadly force. The law permits police officers to ensure their own safety by frisking persons they have detained, thereby subjecting detainees to a form of nonconsensual touching ordinarily deemed highly offensive in our society. In view of the considerable power and authority that police officers possess, it is neither startling nor unexpected that on occasion an officer will misuse that authority by engaging in assaultive conduct. The precise circumstances of the assault need not be anticipated, so long as the risk is one that is reasonably foreseeable. Sexual assaults by police officers are fortunately uncommon; nevertheless, the risk of such tortious conduct is broadly incidental to the enterprise of law enforcement, and thus liability for such acts may appropriately be imposed on the employing public entity.

Here, Sergeant Schroyer was acting within the scope of his employment when he detained plaintiff for erratic driving, when he ordered her to get out of her car and to perform a field sobriety test, and when he ordered her to get in his police car. Then, misusing his authority as a law enforcement officer, he drove her to her home, where he raped her. When plaintiff attempted to resist Sergeant Schroyer's criminal conduct, he continued to assert his authority by threatening to take her to jail. Viewing the transaction as a whole, it cannot be said that, as a matter of law, Sergeant Schroyer was acting outside the scope of his employment when he raped plaintiff.

[W]e hold that when, as in this case, a police officer on duty misuses his official authority by raping a woman whom he has detained, the public entity that employs him can be held vicariously liable. This does not mean that, as a matter of law, the public employer is vicariously liable whenever an on-duty officer commits a sexual assault. Rather, this is a question of fact for the jury. In this case, plaintiff presented evidence that would support the conclusion that the rape arose from misuse of official authority. Sergeant Schroyer detained plaintiff when he was on duty, in uniform, and armed. He accomplished the detention by activating the red lights on his patrol car. Taking advantage of his authority and control as a law enforcement officer, he ordered plaintiff into his car and transported her to her home, where he threw her on a couch. When plaintiff screamed, Sergeant Schroyer again resorted to his authority and control as a police officer by threatening to take her to jail. Based on these facts, the jury could reasonably conclude that Sergeant Schroyer was acting in the [scope] of his employment when he sexually assaulted plaintiff.

Our society has entrusted police officers with enforcing its laws and ensuring the safety of the lives and property of its members. In carrying out these important responsibilities, the police act with the authority of the state. When police officers on duty misuse that formidable power to commit sexual assaults, the public employer must be held accountable for their actions. "'It is, after all, the state which puts the officer in a position to employ force and which benefits from its use.'" (*Thomas v. Johnson* (D.D.C. 1968) 295 F. Supp. 1025, 1032, quoting Jaffe, *Suits Against Governments and Officers: Damage Actions* (1963) 77 Harv. L. Rev. 209, 229.)

3. In *Lisa M. v. Henry Mayo Newhall Memorial Hospital,* 48 Cal.Rptr.2d 510, 12 Cal.4th 291, 907 P.2d 358 (1995), the California Supreme Court refused to extend *Mary M. v. City of Los Angeles* to a sexual battery committed by an ultrasound technician. As in their opinion in *Mary M.,* the court couched the issue in terms of *respondeat superior,* rather than Restatement section 219(2)(d), but emphasized issues similar to those discussed by the U. S. Supreme Court in *Ellerth*:

It is clear, first of all, that California no longer follows the traditional rule that an employee's actions are within the scope of employment only if motivated, in whole or part, by a desire to serve the employer's interests. * * *

* * *

While the employee thus need not have intended to further the employer's interests, the employer will not be held liable for an assault or other intentional tort that did not have a causal nexus to the employee's work. * * *

* * *

Because an intentional tort gives rise to respondeat superior liability only if it was engendered by the employment, our disavowal of motive as a singular test of respondeat superior liability does not mean the employee's motive is irrelevant. An act serving only the employee's personal interest is less likely to arise from or be engendered by the employment than an act that, even if misguided, was intended to serve the employer in some way.

The nexus required for respondeat superior liability—that the tort be engendered by or arise from the work—is to be distinguished from "but for" causation.[4] That the employment brought tortfeasor and victim together in time and place is not enough. We have used varied language to describe the nature of the required additional link (which, in theory, is the same for intentional and negligent torts): the incident leading to injury must be an "outgrowth" of the employment; the risk of tortious injury must be "'inherent in the working environment'" or "'typical of or broadly incidental to the enterprise [the employer] has undertaken'" (*Hinman v. Westinghouse Elec. Co.* (1970) 2 Cal.3d 956, 960, 88 Cal.Rptr. 188, 471 P.2d 988).

Looking at the matter with a slightly different focus, California courts have also asked whether the tort was, in a general way, foreseeable from the employee's duties. Respondeat superior liability should apply only to the types of injuries that are "'as a practical matter are sure to occur in the conduct of the employer's enterprise.'" (*Hinman v. Westinghouse Elec. Co., supra,* 2 Cal.3d at p. 959, 88 Cal.Rptr. 188, 471 P.2d 988.) The employment, in other words, must be such as predictably to create the risk employees will commit intentional torts of the type for which liability is sought.

In what has proved an influential formulation, the court in *Rodgers v. Kemper Constr. Co., supra,* 50 Cal.App.3d at page 618, 124 Cal.Rptr. 143, held the tortious occurrence must be "a generally foreseeable consequence of the activity." In this usage, the court further explained, foreseeability "merely means that in the context of the particular enterprise an employee's conduct is not so unusual or startling that it would seem unfair to include the loss resulting from it among other costs of the employer's business." (*Id.* at p. 619, 124 Cal.Rptr. 143....) The *Rodgers* foreseeability test is useful "because it reflects the central justification for respondeat superior [liability]: that losses fairly attributable to an enterprise—those which foreseeably result from the conduct of the enterprise— should be allocated to the enterprise as a cost of doing business." (*Farmers Insurance Group v. County of Santa Clara* (1995) 11 Cal.4th 992, 1004, 47 Cal.Rptr.2d 478, 906 P.2d 440.)

*   *   *

Was Tripoli's sexual battery of Lisa M. within the scope of his employment? The injurious events were causally related to Tripoli's employment as an ultrasound technician in the sense they would not have occurred had he not been so employed. Tripoli's employment as an ultrasound technician provided the opportunity for him to meet plaintiff and to be alone with her in circumstances making the assault possible. The employment was thus one necessary cause of the ensuing tort. But, as previously discussed, in addition to such "but for" causation, respondeat superior liability requires that the risk of the tort have been engendered by, "typical of or broadly incidental to," or, viewed from a somewhat different perspective, "a generally foreseeable consequence of," Hospital's enterprise.

---

4. The distinction is reflected in the common meaning of "engender": "to bring into being." (Webster's New World Dict. (3d college ed. 1991) p. 450.)

At the broadest level, Hospital argues sex crimes are never foreseeable outgrowths of employment because they, unlike instances of non-sexual violence, are not the product of "normal human traits." Hospital urges us not to "legitimize" sexual misconduct by treating it on a par with mere fights. These generalized distinctions are not, however, compelling. Neither physical violence nor sexual exploitation are legitimate, excusable or routinely expected in the workplace. * * * We are not persuaded that the roots of sexual violence and exploitation are in all cases so fundamentally different from those other abhorrent human traits as to allow a conclusion sexual misconduct is per se unforeseeable in the workplace.

Focusing more specifically on the type of sexual assault occurring here, we ask first whether the technician's acts were "engendered by" or an "outgrowth" of his employment. They were not.

* * *

As with these nonsexual assaults, a sexual tort will not be considered engendered by the employment unless its motivating emotions were fairly attributable to work-related events or conditions. Here the opposite was true: a technician simply took advantage of solitude with a naive patient to commit an assault for reasons unrelated to his work. Tripoli's job was to perform a diagnostic examination and record the results. The task provided no occasion for a work-related dispute or any other work-related emotional involvement with the patient. The technician's decision to engage in conscious exploitation of the patient did not arise out of the performance of the examination, although the circumstances of the examination made it possible. * * *

Our conclusion does not rest on mechanical application of a motivation-to-serve test for intentional torts, which would bar vicarious liability for virtually all sexual misconduct.[5] Tripoli's criminal actions, of course, were unauthorized by Hospital and were not motivated by any desire to serve Hospital's interests. Beyond that, however, his motivating emotions were not causally attributable to his employment. The flaw in plaintiff's case for Hospital's respondeat superior liability is not so much that Tripoli's actions were personally motivated, but that those personal motivations were not generated by or an outgrowth of workplace responsibilities, conditions or events.

Analysis in terms of foreseeability leads to the same conclusion. An intentional tort is foreseeable, for purposes of respondeat superior, only if "in the context of the particular enterprise an employee's conduct is *not so unusual or startling* that it would seem unfair to include the loss resulting from it among other costs of the employer's business." (*Rodgers v. Kemper Constr. Co., supra,* 50 Cal.App.3d at p. 619, 124 Cal.Rptr. 143, italics added.) The question is not one of statistical fre-

5. Because we do not apply a motivation-to-serve test as the sole standard of vicarious liability, our rationale differs from that of most other courts that have considered factually similar cases, although several courts have reached the same result as we do: sexual assault by a medical technician is not within the scope of employment.

quency, but of a relationship between the nature of the work involved and the type of tort committed. The employment must be such as predictably to create the risk employees will commit intentional torts of the type for which liability is sought.

In arguing Tripoli's misconduct was generally foreseeable, plaintiff emphasizes the physically intimate nature of the work Tripoli was employed to perform. In our view, that a job involves physical contact is, by itself, an insufficient basis on which to impose vicarious liability for a sexual assault. To hold medical care providers strictly liable for deliberate sexual assaults by every employee whose duties include examining or touching patients' otherwise private areas would be virtually to remove scope of employment as a limitation on providers' vicarious liability. In cases like the present one, a deliberate sexual assault is fairly attributed not to any peculiar aspect of the health care enterprise, but only to "propinquity and lust"[6]

Here, there is no evidence of emotional involvement, either mutual or unilateral, arising from the medical relationship. Although the procedure ordered involved physical contact, it was not of a type that would be expected to, or actually did, give rise to intense emotions on either side. We deal here not with a physician or therapist who becomes sexually involved with a patient as a result of mishandling the feelings predictably created by the therapeutic relationship, but with an ultrasound technician who simply took advantage of solitude, access and superior knowledge to commit a sexual assault.[7]

Although the routine examination Tripoli was authorized to conduct involved physical contact with Lisa M., Tripoli's assault on plaintiff did not originate with, and was not a generally foreseeable consequence of,

---

6. We part company at this point with the dissenting justices, who would hold summary judgment improper because either the patient's vulnerability or the intimate physical contact inherent in the examination might have encouraged or incited Tripoli to assault her. On the present record, such inferences would be wholly speculative. Lacking evidence the assault was a product of the therapeutic relationship, to impose vicarious liability on a hospital for a technician's deliberate sexual assault on a patient would stretch the rationale of respondeat superior too far. To do so would make the hospital potentially liable, irrespective of its actual fault, whenever an employee used force, coercion or trickery to exploit criminally a patient's physical or psychological vulnerability, vulnerability that is characteristic of hospitalized patients generally. An analysis that, in the field of health care, deems a conscious sexual assault to have arisen from the employment simply because the patient involved was vulnerable, surrendered his or her privacy or submitted to physical contact unusual for strangers in a nonmedical context, would, in effect, expose health care providers to potential liability without fault for sexual assault by virtually any employee on any patient.

7. The American Medical Association has described and distinguished two broad types of sexual misconduct by physicians: first, misconduct arising from the physician's inability properly to contain and control his or her emotional involvement with the patient; and second, conscious exploitation of the physician's status, knowledge and power to coerce or trick the patient into allowing sexual contact. (American Medical Association, Council on Ethical and Judicial Affairs, Council Rep., Sexual Misconduct in the Practice of Medicine (1991) 266 J.Am.Med.Assn. 2741-2742.) Tripoli, of course, was a technician rather than a physician. In any event, his conduct belongs in the second category—conscious exploitation—and we need not decide here whether sexual misconduct of the first type might, under some circumstances, create respondeat superior liability on the employer's part.

that contact. Nothing happened during the course of the prescribed examinations to provoke or encourage Tripoli's improper touching of plaintiff. The assault, rather, was the independent product of Tripoli's aberrant decision to engage in conduct unrelated to his duties. In the pertinent sense, therefore, Tripoli's actions were not foreseeable from the nature of the work he was employed to perform.

Plaintiff contends the battery in this case, like the police officer's rape of a detainee in *Mary M. v. City of Los Angeles, supra,* 54 Cal.3d 202, 285 Cal.Rptr. 99, 814 P.2d 1341, "arose from an abuse of job-created authority." More accurately, Tripoli abused his position of trust, since he had no legal or coercive authority over plaintiff. Assuming an analogy can be fully maintained between *518 authority and trust, *Mary M.* still provides less than compelling precedent for liability here. In *Mary M.,* we held a police officer's assault was a generally foreseeable consequence of his position. "In view of the considerable power and authority that police officers possess, it is neither startling nor unexpected that on occasion an officer will misuse that authority by engaging in assaultive conduct." (*Mary M. v. City of Los Angeles, supra,* 54 Cal.3d at p. 217, 285 Cal.Rptr. 99, 814 P.2d 1341.) We expressly limited our holding: "We stress that our conclusion in this case flows from the unique authority vested in police officers. Employees who do not have this authority and who commit sexual assaults may be acting outside the scope of their employment as a matter of law." (*Id.* at p. 218, fn. 11, 285 Cal.Rptr. 99, 814 P.2d 1341.)

While a police officer's assault may be foreseeable from the scope of his unique authority over detainees, we are unable to say the same of an ultrasound technician's assault on a patient. Hospital did not give Tripoli any power to exercise general control over plaintiff's liberty. He was not vested with any coercive authority, and the trust plaintiff was asked to place in him was limited to conduct of an ultrasound examination. His subsequent battery of the patient was independent of the narrow purpose for which plaintiff was asked to trust him. Whatever costs may be fairly attributable to a police officer's public employer in light of the extraordinary scope of authority the community, for its own benefit, confers on the officer, we believe it would not be fair to attribute to Hospital, which employed Tripoli simply to conduct ultrasound examinations, the costs of a deliberate, independently motivated sexual battery unconnected to the prescribed examination.

In reaching our conclusion we have consulted the three identified policy goals of the respondeat superior doctrine—preventing future injuries, assuring compensation to victims, and spreading the losses caused by an enterprise equitably—for additional guidance as to whether the doctrine should be applied in these circumstances. In this case, however, we have drawn no firm direction from consideration of the first two policy goals. Although imposition of vicarious liability would likely lead to adoption of some further precautionary measures, we are unable to say whether the overall impact would be beneficial to or destructive of the quality of medical care. Hospital and its *amici curiae* predict imposition of respondeat superior liability would lead health care providers to overreact by monitoring, for possible sexual misconduct, every interaction between patient and health care worker. Published research, on the other hand, indicates providers have available several other approaches to preventing sexual misconduct by employees.

As for ensuring compensation, the briefing does not enable us to say with confidence whether or not insurance is actually available to medical providers for sexual torts of employees and, if so, whether coverage for such liability would drastically increase the insurance costs—or, if not, the uninsured liability costs—of nonprofit providers such as Hospital. The second policy consideration is therefore also of uncertain import here; imposing vicarious liability is likely to provide additional compensation to some victims, but the consequential costs of ensuring compensation in this manner are unclear.

Third and finally, we attempt to assess the propriety of spreading the risk of losses among the beneficiaries of the enterprise upon which liability would be imposed. As Hospital points out, this assessment is another way of asking whether the employee's conduct was "so unusual or startling that it would seem unfair to include the loss resulting from it among other costs of the employer's business." (*Rodgers v. Kemper Constr. Co., supra,* 50 Cal.App.3d at p. 619, 124 Cal.Rptr. 143.) For reasons already discussed, we conclude the connection between Tripoli's employment duties—to conduct a diagnostic examination—and his independent commission of a deliberate sexual assault was too attenuated, without proof of Hospital's negligence, to support allocation of plaintiff's losses to Hospital as a cost of doing business. Consideration of the respondeat superior doctrine's basis in public policy, therefore, does not alter our conviction that an ultrasound technician's sexual assault on a patient is not a risk predictably created by or fairly attributed to the nature of the technician's employment.

4. Other courts have also taken a much less accommodating view of scope of employment:

a. In *Moses v. Diocese of Colorado,* 863 P.2d 310 (Colo. 1993), the court held the Diocese of Colorado was not liable in *respondeat superior* for a priest's sexual relationship with a parishioner who had come to him for counseling. Even though the court recognized that "[a] parishioner in pastoral counseling may develop a deep emotional dependence on a priest", *id.* at 328, the Court nevertheless viewed the relationship as both beyond the scope of the priest's counseling duties and done for purely personal reasons, and thus outside the scope of employment. *Id.* at 330. Even though the Court agreed that it might be reasonably foreseeable that the priest might mishandle the emotional dependence arising during counseling, the Court declined to extend vicarious liability to foreseeable acts outside the scope of employment. *Id.* at 330 n.29.

b. In *Thompson v. Everett Clinic,* 860 P.2d 1054 (Wash. App. 1993), the court held that sexual assaults by a doctor were outside the scope of employment because it "emanated from a wholly personal motive of the agent and was done to gratify solely personal objectives or desires of the agent." *Id.* at 1058. The *Thompson* court also rejected what it called "enterprise liability"—liability for acts outside the scope of employment but "still within the risks that inure in the employer's enterprise." *Id.* at 1058 & n.4.

5. In another portion of the opinion in *Stropes v. Heritage House Children's Ctr.,* the court held that Heritage House owed its patients a "non-delegable duty to provide protection and care" similar to that imposed on common carriers. *See also* Restatement § 219(2)(c). As will be discussed in the next chapter, the existence of a non-delegable duty of care is also a basis for holding the employer of an independent contractor liable for the latter's torts.

3. Vice-Principals: Who Acts as the Firm?

Problem 10.7

Exel Logistics, Inc. Exel provides warehousing and logistics services to companies throughout the United States, and is headquartered in Westerville, Ohio. Ginda, an East Indian, worked as a forklift operator at Exel's Proctor and Gamble regional distribution center in Woodland, California ("Woodland RDC"). Ginda contends that during the course of his employment with Exel he was subjected to continuous harassment and discrimination based on his race, national origin and religious beliefs. Ginda also contends that he complained of said harassment and discrimination to his group leaders, to supervisors and to Woodland RDC General Manager Dale Bailey. Following his complaints, Ginda contends that the harassment and discrimination worsened, and that he was ultimately terminated in retaliation for his complaints.

Dale Bailey was the General Manager at the Woodland RDC. As General Manager, Bailey's authority was limited to the *operation* of the Woodland RDC. He had no authority to set employee work rules, wage rates, or fringe benefits. Bailey supervised approximately 120 employees. There was no on-site human resources representative at the Woodland RDC. There was no formal procedure for employees to follow in lodging complaints, other than Exel's "open door policy." As set forth in Exel's "Associate Handbook," an associate could come to any manager at any time with a complaint. In addition, employees at the Woodland RDC were told by Bailey that "if they had any issues or concerns they could see me or schedule an appointment with me."

The only training Bailey received regarding human resource and labor issues was a one day seminar on "union issues and union avoidance." Bailey received no training with respect to the handling of racial harassment, discrimination or retaliation complaints. The only training he received concerning discrimination in general concerned EEOC principles as they pertained to hiring. The only training provided on sexual harassment or employment discrimination was a one day seminar regarding EEOC regulations and hiring and union activities. While Bailey could consult with Burns at Exel's headquarters in Westerville, Ohio concerning human resource issues, he had complete discretion in determining whether to contact Burns. During his tenure at the Woodland RDC, Bailey received approximately one employee complaint every two weeks and could recall contacting Burns on only two occasions. Bailey never informed employees that they could go to Burns with their complaints, nor was he aware of any other individual so informing any employee.

Is Exel possibly subject to punitive damages for the manner in which Bailey handled Ginda's complaints? *See, Ginda v. Exel Logistics, Inc.,* 42 F.Supp.2d 1019 (E.D. Cal. 1999).

Hammerly Oaks, Inc. v. Edwards

958 S.W.2d 387 (Tex. 1997)

OWEN, Justice, delivered the opinion for a unanimous Court.

The sole point of controversy in this case is the award of punitive damages. In Texas, a corporation may be liable for exemplary damages if it committed gross negligence through the actions or inactions of a vice principal. The court of appeals held that there was some evidence that the leasing agent of a corporate owner of an apartment complex was a vice principal and accordingly modified the trial court's judgment which had disregarded the gross negligence and punitive damages findings. *Edwards v. Hammerly Oaks, Inc.,* 908 S.W.2d 270 (Tex.App.—Hous.[1st Dist]1995). We hold that under the facts of this case, the leasing agent was not a vice principal. There are no other findings to sustain the award of punitive damages. The court of appeals erred in modifying the judgment of the trial court, and we therefore modify the judgment of the court of appeals to exclude punitive damages.

I

The plaintiff in this case, Darrell Edwards, was a resident of an apartment complex owned by Hammerly Oaks, Inc. Edwards was accosted by attackers who pulled him into a vacant apartment that adjoined his. Edwards was brutally assaulted. The assailants were Roman Gonzales, who had been hired by Hammerly Oaks as an independent contractor to clean carpets, and Roman Gonzales's companion Gabriel Gonzales.

The acts or omissions of three employees of Hammerly Oaks are at issue. Those employees were Marilyn Montgomery, the leasing agent for the apartments; Rose Britton, the acting general manager of the apartment complex and Montgomery's superior; and Frank Smotek, a courtesy patrol guard and sometimes wallpaper hanger and maintenance man.

The Hammerly Oaks apartments had approximately 520 units, and Roman Gonzales cleaned carpets in preparation for new tenants as units were vacated. Hammerly Oaks had used the services of Roman Gonzales without incident for a considerable period of time before the attack on Edwards. The assault on Edwards occurred on a Tuesday afternoon. The preceding Friday, a vacant apartment next door to Edwards's apartment was being readied for a new tenant, and Roman Gonzales had cleaned the carpets. On Friday night, someone stole Gonzales's cleaning equipment. He reported this to Marilyn Montgomery, the leasing agent, on either Saturday or Monday. Gonzales was upset and told Montgomery that he believed Edwards had taken the cleaning equipment, and Gonzales then stated that he "would like to go over and beat it out of him [Edwards]." Montgomery did not warn Edwards nor did she contact the police or anyone else. She testified that she did not believe that Gonzales had any intention of harming Edwards, that "like any one of us here who [has had] your car broken into or your equipment stolen," the statement was "like...something I could have said, and I am not a violent woman."

On Monday, the day before the attack, Roman Gonzales also told Rose Britton, the acting apartment manager, that he could not finish cleaning apartments that day because his cleaning equipment had been taken. Britton told him that she would have to hire another company and agreed at trial that this meant Roman Gonzales had "lost his job." However, there is no evidence that Gonzales told Britton that Edwards was responsible for taking the equipment, and Gonzales made no threats against Edwards or anyone else in the presence of Rose Britton. There was no mention of Edwards at all to Rose Britton.

The preparations Hammerly Oaks made for new tenants included rekeying the locks, and at the time of the attack, there was no cylinder in the lock on the vacant apartment next to Edwards. Smotek had been seen in the vacant apartment sometime on the afternoon of the attack performing various "make-ready" activities.

As Edwards arrived home from work later that afternoon, the Gonzaleses forced him into the unlocked apartment where they stabbed and severely beat him. During the attack, Frank Smotek entered the vacant apartment and told Edwards that if he had in fact taken the cleaning equipment, he should return it. When Edwards denied any connection with the disappearance of the property, Smotek told the Gonzaleses to leave. They did so, threatening to kill Edwards if he reported the assault. At that point, instead of taking some action to assist Edwards, Smotek began cleaning up the blood on the landing and in the apartment. Smotek did not contact the police nor did he summon emergency medical personnel. Edwards, seriously wounded, made his own way to his apartment and called 911.

Edwards sued Hammerly Oaks, and the jury found negligence and gross negligence. However, the jury refused to find that the Gonzaleses were acting as employees of Hammerly Oaks and also answered "no" to the following question: "If you have found that Frank Smotek willingly participated in the assault of Plaintiff, was Frank Smotek acting in the scope of his employment while engaging in that activity?"[1] Edwards has not challenged these findings. The jury awarded compensatory damages totaling $133,000 and punitive damages in the amount of $375,000. The trial court rendered judgment awarding all the actual damages together with prejudgment interest, but disregarded the findings of gross negligence and punitive damages.

Hammerly Oaks did not appeal the judgment, but Edwards sought to reverse the trial court's failure to award exemplary damages. Edwards urged two theories in the court of appeals. The first was that Hammerly Oaks had a nondelegable duty to keep the vacant apartment locked. The court of appeals concluded

---

1. The jury was instructed:

    An "employee" is acting in the scope of his employment if he is acting in the furtherance of the business of his employer.

    An "employee" is not acting within the scope of his employment if he departs from the furtherance of the employer's business for a purpose of his own not connected with his employment and is [sic] not returned to the place of departure or to a place he is required to be in the performance of his duties.

that Edwards waived this argument because the gross negligence question submitted to the jury did not include the theory of nondelegable duty.

However, the court of appeals agreed with Edwards' alternative argument that the trial court should not have disregarded the jury's findings of gross negligence and punitive damages because there was legally sufficient evidence that Marilyn Montgomery was a vice principal and that she was grossly negligent. Accordingly, the court of appeals modified the trial court's judgment, awarding the punitive damages found by the jury.

We agree with the trial court that the jury's finding of gross negligence should have been disregarded, and we therefore reverse the judgment of the court of appeals in that regard. Because of our disposition of this case, we do not reach the second point of error brought by Hammerly Oaks in this Court, which is that there is no evidence of gross negligence on the part of Marilyn Montgomery.

II

One of the principal cases in Texas on the liability of a corporation for exemplary damages is *Fort Worth Elevators Co. v. Russell*, 123 Tex. 128, 70 S.W.2d 397 (1934), *overruled on other grounds by Wright v. Gifford-Hill & Co.*, 725 S.W.2d 712, 714 (Tex. 1987) (holding that a plaintiff need not secure a finding on the amount of actual damages to recover exemplary damages under the former workers' compensation statute, Tex.Rev.Civ. Stat. Ann. art. 8306, § 5 (Vernon 1967)[2]). In *Fort Worth Elevators,* this Court recounted that there have been three general views in American jurisprudence on whether or when a corporation can be subjected to punitive damages. One view is that there is no liability. A second view, sometimes referred to as the rule of general liability, is that corporations may be required to respond in punitive damages based on the conduct of employees or agents under the doctrine of respondeat superior. Texas has chosen neither of these extremes, but instead has adopted a modified version of what has been called "exceptional liability." The opinion in *Fort Worth Elevators* discussed a number of Texas decisions that have set forth when a corporation will and will not be liable for exemplary damages, and then summarized:

> The Texas rule, reduced to its simplest terms, and applied to a case of gross neglect, means that the default for which punitive damages may be recovered must be that of the corporation, that the grossly negligent act must be the very act of the corporation itself; or, if the act is that of a mere servant or employee as such, then it must have been previously authorized or subsequently must be approved by the corporation.

Id. at 406.

We subsequently embraced section 909 of the Restatement of Torts as stating the general rule in Texas. *King v. McGuff,* 149 Tex. 432, 234 S.W.2d 403, 405 (1950). That section of the Restatement provides:

> Punitive damages can properly be awarded against a master or other principal because of an act by an agent if, but only if,

---

2. Act approved Mar. 28, 1917, 35th Leg., R.S., ch. 103, § 5, 1917 Tex. Gen. Laws 269, 271, repealed by Act approved Dec. 13, 1989, 71st Leg., 2d C.S., ch. 1, § 16.01(7)-(9), 1989 Tex. Gen. Laws 114.

(a) the principal authorized the doing and the manner of the act, or

(b) the agent was unfit and the principal was reckless in employing him, or

(c) the agent was employed in a managerial capacity and was acting in the scope of employment, or

(d) the employer or a manager of the employer ratified or approved the act.

RESTATEMENT OF TORTS § 909 (1939); *see also Purvis v. Prattco, Inc.*, 595 S.W.2d 103, 104 (Tex. 1980) (setting forth these same factors and citing section 909 of the Restatement (Second) of Torts, which is unchanged from the original Restatement of Torts).

Corporations can, of course, "act only through agents of some character." *Fort Worth Elevators*, 70 S.W.2d at 402. This Court has long recognized that the purpose of punitive damages is to protect society by punishing the offender rather than to compensate the injured party. A corollary to that principle of law is that punitive damages are warranted only when the act is that of the corporation rather than the act of its "ordinary servants or agents." Thus, a corporation's liability for punitive damages is placed on very different grounds than respondeat superior.

Fort Worth Elevators also gives us guidance on how to distinguish between the acts of "the corporation itself" and "that of a mere servant or employee." In explaining the dichotomy between the doctrine of respondeat superior and the liability of a corporation for its own actions, our Court has used the construct of "vice principal." A "vice principal" encompasses four classes of corporate agents:

(a) Corporate officers;

(b) those who have authority to employ, direct, and discharge servants of the master;

(c) those engaged in the performance of nondelegable or absolute duties of the master; and

(d) those to whom a master has confided the management of the whole or a department or division of his business.

The Court elaborated on the meaning of "corporate officer," saying that the term was not intended to restrict this class of employees only to corporate officers, per se, but that the term "vice principal" includes one who represents the corporation in its corporate capacity. The title of the employee is thus not dispositive. Nor is the degree of responsibility determinative unless that responsibility falls within the parameters set out in *Fort Worth Elevators* and other decisions of this Court. *See, e.g., Durand v. Moore*, 879 S.W.2d 196, 203 (Tex.App.—Houston [14th Dist.] 1994, no writ) (holding that doorman at a nightclub was not a vice principal even though he had the discretion to decide whom to admit); *Southwestern Bell Tel. Co. v. Reeves*, 578 S.W.2d 795, 800-01 (Tex.Civ.App.—Houston [1st Dist.] 1979, writ ref'd n.r.e.) (holding that "union manager" of a business office was not a vice principal although four supervisors and four service representatives reported to her).

Fort Worth Elevators also identifies some of the nondelegable duties of a corporation. In the context of the employer/employee relationship, these include the "duty to exercise ordinary care to select careful and competent fellow servants or coemployees." *Fort Worth Elevators,* 70 S.W.2d at 401. The jury in *Fort Worth Elevators* had found that the corporation knew that one of its employees was reckless and careless in his work and thus the corporation was liable for punitive damages when that employee was grossly negligent in injuring a coworker. The selection and retention of the reckless employee was a breach of a nondelegable duty.

In this case, Edwards contends that the award of punitive damages should be sustained on either of two bases. The first is that a vice principal of Hammerly Oaks failed to warn Edwards of the threats by Roman Gonzales or to contact the police regarding those threats. The second is that Hammerly Oaks had a nondelegable duty to keep the door of the vacant apartment locked.

We turn first to the question of whether a vice principal failed to respond appropriately to the threats of Roman Gonzales.

III

The parties agree that Rose Britton, as acting manager of the apartments, was a vice principal of Hammerly Oaks. However, as noted above, there is no evidence that any threats against Edwards were conveyed to her. Nor was there any contention that Frank Smotek knew of any threats prior to the attack. Although the gross negligence issue identified the Gonzaleses as possible vice principals, there was no evidence that would support such a finding, and the jury failed to find that they were even employees. Edwards did not raise a point of error in the court of appeals or contend in this Court that the Gonzaleses were vice principals. The only other individual identified in the gross negligence issue as a potential vice principal was Montgomery.

Therefore the central issue is whether Marilyn Montgomery was a vice principal when she failed to do anything about the threats made against Edwards. It is undisputed that Marilyn Montgomery had no authority to hire or to fire employees or to engage general contractors to perform work on behalf of Hammerly Oaks. She did not hire Roman Gonzales, nor did she have the ability to terminate his services, although she did coordinate with him on which apartments needed carpets cleaned and when. Even those limited functions, however, were overseen by Rose Britton.

Nor was Marilyn Montgomery responsible for the management of the apartments or any division of Hammerly Oaks. She did not have the authority to sign leases or to sign checks. Rather, her duties included showing apartments to prospective tenants and preparing paperwork if potential residents were interested in entering into a lease.

Edwards relies on the fact that Marilyn Montgomery was alone in the leasing office when Roman Gonzales threatened Edwards as some evidence that Montgomery was in charge at that moment in time. This Court has held that the trier of fact may draw inferences, but only reasonable and logical ones. The evidence on which Edwards relies is "'meager circumstantial evidence' which could give rise to any number of inferences, none more probable than another." *Blount v. Bordens, Inc.,* 910 S.W.2d 931, 933 (Tex. 1995) (*quoting Litton Indus. Prods. v. Gammage,* 668 S.W.2d 319, 324 (Tex. 1984)). A jury may not infer an ultimate fact from such evidence. Under the theory advanced by Edwards, a jury could conclude that a receptionist or secretary was a vice principal simply because at times, such persons were the only employees of the corporation in the office authorized to converse with the public and to relay information to and from the corporation. The fact that Montgomery was alone in the office when her discussion with Roman Gonzales occurred falls far short of a showing that Montgomery had the authority to hire and fire employees or that she presided over the management of a department of Hammerly Oaks. There is no evidence that Marilyn Montgomery was a vice principal.

IV

The final issue we must address has been raised by Edwards as an alternative basis for affirming the judgment of the court of appeals. Edwards contends that a breach of a nondelegable duty to keep the vacant apartment secured was established as a matter of law and that even though the jury was not asked to consider "nondelegable duty" in answering the negligence or gross negligence issues, the jury's finding of gross negligence can be supported by a court's determination that a breach was conclusively established. Edwards contends that both Frank Smotek and Rose Britton breached nondelegable duties.

* * *

The court of appeals held that Edwards waived his point of error in this regard because of the way the gross negligence issue was submitted to the jury. We agree.

* * *

In sum, the jury was not properly asked to find that the failure to lock the door of the vacant apartment was negligence amounting to a breach of a nondelegable duty nor to find that there was a premises defect. The jury's answer to the gross negligence issue was predicated on its finding of "negligence," and the jury was asked if "such negligence" was also gross negligence. The jury could not have concluded that the negligence it found also amounted to gross negligence. Thus, its finding of gross negligence was properly disregarded by the trial court.

* * *

The court of appeals erred in awarding punitive damages. We accordingly modify the judgment of the court of appeals to delete that award and affirm the judgment in all other respects.

Notes

1. In *Kolstad v. American Dental Association,* 527 U.S. 526 (1999), the Supreme Court discussed the availability of punitive damages under Title VII. As in *Burlington Industries, Inc. v. Ellerth,* the court adopted common law agency principles, subject to a defense of good faith efforts to comply with the requirements of Title VII:

> The common law has long recognized that agency principles limit vicarious liability for punitive awards. This is a principle, moreover, that this Court historically has endorsed. * * *

* * *

Although jurisdictions disagree over whether and how to limit vicarious liability for punitive damages, our interpretation of Title VII is informed by "the general common law of agency, rather than...the law of any particular State." *Burlington Industries, Inc., supra,* at 754 (internal quotation marks omitted). The common law as codified in the Restatement (Second) of Agency (1957), provides a useful starting point for defining this general common law. The Restatement of Agency places strict limits on the extent to which an agent's misconduct may be imputed to the principal for purposes of awarding punitive damages:

> Punitive damages can properly be awarded against a master or other principal because of an act by an agent if, but only if:
>
> > (a) the principal authorized the doing and the manner of the act, or
> >
> > (b) the agent was unfit and the principal was reckless in employing him, or
> >
> > (c) the agent was employed in a managerial capacity and was acting in the scope of employment, or
> >
> > (d) the principal or a managerial agent of the principal ratified or approved the act.

Restatement (Second) of Agency, supra, § 217 C. See also Restatement (Second) of Torts § 909 (same).

The Restatement, for example, provides that the principal may be liable for punitive damages if it authorizes or ratifies the agent's tortious act, or if it acts recklessly in employing the malfeasing agent. The Restatement also contemplates liability for punitive awards where an employee serving in a "managerial capacity" committed the wrong while "acting in the scope of employment." Restatement (Second) of Agency, *supra,* § 217 C; *see also* Restatement (Second) of Torts, *supra,* § 909 (same). "Unfortunately, no good definition of what constitutes a 'managerial capacity' has been found," [2 J. Ghiardi & J. Kircher, Punitive Damages: Law and Practice [§ 24.05, at 14 (1998)], and determining whether an employee meets this description requires a fact-intensive inquiry. *Id.,* § 24.05; 1 L. Schlueter & K. Redden, Punitive Damages, § 4.4(B)(2)(a), p. 182 (3d ed. 1995). "In making this determination, the court should review the type of authority that the employer has given to the employee, the amount of discretion that the employee has in what is done and how it is accomplished." *Id.,* § 4.4(B)(2)(a), at 181. Suffice it to say here that the examples provided in the Restatement of Torts suggest that an employee must be "important," but perhaps need not be the employer's "top management, officers, or directors," to be acting "in a managerial capacity." *Ibid.; see also* 2 Ghiardi, supra, § 24.05, at 14; Restatement (Second) of Torts, § 909, at 468, Comment b and Illus. 3.

Additional questions arise from the meaning of the "scope of employment" requirement. The Restatement of Agency provides that even intentional torts are within the scope of an agent's employment if the conduct is "the kind [the employee] is employed to perform," "occurs substantially within the authorized time and space limits," and "is actuated, at least in part, by a purpose to serve the" employer. Restatement (Second) of Agency, supra, § 228(1), at 504. According to the Restatement, so long as these rules are satisfied, an employee may be said to act within the scope of employment even if the employee engages in acts "specifically forbidden" by the employer and uses "forbidden means of accomplishing results." *Id.,* § 230, at 511, Comment b; *see also Burlington Industries, Inc., supra,* at 756; Keeton, Torts § 70. On this view, even an employer who makes every effort to comply with Title VII would be held liable for the discriminatory acts of agents acting in a "managerial capacity."

Holding employers liable for punitive damages when they engage in good faith efforts to comply with Title VII, however, is in some tension with the very principles underlying common law limitations on vicarious liability for punitive damages—that it is "improper ordinarily to award punitive damages against one who himself is personally innocent and therefore liable only vicariously." Restatement (Second) of Torts, *supra,* § 909, at 468, Comment b. * * *

Applying the Restatement of Agency's "scope of employment" rule in the Title VII punitive damages context, moreover, would reduce the incentive for employers to implement antidiscrimination programs. In fact, such a rule would likely exacerbate concerns among employers that § 1981a's "malice" and "reckless indifference" standard penalizes those employers who educate themselves and their employees on Title VII's prohibitions. Dissuading employers from implementing programs or policies to prevent discrimination in the workplace is directly contrary to the purposes underlying Title VII. The statute's "primary objective" is "a prophylactic one," *Albemarle Paper Co. v. Moody,* 422 U.S. 405, 417, 95 S.Ct. 2362, 45 L.Ed.2d 280 (1975); it aims, chiefly, "not to provide redress but to avoid harm," *Faragher,* 524 U.S., at 806. With regard to sexual harassment, "[f]or example, Title VII is designed to encourage the creation of antiharassment policies and effective grievance mechanisms." *Burlington Industries, Inc.,* 524 U.S., at 764. The purposes underlying Title VII are similarly advanced where employers are encouraged to adopt antidiscrimination policies and to educate their personnel on Title VII's prohibitions.

In light of the perverse incentives that the Restatement's "scope of employment" rules create, we are compelled to modify these principles to avoid undermining the objectives underlying Title VII. Recognizing Title VII as an effort to promote prevention as well as remediation, and observing the very principles underlying the Restatements' strict limits on vicarious liability for punitive damages, we agree that, in the punitive damages context, an employer may not be vicariously liable for the discriminatory employment decisions of managerial agents where these decisions are contrary to the employer's "good-faith efforts to comply with Title VII." 139 F.3d, at 974 (Tatel, J., dissenting). * * *

2. In *Ginda v. Exel Logistics, Inc.,* 42 F.Supp.2d 1019 (E.D. Cal. 1999), the court discussed the vice-principal doctrine:

Under California law, an employer may not be held liable for punitive damages based upon the acts of its employees unless the employer (1) "had advance knowledge of the unfitness of the employee and employed him or her with a conscious disregard of the rights or safety of others," (2) "authorized or ratified the wrongful conduct for which the damages are awarded," or (3) "was personally guilty of oppression, fraud, or malice." Cal.Civ.Code § 3294(b). With respect to a corporate employer, "the advance knowledge and conscious disregard, authorization, ratification or act of oppression, fraud, or malice must be on the part of an officer, director, or *managing agent* of the corporation." *Id.* (emphasis added).

"The determination of whether employees act in a managerial capacity...does not necessarily hinge on their level in the corporate hierarchy. Rather, the critical inquiry is the degree of discretion the employees possess in making decisions that will ultimately determine corporate policy." *Egan v. Mutual of Omaha Ins. Co.,* 24 Cal.3d 809, 823, 169 Cal.Rptr. 691, 620 P.2d 141 (1979). *Egan* arose in the insurance context and concerned whether a claims manager and claims adjuster were acting within their "managerial capacity," for purposes of holding their employer liable for punitive damages. The California Supreme Court held that, "[w]hen employees dispose of insureds' claims with little if any supervision, they possess sufficient discretion for the law to impute their actions concerning those claims to the corporation." *Id.* In the employment context, the fact that an employee reports to a particular individual with the authority to terminate the employee's employment merely reflects that the individual is a supervisor, not that he or she was a managing agent. *Kelly-Zurian v. Wohl,* 22 Cal.App.4th 397, 421, 27 Cal.Rptr.2d 457 (1994). Because the case at bar involves the handling of "claims" in an employment context, both decisions are instructive. Exel's suggestion that the holding in *Egan* is properly limited to the insurance context is without merit. *Egan* is the seminal case on what constitutes a "managing agent" for purposes of § 3294(b), and is consistently cited by courts, including the court in *Kelly-Zurian,* for the standard set forth therein.

Exel accurately notes that in *Kelly-Zurian* the court held that the company administrator who (1) was plaintiff's supervisor, (2) was the highest ranking employee in plaintiff's region, and (3) possessed the authority to terminate plaintiff's employment, was not a "managing agent," where he lacked the authority to set policies, guidelines and salaries. *Kelly-Zurian,* 22 Cal.App.4th at 421-22, 27 Cal.Rptr.2d 457. While the facts are similar in the case at bar, the court in *Kelly-Zurian* was silent as to the defendant administrator's authority concerning the handling of employee complaints. Significantly, there were management employees above the defendant administrator to whom plaintiff complained, and those management employees exercised their discretionary authority regarding the handling of her complaints. Here, it is clear that Bailey had virtually unlimited authority in handling employee complaints. Moreover, the is no evidence that employees at the Woodland RDC were aware of any management employee above Bailey to whom they could complain. Bailey, in effect, embodied both Exel's authority and policy regarding the handling of employee complaints for Exel at the Woodland RDC. The purposeful delegation of such discretionary authority to Bailey is sufficient to create a triable issue of material fact as to whether Bailey was a managing agent under § 3294(b).

3. How would the Restatement and California law apply to the facts of *Ginda v. Exel Logistics, Inc.,* as stated in Problem 10.7? How would *Kolstad v. American Dental Association* apply?

4. Liability for Acts of Partners

Kelsey-Seybold Clinic v. Maclay
466 S.W.2d 716 (Tex. 1971)

WALKER, Justice.

This is a suit for alienation of affections in which the trial court rendered summary judgment for one of the defendants, Kelsey-Seybold Clinic, a medical partnership.

The suit was brought by John Dale Maclay against Dr. Earl J. Brewer, Jr., M.D. and the Clinic. After sustaining the Clinic's motion for summary judgment, the trial court ordered that this part of the case be severed from the suit against Dr. Brewer. Plaintiff appealed to the Court of Civil Appeals, which reversed the trial court's judgment in favor of the Clinic and remanded the cause for trial.

Plaintiff alleged that Dr. Brewer and the Clinic had treated him, his wife and their children for several years; that Dr. Brewer, who is a pediatrician and one of the partners in the Clinic, was the doctor to whom his wife had taken their children; that beginning in late 1966, Dr. Brewer conceived and entered into a scheme to alienate the affections of plaintiff's wife, Mrs. Maria Maclay; that he showered his attentions and gifts upon her until April or May, 1967, when her affections were alienated as a direct result of his actions, causing her to separate from plaintiff on or about July 25, 1967.

Plaintiff further alleged that Dr. Brewer's actions designed to alienate Mrs. Maclay's affections occurred while he was acting as a medical doctor for plaintiff's family and in the course and scope of his employment as a partner in the Clinic; that various acts of undue familiarity occurred both on and off the premises of the Clinic; that prior to April, 1967, the Clinic, through Dr. Mavis Kelsey, one of the senior partners, had knowledge of Dr. Brewer's actions; that at the time this knowledge was acquired, the Clinic was providing medical treatment for plaintiff and his entire family; and that "the partnership approved of, consented to, and ratified and condoned such conduct of its partner, Brewer, and refused to come to the aid of your plaintiff or in any way attempt to halt or disapprove the actions of Brewer."

Dr. Kelsey stated that he had treated plaintiff ten or fifteen years before and that other doctors in the Clinic had treated plaintiff, his wife and children since then. At some time in the Spring of 1967, plaintiff complained to Dr. Kelsey that Dr. Brewer was having an affair with Mrs. Maclay. According to Dr. Kelsey's recollection of this conversation, plaintiff stated that he and his wife had separated. At about the same time Dr. Kelsey received a telephone call from Mrs. Maclay's uncle, who inquired what Dr. Kelsey knew about this affair.' Two or three weeks later plaintiff telephoned Dr. Kelsey a second time.

It was Dr. Kelsey's impression that the purpose of plaintiff's two telephone calls was to seek sympathy. Plaintiff did not ask him to do anything, and he had done nothing. He did not talk with Dr. Brewer about the matter until after this suit was filed. The witness did not believe that anything improper had occurred at the Clinic. If anyone had known of conduct such as that alleged by plaintiff, the partners wouldn't put up with that.' Dr. Kelsey also stated that the Clinic had not adopted a policy of intentionally alienating Mrs. Maclay's affections. A nurse is always present when a female patient is examined or treated by a doctor in the Clinic, but Dr. Kelsey felt that it would be impossible to keep up with the private lives, outside the Clinic, of over fifty doctors.

Plaintiff stated that in his telephone conversation with Dr. Kelsey, he inquired whether the latter was aware that Dr. Brewer had a romantic interest or involvement with his wife. Dr. Kelsey replied that he was aware of the matter and had talked with Mrs. Maclay's uncle about it. The Clinic filed an affidavit by all members of its executive committee, except Dr. Brewer, stating that the committee is charged with responsibility for setting policy for the partnership, that the business of the partnership is that of operating a medical clinic, that Dr. Brewer was not authorized by the partnership at any time to do any act which might result in the alienation of Mrs. Maclay's affections from her husband, and that the partnership had done no act with the purpose, intent or design to alienate her affections.

The bases of liability alleged in the petition are:

(1) that Dr. Brewer's wrongful conduct was in the course and scope of the partnership business and was approved, consented to, ratified and condoned by the Clinic; and

(2) that the Clinic, after notice of the alleged relationship between Dr. Brewer and Mrs. Maclay, failed to take any action.

Plaintiff is thus relying upon the vicarious or partnership liability of the Clinic for the acts of one of the partners and also its liability for breach of a duty owing by the Clinic when it learned of Dr. Brewer's relationship with Mrs. Maclay.

On the question of vicarious liability, [w]e are unwilling to believe that plaintiff seriously expects to prove in a conventional trial that the acts alleged to have been committed by Dr. Brewer were in the course and scope of the partnership business or were either authorized or ratified by the Clinic. Rather than concern ourselves about possible deficiencies in the affidavit filed by the Clinic, we assume for the purpose of this opinion that Dr. Brewer was not acting in the ordinary course of the Clinic's business and that his conduct was neither authorized nor ratified by the partnership. This will enable us to reach questions that may well arise at the trial of the case.

The Court of Civil Appeals reasoned that the summary judgment was improper because the Clinic had not conclusively negated consent on its part to the alleged wrongful conduct of Dr. Brewer. In reaching this conclusion, it relied on our opinion in K & G Oil Tool & Service Co. v. G & G Fishing Tool Service, 158 Tex. 594, 314 S.W.2d 782, where it was stated that:

A non-participating partner is ordinarily not personally liable for the wrongful, tortious or criminal acts of the acting partner unless such acts are within the scope of the partnership's business or were consented to, authorized, ratified or adopted by the non-participating partner.

There was no question of consent in *K & G*, and it was held that the non-participating partner was not liable. Similar statements have been made by other courts in connection with similar holdings. Two courts apparently entertain the view that mere tacit consent is enough to make the non-participating partner liable for the willful tort of the acting partner outside the scope of the partnership business. Their conclusion in this respect appears to be due, at least in part, to an erroneous interpretation of the opinion in *Williams v. F. & W. Grand Five, Ten and Twenty-five Cent Stores*, 273 Pa. 131, 116 A. 652. The plaintiff there was accused of stealing a tooth brush. While being interrogated in defendant's store, she was assaulted by the operative of a private detective agency employed by defendant to guard the store. The trial court rendered judgment on the verdict in favor of the plaintiff, and it was contended on appeal that defendant could not be responsible for an assault committed by the employee of an independent detective agency. The appellate court pointed out that the jury had been instructed to find for the plaintiff if they believed that the manager of the store was present and participated in the acts or permitted the operative to insult and assault the plaintiff when he could and should have protected her. It then observed that the defendant was held responsible not for the acts of the operative but for those of its own manager.

Where a partner proposes to do, in the name or for the benefit of the partnership, some act that is not in the ordinary course of the business, consent by the other partners may constitute his authority to do the act for the partnership. We also recognize that even a willful or malicious act outside the ordinary scope of the partnership business may be so related to the business that tacit consent of the other partners could fairly be regarded as a grant of authority. In this instance, however, Dr. Brewer was acting solely for his own personal gratification. His conduct could not benefit the Clinic in any way, and no one would have supposed that he was acting for the partnership. It is our opinion that in these circumstances the consent' that might be inferred from the silence or inaction of the Clinic after learning of his conduct does not render the Clinic vicariously liable for the damages claimed by plaintiff.

On the basis of the present record and the facts we are assuming in this case, the liability of the Clinic must rest, if at all, upon some theory akin to that recognized by the court in *Williams*. The Clinic was under a duty, of course, to exercise ordinary care to protect its patients from harm resulting from tortious conduct of persons upon the premises. A negligent breach of that duty could subject the Clinic to liability without regard to whether the tortious conduct immediately causing the harm was that of an agent or servant or was in the ordinary scope of the partnership business.

We are also of the opinion that the Clinic owed a duty to the families of its patients to exercise ordinary care to prevent a tortious interference with family relations. This duty relates only to conduct of a partner or employee on the premises of the Clinic or while purportedly acting as a representative of the Clinic elsewhere. Failure to exercise ordinary care in discharging that duty would subject the Clinic to liability for damages proximately caused by its negligence.

The rather meager information in the present record does not necessarily indicate that the Clinic was under a duty to act or that it could have done anything to prevent the damage when Dr. Kelsey first learned of the situation. On the other hand, it does not affirmatively and clearly appear that the Clinic could or should have done nothing. In our opinion the Clinic has failed to discharge the heavy, and in a case of this character virtually impossible, burden of establishing as a matter of law at the summary judgment stage that it is not liable under any theory fairly presented by the allegations of the petition.

The judgment of the Court of Civil Appeals is affirmed.

Notes

1. UPA section 13 provides that a partnership is liable for a partner's wrongful act or omission if the partner acted "in the ordinary course of business of the partnership or with the authority of his co-partners." Instead of applying UPA section 13, the court in *Kelsey-Seybold Clinic v. Maclay* applied common law respondeat superior. Does it make sense to apply the "scope of employment" test to the conduct of a partner?

2. UPA section 14 also holds the partnership responsible for a partner's misapplication of property, where the property *either* was received by the partnership in the course of its business, UPA 14(b), *or* was received by the partner within the scope of his apparent authority, UPA 14(a). What agency principles is UPA Section 14 equivalent to?

3. RUPA section 305(a) *combines* UPA sections 13 and 14(a):

> A partnership is liable for loss or injury caused to a person or for a penalty incurred as a result of actionable conduct by an act or omission of a partner acting in the ordinary course of business of the partnership or with the actual or apparent authority of the partnership.

How does RUPA section 305(a) change the scope of either UPA section 13 or UPA Section 14(a)?

RUPA section 305(b) is the RUPA equivalent of UPA section 14(b).

Kansallis Finance Ltd. v. Fern

Read case and following notes, page 293.

D. Liability of Agents for Wrongful Conduct

1. Civil Liability

Wheeler v. Frito-Lay, Inc.

743 F. Supp. 483 (S.D. Miss. 1990)

BARBOUR, Chief Judge.

This case is before the Court pursuant to Rule 72(a) of the Federal Rules of Civil Procedure on the Application of the Plaintiff to Review the Order of the United States Magistrate denying the Plaintiff's Motion to remand the case to the Circuit Court of Hinds County, Mississippi.

Plaintiff, a Mississippi resident, seeks to recover damages which he allegedly sustained in a collision between his automobile and a truck driven by Defendant Siler, also a Mississippi resident, and owned by Defendant Frito-Lay, a non-resident corporation. Frito-Lay does not dispute that Siler was acting within the scope of his employment at the time of the accident. The complaint alleges that Defendant Siler's negligence was a proximate cause of the injury to Plaintiff and that Defendant Frito-Lay is liable for the acts of its employee Siler under the doctrine of respondeat superior. Plaintiff's complaint prays for a joint and several judgment against both Defendants.

Defendants Frito-Lay and Siler filed a notice of removal to federal court from the Hinds County, Mississippi Circuit Court, alleging that Siler had been fraudulently joined in the suit since the complaint asked for a joint and several judgment against both Defendants and did not ask for an individual judgment against Siler. Plaintiff filed a motion to remand for lack of complete diversity. The Magistrate denied Plaintiff's motion to remand to state court.

Where removal of an action from state to federal court is sought, the party seeking removal must establish a basis for federal jurisdiction. *B., Inc. v. Miller Brewing Co.*, 663 F.2d 545, 549 (5th Cir. 1981). However, the removal of cases in which the federal court may have had original jurisdiction on the basis of diversity of citizenship is subject to limitation, and

[a]ny civil action of which the district courts have original jurisdiction founded on a claim [of diversity of citizenship] shall be removable only if none of the parties in interest properly joined and served as defendants is a citizen of the State in which such action is brought.

28 U.S.C. § 1441(b). Thus, for removal to be proper in this case, it must be established that Siler was a fraudulently joined defendant so that his presence does not defeat diversity of citizenship jurisdiction or bring the limitation of § 1441(b) into play.

In establishing that a defendant to the action has been fraudulently joined, the removing party must show that there has been fraud in the pleading of jurisdictional facts or that there is no possibility that the plaintiff would be able to establish a claim against the allegedly improper party in a state court proceeding. There is no allegation in the instant case that Plaintiff is guilty of fraudulently pleading jurisdictional facts. Therefore, this action was properly removed to federal court only if Plaintiff would not be able to establish a claim against Defendant Siler in a state court action.

Section 242 of the Restatement (Second) of Agency (1957) cited by the Government, simply is not dispositive of the case. Section 242 states:

A master is not subject to liability for the conduct of a servant towards a person harmed as a result of accepting or soliciting from the servant an invitation, *not binding upon the master*, to enter or remain upon the master's premises or vehicle, although the conduct which immediately causes the harm is within the scope of the servant's employment. (emphasis supplied).

The italicized phrase states a premise which is the very question at issue. The comments to this section state that it applies to a servant who, "without authority or apparent authority to do so, permits or invites persons to ride on [the master's vehicle]." In this case apparent authority is an issue, not an assumption.

Whether a case is removable, and implicitly whether it states a cognizable claim against a defendant, is determined by reference to the allegations made in the original pleadings. The court must then evaluate those allegations in the light most favorable to the party opposing removal, resolving all contested issues of fact and law in favor of that party.

In determining if the facts alleged by the pleadings set forth a cognizable claim against the allegedly improper party, the United States Court of Appeals for the Fifth Circuit has set forth the following standard:

> If, having assumed all of the facts set forth by the plaintiff to be true and having resolved all uncertainties as to state substantive law against the defendants, the district court should find that there is no possibility of a valid cause of action being set forth against the in-state defendant(s), only then can it be said that there has been a "fraudulent joinder." However, if there is even a possibility that a state court would find a cause of action stated against any one of the named in-state defendants on the facts alleged by the plaintiff, then the federal court may find that the in-state defendants have been properly joined, that there is incomplete diversity, and that the case must be remanded to the state courts.

B., Inc., 663 F.2d at 550. Thus, applying the above standard, this court must determine whether Plaintiff has stated a claim, recognized under the laws of Mississippi, against Defendant Siler.

Defendant Frito-Lay asserts that, because Plaintiff has cast his claim in terms of the employer-employee relationship, the doctrine of respondeat superior, and has asked for a joint and several judgment against both Defendants, Siler would not be held individually liable for any of the complained of acts and has therefore been fraudulently joined in the complaint in order to defeat diversity.

Under the mandate of *Erie*, the substantive law to be applied in this case is that of Mississippi. The law of Mississippi does impute to the employer the negligence of an employee if such acts occur within the scope of employment. Where such employee negligence is imputed to the employer under the doctrine of respondeat superior, the employer may be held liable. *Granquist v. Crystal Springs Lumber Co.*, 190 Miss. 572, 1 So. 2d 216, 218 (1941). However, the fact that a judgment may be entered against an employer does not absolve the employee of liability for his acts; rather, the doctrine of respondeat superior operates to establish a joint and several liability between both the employer and the employee. While the liability of an employee under respondeat superior may not be individual in the sense that the employee is the only party responsible for the payment of any judgment, the employee nevertheless remains liable for the total amount of any judgment, though such liability will be joint and several with his employer.

In *Southern Mississippi Planning & Development District v. Robertson*, 660 F. Supp. 1057 (S.D. Miss. 1986), the court considered whether the doctrine of respondeat superior absolved corporate employees of liability for allegedly tortious conduct that took place within the scope of their employment. Noting that

> an agent or other employee, merely because of this relationship as an agent or an employee, or because of the additional fact that he has acted at the direction or command of his employer, cannot escape or exonerate himself from liability to a third person for his own negligence,

the court concluded that employees remain individually liable for torts of their own commission despite the fact that employers may also become primarily liable through respondeat superior.

Under the rationale expressed in these cases, the Court cannot conclude that Plaintiff would be unable to assert a claim for relief against Defendant Siler in a state court proceeding merely on the basis of the respondeat superior doctrine. While that doctrine may be used to establish liability on the part of the employer, it does not operate to relieve the employee of liability, and thus, Plaintiff may be able to obtain relief against Defendant Siler in addition to any relief that may be obtained against Defendant Frito-Lay.

Defendant Frito-Lay has asserted that the laws of agency pertaining to acts of a disclosed principal should be applied in this case. Defendant relies on the case of *Gray v. United States Fidelity & Guaranty*, [646 F. Supp. 27 (S.D. Miss. 1986)], wherein the court considered the propriety of removal in a suit brought by a Mississippi resident against a nonresident insurance corporation and its Mississippi agent for breach of contract, gross negligence, and bad faith handling of a claim. Noting that an agent for a disclosed principal incurs no personal liability for a breach of duty or contract between the disclosed principal and a third party, the court found that no cause of action had been stated against an agent where the third party had brought a suit for breach of contract and there were no allegations that the agent acted outside of the scope of his agency. However, where a third party was able to establish separate, tortious conduct by the agent, the agent could be held personally liable. Since the agent was not a party to the insurance contract in question, and since the complaint did not allege any tortious acts by the agent outside of the scope of his employment, no claim for relief had been stated against the agent and removal of the case to federal court was proper.

The facts of *Gray* are distinguishable from the facts of the instant case and therefore preclude this Court from applying the rationale of that decision. The *Gray* suit involved claims that rely on a contractual relationship between the parties: breach of contract, bad faith performance of contractual duties, and grossly negligent performance of contractual duties. In the context of contractual duties, the "disclosed principal" rule does apply, and the agent does not incur personal liability to third parties for acts within the scope of his employment. Conversely, the instant case deals with a tort allegedly committed by the employee. Defendant Siler will remain personally liable for such tortious conduct even if it occurred within the scope of his employment. The application of respondeat superior does not alter this result.

In light of the above cited authority, this Court finds that there is a possibility that a state court could determine that a cause of action has been stated against Defendant Siler. Therefore, he has not been fraudulently joined in this suit. Because Defendant Siler is a proper party to this suit, complete diversity does not exist between Plaintiff and all Defendants, and this Court is without jurisdiction to hear the case. Accordingly, this cause will be remanded to the Circuit Court for the First Judicial District of Hinds County, Mississippi for further proceedings.

Note

Because the master and the servant are jointly and severally liable to a third person injured by the servant's tort, the doctrine of *election of remedies* studied in chapter 1 does not apply. For example, in *Orrock v. Crouse Realtors, Inc.*, 823 S.W.2d 40 (Mo. App. 1991), the plaintiff (Orrock) sued Crouse for breach of contract and misrepresentation based on a misrepresentation by Crouse's agent (Flynn) in the sale of Crouse's property to Orrock. In a previous suit, Orrock had obtained a default judgment against Flynn, the agent. The trial court entered a summary judgment in favor of Crouse on the grounds that Orrock had elected to proceed against the agent, so was precluded from pursuing Crouse as principal. On appeal, the summary judgment was reversed as to the *misrepresentation* cause of action (but not the breach of contract cause of action):

> The applicable rule is that if there is an election to pursue one of two inconsistent theories, mere entry of a judgment bars suit on the second theory. However, if there is an election between two consistent theories, only satisfaction of a judgment bars proceedings under the second theory.

> This case does not involve an election of inconsistent theories. The test of inconsistency is that one theory must allege what the other denies, or that the theory must be repugnant to the other. The plaintiff obtained judgment against the agent and now bring [sic] suit against the principal under the same theories of law. Under these principles it is clear that

> > [A] person injured by the act of an agent for which the principal is liable can bring separate actions against either one.

> Seavey, *Agency* § 95, p. 170 (1964 Hornbook Edition).

Fireman's Fund American Insurance Cos. v. Turner

260 Ore. 30, 488 P.2d 429 (1971)

TONGUE, Justice.

This is an action for indemnity brought by the insurer of an employer against an employee. The purpose of the action is to recover from insurer of the employee the defense costs and amount paid by the insurer of the employer in satisfaction of a judgment against both employer and employee in favor of a third party injured by an automobile owned by the employee and negligently driven by him in the course of his employment. Plaintiff appeals from a judgment in favor of defendant as entered by the court, sitting without a jury.

Plaintiff issued to Oregon Sign & Neon Corporation (Oregon Sign) a policy of liability insurance with limits for personal injury in the sum of $100,000. That policy covered Oregon Sign against liability arising from the operation of vehicles owned by certain employees, including defendant, but did not cover the employees against liability. The policy also contained a subrogation clause in general form, under which plaintiff, as the insurer, was subrogated to the rights of Oregon Sign in the event that plaintiff, as its insurer, made payments under the terms of the policy.

Defendant was the manager of Oregon Sign and carried his own liability under a policy with limits of $10,000 for injury to one person. He was paid a monthly "car allowance" by Oregon Sign for expenses incurred in the operation of his car for business purposes.

While operating his automobile in the course of his employer's business defendant rear-ended another automobile. The party injured in that accident brought an action for personal injuries and recovered judgment in the sum of $9,177.23 and

$75 in costs against both Oregon Sign and defendant, based solely on the doctrine of respondeat superior, without claim of negligence by it as employer.

Plaintiff insurer paid $7,401.76 in satisfaction of that judgment (or 10/11th of that judgment), and expended an additional $1,186 in defending the action. Defendant's insurer contributed the balance (or 1/11th), in satisfaction of that same judgment.

The trial court made the following additional finding of fact:

That the negligence of Robert S. Turner was established at the trial of the cause, and that the Court having heard evidence on the nature of the accident and the conduct of the defendant at the time of said accident finds that the accident resulted from inadvertence [sic] and a mistake of judgment on the part of Robert S. Turner, but that Robert S. Turner at the time of the accident was rendering good and faithful service to his employer.

The trial court also made the following conclusions of law:

That no recovery may be had by an employer against an employee even though such employee is guilty of negligence constituting mere inadvertence [sic] or mistake where the employee is at the time complained of rendering good and faithful service to his employer.

That plaintiff's action may not be maintained because it is against public policy to permit subrogation of a personal injury award.

That each carrier having discharged its pro rata share of the judgment, and each having received a premium therefor no recovery can be had by the one against the other.

Plaintiff, as appellant, contends that it has long been recognized at common law and by most courts, including this court, that an employer held vicariously liable to a third person injured by the negligence of an employee, without negligence on the part of the employer, may seek indemnity against the employee.[3]

Defendant, while recognizing the authorities cited by plaintiff, contends that "considerations of public policy [are] of greater importance than recognition of an out-dated rule of law exercised without regard to its effect." Thus, defendant contends that Oregon Sign, as an employer, knew that it was inevitable that defendant in driving from 24,000 to 36,000 miles each year would have an accident; that defendant obtained insurance coverage to protect it against such accidents and that where, as in this case, there was no drinking or gross negligence, but no more than "mere inadvertent negligence which was within the contemplation of the parties," the employer should not, as a matter of public policy, be entitled to "pass the economic loss off on to the employee when it is foreseeable at the outset."

We may agree that this contention may have considerable merit as a matter of abstract justice, depending upon the circumstances of the particular case. Indeed, the common law rule of indemnity by an employer against his employees has been strongly criticized for much the same reasons. Defendant has cited no cases, however, in which the courts have undertaken to abolish that rule by judicial decision, and perhaps for good reason.

---

3. Restatement (Second) Agency (1958) § 401, comment d; Restatement, Restitution (1937) § 96, comment a.

The "fault concept"—that all persons should be held responsible for the consequences of their wrongful acts, including "inadvertent negligence"—while subject to criticism, is still firmly established as the foundation of tort liability. Exceptions to and modifications of that rule, such as the requirement of gross negligence, rather than simple negligence, as the basis for liability of the driver of an automobile to a guest passenger have usually been adopted as the result of statute, rather than court decision. And while the legislatures, rather than the courts, are ordinarily considered to have the primary responsibility for changes in the law for reasons of public policy, legislation which undertakes to relieve persons from responsibility for their wrongful acts is also usually subject to strong criticism. (Witness the current controversy over proposals for "no-fault" insurance legislation.)

It has been contended that to permit employers to seek such indemnity against their employees would "thwart efficient loss distribution in pursuit of perfecting the fault principle" and that "if this doctrine were carried to its logical conclusion most of our accident loss would ultimately be paid for by the operators of machines or other workmen."

In considering this contention, however, it must be kept in mind that, as a practical matter, few employers seek to exercise such a right of indemnity against their individual employees, and for three good reasons: (a) the adverse effect upon employee morale; (b) the inability of most employees to pay such indemnity; and (c) the opposition of unions. And while in cases involving automobile accidents the insurers of employers may not be inhibited by these considerations, most employees today also carry automobile liability insurance, as in this case. In addition, in this case, defendant was paid a monthly "car allowance" to cover the cost of expenses incurred in the operation of his car for business purposes. This, of course, raises the problem of the exercise by the insurer of an employer of its rights of subrogation and the problem of whether the insurance companies for both employer and employee should contribute to the loss in a case such as this, as considered separately below.

It must also be kept in mind that the rule of vicarious liability of employers, although a court-made rule, is a rule under which persons injured by the wrongful acts of employees may seek recovery against the employer as the one best able to pay and to distribute the resulting loss—all in the absence of any negligence or "fault" on part of the employer. Thus, it is contended, and with some merit, that if such liability without fault is imposed on the employer, it is not contrary to public policy to permit him to seek indemnity against the person at fault, despite the fact that such person may be his employee.

In any event, it is our view that the right of an employer held vicariously liable to a third person injured by the wrongful act of an employee to seek indemnity against the employee is too well established to be abolished at this time by decision of this court as contrary to public policy, at least under the facts and circumstances of this case.

Defendant next contends that even assuming such a right of indemnity, the basis for such a right is the employment contract, with the servant's act being a breach of an implied condition of that contract, and that the extent of the duty of the employee under his contract of employment is "to render faithful service to the employer." Thus, it is contended that the employee should not be held liable to the employer for "mere inadvertent negligence," or "mistake of judgment," so long as he was "rendering good and faithful service to his employer," as found by the trial court in this case. Defendant also contends that "this modern view is accepted in the cases interpreting the Federal Tort Claims Act where indemnity against the negligent employee by the United States is not permitted."

Although many of the authorities speak of the basis for the employer's right of indemnity in terms of a breach by the employee of an implied condition of his employment contract, most authorities recognize a much broader basis for that right, to the effect that any person who, without fault, becomes liable for the wrongful conduct of another is entitled to indemnity against the other and that this extends to all wrongful conduct, including ordinary negligence ("mere inadvertence" or "mistake of judgment").

In any event, the duty of an agent or employee is usually considered to include not only a duty to render "faithful" service, but also a duty to exercise reasonable care in the performance of his duties. Accordingly, and whether the right of an employer to seek indemnity from an employee is to be considered as a right based upon tort or upon implied contract, we hold, in accordance with what we believe to be the weight of authority, as well as our previous decisions, that such a right includes the right to seek indemnity from liability resulting from any and all "wrongful acts" by employees, including ordinary negligence.

[T]he judgment of the trial court must be reversed and the case remanded for proceedings not inconsistent with this opinion.

Note

If the master *ratifies* the servant's wrongful act, would the master be entitled to indemnification from the servant? Does *Rakestraw v. Rodrigues*, page 431, bear on this question?

Yates v. New South Pizza, Ltd.
412 S.E.2d 666 (N.C. 1992)

FRYE, Justice.

On 5 September 1985, plaintiff was a passenger in an automobile owned by Franklin Hobert Simmons and operated by Lisa Dawn Simmons. Donald Lee Powell, a delivery person for defendant, New South Pizza, Ltd., d/b/a Domino's Pizza, ran a stop sign and collided with the Simmons car. As a result of the collision, plaintiff suffered injuries to his head and right wrist, and permanent damage to his left hip. On 26 August 1987, plaintiff executed a covenant not to sue Powell or his insurer in exchange for $25,000 consideration, the amount of coverage under Powell's insurance policy. The covenant expressly reserved all rights to proceed against defendant, Powell's employer, and reads in relevant part:

> It is understood that [plaintiff] contends there are joint tortfeasors in this matter; to wit, Donald Lee Powell and Domino's Pizza, Inc., said joint tortfeasor relationship arising out of the servant-master relationship and [plaintiff] expressly reserves and maintains his right to pursue any

and all claims against Domino's Pizza, Inc. arising out of the incident and that [plaintiff] agrees only not to sue Donald Lee Powell and INA/Action, his vehicular insurance carrier.

The issue before this Court is whether an injured plaintiff is entitled to proceed against an employer on the theory of respondeat superior after having executed, for valuable consideration, a covenant not to sue the negligent employee or his insurer.

At trial, the employer (defendant) admitted that the employee (Powell) was acting within the scope of his employment when the collision occurred but denied that Powell was negligent in causing the collision. Defendant also moved for summary judgment, arguing that the settlement between plaintiff and Powell operated to release defendant from liability as a matter of law. The trial court granted the motion. The Court of Appeals affirmed the trial court, concluding that the covenant not to sue released any claim against defendant under the doctrine of respondeat superior. The court further held that when there is a right of indemnity from another tort-feasor, the Uniform Contribution Among Tort-feasors Act, N.C.G.S. § 1B-1, et seq. (the Act),[1] does not apply.

Plaintiff contends that the Court of Appeals erred in holding that the Act does not apply to the present case. Plaintiff argues that the plain language of the Act includes employer-employee liability, and thus a covenant not to sue the employee does not release the employer pursuant to section 1B-4 of the Act. Defendant contends that the Act is irrelevant to the disposition of this case because, inter alia, an employer is not a tort-feasor within the meaning of the Act.

We agree with plaintiff that section 1B-4 of the Act controls the disposition of this case. Section 1B-4 of the Act provides:

When a release or a covenant not to sue or not to enforce judgment is given in good faith to one or more persons liable in tort for the same injury or the same wrongful death:

(1) It does not discharge any of the other tort-feasors from liability for the injury or wrongful death unless its terms so provide; but it reduces the claim against the others to the extent of any amount stipulated by the release or the covenant, or in the amount of the consideration paid for it, whichever is the greater; and,

(2) It discharges the tort-feasor to whom it is given from all liability for contribution to any other tort-feasor.

The question of whether this provision applies to vicarious liability in the master-servant context is one of first impression for this Court. Other courts, as noted by the Court of Appeals, have not been uniform in interpreting this provision of the Uniform Act. We agree with those courts which have held that this provision does apply to liability that has been vicariously derived. See, e.g., *Alaska Airlines v. Sweat*, 568 P.2d 916, 929 (Alaska 1977) (release of independent contractor negligently performing licensed common carrier's nondelegable duty does not release carrier); *Brady v. Prairie Material Sales, Inc.*, 190 Ill. App. 3d 571, 583,

<hr/>

1. The Uniform Contribution Among Tort-feasors Act was originally promulgated in 1939 by the National Conference of Commissioners on Uniform State Laws. It was revised in 1955. North Carolina adopted the 1955 version in 1967.

546 N.E.2d 802, 810 (2d Dist. 1989), appeal denied, 129 Ill. 2d 561, 550 N.E.2d 553 (1990) ("Since the servant who acts negligently is obviously a person liable in tort, it is reasonable to conclude that the liability of the master, although derivative, is still a form of liability in tort as that term is used in the Contribution Act, and an employer is also a "tortfeasor" as that term is used in the Contribution Act."); [and citing 6 more cases]; *contra, e.g., Mamalis v. Atlas Van Lines, Inc.,* 364 Pa. Super. 360, 528 A.2d 198, aff'd, 522 Pa. 214, 560 A.2d 1380 (1989) (interpreting the 1939 version of the Act); *Craven v. Lawson,* 534 S.W.2d 653 (Tenn. 1976). We hold, therefore, that section 1B-4 applies to master-servant vicarious liability, and that on the facts of this case, the covenant not to sue the employee does not release defendant-employer from liability.

We recognize that at common law this Court held that the release of or covenant not to sue the servant also served to release the master. *Smith v. R.R.,* 151 N.C. 479, 66 S.E. 435 (1909). Since the decision in *Smith,* our legislature has adopted the Uniform Contribution Among Tort-feasors Act. The question becomes, therefore, whether the Act changes this holding in *Smith.* Defendant argues that the Act is not applicable to the present situation because a vicariously liable master is not a wrongdoer and therefore not a "tort-feasor." Although defendant's argument finds support in our case law prior to the adoption of the Uniform Act, we believe the Act broadens the definition of "tort-feasor" to encompass a vicariously liable master. Stated differently, *for purposes of this Act,* a "tort-feasor" is one who is liable in tort.

An analysis of the 1939 Act and its 1955 revision supports our conclusion. The 1939 Act defined "joint tort-feasors" broadly:

> For the purposes of this chapter[,] the term "joint tort-feasors' means two or more persons jointly or severally liable in tort for the same injury to person or property, whether or not judgment has been recovered against all or some of them.

This language clearly includes master-servant vicarious liability. Although this definition was omitted from the 1955 Act,[2] we believe the 1955 Act is consistent with this broad definition. For example, section 1B-1(a) provides as follows:

> Except as otherwise provided in this Article, where two or more persons become jointly or severally liable in tort for the same injury to person or property or for the same wrongful death, there is a right of contribution among them even though judgment has not been recovered against any or all of them.

More importantly, as we have noted, section 1B-4 provides that when a release or covenant not to sue is given in good faith "to one of two or more persons liable in tort for the same injury or the same wrongful death," it does not discharge "any of the other tort-feasors from liability." Clearly, both the master and the servant are "persons liable in tort for the same injury," and "tort-feasors" as

---

2. The term "joint tort-feasor" and its definition were not included in the 1955 version of the Act because the term "joint tort-feasor" in the 1939 Act led to confusion:

> The term "joint tort-feasors' was not used in the Uniform Act in order to avoid confusion in those jurisdictions where persons who act independently, and not in concert, cannot always be joined as defendants.

The term "joint tort-feasor" was replaced with "tort-feasor." Neither the 1955 Uniform Act nor the North Carolina statute defines "tort-feasor."

used in this provision refers to those persons liable in tort. We therefore hold that the provisions of N.C.G.S. § 1B-4 apply to situations involving master-servant vicarious liability, such as in the instant case.

Defendant also suggests that section 1B-1(f) of the Act excludes indemnity actions. We disagree. Section 1B-1(f) reads:

> This Article does not impair any right of indemnity under existing law. Where one tort-feasor is entitled to indemnity from another, the right of the indemnity obligee is for indemnity and not contribution, and the indemnity obligor is not entitled to contribution from the obligee for any portion of his indemnity obligation.

We agree with the Supreme Court of Nevada that nothing in this provision precludes application of the Act to situations involving vicarious liability. *Van Cleave [v. Gamboni Construction Co.]*, 101 Nev. at 529, 706 P.2d at 848. The provision

> simply states that the vicariously liable employer would have a right to indemnity, rather than contribution. This provision merely provides that no contribution exists where indemnity exists.

In its opinion, the Court of Appeals noted that because a right of indemnity remains against a servant who has settled with the injured party, the servant effectively gains nothing. Thus, the underlying policy of the statute to encourage settlements is undermined. We do not agree. Although the Court of Appeals is correct that the servant remains liable to the master, in practice the master may elect not to seek indemnification. This is especially true in cases such as this one where the servant's settlement was for the entire amount of his insurance coverage. Given that the master may choose not to seek indemnity from his servant, who in many cases may be judgment proof, the servant's settlement with the injured party fulfills the underlying policy of the Act.

REVERSED AND REMANDED.

MEYER, J., dissenting [with Exum, C.J., and Whichard, J.]:

The majority errs when it concludes that N.C.G.S. § 1B-4 (governing contribution among tort-feasors) controls the outcome here. Traditional tools of statutory construction require that the principles of common law, rather than the statute, dictate the outcome in this case.

As an initial matter, the majority misconstrues the plain language and intent of N.C.G.S. § 1B-4, concluding that "the Act broadens the definition of 'tort-feasor' to encompass a vicariously liable master." When technical terms or terms of art are used in a statute, they are presumed to have been used with their technical meaning in mind. Where the language of a statute is clear and unambiguous, there is no room for judicial construction, and the Court must give the language its plain and definite meaning and resist temptation to interpolate or superimpose provisions and limitations not contained therein.

Such should be the case with respect to the term "tort-feasor" as used in N.C.G.S. § 1B-4. "Tort-feasor" is defined as "[a] wrongdoer, an individual or business that *commits or is guilty of a tort*." Black's Law Dictionary 1489 (6th ed. 1990) (emphasis added). This Court has evinced an identical view. "To make persons joint tort feasors they must actively participate in the act which causes the injury." *Brown v. Louisburg*, 126 N.C. 701, 703, 36 S.E. 166, 167 (1900).

In short, the majority's conclusion that a vicariously liable defendant is a "tort-feasor" exists in stark contrast to North Carolina law as it has existed for over ninety years as well as in contrast to the law of many other states. The conclusion that New South Pizza, an employer derivatively liable under only the doctrine of respondeat superior, is a "tort-feasor" blurs the significant distinction between vicarious and joint liability and is completely unsupportable given our understanding of that term.

Similarly, the majority errs in its construction of N.C.G.S. § 1B-4 when it infers from the structure of the statute itself that the legislature intended those merely vicariously liable to be "liable in tort" and thus joint "tort-feasors." While the statute's prefatory sentence speaks of "one or more persons liable in tort," the succeeding sub-paragraphs speak with particularity of "other tort-feasors," "the tort-feasor," and "any other tort-feasor." As the majority itself concedes, the term "tort-feasor" is not defined in the Act. Nevertheless, the majority states that necessarily

> both the master and the servant are "persons liable in tort for the same injury," and "tort-feasors" as used in [the Act] refers to those persons liable in tort.

On this basis, the majority concludes that under N.C.G.S. § 1B-4, a master, wholly lacking in active involvement in the alleged tort, is a "tort-feasor" and therefore remains liable notwithstanding the release from liability of the directly culpable servant.

Furthermore the majority is wrong when it states that its interpretation serves the policy and ends of N.C.G.S. § 1B-4. The Uniform Act was enacted to serve two purposes. First, it was intended to "distribute the burden of responsibility equitably among those who are jointly liable and thus avoid the injustice often resulting under the common law." Unif. Contribution Among Tortfeasors Act, 12 U.L.A. commissioners' prefatory note (1955 rev.), at 59 (1975). Second, the Act was designed to encourage settlements.

The majority's decision to impose liability on a vicariously liable principal when the agent has been discharged from liability promotes neither of these goals. The avowed interest in avoiding injustice is already well served by N.C.G.S. § 1B-1(f), which provides that the Act "does not impair any right of indemnity under existing law." Moreover, under the majority's view, incentives for settlement will be lessened: even if a servant and plaintiff enter into a covenant not to sue, the servant remains potentially liable as an indemnitor. The majority's cavalier assertion that "in practice the master may elect not to seek indemnification" is unconvincing not only as an empirical matter, but also given the explicit policy goals of the Act itself.

2. Criminal Liability

State *ex rel.* Van Nguyen v. Berger
199 W.Va. 71, 483 S.E.2d 71 (1996)

RECHT, Judge:

We are presented here with two cases consolidated for purposes of appeal, each requiring us to consider whether a corporate officer is criminally responsible, along with the corporation, for the failure to pay workers' compensation premiums and to file workers' compensation reports within the meaning of W. Va.Code 23-1-16(a) (1995). The defendant Truong Van Nguyen petitions this Court for a writ of prohibition to prevent the Circuit Court of Kanawha County, Judge Irene Berger, from enforcing an order refusing to grant the defendant's motion to dismiss an indictment for multiple violations of W. Va.Code 23-1-16 (1995). Conversely, the State appeals the granting of a motion to dismiss the indictment against defendant Steve A. Rife for multiple violations of W. Va.Code 23-1-16 (1995) by the Circuit Court of Kanawha County, Judge Paul Zakaib, Jr.

I.
FACTS

The defendants in this case were indicted in separate proceedings in the January 1996 term by the Grand Jury for the Circuit Court of Kanawha County. The grand jury returned multiple count indictments against Van Nguyen, in his capacity as president of McDowell Energy, Inc., and Rife, in his capacity as president of Black Rock Mining, Inc., both for failing to pay premiums into the Workers' Compensation Fund as well as failing to file quarterly reports with the Workers' Compensation Commissioner.

The defendants filed motions to dismiss their indictments on the ground that corporate officers cannot be held criminally liable under W. Va.Code 23-1-16 (1995).

The defendants' motions were considered by different circuit judges, one of whom agreed with the defendant Rife and dismissed his indictment, with prejudice; the other of whom denied Mr. Nguyen's motion.

As a result of the circuit court rulings on the defendants' respective motions, Mr. Nguyen petitions this Court for a writ of prohibition to prevent the circuit court from enforcing its order, and the State appeals the dismissal of the indictment against Mr. Rife. Because both cases turn on the same legal issue, we granted both petitions and consolidated them for purposes of appeal.

II.
DISCUSSION

The sole issue raised in both appeals is whether, under the specific provisions of W. Va.Code 23-1-16(a) (1995), a corporate officer can be held criminally responsible for the failure of the corporation to pay workers' compensation premiums as well as the failure to file quarterly reports.

W. Va.Code 23-1-16 (1995) provides, in relevant part:

(a) Any person, firm, partnership, company, corporation or association who, as an employer, is required by the provisions of this chapter to subscribe to the workers' compensation fund, and who knowingly and willfully fails...to make any payment or file a report as required by the provisions of this chapter within the time periods specified by law, is guilty of a felony, and, upon conviction thereof, shall be fined not less than one thousand dollars and not more than ten thousand dollars....Provided, That in the case of a person other than a natural person, the amount of the fine shall be not less than ten thousand dollars nor more than twenty-five thousand dollars.

W. Va.Code 23-1-16 (1995).

The defendants contend that because W. Va.Code 23-1-16(a) (1995) does not specify corporate officers among those who may be responsible for the non-performance of the mandatory requirement of paying workers' compensation premiums and submitting workers' compensation forms, then the statute was not intended to apply to corporate officers. The argument continues that the statute was designed only to apply to sole proprietorships and other enumerated business organizations in their capacity as employers, and not corporate officers, as they are not employers as contemplated within W. Va.Code 23-2-1.[2]

W. Va.Code 23-1-16(a) does impose responsibility upon a corporation and does not specifically mention officers of the corporation, however, the common law rule is entrenched in West Virginia to the extent that "[o]fficers, agents, and directors of a corporation may be criminally liable if they cause the corporation to violate the criminal law while conducting corporate business." Syllabus Point 5, *State v. Childers*, 187 W.Va. 54, 415 S.E.2d 460 (1992). *See also* Syllabus Point 3, *Bowling v. Ansted Chrysler-Plymouth-Dodge, Inc.*, 188 W.Va. 468, 425 S.E.2d 144 (1992) ("An officer of a corporation...may be personally liable for the tortious acts of the corporation, including fraud, if the officer participated in, approved of, sanctioned, or ratified such acts.")

The rationale behind imputing criminal liability to corporate officers, in addition to imposing liability upon the corporation, is that "[t]he existence of a corporate entity does not shield from prosecution corporate agents who knowingly and intentionally cause the corporation to commit crimes, in that a corporation obviously acts, and can act, only by and through its member agents and it is their conduct which criminal law must deter and those agents who in facts are culpable."[3]

---

2. W. Va.Code 23-2-1 provides, in relevant part:

The state of West Virginia and all governmental agencies or departments created by it, including county boards of education, political subdivisions of the state, any volunteer fire department or company and other emergency service organizations as defined by article five [§ 15-5-1 et seq.], chapter fifteen of this code, and all persons, firms, associations and corporations regularly employing another person or persons for the purpose of carrying on any form of industry, service or business in this state, are employers within the meaning of this chapter and are hereby required to subscribe to and pay premium taxes into the workers' compensation fund for the protection of their employees and shall be subject to all requirements of this chapter and all rules and regulations prescribed by the workers' compensation division with reference to rate, classification and premium payment: Provided, That such rates will be adjusted by the division to reflect the demand on the compensation fund by the covered employer.

W. Va.Code 23-2-1(a) (1995).

3. Our jurisprudence relating to an officer's criminal liability is neither unique nor on the cutting edge of new age legal theories. The highest court in New York in 1912 offered possibly the best analysis as to the persona of a corporation:

A corporation [ ] is a mere conception of the legislative mind. It exists only on paper through the command of the Legislature that its mental conception shall be clothed with power. All its power resides in the directors. Inanimate and incapable of thought, action, or neglect, it cannot hear or obey the voice of the Legislature except through its directors. It can neither act nor omit to act except through them. Hence a command addressed to a corporation would be idle and vain unless the Legislature in directing the corporate body, acting wholly by its directors, to do a thing required or not to do a thing prohibited, meant that the directors should not

The common law rule of imputing criminal liability upon corporate officers who are responsible for the criminal violations of the corporation continues as part of the law of this State until and unless the Legislature says otherwise. * * *

If the Legislature intends to alter or supersede the common law, it must do so clearly and without equivocation. * * *

Because the common law in this State is clear that a corporate officer can be held criminally liable for criminal violations of the corporation, does W. Va.Code 23-1-16(a) (1995) contain express language which plainly and without equivocation exempts corporate officers from criminal sanctions when the corporations that they control fail to pay workers' compensation premiums or file timely appropriate reports? The answer is no.

We are assisted in framing this answer by our decision in *Mullins v. Venable,* 171 W.Va. 92, 297 S.E.2d 866 (1982). In *Mullins,* we held that civil liability may be imposed upon corporate officers, under the Wage Payment and Collection Act, to the employees of the corporation. We noted, in support of our holding, that the Wage Payment and Collection Act, W. Va.Code 21-5-15 (1981), imposed criminal penalties, including imprisonment, for willful violations of the bonding provisions in the Act.[5] We construed W. Va.Code 21-5-15 (1981), which is similar in language to W. Va.Code 23-1-16 (1995), to impose criminal liability upon corporate officers from the language "[a]ny person, firm or corporation," despite the absence of corporate officers being specifically mentioned within this provision of the Wage Payment Act. *Mullins,* 171 W.Va. at 95, 297 S.E.2d at 870 (stating that the statute clearly contemplated that "corporate officers may not hide behind the corporate skirt to escape liability for their unlawful mischief"). We reasoned that W. Va.Code 21-5-15 (1981) clearly envisioned "personal liability on the part of corporate officers since imprisonment of the corporation, it having no body, is impossible."[6] *Id.*

---

make or cause the corporation to do what was forbidden, or omit to do what was directed. We think...that when the corporation itself is forbidden to do an act, the prohibition extends to the board of directors and to each director, separately and individually.
People v. Knapp, 206 N.Y. 373, 99 N.E. 841, 844 (1912).
    5. Mullins v. Venable directly involved civil as opposed to criminal responsibility. However, we discussed the range of criminal sanctions that could be imposed upon a corporate officer under the Wage Payment Act.
    6. If we were to adopt the defendants' contention that corporate officers were not intended to be included within the scope of W. Va.Code 23-1-16(a) (1995), because they are not "employers," we would effectively be interpreting the statute so that the only individuals who would be criminally responsible would be sole proprietors and not the constituents of any of the business organizations, including corporations, expressly mentioned in the statute. "It is the duty of a court to construe a statute according to its true intent, and give to it such construction as will uphold the law and further justice. It is as well the duty of a court to disregard a construction, though apparently warranted by the literal sense of the words in a statute, when such construction would lead to injustice and absurdity." Syllabus Point 2, *Click v. Click,* 98 W.Va. 419, 127 S.E. 194 (1925); *accord* Syllabus Point 2, *Pristavec v. Westfield Ins. Co.,* 184 W.Va. 331, 400 S.E.2d 575 (1990). We believe that insulating those who control the business organization from criminal liability would create the absurd result of only subjecting sole proprietors to the imprisonment portion of the penalty. The purpose behind incorporating is to limit the civil and personal liability of the agents, officers, directors, and shareholders in the event that the corporation's performance in the market results in financial losses. The purpose behind incorporating is not to create a shield

We find that *Mullins v. Venable,* while it addresses a different statute within a different act of the West Virginia Code, is still very persuasive, as the language regarding who is liable under W. Va.Code 21-5-15 (1981) is substantively similar to that of W. Va.Code 23-1-16 (1995).

The defendants also contend in support of their position that the legislative rule regarding the enforcement of reporting and payment requirements under the Workers' Compensation Act provides that corporate officers were not intended by the Legislature to be liable for the corporation's failure to pay premiums or file quarterly reports.[7]

The defendants argue that this regulation, which removed the term "officer" from its definition when it amended the previous version, clearly indicates the government's intent not to hold corporate officers responsible for the failure of the corporation to make payments or file reports under W. Va.Code 23-1-16(a) (1995). We disagree.

As we discussed above, if the Legislature desires to alter or supplant the common law, its intent must be plainly and clearly manifested. While the removal of the term "officer" from legislative rule 85 C.S.R. 11 § 2.8 (1993), would, in isolation, lend support to the defendants' argument, we are obliged to observe the other alterations made to the section. Significantly, we note that although the definition of "employer" no longer explicitly includes in its list the term "officer," the Legislature, in amending 85 C.S.R. 11 § 2.8 in 1993, made it clear that the list of persons and entities defined as "employer" was not intended to be an exhaustive list, as evidenced by the addition of the qualifier "but is not limited to" in the definition of "employer." Read in its entirety, then, we cannot say that the Legislature unequivocally expressed an intent to remove officers from the regulation defining "employer."[8]

Finally, the defendants argue that the use of the language "the officer of any corporation" in subsection (b) of W. Va.Code 23-1-16 (1995),[9] is noticeably absent

---

in which to protect those who control the corporation from answering for its actions that may be criminal in nature.

7. 85 C.S.R. 11 § 1.1 (1995) provides:

Scope.—This legislative rule provides for the determination of delinquency and default on the part of emplzoyers regarding reporting and payment requirements, for the enforcement of collection of payments from those requirements, and for enforcement of other required payments.

The term "employer" has the meaning ascribed to that term by W. Va.Code § 23-2-1, which includes, but is not limited to, any individual, firm, partnership, limited partnership, copartnership, joint venture, association, corporation, organization, receiver, estate, trust, guardian, executor, administrator, or any other entity regularly employing another person or persons for the purpose of carrying on any form of industry, service or business in this state.

85 C.S.R. 11 § 2.8 (1993).

8. We do not mean to be so presumptuous as to suggest to the Legislature the model of any statute that might exempt corporate officers and directors from being criminally responsible for criminal offenses of the corporation so as to change the common law. An example, though, might be as follows: "Providing that, liability for violations under this section shall not be imposed upon the officers and directors of the corporation."

9. W. Va.Code 23-1-16(b) (1995) provides:

Any person or firm, or the officer of any corporation, who knowingly and willfully makes a false report or statement under oath, affidavit or certification respecting any information required to be provided under this chapter, shall be guilty of a

from the text of subsection (a), and requires us to apply the maxim of statutory construction known as expressio unius est exclusio alterius, which means the expression of one implies the exclusion of another. We do not believe that subsections (a) and (b) of W. Va.Code 23-1-16 (1995) require us to apply the maxim of expressio unius est exclusio alterius. Although these two subsections are contained within the same section of the West Virginia Workers' Compensation Act, they create separate and distinct offenses, which was made clearer by the Legislature's amendment of the section in 1995, whereby the two offenses were removed from a unified text and placed into separate subsections. The two subsections address mutually exclusive offenses, and each subsection can be read without doing offense to the other. Furthermore, W. Va.Code 23-1-16(a) (1995) is clear and unambiguous in that it does not express an intent to create an exception to our rule under the common law that corporate officers may be liable for the criminal violations of the corporation. Therefore, because W. Va.Code 23-1-16(a) (1995) is not vague or ambiguous, there is no need to construe the statute, and we need not turn to the rules of statutory construction, including the maxim of expressio unius est exclusio alterius.

III.

CONCLUSION

For the foregoing reasons, we find that the Legislature has not expressed a clear intent to exempt corporate officers from criminal liability under W. Va.Code 23-1-16 (1995). We therefore conclude that circuit court's order denying Mr. Nguyen's motion to quash the indictment was proper, and that the circuit court's order granting Mr. Rife's motion to quash the indictment improperly interpreted the statute and misapplied the law.

Writ denied.

Reversed and remanded.

E. Additional Problems

10.8 In a suit for damages for personal injuries, H.T. Chandler, Jr., recovered a judgment against Prairie Livestock Company, Inc. in the amount of $10,000, and the latter appeals. The episode out of which the action arose is correctly described as bizarre. It took place at a public cattle sale and involved three individuals who were cattle buyers, one of whom was Boyce Davis, a buyer for the appellant, Prairie. When Davis entered the stands that surrounded the arena, the other two buyers, James Crenshaw and Willie Mitchell, with whom neither Davis nor Prairie had any connection, were already seated. Mitchell was sitting in the row behind Crenshaw and was occupying a seat behind that occupied by Crenshaw. Davis thought there was a vacant seat in the row in which Crenshaw was sitting and started to enter the row. This required him to get by the seated Crenshaw. Davis was mistaken or the seat he had in mind was filled before he could get to it. When he observed this, Davis jokingly requested Crenshaw (with

---

felony, and, upon conviction thereof, shall be fined not less than one thousand dollars nor more than ten thousand dollars or confined in the penitentiary for a definite term of imprisonment which is not less than one year nor more than three years, or both.

whom he was acquainted) to give him, Davis, his seat and playfully sat down on Crenshaw's lap for a moment. Mitchell, sitting behind Crenshaw, immediately and without warning "goosed" Crenshaw from behind. This caused Crenshaw to react violently by suddenly jumping up and hurling Davis down the aisle steps that descended between the sections of seats. Davis's body, in the course of the fall, struck Chandler, who was sitting on the steps in the aisle a few rows down. Should the judgment be affirmed on appeal? See *Prairie Livestock Co., Inc. v. Chandler*, 325 So. 2d 908 (Miss. 1976).

10.9 Robb was an employee on Hay's farm. During a lull in the harvest season, Hay mentioned that a neighbor, Fain, had owed him $1000 for over two years and that he would like to collect it. Robb said that he would call on Fain to collect the debt if Hay wished and if Hay would give him twenty-five percent of what he recovered. Silent but nodding his head, Hay watched Robb climb in the farm truck and start in the direction of Fain's farm. Robb went directly to Fain's home and demanded payment of the money owed Hay. Fain reluctantly gave Robb $600 to apply on the debt but then called him an obscene name. Robb reacted by knocking Fain to the floor, kicking him, and breaking six ribs. Frightened by the turn of events, Robb raced to the truck to leave. Unfortunately for Fain's pet Shetland pony, Robb hit and killed the pony while quickly backing up the driveway to leave. Afraid to return to Hay, Robb drove to a neighboring town twenty-five miles away and spent three hours in the local tavern bolstering his spirits. Then, while weaving out of the tavern parking lot, Robb negligently ran into Black's automobile, injuring Black. What are the rights and liabilities, if any, of Hay? Explain. (Illinois Bar Examination, July 1980.)

10.10 On July 23, 1976, Elzear Kuehn was driving southbound on Interstate 5. At approximately 6:30 P.M., the Kuehns were in the traffic lane next to the outside lane. As Kuehn's automobile proceeded down a hill, a truck in the outside lane started to pass them. The truck was owned by Inter-City Auto Freight, Inc. and was operated by Richard K. White. When the trailer of the combination pulled even with Kuehn's automobile, the rig swerved left into Kuehn's traffic lane. Kuehn applied his brakes and drove into the lane to his left. Then, Kuehn stepped on the gas, caught up with the truck, and motioned to White to pull over onto the shoulder of the highway. White shook a fist in the direction of Kuehn's automobile and weaved toward Kuehn's car forcing it over into the third lane. Kuehn again accelerated to catch up with the truck. White, followed by the Kuehns, drove onto the right-hand shoulder of the road. White jammed on the brakes of the truck, and Kuehn had to brake hard to keep from driving into the rear of the truck. White got out of the cab of the truck and walked toward Kuehn's car carrying a two-foot metal pipe owned by Inter-City. Kuehn got out of his car and asked White why he had attempted to force the Kuehn automobile off the road. White then swung the pipe at Kuehn's head, knocking Kuehn to his hands and knees, and when Kuehn tried to get up, White hit him again on the head. Will the trucking company be accountable for White's attack on Kuehn? (*See Kuehn v. White*, 24 Wash. App. 274, 600 P.2d 679 (1979).)

10.11 Dawes was engaged in the business of selling automobiles and had in his employ a salesman, Roberts. In response to a telephone call from Perkins, who owned and operated a grocery store, Roberts drove a truck owned by Dawes to the store to show it and try to sell it to Perkins. Roberts asked Perkins to take a test-drive in the truck with him, which Perkins did. Perkins then suggested that Roberts leave the truck with him overnight so that his employee who would be driving the truck might test it. Roberts agreed, and Perkins drove Roberts in the truck to Roberts's hotel. After leaving Roberts at the hotel, Perkins started back to his grocery store. It began to rain and the truck ran out of gasoline. Perkins discovered that the taillights on the truck were not burning, which was previously unknown to Dawes and Roberts. Perkins attempted to flag down automobiles approaching the parked truck, but an automobile owned and operated by Mason collided with the truck, which could not be seen in the rain and darkness. Mason sued Dawes for injuries he sustained. What decision and why? (Illinois Bar Examination, Aug., 1966.)

10.12 Acme Manufacturing Company, a large industrial corporation, owned a fleet of several airplanes for use in its business. It employed several pilots full time, including John Black. The planes were stationed at a privately operated airport near Raleigh, owned and operated by Ace Flying Service, Inc., which also serviced Acme's planes and rented hangar space for their occupancy. Employment of pilots and dispatch of Acme's planes and pilots were the duties of Chief Pilot Burns. Black was ordered to take one of the planes to a small city located several hundred miles away, which had neither commercial airline nor air charter service, in order to pick up potential customers of Acme for an important dinner conference that night in Raleigh with Acme's top management. En route to get his passengers, Black's plane developed mechanical difficulties, forcing him to land at an airport short of his destination. Repairs could not be made in time, so Black attempted unsuccessfully to communicate with Chief Pilot Burns for further instructions. He was also unable to locate their other company pilots. He then telephoned the manager of Ace, who told him that one of the Acme planes was in its hangar and that a pilot employed by Ace was available. Black told the manager to have the Ace pilot ferry the Acme plane to him at once so that he could carry out his mission. While taxing for take off, the Ace pilot negligently rammed the Acme plane into another private plane owned by Innocent, proximately causing extensive damage to both planes. Was the Ace pilot the agent of Acme so as to impose liability on Acme for the damages to Innocent's plane? Explain. (Illinois Bar Examination, July 1981.)

10.13 The defendant, McGary, was deputy marshal of the Town of Friday Harbor. The town issued McGary a badge and identification card, but no other equipment was issued. It was known by the town marshal that McGary had a gun (.38 special) and that he kept it locked in the glove compartment of his automobile. It was also known that McGary occasionally used his own vehicle for police purposes. There was conflicting testimony as to whether McGary was required to have a gun in his possession as deputy marshal. As deputy marshal, McGary was compensated by the Town of Friday Harbor at the rate of $25 per shift. Although McGary was more or less on call twenty-four hours a day, seven days a week, he was not required to come on duty if he wished to decline. On January 28, 1975, Kerri Guard, a seven-year-old girl, was watching a basketball game in Friday Harbor. She was standing on a rock outside the gymnasium and looking through a window at the game. At that time and place, Brian James, the defendant McGary's four-year-old grandson, came up behind Kerri with a gun (which turned out to be McGary's .38 special) and said, "I shoot you, Kerri." Brian fired the weapon, seriously injuring Kerri. Deputy McGary had left his keys in his unattended vehicle, which turned out to be an attraction to his grandson. The town provided no training as to police duties. McGary had previously had five years of experience as a deputy sheriff in San Juan County and twenty-six months of experience as a deputy marshall in the Town of Friday Harbor. A suit was brought against both the Town of Friday Harbor and McGary, and a judgment for damages in the amount of $10,000 was entered. The judgment was paid by the Town of Friday Harbor, which now seeks common-law indemnification against McGary on the theory that the town was a passive joint tortfeasor. Will the town prevail? (See Guard v. Town of Friday Harbor, 22 Wash. App. 758, 592 P.2d 652 (1979).)

10.14 A was the owner and operator of an auto service station in the town of X. He sold at retail the usual petroleum products and small accessories, and he also performed minor repairs on customers' cars. A purchased all his oil and gasoline from Slick Oil Company. There were many signs and emblems displayed on and in the service station extolling the virtues of the products of Slick Oil Company. B was a customer of A and frequently left his car for service and minor adjustments. A had frequently told B that he was one of Slick's best salesmen and that he "had been with Slick Oil for many years." On one occasion when B left his car for service, A wrongfully drove the car on a personal errand and greatly damaged B's car in an accident. B brings an appropriate action against Slick Oil Company for damages to his car. What result and why? (Illinois Bar Examination, Mar. 1969. *See Gizzi v. Texaco*, 437 F.2d 308 (3d Cir. 1971).)

10.15 In a suit for damages for personal injuries, H.T. Chandler, Jr., recovered a judgment against Prairie Livestock Company, Inc. in the amount of $10,000, and the latter appeals. The episode out of which the action arose is correctly described as bizarre. It took place at a public cattle sale and involved three individuals who were cattle buyers, one of whom was Boyce Davis, a buyer for the appellant, Prairie. When Davis entered the stands that surrounded the arena, the other two buyers, James Crenshaw and Willie Mitchell, with whom neither Davis nor Prairie had any connection, were already seated. Mitchell was sitting in the row behind Crenshaw and was occupying a seat behind that occupied by Crenshaw. Davis thought there was a vacant seat in the row in which Crenshaw was sitting and started to enter the row. This required him to get by the seated Crenshaw. Davis was mistaken or the seat he had in mind was filled before he could get to it. When he observed this, Davis jokingly requested Crenshaw (with whom he was acquainted) to give him, Davis, his seat and playfully sat down on Crenshaw's lap for a moment. Mitchell, sitting behind Crenshaw, immediately and without warning "goosed" Crenshaw from behind. This caused Crenshaw to react violently by suddenly jumping up and hurling Davis down the aisle steps that descended between the sections of seats. Davis's body, in the course of the fall, struck Chandler, who was sitting on the steps in the aisle a few rows down. Should the judgment be affirmed on appeal? (See Prairie Livestock Co., Inc. v. Chandler, 325 So. 2d 908 (Miss. 1976).)

Chapter 11

Liability for Wrongful Acts of Independent Contractors

A. Non-Liability for Acts of Independent Contractors

Problem 11.1

Poe employed Allen as his agent for the purpose of locating and purchasing ten mink for breeding purposes. Allen, using his own automobile, drove to Tone's farm and purchased the ten mink. Allen took possession of the ten mink, and left Tone's farm. On his way back to Poe's farm, Allen negligently struck and damaged an automobile driven by Yates. Is Poe subject to liability to Yates for Allen's negligence?

Kane Furniture Corp. v. Miranda

506 So. 2d 1061 (Fla. App. 1987)

RYDER, Acting Chief Judge.

Kane is a furniture store which also sells carpeting. Kane sold its carpet installation business to Perrone in 1975, and since that time, Kane has provided carpet installation services through Perrone's installation business (known as Service) as well as through other independent carpet installers.

For the past ten years, however, Perrone has been the principal carpet installer at Kane's St. Petersburg store. Initially, Kane put Perrone on a two-week probationary period during which Kane inspected Perrone's work to determine that Perrone was qualified. Thereafter, Perrone was given a small work area from which to assign installation jobs. Perrone hired other independent carpet installers, such as Kraus, to complete jobs which he could not perform.

On the morning of Saturday, August 6, 1983, Perrone assigned Kraus two installation jobs from Kane. Kraus completed the installation called for by the jobs around noon. Thereafter, Kraus, in his own truck, drove to a bar with his helper, Kevin Carleton, as a passenger. After drinking for approximately four hours, Kraus attempted to drive Carleton to Kane's warehouse parking lot in order that Carleton could retrieve his car. On the way to the parking lot, Kraus, traveling at a speed in excess of 50 m.p.h., ran a stop sign and collided broadside with the

531

Miranda vehicle. Dr. Miranda's wife, Zenaida Quintos-Miranda, a passenger in the Miranda vehicle, died in a hospital soon after the accident.

This consolidated appeal arose from a wrongful death action which Dr. Romulo Miranda brought against Kane Furniture Corporation and Joseph P. Perrone for the death of Zenaida Quintos-Miranda. Kane appeals from the trial court's final summary judgment finding that Perrone was Kane's employee and that Kraus was Kane's subemployee. Kane appeals the jury verdict finding that Kraus was acting within the scope of his employment at the time of that accident. Kane also appeals the jury verdict award of 2.3 million dollars to Dr. Miranda.

In *Cantor v. Cochran,* 184 So. 2d 173 (Fla. 1966), the Supreme Court of Florida approved the test set out in Restatement (Second) of Agency 220[(2)] (1958) for determining whether one is an employee or independent contractor:

In determining whether one acting for another is a servant or an independent contractor, the following matters of fact, among others, are considered:

(a) the extent of control which, by the agreement, the master may exercise over the details of the work;

(b) whether or not the one employed is engaged in a distinct occupation or business;

(c) the kind of occupation, with reference to whether, in the locality, the work is usually done under the direction of the employer or by a specialist without supervision;

(d) the skill required in the particular occupation;

(e) whether the employer or the workman supplies the instrumentalities, tools, and the place of work for the person doing the work;

(f) the length of time for which the person is employed;

(g) the method of payment, whether by the time or by the job;

(h) whether or not the work is a part of the regular business of the employer;

(i) whether or not the parties believe they are creating the relationship of master and servant; and

(j) whether the principal is or is not in business.

Upon applying the Restatement test to the facts before us, we come to the conclusion that Perrone and Kraus were independent contractors, not employees.

(a) *The extent of control which, by the agreement, the master may exercise over the details of the work.*

It has been said that the extent of control is the most important factor in determining whether a person is an independent contractor or an employee. The right of control as to the mode of doing the work is the principal consideration. If a person is subject to the control or direction of another as to his results only, he is an independent contractor; if he is subject to control as to the means used to achieve the results, he is an employee.

For instance, in *Miami Herald Publishing Co. v. Kendall,* 88 So. 2d 276 (Fla. 1956), the court found that a newspaper carrier was an independent contractor and not an employee. In that case, the Miami Herald had entered into a contract with a newspaper carrier to distribute the Miami Herald within a set territory. The contract among other things provided that the carrier was an independent contractor and that the Miami Herald could not control his method of distributing or handling the newspaper. The contract defined the newscarrier's obligations: he was to furnish the names of new subscribers; to pay money collected to the appellant within a certain time; to present within forty-eight hours claims for shortages in papers; to call to appellant's attention within six days errors in statements; to handle the Miami Herald exclusively; to keep in confidence the names of subscribers; to select a substitute in the event he was unable to make his deliveries and be "responsible" for the substitute; to bear all costs of enforcing the contract; to give bond for his faithful performance of the agreement; to acquaint any successor with the route and list of subscribers; to secure delivery of papers in good condition; and to undertake to increase the number of subscribers.

The Miami Herald set the retail price of the papers and was often the recipient of customer complaints about unsatisfactory delivery of the paper. The Miami Herald, however, did not supervise delivery of the papers. Rather, the court found that the newspaper boy, while making his deliveries, "was acting alone and was a specialist, at least to the extent of following his route, remembering the addresses of subscribers who were in good standing, and collecting and properly accounting for funds coming into his hands." The newsboy was accountable for papers the publisher delivered to him whether or not he collected from the subscriber. The court stated that "we do not doubt that distribution of newspapers is a part of the regular business of the publisher but there is no reason that this cannot be done by independent contractors."

In *T & T Communications* [*v. Dept. of Labor*, 460 So. 2d 996 (Fla. App. 1984)], the court found cable installers to be independent contractors primarily because the company's only concern was with the final product or result. Although the cable installers agreed with the cable company to complete the cable installations pursuant to the cable company's plans and specifications, the installers themselves determined the method by which to accomplish the installation. The court stated that further indicia that they were independent contractors were:

> The fact that cable installers are normally unsupervised[,] are skilled tradesmen[,] provide their own tools and transportation[,] are not employed for any length of time, are paid per installation, and receive no vacation and fringe benefits.

In the instant case, although Kane's salesmen diagrammed the installation layout plan, the carpet installers, Perrone and Kraus, had unbridled discretion in the physical performance of their tasks. Perrone did not report to anyone at Kane and had absolute discretion in contracting out installation jobs. The only instructions Kane gave Perrone were that he and the other carpet installers should be neatly attired and not intoxicated while on the job. Kane also instructed Perrone on customer satisfaction.

Once the carpet installer got the job, he was on his own. He performed his work completely without Kane's supervision or any other involvement. Upon completion of his task, the installer was free to go where he pleased: to another job or, unfortunately, to the local bar.

(b) *Whether or not the one employed is engaged in a distinct occupation or business.*

Carpet installing can be viewed as a distinct occupation. Perrone and Kraus each had their own independent installation businesses. Perrone performed his services through a company which he purchased from Kane in 1975. Kraus performed his services through his own company, Mike's Carpet Service.

(c) *The kind of occupation with reference to whether, in the locality, the work is usually done under the direction of the employer or by a specialist without supervision.*

Carpet installers are skilled workers who routinely perform without supervision. Perrone and Kraus performed work which emanated through Kane sales on an "as needed" basis. Both performed without Kane's supervision. Each was responsible for his own work. Kraus guaranteed his work for one year. Each, personally, was responsible for replacing carpeting he lost or damaged.

(d) *The skill required in the particular occupation.*

Testimony at trial indicated that carpet installers are required to complete an apprenticeship in order to acquire the necessary skill to perform installation. As was aforementioned, Perrone also underwent a two-week probationary period at Kane.

(e) *Whether the employer or the workman supplies the instrumentalities, tools, and the place of work for the person doing the work.*

Perrone and Kraus supplied their own installation equipment: knives, kickers, seaming irons, etc. They owned and insured their own trucks for work. Kane did not reimburse them for mileage and other expenses, such as gasoline.

While Kane supplied Perrone with a small space and telephone from which to assign installation jobs, such accommodations did not make Perrone Kane's employee.

(f) *The length of time for which the person is employed.*

Again, Perrone and Kraus worked for Kane on an "as needed" basis. The time spent on each job varied in length. The installation jobs were assigned on an "A.M. job or P.M. job." Neither was obligated to work exclusively for Kane. Kane was not obligated to use only Perrone and Kraus.

(g) *The method of payment, whether by time or by job.*

While Kane determined the amount Perrone was paid, Perrone was paid strictly on a per yard basis. Kane made its checks out to Perrone's company. Perrone, in turn, paid Kraus and the other installers to whom he had assigned jobs.

Independent contractors are normally paid "per installation" rather than "by time." For instance, in *VIP Tours* [*v. Dept. of Labor*, 449 So. 2d 1307 (Fla. App. 1984)] a tour company was not deemed employer of tour guides using company vehicles who worked on a per job basis. In *T & T Communications*, cable splicers were found to be independent contractors where they were not employed for any length of time, were paid per installation and received no vacation or fringe benefits.

(h) *Whether or not the work is part of the regular business of the employer.*

Kane is engaged in the retail furniture business. As a part of that business, Kane also sells carpeting and advertises installation as included in the purchase price. This is the only factor favoring the conclusion that Perrone and Kraus are employees. With all the other factors pointing to the conclusion that they are independent contractors, this factor alone is insufficient to sustain a holding that they are employees.

(i) *Whether or not the parties believe they are creating the relation of master and servant.*

The parties' intent and course of dealing are important factors in determining their legal status. Clearly, the parties believed they were entering into an independent contractor relationship. Perrone and Kraus paid taxes as the owners of independent carpet installation businesses. Kane did not withhold social security or income taxes. Kane filed a Form "1099" for Perrone which is the IRS tax form a company files for nonemployees. A person who is responsible for paying all taxes due has been found to be an independent contractor.

Both Perrone 'and Kraus were free to accept or reject Kane's work. Perrone and Kraus were also able to work for companies in addition to Kane. Kane was not obligated to use Perrone or Kraus exclusively and, in fact, did not. Both Perrone and Kraus could hire their own employees.

Neither Perrone nor Kraus had employment agreements with Kane. Neither enjoyed the usual amenities associated with an employment relationship: fringe benefits, health care insurance, unemployment compensation, worker's compensation and paid vacations or holidays.

(j) *Whether the principal is or is not in business.*

We concur in Mr. Justice Grimes' opinion in *D.O. Creasman [Electronics v. Dept. of Labor,* 458 So. 2d 894 (Fla. App. 1984)] that "the relevance of this factor is obscure, but for what it is worth, appellant is in business."

Measured against the Restatement criteria, we hold that Perrone and Kraus are independent contractors.

[W]e reverse and set aside the verdict entered herein, vacate the summary final judgment and remand the matter to the trial court with instructions to enter summary judgment for Kane finding that Perrone and Kraus are independent contractors.

Notes

1. A contractor is one who is hired to perform physical services or to accomplish a specified task without being subject to the detailed control of the employer. Restatement Section 2(3) provides that:

> [a]n independent contractor is a person who contracts with another to do something for him but who is not controlled by the other nor subject to the other's right to control with respect to his physical conduct in the performance of the undertaking. He may or may not be an agent.

Even an "employee" may be viewed as an independent contractor, rather than a servant, for tort liability purposes. Although he or she may be an agent for purposes of contract accountability of the employer, he or she may not be a servant but an independent contractor when it comes to the question of whether the employer is liable for misconduct.

2. Are all of the factors of Restatement section 220 (listed in the principal case) of equal weight? If not, which ones are most important? Which are largely evidentiary?

Problem 11.2

Avis Rent-A-Car System Inc., a national car rental business, paid "car shuttlers" to drive cars from one Avis station to another in order to adjust local inventories to meet demand. Car shuttlers were ordinarily servicemen, housewives, and others who were not regularly or permanently employed by Avis and who were recruited informally without interviews or training. A standard form contract was signed by the parties on each occasion of a shuttle which provided that the driver would deliver the car to a designated place at a designated time for the stated fee, that the car would remain in the same condition as when it was received by the driver, that the car was not to be used for any purpose other than transport to the Avis station, and "that this contract in no way constitutes the contractor as an agent or employee" of Avis. The drivers did not wear Avis uniforms like other Avis employees and did not participate in the Avis employment benefit program. Furthermore, Avis did not pay federal employment taxes on the car shuttlers. Were the car shuttlers employees or independent contractors of Avis? See *Avis Rent-A-Car Sys. Inc. v. United States*, 503 F.2d 423 (2d Cir. 1974).

Pamperin v. Trinity Memorial Hospital
144 Wis. 2d 188, 423 N.W.2d 848 (1988)

CALLOW, Justice.

This is a review of an unpublished decision of the court of appeals which affirmed an order of the circuit court dismissing Trinity Memorial Hospital from [an] action brought by Clarence Pamperin to recover damages for the alleged negligence arising out of the care and treatment provided to Pamperin following his admission to Trinity's emergency room. Pamperin argues that Trinity should be liable for the negligence of a radiologist, practicing medicine at Trinity.

Because this case comes to us following motions for summary judgment, the facts before us on review are limited. In essence, they are that on January 3, 1982, Pamperin fell and injured his leg. He was thereafter taken to the emergency room at Trinity where he was examined by Dr. Ronald Schulgit. During the examination, Schulgit requested X-rays be taken of Pamperin's lower right leg. Schulgit read the X-ray, determined there was a minor ankle fracture, splinted the fracture, and then sent Pamperin home.

The next day the X-rays were read at Trinity by Dr. Boex, a radiologist. Boex also determined there was a minor ankle fracture. However, both Boex and Schulgit failed to observe that the X-rays also revealed a comminuted fracture of the proximal tibia at the knee.

[A]t the time Boex read the X-rays, he was an employee of Lakeview Radiologists, S.C. According to Boex, Lakeview is a service corporation which contracted with Trinity to provide diagnostic radiology for Trinity. Under the terms of the contract, Lakeview is to provide twenty-four hour radiological services. Trinity is to provide the physical facilities, equipment, and staff. Although Lakeview is, under the contract, prohibited from engaging in any activity which will impair its ability to provide adequate radiological services, Lakeview is not prohibited from maintaining a separate practice. However, according to Boex, Lakeview provides radiological services only to Trinity.

On May 27, 1986, Pamperin commenced [an] action in the circuit court against Trinity and Schulgit. In the complaint, Pamperin alleged that Trinity and Schulgit were negligent in the care and treatment rendered to Pamperin. Pamperin moved for summary judgment requesting an order that Trinity was vicariously liable for the negligence of Boex.

On October 27, 1986, the circuit court issued a decision granting summary judgment dismissing the malpractice action against Trinity. In reaching this conclusion, the court first held that Boex was an independent contractor. Next, the court noted that, in this case, because there was no allegation that Trinity was negligent in failing to check the credentials of Lakeview, whether the hospital was liable was "a question of agency." However, because the only type of agency relationship which would impose liability was a master-servant agency relationship, Trinity could not be liable for the acts of Boex, an independent contractor.

Pamperin appealed, and the court of appeals affirmed the circuit court's order.

We begin our review by considering Pamperin's assertion that Trinity is responsible for the negligence of Boex under the doctrine of respondeat superior. Essentially, Pamperin contends that Trinity has substantial control over Lakeview and that because of Trinity's retention of control over Lakeview, Boex—as an employee of Lakeview—is a servant of Trinity.

Under the doctrine of respondeat superior, a master is subject to liability for the tortious acts of his or her servant [committed within the scope of employment]. A servant is one who is

> employed to perform service for another in his affairs and who, with respect to his *physical conduct* in the performance of the service, is subject to the other's control or right to control.

Arsand v. City of Franklin, 83 Wis. 2d 40, 45–46, 264 N.W.2d 579 (1978) (emphasis in original). The right to control is the dominant test in determining whether an individual is a servant. However, other factors are considered, including the place of work, the time of the employment, the method of payment, the nature of the business or occupation, which party furnishes the instrumentalities or tools, the intent of the parties to the contract, and the right of summary discharge of employees.

Looking first at the element of control, we conclude that Trinity does not exercise any control over the manner in which Lakeview's radiological services are provided. The very nature of a radiologist's function requires the exercise of independent professional judgment. Accordingly, a hospital is not in a position to, and generally does not, exercise control over a radiologist's performance of his or her professional activities. Although Trinity does require that the Lakeview radiologists be members of Trinity's staff, and although Trinity retains a limited ability to monitor the quality of the care which Lakeview provides, Trinity does not reserve the right of control over the specific techniques employed by the Lakeview radiologists.

Other factors also indicate that Lakeview is not Trinity's servant. Lakeview and Trinity maintain separate offices. Each is responsible for billing and collecting for the costs associated with the particular service each provides. Consistent with this responsibility, Lakeview has final authority in establishing its fees. In addition, Lakeview is required to provide its own malpractice insurance. Finally, Lakeview is not prohibited from serving other hospitals or patients.

The factors listed by Pamperin, including Trinity's right to request review of Lakeview's performance, Trinity's ability to review procedures adopted by Lakeview, its power to approve Lakeview's appointment of a director of the radiology department, as well as the requirement that the Lakeview radiologists be members of Trinity's staff, do not compel the conclusion that Lakeview is Trinity's servant. A number of these factors focus on maintaining professional standards; they do not indicate that a master-servant relationship exists. Other factors noted by Pamperin, particularly the requirement that the Lakeview radiologists be members of Trinity's staff and subject to the hospital's approval, are imposed by statute. In addition, factors which indicate a master-servant relationship, e.g., a fixed monthly salary and withholding of taxes and social security, are not present in this case. The limited control which Trinity has reserved over Lakeview's providing radiological services does not transform Lakeview's relationship with Trinity into a master-servant/relationship. Under the facts of this case, we hold, as a matter of law, that Lakeview—and thus Boex—is not Trinity's servant, i.e., Lakeview is an independent contractor. [T]he doctrine of respondeat superior is not applicable in the present case.

Notes

1. Often, the independent contractor's business is distinct from that of the employer, and in these settings, the independent contractors will be most readily identifiable. Thus, when a merchant hires a painter to paint his or her store, hails a taxicab, or retains a private detective to investigate a competitor, the merchant has employed an independent contractor. So long as the merchant does not exercise too much control over the manner in which the painter, the cab driver, or the detective performs his or her duties, the merchant will be insulated from liability for torts committed by the painter, the cab driver, or the detective.

2. The question of whether one is an employee or an independent contractor may arise in contexts other than tort liability situations. For instance, an employer may prefer to have some individuals characterized as independent contractors to avoid liability for federal employment taxes that must be paid where employees are involved.

3. The last several years have seen the development of the practice of "employee leasing" (also called "staff leasing"). Under employee leasing, a group of employees a company (the "customer") purportedly cease being employees of the customer, and are instead purportedly employed by the employee leasing company. The employee leasing company then provides the customer with personnel to operate the customer's business by "leasing" the same employees back to the

customer. The employee leasing company pays all salaries, all employee benefits, and all state and federal taxes, and provides (and pays) for worker's compensation, but does so out of funds supplied by the customer. Except for this change in the name that appears on paychecks, etc., nothing changes for the employees. They do the same work, and do it in the same way.

The purpose of employee leasing goes beyond the provision of administrative services. Instead, the intent is to achieve some benefit that derives from the purported transfer of employment. Such benefits include (i) avoiding the anti-discrimination provisions of ERISA (the federal statute regulating retirement plans), as well as (ii) lowering insurance and workers' compensation premiums or taxes by changing the size of the workforce. Whether such benefits can be achieved depends on whether the leased employees remain employees of the customer, or in fact have become employees of the employee leasing company.

Wolf v. DaCom, Inc., 499 N.W.2d 728 (Iowa 1993) involved an employee, Wolf, who had been "leased" by DaCom, Inc. (the customer) from Strategic Staff Management (the employee leasing company). Wolf sued DaCom to recover past due commissions, wages, and vacation pay. DaCom claimed that it was not liable to Wolf, arguing that Strategic Staff Management (Strategic), rather than DaCom, had employed Wolf. The court rejected this argument:

> DaCom first contends Wolf is not entitled to recover under the Iowa Wage Payment Collection Act because DaCom was not his employer.
>
> Wolf's claims for unpaid wages and unpaid commissions are controlled in part by the Iowa Wage Payment Collection Act. Under [that Act], an employer is defined as a person who "employs for wages a natural person." "Wages" is defined as compensation owed by an employer for "labor or services rendered by an employee." DaCom relies upon several rulings which, in the context of the Internal Revenue Code, define an "employer" as the person who actually pays the wages.
>
> In the context of workers' compensation, our supreme court has considered the factors relevant in determining whether an employer-employee relationship exists under [Iowa Wage Payment Collection Act]. Factors to be considered include: ... (1) the right of selection, or to employ at will, (2) responsibility for the payment of wages by the employer, (3) the right to discharge or terminate the relationship, (4) the right to control the work, and (5) identity of the employer as the authority in charge of the work or for whose benefit the work is performed. In addition, the intention of the parties as to the relationship they are creating should also be considered. In general, the court looks to who has the "right of control." Here, the identity of the employer, and not the employee, is at issue. Nevertheless, the above case law provides much guidance in determining whether DaCom was an "employer" under [the Iowa Wage Payment Collection Act].
>
> DaCom contends its employees were terminated and then immediately rehired by Strategic on January 1, 1990. However, the employees of DaCom were never informed they had been terminated by DaCom and rehired by Strategic. While Strategic handled the payroll and other employee benefits, we find DaCom never abdicated its role as the actual employer.
>
> [T]he president of DaCom, testified Strategic performed only administrative functions. [DaCom] retained the right to make decisions regard-

ing hiring, firing, and setting compensation. Further, all monies for workers' compensation insurance, compensation, vacation benefits, sick leave, and employer contributions for 401K plans were paid by DaCom. [DaCom's President] testified that if DaCom did not put money into the account from which Strategic drew to pay employees, Strategic would not pay the employees.

We also note the language found in the March 22, 1990 confidentiality agreement. In this agreement, DaCom is referred to as "Company," and Wolf is referred to as "Employee." The agreement states, in relevant part: "WHEREAS, Employee is *employed by the Company* in a capacity in which Employee may become acquainted with such information and may in fact contribute thereto..." (emphasis added). Strategic is mentioned nowhere in this document which was executed almost four months after Strategic allegedly rehired the DaCom employees.

DaCom retained the right of control over all major decisions made regarding its employees. There is no evidence Strategic and the employees, including Wolf, ever intended to create an employer-employee relationship. The fact Strategic issued the paychecks is not at all controlling. We will not allow DaCom to hide behind Strategic and avoid liability for Wolf's claims. DaCom's contention that Wolf has sued the wrong party is without merit.

B. Duties in Selecting and Supervising Independent Contractors

King v. Loessin
572 S.W.2d 87 (Tex. Civ. App. 1978)

COLEMAN, Chief Justice.

The question is whether the action of a purported agent is chargeable to the defendant where the purported agent is the employee of a corporation who was employed to do investigative work for the defendant.

Delcer King, appellant, contracted with Smith Protective Services, Inc. to investigate a number of his competitors in the equipment business. Smith's employee, Thompson, along with another employee burglarized the offices of appellee in order to obtain certain sales invoices. Appellee sued Smith Protective Services, Inc., Cal Meyers, the investigations manager for Smith, and appellant, King, for damages incurred as a result of the alleged break-in.

It is undisputed that Thompson entered the premises of Loessin without permission of Loessin and removed certain items. The appellant contends that the plaintiff failed to prove that Thompson was an agent of King at the time of the trespass and that he was acting within the course and scope of his employment.

A contract between King and Smith Protective Services, Inc., is in evidence. It reflects that King contracted with Smith to conduct certain investigative services and agreed that the services would be performed by licensed investigators if required by law.

There was testimony that Mr. King told Mr. Meyers, who was acting for Smith Protective Services, Inc. that he desired an investigation of tool thefts and sabotage at his John Deere Tractor Agency and certain other matters. In particular, he wanted to determine who was selling parts to a competitor "at a [lower] cost than what was the normal rule within his area." Mr. Meyers testified that King explained to him what was required in order to satisfy the John Deere people that someone was infringing upon his region. Meyers stated that King told him that the only thing that would satisfy the John Deere people would be an invoice showing a 20% discount and that he wanted to secure one of those invoices. "He didn't particularly care how he went about getting it and said money was no object."

Mr. Meyers testified that while Mr. King did not specifically discuss a violation of the law in connection with the investigation, he did stipulate that he didn't particularly care how he went about getting the information he needed. Mr. Meyers hoped that his employees would not exceed the law because they had been warned not to, but he stated that he had given Mr. Jerry Dolly permission to discuss the matter with Mr. King. Mr. Meyers stated that he told Mr. King that if anything criminal came up he was going to have to bear the burden if he was going to coach the Smith investigators.

Mr. Thompson was a Smith employee before the contract with King was executed. Thompson took his instructions from Meyers. Mr. Thompson testified that he went with Jerry Dolly to see Delcer King and that Dolly did all the talking. He didn't hear Mr. King say anything about committing a burglary. Mr. Dolly gave him his instructions. Thompson admitted that he burglarized the Loessin Implement Company located in Weimar, Colorado County, Texas. He reported to Mr. Meyers after he "pulled the burglary." Meyers paid him for "conducting such burglary" with a Smith Protective Services, Inc. payroll check.

There is nothing in the testimony of Mr. King which would support the conclusion that he had any right to control Smith as to the method or means by which the work contracted for was to be accomplished. There is no testimony that King in fact instructed either Meyers, Thompson, or Dolly concerning the methods to be used in conducting the investigations.

A crucial question for determination is whether Smith Protective Services, Inc. was an independent contractor or whether the corporation and its employees had the status of agents or employees of King. The written agreement merely provides that Smith Protective Services, Inc. will be compensated at the rate of $20 per hour plus expenses for its investigative services. It does not specify the services to be rendered.

An employer is not responsible for the acts or omissions of an independent contractor and his subcontractors or servants, committed in the prosecution of work that is not in itself unlawful or attended with danger to others. The doctrine of respondeat superior has no application.

A person who contracts with another to perform a service unlawful in itself, even as an independent contractor, is responsible in damages for injury which might result from the performance of that service.

There is evidence which will support an implied fact finding of contemplated illegal activity on the part of Smith Protective Services, Inc. in conducting the investigation and of authorizing such activity if necessary to the successful completion of the investigation. This fact will be presumed found in support of the trial court's judgment. Under such circumstances the employer would not be insulated from liability by reason of the fact that the person perpetrating the offense might otherwise enjoy the status of an independent contractor.

Note

A person who directs another to take an action is subject to liability for the consequences

> result[ing] from his directions [to the same extent] as he would be [liable] for his own personal conduct if, with knowledge of the conditions, he intends the conduct, or if he intends its consequences.

Restatement § 212.

Problem 11.3

Homebuilder often employs Carpenter, an independent contractor, to frame windows on homes under construction. As Homebuilder knows, Carpenter has a violent temper, and often gets into fights with other workers. While out on a job, Woodworker borrows Carpenter's saw without his permission, and accidentally breaks it. Woodworker becomes enraged, and hits Woodworker on the head with a hammer, severely injuring him. Is Homebuilder subject to liability to Woodworker for Carpenter's attack?

Redinger v. Living, Inc.
689 S.W.2d 415 (Tex. 1985)

CAMPBELL, Justice.

Louis Redinger sued Living, Inc., the general contractor, and Bobby Baird, an independent contractor, for damages resulting from an injury to Redinger's finger. The trial court rendered judgment for Redinger based on jury findings that Baird and Living, Inc. [were each] negligent. The court of appeals reversed and remanded for a new trial.

Living, Inc. was the general contractor on the building construction site. Bobby Baird was the dirt hauling subcontractor, and Redinger was an employee of a plumbing subcontractor. David Yargo, the superintendent for Living, Inc., was preparing the site for a subcontractor to pour concrete. When the concrete trucks arrived, piles of dirt placed by Baird blocked the route to the work area. Yargo ordered Baird to move the dirt. As he was moving the dirt, the box blade of his tractor crushed Redinger's left index finger.

[T]he jury found that Living, Inc. was negligent in allowing Bobby Baird to operate his tractor while Louis Redinger and others were working in the area and also for failing to warn.

Living, Inc. contends the court of appeals erred in failing to render judgment that Redinger take nothing against it because Living, Inc., a general contractor, does not have a duty to Redinger, an employee of a subcontractor.

We will first consider whether a general contractor has a duty to a subcontractor's employee, and, if so, whether there is evidence in this case that the duty was breached. An owner or occupier of land has a duty to use reasonable care to keep the premises under his control in a safe condition. A general contractor on a construction site, who is in control of the premises, is charged with the same duty as an owner or occupier. This duty to keep the premises in a safe condition may subject the general contractor to direct liability for negligence.

The general rule is that an owner or occupier does not have a duty to see that an independent contractor performs work in a safe manner. However, when the general contractor exercises some control over a subcontractor's work he may be liable unless he exercises reasonable care in supervising the subcontractor's activity. We adopt the rule enunciated in the Restatement (Second) of Torts:

> One who entrusts work to an independent contractor, but who retains the control of any part of the work, is subject to liability for physical harm to others for whose safety the employer owes a duty to exercise reasonable care, which is caused by his failure to exercise his control with reasonable care.

Restatement (Second) of Torts § 414 (1977).

This rule applies when the employer retains some control over the manner in which the independent contractor's work is performed, but does not retain the degree of control which would subject him to liability as a master. Restatement (Second) of Torts § 414, comment a (1965). The employer's role must be more than a general right to order the work to start or stop, to inspect progress or receive reports. *Id.*, comment c.

> He may retain only the power to direct the order in which the work shall be done, or to forbid its being done in a manner likely to be dangerous to himself or others. Such a supervisory control may not subject him to liability under the principles of Agency, but he may be liable under the rule stated in this Section unless he exercises his supervisory control with reasonable care so as to prevent the work which he has ordered to be done from causing injury to others.

Id., comment a.

There is evidence that Living, Inc. retained the power to direct the order in which the work was to be done and to forbid the work being done in a dangerous manner. When the concrete trucks arrived at the site, Yargo ordered Baird to immediately move the dirt to another location. Yargo exercised supervisory control by coordinating the work performed by two subcontractors. Living, Inc. owed a duty to Redinger to exercise this supervisory control in a reasonable manner.

There is evidence that Living, Inc. negligently exercised this control. The dirt was located within one to five feet of an area where Redinger and employees of other subcontractors were working. While Baird was moving the dirt, his backhoe operated within one to five feet of Redinger and the other workers. There is evidence to support the jury finding that Living, Inc. was negligent in allowing Bobby Baird to operate his tractor while Redinger was working in the area and in failing to warn Redinger. We agree with the court of appeals that Living, Inc. owed a duty to Redinger to exercise reasonable care.

We affirm the judgment of the trial court.

Notes

1. An employer must exercise the same care in the selection and supervision of an independent contractor as in that of a servant Under Restatement section 213:

> A person conducting an activity through servants *or other agents* is subject to liability for harm resulting from his conduct if he is negligent or reckless:
>
>> (a) in giving improper or ambiguous orders of in failing to make proper regulations; or
>>
>> (b) in the employment of improper persons or instrumentalities in work involving risk of harm to others:
>>
>> (c) in the supervision of the activity; or
>>
>> (d) in permitting, or failing to prevent, negligent or other tortious conduct by persons, whether or not his servants or agents, upon premises or with instrumentalities under his control.

Restatement § 213.

2. In addition to these general duties, the employer of an independent contractor has additional responsibilities in certain circumstances. As provided in section 413 of the Restatement (Second) of Torts:

> One who employs an independent contractor to do work which the employer should recognize as likely to create, during its progress, a peculiar unreasonable risk of physical harm to others unless special precautions are taken, is subject to liability for physical harm caused to them by the absence of such precautions if the employer
>
>> (a) fails to provide in the contract that the contractor shall take such precautions, or
>>
>> (b) fails to exercise reasonable care to provide in some other manner for the taking of such precautions.

Restatement (Second) of Torts § 413. For example, in *Wilson v. Good Humor Corp.*, 757 F.2d 1293 (D.C. Cir. 1985), Good Humor hired independent contractors to operate the familiar ice cream trucks used for curbside vending of ice cream to children. The court held that, in light of Good Humor's knowledge of the peculiar risks to children, Good Humor should be liable for a failure to take *any* steps to ensure that the necessary special precautions were taken. For additional discussion of the peculiar risk doctrine, see *Huddleston v. Union Rural Electric Ass'n*, page 554.

C. Non-Delegable Duties

Problem 11.4

Borrower borrowed money from Bank to buy a car. When Borrower defaulted in the payment of her note to Bank, it hired Recovery Service to repossess the car. Recovery Service sent two servants to Borrower's home, where they found the car, parked in Borrower's driveway. After they had hooked the car to a tow truck, Borrower came outside, and demanded that they stop. They refused, got into the tow truck, and started pulling away. Borrower jumped into the car, and locked herself in. When Borrower refused to leave, they towed the car off with Borrower inside. They parked the car in Recovery Service's fenced repossession yard and padlocked the gate. Borrower was left in the car, with a Doberman pinscher guard dog loose in the repossession yard. Eventually, Borrower was rescued by her husband and police. Even after learning of the circumstances of the repossession, Bank kept the car.

a. Is Bank subject to liability to Borrower for any torts that were committed in the repossession of the car? *See, M-Bank El Paso, N.A. v. Sanchez,* 836 S.W.2d 151 (Tex. 1992).

b. If Bank is held liable to Borrower, must Recovery Service indemnify Bank for its losses?

Kleeman v. Rheingold
81 N.Y.2d 270, 598 N.Y.S.2d 149, 614 N.E.2d 712 (1993)

TITONE, Judge.

In a prior action brought to recover damages for alleged medical malpractice, plaintiff was non suited for failure properly to serve the defendant doctor before the Statute of Limitations on her claim expired. The threshold issue in this second malpractice action, which was brought by plaintiff against the lawyers she retained to prosecute the first, is whether an attorney may be held vicariously liable to his or her client for the negligence of a process server whom the attorney has hired on behalf of that client.

According to the allegations in the present complaint, plaintiff, a victim of alleged medical malpractice, had originally retained defendant and his law firm to pursue her claim against Dr. Neils Lauersen. With only five days remaining before the Statute of Limitations on the claim would expire, defendant promptly prepared a summons and complaint. On November 5, 1978, two days before the Statute of Limitations was to run, defendant delivered the prepared documents to Fischer's Service Bureau, a process service agency regularly used by defendant's law firm, with the instruction that process was to be served "immediately." It is undisputed that Fischer's, not defendant, selected the licensed process server who would actually deliver the papers and that Fischer's and the process server, rather than defendant, determined the precise manner of effecting service.

Although the process server used by Fischer's apparently delivered the papers on time, plaintiff's medical malpractice claim was ultimately dismissed when a traverse hearing revealed that the process server had given the papers to Dr. Lauersen's secretary rather than Dr. Lauersen himself. By the time the traverse hearing was held, the Statute of Limitations had expired and plaintiff had no further legal recourse against the allegedly negligent doctor. Defendants then attempted to recover on plaintiff's behalf by "alleging various and different theories of liability against certain other parties." (Plaintiff's verified complaint P 11.3) These claims, however, were all resolved against plaintiff in January of 1987.

Plaintiff subsequently commenced the present legal malpractice action against defendant and his law firm, claiming that they should be held liable for the negligence of the process server who had been retained to serve Dr. Lauersen on plaintiff's behalf. Defendants moved for summary judgment and plaintiff cross-moved. Plaintiff argued that defendants' liability could be predicated on a nondelegable duty of attorneys to exercise care in assuring proper service of their clients' legal process. Alternatively, plaintiff argued that the process server was defendants' agent and that, under settled agency law principles, they could therefore be held accountable for the process server's wrongful acts. Finally, plaintiff contended that defendants should be held liable because of their own negligence in selecting a process serving agency that was "not a particularly respected or reliable entity," in failing to supervise or monitor the work of that agency and, finally, in neglecting to file the summons and complaint with the appropriate County Clerk so as to obtain a 60-day toll of the Statute of Limitations on plaintiff's claim pursuant to CPLR 203(b)(5).

The trial court rejected all of plaintiff's arguments. [T]he court concluded that a process server is an "independent contractor" rather than an agent of the employing attorney, since "[t]he attorney does not have control over the manner in which the task is performed." (148 Misc.2d 853, 855, 562 N.Y.S.2d 915.) Accordingly, the court held, the relationship between the process server and the attorney here did not provide a cognizable basis for holding the latter vicariously liable for the acts of the former. On reargument, the court also rejected plaintiff's claims regarding defendants' failure to supervise the process server, holding that defendants' duty was satisfied when they took the necessary steps to commence the action by retaining the services of a licensed process server.

On plaintiff's appeal, a divided Appellate Division affirmed for essentially the same reasons. 185 A.D.2d 118, 585 N.Y.S.2d 733.

The general rule is that a party who retains an independent contractor, as distinguished from a mere employee or servant, is not liable for the independent contractor's negligent acts. Although several justifications have been offered in support of this rule, the most commonly accepted rationale is based on the premise that one who employs an independent contractor has no right to control the manner in which the work is to be done and, thus, the risk of loss is more sensibly placed on the contractor.

Despite the courts' frequent recitation of the general rule against vicarious liability, the common law has produced a wide variety of so-called "exceptions". Indeed, it has been observed that the general rule "is now primarily important as a preamble to the catalog of its exceptions" (*Pacific Fire Ins. Co. v. Kenny Boiler & Mfg. Co.*, 201 Minn. 500, 503, 277 N.W. 226, 228). These exceptions, most of which are derived from various public policy concerns, fall roughly into three basic categories: negligence of the employer in selecting, instructing or supervising the contractor;[1] employment for work that is especially or "inherently" dan-

---

1. Notably, although often classified as an "exception," this category may not be a true exception to the general rule, since it concerns the employer's liability for its own acts or omissions rather than its vicarious liability for the acts and omissions of the contractor.

gerous; and, finally, instances in which the employer is under a specific nondelegable duty.[2]

The exception that concerns us here — the exception for nondelegable duties — has been defined as one that "requires the person upon whom it is imposed to answer for it that care is exercised by anyone, even though he be an independent contractor, to whom the performance of the duty is entrusted" (Restatement [(Second) of Torts,] ch 15, topic 2, Introductory Note, at 394, quoted in *Feliberty v. Damon*, 72 N.Y.2d at 118–119, 531 N.Y.S.2d 778, 527 N.E.2d 261). The exception is often invoked where the particular duty in question is one that is imposed by regulation or statute. However, the class of duties considered "nondelegable" is not limited to statutorily imposed duties. To the contrary, examples of nondelegable common-law duties abound.

There are no clearly defined criteria for identifying duties that are nondelegable. Indeed, whether a particular duty is properly categorized as "nondelegable" necessarily entails a sui generis inquiry, since the conclusion ultimately rests on policy considerations.

The most often cited formulation is that a duty will be deemed nondelegable when "'the responsibility is so important to the community that the employer should not be permitted to transfer it to another'" (*Feliberty v. Damon, supra,* 72 N.Y.2d at 119, 531 N.Y.S.2d 778, 527 N.E.2d 261, *quoting* Prosser and Keeton, *op. cit.,* at 512). This flexible formula recognizes that the "privilege to farm out [work] has its limits" and that those limits are best defined by reference to the gravity of the public policies that are implicated (5 Harper, James and Gray, Torts § 26.11, at 73 [2d ed.]).

Viewed in the light of these principles, the duty at issue here — that owed by an attorney to his or her client to exercise care in the service of process — fits squarely and neatly within the category of obligations that the law regards as "nondelegable." Manifestly, when an individual retains an attorney to commence an action, timely and accurate service of process is an integral part of the task that the attorney undertakes. Furthermore, proper service of process is a particularly critical component of a lawyer's over-all responsibility for commencing a client's lawsuit, since a mistake or oversight in this area can deprive the client of his or her day in court regardless of how meritorious the client's claim may be. Given the central importance of this duty, our State's attorneys cannot be allowed to evade responsibility for its careful performance by the simple expedient of "farming out" the task to independent contractors.

The existence of an extensive and comprehensive Code of Professional Responsibility that governs the obligations of attorneys to their clients reinforces our conclusion. Under the Code, a lawyer may not "seek, by contract or other means, to limit prospectively the lawyer's individual liability to a client for malpractice" (DR 6-102, 22 NYCRR 1200.31). Moreover, the Code forbids lawyers from "[n]eglect[ing] legal matter[s] entrusted to [them]" (DR 6-101[a][3], 22 NYCRR 1200.30[a][3]), enjoins them to assist in "secur[ing] and protect[ing] available legal rights" (EC 7-1) and requires them to represent their clients as

---

2. A fourth category—i.e., cases in which the employer is held liable for risks "inherent in the work itself"—has been identified by one noted commentator (Prosser and Keeton, [Torts § 71], at 515–516) [(5th ed.)].

zealously as the "bounds of the law" permit (Canon 7). All of the latter ethical and disciplinary considerations are implicated when a client's lawsuit is undermined—or even defeated—as a consequence of carelessness in the service of process.

Our conclusion is also supported by the perceptions of the lay public and the average client, who may reasonably assume that *all* of the tasks associated with the commencement of an action, including its formal initiation through service of process, will be performed either by the attorney or someone acting under the attorney's direction. While it may be a common practice among attorneys to retain outside agencies like Fischer's to assist them in effecting service, that custom is not necessarily one of which the general public is aware. Even where a client is expressly made aware that a process serving agency will be retained, it is unlikely that the client will understand or appreciate that the process serving agency's legal status as an "independent contractor" could render the retained attorney immune from liability for the agency's negligence. Under established principles, the client's reasonable expectations and beliefs about who will render a particular service are a significant factor in identifying duties that should be deemed to be "nondelegable".

Finally, we conclude that permitting lawyers to transfer their duty of care to process servers would be contrary to sound public policy. In this State, licensed attorneys have been granted an exclusive franchise to practice law, with the understanding that they have both the specialized knowledge and the character required to represent clients in a competent, diligent and careful manner. Under this system, lawyers are authorized to hold themselves out as being uniquely qualified to manage their clients' legal affairs, a task that unquestionably includes the commencement of lawsuits. While it is true that the State also licenses non-lawyers to perform certain discrete, law-related tasks such as service of process, the existence of that licensing system certainly does not evince a governmental intent to relieve attorneys of the responsibilities implicit in their franchise. To the contrary, the purpose of the licensing system for process servers is to "combat a continuing and pervasive problem of unscrupulous service practices" in order to protect *defendants* who might otherwise be deprived of their day in court or be victimized by "fraudulent default judgments" (*Matter of Barr v. Department of Consumer Affairs*, 70 N.Y.2d 821, 822, 523 N.Y.S.2d 435, 517 N.E.2d 1321). That purpose is obviously unrelated to the entirely separate goal of assuring clients who are would-be *plaintiffs* that their process will be timely served in a manner that complies with the complex requirements of CPLR articles 2 and 3, as well as with the numerous other statutory provisions relating to commencement of actions (see, e.g., Business Corporation Law §§ 304–308) and the formidable body of case law illuminating those statutes. The responsibility for achieving that goal—and the liability for negligent failures to achieve it—must remain squarely on the shoulders of trained and licensed attorneys who, as members of a "learned profession," alone have the necessary knowledge and experience to protect their clients' rights.

Before closing, we note that, contrary to the concurrer's suggestion that our ruling has a far broader application, the nondelegable duty of care that we have recognized in this case is limited to the discrete and unique function of commencing an action through service of process. Furthermore, the duty extends only to clients who have retained an attorney for the purpose of commencing a lawsuit.

We do not decide here the entirely separate question of an attorney's liability for the wrongs that a retained process server may commit against a potential defendant or another third party. Nor do we consider the right of an attorney who has been held liable for the negligence of a retained process server to pursue whatever contractual or tort remedies that the attorney may have against that process server. We hold only that an attorney has a nondelegable duty to his or her clients to exercise due care in the service of process and that, accordingly, an attorney may be held liable to the client for negligent service of process, even though the task may have been "farmed out" to an independent contractor.[3]

In view of this conclusion, it is evident that the courts below erred in granting defendants' motion for summary judgment dismissing the complaint. If there was negligence in the effort to effect service of process in plaintiff's failed action against Dr. Lauersen, plaintiff is entitled to hold defendant vicariously liable, and she may recover in damages if she can demonstrate that this negligence was the proximate cause of any pecuniary injury she sustained. We note, however, that plaintiff is not herself entitled to summary judgment on the liability question at this point in the litigation, since she still must demonstrate both that the retained process server acted negligently and that she would have prevailed in the underlying action against Lauersen if the negligence had not occurred. Thus, the denial of plaintiff's cross motion for partial summary judgment was proper. Finally, since we are holding that neither party is entitled to summary judgment on plaintiff's single cause of action for legal malpractice, we need not now consider the viability of the other theories that plaintiff has advanced to support defendants' liability.[4] At this point in the litigation, it suffices to hold that defendants' nondelegable duty to plaintiff provides a legally viable basis for imposing liability on them.

Accordingly, the order of the Appellate Division should be modified, with costs to plaintiff, by denying defendants' motion for summary judgment dismissing the complaint and, as modified, affirmed.

BELLACOSA, Judge (concurring).

While I agree with the Court's result, I am unable to join in the broad rationale upon which it is premised. This case should be more prudently resolved on the narrower ground that questions of fact exist as to whether the defendant law firm was negligent in choosing its process server and in failing to obtain an automatic 60-day extension under CPLR 203(b)(5).

The remedial rescue device, CPLR 203(b)(5), which has been described as the "skyscraper on the statute of limitations landscape" (Siegel, N.Y. Practice,

---

3. Contrary to the concurrer's concern about the practical implications of our holding, we find nothing untoward or "unrealistic" about a rule that holds practicing attorneys responsible to their clients for the negligence of the process servers they choose to retain. Further, we see no sound reason for permitting attorneys who happen to use outside process servers to escape liability while attorneys who use in-house staff to perform the same functions can be held liable under ordinary principles of respondeat superior.

4. In response to the concurrence, however, we find it necessary to note that the theory of liability we have approved herein is not interchangeable with the theories of liability the concurrer would permit, since the latter requires plaintiff to prove that defendants were negligent in their own right while the former does not. Thus, contrary to the concurrer's contention, this case may not be resolved on the narrower ground the concurrence advances without the need to address the vicarious liability question that plaintiff's appeal presents.

at 56 [2d ed 1991]), was enacted to aid attorneys, such as the defendants, whose clients are faced with the imminent running of the Statute of Limitations. The allegations with respect to defendants' failure to take advantage of this statutory remedy raise questions of fact barring dismissal of the plaintiff's complaint.

Also, since attorneys may be liable for their own negligence in selecting a particular process server, and since plaintiff alleges that the entity chosen by defendants, Fischer's Service Bureau, Inc., had a reputation for poor and sloppy service, there are fact issues here which suffice to defeat defendants' summary judgment motion for dismissal.

The Court's result is reached instead by classifying service of process, for the first time, as a nondelegable duty of the attorney. This rationale opens up an unrealistic and undue liability channel not only with respect to the relationship of attorneys to process servers but, by analogous extension, also to many other relationships in which attorneys retain specialists and experts in the discharge of their professional obligations to clients.

This broad new rule requires, in effect, that an attorney inquire beyond any facially sufficient affidavit of service of process to verify personally the facts that underlie it. This contradicts the justification and practicality for the long-standing practice of utilizing and relying on independent process servers. For practical purposes, it will compel attorneys to assume the role of process servers themselves. While many large firms already have such in-house operatives, attorneys practicing in small firms and solo practitioners may now also have no choice but to hire in-house process servers so that the lawyers can always maintain direct supervision and control over them. No other way is left to avoid potential liability to disgruntled or harmed clients. Since the ordinary question-of-fact path is available through which plaintiff's cause may proceed beyond summary judgment, I see no justification or necessity for paving this boulevard route to that same result.

Notably, the rule that would make an attorney liable for the acts of an outside process server on the basis announced in this case also conflicts with the useful teachings of several of our lower courts and at least one sibling State. They continue the classification of "outside" process servers as independent contractors. This approach is prudent because attorneys in these situations have no effective control over the particular manner in which selected process servers do their jobs. The long-standing classification of process servers as independent contractors should be retained, with the result that attorneys would not be liable to plaintiff on a respondeat superior basis for the negligent acts of process servers.

Accordingly, I would modify to deny defendants' motion for summary judgment but on the more narrowly expressed basis.

Notes

1. The concurring opinion argues that the law firm could be held liable for its own negligence in selecting the process server. On what basis does the dissent disagree with the majority?

2. Under Restatement (Second) of Agency section 214

> A master or other principal who is under a duty to provide protection for or to have care used to protect others or their property and who confides the performance of such duty to a servant *or other person* is subject to liability to others for harm caused to them by the failure of such agent to perform the duty.

See also Restatement (Second) of Agency section 251(a) (principal "subject to liability for physical harm caused by the negligence of a servant or non-servant agent in the performance of an act which the principal is under a duty to have performed with care").

3. As indicated by the court in *Kleeman v. Rheingold,* non-delegable duties often arise where a statute imposes a duty. For example, in *M-Bank El Paso, N.A. v. Sanchez,* 836 S.W.2d 151 (Tex. 1992), the Texas Supreme Court held that Section 9-503 of the Uniform Commercial Code, which authorizes "self-help" repossession of collateral, imposes on the secured party a non-delegable duty of peaceable repossession:

> [UCC Section 9-503] gives a secured party two choices: it may repossess the collateral "if this can be done without breach of the peace," or it may take legal action. If the secured party chooses the first of those options, it runs the risk that the repossession may, in fact, breach the peace. When that happens, the secured party may be held liable in tort.

> The rule imposing liability on secured parties for breaches of the peace is based on longstanding policy concerns regarding the exercise of force or violence. The preservation of peace, courts recognize, "is of more importance to society than the right of the owner of a chattel to get possession of it." *Willis v. Whittle,* 82 S.C. 500, 64 S.E. 410 (1909).

> As a general rule, when a duty is imposed by law on the basis of concerns for public safety, the party bearing the duty cannot escape it by delegating it to an independent contractor. Section 424 of the Restatement (Second) of Torts (1965) provides:

> > One who by statute or by administrative regulation is under a duty to provide specified safeguards or precautions for the safety of others is subject to liability to the others for whose protection the duty is imposed for harm caused by the failure of a contractor employed by him to provide such safeguards or precautions.

Comment a to section 424 further explains that a duty to take safety precautions cannot be delegated to an independent contractor:

> > The rule stated in this Section applies whenever a statute or an administrative regulation imposes a duty upon one doing particular work to provide safeguards or precautions for the safety of others. In such a case the employer cannot delegate his duty to provide such safeguards or precautions to an independent contractor.

> We believe that section 9-503 of the UCC imposes a duty on secured creditors pursuing nonjudicial repossession to take precautions for public safety. Applying section 424 of the Restatement, a secured creditor is prohibited from delegating this duty to an independent contractor.

A secured creditor certainly has a strong interest in obtaining collateral from a defaulting debtor. That interest, however, must be balanced against society's interest in the public peace. If a creditor chooses to pursue self-help, it must be expected to take precautions in doing so. If this burden is too heavy, the creditor may seek relief by turning to the courts.

Because the Bank chose to pursue nonjudicial repossession, it assumed the risk that a breach of the peace might occur. Under section 424 of the Restatement (Second) of Torts, the Bank remains liable for breaches of the peace committed by its independent contractor.

836 S.W.2d at 152–54. The dissent argued as follows:

If the plaintiff in this case goes back to trial and proves that the repossessor committed a breach of the peace, then the bank which hired the contractor is liable. Liability is absolute and extreme. The bank has no defenses, outside of proving that no breach of the peace occurred. Even if the bank had no knowledge of the contractor's actions, the bank cannot defend. Even if the bank expressly ordered the contractor to proceed cautiously, the bank cannot protest.

Why has the court created such unyielding liability? The facts in this case certainly invite such a response. They are egregious. No repossessor has the right to breach the peace, and certainly not so blatantly as the facts here indicate.

But as disturbing as the facts are, I cannot join in this decision. [T]he decision has unjustifiably severe consequences for creditors who hire independent contractors to enforce their rights.

836 S.W.2d at 155 (Cook, J. dissenting).

3. In *Braud v. Theriot*, 170 So. 2d 679 (La. App. 1964), the defendant employed Chitty, who appeared to be an independent contractor, to fill a bayou that ran between the defendant's and the plaintiff's land and to substitute a drainage ditch five to six feet deep. Without the plaintiff's permission, Chitty went on the plaintiff's land and dug the ditch, which was later determined to encroach on the plaintiff's land to a depth of three to ten feet and for a length of twenty-two feet.

Defendant paid Chitty for the work done by him subsequent to the completion of the undertaking, without protesting the agent's violation of any authority to perform the excavation in the manner in which it was done, and certainly this must be regarded as a condonation of the agent's action. Accordingly, we are of the opinion Defendant is liable for the damages sustained by Plaintiff because of the trespass committed by Defendant through his agent, Chitty.

4. In *Lipman Wolfe & Co. v. Teeples & Thatcher, Inc.*, 268 Or. 578, 522 P.2d 467 (1974), a department store engaged an independent contractor to remodel its premises. During the course of the work, the independent contractor negligently failed to use barriers to keep shoppers out of the area being remodeled. When the department store was held liable to a shopper who had slipped and fallen, the store sought indemnification from the independent contractor. The Oregon Supreme Court applied the common-law test for indemnification:

(i) was the person (the "plaintiff") seeking indemnification legally obligated to a third party;

(ii) was the person ("defendant") from whom indemnification was sought also liable to that party; and

(iii) as between the two, was it more equitable for the defendant to discharge the obligation to the third person?

In *Lipman Wolfe & Co.,* the department store was liable to the shopper on the basis of a non-delegable duty owed by occupiers of land to invitees, but was not directly negligent. The independent contractor was liable to the shopper for its own negligence. As between the two, it was more equitable that the liability be borne by the party actively at fault, the independent contractor.

5. How would the *Lipman Wolfe & Co.* apply where the employer of the independent contractor had ratified the latter's tort?

Problem 11.5

Good Humor has been engaged in the street sale of ice cream products for well over 35 years. Until recently, it owned and maintained its ice cream trucks and it employed drivers to vend its products. Good Humor recognized that curbside sales of ice cream created special hazards for its customers, especially children. The company conducted an extensive safety program designed to orient its employees towards the dangers of curbside sale and methods of operation that minimize those dangers. For example, it instructed employees to help children in crossing the street. It also instructed employees not sell near busy roadways.

Recently, Good Humor changed its relationship with it vendors. Vendors now purchased their trucks from Good Humor, with the aid of Good Humor financing. The vendors entered into a "vendor's agreement" authorizing them to sell Good Humor products which they bought wholesale from Good Humor. The vendors could sell ice cream at any price and at any location, they were not on the company payroll, and Good Humor did not supervise their day-to-day activities. At the same time, Good Humor stopped its entire safety programs.

Williams, a Good Humor vendor, parked his Good Humor truck on a high-traffic thoroughfare after dark, and began ringing the distinctive Good Humor jingle bells. That Rosita and her daughter Tomikia were visiting Rosita's aunt, who lived across the street from the parked Good Humor truck. On hearing Good Humor's distinctive bells, Tomikia's cousins got ice cream money and ran across the street. Tomikia followed them, and was hit by a car.

a. Assuming that Williams was negligent, is Good Humor subject to liability for the accident?

b. Would your answer change if the vendor's agreement required Williams not to sell on busy streets or after dark?

c. Would your answer change if Good Humor had continued its safety program, and required all its vendors, including Williams, to attend it?

See Wilson v. Good Humor Corp., 757 F.2d 1293 (D.C. Cir. 1985).

Huddleston v. Union Rural Electric Association
841 P.2d 282 (Colo. 1992)

Justice LOHR delivered the Opinion of the Court.

This case arises out of an airplane accident and presents issues concerning the scope of the "inherently dangerous activity" exception to the rule that one who employs an independent contractor is not liable for torts committed by the independent contractor or its servants. In an action by the children of a passenger killed in a crash of a single engine plane against Union Rural Electric Association (UREA), which engaged a contract flight service to make the wintertime mountain flight that resulted in the passenger's death, the district court entered judgment for the plaintiffs based on a jury verdict. The Colorado Court of Appeals reversed and directed that the action be dismissed. *Huddleston v. Union Rural Elec. Ass'n,* 821 P.2d 862 (Colo. App. 1991). The court held that as a matter of law the activity of the contractor was not inherently dangerous and that the district court therefore erred in denying the motion of UREA for a directed verdict. *Id.*

I

Some of the pertinent facts have been stipulated, and others appear in the record without contradiction. UREA is a rural electric cooperative corporation that supplies power to customers in certain Colorado counties along the front range. Early in 1987, legislation proposed by UREA was pending in the Colorado General Assembly, and UREA had hired an organization of which James Huddleston was a part to provide lobbying services. In furtherance of the effort to secure passage of the legislation, UREA wished to seek the support of other rural electric cooperatives. One such organization was San Miguel Power Association, which served certain areas on Colorado's western slope. At least a week before a meeting of the board of directors of San Miguel Power Association scheduled for January 28, 1987, in Nucla, Colorado, UREA's executive secretary called Charles L. Brooks, who operated a charter airplane service, and arranged for him to transport UREA representatives to the meeting. They agreed on the use of a single engine aircraft. On January 28, Brooks piloted a single engine Cessna aircraft on a trip from the Jefferson County airport, with Nucla as the destination. On board were two directors of UREA and James Huddleston. The plane subsequently crashed into a mountain near Nucla killing all occupants of the aircraft.

Judith Huddleston, the wife of decedent James Huddleston, brought this action in Boulder County District Court as parent and next friend of the couple's two children, Jami N. Huddleston and Jenifer B. Huddleston. The plaintiffs asserted a claim for negligent hiring of pilot Brooks and also asserted that UREA was accountable for Brooks' negligence on the basis of respondeat superior because the activity in which Brooks was engaged was "inherently dangerous," thereby qualifying for an exception to the general rule that an employer of an independent contractor is not liable for injuries resulting from the negligence of the contractor.

UREA moved to dismiss the claim grounded on respondeat superior on the basis that as a matter of law "aviation is not inherently dangerous and the operation of a charter service does not subject the party who charters the plane to vicarious liability." As part of the same motion, UREA sought summary judgment on the negligent hiring claim. The district court granted the motion for summary judgment on the negligent hiring claim.[3] It concluded, however, that it could not find as a matter of law that the activity in question was not inherently dangerous, and therefore denied the motion to dismiss the respondeat superior claim.

The case was tried to a jury. Prior to trial, the parties stipulated that the crash that caused the death of James Huddleston occurred as a direct and proximate result of the negligence of Brooks. They also stipulated that Brooks was an independent contractor and not an employee of UREA.

After presentation of all the evidence, UREA moved for a directed verdict, again asserting that as a matter of law the activity in which Brooks was engaged was not inherently dangerous. The district court denied the motion, and the jury subsequently returned a verdict for the plaintiffs in the amount of $525,000. The court entered judgment against UREA based on the jury verdict.

UREA appealed to the Colorado Court of Appeals. The court held that "the proper test to determine whether an activity is 'inherently dangerous' is whether danger 'inheres' in performance of the activity no matter how skillfully performed" and that "if there is a way to perform the...activity without danger,... then the activity is not 'inherently dangerous.'" *Huddleston*, 821 P.2d at 864 (citations omitted). Relying on the proposition that construction of a contract is a matter of law for a court to decide, the court then defined the activity for which Brooks was hired according to its interpretation of the agreement between Brooks and UREA. It found that the parties had agreed that Brooks would safely transport Huddleston to Nucla by a single engine airplane, and that Brooks was not required by contract to proceed with the flight in the event of adverse weather conditions. Taking notice that air transportation, in general, is far safer than automobile transportation, and applying what it found to be the proper test for determining whether an activity is inherently dangerous, the court held that reasonable minds had to agree that the contracted-for activity was not inherently dangerous. Therefore, according to the court of appeals, "UREA was not vicariously liable under the 'inherent danger' exception to the general rule of employer non-liability," and the district court erred in denying UREA's motion for a directed verdict. *Id.*

II

In *Western Stock Center, Inc. v. Sevit, Inc.*, 195 Colo. 372, 578 P.2d 1045 (1978), we again recognized the "inherently dangerous activity" exception to the general rule that employers of independent contractors are not liable for the torts of their contractors. See *Garden of the Gods Village v. Hellman*, 133 Colo. 286, 295, 294 P.2d 597, 602 (1956). We now reaffirm the inherently dangerous activity exception[5] and further articulate guidelines for its application. We consider first the policy objectives behind the exception and then the legal bases from which the exception is derived. We conclude that the court of appeals misinterpreted the exception in this case.

---

3. The plaintiffs did not appeal the dismissal of the negligent hiring claim.
5. Although the inherently dangerous activity exception is well established at common law, no consistent and uniform definition of "inherently dangerous activity" has emerged.

A

The inherently dangerous activity exception is based on two primary policy concerns. The first is that employers whose enterprises directly benefit from the performance of activities that create special and uncommon dangers to others should bear some of the responsibility for injuries to others that occur as a result of the performance of such activities. See *Fleming James, Jr., Vicarious Liability*, 28 TUL. L. REV. 161, 169–70, 172 (1954) S.C. (explaining that a policy behind vicarious liability in general has been that those for whose benefit and at whose direction risks are imposed on others should share the cost of losses incurred as a result of such risks).[6] This accords with basic intuitions of fairness, and it is also consistent with what is often efficient economically.[7] The second is that it is sound public policy with regard to inherently dangerous activity "to have another layer of concern in order to try to ensure that activity that is inherently dangerous gets enough attention so that we reduce the number of people who are injured." Tr. at 158–59, *Huddleston v. Union Rural Electric Ass'n* (Boulder County Dist.Ct. Feb. 6, 1990) (No. 88CV2012) (Bellipanni, J., ruling from the bench on defendant's motion for a directed verdict). In other words, with regard to inherently dangerous activities, it is desirable that employers have an added incentive to encourage their independent contractors to take all reasonably feasible precautions against injury to others.

B

As a general rule, a person hiring an independent contractor to perform work is not liable for the negligence of the independent contractor. In *Garden of the Gods*, however, this court adopted the widely recognized rule that

> [w]hen work to be done is dangerous in itself, or is of a character inherently dangerous unless proper precautions are taken, an employer cannot evade liability by engaging an independent contractor to do such work.

Garden of the Gods, 133 Colo. at 295, 294 P.2d at 602. In *Western Stock*, we drew upon section 427 of the *Restatement (Second) of Torts* and described an inherently dangerous activity as one "'involving a special danger to others which the employer knows or has reason to know to be inherent in or normal to the work,'" *Western Stock*, 195 Colo. at 378, 578 P.2d at 1050 (quoting from sec-

---

6. A closely related concern is that if an employer has the ability to select an independent contractor who is responsibly insured, either through itself or a third party, for carrying on activities that create special and uncommon dangers to others, then it is desirable to have a rule of law that encourages employers to select such a contractor. *See* Clarence Morris, *The Torts of an Independent Contractor*, 29 ILL.L.REV. 339, 342–43 (1934).

7. *See* Alan O. Sykes, *The Economics of Vicarious Liability*, 93 YALE L.J. 1231, 1271–73 (1984). Sykes defines the relative efficiency of a liability rule by applying the following analysis: "[rule] A is efficient relative to [rule] B if the members of society who prefer A to B can compensate the members of society who prefer B to A and remain better off themselves." *Id.* at 1232 n. 5. Sykes reasons that if the activity in question requires particular precautions, the employer can require them by contract and provide that failure to undertake them will result in some adequately severe penalty. *Id.* at 1272. Furthermore, because many inherently dangerous activities present inexpensive opportunities for the employer to verify that precautions are being observed, "[v]icarious liability is clearly efficient for many inherently dangerous activities." *Id.* at 1271–72.

tion 427 of the Second Restatement), but then added, somewhat paradoxically, that the work or activity "must only present a foreseeable and significant risk of harm to others if not carefully carried out." *Id.* We now are persuaded that Western Stock does not adequately identify the legal criteria by which to determine whether an activity may properly be characterized as "inherently dangerous" for purposes of the rule of vicarious liability. Instead of relying solely upon Western Stock as the standard for resolving whether an activity is inherently dangerous, we must therefore look to several provisions of the *Restatement (Second) of Torts* and related case law to supply the appropriate analytical framework for answering that question.

Section 427 of the *Restatement (Second) of Torts* carves out a limited exception to the general rule of nonliability for the negligence of an independent contractor by providing as follows:

> One who employs an independent contractor to do work involving a *special danger* to others which the employer knows or has reason to know to be inherent in or normal to the work, or which he contemplates or has reason to contemplate when making the contract, is subject to liability for physical harm caused to such others by the contractor's failure to take reasonable precautions against such danger. (Emphasis added.)

As framed, section 427 creates a rule of vicarious liability making the employer liable for the negligence of the independent contractor in failing to guard against a special danger, irrespective of whether the employer has itself been at fault. See *Restatement (Second) of Torts*, introductory note at 394. However, this rule of vicarious liability "applies only where the harm results from the negligence of the contractor in failing to take precautions against the danger involved in the work itself, which the employer should contemplate at the time of his contract," *id.* § 427 cmt. d, and does not apply "where the negligence of the contractor creates a new risk, not inherent in the work itself or in the ordinary or prescribed way of doing it, and not reasonably to be contemplated by the employer." *Id.* Section 427, in other words, does not apply to the "'collateral negligence,'" *id.*, of the independent contractor.

Although the comments to section 427 of the *Restatement (Second) of Torts* do not define "special danger," *id.* § 427, helpful insight into the meaning of this term can be gleaned from other sections of the *Restatement*, such as section 416, which is closely related to section 427 and represents a different form of the same general principle stated in section 427. *See id.* § 416 cmt. a. Section 416 of the *Restatement (Second) of Torts* states:

> One who employs an independent contractor to do work which the employer should recognize as likely to create during its progress a *peculiar risk* of physical harm to others unless special precautions are taken, is subject to liability for physical harm caused to them by the failure of the contractor to exercise reasonable care to take such precautions, even though the employer has provided for such precautions in the contract or otherwise. (Emphasis added.)

Comment d to section 416 defines a "peculiar risk" as

> a risk differing from the common risks to which persons in general are commonly subjected by the ordinary forms of negligence which are usual in the community.

Comment b to section 416 incorporates by reference comment b to section 413 with respect to the meaning of both "peculiar risk" and "special precautions."[9] When these comments are read together, it is clear that the independent contractor's failure to take precautions against an ordinary or customary danger does not create the type of "special or peculiar danger" to which the "inherently dangerous" activity exception applies. *Id.* § 413 cmt. b. Rather, it is the work itself, or the particular circumstances under which the work is to be performed, that must create the special type of danger that is not ordinarily present in the type of activities to which persons are generally subjected in the community. For purposes of the "inherently dangerous" activity exception, therefore, the focus is on dangers recognizable in advance or contemplated by the employer as being "inherent" in the activity, or the circumstances of performance, when carried out in its ordinary way, and not on risks created by or following from the contractor's unforeseeable departure from the ordinary or prescribed way of performing the work under the circumstances.

Against this backdrop of the *Restatement (Second) of Torts* and related case law, we conclude that an activity will qualify as "inherently dangerous" when it presents a special or peculiar danger to others that is inherent in the nature of the activity or the particular circumstances under which the activity is to be performed, that is different in kind from the ordinary risks that commonly confront persons in the community, and that the employer knows or should know is inherent in the nature of the activity or in the particular circumstances under which the activity is to be performed. In addition, although an activity may be inherently dangerous, an employer will not be liable for injuries caused by the collateral negligence of its independent contractor in performing that activity.

C

The court of appeals held that because the activity for which Brooks was hired could have been performed without danger, such activity could not have been inherently dangerous.

This, however, is not the correct test, for an activity may be inherently dangerous even if it can be performed safely by taking proper precautions, *Restate-*

---

9. Although § 413 of the *Restatement (Second) of Torts* is not directly applicable in this case (§ 413 falls under chapter 15, topic 1, "Harm Caused by Fault of Employers of Independent Contractors," whereas §§ 416 and 427 fall under chapter 15, topic 2, "Harm Caused by Negligence of a Carefully Selected Independent Contractor"), comment b to § 413 provides some additional insight into the meaning of "peculiar risk," a term common to both §§ 413 and 416:

> This Section is concerned with special risks, peculiar to the work to be done, and arising out of its character, or out of the place where it is to be done, against which a reasonable man would recognize the necessity of taking special precautions. The situation is one in which a risk is created which is not a normal, routine matter of customary human activity, such as driving an automobile, but is rather a special danger to those in the vicinity, arising out of the particular situation created, and calling for special precautions. "Peculiar" does not mean that the risk must be one which is abnormal to the type of work done, or that it must be an abnormally great risk. It has reference only to a special, recognizable danger arising out of the work itself.

Id. § 413 cmt. b. Many courts treat the terms "peculiar risk" and "special danger" as being equivalent.

ment (Second) of Torts § 427 cmt. b ("[i]t is not...necessary to the employer's liability that the work be of a kind which cannot be done without a risk of harm to others"). In other words, the court of appeals erred by selecting a test that requires an activity to be more dangerous than it needs to be in order to be classified as inherently dangerous for the purpose of applying the inherently dangerous activity exception to the general rule that employers are not liable for the torts of their independent contractors.[10]

III

Once the correct standard by which to determine whether an activity is inherently dangerous has been identified, it is still necessary to define the activity to which that standard should be applied. The court of appeals took the approach that the activity to which the standard is to be applied should be defined by the independent contractor's contractual obligations to the employer.

In *Western Stock*, we held that when the inherently dangerous activity exception is applicable, "'the law invokes the theory of respondeat superior, imposing the master-servant relationship upon the parties engaged in the activity.'" *Western Stock*, 195 Colo. at 378, 578 P.2d at 1050 (*quoting Epperly v. City of Seattle*, 65 Wash.2d 777, 399 P.2d 591 (1965)). Under the theory of respondeat superior, "[a]n employer may be held responsible for tortious conduct by an employee only if the tort is committed within the course and scope of employment." *Destefano v. Grabrian*, 763 P.2d 275, 286 (Colo. 1988). Generally, "[a]n employee is acting within the scope of his employment if he is engaged in the work which has been assigned to him by his employer or he is doing what is necessarily incidental to the work which has been assigned to him or which is customary within the business in which the employee is engaged." *Id.* at 287. Moreover, it is widely recognized that "[i]f the tortious act is within or incident to an employee's authorized duties, the employer is liable even if the employee acted in violation of the employer's instructions." *Fahey v. Rockwell Graphic Systems, Inc.*, 20 Mass.App.Ct. 642, 482 N.E.2d 519, 527 (1985), rev. denied, 396 Mass. 1103, 485 N.E.2d 188 (1985). In short, "[a]n act, although forbidden, or done in a forbidden manner, may be within the scope of employment," *Restatement*

---

10. The test employed by the court of appeals seems more appropriately suited to determining whether an activity is abnormally dangerous within the meaning of § 520 of the Second Restatement. *See Restatement (Second) of Torts* § 520 (1976) ("In determining whether an activity is abnormally dangerous, the following factors are to be considered:... (c) inability to eliminate the risk by the exercise of reasonable care;"). A few other jurisdictions appear also to have taken this approach. *See, e.g., Eastern Airlines v. Joseph Guida & Sons Trucking Co.*, 675 F.Supp. 1391, 1396 (E.D.N.Y. 1987) ("[I]n order for the work to be inherently dangerous, it must be '"attended with danger, no matter how skillfully or carefully it is performed."'") (*quoting Carmel Associates, Inc. v. Turner Construction Co.*, 35 A.D.2d 157, 314 N.Y.S.2d 941 (1st Dep't 1970) (*quoting Janice v. New York*, 201 Misc. 915, 107 N.Y.S.2d 674, 679 (1957))); *Ft. Lowell-NSS Ltd. Partnership v. Kelly*, 166 Ariz. 96, 800 P.2d 962, 971 (1990) (in order to be inherently dangerous, "work must involve a risk of harm that cannot be eliminated by exercising reasonable care"); *Smith v. Zellerbach*, 486 So.2d 798, 802 (La.App. 1986) ("The critical inquiry in determining whether an activity is 'inherently or intrinsically dangerous,' and therefore non-delegable, is whether it can be made safe when it is performed in a proper and workmanlike manner."), *cert. denied*, 489 So.2d 246 (La. 1986). *Cf. Balagna v. Shawnee County*, 233 Kan. 1068, 668 P.2d 157, 168 (1983) (implying that if a type of work is safe when proper precautions are taken, then it cannot be inherently dangerous). This, however, is not the law in Colorado.

(Second) of Agency § 230 (1958), and "[a] master cannot avoid responsibility for the negligence of a servant by telling him to act carefully." *Id.* § 230 cmt. b.

In the case before us, therefore, it is not dispositive if UREA's agreement with Brooks required that Brooks carefully or safely transport Huddleston to Nucla aboard a single engine plane. Rather, if the negligence of Brooks occurred while Brooks was acting within the scope of the work for which he was hired, and if the negligence was not collateral to that work, then, if it was recognizable to UREA that the work as performed would be inherently dangerous, even if the negligence of Brooks violated his contractual obligations and UREA's express instructions, UREA would still be liable under the inherently dangerous activity exception for injuries directly and proximately caused to third persons by such negligence.[14] If this were not the rule, an employer could always avoid liability under the inherently dangerous activity exception simply by inserting into its agreements standard language to the effect that its independent contractor promises to perform safely and to take all necessary precautions. Consequently, when determining whether the work that an independent contractor was hired to perform was inherently dangerous, the trier of fact must take into account more than just the manner in which an oral or written contract legally obligates the contractor to perform such work. The important point is that while an independent contractor may have a legal obligation to take a particular precaution as a matter of contract law, as a matter of fact the employer may nevertheless know or contemplate, or may nevertheless have reason to know or to contemplate, that the work to be performed is inherently dangerous. The court of appeals erred, therefore, insofar as it defined the activity in question only or primarily according to the terms of Brooks' contractual obligations, rather than in terms of what, as a matter of fact, UREA knew or had reason to know about the type of dangers associated with the work it was hiring Brooks to perform. *Cf. Ballinger v. Gascosage Elec. Coop.,* 788 S.W.2d 506, 511 (Mo. 1990) (explaining that under the inherently dangerous activity exception, the employer "remains liable for the torts of the contractor[ ] simply for commissioning the activity. The liability attaches without any need for showing that the employer is in any respect negligent. It is purely vicarious.").

IV

Having determined that the court of appeals erred in its definition of inherently dangerous activity, and that it also erred by applying that definition to an activity defined only or primarily according to an interpretation of Brooks' contractual obligations, we now address whether the plaintiffs produced sufficient evidence at trial to create an issue of fact for the jury as to whether all the elements of the inherently dangerous activity exception were proven by a preponderance of the evidence.

---

14. *Cf. Restatement (Second) of Torts* § 416 cmt. c ("[§ 416] deals with the liability of one who employs an independent contractor to do such work [i.e., work that creates a peculiar danger to others unless special precautions are taken], even though he stipulates in his contract or in a contract with another independent contractor that the precautions shall be taken," and "the fact that the contract contains express stipulations for the taking of adequate precautions and that the contractor agrees to assume all liability for harm caused by his failure to do so, does not relieve his employer from the liability stated in this section."); *id.* § 416 cmt. a (explaining that there is a "close relation" between the rules stated in §§ 416 and 427, and that they "represent different forms of statement of the same general rule").

We acknowledge that the determination of whether an activity is inherently dangerous will ultimately depend on the state of the evidence bearing on that issue. Depending on the state of the evidence, a court may or may not be required to rule as a matter of law that the activity does or does not qualify as inherently dangerous. If the state of the evidence is such that when viewed in a light most favorable to the plaintiff, the court is convinced that a jury could not find that all the following elements have been proven by a preponderance of the evidence, then it should direct a verdict against the plaintiff and in favor of the employer:

(1) that the activity in question presented a special or peculiar danger to others inherent in the nature of the activity or the particular circumstances under which the activity was to be performed;

(2) that the danger was different in kind from the ordinary risks that commonly confront persons in the community;

(3) that the employer knew or should have known that the special danger was inherent in the nature of the activity or in the particular circumstances under which the activity was to be performed; and

(4) that the injury to the plaintiff was not the result of the collateral negligence of the defendant's independent contractor.

Of course, if a jury could reasonably find from the evidence, when viewed in the light most favorable to the plaintiff, that all of the above elements have been proven by a preponderance of the evidence, then the issue of whether the activity is inherently dangerous should be submitted to the jury.

At trial, the plaintiffs' expert witness on aviation testified that in light of the particular circumstances surrounding the flight in question, it was his opinion that the flight was "very dangerous" if it was not carefully carried out. The jury also heard evidence to the effect that Brooks was hired to fly a single engine airplane, that such an airplane was unpressurized and uncertified for flights into icy conditions, that flying in the Colorado mountains safely in the wintertime requires a skilled understanding of sometimes difficult and unpredictable weather patterns, that the airport at Nucla did not have a Federal Aviation Administration approved instrument approach procedure, that Brooks filed an instrument flight plan, and that representatives of UREA took into consideration the risk involved in flying a small plane in the wintertime in the mountains of Colorado. The jury also heard evidence to the effect that the type of aircraft flown by Brooks is a good, reliable "work horse type airplane" capable of safely flying in Colorado all year around under proper conditions. There was no evidence introduced that, in general, Brooks was not a capable pilot.

We are satisfied that contracting with a charter airplane service to fly passengers in the wintertime is not per se an inherently dangerous activity. However, when the evidence bearing on the particular circumstances under which the flight was to be performed in this case is viewed in a light most favorable to the plaintiff, we are also convinced that the evidence created an issue of fact for the jury as to whether all the elements of the "inherently dangerous activity" exception to the general rule of nonliability for the negligence of an independent contractor were proven by a preponderance of the evidence.

V

Our last step is to consider whether the jury was properly instructed on the meaning of "inherently dangerous activity," and on how to apply that concept in this case. We conclude that it was not.

Understandably, the trial court relied heavily on the precise language employed in Western Stock (part of which we characterize today as "somewhat paradoxical") and was reluctant even to attempt to dissect into its individual elements the meaning of section 427 of the *Restatement (Second) of Torts.* As a result the jury was not instructed to consider separately any of the elements of the inherently dangerous activity exception that we identify today, and the jury was given no instruction at all on the issue of whether the accident was caused by the collateral negligence of Brooks. The jury instructions in this case were therefore "'so erroneous or so confusing or misleading as probably to lead the jury into error of such proportion as to require a new trial.'" *Rego Co. v. McKown-Katy,* 801 P.2d 536, 539 (Colo. 1990) (*quoting Coleman v. United Fire and Casualty Co.,* 767 P.2d 761, 764 (Colo.App. 1988)).

VI

For the foregoing reasons, we reverse the judgment of the court of appeals and remand to that court with directions to order a new trial.

CHIEF JUSTICE ROVIRA DISSENTING [JOINED BY JUSTICE VOLLACK]

Contrary to the majority, it is my opinion that rather than refining the circumstances and manner in which the inherently dangerous exception is to apply, we should take this opportunity to repudiate that doctrine and overrule the prior decisions of this court adopting it. I would do so for a number of reasons. First, I am of the opinion that, to the extent the policy considerations that gave rise to this exception are justifiable, they are neither adequately nor properly advanced by invocation of the inherently dangerous exception. Second, though the exception may appear desirable in the abstract, when its practical implications and potential applications are considered, it is revealed to be impractical. Third, the costs that are imposed as a result of this exception far outweigh any incremental benefits that are to be gained by adherence to it. Finally, it is my view that the inherently dangerous exception is itself unnecessary, as clearer more predictable theories of liability are available to address the policy considerations that purportedly support the inherently dangerous doctrine. Therefore, I respectfully dissent.

I

The majority opinion refines the rule adopted by this court in *Western Stock Ctr. v. Sevit, Inc.,* 195 Colo. 372, 578 P.2d 1045 (1978), and *Garden of the Gods Village v. Hellman,* 133 Colo. 286, 294 P.2d 597 (1956), which recognized an exception to the general rule that an employer of an independent contractor is not liable for torts committed by the independent contractor. That exception provides that liability may be imposed on the employer based on the theory of vicarious liability so long as the torts occur while the independent contractor is engaged in an "inherently dangerous" activity on behalf of the employer. As refined by the majority, an "inherently dangerous" activity is one that presents a special or peculiar danger to others that is inherent in the nature of the activity or the particular circumstances under which the activity is to be performed, that is different in kind from the ordinary risks that commonly confront persons in the community, and that the employer knows or should know is inherent in the nature of the activity or in the particular circumstances under which the activity is to be performed.

The majority finds that this rule of vicarious liability is justified on the bases of two primary policy considerations. One such consideration is the propriety of establishing "another layer of concern in order to try to ensure that activity that is inherently dangerous gets enough attention so that we reduce the number of people who are injured." The other policy rationale is that employers whose enterprises directly benefit from the performance of activities that create special and uncommon dangers to others should bear some of the responsibility for injuries to others that occur as a result of the performance of such activities. Although I acknowledge that these goals are desirable, I do not agree that the inherently dangerous exception to the general rule advances them.

It is axiomatic that reducing the number of injuries which result from the performance of inherently dangerous activities is a desirable end. Indeed, this policy is merely one way to express one of the primary functions of tort law, *i.e.*, creating the incentive to prevent the occurrence of harm. Simply identifying this policy, however, begs the question whether, and at what cost, a particular rule of tort law may further this end.

The inherently dangerous exception to the general rule of nonliability does not necessarily insure that inherently dangerous activities will be performed any more safely than in the absence of this exception. This is so for at least three reasons. First, because the inherently dangerous exception creates no new obligations or duties on the part of the employer than would otherwise be applicable, it does not directly create the incentive on the part of the employer to more carefully select, instruct, or provide for the independent contractor. Second, because independent contractors—by definition—discharge their activities free from the control and supervision of their employer, there is no reason to assume that the imposition of vicarious liability on the employer will, or could, have a significant impact on the safety with which an independent contractor performs the inherently dangerous activity. *See Restatement (Second) of Agency* § 2(3) (1958) ("An independent contractor is a person who contracts with another to do something for him but who is not controlled by the other nor subject to the other's right to control with respect to his physical conduct in the performance of the undertaking."). Consequently, any additional safety incentives that may be created by imposition of the inherently dangerous exception could, by the very nature of the employer/independent contractor relationship, be only minimal. Finally, given that the inherently dangerous exception imposes liability on the employer, and not the independent contractor, it cannot be said that the rule creates any additional incentives on the independent contractor to perform the work any more safely than otherwise would be the case. In light of these observations, I am left with considerable doubt as to whether the inherently dangerous exception can be said to further the first policy rationale that purportedly justifies it, *i.e.*, the avoidance of harm.

II

The propriety of abolishing the exception is similarly warranted on the grounds that the rule itself creates extremely impractical expectations on potential employers of independent contractors. The second policy justification thought to support the inherently dangerous exception identified by the majority is that employers whose enterprises directly benefit from the performance of activities that create special and uncommon dangers to others should bear some of the responsibility for injuries to others that occur as a result of the performance of such activities. While such a principle may seem perfectly logical, its impracticalities can clearly be seen by recognizing the wide range of circumstances to which the inherently dangerous exception applies.

It is important to note that "employers whose enterprises directly benefit" from inherently dangerous activities include not only large corporations, multimillion dollar manufacturers, and general contractors harnessing the expertise of many independent contractors. The "enterprises" which may benefit from the performance of inherently dangerous work can be as commonplace as a homeowner contracting to have his or her home painted. *See Rohlfs v. Weil*, 271 N.Y. 444, 3 N.E.2d 588 (1936) (affirming appellate court's finding that a jury could properly impose vicarious liability on an employer who contracted with an independent contractor for painting services when a pedestrian passing near a scaffold used to complete the painting was injured by falling objects from the scaffold); *Mackey v. Campell Constr. Co.*, 101 Cal.App.3d 774, 162 Cal.Rptr. 64 (1980) (affirming the imposition of vicarious liability on an employer for injuries sustained by an independent contractor's servant who was injured when he fell from a scaffold while attempting to move it). In such a circumstance, it seems highly impractical to impose liability on a homeowner for the negligence of an independent contractor when the very reason for hiring the contractor may be the acknowledged lack of expertise, knowledge, and experience required to correctly perform the inherently dangerous activity. To what extent can it reasonably be expected that such activities will be undertaken more safely as a result of imposing liability on a party who may very well be completely ignorant with respect to the proper way to perform the task and wholly unknowing respecting possible safety measures that might be taken? Moreover, even if one accepts the notion that innocent persons injured as a result of inherently dangerous activities should not go uncompensated, to what extent does it make sense to impose the burden of compensation on the homeowner contracting for painting services?

III

Such doubts should, in and of themselves, create considerable apprehension regarding the desirability of maintaining this rule. This skepticism is enhanced, however, after recognition is given to the fact that any minimal safety gains that may result from invocation of this rule are far outweighed by the significant uncertainties and costs imposed by the exception.

As we recognized in *Western Stock Ctr.*, the question of what constitutes an inherently dangerous activity is a difficult one. The inconsistencies and ambiguities that have resulted from the adoption of the inherently dangerous rule have led to a line of cases that is, as one commentator has noted, "divided against itself without reason." James B. McHugh, *Note, Risk Administration in the Marketplace: A Reappraisal of the Independent Contractor Rule*, 40 U.CHI.L.REV. 661, 665 (1973).

Given the seeming contradictions evidenced by the cases regarding what is or is not an inherently dangerous activity, it is safe to assume that this exception often will provide no warning to prospective employers of independent contractors respecting their potential liabilities. Again, this fact tends to repudiate the notion that the inherently dangerous exception would enhance the safety with which inherently dangerous activities are undertaken.

Further, any minimal benefits provided by the exception are outweighed by the significant costs that it imposes on employers and consumers alike. There can be little doubt that independent contractors who engage in inherently dangerous activities should be insured for any injuries that might result from their activities. Naturally, the cost of such insurance will be passed on to those who employ these contractors. This increased cost carried by the employer will in turn be passed on to his or her consumers. With the inherently dangerous exception, however, the law now imposes upon prudent employers the obligation to insure against the potential negligence of their independent contractors. As stated above, however, responsible independent contractors should also insure against their negligence. The result is that all independent contractors who engage in inherently dangerous activities will now be "double insured"—resulting in increased and unnecessary costs both to the employer of independent contractors and to the ultimate consumer. Moreover, because of the confusion regarding what an inherently dangerous activity might be, it would be reasonable to assume not only that many independent contractors will be double insured, but that many employers will be obtaining insurance for the activities of their independent contractors when such insurance may in fact be unnecessary. Once again, any minimal safety benefits that may result from the inherently dangerous exception will be outweighed both by the uncertainties and costs imposed by the exception.

IV

It could be argued, of course, that the costs, uncertainties, and impractical expectations which attend the inherently dangerous rule adequately could be avoided by properly restricting the scope of the inherently dangerous exception. This is, in fact, precisely what the majority opinion purports to do. The majority, after articulating the proper test to apply in determining what activities are inherently dangerous, seeks to restrict the overly broad test set forth in *Western Stock Ctr.* Examination of the majority opinion, however, reveals the intrinsic difficulty in attempting to restrict the coverage of the rule and thereby avoid the problems identified above. This can most clearly be seen simply by looking to the facts of the case before us. It is certainly possible that in the present case, a jury applying the inherently dangerous exception could find that a special or peculiar danger was presented by flying a single-engine plane in a mountainous area during poor weather and thus, hold UREA liable for pilot Brook's negligence. This alone reinforces my views regarding the propriety—or lack thereof—in maintaining this rule. I am bothered even more, however, after consideration is given to the fact that in this case, the court of appeals noted that "[s]tatistics show that air transportation is far safer than automobile transportation." *Huddleston v. Union Rural Elec. Ass'n*, 821 P.2d 862, 866 (Colo.App. 1992). Thus, it would be entirely safe to assume that a jury could also find that hiring a taxicab or bus service to transport people through the mountains is an inherently dangerous activity. If such a finding is indeed possible, I think that such a fact speaks for itself regarding the majority's success in its effort to "supply the appropriate analytical framework for answering" the question of what an inherently dangerous activity is.

V

Though I acknowledge the desirability of achieving the policy consideration which are thought to support the inherently dangerous exception, I would nevertheless abolish the inherently dangerous exception not only for the reasons stated above, but also based on my view that the exception is wholly unnecessary to attain those policies. In its stead, I would favor application of the principles developed in the area of negligent hiring.[1] Doing so would more appropriately create the incentives on the part of independent contractors to properly perform their activities safely, because good safety records could more reasonably be expected to translate into the confidence required to hire independent contractors. In addition, such a rule would squarely place the obligation on employers to ensure that the independent contractors whom they hire are adequately qualified and sufficiently responsible to properly discharge their duties.

Therefore, I dissent.

Notes

1. As noted in *Huddleston v. Union Rural Electric Ass'n,* courts use the terms "inherent danger," "special danger" and "peculiar risk" interchangeably.

2. As discussed in connection with *Redinger v. Living Well, Inc.,* page 542, an employer has a duty to provide for the taking special precautions necessary to avoid peculiar risks. *See* Restatement (Second) of Torts § 413. As discussed in *Huddleston v. Union Rural Electric Ass'n,* an employer who satisfies its duty Under section 413 *remains* liable for the independent contractor's negligence in taking such precautions. *See* Restatement (Second) of Torts §§ 416 & 427. Should the inherent danger/peculiar risk doctrine apply to hold the non-negligent employer liable?

3. What determines whether a risk is "normal" or "peculiar," and thus imposing on the employer of the independent contractor a non-delegable duty to provide precautions?

> This Section is concerned with special risks, peculiar to the work to be done, and arising out of its character, or out of the place where it is to be done, against which a reasonable man would recognize the necessity of taking special precautions. The situation is one in which a risk is created which is *not a normal, routine matter of customary human activity,* such as driving an automobile, but is rather a special danger to those in the vicinity, arising out of the particular situation created, and calling for special precautions. *"Peculiar" does not mean that the risk must be one which is abnormal to the type of work to be done, or that it must be an*

---

1. *Restatement (Second) of Agency* § 213 (1958) provides: A person conducting an activity through servants or other agents is subject to liability for harm resulting from his conduct if he is negligent or reckless: (a) in giving improper or ambiguous orders of [sic] in failing to make proper regulations; or (b) in the employment of improper persons or instrumentalities in work involving risk of harm to others: (c) in the supervision of the activity; or (d) in permitting, or failing to prevent, negligent or other tortious conduct by persons, whether or not his servants or agents, upon promises or with instrumentalities under his control.

abnormally great risk. It has reference only to a special, recognizable danger arising out of the work itself.

Restatement (Second) of Torts § 413 comment b (emphasis added).

A "peculiar" risk is a risk differing from the common risks to which persons in general are commonly subjected by the ordinary forms of negligence which are usual in the community. It must involve some special hazard resulting from the nature of the work done, which calls for special precautions. Thus, if a contractor is employed to transport the employer's goods by truck over the public highway, the employer is not liable for the contractor's failure to inspect brakes on his truck, or for his driving in excess of the speed limit, because the risk is in no way a peculiar one, and only an ordinary precaution is called for. But if the contractor is employed to transport giant logs weighing several tons over the highway, the employer will be subject to liability for the contractor's failure to take special precautions to anchor them on his trucks.

Restatement (Second) of Torts § 416 comment d.

As indicated in the dissent in *Huddleston v. Union Rural Electric Ass'n,* the cases are often inconsistent. First, the question of what is not a "normal, routine matter of customary human activity, such as driving an automobile", Restatement (Second) of Torts § 413 comment b. Second, many cases arise out of suits by an injured employee of the independent contractor against the employer of the independent contractor. As discussed in Note 2 to *Brandt v. Missouri Pacific Railroad Co.,* page 569, these cases raise difficult problems of coordination with the laws of employer liability and/or workers' compensation. Where courts fail to recognize these problems and address them directly, the result is often an anomalous interpretation of the inherent danger/special risk doctrine.

4. In *Lipman Wolfe & Co. v. Teeples & Thatcher, Inc.,* 268 Or. 578, 522 P.2d 467 (1974), Lipman Wolfe & Co. owed a large department store. Lipman contracted with an independent contractor, Teeples & Thatcher, Inc., for remodeling in the store. While Teeples was laying tile in front of the store's elevators, a customer fell and was injured when she stepped in a slippery substance spread on the floor in preparation for laying tile. Teeples was found negligent in failing to place or maintain adequate barriers around the area where it was laying tile. The court found that Lipman was vicariously liable for Teeples' negligence:

We have never decided the basis for a storekeeper's liability or that of any other possessor of land for injuries to a customer caused by a condition negligently created by an independent contractor employed by the storekeeper.

Other courts and writers have placed a storekeeper's liability in these circumstances upon two different bases—personal liability for failing to supervise the work of the independent contractor and vicarious liability for the negligence of the independent contractor. Some decisions seemingly have relied upon a combination of the two without distinguishing between them.

We are surprised at the confusion existing in this small corner of the law. Harper and James write of the confusion thusly:

As to invitees, some cases proceed on the reasoning that the land occupier's duty is nondelegable, so that he will be held vicariously for the contractor's negligence at least where that results in an unreasonably dangerous condition of the premises. Other cases rest liability on the occupier's own duty to supervise, inspect, etc. work done or operations carried out by the independent contractor. Many opinions draw on both lines of reasoning without apparently realizing the distinctions between them.

2 Harper and James, Law of Torts, 1407 n. 51, 26.11 (1956).

We have concluded that the most logical and desirable basis for liability is the vicarious basis: that is, to apply the doctrine of respondeat superior and hold the storekeeper liable for the negligence of the contractor. We reach this conclusion for several reasons. The storekeeper, of course, has the duty to have its premises in a reasonably safe condition for the reception of its customers. The storekeeper is liable for the negligence of its own employees who fail to keep the store in a reasonably safe condition. When a contractor is brought in to remodel or repair and the store permits customers to continue to enter the premises the danger to customers increases. Under such circumstances it would be inconsistent to hold that a storekeeper can escape liability by asserting that the increased danger to its customers was created by an independent contractor and, therefore, the storekeeper is not liable.

In addition to vicarious liability being imposed because of the duty of a storekeeper to keep its premises in a safe condition for its customers another accepted principle points to adopting vicarious liability. In *Gordon Creek Tree Farms v. Layne*, 230 Or. 204, 220, 368 P.2d 737, 741 (1962), we stated this principle as follows:

> It is well settled that an employer who orders work to be performed from which, in the natural course of things, injurious consequences must be expected to arise unless means are adopted by which such consequences may be prevented, is bound to see that necessary precautions are taken to prevent injury and such person can not by employing some other person relieve himself of his liability to do what is necessary to prevent the work from becoming wrongful.

> Another reason why we prefer the doctrine of vicarious liability is that placing a duty upon a storekeeper to closely supervise its remodeling contractor appears to us to be unrealistic. Unless the business or the particular project is large enough to employ one or more persons whose exclusive duties are to supervise the work, the contractor is usually in a better position to protect the storekeeper's customers. The testimony in this case was that the employees of Artcraft worked so fast that the barricade had to be practically a rolling barricade. If the storekeeper had a duty to supervise, the storekeeper would have to employ a person whose sole duties were to constantly inspect the tile layer's work to be certain that the successive barricades were adequate.

5. Work that is not inherently dangerous, or does not inherently require special precautions, may *become* such because of the way the independent contrac-

tor performs it. If the employer knows how the independent contractor will perform the work, Restatement (Second) of Torts sections 413, 416, and 427 will apply. *E.g.,* Restatement (Second) of Torts 416, comment e.

> [O]rdinary hauling by a truck is not inherently dangerous; and therefore a shipper is under no duty to ascertain whether the motor carrier has complied with the motor vehicle laws or to inquire into the nature and adequacy of his equipment.

> [A]lthough a truck may not in itself be considered a dangerous instrumentality, its operation in hauling by a drunk driver is an inherently dangerous undertaking. It should be analogous that the hauling of wheat on wet pavement in an overloaded tractor-trailer which has no speedometer, defective brakes, deficient springs, threadbare tires, and which evidence revealed to be in such poor mechanical condition that it would be unsafe to drive if unloaded, may likewise be an inherently dangerous undertaking.

Hudgens v. Cook Industries, Inc., 521 P.2d 813 (Okla. 1974).

6. Regarding the "collateral risk" doctrine referred to in *Huddleston v. Union Rural Electric Ass'n,* read Note 1 to *Brandt v. Missouri Pacific Railroad Co.,* page 571.

7. Recall that the court in *Strophes v. Heritage House Children Center,* page 485, imposed a non-delegable duty to avoid what it perceived as the strictures of the scope of employment doctrine. *See* Note 3 to *Strophes v. Heritage House Children's Ctr.,* page 491.

Brandt v. Missouri Pacific Railroad Co.

787 S.W.2d 781 (Mo. App. 1990)

KAROHL, Judge.

Kenneth Brandt sued defendants for personal injuries he suffered while working as an employee of C.E. Jarrell & Associates. Jarrell & Associates contracted with defendants, owners and occupiers of a twenty-two story office building, to install gas boilers to convert the heating system. He alleged performance of the contract necessarily involved an inherently dangerous activity. Two trial judges determined the activity which caused Brandt's injuries was not inherently dangerous. Each judge found "the undisputed facts of the present case constitute mere negligence which could have been prevented by routine precautions of a kind that a careful contractor would be expected to take." Both judges granted summary judgment for some of the defendants.

Brandt concedes that as a general rule one who contracts with an independent contractor is not liable for the negligent acts of the independent contractor. He relies on an exception to the general rule, the inherent danger doctrine.

Our task in the present case is not confined to determining whether the facts developed during discovery would support submitting plaintiff's theory of liability. Liability was alleged on the theory that an employer has a non-delegable duty imposed by law where performance of the contract necessarily involves inherently dangerous activity. Brandt's appeal is from summary judgments in favor of defendants. He claims the trial courts erred in granting summary judgments because application of the inherently dangerous doctrine depends upon questions of fact which remain in dispute. Summary judgment is proper only if summary judgment facts developed in discovery, together with affidavits, show there is no genuine issue as to any material fact and that defendants are entitled to judgment as a matter of law.

The parties agreed that defendants owned, operated, managed, leased or controlled a twenty-two story office building in downtown St. Louis. Defendant, Missouri Pacific Railroad Company, as lessee of Bakewell Corporation, contracted with Jarrell& Associates to install a flue pipe from the basement to the top of the building. Jarrell & Associates was prepared to use its pipe-threading machine as a hoist to lower the flue pipe into an existing duct in the building. Three employees of Jarrell & Associates, including plaintiff, were on the roof of the building preparing to test the hoist. The machine rested on a tripod. When plaintiff activated the machine as part of the test the machine lurched. One of the three legs struck his hip. It threw him up and across the roof. He landed ten feet away on his neck and shoulder. The tripod legs were not secured in any way. It was the intention of Jarrell & Associates to use the pipe-threading machine as a hoist to lower sections of pipe from the roof down through existing duct work and to lower employees in a swing seat in a similar manner to make connections of the sections of pipe. The parties do not dispute any of these facts.

The question in the present appeal narrows to whether on the above undisputed facts both trial courts could determine, as a matter of law, Brandt was injured performing work which was not inherently dangerous. If, at the time of the injury, Brandt was performing work from a position of safety and the casualty could have been avoided by ordinary care in the performance of his duties then the decision was available as a matter of law. Under the circumstances it is irrelevant to the application of the inherently dangerous doctrine that Brandt was working on a tall building, that there was a hole from the basement to the roof thirty-six inches in diameter, that materials had been delivered to the roof by helicopter, and Jarrell & Associates intended to lower materials from the roof to the basement with a pipe-threading machine used as a hoist. These are the facts which Brandt contends remain in dispute and from which a trier of fact could determine the activity was inherently dangerous. However, the unsecured tripod could have caused the same events if activated at ground level. Brandt did not fall off the roof. He did not fall down the airshaft. He was not injured by a helicopter. If the use of the pipe-threading machine as a hoist was a dangerous misuse, the fact remains it was not being used as a hoist at the time of casualty. The negligence and sole cause of injury was failure to secure the legs. The event was one which occurred under conditions not inherently dangerous.

Work is not inherently dangerous unless it started with danger and required preventive care to make safety [sic]. Under the present facts the work Brandt was performing, testing the hoist, started with safety and required negligence to make danger. If the legs of the tripod had been secured Brandt would not have been injured. Defendants may have anticipated inherent danger in lowering employees of an independent contractor down through duct work. There may have been a duty arising from anticipation of such danger to insure use of a safer method for such activity. However, Brandt was not injured under these circumstances. Defendants are not liable under the doctrine for failing to anticipate that the legs of the tripod would not be secured before the machine was tested. The doctrine is not applicable merely because some of the work under the contract includes inherently dangerous activity. On undisputed facts the particular activity being performed at the time of the injury was not inherently dangerous. The doctrine as an exception to the general rules does not apply as a matter of law.

We affirm.

Notes

1. The doctrine applied in *Brandt* is the collateral risk or collateral negligence doctrine, under which a non-negligent employer is *not* liable for an independent contractor's negligence where

> (a) the [independent] contractor's negligence consists solely in the improper manner in which he does the work, and

> (b) [the independent contractor's conduct] creates a risk of harm *which is not inherent in or normal to the work*, and

> (c) the employer had no reason to contemplate the contractor's negligence when the contract was made.

Restatement (Second) of Torts § 426 (emphasis added). By definition, if a risk is not inherent in the work, then Restatement (Second) of Torts sections 413 and 416 and 427 do not impose a non-delegable duty on the employer. The fact that the work may have involved some *other* risk that required special precautions is irrelevant.

2. The plaintiff in *Brandt* was an employee of the independent contractor employed to do the work. Whether the special precaution/inherent danger doctrines of Restatement (Second) of Torts sections 413, 416, and 427 can be applied to hold an employer of an independent contractor liable to the employees of the independent contractor is a matter of some debate. The problem arises because the negligent independent contractor generally will *not* be liable to its own employees. Assuming a *workers' compensation* regime applies *and* that the independent contractor provided workers' compensation insurance, that insurance is the employee's *sole* remedy *as against the independent contractor* (but not as against others). If *no* workers' compensation regime is in place, an employee is deemed *at common law* to have *assumed* risks *inherent* to the work.

In either case, the issue is whether the employee should be able to proceed against the employer of the independent contractor. If the employer had undertaken the assigned task directly, it would have been similarly insulated from liability. *See Wagner v. Continental Casualty Co.*, 143 Wis. 2d 379, 421 N.W.2d 835 (1987). Unfortunately, many of the cases do not confront the issue directly, but instead apply the inherent danger/special precaution doctrine in a distorted manner. Such cases hold that *because* the risk was *inherent* in the work, it was *not* a *peculiar* risk requiring *special* precautions. E.g., *Micheletto v. State*, 798 P.2d 989 (Mont. 1990). This reasoning seems to harken back to the assumption of the risk doctrine. As discussed in *Huddleston v. Union Rural Electric Ass'n*, page 554, the basis of the inherent danger/special precaution rule is that the employer has a non-delegable duty as to risks inherent in the work that require special precautions. Consider the following statement by Justice Hunt, dissenting in *Micheletto v. State*, 798 P.2d 989 (Mont. 1990) (Hunt, J., dissenting):

> [F]or the reasons stated in my dissent in *Kemp v. Bechtel Constr. Co.*, 221 Mont. 519, 528–34, 720 P.2d 270, 276–80 (1986), I must dis-

sent from the Majority's conclusion that trenching is not an inherently dangerous activity.

Trenching is precisely the type of inherently dangerous activity envisioned by the Restatement (Second) of Torts 416 and 427 (1977). By its very nature, trenching is "likely to create during its progress a peculiar risk of physical harm to others unless special precautions are taken." Restatement [(Second) of Torts] 416. Further, trenching involves "a special danger to others which the employer knows or has reason to know to be inherent in or normal to the work." Restatement [(Second) of Torts] 427. The danger inherent in or normal to trenching is exactly the type that appears in the present case—the risk that an excavation might collapse upon and injure an individual inside the trench.

The Majority apparently believes that trenching is not inherently dangerous because "standard" precautions, rather than "special" precautions, can be taken to prevent or lessen the perils of excavating. However, as I noted in my dissent in *Kemp,* the special precautions contemplated by the Restatement are precautions specially designed to counter the peculiar risks inherent in the activity, not extraordinary precautions. Indeed, the safeguards that may be taken to prevent the dangers inherent in trenching are "ordinary in the sense that a reasonably cautious contractor would take them." What makes the precautions "special" in trenching is that they are needed to lessen the dangers inherent in or normal to the activity.

The Majority confuses the idea of "standard" precautions with the idea of "standard" activity, *i.e.,* activity that is not inherently dangerous. The fact that "standard" rather than extraordinary safeguards may counter the risks inherent in trenching does not mean that trenching itself is "standard" activity.

D. Apparent Authority/Estoppel

Problem 11.6

Patient entered Hospital for the delivery of her first child. Before entering Hospital, Patient consulted with Obstetrician about anesthesia. On the advice of Obstetrician Patient, decided to have an epidural, which would numb her from the waist down. Patient did not know in advance who would administer the epidural.

Patient also made arrangements to go to Hospital through Obstetrician. Hospital aggressively marketed its services to the public. According to its advertising, it offered

(i) the most technically sophisticated birthplace in the region,

(ii) a special anesthesiology team, experienced and dedicated exclusively to OB patients, and

(ii) a medical staff that included specialists in obstetrical anesthesiology, who were experts in the administration of epidural anesthesia.

At some point during her labor, one of Hospital's staff physicians, Anesthesiologist, came into Patients room. He explained the epidural procedure and how it would make her feel. He told her that he would stick the tubing for the epidural in her lower back and then she would feel numbness from the waist down.

Anesthesiologist then began the epidural procedure. As Patient sat on the bed and leaned forward, Anesthesiologist began inserting the epidural tubing. Anesthesiologist first inserted the tubing near the top of Patients neck. Shortly thereafter, Anesthesiologist removed the epidural tubing because it did not take and then reinserted it in Patients lower back.

Soon after the delivery of her healthy baby, Patient began to have headaches which recur every four to six weeks. When the headaches occur, Patient is very sensitive to light and sound. In addition to the headaches, she also feels a numbness in her back where epidural was administered.

Assume that Anesthesiologist was negligent in administering the epidural. Assume further that Anesthesiologist is an independent contractor. Is Hospital subject to liability to Patient for Anesthesiologist's negligence? *See Sword v. NKC Hospitals, Inc.,* 714 N.E.2d 142 (Ind. 1999).

Sampson v. Baptist Memorial Hospital System

940 S.W.2d 128 (Tex. App. 1996), *rev'd* 969 S.W.2d 945 (Tex. 1998)

RICKHOFF, Justice.

Appellant, Rhea Sampson ("Sampson"), appeals from a summary judgment granted in favor of appellee, Baptist Memorial Hospital System ("BMHS"), in a medical negligent treatment action. Although BMHS' evidence included both posted signage and an executed consent to treatment form stating "each physician is an independent contractor," Sampson contends the summary judgment was erroneously granted because a genuine issue of material fact was raised as to whether Dr. Mark Zakula, the emergency room attending physician ("Zakula"), was an employee or ostensible agent of BMHS. We reverse the judgment of the trial court and remand the cause for trial.

FACTS

Sampson was bitten on the arm by an unknown insect on March 23, 1990, and was taken to the emergency room at Southeast Baptist Hospital, an affiliate of BMHS. Sampson was treated by Dr. Susan Howle, who diagnosed Sampson as having a reaction to an insect, gave her a shot of Benadryl, a shot of pain medication and two prescriptions for pain and swelling and released her. Early in the morning on March 25, 1990, Sampson returned to the hospital by ambulance and was seen by Zakula, who confirmed Howle's diagnosis, gave Sampson some additional shots and released her at approximately 3:00 a.m. Approximately fourteen hours later, Sampson was taken to a different hospital and admitted to the intensive care ward in septic shock. The insect that had bitten Sampson was then identified as a brown recluse spider.

Sampson brought suit against Howle and Zakula claiming negligent treatment. Sampson also sued BMHS contending, among other claims, that BMHS was vicariously liable for the negligence of Zakula because he was an employee or ostensible agent of BMHS.

BMHS moved for summary judgment on Sampson's vicarious liability and negligent treatment claims. The trial court granted the summary judgment in favor of BMHS and severed these claims from the remaining action, thereby making the summary judgment final for purposes of appeal.[1] Sampson appeals the trial court's judgment contending that a genuine issue of material fact was raised as to whether Zakula was an employee or ostensible agent of BMHS.

STANDARD OF REVIEW

In order to prevail on summary judgment, the movant must disprove at least one of the essential elements of each of the plaintiff's causes of action. This burden requires the movant to show that no genuine issue of material fact exists and that the movant is entitled to judgment as a matter of law. In determining whether a material fact issue exists to preclude summary judgment, evidence favoring the non-movant is taken as true, and all reasonable inferences are indulged in favor of the non-movant. Any doubt is resolved in favor of the non-movant.

Where the non-movant opposes a summary judgment based upon an affirmative defense, the non-movant must produce sufficient summary judgment evidence to raise a question of fact as to each element of the affirmative defense in order to avoid summary judgment. The movant is not required to negate every possible issue of law and fact that could have been raised by the non-movant, but rather the burden of raising and producing sufficient evidence with respect to affirmative defenses is on the non-movant.

RESPONDEAT SUPERIOR

In general, an employer is not legally responsible for the negligent acts of an independent contractor. Physicians are generally considered to be independent contractors with regard to hospitals at which they have staff privileges. Thus, it would generally follow that a hospital is not liable for the negligent acts of independent physicians. Stated differently, under the general rule, no respondeat superior liability attaches where a physician is an independent contractor rather than an employee of the hospital.

The standard test for distinguishing between an independent contractor and employer/employee situation is whether the employer retains the right to control the performance of the individual. It is the right to control, not actual control, which is determinative, and the right to control must extend to both the means and details of the work, as well as the end result.

[The court reviewed the evidence, and concluded:]

[W]e agree with the trial court that the summary judgment evidence showed that Zakula was not an employee of BMHS.

---

1. During oral argument, Sampson's attorney commented that the trial judge, the Hon. David Peeples, parenthetically remarked that this would be a suitable issue for our court to resolve. We suspect he actually meant by this surplusage that the Texas Supreme Court should resolve the issue since it will impact so many relationships in the medical field. We have, therefore, advanced a more complete explication than we ordinarily would.

OSTENSIBLE AGENCY

In addition to contending that Zakula was an employee of BMHS, Sampson also asserted, in the alternative, that Zakula was BMHS' ostensible agent.

1. Vicarious Liability Theories and Burden in Summary Judgment Setting

Whether labeled "ostensible agency," "apparent authority," or "agency by estoppel," two distinct theories of vicarious liability have been recognized by this court and by various courts in other jurisdictions to impose liability on a hospital for the negligence of emergency room physicians. One of these theories is based on § 267 of the Restatement (Second) of Agency,[2] referred to herein as "agency by estoppel," while the other theory is based on § 429 of the Restatement (Second) of Torts,[3] referred to herein as "apparent agency." Since prior cases have not always succinctly drawn a distinction between these two theories, it is important to carefully analyze the language of the cases to determine the theory applied, rather than relying on the label attached.

Vicarious liability based on the "agency by estoppel" theory is generally more difficult to prove because a representation or holding out and actual reliance must be shown. Agency by estoppel is comprised of the following three elements:

(1) a third party has a reasonable belief in an agent's authority;

(2) the belief is generated by some holding out by act or neglect of the principal; and

(3) the third party justifiably relies on the representation of authority.

In applying the theory, however, courts have fought against a rigorous application of the elements in order to achieve what has been perceived by one commentator as a result-oriented outcome favorable to the plaintiff. Martin C. McWilliams, Jr. & Hamilton E. Russell, III, *Hospital Liability for Torts of Independent Contractor Physicians*, 47 S.C. L.Rev. at 451. In reaching this result, the commentator contends these courts "assume away or ignore great chunks of the required analysis." *Id.*

Under apparent agency, the alternative theory for holding a hospital vicariously liable for the negligence of its emergency room physicians, only two elements are required to be shown:

(1) the patient must look to the hospital, rather than the individual physician, for treatment; and

---

2. Section 267 provides:
   One who represents that another is his servant or other agent and thereby causes a third party justifiably to rely upon the care or skill of such apparent agent is subject to liability to the third person for harm caused by the lack of care or skill of the one appearing to be a servant or other agent as if he were such.
   RESTATEMENT (SECOND) OF AGENCY § 267 (1958).
3. Section 429 provides:
   One who employs an independent contractor to perform services for another which are accepted in the reasonable belief that the services are being rendered by the employer or by his servants, is subject to liability for physical harm caused by the negligence of the contractor in supplying such services, to the same extent as though the employer were supplying them himself or by his servants.
   RESTATEMENT (SECOND) OF TORTS § 429 (1965).

(2) the hospital must "hold out" the physician as its employee.

Therefore, under this theory, reliance need not be shown.

Both agency by estoppel and apparent agency are affirmative defenses. Therefore, Sampson had the burden of producing summary judgment evidence sufficient to raise an issue of fact as to each element of these defenses in order to successfully oppose summary judgment.

2. Evidence in the Instant Case

BMHS attached to its motion for summary judgment the affidavit of James Potyka, M.D., who stated:

(1) he is an emergency room physician and had worked in BMHS emergency rooms for 22 years;

(2) it was his expert opinion that Dr. Zakula was ultimately responsible for Sampson's treatment;

(3) Dr. Zakula was not a hospital employee;

(4) all physicians working at the hospital are independent, licensed physicians as evidenced by the consent forms signed by patients prior to treatment;

(5) there is signage in the emergency room that notifies patients that the emergency room physicians are independent contractors and that the signage was in place when Sampson was in the emergency room; and

(6) BMHS did not collect or retain fees for the physicians' services, instead the physicians bill for the services they provide.

BMHS also presented copies of the consent forms allegedly executed by Sampson as summary judgment evidence. The consent forms acknowledge that the physicians providing professional services are independent contractors and that the hospital is not responsible for their judgment or conduct.[4]

Sampson attached her personal affidavit to her response. In her affidavit, Sampson stated:

---

4. The acknowledgment contained in paragraph 3 of the consent to treatment form provides:

I acknowledge and agree that Baptist Medical Center, Northeast Baptist Hospital, Southeast Baptist Hospital, North Central Baptist Hospital and any Hospital operated as a part of Baptist Memorial Hospital System, is not responsible for the judgment or conduct of any physician who treats or provides a professional service to me, but rather each physician is an independent contractor who is self-employed and is not the agent, servant or employee of the hospital. I further understand that other physicians may be called upon to provide care, either directly (as consultants) or indirectly through professional services (i.e. radiology, Pathology, EKG interpretations, Anesthesiology). These physicians are also independent contractors who are self-employed and are not the agents, servants or employees of the hospital. It is also understood that for emergency or unscheduled services, the hospital may aid my selection of physicians by an established "on-call" roster provided through each department of the hospital. These physicians are also independent contractors who are self-employed and are not the agents, servants, or employees of the hospital. I further agree the hospital is not responsible for the judgment or conduct of any of the physicians identified above.

(1) she did not see any signs stating that the doctors were not employees of BMHS;

(2) she was never told that the doctors were not employees;

(3) she believed the doctors were employees;

(4) she was not given a choice as to which doctor would treat her;

(5) she asked only for treatment not for a specific doctor; and

(6) she did not recall being shown the consent form nor did she recall signing the document.

Although Sampson admitted in her deposition that she was mentally alert upon her presentation at the hospital for treatment, she also stated that she was in a lot of pain, and she did not remember what happened once she arrived at the emergency room.

3. Analysis

We initially analyze whether the summary judgment was properly granted under the apparent agency theory of vicarious liability. In order to defeat BMHS' motion under this theory, Sampson was required to produce sufficient summary judgment evidence to raise an issue of fact as to each of the following elements:

(1) the patient must look to the hospital, rather than the individual physician, for treatment; and

(2) the hospital must "hold out" the physician as its employee.

Sampson stated in her affidavit that she arrived at BMHS and asked for treatment not for a specific doctor. BMHS did not controvert this statement; therefore, Sampson's affidavit contained sufficient summary judgment evidence to raise an issue of fact as to whether Sampson looked to the hospital, not Dr. Zakula, for treatment.

With respect to the second element, the increasing trend among the courts in other jurisdictions is to hold this second requirement to be satisfied when the hospital holds itself out to the public as a provider of emergency medical services. These courts note modern-day hospitals have become large, well-run businesses that spend enormous dollars competitively advertising their services to induce patients to utilize their services. Therefore, courts generally imply the "holding out" requirement from the circumstances where the hospital offers emergency services. The courts also note, however, that a different result may follow where the hospital provides notice to the patient, thereby eliminating the implication that the physician is an employee. In the instant case, BMHS contended that sufficient notice was provided to make the general inference that BMHS held Dr. Zakula out as an employee unreasonable. BMHS contended such notice was provided by the signs posted on the emergency room walls and the consent forms executed by Sampson.

Although Dr. Potyka did state in his affidavit that there was signage in the emergency room regarding the independent status of the emergency room physicians, Sampson stated that she did not see any signs. There was no evidence presented by BMHS regarding the number or conspicuousness of the signs. Therefore, we find Sampson's affidavit raises a question of fact as to whether the signs were sufficient notice.

With respect to the consent forms, Sampson stated that she did not recall being shown the consent form nor did she recall signing the document. In *Paramount Nat. Life Ins. Co. v. Williams*, 772 S.W.2d 255, 262 (Tex.App.— Houston [14th Dist.] 1989, writ denied), the court of appeals held that a disclaimer in a document was insufficient to negate the apparent authority with which an insurance company had clothed its agent. The court noted that it was unreasonable to expect a sixty-four year old uneducated woman to understand the limitation on the agent's authority in that instance. *Id.* Similarly, we find that the nature of the circumstances under which Sampson sought emergency room services coupled with her statement that she did not recall signing the consent forms were sufficient to raise a question of fact as to whether Sampson was in a position to understand the terms of the forms.

Although we find that an issue of fact was raised in the instant case as to each element of the defense of apparent agency, we feel compelled by the manner in which the law has developed in this area to take our analysis one step further.

In the initial opinion issued by this court in this area, we reversed a summary judgment granted in favor of BMHS asserting that the simple fact that the emergency room physician "manifested the authority of a competent physician placed the fact issue of ostensible agency in issue." *Smith v. Baptist Memorial Hosp. System*, 720 S.W.2d 618, 625 (Tex.App.—San Antonio 1986, writ ref'd n.r.e.). We then implied that irrespective of any other fact, if a hospital includes an emergency room as part of its facilities, the appearance of agency is sufficient to defeat a summary judgment, asserting:

> Sound public policy demands that when an institution calls itself a "full service hospital" and includes an emergency room as part of its facilities, that institution makes a special statement to the public when it opens its emergency room to provide emergency care for people. An agency by estoppel is established by creating the effect that the appearance that hospital's agents, not independent contractors, will provide medical care to those who enter the hospital. The appearance is what the patient observes and which he relies upon when entering a full-service hospital.

Id. at 625 (citations omitted). We cited with approval the decision in *Hannola v. City of Lakewood*, 68 Ohio App.2d 61, 426 N.E.2d 1187, 1190 (1980), wherein it was held that a hospital would be liable to an injured patient for acts of malpractice committed in its emergency room regardless of any contractual arrangements with independent contractors, provided that proximate cause and damages were present. We then concluded that the rationale employed in *Hannola* was simple:

> the patient who relies on the ostensible agency might have acted differently with knowledge that there was no actual agency.

Id. We agreed with that approach, concluding

> [a] person who is ill or injured and needs treatment will turn to his local hospital to provide it regardless of prior notice that the physicians are independent contractors. After all, the injured or ill person chooses [the hospital] not the [emergency room physician] for treatment.

Id. These last two sentences imply that even if actual prior notice of the existence of an independent contractor relationship was provided, the hospital would remain vicariously liable.

After the summary judgment in the Smith case was reversed, the case was tried to a jury, and the trial court's judgment entered after the jury's verdict was again appealed to this court. *Baptist Memorial Hosp. System v. Smith,* 822 S.W.2d 67 (Tex.App.—San Antonio 1991, writ denied). In the second appeal, we first rejected the hospital's contention that the doctrines of ostensible agency and agency by estoppel were not recognized in Texas under the factual circumstances of that case. We relied upon the law of the case and our prior decision in light of the Supreme Court's denial of the application for writ of error in the prior case. We then addressed the hospital's challenge to the sufficiency of the evidence to support the jury's finding of ostensible agency. We held the evidence to be sufficient to support the finding, noting the following:

(1) the emergency room receptionist collected the fees for the physician;

(2) the patient would not likely know the relationship between the contracting physicians and the hospital;

(3) the patient requested to be seen by an emergency room physician because he had no personal physician, and the admitting clerk asked the patient if he wanted to see one of "our" doctors;

(4) no notices in the emergency room advised patients about the contractual arrangement;

(5) the hospital expected the emergency room physicians to render proper care to emergency room patients;

(6) the permission to treat form referred only to the hospital and the "chosen physician" and not the specific emergency room treating physician; and

(7) BMHS advertised its hospital emergency rooms as being staffed 24 hours a day by licensed physicians.

The language in the second *Smith* opinion seems to depart from the concept introduced in the first decision that ostensible agency can arise simply from the nature of emergency room services, *i.e.,* the imposition of liability based on public policy when a "full service hospital" provides emergency room services. In the second opinion, we noted that there were no notices in the emergency room advising patients that the physicians were independent contractors. In addition, we referred to the murky relationship between the hospital and the emergency room physicians created by the hospital's failure to notify or draw the patient's attention up front to the contractual nature of the service arrangement. This language implies that where the patient is notified prior to receiving services and signs are conspicuously posted, the "holding out" element of vicarious liability would be absent. Thus, the two opinions appear to be in conflict as to the effect prior notice of the contractual relationship should have.

Seizing upon the language in the second *Smith* opinion, hospitals, like BMHS, will continue to take actions in an effort to provide sufficient notice to negate the "holding out" element. Although we have found a fact issue regarding the sufficiency of the notice in the instant case, we anticipate future cases in which the summary judgment evidence will show as a matter of law that prior notice of the contractual relationship was given by the hospitals. Thus, we take an additional step in our analysis to consider whether notice provided in consent forms and posted in emergency rooms can ever be sufficient to negate a hospital's "holding out" given the exigencies of the circumstances in which patients seek emergency medical treatment.

In *Clark v. Southview Hospital & Family Health Ctr.*, 628 N.E.2d at 54 & n. 1, the Ohio Supreme Court asserted that notice that care is being provided by independent practitioners must be provided at a meaningful time. Contrary to the dissenting justice's contention in *Pamperin v. Trinity Memorial Hosp.*, 423 N.W.2d at 861 (Steinmetz, J., dissenting), the court then stated that posting signs in an emergency room will rarely provide the patient with the ability to choose at a meaningful time. *Clark v. Southview Hospital & Family Health Ctr.*, 628 N.E.2d at 54 n. 1. Quoting one commentator's criticism of the *Pamperin* dissent, the court concluded:

> The plaintiff, who by definition is injured and under stress, is relying upon the hospital to provide the services that the hospital has held out that it can provide. The plaintiff's reliance upon the hospital's competence has been demonstrated by her walking (or being wheeled) into the emergency room. Simply informing her that some doctors and staff have a different technical relationship with the hospital than the one she expected does not lessen the reasonableness of her reliance upon the hospital. Even if the patient understood the difference between an employee and an independent-contractor relationship, informing her of the nature of the relationship after she arrives is too late. The purpose of any notice requirement is to impart knowledge sufficient to enable the plaintiff to exercise an informed choice. The signs suggested by the dissent are too little, too late.

Id. (quoting Note, *Pamperin v. Trinity Memorial Hospital and the Evolution of Hospital Liability: Wisconsin Adopts Apparent Agency*, 1990 WIS. L. REV. 1129, 1147 (1990)).

Preventing hospitals from avoiding liability by notifying a patient upon presentation at the emergency room of a physician's independent status, however, would merely be one more judicial step in eliminating the liability loopholes currently available to hospitals in the emergency room setting. The preclusion of last minute notification could simply lead to more far-reaching general notices by hospitals contained in advertisements and other literature in an effort to avoid vicarious liability. Now, we see this as an unavailing step. Because we do not believe hospitals should be allowed to avoid such responsibility, we encourage the full leap—imposing a nondelegable duty on hospitals for the negligence of emergency room physicians.

Emergency rooms are aptly named and vital to public safety. There exists no other place to find immediate medical care. The dynamics that drive paying patients to a hospital's emergency rooms are known well. Either a sudden injury occurs, a child breaks his arm or an individual suffers a heart attack, or an existing medical condition worsens, a diabetic lapses into a coma, demanding immediate medical attention at the nearest emergency room. The catch phrase in legal nomenclature, "time is of the essence," takes on real meaning. Generally, one cannot choose to pass by the nearest emergency room, and after arrival, it would be improvident to depart in hope of finding one that provides services through employees rather than independent contractors. The patient is there and must rely on the services available and agree to pay the premium charged for those services.

The rationale for the imposing a nondelegable duty in this situation has previously been set forth by the New York Supreme Court in *Martell v. St. Charles Hosp.* as follows:

> This Court is of the further opinion that even with the knowledge that emergency room physicians were independent contractors, and not hospital employees, an individual requiring emergency room medical care, given a choice, would opt for the emergency room of the hospital which that individual perceived to have the better reputation. It is the hospital's location and reputation which draw patients to its emergency room, as well as the exigencies of the moment, and, in this regard, the contractual relationship between the hospital and the emergency room physicians is irrelevant as a practical matter.

>   *   *   *

> In this Court's opinion it is public policy, and not traditional rules of the law of agency or the law of torts, which should underlie the decision to hold hospitals liable for malpractice which occurs in their emergency rooms. In this regard the observation of former United States Supreme Court Justice Oliver Wendell Holmes is apt: "The true grounds of decision are consideration of policy and of social advantage, and it is vain to suppose that solutions can be attained merely by logic and the general propositions of law which nobody disputes. Propositions as to public policy rarely are unanimously accepted, and still more rarely, if ever, are capable of unanswerable proof." (Shriver, The Judicial Opinions of Oliver Wendell Holmes, page 65).

523 N.Y.S.2d at 352.[5] The Supreme Court of Alaska has imposed such a duty. *Jackson v. Power,* 743 P.2d at 1384–85. The duty was imposed in *Jackson* after the court noted that a hospital licensed as a "general acute care hospital" is required to "insure that a physician is available to respond to an emergency at all times." *Id.* at 1382. The court held that the duty to provide physicians for emergency care is non-delegable and that a hospital may not shield itself from responsibility for the negligent performance of such care. *Id.* at 1385.

Similarly, a hospital licensed as a general hospital in Texas must make physicians available for emergency services and have an emergency service with appropriate facilities. 25 Tex. Admin. Code § 133.21 (West 1996) (adopting rule contained in publication entitled Hospital Licensing Standards which requires emergency service under rule 1-14.1.1 and the provision of physicians for emergencies under rule 1-14.1.6). In addition, hospitals accredited by the Joint Commission on Accreditation of Healthcare Organizations ("JCAHO") must provide emergency medical services. David W. Lovisell, J.D. & Harold Williams, M.D., L.L.B., Medical Malpractice 16B-10 (Matthew Bender 1996). Although there are differing levels of emergency services that can be provided under JCAHO guidelines, each level recognizes the hospital's responsibility to respond to a patient presented to its facility in a crisis situation. Id. at 16B-6–16B-7.

---

5. In the instant case, Sampson admitted that she initially went to Southeast Baptist because it was closest. She was taken to Southeast Baptist the second time by EMS. The third time she elected to go to Southwest General, where she was admitted to intensive care.

During oral argument, BMHS contended the imposition of this type of liability conflicts with the prohibition on the corporate practice of medicine. Tex.Rev.Civ. Stat Ann. art. 4495b, § 3.08(1) (Vernon Supp. 1996). BMHS asserted that since it cannot control the professional services rendered by physicians, it should not be held liable for their negligent acts. This same contention has been asserted by hospitals seeking to avoid responsibility under vicarious liability theories.[6] Various reasons have been advanced to reject this contention.

In *Hardy v. Brantley*, the Mississippi Supreme Court noted that the law permitted a hospital to be liable for the actions of a nurse, even though hospitals cannot be licensed as an R.N.; therefore, the court reasoned there was no reason to permit the corporate practice of medicine prohibition to otherwise bar liability for physicians' actions. 471 So.2d at 373. In addition, the court reasoned that imposing liability on hospitals is no different than imposing liability on the professional corporations through which physicians practice since such professional corporations similarly are not entitled to be licensed to practice medicine. *Hardy*, 471 So.2d at 373.

Applying this same reasoning under Texas law, Texas hospitals have been held liable for the negligence of residents and nurses who were paid employees of the hospitals. In addition, a physician in Texas may practice medicine through a professional association, which is held jointly and severally liable for acts of professional negligence. Therefore, the corporate practice of medicine prohibition should not be successful in shielding a hospital from liability for the negligence of emergency room physicians.

We are concerned that the imposition of this nondelegable duty may cause unintended and undesirable economic ramifications, including the closure of emergency rooms. We note, however, that the same policy concerns were advanced in connection with the imposition of vicarious liability, and at least one commentator has noted that the empirical evidence does not support this fear. Jim M. Perdue, *Medical Malpractice and Hospital Liability in Texas*, in STATE BAR OF TEXAS PROF. DEV. PROGRAM, 10 ADVANCED PERSONAL INJURY LAW COURSE Q, Q-65 (1994). Furthermore, we note that hospitals are in a position to protect against these losses through insurance; whereas, the patient is without similar control.

At a time when hospitals are engaged in sophisticated managed care structuring and advertising in an effort to induce patients and insurance companies to use their services, we contend that hospitals must accept the responsibility that attaches to the services it undertakes to generate revenues. While public policy and fundamental fairness indicate this result, it is dictated by the simple fact that an injured party must rely on a hospital's emergency room because there is no other place to go.

CONCLUSION

Because we find material fact issues were raised with respect to the defense of apparent agency, we reverse the judgment of the trial court and remand the cause for trial.

---

6. The prohibition of the corporate practice of medicine is the law in all states except Nebraska and Missouri. Martin C. McWilliams, Jr. & Hamilton E. Russell, III, *Hospital Liability for Torts of Independent Contractor Physicians*, 47 S.C. L. REV. at 431.

DUNCAN, Justice, dissenting.

I respectfully dissent for the following reasons:

1. Section 429 of the Restatement (Second) of Agency, the "apparent agency" legal theory upon which the majority relies in reversing this summary judgment:

> a. was not pleaded or argued by either party in the trial court (either in a petition or answer or in a motion for summary judgment or response) and was not briefed or argued by either party in this court; rather, in the trial court and this court, the parties have argued whether Texas' ostensible agency law— which they have consistently used interchangeably with "apparent authority" and "agency by estoppel"—mandates or precludes the summary judgment;

> b. does not reflect Texas law, was not adopted by this court in *Baptist Memorial Hosp. Sys. v. Smith,* 822 S.W.2d 67, 72–73 (Tex.App.— San Antonio 1991, writ denied), and, as far as I have been able to determine, has not been adopted by any Texas court; and

> c. is, in fact, completely inconsistent with Texas independent contractor law, which rests upon the right to control, as reflected in the leading case of *Redinger v. Living, Inc.,* 689 S.W.2d 415, 418 (Tex. 1985).

2. Even under the apparent agency theory adopted by the majority, "the hospital must 'hold out' the physician as its employee." But Baptist has conclusively demonstrated that it did not hold out its emergency room physicians as its employees; to the contrary, short of shutting down its emergency room, it did all it could reasonably have done to notify patients that its emergency room physicians were not its employees. There simply is no evidence in this record raising a fact issue on this element of Sampson's affirmative defense, and the majority cites none. Rather, the majority reverses the summary judgment because "Sampson's affidavit raises a question of fact as to whether the signs were sufficient notice" to her and "whether [she] was in a position to understand the terms of the forms." The majority's reasons for reversing the summary judgment thus go only to Sampson's belief— reasonable or otherwise—which is irrelevant and immaterial in the absence of some holding out by Baptist.

3. Under the controlling Texas law of ostensible agency, the record conclusively establishes that Baptist did not, by any act or omission, generate a belief in Sampson that its emergency room physicians were its employees or agents; rather, it did all it reasonably could have done (short of shutting down its emergency room) to ensure that she did not hold this belief. Under these circumstances, Baptist is entitled to summary judgment.

But as the majority's expansive dicta—its encouragement of "the full leap"— makes clear, none of these procedural and substantive obstacles to reversal are even relevant to the members of the majority. The simple reason this summary judgment has been reversed is because they believe that the hospital should be liable for its emergency room physicians' negligence as a matter of "public policy and fundamental fairness." The first half of the opinion is, therefore, just an exercise in creating a fact issue to justify a reversal.

The members of the majority apparently believe it is this court's role to unilaterally impose its views of good "public policy," and what it perceives to be "fundamental fairness," on Texas citizens. I, on the other hand, believe it is our role to apply the law enunciated by the higher courts and the legislatures to the best of our ability. Accordingly, I would leave this difficult policy decision—with its far-reaching social and economic ramifications—to the Texas Legislature. In short, I would hold that no material issues of fact are presented in this record under the controlling Texas law and affirm the summary judgment.

Notes

1. As indicated in the principal case, when deciding whether hospitals can be liable for the torts of doctors who were independent contractors, courts often apply Restatement (Second) of Agency section 267 and Restatement (Second) of Torts section 429.

Under Restatement (Second) of Agency section 267:

> One who represents that another is his servant or other agent and thereby causes a third party justifiably to rely upon the care or skill of such apparent agent is subject to liability to the third person for harm caused by the lack of care or skill of the one appearing to be a servant or other agent as if he were such.

Restatements § 267. Contrast Section 267 with Restatement (Second) of Torts section 429:

> One who employs an independent contractor to perform services for another which are accepted in the reasonable belief that the services are being rendered by the employer or by his servants, is subject to liability for physical harm caused by the negligence of the contractor in supplying such services, to the same extent as though the employer were supplying them himself or by his servants.

Restatement (Second) of Torts § 429.

2. In *Baptist Memorial Hospital System v. Sampson*, 969 S.W.2d 945, 948–49 (Tex. 1998), the Texas Supreme Court reversed the holding of the Court of Appeals in the principal case. The Texas Supreme Court reasoned:

> We first reject the court of appeals' conclusion that there are two methods, one "more difficult to prove" than the other, to establish the liability of a hospital for the malpractice of an emergency room physician. Our courts have uniformly required proof of all three elements of section 267 to invoke the fiction that one should be responsible for the acts of another who is not in fact an agent acting within his or her scope of authority. As we have explained:
>
>> Apparent authority in Texas is based on estoppel. It may arise either from a principal knowingly permitting an agent to hold herself out as having authority or by a principal's actions which lack such ordinary care as to clothe an agent with the indicia of authority, thus leading a reasonably prudent person to believe that the agent has the authority she purports to exercise....
>>
>> A prerequisite to a proper finding of apparent authority is evidence of conduct by the principal relied upon by the party as-

serting the estoppel defense which would lead a reasonably prudent person to believe an agent had authority to so act.

Ames v. Great S. Bank, 672 S.W.2d at 450.... Thus, to establish a hospital's liability for an independent contractor's medical malpractice based on ostensible agency, a plaintiff must show that

(1) he or she had a reasonable belief that the physician was the agent or employee of the hospital,

(2) such belief was generated by the hospital affirmatively holding out the physician as its agent or employee or knowingly permitting the physician to hold herself out as the hospital's agent or employee, and

(3) he or she justifiably relied on the representation of authority.

While a few courts of appeals have referred to section 429, it has never before been adopted in this state by any appellate court. To the extent that the Restatement (Second) of Torts section 429 proposes a conflicting standard for establishing liability, we expressly decline to adopt it in Texas.

Next, we reject the suggestion of the court of appeals quoted above that we disregard the traditional rules and take "the full leap" of imposing a nondelegable duty on Texas hospitals for the malpractice of emergency room physicians. Imposing such a duty is not necessary to safeguard patients in hospital emergency rooms. A patient injured by a physician's malpractice is not without a remedy. The injured patient ordinarily has a cause of action against the negligent physician, and may retain a direct cause of action against the hospital if the hospital was negligent in the performance of a duty owed directly to the patient.

*   *   *

Even if Sampson's belief that Dr. Zakula was a hospital employee were reasonable, that belief, as we have seen, must be based on or generated by some conduct on the part of the Hospital. * * * The summary judgment proof establishes that the Hospital took no affirmative act to make actual or prospective patients think the emergency room physicians were its agents or employees, and did not fail to take reasonable efforts to disabuse them of such a notion. As a matter of law, on this record, no conduct by the Hospital would lead a reasonable patient to believe that the treating emergency room physicians were hospital employees.

3. In *Sword v. NKC Hospitals, Inc.,* 714 N.E.2d 142 (Ind. 1999), the Indiana Supreme Court took the path rejected by the Texas Supreme Court in *Baptist Memorial Hospital System v. Sampson. Sword v. NKC Hospitals, Inc.* involved a claim that a hospital (Norton) was liable for the alleged negligence of a "staff" anesthiologist (Dr. Luna) in administering anesthesia to a woman (Sword) who was delivering a baby. Even though Sword and her obstetrician had chosen Norton, the Court reversed a summary judgment in favor of Norton:

In the present case, Sword argues that, under the doctrine of apparent or ostensible agency, Norton is vicariously liable for the actions of its apparent agent Dr. Luna, whom the parties agree was an independent contractor. The Court of Appeals held that Dr. Luna could be an apparent agent of Norton, and that there were genuine issues of material fact in dispute on this question. * * * We agree with the conclusion of the Court of Appeals and now, in the specific context of a hospital setting, expressly adopt the formulation of apparent or ostensible agency set forth in the Restatement (Second) of Torts section 429.

Under Section 429, as we read and construe it, a trier of fact must focus on the reasonableness of the patients belief that the hospital or its employees were rendering health care. This ultimate determination is made by considering the totality of the circumstances, including the actions or inactions of the hospital, as well as any special knowledge the patient may have about the hospitals arrangements with its physicians. We conclude that a hospital will be deemed to have held itself out as the provider of care unless it gives notice to the patient that it is not the provider of care and that the care is provided by a physician who is an independent contractor and not subject to the control and supervision of the hospital. A hospital generally will be able to avoid liability by providing meaningful written notice to the patient, acknowledged at the time of admission. Under some circumstances, such as in the case of a medical emergency, however, written notice may not suffice if the patient had an inadequate opportunity to make an informed choice.

As to the meaning and importance of reliance in this specific context, we agree with the cases that hold that if the hospital has failed to give meaningful notice, if the patient has no special knowledge regarding the arrangement the hospital has made with its physicians, and if there is no reason that the patient should have known of these employment relationships, then reliance is presumed.

Applying this test here, we conclude that there are genuine material issues of fact in dispute as to whether Dr. Luna was an apparent or ostensible agent of Norton and whether Norton may be held liable for any of Dr. Lunas asserted negligent acts. First, there is nothing in this record which indicates that the hospital did anything to put plaintiff on notice that it was her physician, an independent contractor, who was responsible for her medical care and not the hospital.[16] Second, this is clearly not a case where plaintiff selected her own anesthesiologist prior to admission, for she specifically testified that she did not know who would administer the epidural until just before the procedure, and if she had any special knowledge of the hospitals employment arrangement with Dr. Luna or with the hospitals general employment practices with respect to

---

16. In a deposition colloquy, counsel made a general reference to a document titled Condition of Admission and Authorization for Treatment, which assertedly informed plaintiff that her physician is not an employee of the hospital, and that the hospital is not liable for any acts of the practicing physician. That document, however, is not in the record, and no witness testified regarding that document. Nevertheless, even assuming the accuracy of counsel's representations during this colloquy, it is far from clear that this document would constitute sufficient notice of the relationship between the hospital and the physician within the meaning of the rule we articulate today. In fact, it is likely insufficient notice if it is the sole source of notice and if plaintiff did not read or sign that form until she arrived at the hospital in active labor.

physicians, it is not apparent on this record. Finally, Norton held itself out, through an extensive advertising campaign, as a full-service hospital which specializes in obstetric care.

Based on this record and under Section 429 as we construe it today, there are clearly genuine issues of material fact as to whether Dr. Luna is an apparent agent of Norton. The trial court erred when it entered summary judgment for defendant on this issue.

4. As between the three approaches taken in the opinions discussed above, which approach offers the most plausible basis for hospital liability where the hospital, instead of the patient, selects the doctor who supplies negligent medical services? Which approach is better from a policy standpoint? Do you agree with the statement by Justice Duncan, in his dissent in *Sampson v. Baptist Memorial Hospital System,* that only legislatures, and not courts, should decide matters of policy?

Volkman v. DP Associates
48 N.C. App. 155, 268 S.E.2d 265 (1980)

Plaintiffs brought suit alleging that they entered into a contract with DP Associates for construction advice in building a residence and that the contract was breached with damages resulting to them. Plaintiffs brought suit against DP Associates, which they alleged was a partnership, David L. McNamee and Philip E. Carroll as individuals, who were alleged to be partners in DP Associates. Before any answers were filed, interrogatories were served on plaintiffs by defendant Carroll. These interrogatories sought information on what basis plaintiffs made their claim that Carroll was a partner with McNamee in DP Associates.

Plaintiffs answered defendants' interrogatories indicating the following. At an early meeting in 1976, McNamee informed Mr. Volkman, who was authorized to act for his wife, that "he either had just commenced business, or was going into business with Philip E. Carroll." Subsequently, Mr. Volkman received correspondence from McNamee on DP Associates letterhead, and he assumed the "DP" was derived from the given names of the individual defendants, David and Philip. Prior to the signing of the contract, McNamee introduced Carroll to Mr. Volkman at the DP Associates' office where Carroll said, "I hope we'll be working together." Carroll identified McNamee as the person primarily concerned with Volkman's business with DP Associates but that he would also be available.

Mr. and Mrs. Volkman reviewed the written contract in the DP Associates office on 21 January 1977 with McNamee. McNamee suggested it might be advantageous to use a straight contractor's form to clearly identify DP Associates as acting as virtual general contractor. He then left the room saying, "I will ask Phil," and when he returned, he said they would use the contract with initialed modifications. After the signing of the contract but before construction of the house began, Mr. Volkman was in the office of DP Associates and again saw and conversed with Carroll who said to him in the course of the conversation, "I am happy that we will be working with you." During construction, Mr. Volkman visited the office of DP Associates on numerous occasions and saw Carroll there. During one visit, he expressed concern about construction delays to Carroll, who told him not to worry because McNamee would take care of it. Mr. and Mrs. Volkman have no documents tending to show a partnership existed. All money was paid to DP Associates. They never saw Carroll on the construction site and knew of no other construction supervised by Carroll. They understood they were purchasing Carroll's services and construction expertise through DP Associates.

Carroll moved for summary judgment on the basis that the pleadings, affidavits and answers to interrogatories showed that Carroll was not a partner in DP Associates. An affidavit by McNamee supporting the motion for summary judgment states that McNamee is not and never has been in partnership with Carroll and that Carroll received no income, profits, salary or other remuneration from the Volkman job.

The trial court entered an order dismissing Carroll as a party defendant because no issue was raised as to whether Carroll was a partner in DP Associates. Plaintiffs appeal.

VAUGHN, Judge.

The question raised on this appeal is not whether plaintiffs proved that Carroll was a partner. That burden will be upon plaintiffs when they go to trial. The question is whether defendant carried his burden of showing there was no genuine issue as to whether Carroll was a partner. The answers to the interrogatories indicate that there is at least a question as to whether Carroll was a partner. If at trial plaintiffs are unable to prove a partnership in fact, they may be able to show that Carroll should be held as a partner by estoppel or under the agency theory of apparent authority.

The Uniform Partnership Act as adopted in this State provides that "[t]he law of estoppel shall apply." [UPA 4(2).] The essentials of equitable estoppel or estoppel *in pais* are a representation, either by words or conduct, made to another, who reasonably believing the representation to be true, relies upon it, with the result that he changes his position to his detriment. "[I]t is essential that the party estopped shall have made a representation by words or acts and that someone shall have acted on the faith of this representation in such a way that he cannot without damage withdraw from the transaction." 2 Williston, Sales 312 (rev. ed. 1948).

As well as making the "law of estoppel" expressly applicable to partnerships, the Uniform Partnership Act as adopted in this State sets forth in more detail the conditions for liability as a partner by estoppel in [UPA section 16] which provides:

> Partner by estoppel—(a) When a person, by words spoken or written, by conduct, or by contract, represents himself, or consents to another representing him to anyone, as a partner in an existing partnership or with one or more persons not actual partners, he is liable to any such person to whom such representation has been made, who has, on faith of such representation, given credit to the actual or apparent partnership, and if he has made such representation or consented to its being made in a public manner, he is liable to such person, whether the representation has or has not been made or communicated to such person so giving credit by or with the knowledge of the apparent partner making the representation or consenting to its being made.

> (1) When a partnership liability results, he is liable as though he were an actual member of the partnership.

(2) When no partnership liability results, he is liable jointly with the other persons, if any, so consenting to the contract or representation as to incur liability, otherwise separately.

Liability by estoppel may result either from defendant Carroll's representation of himself as a partner "by words spoken or written" or "by conduct" or defendant Carroll's "consent" to such a representation by another. The pleadings and answers to interrogatories of Mr. and Mrs. Volkman indicate they may be able to show that Carroll by his oral statements to them and conduct in their presence and by his consent to the representations of McNamee to the Volkmans, some of which were in the presence of Carroll, represented himself as a partner and should be estopped to deny such association. They may be able to show further they relied upon these representations not knowing them to be false and that based upon the representations of Carroll and McNamee, the Volkmans changed their position and were thereby damaged. Defendant has failed to show that there can be no question of fact on the issue of partnership by estoppel.

In addition to an estoppel theory of liability, Carroll may be liable under apparent or ostensible authority, a theory of agency law applicable to partnerships. [UPA 4(3).] There is virtually no difference between estoppel and apparent authority. Both depend on reliance by a third person on a communication from the principal to the extent that the difference may be merely semantic. Despite its title, "Partner by Estoppel," [UPA section 16] "provides for a form of liability more akin to that of apparent authority than to estoppel." Painter, *Partnership by Estoppel*, 16 Vand. L.J. 327, 347 (1963). If this view is taken, the liability of the person seeking to deny partner status is not based on estoppel to deny agency or authority but on the objective theory of contract law, *i.e.*, a person should be bound by his words and conduct. Thus, when Carroll told Mr. Volkman, "I am happy that we will be working with you" and conducted himself as he did in the DP Associates office in the presence of Mr. Volkman, the trier of facts may find he was indicating a willingness to be bound by the statements and acts of McNamee, that Carroll held himself out as a partner of McNamee in DP Associates, that McNamee had apparent authority to act for Carroll and that the Volkmans reasonably relied upon this holding out. If so, he is bound as if he directly dealt with the Volkmans.

It was error for the trial court to grant summary judgment for defendant Carroll. Defendant has not conclusively shown that plaintiffs cannot possibly prove a claim against him because of an estoppel to deny the liability or because of his holding out to the Volkmans of apparent authority in McNamee to act in his behalf as a partner.

Reversed and Remanded.

Notes

1. Why does *Volkman* apply general principles of estoppel and apparent authority *via* UPA section 4 instead of applying only UPA Section 16?

2. RUPA section 308 parallels UPA section 16, except that it calls persons liable under that section "purported partners," rather than "partners by estoppel"(see Professor Painter's analysis referred to in *Volkman*). The only other changes to UPA section 16 are for the purpose of clarification.

E. Additional Problems

11.7. On October 15, 1973, Ricky Clark, then sixteen years old, was watching the demolition of a five-story building located at the intersection of 63rd Street and Harper Avenue in Chicago. Clark watched the work while he stood on the west sidewalk of Harper. The demolition site across the street was owned by the city. The demolition was performed by Virgil Kitchens, subcontractor to Anthony Hall, who was awarded the demolition contract by the city. Kitchens's crane consisted of several vertical crane sections of reinforced angle iron measuring in total about eighty-five feet in height over the control cabin and engine housing. A movable boom of similar construction and measuring about eighty-five feet in length was attached to the base section of the crane. For demolition work, Kitchens used a hinged bucket with teeth known as a clam bucket, which he suspended by cable from the end of the boom. The bucket could bite off brick from the top of a building, and as the crane was rotated, transport it for deposit on the ground. On this day, Kitchens was biting off brick and a portion of a fire escape. The crane was operated from the middle of Harper Avenue. After Kitchens deposited debris on a lot near the building, he raised the bucket about ten feet and started to swing the boom around quickly toward the building. The boom collapsed, and fell toward the west sidewalk. It struck Clark who was about eighty feet from Kitchens. Clark suffered severe injuries. Assuming that sovereign immunity will not bar Clark's action, is the city of Chicago subject to liability for Clark's injuries? *See Clark v. City of Chicago,* 88 Ill. App. 3d 760, 410 N.E.2d 1025 (1980).

11.8. The United States contracted with a joint venture or it to paint and to maintain various radar domes (radomes). The contract contained numerous provisions regarding safety and allocation of responsibility. Under the term of the contract, radome crew members were to have a minimum of one year's actual experience. The contractor was given the responsibility to select and to supervise its employees. The government reserved the right to inspect, to oversee performance of the contract, and to suspend or to terminate the contract, but it was not required to do so. Dennis Rooney was employed by the joint venture without the minimum experience required by the contract and was assigned with three other employees to paint radomes at Mt. Tamalpais Air Force Base in Mill Valley, California. The supervisor of the crew left the jobsite after the first day. An engineering technician for the Air Force was present at the radome site, however, on October 20, 1971, the third day of work at that job, Rooney apparently failed to tie in to the safety line after ascending the dome. He somehow slipped and fell from the fifty-five-foot radome to a catwalk fifteen feet above the ground. He was severely injured. Will the United States have liability for the injuries to Rooney? *See Rooney v. United States,* 634 F.2d 1238 (9th Cir. 1980).

11.9. The plaintiff, Hill, had purchased certain furniture from Grant's that, she testified, showed nicks, scratches, and gouges on delivery. She reported this to Grant's and was assured that someone would be sent to fix it. She then received a call from a man who said he was from Grant's, and an appointment was made. When the defendant, Newman, arrived at her home, he identified himself as the man from Grant's Furniture Store who had come to fix the furniture. She admitted him and he proceeded to repair the defects. The plaintiff said that Newman sprayed the furniture with some "bad smelling stuff"—a lacquer. On completion of the work, the plaintiff followed Newman out the door and remained on the porch talking to a friend. A few minutes later, she reentered her apartment to answer the telephone, and as she picked up the receiver, there was an explosion. The plaintiff's clothes caught on fire, with resultant serious burns to her body. Newman was not a regular employee of Grant's, but was a furniture repairman who was contacted when there were problems with furniture delivered by Grant's. The plaintiff sued Newman, individually and doing business as Nuwood Furniture Service, and Grant's Furniture. Grant's first argues that Newman was an independent contractor and that it is not vicariously liable for his negligence. Will Grant prevail? Why? *See Hill v. Newman,* 126 N.J. Super. 557, 316 A.2d 8 (1973).

Chapter 12

Borrowed Servant Doctrine

A. Liability of Special Employer

A common situation in commercial settings is the presence of two or more employers. For example, contractors undertaking construction projects often bring in "subcontractors" to help with the work. The construction sites are busy places, filled with the employees of the contractor and with the employees of the various subcontractors. The contractor, through its servants, directs and coordinates the activities of all the subcontractors. Thus, both parties are involved in the continued direction and supervision of the work. If the servant of one of the subcontractors causes a tort loss to a plaintiff, will the contractor be liable to the injured person? The contractor will argue it is not liable because the subcontractor was an *independent contractor*. If the plaintiff loses on the independent contractor issue, plaintiff may then argue that the contractor should be liable on the basis that it had "borrowed" the subcontractor's servant.

In cases discussing the "borrowed servant doctrine," the original and regular employer of the servant—the subcontractor in the above scenario—is called the "general employer." The party found to have borrowed the servant—possibly the contractor in the above scenario—is called the "special employer."

Problem 12.1

Herndon owned a bulldozer and employed Flowers to operate it. McCullough, a nearby landowner, asked Flowers to do some work on a ditch. Herndon gave Flowers permission to do the work, but charged McCullough $200. While Flowers was working, McCullough came by and asked him to knock down a tree also. When Flowers knocked down the tree, it fell into a nearby road and into Wilson's path. Assuming that Flowers was negligent in the manner in which he knocked down the tree, is McCullough subject to liability to Wilson on account of Flowers' negligence? *See Wilson v. McCullough,* 180 Ga. App. 579, 349 S.E.2d 751 (1986).

Paoli v. Dave Hall, Inc.

462 A.2d 1094 (Del. Super. 1983)

O'HARA, Judge.

Cross-motions for summary judgment have been advanced by defendant Dave Hall, Inc. ("Hall") and defendants Donald F. Deaven, Inc. ("Deaven") and William C. Zern ("Zern"). The issues upon which the parties seek summary adjudication concern 1) whether Zern, a crane operator in the service of equipment owner Deaven and leased by him to general contractor Hall to operate said crane, was, in fact, a "loaned employee" of the latter during the incident giving rise to this lawsuit, and 2) whether Deaven and Zern are entitled to indemnity from Hall in the event liability for negligence is assessed against them.

The underlying action is one for personal injuries arising in the following manner. In accordance with a contract entered into with E.I. DuPont de Nemours & Company, Hall was in the progress of constructing a pharmacological laboratory in Newark, Delaware. In order to complete the roof of said structure, Hall leased from Deaven a crane to lift prefabricated, triangular shaped trusses onto the perimeter walls. Deaven likewise supplied an operator, Zern, to the job site to man this equipment. In undertaking this construction procedure, Zern placed the trusses along the length of the building's concrete walls, with each truss braced and connected to the adjacent truss.

Midway through this procedure, Hall's foreman instructed Zern to begin depositing plywood bundles on the trusses. The first bundle was placed thereupon without incident; the second, however, was not, and as a result the trusses toppled over and the walls of the building collapsed, injuring plaintiff Dominick A. Paoli, Sr., who was thrown from the scaffolding on which he was standing.[2]

At this juncture there is a factual dispute as to what precisely occurred during placement of the second bundle of trusses [sic] to cause the structure to collapse. Zern explained the incident as follows:

> The bundles were on the outside of the building. I was signaled to pick the bundle up and send it up to the roof, which I did. I got it up to the roof in the position they wanted. They wanted me to lower it on the roof. I lowered it on the roof. And they held me there. I—the bundle was on the roof completely, but I still had the majority of the weight. And at that point they wasn't ready for me to release the full load yet; so I locked the crane in position and waited. They gave me the signal to let it down; I let it down. And I am not sure exactly who was the man unhooking. I released it. He gave me a signal to release it. I give him the weight. He reached up to unhook me. And that's when the trusses fell. So I seen movement, I picked back up on the load, I thought maybe he would hang on to the load. And the building fell. I swung back over, let the plywood down and that was it.

---

2. At the time of the accident, plaintiff was an employee of John W. Walker Construction Co., a sub-contractor of defendant Hall.

Earl Bowman, a Hall employee who witnessed the event, offered a different account of Zern's actions:

> He started to let it down. It got closer to the truss so it looked like he was letting it down and then at the last minute he swung it to the south but at this time it was close enough to the trusses where it must—to come down on this teeter-totter a bit and come down and hit a couple trusses and bounced against them.

The evidence is similarly controverted with respect to Zern's reliance on hand signals from the Hall employees.

On their motion for summary judgment, defendants Deaven and Zern seek to have any liability for negligence assessed against Zern imputed to Hall under the borrowed-servant or loaned employee doctrine. The proper inquiry in determining whether the doctrine is applicable appears in *Richardson v. John T. Hardy & Sons, Inc.*, Del. Supr. 182 A.2d 901 (1962):

> Whether or not a loaned employee becomes the employee of the one whose immediate purpose he serves is always a question of fact, and depends upon whether or not his relationship to the specific employer has the usual elements of the employer-employee status. Fundamentally, it is not important whether or not he remains the employee of the general employer as to matters generally. What is important to determine is, with respect to the alleged negligent act in question, whether or not he was acting in the business of and under the direction of the general or the specific employer. This is almost always determined by which employer has the right to control and direct his activities in the performance of the act allegedly causing the injury, and whose work is being performed.

Furthermore, in the instant case, Hall directs the Court's inquiry to the presumption that an owner of heavy rented equipment, who supplies to the lessor an operator therefor, retains control over the actual operation of the equipment, and in the actual operation thereof, the operator remains the employee of the owner. *Brittingham v. American Dredging Company*, Del. Supr., 262 A.2d 255 (1970).

Although both *Richardson* and *Brittingham* involved the lease of heavy equipment, the above cited presumption was conclusive in neither case; in *Richardson* it did not even attach since the Court found that the negligence charged was not an act of actual operation of the machine. Specifically, *Richardson* involved an action against the lessor of a backhoe for injuries sustained by the lessee's foreman when the side wall of a trench collapsed on him. The Court therein ruled that the alleged negligence of the machine's operator in piling the dirt too close to the trench was not imputable to the lessor, who had furnished [the] operator and paid his wages, where 1) the operator was instructed where and how deep to dig the ditch by the foreman; 2) the foreman staked out the ditch for the operator's guidance; and 3) the foreman directed the operator on which side of the trench to pile the dirt removed. This conclusion was dictated by the fact that the negligence cited was not an act of actual operation of the machine, but rather the act of piling the dirt too close to the mouth of the trench.

The *Brittingham* case, on the other hand, did involve negligent operation of the heavy rental equipment itself. However, *Brittingham* was not an action *against* a lessor for his operator's negligence, but rather a suit brought *by* the owner/lessor against the lessee dredging company for damage to a bulldozer by imputing the operator's alleged negligence to the lessee, presumably under the borrowed servant doctrine. While the Court therein acknowledged the presumption against the owner/lessor of equipment, it further cited evidential considerations which support the presumption as well as those tending to defeat it:

> The evidence in the case at bar is that the plaintiff selected the operator of the machine, retained the right to discharge him, retained the right to determine and supervise the method of operating the machine, paid the operator's wages, and paid for the upkeep and maintenance of the machine. The evidence further shows that defendant could not, and did not, attempt to control the actual operation of the machine; could not discharge the operator but only complain to plaintiff about him and had no responsibility for the upkeep and care of the machine.

Inasmuch as the authority of the lessee therein was limited to instructing the operator as to the area in which he was desired to work and the result he was to accomplish, the *Brittingham* Court declined to impute the operator's negligence to lessee under the borrowed servant doctrine.

Thus, under *Richardson* and *Brittingham*, this Court's inquiry reduces itself to whether the negligence charged involved actual operation of Deaven's crane, in which case there is a presumption that Zern remained the owner's employee for purposes of liability, or some other attendant act involving the control or discretion of Hall or his crew, thereby imputing liability to the lessee under the borrowed servant doctrine. At this juncture, the Court notes that plaintiffs allege that Zern was negligent as follows:

> (a) In operating the crane to lift bundles of plywood sheets from the ground to the level of the then height of the partially constructed building, he allowed one or more of said bundles each weighing approximately 1,500 pounds to drag across and strike trusses which had been installed as part of the construction of said building causing the trusses to topple over and push out the walls of the building;
>
> (b) By placing the bundles of plywood in a concentrated portion of the building resulting in the overloading of the trusses.

The first act articulated above suggests that the negligence occurred in the actual operation of the equipment. However, the latter basis of liability, involving placement of the bundles, indicates negligence in the exercise of judgment or discretion. Moreover there is evidence of record that the placing of plywood bundles was determined by Hall's crew and that operator Zern performed said act at their direction, a situation factually analogous to *Richardson*.

The parties admit that there is a factual dispute as to how the incident occurred; however, Hall asserts that the only material fact is that Zern alone controlled the actual operation of the machine. With that contention the Court does not agree, noting that said fact was not dispositive in *Richardson*.

In sum, the applicability of the borrowed servant doctrine with respect to defendant Zern is an issue ripe for jury determination. Under no circumstances will summary judgment be granted when there is a reasonable indication that a material fact is in dispute.

Notes

1. If, as *Paoli v. Dave Hall, Inc.* indicates, borrowed servant questions depend on the presence or absence of the customary indicators of the master-servant relation, are the factors studied in chapter 8, "Liability for Acts of Independent Contractors," relevant here?

2. In *Progressive Construction v. Indiana & Michigan Electric,* 533 N.E.2d 1279 (Ind. App. 1989), the court set forth the following general tests to determine the liability of the special employer for the negligent acts (there, a collision) of a borrowed servant:

> [T]hree related analyses have been developed:
>
> (1) the "whose business" test which seeks to discern whether the tortfeasor was furthering the business of the special or general employer at the time of the collision;
>
> (2) the "control" test which attempts to determine which employer had the right to control the specific act in question; and
>
> (3) the "scope of business" test which attempts to determine if the work being done by the servant is within the scope of the business of the special employer.

3. Under the facts of Problem 12.1, the trial court entered summary judgment in favor of a landowner (McCullough) who borrowed a bulldozer owned by Herndon and operated by Herndon's servant, Flowers. In *Wilson v. McCullough,* 180 Ga. App. 579, 349 S.E.2d 751 (1986), the summary judgment was upheld on appeal:

> McCullough gave Flowers no instructions with regard to the method or manner he was to use to complete the task, and McCullough exercised no control over when or how Flowers did the work. McCullough was not present when Flowers chose to do the job and when the tree fell.
>
> As noted by the trial court, it was undisputed that Flowers was regularly employed by Herndon. It is clear that Flowers was not a borrowed servant. [McCullough] in no way directed the time, manner, or method Flowers was to use in accomplishing the task at hand. Since, at the time of the injury, Flowers was not subject to McCullough's orders and control and was not liable to be discharged by him for misconduct or disobedience to orders, Flowers was not McCullough's servant.
>
> Rather than a servant, Flowers was more like an independent contractor, one who carried on an independent business and who contracted with McCullough to perform services, answerable only for the result and not under McCullough's control as to time, method, or manner of doing the work.

4. Why would a general employer *both* rent equipment to a third person *and* supply an operator to run the equipment? Suppose the third person instructs the operator to use the equipment in a manner that the operator knows is dangerous. Would the general employer expect the servant to ignore the orders? Should it make any difference whether the general employer is in the *business* of renting equipment/operator teams? *See* Restatement 227 comment c.

5. As indicated in *Paoli v. Dave Hall, Inc.*, even where the putative special employer is found *not* to have borrowed the general employer's servant, the "special employer" may be liable for his or her *own* negligence in selecting, retaining, or supervising the servant.

Parker v. Vanderbilt University

767 S.W.2d 412 (Tenn. App. 1988)

CANTRELL, Judge.

This is a medical malpractice action against multiple defendants. Plaintiff Richard O. Parker emerged from surgery with severe brain damage and has since remained in a coma.

During the evening of June 17, 1984, plaintiff Richard O. Parker was shot in the back with a small caliber handgun as he tried to escape from an armed robber. He was taken to Nashville General Hospital, a hospital operated by the Metropolitan Government of Nashville and Davidson County.

The surgical staff at Nashville General was furnished by Vanderbilt University under a contract with the Metropolitan Government. On the evening in question, Drs. Powell, Kreuger, Alexander and Peacock were on duty in the operating room at General. Sandra Conner, a nurse anesthetist employed by the Metropolitan Government, and Rebecca Murphy, a student nurse anesthetist at the Middle Tennessee School of Anesthesia, provided the anesthesia services in the operation room. Dr. Ildefonso Alcantara headed the department of anesthesia services for General, but he was not present at the hospital on the evening of June 17, 1984.

At the time of his admission, Mr. Parker was able to walk and his vital signs were stable. After an examination in the emergency room, Mr. Parker was taken to the operating room for surgery.

After Mr. Parker was sedated and given oxygen by mask for approximately five minutes, Ms. Murphy inserted an endotracheal tube into Mr. Parker's throat. The tube was to supply oxygen to Mr. Parker during the operation. The complaint alleges that the tube entered Mr. Parker's esophagus rather than his trachea and he was therefore deprived of oxygen for approximately twelve minutes. Within five minutes, Mr. Parker's blood pressure and heart rate dropped dramatically. His abdomen had been opened and the surgical team noticed that his blood was dark and his stomach distended. As his heart rate continued to drop, the anesthetists administered atropine and bicarbonate and one of the surgeons started pressing Mr. Parker's chest to restore circulation. Ms. Conner removed the endotracheal tube and replaced it with another. At approximately the same time, one of the surgeons opened Mr. Parker's chest and started heart massage. Within seven minutes after Mr. Parker's heart rate began to fall, his blood pressure and heart rate were restored. However, during the twelve minute period when his lungs were deprived of oxygen, he suffered severe brain damage.

Mr. Parker, through his next of kin and limited guardian, filed an action against Nashville General Hospital, the Metropolitan Government of Nashville and Davidson County, Vanderbilt University, five Vanderbilt doctors, Sandra Conner, Rebecca Murphy, Middle Tennessee School of Anesthesia, Inc. and Dr. Alcantara.

On October 8, 1986, the trial court dismissed Dr. Alcantara on a motion for summary judgment. The plaintiffs voluntarily dismissed one of the Vanderbilt doctors and, on June 9, 1987, the trial judge dismissed Vanderbilt University and the remaining Vanderbilt doctors on a motion for summary judgment. The plaintiffs then voluntarily dismissed the remaining defendants. An order to that effect was entered by the trial judge on July 29, 1987.

The cause of action asserted by the plaintiffs is described in the complaint as follows:

> As a result of the careless placement of the endotracheal tube and/or failure to recognize the problem and correct it for so long a period of time, Richard O. Parker suffered profound irreversible brain damage.

Thus, the plaintiffs allege two acts of negligence: the first is the misplacement of the tube, and the second is the failure to recognize the problem and to take prompt action to correct it.

The parties disagree as to whether the endotracheal tube was actually misplaced. Although the record in this court does not show that the tube was misplaced, that is one inference to be drawn from the proof on file.

As to all the appellees (Dr. Alcantara, Vanderbilt University, Drs. Powell, Kreuger, Alexander, and Peacock), their responsibility for the misplacement of the tube must result from some theory of vicarious liability. We will deal with that aspect of the case first.

One legal theory by which vicarious liability has been placed on a surgeon is the so-called "Captain of the Ship Doctrine." The analogy was first used in the case of *McConnell v. Williams*, 361 Pa. 355, 65 A.2d 243 (1949), where the court said,

> He [the surgeon] is in the same complete charge of those who are present and assisting him as is the captain of a ship over all on board.

Taken to the extreme, this logic would impose absolute liability on a surgeon for the negligent acts of every person connected with the surgery. However, the facts and holding of *McConnell* do not seem to indicate the beginning of a revolution. The court simply held that there was a factual question for the jury as to whether, under familiar agency principles, the obstetrician could be vicariously liable for the negligence of an assisting intern.

In later cases, the Pennsylvania courts relied on the Captain of the Ship Doctrine to expand the liability of surgeons to acts of subordinates occurring outside of the operating room. But, in more recent cases, the courts in Pennsylvania have redefined the doctrine so that, now, it more nearly resembles the "borrowed servant" concept. In *Collins* [*v. Hand*, 431 Pa. 378, 246 A.2d 398 (1968)], the court said:

> The crucial test in determining whether an employee furnished to another becomes a servant of the one to whom he is loaned is whether he passes under the latter's right of control with regard not only to the work to be done but also as to the manner of performing it.

With the concept taking on so many shades of meaning in the state of its origin, it is not surprising that other states have had difficulty in defining it. While referring to the doctrine in several cases, the Tennessee courts have not attempted to formulate a definition. In two unreported cases, the Western Section of the Court of Appeals has rejected the Captain of the Ship Doctrine after failing to find its precise meaning.

We are of the opinion that the use of the term "Captain of the Ship" with respect to the liability of a surgeon for the negligent acts of others in or around the operating room is unnecessarily confusing and should be avoided. We think the surgeon's liability for the acts of others should rest on the more familiar concepts of master and servant; "[o]perating surgeons and hospitals are subject to the principles of agency law which apply to others." *Sparger v. Worley Hospital, Inc.*, 547 S.W.2d 582, 585 (Tex. 1977).

Under Tennessee law, a master is liable for his servant's negligence solely on the doctrine of respondeat superior. That doctrine is based upon the principle "that the wrong of the [servant] is the wrong of his employer." To hold the master liable, it must be established "that the servant shall have been on the superior's business, acting within the scope of his employment."

When does a master-servant relationship exist? The Tennessee cases indicate that

> the right to control the "result' is not determinative of the existence of the relation of master and servant, but the actual control of means and method is.

Thus, one test employed to determine whether a person is a servant of another involves an inspection of the amount of control exerted over the "means and method" of the work of the putative servant.

An employee of one employer may become the servant of another. The test to determine whether an employee is a loaned servant of another employer was set out in *Gaston v. Sharpe*, 179 Tenn. 609, 168 S.W.2d 784 (1943). In *Gaston*, the court said:

> [A] servant at a particular time may remain under the control of his general employer for some purposes and yet be under the control of a special employer for others. Likewise it sometimes happens that a particular work in which the servant is engaged may be properly considered as the work or business of both the general employer and the special employer.

> The question is difficult. It is considered at some length in Restatement of Agency, 227. We take the following from [the] Restatement as a satisfactory rule:

>> Since the question of liability is always raised because of some specific act done, the important question is not whether or not he remains the servant of the general employer as to matters generally, but whether or not, as to the act in question, he is acting in the business of and under the direction of one or the other. It is not conclusive that in practice he would be likely to obey the directions of the general employer in case of conflict of orders. The question is as to whether it is understood between him and his employers that he is to remain in the allegiance of the first as to a specific act, or is to be employed in the business of and subject to the direction of the temporary employer as to the details of such act. This is a question of fact in each case.

There were four doctors present in the operating room on the night of Mr. Parker's operation. All four were receiving their surgical training through the Vanderbilt University residency program. Dr. Powell was the chief resident in surgery at General. He was in charge of and directed the surgical procedures involving Mr. Parker. Dr. Kreuger, the senior resident in surgery, performed the operation. Drs. Alexander and Peacock assisted the chief resident and the senior resident.

The student nurse, Ms. Murphy, conducted the insertion of the endotracheal tube. She was working under the supervision of Ms. Conner, a certified registered nurse anesthetist. Ms. Murphy was a registered nurse also and a student at Middle Tennessee School of Anesthesia. She had hospital privileges to administer anesthesia and was paid by General for her work. She had performed fifty-two intubations prior to the night in question.

Ms. Murphy and Ms. Conner were working under protocols developed by Dr. Alcantara, the chief of anesthesiology at General. The protocols authorized the anesthetist to administer anesthesia to surgical patients in Dr. Alcantara's absence. In part, the protocol provided:

> A nurse anesthetist shall administer anesthesia to a patient in accordance with the general standard principles of anesthesiology to the best of his/her knowledge and belief, and along the guidelines of the anesthesia services of the Department of Anesthesia, and as directed and/or advised by the anesthesiologist-in-charge, if any.

> The attending physician/surgeon's preference in the way of anesthesia will be honored provided the preferred way of anesthesia is generally compatible with the guideline of the Department of Anesthesia, and the general standard principles of anesthesiology. Otherwise, the nurse anesthetist will proceed with his/her own chosed [sic] way of anesthesia.

> A nurse anesthetist will never be forced to administer anesthesia to a patient against his/her own will based upon a reasonable rationale except that, by the discretion of the attending physician/surgeon with full responsibility, the situation is such that an immediate surgical intervention with anesthesia is warranted regardless of the consequences. In case an anesthesiologist is not available for the above matter, the nurse anesthetist will either follow the attending physician/surgeon's decision or withdraw from the case by his/her own judgment with the exception of an emergency case.

A nurse anesthetist is a highly trained specialist acquiring skills in the course of his or her training that a surgeon does not possess. In this case, the nurse anesthetists were assigned by General Hospital according to a call schedule developed and implemented by the hospital. The surgeons did not select the drugs used to put the patient to sleep nor did they oversee or direct the procedures used by the nurse anesthetists.

If we are correct in the conclusions we have reached in regard to the application of the Captain of the Ship Doctrine, a surgeon is responsible for the negligence of third persons only when those persons are the servants of the surgeon and engaged in the surgeon's business.

Under the general principles we have discussed, the question in this case is whether the surgeon exercised control over the means and method of the nurse

602   AGENCY, PARTNERSHIPS AND LIMITED LIABILITY COMPANIES

anesthetists. This is a question of fact. If the essential facts are undisputed, however, and the movant shows that he is entitled to judgment as a matter of law, summary judgment is proper.

In this case, we are of the opinion that the undisputed facts in the record show that the nurse anesthetists were not the servants of the doctors in the operating room. The doctors did not select the individuals involved in the administration of the anesthesia. They were selected in accordance with the policy of General Hospital. The drugs and procedures used by the nurse anesthetists were governed by hospital policy. The protocol under which the nurse anesthetists operated provided that the administration of anesthesia would be governed by standard principles of the anesthesiology department of the hospital. Any direction by the surgeon would be honored only so long as it was compatible with the guidelines of the Department of Anesthesia. If the two conflicted, the nurse anesthetist must withdraw from the case (except in an emergency).

The plaintiffs rely on the testimony of Dr. Alcantara that in his absence the nurse anesthetist is under the direct control of the surgeon. This conclusion is confirmed by the protocol. Nurse Conner also testified that she considered herself under the direction of the doctors present at the surgery. Ms. Murphy stated that she believed that the doctors could control her actions. However, these statements refer to the general chain of command in the operating room—to the right to control the result, and not to the actual control over the means and method of administering the anesthesia. There is no testimony in this record that the surgeons in the operating room had power over the means and method of inserting the endotracheal tube.

Recent cases from other jurisdictions recognize the distinction we have drawn in this case. In *Fortson v. McNamara*, 508 So. 2d 35 (Fla. 1987), the court said:

> While we agree that a surgical nurse, under the direct supervision of the surgeon, who acts according to the surgeon's specific directions, is certainly the servant of the surgeon, we are not willing to place a nurse anesthetist in this category, particularly where there is no showing that the surgeon directed the procedures to be utilized by the nurse anesthetist or had a genuine opportunity to alter the course of events.

In *Kemalyan v. Henderson*, 45 Wash. 2d 693, 277 P.2d 372 (1954), the court held that a surgeon was not liable as the master of an anesthetist where the anesthetist

> knew considerably more about administering an anesthetic than he did, and he left completely to her discretion the administration of the ether to the plaintiff.

We conclude that the nurse anesthetists in this case were not servants of the surgeons.

The judgment of the court below is affirmed and the cause is remanded to the Circuit Court of Davidson County for any further necessary proceedings.

Notes

1. The question of when a medical professional is another's servant is difficult at best. The Captain of the Ship Doctrine resolves those problems by hold-

ing the surgeon *per se* liable for negligent acts occurring during an operation. Is there a difference between the position of the surgeon in *Parker v. Vanderbilt University* and that of the hospital in *Pamperin v. Trinity Memorial Hospital*, page 536?

2. The Captain of the Ship Doctrine has largely been rejected in favor of the application of general borrowed servant analysis. *See* Price, *The Sinking of the "Captain of the Ship": Reexamining the Vicarious Liability of an Operating Surgeon for the Negligence of Assisting Hospital Personnel*, 10 J. Legal Med. 323 (1989).

B. Liability of the General Employer

Up until now, we have seen the borrowed servant doctrine used as a *sword* by the plaintiff to impose on the special employer liability for the acts of the borrowed servant. The borrowed servant doctrine often is used as a *shield* to protect the *general* employer from liability.

Problem 12.2

Hazlett, a wholesale and retail seller of gasoline, was interested in buying a used truck from Byers Company. Byers Company lent the truck and a driver, Lewis, to Hazlett for one week to demonstrate that the truck would do Hazlett's work. The truck was equipped with three gasoline tanks, which were loaded with gasoline for delivery to a customer. Lewis began unloading the gasoline even though there was an open fire nearby. Some gasoline overflowed and then exploded, killing plaintiff's husband. Is Hazlett subject to liability for the negligence of Lewis? Is Byers Company? *See, Gordon v. S.M. Byers Motor Car Co.*, 309 Pa. 453, 164 A. 334 (1932).

Jefferson Smurfit Corp. v. JBS, Inc.
546 So. 2d 30 (Fla. App. 1989)

SHIVERS, Judge.

Jefferson Smurfit Corporation (Smurfit) appeals the summary judgments against it on its action in negligence.

Smurfit is in the business of manufacturing corrugated boxes. Smurfit contacted Handi-Man Industrial Temporary Help Service (Handi-Man), which is in the business of providing temporary labor, and requested four temporary workers. Handi-Man did not provide a supervisor and did not supervise any of the work performed by the workers. David Lott, the general manager at Handi-Man, stated in an affidavit that Smurfit had the right to (1) control the work assignments, (2) terminate the employment of the workers with or without cause, and (3) establish work hours, breaks, and lunches. He also stated that Handi-Man pays the workers $3.35 an hour for every hour Smurfit assigned and then Handi-Man bills Smurfit for those hours at $5.50 per hour.

When the four workers arrived at Smurfit on April 7, Mr. Holton, the floor supervisor, gave them some brooms and told them to sweep up around the outside of a nearby warehouse. Mr. Holton stated upon deposition that he instructed the men that they were not to smoke inside any building. He stated that after the workers began their tasks, he checked on them about every two hours or so.

Later that morning, the nearby warehouse where two of the workers were working caught fire. Holton said that one of the employees told him that Vincent Singleton had thrown down a cigarette or a match in some of the boxes and then had run off.

After a hearing, summary final judgment was entered in favor of Handi-Man on the negligence count. The court found that

> Vincent Singleton, who allegedly negligently discarded a cigarette causing the destruction by fire of Jefferson Smurfit warehouse and its contents, was the borrowed employee of Jefferson Smurfit.

The question presented by this case is whether the borrowed servant doctrine applies to a borrowing employer as a matter of law when a borrowing employer seeks damages from a temporary labor service resulting from the tortious acts of a worker supplied by the temporary labor service.

In applying the borrowed servant doctrine to attach liability under the theories of respondeat superior and vicarious liability, the Florida Supreme Court held in *Postal Telegraph and Cable Co. v. Doyle*, 123 Fla. 695, 167 So. 358 (1936) that

> [i]t is competent for a principal to loan or farm out his servant to a third party, and if such third party has complete dominion over the servant, and directs his conduct at all times, he will be held responsible for his derelictions even though the principal is paying his salary; but this rule does not hold good if the principal in any way withholds control over him.

Smurfit asserts that it did not have complete dominion over Singleton because Handi-Man chose Singleton for the job, paid Singleton, and could have pulled Singleton off the job. It asserts that Handi-Man hired Singleton and Smurfit hired Handi-Man to provide a service.

> It sometimes happens that one wishes a certain work to be done for his benefit and neither has persons in his [employ] who can do it nor is willing to take such persons into his general service. He may then enter into an agreement with another. If that other furnishes him with the men to do the work and places them under his exclusive control in the performance of it, those men become *pro hac vice* servants of him to whom they are furnished. But, on the other hand, one may prefer to enter into an agreement with another that that other, for a consideration, shall himself perform the work through servants of his own selection, retaining the direction and control of them. In the first case, he to whom the workmen are furnished is responsible for their negligence in the conduct of the work, because the work is his work and they are for the time his workmen. In the second case, he who agrees to furnish the completed work through servants over whom he retains control is responsible for their negligence in the conduct of it, be-

cause, though it is done for the ultimate benefit of the other, it is still, in its doing, his own work. To determine whether a given case falls within the one class or the other we must inquire whose is the work being performed—a question which is usually answered by ascertaining who has the power to control and direct the servants in the performance of their work.

Standard Oil Co. v. Anderson, 212 U.S. 215, 221, 29 S. Ct. 252, 254, 53 L. Ed. 480, 483 (1909). In this [sic] case Standard Oil contracted with a stevedore to load a ship and it provided the stevedore with some of the equipment and the winchman to do so. The winchman was in the general employ of Standard Oil which hired him, paid him, and could discharge him. A gangman and others were employed by the stevedore. The Court found that the winchman, who negligently failed to observe a gangman's signals in the lowering of oil cases into a ship's hold, was the rightful employee of Standard Oil under the facts of the case. The Court stated that the winchman's obedience with the gangman's signals was more a cooperation with one large, general task than it was evidence of subordination to the stevedore's gangman. The Court concluded that

> the mere fact that a servant is sent to do work pointed out to him by a person who has made a bargain with his master does not make him that person's servant; more than that is necessary to take him out of the relation established by the only contract which he has made, and to make him a voluntary subject of a new sovereign.

Though *Standard Oil* is not directly controlling on the instant issue, its instruction guides our conclusion that the question of whether Singleton was under the control and direction of Smurfit, for purposes of applying the borrowed servant doctrine to immunize Handi-Man, was a question that presented a material issue of fact which cannot be disposed of by summary judgment.

REVERSED and REMANDED.

Notes

1. Would the result in *Jefferson Smurfit Corp. v. JBS, Inc.,* have been different if Singleton (the Handi-Man temporary worker) had negligently injured a third person while working at Smurfit? Could Singleton's act be within the scope of employment of *both* Smurfit and Handi-Man?

2. In *Jefferson Smurfit Corp. v. JBS, Inc.,* the court indicates that the special employer must have assumed *complete* control over the borrowed servant before *either* the special employer will become liable *or* the general employer will be relieved of liability. Is that consistent with *Paoli v. Dave Hall, Inc.,* and *Parker v. Vanderbilt University?*

3. In *Charles v. Barrett,* 233 N.Y. 127, 137 N.E. 199 (1922), Steinhauser, who was in the trucking business, leased Adams Express Company, the defendant, a van and a driver ("chauffeur"). Adams Express loaded the van and sealed it at the point of departure and unsealed and unloaded it at the point of destination. While the chauffeur was driving the van in between, the van struck and killed the plaintiff's son. The court held that truck and driver were not borrowed servants, but remained in the general employer's service:

In between the point of departure and destination, the truck remained in the charge of the chauffeur without interference or supervision. There was no such change of masters as would relieve Steinhauser of liability if the driver of the van had broken the seals and stolen the contents. By the same token, there was no such change as to relieve liability for other torts committed in the conduct of the enterprise. Where to go and when to go could be determined for the driver by [Adam Express'] commands. The duty of going carefully, for the safety of the van as well as for that of wayfares, remained a duty to the master at whose hands he had received possession. Neither the contract nor its performance shows a change of control so radical as to disturb that duty or its incidence. The rule now is that as long as the employee is furthering the business of his general employer by the service rendered to another, there will be no inference of a new relation unless command has been surrendered and no inference of its surrender from the mere fact of its division.

4. Is it possible for the general and special employers to *share* control of a single servant, so that *both* can be held liable for the servant's tort within the scope of both employments?

Strait v. Hale Construction Co.

26 Cal. App. 3d 941, 103 Cal. Rptr. 487 (1972)

KERRIGAN, Associate Justice.

Two lawsuits were filed against three defendants as a result of a collision between a tractor (earthmover) and a truck on September 6, 1966, at the intersection of Route 115 and Allbright Street in the County of Imperial. The truck driver (Oliver Strait) was seriously injured in the collision and sued to recover damages for his injuries. The truck owner (Topham & Sons, a corporation) sued for the property damage to its truck. The earthmover was owned by a farmer (William E. Young, Jr.) and was being operated by his employee (Miguel Hurtado). Young had let the tractor and the operator (Hurtado) to a road construction firm (Hale Construction Company, as co-partnership). At the time of the accident, the road builder (Hale) was converting Allbright Street from a dirt road to a paved street.

The two actions against the farmer, the tractor operator and road builder (Young, Hurtado and Hale) were consolidated for trial. The jury awarded the truck driver $225,700 and the truck owner $8,603 against all defendants. This appeal ensued.

The crucial problem involves the vicarious liability, if any, of the general employer (Young) and the special employer (Hale) for the negligence of the borrowed servant (Hurtado). The general employer claims that the court erred in instructing the jury as a matter of law that he was liable for the loaned servant's negligence. The special employer claims that the trial court erred in denying its motions for nonsuit, directed verdict and judgment notwithstanding the verdict and in leaving the issue of vicarious liability to the jury.

Hale Construction Company is a firm specializing in road and airport work. It entered into a contract with the County of Imperial and the federal government to do the work on Allbright Street. The job consisted of preparing Allbright Street for eventual hardtop surfacing. This required excavating dirt from some areas and building-up other areas which, in turn, required the use of earthmoving machines commonly called rigs.

After the road firm undertook the Allbright Street job, it found it was falling behind in its work schedule. Hale was under a completion deadline with a penalty of $100 per day. Initially, Hale had the use of 3 John Deere 50-10 tractors (earthmovers or rigs). One was owned by Hale and operated by its own employee. The other two were rented, with the operators being provided by the equipment owners. Someone told Hale that Young owned a 50-10 tractor. To accelerate construction, Hale contacted Young about letting the rig with an operator.

Young is a farmer living near Calipatria in Imperial County. He uses the earthmover in connection with his extensive farming operations. He had never leased out the rig or operator prior to being contacted by the road builder. Inasmuch as the machine was not then being utilized in farming operations, he agreed to rent the rig and supply Hurtado as the operator for $18 an hour. Young was to pay Hurtado $5 an hour to operate the rig from the $18 hourly rental.

In addition to a construction superintendent, the Allbright Street job was under the direct supervision of Raymond Hale, a general partner and officer of Hale Construction Company. Hale had a grade checker located at the place where the dirt was to be removed by the various tractor operators, as well as a dump boy at the site where the dirt was to be deposited by them. The grade checker would tell the rig operators where to cut and how deep to cut and the dump boy instructed them where and how to deposit the removed dirt. In removing and dumping the earth, it was necessary for the rigs to cross Route 115—a through highway—where it intersects with Allbright. Entrances to the highway on both sides of Allbright were posted with stop signs. In hauling dirt from a removal point west of the intersection to the dumpsite at a point east of the intersection, Hurtado collided with the truck being driven by Strait and owned by Topham & Sons which was proceeding north on Route 115.

Turning to the legal aspects of the two lawsuits, cases involving the application of the *loaned servant rule* have not always been uniform in the results obtained. This observation is not new or novel. In 1928, an illustrious jurist came to the same conclusion when he wrote: "The law that defines or seeks to define the distinction between general and special employers is beset with distinctions so delicate that chaos is the consequence. No lawyer can say with assurance in any given situation when one employment ends and the other begins. The wrong choice of defendants is often made, with instances, all too many, in which justice has miscarried." Cardozo, A Ministry of Justice, [1921] 35 Harv. L. Rev. 113, 121. The passage of time has not eliminated the confusion. Courts have refused to attempt to differentiate and harmonize the case law on the grounds that to do so would merely add to the confusion; for the most part, the decisions have been characterized as irreconcilable.

The difficulty in determining the issue as to whether the general employer or the special employer, or both, should be liable for the tort of the loaned servant arose out of the test governing its application. In determining the vicarious liability issue, the courts have uniformly applied the *test of control*, i.e., which employer had actual control or the right of control—the power to direct the borrowed servant in the details of the work at the time the tort occurred? In adopting the control theory and in weighing the elements of control, courts were inexorably driven to the expedience of making and accepting disparate refinements, ethereal in substance and revolting in reason, in order to reach any semblance of reconciliation of the results flowing from the borrowed servant cases.

As in other jurisdictions, California courts applied the control test with varying results. In 1922, it was held that when a master (general employer) hires out under a rental agreement the services of his employee (loaned servant) for the operation of an instrumentality owned by the master, together with the use of the instrumentality, without relinquishing to the hirer (special employer) the power to discharge such servant, the legal presumption is that, although the hirer directs the servant where to go and what to do in the performance of the work, the servant who is the operator of the instrumentality employed in the doing of the work, remains, in the absence of an agreement to the contrary, the servant of the general employer insofar as concerns the manner and method of operating the instrumentality, and the general employer is solely liable for the servant's negligence in the operation of such instrumentality. *Billig v. Southern Pacific Co.*, 189 Cal. 477, 485–486, 209 P. 241. In accord are other authorities holding that if the special employer does not have power to discharge the servant even though he directs the servant where to go and what to do in performance of the work, the servant, as operator of the instrumentality employed in the doing of the work, remains the employee of the general employer, with the latter being responsible under the doctrine of respondeat superior for the servant's negligence.

Conversely, the proposition has been propounded that an employee may be the general servant of one person and may be hired to another for a special service, and when he is subject wholly to the direction and control of the special employer, the latter, not the general employer, is liable for the borrowed servant's negligence; but to escape liability for the negligence of a servant whose services have been rented or hired to another, the general employer must resign full control of the servant for the time being. In those cases where the special employer may be liable, the paramount consideration is whether the alleged special employer exercises control of the details of the work; such control strongly supports an inference that a special employment exists. If one employer hires out either the services of his employee to another employer or rents an instrumentality and an employee to operate it, the second or special employer may become temporarily liable for his tortious actions under the "borrowed servant" rule.

With the development of the borrowed servant doctrine, another line of cases appeared suggesting that instead of imposing liability solely on the general employer or only on the special employer, a third alternative should be considered, to wit, both could be held liable. Under these authorities, the control factor was still utilized as the primary test in determining vicarious liability. A general and special employer may both be held liable for the employee's negligence where each had some power, not necessarily complete, of direction and control; the control need not be exercised; it is deemed sufficient if the right to direct the details of the work existed. Where, at the time of the accident, both the general and the special employer exerted some measure of control over the employee, both may be held liable for the employee's negligence.

Consequently, three possible results have flowed from the application of the control test in the borrowed servant cases: (1) liability of the general employer; (2) liability of the special employer; and (3) liability of both employers.

Capably recognizing the inconsistencies in the decisions resulting from the application of the control test in the loaned servant cases, Young (general employer) claims that the trial court committed serious error in ruling, as a matter of law, that he was responsible for Hurtado's negligence. Young predicates his claim of error on the evidence indicating that he did not exercise any control over Hurtado on the Allbright Street job and, in fact, never visited the job or gave the rig operator any instructions or directions whatsoever, except to follow Hale's orders. Similarly, Hale (special employer) claims that its firm did not exercise any significant control over Hurtado so as to be vicariously responsible for his tort. In support of its argument, Hale contends that the essential element of control is the right to discharge the employee, as contrasted with the giving of mere information or general signals as to where the instrumentality should be used, and that it did not have the right to fire Hurtado.

Turning first to Hale's contention, the paving firm relies on *Billig v. Southern Pacific Co.*, and its progeny, holding that where a special employer does not enjoy the right to discharge the borrowed servant, only the general employer is liable for his negligence. While the *Billig* court held that the special employer was not liable under the doctrine of respondeat superior, in doing so, it utilized the following language:

> [T]he application of the doctrine of respondeat superior in any given case depends upon the power of control which the superior possesses, and which for the protection of third persons he is required to exercise, over the conduct and activities of his subordinates. Consequently the doctrine has application only in cases where the power of control exists, and such power does not exist in a situation where the special employer has no voice in the selection or retention of the negligent subordinate.

In answer to Hale's argument to the effect that it did not possess the power to discharge Hurtado and that its checker and dump boy merely gave him signals or directions as to where to remove the dirt and where to deposit it, it should be emphasized that if the ultimate determination of liability in borrowed servant cases is controlled by the doctrine of respondeat superior, then the policy considerations underlying respondeat superior must also be examined.

As early as 1947, the California Supreme Court defined the public policy factors underlying an employer's vicarious liability in the following terms:

> The principle justification for the application of the doctrine of respondeat superior in any case is the fact that the employer may spread the risk through insurance and carry the cost thereof as part of his costs of doing business.

Johnston v. Long, 30 Cal. 2d 54, 64, 181 P.2d 645, 651. Twenty-three years later, the same court amplified the policy factors underlying the doctrine imposing liability without fault in *Hinman v. Westinghouse Elec. Co.*, 2 Cal. 3d 956, 959–960, 471 P.2d 988, in the following language:

> Although earlier authorities sought to justify the respondeat superior doctrine on such theories as "control' by the master of the servant, the

master's "privilege' in being permitted to employ another, the third party's innocence in comparison to the master's selection of the servant, or the master's "deep pocket' to pay for the loss, "the modern justification for vicarious liability is a rule of policy, a deliberate allocation of a risk. The losses caused by the torts of employees, which as a practical matter are sure to occur in the conduct of the employer's enterprise, are placed upon that enterprise itself, as a required cost of doing business. They are placed upon the employer because, having engaged in an enterprise which will, on the basis of past experience, involve harm to others through the torts of employees, and sought to profit by it, it is just that he, rather than the innocent injured plaintiff, should bear them; and because he is better able to absorb them, and to distribute them, through prices, rates or liability insurance, to the public, and so to shift them to society, to the community at large.'

In an expert critique, a legal source points out why the control justification for liability should be discarded in the dual employer situation just as it has been abandoned in the single employer situation. In the case of a borrowed servant, both the general employer and special employer share control; while the general employer can fire the employee, the special employer can dismiss him from the particular job; while the general employer can direct the borrowed servant in the general use of the instrumentality, the special employer directs him on the particular aspects of the job at hand; control is thus actually split and it is a test without meaning. *Borrowed Servants and the Theory of Enterprise Liability*, [1967] 76 Yale L.J. 807; *see also* Smith, *Scope of the Business: The Borrowed Servant Problem*, [1940] 38 Mich. L. Rev. 1222, 1228–31.

Liability in borrowed servant cases involves the exact public policy considerations found in sole employer cases. Liability should be on the persons or firms which can best insure against the risk, which can best guard against the risk, which can most accurately predict the cost of the risk and allocate the cost directly to the consumers, thus reflecting in its prices the enterprise's true cost of doing business.

Control, then, at least in the narrow sense suggested by Hale, is not dispositive of this case. The theory having greater integrity in respondeat superior cases is allocation of risk.

In light of the policy factors underlying respondeat superior, it is inconceivable that Hale should escape liability. A special employment relationship with Hurtado was conclusively established. Obviously, the resurfacing work being accomplished was within the regular scope of Hale's business. Hale was to profit from this job. Hale understood the risks inherent in construction work and was in a position to guard against, and insure against, such risks. Consequently, Hale was not at all prejudiced by the trial court's ruling allowing the question of its liability to go to the jury. To the contrary, the court could have instructed the jury, in view of the foregoing policy factors, that the road builder was vicariously liable for Hurtado's negligence as a matter of law.

Finally, Young (general employer) urges that the trial court committed prejudicial error in ruling as a matter of law that Hurtado was his agent at the time of the accident. He contends the facts of the case are susceptible to more than one inference as to the relationship between him [*sic*] and Hurtado, and the agency issue therefore required jury resolution.

For an employer to be vicariously liable for the negligent acts of his servant, the servant must have been acting within the scope of his duties. Young seems to contend that when Hurtado was working for Hale, he was not necessarily working for Young. But as Young concedes, an employee can have more than one employer, both of whom may be simultaneously liable for a negligent act of the employee.

This is just such a case, Young owned the tractor and was profiting from the renting of the rig, as well as Hurtado's employment with Hale. Young reserved the right to dismiss Hurtado. This analysis of Young's liability does not contradict the earlier discussion holding Hale liable despite previous case law that may not have held Hale liable. In those cases the court held the general employer liable as a matter of law. The language questioned previously in those cases does not bear on that issue, but whether the special employer should also be liable. Their holdings as to the general employer's initial liability are sound.

Young urges he should not be liable to the plaintiffs inasmuch as he is not in the business of renting heavy equipment and furnishing an operator. But the policy factors heretofore discussed weigh as heavily on Young as on Hale. While Young is a farmer and not directly engaged in letting construction equipment and providing an operator, his agriculture venture can be equated with any other enterprise engaged in business for profit. Farming in California can be big business. Tractors are driven on highways frequently and infrequently in agriculture production. One cannot expect to put a $25,000 rig and driver to work on a public highway—a place fraught with danger—without incurring liability for the operator's negligence. If Young did not feel he had sufficient control of the working conditions or sufficient knowledge of the construction business to guard against the risks, he could have contracted for specific indemnity or obtained the appropriate liability insurance.

In conclusion, it should be parenthetically noted that Hale (special employer) and Young (general employer) have filed cross-complaints against the other based on implied indemnity. In any future trial, the joint tortfeasors will then be accorded the opportunity to show, on equitable principles, why the other should be held primarily liable for Hurtado's negligence. In this connection, Young argues that Hale should have had a flagman on duty to warn drivers on Route 115 of the construction work being done on Allbright Street and of the heavy equipment crossing the main highway, or a flagman to direct the rig operator's crossing the highway, and that the failure to provide a flagman was the actual and proximate cause of this accident. Assuming, without deciding, that Hale had such a duty or assuming that even if Hale had no such duty, Young will have an opportunity to establish in his action for indemnity that Hale was primarily responsible for the injuries and damages incurred by the plaintiffs herein, particularly in view of the evidence indicating Young played a passive role in the events culminating in plaintiffs' damages. However, the merits of the indemnity actions are not before us and patently cannot be resolved in this appeal.

The judgment is affirmed.

Notes

1. In *DePratt v. Sergio,* 102 Wis. 2d 141, 306 N.W.2d 62 (1981), the court addressed the question of whether borrowed servant liability should necessarily

be an either-or question, with only *one* of the general and the special employers liable:

> Under the borrowed servant rule, the borrowing master, not the loaning master, is liable for the negligent acts of a loaned servant if the loaned servant becomes the servant of the borrowing master. This result is reached even though the loaned servant remains in the employ of the loaning master and is acting within the scope of his employment with the loaning master. Thus when a servant is loaned, either the loaning master or the borrowing master, not both masters, will be held vicariously liable for the servant's tort.

[T]he circuit court concluded that the [servant] had become the employee of [the borrowing employer], so that only [the borrowing employer] bore liability for the [servant's] negligent conduct.

On appeal from an order and a portion of the judgment the court of appeals affirmed. We granted review to decide an issue not specifically presented to the circuit court or to the court of appeals: Should Wisconsin abandon the borrowed servant rule and adopt the concept of dual liability. Under the dual liability approach, which the plaintiff urges us to adopt, both the borrowing employer and the loaning employer may be held liable in tort to a third party who sustains injuries caused by the negligence of the loaned employee when the loaning employer retains broad control over the loaned employee (such as the right to discharge the employee) and the borrowing employer has control over the details of the loaned employee's work.

The plaintiff attacks the borrowed servant rule on two grounds: first, that the borrowed servant rule is theoretically unsound, i.e., that an underlying premise of the borrowed servant rule is difficult to apply.

The plaintiff contends that the borrowed servant rule is premised on the concept that the master who has control over the servant and derives benefit from the servant should be exclusively liable for the negligent acts of the loaned servant. This premise, that one master can thus be selected to be exclusively liable for the torts of the servant, is weak because both the borrowing and loaning masters have some control over the servant; the loaned servant acts within the scope of employment of both masters; and both masters derive some benefit from the servant's work. Calling our attention to this weakness, the plaintiff asserts that justice and common sense indicate that an equitable system for allocating responsibility and liability between the two masters should replace the current rule imposing exclusive liability on one of the masters. Under the entrepreneur or enterprise theory of liability both employers should be responsible to the injured party because both exercise a degree of control, both profit from the employee's conduct, and both are capable of planning for and transferring the losses incurred. Under the dual liability approach the injured party, for whom the doctrine of respondeat superior was designed, would enjoy greater assurance of recovery.

The plaintiff further contends that the borrowed servant rule is difficult to apply. The plaintiff argues that when the tests to determine whether a loaned servant becomes the servant of the borrowing master are applied to particular fact situations, the results are not predictable or consistent. We acknowledge that this criticism is well founded. We have said that while the tests or rule to determine whether a loaned employee retains employment with his original employer or becomes the employee of the borrowing employer

> are readily comprehensible, when applied to specific factual situations, the distinctions are sometimes slight and the decisions well-nigh irreconcilable.

We concede that the traditional borrowed servant rule has deficiencies in theory and in application. We conclude, however, that the dual liability approach, although having some merit, does not offer a simple and easily applicable alternative to the borrowed servant rule, and we decline to substitute it for the present rule. If we were to adopt the dual liability approach as explained and urged by the plaintiff, the courts would have to decide when each employer retained sufficient control—or when each employer retained sufficient indicia of the master-servant relation—to subject that employer to liability for the negligent conduct of the loaned employee. Similarly courts would have to decide how responsibility and liability should be allocated to each employer. One way of allocating responsibility and liability between the employers is on the basis of their degree of control over the employee's conduct. This dual liability control test might prove similar to the borrowed servant control test used now to determine which employer is exclusively liable.

We have found no support nor have we been furnished any authority to suggest that the dual liability approach would afford greater certainty or precision in its application than the current approach. It appears that the preferred replacement would create a new area of uncertainty in the law and might force a change in business practices of borrowing and loaning employers, the purchase of additional insurance, and the negotiation of indemnity agreements. Also the dual liability approach might, instead of diminishing unfairness, add unfairness in an already troubled area. For example, if we were to adopt the dual liability approach in the instant case and view both [the loaning and the borrowing employers] as liable to the injured plaintiff for the tort of the [servant], [the loaning employer] would have to pay the entire judgment. [The borrowing employer's] liability to the injured plaintiff, an employee of [the borrowing employer], is limited to worker's compensation benefit; [the loaning employer] could not require contribution from [the borrowing employer] even if [the borrowing employer] was substantially more at fault than [the loaning employer]. Until a more satisfactory solution is developed as to the liability of the borrowing and loaning employers for the torts of a loaned employee than the broadly stated dual liability approach urged by the plaintiff, we decline to abandon the borrowed servant rule which, although troublesome, has been followed by this court for many years.

Decision of the court of appeals affirmed.

2. In the cases so far considered, the courts have focused on the question of which possible employer had *actual control* of the servant's acts at the time of the tort. Is the master's responsibility in respondeat superior for the torts of the

servant committed within the scope of employment based on the master's control or the master's *right* of control? May both the general and the special employers have the right to control the borrowed servant's conduct?

City of Somerset v. Hart
549 S.W.2d 814 (Ky. 1977)

LUKOWSKY, Justice.

This is an appeal by the Hospital and its alter ego, the City, from their share of a $28,144.38 malpractice judgment in favor of Hart. The verdict of the jury apportioned the recovery forty percent or $11,257.75 against the operating surgeon and sixty percent or $16,886.63 against the Hospital and the City. The surgeon has paid his share and gone forth rejoicing.

In July of 1970 Hart was afflicted with a kidney stone. Surgery was indicated and Hart was admitted to the Hospital.

Hart was taken to the operating room and given a general anesthetic. The surgeon opened his abdomen and exposed the ureter and bladder. After the stone was removed, the surgeon closed. This is the first time Hart had undergone abdominal surgery.

Hart's hospital recuperation was uneventful. He was seen by his surgeon postoperatively at four and six weeks and discharged. On each occasion he complained of pain and was told that this was not abnormal. For about three months the pain remitted and then it exacerbated. In August of 1971 he was referred to another surgeon who examined him and took x-rays. The x-rays revealed a bladder stone from which a scalpel blade protruded. A second major operation was performed and the stone and blade were removed.

Obviously, the part of the Hospital in the first operation becomes the subject of scrutiny.

The Hospital supplied the operating room and staffed it with a supervisor, a scrub nurse and a circulating nurse. This staff was selected, paid and generally supervised by the Hospital. The staff was required to set up the room, lay out the instruments, including scalpels with blades attached, hand instruments to the surgeon and generally assist him during the operation. The operating surgeon was authorized to supervise and direct the staff in the operating room.

The Hospital supplied the instruments in the form of an instrument pack. This pack is a set of instruments of a type and number prescribed by the Hospital sufficient to perform the operation scheduled by the surgeon. The packs are assembled by employees of the Hospital. The rules of the Hospital do not require that the number of instruments be verified by their operating room staff by either a preoperation or preclosing instrument count. However, the Hospital does require its operating room staff to make a post operation count at the time the instruments are cleaned, to keep count of the number of scalpel blades used and to report any deficiency. No such report was made here either to the hospital administration or the operating surgeon.

The only assignment of error by the Hospital worthy of discussion is that the operating room staff are the borrowed servants of the surgeon and that the Hospital as their general employer is not liable for their negligence. Hart's response to this assignment of error is that there is distinction between administrative and medical acts, that the Hospital is the master in regard to administrative and medical acts, that the surgeon is the master in regard to medical acts, and that the failure to account for a scalpel blade is an administrative omission chargeable to the Hospital. The parties rely on a plethora of cases, most of which are discussed in an annotation, "Liability of Hospital for Negligence of Nurse Assisting Operating Surgeon," 29 A.L.R.3d 1065 (1970). We find both submissions to be superficial.

The borrowed servant doctrine frequently rears its head in malpractice cases primarily because of the relationship between hospital employees and attending staff physicians and surgeons. In few other areas where the doctrine of respondeat superior may be potentially applicable is the issue of control as crucial or as difficult to resolve as it is in many of the doctor-hospital relationships. Although hospital employees are primarily servants of the hospital and not of the doctor the familiar rule of agency law that a servant may serve two masters simultaneously, and at times only momentarily, comes into play when interns, nurses or other hospital personnel assist a physician or surgeon as he treats a patient. Restatement of Agency 2d, Secs. 226, 227 (1957).

A dangerous tendency exhibited in some of the borrowed servant malpractice cases is to blindly hold that because a nurse or other hospital employee was lent to a physician or surgeon so as to render him liable under the doctrine of respondeat superior for the employee's negligence, the hospital by reason of the loan necessarily ceased to be liable. Sometimes, even though the question may be left to the jury as to which was liable, doctor or hospital, the assumption is clearly that only one of them could have been liable because the hospital employee could not simultaneously have been the servant of both. This is to ignore the legal principle that a person may be the servant of two masters, not joint employers, at one time as to one act, if the service to one does not involve the abandonment of the service to the other. Restatement of Agency, 2d, Sec. 226 (1957).

Frequently, if not most often, the hospital nurse or other employee who is temporarily lent to the physician or surgeon, in every realistic sense continues to carry on her hospital duties. Her work is of mutual interest to both of two employers, the physician or surgeon and the hospital, and is performed to effect their common purpose. The doctrine of respondeat superior is therefore equally applicable to both employers.

The failure of courts to more generally perceive this is probably due to an unarticulated feeling that it would be unjust to impose liability on the hospital where the nurse has only obeyed the orders of her superior, the physician or surgeon. We recognize that the nurse's duty to obey such orders exculpates her and her hospital employer from responsibility for the results of the competent execution of the orders, unless the orders are so obviously improper that the ordinarily prudent nurse would not obey them. When exculpation is the result, it is so because the nurse's obedience to the orders does not constitute negligence, and consequently, there is no basis for vicarious liability of the hospital. This is far different from a general and uncritical elimination of the hospital's liability under the doctrine of respondeat superior solely because the nurse or other employee was lent to the physician or surgeon.

It is beyond cavil in this case that the accurate accounting for scalpel blades is "of mutual interest to both" the surgeon and the hospital, that such an accounting "effects their common purpose," i.e., the cure of the patient, and that the surgeon issued no orders to the operating room staff in regard to the accounting for scalpel blades which conflicted with those of the Hospital. Consequently, the operating room staff acted as servants of both the surgeon and the hospital as a matter of law.

The judgment is affirmed.

Notes

1. Courts are increasingly applying Restatement section 226, especially in the hospital context. *See* Reuter, *Toward a More Realistic and Consistent Use of Respondeat Superior in the Hospital*, 29 St. Louis U.L.J. 601 (1985).

2. Consider, for example, In *Gordon v. S.M. Byers Motor Car Co.*, 309 Pa. 453, 164 A. 334 (1932), the court applied Restatement section 226. Under facts of Problem 12.2, the court held that both general employer, Byers Company, and the special employer, Hazlett, were liable for the negligence of the drive of a gasoline tank truck, Lewis:

> While manipulating the mechanism on the truck, Lewis was acting in the course of his employment and instructions, actual or implied, from Byers Company as part of the demonstration of the performance of the truck. In his efforts to deliver the gasoline to Hazlett's customer, he was carrying out Hazlett's instructions. Thus, Lewis, in the sale service of Byers Company as demonstrator, was transferred to the service of Hazlett to also do his work as directed by him. The employment involved a double service. Hazlett testified that he had direction and control over Lewis only for the delivery of the gasoline. While demonstrating the truck, Lewis was assisting in making a sale of the truck for the Byers Company. He was acting for both parties according to their common understanding; the power of control as to one part of his work was in Byers Company and, so to the other part, in Hazlett.

> The next question is whether Lewis's acts that resulted in the explosion were performed on behalf of both? Was he acting pursuant to directions from each? He was promoting the interest of Byers Company in manipulating the machinery on the truck to cause the gasoline to flow, for obviously, if the mechanism on the truck would not discharge the load, Hazlett would not wish to purchase the truck. Lewis was also complying with specific instructions in delivering the gasoline. The Byers Company controlled Lewis as demonstrator for the purpose of selling the truck, and Hazlett controlled him in delivering the gasoline. While breach of Lewis's duty to either alone would not have involved the other in responsibility for damage, he was negligent in doing an act for the account of both; they are joint tortfeasors.

3. *Ward. v. Gordon*, 999 F.2d 1399 (9th Cir. 1993) involved an active-duty U.S. Army physician (Gordon) assigned to a private hospital for a surgical residency.

> The key consideration [in determining whether Gordon has become the Hospital's borrowed servant] is whether the Hospital had "control in fact or the right to control [Gordon's] physical conduct in the performance of his duties." *See [Pichler v. Pacific Mechanical Constructors,* 1 Wash. App. 447, 462 P.2d 960, 963 (1969)].

The problem is that Gordon's duties were multifaceted. He was responsible for assisting or performing surgical/clinical procedures as assigned by and under the supervision of members of the staff of Children's Hospital, and at the same time, Gordon quite literally had a duty to his country: to complete satisfactorily the residency program. Fortunately for Gordon, his duties were such that they could be discharged concurrently.

The district court found that Gordon was acting as a borrowed servant at the time of the alleged negligence. The United States assigned Gordon to the residency program at Children's and had the right to recall him. Gordon's immediate supervision in the performance of his duties as a surgical resident, however, came from employees of the Hospital, not from military personnel. The fact that Gordon remained subject to the Uniform Code of Military Justice and could be recalled by the Army does not undermine the district court's conclusion.

The district court did not err in concluding that Gordon was a borrowed servant under Washington law.

V.

The district court erred, however, in its analysis of the consequences that flow from Gordon's borrowed servant status. According to the district court, Gordon necessarily exceeded the scope of his employment with the government by acting as the Hospital's servant. Not so. Military personnel act within the scope of their government employment if they act "in the line of duty." 28 U.S.C. § 2671. "'Line of duty' is defined in turn by the applicable state law of respondeat superior."

Gordon acted precisely and only as the government expected and required him to act. Gordon cannot be said to have exceeded the scope of his government employment or to have acted other than in the line of duty merely because he acted in the interests of Children's Hospital. The interests of Gordon's other "master," the United States Government, were not compromised, but rather were furthered—and furthered in a foreseeable and foreseen manner—by Gordon's service to the hospital. Gordon acted within the scope of his government employment. The Liability Reform Act therefore requires substitution of the United States in place of Gordon as a party defendant. 28 U.S.C. s 2679(b)(1).

VI.

We next consider how Gordon's status as a borrowed servant of Children's Hospital affects Ward's ability to recover from the United States. The district court apparently assumed that Gordon's status necessarily would preclude a finding that the United States is liable for his negligence. This assumption is invalid. Although a "lending employer" such as the United States can escape liability for the negligence of a "loaned" servant, nothing in the law of Washington compels that result. Washington law recognizes that an individual simultaneously can be the servant of both the "lending" and the "borrowing" master.

"A person may be the servant of two masters, not joint employers, at one time as to one act, if the service to one does not involve abandonment of the service to the other." Restatement (Second) of Agency § 226 (1957). Where, as here, a servant acts within the scope of his employment for both masters, both may "be responsible for an act which is a breach of duty to one or both of them." Restatement (Second) of Agency § 226 cmt. a (1957).

On remand, the district court ultimately may be called upon to determine whether Gordon's status as a borrowed servant of Children's Hospital may be used by the Government as a shield to its own liability. If so, the Government likely will find itself in the difficult and unenviable position of arguing that although Gordon acted in furtherance of the government's business and in the "line of duty," he nevertheless "abandoned" his service to the government, see Restatement (Second) of Agency s 226. Prudential concerns constrain us from addressing that argument today.

999 F.2d 1402–04.

C. Additional Problems

12.3 On October 31, 1967, plaintiff appellee, Hiroshi Nakagawa, an employee of Johnson Pacific Company (Johnson Pacific), was working on the roof of the Maui Community College Building when he was struck by a bucket of cement. The cement bucket was being lifted to the roof of the building by a crane owned by the defendant appellant, Helen Apana, and operated by Rusty Apana. Rusty's signalman was Joseph Kaiwi. Both Kaiwi and Rusty Apana were the defendant's employees. Suit was filed against the owner of the crane for the negligence of its employees on the theory of respondeat superior. The defendant was the general employer of Kaiwi and Rusty Apana. Kaiwi and Apana were paid wages by the defendant. The defendant rented two cranes to Johnson Pacific with four employees to operate them, two operators and two signalmen. The defendant's employees maintained and operated the cranes. Both Kaiwi and Apana were trained in their particular operations of crane operator and signalmen. The training was conducted at the defendant's yard with the defendant's equipment. The manner in which Kaiwi and Apana operated the crane was left entirely to them. Kaiwi and Rusty Apana were expected to get the concrete up on the roof and to the places indicated by the foreman of Johnson Pacific. When the foreman indicated he was ready for the next bucket of concrete and where it was to be placed, Kaiwi, the signalman, would give the necessary hand signals to Rusty Apana, the crane operator. The power to substitute was in the defendant, since Rusty Apana told Kaiwi immediately following the accident to stay off the roof. The period of employment was short; they were called in for a one-day pour. The defendant claims that the evidence requires a finding that at the time of the accident in which the plaintiff was injured, the crane operator and signalman were employees of and under the supervision and control of Johnson Pacific. Will the defendant prevail? (See *Nakagawa v. Apana*, 52 Hawaii 379, 477 P.2d 611 (1970).)

12.4 On September 4, 1962, the defendant Keolian, a uniformed guard in the employ of the defendant Heidt's Protective Service, Inc., apprehended the plaintiff, Mary Nash, as she was leaving the store of the defendant Sears, Roebuck and Company. Keolian was given detailed instructions by both Heidt's and Sears concerning the performance of his duties for Sears. Both retained the right to supervise, direct, and discharge him from further service for Sears. One of Heidt's witnesses testified it had the right to pull a guard assigned to Sears off the job while he was at Sears and to replace him with someone else. Heidt's retained the right to continue to supervise Keolian to the extent it chose to do so. Keolian worked side by side with and for Sears's employees. He was expected to respond to intelligence received from other Sears's employees, though he had been instructed not to arrest unless he himself witnessed a shoplifting incident. Keolian purportedly acted on the information of a Sears's salesperson who allegedly witnessed a woman, identified by her as the plaintiff, shoplifting. When Keolian confronted the plaintiff and requested her to accompany him to the store, she refused and started to walk away. Keolian shoved her to the ground, straddled her body, and pinned her arms above hear head. When the police arrived, both Keolian and Nash were taken to the station and subsequent search and investigation proved the shoplifting charge to be without foundation. The plaintiff sued Sears, Heidt's, and Keolian on the theories of false arrest, false imprisonment, and assault and battery. Sears and Heidt's filed cross claims respectively seeking indemnification should the plaintiff recover. Against whom should the plaintiff win judgment? (*See Nash v. Sears, Roebuck & Co.*, 383 Mich. 136, 174 N.W.2d 818 (1970).)

Chapter 13

Ownership of the Firm

A. Ownership of the Firm versus Ownership of Assets

Problem 13.1

Alice, Paula, and Brenda are partners in a dairy farm called "APB Farms." Except for an agreement to be partners, and to devote full time to APB Farms, the partners have no other agreements with respect to partnership business or affairs.

Connie has a $100,000 judgment against Paula, individually. Connie has discovered that Paula's only non-exempt asset is her interest in APB Farms. To enforce her judgment, Connie sent the sheriff out to execute on Connie's share of APB Farms' real estate, equipment and cattle. The partners got wind of what was going to happen. Individually, and on behalf of APB Farms, Alice, Brenda and Paula have sued Connie and the sheriff, seeking temporary and permanent injunctions against their interference with partnership property of APB Farms. What result?

Problem 13.2

Beach and Anderson entered into an oral partnership agreement to own and operate an amusement center in Brainerd, Minnesota, called Vacationland Park. Together they purchased real estate for the venture and constructed a go-cart track. Shortly after opening, the parties disagreed on the management of the center. As a result of the disputes, during the next two years they agreed to alternate management of the park. When the parties were still unable to agree to terms of a written partnership agreement, Beach filed suit for dissolution of the oral partnership.

At a deposition, Beach, Anderson and their attorneys negotiated a settlement, which was stipulated before the court reporter. Anderson agreed to sell, and Beach agreed to buy, Anderson's interest in the partnership and its property for $85,000.

Anderson then changed his mind about the settlement. Andersen argues that the settlement in not enforceable. He reasons that, because the partnership owns real estate, an oral settlement violates the Statute of Frauds. Andersen also argues that his wife did not agree to release any marital interest in partnership property. What result? *See, Beach v. Anderson,* 417 N.W.2d 709 (Minn. App. 1988).

Putnam v. Shoaf

620 S.W.2d 510 (Tenn. App. 1981)

NEARN, Judge.

This dispute is over the sale of a partnership interest in the Frog Jump Gin Company.

The Frog Jump Gin had operated for a number of years showing losses in some years and profits in others. In the time immediately preceding February, 1976, it appears that the gin operated at a loss. Originally, the gin was operated as an equal partnership between E. C. Charlton, Louise H. Charlton, Lyle Putnam and Carolyn Putnam. In 1974 Mr. Putnam died and Mrs. Putnam, by agreement, succeeded to her husband's interest. The gin operated under that control and management until February 19, 1976, when Mrs. Putnam desired to sever her relationship with the other partners in Frog Jump Gin. At that time the gin was heavily indebted to the Bank of Trenton and Trust Company, and Mrs. Putnam desired to be relieved of this liability. John A. and Maurine H. Shoaf displayed an interest in obtaining Mrs. Putnam's one-half interest in the partnership. An examination by the Shoafs of the financial records of the gin, evidenced by a statement from the gin bookkeeper, indicated a negative financial position of approximately $90,000.00. The Shoafs agreed to take over Mrs. Putnam's position in the partnership if Mrs. Putnam and the Charltons would each pay $21,000.00 into the partnership account. The Shoafs agreed to assume personal liability for all partnership debts, including Putnam's share of any partnership debts made prior to their coming into the partnership, although the Uniform Partnership Act would only make him [sic] personally liable for debts made after his [sic] entry into the partnership unless he agreed to more. *See* [UPA § 17]. Both the Charltons and Mrs. Putnam paid their respective amounts into the partnership account, and Shoaf [sic] assumed all partnership obligations as aforesaid.

At the time of this agreement the known assets of the Frog Jump Gin consisted primarily of the gin, its equipment, and the land upon which they were located. All gin assets, including the land, were held in the name of the partnership. Mrs. Putnam conveyed her interest in the partnership to the Shoafs by means of a quit claim deed. Upon Shoafs' assumption of the position of a partner, the services of the old bookkeeper were terminated and a new bookkeeper was hired.

In April, 1977, with the assistance of the new bookkeeper, it was learned that the old bookkeeper had engaged in a scheme of systematic embezzlement from the Frog Jump Gin Company from the time of Mr. Putnam's death until the bookkeeper's services were terminated. This disclosure led to suits being filed by the gin against the bookkeeper and the banks that had honored checks forged by the bookkeeper. There is no need to go into the details of all that litigation. Suffice it to say that Mrs. Putnam was allowed to intervene claiming an interest in any fund paid by the banks and the upshot of it all was a judgment paid into Court by the banks in excess of $68,000.00. One-half of that sum, by agreement, has been paid to the Charltons as owners of a one-half interest in the gin, and the other half is the subject of this dispute between the Shoafs and Mrs. Putnam's estate. She has died pending this litigation and the case revived.

Mrs. Putnam had died before the hearing of the case, thus the only proof before the Trial Judge on the issue at hand was the pleadings, the documents signed by the parties of interest and the deposition of Mr. Shoaf. The Trial Judge dismissed the claim of Putnam and held that Mrs. Putnam had no interest in the fund. The Putnam estate has appealed, citing numerous alleged "issues."

The basis of the Trial Judge's decision was that Mrs. Putnam intended to convey all of her interest in the partnership to Shoaf and, therefore, the Court could not reform the sale and hold that the unknown right of action against the banks for payment of forged checks was not conveyed by Mrs. Putnam in the conveyance to the Shoafs.

The conveyance between Mrs. Putnam and the Shoafs is evidenced by what is styled a "Quitclaim Deed" executed by Mrs. Putnam on February 19, 1976, which is as follows:

FOR AND IN CONSIDERATION of the sum of One Dollar ($1.00), cash in hand paid, the receipt of which is hereby acknowledged, and the assumption by Grantees of all Grantor's obligations arising or by virtue of her partnership interest in the Frog Jump Gin Company, including three notes to Bank of Trenton and Trust Company, I, CAROLYN B. PUTNAM, a widow, have this day bargained and sold and by these presents do hereby sell, transfer, convey and forever quitclaim unto JOHN A. SHOAF and wife, MAURINE H. SHOAF, their heirs and assigns, all the right, title and interest (it being a one-half (1/2) undivided interest) I have in and to the following described real and personal property located in the 25th Civil District of Gibson County, Tennessee, and described as follows; to-wit:

(The legal description of the real property follows.)

PERSONAL PROPERTY:

All of the personal property and machinery in said Frog Jump Gin Company's buildings and on said properties described and used in the operation of its cotton gin plant on the above described parcel of land, including two Moss Gordin 75 saw gin stands; one Overhead incline cleaner; stick and green leaf machine; two Moss Gordin lint cleaners; two Mitchell Feeders; two Mitchell burners; one Hardwick Etter all steel press; condensers; fans; motors; pulleys; shafting; all piping; belting and machinery and appliances and other personal property, including all cotton trailers, on said parcel of land and used in connection with the operation of said cotton gin, accounts receivable, inventory and all other assets of Frog Jump Gin Company.

TO HAVE AND TO HOLD the said real and personal property with the appurtenances, estate, title and interest thereto belonging unto the said John A. Shoaf and wife, Maurine H. Shoaf, their heirs and assigns, forever.

Witness my signature this the 19th day of February, 1976.

On the same day Mrs. Putnam and the Charltons executed the following agreement:

This Agreement made and entered into on this the 19th day of February, 1976, by and between E. C. Charlton and wife, Louise H. Charlton, party of one part, and Carolyn B. Putnam, party of the other part, all of Trenton, Gibson County, Tennessee;

WITNESSETH: THAT WHEREAS, the parties have heretofore been conducting a business, as partners, under the firm name and style of Frog Jump Gin Company; and

WHEREAS, Carolyn B. Putnam has agreed to pay into the partnership the sum of Twenty-one Thousand Dollars ($21,000.00), the receipt of which is hereby acknowledged, and has sold and conveyed her interest in the partnership to John A. Shoaf and wife, Maurine H. Shoaf.

NOW, THEREFORE, it is mutually agreed that the partnership be and hereby is dissolved. It is further mutually agreed that the parties do hereby release and forever discharge each other from any and all claims and demands on account of, connected with, or growing out of the said partnership, or the division of the assets thereof; and it is expressly understood and agreed that Carolyn B. Putnam is completely released and discharged from any and all liability, debts, or causes of action of the Frog Jump Gin Company, presently existing, contingent, or otherwise, including notes owed to Bank of Trenton and Trust Company, and that E. C. Charlton and wife, Louise H. Charlton, assume all liability and indebtedness of the said partnership and covenant to indemnify and save harmless the said Carolyn B. Putnam in the premises.

In Witness Whereof, the parties have hereunto set their signatures, this day and date first above written.

At approximately the same time, Mrs. Putnam obtained from the Bank of Trenton a complete release from all personal liability for note indebtednesses to the Bank in the face amount of $105,000.00 in consideration of the Shoafs' assumption of all obligations of the Frog Jump Gin.

Counsel for Putnam argues that the proof shows there was no meeting of the minds to convey the unknown asset of the claim against the bank, first because its existence was admittedly unknown by both parties and second, the quit claim deed makes no mention of cash or money in the bank and the items that are there mentioned are in fact physical assets, readily ascertainable items that could be identified for the purpose of securing loans and paying debts. Further, counsel argues that the words "all other property" used in the quit claim deed must be construed in accordance with the true intent of the parties.

First, we must discover the nature of the ownership interest of Mrs. Putnam in that which she conveyed. Under the Uniform Partnership Act, her partnership property rights consisted of her (1) rights in specific partnership property, (2) interest in the partnership and (3) right to participate in management. [UPA § 24]. The right in "specific partnership property" is the partnership tenancy possessory right of equal use or possession by partners for partnership purposes. This possessory *right* is incident to the partnership and the possessory right does not exist absent the partnership. The possessory right is not the partner's "*interest*" in the assets of the partnership. [UPA § 25]. The real interest of a partner, as opposed to that incidental possessory right before discussed, is the partner's interest in the partnership which is defined as "his share of the profits and surplus and the same is personal property." [UPA § 26]. Therefore, a co-partner owns no personal specific *interest* in any specific property or asset of the partnership. The *partnership* owns the property or the asset. [UPA § 8]. The partner's interest is an undivided interest, as a co-tenant in all partnership property. [UPA § 25]. That interest is the partner's pro rata share of the net value or deficit of the partnership. [UPA § 26]. For this reason a conveyance of partnership property held in the name of the partnership is made in the name of the partnership and not as a conveyance of the individual interest of the partners. *See* [UPA § 8].

This being true, all Mrs. Putnam had to convey was her interest in the partnership. Accordingly, she had no specific interest in the admittedly unknown choses in action to separately convey or retain. Therefore, the determinative question is: Did Mrs. Putnam intend to convey her interest in the partnership to the Shoafs? There can be no doubt that such was the intent of Mrs. Putnam, as she had no other interest to convey. To give any other intent to the actions of Mrs. Putnam would require a fraudulent intent on her part, which intent certainly did not exist. Therefore, the intent of Mrs. Putnam was to convey the interest she owned which was "her share of the profits and surplus." [UPA § 26].

Since neither the Shoafs nor Mrs. Putnam knew of the embezzlement by accountant Bennie Johnston, there can be no doubt that neither the Shoafs nor Mrs. Putnam knew of the valuable asset that the partnership possessed in its claim against the banks. However, it was the partnership's asset and not her personal asset. Just as she could not have retained it, had she known of it, and at the same time conveyed her partnership interest, we cannot now say she conveyed her partnership interest in 1976, but is still entitled to a share in it. This situation is no different from a hypothetical oil discovery on the partnership real property after transfer of a partnership interest with neither party believing oil to be present at the time of the conveyance. The interest in the real property always was and remained in the partnership. Of course, the transferor would not have transferred his partnership *interest* had he known of the existence of oil on partnership property; but, mutual ignorance of the existence of the oil would not, in our opinion, warrant a "reformation" of the contract for sale of the partnership interest, or warrant a decree in favor of the transferor for a share of the value of the oil.

It is inescapable to us that the interest in the choses in action remained in the partnership at all times regardless of the composition of the partners; and, it is equally inescapable that Mrs. Putnam intended to convey her partnership interest.

This is not a case of mutual mistake but one of mutual ignorance. They are not necessarily the same thing. Those cases cited by appellant as authority for a reversal of the Chancellor...are not applicable to the facts of this case. The results in those cases are primarily based on the finding that the transferor could not have intended to convey that which the transferee received for less than valuable consideration. In this case Mrs. Putnam had to intend to convey her interest in the partnership. Hindsight now shows that it had more value than either party thought. But, hindsight is not a basis for a money judgment, a revision or a reformation. We wonder what would be the position of Mrs. Putnam, or the estate, had the Frog Jump Gin failed, leaving a sizeable deficit, even after the influx of the bank's refund. Would she accept a partner's share of the Frog Jump Gin's liabilities for a share of the bank's refund? The question answers itself and we pose it only to show that she did not have a specific interest in any specific assets of the Frog Jump Gin, either to retain or convey. All she had was a partner's interest in a "share of the profits" (and losses) which she certainly intended to convey.

In looking at the pleadings we note that in Mrs. Putnam's complaint it states that she "sold her undivided one-half interest to John Shoaf and wife, Maurine H. Shoaf."

We also note that in the agreement made with the Charltons, on the same day, she stated that she had "sold and *conveyed her interest in the partnership* to John Shoaf and wife, Maurine H. Shoaf."

We hold that the evidence does not preponderate against the Trial Judge's finding regarding interest.

The result is the judgment below is affirmed with costs of appeal adjudged against the Putnam estate.

Notes

1. UPA section 25(1) specifies that the partners are co-owners of "specific partnership property," holding in a tenancy in partnership. Under UPA Section 25, the rights of partners as tenants–in–partnership of specific partnership property are very narrow. A partner has the right to possess partnership property for partnership purposes only. UPA § 25(2)(a). Moreover, a partner's rights as a tenant–in–partnership cannot separately be conveyed or attached for individual (non-partnership) purposes. The only property right of a partner that can be *individually* conveyed is the interest in the partnership — the partner's share of profits and surplus.

2. The UPA does not define what it means by either "profits" or "surplus." *Putnam v. Shoaf* indicates that the interest in the partnership is an undivided interest in all of the partnership property, taken as a whole, and not in any individual part. This view is supported by the Comment to UPA section 25:

> A partner has a beneficial interest in partnership property *considered as a whole.* As profits accrue, he has a right to be paid his proportion, and on winding up of the business, after obligations due third persons have been met, he has a right to be paid in cash *his share of what remains of the partnership property.* These rights considered as a whole are his interest in the partnership; and this beneficial interest he may assign in whole or in fractional part, as is indicated in section 27.

UPA § 25 Official Comment (emphasis added). Based on this Comment, what does UPA section 26 mean by "profits"? What does it mean by "surplus"?

3. In *Beach v. Anderson*, 417 N.W.2d 709 (Minn. App. 1988), the court rejected the argument that the sale of an interest in a partnership that owns real estate is subject to the Statute of Frauds:

> Anderson argues that the statute of frauds applies because the stipulation involved the transfer of real estate, but the stipulation clearly transfers the "partnership interest" ...
>
> As a contract for the sale of a partnership interest, [UPA section 26] applies:
>
> > A partner's interest in the partnership is that partner's share of the profits and surplus, and the same is *personal property.* (Emphasis added.)
>
> From this language it is evident that the conveyance of deeds and "other such documentation" connected to real estate transfer is merely ancillary to the partnership transfer. This is not a stipulation for the sale of land within the statute of frauds, as Anderson would characterize it.

Real estate owned by a partnership is considered personalty. Under [UPA section 26], once a partnership acquires realty with partnership funds and for partnership purposes, it then becomes personalty for all purposes.

* * *

Under this analysis the statute of frauds does not apply. . . .

4. *Beach v. Anderson*, 417 N.W.2d 709 (Minn. App. 1988), also involved the questions of a spouse's marital rights in partnership property:

Anderson also raises the issue of whether his wife can be required to join him in signing a quit-claim deed. [UPA section 25(2)(e)] states:

A partner's right in specific partnership property is not subject to dower, curtesy, the statutory interest of a surviving spouse, or allowances to a surviving spouse, heirs or next of kin.

Therefore, it does not appear that Kim Anderson has any individual interest in the property, because she is not personally interested in the partnership. We remand to the trial court for consideration of an appropriate order effectuating the transfer pursuant to the agreement.

5. Courts and commentators have not been receptive to the intent of the UPA to create a new estate in land—the tenancy in partnership. *See* Rosin, *The Entity-Aggregate Dispute: Conceptualism and Functionalism in Partnership Law*, 42 ARK. L. REV. 395 (1989). Many courts and commentators argue (as did *Putnam v. Shoaf* in *dicta*) that, under the UPA, the partnership itself owns partnership property. They reason that UPA section 25(2) so limits partners' rights as to leave them no real "ownership" in the traditional sense. Instead, all the partner owns is an interest in the partnership itself.

6. On the other hand, it is clear that the drafters of the UPA did not consider a partnership to be an entity—a legal person—separate from its partners. If the partnership is not a person capable of owning property, who owns partnership property? How does the UPA make it clear that partnership property must be dedicated to partnership purposes only?

7. The RUPA rejected the UPA's concept of partners as tenants–in–partnership of specific partnership. Consistent with the RUPA's general entity-oriented approach, title to partnership property vests in the partnership itself. RUPA §§ 203 & 204. Despite this change in approach, the substance of UPA section 25(2) remains unchanged—partners have no *transferable* interest in partnership property. RUPA § 501.

8. The RUPA's treatment of UPA Section 25's "property rights of a partner" is equivalent to that of the UPA, but somewhat confusing. First, the RUPA section 501 renames the UPA's "interest in the partnership" a "*transferable* interest in the partnership:"

The only transferable interest of a partner in the partnership is the partner's share of the profits and losses of the partnership and the partner's right to receive distributions.

RUPA § 501. Section 101(9) of the RUPA further confuses this by defining "interest in the partnership" in a different manner than that term is used under the UPA:

"Partnership interest" or "interest in the partnership" means *all* of a partner's interests in the partnership, including the partner's transferable interest *and all management and other rights.*

RUPA § 101(9). The RUPA's intent is to distinguish between a partner's transferable "economic interests" (the transferable interest in the partnership), and a partner's other rights as partner, which are not transferable:

A partner's "transferable interest" is a more limited concept [than a partner's interest in the partnership] and means only his share of the profits and losses and right to receive distributions, that is, the partner's *economic interests.* See Section 502 and Comment. Compare RULPA § 101(10) ("partnership interest" includes partner's economic interests only).

RUPA § 101 Comment (emphasis added).

B. Distributions on Liquidation

1. In General

Problem 13.3

Chandler, Joey and Ross are partners in "Bones and Stones" a gift shop in the Paleontology Museum. Except for an agreement to be partners, and to make the capital contributions and loans described below, there is no other agreement among the partners as to partnership business or affairs. At the time Bones and Stones was formed, the partners made the following capital contributions:

Partner	Amount
Chandler	$1,000
Joey	1,000
Ross	3,000

At the same time, Bones and Stones also borrowed $10,000 from Bank.

a. Prepare a balance sheet for Bones and Stones as of its formation. As of the same date, prepare Capital Accounts for each of the partners. If the partnership were liquidated at that time, how would partnership assets be distributed under the UPA to the Bank and to each of the partners? Under the RUPA?

b. Assume that Bones and Stones has operated for a year, during which no distributions have been made to the partners, and no capital contributions have been returned. As of the end of its first year,

(i) Bones and Stones has total assets valued at $20,000.00, and total liabilities of $12,000.00, and

(ii) Bones and Stones is current on all interest owed to partners and non–partners.

Prepare a balance sheet for Bones and Stones as of that date. Prepare Capital Accounts for each of the partners as of the same date. If Bones and Stones were to be liquidated at that time, what amounts would be distributed under the UPA to Bank and to each of the partners? Under the RUPA?

c. Assume instead that the total liabilities of Bones and Stones as of the end of its first year instead totaled $18,000. Prepare a balance sheet for Bones and Stones as of that date. Assuming that no distributions have been made to the partners, and no capital contributions have been returned, prepare Capital Accounts for each of the partners as of the same date. If Bones and Stones were to be liquidated at that time, what amounts would be distributed under the UPA to the Bank and to each of the partners? Under the RUPA?

d. Assume instead that the total liabilities of Bones and Stones as of the end of its first year instead totaled $21,000. Prepare a balance sheet for Bones and Stones as of that date. Assuming that no distributions have been made, and no capital contributions have been returned, prepare Capital Accounts for each of the partners as of the same date. If Bones and Stones were to be liquidated at that time, what amounts would be distributed under the UPA to the Bank and to each of the partners? Under the RUPA?

Parker v. Northern Mixing Co.

756 P.2d 881 (Alaska 1988)

RABINOWITZ, Chief Justice.

A partnership dissolved, and the partners sued each other over the proper distribution of assets and losses. This appeal raises legal issues regarding awards of prejudgment interest and the sharing of partnership losses. The parties also challenge factual findings of the superior court concerning specific aspects of the partnership agreement, various elements of damages, and disputes over items allowed and disallowed in the final accounting.

Early in 1984, long-time acquaintances Douglas Guthrie ("Douglas") and Daniel Mark Parker, III ("Ike") discussed the possibility of operating an asphalt plant in the central Kenai Peninsula area. Ike had considerable experience in the asphalt paving business and, in 1983, he established his present business, Parker Paving Corporation ("PPC"). Douglas is employed as a salesman by Guthrie Machinery Company ("GMC"), a corporation owned by his father, C.J. Guthrie ("C.J."), which sells new and used asphalt plants and accessories.

In June 1984, Douglas, Ike, and C.J. orally agreed to purchase an asphalt plant located in Kamloops, British Columbia. After transporting the plant to Soldotna, they would commence operations to supply asphalt to PPC. The terms of this agreement are disputed. Douglas and C.J. ("the Guthries") claim that C.J. individually or through GMC would supply start-up capital for the asphalt venture (known as Northern Mixing Company or "NMC"), and that C.J.'s advance would be replaced by permanent financing provided by an institutional lender. The Guthries also claim that, pursuant to the agreement: Douglas and Ike would be equally responsible for repayments of the permanent financing and would each provide financial statements, security for his share of the financing, and a statement of work in progress; Douglas and Ike would manage NMC and each own 40% of the corporate stock; and Douglas would be paid $2,500 per month for managing the operation of the asphalt plant. Finally, they claim that C.J. was to own the remaining 20% of the corporate stock in return for securing the financing, and that Ike agreed to make available his and PPC's financial statements and to furnish real property in Oregon as security.

Ike agrees that C.J. was to secure financing for NMC and that NMC was intended to be a corporation. Ike further agrees that he and Douglas were to be responsible for the business, but he disputes any agreement that he was to provide security or any financial statements in connection with long-term financing of NMC or that Douglas was to receive any additional compensation for his participation in managing the business.

The superior court found that all the parties expected C.J. to be able to secure long-term financing to replace his initial investment. It found further that Ike would provide financial information to aid the financing, but that Ike's obligation to provide security arose only when a likely source of financing had been identified. The superior court also found that, although the reasonable value of Douglas's services for the period during which he worked was $2,500 per month, "there was no meeting of the minds among the principals of NMC" to pay him a salary in that or any other amount.

The asphalt plant operated for only about two months, in 1984. When the parties decided to discontinue the business relationship in the winter of 1984–85, they were not able to reach an agreement concerning the allocation of NMC's assets, profits, and liabilities.

The Guthries filed a complaint against Ike in superior court seeking possession of the asphalt plant, damages for diminution in the plant's value equal to its reasonable rental value while in Ike's possession, and an accounting of all income and disbursements of NMC. C.J. (through GMC) claimed expenses of $93,477.16 incident to the original financing of NMC, of which $84,829.09 is acknowledged by Ike as properly chargeable to NMC. Included in the $6,022.84 of disputed charges[2] are a fine and attorney's fees incurred as a result of operating the asphalt production plant without a required environmental permit, and certain credit card charges. C.J. also claimed $19,863.68 in interest on his advances, all of which Ike disputes. Ike (through PPC) in turn claimed expenses incident to operation of NMC of $151,291.66, of which $95,413.39 is acknowledged by the Guthries as chargeable to NMC. Included in the $55,878.27 of disputed charges are trucking and equipment rental charges, land rent, approximately $22,000 for rock, certain payroll charges, and the cost of repair work—application of a "slurry coat" to a finished project—necessitated by the plant's production of some faulty batches of asphalt. PPC also owes NMC $92,320.00 for asphalt produced and sold to PPC in 1984.

The superior court found that the fine, attorney's fees, and the cost of the repair work were properly charged against the business. Pursuant to its finding that NMC, although intended ultimately to be a corporation, was a *de facto* partnership of Ike and Douglas, the superior court applied Alaska's Uniform Partnership Act to settle their rights and liabilities.[3] The superior court found that the partnership was dissolved during the winter of 1984–85 due to the parties' inability

---

2. This figure, stated by the superior court, appears incorrect since $93,477.16 − $84,829.09 = $8,648.07.

3. The specific provision applied by the superior court was [UPA section 40].

to reach an agreement for the operation of the asphalt plant in 1985. According to the superior court, neither party was at fault in causing the dissolution of the partnership since either could terminate it at will under [UPA section 31(1)(b)].

The court determined that C.J. was at all material times a creditor of NMC based on his furnishing the start-up capital for the company, that he never became a shareholder because NMC never issued any stock or operated as a going business, and that although he was to share in NMC's gross returns, he was not for that reason alone a partner.[5] The superior court further found that there was no agreement by the partnership or its individual partners to pay C.J. any interest.

The superior court determined that the partnership's sole assets were the plant itself and related equipment, and the accounts receivable from PPC. Based on C.J.'s testimony, the court's valuation of the plant was $76,887.73, and the PPC receivable was $92,320.00. NMC's total asset value, including prejudgment interest of $13,625.28, was thus $182,833.01.[7] The amount owed C.J., NMC's sole creditor, was established as $88,956.40. As indicated previously, the court found that there were no agreements between Ike and Douglas concerning compensation for each other's services and concluded that, because NMC produced no profits for distribution, the only sums due the partners were for their contributions. Douglas contributed services valued at $7,500 and Ike contributed services, equipment and expenditures of $134,477.62.

The superior court's accounting for the partnership under [UPA section 40] was thus as follows:

ASSETS OF NMC

Plant	$ 76,887.73
PPC Receivable	$ 92,320.00
Prejudgment Interest	$ 13,625.28
TOTAL	$182,833.01

AMOUNT DUE CREDITOR

C.J. Guthrie d/b/a GMC	$ 88,956.40

BALANCE AVAILABLE FOR
PARTNER'S CONTRIBUTIONS $ 93,876.61

PRO-RATA DISTRIBUTION TO PARTNERS
(56.52% of Contribution)

Douglas Guthrie	$ 4,960.00
Ike Parker	$ 88,916.61

Accordingly, the net liability/recovery of the parties was calculated as:

Ike Parker d/b/a/ PPC

Prejudgment Interest	($ 13,625.28)
Account Payable NMC	(92,320.00)
Return of Contribution	88,916.61
Balance — Contribution	($ 17,028.67)

---

5. The court cited [UPA section 7(3)] in support of this conclusion.

7. Upon motion for reconsideration, the superior court amended its original Findings of Fact, Conclusions of Law and Order to include prejudgment interest.

<u>Douglas Guthrie</u>

Return of Contribution	$ 4,960.00

<u>C.J. Guthrie</u>

Value of Plant	$ 76,887.73
Balance Due — Cash	$ 12,068.67

Finally, the superior court rejected all claims of the parties against each other, except those included in the accounting. The court concluded in particular that neither party's actions support a claim for breach of any joint venture or partnership agreement since the partnership was at will and no specific agreement existed; that GMC was not a seller of goods to NMC or to either of its partners; and that the Guthries have no claim for punitive damages because Ike's conduct was not willful or malicious. Therefore, the superior court ordered:

1. Judgment for NMC against Ike in the amount of $17,028.67;

2. Judgment for Douglas against NMC in the amount of $4,960.00

3. Transfer by NMC, Douglas, and Ike to C.J. of all rights, title and interest in the plant in satisfaction of all of C.J.'s claims (except as otherwise provided in the court's order);

4. Judgment for C.J. against NMC of $12,068.67.

The superior court also ordered each party to bear its own costs and attorney's fees based on its view that neither party "prevailed" as that term is used in Civil Rules 79 and 82.

This appeal and cross-appeal followed.

Partners are entitled to repayment of their contributions only *after* other liabilities of the partnership (i.e., those owing to creditors other than partners and to partners other than for capital and profits) are satisfied. *See* [UPA § 40(b)II].

Ike contends that it necessarily follows from the "undisputed evidence" that the parties agreed to share partnership profits equally that they also agreed to share losses equally. Accordingly, he argues, the superior court erred in allocating NMC's liabilities between the parties based on the amounts of their respective capital contributions. We reverse the superior court's determination of the repayment of capital contributions.

The capital account of a partnership is, by definition, the difference between its assets and liabilities. The partnership had total assets of $182,833.01. From this amount $88,956.40 was due to its sole creditor, C.J. Guthrie.[A] The partnership's remaining assets thus totaled $93,876.61. Each partner made the following contributions to capital:

Parker	$134,477.62
Guthrie	7,500.00[14]
Total Capital	$141,977.62

A. [Note by editors.] Earlier in its opinion, the court had affirmed the trial court's finding that C.J. Guthrie was not a partner.

14. This amount is disputed and in accordance with this opinion is remanded for further findings.

Since only $93,876.61 in partnership assets remained after paying C.J., the partnership suffered a loss of $48,101.01.

Since there was no agreement to the contrary, [UPA section 18(a)] determines the division of this loss between the parties: "each partner shall contribute towards the losses, whether of capital or otherwise according to the partner's share in the profits." Since the partners agreed to share profits equally, the loss sustained by the partnership capital account should be shared equally. Thus:

$$\$48,101.01 \div 2 = \$24,050.50.$$

Guthrie's capital account:

$ 7,500.00	Capital contribution
($ 24,050.50	1/2 of loss
($ 16,550.50)	

Parker's capital account:

$134,477.62)	Capital contribution
($ 24,050.50)	1/2 of loss
$110,427.12	

Guthrie must therefore pay $16,550.50 to the partnership. When he makes that payment his capital account will be zero, the net assets of the partnership will be $110,427.12, and Parker's capital account will remain at $110,427.12.[17]

In view of the foregoing we reverse the superior court's pro rata repayment of capital contributions.

Notes

1. Guthrie was required to contribute $16,550.50 to equalize losses, including capital losses. After Guthrie makes that contribution, and Parker is paid $110,427.12, how much will each partner have lost?

2. Is the method of settlement of accounts used by the court in the principal case consistent with UPA section 40?

Note on Firm Financial Statements

When a firm liquidates, it must settle its accounts and distribute its assets. It converts its assets into cash, and uses the cash to pay its creditors. The firm then distributes whatever is left among its owners according to their rights.

In studying the liquidation process, it's useful to consider two common financial statements, the Balance Sheet and the Statement of Income. It is important to remember that we are looking at financial statements from a *legal* perspective. Our focus is the *legal* rights of the owners of the firm. Financial statements can give us information than can help us determine how the owners' legal rights should be applied.

---

17. In other words Guthrie must pay $16,550.50 to NMC, rather than receive back $4,960.00.

The Balance Sheet

A Balance Sheet sets out the financial condition of a firm *as of* a specific date. A Balance Sheet shows the firm's assets on that date, as well as the "equities" against those assets. *Equities* are legal or equitable claims against the firm's assets. As such, the Balance Sheet tells us how the firm's assets would be distributed if the firm were liquidated on that date.

There are two general types of equities, "Liabilities" and "Owners' Equity." *Liabilities* are amounts owed to creditors of the firm. *Total* Liabilities is the aggregate amount that would be necessary to repay the firm's obligations to its creditors if the firm were liquidated as of the date of the Balance Sheet. *Owners' Equity* represents the portion of firm assets that would not be required to repay creditors, and is thus available for distribution to the firm's owners.

The fundamental Balance Sheet equation is

Total Assets = Total Liabilities + Owners' Equity (*Equation 1*)

Balance Sheets are often presented in side-by-side columns. The left-hand column lists all firm assets. The right-hand column lists its Liabilities and its Owners' Equity. Because the total of each column must be the same as that of the other column (Equation 1), the two columns of a Balance Sheet "balance" each other.

Recall that Owners' Equity represents the portion of firm assets that would not be required to repay creditors. By definition, then

Owners' Equity = Total Assets − Total Liabilities (*Equation 2*)[A]

When a firm has more than one owner, especially when it has different classes of owners, the firm's balance Sheet often divides Owners' Equity among the owners (or the different classes). For example, in *partnership* accounting, firms often set up accounts that measure each partner's share of Owners' Equity.

As we saw in *Parker v. Northern Mixing Co.*, owners' claims against firm assets can arise in different ways. Under the UPA, partners have claims for contributions they have made to the property of the partnership, as well as claims for profits. UPA §§ 18(a)–(b), 40(b).

The RUPA provides for "a rudimentary system"[B] of accounting for the financial claims of partners as partners. Under RUPA section 401(a), each partner is "deemed to have" an account that is (i) *credited with* the partner's contributions and share of profits and (ii) *charged with* distributions to the partner and the partner's share of losses. On liquidation, partners with net credits in their accounts are entitled to distributions, while those with net charges must make additional contributions. RUPA §§ 807(a)–(b).

A partner's account with a partnership is commonly called a "Capital Account." This is something of a misnomer in that the account includes not only claims for contribution of capital, but also claims for profits. Partners may not have made contributions in the same proportion as they share profits. Thus, a

---

A. Note that Equation 2 is equivalent to Equation 1.
B. RUPA § 401 Comment 2.

"Capital Account" with separate entries for contributions and profits is the most helpful.[C]

The Statement of Income.

At this point you may be wondering how the Statement of Income fits in. A Balance Sheet is like a *photograph*; it shows the firm's financial position *as of a specific date*. A Statement of Income shows the results of a firm's operations *over a specific period of time*. If a Balance Sheet is a photograph, a Statement of Income is a *movie* that shows the firm's revenues, expenses and net income during that period. The Statement of Income reflects the following equation:

$$\text{Income} = \text{Revenues} - \text{Expenses} \quad \textit{(Equation 3)}$$

Statements of Income often use the terms *earnings* or *profits* instead of the term income. Where a firm's revenues in a period exceed its expenses in that period, the firm has positive income (profits or earnings) (Equation 3). Where a period's expenses exceed its revenues, the firm has negative income—it has incurred a loss for the period.

Linking the Statement of Income and the Balance Sheet.

For most purposes, the Statement of Income and the Balance Sheet are not connected to each other. A Statement of Income describes what happened during a period, and is not concerned with the financial condition of the firm at the beginning of the period, or at its ending. Similarly, a Balance Sheet shows the firm's financial condition as of a specific date, and does not reflect how it got there.

Logically, however, the Statement of Income explains changes in the firm's assets, its liabilities and its Owners' Equity. Thus, the Statement of Income for a period is the "bridge" that connects the Balance Sheets at the beginning and at the end of the period.

> *Example.* Suppose that a firm begins a period with Owners' Equity of $100,000, and has income of $100,000 during the period. An income of $100,000 means that the firms receipts of assets (revenues) exceed its expenditures of assets (expenses) by $100,000 (Equation 3). That is, the firm's Total Assets increased by $100,000. All other things being equal, we would expect that Owners' Equity at the end of the period would increase by the same amount (Equation 2).

At this point, we need to recognize that the Statement of Income may not account for all increases and decreases in firm assets. A firm's assets can decrease without the firm paying off a liability or incurring an expense on its Statement of Income. For example, a firm may distribute money or property to its owners. By the same token, the owners can contribute additional money or property to the firm. That would increase the firm's assets without borrowing from a creditor or realizing revenue.

C. Depending on the jurisdiction, and the type of firm, separating claims for contributions of capital and claims for profits may be important in determining the right to interim distributions.

In this connection, note that the partner accounts of RUPA section 401(a) take into account both contributions and distributions, as well as profits and losses.

Problem 13.4

You represent Xiu, one of two partners in the law firm of Xiu & Nguyen, LLP, which is insolvent. The partnership has $1,000,000 in generally available assets and $100,000 in a segregated trust fund from which it can pay malpractice judgments. It also has the following debts:

> $500,000   lease payments owed to Lessor
> $250,000   accounts payable owed to Suppliers
> $250,000   bank loan owed to Bank
> $1,000,000   malpractice judgment in favor of Client

The $1,000,000 malpractice judgment was based on the professional negligence of Nguyen in a matter in which Xiu was not involved. Assume that Xiu had no power or duty to supervise or control Nguyen. Also assume that Nguyen and Xiu both have personal assets which could pay the foregoing indebtedness.

a. If Xiu & Nguyen, LLP is a Texas registered limited liability partnership, how will Nguyen want to distribute assets? How will Xiu want them distributed?

b. If Xiu & Nguyen is an LLP under the RUPA, how will Nguyen want to distribute assets? How will Xiu want them distributed? See RUPA § 306(c), 807(b).

c. As a matter of public policy, is the Texas or the RUPA statutory model of liability more desirable than the other? Remember that, under either statute, if the partnership cannot pay the malpractice judgment, Client can recover against Nguyen. However, if the partnership does not pay Lessor, Suppliers or Bank, they have no one else who will be liable under the California statute. In Texas, of course, they could sue the partners individually.

2. Service Partners

Problem 13.5

Capital and Labor form a partnership to run a convenience store. Capital owns a suitably located building, and agrees to let the partnership use the building rent-free. In order to buy the inventory, the partnership borrows $20,000 from Bank. Labor agrees to devote full-time and best efforts to the partnership business. Capital, a doctor, will not work in the partnership business. Capital and Labor agree to share profits equally. Except as described above, Capital and Labor have no other agreements concurring the partnership, its business or affairs.

a. Six months later, the store is not successful, and Capital and Labor decide to liquidate the partnership. The partnership's sole property consists of inventory worth $10,000. The partnership's sole creditor is Bank, which is still owed $20,000 (assume that the partnership is current on interest payments to Bank). Determine the relative rights and obligation of Bank and to each of the partners.

b. Suppose that, instead of borrowing the start-up funds from Bank, *Capital* advanced (loaned) the partnership $20,000. Determine the relative rights and obligation of Bank and to each of the partners.

c. Suppose that the partnership does not borrow the $20,000 from either Bank or Capital. Instead, Capital contributes $20,000 cash to the partnership. Determine the relative rights and obligation of Bank and to each of the partners.

Becker v. Killarney

177 Ill. App. 3d 793, 532 N.E.2d 931 (1988)

Justice SCOTT:

It is rare that parties come together, form a partnership, and plan to lose money in their endeavors. Nevertheless, the old saw teaches that the "best laid plans of mice and men" will occasionally go awry. This is the legal culmination of just such an ill-fated endeavor.

Prior to June 1975, First Federal Savings and Loan Association of Peoria advanced money for the expansion of the Voyager Inn, an existing hotel in downtown Peoria. Before the expansion was complete, First Federal had taken possession of the property as mortgagee. Thereupon, First Federal entered into negotiations with G. Raymond Becker, one of the plaintiffs, to strike a deal under which Becker would take over the parcel and complete the hotel addition. In furtherance of that deal, Becker formed the partnership which was to become the subject of the instant dispute.

Becker assembled a partnership team that included parties with various skills and services that could be valuable to the enterprise. He himself was a developer and president of a construction company, Gordon E. Burns was an architect, John P. Dailey was a financier, John C. Parkhurst was an attorney, and Rosel was the prospective hotel manager. These original five partners entered into a formal written agreement on June 20, 1975. None of the original five partners funded the partnership with any cash capital, but each agreed to contribute his services; the evidence adduced in the trial court establishes that the five partners did so throughout the partnership's operation of the hotel.

With the exception of Rosel, and his successor White, who also managed the hotel, the original partners were not compensated for their services. Salaries were prohibited by the partnership agreement. The cash contributions necessary to get the partnership off the ground came from Thomas Killarney and Bernard Feely. Within months following the original formation of the partnership, Killarney had contributed $160,000 for an 8% interest and Feely had contributed $100,000 for a 5% interest. Both Killarney and Feely had been previous business associates of Becker, and both signed identical amendments to the partnership agreement setting forth the rights and obligations of the new partners.

The project proceeded, aided by a $10,500,000 non-recourse first mortgage loan from First Federal and credit extended by the contractor, Becker Bros., Inc.,

Becker's construction company. The capital contribution of Killarney and Feely provided working capital for the partnership. It appears, however, that the hotel, once constructed and open, was something less than a commercial success. After the hotel had been open for some time, it became necessary to negotiate an additional $500,000 loan from First Federal to be used as working capital. Indeed, the hotel consistently lost money, not just tax shelter losses but real cash losses, and the losses increased as time passed. In August of 1979, the partners were assessed $100,000 according to their respective interests, in order to raise money to pay the bills. Again in April of 1980, a second assessment of $100,000 was necessary, and all the partners paid their percentage shares.

As the losses mounted, in September 1984 the hotel property was transferred back to First Federal. Unlike the original mortgage loan, not all obligations of the partnership feature non-recourse agreements to protect the partners. A dispute arose as to the obligations of the various partners to pay for these partnership debts and the subject lawsuit resulted. In the circuit court of Peoria County, four of the original partners, Becker, Burns, Dailey and Parkhurst, complained for a money judgment against the two defendant partners, Killarney and Feely, for their shares of the partnership debts. The defendant partners counterclaimed, alleging that the plaintiffs owed money to the partnership. After a trial extending for a period of weeks, the Peoria court entered judgment against the plaintiffs and for the defendants. The plaintiffs appeal that judgment.

The circuit court concluded the law required that the partnership capital accounts of Killarney and Feely should reflect their cash contributions and be applied to their share of the net loss; that is, the net losses of the partnership should be calculated according to each partner's percentage commencing with the first dollar of loss, and not simply those losses which exceeded the original capital contributions of Killarney and Feely. The plaintiffs, those partners who contributed services rather than cash to the partnership, believe the circuit court erred in permitting the "cash partners" to apply their original investment totaling $260,000 against their share of the losses.

In Illinois, the relations among partners are governed by the Uniform Partnership Act. [UPA section 40] provides for the settling of accounts between the parties. The circuit court, relying on the statute, concluded that the $260,000 capital contribution of the "cash partners," Killarney and Feely, was a liability of the partnership and therefore subject to contributions from all the partners for payment.

The plaintiffs urge that such an unbending application of the statute yields an unfair and inequitable result. Killarney and Feely, the cash partners, receive a preference in the payment of their contribution to the partnership because that contribution was made in cash, but Becker, Dailey, Burns and Parkhurst receive no payment for their contribution because it was made in the form of services. One might reasonably assume that the partners themselves determined the services, skill and know-how of the plaintiffs to be of proportionate value of the partnership as the partners' shares of the profits; there was no preference in sharing profits (or losses) for those who contributed cash as opposed to services.

The "service partners" urge that equity and fairness demand that their contribution of services, skill, know-how or sweat-equity, however it be labeled, must be accounted for in the same manner as the cash contribution of the "cash partners." The plaintiffs cite no provision of the Uniform Partnership Act in support of their position, but argue instead that where the Act is silent, the general principles of law and equity apply ([UPA § 5]), and equity would militate against this unjust enrichment of the defendants. The plaintiffs rely on the California court's decision in *Kovacik v. Reed* (1957), 49 Cal. 2d 166, 315 P.2d 314, as the correct rule of law in cases such as this.

The *Kovacik* court, while recognizing the general rule with respect to loss sharing among partners, also notes:

> it appears that in the cases in which the above stated general rule has been applied, each of the parties had contributed capital consisting of either money or land or other tangible property, or else was to receive compensation for services rendered to the common undertaking which was to be paid before computation of the profits or losses. Where, however, as in the present case, one partner or joint adventurer contributes the money capital as against the other's skill and labor, all the cases cited, and which our research has discovered, hold that neither party is liable to the other for contribution for any loss sustained. Thus, upon loss of the money the party who contributed it is not entitled to recover any part of it from the party who contributed only services. (I)n such a situation, the parties have, by their agreement to share equally in profits, agreed that the value of their contributions—the money on the one hand and the labor on the other—were likewise equal; it would follow that upon the loss, as here, of both money and labor, the parties have shared equally in the losses.

We find the rationale set forth in *Kovacik* to be persuasive, inconsistent with no express provision of the Uniform Act, and consistent with long-held equitable principles which form the foundation of our jurisprudence.

The defendant would have us conclude that *Kovacik* is inconsistent with [UPA section 40]. We disagree. While the liabilities of the partnership may well include payments "owing to partners in respect of capital," we do not agree that such capital cannot be intangibles such as special skills or know-how as well as tangibles such as cash. In fact, it is more likely that the parties "by their agreement to share equally in profits, agreed that the value of their contributions—the money on the one hand and the labor on the other—were likewise equal." *Kovacik*, 315 P.2d at 316.

Likewise, we find no inconsistency between the *Kovacik* rule and the express provisions of the partnership agreement itself. Defendants' expert finds such an inconsistency in a provision in the two agreement amendments which reads as follows:

> Additional cash contributions of capital may be made by any or all of the partners from time to time and any such cash contributions shall be returned to such partners before any distribution of assets is made upon the sale of assets or dissolution of the partnership.

The experts who testified were not unanimous as to the meaning and application of the quoted provision. It is ambiguous, but in its ambiguity, it is not inconsistent with the unique rule of *Kovacik*.

For the reasons stated, we agree that in cases such as this, the *Kovacik* rule should apply. Equity requires that the value of services be recognized and capitalized, so as to prevent unjust enrichment. Absent an agreement to the contrary, and we find no such agreement under the instant facts, *Kovacik* should apply. We direct the circuit court to apply the principles therein and enter judgment accordingly.

REVERSED AND REMANDED.

Notes

1. *Becker v. Killarney* reasons that because the capital and service partners agreed to share profits equally, the partners must have viewed their "contributions" to the partnership as being equal. Yet partners can "contribute" in more than one way. First, they can contribute to the partnership's *profit-producing potential*. Second, they can contribute directly to the partnership's *wealth*. A contribution to profit-producing potential indirectly can increase the partnership's wealth, but only to the extent that potential is *realized* as actual profits.

2. In the case of a capital/service partnership, one partner "contributes" only property, and the other only services. What, if anything, does the fact that the partners share profits equally imply about the partner's relative contributions to the partnership's profit-producing potential? Their relative contributions to the partnership's wealth?

3. In each of the variations of Problem 13.2, what did each of Capital and Service contribute to the partnership's profit-producing potential? To its wealth?

4. The RUPA is more clear concerning the nature of the "contributions" that rise to rights to distributions. RUPA section 401(a) provides that each partner's implicit account "must be credited with an amount equal to the cash plus the value of any other property, net of the amount of any liabilities, the partner contributes to the partnership." Comment 3 to RUPA section 401 notes that the accounting rules of section 401(a) apply even where a partner contributes little or no capital. That Comment suggests that those who think that that result is not fair should "take advantage of their power to vary by agreement the allocation of capital losses." RUPA § 401 Comment 3.

Parker v. Northern Mixing Co. (Part 2)
756 P.2d 881 (Alaska 1988)

[Re-read the *facts* set out at pages 629–32.]

Ike contends that the superior court erred in crediting Douglas for a partnership contribution of $7,500 in services. He argues that such credit is contrary to the court's express finding that, although Douglas worked full time running the asphalt plant for approximately three months in 1984 and the reasonable value of his services was $2,500 per month, "there was no meeting of the minds among the principals of NMC that he be paid a salary in that or any other amount."

In *Schymanski v. Conventz*, 674 P.2d 281, 284–85 (Alaska 1983), this court distinguished between non-cash capital contributions to a partnership and remuneration for ordinary services:

> The general rule is that, in the absence of an agreement to such effect, a partner contributing only personal services is ordinarily *not* entitled to any share of partnership capital pursuant to dissolution. Personal

services may, however, qualify as capital contributions to a partnership where an express or implied agreement to such effect exists.

To be distinguished from non-cash capital contributions to a partnership is compensation or remuneration for a partner's services performed in the course of day-to-day affairs of the partnership. In the absence of an agreement to provide for such compensation, remuneration for a partner's services performed in the course of partnership affairs is prohibited by statute.[12]

In light of *Schymanski*, it seems clear that the superior court meant, by its finding that no meeting of the minds occurred regarding payment of any *salary* to Douglas, that the parties entered no agreement that would lift the [UPA section 18(f)] proscription against compensation for acting in the partnership business. That does not, however, necessarily answer the question of whether the court found an express or implied agreement that Douglas's services would qualify as capital contributions to the partnership. Douglas argues that the superior court could reasonably have found such an implied agreement since he was to operate the plant full time, whereas Ike had other employment and income.

The superior court made no specific findings as to the existence of an agreement to treat Douglas's services as capital contributions. The court did, however, find that

[t]here were no agreements between the partners for compensation for either's services. There are no profits to be distributed. Consequently the only sums due the partners are with respect to their contributions.

The superior court then proceeded to find that Douglas "contributed services to the joint venture in the amount of $7,500," and that Ike "contributed services, equipment and expenditures" totalling $134,477.62. From these findings collectively, it could be inferred that the superior court found an implied agreement between Douglas and Ike that their services would constitute capital contributions to NMC.

Given the foregoing, however, we conclude that the question of the existence or non-existence of such an agreement should be remanded to the superior court for explicit findings of fact as to whether it was agreed that Douglas's services would constitute capital contributions.

Notes

1. UPA section 18(f) says that a partner may not receive remuneration for acting in the partnership business. In *Parker v. Northern Mixing Co.*, did the trial court indirectly compensate Guthrie (the service partner) for services? Suppose the *Parker* partnership had lasted 12 — or even 24 or 36 — months before dissolving. What would Guthrie's implied capital contribution be by then?

2. Just as a partner is not entitled to remuneration for acting in the partnership business, a partner contributing capital is not entitled to *interest* on that capital until after the date the capital was to be repaid (generally, after dissolu-

---

12. [UPA section 18(f)] provides, with an exception not here relevant, that subject to any agreement between the partners, no partner is entitled to remuneration for acting in the partnership business.

tion). The theory in the case of contributions of both capital and services is that partners are compensated for those contributions by a share of the profits.

C. Interim Distributions

Problem 13.6

Dick, Jane and Sally are members of Run, Spot, Run, LLC, a member-managed limited liability company under the Uniform Limited Liability Company Act. The members have made the following unreturned contributions to the capital of Run, Spot, Run: Dick, $70,000; Jane, $20,000 and Sally, $10,000. The operating agreement provides for Dick and Jane to be members, for the agreed capital contributions, and for member management. The operating agreement has no other relevant provisions.

Dick proposes that Run, Spot, Run make an interim distribution to the members of $32,000. Both Jane and Sally oppose the proposed distribution.

a. Is the distribution approved by the members? *See* ULLCA §§ 404(a) and 404(c). Would your answer change if Run, Spot, Run were organized under the Delaware LLC Act? *See* Del. LLC Act § 18-402.

b. As of the time of the proposed distribution, Run, Spot, Run, the fair value of its assets is $200,000, and its has total liabilities (other than liabilities to members for the return of contributions) of $176,000. Is the proposed distribution proper under the ULLCA? What would be the effect of an improper distribution? *See* ULLCA §§ 406–07. Would your answer change if Run, Spot, Run were organized under the Delaware LLC Act? *See* Del. LLC Act § 18-607.

c. Assuming that a distribution of $24,000 is both proper, and properly agreed to by the members, how should it be divided among them, equally or in proportion to their capital contributions? *See* ULLCA § 405(a). Would your answer change if Run, Spot, Run were organized under the Delaware LLC Act? *See* Del. LLC Act § 18-504.

Brooke v. Mt. Hood Meadows Oreg., Ltd.

81 Or.App. 387, 725 P.2d 925 (1986)

BUTTLER, Presiding Judge.

Plaintiffs are three of 18 limited partners in Mt. Hood Meadows, Oreg., Ltd., a limited partnership established to carry on the business of constructing and operating a winter sports development in the Hood River Meadows area of the Mt. Hood National Forest. They brought this action against the general partner, Mt. Hood Meadows Development Corp., and the partnership for money had and received. [A]fter a trial on the merits, the court awarded judgment to plaintiffs.

The question is whether plaintiffs, as limited partners, have a right to compel the general partner to distribute to them all of the profits allocated to them under the provisions of the partnership agreement. For the years in which profits were earned after 1974, the general partner's board of directors voted to distribute only 50 percent of the limited partners' taxable profits. The remaining profits were retained and reinvested in the business. The trial court held that the general partner had no authority to retain profits and ordered that it distribute annually to all limited partners cash equal to the profits allocated to them.

[Article X[B] of the limited partnership agreement provides] that all management decisions of the partnership be the responsibility of the general partner and that the limited partners have no right to take part in the control of the business. That provision protects the limited partners from becoming liable as general partners. [ULPA § 7.] Management of the business necessarily includes decisions regarding the management of profits, unless the parties have specified otherwise in the limited partnership agreement.

Article VII[2] of the agreement defines the partners' interest in the capital of the partnership. Article VI of the agreement describes each limited partner's interest in the profits.

> Each limited partner shall be entitled to a portion of the remainder of the profits after payment to the general partner as specified above, which bears the same ratio to such remainder as such limited partner's capital contribution bears to the total capital contribution of the limited partners.

A partner's interest in the capital of the partnership is made up of the partner's capital contributions and, in part, his share of undistributed profits. That is

---

B. [Note by editors] Article X of the limited partnership agreement provides:
"POWERS AND RESPONSIBILITIES, COMPENSATION
"Management and control of the partnership business shall be vested exclusively in the general partner, who, except as otherwise herein provided, shall have all the rights and powers and be subject to all the restrictions and liabilities of a general partner. The general partner shall have the power to borrow funds for the partnership's business and to pledge, mortgage, assign or otherwise hypothecate any or all properties of the partnership to secure such borrowings.
"None of the limited partners shall have any voice or take any part in the control or management of the business of the partnership nor shall any limited partner have any power or authority to act for or on behalf of the partnership in any respect whatever; provided that nothing herein contained shall in any way affect the rights of the limited partners to dissolve the partnership as provided in Article XI hereof."
2. Article VII provides:
"CAPITAL, ADDITIONAL CAPITAL, RETURN OF CAPITAL
"The partners' interest in the capital of the partnership shall be in the proportions in which the agreed capital contributions of each, increased by his share of profits, gains, credits, and additional capital contributions and decreased by his share of losses, expenses, deductions and withdrawals bears to the aggregate capital contributions of all partners so increased or decreased, as the case may be.
"The partners shall not be required to make capital contributions in addition to those herein provided for unless further capital contributions are unanimously agreed upon by all the partners, general and limited.
"The contributions of each partner shall be returned upon dissolution and termination of the partnership only as provided in Article XIV."
"The partners' interest in the capital of the partnership shall be in the proportions in which the agreed capital contributions of each, increased by his share of profits, gains, credits, and additional capital contributions and decreased by his share of losses, expenses, deductions and withdrawals bears to the aggregate capital contributions of all partners so increased or decreased, as the case may be."

what, in accounting terms, constitutes a partner's capital account. Although Article VI, the only section of the agreement that addresses the partners' right to profits, describes the percentage of profits to which each partner is "entitled," it does not address the distribution of profits; it merely provides the method of calculating and allocating profits. We conclude that the agreement contains no provision expressly directing the general partner to distribute profits to the limited partners.

Plaintiffs argue that the authority to retain profits is one that must be granted expressly to the general partner and that, in the absence of a grant, is presumed to have been withheld. That proposition is too broad. With certain exceptions and unless otherwise agreed, a broad grant of authority to manage a business, such as that applicable here, includes the authority to conduct all affairs reasonably necessary or incidental to the expressly authorized business. Decisions regarding the management, including the distribution, of profits fall within that broad authority.

Profit is an accounting concept; its allocation takes place in the partnership books, and it may bear little or no relationship to cash on hand. Each partner is taxed on his distributable share of the profits, regardless of whether cash is actually distributed or whether it is available for distribution. For that reason, the partnership agreement must specify how the profits are to be allocated.

The availability of cash for distribution, however, depends strictly on management's operation of the business. The business' future cash needs are also determined by management. That is why the decision as to how much, if any, of a limited partner's share of the profits is to be distributed is a management decision. If a limited partner were to take part in that aspect of the control of the business, the partner would risk the loss of his limited liability.

A limited partner's position is analogous to that of a corporate shareholder, whose role is that of an investor with limited liability, and with no voice in the operation of the enterprise. With limited exceptions, which do not include control over the distribution of profits, a limited partner who takes part in the control of the business may be held liable as a general partner. A general partner's relationship to the limited partners is analogous to the relationship of a corporate board of directors to the corporate shareholders; the general partner functions as a fiduciary with a duty of good faith and fair dealing. Like the corporate director's fiduciary responsibility to the shareholders for the declaration of dividends, the general partner's duty to the limited partners in the distribution of profit is discharged by decisions made in good faith that reflect legitimate business concerns. There is no contention here that the general partner acted in bad faith in failing to distribute all of the profits.

The limited partners' right to a share of the profits of the partnership under [ULPA § 10(2)] is unrestricted; however, in the absence of a provision to the contrary in the partnership agreement, the right to a distribution of that share is subject to the good faith judgment of the general partner. The agreement is not ambiguous and contains no provision that would give plaintiffs the right to demand payment for undistributed profits.

Accordingly, the trial court erred in denying defendants' motion for judgment on the pleadings.

Reversed and remanded for entry of judgment for defendants.

Notes

1. ULPA section 2 requires a limited partnership's certificate of limited partnership to state the "share of the profits or the other compensation by way of income which each limited partner shall receive by reason of his contribution," ULPA § 2(1)(a)IX. Under ULPA section 15,

> A limited partner may receive from the partnership the share of the profits or the compensation by way of income stipulated for in the certificate; provided, that after such payment is made,... the partnership assets are in excess of all liabilities of the partnership except liabilities to limited partners on account of their contributions and to general partners.

ULPA § 15. Is the principal case's interpretation of a limited partner's rights consistent with ULPA section 15? On what basis could you argue that it is? That it is not?

2. Under RULPA sections 503 and 504, both profits and losses (RULPA §503) and distributions of cash and other assets (RULPA § 504) are to be allocated among the partners in the manner(s) provided in writing in the partnership agreement. Where the partnership agreement is silent, both profits and losses, and distributions are each to be allocated

> on the basis of the value, as stated in the partnership records required to be kept pursuant to Section 105, of the contributions made by each partner to the extent they have been received by the partnership and have not been returned.

RULPA §§ 503 & 504. Note that the default profit and loss sharing ratios under RULPA sections 503 and 504 are according to the partner's contributions. By way of contrast, under both the UPA and the RUPA, the default rule is that partners share profits is equally, and share losses in the same proportion as they share profits.

RULPA section 601 addresses the question of a partner's right to "interim distributions" — distributions made "before [the partner's] withdrawal from the limited partnership and before the dissolution and winding up thereof," RULPA § 601. As a general rule partners are only *entitled* to interim distributions "to the extent and at the times or upon the happening of the events specified in the partnership agreement." *Id.*

3. UPA section 18(a) provides as follows:

> Each partner shall be repaid his contributions, whether by way of capital or advances to the partnership property and share equally in the profits and surplus remaining after all liabilities, including those to partners, are satisfied; and must contribute towards the losses, whether of capital or otherwise, sustained by the partnership according to his share in the profits.

Is it clear from UPA section 18(a) that a partner has only the right to be *allocated on the books of the partnership* a share of its profits? Reread Note 2 to *Putnam v. Shoaf,* page 622. How does the Comment to UPA section 25 bear on this question?

4. Under RUPA section 401(a) restates the partner's rights to profits and losses:

Each partner is *deemed to have an account* that is:

(1) *credited with* an amount equal to the money plus the value of any other property, net of the amount of any liabilities, the partner contributes to the partnership and the partner's share of the partnership profits; and

(2) *charged with* an amount equal to the money plus the value of any other property, net of the amount of any liabilities, distributed by the partnership to the partner and the partner's share of the partnership losses.

RUPA § 401(a) (emphasis added). The Comment to RUPA section 401 emphasizes the difference between a partner's right to have profits credited to the partner's account and rights to interim distributions:

Absent an agreement to the contrary, however, a partner does not have a right to receive a current distribution of the profits credited to his account, the interim distribution of profits being a matter arising in the ordinary course of business to be decided by majority vote of the partners.

RUPA § 401 Comment.

5. One of the advantages of partnerships, limited partnerships and limited liability companies is that, for federal income taxation purposes, they are taxed as partnerships, unless they elect to be taxed as associations taxable as corporations. Under partnership taxation, there is no entity-level taxation of income; instead, firm owners—partners for tax purposes—are individually taxed on their shares of partnership income. As the principal case illustrates, partnership taxation also exposes firm owners to the risk that the firm will not distribute cash to assist the owners in paying their taxes. Firm income is property of the firm. In the absence of a contrary agreement, the decision to distribute firm property is a business decision, to be decided by a majority of the firm's managers. Thus, while owners must pay federal income taxes on partnership income, the firm may not distribute cash sufficient to pay those taxes.

D. Rights of Assignees and Creditors

1. Assignments

Problem 13.7

Alice, Paula, and Brenda are partners in a dairy farm called "APB Farms." Except for an agreement to be partners, and to devote full time to APB Farms, the partners have no other agreements with respect to partnership business or affairs.

Connie has a $100,000 judgment against Paula, individually. Paula's only non-exempt asset is her interest in APB Farms. Paula settles with Connie by assigning to her half of Paula's interest in APB Farms.

a. Did the assignment dissolve APB Farms?

b. Is Connie now a partner in APB Farms?

c. Did the assignment entitle Connie to take possession of half of Paula's share of the cattle owned by APB Farms?

d. After the assignment to Connie, APB Farms continues its practice of reinvesting all profits in the business.

(1) May Connie sue the partners for an injunction forcing them to make distributions?

(2) May Connie bring a direct or a derivative suit for breach of fiduciary duty?

e. What rights does Connie have as an assignee?

Bauer v. The Blomfield Company/Holden Joint Venture
849 P.2d 1365 (AK 1993)

Before RABINOWITZ, C.J., and BURKE, MATTHEWS, COMPTON and MOORE, JJ.

OPINION

BURKE, Justice.

William J. Bauer, assignee of a partnership interest, sued the partnership and the individual partners, claiming that partnership profits were wrongfully withheld from him. The superior court granted summary judgment to the partnership and individual partners, and dismissed Bauer's complaint with prejudice. We affirm.

I

In 1986 William Bauer loaned $800,000 to Richard Holden and Judith Holden. To secure the loan, the Holdens assigned to Bauer "all of their right, title and interest" in a partnership known as the Blomfield Company/Holden Joint Venture. The other members of the partnership—Charles Alfred (Chuck) Blomfield, Patricia A. Blomfield, Charles Anthony (Tony) Blomfield and Richard H. Monsarrat—consented to the assignment. According to the consent document, their consent was given "[p]ursuant to AS 32.05.220 [*i.e.*, UPA § 27]."[1]

When the Holdens defaulted on the loan, Bauer sent the following notice to the partnership members:

---

1. AS 32.05.220 provides:

(a) A conveyance by a partner of a partner's interest in the partnership does not by itself dissolve the partnership, nor as against the other partners in the absence of agreement, entitle the assignee, during the continuance of the partnership, to interfere in the management or administration of the partnership business or affairs, or to require any information or account of partnership transactions or to inspect the partnership books, but it entitles the assignee to receive in accordance with the assignee's contract the profits to which the assigning partner would otherwise be entitled.

(b) In the case of a dissolution of the partnership, the assignee is entitled to receive the assignor's interest and may require an account from the date only of the last account agreed to by all of the partners.

William Bauer hereby gives notice that he is exercising his rights to receive all distributions of income and principal from the Blomfield Company/Holden Joint Venture Partnership.

Thereafter, for a time, the partnership income share payable to the Holdens was paid monthly to Bauer.

In January, 1989 the partners stopped making income payments to Bauer. They, instead, agreed to use the income of the partnership to pay an $877,000 "commission" to partner Chuck Blomfield. Bauer was not a party to this agreement; he was notified of the agreement after the fact by means of a letter dated January 10, 1989. Bauer was not asked to consent to the agreement, and he never agreed to forego payment of his assigned partnership income share or to pay part of the "commission" to Blomfield. The amount Bauer would have received, had the "commission" not been paid, was $207,567.

Blomfield's $877,000 commission represented five percent of the increased gross rental income earned by the partnership from lease extensions obtained from the state by Blomfield on partnership properties leased by the state. These and other lease extensions were obtained when a private claim made against the state by Chuck Blomfield and Patricia Blomfield for $1,900,000 was settled. Other lease extensions thus obtained were on properties not owned by the partnership; these properties were owned by the Blomfields and were leased by them to the state. One of the conditions upon which Chuck and Patricia Blomfield based their settlement was the agreement of the partners to pay Chuck Blomfield an $877,000 commission for the lease extensions that he obtained on the partnership's properties.

II

Insisting that his assigned right to the Holdens' share of the partnership's income had been violated, Bauer filed suit in superior court against the partnership and all of the partners except the Holdens. Bauer sought declaratory and injunctive relief, and damages. His various claims were dismissed, with prejudice, when the court concluded that Bauer's assignment from the Holdens did not make him a member of the partnership. Therefore, he was not entitled to complain about a decision made with the consent of all the partners. This appeal followed.

III

The assignment to Bauer of the Holdens' "right, title and interest" in the partnership, did not, in and of itself, make Bauer a partner in the Blomfield Company/Holden Joint Venture. See [UPA § 27]. We are unpersuaded by Bauer's argument that he should be considered a de facto partner.

As the Holdens' assignee, Bauer was not entitled "to interfere in the management or administration of the partnership business or affairs, or to require any information or account of partnership transactions or to inspect the partnership books." [UPA § 27(a)].[2]

---

2. We are unwilling to hold that partners owe a duty of good faith and fair dealing to assignees of a partner's interest. To do so would undermine the clear intent of [UPA § 27(a)]. Partners should be able to manage their partnership without regard for the concerns of an assignee, who may have little interest in the partnership venture. As commentators have explained:

The UPA rules concerning assignment of partnership interests and the rights of as-

The "interest" that was assigned to Bauer was the Holdens' "share of the [partnership's] profits and surplus." [UPA § 26].[3] The assignment only entitled Bauer to "receive...the [partnership] profits to which the [Holdens] would otherwise be entitled." [UPA § 27(a)] (emphasis added). Because all of The Blomfield Company/Holden Joint Venture partners agreed that Chuck Blomfield was entitled to receive an $877,000 commission, to be paid out of partnership income, we agree with the superior court's conclusion that there were no partnership profits which the Holdens, and thus Bauer, were entitled to receive until the commission was fully paid.

AFFIRMED.

MATTHEWS, Justice, with whom RABINOWITZ, Chief Justice, joins, dissenting.

It is a well-settled principle of contract law that an assignee steps into the shoes of an assignor as to the rights assigned.[1] Today, the court summarily dismisses this principle in a footnote and leaves the assignee barefoot.

The court's analysis, set out in three cursory paragraphs is this:

(1) Bauer was not a partner;

(2) Bauer, as an assignee, was not entitled to interfere in the management of the partnership;

(3) Bauer's assignment entitled him to receive only the profits the Holdens would have received; and

(4) Bauer was due nothing because no profits were distributed.

These statements are generally correct as far as they go. However, they do not address the issue in dispute: whether the partners owe Bauer a duty of good faith and fair dealing.

The court is correct to state that Bauer's assignment entitles him to nothing if the partnership decides to forego a distribution. However, this statement leaves unanswered the crucial question that must first be asked: was the partners' decision to pay Blomfield a "commission," thereby depleting profits for distribution, a decision made in good faith? Until this question is answered, we cannot know if Bauer was unjustly deprived of that to which he is entitled.

---

signees balance the interests of assignees, assignors, and nonassigning partners in a way that is suited to the very closely held business. Although the assignee's impotence obviously limits the market value of the partners' interest, the partners need to be protected from interference by unwanted strangers.
ALAN R. BROMBERG AND LARRY E. RIBSTEIN, PARTNERSHIP § 3:61 (1988).

3. [UPA § 26] provides: "A partner's interest in the partnership is the partner's share of the profits and surplus."

1. 6A C.J.S. Assignments § 88 (1975) ("An assignee stands in the shoes of the assignor and ordinarily obtains only the rights possessed by the assignor at the time of the assignment, and no more."); United States v. American Nat'l Bank, 443 F.Supp. 167, 174 (N.D.Ill.1977) ("The assignee stands in the shoes of its assignor."); Massey-Ferguson Credit Corp. v. Brown, 173 Mont. 253, 567 P.2d 440, 444 (1977) ("An assignee stands in the shoes of the assignor...."); see also id. § 73 ("A valid assignment generally operates to vest in the assignee the same right, title, or interest that the assignor had in the thing assigned...."); id. § 76 ("Unless a contrary intention is manifest or inferable, an assignment ordinarily carries with it all rights, remedies, and benefits which are incidental to the thing assigned....").

The court dismisses the main issue in a short footnote, stating "[w]e are unwilling to hold that partners owe a duty of good faith and fair dealing to assignees of a partner's interest." The court reasons that to find such a duty "would undermine the clear intent of AS 32.05.220(a). Partners should be able to manage their partnership without regard for the concerns of an assignee...." The court is correct in noting that Bauer has no management rights in the partnership. Bauer's attempt to enforce his right to profits under the assignment is not, however, an interference with the management of the partnership. Requiring the partners to make decisions regarding distributions in good faith does not interfere with management, it merely requires that the partners fulfill their existing contractual duties to act in good faith.

I further disagree with the court's interpretation of the intent of the statute. The statute's intent is to assure that an assignee does not interfere in the management of the partnership while receiving "the profits to which the assigning partner would otherwise be entitled." [UPA § 27(a)]. As interpreted by the court, the statute now allows partners to deprive an assignee of profits to which he is entitled by law for whatever outrageous motive or reason. The court's opinion essentially leaves the assignee of a partnership interest without remedy to enforce his right.[2]

Upon formation of the Blomfield Company/Holden Joint Venture, a contractual relationship arose among the partners.[3] This court has held that a covenant of good faith and fair dealing is implied in all contracts.[4] We have noted that the basis for imposing this duty "is a hybrid of social policy and an effort to further the expectations of the contracting parties that the promises will be executed in good faith." *Alaska Pacific,* 794 P.2d at 947. The duty of good faith and fair dealing "requires 'that neither party...do anything which will injure the right of

---

2. The court notes that the Uniform Partnership Act balances the rights of assignees, assignors, and nonassigning partners. One of the ways in which the UPA accomplishes this is to provide the assignee with the right to petition a court for dissolution of the partnership. The UPA states that upon application of an assignee, the court must decree a dissolution if the partnership was a partnership at will at the time of assignment. UPA § 32(2)(b). Although the Alaska Partnership Act was copied from the UPA, due to an error in cross-referencing, it is unclear that an assignee in Alaska has the right to apply for a dissolution. Thus he may be deprived of one of the "balances" that the UPA sets up for his protection.

3. *See* Alan A. Bromberg & Larry E. Ribstein, Partnership § 1.01, at 1:11 (1988) ("Fundamentally, general partnership is a contractual relationship among the partners."); *Grimm v. Pallesen,* 215 Kan. 660, 527 P.2d 978, 982 (1974) ("'It...has been repeatedly declared that a man cannot be made a partner against his will, by accident, or by the conduct of others, for the reason that partnership is a matter of contract.'") (*quoting Wade v. Hornaday,* 92 Kan. 293, 140 P. 870, 871 (1914)); *Eder v. Reddick,* 46 Wash.2d 41, 278 P.2d 361, 365 (1955) ("A contract of partnership, either express or implied, is essential to the creation of the partnership relationship."); *Preston v. State Indus. Accident Comm'n,* 174 Or. 553, 149 P.2d 957, 961 (1944) ("'Our law has always treated the partnership relation as founded in voluntary contract.'") (*quoting Call v. Linn,* 112 Or. 1, 228 P. 127, 129 (1924)).

4. *Alaska Pacific Assurance Co. v. Collins,* 794 P.2d 936, 947 (Alaska 1990) ("A covenant of good faith and fair dealing is an implied component of all contracts as a matter of law."); *Alyeska Pipeline Serv. Co. v. H.C. Price Co.,* 694 P.2d 782, 788 (Alaska 1985) ("Parties to a contract have mutual obligations of good faith and fair dealing."); *Guin v. Ha,* 591 P.2d 1281, 1291 (Alaska 1979) ("In every contract...there is an implied covenant of good faith and fair dealing...."); *see also* Restatement (Second) of Contracts § 205 (1981) ("Every contract imposes upon each party a duty of good faith and fair dealing in its performance and its enforcement.").

the other to receive the benefits of the agreement.'" *Klondike Indus. Corp. v. Gibson*, 741 P.2d 1161, 1168 (Alaska 1987) (*quoting Guin*, 591 P.2d at 1291).

One element of the contract between the Holdens and the partnership is the Holdens' right to receive their share of profits when a distribution is made. As an element of the partnership contract, this right is accompanied by the duty of the parties to deal fairly and in good faith. The partnership has a right to decide not to make a distribution, but in making this decision, the partnership must act in good faith.[5]

The Holdens assigned to Bauer that part of the partnership contract that entitled the Holdens to receive distributions. Under the law of assignments, Bauer steps into the shoes of the Holdens as to this distribution right. Accompanying this contract right is the partners' duty to act in good faith. Thus, as the assignee of that element of the contract, the partners owe Bauer a duty of good faith and fair dealing in deciding whether to make a distribution.

Holding that, as a matter of law, the partners owe Bauer a duty of good faith when deciding whether to make a distribution does not resolve the dispute in this case. Whether the decision to pay the "commission" in lieu of making a distribution was made in good faith is a factual question. As the moving party on a motion for summary judgment, the burden is on the partnership to demonstrate that no genuine issue existed as to whether the decision to pay the 5% "commission" was made in good faith.[6] The partnership presented little to no evidence on this issue.[7] This court should thus remand to the superior court for a factual determination of whether or not the decision by the partners to pay Blomfield's "commission" was made in good faith.

---

5. *See Brooke v. Mt. Hood Meadows Oreg.*, Ltd., 81 Or.App. 387, 725 P.2d 925, 929 (1986) ("Like the corporate director's fiduciary responsibility to the shareholders for the declaration of dividends, the general partner's duty to the limited partners in the distribution of profit is discharged by decisions made in good faith that reflect legitimate business concerns."); *see also Betz v. Chena Hot Springs Group*, 657 P.2d 831, 835 (Alaska 1982) ("Absent bad faith, breach of a fiduciary duty, or acts contrary to public policy, we will not interfere with the management decisions of the firm."); Steven J. Burton, *Breach of Contract and the Common Law Duty to Perform in Good Faith*, 94 Harv.L.Rev. 369, 385–86 (1980) ("The good faith performance doctrine may be said to permit the exercise of discretion for any purpose—including ordinary business purposes—reasonably within the contemplation of the parties.").

6. *McGee Steel Co. v. State ex rel. McDonald Indus. Alaska, Inc.*, 723 P.2d 611, 615 (Alaska 1986) ("The moving party bears the burden of demonstrating the absence of any genuine issue of material fact and its entitlement to judgment as a matter of law."); *Stanfill v. City of Fairbanks*, 659 P.2d 579, 581 (Alaska 1983) ("In ruling on a motion for summary judgment, all reasonable inferences must be drawn in favor of the non-moving party and against the movant. The burden of proving the absence of any genuine issues of material fact is upon the moving party.").

7. In support of its contention that the decision to pay the "commission" was fair, the partnership argued that the amount paid to Blomfield was the "standard" rate. The only evidence presented by the partnership was the testimony of Blomfield himself that a 5% "commission" was standard. One should view this with some skepticism as Blomfield was dealing with a tenant who was already in the building and did not have to be located or persuaded to move in. Furthermore, the rate Blomfield received is greater than 5% as the rent on which the "commission" is based is a future stream of income, not a present lump sum. After discounting future rental income to its present value, Blomfield's "commission" is greater than 5%.

The court's decision today effectively leaves an assignee with no remedy to enforce his right to receive partnership profits. Without such a remedy, his assignment becomes worthless. As I believe this result is contrary to basic contract and assignment law, I dissent from the court's opinion.

Notes

1. RUPA section 503 sets forth the rights of a transferee of a partner's transferable interest in the partnership. Like UPA section 27, the RUPA gives the assignee only

(i) the right to receive distributions to the transferor, RUPA § 503(b)(1)

(ii) the right to receive the net amount distributable to the transferor on dissolution and winding up, RUPA § 503(b)(2), and

(iii) the right to seek a judicial determination, under RUPA section 801(6), that it is equitable to wind up the partnership, RUPA § 503(b)(3).

A transferee does not become a partner solely by virtue of the transfer, and the transferor "retains the rights and duties of a partner other than the interest in the distributions transferred." RUPA § 503(c). A transferee has no right, as such, to participate in the management or conduct of partnership business, to obtain information about partnership transactions, or to inspect or copy partnership books or records. RUPA § 503(a)(3).

2. Even though a transferee has no right to participate in the management or conduct of the business, does it follow that the partners do not owe fiduciary duties to the transferee? Alternatively, do the partners their fiduciary duties to *the partnership*? See *Life Care Centers of America, Inc. v. Charles Town Associates Ltd. Partnership*, page 47.

3. Would the court in *Labowitz v. Dolan*, page 367, agree with the reasoning of Justice Matthews in his dissenting opinion of in *Bauer v. The Blomfield Company/Holden Joint Venture*? Would the *Labowitz* court have agreed with Justice Matthews' recommendation of a remand to determine if the partners had acted in good faith?

2. Charging Orders

Problem 13.8

Alice, Paula, and Brenda are partners in a dairy farm called "APB Farms." Except for an agreement to be partners, and to devote full time to APB Farms, the partners have no other agreements with respect to partnership business or affairs.

Connie has a $100,000 judgment against Paula, individually. Paula's only non-exempt asset is her interest in APB Farms.

a. May Connie go to a court of competent jurisdiction, and ask the court to enter a charging order against Paula's interest in APB Farms? Does the charging order entitle Connie to half of Paula's share of partnership property?

b. Now suppose that two quarters have passed, and that Connie has received pursuant to her charging order an aggregate amount sufficient to pay the judgment, plus interest. Will Connie be entitled to half of future distributions to Paula from APB Farms?

c. Suppose instead that APB Farms has made no distributions to its partners for over a year. The partners have told Connie that, for the foreseeable future, they plan to reinvest all profits in the business. Should the court grant Connie's motion to foreclose on the charging order? What is the effect of such a foreclosure?

d. Suppose that APB Farms changes it policy, and begins to pay partners, including Paula, a monthly salary of $3,000. Paula refuses to pay Connie half of her salary. Connie goes to the court that entered the charging order, and asks for an order directing APB Farms to pay half of Paula's salary to Connie. Should the court enter the order?

e. Now suppose that, at the foreclosure sale, Connie bids the amount of her judgment, with interest, and is the high bidder. What happens to the judgment? What are Connie's rights against APB Farms?

91st Street Joint Venture v. Goldstein

114 Md.App. 561, 691 A.2d 272 (Ct. Spec. App. 1997)

EYLER, Judge.

The question presented by this appeal is whether the Circuit Court for Baltimore County erred in vacating a charging order pursuant to which it had appointed a receiver to transfer a joint venture interest. We hold that the trial court possessed broad discretion to fashion the charging order and to review for basic fairness the transfer of the debtor's interest, and that it did not abuse its discretion in vacating the charging order and refusing to ratify the transfer. Accordingly, we shall affirm the judgment of the trial court.

FACTS

On July 25, 1994, the trial court granted a petition by appellants, 91st Street Joint Venture, a joint venture and a Maryland general partnership, Joint Venture Holding, Inc., and Princess Hotel Ltd. Partnership, to confirm an arbitrator's award. Appellants and Edward S. Goldstein, appellee, are the joint venturers in 91st Street Joint Venture. A dispute between appellants and appellee regarding capital calls required under the joint venture agreement was the subject of the arbitrator's award. Pursuant to that award, appellee's interest in the joint venture was reduced to 0.2022%, and a judgment, representing fees and expenses incurred in the arbitration, was entered in favor of appellants against appellee in the amount of $55,938.08.

On August 5, 1994, the trial court entered a charging order against appellee's 0.2022% interest in 91st Street Joint Venture. The order appointed William A. Hahn, Jr., an attorney, as receiver, for the sole purpose of effectuating a transfer, assignment, and/or conveyance to the joint venture of appellee's interest therein in the event that the judgment remained unsatisfied more than 15 days after service of the order on appellee. On August 18, 1994, appellee noted an appeal to this Court. On August 23, 1994, the trial court entered an order staying enforcement of the judgment and fixed a supersedeas bond in the amount of $56,000.

On September 21, 1994, the trial court amended its order staying enforcement of judgment. In that order, the court increased the amount of the bond to $61,600. Appellee posted a cash bond in [that amount] on October 20, 1994. We dismissed appellee's appeal for lack of prosecution on our own motion on June 6, 1995, and the mandate issued on July 5, 1995.

On February 1, 1996, appellants sought and obtained an order dissolving the stay of enforcement of the judgment. On February 23, 1996, William Hahn filed a report with the Clerk of the Circuit Court stating that he had assigned appellee's joint venture interest to the appellants, valued by an independent accounting firm at $28,950, in partial satisfaction of the judgment. On the same day, appellants filed a petition to release part of appellee's bond and to retain it in an amount sufficient to satisfy the unsatisfied portion of the judgment. The judgment with interest at that time was $64,752.83, and the amount deposited in the Clerk's Office was $63,501.09, representing the cash bond plus accrued interest.

On March 6, 1996, appellee filed an opposition to appellants' petition, a motion to release the bond, distribute the funds, and vacate the charging order, and exceptions to the receiver's report. At a hearing on March 27, 1996, the trial court orally granted appellee's exceptions and motion to vacate the charging order and denied appellants' petition to release part of the bond. The rulings were subject to the condition that, by April 8, 1996, appellee deposit into the court additional cash to cover the deficit between the amount held in the Clerk's registry and the amount necessary to satisfy the judgment with accrued interest. The court indicated that, if the judgment was not fully satisfied by April 8, 1996, the court would approve the transfer of appellee's interest to appellants on that date. Appellee paid the deficiency into the Clerk's registry on March 27, 1996. [T]he trial court entered an order, dated May 22, granting appellee's exceptions and his motion to vacate the charging order and denying appellants' petition to release part of the bond. Appellants filed a timely appeal from the court's written order.

QUESTION PRESENTED

The parties pose several questions to this Court but, in essence, inquire whether the trial court erred in setting aside the receiver's transfer of appellee's partnership interest and in vacating the charging order and terminating the receivership.

DISCUSSION

A charging order is the statutory means by which a judgment creditor may reach the partnership interest[1] of a judgment debtor. *Bank of Bethesda v. Koch*, 44 Md.App. 350, 354, 408 A.2d 767 (1979). Prior to its availability, the courts would resort to common law procedures for collection that were ill-suited for reaching partnership interests. Gose, *The Charging Order Under the Uniform Partnership Act*, 28 Wash.L.Rev. 1 (1953). Typically, despite the fact that individual partners do not have title in partnership property, partnership property would be seized under writs of execution; the debtor partner's interest in the

---

1. A joint venture and a partnership are indistinguishable for all purposes relevant to the case before us.

partnership would be sold, often to the judgment creditor, subject to the payment of partnership debts and prior claims of the partnership against the debtor partner; and the sale of the debtor partner's interest would result in compulsory dissolution and winding up of the partnership. As noted by at least one jurist, "[a] more clumsy method of proceeding could hardly have grown up." *Id.* (quoting Lord Justice Lindley of the English Court of Appeal, *Brown Janson & Co. v. Hutchinson & Co.*, 1 Q.B. 737 (1895)).

The charging order solution to this procedural nightmare appeared first in the Partnership Act adopted in England in 1890, and then in the 1914 Uniform Partnership Act (UPA) at § 28. Maryland adopted, unrevised, § 28 of the UPA in 1916. [UPA § 28] provides as follows:

[UPA § 28]. Partner's interest subject to charging order

[(1)] Authority of court. — On due application to a competent court of any judgment creditor of a partner, the court which entered the judgment, order or decree, or any other court, may charge the interest of the debtor partner with payment of the unsatisfied amount of the judgment debt with interest thereon; and may then or later appoint a receiver of his share of the profits, and of any other money due or to fall due to him in respect of the partnership, and make all other orders, directions, accounts and inquiries which the debtor partner might have made, or which circumstances of the case may require.

[(2)] Redemption of interest. — The interest charged may be redeemed at any time before foreclosure or in case of a sale being directed by the court may be purchased without thereby causing a dissolution:

[(a)] With separate property, by any one or more of the partners; or

[(b)] With partnership property, by any one or more of the partners with the consent of all the partners whose interests are not so charged or sold.

(c) Partner's interest in partnership not deprived by title. — Nothing in this title shall be held to deprive a partner of his right, if any, under the exemption laws, as regards his interest in the partnership.

By its express terms, [UPA § 28(1)] empowers the trial court to

(1) charge the interest of the partner, thereby creating a lien upon the interest;

(2) appoint a receiver of any monies due the debtor partner; and

(3) "make all other orders, directions, accounts and inquiries which the debtor partner might have made, or which circumstances of the case may require."

Also implicit in the statute is that any orders "which circumstances of the case may require" is broad enough to include the power to order a judicial sale of the property subject to the right of redemption prior to foreclosure. In the jurisdictions which have adopted § 28 of the UPA, there is general agreement that the charging order is now the judgment creditor's exclusive method of reaching a partner's interest in a partnership and that the creditor may no longer execute directly on partnership property.

While the statute sets forth the general goals and parameters of the charging order remedy, it does not delineate the particular procedures to be utilized in achieving those goals. Section [UPA § 28] does not set forth any procedures to be followed (regarding, for example, any ultimate sale of the partnership interest) once the charging order is in place.

Similarly, Rule 2-649 is drafted in very general terms:

Rule 2-649. CHARGING ORDER

(a) Issuance of Order. — Upon the written request of a judgment creditor of a partner, the court where the judgment was entered or recorded may issue an order charging the partnership interest of the judgment debtor with payment of all amounts due on the judgment. The court may order such other relief as it deems necessary and appropriate, including the appointment of a receiver for the judgment debtor's share of the partnership profits and any other money that is or becomes due to the judgment debtor by reason of the partnership interest.

*   *   *

Further, case law regarding the charging order does not shed any light on the appropriate procedures for effecting a transfer of a debtor partner's interest under a charging order. Indeed, despite its lengthy existence in Maryland law, we have been able to uncover only six published opinions that even mention the charging order. In *Hatzinicolas v. Protopapas*, 314 Md. 340, 347 n. 5, 550 A.2d 947 (1988), the Court of Appeals mentioned the charging order in a footnote and only to remark that the case before it did not concern a charging order. *In M. Lit, Inc. v. Berger*, 225 Md. 241, 170 A.2d 303 (1961), the Court of Appeals similarly mentioned the charging order only in passing because the judgment creditor had failed to establish the existence of a partnership. *O.C. Partnership v. Owrutsky*, 88 Md.App. 507, 596 A.2d 76 (1991), while involving the issue of the legal effect of a charging order against a debtor partner's interest, was concerned with the valuation of the partner's interest rather than with the charging order mechanism. In only three cases, *Leventhal v. Five Seasons Partnership*, 84 Md.App. 603, 581 A.2d 449 (1990), *Rector v. Azzato*, 74 Md.App. 684, 539 A.2d 1162 (1988),[2] and *Bank of Bethesda v. Koch*, 44 Md.App. 350, 408 A.2d 767 (1979), have we discussed the nature of the charging order in any detail. None of those cases delineates the scope of the trial court's powers in fashioning relief under the charging order.

---

2. We note that although we applied [UPA § 28] in *Rector*, that case involved a limited partnership and was governed by [RULPA § 703]. Unlike the UPA and the corresponding section of the [Revised] Uniform Limited Partnership Act ([R]ULPA), [RULPA § 703] provides the judgment creditor with a somewhat more limited remedy than that provided for in the UPA and ULPA. More specifically, [RULPA § 703] provides that,

[o]n application to a court of competent jurisdiction by any judgment creditor of a partner, the court may charge the partnership interest of the partner with payment of the unsatisfied amount of the judgment with interest. To the extent so charged, the judgment creditor has only the rights of an assignee of the partnership interest. This title does not deprive any partner of the benefit of any exemption laws applicable to his partnership interest.

We note the foregoing for purposes of accuracy only. We view the discussion in *Rector* regarding charging orders generally to be both relevant and correct.

Apparently, Maryland is not alone in the paucity of its authority on this subject. In 1953, Professor J. Gordon Gose, in his very insightful and lucid discussion of the charging order, stated that one explanation for the dearth of case law on the subject could be that the statute works so well it presents no problems for those implementing it. 28 Wash. L.Rev., *supra*, at 5. He goes on to state that

> [o]ther evidence, however, suggests that the paucity and serenity of the decisions conceal a number of deficiencies in the statute, particularly in the United States. Casual conversations with American judges and lawyers reveal not only a general unfamiliarity with the statute but also a lack of familiarity with its theory and meaning on the part of those who try to apply it. Such confusion is wholly understandable. Although the statute, when read generally with some understanding of its background, may appear to be satisfactory, it fairly bristles with unanswered questions when it is closely scrutinized. In contrast to statutes pertaining to more conventional enforcement proceedings such as executions, attachments and garnishments, the charging order statute is couched in the most general terms. Neither Section 28 of the Uniform Act nor its English counterpart contains a detailed statement of the procedure for obtaining or the consequences which result from a charging order. The English have something of an advantage in that a "charging order" procedure is prescribed in the Judgment Acts of 1838....In the United States, however, the "charging order" procedure was a complete innovation and none of the procedural doubts has been squarely resolved by statute or court rule so far as the author has been able to ascertain.

Id. at 5–6. Since the publication of that 1953 article, the case law on the subject remains relatively undeveloped. The general understanding and implementation of the charging order, however, seems to be consistent with the view expressed by Professor Gose in 1953:

> [T]he [charging order] statute apparently contemplates a highly flexible and elastic procedure under which the court may employ a charging order, a receivership of the debtor partner's interest, a sale of that interest, and a wide range of orders for accounting or for other purposes "which the circumstances of the case may require." Fundamentally, the act seems to proceed on the theory that the primary method for satisfying the creditor's judgment shall be by means of an order diverting the debtor partner's share of the profits to his creditor in a manner somewhat like that used in garnishment proceedings. If this method is ineffectual there is another more drastic course of action mentioned—a sale of the debtor's interest in the partnership. The other things provided for—appointment of a receiver and the taking of accounts and the making of such orders as the "circumstances of the case may require"—appear to be designed simply as aids to these two basic methods of collecting. The use of these subsidiary aids to the collecting process certainly should be regarded as permissive rather than compulsory. There is no apparent necessity for the appointment of a receiver, if effective collection would result from the mere issuance of an order requiring the partners to pay directly to the creditor the amounts which otherwise would go to the debtor partner. The receiver in such a case would serve no useful function but would merely add to the expense and complexity of the proceeding.

Id. at 10.

Among the cases we have found that discuss the charging order procedure in any detail, there seems to be at least implicit agreement with Professor Gose's observation that the charging order statute provides two basic collection methods:

(1) the diversion of the debtor partner's profits to the judgment creditor; and

(2) the ultimate transfer of the debtor partner's interest should the first collection method prove unsatisfactory.

Appellants argue that the trial court had entered a valid charging order pursuant to [UPA § 28]. They argue that the charging order empowered the receiver to effect an assignment of appellee's interest in the partnership without further order of court and that the receiver did effect the assignment as reflected in his report on February 23, 1996.

[W]e understand appellants to argue that the charging order itself was a final judgment which triggered the thirty day limit on the trial court's revisory powers.

A review of the express terms of the charging order tends to support appellants' argument. The order provides in pertinent part as follows:

ORDERED, that William A. Hahn, Jr. be and he is hereby appointed as a Receiver for the limited purpose of effectuating a transfer, assignment and/or conveyance to the Joint Venture of Edward S. Goldstein's 0.2022 percent interest in the Joint Venture, provided that the judgment amount remains unsatisfied after the expiration of fifteen (15) calendar days after service of this Order is made upon Edward S. Goldstein; and it is further

ORDERED, that the Receiver may effectuate said transfer, assignment and/or conveyance to the Joint Venture upon receipt of written notice from the Judgment Creditor's counsel that the judgment amount remains unsatisfied after the expiration of the fifteen (15) calendar day period as aforementioned; and it is further

ORDERED, that the Receiver shall be provided with such other power and authority as may be necessary to effectuate the complete assignment, transfer and/or conveyance of Edward S. Goldstein's 0.2022 percent interest without further order of this Court....

A literal reading of the charging order suggests that the order conclusively determined the rights of the parties in that it directed the receiver to assign or transfer appellee's interest in the joint venture, subject only to the condition precedent of a fifteen day default, and without further order of the trial court. By its terms, the order left nothing more for the trial court to do. Without considering more, the charging order would seem to have put appellee out of court, and consequently, to have constituted a final judgment. Under this view of the charging order, it was a final judgment entered on the docket on August 8, 1994, and enrolled as of September 7, 1994, and could be disturbed only for fraud, mistake or irregularity after that date.

For reasons set forth below, we hold that appellee's interest that was the subject of the charging order was subject to redemption by appellee and the assignment was subject to ratification by the trial court. Further, it could be challenged by appellee through the filing of exceptions. Accordingly, the charging order was not a final order which concluded the matter between the parties at the time it was issued by the court, and it was subject to revision at any time prior to the entry of a final judgment.

As we stated earlier, § 28 of the UPA is drafted in the most general terms and provides courts with very little guidance regarding particular procedures that should be used to further the goals of the charging order. The generality of its terms could be read to sanction the fashioning of charging order procedures on a case-by-case basis and without regard to collection procedures already in place with respect to judgment debtors generally. A better explanation for the generality is the fact that § 28 was drafted to fit the differing procedures of all jurisdictions within the United States. We view this latter explanation as the more likely one. Further, we view it as just an unfortunate circumstance that § 28 was adopted in Maryland and most other jurisdictions without any additional elaboration of procedure.

In every published opinion we have been able to uncover that implicitly or explicitly has approved the transfer of the debtor partner's interest, the transfer has taken place according to established procedures for a judicial sale, or in one instance, for strict foreclosure.[4] *See Hellman,* 233 Cal.App.3d at 848–49, 284 Cal.Rptr. 830 (foreclosure sale as distinguished from execution sale); *Madison Hills Ltd.,* 644 A.2d at 368–70 (strict foreclosure); *Nigri v. Lotz,* 453 S.E.2d at 783 (judicial sale); *Tupper,* 494 P.2d at 1278 (judicial sale); *Birchwood Builders,* 573 A.2d at 185–86 (judicial sale). Indeed, all of the foregoing cases presume without deciding that the ordering of a sale is something that the trial court may do as a supplement to charging the interest of the partnership and appointing a receiver for profits. We concur but hold that any transfer of the debtor partner's interest is to take place pursuant to the rules governing judicial sales.

Forced sales prescribed by the Maryland Rules fall into three general categories: (1) execution or sheriff's sales, (2) judicial sales, or (3) sales pursuant to foreclosure of mortgages or other security devices or liens created by statute providing for foreclosure in the manner specified for foreclosure of mortgages. This third category includes mortgages that contain a power of sale, a consent to decree, both, or neither. The Maryland Rules prescribe pre-sale and post-sale procedures for all such forced sales. More specifically, all such forced sales are subject to challenge by the filing of exceptions and are required to be ratified by the trial court. No such sales are final until ratified.

Although Rule 2-649(a) gives the court broad discretion to "order such other relief as it deems necessary and appropriate," we do not read it to give the court the authority to fashion procedures for the transfer of the debtor partner's interest without regard to those procedures set forth in the Maryland Rules. A better reading of Rule 2-649 is that it provides the court with the authority to utilize

---

4. Prior to the enactment of statutes authorizing foreclosure sales, the equitable remedy of "strict foreclosure" was the method by which a mortgagee extinguished the mortgagor's right of redemption in the mortgaged property. In such a proceeding, no sale of the mortgaged property took place, but instead, the equity court determined the amount due the mortgagee and passed a decree naming a date for the sum named in the decree to be paid, or the mortgagor's right to redeem would forever be taken away. While strict foreclosure remains a viable, if little used, procedure for foreclosing mortgages, it does not apply to the enforcement of judgment liens. Strict foreclosure is premised on the fact that legal title to the property already rests in the mortgagee and, by extinguishing the mortgagor's right of redemption, the mortgagee merely is clearing its title to the property.

any of the procedures available under Maryland law. The one procedure currently available for the transfer of the debtor partner's interest is the judicial sale. Any other reading of Rule 2-649 would lead us to conclude that the Court of Appeals did not intend to protect the partnership interest with the same types of procedural safeguards it provides for other types of property. We can ascertain no rationale for such unfavorable treatment, and, indeed, such a reading would be at odds with the right of redemption provided in [UPA § 28(2)]. Further, our holding is consistent with the view expressed by other courts, which is that any transfer of the debtor partner's interest should occur under judicial supervision.

Relying on *Leventhal*, 84 Md.App. at 606, 581 A.2d 449, appellants argue that [UPA § 28] gives the receiver the power to do whatever appellee could have done, including assign appellee's interest. That interpretation of [UPA § 28] arguably removes the charging order remedy from the confines of the post-sale procedures of Title 14, Chapter 300. *Leventhal*, however, is not on point, but instead, involved the general question of the powers of a receiver to protect the value of the partnership interest and, specifically, the issue of a receiver's standing to petition the trial court for dissolution of a partnership. The holding in *Leventhal* is consistent with our reading of [UPA § 28].

Section [UPA § 28] empowers the trial court to "make all other orders, directions, accounts and inquiries which the debtor partner might have made, or which the circumstances of the case may require." See also Rule 2-649 (providing that "[t]he court may order such other relief as it deems necessary and appropriate, including the appointment of a receiver for the judgment debtor's share of the partnership profits and any other money that is or becomes due to the judgment debtor by reason of the partnership interest") (emphasis added). Indeed, the phrasing of [UPA § 28(1)] and of Rule 2-649 suggests that the role contemplated for a receiver appointed pursuant to a charging order is a very limited role, i.e., confined to the receipt of moneys due the debtor partner as a result of his partnership interest. While [UPA § 28] does give the trial court the authority to vest the receiver with additional powers, it does not give the court the authority to exempt a transfer of the debtor partner's interest from the procedures set forth in the Maryland Rules.

Given that the transfer was subject to challenge and review and was not final until ratified by the trial court, the charging order authorizing the transfer was not a final order, and was subject to revision at any time prior to the entry of a final judgment. Moreover, the trial court could not have ratified the transfer unless the court was satisfied that the sale was fairly and properly made. At the March 27, 1996 hearing on appellee's exceptions to the receiver's report and on the parties' various outstanding motions, the trial court noted that substantially all of the judgment was secured by a cash bond that had been posted by appellee in order to stay execution of the judgment during the pendency of the initial appeal. At the time the cash was deposited into the Clerk's registry, it was enough to cover the judgment plus a year's worth of interest. Although our mandate in the first appeal had issued on July 5, 1995, appellants did not seek to dissolve the stay and execute on their judgment until February of 1996. In the interim, enough interest on the judgment had accrued so that there was a deficiency of a little over twelve hundred dollars between the judgment and the cash bond. Appellants' counsel admitted that appellants' primary objective in seeking to execute on the charging order was to obtain a "business divorce." Indeed, appellants' counsel argued that the trial court should assist appellants in this endeavor.

Rather than permit the charging order to be used for this purpose, the trial court gave appellee an additional twelve days within which to deposit the deficiency into the Clerk's registry and thereby redeem his interest. The trial court's actions in this regard did not constitute an abuse of discretion, given the particular circumstances of this case. We agree with Professor Gose that the primary means of satisfying a judgment from a partnership interest should be the receipt and distribution of any income or profits due the debtor partner, and that, ordinarily, sale of the interest should not be resorted to unless the judgment could not be satisfied in that manner within a reasonable period of time. Gose, *supra*, 28 Wash. L.Rev. at 16.[7]

Given our interpretation of the charging order, we disagree with appellants that appellee was estopped from challenging the charging order. Although an order appointing a receiver is one of the limited types of interlocutory orders from which a party may take an immediate appeal, appellee was free to challenge the assignment by filing exceptions under Rule 14-305(d). To be sure, appellee did not challenge the charging order as expeditiously as he might have, but instead, waited until the last possible moment to challenge it. Accordingly, the equities are not overwhelmingly in his favor. That fact notwithstanding, the trial court did not abuse its discretion in considering the challenge when it did.

Finally, appellants argue that the court erred in vacating the charging order *nunc pro tunc* because that phrase is properly used only to correct clerical errors and not to correct judicial error. We agree. The phrase *nunc pro tunc* signifies a thing that is done now which has the same legal force and effect as if done at the time it ought to have been done. It is properly used only to correct clerical errors. In this case, the entry of the charging order was not merely a clerical error and could not be vacated *nunc pro tunc*. Accordingly, we will modify the judgment to strike the phrase *nunc pro tunc*.[8]

JUDGMENT AFFIRMED IN PART AND MODIFIED IN PART IN ACCORDANCE WITH THE OPINION OF THE COURT; APPELLANTS TO PAY THE COSTS.

Notes

1. RUPA section 504(b) clarifies UPA section 28 by providing an express right to foreclosure of the charging order by sale of the charged interest in the partnership.

---

7. Indeed, although not well-developed on the record, there was a reference below to the fact that the debtor partner was owed a 1.1 million dollar developer's fee under the joint venture agreement. If that fee was due to be paid in a timely fashion, the judgment should have been satisfied out of the fee.

8. Appellee had argued below for the inclusion of the phrase *nunc pro tunc* because he was concerned that appellants would use the existence of the charging order to deny appellee a 1.1 million dollar developer's fee that he was owed pursuant to the terms of the joint venture agreement. As a preliminary matter, the joint venture agreement, which was included in its entirety in the record, indicates that the developer's fee is for services rendered and does not seem to be conditioned upon appellee's continued status as a partner. In any event, the charging order did not interrupt appellee's status as partner, but instead, merely constituted a lien upon his interest. Appellee never ceased to be a partner by virtue of the charging order.

2. Why doesn't a foreclosure on the charging order interfere with the rights of the other partners?

PB Real Estate, Inc. v. DEM II Properties

50 Conn.App. 741, 719 A.2d 73

Before SCHALLER, FRANCIS X. HENNESSY and SHEA, JJ.

SHEA, Judge.

The Connecticut Limited Liability Company Act, General Statutes §§ 34-100 to 34-242, inclusive, was adopted in 1993 and is generally similar to the model act promulgated in 1995 by the Uniform Laws Commissioners.

> The allure of the limited liability company is its unique ability to bring together in a single business organization the best features of all other business forms—properly structured, its owners obtain both a corporate-styled liability shield and the pass-through tax benefits of a partnership.

Unif. Limited Liability Company Act, prefatory note, 6A U.L.A. 426 (1995). The central issue in this appeal is the extent to which that liability shield protects the interest of a member of a limited liability company against a judgment creditor when the basis for the judgment is an obligation unrelated to the activities of the company. Under the circumstances of this case, we conclude that it raises no barrier to the satisfaction of such a judgment from the member's interest in the company.

After obtaining a deficiency judgment resulting from a mortgage foreclosure against the defendants, Edward J. Botwick, David J. Kurzawa and DEM II Properties[1], the plaintiff, PB Real Estate, Inc., applied, pursuant to General Statutes (Rev. to 1995) § 34-66(1)[2], for a charging order directed to Botwick & Kurzawa, LLC, a limited liability company (LLC) engaged in the practice of law. The plaintiff was attempting to satisfy the judgment from any payments becoming due to the individual defendants, each of whom owns one half of the LLC. The trial court granted the application and directed the LLC to pay to the plaintiff

---

1. The named defendant, DEM II Properties, is named as an appellant in the docketing statement filed with this appeal. See Practice Book § 63-4(a)(4). There is no indication, however, that it is aggrieved by the issuance of the turnover order, which is the subject of this appeal. No brief has been filed on behalf of this defendant. We refer in this opinion to Edward J. Botwick and David J. Kurzawa as the defendants.

2. General Statutes (Rev. to 1995) § 34-66(1) provides:

    On due application to a competent court by any judgment creditor of a partner, the court which entered the judgment, order, or decree, or any other court, may charge the interest of the debtor partner with payment of the unsatisfied amount of such judgment debt with interest thereon; and may then or later appoint a receiver of his share of the profits, and of any other money due or to fall due to him in respect of the partnership, and make all other orders, directions, accounts and inquiries which the debtor partner might have made, or which the circumstances of the case may require.

This provision was repealed by No. 95-341 of the 1995 Public Acts, which became effective on July 1, 1997. The plaintiff's motion for a charging order was granted on November 11, 1996.

present and future shares of any and all distributions, credits, drawings, or payments due[3] to the defendant[s]...until the judgment is satisfied in full....

The order also directed the LLC to furnish to the plaintiff for examination a copy of the LLC agreement and various financial information.

Pursuant to General Statutes § 52-356b (b)[4], the plaintiff applied for a turnover order, claiming that the LLC had not fully complied with the charging order because the 1996 profit and loss statement indicated that a portion of the item designated on the statement as "legal staff" expense appeared to have been paid to the defendants, contrary to the directive in the charging order that all distributions should be paid to the plaintiff. After an evidentiary hearing, the trial court granted the application for a turnover order. The LLC appeals from that order and raises two issues:

(1) whether certain payments it made to the defendants, the sole owners, managers and members of the LLC, were properly the subject of a turnover order; and

(2) whether the turnover order exceeds the scope of the statute authorizing such orders with respect to an LLC.

We resolve both issues against the LLC and affirm the order of the trial court.

I

The trial court found that, since the date of the charging order, the LLC had paid approximately $28,000 to each of two defendants. The court rejected the defendants' claim that those payments were merely compensation for their services to the LLC as lawyers and were similar to the wages paid to other employees of the firm. The payments to the defendants were not shown in the "salary" column of the business record where payments to employees of the law firm are recorded but were listed separately under their initials. The 1996 tax returns of the individual defendants indicated that they received little or no wages, but they reported significant earnings from self-employment. The trial court concluded that the payments made by the law firm to the defendants were "distributions" that were subject to the charging order.

The LLC does not dispute the underlying facts on which the trial court relied in reaching that conclusion. Even without such a concession, we conclude that

---

3. The trial court observed that the phrase, "distributions, credits, drawings, or payments due" in the charging order may be broader than the definition of a member's limited liability company interest in General Statutes § 34-101(10)

a member's share of the profits and losses of the limited liability company and a member's right to receive distributions of the limited liability company's assets....

The court restricted the scope of the turnover order to payments found to have been "distributions."

4. General Statutes § 52-356b (b) provides:

The court may issue a turnover order pursuant to this section, after notice and hearing or as provided in subsection (c), on a showing of need for the order. If the order is to be directed against a third person, such person shall be notified of his right pursuant to section 52-356c to a determination of any interest claimed in the property."

the evidence adequately supports the facts set forth in the memorandum of decision. The LLC contends, nevertheless, that several provisions of the Connecticut Limited Liability Company Act preclude the conclusion that the challenged payments were distributions.

II

The LLC claims that the trial court incorrectly failed to limit the turnover order to the "rights of an assignee of the member's limited liability company interest," as provided by General Statutes § 34-171[5] in defining the rights of a judgment creditor. That statute provides that,

> [t]o the extent so charged, the judgment creditor has only the rights of an assignee of the member's limited liability company interest.

The phrase, "[l]imited liability company membership interest," is defined by General Statutes § 34-101(10)[6] to mean

> a member's share of the profits and losses of the limited liability company and a member's right to receive distributions of the limited liability company's assets, unless otherwise provided in the operating agreement.

The operating agreement for the LLC provides that

> all distributions...shall be made at such time as determined by the Manager,[7]

who consists solely of the two owners. They maintain that they have authorized no distributions, and therefore, the court's finding that the $28,000 each of them has received was a distribution is contrary to General Statutes § 34-158, which provides in part that

---

5. General Statutes § 34-171 provides:
   On application to a court of competent jurisdiction by any judgment creditor of a member, the court may charge the member's limited liability company interest with payment of the unsatisfied amount of the judgment with interest. To the extent so charged, the judgment creditor has only the rights of an assignee of the member's limited liability company interest. Nothing in sections 34-100 to 34-242, inclusive, shall be held to deprive a member of the benefit of any exemption provided by law applicable to such person's limited liability company membership interest.

6. General Statutes § 34-101(10) provides:
   'Limited liability company membership interest' or 'interest' or 'interest in the limited liability company' means a member's share of the profits and losses of the limited liability company and a member's right to receive distributions of the limited liability company's assets, unless otherwise provided in the operating agreement.

7. Article VIII, § 8.2 of the operating agreement provides:
   Except as provided in Section 7.3(c), all distributions of cash or other property shall be made to the Members pro rata in proportion to the respective Capital Interests of the Members on the record date of such distribution. [E]xcept as provided in Section 8.4, all distributions of Distributable Cash and property shall be made at such time as determined by the Manager. No Member shall have the right to demand and receive property other than cash irrespective of the nature of its Capital Contribution. All amounts withheld pursuant to the Code or any provisions of state or local tax law with respect to any payment or distribution to the Members from the Company shall be treated as amount[s] distributed to the relevant Member or Members pursuant to this Section 8.2.

[a] member is entitled to receive distributions…from a limited liability company to the extent and at the times or upon the happening of the events specified in the operating agreement or at the times determined by the members or managers pursuant to section 34-142.[8]

It defies common sense for the defendants, who jointly comprise the "Manager," to contend that the payments they made to themselves from the assets of their LLC do not constitute distributions, simply because they never voted to order such distributions. The operating agreement requires that distributions "shall be made at such time as determined by the Manager," but does not specify any formal procedure for authorizing distributions. General Statutes § 34-142(a) requires

the affirmative vote, approval or consent of…more than one-half by number of the managers

to decide matters connected with the LLC, but these are alternatives. The defendants can hardly deny that they approved or consented to the payments they received from the LLC, which they own and control. Neither § 34-142(a) nor General Statutes § 34-158[9], which authorizes distributions

at the times determined by the members or managers pursuant to section 34-142,[10]

raises any barrier to the finding of the court that the payments to the defendants constituted distributions subject to the charging order they have disregarded.

Furthermore, the definition in § 34-101(10) of a member's limited liability company interest, which § 34-171 makes available for satisfaction of a judgment, includes "a member's share of the profits and losses" of the company as well as "distributions of the…company's assets.…" Although the defendants at trial presented a profit and loss statement for 1996 showing a net profit of only $23.44, that result was achieved only by treating the payments of $28,000 to each of them as expenses for wages. If those payments were neither distributions, as the defendants contend, nor wages, as the trial court found, they would have to be considered profits. The plaintiff claims that, as an assignee of the defendants' shares thereof, it would be entitled to satisfy its deficiency judgment from those profits even if the payments made to the defendants had not been approved in accordance with the operating agreement. The defendants contend, however, that General Statutes § 34-170(a)(2), providing that

---

8. General Statutes § 34-142(a) provides in relevant part that "the affirmative vote, approval or consent of…more than one-half by number of the managers, if management of the limited liability company is vested in managers, shall be required to decide any matter connected with the business or affairs of the limited liability company."

9. General Statutes § 34-158 provides:

Except as provided in sections 34-159 and 34-210, distributions of cash or other assets of a limited liability company shall be allocated among the members and among classes of members in the manner provided in the operating agreement. If the operating agreement does not so provide, the distributions shall be made on the basis of the value of the contributions made by each member to the extent they have been received by the limited liability company and have not been returned. A member is entitled to receive distributions described in this section from a limited liability company to the extent and at the times or upon the happening of the events specified in the operating agreement or at the times determined by the members or managers pursuant to section 34-142.

10. See footnote 8.

> an assignment entitles the assignee to receive, to the extent assigned, only the distributions to which the assignor would be entitled

indicates otherwise. The trial court did not consider the issue of a possible inconsistency between that provision and the definition of a member's interest in § 34-101(10), nor shall we do so in view of our agreement with the court's conclusion that the payments received by the defendants were distributions subject to the charging order.

The judgment issuing the turnover order is affirmed.

In this opinion the other judges concurred.

Notes

1. The ULLCA is similar to the RUPA with respect to the rights of members, their transferees, and charging orders. *See* ULLCA §§ 101(5)–(6), 501–04.

2. The ULLCA differs from both the UPA and the RUPA in that it calls the interest in the firm (UPA) or the transferable interest in the firm (RUPA) the member's "distributional interest." ULLCA § 101(6). ULLCA section 101(5) defines distributions in a manner similar to RUPA section 101(3).

3. In its opinion, the court notes that a member's LLC interest includes a "share of the profits and losses," but does not address the question of whether the holder of a charging order has a right to receive all profits allocated to the member whose interest has been charged. How would the court in *Bauer v. The Blomfeld Company/Holden Joint Venture* have analyzed that issue? Should the same result be reached under the Connecticut LLC Act? Under the Uniform LLC Act?

4. Connecticut LLC Act section 34-171 provides for charging orders on LLC interests:

> On application to a court of competent jurisdiction by any judgment creditor of a member, the court may charge the member's limited liability company interest with payment of the unsatisfied amount of the judgment with interest. To the extent so charged, the judgment creditor has only the rights of an assignee of the member's limited liability company interest. * * *

Note that the trial court relied on Connecticut General Statute section 34-66(1)—Connecticut's version of UPA 28(1)—which entitles a judgment creditor holding a charging order to receive the member's

> share of the profits, and of any other money to due or to fall due to him in respect of the partnership.

Why would the trial court have relied on the partnership statute, rather than the LLC statute in framing its charging order?

5. Suppose that the operating agreement provides for the payment of salaries to members who are employed by the LLC. Would a judgment creditor with a charging order be entitled to the amounts paid as salary under Connecticut LLC Act section 34-171? Under Connecticut UPA section 34-66(1) [UPA section 28(1)]?

3. Right to Dissolution

Problem 13.9

Alice, Paula, and Brenda are partners in a dairy farm called "APB Farms". Except for an agreement to be partners, and to devote full time to APB Farms, the partners have no other agreements with respect to partnership business or affairs. Paula has assigned to Connie half of Paula's interest in APB Farms. After the assignment, APB Farms tells Connie that, for the foreseeable future, they will continue their practice of reinvesting all its profits in the business, and will make no distributions. May Connie sue in a court of competent jurisdiction for a decree dissolving or liquidating APB Farms?

Baybank v. Catamount Construction, Inc.
693 A.2d 1163 (N.H. 1997)

JOHNSON, Justice.

The defendants, Catamount Construction, Inc., Sunset Construction Co., Eugene R. Connor, M. Patricia Connor, John H. Connor, and Marilyn A. Connor, appeal an order of the Superior Court (Perkins, J.) granting plaintiff Baybank a charging order and other relief against two of the defendants' interests in a limited partnership.

Baybank obtained a judgment in superior court against defendants Eugene and John Connor (the Connors) as guarantors on a promissory note made by defendant Catamount Construction, Inc. In an effort to satisfy its judgment, Baybank sought to reach the Connors' interests in East Street Associates Limited Partnership (East Street), in which the Connors are limited partners. Baybank requested a charging order against the Connors' interests in East Street, the appointment of a receiver for any monies due the Connors as limited partners in East Street, and, if the judgment was not satisfied within fourteen days, dissolution of East Street. The Connors responded by conceding that Baybank would be entitled to a charging order under [the RULPA], but objecting to the additional relief sought. The superior court granted Baybank a charging order and further ordered that

> East Street Limited Partnership be dissolved and a receiver appointed to dispose of [the Connors'] interest in the limited partnership to satisfy the judgment debt.

On appeal, the defendants challenge the trial court's authority to order the additional relief, particularly the dissolution of East Street. Specifically, the defendants contend that the trial court erred in importing creditors' rights and remedies found in the Uniform Partnership Act (UPA) into the [Revised] Uniform Limited Partnership Act ([RULPA]).

The trial court ruled that it had broad equitable power to grant the additional relief under [UPA § 28], which provides:

> On due application to a superior court by any judgment creditor of a partner, the court may charge the interest of the debtor partner with payment of the unsatisfied amount of such judgment debt with interest

thereon: and may then or later appoint a receiver of his share of the profits, and of any other money due or to fall due to him in respect to the partnership, and make all other orders, functions, accounts and inquiries which the circumstances of the case may require.

[UPA § 28]. Citing [UPA § 6], which states that the UPA

shall apply to limited partnerships except insofar as the statutes relating to such partnerships are inconsistent herewith,

the trial court concluded that it should apply the UPA to East Street to the extent that the UPA did not conflict with the [RULPA]. Finding no conflict between [UPA § 28] and anything in the [RULPA], the court applied the UPA provision to East Street.

In addition, the trial court based its order of dissolution on [UPA § 32, II(b),] which provides:

The court shall decree a dissolution on the application of the purchaser of a partner's interest under [UPA § 27] or [UPA § 28:]

*   *   *

(b) At any time if the partnership was a partnership at will when the interest was assigned or when the charging order was issued.

Again, the court found that this section did not conflict with anything in [the RULPA] and was therefore applicable to East Street.

The defendants urge us to hold that the rights of judgment creditors of limited partners are limited to those set forth in [the RULPA], and that it was error for the trial court to import any of the remedial provisions of [the UPA] into [the RULPA]. We decline to adopt this position as we are persuaded by the weight of authority from other jurisdictions and scholarly commentary that the legislature did not intend to preclude a creditor with a charging order on a limited partnership interest from enforcing that interest if necessary. We are also convinced, however, that the legislature did not intend such a creditor to have the remedies ordered by the trial court.

The statutory remedy of a charging order was designed to prevent the personal creditors of a limited partner from disrupting the partnership business by seizing partnership assets on execution. The statutory remedy forces a judgment creditor to look solely to the debtor's partnership interest, which the [RULPA] defines as

a partner's share of the profits and losses of a limited partnership and the right to receive distributions of partnership assets,

[RULPA § 101(10)], rather than to partnership assets, to satisfy a partner's personal debt.

In effect, the charging order leaves the partnership intact but diverts to the judgment creditor the stream of profits that would otherwise flow to the debtor partner.

Weinberger, *Making Partners Pay Child Support: The Charging Order at 100*, 27 Hous.L.Rev. 297, 302 (1990).

The defendants conceded that their interests in East Street could have been charged under [the RULPA]. We therefore affirm the portion of the trial court's order that charged the Connors' interests in East Street. The question before us is whether the additional remedies, particularly dissolution, ordered by the trial court are available to a creditor of a limited partner. As noted above, the UPA provides that it "shall apply to limited partnerships except insofar as the statutes relating to such partnerships are inconsistent herewith." UPA § 6(2). The [RULPA] provides that "[i]n any case not provided for in this chapter the provisions of the Uniform Partnership Act shall govern." [RULPA § 1105]. Although the parties disagree on whether the later-enacted [RULPA § 703] applies to the exclusion of [the UPA], we find it unnecessary to decide this issue since we would arrive at our holding in this case regardless of which provision we applied.

We first address the defendants' contention that the appointment of a receiver and sale of a charged partnership interest are unauthorized under the charging order provision of the [RULPA]. That section, entitled "Rights of Creditor," provides:

> On application to a court of competent jurisdiction by any judgment creditor of a partner, the court may charge the partnership interest of the partner with payment of the unsatisfied amount of the judgment with interest. To the extent so charged, the judgment creditor has only the rights of an assignee of the partnership interest. This chapter does not deprive any partner of the benefit of any exemption laws applicable to his partnership interest.

[RULPA § 703]. As observed by the court in *Madison Hills Ltd. v. Madison Hills, Inc.,* 35 Conn.App. 81, 644 A.2d 363, 367 (1994), this section does not provide a method for enforcing the charging order. The significance of this omission becomes apparent in a case such as that before us, in which Baybank alleges that a charging order alone would never divert enough money to Baybank to satisfy even the accruing interest on the judgment debt. It is in precisely such situations that courts have been most inclined to enforce the creditor's rights through foreclosure on the charged interest. We therefore find that [RULPA § 703] does not "provide[ ] for," within the meaning of [RULPA § 1105], a case such as this, and that the legislature intended that reference be made to the UPA for the means of enforcing the creditor's rights in the charged partnership interest. See *Madison Hills,* 644 A.2d at 368 (finding that where only the UPA, and not the [RULPA], provides means of enforcing a charging order, the charging order provision of the [RULPA] "relies on rather than conflicts with" the UPA provision).

We also find that [RULPA § 703] is not inconsistent with the remedial provisions of [UPA § 28], since, as the *Madison Hills* court noted,

> the purpose of the charging order provisions under both statutes is to balance the need to protect the orderly operation of the partnership and the rights of creditors.

644 A.2d at 368–69. In most cases, neither the appointment of a receiver to collect the debtor partner's share of distributed profits, nor the sale of the debtor partner's interest in the partnership, as opposed to partnership assets, would unduly interfere with the running of the partnership business. Thus, we hold that a court may properly look to [UPA § 28] for the means to enforce a charging order under [RULPA § 703] when the latter remedy alone would be insufficient.

The trial court, however, did not actually grant the type of relief contemplated by [UPA § 28]. Although the trial court purported to order the appointment of a receiver "to dispose of the guarantors' interest in the limited partner-ship to satisfy the judgment debt," such relief would have been unnecessary in light of the trial court's order that the partnership be dissolved. In fact, it appears that the receiver and court-ordered sale were not intended to be in aid of the charging order but in aid of dissolution.

A review of the transcript of the hearing on Baybank's motion reveals that what was really at issue was Baybank's attempt to liquidate the primary asset of the limited partnership, a piece of real estate located in Tewksbury, Massachu-setts, and satisfy its judgment out of the proceeds thereof. At one point, counsel for Baybank stated,

> the basic process that we're asking the court to do is to award the charg-ing order for the judgment amount which is what the defendants con-fessed that we're entitled to, *but then to go the next step which is to order*—to make sufficient findings to order that a *judicial dissolution* of this partnership, given its history, given its stated purpose under oath, given its ultimate frustration of that purpose, to dissolve that partner-ship, *to allow the underlying property or the interest in the partnership and then the underlying property to be sold* so that the cash gets freed up, the debt gets paid so the interest ticker now does not outstrip the in-come that can be earned from the partnership. . . .

(Emphasis added.) Such an application of partnership property to pay the per-sonal debts of a partner, however, is precisely what the charging order provisions of the [RULPA] and the UPA are intended to prevent. Neither the [RULPA] nor the UPA charging order provision allows a creditor such as Baybank to satisfy its judgment out of partnership assets.

Nor is Baybank entitled to the dissolution of East Street. The trial court erred by ordering dissolution under [UPA § 32(2)(b)]. First, that provision allows the court to order dissolution

> on the application of the purchaser of a partner's interest under [UPA § 27] or [UPA § 28].

[UPA § 32(2)(b)]. Baybank is not such a purchaser, however, because the defen-dants' partnership interests were never foreclosed upon. Baybank is merely a creditor with a charging order on the defendants' limited partnership interests and, as such, is not entitled under the terms of [UPA § 32(2)], to petition for dis-solution of East Street.

Moreover, on the issue of judicial dissolution, the [RULPA] is neither silent nor consistent with the UPA, which leaves no occasion to import the provisions of [UPA § 32] into [the RULPA]. Judicial dissolution of a limited partnership is provided for in[RULPA § 802], which states that "[o]n application by or for a partner, the superior court may decree dissolution of a limited partnership when-ever it is not reasonably practicable to carry on the business in conformity with the partnership agreement." [RULPA § 802]. Thus, the availability of judicial dis-solution under the terms of the [RULPA] is much more limited than under the UPA. *Cf.* [UPA § 32(2)]. Limited recourse to judicial dissolution for limited part-nerships reflects basic structural differences between the two types of entities. *See* A. Bromberg, Crane and Bromberg on Partnership § 90B(a), at 516 (1968) (not-ing that there are differences between dissolution of general and limited partnerships and finding it "not surprising that in some aspects of continuity, limited partnerships resemble corporations more closely than they do general partnerships"). In short, the [RULPA] is inconsistent with the UPA on this issue, and the trial court therefore erred in applying the UPA.

Baybank argues that even if the superior court erred in basing its order of dissolution on [UPA § 32(2)(b)], the same result could have been reached under either [RULPA § 802] or [UPA § 32(1)(f)], which provides that a court may order dissolution on application by or for a partner when "[o]ther circumstances render a dissolution equitable." Thus, Baybank urges us to affirm the trial court's order on the ground that a correct result reached on mistaken grounds should be sustained if there are valid alternative grounds to support it. We conclude, however, that dissolution was not authorized under either [RULPA § 802] or [UPA § 32(1)(f)].

First, as with [UPA § 32(2)], we find no occasion to import the provisions of [UPA § 32(1)] into the [RULPA], which speaks plainly and comprehensively on the issue of dissolution of a limited partnership. As for [RULPA § 802], it requires that a petition for dissolution be made "by or for a partner." [RULPA § 802]. Baybank, as a judgment creditor, lacked standing to seek judicial dissolution under this section. As a creditor holding a charging order, Baybank has, to the extent of the interest charged, "only the rights of an assignee of the partnership interest." [RULPA § 703]. Under [RULPA § 702],

[a]n assignment of a partnership interest does not...entitle the assignee to become or to exercise any rights of a partner.

[RULPA § 702] (emphasis added). This explicit statutory limitation on the rights of assignees precludes Baybank from acting "by or for" the Connors in petitioning for dissolution of East Street.

Nor do we believe, as Baybank argues, that a receiver appointed under [UPA § 28] could petition "by or for a partner" for dissolution. That section provides that the court "may then or later appoint a receiver of [the debtor partner's] share of the profits, and of any other money due or to fall due to him in respect to the partnership, and make all other orders, functions, accounts and inquiries which the circumstances of the case may require." [UPA § 28(1)]. Under our reading of this section, the express purpose for which a receiver may be appointed is to collect whatever money the partnership distributes that would otherwise have gone to the debtor partner. It is the court, not the receiver, that is authorized by the statute to "make all other orders, functions, accounts and inquiries." [UPA § 28(1)]. Therefore, we are not persuaded by *Leventhal v. Five Seasons,* 84 Md.App. 603, 581 A.2d 449 (Spec.1990), for the proposition that a receiver may petition for dissolution because the receiver "stands in the shoes of the debtor/partner." 581 A.2d at 452. That assertion appears to have been based on the premise that

[t]he receiver may do whatever the debtor partner could do by way of orders, directions, accounts, or inquiries,

581 A.2d at 451 (quotation omitted), a premise not supported by our reading of the statute.

Moreover, even if Baybank could petition on behalf of the Connors for dissolution of East Street, we find that the conditions for judicial dissolution under [RULPA § 802] are not met in this case. Baybank argues that it is not reasonably practicable for East Street to carry on its business in conformity with its partnership agreement because East Street does not generate and distribute to its limited partners enough income to meet even the interest payments on the Connors' judgment debt. Even if we were to accept Baybank's statement that "the purpose of every partnership is to make a profit for its partners," however, we fail to see how East Street's alleged inability to distribute enough income to its partners to enable them to pay their personal debts renders the partnership unprofitable.

Finally, Baybank argues that allowing the Connors to use East Street as a shield against their personal creditors would be contrary to reason and against public policy. Baybank therefore asks us to read an exception into the statutory scheme to address the Connors' alleged attempt to defraud Baybank by transferring the Tewksbury property into East Street. We decline to do so. We note that the case upon which Baybank primarily relies, *Taylor*, 190 Cal.App.2d 700, 12 Cal.Rptr. 323, involved an alleged fraudulent transfer of property out of a partnership, not into one. 12 Cal.Rptr. at 330. In that case, the issue was the frustration of the charging order remedy when the fraudulent transfer of partnership assets ensured that there would be no profits or surplus from which the charging creditor could be satisfied. *Id.*

In the instant case, the value of the Connors' partnership interests, the only assets to which Baybank is entitled to look for satisfaction of its judgment, has not been placed beyond Baybank's reach. The purposes of [RULPA § 703] and [UPA § 28] have not been frustrated. To the extent that Baybank believes the initial conveyance of the Tewksbury property from the Connors to East Street to have been fraudulent, its recourse lies in fraudulent conveyance law, not in a judicially created exception to the partnership statutes.

Since we find that Baybank had no standing to seek judicial dissolution of East Street, we need not address the parties' arguments regarding the proper parties to such a proceeding. We hold that the trial court erred in ordering dissolution of East Street, and we reverse that portion of the trial court's order. Since it appears that the trial court ordered the appointment of a receiver solely to assist in the dissolution of East Street, rather than for purposes authorized under the [RULPA], by reference to UPA, we vacate that portion of the trial court's order and remand for further proceedings not inconsistent with this opinion.

Affirmed in part: reversed in part: vacated in part: remanded.

All concurred.

Notes

1. UPA

a. UPA section 31 gives *partners* the power to dissolve the partnership at any time. UPA §§ 31(1)(b), 331(2). A dissolution is rightful when the partners had not agreed to a "definite term or particular undertaking." UPA § 31(1)(b). Such a partnership is referred to as a partnership "at will". On dissolution, the partnership begins the process of winding-up the partnership business, and distributing cash to the partners. UPA §§ 29, 38(1).

b. UPA section 32(2) gives courts power to dissolve a partnership at the request of "purchasers" of a partner's interest in the partnership.

2. RUPA

a. One of the major changes made by the RUPA is to distinguish between the withdrawal, or dissociation, of a partner and dissolutions. *Compare* RUPA §§ 601 & 603 *with* RUPA § 801 The "D-word" applies only when the partnership is required to liquidate. Where the partnership will not be dissolved after a partner dissociation, the partner has the right to have the partner's interest in the partnership purchased by the partnership. RUPA § 701.

b. The RUPA expands the right to equitable dissolution of at-will partnerships to include all transferees, rather than just purchasers. *Compare* UPA § 32(2) *and* RUPA § 801(6). Interestingly enough, the RUPA does not provide for a court-ordered *dissociation* of a partner at the request of a transferee of that partner's interest in the partnership.

3. ULPA

a. Under the ULPA, a limited partner has only a limited right to a return of his or her contribution, ULPA §§ 10(2) & 16(2), or to dissolution if the contribution is not returned, ULPA § 16(3).

b. Section 19 sets forth the rights of assignees of a limited partner's interest in the partnership. Under ULPA § 19(3), an assignee who does not become a substitute limited partner retains the right to distributions, *including the right to a return of the assignor's contribution.*

c. Interestingly enough, ULPA section 19(3) does not require a court order before the assignee has a right to return of the assignor's contribution. Why not? What differences between the rights of partners and of limited partners might account for this?

d. ULPA section 22 allows judgment creditors of a *limited partner* the right to an order charging the interest in the partnership of the limited partner.

e. The ULPA has no provisions relating to a general partner's interest in the partnership, its assignment, or charging orders with respect to. Why not? Where would you look to find such provisions? *See,* ULPA § 9(1); UPA § 6(2).

4. RULPA

a. What changes, if any, does the RULPA make in the rights of *limited* partners, their assignees and their judgment creditors? *See,* RULPA §§ 603–04, 702–04, 902.

b. What changes, if any, does the RULPA make in the rights of *general* partners, their assignees and their judgment creditors? *See,* 101(8), 101(10), 402–04, 602, 702–03, 802, 1105.

E. Additional Problems

13.10. A and B were partners operating a farm implement business. The business was quite profitable and had a steady growth for ten years. B, for a valuable consideration, sold his interest in the business and executed an assignment of his interest to C. C wanted to enter into active participation in the business as a partner and so informed A. A told C that C was not and could not become a partner, that the partnership was not dissolved, and that C could not interfere in the business or obtain any information about partnership transactions or inspect the partnership books. C consults you as to his rights under the circumstances. Advise him. (Illinois Bar Examination, July 1981.)

13.11 Brothers X, Y, and Z were partners who owned and operated a successful company in the business of manufacturing widgets (with a term of about twenty-five years yet to run under the original partnership agreement). Partner X encountered serious personal financial problems. Judgment creditor A obtained a court decree charging X's partnership interest. X owed A a debt of $50,000.

a. Z immediately appeared in court and petitioned the court to allow Z to redeem X's charged interest by purchasing it. Z offered to pay $40,000. Evidence from expert testimony established the sale value of the charged interest to be at least $100,000 (if there were an interested purchaser). A objected to the sale, but the court ordered the sale to Z for $40,000. On reconsideration after motion by A, the court vacated its order and disapproved the sale to Z.

b. A then moved the court to order a foreclosure sale. It was established that X's interest would have to be charged for about four or five years to satisfy the debt to A. The court allowed the motion and ordered an auction sale, which was adequately publicized. There were only two sealed bids received by the court:

(1) a bid of $40,000 from Z and

(2) a bid of $50,000 from A.

The court allowed the purchase by A at $50,000, and an appropriate order was entered. A simply expunged X's debt from A's records.

c. On the day after this last order was entered, X, Y, and Z met and voted unanimously (3–0) to dissolve the business. The business was liquidated. After payment of partnership creditors and the return of the contributions of X, Y, and Z, only $15,000 remained, which was divided equally between Y, Z, and A.

d. Please answer the following:

(1) Should the court have allowed Z to redeem X's charged interest for $40,000?

(2) Should the court have ordered the foreclosure sale of X's interest? If so, what amount should the court have required in order to direct the sale?

(3) How will A argue that the dissolution and liquidation were improper, and what remedy should he have?

13.12. Able and Baker orally agreed to engage together in building houses for sale. Pursuant to their agreement, Able would furnish all necessary capital to acquire the land and to pay for the construction of the houses, and Baker, who was a contractor by trade, would not contribute any capital but would keep the books and furnish his knowledge, skill, and supervision. All profits would be shared equally between them. Baker selected a lot that was purchased for $20,000 with funds furnished by Able. Title to the lot was taken in Able's name. Able also deposited $95,000 in a joint bank account with Baker from which Baker drew funds to pay for the materials and labor used in the construction of a house on the lot. The funds deposited by Able to the account were not sufficient to complete the house, and Baker advanced $5000 of his own funds to pay the final construction costs when Able refused to make any further deposits to the account. The house and lot were thereafter sold by Able for $180,000. Able delivered a deed to the purchaser and deposited the $180,000 in his own account without paying expenses of sale he incurred in the amount of $4000. Baker immediately demanded that Able pay over to him $90,000, representing one half of the proceeds of the sale, as well as the $5000 he advanced with interest from the date of the advance. Baker's demand for payment was refused by Able who informed Baker that he no longer wanted to have any further dealings with him. Baker promptly brought an action to recover the sums claimed due him, and the foregoing facts were proved. How should the court rule on disposition of the $180,000 proceeds of sale? Give reasons. (Illinois Bar Examination, July 1982.)

13.13 In 1975, four parties entered into a limited partnership for the manufacturer and distribution of widgets in Chicago, Illinois. The four parties drafted two documents without the assistance of legal counsel—a partnership contract and a certificate of limited partnership. Accordingly, a certificate of limited partnership was filed in the appropriate state office in Springfield, Illinois, describing the Jones, Johnson and Company as a limited partnership. The certificate, which was complete enough to comply with the limited partnership law in effect, provided that there would be two general partners—Smith, whose contribution was $20,000 in cash, and Jones, whose contribution was 0—and two limited partners—Adams, whose contribution was $30,000 in cash and Johnson, whose contribution was $40,000 in services to the firm. The written partnership contract provided that the partnership was to last for a period of ten years from January 1, 1975 to December 31, 1984; that Jones was to serve as manager of the business; that Johnson was to be employed as assistant manager; and that profits were to be shared equally between the four partners. In 1975, the partnership did well enough to permit Jones to pay himself a salary of $30,000 and to pay Johnson a salary of $20,000. There was also a $10,000 profit that was kept in the partnership rather than distributed to the partners by the consensus of the four partners. The partnership purchased some machinery and paid off some of its loans. In 1976, 1977, 1978, 1979, and 1980, the company lost $5000 each year. Jones had continued to pay himself $30,000 annually and to pay Johnson $20,000 annually. Thus, on January 1, 1981, the financial picture of the business and its partners was as follows:

(1) The partnership had assets of approximately $70,000. Its liabilities totaled approximately $95,000.

(2) Smith had assets that could be reached by creditors totaling about $75,000. He had no liabilities.

(3) Jones had assets that could be reached by creditors totaling $50,000. He had liabilities totaling $80,000.

(4) Adams had assets that could be reached by creditors totaling about $90,000. He had liabilities totaling about $100,000.

(5) Johnson had assets that could be reached by creditors totaling about $500,000. He had no liabilities.

If the limited partnership were to be dissolved and liquidated, what would each partner be entitled to receive or required to pay to settle the accounts among the partners? *Compare* ULPA §§ 16 & 23 *with* RULPA §§ 101(10), 503, 504, 604, 606 & 804.

Chapter 14

Dissociation of Agents from the Firm

A. Voluntary Terminations

Problem 14.1

Tutt, a meat processor, employed Jason in 1976 to purchase livestock for him. From the beginning of his employment by Tutt, Jason purchased beef cattle from Pace, who operated a stockyard. After a purchase, Pace would bill Tutt, who then forwarded his check in full payment. Tutt had instructed Jason that at no time was he to purchase any sheep from Pace. During the period from 1976 through 1980, Jason purchased over 5000 head of cattle for Tutt's account. On February 14, 1981, Tutt became angry with Jason and discharged him, refusing to pay Jason any of the severance pay to which Jason thought he was entitled. Jason, smarting at his discharge, told Pace on February 20 to forward 100 sheep to Tutt. Tutt refused delivery of the sheep and refused to pay on the ground(s) (a) he had expressly ordered Jason never to purchase sheep and (b) he had discharged Jason on February 14. What decision? Give reasons. (Illinois Bar Examination, Feb. 1981).

Problem 14.2

Clark sued Perino and Perino's employer, IBM Corporation. Clark was represented by Parker and his law firm. On May 10, 1994 Parker recommended that Clark settle the suit $25,000. Clark says that she told Parker that she would not settle for that amount. She also says that at that time, she discharged Parker as her attorney. Clark's husband confirms hearing her fire Parker. Parker claims that Clark did not fire him on May 10, 1994. He also claims that nine days later, on May 19, 1994, Clark specifically authorized him to accept a settlement offer of $25,000. On that date, Parker negotiated a settlement with Scott, counsel for Perino and IBM. When Parker sent Clark the settlement documents for her signature, she wrote him a letter rejecting the $25,000 settlement. The letter also set forth her conditions for a settlement. The letter continued

> [i]f you and your firm do not present the [conditions listed] to Perino/IBM, it is my wish that you and your firm no longer represent me in this matter....

In August 1994, Parker and his firm moved to withdraw as counsel of record, and their motion was granted on September 8, 1994.

Scott states that he had no notice that Clark disputed Parker's authority to enter into a settlement agreement on her behalf until he received Parker's motion to withdraw.

Assume that Parker would be deemed to have apparent authority to settle their suit if he was still Clark's attorney. Assume further that Clark did discharge Parker and his law firm on May 10. Should the trial court enforce the oral settlement agreement between Scott and Parker? *See Clark v. Perino,* 235 Ga.App. 444, 509 S.E.2d 707 (App. Ct. 1998).

Zukaitis v. Aetna Casualty & Surety Co.
195 Neb. 59, 236 N.W.2d 819 (1975)

BLUE, District Judge.

This is an action for a declaratory judgment brought to determine whether defendant-appellee, the Aetna Casualty and Surety Company, is obligated under its professional liability insurance policy to defend plaintiff-appellant, Raymond R. Zukaitis, in a medical malpractice suit.

Raymond R. Zukaitis was a physician practicing medicine in Douglas County, Nebraska. Aetna issued Dr. Zukaitis a policy of professional liability insurance through its agent, the Ed Larsen Insurance Agency, Inc. This policy was for a period from August 31, 1969, to August 31, 1970.

On August 7, 1971, Dr. Zukaitis received a written notification of a claim for malpractice which allegedly occurred on September 27, 1969. On August 10, 1971, Dr. Zukaitis telephoned the Ed Larsen Insurance Agency. At the request of the agency the written claim was forwarded to it by Dr. Zukaitis. This was received on August 11, 1971, and was erroneously referred to the St. Paul Fire and Marine Insurance Company on that date by the agency.

Dr. Zukaitis was insured with St. Paul Fire and Marine Insurance Company from August 31, 1970, to August 31, 1971. But on the date of the alleged malpractice, he was insured with Aetna. Apparently without notice to Dr. Zukaitis, the agency contract between Ed Larsen Insurance Agency and Aetna had been canceled effective August 1, 1970. At the time the agency placed Dr. Zukaitis' insurance with St. Paul.

On November 22, 1971, a malpractice action was brought against Dr. Zukaitis based on the alleged malpractice of September 27, 1969. Attorneys for St. Paul undertook the defense of the lawsuit. On January 25, 1974, St. Paul discovered that it was not the insurance carrier for Dr. Zukaitis on September 27, 1969, the date of the alleged malpractice, and advised Aetna of this at that time. Dr. Zukaitis was also advised of this, and the attorney retained for St. Paul to represent Dr. Zukaitis withdrew. Dr. Zukaitis made demand upon Aetna on May 28, 1974, for it to undertake the defense of Dr. Zukaitis, but this demand was refused.

Dr. Zukaitis retained his own attorney to represent him in the malpractice case. A motion for summary judgment was filed by Dr. Zukaitis in that case, which motion was sustained. This action for a declaratory judgment against

Aetna therefore resolved itself into an effort to recover attorney's fees and costs. The District Court found for Aetna.

Aetna contends that it is relieved from its obligation to Dr. Zukaitis since notice was not given as required by paragraph 4(b) of the policy which provides: "If claim is made or suit is brought against the insured, the insured shall immediately forward to the company every demand, notice, summons or other process received by him or his representative."

Dr. Zukaitis contends that under the circumstances, notice to Aetna was given within a reasonable period in that the agent who wrote the policy was given notice.

This court has previously construed provisions of insurance policies similar to the one here. In *Keene Coop. Grain & Supply Co. v. Farmers Union Ind. Mut. Ins. Co.*, 177 Neb. 287, 128 N.W.2d 773, it is stated:

> The word "immediate" in referring to the notice required in an insurance policy means with reasonable celerity, with reasonable and proper diligence, and what is a reasonable time depends upon all the facts and circumstances of each particular case.

Ordinarily notice to a soliciting agent who countersigns and issues policies of insurance is notice to the insurance company. Restatement, Agency 2d, § 127. This is also true even if the agent forwards the notice to the wrong company. At 44 Am. Jur. 2d, Insurance, § 1468 p. 336, it is stated:

> Also, an insured who has promptly given notice of an accident to the general agent that issued the policy, and has also promptly delivered process to him, has been held not required to do anything further, although in each instance the agent by mistake forwarded the papers to the wrong company.

The question then is whether this is true after the agency contract between the insurance company and the agent has been terminated as it was in this case. To answer this, it is necessary to refer to the general law of agency.

The rule is that a revocation of the agent's authority does not become effective as between the principal and third persons until they receive notice of the termination.

Here, Dr. Zukaitis did what most reasonable persons would do in the situation; he notified the agent who sold him the policy. There is no evidence that notice of the termination was sent to him or that he knew the agency contract had been canceled.

It is stated in 3 Couch on Insurance 2d, § 26:50, p. 513:

> When the insurer terminates the agency contract, it is its duty to notify third persons, such as the insureds with whom the agent dealt, and inform them of such termination. If it does not so notify and such third persons or insureds deal with the agent without notice or knowledge of the termination, and in reliance on the apparently continuing authority of the agent, the insurer is bound by the acts of the former agent.

The following appears in 3 Couch on Insurance 2d, § 26:50, p. 515:

> The principle of the carrying over of the authority of an agent after termination with respect to third persons having no notice or knowledge thereof has been applied so as to bind the insurer when the third person

dealt with the apparent agent by contracting with him, or by forwarding or delivering to him suit papers and proofs of loss.

A case involving similar facts as the case presented here is *Yannuzzi v. United States Cas. Co.*, 19 N.J. 210, 115 A.2d 557. The insureds in that case were sued as the result of an accident which occurred on December 9, 1951. After insureds were served with the suit papers on October 16, 1952, they forwarded them to the agent who sold them an automobile accident insurance policy. The agency forwarded the suit papers to the wrong insurance company. The agency contract had been terminated effective January 1, 1952. The insurance company claimed the insureds did not comply with a condition of the policy requiring them to immediately forward to insurer every summons or other process. The New Jersey Supreme Court held that the insureds complied with this provision when they sent the suit papers to the agent from whom insureds had received the policy even though the agency relationship had been terminated. The New Jersey Court set out the following applicable statement from *Southern Life Ins. Co. v. McCain*, 96 U.S. 84, 24 L. Ed. 653:

> No company can be allowed to hold out another as its agent, and then disavow responsibility for his acts. After it has appointed an agent in a particular business, parties dealing with him in that business have a right to rely upon the continuance of his authority, until in some way informed of its revocation.

> We conclude that under the facts and circumstances of this case, the notice given by the plaintiff to the agent of the defendant constitutes notice to the defendant and would obligate defendant to carry out the terms of its insurance contract with plaintiff. The District Court was in error when it determined to the contrary.

Notes

1. The principal may at any time *revoke* his or her consent to action on his or her behalf by the agent. Restatement § 118 & comments a & b. The authority of an agent to act for the principal terminates when the principal "manifests" to the agent that the principal no longer consents, *or* when the agent has *notice* the principal no longer consents. Restatement § 119. The agent will have notice when the agent knows, has reason to know, should know, or has been given a notification, of the principal's lack of consent. Restatement §§ 9(1) & 134. Recall that the agent will be affected by notice to the *agent's* agents under the principles discussed in chapter 3.

2. The agent may in a similar manner *renounce* the agency and withdraw his or her consent to act on behalf of the principal. Restatement §§ 118, 119, & 134.

3. Termination of the agent's authority terminates all power of the agent to affect the principal's legal relations, except apparent authority and emergency authority. Restatement § 124A. The extent of the agent's remaining *apparent authority* depends on the attendant circumstances, including the nature of the agency.

4. *Lingering Apparent Authority of General Agents.* As indicated in *Zukaitis v. Aetna Casualty & Surety Co.*, a *general* agent continues to have *apparent authority* to bind the (former) principal to a third person *despite* a voluntary termi-

nation of the agency relationship until such time as the third person has *notice* of the termination. Restatement § 127. That is, apparent authority continues until the third person (or the appropriate agent of the third person) knows, has reason to know, should know, or has been given a notification of the termination. Restatement § 135.

Notification *by publication* in a newspaper of general circulation in the place where the agency had regularly been carried on is effective to terminate the (former) general agent's apparent authority as to all third persons *except* certain limited classes of persons. Restatement § 136(3). Notification by publication is *not* effective where:

(a) the third person had previously extended or received *credit* to or from the principal through the general agent;

(b) the third person had "specially accredited" the agent to the third person (a principal specially accredits an agent by inviting a third person to deal with the agent, *cf.* Restatement 128 comment a);

(c) the principal should have known that the agent had already begun to deal with the third person; or

(d) where the principal has entrusted the agent with an "indicia of authority" (a power of attorney or other writing given to the agent for the purpose of evidencing the agent's authority, Restatement 130).

Restatement § 136(2). Why should notification by publication be required for the above classes of third persons, but not as to other kinds of third persons?

5. *Lingering Apparent Authority of Special Agents.* Where the agent has *not* been held out as a general agent, the agent generally has *no* lingering apparent authority. Restatement § 132. A special agent will have lingering apparent authority *only* where

(a) the principal has specially accredited the agent to the third person;

(b) the principal has *notice* that the agent has begun to deal with the third person; or

(c) the principal has entrusted the agent with an indicia of authority.

Restatement § 132. Why should special and general agents be treated differently? Given that it would be next to impossible to notify all persons who might rely on the agent's possession of an indicia of authority, how can the principal cut off the (former) agent's apparent authority?

6. Suppose Husband had established a credit account at Department Store to which Wife was authorized to charge purchases. Husband decides that Wife is spending too much money, and informs Department Store not to extend further credit to her, but does not tell Wife this. Wife charges further merchandise to the account, and Department Store demands payment from Husband.

Recall that an agent continues to have (actual) authority to bind the principal until such time as the agent has notice that the principal no longer consents to action by the agent. May Department Store, which had notice that Husband no longer consented to Wife acting on his behalf, hold Husband responsible under Wife's actual authority?

One well-known Canadian case concluded that Department Store could hold Principal liable. *Robert Simpson Co. v. Godson*, 1 D.L.R. 454 (Can. 1937). *But see* Restatement § 125 comment c (while the agent has authority to bind the principal, third persons with notice of the principal's lack of consent can acquire no rights against the principal).

7. Because the authority of an agent to act on behalf of the principal is based on the principal's consent for the agent so to act, the agent's authority to act sometimes terminates *by implication.* Implied terminations arise when the agent should realize that, in light of intervening events, the principal would no longer consent to action by the agent if the principal knew of the events. For example, the occurrence of the following events (among others) may call into question the continued consent of the principal:

(a) A change in value of the subject matter of the agency or a change in business conditions, Restatement § 109;

(b) the loss or destruction of the subject matter of the agency or the termination of the principal's interest in it, Restatement § 110;

(c) a change of law of which the agent has notice and which causes the execution of his or her authority to be illegal, or which otherwise materially changes the effect of its execution, Restatement § 116;

(d) the bankruptcy or substantial impairment of the assets or credit of the agent or the principal of which the agent has notice, Restatement §§ 113, 114; and

(e) the outbreak of war of which the agent has notice, Restatement § 115.

8. In *Clark v. Perino*, 235 Ga.App. 444, 509 S.E.2d 707 (App. Ct. 1998), Clark had sued Perino and IBM Corporation. Clark sought to avoid a settlement of the suit by her lawyer, Parker, by claiming that she had discharged him before he made the agreement. The court held that, even if Clark had in fact discharged Parker, Scott (the lawyer for Perino and IBM) did not know Parker was no longer her attorney, so she was bound by Parker's settlement:

> Clark does not dispute that Parker entered into a settlement on her behalf on May 19, 1994, but claims that at the time he entered into the settlement Parker was no longer her attorney and thus had no authority to act on her behalf. While there is a dispute in the record as to when Clark discharged Parker, for purposes of this appeal we must accept her statement that she fired him nine days before the settlement was entered.
>
> While prior Georgia cases addressing the enforceability of settlement agreements have not addressed an instance when a client claims to have terminated her attorney prior to a settlement, under general principles of agency law,
>
> > [t]he termination of authority does not thereby terminate apparent authority.
>
> Restatement, Law of Agency 2d, § 124A. As the comments to the Restatement explain,
>
> > If there was apparent authority previously, its existence is unaffected until the knowledge or notice of the termination of authority comes to the third person, except when all agency powers are terminated without notice by death, loss of capacity by

the principal or an event making the authorized transaction impossible.

Id. at comment a.

It is undisputed that no one communicated to Scott that Parker had been discharged or that any limitation on his authority existed. To the contrary, Parker was Clark's attorney of record in the case, and Scott was entitled to rely on Parker's apparent authority to enter into a settlement on her behalf.

In other words, where the dispute as to an agreement is not between opposing parties but is, rather, between the attorney and client over the attorney's authority, and where the opposite party is ignorant of any limitation upon the attorney's authority, the client will be bound by his attorney's actions.

Brumbelow v. Northern Propane Gas Co., 251 Ga. at 676, 308 S.E.2d 544. * * *

Therefore, even if Clark had fired Parker prior to the settlement, this fact alone does not render the settlement unenforceable where opposing counsel had no notice of the termination when the settlement was entered.

In making this ruling, we are mindful that this Court previously has raised concerns about the harshness of a doctrine binding a client to a settlement he did not authorize. It may seem harsher still to hold that a client may be bound to an agreement entered into by an attorney whom he no longer employs. However, the rule outlined in *Brumbelow* focuses on the interests of opposing parties and puts the burden of communicating any limitation of an attorney's authority on the party seeking to disavow the settlement. * * *

Therefore, we are bound by *Brumbelow,* as well as general principles of agency law, to hold that where an opposing party has not received notice that an attorney's authority has been terminated, or otherwise limited, he may rely upon the attorney's apparent authority to bind his client.

B. Terminations by Operation of Law

1. Death

Problem 14.3

Father gave Son a written power of attorney that specifically authorized Son to change Father's bank accounts to add Son's name as joint tenant. Son went down to the Bank. After showing Bank his written power of attorney, Son closed the bank accounts in Father's name, and opened new bank accounts in the names of Father and Son as joint tenants with right of survivorship. Unknown to Son or to Bank, Father had died a half-hour before Son got to the Bank. Assume that, if the transfer to the new bank account was effective, the money in Father's bank accounts would not pass via his will, but would vest in Son as surviving joint tenant. Did Son take the funds, or must the funds pass under Father's will?

Estate of Krempasky

501 A.2d 681 (Pa. Super. 1985)

WATKINS, Judge:

This case comes to us on appeal from the Court of Common Pleas of Cambria County and involves the issue as to whether a valid joint tenancy with the right of survivorship was created in certain certificates of deposit prior to a decedent's death.

The decedent, Elizabeth Krempasky, died on June 8, 1979 at 2:45 P.M. while a patient at a hospital. She was 82 years of age at the time of her death. She died of heart failure and cardiovascular disease. In her will she devised the residue of her estate to her niece, Lydia Elizabeth Vrablova Wanamaker, who was also appointed executrix. The decedent had four bank certificates of deposit worth $5,000 each which she kept in a metal box at her home. The executrix testified at trial that the certificates of deposit were not found in the metal box after decedent's death. Upon further inquiry the executrix discovered that the name of Anna A. Parana had been added to the four certificates on the very day of her death. The executrix then filed a petition requesting that the certificates of deposit be ordered returned to the estate as estate property. After hearing, the court below denied the petition and directed a verdict in favor of Parana. After exceptions to the order were dismissed by the court below, the executrix took the instant appeal.

[T]he name of Anna A. Parana was added to the instruments by the bank on the very day of the decedent's death. The name was added pursuant to an authorization form containing the decedent's signature and brought to the bank by Anna Parana. Anna Parana had also prepared the authorization forms. A bank official testified that Anna Parana had brought the form to the bank in the "late afternoon," "about 3 o'clock" on the date of the decedent's death and the name of Anna Parana was added to the instrument between 3:00 P.M. and 4:00 P.M. when the bank closed. However, the testimony also revealed that the decedent died on June 8, 1979 at 2:45 P.M. Thus, when the addition of the other name to the certificates took place the decedent was dead.

> It is well established as the general rule that the death of the principal operates, as an instantaneous and absolute revocation of the agent's authority or power, unless the agency is coupled with an interest. Hence, any act done by the agent, as such, after the principal's death will not affect the estate of the latter.

3 Am. Jur. 2d 453 § 51. It is well settled that the death of the principal puts an end to the agency and terminates the agent's authority to act for the principal unless the agency is coupled with an interest. In our case the decedent died before [the agent] created the joint tenancy. Anna Parana had no interest in the certificates of deposit at the time of the decedent's death. Thus, her death terminated both Parana's and the bank's authority to change the account. For that reason we agree with the appellant's contention that the four certificates of deposit belong to the decedent's estate.

Notes

1. At common law, death terminates *all* power of the agent to bind the principal, both authority and *apparent authority*, *without notice* to either the agent

or the third person dealing with the agent. Restatement §§ 120 & comment c, 124A comment a; *cf.* Restatement § 133. Comment a to Restatement section 120 gives the rationale for this rule:

> Agency is a personal relation, necessarily ending with the death of the principal; the former principal is no longer a legal person with whom there can be legal relations. One cannot act on behalf of a non-existent person.

2. The common law rule terminating without notice all power of the agent to act on behalf of a dead principal puts agents in a double bind. So long as the principal lives, the agent is under a duty to act on behalf of the principal. An agent without notice of the principal's death will believe he or she is still required to act. Because the agent will no longer be able to bind the principal (*or his or her estate*), the agent contracting with a third person will breach his or her implied *warranty* of authority under Restatement section 329. Other than by refusing to consent to an agency relationship, how may the agent protect himself or herself against the death of the principal?

3. The harshness of the common law rule regarding the effect of the principal's death on an agent's power to bind a principal has been criticized, even by the Restatement. Restatement § 120 comment a. Later in this chapter we will discuss *statutory modifications* of the common law rule.

4. When does death occur?

> From ancient times down to the recent past it was clear that, when the respiration and heart stopped, the brain would die in a few minutes; so the obvious criterion of no heart beat as synonymous with death was sufficiently accurate. In those times the heart was considered to be the central organ of the body; it is not surprising that its failure marked the onset of death. This is no longer valid when modern resuscitative and supportive measures are used. These improved activities can now restore "life" as judged by the ancient standards of persistent respiration and continuing heart beat. This can be the case even where there is not the remotest possibility of an individual recovering consciousness following massive brain damage.

Ad Hoc Committee of the Harvard Medical School, "A Definition of Irreversible Coma," 205 J. A.M.A. 337, 339 (1968). *See also In re Quinlan*, 70 N.J. 10, 355 A.2d 647, 656, *cert. denied* 429 U.S. 922 (1976) ("Developments in medical technology have obfuscated the use of the traditional definition of death").

2. Incapacity

Campbell v. United States
657 F.2d 1174 (Ct. Cl. 1981)

FRIEDMAN, Chief Judge:

This is another chapter in the continuing saga of attempts by the Internal Revenue Service to limit the use of "flower bonds" to pay federal estate taxes. Flower bonds are United States Treasury bonds that were issued a number of years ago at interest rates substantially below current ones and therefore sell significantly below par, but that may be redeemed at par before maturity to pay federal estate taxes.

The bonds were purchased for the decedent soon after he became comatose and shortly before he died, pursuant to a power of attorney executed several years earlier. The government contends that the power of attorney lapsed when the decedent became comatose, that the purchase of the bonds on his behalf was ineffective, and that the decedent therefore was not the "owner" of the bonds when he died which, under the governing regulation, is a condition to the early redemption of the flower bonds at par to pay estate taxes.

In 1965, the decedent, Lionel L. Campbell ("Campbell"), while in good health, gave his son ("Campbell Junior") "a full and universal power of attorney" authorizing Campbell Junior "to do any and every act, and exercise any and every power" that Campbell could do or exercise through any other person. On December 9, 1976, Campbell, then 73 years old, was "stricken with a cerebral hemorrhage, and became permanently and irreversibly mentally incompetent, remaining so until his death." He died 24 days later on January 2, 1977.

On December 10, the day after Campbell was stricken, Campbell Junior purchased, at a substantial discount and with Campbell's funds, a United States Treasury bond, in the face amount of $200,000, bearing interest at 3=t=1=/=2=u percent per annum, and maturing on November 15, 1998. In purchasing the bond, Campbell Junior intended to act as agent and attorney for his father, although he was fully aware of his father's medical condition.

The only question before us is whether the bonds were actually owned by Campbell at his death. The government contends that when Campbell became "permanently and irreversibly mentally incompetent" following his stroke, the effect was to terminate Campbell Junior's "authority to act on decedent's behalf in effecting a bond purchase." Under the government's theory, therefore, Campbell Junior's purchase of the bond for his father was ineffective.

A preliminary question is whether state or federal law determines whether Campbell Junior's power of attorney terminated when his father became comatose. Plaintiff urges that state law governs; the government invokes federal law. We conclude that we should look to Texas law to decide the question.

Although there is no Texas authority dealing with this specific question, Texas law indicates that Texas courts would hold that when Campbell became comatose, the power of attorney did not immediately terminate but rather continued effective for some brief period, subject to disaffirmance by Campbell's executrix after his death. This is also the view of most of the federal courts that have considered the question under the laws of other states.

It is settled in Texas that when a principal is adjudicated insane, the authority of his agent to act for him is terminated. In *Jensen v. Kisro*, 547 S.W.2d 65 (Tex. Civ. App. 1977), the court refused to hold that a power of attorney, pursuant to which the decedent's stock had been sold shortly after she entered a hospital in a "disabled" condition and while she was "very, very sick" had been terminated, since these two circumstances "cannot be held to establish that on (the date of the conveyance) she lacked the mental capacity to sell the stock." *Id.* [at] 67.

The government relies heavily upon the Restatement (Second) of Agency. Section 122(1) of the Restatement states:

Except as stated in the caveat, the loss of capacity by the principal has the same effect upon the authority of the agent during the period of incapacity as has the principal's death.

The caveat states that

(t)he Institute expresses no opinion as to the effect of the principal's temporary incapacity due to a mental disease.

The comments add little to defining temporary incapacity:

(T)he agent of one who becomes mentally incompetent to act on his own account or to appoint an agent does not necessarily lose authority to act for the principal. Very brief periods of insanity caused by temporary mental or physical illness of the principal do not destroy the power of a previously appointed agent to act in his behalf. The matter is too amorphous for a statement of a definite rule.

Comment on Caveat.

In refusing to accept the Restatement as a basis for holding in a flower bond case that under New York law a power of attorney was terminated when the decedent became comatose shortly before the bonds were purchased, the Second Circuit pointed out in [*United States v. Manny*, 645 F.2d 163, 168 (2d Cir. 1981)]:

The difficulty with the Restatement analysis is that at the time of acting the agent cannot tell whether the incapacity will be temporary or permanent. [D]ecedents could have recovered from their comatose conditions and survived. We are persuaded that the Restatement provisions are best construed as depriving agents of capacity only where the incapacity of their principals is known to be permanent from the outset; mental or physical incapacity which does not preclude recovery should render the interim acts of the agent voidable rather than void. This reading is wholly consistent with the weight of New York cases in point and preserves the salutary principle that those temporarily unable to act for themselves should be able to benefit from favorable acts which their agents take during their incapacity.

In *Manny*, which involved two consolidated cases similar to the present case, the court held that in both cases the disability resulting from the decedent's comatose state rendered the purchase of flower bonds voidable and not void and that since the executors had not rejected the purchase by the agent, the decedent was the owner of the bonds when he died. In one of the cases the bonds were purchased 10 days after the decedent lapsed into a coma; he died 8 days after the purchase. In the other case the bonds were purchased 5 days after a stroke rendered the decedent semi-comatose, disoriented, and confused; he died 3 days after the purchase. Those two cases are strikingly similar to the present case, in which the bonds were purchased the day after Campbell became comatose, and Campbell died 24 days after the purchase.

We agree with the reasoning of *Manny* and follow it. Although *Manny* dealt with New York rather than Texas law, there is no reason to think that the two states would reach different conclusions on this issue.

The government stresses the stipulation in the present case that when Campbell suffered his stroke and became comatose, he "became permanently and irreversibly mentally incompetent, remaining so until his death." When Campbell suffered his stroke, however, his son could not then have been certain that his father's incapacity was permanent. Here, as was the case when the bonds were purchased in *Manny*, Campbell Junior, when he purchased the bond one day after his father's stroke, could not know whether incapacity would be permanent or only temporary.

The government points to a Texas statute providing that a power of attorney does not terminate upon the "disability or incompetence of the principal" if the power "contains the words "this power of attorney shall not terminate on disability of the principal' or similar words showing the intent of the principal that the power shall not terminate on his disability." Tex. Prob. Code Ann. art. 36A (Vernon) (1980). The inference the government draws from this provision, however, that without such words the power terminates upon disability does not follow.

On its face the statute merely provides a method by which a principal may enable his agent to continue to act for him even after the principal has become disabled. The statute does not provide that without such language, the power immediately terminates if the principal becomes comatose. The government relies solely upon the language of the statute. Standing alone, this statute does not outweigh the arguments previously set forth that support the conclusion we have reached.

Thus, under Texas law, Campbell Junior's purchase of the bond for his father, like any other contract or conveyance executed on behalf of a person lacking mental capacity, was a voidable and not a void act. Upon Campbell's death, only Campbell's heirs, devisees, or personal representatives could have disaffirmed the purchase. The government would not have the power to disaffirm the flower bond purchase.

Since Campbell's estate did not repudiate the purchase and, in fact, ratified it by submitting the bond for early redemption, the purchase remained valid and enforceable. Consequently, under Texas law, Campbell was the owner of the bond at his death.

In so holding, we decide only this case, in which the bond was purchased the day after the decedent became comatose and less than 4 weeks before he died. We express no opinion on whether the result would be the same if the purchase was not made until a substantial time after the decedent became comatose, during which period a guardian could have been appointed, or if the decedent survived the purchase for an extended time.

The plaintiff is entitled to recover. Because we hold that the government is required to redeem at par the portion of the flower bond necessary to pay the estate tax, plaintiff is entitled to recover damages it suffered as a result of the government's refusal to redeem the bond. The case is remanded to the Trial Division to determine the amount of such damages.

Notes

1. The principal's loss of capacity also terminates by operation of law all power of the agent to act on behalf of the principal. Restatement § 122. As indicated in *Campbell v. United States*, incapacity raises even more questions than does death. If temporary loss of capacity does not *necessarily* terminate agency

power, how does an agent know whether the incapacity is temporary or permanent? Moreover, short of a declaration by a court, the question of *when* the principal has become incapacitated is far from certain:

> [M]ental disease causing insanity has no definite boundary at which a person loses capacity. Thus, one may have capacity to make a will without having capacity to conduct an intricate business transaction. Even where there is a pronounced mental incompetency, there may be ratification of previously executed transactions during lucid intervals. The matter is too amorphous for a statement of a definite rule.

Restatement § 122 comment d.

2. What happens to the affairs of someone suffering from an extended lack of capacity, such as a coma? The traditional response is for a court to declare the person incompetent and to appoint a guardian of both the incompetent and the incompetent's estate. At common law there is no non-judicial alternative. Even though a (previously executed) general power of attorney could be invaluable in just this context, the common law rule terminates the power of attorney just when it is needed most. Here again, the result has been changed by statutory modification of the common law rule (see below).

3. In addition to the death or incapacity of the principal, a number of other occurrences will terminate by operation of law an agent's power to act on behalf of the principal: (i) the impossibility of performing the agency, Restatement § 124, and (ii) the death or incapacity of the *agent*, Restatement §§ 121, 122.

3. Statutory Responses

Powers of Attorney

Under section 4 of the Uniform Durable Power of Attorney Act (1979), the death or incapacity of a principal who has executed a *written power of attorney* does not revoke or terminate either

(i) the *authority* of agent without knowledge of the principal's death or incapacity to act under the power of attorney *or*

(ii) the *apparent authority* of the agent as to third persons without knowledge of the principal's death or incapacity.

Note that where the third person, but not the agent, knows of the death or incapacity, we have a situation similar to that in *Robert Simpson Co. v. Godson* (discussed earlier in this chapter). As of November 1, 1999, the Uniform Durable Power of Attorney Act has been adopted in 49 jurisdictions.

All Agency Powers

Under section 2356 of the California Civil Code (1985), both authority and apparent authority continue until the agent and third person, respectively, know of the death or incapacity of the principal.

Durable Powers of Attorney

A majority of states have statutes authorizing *durable powers of attorney* to survive the incapacity or disability of the principal. *E.g.,* UNIF. DURABLE POWER

OF ATTORNEY ACT § 2 (1987). A durable power of attorney is a written power of attorney that *expressly provides* that the power will not be affected by the subsequent disability or incapacity of the principal. *Id.* § 1.

As discussed in chapter 2, the utility of general powers of attorney is limited by problems of defining the scope of the power. Unless specifically granted by the power, an act by the agent/attorney-in-fact *outside* the ordinary course of business may not be effective.

Durable Health-Care Powers of Attorney

One highly uncertain question at common law is the power of an agent/attorney-in-fact to make *health-care* decisions on behalf of a comatose principal, especially decisions to refuse medical treatment, life support, or even food and water. As a part of the "Living Will" movement, many states have adopted statutes authorizing *durable health-care* powers of attorney under which a person may appoint a health-care agent to make such decisions on his or her behalf when he or she no longer has the capacity to make them. *E.g.,* TEX. CIV. PRACTICE & REMEDIES CODE §§ 135.001-135.018 (Vernon's Supp. 1992). Generally, at the time a durable health-care power of attorney is executed, the principal also executes a "Living Will"—a directive indicating his or her wishes regarding the continuance of medical treatment, life support, food, and water. *Id.* §§ 135.012.

C. Irrevocable Agencies

Problem 14.4

Kane lost his executive position and was badly in need of money to meet a number of debts.

(i) A friend, Dore, loaned him $1000 but wanted some kind of protection. Kane wrote Dore a letter stating, "If I do not repay the $1000 on December 31, 1978, you may come to my house, take my GE electric refrigerator, sell it, and apply the proceeds on the debt."

(ii) Another friend, Chase, loaned Kane $500, and Kane delivered to Chase a diamond ring and a note stating, "If I do not repay the $500 on December 31, 1978, you may sell this ring and apply the proceeds on the debt."

(iii) Kane took his piano to a piano dealer, Sarle, and told him, "You have my authority to sell this piano for $750 and to retain $250 as a commission."

Subsequently, Kane became angry with Dore, Chase, and Sarle. On December 15, 1978, he wrote each a letter revoking the authority to sell that he had given to each of them. On December 24, Kane died suddenly of a heart attack. On December 28, Sarle, without knowledge of Kane's death, sold the piano to Ware, an innocent purchaser. Determine the rights, if any, of Dore, Chase, Sarle, and Ware (a) because of the letters and (b) because of Kane's death. Explain. (Illinois Bar Examination, Feb. 1979.)

1. Voluntary Terminations

Lee v. O'Brien

21 Md. App. 165, 319 A.2d 614 (1974)

POWERS, Judge.

The death on 16 February 1969 of Letitia N. Lee terminated her rights as beneficiary in a farm of some 193 acres in Howard County conveyed in trust by her mother in 1914. Upon Mrs. Lee's death it became the duty of Mercantile-Safe Deposit & Trust Company, the trustee, to have the property appraised by two or more disinterested and qualified persons, and to offer it at private sale, at 90% of the appraised value, to each of Mrs. Lee's children, one by one, in the order of their age.

The four surviving children of Mrs. Lee were three daughters—Hannah Lee Sharp, Laura L. O'Brien, and Neville Lee Worthington—and one son, M. L. Dawson Lee, Jr. After the trustee made the offer to Mrs. Sharp, all four children joined in requesting the trustee to convey the property to all of them as tenants in common, each to own an undivided one fourth interest. The trustee concluded that such a conveyance would be a proper exercise of its trust responsibilities, and agreed to the request.

Simultaneously with the conveyance, the four children entered into an agreement, dated 9 July 1969, to which the trust company was also a party. The agreement was recorded with the deed among the Land Records of Howard County. Subsections 6(b) and 6(c) are as follows:

(b) That by this agreement said parties and their respective spouses do hereby constitute, nominate and appoint Hannah Lee Sharp of Montgomery County, Maryland (one of the parties hereto) to be their true, sufficient, and lawful attorney, for them and in their name, place and stead, to grant and convey the property described in said deed of May 18, 1914, as a whole or in parcels, from time to time; and she shall have the sole right and authority to determine, when to sell and convey, to whom to sell and convey and at what price and upon what terms to sell and convey. Such sale or sales may be to such person or persons or to any body corporate, its successors and assigns as she shall determine.

(c) That in the event the said Hannah Lee Sharp shall die before having disposed of all of said property in accordance with the power and authority hereby conferred upon her, the parties hereto do hereby constitute, nominate and appoint Laura L. O'Brien, of Baltimore County, State of Maryland, one of the parties hereto, to be their true, sufficient and lawful attorney to act for them, in the place and stead of the said Hannah Lee Sharp then deceased, with the same powers, duties and authority as herein conferred upon the said Hannah Lee Sharp.

The agreement provided that all expenses in connection with the transfer of title and expenses accruing on the property as a whole, such as taxes and insurance, would be borne equally by the four children, and that they would participate equally in the net proceeds derived from any sale or sales of the property.

Hannah died in December, 1971. The succeeding events, as stated in appellant's brief and agreed to by appellees as reasonably accurate and correct, were:

[I]n June 1972, Perkins (Counsel for Laura and for Hannah's estate) forwarded to Dawson's counsel a firm contract for the purchase of the property by Urban Systems Development Corporation (USDC), which was prepared for the signatures of Dawson, Laura, George T. Sharp and the Sharp Estate as the sellers. At this time Perkins requested that Dawson indicate, among other things, whether or not the price (approximately $550,000) was acceptable. On July 13, 1972, Dawson's counsel informed Perkins that the offer was not acceptable to Dawson, and Perkins asked what counter-offer Dawson would make and consider to be an acceptable price. Dawson's counsel informed Perkins that Dawson was not desirous of making or suggesting any counter-offer, as the price was not "in the ballpark.'

By letter dated August 15, 1972, Perkins presented to Dawson's counsel a revised agreement of sale with USDC still listing Dawson individually as one of the sellers, with the same purchase price as the initial agreement. On August 24, 1972, Dawson's counsel informed Perkins that since (the) purchase price had not changed, the offer was still unacceptable. During this conversation, Perkins made no mention of the existence of a third purported agreement of sale dated August 23, 1972. With a letter dated August 25, a copy of this Agreement was received from Perkins by Dawson's counsel by mail on August 28, 1972, which was the first knowledge of said agreement by Dawson or his counsel. This Agreement was signed by Laura individually and as attorney in fact for Dawson, by George T. Sharp individually and as Personal Representative of the Estate of Hannah. The purchase price was still the same as that set forth in the preceding proposed agreements. On August 28th, counsel for Dawson notified Perkins as counsel for all other parties "seller' that Dawson did not believe that the agreement of August 23, 1972 was binding upon him.

In his complaint Dawson prayed that the court declare whether the designation of Laura as attorney-in-fact was terminated prior to the contract with Urban Systems and whether her execution of it was in derogation of his rights; [and] that Laura be enjoined from acting further as attorney-in-fact and Urban Systems be enjoined from acting in any manner in respect to its purported interest under the contract.

On 23 July 1973 the chancellor filed an opinion and decree declaring "that the agreement of July 9, 1969 is a valid subsisting agreement and now in full force and effect and binding upon the Plaintiff [and entering a summary judgment in favor of the defendant].

The appeal before us was taken from that decree. In his brief appellant presents these questions: Was the power of attorney granted in the Agreement of July 9, 1969 revocable by Appellant? Has the Agreement of July 9, 1969 terminated, thus terminating the designation of Appellee, Laura L. O'Brien, as attorney in fact?

The agreement which created the agency or power of attorney in Hannah, and upon her death, in Laura, was silent both as to expiration and as to revocation. Therefore it continued in effect among the parties until lawfully terminated by breach, by action of a party, by agreement of the parties, by operation of law, or by accomplishment of its purpose.

In *Attrill v. Patterson*, 58 Md. 226 (1882), Attrill owned a majority stock interest in a corporation chartered in Louisiana to furnish gas service in New Orleans. Its franchise claims conflicted with those of the New Orleans Gas Light Company. Attrill asked Patterson to go to New Orleans to negotiate a compromise with the other company. He said, "if there is a good negotiation effected, you shall have $50,000.00.' Patterson negotiated for a period of three to four months, but failed to effect a compromise. Attrill terminated Patterson's services, engaged counsel, and filed suit. Attrill's company prevailed in its franchise claims, after which Attrill and others, without any participation by Patterson, dictated the terms of a merger of the two companies.

Patterson sued Attrill for $50,000.00 plus interest, claiming that Attrill could not discharge him without paying him. The court said:

> It may be laid down, as a general rule, that an agent's authority to act for a principal, is always revocable at the will of the principal; and may at any time be put an end to by withdrawing the authority; unless the authority be coupled with an interest; or has been conferred on the agent for a valuable compensation moving from him to the principal.

What constitutes an authority coupled with an interest, the decisions without exception, are agreed about. In *Hunt v. Rousmanier*, [8 Wheat. 174], Chief Justice Marshall says, it "is an interest in the thing itself on which the power is to be exercised, and not an interest in that which is to be produced by the exercise of the power."

The same rule is now the doctrine of all the text books.

In *Smith v. Dare*, 89 Md. 47, 42 A. 909 (1899), the owners of a farm appointed Smith as agent to attend the farm, collect rents when due, and refund same to the owners, after deducting such money as is necessary for the benefit of the farm, but "not to advance any rents before due, except when absolutely convenient.' Smith advanced the owners more than the net rents he collected from the tenant. The owners revoked the power of attorney, and conveyed the farm to another, in trust. Smith filed suit for the appointment of a receiver to collect the rents, and apply them on account of the sums he had advanced. In discussing the nature of Smith's agency the Court of Appeals said:

> There is no implication to be found anywhere in the contract that his authority, or any part of it, was conferred upon him as a security for indebtedness due to him or thereafter to become due him from the Dares, or that he paid anything for his agency or for any of the powers that were conferred on him. This case, therefore, falls within the principles laid down in *Hunt v. Rousmanier* and in *Attrill v. Patterson*.

In *Howard v. Street*, 125 Md. 289, 93 A. 923 (1915), the Court of Appeals reaffirmed the law as stated in *Attrill v. Patterson* and *Smith v. Dare*. In *Piper v. Wells*, 175 Md. 326, 2 A.2d 28 (1938), dealing with a real estate brokerage contract, clearly not coupled with an interest, the Court of Appeals recognized the power of a principal to revoke an agency, though not necessarily the right to do so without incurring liability.

In Mechem's Law of Agency, Second ed. § 570, the author describes two kinds of interests which may be coupled with an agency to make it irrevocable. One is,

An interest, not amounting to a property or estate in the thing itself, but still an interest in the existence of the power or authority to act with reference to it, not for the purpose of earning a commission by the exercise of the power, but because the agent has parted with value, or incurred liability, or assumed obligations, at the principal's request or with his consent, looking to the exercise of the power as the means of reimbursement, indemnity or protection.

The other is,

An interest or estate in the thing itself, concerning which the power is to be exercised, arising from an assignment, pledge or lien created by the principal, coupled with which is the power to deal with the thing itself in order to make the assignment, pledge or lien effectual.

The author goes on to say, in § 571,

The(y) differ from each other only in the fact that, in the latter, the agent has an estate or interest in the subject matter of the power, while in the former his interest is rather in his right to exercise the power over the thing, in order to make it available for the security or protection contemplated.

In the facts of the case under consideration, each of the four children of Letitia N. Lee became the owner of an undivided one fourth interest in the property. The power given in the agreement to Hannah, and later to Laura, neither enhanced nor diminished the share of the agent, or of any principal. As far as Dawson was concerned, the subject matter of the power he granted to the agent was his one fourth share in the property. The agent received no interest in that subject matter. There was no valuable compensation moving from the agent to Dawson in return for which the power was conferred on the agent. There was no liability incurred, or obligation assumed by the agent which required the security of the power as a means of reimbursement, indemnity, or protection.

In short, the agreement among the four children surely created an agency, but not an agency coupled with an interest, nor one given for valuable compensation moving from the agent to the principal, nor one given to secure to the agent reimbursement for liabilities incurred or obligations assumed. The agency was not irrevocable. Restatement of Agency 2d says, in § 118:

Authority terminates if the principal or the agent manifests to the other dissent to its continuance.

Comment b. under § 118 says:

The principal has power to revoke and the agent has power to renounce, although doing so is in violation of a contract between the parties and although the authority is expressed to be irrevocable.

We hold that as between Dawson as the principal and Laura as the agent, Dawson revoked Laura's authority when he rejected the first contract she submitted. That rejection clearly manifested to Laura his dissent to the continuance of her sole right and authority to determine at what price and upon what terms to sell and convey Dawson's property. The filing of this suit by Dawson, asking that Laura be enjoined from acting further as his attorney in fact is, to say the least, another manifestation that he dissented to the continuance of her authority.

In our view of the law, Dawson had revoked Laura's authority to sell his share of the property, and the court erred in holding to the contrary.

Decree reversed, and remanded for passage of a decree in accordance with this opinion.

Notes

1. Because the principal entrusts the agent with the power to bind him or her, the principal generally has the power to revoke at any time the agent's power to act on his or her behalf. Even where the principal and the agent have agreed that the agency would be irrevocable, or where the exercise of the power to revoke would otherwise violate a contract between the principal and the agent, the principal retains the power to revoke at will. Restatement § 118 comment b. The principal might well be liable in *damages* for revoking the agency in violation of the contract, but the principal nevertheless could revoke the agency.

As indicated in *Lee v. O'Brien*, the only agency powers that were irrevocable *by voluntary act* were (i) powers coupled with an interest in the subject matter of the power, and (ii) powers given for consideration or as security.

2. *Powers Coupled with an Interest.* An agent's power was coupled with an interest, and thus irrevocable, only where the agent had a *separate* interest in the subject matter of the power that arose *independently* of the agency power. An interest only in the *proceeds*, or the result of the exercise of the power, was insufficient. A typical example would be a creditor with a *mortgage or other lien* on Blackacre to secure repayment of debt, and who is also given a *power to sell* Blackacre on default (without a power of sale, the creditor would have to go to court to have the mortgage foreclosed).

In *Lee v. O'Brien,* the agent and all the principals owned interests in the property, yet the court held that the power of sale was *not* irrevocable. What did the court view as the *subject matter* of the power of sale?

3. *Powers Given for Consideration or as Security.* As the opinion in *Lee v. O'Brien* indicates, a power given for consideration or as security may not be revoked by the principal's voluntary act. Restatement section 138 defines a power given as security as a power

> created in the form of an agency authority, but held for the benefit of the power holder or a third person and given to secure the performance of a duty or to protect a title, either legal or equitable, such power being given when the duty or title is created or given for consideration.

For example, if Debtor gives Creditor a power to sell Blackacre, but Creditor has no lien or other interest in Blackacre, other than the power to sell it on default, Creditor's power would not be coupled with an interest, but would be given for consideration or as security. Thus, Debtor could not *by voluntary act* revoke Creditor's power of sale.

Recall the circumstances under which the *Lee v. O'Brien* power of sale was given. The property was the corpus of trust of which Letitia N. Lee was the beneficiary. On the death of Letitia, the terms of the trust required the trustee to offer to sell the property serially to each of the children, starting with the oldest. Hanna was the oldest, and the trustee first offered the property to her. At that point the children agreed to take undivided interests in the property, with Hanna, and then Laura (presumably the next oldest), to have the power to sell all their shares in the property. If the *quid pro quo* for Hanna's agreement to give up her prior right to purchase the property was the agreement by the others giving her the power to sell the entire property, was the power of sale given for consideration?

2. Terminations by Operation of Law

Problem 14.5

Helm owned a farm, Grasmere, that he wanted to sell. He authorized Payne, a licensed real estate broker, to sell Grasmere for not less than $200,000, the authority to continue for one year and not to terminate on Helm's death or incapacity. On January 2, 1979, Helm executed an "Irrevocable Power of Attorney" for one year to Payne, authorizing him to sell and execute a deed to the farm at a sale price of $200,000. The power of attorney authorized Payne to retain as a commission six percent of the sale price of the farm when sold. Thereafter, Payne used his own funds to advertise the farm for sale. On April 2, Helm suffered a severe stroke. On proper application in the proper court, Helm was adjudged to be an incompetent on May 1. Payne had no knowledge of the adjudication. On June 4, Payne found a buyer for the farm at a price of $220,000. Assume that on July 13, when settlement is to take place, Payne learns for the first time that Helm has been adjudged incompetent. Payne shows the buyer's attorney his power of attorney to sell, which is sufficient in form under the applicable statute to evidence Payne's authority to convey the principal's title to the farm. Can Payne convey good title to the farm? Explain fully. (Illinois Bar Examination, July 1979 [adapted].)

Fidelity Bank v. Gorson
296 Pa. Super. 1, 442 A.2d 265 (1982)

CAVANAUGH, Judge.

These cases involve appeals from court orders upon petitions to open and strike judgments which were entered upon a promissory note by The Fidelity Bank against S. Marshall Gorson, The Estate of Joseph N. Gorson and Harry F. Glazer, individually and trading as Gorson Enterprises. The note was an unsecured demand note in the amount of three million dollars dated May 23, 1978. It contained a provision empowering Fidelity to confess judgment against the maker at any time before or after maturity. A confession of judgment was entered on the note on January 11, 1980. [T]he executors of the Estate of Joseph N. Gorson, who had been a maker of the note but had deceased, filed petitions to strike the judgment. The court denied the petitions.

Joseph N. Gorson was one of the makers of the judgment noted dated May 23, 1978. He died on February 4, 1979. Judgment was entered against the Estate on January 11, 1980. This appeal is from the refusal of the lower court to strike judgment on a demand note after the death of the maker. On close analysis we are unable to accept Fidelity's conclusion that the cases distinguish between situations where the right to confess judgment is contingent upon a default which occurs after the maker's death, and the right to enter judgment on a note (as here) not contingent upon a default, and that they permit the entry of judgment in the latter situation. A reading of the cases does not make such a distinction cognizable under Pennsylvania law. Rather, the cases indicate that the maker's demise terminates the warrant of attorney to confess judgment. It is true that the early case of *Webb v. Wiltbank*, 1 Clark 324, 2 Pa. L.J. 303 (1842) is cited by the lower court as support for the principle that the death of the maker does not void the warrant to confess. However, this authority is merely a brief summary of a lower court decision and in light of later pronouncements by the Pennsylvania Supreme Court is of doubtful authority.

It is also true that the validity of the "death voids warranty" principle has been questioned. In *Brennan v. Ennis*, 219 Pa. Super. 291, 280 A.2d 605 (1971), the court stated:

> Cases citing the general rule that judgment cannot be entered by confession after the maker's death have done so without discussion of any underlying rationale. And recent cases have placed possible reasons for the rule in question. *See Mid-City Federal Savings and Loan Ass'n of Phila. v. Allen*, 413 Pa. 174, 196 A.2d 294 (1964); Restatement of Agency 2d, §§ 138, 139(1)(d).

Indeed, in *Mid-City Federal* cited by the *Brennan* decision as one of the cases questioning the authority of the no entry of judgment after the maker's death line of cases, Justice Eagen wrote in a case involving mental incompetency of the maker:

> A power of attorney to confess judgment for a proper consideration is security to the creditor, is coupled with an interest and is irrevocable. The entry of the judgment is not a new act of the debtor, but is a legal result beyond his control. Lunacy will not revoke a power of attorney to confess judgment, which was valid when executed.

From this it is argued that the proper rule is that an irrevocable power which was validly granted and which requires no further occurrence to become operative does not terminate upon the grantor's death or incompetence. It is contended that while the authority in a note that permits confession of judgment after a default might expire on the death of the maker, the authority in a note which, as here, permits the entry of judgment at any time does not.

[handwritten margin note: Rule proposed by Fidelity]

Despite the report of the early *Wiltbank* case and the question raised in *Brennan* we hold that it is the law of Pennsylvania that the death of the maker revokes the warrant to confess judgment even for the purposes of security and even if the warrant is not contingent upon a default under the obligation. In so holding we are persuaded by the following line of cases which support our conclusion.

In *Lanning v. Pawson*, 38 Pa. 480, 486 (1861), it was held that:

> It was manifestly very proper to strike off the judgment that had been entered on the warrant of attorney, on the fact being found that the defendant was dead before it was entered.

In *Stucker v. Shumaker*, 290 Pa. 348, 351, 139 A. 114 (1927), it was stated that:

> The warrant to confess lost its efficacy when the maker died.

Nor can we accept Fidelity's claim that even if the death of the maker prevents the holder from executing on the note, that entry of judgment for security purposes only is permissible. We do not find this distinction to be supported by the cases. Rather, the language of our Supreme Court is absolute. In *Strucker v. Shumaker*, the court stated "the warrant to confess lost its efficiency when the maker died."

The order of the lower court is reversed and the judgment entered in favor of Fidelity Bank against the Estate of Joseph N. Gorson, Deceased, is ordered stricken.

SPAETH, Judge, dissenting:

Professor Seavey noted in his article, Termination by Death of Proprietary Powers of Attorney, 31 Yale Law Journal 283, 286 (1921), that

> [t]he first case in the United States raising the question of the termination of [an agency] power by death of the grantor was that of *Bergen v. Bennett* in which Chancellor Kent held that a power of sale in a mortgage was a "power coupled with an interest" and was not affected by the death of the mortgagor. It was *Hunt v. Rousmanier's Administrators*, however, which proved to be the foundation of later American cases.

In *Hunt v. Rousmanier's Administrators*, 8 Wheat. 174, 5 L. Ed. 589 (1823), Rousmanier had given Hunt a power of attorney to sell certain vessels as security for the repayment of a loan. Rousmanier died insolvent without having repaid the loan. [The ships were at sea at that time. Hunt took possession of them on their return and offered the intestate's interest in them for sale. The defendants objected.] When Hunt sued to recover, Rousmanier's administrator demurred. The lower court sustained the demurrer. Although Chief Justice Marshall reversed the order of the lower court and remanded the case for argument on the issue of mutual mistake, he outlined the law of agency as applied to a power of attorney held as security for a debt:

> This instrument contains no words of conveyance or of assignment, but is a simple power to sell and convey. As the power of one man to act for another depends on the will and license of that other, the power ceases when the will, or this permission, is withdrawn. The general rule, therefore, is, that a letter of attorney may, at that time, be revoked by the party who makes it; and is revoked by his death. But this general rule, which results from the nature of the act, has sustained some modification. Where a letter of attorney forms a part of a contract, and is a security for money, or for the performance of any act which is deemed valuable, it is generally made irrevocable in terms, or if not so, is deemed irrevocable in law. Although a letter of attorney depends, from its nature, on the will of the person making it, and may, in general, be recalled at his will, yet, if he binds himself for a consideration, in terms, or by the nature of his contract, not to change his will, the law will not permit him to change it. Rousmanier, therefore, could not, during his life, by any act of his own, have re-

voked this letter of attorney. But does it retain its efficacy after his death? We think it does not. We think it well settled, that a power of attorney, though irrevocable during the life of the party, becomes extinct by his death.

The legal reason of the rule is a plain one. It seems founded on the presumption that the substitute acts by virtue of the authority of his principal, existing at the time the act is performed; and on the manner in which he must execute his authority, as stated in *Coombes'* case. In that case it was resolved that "when any has authority as attorney to do any act, he ought to do it in his name who gave the authority." The reason of this resolution is obvious. The title can, regularly, pass out of the person in whom it is vested, only by a conveyance in his own name; and this cannot be executed by another for him, when it could not, in law, be executed by himself. A conveyance in the name of a person who was dead at the time, would be a manifest absurdity.

This general rule, that a power ceases with the life of the person giving it, admits of one exception. If a power be coupled with an "interest," it survives the person giving it, and may be executed after his death.

As this proposition is laid down too positively in the books to be controverted, it becomes necessary to inquire what is meant by the expression, "a power coupled with an interest." Is it an interest in the subject on which the power is to be exercised, or is it an interest in that which is produced by the exercise of the power? We hold it to be clear that the interest which can protect a power after the death of a person who creates it, must be an interest in the thing itself. In other words, the power must be engrafted on an estate in the thing.

[T]he substantial basis of the opinion of the court on this point, is found in the legal reason of the principle. The interest or title in the thing being vested in the person who gives the power, remains in him, unless it be conveyed with the power, and can pass out of him only by a regular act in his own name. The act of the substitute, therefore, which, in such a case, is the act of the principal, to be legally effectual, must be in his name, must be such an act as the principal himself would be capable of performing, and which would be valid if performed by him. Such a power necessarily ceases with the life of the person making it. But if the interest, or estate, passes with the power, and vests in the person by whom the power is to be exercised, such person acts in his own name. The estate, being in him, passes from him by a conveyance in his own name. He is no longer a substitute, acting in the place and name of another, but is a principal acting in his own name, in pursuance of powers which limit his estate. The legal reason which limits power to the life of the person giving it, exists no longer, and the rule ceases with the reason on which it is founded. The intention of the instrument may be effected without violating any legal principle.

Finding that "the power given in this case is a naked power of attorney, not coupled with an interest," the Chief Justice concluded that Hunt's interest did not survive the death of Rousmanier. Thus Hunt lost his position as a secured party despite the parties' undisputed intention to the contrary.

Since 1823, when *Hunt v. Rousmanier's Administrators* was decided, many courts "have seen the equity of the situation and have attempted to avoid the consequences of Marshall's opinion."

> The result has been great confusion: The courts are not at all clear, save in England, as to what constitutes a power coupled with an interest. In many cases the American courts have used "power coupled with an interest" as meaning a contractual power. When a square determination as to the termination of the power by death has been presented, there are a variety of holdings. Thus where a legal title to real estate is given to a power holder, it is everywhere held that the title survives. Where there is a legal lien upon real property, it would seem that the existence of the lien should be held to create an interest and make the power nonterminable. But some of the courts, finding that the power of sale can not be exercised in the name of the mortgagee, hold that the power terminates with the death of the mortgagor. Where there is less than a lien, the courts have generally held that the power does not survive upon the ground that the power can not be exercised in the name of a dead man.

Seavey, *supra* at 297.

This confusion is apparent in the Pennsylvania cases. While many cases accord with the majority's view, others have held the power of attorney to survive the grantor's death. In *Key's Estate*, 137 Pa. 565, 20 A. 710 (1890), Daniel Keys died after having executed a power of attorney to his sister authorizing her to collect the proceeds from a real estate sale and to keep so much of the money as necessary to repay a debt he owed her. Upholding the power, the Court stated:

> The manifest purpose of Daniel Keys was to specifically appropriate so much of his share in his brother's estate as was necessary to pay the indebtedness therein mentioned; and, to that end, he invested his sister with full authority to receive the money that was coming to him from the land that was then about being sold, and credit the same on account of that indebtedness. There is nothing in the evidence to indicate any other intention. The land referred to in that and subsequent letters is undoubtedly the same that was shortly afterwards sold under the proceedings in partition, and the money in court is part of the proceeds of that sale. What, then, was the effect of the power of attorney and accompanying letter, both of which appear to have been delivered to appellant at the same time? Without pausing to inquire what is necessary to constitute a power coupled with an interest, and wherein it differs from a specific appropriation of property, or the proceeds thereof, to the payment of a particular debt, or for any other special purposes, we are of opinion that the power of attorney and letter above quoted operated as an equitable assignment to appellant of so much of Daniel Keys's interest in the estate of his brother John as would be sufficient to pay the indebtedness of $250, and interest, specified in the letter. To that extent, appellant thereby acquired a vested right to the purchase money raised by the sale in partition, and that right was not divested by the subsequent death of Daniel Keys in April, 1887.

For cases upholding a power of attorney after the grantor's death where the grantor had delivered to the holder the property securing the debt, *see Fisher v.*

New York & Middle Coal Field R. & Coal Co., 31 Wkly. Notes Cas. 502 (1892), and *Droste's Estate*, 9 Wkly. Notes Cas. 224 (1880).

The present case is of course distinguishable from such cases. Fidelity Bank was neither equitably assigned nor given possession of specific property as security for the debt. But such requirements seem archaic. Fidelity's power of attorney was "coupled with an interest" insofar as its exercise was to benefit the holder and not the creator. Had Fidelity taken control of property sufficient to secure its three million dollar debt, it is unlikely that Gorson Enterprises could have been maintained as a going business. The effect of the majority opinion is to interfere with, if not make unavailable, a sensible commercial device.

The American Law Institute's treatment of the problem of irrevocable agency reflects such commercial considerations. Instead of defining when a power is "coupled with an interest," Restatement (Second) Agency emphasizes the concept of security. Section 138 provides:

§ 138. Definition

A power given as security is a power to affect the legal relations of another, created in the form of an agency authority, but held for the benefit of the power holder or a third person and given to secure the performance of a duty or to protect a title, either legal or equitable, such power being given when the duty or title is created or given for consideration.

Section 139 defines the circumstances in which a power given as security may be terminated:

§ 139. Termination of Powers Given as Security

(1) Unless otherwise agreed, a power given as security is not terminated by:

(a) revocation by the creator of the power;

(b) surrender by the holder of the power, if he holds for the benefit of another;

(c) the loss of capacity during the lifetime of either the creator of the power or the holder of the power; or

(d) the death of the holder of the power, or, if the power is given as security for a duty which does not terminate at the death of the creator of the power, by his death.

(2) A power given as security is terminated by its surrender by the beneficiary, if of full capacity; or by the happening of events which, by its terms, discharges the obligations secured by it, or which makes its execution illegal or impossible.

In the Comment to Section 139 it is said:

d. Death. If the power holder dies, a court of equity will direct the exercise of the power for the benefit of the beneficiary. If the creator of the power dies and the power is given to secure the performance of a duty not terminated by the death of the power giver, the power survives.

Among the illustrations to the Section are the following:

702 AGENCY, PARTNERSHIPS AND LIMITED LIABILITY COMPANIES

5. P sells shares in a corporation to A and delivers to A his share certificate, and a power of attorney to transfer the shares upon the books of the corporation. P dies before the shares are transferred upon the books. A's power to make the transfer is not terminated.

6. P borrows money from A and as security gives A a power, in case of P's default in payment, to collect a debt owned by T to P and to pay himself out of the proceeds. A's power to collect the debt is not affected by the death of P.

7. P borrows money from A, and as security in case of nonpayment, gives A a power of attorney to take and sell certain ships belonging to P, then at sea. P makes default in payment, and A takes possession of the ships in pursuance of the power. P dies. A can now sell the ships, notwithstanding P's death.

This formulation of the law first appeared in Preliminary Draft #54, which was issued by the American Institute of Law in 1932 (Professor Seavey acting as Reporter). The draft was accompanied by an explanatory Note to the Council, which stated:

> Note to the Council: This Section is a departure from the corresponding Sections in the Second Tentative Draft (§§ 233, 234 and 235) in that it states that a power given for security is not terminated by the death of the power giver. These Sections were written in light of the case of *Hunt v. Rousmanier*, 8 Wheat. 174 [5 L. Ed. 589] (1823). The American courts have professed to follow the authority of this case but have distinguished the cases involving the point so that it may be fairly said that today in substantially all situations in which a power has been given, the death of the giver of the power does not terminate it. The only cases in which it can be said to have any remaining validity are those where the power is given in reference to land and in which the court finds that it was not intended to give either an equitable interest in the land or a lien upon it. The cases holding that the power terminates upon the death of the giver are almost all fifty years old or more, and the rule does not accord with the modern idea that one having a power in regard to something has an interest in it. It may fairly be said therefore that with the change of view in regard to the creation of an interest in things, in every case where a power of this sort is created, the rule as stated satisfies the requirement of Marshall in *Hunt v. Rousmanier*, that in order to survive a power must be coupled with an interest. The views of the Reporter upon this matter were expressed in 31 Yale Law Journal 283 (1922). The more recent case of *Mulloney v. Black*, 244 Mass. 391 [138 N.E. 584] (1923) is typical since, although citing *Hunt v. Rousmanier*, it held that a power to appropriate money due the power giver was not terminated by his death. The original sections purported to follow *Hunt v. Rousmanier* but a critical examination of them shows that their meaning is substantially similar to that of the present Section. It appears to the Reporter that it will serve the profession better to state frankly that the law as to these powers has become consistent with the law of contracts and property.

In my opinion, the American Law Institute has stated the better rule, and we should adopt it. I acknowledge that doing so would be inconsistent with some cases. But it would be consistent with others, and would bring our law up-to-date by recognizing the practical considerations of the commercial world.

As to the Estate of Joseph N. Gorson, the order of the lower court should be affirmed.

Notes

1. As stated in the extract from *Hunt v. Rousmanier's Administrators* (set forth in the *Fidelity Bank v. Gorson* dissent), at common law *only* powers coupled with an interest survived the death of the principal. Although powers given for consideration or as security could not be revoked by *voluntary act* of the principal, such powers were revoked by the *death* of the principal unless they were *also* coupled with an interest in the subject matter.

2. The question of whether powers given for consideration or as security should survive the death of the principal is one in which the Restatement did not *restate* existing law, but tried to *reform* it. Under Restatement section 139, a power given as security *not only* is irrevocable *by voluntary act*, but *also* is not revoked by the principal's *death*, regardless of whether the power is coupled with an interest. As indicated by the extract from the Reporter's Notes (set forth in the *Fidelity Bank v. Gorson* dissent), the Reporter's position was that the common law rule had been so eroded by the willingness of courts to find equitable titles or liens in the power-holder as to retain no meaning.

Consider, for example, the case of *Chrysler v. Blozic*, 267 Mich. 497, 255 N.W. 399 (1934). Steve Blozic was insured under a group life and disability insurance policy, with Frank Blozic as his named beneficiary. Blozic came down with tuberculosis and was hospitalized in County's hospital. Blozic executed a power of attorney appointing County as his agent to collect all sums due him under his insurance policy and to apply them to repay the expenses of his hospitalization. Blozic died before a *disability claim* could be filed on his behalf. Both Frank Blozic (the named beneficiary) and the County submitted claims for the insurance benefits. Because at the time of the assignment Blozic was already entitled to disability benefits under the policy, the court held that the power of attorney amounted to a "crude" assignment of those benefits, so that it survived Blozic's death. Is *Chrysler v. Blozic* consistent with *Hunt v. Rousmanier's Administrators*?

3. As *Fidelity Bank v. Gorson* indicates, the common law rule that only powers coupled with an interest survive the death of the principal largely retains its vitality; like Mark Twain, the reports of its death have been exaggerated.

D. Post-Termination Fiduciary Duties

Problem 14.6

Adam was employed by Bob to secure uranium leases for Bob. There was no agreement between them about any of the terms of the employment except about the salary. Adam worked for five weeks acquiring leases, during which time he learned of Rockacre, which was available for leasing. Adam was also informed that Rockacre contained valuable deposits of uranium and that recent tests indicated that it was a most valuable discovery. Subsequently, Adam notified Bob that he was quitting his job and immediately acquired a lease on Rockacre in his own name. Bob brought an appropriate action against Adam, claiming the Rockacre lease and asking that it be assigned to him. What decision? Why? (Illinois Bar Examination, Mar. 1969.)

Prudential Insurance Company v. Crouch
606 F. Supp. 464 (S.D. Ind. 1985)

DILLIN, District Judge.

The plaintiff, Prudential Insurance Company of America (Prudential), seeks relief in this cause of action against the defendant, Gregory M. Crouch (Crouch), in the form of a declaratory judgment, injunctive relief and damages. Prudential alleges that following Crouch's resignation from Prudential, he breached an implied covenant of good faith and breached an alleged fiduciary duty to Prudential in causing the termination of certain whole life insurance policies sold or serviced by him while a Prudential agent.

Crouch was employed by Prudential as a District Agent, selling Prudential life insurance policies exclusively, from August 9, 1974 to August 17, 1984. While a Prudential agent, Crouch developed a substantial clientele and upon his resignation, Crouch took with him a list of his client's names and addresses. This client list included Prudential policyholders whose policies were purchased through Crouch or were serviced by Crouch. Crouch returned all other property which may have belonged to Prudential at the time of his resignation.

On August 16, 1984, Crouch became a Career Agent employed by State Mutual Life Assurance Company and its wholly owned subsidiary SMA Life Assurance Company (SMA). Crouch solicited and sold insurance on behalf of SMA to his former Prudential clients. In some instances Crouch encouraged his clients to terminate their Prudential whole life insurance policies if they had a surrender value. In other instances, Crouch encouraged his clients to allow their Prudential policies to lapse by failing to pay premiums as they fell due so they could then purchase insurance through SMA.

At the time of the hearing on Prudential's motion for a preliminary injunction, Crouch had succeeded in replacing approximately fifty Prudential policies with SMA policies.

Briefly, Crouch received compensation in the form of commissions on insurance policies he sold and serviced.

Upon termination of the agent's employment with Prudential, no further commissions are paid even though premiums subsequently may be received under those policies.

Neither the Agent's Agreement nor the Collective Bargaining Agreement expressly prohibits Prudential agents from engaging in replacement activities or otherwise soliciting or selling insurance to Prudential policyholders following termination of their employment with Prudential. Crouch's Agent's Agreement contains only the following provisions respecting his duties to Prudential following termination of employment:

Sec. 7(a) That upon termination of this Agreement either by myself or the Company, or at any other time upon request by the Company, I will immediately submit said books and records for an inspection and accounting, to be made in accordance with the rules of the Company then in force.

(b) That all books, records, and supplies furnished to me by the Company shall be the property of the Company; and that, upon the termination of this Agreement, I will hand over said books, records, and supplies to a proper representative of the Company.

Although Crouch returned Prudential's property upon termination of his employment, Crouch took with him the names and addresses of his clients. Crouch's client list contained no other information except names and addresses.

Prudential makes no claim against Crouch under Section 7, above, and does not seek to enjoin Crouch from using the client list in selling additional insurance to his former Prudential clients. Rather, Prudential seeks to prevent Crouch from inducing or endeavoring to induce his former clients to cancel their Prudential policies or to allow them to lapse by nonpayment of premiums in order that Prudential policies may be replaced by other insurance policies sold by or through Crouch's employment. Prudential argues that during Crouch's employment, Crouch made an implied promise of good faith and became subject to a fiduciary duty to Prudential and that these obligations survived the termination of the employment relationship to proscribe Crouch's replacement activities.

Alternatively, Prudential relies upon the general rule of agency law that every agent owes a fiduciary duty to his principal to act with good faith and loyalty in furtherance of the principal's interests. This fiduciary duty precludes the agent from engaging in conduct dealing with the subject matter of the agency for his own benefit or in derogation of the interests of his principal. Upon termination of the agency, the fiduciary duty generally no longer applies and the former agent may compete with his former principal. Nevertheless, it is universally recognized that the agent, following termination of the agency, may not use trade secrets or other confidential information acquired during the agency in a manner which is detrimental to the principal's interests in the subject matter of the agency. Additionally, an agent is bound by his fiduciary relationship to refrain from interfering with the principal's ability to accomplish the purpose of the agency. *Trice v. Comstock*, 121 Fed. 620 (8th Cir. 1903).

This latter principle, although stated in broad language by the court in *Trice*, has been narrowly applied. The duty of an employee to a former employer must be considered alongside the common-law right of an employee to compete against his former employer. The continuing duty described in *Trice* does not abrogate the right to compete, even "steal" clients following termination of employment. Rather, the rule in *Trice* is applied only to prohibit an employee from completing transactions, which the employee negotiated during his employment, for his own benefit following termination of employment. This application of the rule in *Trice* is consistent with the law in Indiana which recognizes the right to compete against one's former employer absent contractual or statutory restrictions.

In the present case, therefore, the "purpose of the agency" must be viewed in terms of the "transactions" which Crouch was employed to complete on behalf of Prudential. Crouch was employed to sell and service insurance policies so that Prudential would receive the premiums thereunder. With respect to each insurance policy sold or serviced by Crouch, the "purpose of the agency" or the "transaction" was completed when the premium was paid to Prudential. Each sale of a new policy or renewal of an existing policy is represented by the payment of a premium and constitutes a separate transaction. Under the continuing fiduciary duty owed by Crouch to Prudential, therefore, Crouch is prohibited from negotiating any sale (either original sale or renewal) of a life insurance policy during his employment with Prudential and then completing that sale after his resignation by receiving the premium payment for his own or his new employer's benefit.

Again, consistent with the common-law right to compete against one's former employer, Crouch is otherwise free to engage in replacement activities after termination of his employment which may include inducing his former clients to allow their Prudential policies to lapse.

For the foregoing reasons, therefore, Prudential is not entitled to injunctive relief and its motion for a preliminary injunction will be denied.

Note

Fiduciary duties arise out of certain relationships, such as the agency relationship. It follows that most such duties, including most aspects of the duty of loyalty, must necessarily terminate when the relationship terminates. Thus, in *Prudential Insurance Co.*, the agent was no longer, in the absence of an agreement to the contrary, prohibited from competing with the principal. *See* Restatement § 396(a).

ABKCO Music, Inc. v. Harrisongs Music, Ltd.
722 F.2d 988 (2d Cir. 1983)

PIERCE, Circuit Judge:

Background

A. *Events Leading to Liability Trial*

On February 10, 1971, Bright Tunes Music Corporation (Bright Tunes), then copyright holder of the song "He's So Fine," composed by Ronald Mack, brought this copyright infringement action against former member of the musical group "The Beatles" George Harrison, and also against related entities ("Harrison Interests"),[1] alleging that the Harrison composition "My Sweet Lord" ("MSL") infringed the Ronald Mack composition "He's So Fine" ("HSF").

When this action was commenced, the business affairs of The Beatles, including Harrison Interests, were handled by ABKCO Music, Inc. (ABKCO) and Allen B. Klein, its President and "moving spirit."[3] ABKCO was Harrison's business

---

1. Suit was brought against Harrisongs Music, Ltd. (Harrison's English company), Harrisongs Music, Inc. (Harrison's American company), Apple Records Inc.

3. References to "ABKCO" or to "Klein" are to include ABKCO Music, Inc., its parent ABKCO Industries, Inc., and Allen B. Klein. [ABKCO]

manager during the initial stages of the copyright liability action herein, at which time the litigation was handled for Harrison by ABKCO's General Counsel.

The following events preceded the instant appeal. Shortly after this action was commenced in February, 1971, Klein (representing Harrisongs Music, Inc. and George Harrison) met with Seymour Barash (President and major stockholder of Bright Tunes) to discuss possible settlement of this lawsuit.[4] Thus, in 1971, Klein was acting on behalf of Harrison Interests in an effort to settle this copyright infringement claim brought by Bright Tunes, although no settlement resulted.

Subsequent to the Klein-Barash meeting, Bright Tunes went into "judicial dissolution proceedings." This infringement action was placed on the district court's suspense calendar on March 3, 1972, and was resumed by Bright Tunes (in receivership) in early 1973. Also in early 1973 (March 31), ABKCO's management contract with The Beatles expired. Bitter and protracted litigation ensued between The Beatles and ABKCO over the winding down of management affairs—a dispute that ended in 1977 with The Beatles paying ABKCO $4.2 million in settlement.

There is some disagreement as to whether further settlement negotiations took place between Harrison Interests and Bright Tunes between 1973 and mid-1975. It appears undisputed, however, that Harrison Interests' attorney at least initiated settlement talks in the late summer of 1975; that in the period October 1975 through February 1976, settlement discussions took place between Bright Tunes' counsel and counsel for Harrison Interests regarding settlement of this infringement action (an offer by Harrison Interests based on United States royalties); and that those discussions were in the 50%/50% or 60%/40% range. These discussions culminated in a $148,000 offer by Harrison Interests in January of 1976 (representing 40% of the United States royalties).

At about the same time (1975), apparently unknown to George Harrison, Klein had been negotiating with Bright Tunes to purchase all of Bright Tunes' stock. That such negotiations were taking place was confirmed as early as October 30, 1975, in a letter from Seymour Barash (Bright Tunes' former President) to Howard Sheldon (Bright Tunes' Receiver), in which Barash reported that there had been an offer from Klein for a substantial sum of money. The same letter observed that "[Klein] would not be interested in purchasing all of the stock of Bright Tunes if there was any doubt as to the outcome of this litigation."

In late November 1975, Klein (on behalf of ABKCO) offered to pay Bright Tunes $100,000 for a call on all Bright Tunes' stock, exercisable for an additional $160,000 upon a judicial determination as to copyright infringement. In connection with this offer, Klein furnished to Bright Tunes three schedules summarizing the following financial information concerning "My Sweet Lord:" (1) domestic royalty income of Harrisongs Music, Inc. on MSL; (2) an updated version of that first schedule; and (3) Klein's own estimated value of the copyright, including an estimate of foreign royalties (performance and mechanical) and his assessment of the total worldwide future earnings.

---

4. At this meeting Klein suggested purchasing the entire Bright Tunes catalogue (which included HSF) as a means of resolving the lawsuit, although apparently no precise dollar amount was mentioned. At the same time, Klein informed Barash that Harrison was unwilling to admit to copyright infringement.

Barash considered the Klein offer only a starting point. He thought that a value of $600,000 was more accurate and recommended a $200,000 call, based on a $600,000 gross sales price. Also in December 1975, Barash noted, in a letter to counsel for the Peter Maurice Co., that Harrison Interests' counsel had never furnished a certified statement of worldwide royalties of MSL, but that Bright Tunes had been given that information by Klein.

Shortly thereafter, on January 19, 1976, Barash informed Howard Sheldon (Bright Tunes' Receiver) of the Klein offer and of the Bright Tunes stockholders' unanimous decision to reject it. Barash noted that "[s]ince Mr. Klein is in a position to know the true earnings of 'My Sweet Lord,' his offer should give all of us an indication of the true value of this copyright and litigation." Sheldon responded in a letter dated January 21, 1976, noting that Harrison's attorneys were informed that no settlement would be considered by Bright Tunes until total sales of MSL were determined after appropriate figures were checked.

On January 30, 1976, the eve of the liability trial, a meeting was held by Bright Tunes' attorney for all of Bright Tunes' stockholders (or their counsel) and representatives of Ronald Mack. The purpose of the meeting was to present Bright Tunes with an offer by Harrison Interests of $148,000, representing 40% of the writers' and publishers' royalties earned in the United States (but without relinquishment by Harrison of the MSL copyright). At the time, Bright Tunes' attorney regarded the offer as "a good one." The Harrison offer was not accepted, however. Bright Tunes raised its demand from 50% of the United States royalties, to 75% worldwide, plus surrender of the MSL copyright. The parties were unable to reach agreement and the matter proceeded to trial.

B. Liability Trial and Events Thereafter

A three-day bench trial on liability was held before Judge Owen on February 23-25, 1976. On August 31, 1976 (amended September 1, 1976), the district judge rendered a decision for the plaintiff as to liability, based on his finding that "My Sweet Lord" was substantially similar to "He's So Fine" and that Harrison had had access to the latter. The issue of damages and other relief was scheduled for trial at a later date.

Following the liability trial, Klein, still acting for ABKCO, continued to discuss with Bright Tunes the purchase of the rights to HSF. During 1977, no serious settlement discussions were held between Bright Tunes and Harrison Interests. Indeed, the record indicates that throughout 1977 Bright Tunes did not authorize its attorneys to give Harrison a specific settlement figure. By November 30, 1977, Bright Tunes' counsel noted that Klein had made an offer on behalf of ABKCO that "far exceeds any proposal that has been made by the defendants."[6]

On February 8, 1978, another settlement meeting took place, but no agreement was reached at that meeting. Although it appears that everyone present felt that the case should be settled, it also appears that there were no

---

6. In a letter dated November 30, 1977 from Bright Tunes' counsel to the attorney for the estate of composer Ronald Mack, Tenenbaum and Sheldon, Klein's offer was set forth in detail: acquisition of the rights to HSF, including Bright Tunes' damages claim against Harrison Interests herein, in exchange for (1) payment of $150,000 to the estate of Ronald Mack (ten-year annuity of $15,000 per year); (2) payment to Bright Tunes' Receiver of $350,000 [plus an amount for legal fees].

further settlement discussions between Harrison Interests and Bright Tunes subsequent to that date. The Bright Tunes negotiations with ABKCO, however, culminated on April 13, 1978, in a purchase by ABKCO of the HSF copyright, the United States infringement claim herein, and the worldwide rights to HSF, for $587,000, an amount more than twice the original Klein (ABKCO) offer. This purchase was made known to George Harrison by Klein himself in April or May of 1978. Harrison "was a bit amazed to find out" about the purchase.

C. Damages Proceedings

On July 17, 1978, ABKCO adopted Bright Tunes' complaint and was substituted as the sole party plaintiff in this action. In May 1979, Harrison Interests obtained leave to assert affirmative defenses and counterclaims against Klein and ABKCO for alleged breaches of fiduciary duty relating to the negotiation for and purchase of the Bright Tunes properties.[8] An eight-day bench trial was held on damages and counterclaims between August 27 and October 15, 1979.

The damages decision was filed on February 19, 1981. Having determined that the damages amounted to $1,599,987, the district judge held that ABKCO's conduct over the 1975-78 period limited its recovery, substantially because of the manner in which ABKCO had become a plaintiff in this case. Particularly "troublesome" to the court was "Klein's covert intrusion into the settlement negotiation picture in late 1975 and early 1976 immediately preceding the trial on the merits." 508 F. Supp. at 802. He found, *inter alia,* that Klein's status as Harrison's former business manager gave special credence to ABKCO's offers to Bright Tunes and made Bright Tunes less willing to settle with Harrison Interests either before or after the liability trial. Moreover, the court found that in the course of negotiating with Bright Tunes in 1975-76, Klein "covertly furnished" Bright Tunes with certain financial information about MSL which he obtained while in Harrison's employ as business manager. The foregoing conduct, in the court's view, amounted to a breach of ABKCO's fiduciary duty to Harrison. The court held that although it was not clear that "but for" ABKCO's conduct Harrison Interests and Bright Tunes would have settled, he found that good faith negotiations had been in progress between the parties and Klein's intrusion made their success less likely, since ABKCO's offer in January 1976 was viewed by Bright Tunes as an "insider's disclosure of the value of the case." Consequently, the district judge directed that ABKCO hold the "fruits of its acquisition" from Bright Tunes in trust for Harrison Interests, to be transferred to Harrison Interests by ABKCO upon payment by Harrison Interests of $587,000 plus interest from the date of acquisition.

---

8. Specifically, Harrison Interests alleges that the following conduct by Klein and ABKCO constituted such breaches of duty: (1) clandestine interference with Harrison Interests' settlement efforts; (2) covert furnishing of MSL financial data to Bright Tunes in connection with ABKCO's own efforts to obtain the HSF copyright; (3) covert furnishing to Bright Tunes of Klein's personal estimates of MSL financial expectations; (4) side-switching in the present litigation; (5) use of information acquired as a fiduciary in prosecuting this action after the purchase of HSF; and (6) use of confidential information to compete with Harrison Interests and wrongful appropriation of an opportunity rightfully belonging to Harrison Interests.

ABKCO's Arguments on Appeal

[ABKCO argues on appeal that it] did not breach its fiduciary duty to Harrison because (a) no confidential information was improperly passed from ABKCO to Bright Tunes during the negotiations to purchase HSF, and (b) there was no causal relationship between ABKCO's actions and Harrison Interests' failure to obtain settlement.

A. *Breach of Fiduciary Duty*

There is no doubt but that the relationship between Harrison and ABKCO prior to the termination of the management agreement in 1973 was that of principal and agent, and that the relationship was fiduciary in nature. The rule applicable to our present inquiry is that an agent has a duty "not to use confidential knowledge acquired in his employment in competition with his principal." *Byrne v. Barrett,* 268 N.Y. 199, 206, 197 N.E. 217, 218 (1935). This duty "exists as well after the employment is terminated as during its continuance." *Id.; see also* Restatement (Second) of Agency § 396 (1958). On the other hand, use of information based on general business knowledge or gleaned from general business experience is not covered by the rule, and the former agent is permitted to compete with his former principal in reliance on such general publicly available information. Restatement (Second) of Agency § 395 comment b (1958). The principal issue before us is whether the district court committed clear error in concluding that Klein (hence, ABKCO) improperly used confidential information, gained as Harrison's former agent, in negotiating for the purchase of Bright Tunes' stock (including HSF) in 1975-76.

One aspect of this inquiry concerns the nature of three documents—schedules of MSL earnings—which Klein furnished to Bright Tunes in connection with the 1975-76 negotiations. Although the district judge did not make a specific finding as to whether each of these schedules was confidential, he determined that Bright Tunes at that time was not entitled to the information. It appears that the first of the three schedules may have been previously turned over to Bright Tunes by Harrison. The two additional schedules which Klein gave to Bright Tunes (the detailed updating of royalty information and Klein's personal estimate of the value of MSL and future earnings) appear not to have been made available to Bright Tunes by Harrison. Moreover, it appears that at least some of the past royalty information was confidential. The evidence presented herein is not at all convincing that the information imparted to Bright Tunes by Klein was publicly available.

Another aspect of the breach of duty issue concerns the timing and nature of Klein's entry into the negotiation picture and the manner in which he became a plaintiff in this action. In our view, the record supports the position that Bright Tunes very likely gave special credence to Klein's position as an offeror because of his status as Harrison's former business manager and prior coordinator of the defense of this lawsuit. *See, e.g.,* letter from Barash to Sheldon, dated January 19, 1976 ("Since Mr. Klein is in a position to know the true earnings of My Sweet Lord, his offer should give all of us an indication of the true value of this copyright and litigation."). To a significant extent, that favorable bargaining position necessarily was achieved because Klein, as business manager, had intimate knowledge of the financial affairs of his client. Klein himself acknowledged at trial that his offers to Bright Tunes were based, at least in part, on knowledge he had acquired as Harrison's business manager.

Under the circumstances of this case, where there was sufficient evidence to support the district judge's finding that confidential information passed hands, or, at least, was utilized in a manner inconsistent with the duty of a former fiduciary at a time when this litigation was still pending, we conclude that the district judge did not err in holding that ABKCO had breached its duty to Harrison.

We find this case analogous to those "where an employee, with the use of information acquired through his former employment relationship, completes, for his own benefit, a transaction originally undertaken on the former employer's behalf." *Group Association Plans, Inc. v. Colquhoun*, 466 F.2d 469, 474 (D.C. Cir. 1972). In this case, Klein had commenced a purchase transaction with Bright Tunes in 1971 on behalf of Harrison, which he pursued on his own account after the termination of his fiduciary relationship with Harrison. While the initial attempt to purchase Bright Tunes' catalogue was several years removed from the eventual purchase on ABKCO's own account, we are not of the view that such a fact rendered ABKCO unfettered in the later negotiations. Indeed, Klein pursued the later discussions armed with the intimate knowledge not only of Harrison's business affairs, but of the value of this lawsuit—and at a time when this action was still pending. Taking all of these circumstances together, we agree that appellant's conduct during the period 1975-78 did not meet the standard required of him as a former fiduciary.

In so concluding, we do not purport to establish a general "appearance of impropriety" rule with respect to the artist/manager relationship. That strict standard—reserved principally for the legal profession—would probably not suit the realities of the business world. The facts of this case otherwise permit the conclusion reached herein. Indeed, as Judge Owen noted in his Memorandum and Order of May 7, 1979 (permitting Harrison Interests to assert counterclaims), "The fact situation presented is novel in the extreme. Restated in simplest form, it amounts to the purchase by a business manager of a known claim against his former client where, the right to the claim having been established, all that remains to be done is to assess the monetary award." We find these facts not only novel, but unique. Indeed, the purchase, which rendered Harrison and ABKCO adversaries, occurred in the context of a lawsuit in which ABKCO had been the prior protector of Harrison's interests. Thus, although not wholly analogous to the side-switching cases involving attorneys and their former clients, this fact situation creates clear questions of impropriety. On the unique facts presented herein, we certainly cannot say that Judge Owen's findings and conclusions were clearly erroneous or not in accord with applicable law.

Appellant ABKCO also contends that even if there was a breach of duty, such breach should not limit ABKCO's recovery for copyright infringement because ABKCO's conduct did not cause the Bright Tunes/Harrison settlement negotiations to fail. Appellant urges, in essence, that a finding of breach of fiduciary duty by an agent, to be actionable, must be found to have been the proximate cause of injury to the principal. We do not accept appellant's proffered causation standard. An action for breach of fiduciary duty is a prophylactic rule intended to remove all incentive to breach—not simply to compensate for damages in the event of a breach. Having found that ABKCO's conduct constituted a breach of fiduciary duty, the district judge was not required to find a "but for" relationship between ABKCO's conduct and lack of success of Harrison Interests' settlement efforts.

[On] the facts herein, we agree that a constructive trust on the "fruits" of ABKCO's acquisition was a proper remedy.

[We] affirm, with modification,* the decisions of the district court, and remand [for further proceedings] consistent with this opinion.

Notes

1. During the term of the agency, the agent may not use or communicate confidential information belonging to the principal "in competition with or to the injury of the principal, on [the agent's] own account or on behalf of another." Restatement § 395. The agent's duty regarding confidential information—trade secrets and customer lists—is one of the few duties that survive termination of the agency relationship. Restatement § 396(b).

2. An agent may compete with the principal *after* termination of the relationship. The issue in most post-termination competition cases is whether the agent in competing used confidential information proprietary to the principal or only "general information concerning the method of business of the principal and the names of customers retained in [the agent's] memory." Restatement § 396(b).

E. Additional Problems

14.7. On June 10, 1978, a cattleman named Flood borrowed $5000 from Aherin. As a condition of the loan, Flood orally agreed with Aherin that should Flood fail to repay the loan on or before November 15, 1978, Aherin would be authorized to sell twenty head of Flood's registered black Angus cattle as repayment for the amount of the loan. On the morning of November 16, 1978, Flood was in default, so Aherin took possession of twenty head of cattle from the herd. The next day, on hearing of Aherin's action, Flood became excited and telephoned Aherin, urgently requesting that Aherin not sell the cattle but extend the time of payment. Aherin refused the request. The same day Flood died of a heart attack. On November 26, 1978, Aherin entered into a contract with Thomas by which he agreed to sell Thomas the twenty head of cattle at a fair market price of $10,000. At the time the contract was made, Thomas knew of Flood's death and that Aherin was relying on his earlier agreement with Flood. Before Aherin could deliver the cattle to Thomas and receive the agreed price of $10,000, the administrator of Flood's estate brought an action against Aherin alleging the foregoing facts and praying for a judgment requiring Aherin to return the cattle. What decision? Give reasons. (Illinois Bar Examination, July 1979.)

14.8. William Mubi commenced a civil suit against Walter and Jane Tribble for personal injuries and property damages resulting from a motor vehicle collision. On August 5, 1970, after this action was filed, defendants through their attorney filed an answer and an offer of judgment in the amount of $3150. Under rule 68 of the rules of civil procedure, this offer had to be accepted, if at all,

---

* [Note by the editors.] In an omitted portion of the opinion, the court modified the scope of the constructive trust on grounds not affecting the included portion of the opinion.

within ten days or it would be deemed withdrawn. Rule 68 makes the offer irrevocable for ten days and requires acceptance to be in writing within that time. Mubi died at approximately 9:00 A.M. on August 11, 1970, six days after the offer was made. Before his death, he advised his wife, Sharon, to accept the offer of settlement of $3150, and she in turn advised the secretary of Mubi's attorney, Spillman, that the offer was accepted. Because Spillman was out of town on vacation, he did not receive the notice of the offer of judgment until 2:00 P.M. on August 11, at which time Spillman authorized an office associate to immediately accept the offer of judgment pursuant to rule 68. The acceptance was duly mailed to the defendants on August 11, 1970, and was received in due course. While the decision to accept the offer was communicated to Mubi's attorney before Mubi died, the written acceptance as required by rule 68 was not made until after Mubi died. Was the acceptance effective? (*See Mubi v. Broomfield,* 108 Ariz. 39, 492 P.2d 700 (1972).)

14.9. Peters owned a mill in which he manufactured cotton sheets. He employed Adams as his general purchasing agent to buy supplies for the mill on sixty-day credit. Adams purchased twenty-five bales of raw cotton from Tidd on thirty-day credit, the usual terms for that kind of purchase. Adams, although acting for Peters, did not disclose his agency but purchased the cotton in his own name. The day before Adams contracted to buy the cotton, Peter's factory burned down, although neither Adams nor Tidd knew of this or had any reason to know of it at the time the contract was executed. Adams refused to accept or pay for the cotton. Tidd learned that Adams was Peters' agent. Tidd brought an appropriate action to recover from Peters. What decision? Give reasons. (Illinois Bar Examination, Mar. 1957.)

Chapter 15

Dissociation of Owners from the Firm

A. Power to Withdraw or to Dissolve

Problem 15.1

Nina, Pinta and Maria are owners of a firm doing business as Columbus Racquetball Club. Except as set forth below, the owners have no written or oral agreements as to the firm or its business or affairs. At the time the business was formed, the owners made the contributions to the capital of the firm set forth below:

Owner	Contribution to Capital
Nina	$ 20,000
Pinta	10,000
Maria	50,000

After 5 years of operations, Columbus Racquetball Club has a modest, but growing, clientele. Maria writes to Nina and Pinta indicating that she is withdrawing from the firm, effective immediately. In the same letter, Maria demands that the firm be dissolved, its business and affairs be wound up, its assets liquidated and any balance distributed among the owners according to their respective rights.

a. Assume that the firm is a partnership organized under the UPA, with Nina, Pinta and Maria are partners. Discuss the respective rights of the partners. Be sure to address the following:

(1) Is Maria still a partner?

(2) If Nina and Pinta wish to continue the business of Columbus Racquetball Club without liquidation, can they do so over Maria's objections?

(3) If Nina and Pinta may rightfully continue the business without liquidation, what are Maria's rights and obligations as against Pinta and Nina?

b. Assume instead that the firm is a partnership is organized under the RUPA, with Nina, Pinta and Maria are partners. In what manner, if any, would the rights and obligations of Pinta, Nina and Maria change from those discussed in 15.1.a?

c. Assume instead that the firm is a partnership is organized under the Texas Revised Partnership Act, with Nina, Pinta and Maria are partners. In what manner, if any, would the rights and obligations of Pinta, Nina and Maria change from those discussed in 15.1.a?

d. Assume instead that the firm is a member-managed limited liability company organized under the ULLCA, with Nina, Pinta and Maria as members. In what manner, if any, would the rights and obligations of Pinta, Nina and Maria change from those discussed in 15.1.a?

(1) Is Maria still a member?

(2) If Pinta and Nina wish to continue the business of Columbus Racquetball Club without liquidation, can they do so over Maria's objections?

(3) If Pinta and Nina may rightfully continue the business without liquidation, what are Maria's rights and obligations as against Pinta and Nina?

e. Assume instead that the firm is a member-managed limited liability company organized under the Delaware LLC Act, with Nina, Pinta and Maria as members. In what manner, if any, would the rights and obligations of Pinta, Nina and Maria change from those discussed in 15.1.d?

Problem 15.2

The facts are otherwise as stated in Problem 15.1, except that the owners had contracted, in the applicable agreement, with respect to either (i) withdrawal of an owner or (ii) the term of the firm. In what manner, if any, would the rights and obligations of Nina, Pinta and Maria change from those discussed in each of the various parts of Problem 15.1?

a. The owners agreed that the term of the firm was ten years.

b. The owners agreed that for ten years none of the owners would withdraw from the firm.

c. The firm would neither be dissolved, nor its affairs wound up, until a majority–in–interest of the owners agreed to do so.

Problem 15.3

Dwight L.P. is a properly formed limited partnership under the RULPA created to purchase, renovate, and sell the historic Dwight Building in the downtown preservation district. The sole general partner of Dwight L.P. is Able, Inc. The Dwight L.P. partnership agreement provides that it will continue its operations until such time as the Dwight Building is renovated and sold.

Initially, Able estimated that it would cost $10 million to purchase and renovate the Dwight Building in a way that would maintain its unique architectural elements. Able's financial plan for the limited partnership was to admit limited partners who would contribute a total of $1 million to the partnership and then to obtain an additional $9 million in financing from a bank. Able found 10 local investors who contributed $100,000 each to join the partnership as limited partners.

Now, one year after formation of Dwight L.P., the Dwight Building renovation project has run into financial difficulty. Able failed to take into account the special requirements that the city imposed on materials and workmanship in the historic district and therefore seriously, but not fraudulently, underestimated the renovation costs of the Dwight Building. As a result, the $10 million financing has been spent, and the renovation is only three-fourths complete. The limited partners have retained a reputable independent architectural consultant who has informed them that the project can be completed for an additional $2.5 million and upon completion, the building will probably be worth $13.5 million.

In the two weeks since the limited partners and Bank were informed of the financial situation, Bank, Able, and the limited partners have had a series of meetings. Able wants to complete the project but has no capital to contribute. Bank is unwilling to grant another loan to the partnership. Able is pressuring the limited partners to make additional capital contributions to cover the costs of completion. None of the limited partners wants to contribute any additional funds, and they are not obligated to do so under the limited partnership agreement. Able has threatened to dissolve the limited partnership unless the limited partners can come up with the additional funds required within the next 10 days.

a. Can Able carry out its threat to dissolve the limited partnership, and, if so, what options, if any, do the limited partners have as a result? Explain.

b. Last week, Historical Society contacted Able and offered $10 million to Dwight L.P. to purchase the Dwight Building in its present uncompleted state. Historical Society has full information about the project, and its offer is firm. Because Able does not want to sell the building until it has been fully restored as originally intended, Able has rejected the offer without notifying the limited partners either of the offer or of Able's rejection. The limited partners found out about Historical Society's offer and Able's failure to inform them of the offer. The limited partners believe they can no longer trust Able to run the partnership. They are now united in their desire to take one or more of the following actions:

(1) to dissolve the limited partnership; or

(2) to remove Able as general partner and elect a new general partner;

Assuming that the limited partnership agreement contains no provisions that would affect your answer, may the limited partners take either of the above actions?

c. Suppose that the firm were organized as a limited liability company under the ULLCA. How would you answer questions a and b?

(1) If Able were a member in a member-managed LLC in which the ten investors were also members?

(2) If Able were manager of a manager-managed LLC in which the ten investors were members but not managers?

d. Suppose that the firm were organized as a limited liability company under the Delaware LLC Act. How would you answer question c?

e. What if the firm were organized as a partnership under the RUPA, and Able and the ten investors were partners?

(Questions a and b are based on the Multistate Essay Exam, February 2000).

Canter's Pharmacy, Inc. v. Elizabeth Associates
578 A.2d 1326 (Pa. Super. 1990)

CIRILLO, President Judge:

Westbrook Pharmacy and Surgical Supply ("Westbrook") appeals from an order entered on June 2, 1989, in the Allegheny County Court of Common Pleas granting Elizabeth Associates' motion to stay the proceedings pending arbitration.

On January 7, 1987, Schneider Health Services, Inc. ("SHS"), Orrie M. Rockwell, Jr., and Westbrook entered into a partnership agreement for the purpose of operating a personal care facility in Elizabeth, Pennsylvania. The partnership was conducted under the name of Elizabeth Associates ("Elizabeth"). The partnership agreement contained an arbitration provision:

> *Arbitration.* If for any reason the Partners cannot agree in a matter or matters of Partnership affairs, the dispute shall be decided by a majority decision of three (3) arbitrators, by which the Partners agree to abide. Each Partner shall have the right to appoint one arbitrator. The decision of the arbitrators shall be final, and the cost of the same shall be borne equally by the Partners.

After the partnership commenced operations, it began to suffer financial losses which required, pursuant to the agreement, additional capital contributions by the partners. Disputes arose concerning the extent of the losses and the management of the partnership. In sum, Westbrook refused to contribute any additional operating capital.

On January 24, 1989, Elizabeth instituted a civil action in the Allegheny County Court of Common Pleas against Westbrook to recover capital contributions allegedly owed by Westbrook to the partnership. On March 7, 1989, Westbrook responded by answering Elizabeth's complaint and filing a counterclaim against Elizabeth seeking equitable relief in the form of a partnership accounting and a dissolution of the partnership. Subsequently, on March 8, 1989, Westbrook commenced a separate equity action alleging various breaches of the partnership agreement. Elizabeth did not respond to this separate equity action.

On March 28, 1989, the trial court granted Westbrook's petition to consolidate the civil action commenced by Elizabeth with the equity actions instituted by Westbrook. On May 10, 1989, Elizabeth filed a motion to stay the consolidated proceedings pending arbitration pursuant to the arbitration provision in the partnership agreement. On June 2, 1989 the trial court entered an order staying the proceedings pending arbitration, and this timely appeal followed. Westbrook presents one issue for our consideration:

> When a contract contains a provision that all disputes arising under the contract will be decided by Arbitration, can the parties, by their conduct, waive or revoke the Arbitration provision and resort to suit under the jurisdiction of the Court of Common Pleas?

It is well settled that when one party to an agreement seeks to prevent the other from proceeding to arbitration, our inquiry is limited to determining whether an agreement to arbitrate was entered into and whether the dispute involved is within the scope of the arbitration provision.

Westbrook maintains that since its separate equity action seeking dissolution of the partnership cannot be heard in arbitration that these consolidated actions are not subject to arbitration.

It is clear that in certain circumstances a partnership may be dissolvable by the express will of any partner at any time. As the following discussion will illustrate, Westbrook's filing of an equity action seeking a dissolution effectively expressed its desire to dissolve the partnership at-will.

> Dissolution of a partnership is caused under [UPA section 31(1)(ii)] "by the express will of any partner." The expression of that will need not be supported by any justification. *If no "definite term or particular undertaking* [is] *specified in the partnership agreement," such an at-will dissolution does not violate the agreement between the partners; indeed, an expression of a will to dissolve is effective as a dissolution even if in contravention of the agreement.* We have recognized the generality of a dissolution at will. If the dissolution results in breach of contract, the aggrieved partners may recover damages for the breach and, if they meet certain conditions, may continue the firm business for the duration of the agreed term or until the particular undertaking is completed.

Girard Bank v. Haley, 460 Pa. 237, 243, 332 A.2d 443, 446-47 (1975) (emphasis added). The concept is simple: one cannot be coerced to remain in a partnership against his or her wishes.

Also, it is significant that the dissolution of a partnership does not mean that the partnership ceases doing business; rather dissolution "is the change in the relation of the partners caused by *any partner* ceasing to be associated in the carrying on, as distinguished from the winding up, of the business." [UPA § 29](emphasis added). Here, although the partners drafted a provision concerning the termination of the partnership, the agreement is silent as to dissolution.

The termination of a partnership is markedly different from the dissolution of a partnership. When a partnership has terminated it ceases doing business; when a partner effects a dissolution it simply means that partner is no longer associated with the business of the partnership.[i] Consequently, since the instant agreement does not concern the dissolution of the partnership, the relevant provisions of the [UPA] will control.

We must now determine if this partnership was for a definite term or for a particular undertaking. Once again, if the partnership was for an indefinite term or not for a particular undertaking, Westbrook was free to dissolve the partnership at-will without violating the agreement. [UPA § 31(1)(b)]. A review of the partnership agreement reveals that the partnership is not for a fixed term, and its purpose is set forth as follows:

---

i. The authors of the Uniform Partnership Act suggest the following delineation in distinguishing among various terms which apply to that process which leads to the final settlement of all partnership affairs: "Dissolution" designates that point in time when the partners cease to carry on the business together; "termination" is the point in time when all the partnership affairs are wound up; and "winding up" or "liquidation" is the process of settling partnership affairs after dissolution. This is judicially recognized as the correct sequence of events. [UPA § 30.]

The purpose of the Partnership shall be renovation, equipping and operation of a large personal care facility to be known as Old Elizabeth Manor and to be located at 310 Third Street, Elizabeth, Pennsylvania and to do and perform any and all other acts as shall be necessary or incidental thereto.

In *Haley*, the partnership's purpose was to maintain and lease buildings on a tract of real property. The supreme court found that this undertaking was general and could not be said to set forth a "particular undertaking" within the meaning of the Act.

A "particular undertaking" under the statute must be capable of accomplishment at some time, although the exact time may be unknown and unascertainable at the date of the agreement. Leasing property, like many other trades or businesses, involved entering into a business relationship which may continue indefinitely; there is nothing "particular" about it.

The purpose of the instant partnership was to renovate, equip and operate a personal care facility. Operating a personal care facility, like leasing property, may continue indefinitely; there is nothing particular about it. Accordingly, Westbrook's decision to dissolve was not in violation of the agreement.

Having concluded that Westbrook did not violate the agreement when it effected a dissolution of the partnership, we further find that these parties should not be forced into arbitration. Since an expression of a will to dissolve is effective as a dissolution, Westbrook's equity action seeking dissolution effectively caused a dissolution of the partnership. Arbitration, by its very nature, presupposes the existence of a dispute and an ability to decide in favor of one party and against another. Clearly, when a party has an unqualified right to dissolve a partnership at-will there is nothing to arbitrate. Indeed, arbitration, in this case, would be futile. Therefore, since Westbrook's decision to dissolve at-will is not subject to arbitration, the trial court erred in staying these proceedings pending arbitration.

Order reversed.

Notes

1. A partnership in which there is no agreed definite term or particular undertaking is often called an "at will" partnership. This is the way such partnerships are defined in Section 101(8) of the RUPA.

2. Under the UPA, even where there was an agreed definite term of particular undertaking, a partner nevertheless has the power to dissolve a partnership at any time. UPA § 31(2). As the court in *Canter's Pharmacy, Inc. v. Elizabeth Associates* put it

The concept is simple: one cannot be coerced to remain in a partnership against his or her wishes.

Because partners are liable for partnership obligations, allowing them to dissolve even a partnership for a term or undertaking allows them to avoid additional liability on new partnership obligations. As discussed in *Bradford v. First National Bank* (Chapter 16), partners must notify third persons that they are no longer associated with the business.

3. Under the UPA, the fact that a partnership has dissolved does not mean that it has terminated. As used in the UPA, "dissolution" means that the partners are no longer "associated in the carrying on as distinguished from the winding up of the [partnership's] business." UPA § 29. Despite dissolution, the partners remain partners until the winding up of partnership affairs is completed. UPA § 30.

4. In *Page v. Page,* 55 Cal.2d 192, 359 P.2d 41, 10 Cal.Rptr. 643 (1961) (*en banc*), there was no express agreement as to the term of the partnership. The partners operated a linen supply business from 1949 through the first quarter of 1959. The business lost money each year until 1958 (losing a total of about $62,000). In 1958, about $4000 was earned in profit; and about $2000 profit was earned in the first quarter of 1959. One creditor held a $47,000 demand note on the partnership. When one partner tried to dissolve the partnership, the other claimed an implied agreement to remain partners until the partnership business had paid off its obligations to creditors. The Court rejected this argument:

> Defendant testified that the terms of the partnership were to be similar to former partnerships of plaintiff and defendant, and that the understanding of these partnerships was that
>
> > we went into partnership to start the business and let the business operation pay for itself, put in so much money, and let the business pay itself out.
>
> There was also testimony that one of the former partnership agreements provided in writing that the profits were to be retained until all obligations were paid.
>
> Upon cross-examination defendant admitted that the former partnership in which the earnings were to be retained until the obligations were repaid was substantially different from the present partnership. The former partnership was a limited partnership and provided for a definite term of five years and a partnership at will thereafter. Defendant insists, however, that the method of operation of the former partnership showed an understanding that all obligations were to be repaid from profits. He nevertheless concedes that there was no understanding as to the term of the present partnership in the event of losses. He was asked:
>
> > (W)as there any discussion with reference to the continuation of the business in the event of losses?
>
> He replied,
>
> > Not that I can remember.
>
> He was then asked,
>
> > Did you have any understanding with Mr. Page, your brother, the plaintiff in this action, as to how the obligations were to be paid if there were losses?
>
> He replied,
>
> > Not that I can remember. I can't remember discussing that at all. We never figured on losing, I guess.

Viewing this evidence most favorably for defendant, it proves only that the partners expected to meet current expenses from current income and to recoup their investment if the business were successful.

Defendant contends that such an expectation is sufficient to create a partnership for a term under the rule of *Owen v. Cohen*, 19 Cal.2d 147, 150, 119 P.2d 713. In that case we held that when a partner advances a sum of money to a partnership with the understanding that the amount contributed was to be a loan to the partnership and was to be repaid as soon as feasible from the prospective profits of the business, the partnership is for the term reasonably required to repay the loan. It is true that *Owen v. Cohen, supra,* and other cases hold that partners may impliedly agree to continue in business until a certain sum of money is earned (*Mervyn Investment Co. v. Biber*, 184 Cal. 637, 641-642, 194 P. 1037), or one or more partners recoup their investments (*Vangel v. Vangel*, 116 Cal.App.2d 615, 625, 254 P.2d 919), or until certain debts are paid (*Owen v. Cohen, supra,* 19 Cal.2d at page 150, 119 P.2d at page 714), or until certain property could be disposed of on favorable terms (*Shannon v. Hudson*, 161 Cal.App.2d 44, 48, 325 P.2d 1022). In each of these cases, however, the implied agreement found support in the evidence.

In *Owen v. Cohen, supra,* the partners borrowed substantial amounts of money to launch the enterprise and there was an understanding that the loans would be repaid from partnership profits. In *Vangel v. Vangel, supra,* one partner loaned his co-partner money to invest in the partnership with the understanding that the money would be repaid from partnership profits. In *Mervyn Investment Co. v. Biber, supra,* one partner contributed all the capital, the other contributed his services, and it was understood that upon the repayment of the contributed capital from partnership profits the partner who contributed his services would receive a one-third interest in the partnership assets. In each of these cases the court properly held that the partners impliedly promised to continue the partnership for a term reasonably required to allow the partnership to earn sufficient money to accomplish the understood objective. In *Shannon v. Hudson, supra,* the parties entered into a joint venture to build and operate a motel until it could be sold upon favorable and mutually satisfactory terms, and the court held that the joint venture was for a reasonable term sufficient to accomplish the purpose of the joint venture.

In the instant case, however, defendant failed to prove any facts from which an agreement to continue the partnership for a term may be implied. The understanding to which defendant testified was no more than a common hope that the partnership earnings would pay for all the necessary expenses. Such a hope does not establish even by implication a 'definite term or particular undertaking' as required by section 15031, subdivision (1)(b) of the Corporations Code. All partnerships are ordinarily entered into with the hope that they will be profitable, but that alone does not make them all partnerships for a term and obligate the partners to continue in the partnerships until all of the losses over a period of many years have been recovered.

359 P.2d at 42-44.

Note on Withdrawal and Dissolution in Partnerships

UPA

Right to Liquidation

Under the UPA, on dissolution of the partnership, *each* partner generally has the right to have partnership affairs wound up. Winding up involves

a. the completion of unfinished partnership business, *cf.* UPA § 33,

b. the liquidation of partnership property and the discharge or partnership obligations, UPA § 38(1)

c. the settlement of partnership accounts, UPA § 40, and

d. the payment in cash of the net amount due each partner, UPA § 38(1).

Right to Continue Partnership Business under UPA Section 38(2)

Under UPA section 38(2), a partner loses the right to liquidation when the partner has "caused dissolution wrongfully"—or "in contravention of the partnership agreement".

Although the UPA could be drafted more clearly, for purposes of section 38(2), a partner "wrongfully causes dissolution" when the partner voluntarily dissolves the partnership before the completion of an agreed definite term or particular undertaking. Under section 31(1)(b), where the partners have not agreed to a definite term or particular undertaking, any partner may by "express will" dissolve the partnership "*without violation of the agreement between the partners*".

Under section 31(2), a partner who by express will dissolves the firm does so "in contravention of the partnership agreement" when "the circumstances do not permit a dissolution under any other provision of [section 31]." Given the language of section 31(b), a dissolution by express will is wrongful (contravenes the agreement) only when it occurs before the completion of an agreed definite term or particular undertaking. Note that section 38(2)(b) allows the other partners to continue the partnership business only for the remainder of "the agreed term of the partnership."

Unless the partnership agreement provides otherwise, the consent of *all* of the other ("innocent") partners is required before the business can be continued under UPA section 38(2). That is, *each* of the innocent partners has the right to liquidation. UPA § 38(2)(a)(I).

If the innocent partners elect to continue the partnership business, the partner wrongfully causing dissolution loses the right to liquidation. Instead, the partner wrongfully causing dissolution is only entitled to be paid the value of the partner's interest in the partnership, but without including any value for goodwill of the partnership business, and less any damages. UPA § 38(2)(c).

In addition, the partner wrongfully causing dissolution must be *released* from existing liabilities of the partnership. UPA § 38(2)(c)II.

Continuation of Business, not Continuation of Partnership

Under the UPA, any change in partner composition technically works a dissolution of the existing partnership. Where the partners continue the business without winding up partnership affairs, they do so as a new, different, partnership. RUPA § 801 Comment 1.

RUPA

Dissociation and Dissolution.

One of the main contributions of the RUPA is greater continuity of the partnership entity. The RUPA distinguishes between the "dissociation" of a partner, section 601, and "dissolution" of the partnership, section 801. When a partner dissociates from the partnership, that partner is no longer associated in the carrying on of business by the partnership. RUPA § 601 Comment 1.

Where the remaining partners are permitted to continue doing business without a winding up, there is no reason why they should not be viewed as *continuing* their association with each other. Put in entity terms, although one partner is no longer associated with the carrying on of business by the partnership entity, the partnership entity continues despite the dissociation.

Under the RUPA, "dissolution" occurs only on the occurrence of an event that requires the winding up of partnership business. RUPA § 801 & Comment 1.

Unqualified Power to Dissociate

Under RUPA section 601(1), partners have an unqualified power to dissociate from a partnership—to withdraw by express will, RUPA § 601(1). A partner may dissociate even though that withdrawal is "wrongful" as to the other partners. RUPA § 602(a). Partners may not contract away or vary their power to dissociate, except to require written notice. RUPA § 103(b)(6).

Power to Dissolve—Partnerships at Will

Under the RUPA, a partners power to dissolve a partnership by express will is more limited. In a partnership at will—a partnership without an agreed definite term or particular undertaking, RUPA § 101(8)—a partner's withdrawal by express will dissolves the partnership.[B] RUPA § 801(1). Unlike the power to dissociate, a partner may contract away the power to dissolve a partnership at will. RUPA § 103. Moreover, at any time before winding up of the partnership business is complete, all the partners may waive the right to have the partnership's business wound up. RUPA § 802(b).

Continuation after an Early Dissociation from a Partnership for a Definite Term or a Particular Undertaking

Under the RUPA, where the partners have agreed to a definite term or particular undertaking, no single partner has the power to dissolve the partnership before the expiration of the term or the completion of the undertaking. Despite any agreed definite term or specific undertaking, each partner retains the power to *dissociate* by express will at any time, RUPA §§ 601(1) & 602(a), but any withdrawal before the expiration of the definite term or the

---

B. Technically, the partnership dissolves on *notice* of the partner's express will to withdraw. RUPA § 801(1).

completion of the specific undertaking would generally be *wrongful*. RUPA § 602(b)(2)(i).

Recall that, under the UPA, after an early withdrawal from a partnership for a definite term or a specific undertaking, continuing the partnership business without liquidation requires the concurrence of *all* the remaining partners. UPA §§ 38(2)(a) & 38(2)(b). Under the RUPA, the partnership is not dissolved after an early withdrawal, except upon the express will of *at least half* of the other partners. RUPA § 801(2)(i). On the other hand, any of the other partners may *rightfully* withdraw from the partnership after another partner's wrongful dissociation, bankruptcy or death (or similar event for partners who are not natural persons). RUPA § 602(b)(2)(i).

When there is no dissolution of the partnership, the partnership must purchase the withdrawing partner's interest in the partnership. RUPA §§ 603(a), 701(a). The partnership must also *indemnify* the withdrawing partner against partnership liabilities. RUPA § 701(d).

Wrongful Dissociation

Under RUPA section 602, a partner's dissociation is wrongful only if:

(1) the dissociation violates the partnership agreement, RUPA § 602(b)(1), or

(2) before the expiration of a definite term or the completion of a specific undertaking, a partner dissociates by express will, is judicially expelled, becomes bankrupt, or (if a legal entity and not a natural person) willfully dissolves or terminates, RUPA § 602(b)(2).

The chief consequence of a wrongful dissociation is that the wrongfully dissociating partner is liable for damages. RUPA § 602(c). In addition, partners who wrongfully dissociate before the expiration of a definite term or specific undertaking are not entitled to payment for the partner's interest in the partnership until the expiration of the term or the completion of the undertaking. RUPA § 701(h).

Texas Revised Partnership Act

Withdrawal

The basic structure of the Texas Revised Partnership Act ("TRPA") is similar to that of . Under the TRPA, partners have the power to withdraw at any time, TRPA §§ 6.01(b)(1) & 6.02(a), and that power may not be contracted away, TRPA § 1.03(b)(5). A partner's withdrawal is wrongful if it breaches the partnership agreement. TRPA § 6.02(b)(1). A withdrawal is also wrongful where the partner has withdrawn prior to

(a) the expiration of any agreed definite term,

(b) the completion of an agreed particular undertaking, or

(c) the occurrence of an agreed specified event.

Winding Up

Unless the partnership agreement provides others, TRPA § 1.03, where there is no agreed definite term, particular undertaking or specified event upon which the partnership is to be wound up:

(a) A majority-in-interest, TRPA § 1.01(10), of the partners[C] may voluntarily dissolve the partnership. TRPA § 8.01(a).

(b) A partner who has not agreed not to withdraw may request a winding up of the partnership, but the partnership will not be wound up if a majority-in-interest of the partners agree to continue the partnership. TRPA § 8.01(g). TRPA section 8.01(g) provides for an implied election to continue:

> The continuation of the business by the other partners or by those who habitually acted in the business before the notice, other than the partner giving the notice, without any settlement or liquidation of the partnership business, is prima facie evidence of an agreement to continue the partnership.

TRPA § 8.01(g) (last sentence).

Where a partner withdraws, and the partnership is not required to be wound up, the partnership must purchase the interest of the withdrawing partner. TRPA § 7.01(a).

Note on Withdrawal and Dissolution in Limited Partnerships

Withdrawal

General Partners

Under the RULPA, a general partner may withdraw at any time. RULPA §§ 402(1), 602. In addition, a general partner involuntary "withdraws" as a general partner when "removed as a general partner *in accordance with the partnership agreement.*" RULPA § 402(3).

A withdrawal by a general partner dissolves the limited partnership, except in two circumstances. RULPA § 801(4).

a. First, dissolution can be avoided where

(i) there is at least one remaining general partner,

(ii) a written partnership agreement permits the business of the limited partnership to be carried on by the remaining general partner(s), and

(iii) the remaining general partners carry on the business of the limited partnership. RULPA § 801(5) ("unless" clause).

b. Second, within 90 days of a general partner's withdrawal, all the partners agree

(i) to continue the business of the limited partnership, and

(ii) to the appointment of one or more additional general partners "if necessary or desired". RULPA §801(5) ("but" clause).

Limited Partners

Under RULPA section 603, a limited partner may withdraw from a limited partnership

---

C. Technically, a majority-in-interest of the partners who have not assigned their interests

(a) at the time or one the happening of events specified in the partnership agreement, and

(b) on at least 6 month's notice to the general partners, where the agreement specifies neither

(i) a time or the happening of an event allowing a limited partner to withdraw, nor

(ii) a definite time for dissolution and winding up of the limited partnership. RULPA 603.

Unless the partnership agreement provides otherwise, the withdrawal of a limited partner does not dissolve the limited partnership. RULPA §§ 801(2), (4). Why?

Distributions on Withdrawal

Under RULPA § 604, a withdrawing partner is entitled to receive

(a) any distribution to which the withdrawing partner may be entitled under the partnership agreement, and

(b) unless the partnership provides otherwise the fair value of the withdrawing partner's interest in the partnership.

Note on Withdrawal and Dissolution in LLC's

Uniform Limited Liability Company Act

In General

Unless the operating agreement provides otherwise, a member of an LLC has the power to withdraw at any time. ULLCA §§ 601(1), 602(a). This is true, even where the members have agreed to remain members until the expiration of a term specified in the operating (a "term company"). ULLCA § 602(a) & Comment. A member who withdraws in breach of the operating agreement, or before the expiration of the specified term of a term company, has wrongfully dissociated from the LLC.

Unlike a partnership, a member has no right to unilaterally cause dissolution of the LLC, unless the operating agreement provides otherwise. ULLCA §§ 103, 801(2).

Delaware Limited Liability Company Act

Members

Instead of using either "withdrawal" or "dissociation", the Delaware LLC Act ("DLLCA") uses the term "resignation". Under the DLLCA, a member may not resign from an LLC prior to its dissolution and winding up, except to the extent permitted by the LLC agreement. DLLCA § 603. Where the LLC agreement permits it, a member may resign. *Id.* Unless the LLC agreement provides otherwise, a resigning member is entitled to receive the fair value of the members interest in the LLC as of the date of the resignation.

On the resignation of a member, unless the LLC Agreement otherwise provides, the LLC shall be continued without dissolution, unless within 90 days members owning a majority of the profits interest agree in writing to dissolve the LLC. DLLCA § 18-801(b).

Managers

By written notice to the members and other managers, a manager[A] may resign as manager at any time. DLLCA § 18-602. Even where the LLC agreement provides that the manager has no right to resign as manager, the manager has the power to do so, but is liable in damages. *Id.*

B. Expulsions

Problem 15.4

Levy, was a physician engaged in the practice of medicine as a partner in Nassau Queens Medical Group. By a majority vote of the partnership executive committee, Levy was expelled from the partnership on the ground that he was more than 70 years of age. The partnership agreement provided that a partner who was 70 years old or older could be terminated by a majority vote. Levy argues that the partners terminated him in bad faith. Other partners over the age of 70 were not expelled from the partnership. Levy believes that the real reason for the termination was Levy's criticisms of partnership decisions. *See Levy v. Nassau Queens Medical Group*, 102 A.D.2d 845, 476 N.Y.S.2d 613 (1984).

Bohatch v. Butler Binion
977 S.W.2d 543 (Tex. 1998)

ENOCH, Justice, delivered the opinion of the Court, in which GONZALEZ, OWEN, BAKER, and HANKINSON, Justices, join.

Partnerships exist by the agreement of the partners; partners have no duty to remain partners. The issue in this case is whether we should create an exception to this rule by holding that a partnership has a duty not to expel a partner for reporting suspected overbilling by another partner. The trial court rendered judgment for Colette Bohatch on her breach of fiduciary duty claim against Butler & Binion and several of its partners (collectively, "the firm"). The court of appeals held that there was no evidence that the firm breached a fiduciary duty and reversed the trial court's tort judgment; however, the court of appeals found evidence of a breach of the partnership agreement and rendered judgment for Bohatch on this ground. We affirm the court of appeals' judgment.

I. FACTS

Bohatch became an associate in the Washington, D.C., office of Butler & Binion in 1986 after working for several years as Deputy Assistant General

---

A. Recall that a member may be a manager of a Delaware LLC. DLLCA § 18-402. A person who is both a member and a manager has all the rights and powers, and is subject to the restrictions, of members and of managers. DLLCA § 18-403.

Counsel at the Federal Energy Regulatory Commission. John McDonald, the managing partner of the office, and Richard Powers, a partner, were the only other attorneys in the Washington office. The office did work for Pennzoil almost exclusively.

Bohatch was made partner in February 1990. She then began receiving internal firm reports showing the number of hours each attorney worked, billed, and collected. From her review of these reports, Bohatch became concerned that McDonald was overbilling Pennzoil and discussed the matter with Powers. Together they reviewed and copied portions of McDonald's time diary. Bohatch's review of McDonald's time entries increased her concern.

On July 15, 1990, Bohatch met with Louis Paine, the firm's managing partner, to report her concern that McDonald was overbilling Pennzoil. Paine said he would investigate. Later that day, Bohatch told Powers about her conversation with Paine.

The following day, McDonald met with Bohatch and informed her that Pennzoil was not satisfied with her work and wanted her work to be supervised. Bohatch testified that this was the first time she had ever heard criticism of her work for Pennzoil.

The next day, Bohatch repeated her concerns to Paine and to R. Hayden Burns and Marion E. McDaniel, two other members of the firm's management committee, in a telephone conversation. Over the next month, Paine and Burns investigated Bohatch's complaint. They reviewed the Pennzoil bills and supporting computer print-outs for those bills. They then discussed the allegations with Pennzoil in-house counsel John Chapman, the firm's primary contact with Pennzoil. Chapman, who had a long-standing relationship with McDonald, responded that Pennzoil was satisfied that the bills were reasonable.

In August, Paine met with Bohatch and told her that the firm's investigation revealed no basis for her contentions. He added that she should begin looking for other employment, but that the firm would continue to provide her a monthly draw, insurance coverage, office space, and a secretary. After this meeting, Bohatch received no further work assignments from the firm.

In January 1991, the firm denied Bohatch a year-end partnership distribution for 1990 and reduced her tentative distribution share for 1991 to zero. In June, the firm paid Bohatch her monthly draw and told her that this draw would be her last. Finally, in August, the firm gave Bohatch until November to vacate her office.

By September, Bohatch had found new employment. She filed this suit on October 18, 1991, and the firm voted formally to expel her from the partnership three days later, October 21, 1991.

The trial court granted partial summary judgment for the firm on Bohatch's wrongful discharge claim, and also on her breach of fiduciary duty and breach of the duty of good faith and fair dealing claims for any conduct occurring after October 21, 1991 (the date Bohatch was formally expelled from the firm). The trial court denied the firm's summary judgment motion on Bohatch's breach of fiduciary duty and breach of the duty of good faith and fair dealing claims for conduct occurring before October 21, 1991. The breach of fiduciary duty claim and a breach of contract claim were tried to a jury. The jury found that the firm breached the partnership agreement and its fiduciary duty. It awarded Bohatch $57,000 for past lost wages, $250,000 for past mental anguish, $4,000,000 total in punitive damages (this amount was apportioned against several defendants), and attorney's fees. The trial court rendered judgment for Bohatch in the amounts found by the jury, except it disallowed attorney's fees because the judgment was based in tort. After suggesting remittitur, which Bohatch accepted, the trial court reduced the punitive damages to around $237,000.

All parties appealed. The court of appeals held that the firm's only duty to Bohatch was not to expel her in bad faith. The court of appeals stated that

'[b]ad faith' in this context means only that partners cannot expel another partner for self-gain.

Finding no evidence that the firm expelled Bohatch for self-gain, the court concluded that Bohatch could not recover for breach of fiduciary duty. However, the court concluded that the firm breached the partnership agreement when it reduced Bohatch's tentative partnership distribution for 1991 to zero without notice, and when it terminated her draw three months before she left. The court concluded that Bohatch was entitled to recover $35,000 in lost earnings for 1991 but none for 1990, and no mental anguish damages. Accordingly, the court rendered judgment for Bohatch for $35,000 plus $225,000 in attorney's fees.

II. BREACH OF FIDUCIARY DUTY

We have long recognized as a matter of common law that

[t]he relationship between...partners...is fiduciary in character, and imposes upon all the participants the obligation of loyalty to the joint concern and of the utmost good faith, fairness, and honesty in their dealings with each other with respect to matters pertaining to the enterprise.

Fitz-Gerald v. Hull, 150 Tex. 39, 237 S.W.2d 256, 264 (1951) (quotation omitted). Yet, partners have no obligation to remain partners;

at the heart of the partnership concept is the principle that partners may choose with whom they wish to be associated.

Gelder Med. Group v. Webber, 41 N.Y.2d 680, 394 N.Y.S.2d 867, 870-71, 363 N.E.2d 573, 577 (1977). The issue presented, one of first impression, is whether the fiduciary relationship between and among partners creates an exception to the at-will nature of partnerships; that is, in this case, whether it gives rise to a duty not to expel a partner who reports suspected overbilling by another partner.

At the outset, we note that no party questions that the obligations of lawyers licensed to practice in the District of Columbia—including McDonald and Bohatch—were prescribed by the District of Columbia Code of Professional Responsibility in effect in 1990, and that in all other respects Texas law applies. Further, neither statutory nor contract law principles answer the question of whether the firm owed Bohatch a duty not to expel her. The Texas Uniform Partnership Act, Tex. Rev. Civ. Stat. Ann. art. 6701b, addresses expulsion of a partner only in the context of dissolution of the partnership. *See id.* §§ 31, 38. In this case, as provided by the partnership agreement, Bohatch's expulsion did not dissolve the partnership. Additionally, the new Texas Revised Partnership Act, Tex. Rev. Civ. Stat. Ann. art. 6701b-1.01 to -11.04, does not have retroactive effect and thus does not apply. *See id.* art. 6701b-11.03. Finally, the partnership agreement contemplates expulsion of a partner and prescribes procedures to be followed, but it does not specify or limit the grounds for expulsion. Thus, while Bohatch's claim that she was expelled in an improper way is governed by the partnership agreement, her claim that she was expelled for an improper reason is not. Therefore, we look to the common law to find the principles governing Bohatch's claim that the firm breached a duty when it expelled her.

Courts in other states have held that a partnership may expel a partner for purely business reasons. Finally, many courts have held that a partnership can expel a partner without breaching any duty in order to resolve a "fundamental schism." *See Waite [v. Sylvester,* 131 N.H. 663, 560 A.2d 619, 623 (1989)] (concluding that in removing partner as managing partner "the partners acted in good faith to resolve the 'fundamental schism' between them"); *Heller v. Pillsbury Madison & Sutro,* 50 Cal.App.4th 1367, 58 Cal.Rptr.2d 336, 348 (1996) (holding that law firm did not breach fiduciary duty when it expelled partner who was not as productive as firm expected and who was offensive to some of firm's major clients); *Levy v. Nassau Queens Med. Group,* 102 A.D.2d 845, 476 N.Y.S.2d 613, 614 (1984) (concluding that expelling partner because of "[p]olicy disagreements" is not "bad faith").

The fiduciary duty that partners owe one another does not encompass a duty to remain partners or else answer in tort damages. Nonetheless, Bohatch and several distinguished legal scholars urge this Court to recognize that public policy requires a limited duty to remain partners—*i.e.,* a partnership must retain a whistleblower partner. They argue that such an extension of a partner's fiduciary duty is necessary because permitting a law firm to retaliate against a partner who in good faith reports suspected overbilling would discourage compliance with rules of professional conduct and thereby hurt clients.

While this argument is not without some force, we must reject it. A partnership exists solely because the partners choose to place personal confidence and trust in one another. Just as a partner can be expelled, without a breach of any common law duty, over disagreements about firm policy or to resolve some other "fundamental schism," a partner can be expelled for accusing another partner of overbilling without subjecting the partnership to tort damages. Such charges, whether true or not, may have a profound effect on the personal confidence and trust essential to the partner relationship. Once such charges are made, partners may find it impossible to continue to work together to their mutual benefit and the benefit of their clients.

We are sensitive to the concern expressed by the dissenting Justices that

retaliation against a partner who tries in good faith to correct or report perceived misconduct virtually assures that others will not take these appropriate steps in the future.

However, the dissenting Justices do not explain how the trust relationship necessary both for the firm's existence and for representing clients can survive such serious accusations by one partner against another. The threat of tort liability for expulsion would tend to force partners to remain in untenable circumstance— suspicious of and angry with each other—to their own detriment and that of their clients whose matters are neglected by lawyers distracted with intra-firm frictions.

Although concurring in the Court's judgment, Justice Hecht criticizes the Court for failing to

> address *amici*'s concerns that failing to impose liability will discourage attorneys from reporting unethical conduct.

To address the scholars' concerns, he proposes that a whistleblower be protected from expulsion, but only if the report, irrespective of being made in good faith, is proved to be correct. We fail to see how such an approach encourages compliance with ethical rules more than the approach we adopt today. Furthermore, the *amici*'s position is that a reporting attorney must be in good faith, not that the attorney must be right. In short, Justice Hecht's approach ignores the question Bohatch presents, the *amici* write about, and the firm challenges—whether a partnership violates a fiduciary duty when it expels a partner who in good faith reports suspected ethical violations. The concerns of the *amici* are best addressed by a rule that clearly demarcates an attorney's ethical duties and the parameters of tort liability, rather than redefining "whistleblower."

We emphasize that our refusal to create an exception to the at-will nature of partnerships in no way obviates the ethical duties of lawyers. Such duties sometimes necessitate difficult decisions, as when a lawyer suspects overbilling by a colleague. The fact that the ethical duty to report may create an irreparable schism between partners neither excuses failure to report nor transforms expulsion as a means of resolving that schism into a tort.

We hold that the firm did not owe Bohatch a duty not to expel her for reporting suspected overbilling by another partner.

III. BREACH OF THE PARTNERSHIP AGREEMENT

The court of appeals concluded that the firm breached the partnership agreement by reducing Bohatch's tentative distribution for 1991 to zero without the requisite notice. The firm contests this finding on the ground that the management committee had the right to set tentative and year-end bonuses. However, the partnership agreement guarantees a monthly draw of $7,500 per month regardless of the tentative distribution. Moreover, the firm's right to reduce the bonus was contingent upon providing proper notice to Bohatch. The firm does not dispute that it did not give Bohatch notice that the firm was reducing her tentative distribution. Accordingly, the court of appeals did not err in finding the firm liable for breach of the partnership agreement. Moreover, because Bohatch's damages sound in contract, and because she sought attorney's fees at trial under section 38.001(8) of the Texas Civil Practice and Remedies Code, we affirm the court of appeals' award of Bohatch's attorney's fees.

*   *   *

We affirm the court of appeals' judgment.

HECHT, Justice, concurring in the judgment.

The Court holds that partners in a law firm have no common-law liability for expelling one of their number for accusing another of unethical conduct. The dissent argues that partners in a law firm are liable for such conduct. Both views are unqualified; neither concedes or even considers whether "always" and "never" are separated by any distance. I think they must be. The Court's position is directly contrary to that of some of the leading scholars on the subject who have appeared here as *amici curiae*. The Court finds *amici*'s arguments "not without some force", but rejects them completely. I do not believe *amici*'s arguments can be rejected out of hand. The dissent, on the other hand, refuses even to acknowledge the serious impracticalities involved in maintaining the trust necessary between partners when one has accused another of unethical conduct. In the dissent's view, partners who would expel another for such accusations must simply either get over it or respond in damages. The dissent's view blinks reality.

The issue is not well developed; in fact, to our knowledge we are the first court to address it. It seems to me there must be some circumstances when expulsion for reporting an ethical violation is culpable and other circumstances when it is not. I have trouble justifying a 500-partner firm's expulsion of a partner for reporting overbilling of a client that saves the firm not only from ethical complaints but from liability to the client. But I cannot see how a five-partner firm can legitimately survive one partner's accusations that another is unethical. Between two such extreme examples I see a lot of ground.

This case does not force a choice between diametrically opposite views. Here, the report of unethical conduct, though made in good faith, was incorrect. That fact is significant to me because I think a law firm can always expel a partner for bad judgment, whether it relates to the representation of clients or the relationships with other partners, and whether it is in good faith. I would hold that Butler & Binion did not breach its fiduciary duty by expelling Colette Bohatch because she made a good-faith but nevertheless extremely serious charge against a senior partner that threatened the firm's relationship with an important client, her charge proved groundless, and her relationship with her partners was destroyed in the process. I cannot, however, extrapolate from this case, as the Court does, that no law firm can ever be liable for expelling a partner for reporting unethical conduct. Accordingly, I concur only in the Court's judgment.

* * *

II.

A

Butler & Binion argues that its expulsion of Bohatch did not breach its fiduciary duty. No one questions that the obligations of the lawyers licensed to practice in the District of Columbia—including McDonald and Bohatch—were prescribed by the District of Columbia Code of Professional Responsibility in effect in 1990, and that in all other respects Texas law applies.

Of the three possible sources of governing Texas law—statute, contract, and common law—only one applies here. Butler & Binion argues that it did not violate the Texas Uniform Partnership Act in effect throughout the events of this case (but since repealed), Law of May 9, 1961, 57th Leg., R.S., ch. 158, 1961 Tex. Gen. Laws 289, formerly Tex. Rev. Civ. Stat. Ann. art. 6132b (Vernon 1970). But Bohatch responds that TUPA does not determine her claims because it spoke to expulsion of a partner only in the context of a partnership's dissolution. *See id.* art. 6132b, §§ 31 & 38. In this case, as provided by the partnership agreement, Bohatch's expulsion did not dissolve the partnership, and thus the statute does not directly answer Bohatch's claims. The partnership agreement contemplates expulsion of a partner and prescribes procedures to be followed, but it does not specify or limit the grounds for expulsion. Bohatch's claim that she was expelled in an improper way is governed by the partnership agreement, but her claim that she was expelled for an improper reason is not. Thus, the principles governing Bohatch's claim that her expulsion was a breach of fiduciary duty must be found in the common law.

We have long recognized that

'[t]he relationship between joint adventurers, like that existing between partners, is fiduciary in character, and imposes upon all the participants the obligation of loyalty to the joint concern and of the utmost good faith, fairness, and honesty in their dealings with each other with respect to matters pertaining to the enterprise.'

Fitz-Gerald v. Hull, 150 Tex. 39, 237 S.W.2d 256, 264 (Tex.1951)(*quoting* 30 AM.JUR. Joint Adventures § 34 (____)). But we have never had occasion to apply this duty in the situation of a partner's expulsion. A few other appellate courts have done so. None has held that a partnership breached its fiduciary duty to a partner by expelling the partner. Only one has held that an expelled partner stated a claim for breach of fiduciary duty. [*Winston & Strawn v. Nosal*, 279 Ill.App.3d 231, 215 Ill.Dec. 842, 847-849, 664 N.E.2d 239, 244-246 (1996)].

The courts have not had much difficulty holding that a partnership may expel a partner for purely business reasons. In *Leigh [v. Crescent Square, Ltd.*, 80 Ohio App.3d 231, 608 N.E.2d 1166 (1992)], for example, a limited partnership formed to rehabilitate an apartment complex expelled a general partner, one Leigh, for misconduct in connection with the partnership's affairs. The court held that the partnership's failure to give Leigh notice of his impending ouster was not a breach of fiduciary duty. The court explained:

We find that a general partner's fiduciary duty applies only to activities where a partner will take advantage of his position in the partnership for his own profit or gain. Taking into account the general partners' past problems and the previous litigation wherein Leigh was found to have acted in contravention of the partnership's best interests, the ouster was instituted in good faith and for legitimate business purposes.

608 N.E.2d at 1170.

At least in the context of professional partnerships, the courts have uniformly recognized that a partner can be expelled to protect relationships both inside the firm and with clients. In *Holman [v. Coie*, 11 Wash.App. 195, 522 P.2d 515 (1974)], a law firm expelled two partners, both sons of a retired partner, because they had been contentious members of the executive committee, and because one of them, as a state senator, had made a speech offensive to a major client. The court held that while the partners remaining in the firm owed the expelled partners a fiduciary duty,

the personal relationships between partners to which the terms 'bona fide' and 'good faith' relate are those which have a bearing upon the business aspects or property of the partnership and prohibit a partner, to-wit, a fiduciary, from taking any personal advantage touching those subjects. Plaintiffs' claims do not relate to the business aspects or property rights of this partnership. There is no evidence the purpose of the severance was to gain any business or property advantage to the remaining partners. Consequently, in that context, there has been no showing of breach of the duty of good faith toward plaintiffs.

522 P.2d at 523 (citations omitted). *Cf. Waite [v. Sylvester*, 131 N.H. 663, 560 A.2d 619, 623 (1989)] (concluding that in removing a partner as managing partner "the partners acted in good faith to resolve the 'fundamental schism' between them").

Likewise, in *Heller [v. Pillsbury Madison & Sutro*, 50 Cal.App.4th 1367, 58 Cal.Rptr.2d 336 (1996),] the court held that a law firm was not liable for expelling Heller, a partner, who was not as productive as the firm expected and who was offensive to some of the firm's major clients. The court wrote:

Although partners owe each other and the partnership a fiduciary duty, this duty 'applies only to situations where one partner could take advantage of his position to reap personal profit or act to the partnership's detriment.'

Heller, 58 Cal.Rptr.2d at 348 (*quoting Leigh*, 608 N.E.2d at 1170). The court added:

More importantly, even with evaluating the evidence in the light most favorable to Heller, the evidence shows that the Executive Committee expelled Heller because of a loss of trust in him. "The foundation of a professional relationship is personal confidence and trust. Once a schism develops, its magnitude may be exaggerated rightfully or wrongfully to the point of destroying a harmonious accord. When such occurs, an expeditious severance is desirable...."

Id. (*quoting Holman*, 522 P.2d at 524).

In *Lawlis [Lawlis v. Kightlinger & Gray*, 562 N.E.2d 435 (Ind.App.1990)], the court stressed the importance of a law firm's reputation in holding that the firm was not liable for expelling a partner, one Lawlis, following his successful struggle against alcoholism. The court observed that had the firm acted in bad faith or with a predatory purpose, it would have violated both the partnership agreement and its fiduciary duty, but the court limited actionable conduct to partners' attempting to obtain a personal financial advantage from the expulsion. The court explained:

The lifeblood of any partnership contains two essential ingredients, cash flow and profit, and the prime generators of that lifeblood are "good will" and a favorable reputation. The term "good will" generally is defined as the probability that old customers of the firm will resort to the old place of business where it is well-established, well known, and enjoys the fixed and favorable consideration of its customers. An equally important business adjunct of a partnership engaged in the practice of law is a favorable reputation for ability and competence in the practice of that profession. A favorable reputation not only is involved in the retention of old clients, it is an essential ingredient in the acquisition of new ones. Any condition which has the potential to adversely affect the good will or favorable reputation of a law partnership is one which potentially involves the partnership's economic survival. Thus, if a partner's propensity toward alcohol has the potential to damage his firm's good will or reputation for astuteness in the practice of law, simple prudence dictates the exercise of corrective action, as in Holman, since the survival of the partnership itself potentially is at stake.

Lawlis, 562 N.E.2d at 442 (citations omitted).

In *Levy [v. Nassau Queens Medical Group,* 102 A.D.2d 845, 476 N.Y.S.2d 613 (1984)], a medical partnership claimed that it expelled a partner, Dr. Levy, because the partnership agreement allowed for expulsion of partners over seventy years of age. Dr. Levy countered that he had been expelled for being critical of partnership policies. The court held that even if Dr. Levy were right, the partnership did not breach any duty owed him. While bad faith may be actionable, there must be some showing that the partnership acted out of a desire to gain a business or property advantage for the remaining partners. Policy disagreements do not constitute bad faith since

> at the heart of the partnership concept is the principle that partners may choose with whom they wish to be associated.

Levy, 476 N.Y.S.2d at 614 (*citing Holman* and *Gelder,* citations omitted).

Despite statements in these cases that partners cannot expel one of their number for personal profit, in each instance the expelling partners believed that retaining the partner would hurt the firm financially and that the firm—and thus the partners themselves—stood to benefit from the expulsion. It is therefore far too simplistic to say, as the court of appeals held, that partners cannot expel a partner for personal financial benefit; if expulsion of a partner to protect the firm's reputation or preserve its relationship with a client benefits the firm financially, it perforce benefits the members of the firm. If expulsion of a partner can be in breach of a fiduciary duty, the circumstances must be more precisely defined.

The New York Court of Appeals—the only high court to have addressed the topic—has expressed hesitation in specifying whether and when expulsion of a partner breaches fiduciary duties. In *Gelder [Medical Group v. Webber,* 41 N.Y.2d 680, 394 N.Y.S.2d 867, 363 N.E.2d 573 (1977)], a surgeon, a certain Dr. Webber, was expelled from a medical partnership because his personal and professional conduct had become abrasive and objectionable to his partners. Dr. Webber's psychiatrist described him as

> a perfectionist who was a 'rather idealistic sincere, direct, frank individual who quite possibly could be perceived at times as being somewhat blunt.'"

394 N.Y.S.2d at 868-870, 363 N.E.2d at 575-576. The court held that expulsion in accordance with the partnership agreement was proper. The court added:

> Assuming, not without question, that bad faith might limit the otherwise absolute language of the agreement, the record does not reveal bad faith. Embarrassing situations developed, affecting the physicians and their patients, as a result of Dr. Webber's conduct, however highly motivated his conduct might have been. It was as important, therefore, in the group's eyes, as anything affecting survival of the group that it be disassociated from the new member's conflict-producing conduct. Indeed, at the heart of the partnership concept is the principle that partners may choose with whom they wish to be associated.
>
> Even if bad faith on the part of the remaining partners would nullify the right to expel one of their number, it does not follow that under an agreement permitting expulsion without cause the remaining partners

have the burden of establishing good faith. To so require would nullify the right to expel without cause and frustrate the obvious intention of the agreement to avoid bitter and protracted litigation over the reason for the expulsion. Obviously, no expulsion would ever occur without some cause, fancied or real, but the agreement provision is addressed to avoiding the necessity of showing cause and litigating the issue. On the other hand, if an expelled partners [sic] were to allege and prove bad faith going to the essence, a different case would be presented.... In his affidavits Dr. Webber has not shown even a suggestion of evil, malevolent, or predatory purpose in the expulsion. Hence, he raises no triable issue on this score.

Gelder, 394 N.Y.S.2d at 869-871, 363 N.E.2d at 576-577 (emphasis added; citations omitted). The court did not suggest what it might consider "bad faith going to the essence" or an "evil, malevolent, or predatory purpose".

In only one case has an appellate court confronted circumstances which it believed might give rise to liability for a breach of fiduciary duty in expelling a partner. In *Nosal*, an attorney claimed that he had been expelled from his firm because of his insistence on his right under the partnership agreement to inspect firm records which he believed would show misconduct by the firm's management. The court reversed summary judgment for the firm, holding that Nosal's evidence raised a fact issue that his expulsion was in breach of the fiduciary duty owed him. *Nosal*, 215 Ill.Dec. at 849, 664 N.E.2d at 246.

Scholars are divided over not only how but whether partners' common-law fiduciary duty to each other limit expulsion of a partner. There is also disagreement over the impact of the Revised Uniform Partnership Act. Nine distinguished law professors... have argued in *amicus curiae* briefs that expulsion of a partner in bad faith is a breach of fiduciary duty, and that expulsion for self-gain is in bad faith, but so is expulsion for reporting unethical conduct. From a canvass of the various commentators' arguments it is fair to say that the law governing liability for expulsion of a partner is relatively uncertain.

B

No court has considered whether expulsion of a partner from a law firm for reporting unethical conduct is a breach of fiduciary duty. Several courts have concluded that expulsion to remedy a fundamental schism in a professional firm is not a breach of fiduciary duty. There is hardly a schism more fundamental than that caused by one partner's accusing another of unethical conduct. If a partner can be expelled because of disagreements over nothing more significant than firm policy and abrasive personal conduct, as cases have held, surely a partner can be expelled for accusing another partner of something as serious as unethical conduct. Once such charges are raised, I find it hard to imagine how partners could continue to work together to their mutual benefit and the benefit of their clients. The trust essential to the relationship would have been destroyed. Indeed, I should think that a lawyer who was unable to convince his or her partners to rectify the unethical conduct of another would choose to withdraw from the firm rather than continue in association with lawyers who did not adhere to high ethical standards.

But I am troubled by the arguments of the distinguished *amici curiae* that permitting a law firm to retaliate against a partner for reporting unethical behavior would discourage compliance with rules of conduct, hurt clients, and contravene public policy. Their arguments have force, but they do not explain how a relationship of trust necessary for both the existence of the firm and the representation of its clients can survive such serious accusations by one partner against another. The threat of liability for expulsion would tend to force partners to remain in untenable circumstances—suspicious of and angry with each other—to their own detriment and that of their clients whose matters are neglected by lawyers distracted with intra-firm frictions. If

> at the heart of the partnership concept is the principle that partners may choose with whom they wish to be associated,

Gelder, 394 N.Y.S.2d at 870-871, 363 N.E.2d at 577, surely partners are not obliged to continue to associate with someone who has accused one of them of unethical conduct.

This very difficult issue need not be finally resolved in this case. Bohatch did not report unethical conduct; she reported what she believed, presumably in good faith but nevertheless mistakenly, to be unethical conduct. * * * Pennzoil's conclusion that Butler & Binion's fees were reasonable, reached after being made aware of Bohatch's concerns that McDonald's time was overstated, establishes that Butler & Binion did not collect excessive fees from Pennzoil. A fee that a client as sophisticated as Pennzoil considers reasonable is not clearly excessive simply because a lawyer believes it could have been less. Bohatch's argument that Pennzoil had other reasons not to complain of Butler & Binion's bills is simply beside the point. Whatever its motivations, Pennzoil found the bills reasonable, thereby establishing that McDonald had not overbilled in violation of ethical rules. Bohatch's argument that Pennzoil's assessment of the bills was prejudiced by Butler & Binion's misrepresentations about her is implausible. There is nothing to suggest that Pennzoil would have thought clearly excessive legal fees were reasonable simply because it did not like Bohatch.

Bohatch's real concern was not that fees to Pennzoil were excessive— she had never even seen the bills and had no idea what the fees, or fee arrangements, were—but that McDonald was misrepresenting the number of hours he worked. The District of Columbia Code of Professional Responsibility at the time also prohibited lawyers from engaging in "conduct involving dishonesty, fraud, deceit or misrepresentation." *Id.* DR 1-102(A)(4). But there is no evidence that McDonald actually engaged in such conduct. At most, Bohatch showed only that McDonald kept sloppy time records, not that he deceived his partners or clients. Neither his partners nor his major client accused McDonald of dishonesty, even after reviewing his bills and time records. Bohatch complains that Butler & Binion did not fully investigate McDonald's billing practices. Assuming Butler & Binion had some duty to investigate Bohatch's charges, it discharged that duty by determining that Pennzoil considered its bills reasonable. (The district court, as the court of appeals noted, excluded evidence that Paine and McDonald himself went so far as to report the charges against McDonald to the lawyer disciplinary authority, which exonerated him.)

Even if expulsion of a partner for reporting unethical conduct might be a breach of fiduciary duty, expulsion for mistakenly reporting unethical conduct cannot be a breach of fiduciary duty. At the very least, a mistake so serious indicates a lack of judgment warranting expulsion. No one would argue that an attorney could not be expelled from a firm for a serious error in judgment about a client's affairs or even the firm's affairs. If Bohatch and McDonald had disagreed over what position to take in a particular case for Pennzoil, or over whether Butler & Binion should continue to operate its Washington office, the firm could have determined that she should be expelled for the health of the firm, even if Bohatch had acted in complete good faith. Reporting unethical conduct where none existed is no different. If, as in Gelder, a partner can be expelled for being blunt, surely a partner can be expelled for a serious error in judgment.

Butler & Binion's expulsion of Bohatch did not discourage ethical conduct; it discouraged errors of judgment, which ought to be discouraged. Butler & Binion did not violate its fiduciary duty to Bohatch.

* * *

I do not disagree with the Court's treatment of Bohatch's claim for breach of contract. Accordingly, I concur in the Court's judgment but not in its opinion.

SPECTOR, joined by PHILLIPS, Chief Justice, dissenting.

[W]hat's the use you learning to do right when it's troublesome to do right and ain't no trouble to do wrong, and the wages is just the same?

—The Adventures of Huckleberry Finn

* * *

The majority views the partnership relationship among lawyers as strictly business. I disagree. The practice of law is a profession first, then a business. Moreover, it is a self-regulated profession subject to the Rules promulgated by this Court.

* * *

I believe that the fiduciary relationship among law partners should incorporate the rules of the profession promulgated by this Court. Although the evidence put on by Bohatch is by no means conclusive, applying the proper presumptions of a no-evidence review, this trial testimony amounts to some evidence that Bohatch made a good-faith report of suspected overbilling in an effort to comply with her professional duty. Further, it provides some evidence that the partners of Butler & Binion began a retaliatory course of action before any investigation of the allegation had begun.

In light of this Court's role in setting standards to govern attorneys' conduct, it is particularly inappropriate for the Court to deny recourse to attorneys wronged for adhering to the Disciplinary Rules. I would hold that in this case the law partners violated their fiduciary duty by retaliating against a fellow partner who made a good-faith effort to alert her partners to the possible overbilling of a client.

* * *

The Court's writing in this case sends an inappropriate signal to lawyers and to the public that the rules of professional responsibility are subordinate to a law firm's other interests. Under the majority opinion's vision for the legal profession, the wages would not even be the same for "doing right"; they diminish considerably and leave an attorney who acts ethically and in good faith without recourse. Accordingly, I respectfully dissent.

Notes

1. The UPA provides that

> Dissolution is caused:
>
> > (1) Without violation of the agreement between the partners,
>
> > * * *
>
> > (d) By the expulsion of any partner from the business *bona fide* in accordance with such a power conferred by between the partners.

UPA § 31(1)(d)(emphasis added). In *Bohatch v. Butler & Binion,* the court framed the issue as the extent of a *fiduciary duty* in expelling a partner. In his dissenting opinion, Justice Hecht reasoned that, because the partnership agreement that the partnership would not dissolve after an expulsion, the Texas version of UPA section 31(1)(d) did not apply. Would you agree? How could you interpret the partnership agreement to be consistent with the UPA?

2. Under RUPA section 601(3), a partner is dissociated from the partnership on "the partner's expulsion pursuant to the partnership agreement." Although RUPA section 601(3) does not by its terms require that an expulsion be done in good faith, recall that, under that under the RUPA:

> A partner shall discharge the duties to the partnership and the other partners under this [Act] or under the partnership agreement and *exercise any rights consistently with the obligation of good faith and fair dealing.*

RUPA § 404(d) (emphasis added). Note, however, that under RUPA section 404(a), the 404(d) obligation of good faith and fair dealing is not a *fiduciary* obligation. If RUPA section 404 had applied in *Bohatch v. Butler & Binion,* would the result have been different? Why or Why not?

3. In *Levy v. Nassau Queens Medical Group,* 102 A.D.2d 845, 476 N.Y.S.2d 613 (1984), a doctor was expelled from a medical partnership. Levy was expelled from the partnership on the ground, purportedly because he was more than 70 years of age. Levy claimed that the partners had expelled him in bad faith because he often criticized partnership decisions.

> The purpose of the termination clause was to provide a simple, practical and speedy method of separating a partner from the partnership, and in the absence of undue penalty or unjust forfeiture, the court may not frustrate this purpose. While bad faith may be actionable, there must be some showing that the partnership acted out of a desire to gain a business or property advantage for the remaining partners. Policy disagreements do not constitute bad faith since "at the heart of the partnership concept is the principle that partners may choose with whom they wish to be associated."

Note on Effect of Expulsion

UPA

Under UPA section 38(1), when dissolution is caused by "the expulsion of a partner, bona fide under the partnership agreement," the expelled partner loses the right to liquidation. So long as the expelled partner is *discharged* from partnership obligations, the expelled partner is only entitled to "receive in cash the net amount due him." *Id.* Presumably, all the other partners retain the right to liquidation (unless the agreement otherwise provides).

RUPA

As discussed earlier, the expulsion of a partner under the partnership agreement dissociates the partner. RUPA § 601(3). An expelled partner no longer has the right to dissolve the partnership. RUPA § 801(1). Instead, the expelled partner has the right to have the expelled partner's interest in the partnership to be purchased, RUPA § 701(a), and to be *indemnified* against partnership liabilities, RUPA § 701(d).

Note on Expulsions in Limited Partnerships and Limited Liability Companies

Limited Partnerships

Under RULPA § 402(3), a general partner is withdrawn and "cease to be a general partner" when the general partner

is removed in accordance with the partnership agreement[.]

Limited Liability Companies

ULLCA. Under ULLCA § 601(4), a member can be dissociated from the LLC based on

the member's expulsion pursuant to the operating agreement.

Delaware LLC Act. The Delaware LLC Act has no express provisions for expulsion of members pursuant to a limited liability company agreement. However, recall that the policy of the Delaware LLC Act is

to give maximum effect to the principle of freedom of contract and to the enforceability of limited liability company agreements.

Del. LLC Act § 18-1101(b).

C. Judicial Dissolutions

1. Owner Rights

Problem 15.5

A general partnership for the operation of an insurance business was formed for a five-year term in 1934 with ten partners. Partner Brown held the majority interest in the business, with the other nine partners sharing the remainder. The partnership agreement provided that Brown would set the salaries of the partners, that the admission of a new partner would require the affirmative vote of a majority in number of the partners, and that all other decisions would be made by an affirmative vote of a majority in interest of the partnership. Brown proposed the admission of Moore as a new partner, but it was defeated by a 7-3 vote. Thereafter, Brown reduced the salaries of the seven plaintiffs by fifty percent. The seven plaintiffs sued for a dissolution of the partnership, and the trial court granted it. What decision on appeal? *See Potter v. Brown*, 328 Pa. 554, 195 A. 901 (1938).

Monteleone v. Monteleone
147 Ill. App. 3d 265, 497 N.E.2d 1221 (1986)

Justice McMorrow:

Nick Monteleone and Lorenzo Monteleone (Nick and Lorenzo) appeal from the order of the judicial sale of the Monte Auto Body Shop, of which Nick and Lorenzo are partners in conjunction with Jerry Monteleone (Jerry). The primary question presented for our review is whether the trial court erred in ordering a judicial sale of the partnership assets prior to adjudicating whether Nick and Lorenzo have a right to retain the partnership business and reimburse Jerry for the value of his interest in the partnership, on the ground that Jerry wrongfully terminated the partnership.

Jerry instituted proceedings to dissolve his partnership with Nick and Lorenzo in the Monte Auto Body Shop on January 5, 1984. Thereafter Nick and Lorenzo filed an answer to Jerry's complaint and presented a counter-claim requesting dissolution of the partnership and recognition of their right to continue the business and to reimburse Jerry for his interest in the partnership, less damages for his wrongful termination of the partnership.

It is undisputed between the parties that Jerry, Nick, and Lorenzo formed an oral partnership in April 1979 to own and operate an automobile body repair business named Monte Auto Body Shop in Melrose Park, Illinois. Jerry, Nick, and Lorenzo dispute who among them caused the dissolution of partnership.

Jerry stated in his complaint that Nick and Lorenzo "wrongfully executed from the partnership premises" on or about October 31, 1983, thereby effecting a dissolution of the partnership. He alleged that Nick and Lorenzo subsequently failed to conclude partnership business, but instead continued to operate the auto body shop partnership without complying with the requirements of section 38(2)(b) of the Uniform Partnership Act. Jerry's pleading requested dissolution of the partnership. This behavior included, in essence, misappropriation of partnership funds, failure to contribute to the operation of the business, a wrongful demand that Jerry's son be made a partner in the business and that a certain employee be immediately discharged, and refusal to return partnership books and records. They stated that after the partnership "was dissolved in October of 1983 [by Jerry's wrongful termination]," Nick and Lorenzo, "being a surviving majority, formed a new partnership." Apparently this enterprise operates under the name Monte Auto Body Shop in the same location as the presently disputed partnership and continues ownership and operation of that partnership in auto body repair work. Based upon these allegations, Nick and Lorenzo requested that the court declare the partnership dissolved by virtue of Jerry's wrongful conduct in October 1983, the value of partnership assets to be determined as of October 1983, Nick and Lorenzo be permitted to purchase Jerry's interest, Nick and Lorenzo "be decreed to be the surviving partners and to continue the partnership business," an accounting to be performed, and Jerry "be assessed all damages and costs incurred by the partnership and/or [Nick and Lorenzo]" because of Jerry's wrongful termination of the partnership.

Although hearings on the parties' allegations had commenced, the trial court never made a final adjudication of the merits of their claims. Thereafter Jerry filed a motion requesting that the court order a judicial sale of partnership assets prior to the court's decision on the issues of the parties' interests in the business, the dissolution of the partnership and its wrongful termination, and the parties' rights upon dissolution. Following a briefing and oral argument, the trial court granted the motion in a written order for the judicial sale of partnership assets. The court's order found that the partnership was dissolved over two years ago. Based upon "the obvious dispute concerning the value of assets," the court ordered a judicial sale of "all of the partnership assets" with directions that, following the sale, "the sheriff shall * * * hold the proceeds subject to confirmation and appropriate proceeds order by this court based upon reasonable value and other equitable and legal considerations * * * ." The court found no just reason to delay enforcement of or appeal from its order of judicial sale. The timely expedited appeal of Nick and Lorenzo followed.

As previously noted, the primary question presented for our review is whether the court could properly order a judicial sale of the "partnership assets" of Monte Auto Body Shop prior to a determination of the claim of Nick and Lorenzo that they could continue operation of the partnership business because of Jerry's wrongful termination of the partnership.

Under section 38(2)(b) of the Uniform Partnership Act, innocent partners have the right to continue partnership business where another partner has wrongfully terminated the partnership. Nick and Lorenzo thus may have the right to continue ownership and operation of the Monte Auto Body Shop partnership, if they are able to establish at a subsequent proceeding that Jerry's conduct constituted a wrongful termination of the partnership.

The rights of partners upon a partner's wrongful termination of the partnership are governed by section 38(2) of the Uniform Partnership Act. This section provides in relevant part:

(2) When dissolution is caused in contravention of the partnership agreement the rights of the partners shall be as follows:

(a) Each partner who has not caused dissolution wrongfully shall have,

II. The right, as against each partner who has caused the dissolution wrongfully, to damage for breach of the agreement.

(b) The partners who have not caused the dissolution wrongfully, if they all desire to continue the business in the same name, either by themselves or jointly with others, may do so, during the agreed term for the partnership and for that purpose may possess the partnership property, provided they secure the payment by bond approved by the court, or pay to any partner who has caused the dissolution wrongfully, the value of his interest in the partnership at the dissolution, less any damages recoverable under clause (2a II) of this section, and in like manner indemnify him against all present or future partnership liabilities.

(c) A partner who has caused the dissolution wrongfully shall have:

II. If the business is continued under paragraph (2b) of this section the right as against his co-partners and all claiming through them in respect of their interests in the partnership, to have the value of his interest in the partnership, less any damages caused to his co-partners by the dissolution, ascertained and paid to him in cash, or the payment secured by bond approved by the court and to be released from all existing liabilities of the partnership; but in ascertaining the value of the partner's interest the value of the good will of the business shall not be considered.

A partner's conduct is considered "wrongful" when it is taken in derogation of the duties imposed either explicitly by the partnership agreement or implicitly by virtue of the nature of the partnership itself. The Uniform Partnership Act empowers a court to order partnership dissolution whenever, for example, a "partner has been guilty of such conduct as tends to affect prejudicially the carrying on of the business, [or whenever a] partner willfully or persistently commits a breach of the partnership or agreement, or otherwise so conducts himself in matters relating to the partnership business that it is not reasonably practicable to carry on the business in partnership with him." [UPA § 32(1)(c), (1)(d)].

Nick and Lorenzo alleged in their counter-claim that the oral partnership between Nick, Lorenzo, and Jerry specified that "each partner would contribute equally to the capital and equally share all profits and losses and further, that each partner would contribute an equal amount of labor to the operation of the partnership, and each partner would receive weekly compensation for his labor." Their pleading then alleged in substance that Jerry had violated this agreement in several specified respects. They claimed before the trial court and in this appeal that these allegations also constituted a breach of Jerry's fiduciary duties to the partnership.

Jerry concedes in this appeal that for the purposes of analysis, "we must assume that took draws in excess of his percentage of ownership and committed the conduct alleged in the counter-claim." In our opinion these allegations in the counter-claim of Nick and Lorenzo were sufficient to state a claim that Jerry's behavior was in contravention of the partnership agreement or a breach of Jerry's fiduciary duties, and would amount to "wrongful termination" of the partnership. Such alleged wrongful termination of the partnership is sufficient to order dissolution of the partnership and to recognize the right of Nick and Lorenzo to continue operation of the business rather than be subjected to the possibility of a contrived judicial sale from which they would receive a monetary payment for their respective interests in the partnership. (See [UPA § 38(2)].) As a result, the court's order of judicial sale of the partnership before a finding of whether Jerry wrongfully terminated his participation in the partnership was premature, and amounted to reversible error.

Jerry argues that his conduct, even if it amounts to wrongful termination, would not justify the continuation of the partnership business by Nick and Lorenzo, because the oral partnership agreement between them was not for a fixed term and was therefore a partnership at will. See [UPA § 31].

We find this argument unpersuasive. Section 38 of the Uniform Partnership Act does not explicitly limit the rights of innocent partners conferred in the provision to those partners who have agreed to a partnership for a fixed term. Furthermore, the fact that subsection (2) permits the innocent partners to "continue the business in the same name during the agreed term for the partnership" is not reasonably interpreted, in our view, as a limitation upon the application of section 38 solely to fixed-term partnerships. Instead it recognizes that the term originally agreed upon by the partners (here, at will) shall remain in effect during the innocent partners' continuation of the partnership business.

In our view section 38 does not contemplate that Nick and Lorenzo should be precluded from continuing the partnership business under these circumstances merely because their oral agreement set no fixed date for the termination of the partnership.

Parenthetically we also find without merit Jerry's contention that, in the interest of judicial economy, a judicial sale is preferable to a hearing wherein the parties present evidence of the appraised value of partnership assets. Section 38(2) accords to innocent partners the right to continue the partnership enterprise, rather than to share in the proceeds of sale or liquidation of the partnership estate.

REVERSED AND REMANDED.

Notes

1. Under UPA section 31(6), a partnership can be dissolved by a court decree under section 32. UPA section 32(1) permits a partner to petition a court to dissolve the partnership, among other reasons, where:

* * *

(c) A partner has been guilty of such conduct as tends to affect prejudicially the carrying on of the business,

(d) A partner wilfully or persistently commits a breach of the partnership agreement, or otherwise so conducts himself in matters relating to the partnership business that it is not reasonably practicable to carry on the business in partnership with him.

* * *

UPA § 32(1).

2. Judicial dissolution of a partnership under UPA section 32(1)(c) or (d) is an equitable remedy that speaks to the discretion of the trial court:

[A]n action of a partner which is merely trifling in nature or a temporary grievance without permanent damage does not form adequate grounds for dissolution. Rather the conduct must be legally substantial and evidence either gross misconduct or want of good faith or cause serious and permanent injury to the partnership.

Wood v. Holiday Mobile Home Resorts, Inc., 128 Ariz. 274, 625 P.2d 337, 343 (App. 1980) (action of general partner in mortgaging partnership property without authority and in taking unauthorized management fees justified court dissolution of limited partnership).

3. In *Monteleone v. Monteleone,* the partnership was a partnership at will. As discussed in the Note on Withdrawal and Dissolution in Partnerships, earlier in this Chapter, the UPA section 38(2) right to continue applies only where a partner has voluntarily dissolved a partnership before the expiration of an agreed definite term or the completion of an agreed particular undertaking. One might ask the purpose of allowing judicial dissolution; after all, all partners have the power to withdraw at any time. Remember that the exercise of the power to withdraw will be wrongful where the partnership is for an unexpired definite term or an incomplete particular purpose. In such a partnership, petitioning for judicial dissolution allows the other partners an early out that is not wrongful. This not only entitles them to demand liquidation of the partnership, it also protects them from being liable in damages for wrongful dissolution.

4. The *Monteleone v. Monteleone* court interpreted UPA section 38(2) to allow continuation of the business where the partnership was dissolved because if misconduct by another partner. *Monteleone* is not an isolated case. Courts often allow continuation in circumstances involving partner misconduct, applying what might be called *"section 38(1 1/2)."* That is, they purport to apply UPA section 38(2) to UPA section 32(1) court dissolutions on account of partner misconduct.

5. The RUPA judicial expulsion provision is section 601(5), which provides as follows:

A partner is dissociated from the partnership upon the occurrence of any of the following events:

* * *

(5), on application by the partnership or another partner, the partner's expulsion by judicial determination because:

(i) the partner engaged in wrongful conduct that adversely and materially affected the partnership business;

(ii) the partner willfully or persistently committed a material breach of the partnership agreement or of a duty owed to the partnership or to the other partners under Section 404; or

(iii) the partner engaged in conduct relating to the partnership business which makes it not reasonably practicable to carry on the business in partnership with the partner.

Again, a partner expelled under RUPA section 601(5) loses the right to dissolve the partnership. UPA § 801(1). Thus, the RUPA has adopted the result of the *Monteloene v. Monteleone* line of cases.

5. In *Monteleone v. Monteleone,* the partners engaged in "self-help." Even though the partnership agreement did not permit expulsion by the partners, they expelled their brother by locking him out of the partnership business. Moreover, the partners did not first apply to the court to dissolve the partnership. That is, they acted without the benefit of a court's review of the facts. As a policy matter, should the law require partners who have not bargained for a right to expel to go before a court to prove the justness of their "cause" before they exclude another partner?

6. As discussed in *Cadwalader, Wickersham & Taft v. Beasley,* page 749, a wrongful exclusion of another partner breaches the fiduciary duties owed by the excluding partners.

7. In addition to judicial expulsions, partners may also seek a judicial dissolution under other circumstances. Under the UPA section 32(1), partners may petition the court to dissolve the partnership

(e) The business of the partnership can only be carried on at a loss,

(f) Other circumstances render a dissolution equitable.

Under the RUPA section 801(5), partners may have a partnership dissolved by a judicial determination that

(i) the economic purpose of the partnership is likely to be unreasonably frustrated;

(ii) another partner has engaged in conduct relating to the partnership business which makes it not reasonably practicable to carry on the business in partnership with that partner; or

(iii) it is not otherwise reasonably practicable to carry on the partnership business in conformity with the partnership agreement;

Note on Judicial Dissolution in Limited Partnerships and Limited Liability Companies

Limited Partnerships

The RULPA has no provisions permitting the expulsion or involuntary *withdrawal* of a general partner.

RULPA section 802 allows any partner to petition a court for *dissolution* of the limited partnerships

whenever it is not reasonably practical to carry on the business in conformity with the partnership agreement.

Limited Liability Companies

ULLCA

ULLCA section 601(6) permits partners to seek a judicial expulsion of a member who has

(i) Engaged in wrongful conduct that adversely and materially affected the company's business;

(ii) Willfully or persistently committed a material breach of the operating agreement or of a duty owed to the company or the other members under Section 409; or

(iii) Engaged in conduct relating to the company's business which makes it not reasonably practicable to carry on the business with the member[.]

ULLCA section 801(b)(4) allows a member or a dissociated member to petition a court for dissolution of the LLC based on a judicial determination that:

(i) The economic purpose of the company is likely to be unreasonably frustrated;

(ii) Another member has engaged in conduct relating to the company's business that makes it not reasonably practicable to carry on the company's business with that member;

(iii) It is not otherwise reasonably practicable to carry on the company's business in conformity with the articles of organization and the operating agreement;

(iv) The company failed to purchase the petitioner's distributional interest as required by Section 701; or

(v) The managers or members in control of the company have acted, are acting, or will act in a manner that is illegal, oppressive, fraudulent, or unfairly prejudicial to the petitioner[.]

Delaware LLC Act

The Delaware LLC Act has no provisions permitting the judicial expulsion or withdrawal of a member.

Under Delaware LLC Act section 18-802 a member *or a manager* may petition a court for dissolution of an LLC

whenever it is not reasonably practical to carry on the business in conformity with the limited liability company agreement.

2. Assignee Rights

Problem 15.6
Read Problem 13.9 at page 667.

Baybank v. Catamount Construction, Inc.
Read case and following notes at page 667.

D. Fiduciary Limits on Rights to Dissolve or to Dissociate

Problem 15.7

George and H.B. are partners in Santa Maria Linen Supply, which was formed in December, 1949, for the purpose of conducting a linen supply business in Santa Maria, California. The partners agreed that George would act as managing partner. During the first two years, each partner contributed approximately $43,000 to the partnership. The partners have no other written or oral agreements regarding the partnership or its affairs.

From 1949 to 1957, the partnership lost approximately $62,000. During 1958, Vandenberg Air Force Base opened nearby, and business began to improve. The partnership earned $3,824.41 in 1958 and $2,282.30 in the first three months of 1959. The partnership's chief obligations are $47,610.32 owed to Mission Supply Service on open account, and $12,794.21 owed to Bank of America.

Mission Supply Service, which is wholly owned by George, has sold the partnership all linen and machinery used in the day-to-day operation of its business from Mission Supply Service, . Since 1949, the partnership has paid Mission Supply Service a total of $234,11434. The proceeds of the loans from Bank of America was used to pay Mission Supply Service

In April, 1959, George dissolved the partnership, and demanded that it be liquidated. H.B. argues that George is acting in bad faith, and is attempting to use his superior financial position to appropriate the now profitable business of the partnership. H.B. believes that the amount owed Mission Supply Service may make it difficult to sell the business as a going concern. He fears that upon dissolution he will receive very little and that George will receive a business that has become very profitable because of the . H.B. charges that George was content to share the losses but now that the business has become profitable, he wishes to keep all the gains. See Page v. Page, 55 Cal.2d 192, 359 P.2d 41, 10 Cal. Rptr. 643 (1961)(en banc).

Cadwalader, Wickersham & Taft v. Beasley

728 So.2d 253 (Fla. Dist. Ct. App. 1998)

POLEN, Judge.

We grant CW & T's motion for rehearing in part as it pertains to the trial court's award of punitive damages, and substitute the following in lieu of our original opinion:

In case numbers 96-2805 and 97-380, Cadwalader, Wickersham & Taft (CW & T), a New York law firm, appeals from a final judgment awarding return of capital, interest, profits, and punitive damages to its former partner, James Beasley (Beasley), for wrongful expulsion. CW & T appeals all aspects of the award except for the return of the paid-in capital with interest. Beasley cross-appeals the court's refusal to award him any interest in the firm's goodwill. In case numbers 96-3818 and 97-146, CW & T appeals from an award of attorney's fees and costs to Beasley. On our own motion, we consolidate all four cases at this time. We reverse as to the award of profits, attorney's fees and costs, but affirm as to all other points raised by both parties.

Beasley laterally transferred to become a partner at CW & T in its Palm Beach office in 1989. After his arrival, the Palm Beach office suffered from internal discord and, by 1994, the office was operating at a loss. In response to this situation, the firm's management committee began discussions regarding the termination of up to 30 partners nationwide, including the Palm Beach partners. During this time, and allegedly unbeknownst to CW & T, Beasley was planning to leave the firm. He met secretly with associates in CW & T's Palm Beach office about leaving with him.

The management committee eventually held a day-long meeting on August 7, 1994. Prior to the meeting, the committee members were asked to submit lists of less productive partners to be considered for possible termination. All of the Palm Beach partners were identified on the lists actually submitted. A tentative vote was reached at that meeting and, later that month, the committee formally decided to close its Palm Beach office by year-end 1994. It informed its partners, including Beasley, of its decision on August 30, 1994.

After the announcement, Beasley retained Professor Robert Hillman, who opined that CW & T, pursuant to the partnership agreement, lacked the legal authority to expel him from the partnership. In response to this opinion, CW & T sent a memorandum to Beasley informing him that he was still a partner in the firm. It then offered Beasley either relocation within the firm but in the New York or Washington, D.C. offices, or, a compensation/severance package which included his return of capital, departure bonus, and full shares through December 31, 1994. He was presented with a written withdrawal agreement confirming the same. Beasley, a member of both the Florida and New York bars, rejected the same as impractical.

Settlement negotiations between CW & T and Beasley then continued. On November 9, he sued the firm for fraud and breach of fiduciary duty, among other counts. On November 10, 1994, CW & T sent a letter to Beasley informing him to vacate the premises by 5:00 p.m. the next day. The letter specifically prohibited him from continuing to represent himself as associated with the firm.

After a nine-day bench trial, Judge Cook authored a meticulous and, we believe, exceptionally well-reasoned final judgment. He found that CW & T was authorized to close the Palm Beach office pursuant to the partnership agreement, and that Beasley would have voluntarily left CW & T by year-end 1994 in any event. Nevertheless, since the partnership agreement lacked provisions for the expulsion of a partner except in one limited situation,[1] he found that CW & T had anticipatorily breached the partnership agreement when it announced its plans to close the Palm Beach office in August, and then actually breached the agreement when it sent him the November 10, 1994 letter. The final judgment awarded Beasley his paid-in capital plus interest (which CW & T does not dispute), his percentage interest in the firm's accounts receivables and assets and interest thereon, and punitive damages, all totaling $2.5+ million. The later judgment awarded Beasley's attorneys fees and costs. These amounts are broken down as follows:

Beasley's paid-in capital of $194,193, plus interest at the rate as defined in the partnership agreement to the date of judgment [$42,199]	$ 236,392.00
his percentage interest in the firm's accounts receivable, work-in-progress, office building and other assets	$ 867,110.00
his profits attributable to the use of his right in the property of the dissolved partnership	$ 935,261.52
punitive damages	$ 500,000.00
attorney's fees and costs	$1,108,247.92

The court, however, rejected Beasley's claims for future lost income and retirement benefits. The appeals and cross-appeal, as set forth above, ensued.

---

1. Paragraph F(4) of the agreement provided for expulsion where a partner experienced sudden and total disability, a provision not implicated in this case.

I. WHETHER BEASLEY WAS EXPELLED OR VOLUNTARILY WITHDREW

Under New York Partnership Law's adoption of the Uniform Partnership Act (UPA), partners have no common law or statutory right to expel or dismiss another partner from the partnership; they may, however, provide in their partnership agreement for expulsion under prescribed conditions which must be strictly applied. *Gelder Med. Group v. Webber*, 41 N.Y.2d 680, 394 N.Y.S.2d 867, 363 N.E.2d 573 (1977); [UPA § 31(1)(d)]. Absent such a provision, as here, the removal of a partner may be accomplished only through dissolution of the firm.

The evidence supports Judge Cook's finding that CW & T intended to remove Beasley as a partner in the firm when it announced it was closing its Palm Beach office by year-end 1994. This finding, in turn, supports the conclusion that CW & T anticipatorily expelled Beasley from the firm.

In reaching this conclusion, we necessarily reject CW & T's argument that Beasley voluntary withdrew from the firm rather than having been expelled. Beasley had been practicing exclusively in South Florida for 22 years, where he built a substantial client base. As the trial court observed, to suddenly uproot to New York or Washington and leave his clients and contacts behind, as the court suggested, would have severely diminished his rainmaking abilities. Under these circumstances, we conclude that his rejecting the offer as impractical was not tantamount to a voluntary withdrawal.

Even assuming that CW & T did not anticipatorily breach the agreement on August 29, 1994, we conclude that the November 10, 1994 letter actually expelled him. Even though CW & T notes that Beasley planned on eventually leaving the firm even before it announced the decision to close the Palm Beach office, and that he most likely would not have stayed past 1994, the record does not reflect that he actually had definite plans to leave.

We further reject CW & T's argument that Beasley's suing the firm on November 9, 1994 was tantamount to a voluntary withdrawal. Since CW & T does not dispute the lack of frivolousness of Beasley's lawsuit, but merely takes issue with its allegations, we find its argument unpersuasive.

II. THE AWARD OF INTEREST

CW & T then argues the trial court erred in finding that a dissolution occurred and contends that, as a "withdrawn partner" pursuant to the agreement, Beasley was entitled to only his paid-in capital. Even if dissolution had occurred, it argues he still only would be entitled to an amount significantly less than that awarded to him. Beasley disputes that he was a "withdrawn" partner pursuant to the agreement, and contends that dissolution was mandated.

Under the partnership agreement, a "withdrawn Partner" is anyone "who was a Partner under this or a prior Firm Agreement." More specifically, the agreement provides that a partner, upon 60 days written notice, may withdraw from the firm at the end of any fiscal year. CW & T argues that, under these provisions, Beasley was technically a withdrawn partner and, thus, was only entitled to his capital contribution plus interest under Paragraph F(2)(a)(i) of the agreement. We, instead, agree with Judge Cook that the term "withdrawn" neither contemplated nor encompassed a partner expelled in the same manner as Beasley, especially since Beasley never provided any written notice of a voluntary with-drawal, and since CW & T conceded at trial that it did not treat Beasley as a "withdrawn partner" after his departure.

Antidissolution Provision

CW & T then argues that concluding a dissolution occurred would conflict with that portion of the agreement which states,

> Neither withdrawal of a Partner nor the death of a Partner, *nor any other event* shall cause dissolution of the Firm [unless 75% of the re-maining partners agreed in writing].

(Emphasis added.) It reasons that expulsion of a partner, however wrongful, is an "event" for purposes of this antidissolution clause. We disagree, for to construe this anti-dissolution provision strictly would recognize an implicit expulsion pro-vision where no provision exists. Such an interpretation would be inconsistent with existing law.

Even if the provision were broad enough to cover expulsions, we believe Beasley would still be allowed to seek dissolution of the partnership. Under New York law, any partner has the right to a formal accounting as to partnership affairs if he is wrongfully excluded from the partnership business or possession of its property by his co-partners, or "[w]henever other circumstances render it just and reasonable." [UPA § 22(d)]. Thus, a wrongful exclusion of one partner by a co-partner from par-ticipation in the conduct of the business may be grounds for judicial dissolution.

Since Beasley was expelled, his damages are to be assessed under [UPA § 40], and not under the partnership agreement. Since there is competent, substantial evidence in the record to support both the method and result used to calculate his interest in the firm's assets, we affirm the award of interest in the amount of $867,110.00.

* * *

IV. THE IMPOSITION OF PUNITIVE DAMAGES

CW & T then argues that the court's award of punitive damages was both unwarranted and erroneous as a matter of law. It asserts that the court's failure to award Beasley compensatory damages on his breach of fiduciary duty claim barred an award of punitive damages under New York law. Under New York law, the nature of the conduct which justifies an award of punitive damages is conduct having a high degree of moral culpability, or, in other words, conduct which shows a "conscious disregard of the rights of others or conduct so reckless as to amount to such disregard." *Home Ins. Co. v. American Home Products Corp.*, 75 N.Y.2d 196, 551 N.Y.S.2d 481, 550 N.E.2d 930, *answer to certified question conformed to* 902 F.2d 1111 (2d Cir.1990).... CW & T is correct in ar-guing that punitive damages are generally recovered only after compensatory damages have been awarded; however, since the purpose of punitive damages is to both punish the wrongdoer and deter others from such wrongful behavior, as a matter of policy, courts have the discretion to award punitive damages even where compensatory damages are found lacking.

We believe CW & T should not be insulated from the consequences of its wrongdoing simply because Beasley suffered no compensatory damages. As the court found, CW & T was participating in a clandestine plan to wrongfully expel some partners for the financial gain of other partners. Such activity cannot be said to be honorable, much less to comport with the 'punctilio of an honor.'

Because these findings establish that CW & T consciously disregarded the rights of Beasley, we affirm the award of punitive damages.

* * *

AFFIRMED in part; REVERSED in part and REMANDED for further proceedings in accordance with this opinion.

STEVENSON and SHAHOOD, JJ., concur.

Notes

1. The trial court's opinion makes it clear that the expulsion of Beasley from Cadwalader, Wickersham & Taft was part of the firm's response to declining profits and increasing discontent among the more productive partners:

> In 1993, the Palm Beach office operated at a loss for the first time since 1989. At the same time, the share value[1] of CW & T also declined by over $11,000.00 per share from the previous year. This decline in profitability concerned some of the CW & T partners, especially some of those who were lateral transfers from other firms. As a result, by vote of the firm, the management committee changed substantially at the end of 1993 and only four of the twelve management committee members were reelected for 1994. * * *

> During the spring and early summer of 1994, the management committee was proceeding with its' annual compensation review. In that process, the management committee sought to reward more productive partners by increased shares and to reduce the shares of less productive partners. However, 1994 was not a good year for CW & T and the share value decreased almost $15,000.00 per share. Several younger, more productive partners were very upset with their compensation and the fall of CW & T's per share value which threatened its' standing as a "top ten firm" in such publications as The American Lawyer. These partners conducted a series of three meetings in July, culminating in a group of fifteen partners presenting their position to the management committee through Karsten Giesecke, who was a member of both the disgruntled partner group and the management committee. Although there were no specific threats to leave the firm unless compensation was increased, as Robert Link testified, it was made clear to the management committee that if changes were not made quickly, he was going to leave. It also seemed clear that others in the group were of a like mind and that the management committee was lead to appreciate this. Thus was born "Project Right Size."

---

1. The equity partners of CW & T are compensated by shares, the value of which varies from year to year depending on the firm's profits. The number of shares to which a partner is entitled also varies from year to year and is set by the management committee in a yearly compensation review which in the pertinent years was announced in July.

In short, "Project Right Size" was aimed at identifying less productive partners for elimination from the partnership. While it is clear that the Palm Beach office was of concern to the management committee before "Project Right Size" reared its head, I find that as Giesecke testified, ultimately the closing of the Palm Beach office became integrated into "Project Right Size", with the common purpose being to improve compensation to the remaining partners and to retain the disgruntled more productive partners (*see* Giesecke deposition at pages 72 and 81). As "Project Right Size" continued on its course, numerous computer runs were generated for the management committee at Mr. Giesecke's instigation, analyzing the financial impact of terminating from ten to thirty partners.[2]

The watershed of the project was a clandestine all day management committee meeting held on Sunday, August 7, 1994, at the Marriot Hotel in Manhattan. Prior to the meeting, Cochair Donald Glascoff had asked all management committee members to submit lists of less productive partners for discussion as to possible termination. Only five of the twelve members chose to submit such a list. Plaintiff's exhibit # 203 and Defendant's exhibit # 596 contain the names of all of the partners appearing on the lists and the number of times they appeared. All of the Florida partners appeared on at least three lists and one appeared on all five. The Marriot meeting resulted in seventeen partners being identified for expulsion from the partnership, including all of the Florida partners. The final management committee vote to close the Florida office was taken August 29, 1994. In this same July and August time period, the management committee also decided to create a bonus pool to further compensate the more productive partners. Several bonuses were paid, including $250,000,00 to Robert Link.

Beasley v. Cadwalader, Wickersham & Taft, No. CL 8646 "AJ", 1996 WL 438777 at *1-*2 (Fla.Cir.Ct. July 23, 1996), *aff'd in part and, on other grounds, rev'd in part, Cadwalader, Wickersham & Taft v. Beasley,* 728 So.2d 253 (Fla. Dist. Ct. App. 1998). The trial court found that the firm's expulsion of Beasley justified punitive damages:

The facts relevant to the punitive damage determination are as follows:

1. The partnership agreement contains no clause authorizing the expulsion of a partner from the firm.

2. In addition to the clear language of the partnership agreement, the management committee had Mr. Robertson's legal memorandum which told them that they did not have the authority to expel partners (plaintiff's exhibit # 221).

3. Management committee members testified that they had not even read the partnership agreement to determine what it said about expelling partners prior to determining to take such action.

---

2. These documents were treated as confidential by the management committee and were not shared with most of the other partners. However, they were shared with at least one nonmanagement committee partner, Robert Link, one of the most productive partners and a prime member of what CW & T's management consultant has termed "the young Turks".

4. CW & T is a partnership of highly skilled attorneys and includes experts on partnership law. These experts were not consulted before partners were expelled.

5. The expulsion was for the express purpose of increasing the compensation available to the other partners.

The management committee's action in expelling the partners was poignantly justified by Cochair Fritts when he explained:

> We had a bunch of extraordinarily productive partners. It was known around the firm that from time to time those partners were offered positions in other firms. There was a fear, there is a fear, there always will be a fear, that highly productive partners, this doesn't relate just to 1993 or 1994, it goes back lots of years highly productive partners can leave, go to another place and get more money.
>
> And life is not made up of love, it is made up of fear and greed and money—how much you get paid in large measure. Unless we didn't get Cadwalader's profitability to where it was with our competitors' firms, my great fear was that people were going to leave and that we would then not be able to sustain ourselves."
> (Fritts deposition page 95, lines 10 through 25, docket # 132)

While life in the market place may well be made up of fear, greed and money, life in a partnership is not so composed. As Justice Cardozo observed in *Meinhard, supra,* at page 462,

> For each the venture had its phases of fair weather and foul. The two were in it jointly, for better or worse.

When the partnership encounters foul weather, the partners must either all stay the course or all abandon it. Under the facts of this case, it was a gross breach of fiduciary duty for some partners to throw others overboard for the expediency of increased profits. I find that these facts establish at least conduct which was so reckless as to amount to a conscious disregard for the rights of Beasley and the other expelled partners.

Id. at *7.

2. The Cadwalader, Wickersham & Taft partnership agreement provided that the firm could only be dissolved by a vote of 75% of the partners. Under the UPA,

a. Would such a provision be effective to prevent a technical dissolution after a partner withdraws from the firm? *See* UPA §§ 29, 31.

b. Would such a provision be effective to prevent the winding up and liquidation of the partnership? *See* UPA § 38(1).

How would you answer those questions under the RUPA? *See* RUPA §§ 103, 801.

3. Why did the court refuse to enforce the anti-dissolution provision? Given the court's interpretation of the anti-dissolution provision, could Beasley have insisted on the liquidation of the partnership?

4. In *Page v. Page,* 55 Cal.2d 192, 359 P.2d 41, 10 Cal. Rptr. 643 (1961)(*en banc*), a partner claimed that the managing partner of the partnership had acted in bad faith in dissolving a partnership. Although that issue was not before the

court, the California Supreme Court commented on the role of fiduciary duties in connection with dissolution of a partnership:

> Defendant contends that plaintiff is acting in bad faith and is attempting to use his superior financial position to appropriate the now profitable business of the partnership. Defendant has invested $43,000 in the firm, and owing to the long period of losses his interest in the partnership assets is very small. The fact that plaintiff's wholly-owned corporation holds a $47,000 demand note of the partnership may make it difficult to sell the business as a going concern. Defendant fears that upon dissolution he will receive very little and that plaintiff, who is the managing partner and knows how to conduct the operations of the partnership, will receive a business that has become very profitable because of the establishment of Vandenberg Air Force Base in its vicinity. Defendant charges that plaintiff has been content to share the losses but now that the business has become profitable he wishes to keep all the gains.

> There is no showing in the record of bad faith or that the improved profit situation is more than temporary. In any event these contentions are irrelevant to the issue whether the partnership is for a term or at will. Since, however, this action is for a declaratory judgment and will be the basis for future action by the parties, it is appropriate to point out that defendant is amply protected by the fiduciary duties of co-partners.

> Even though the Uniform Partnership Act provides that a partnership at will may be dissolved by the express will of any partner (Corp.Code, § 15031, subd. (1) (b)), this power, like any other power held by a fiduciary, must be exercised in good faith.

> We have often stated that

>> partners are trustees for each other, and in all proceedings connected with the conduct of the partnership every partner is bound to act in the highest good faith to his copartner, and may not obtain any advantage over him in the partnership affairs by the slightest misrepresentation, concealment, threat, or adverse pressure of any kind.

> *Llewelyn v. Levi,* 157 Cal. 31, 37, 106 P. 219, 221.... Although Civil Code § 2411,[1] embodying the foregoing language, was repealed upon the adoption of the Uniform Partnership Act, it was not intended by the adoption of that act to diminish the fiduciary duties between partners.

> A partner at will is not bound to remain in a partnership, regardless of whether the business is profitable or unprofitable. A partner may not, however, by use of adverse pressure 'freeze out' a co-partner and appropriate the business to his own use. A partner may not dissolve a partnership to gain the benefits of the business for himself, unless he fully compensates his co- partner for his share of the prospective business opportunity. In this regard his fiduciary duties are at least as great as those of a shareholder of a corporation.

---

1. Now Corporations Code, § 15017.

In the case of *In re Security Finance Co.,* 49 Cal.2d 370, 376-377, 317 P.2d 1, 5 we stated that although shareholders representing 50 per cent of the voting power have a right under Corporations Code, § 4600 to dissolve a corporation, they may not exercise such right in order 'to defraud the other shareholders (citation), to 'freeze out' minority shareholders (citation), or to sell the assets of the dissolved corporation at an inadequate price (citation).'

Likewise in the instant case, plaintiff has the power to dissolve the partnership by express notice to defendant. If, however, it is proved that plaintiff acted in bad faith and violated his fiduciary duties by attempting to appropriate to his own use the new prosperity of the partnership without adequate compensation to his co-partner, the dissolution would be wrongful and the plaintiff would be liable as provided by subdivision (2)(a) of Corporations Code, § 15038 (rights of partners upon wrongful dissolution) for violation of the implied agreement not to exclude defendant wrongfully from the partnership business opportunity.

359 P.2d at 44.

5. Suppose that, in *Mongteleone v. Monteleone,* page 742, the court had found that Jerry had not engaged in wrongful conduct justifying a judicial dissolution of the partnership. In that event, would Nick and Lorenzo have been liable for wrongful exclusion?

Konover Development Corp. v. Zeller
228 Conn. 206, 635 A.2d 798 (Conn. 1994.)

BORDEN, Justice.

The dispositive issue in this appeal is the standard of proof required, under the circumstances of this case, in a breach of contract action by a general partner against a limited partner. The defendant appeals from the judgment, after a jury trial, in favor of the plaintiff on the complaint and on the defendant's counterclaim. The defendant claims that the trial court improperly: (1) instructed the jury on the extent of the plaintiff's fiduciary duty; (2) instructed the jury on the burden of proof by which a fiduciary must prove fair dealing; [and (3)] enforced provisions of a partnership agreement that are void as a matter of public policy.

The plaintiff, Konover Development Corporation, the general partner in a limited partnership with the defendant limited partner, A. James Zeller, brought this action claiming that the defendant had failed to pay debts according to the partnership agreement. The defendant filed a counterclaim alleging, inter alia, that the plaintiff had breached its fiduciary duty to the defendant.[2] The jury returned a verdict for the plaintiff on both the complaint and the counterclaim, and the trial court rendered judgment accordingly. This appeal followed.

The jury could reasonably have found the following facts. In April, 1986, the plaintiff and the defendant, together with Alan Temkin, executed a written agree-

---

2. The defendant's counterclaim contained five counts. The trial court directed a verdict in favor of the plaintiff on all but the third count. The defendant did not appeal from the judgment on the directed verdict on the other counts.

ment to form a limited partnership called Torringford Commercial Associates Limited Partnership (partnership). The purpose of the partnership was to merge parcels of land owned by Temkin and the defendant with four additional parcels, and construct a shopping mall in Torrington. The limited partnership agreement named the plaintiff as the general partner with a 50 percent interest, and Temkin and the defendant as limited partners with 29 percent and 21 percent interests, respectively. The agreement provided that expenses would be shared, with the general partner contributing 50 percent and the limited partners contributing 50 percent collectively. The agreement further required the limited partners to authorize, in advance and in writing, any partnership expenditures exceeding $75,000.

At the time of the partnership formation, Temkin owned a twenty-eight acre parcel of land and the defendant owned a four acre adjoining parcel. The defendant and Temkin conveyed options on their parcels to the partnership. The option on the parcel owned by Temkin provided for a purchase price of $464,000 and expired on December 31, 1988. The partnership also acquired options on the four additional parcels needed to complete its plans, and later, it acquired an option on an additional parcel. The partnership intended to exercise its options upon the project receiving approvals by local zoning and wetlands authorities.

The project began with the advantage of a 1970 approval by the Torrington planning and zoning commission of Temkin's land for the development of a shopping center. The plaintiff's legal counsel, however, noticed a defect in the approval that required the partnership to resubmit the previous application. After the application received renewed approval, the partnership submitted to the Torrington inland wetlands and planning and zoning commissions a new application, involving all of the parcels, for approval of an enclosed shopping mall of approximately 300,000 square feet.

While the application was pending, Temkin decided to withdraw from the partnership. In February, 1988, for $1.3 million, Temkin sold the defendant his interest in the partnership and the twenty-eight acre parcel that the partnership held under option. That transaction left the defendant and the plaintiff with equal shares in the partnership.

Since the formation of the partnership, property values in Torrington had risen rapidly. As a result, a disagreement arose between the plaintiff and the defendant regarding the purchase price to be paid by the partnership for the twenty-eight acre parcel that the defendant had purchased from Temkin. The defendant wanted more than $1 million for the parcel, while the plaintiff insisted on the $464,000 option price. As an alternative, however, the plaintiff proposed that the partnership take advantage of the increased property values by exercising its options on parcels it could acquire below market value, reselling them at a profit, and then dissolving the partnership and abandoning the development plans. The defendant rejected the plaintiff's proposal.

This disagreement led to a series of negotiations between the plaintiff and the defendant that eventually culminated in the letter agreement of November 14, 1988, that gave rise to this lawsuit.[3] The letter, written by the plaintiff and

---

3. The letter agreement of November 14, 1988, portions of which were subsequently incorporated into the partnership agreement, covers five single spaced pages and includes twelve numbered paragraphs.

countersigned by the defendant, stated that the partnership agreed to increase the purchase price of the twenty-eight acre parcel from $464,000 to $1,000,000, but that the partnership would only exercise its option to acquire the parcels in order to go forward with the proposed mall. Furthermore, the defendant would receive a development fee of 1 percent of the total project costs, and the plaintiff would finance the project's entire carrying costs, including reimbursement to the defendant for his expenses in acquiring and carrying the optioned properties when it became necessary to execute options in the defendant's own name.

In exchange, the defendant agreed that if the plaintiff, in its sole discretion, determined that the project were no longer feasible, the defendant would reimburse the plaintiff for all of the plaintiff's "out-of-pocket" expenditures. The plaintiff would then withdraw from the partnership, leaving the defendant with a 100 percent interest in the partnership and full ownership of all real estate, permits and property rights. The letter agreement, therefore, in effect, permitted the plaintiff to terminate the partnership if it determined that the project were no longer feasible, and provided that the defendant would own all of the partnership assets and would be obligated to reimburse the plaintiff for all of its partnership expenditures.

Furthermore, the letter authorized the plaintiff to expend more than $75,000 in support of the project, purportedly in accordance with the original partnership agreement's requirement that limited partners authorize such expenditures. On August 11, 1989, by amendment to the partnership agreement, the partners formalized the essential terms of the letter agreement.

In the interim, the partnership encountered outside problems. A neighborhood group opposed the development plans and precipitated costly additional

---

Paragraph 1 states in pertinent part:
We [the plaintiff] agree to enter into a new option with you [the defendant] regarding this property [the twenty-eight acre parcel formerly owned by Temkin]...and which option shall specify a purchase price of One Million Dollars ($1,000,000).
Paragraph 7 states in pertinent part:
KDC [the plaintiff] agrees to execute an amendment to the Agreement to provide that KDC, as Managing General Partner of TCALP [the partnership], can only exercise TCALP's options on the various properties which comprise the proposed Litchfield Hills Mall project in conjunction with the development of said project, it being understood and agreed that KDC will not have the right to exercise said options solely for the purpose of effectuating a liquidation of said properties if the project is deemed by KDC to be infeasible. *In consideration of the foregoing, you agree to reimburse KDC, at such time as KDC determines in its sole discretion that the proposed project is no longer feasible, for any and all out-of-pocket expenses incurred by KDC with respect to the project....*
(Emphasis added). Paragraph 10 states:
This letter serves to document your authorization, as required by Article 3, Section 2 of the agreement, for TCALP to expend more than Seventy-Five Thousand Dollars ($75,000) in support of the project.
Paragraph 11 states:
Additionally, it is understood and agreed that Article VII, Paragraph 1 of the Partnership Agreement shall be amended to provide for a development fee of 3%, of which fee you shall receive one-third (1/3).

legal procedures. In addition, the partners had difficulty locating tenants interested in occupying the proposed development. Finally, in July, 1988, the inland wetlands commission issued a ruling that denied in part the partnership's application to develop the properties and significantly reduced the mall's proposed parking space. The partnership amended its plans and resubmitted them to the inland wetlands commission, but the commission's ruling on the amended plan still substantially restricted the proposed parking area.

As a result, the partners reduced the size of the proposed development. They changed the plan from a 300,000 square foot enclosed mall to a 200,000 square foot strip shopping center. They believed that the partial approval by the inland wetlands commission would accommodate the strip shopping center and that they would not be required to return to the commission for further approval. The inland wetlands commission and the planning and zoning commission, however, ordered new applications.

At that point, the plaintiff decided that the project was no longer feasible. The plaintiff determined that the cost of developing new applications, combined with carrying costs, litigation costs, delay and uncertainty, outweighed the potential benefit of completing the development. On February 7, 1990, the plaintiff advised the defendant of its decision, and on February 22, 1990, the plaintiff formally requested reimbursement for its out-of-pocket expenses according to the amended partnership agreement. The plaintiff fixed these expenses at nearly $1.1 million. The defendant did not acknowledge any debt to the plaintiff. At that time, the defendant owned all the properties that had been the subject of the partnership agreement, and the following year he entered into a contract to sell them for approximately $4.3 million.

Thereafter, the plaintiff brought this action for breach of contract, seeking recovery of the alleged debt under the partnership agreement. The defendant denied the debt and filed a counterclaim for breach of fiduciary duty. On June 24, 1992, the jury returned a verdict for the plaintiff on both the complaint and the counterclaim, awarding damages of $1,052,663.67. The trial court rendered judgment accordingly.

I

The defendant first claims that the jury instructions did not properly impose a fiduciary duty on the plaintiff. Specifically, the defendant argues that the trial court charged the jury that the law required the plaintiff to act reasonably in its determination that the project was infeasible, rather than under the heightened standard imposed on a fiduciary. Furthermore, the defendant argues that the trial court improperly instructed the jury to evaluate the plaintiff's determination of the project's feasibility using a preponderance of the evidence standard. The defendant contends that as a fiduciary the plaintiff had the burden to prove by clear and convincing evidence that its determination had been made in good faith.

B

We next consider the defendant's claim that the jury instructions failed to impose a fiduciary duty on the plaintiff's decision to terminate the partnership because the project was no longer feasible.

The defendant argues in effect that the basic principle articulated by this court in *Dunham v. Dunham*, 204 Conn. 303, 528 A.2d 1123 (1987), applies, namely, that the plaintiff, as a fiduciary with respect to the defendant, was required to prove that it made its decisions with the utmost regard for the defendant's interests. The plaintiff responds, however, that under the terms of the partnership agreement, as amended pursuant to the letter agreement of November 14, 1988 the plaintiff's fiduciary duty did not extend to its decision to withdraw from the partnership. Specifically, the plaintiff argues that the partners entered into an arm's length agreement to modify their rights and obligations under the partnership agreement and that the exercise of such bargained for rights was not fiduciary in nature. Accordingly, the plaintiff argues that its determination of infeasibility and the defendant's failure to reimburse the plaintiff's expenses gave rise to an ordinary breach of contract dispute, and that, therefore, the trial court's instructions were correct.

We reject both the plaintiff's and the defendant's positions. We hold, instead, that, under the circumstances of this case:

(1) the plaintiff's decisions regarding the project's feasibility and withdrawal from the partnership, pursuant to the letter agreement, were impressed with a fiduciary duty; but

(2) the exercise of that duty was to be viewed in light of all of the facts of the case, including whether

(a) the plaintiff had made full and frank disclosure of the relevant information,

(b) whether the consideration received by the defendant pursuant to the letter agreement was adequate,

(c) whether the defendant had access to competent, independent advice with regard to the letter agreement, and

(d) the relative degrees of sophistication and bargaining power between the parties with respect to the letter agreement.

Both parties agree that, as general and limited partners, they were bound in a fiduciary relationship. In general, partners act as trustees toward each other and toward the partnership.[9] Moreover, the general partner of a limited partnership

---

9. [ULPA § 9] provides:
GENERAL POWERS AND LIABILITIES OF GENERAL PARTNERS.

(a) Except as provided in this chapter or in the partnership agreement, a general partner of a limited partnership shall have all the rights and powers and be subject to all the restrictions of a partner in a partnership without limited partners.

(b) Except as provided in this chapter, a general partner of a limited partnership shall have all the liabilities of a partner in a partnership without limited partners to persons other than the partnership and the other partners. Except as provided in this chapter or in the partnership agreement, a general partner of a limited partnership shall have all the liabilities of a partner in a partnership without limited partners to the partnership and to the other partners.

[UPA § 21(1)] provides in pertinent part:
ACCOUNTING BY PARTNER.

(1) Every partner must account to the partnership for any benefit, and hold as trustee for it any profits derived by him without the consent of the other partners from any transaction connected with the formation, conduct, or liquidation of the partnership or from any use by him of its property.

This statutory language was intended to incorporate the fiduciary relationship as described by Chief Judge Benjamin Cardozo in *Meinhard v. Salmon,* 249 N.Y. 458, 464, 164 N.E. 545 (1928):

Many forms of conduct permissible in a workaday world for those acting at arm's

has the fiduciary duty "'of rendering true accounts and full information about anything which affects the partnership.'" *Williams v. Bartlett,* 189 Conn. 471, 482 n. 8, 457 A.2d 290 (1983). We have stated that a

> fiduciary or confidential relationship is characterized by a unique degree of trust and confidence between the parties, one of whom has superior knowledge, skill or expertise and is under a duty to represent the interests of the other.... The superior position of the fiduciary or dominant party affords him great opportunity for abuse of the confidence reposed in him. (Citations omitted.)

Dunham v. Dunham, supra, 204 Conn. at 322, 528 A.2d 1123.

"Once 'a [fiduciary] relationship is found to exist, the burden of proving fair dealing properly shifts to the fiduciary.'" *Id.* This means that the plaintiff had the burden to prove "that [it] had dealt fairly with the [defendant]." *Id.* at 323, 528 A.2d 1123.

The defendant argues that the jury instructions failed to extend the fiduciary relationship to the plaintiff's decision that the project was infeasible. The defendant contends that while the jury instructions recognized a general fiduciary duty, they stated that the law only required the plaintiff to act reasonably in its determination that the project was infeasible, rather than under the higher standard imposed on a fiduciary.

The court properly charged the jury with respect to the general principles of the fiduciary duty that the plaintiff owed to the defendant and, further, the trial court initially properly instructed the jury that the plaintiff was required to "make the decision [to terminate the partnership] as a fiduciary." The trial court stated that "[t]he plaintiff is a general partner and owes a fiduciary duty to its limited partner." The court defined a fiduciary as a "trustee" who must act in "scrupulous good faith and candor." Furthermore, in accordance with the defendant's request, the trial court charged the jury with the traditional portrait of fiduciary dealings:

> [The fiduciary] must act honestly, and with the finest and undivided loyalty to the trust, not merely with that standard of honor required of men dealing at arm's length and the workaday world, but with a punctilio of honor the most sensitive.

This was an accurate statement of the fiduciary relationship.

We are persuaded, however, that the trial court improperly diluted the effect of its instruction when the court focused the jury's attention on the application of that duty to the plaintiff's decision to terminate the project because of the plaintiff's belief that the project was no longer feasible. The trial court unduly attenuated that duty by instructing the jury that the plaintiff complied with its fiduciary

---

length, are forbidden to those bound by fiduciary ties. A trustee is held to something stricter than the morals of the marketplace. Not honesty alone, but the punctilio of an honor the most sensitive, is then the standard of behavior. As to this there has developed a tradition that is unbending and inveterate. Uncompromising rigidity has been the attitude of courts of equity when petitioned to undermine the rule of undivided loyalty by the 'disintegrating erosion' or particular exceptions.... Only thus has the level of conduct for fiduciaries been kept at a level higher than that trodden by the crowd.

See generally H. Reuschlein & W. Gregory, The Law of Agency and Partnership (1990) p. 278.

duty so long as its decision that the project was infeasible was reasonable. In particular, the court instructed:

> Notwithstanding the existence of a fiduciary duty as a general proposition, a general partner and limited partner can bargain for whatever terms they want in a contract so long as they are not illegal or against public policy. The exercise by the plaintiff of the contractual right it bargained for and obtained would not be a breach of its duty under the contract, provided the decision was made reasonably based upon a careful review of the relevant information the general partner had before it.

By stating that the plaintiff had met its fiduciary duty simply by making the decision "reasonably based upon a careful review of the relevant information [the plaintiff] had before it," the court impermissibly reduced the level of the plaintiff's duty to make its decision. The plaintiff, as a fiduciary, had the duty to deal fairly with the defendant, not simply to act reasonably based upon the relevant information.

The court's instruction in effect transformed the plaintiff's fiduciary duty into the duty to make a reasonable business decision. While a decision by the plaintiff to terminate the project, reached on the basis of its fiduciary duty to the defendant, would undoubtedly have been "reasonable," the converse, which the instruction necessarily implied, was not necessarily also true. That is, the duty to make a "reasonable" business decision based upon all the circumstances was not necessarily the equivalent of a duty to deal fairly, as a fiduciary, with the defendant.

Having concluded that the trial court improperly instructed the jury regarding the plaintiff's fiduciary duty to the defendant in deciding to terminate the partnership, we turn to the question of the general principles that governed such a decision under the circumstances of this case. We reject the defendant's argument that the traditional principles of fiduciary duty as expressed in *Dunham v. Dunham, supra,* govern, because those principles do not adequately take into account the factors that are relevant to the complex commercial transaction involved in this case. We also reject the plaintiff's argument that no fiduciary principles applied to the parties' contractual provision regarding termination of their partnership, because at least under the facts of this case, in which the decision to terminate had adverse, concrete financial consequences that flowed foreseeably and directly from that decision, the plaintiff's position gives inadequate deference to the parties' preexisting fiduciary relationship. We choose, instead, a middle ground that affords an appropriate degree of flexibility and deference to the parties' contractual arrangement as well as an appropriate degree of deference to their fiduciary relationship.

With regard to the defendant's position, we recognize that the fiduciary relationship is not singular. The relationship between sophisticated partners in a business venture may differ from the relationship involving lay people who are wholly dependent upon the expertise of a fiduciary. Fiduciaries appear in a variety of forms, including agents, partners, lawyers, directors, trustees, executors, receivers, bailees and guardians.[11] "[E]quity has carefully refrained from defining a fiduciary

---

11. "[V]arious types of fiduciaries have evolved over the centuries. Trustees, administrators, and bailees are of ancient origin, whereas agents appeared only at the end of the eighteenth century. In the business realm, the fiduciary duties of partners, corporate directors, and officers originated with the formation of partnerships and corporations, but major-

relationship in precise detail and in such a manner as to exclude new situations." *Harper v. Adametz,* 142 Conn. 218, 225, 113 A.2d 136 (1955). Simply classifying a party as a fiduciary inadequately characterizes the nature of the relationship.

None of the cases upon which the defendant relies involved complex commercial transactions between sophisticated parties with significant bargaining power. *Dunham v. Dunham, supra,* the case upon which the defendant principally relies for his description of fiduciary obligations, is factually distinct from the case at hand. In *Dunham,* one son, an attorney, had performed the family's estate planning and had drafted his mother's will, which left him substantial assets and named him executor of the estate. He then consolidated the entire family's property in his name, leaving a second son with virtually nothing. The trial court correctly instructed the jury that if it found a fiduciary relationship, the burden shifted to the attorney son to prove fair dealing. *Dunham* relies, in turn, on cases whose circumstances are also different from the case at hand. Many of the cases involved disputes between family members. Typically, one party had depended on the other and had been defrauded. Thus, *Dunham* does not resolve the question in this case.

The plaintiff's position, however, goes too far in the other direction. We agree with the plaintiff that, in general, the rights and duties of partners are subject to agreement between the partners.

> It is the 'general rule...that competent persons shall have the utmost liberty of contracting and that their agreements voluntarily and fairly made shall be held valid and enforced in the courts.'

Real Estate Listing Service, Inc. v. Real Estate Commissions, 179 Conn. 128, 137, 425 A.2d 581 (1979). The parties may agree to such things as unequal or variable sharing of profits, compensation in addition to profit sharing, or different classes of partners with different rights and duties. II A. Bromberg & L. Ribstein, Partnership (1994) § 6.01, p. 6:4. We are not persuaded, however, by the caselaw upon which the plaintiff relies.[13]

---

ity shareholders were not subjected to fiduciary duties until this century. Union leaders were cast in the fiduciary role at a still later date, when they acquired the statutory power to represent workers in negotiations with management. The twentieth century is witnessing an unprecedented expansion and development of the fiduciary law. For example, physicians and psychiatrists have recently become members of the fiduciary group, and one commentator has suggested trust law as a model for the relations between the state, parents, and children." T. Frankel, "Fiduciary Law," 71 Cal.L.Rev. 795 (1983).

13. The plaintiff relies on an Illinois Appellate Court decision holding that "when the partners have entered into an arm's length transaction in order to effect dissolution, their relationship is not fiduciary in character." Hamilton v. Williams, 214 Ill.App.3d 230, 158 Ill.Dec. 91, 103, 573 N.E.2d 1276, 1288, cert. denied, 141 Ill.2d 540, 162 Ill.Dec. 488, 580 N.E.2d 114 (1991). In *Hamilton,* however, the partnership had already been formally dissolved and the partners were in an arbitration proceeding regarding the division of partnership assets before the incident occurred which the limited partners claimed constituted a breach of fiduciary duty. Thus, the claimed breach occurred after their dissolution was complete and when the parties were dealing at arms length. The plaintiff in this case, however, was still the general partner when the alleged breach of fiduciary duty occurred. The claimed breach related to the plaintiff's decision to withdraw, not to its behavior after withdrawal.

The plaintiff also relies on *Furman v. Cirrito,* 828 F.2d 898 (2d Cir.1987), to support its contention that the terms of the agreement supersede any fiduciary obligation. In *Furman,* the limited partners alleged that the general partners had used powers granted by the partnership agreement to engage in a pattern of criminal wrongdoing in violation of the Racketeer Influenced and Corrupt Organizations Act, 18 U.S.C. §§ 1961 through 1968 (RICO). In

Furthermore, we are not convinced, as a matter of policy, that the terms of a partnership agreement, even given due deference to the provisions of freedom of contract, necessarily negate the fiduciary relationship that inheres in the partnership. At the least, such a requirement is inappropriate in circumstances such as these, in which the termination by the general partner will inevitably result in substantial financial obligations from the limited to the general partner. In such circumstances the better course is to maintain the fiduciary relationship, but to make clear that, in determining whether the general partner has dealt fairly with the limited partner, the factfinder should take into account all of the circumstances surrounding their business relationship.

This position is consistent with the conclusions reached by other courts, which have likewise held that the terms of a limited partnership agreement cannot negate the fiduciary duty. *See, e.g., Wartski v. Bedford,* 926 F.2d 11 (1st Cir.1991) (fiduciary duty of partners is integral part of partnership agreement, whether or not expressly set forth therein, and cannot be negated by partnership agreement); *Labovitz v. Dolan,* 189 Ill.App.3d 403, 406, 136 Ill.Dec. 780, 545 N.E.2d 304, cert. denied, 129 Ill.2d 564, 140 Ill.Dec. 672, 550 N.E.2d 557 (1990) (general partner had breached its fiduciary duty because duty existed concurrently with obligations set forth in partnership agreement and could not be destroyed by agreement that gave general partner "sole discretion" over "availability of Cash Flow for distribution to partners").

Commentators have acknowledged that the fiduciary relationship in a commercial limited partnership may differ from other fiduciary relationships.

Categorical prohibitions of conflicting interests might be a coherent response [to problems of divergent interests endemic to the limited partnership form]...but a potentially fatal one as well for whatever assumed benefits of flexibility in capital formation the form provides. Categorical permission for conflicting interests might also be a coherent response, but one running all the risks that 'fiduciary ideology' is supposed to prevent. What is desired is a scheme for containing conflicts, a fairness-promoting regime that ensures, to the extent possible, that investors in the limited partnership are not being exploited, overreached, or taken advan-

---

upholding dismissal of the action for failure to state a claim, the Second Circuit Court of Appeals stated that "[e]ven terms [of a partnership agreement] which permit self-dealing by a partner will be enforced." Id., at 901. The dispositive issue, however, was the plaintiffs' failure to allege facts of a pattern of criminal activity sufficient to create liability under RICO, not the interpretation of the agreement.

Moreover, in making the claim about self-dealing in partnerships, the court relied on *Riviera Congress Associates v. Yassky,* 18 N.Y.2d 540, 548, 277 N.Y.S.2d 386, 223 N.E.2d 876 (1966), for its authority. *Riviera Congress Associates* is often cited for the "anything goes" position toward partnership agreements, but the propriety of its use in this regard is debatable. D. Reynolds, "Loyalty and the Limited Partnership," 34 Kan.L.Rev. 1, 28 (1985); *Furman v. Cirrito, supra,* at 905 (Pratt, J., dissenting). *Riviera Congress Associates* was a victory for the limited partners in their suit against general partners for claimed self-dealing. The court in *Riviera Congress Associates* concluded that provisions authorizing self-dealing were not ipso facto impermissible, but remanded the case for a determination of whether the general partners in that case had acted in good faith. The court also reaffirmed the principle that general and limited partners are bound in a fiduciary relationship. *Riviera Congress Associates v. Yassky, supra,* 18 N.Y.2d at 547, 548, 277 N.Y.S.2d 386, 223 N.E.2d 876.

tage of by the managers of their money. (Citations omitted; internal quotation marks omitted.)

D. Reynolds, "Loyalty and the Limited Partnership," 34 Kan.L.Rev. 1, 26 (1985); *see also* II A. Bromberg & L. Ribstein, supra, § 6.07, p. 6:70 (arguing for more flexible application of rules of fiduciary duty to commercial partnerships based upon availability of "extrajudicial controls, including joint management by the partners, the relatively equal expertise of the partners, the terminability of the relationship, and the alignment of incentives of the partners through profit sharing and personal liability for partnership debts").

We agree with the thrust of these commentaries that, in general, in the context of a commercial limited partnership the fiduciary relationship must be flexible enough to ensure that partners with diverse interests will be able to craft and rely on a partnership agreement that reflects their common interests. The law should recognize that an overly strict interpretation of partnership loyalty might stifle the limited partnership form, and enable a limited partner to exploit its status as beneficiary to hold a general partner hostage to the partnership. We also recognize, however, that an active general partner may use its position in the partnership for its advantage at the expense of a passive limited partner, and that, therefore, wise public policy counsels the retention of the fiduciary principle. We must search for a balance between flexibility and fidelity.

The courts of Illinois have developed a framework, which we endorse, that accommodates this need for balance. In *Brown v. Commercial National Bank of Peoria*, 42 Ill.2d 365, 247 N.E.2d 894, cert. denied, 396 U.S. 961, 90 S.Ct. 436, 24 L.Ed.2d 425 (1969), *reh. denied*, 396 U.S. 1047, 90 S.Ct. 680, 24 L.Ed.2d 693 (1970), the Supreme Court of Illinois held that, in the context of a claim that a bank had breached its fiduciary duty in dealings with a financially sophisticated beneficiary, the fiduciary's responsibility to establish that the transaction was fair was to be considered in light of all the circumstances.

Important factors in determining whether a particular transaction is fair include a showing by the fiduciary:

(1) that he made a free and frank disclosure of all the relevant information he had;

(2) that the consideration was adequate; and

(3) that the principal had competent and independent advice before completing that transaction. (Internal quotation marks omitted.)

Id. at 369, 247 N.E.2d 894. We make explicit an additional factor that the Illinois court implicitly included in its analysis:

(4) the relative sophistication and bargaining power among the parties.

This framework retains the principle of fiduciary honor, but also reflects the many different kinds of parties that enter into fiduciary relationships by requiring, in the calculus of the factors that constitute fair dealing, consideration of the nature of the relationship between the parties. It protects passive investors while preserving the flexibility required in commercial relationships. The trial court's instructions to the jury did not reflect this analysis, and a new trial is therefore required.

C

We also agree with the defendant's claim that the trial court improperly instructed the jury to evaluate the plaintiff's determination of the project's feasibility by a preponderance of the evidence standard. The defendant contends that the plaintiff, as a fiduciary, bore the burden to prove by clear and convincing evidence that it made its decision in good faith.

Proof of a fiduciary relationship imposes a twofold burden on the fiduciary. First, the burden of proof shifts to the fiduciary; and second, the standard of proof is clear and convincing evidence.

> Once a fiduciary relationship is found to exist, the burden of proving fair dealing properly shifts to the fiduciary.... Furthermore, the standard of proof for establishing fair dealing is not the ordinary standard of proof of fair preponderance of the evidence, but requires proof either by clear and convincing evidence, clear and satisfactory evidence or clear, convincing and unequivocal evidence. (Citations omitted; internal quotation marks omitted.)

Dunham v. Dunham, supra 204 Conn. at 322-23, 528 A.2d 1123.

The jury instructions in this case replaced the plaintiff's burden to prove fair dealing by clear and convincing evidence with the ordinary civil standard of proof by charging that

> the plaintiff must prove the allegations of its complaint by a fair preponderance of the evidence.... The party having the burden of proof on the complaint or counterclaim must prove it by the better and weightier evidence.

The court then defined "fair preponderance" of evidence as that which induces a "reasonable belief that it is more probable than not that the fact that [is] in issue is true." Upon retrial, the court should instruct the jury on the burden of proof in accordance with the rule of *Dunham v. Dunham, supra.*

II

The defendant further claims that certain provisions of the partnership agreement are unenforceable as against public policy. In particular, the defendant claims that the terms of the agreement permitting the plaintiff to withdraw from the partnership and receive reimbursement for its expenses if, in its sole discretion, it determined that the project were infeasible, cannot be enforced because they permitted the general partner to manipulate the partnership to its own advantage.

This court has refused to enforce contract provisions that violate public policy. We are not persuaded, however, that this partnership agreement, which granted the general partner sole discretion to determine the feasibility of continuing the enterprise, violated public policy. A provision of a partnership agreement does not violate public policy simply because it is susceptible of an application that is advantageous to one partner and disadvantageous to another. The defendant has failed to advance any cogent reason to persuade us otherwise.

The judgment is reversed and the case is remanded for a new trial.

Notes

1. How does the definition of good faith and fair dealing adopted by the Connecticut Supreme Court in *Konover Development Corp. v. Zeller* compare to that adopted in *Bohatch v. Butler & Binion*, page 728?

2. In *Konover Development Corp. v. Zeller*, why should the plaintiff have a fiduciary duty imposed on its exercise of its contractual right in its sole discretion to withdraw and receive reimbursement?

    a. Does the exercise of that right necessarily involve the plaintiff's use of its power to act on behalf of the partnership or the other partners?

    b. In *Konover Development Corp. v. Zeller*, was Konover Development Corporation trying to improper advantage of Zeller?

Problem 15.8
Read Problem 16.10, at page 829.

Rosenfeld, Meyer & Susman v. Cohen
Read case and following notes, at page 830.

E. Additional Problems

15.9. A and B were partners opening an insurance business. The written partnership agreement provided, among other things, that the partnership would only be dissolved in case of death or by the mutual agreement of the partners. After a disagreement between the partners, A left the partnership premises, moved to a new location, and began doing business on his own account. Has the partnership been dissolved under the UPA? Under the RUPA (based on Illinois Bar Examination, July 1980.)

15.10 In 1975, four parties entered into a limited partnership for the manufacturer and distribution of widgets in Chicago, Illinois. The four parties drafted two documents without the assistance of legal counsel - a partnership contract and a certificate of limited partnership. Accordingly, a certificate of limited partnership was filed in the appropriate state office in Springfield, Illinois, describing the Jones, Johnson and Company as a limited partnership. The certificate, which was complete enough to comply with the limited partnership law in effect, provided that there would be two general partners - Smith, whose contribution was $20,000 in cash, and Jones, whose contribution was 0 - and two limited partners -Adams, whose contribution was $30,000 in cash and Johnson, whose contribution was $40,000 in services to the firm. The written partnership contract provided that the partnership was to last for a period of ten years from January 1, 1975 to December 31, 1984; that Jones was to serve as manager of the business; that Johnson was to be employed as assistant manager; and that profits were to be shared equally between the four partners. In 1975, the partnership did well enough to permit Jones to pay himself a salary of $30,000 and to pay Johnson a salary of $20,000. There was also a $10,000 profit that was kept in the partnership rather than distributed to the partners by the consensus of the four partners. The partnership purchased some machinery and paid off some of its loans. In 1976, 1977, 1978, 1979, and 1980, the company lost $5000 each year. Jones had continued to pay himself $30,000 annually and to pay Johnson $20,000 annually. Thus, on January 1, 1981, the financial picture of the business and its partners was as follows:

(1) The partnership had assets of approximately $70,000. Its liabilities totaled approximately $95,000.

(2) Smith had assets that could be reached by creditors totaling about $75,000. He had no liabilities.

(3) Jones had assets that could be reached by creditors totaling $50,000. He had liabilities totaling $80,000.

(4) Adams had assets that could be reached by creditors totaling about $90,000. He had liabilities totaling about $100,000.

(5) Johnson had assets that could be reached by creditors totaling about $500,000. He had no liabilities.

Questions:

a. Should Johnson want out of this business? Why? If so, what should he do? Can he obtain a dissolution of the business by decree of court? Why?

b. If Smith wants out of this business, how should he argue? Can he obtain a dissolution by decree of court? Why?

Chapter 16

Dissolution and Winding Up of the Firm

As discussed in Chapter 15, when an owner dies or withdraws, a firm faces two diametrically opposed possibilities. One is that the firm will continue to operate; the other is that the firm must wind-up its business. Which of these two paths is taken depends upon a few key factors:

1. the firm's organizational form, and the default provisions of the applicable statute;

2. the terms of any agreement among the owners;

3. the circumstances that triggered the withdrawal, and the current relations between the withdrawing partner and the remaining partners; and

4. whether the business is sufficiently profitable to warrant a continuation of its business.

Although in the real world, businesses that are well planned and/or profitable do not suffer the fate of being liquidated and terminated after the withdrawal of an owner, the emphasis of this chapter will be upon firms that do wind up their business.

A. Liquidation v. Buyout

Problem 16.1

Hunt, as sole proprietor, was engaged in the manufacture and sale of lead shot for shotgun shells under the name West Coast Shot Manufacturing Company. Hunt had invented a "miner" and special equipment to recover used shot from trap shooting fields which was then melted down to produce new shot for sale on the market.

In the spring of 1972 Nicholes met Hunt in Medford, Oregon, and they orally agreed to form an equal partnership for the mining, manufacture, and sale of shot. Nicholes purchased a one-half of Hunt's existing business for $50,000, payable in installments. Hunt was to devote his best effort to the business. No written partnership agreement was ever signed.

While the new venture was a financial success, there was considerable dissension between the partners. Although it seemed that the partners had "pretty well patched everything up," on May 28, 1973, Hunt phoned Nicholes and told him that their "business relationship was at an end." On May 31, 1973, Hunt sent Nicholes a letter confirming the "termination of our business relationship". Over the objections of Nicholes, Hunt has continued to operate the business for his own account.

Nicholes and Hunt each claim to be entitled to buy the 50 percent share of the other partner and continue the business as a sole proprietor. Assuming that the partners have no written or oral agreement that might affect your answer, what result? *See Nicholes v. Hunt,* 273 Or. 255, 541 P.2d 820 (1975).

Dreifuerst v. Dreifuerst
90 Wis. 2d 566, 280 N.W.2d 335 (1979)

BROWN, Presiding Judge

The plaintiffs and the defendant, all brothers, formed a partnership. The partnership operated two feed mills, one located at St. Cloud, Wisconsin and one located at Elkhart Lake, Wisconsin. There were no written Articles of Partnership governing this partnership.

On October 4, 1975, the plaintiffs served the defendant with a notice of dissolution and wind-up of the partnership. The action for dissolution and wind-up was commenced on January 27, 1976. The dissolution complaint alleged that the plaintiffs elected to dissolve the partnership. There was no allegation of fault, expulsion or contravention of an alleged agreement as grounds for dissolution. The parties were unable, however, to agree to a winding-up of the partnership.

Hearings on the dissolution were held on October 18, 1976 and March 4, 1977. Testimony was presented regarding the value of the partnership assets and each partner's equity. At the March 4, 1977 hearing, the defendant requested that the partnership be sold pursuant to [UPA section 38(1)], and that the court allow a sale, at which time the partners would bid on the entire property. By such sale, the plaintiffs could continue to run the business under a new partnership, and the defendant's partnership equity could be satisfied in cash.

On February 20, 1978, the trial court, by written decision, denied the defendant's request for a sale and instead divided the partnership assets in-kind according to the valuation presented by the plaintiffs. The plaintiffs were given the physical assets from the Elkhard Lake mill, and the defendant was given the physical assets from the St. Cloud mill. The defendant appeals this order and judgment dividing the assets in-kind.

Under [UPA section 29], a partnership is dissolved when any partner ceases to be associated in the carrying on of the business. The partnership is not terminated, but continues, until the winding-up of partnership is complete. [UPA section 30]. The action stated by the plaintiffs, in this case, was an action for dissolution and wind-up. The plaintiffs were not continuing the partnership and, therefore, [UPA sections 41 and 42] do not apply. The sole question in this case is whether, in the absence of a written agreement to the contrary, a partner, upon dissolution and wind-up of the partnership, can force a sale of the partnership assets.

At the outset, we note, and the parties agree, that the appellant was not in contravention of the partnership agreement since there was no partnership agreement. The partnership was a partnership at will. They also agree there was no written agreement governing distribution of partnership assets upon dissolution and wind-up. The dispute, in this case, is over the authority of the trial court to order in-kind distribution in the absence of any agreement of the partners.

[UPA section 38(1)] provides:

> When dissolution is caused in any way, except in contravention of the partnership agreement, each partner, as against his copartners and all persons claiming through them in respect to their interests in the partnership, *unless otherwise agreed*, may have the partnership property applied to discharge its liabilities, and the surplus applied to pay *in cash* the net amount owing to the respective partners. [Emphasis supplied.]

The appellant contends this statute grants him the right to force a sale of the partnership assets in order to obtain his fair share of the partnership assets in cash upon dissolution. He claims that in the absence of an agreement of the partners to in-kind distribution, the trial court had no authority to distribute the assets in-kind. He is entitled to an in-cash settlement after judicial sale.

The respondents contend the statute does not entitle the appellant to force a sale and grants the trial court the power to distribute the assets in-kind if in-kind distribution is equitably possible and doesn't jeopardize the rights of creditors.

We do not believe that the statute can be read in any way to permit in-kind distribution unless the partners agree to in-kind distribution or unless there is a partnership agreement calling for in-kind distribution at the time of dissolution and wind-up.

A partnership at will is a partnership which has no definite term or particular undertaking and can rightfully be dissolved by the express will of any partner. [UPA section 31(1)(b)]. In the present case, the respondents wanted to dissolve the partnership. This being a partnership at will, they could rightfully dissolve this partnership with or without the consent of the appellant. In addition, the respondents have never claimed the appellant was in violation of any partnership agreement. Therefore, neither the appellant nor the respondents have wrongfully dissolved the partnership.

Unless otherwise agreed, partners who have not wrongfully dissolved a partnership have a right to wind up the partnership. [UPA section 37]. Winding-up is the process of settling partnership affairs after dissolution. Winding-up is often called liquidation and involves reducing the assets to cash to pay creditors and distribute to partners the value of their respective interests. Thus, lawful dissolution (or dissolution which is caused in any way except in contravention of the partnership agreement) gives each partner the right to have the business liquidated and his share of the surplus paid *in cash*. In-kind distribution is permissible only in very limited circumstances. If the partnership agreement permits in-kind distribution upon dissolution or wind-up or if, at any time prior to wind-up, all partners agree to in-kind distribution, the court may order in-kind distribution. While at least one court has permitted in-kind distribution, absent an agreement by all partners, *Rinke v. Rinke*, 330 Mich. 615, 48 N.W.2d 201 (1951), the court's holding in that case was limited. In *Rinke*, the court stated:

The decree of the trial court provided for dividing the assets of the partnerships rather than for the sale thereof and the distribution of cash proceeds. Appellants insist that such method of procedure is erroneous and not contemplated by the Uniform Partnership Act. Attention is directed to Section 38. Construing together pertinent provisions of the statute leads to the conclusion that it was not the intention of the legislature in the enactment of the Uniform Partnership Act to impose a mandatory requirement that, under all circumstances, the assets of a dissolved partnership shall be sold and the money received therefore divided among those entitled to it, particularly so, as in the case at bar, where there are no debts to be paid from the proceeds. *The situation disclosed by the record in the present case is somewhat unusual in that no one other than the former partners is interested in the assets of the businesses. In view of this situation and of the nature of the assets*, we think that the trial court was correct in apportioning them to the parties. There is no showing that appellants have been prejudiced thereby. [(Emphasis supplied.)]

The Michigan court's holding was limited to situations where:

(1) there were no creditors to be paid from the proceeds,

(2) ordering a sale would be senseless since no one other than the partners would be interested in the assets of the business, and

(3) an in-kind distribution was fair to all partners.

That is not the case here. There was no showing that there were no creditors who would be paid from the proceeds, nor was there a showing that no one other than the partners would be interested in the assets. These factors are important if an in-kind distribution is to be allowed. [UPA section 38 is] intended to protect creditors as well as partners. In-kind distributions may affect a creditor's right to collect the debt owed since the assets of the partnership, as a whole, may be worth more than the assets once divided up. Thus, the creditor's ability to collect from the individual partners may be jeopardized. Secondly, if others are interested in the assets, a sale provides a more accurate means of establishing the market value of the assets and, thus, better assuring each partner his share in the value of the assets. Where only the partners are interested in the assets, a fair value can be determined without the necessity of a sale. The sale would be merely the partners bidding with each other without any competition. This process could be accomplished through negotiations or at trial with the court as a final arbitrator of the value of the assets. With these policy considerations in mind, we think the Michigan court's holding in *Rinke* was limited to the facts of that case. Those facts not being present in this case, we do not feel an in-kind distribution in this case was proper.

However, even assuming the respondents in this case can show that there are no creditors to be paid, no one other than the partners are interested in the assets, and in-kind distribution would be fair to all partners, we cannot read [UPA section 38] as permitting an in-kind distribution under any circumstances, unless all partners agree. [UPA section 38 is] quite clear that if a partner may force liquidation, he is entitled to his share of the partnership assets, after creditors are paid *in cash*. To the extent that *Rinke v. Rinke* creates an exception to cash distribution, we decline to adopt that exception. We, therefore, must hold the trial court erred in ordering an in-kind distribution of the assets of the partnership.

The last question that arises is whether the appellant can force an actual sale of the assets or whether the trial court can determine the fair market value of the assets and order the respondents to pay the appellant in cash an amount equal to his share in the assets.

As discussed above, a sale is the best means of determining the true fair market value of the assets. Generally, liquidation envisions some form of sale. Since the statutes provide that, unless otherwise agreed, any partner who has not wrongfully dissolved the partnership has the right to wind up the partnership and force liquidation, he likewise has a right to force a sale, unless otherwise agreed. While judicial sales in some instances may cause economic hardships, these hardships can be avoided by the use of partnership agreements.

Judgment reversed and cause remanded for further proceedings not inconsistent with this opinion.

Notes

1. As discussed in Chapter 15, under UPA section 38(1), unless a partner has wrongfully dissolved a partnership for a definite term or particular undertaking, partners have the right to winding up of the partnership business following a dissolution of the partnership. Notwithstanding the dissolution of the partnership, partners remain liable for all partnership obligations. UPA § 36(1). Winding up partnership affairs is important because the process of winding up discharges partnership obligations. First, the partnership completes "unfinished business"—transactions begun, but not completed, before dissolution. Cf., UPA § 33. Second, partnership property is applied to discharge partnership liabilities. UPA § 38(1).

2. As discussed in Chapter 15, the RUPA generally continues the rule that partners are entitled, not only to dissociate from the partnership, but also to a winding up of its business. RUPA § 801(1), 807(1)

3. In *Dreifuerst v. Dreifuerst,* one of the partners urged the court to divide partnership assets *in kind,* by giving each partner one of the partnership's two mills. Distributions in kind are disfavored. Under the UPA, the general rule is that winding up necessarily involves a *liquidation,* or sale, of partnership assets:

a. First, the partnership must generate the cash necessary to discharge partnership liabilities, as required by UPA section 38(1). Often a proposal, such as the one in *Dreifuerst v. Dreifuerst,* contemplates that partnership obligations will not be discharged, but only assumed by the partners continuing the business. This leaves the other partners liable for those obligations. See the discussion later in this Chapter.

b. Second, partners are entitled to receive *in cash* their respective shares of the surplus remaining after discharging partnership liabilities. UPA § 38(1).

c. As discussed in *Dreifuerst v. Dreifuerst,* one of the rationales of the rule requiring liquidation by sale is that a sale—particularly a competitive, auction sale—is the best way to determine the true market value of partnership assets.

4. Note that the RUPA generally continues the liquidtion by sale rules under the UPA. Under RUPA section 402:

A partner has not right to receive, and may not be required to accept, a distribution in kind.

RUPA section 807(a) continues the rule of UPA section 38(1):

In winding up a partnership's business, the assets of the partnership, including the contributions of the partners required by this section, must be applied to *discharge its obligations to creditors,* including, to the extent permitted by law, partners who are creditors. Any surplus must be applied to pay *in cash* the net amount distributable to partners in accordance with their right to distributions under subsection (b).

RUPA § 807(a) (emphasis added).

5. How would the principles discussed in *Dreifuerst v. Dreifuerst* apply to the facts of problem 16.1? How could Hunt and Nicholes have protected their interests at the time they formed their partnership?

In Re Estate of Bolinger
292 Mont. 97, 971 P.2d 767 (Mont. 1998)

Hal Bolinger filed a petition for probate of the will of his son, Harry Albert Bolinger, III(Bud), in the District Court for the Eighteenth Judicial District in Gallatin County. The decedent's three children, as well as the personal representative who had been appointed prior to the discovery of the will, contested the will and asserted, among other things, that the decedent's estate was entitled to a share of the partnership that they claim Hal had formed with Bud. The District Court concluded that a partnership existed and awarded the estate half of the value of the partnership assets. Hal and his spouse appeal and the estate cross-appeals.

*   *   *

FACTUAL BACKGROUND

Harry Albert Bolinger, III (Bud) died March 25, 1995. He was survived by his three adult children, as well as his father and stepmother. Intestacy proceedings were initiated, and in April 1995 Deborah Reichman became personal representative of the estate.

On July 13, 1995, H.A. Bolinger (Hal), Bud's father, submitted a will for probate and petitioned the District Court for appointment as personal representative. The will, which was prepared in 1984, left all of Bud's estate to Hal and nominated him as the personal representative. In the event that Hal failed to survive Bud, the will named Marian Bolinger, Hal's wife, as the sole beneficiary. On November 1, 1995, Hal withdrew his request to be appointed personal representative and suggested that Marian, who was also nominated by the will, be named personal representative.

After a hearing, and based on all the evidence before it, on December 18, 1996, the District Court made findings of fact and conclusions of law in response to the summary judgment motion. It stated that

[I]n the interest of judicial economy, the Court feels it advisable to make detailed findings at this time, to assist in determining other issues which may hereafter need to be determined.

Most of the District Court's findings and conclusions pertained to the terms of the will, but in addition, the District Court found that Hal and Bud had entered into a written partnership agreement in 1968. It found that despite the express ten-year term of the agreement, Hal and Bud operated the ranch as a partnership until Bud's death. * * * It went on to find that there were no written documents regarding the terms of the alleged agreement, and that Marian, the only witness to Hal and Bud's agreement, had described the extent of the agreement as a statement by Hal and subsequent acknowledgment by Bud that he would "have to pay his share."

Based on the District Court's findings, the estate made a second motion for partial summary judgment in January 1997. It contended that the findings established the existence of a partnership and that the District Court should order an accounting of the partnership. * * * In response, Hal and Marian contended that their affidavits established genuine issues of fact regarding...the existence of a partnership....

On February 25, 1997, the District Court concluded that the alleged agreement between Hal and Bud...was not specific and, therefore, was unenforceable as a matter of law. The District Court also concluded, based on Hal's testimony, that a partnership existed. Accordingly, it granted the motion for partial summary judgment and ordered that an accounting be performed.

The accounting was eventually performed and considered by the District Court at a hearing in May 1997. On September 3, 1997, the District Court issued its findings of fact, conclusions of law, and judgment pursuant to the accounting, in which it determined the amount of ranch property that should be credited to the estate. Based on its interpretation of the partnership agreement, the District Court concluded that the land on which the partnership operation was conducted was never intended to be an asset of the partnership and excluded its value from the determination of the estate's interest. The division and valuation of the remaining partnership assets relied, in large part, on the fact that Hal and Marian had refused to respond to Reichman's discovery requests and the District Court's subsequent orders to compel, so that they were estopped from contesting the values or division arrived at by the District Court.

The judgment awarded Bud's estate included one-half the market value of the partnership cattle and equipment....Finally, the District Court held that the judgment constituted a lien against all personal property of the partnership.

* * *

ISSUE 5

Did the District Court err when it awarded one-half of the market value of the ranch equipment and cattle to the estate?

Appellants contend that the 1968 partnership agreement established the value of the partnership and that the terms of the agreement should govern the amount to which the estate is entitled. They assert that the District Court erred when it did not follow the terms of the agreement but instead awarded the estate one-half of the market value of the partnership property.

Montana law provides that when a partnership agreement exists, it controls the rights and duties of partners. See [RUPA § 103.] Moreover, when partners continue a partnership beyond the expiration of the partnership agreement, their rights and duties remain the same as they were at the expiration of the agreement, effectively extending the force of the agreement to the partnership for as long as the partners continue the business or until they modify the agreement. See [RUPA § 406.]

The partners' right to control their relationship via the agreement, and in particular to restrict the value of their respective shares upon death or dissolution, is so well-established that courts will enforce a value in the agreement even if the value to which a partner is entitled is substantially lower than the actual market or book value of his share. For such a limitation to be valid, however, the partners must have explicitly agreed to a value of their potential share at something other than fair market value.

Here, the agreement establishes a value ($47,790.30) for the partnership and states that that value shall control in the event of a sale or dissolution of the partnership. The terms also state that the partners shall, for the duration of the agreement, arrive annually at a new and updated value, which will serve for the following year as the value of the partnership. In the event of Hal's or Bud's death, the agreement gives the surviving partner the right to purchase the deceased partner's interest at the value established in the agreement, with one-fourth of the purchase price due within six months of the death. However, the terms set forth were not followed.

First, Hal and Bud did not reestablish a different value for the partnership as contemplated in the agreement. Therefore, the only value established by the partnership is the original 1968 amount of $47,790.30, an amount which neither of the parties suggests reflects its present value. Second, Hal has made no effort to purchase Bud's interest in the partnership.

A partnership agreement is essentially a contract between the partners and, therefore, is to be interpreted and applied in accordance with principles of contract law. Where language in a contract is clear and unambiguous, it is a court's duty to simply apply the language. On the one hand, the contract is absolutely clear and unambiguous as to what the parties intended regarding the partnership's valuation and, likewise, as to what that value was at the time that they entered the agreement. This issue turns, however, on the fact that the parties' failure to comply with the agreement and to reassess the value of the partnership conflicts with their expression of intent and creates now a manifest ambiguity as to the value of the partnership thirty years after its creation.

Other courts have had to interpret and apply ambiguous partnership agreements similar to the one here when partners failed to establish a value for partnership property. In each case, the court held that fair market value at the time of the partner's death should apply.

Chapman [v. Dunnegan (Mo.Ct.App.1984), 665 S.W.2d 643] involved facts very similar to this case. The partnership agreement called for the partners to value the real estate owned by the partnership on an annual basis; additional language which is not present in Hal's and Bud's agreement stated that if in a given year the partners failed to value the property, the previous year's value stood. Like here, however, the partners failed to follow the terms of the agreement and never established a value for the property. The estate urged that a fair market value should be assigned to the property, while the remaining partners contended that its book value should control. The court provided the following analysis:

The partners' failure to comply with the expressed method for valuing partnership real estate was, in effect, an abandonment of that method and left the partnership agreement without a provision for valuing partnership real estate. In the absence of a provision in the partnership agreement, the relevant provisions of the [statute]...are persuasive. [The statute] provides that the legal representatives of a deceased partner shall receive "an amount equal to the value of his interest in the dissolved partnership" at the time of dissolution.... The prevailing view among [other] courts is that, upon the dissolution of a partnership by death, fair market value must be used to evaluate the deceased partner's interest if the partnership agreement does not specify the method of valuing partnership assets or the method provided was not complied with.

The rationale for this view is not difficult to understand.... [A] fair market value represents the real value of the partnership holdings—the value that the partners would receive if they sold the business. At common law, when a partner died or retired, surviving partners were required to liquidate the business and distribute the proceeds. The Uniform Partnership Act permits the surviving partners to continue the business, but requires them to pay to the decedent's legal representatives the value of the decedent's interest.... Measuring "the value of his interest" at its actual fair market value, when no other method is expressed, is the only sensible method to preserve the estate's right to the decedent's fair share.

Chapman, 665 S.W.2d at 649-50 (citations omitted).

Appellants contend that insofar as the agreement here establishes a value, it has more force and is thus distinguishable from the agreements in the cases above which either did not establish a value or referred only to an imprecise valuation term. As in *Chapman,* however, Hal and Bud essentially abandoned their method of valuation, the effect of which was to abandon whatever explicit agreement they reached regarding the 1968 valuation and its potential ability to serve as (*i.e.,* limit) the value for the partnership in subsequent years. It was clearly not their intent that the 1968 figure would serve as the value in future years, nor should we now default to that value simply because they failed to establish a new one. Rather, like in *Chapman,* we are guided by the statute, which suggests that upon dissociation a partner is entitled to the greater of either the liquidation value or the fair market value at the date of dissociation. See § 35-10-619(2), MCA [RUPA § 701(b).][A] While the statute is not directly applicable here, we note

---

A. [by the Editors] Section 35-10-619(2), MCA differs from RUPA section 701(b) in that it specifies that:

In either case, the selling price of the partnership assets must be determined on the basis of the amount that would be paid by a willing buyer to a willing seller, neither being under any compulsion to buy or sell, and with knowledge of all relevant facts.

MCA § 35-10-619(2)(b). RUPA section 701(b) uses "buyout" price instead of "selling" price, and does not refer to "fair market value." As explained in Comment 3 to RUPA section 701:

The terms 'fair market value" or "fair value" were not used because they are often considered terms of art having a special meaning depending on the context, such as in tax or corporate law. "Buyout price" is a new term. It is intended that the term be developed as an independent concept appropriate to the partnership buyout sit-the policy reflected therein and we agree with the court's rationale in *Chapman* and its conclusion that fair market value at the time of a partner's death should apply when partners have failed to comply with the terms of their agreement and are thus left without an explicitly agreed upon value for the partnership. Accordingly, we affirm the District Court's award to the estate of fair market value for the partnership assets.

Note

1. UPA section 38(1) provides that the partners' rights to winding up of partnership business apply only "unless otherwise agreed." UPA § 38(1). Under RUPA section 103(a), the partnership agreement governs the relations among partners, except as limited by RUPA section 103(b). RUPA section 103(b) does not limit the ability of partners to override RUPA section 807(a).

2. In *In Re Estate of Bolinger,* the court did not order liquidation by sale of the partnership's property, but instead directed that Bud's interest in the firm was to be *purchased,* not at the price set in the partnership agreement, but rather at the price required by RUPA section 701(b).

> a. If the partnership agreement had failed, why didn't the court order liquidation by sale? Would the result have been different if the case had arisen under the UPA?

> b. Based on *Dreifuerst v. Dreifuerst,* page 772, and the following notes, what are the disadvantages of the court's approach?

3. In *Chapman v. Dunnegan,* 665 S.W.2d 643 (Mo.Ct.App.1984), the partnership agreement provided that, if the partners failed to revalue the partnership, then the prior year's value would carryforward. Why did the court ignore the agreement, and value the interest under UPA sections 38(a) and 40?

4. If you had represented Hunt in Problem 16.1, how could you have drafted a partnership agreement to avoid the problems confronted in *In Re Estate of Bolinger* and *Chapman v. Dunnegan?*

5. Under the RUPA, where the partnership will not be wound up, the partnership is obligated to purchase the interest of the dissociated partner. RUPA §§ 603. 701. Under RUPA section 701(b):

> The buyout price of a dissociated partner's interest is the amount that would have been distributable to the dissociating partner under Section 807(b) if, on the date of dissociation, the assets of the partnership were sold at a price equal to *the greater of* the liquidation value *or* the value based on a sale of the entire business as a going concern without the dissociated partner and the partnership were wound up as of that date.

RUPA § 701(b). RUPA section 701 provides a mechanism for the partnership, and the dissociating partner (or that partner's representative) to agree on the buyout price. If the parties are unable to agree, the dissociated partner has the right to ask a court to determine the buyout price. RUPA § 701(I).

---

uation, while drawing on valuation principles developed elsewhere.
Also, MCA § 35-10-619(2) uses the term "selling price" instead of "buyout price."

Creel v. Lilly
354 Md. 77, 729 A.2d 385 (1999)

Opinion by Chasanow, J.

The primary issue presented in this appeal is whether Maryland's Uniform Partnership Act (UPA)[A] permits the estate of a deceased partner to demand liquidation of partnership assets in order to arrive at the true value of the business. Specifically, Petitioner (Anne Creel) maintains that the surviving partners have a duty to liquidate all partnership assets because

(1) there is no provision in the partnership agreement providing for the continuation of the partnership upon a partner's death and

(2) the estate has not consented to the continuation of the business.

Respondents (Arnold Lilly and Roy Altizer) contend that because the surviving partners wound up the partnership in good faith, in that they conducted a full inventory, provided an accurate accounting to the estate for the value of the business as of the date of dissolution, and paid the estate its proportionate share of the surplus proceeds, they are under no duty to liquidate the partnership's assets upon demand of the deceased partner's estate.

As discussed in more detail in Part II.A., *infra*, UPA, which has governed partnerships in this State for the past 80 years, has been repealed since this litigation commenced. The Act that now governs Maryland partnerships is the Revised Uniform Partnership Act (RUPA)[B] which was adopted in July 1998 with a phase-in period. Therefore, until December 31, 2002, both UPA and RUPA will coexist, with § 9A-1204 determining which Act applies to a particular partnership's formation, termination, and any other conflict that may arise.

At the outset we note there is a partnership agreement in the instant case that, while somewhat unclear, seems to provide for an alternative method of winding up the partnership rather than a liquidation of all assets. The circuit court and intermediate appellate court both found the agreement unclear as to dissolution and winding up of the business upon the death of a partner and correctly turned to UPA as an interpretative aid. In looking specifically at the trial court's order, the trial judge referred to the partnership agreement and UPA but was not explicit as to which one he primarily relied on in holding that a forced sale of all assets was not required in this case. Regardless, the trial judge's interpretation of the partnership agreement and holding are in conformity with UPA.

Due to our uncertainty as to whether the trial court's holding was based primarily on the partnership agreement or UPA, and also because clarification of the liquidation issue implicates other aspects of partnership law, we will ex-

A. [By the Editors]. The Maryland version of the Uniform Partnership Act is found in Maryland Code (1975, 1993 Repl. Vol., 1998 Supp.), Corporations and Associations Article, §§ 9-101 *et seq.*

B. [By the Editors]. The Maryland version of the Revised Uniform Partnership Act is found in Maryland Code (1975, 1993 Repl. Vol., 1998 Supp.), Corporations and Associations Art. §§ 9A-101 *et seq.*

amine not only the partnership agreement itself, but also Maryland's UPA and applicable case law, the cases in other jurisdictions that have interpreted the liquidation issue under UPA, and the newly adopted RUPA. For the reasons stated in this opinion, we concur in the finding of the courts below that Respondents are under no duty to "liquidate on demand" by Petitioner, as UPA does not mandate a forced sale of all partnership assets in order to ascertain the true value of the business. Winding up is not always synonymous with liquidation, which can be a harsh, drastic, and often unnecessary course of action. A preferred method in a good faith winding up, which was utilized in this case, is to pay the deceased partner's estate its proportionate share of the value of the partnership, derived from an accurate accounting, without having to resort to a full liquidation of the business. To hold otherwise vests excessive power and control in the deceased partner's estate, to the extreme disadvantage of the surviving partners. Thus, on this issue, we affirm the judgment of the Court of Special Appeals.

* * *

I. BACKGROUND

On approximately June 1, 1993, Joseph Creel began a retail business selling NASCAR racing memorabilia. His business was originally located in a section of his wife Anne's florist shop, but after about a year and a half he decided to raise capital from partners so that he could expand and move into his own space. On September 20, 1994, Mr. Creel entered into a partnership agreement—apparently prepared without the assistance of counsel—with Arnold Lilly and Roy Altizer to form a general partnership called "Joe's Racing." * * *

* * *

The three-man partnership operated a retail store in the St. Charles Towne Center Mall in Waldorf, Maryland. For their initial investment in Joe's Racing, Mr. Lilly and Mr. Altizer each paid $6,666 in capital contributions, with Mr. Creel contributing his inventory and supplies valued at $15,000. Pursuant to the partnership agreement, Mr. Lilly and Mr. Altizer also paid $6,666 to Mr. Creel ($3,333 each) "for the use and rights to the business known as Joe's Racing Collectables." The funds were placed in a partnership bank account with First Virginia Bank-Maryland. All three partners were signatories to this account, but on May 19, 1995, unknown to Mr. Lilly and Mr. Altizer, Mr. Creel altered the account so that only he had the authority to sign checks. It was only after Mr. Creel's death that Mr. Lilly and Mr. Altizer realized they could not access the account funds, which were frozen by the bank upon Mr. Creel's passing. Moreover, on approximately February 20, 1995, Mr. Creel paid a $5,000 retainer to an attorney without his partners' knowledge. He wanted the attorney to prepare documents for the marketing of franchises for retail stores dealing in racing memorabilia.

Joe's Racing had been in existence for almost nine months when Mr. Creel died on June 14, 1995. Mrs. Creel was appointed personal representative of his estate. In this capacity, and acting without the knowledge of the surviving partners, Mrs. Creel and the store's landlord agreed to shorten the lease by one month so that it expired on August 31, 1995. June, July, and August's rent was paid by Mr. Lilly and Mr. Altizer.

In accordance with [UPA section 31(4)],[3] Joe's Racing was automatically dissolved upon Mr. Creel's death and because the partnership agreement did not expressly provide for continuation of the partnership nor did his estate consent to its continuation, the surviving partners were required under UPA to wind up the business. *See* [UPA §§ 30 and 38(a).] In order to pay debts and efficiently wind up the partnership affairs, Mr. Lilly and Mr. Altizer requested that Mrs. Creel and the bank release the funds in the partnership account ($18,115.93 as of July 13, 1995). Their request was refused and it was at this point that litigation commenced. We adopt the following procedural history of this case, as detailed in the unreported opinion of the Court of Special Appeals:

> Not receiving a favorable response, the surviving partners, on behalf of Joe's Racing, brought an action in the District Court against Mrs. Creel, individually and as personal representative of her late husband's estate, and First Virginia Bank-Maryland. * * *

> In the meantime, [Mrs. Creel] had filed in the circuit court a complaint seeking an accounting and a declaratory judgment against Messrs. Lilly and Altizer, individually and doing business under the name "Good Old Boys Racing." She asserted that, instead of winding up the affairs of Joe's Racing in accordance with her demand, Lilly and Altizer continued the partnership business under a new name, using the assets of the partnership. * * * [Mr. Lilly and Mr. Altizer] later filed an Amended Complaint/Counter Complaint for Declaratory Relief, naming Mrs. Creel, as Personal Representative, as the sole defendant, seeking, *inter alia*, a declaration as to the amounts the Estate of Joseph Creel was entitled to by way of return of capital contributions and as Joseph Creel's share of the net value of the partnership as of the time of dissolution.

*   *   *

> The court also found that the surviving partners sought to wind up and close out the partnership and took all reasonable steps to do so, and that there was no breach by them of any fiduciary duty to the Estate. The lease on the store premises occupied by the partnership expired on 31 August 1995, and on that date Mr. Lilly conducted an inventory of all merchandise in the store. Based on that inventory, an accountant computed the value of the partnership business; Mrs. Creel was invited to review the books and records and retain her own accountant or appraiser if she questioned [Mr. Lilly or Mr. Altizer's] figures. *She declined to do so. After 31 August 1995, Messrs. Lilly and Altizer ceased doing business as Joe's Racing and began doing business together under the name 'Good OLE Boys Racing.'*

> *The court accepted the valuation prepared by [Mr. Lilly and Mr. Altizer's] accountant as the correct value of the partnership assets as of 31 August 1995, and found that the surviving partners fully disclosed and delivered to the Estate all records of the financial affairs of the Joe's Rac-*

---

3. [UPA section 31(4)] states in pertinent part:
   "Dissolution is caused:
   * * *
   (4) By the death of any partner[.]"

ing partnership up to 31 August 1995, which the court took to be the end of the winding up period. Rejecting [Mrs. Creel's] assertions

> (1) that [Mr. Lilly and Mr. Altizer] were obligated to liquidate the partnership assets in order to wind up the partnership;

> (2) that [Mr. Lilly and Mr. Altizer], instead of winding up the partnership by liquidating its assets, misappropriated partnership assets, i.e., inventory to make a profit, for which they were obligated to account; *and*

> (3) that the Estate was entitled to 52% of such profits,

the court declared that the Estate was entitled to a total of $21,631....

*   *   *

On the basis of those findings, the court ordered that [Mrs. Creel] could withdraw the funds deposited in court by the bank and that [Mr. Lilly and Mr. Altizer] should pay [Mrs. Creel] the difference between the amount of those funds and $21,631.00. (Emphasis added).

The Court of Special Appeals affirmed the judgment of the Circuit Court for Charles County, finding that under UPA "winding up" does not always mean "liquidate;" therefore, Joe's Racing had no duty to sell off all of its assets in a liquidation sale. * * *

II. DISCUSSION AND ANALYSIS
A.

We begin our analysis by reviewing the law of partnership as it pertains to the issues in this case. Maryland enacted UPA in 1916. Section 9-101(g) [*see* UPA § 6] defines a partnership as

> an association of two or more persons to carry on as co-owners [of] a business for profit.

There is no requirement that the partnership be formally established with a writing; so long as this definition is met, a partnership exists whether the parties intend it to or not. However, the

> general rule is that the partnership agreement governs the relations among the partners and between the partners and the partnership. The provisions of [UPA] govern to the extent the partnership agreement does not provide otherwise.

John W. Larson et al., *Revised Uniform Partnership Act Reflects a Number of Significant Changes*, 10 J. PARTNERSHIP TAX'N 232, 233 (1993)(footnote omitted).

A partnership is either (1) for a definite term or a particular undertaking or (2) at will, which means the business has no definite term or particular undertaking. *See*...[RUPA § 101(8)]. An at-will partnership continues indefinitely and can be dissolved by the express will of any partner or automatically by the happening of a specific event as mandated by UPA, such as the death of a partner. *See*...[UPA § 31(4).] Under UPA, partners may avoid the automatic dissolution of the business upon the death of a partner by providing for its continuation in their partnership agreement. Sophisticated partnerships virtually always use carefully drafted partnership agreements to protect the various partners' interests by providing for the continuation of the business, the distribution of partnership assets, etc., in the face of various contingencies such as death. Less sophisticated partnerships, however, are often operating under oral terms or a "homemade" agreement that does not contain protections for the partners or the business.

While the death of a partner automatically dissolves the partnership unless there is an agreement stating otherwise, the partnership is not terminated until the winding-up process is complete. *See...* [UPA § 30].... Winding up is generally defined as

> getting in the assets, settling with [the] debtors and creditors, and appropriating the amount of profit or loss [to the partners].

Comp. of Treas. v. Thompson Tr. Corp., 209 Md. 490, 501-02, 121 A.2d 850, 856 (1956)(quoting *Lafayette Trust Co. v. Beggs*, 107 N.E. 644, 645 (N.Y. 1915)). The surviving partners have the right to wind up the partnership or the deceased partner's representative may obtain a winding up through the courts. *See* [UPA § 38]. [UPA Section 38] details the winding-up procedures and whether Subsection (a) or (b) applies depends on whether dissolution was caused in contravention of the partnership agreement or not, wrongfully, etc. The winding-up procedure that applies in this case is found in [UPA Section 38(a)], which states in pertinent part:

> When dissolution is caused in any way...each partner...unless otherwise agreed, may have the partnership property applied to discharge its liabilities, and the surplus applied to pay in cash the net amount owing to the respective partners.

Historically, under many courts and commentators' interpretation of UPA, when a partner died and the partnership automatically dissolved because there was no consent by the estate to continue the business nor was there a written agreement allowing for continuation, the estate had the right to compel liquidation of the partnership assets. Reducing all of the partnership assets to cash through a liquidation was seen as the only way to obtain the true value of the business. However, while winding up has often traditionally been regarded as synonymous with liquidation, this "fire sale" of assets has been viewed by many courts and commentators as a harsh and destructive measure. Consequently, to avoid the drastic result of a forced liquidation, many courts have adopted judicial alternatives to this potentially harmful measure.

Over time, the UPA rule requiring automatic dissolution of the partnership upon the death of a partner, in the absence of consent by the estate to continue the business or an agreement providing for continuation, with the possible result of a forced sale of all partnership assets was viewed as outmoded by many jurisdictions including Maryland. The development and adoption of RUPA by the National Conference of Commissioners on Uniform State Laws (NCCUSL) mitigated this harsh UPA provision of automatic dissolution and compelled liquidation.

* * *

* * * Critically, under RUPA the estate of the deceased partner no longer has to consent in order for the business to be continued nor does the estate have the right to compel liquidation.

Like UPA, RUPA is a "gap filler" in that it only governs partnership affairs to the extent not otherwise agreed to by the partners in the partnership agreement. * * *

Along with 18 other states,[5] Maryland has adopted RUPA, effective July 1, 1998, with a phase-in period during which the two Acts will coexist. As of January 1, 2003, RUPA will govern all Maryland partnerships. *See* § 9A-1204. In adopting RUPA, the Maryland legislature was clearly seeking to eliminate some of UPA's harsh provisions, such as the automatic dissolution of a viable partnership upon the death of a partner and the subsequent right of the estate of the deceased partner to compel liquidation. In essence, the NCCUSL drafted RUPA to reflect the emerging trends in partnership law. RUPA is intended as a flexible, modern alternative to the more rigid UPA and its provisions are consistent with the reasonable expectations of commercial parties in today's business world.

B.

As discussed earlier, the traditional manner in which UPA allows for the continuation of the partnership upon the death of a partner is to either obtain the consent of the deceased partner's estate or include a continuation clause in the partnership agreement. There have been several cases in other jurisdictions, however, where neither of these conditions was met and the court elected another option under UPA instead of a "fire sale" of all the partnership assets to ensure that the deceased partner's estate received its fair share of the partnership. These jurisdictions have recognized the unfairness and harshness of a compelled liquidation and found other judicially acceptable means of winding up a partnership under UPA, such as ordering an in-kind distribution of the assets or allowing the remaining partners to buy out the withdrawing partner's share of the partnership.

While the following cases have not involved the specific situation that we are faced with here — dissolution upon the death of a partner — the options the various courts have adopted to avoid a compelled liquidation of all partnership assets are equally applicable to the instant case. A dissolution is a dissolution and a winding-up process is a winding-up process, no matter what the underlying reason is for its occurrence. The reason for the dissolution is relevant when liabilities are being apportioned among partners, such as in a wrongful dissolution, but such is not the concern in the instant case. Many of these cases also involve a continued partnership, as opposed to a successor partnership like Good OLE Boys, but again the various courts' reasons for not compelling a sale of all assets in order to arrive at the true value of the business are equally applicable to the instant case.

We look to the case law of other jurisdictions because this is a case of first impression in Maryland. The Maryland cases cited by Petitioner and Respondent in their briefs and during arguments are inapposite and offer little assistance in the task before us. We now turn to a discussion of out-of-state cases that have confronted the issue of whether, under UPA, a compelled liquidation in a dissolution situation is always mandated or whether there are other judicially acceptable alternatives.

---

5. To date, RUPA has been adopted in the following states: Alabama, Arizona, California, Colorado, Connecticut, District of Columbia, Florida, Minnesota, Montana, Nebraska, New Mexico, North Dakota, Oklahoma, Oregon, Texas, Virginia, West Virginia, and Wyoming. BUSINESS AND NONPROFIT ORGANIZATIONS AND ASSOCIATIONS LAWS 6 U.L.A. 1 (1998 Supp.). The National Conference of Commissioners on Uniform State Laws refers to the revised act as "Uniform Partnership Act (1996)." Maryland adopted the act as the "Revised Uniform Partnership Act," or RUPA, as we refer to it in this opinion.

1. In-Kind Distribution

We first examine the cases where the court elected to order an in-kind distribution rather than a compelled liquidation in order to ascertain the true value of the partnership. An in-kind distribution is the actual division and distribution of the physical assets themselves. *See* BLACK'S LAW DICTIONARY 475 (6th ed. 1990)(defining "[d]istribution in kind" as "[a] transfer of property 'as is'").

In *Nicholes v. Hunt*, the parties orally agreed to form a partnership for the manufacture and sale of shot. 541 P.2d 820, 822-23 (Or. 1975). The relationship between the two partners quickly soured, with Nicholes alleging that he was being wrongfully excluded from the business by Hunt. Nicholes sought a dissolution decree, requesting that the partnership assets be liquidated at a sale. In holding that the partnership assets could be apportioned without resorting to a sale, the Supreme Court of Oregon stated:

> *There is no express provision in [UPA] which establishes liquidation by sale as the exclusive mode of distributing partnership assets after dissolution.* Although the basic rule is that any partner has the right to force liquidation by sale, the rule has been subject to criticism....

Nicholes, 541 P.2d at 827 (emphasis added).

The court went on to quote extensively from a law review article, stating in pertinent part:

> '*[T]he liquidation right will be injurious to the business in many, perhaps in most, cases. One authority has described it as "ruinous."* Whether it really is depends on the relative value of the business sold and the business retained. Such values are partly subjective and partly influenced by specific facts. But, it is rare that a small business, which is the kind most partnerships are, can be sold for as much as the owners think it is worth to themselves. This is true if it is disposed of intact as a going concern, and even more so if it is sold piecemeal. *In short, the likelihood of loss of value is great enough to require every partnership to look to the ways of denying or restricting the liquidation right.*' (Emphasis added).

Nicholes, 541 P.2d at 827 (quoting Alan R. Bromberg, *Partnership Dissolution—Causes, Consequences, and Cures*, 43 TEX. L. REV. 631, 647-48 (1965)(footnote omitted)).

In support of its holding, the Oregon court looked to the Michigan case of *Rinke v. Rinke*, 48 N.W.2d 201 (Mich. 1951). *Rinke* involved two withdrawing partners seeking dissolution of two family partnerships, one a hardware and appliance business and the other dealing with the sale and servicing of automobiles. In upholding the trial court's decree that divided the partnership's assets rather than mandating a sale and the distribution of cash proceeds, the Supreme Court of Michigan held:

> Appellants insist that [dividing the assets] is erroneous and not contemplated by the [U]niform [P]artnership [A]ct....*Constructing together pertinent provisions of the statute leads to the conclusion that it was not the intention of the legislature in the enactment of the Uniform Partnership Act to impose a mandatory requirement that, under all circumstances, the assets of a dissolved partnership shall be sold and the money received therefor divided among those entitled to it....* The situation dis-

closed by the record in the present case is somewhat unusual in that no one other than the former partners is interested in the assets of the businesses. In view of this situation and of the nature of the assets, we think that the trial court was correct in apportioning them to the parties. There is no showing that appellants have been prejudiced thereby. (Emphasis added).

Rinke, 48 N.W. 2d at 207.

Two other cases where the court ordered an in-kind distribution rather than a liquidation sale are *Logoluso v. Logoluso*, 43 Cal.Rptr. 678 (Cal. Dist. Ct. App. 1965) and *Kelley v. Shay*, 55 A. 925 (Pa. 1903). *Logoluso* involved a dissolution proceeding of a farming partnership. The Respondents argued that in the absence of an agreement of the partners authorizing a distribution of assets in kind, the trial court only had the authority to order a sale of the partnership assets. In upholding the trial court's order of an in-kind distribution of the partnership assets, the California court declared:

[W]e hold that in a partnership dissolution action a court has authority to make distribution of partnership...property in kind. *** [I]t is not necessary to hold a sale in order to satisfy partnership obligations. Absent a compelling necessity to satisfy partnership obligations, a public sale of assets can be justified only if it is found that distribution in kind would result in great prejudice to the parties. (Emphasis added).

Logoluso, 43 Cal.Rptr. at 682.

Kelley dealt with the ownership of stock in a natural gas company, apparently not controlled by the partnership. The Supreme Court of Pennsylvania found that one partner would have an advantage over the other in bidding for the stock, and thus ordered it to be distributed in kind. The court looked to equity principles in holding:

Equity and good conscience, therefore, require that in the present case the stock should be divided in kind, rather than that it should be sold and the proceeds divided.

Kelley, 55 A. at 927. For another case where a court relied on equitable principles in refusing to order a liquidation, *see also Gelphman v. Gelphman*, 50 P.2d 933, 936 (Kan. 1935)(holding that in the absence of a specific request at trial to sell the partnership assets, "[I]t was competent for the court, sitting as a court of equity, to adjudge the disposition of the partnership property, to order conveyances of partnership property, and to make division of partnership assets.").

2. Buy-Out Option

We turn to the line of cases where the court allowed the remaining partners to buy out the withdrawing partner's interest in the partnership, rather than mandate a forced sale of assets to derive the true value of the business.

In *Gregg v. Bernards*, 443 P.2d 166[, 167] (Or. 1968), Gregg appealed from a decree that dissolved the partnership and vested in Bernards the title to a race horse, the main partnership asset, upon payment by Bernards to Gregg the value of his partnership interest and also his share of the profit. The Supreme Court of Oregon affirmed the trial court's alternative resolution—a buy-out option—to a forced sale of the race horse.

Goergen v. Nebrich also involved a court refusing to order a public sale of the partnership assets in a dissolution situation and instead mandating a buy-out option. 174 N.Y.S.2d 366 (N.Y. Sup. Ct. 1958). Dissolution of the two-person partnership was sought on the basis of one partner's incompetency due to illness. After the decree was entered, the incompetent partner died and his estate wanted a public sale of all partnership assets. The New York court held that the partnership assets must be properly appraised to ascertain the true value of the business, but stated that

> this does not mean that there must be a...sale of the partnership assets.

Goergen, 174 N.Y.S.2d at 369. The court held that because the surviving partner wanted to continue the business,

> it would be inequitable and unfair to the surviving partner to have a public sale.

Goergen, 174 N.Y.S.2d at 369. The court then went on to outline its alternative proposal to a sale of the assets:

> The legal representative of the deceased partner will be fully protected by a disinterested appraisal of the assets of the former partnership and by receiving decedent's share on the purchase of the deceased partner's assets by the surviving partner at the appraisal price. For this purpose, the Court will appoint two qualified, disinterested appraisers to make an appraisal of the firm's assets and upon the filing with the Court of such appraisals and the final accounting... *the Court will approve the sale of the deceased partner's interest to the surviving partner* providing that cash is paid for said interest. If the surviving partner is unable to do this, then it will be necessary, in the interest of justice to order a public sale. (Emphasis added).

Goergen, 174 N.Y.S.2d at 369-70.

Similarly, in *Fortugno [v. Hudson Manure Company*, 144 A.2d 207, 219 (N.J. Super. Ct. App. Div. 1958)], the court adopted what it called a "novel" alternative to a forced sale of the partnership assets. As in *Goergen*, the New Jersey court was willing to adopt the alternative proposal, but if it was not executed properly by the partners, then a liquidation sale would be ordered. The court held:

> [R]ecognizing that a forced sale of the partnership will destroy a great part of the value of the business[,] we approve the alternative proposal....If the opposing partners will agree to the entry of an order for the appraisal of the partnership under the direction of the court and directing them to pay [the withdrawing partner] one-eighth of the valuation determined upon, such an order will be entered. Otherwise, there will be a liquidation by sale of all the partnership assets....(Emphasis added).

Fortugno, 144 A.2d at 219.

Another case in which the court ordered a buy-out option rather than a forced sale of assets is *Wanderski v. Nowakowski*, 49 N.W.2d 139 (Mich. 1951). Nowakowski was not required to liquidate the partnership's assets, pay off creditors, and then settle accounts between himself and the withdrawing partner, Wanderski. Instead, he was entitled to continue operations, provided that he paid

Wanderski the fair value of his interest in the partnership as of the date of dissolution. The Supreme Court of Michigan allowed Nowakowski this alternative to a forced sale, even though their partnership agreement did not contain any provision regarding the continuation of the business after dissolution. *Wanderski*, 49 N.W.2d at 142-44.

C.

In applying the law discussed in Part II.A. and B. to the facts of this case, we want to clarify that while UPA is the governing act, our holding is also consistent with RUPA and its underlying policies. The legislature's recent adoption of RUPA indicates that it views with disfavor the compelled liquidation of businesses and that it has elected to follow the trend in partnership law to allow the continuation of business without disruption, in either the original or successor form, if the surviving partners choose to do so through buying out the deceased partner's share.

In this appeal, however, we would arrive at the same holding regardless of whether UPA or RUPA governs. Although our holding departs from the general UPA rule that the representative of the deceased partner's estate has a right to demand liquidation of the partnership, as we discuss in this subsection, *infra*, our position of "no forced sale" hardly represents a radical departure from traditional partnership law. The cases discussed in Part II.B., *supra*, many of which arose early in UPA's existence, illustrate the lengths other courts have gone to in order to avoid a compelled liquidation and adopt an alternative method for ascertaining the true value of a partnership. With that background, we turn to a discussion of the two issues Mrs. Creel raises in this appeal.

1. Compelled Liquidation Issue

The first issue is whether the Creel estate has the right to demand liquidation of Joe's Racing where its partnership agreement does not expressly provide for continuation of the partnership and where the estate does not consent to continuation. Before we move on to our analysis of the compelled liquidation issue, we point out that our finding that Good OLE Boys is a successor partnership, rather than a continuation of Joe's Racing, does not negate the need for a complete discussion of this issue. Unless there is consent to continue the business or an agreement providing for continuation, upon the death of a partner the accurate value of the partnership must be ascertained as of the date of dissolution and the proportionate share paid to the deceased partner's estate, no matter if we are dealing with a subsequent new partnership or a continuation of the original business. If a compelled liquidation of all partnership assets is seen as the only way to arrive at its true value, then property from the original partnership will have to be sold whether the present business is a continuation or a successor business; regardless, the potential harm of such a "fire sale" affects both equally.

a.

Because a partnership is governed by any agreement between or among the partners, we must begin our analysis of the compelled liquidation issue by examining the Joe's Racing partnership agreement. We reiterate that both UPA and RUPA only apply when there is either no partnership agreement governing the partnership's affairs, the agreement is silent on a particular point, or the agreement contains provisions contrary to law. * * *

The pertinent paragraph and subsections of the Joe's Racing partnership agreement are as follows:

7. Termination

(a) That, at the termination of this partnership a full and accurate inventory shall be prepared, and the assets, liabilities, and income, both in gross and net, shall be ascertained: the remaining debts or profits will be distributed according to the percentages shown above in the 6(e).

* * *

(d) Upon the death or illness of a partner, his share will go to his estate. If his estate wishes to sell his interest, they must offer it to the remaining partners first.

Even though the partnership agreement uses the word "termination," paragraph 7(a) is really discussing the dissolution of the partnership and the attendant winding-up process that ultimately led to termination. Paragraph 7(a) requires that the assets, liabilities, and income be "ascertained," but it in no way mandates that this must be accomplished by a forced sale of the partnership assets. Indeed, a liquidation or sale of assets is not mentioned anywhere in 7(a).

In this case, the winding-up method outlined in 7(a) was followed exactly by the surviving partners: a full and accurate inventory was prepared on August 31, 1995; this information was given to an accountant, who ascertained the assets, liabilities, and income of the partnership; and finally, the remaining debt or profit was distributed....

Mrs. Creel argues that the partnership agreement does not address the winding-up process and that we should look to UPA's default rules to fill in this gap. Her contention is incorrect. We only turn to UPA and its liquidation rule if there is no other option, and such is clearly not the case here. While this partnership agreement was drafted without the assistance of counsel and is not a sophisticated document that provides for every contingency, if it states the intention of the parties it is controlling. * * *

Thus, when we look to the intention of the parties as reflected in 7(a) of the partnership agreement, the trial judge could conclude that the partners did not anticipate that a "fire sale" of the partnership assets would be necessary to ascertain the true value of Joe's Racing. Paragraph 7(a) details the preferred winding-up procedure to be followed, to include an inventory, valuation, and distribution of debt or profit to the partners.

Moreover, paragraph 7(d), which discusses what happens to a partner's share of the business upon his death, also makes no mention of a sale or liquidation as being essential in order to determine the deceased partner's proportionate interest of the partnership. On the contrary, 7(d) appears to be a crude attempt to draft a "continuation clause" in the form of a buy-out option by providing that the deceased partner's share of the partnership goes to his estate, and if the estate wishes to sell this interest it must first be offered to the remaining partners. *See* [RUPA § 701], which details the purchase of the dissociated partner's interest. In contrast to consenting to the continuation of the business, Mrs. Creel made it plain that she wanted the business "dissolved and the affairs of the company wound up;" however, this does not mean a liquidation was required. Particularly in light of Maryland's recent adoption of RUPA, paragraph 7(d) of the partnership agreement can be interpreted to mean that because Mrs. Creel did not wish to remain in business with Lilly and Altizer, they had the option to buy out her deceased husband's interest.

In short, when subsections (a) and (d) of paragraph 7 are read in conjunction, it is apparent that the partners did not intend for there to be a liquidation of all partnership assets upon the death of a partner. Paragraph 7(a) delineates the winding-up procedure, which was methodically followed by Lilly and Altizer. Paragraph 7(d) dictates what happens to the partnership in the event of a partner's death, and it can be interpreted as allowing a buy-out option if the deceased partner's estate no longer wishes to remain in business with the surviving partners, as was clearly the case here. Therefore, the trial judge could have concluded that Lilly and Altizer exercised this 7(d) buy-out option, and subsequently began a new partnership, when they followed the winding-up procedure dictated by 7(a) and presented the Creel estate with its share of Joe's Racing.

Assuming *arguendo* that the Joe's Racing partnership agreement cannot be interpreted as outlining an alternative to liquidation in winding up the partnership in the event of a dissolution caused by a partner's death, we still find that a sale of all partnership assets is not required under either UPA or RUPA in order to ascertain the true value of the business. Support for this is found in Maryland's recent adoption of RUPA, which encourages businesses to continue in either their original or successor form, and also the holdings of out-of-state cases where other options besides a "fire sale" have been chosen when a partnership is dissolved under UPA. *See* full discussions in Part II.A. and B., *supra*.

We agree with the trial court and the intermediate appellate court that there is nothing in Maryland's UPA, in particular [UPA sections 37 and 38], or any of our case law that supports an unequivocal requirement of a forced sale in a situation akin to the instant case. * * *

b.

We find it is sound public policy to permit a partnership to continue either under the same name or as a successor partnership without all of the assets being liquidated. Liquidation can be a harmful and destructive measure, especially to a small business like Joe's Racing, and is often unnecessary to determining the true value of the partnership. *See Arnold v. Burgess*, 747 P.2d 1315, 1322 (Idaho Ct. App. 1987)("A forced sale of partnership assets will often destroy a great part of the value of the business and may prevent the continuation of a valuable source of livelihood for former partners."). We now explore the "true value of the partnership" issue and whether liquidation is the only way to obtain it.

In the instant case, per paragraph 7(a) of the partnership agreement and [UPA § 43], the Creel estate had the right to ask the surviving partners for an accounting of Mr. Creel's interest in Joe's Racing as of the date of dissolution. * * *

> [t]he right to an accounting is not a right to force the winding up partners to liquidate the assets. The personal representative of a deceased

partner is entitled to receive, on behalf of the estate, as an ordinary creditor, the value of the decedent's partnership interest as of the date of dissolution, *i.e.*, the date of the decedent's death. (Emphasis added).

In accordance with both the partnership agreement and UPA, Lilly and Altizer provided Mrs. Creel with an accounting, which was based on the valuation performed by the accountant they hired. Mrs. Creel contends that this accounting did not reflect the true value of Joe's Racing, and as a result the estate did not receive its proportionate share of the partnership.

First, we note that Mrs. Creel did not contest the figures that the surviving partner's accountant derived until approximately a year and a half after her husband's death and one month before trial. At this late date, Mrs. Creel made a request for a court-appointed auditor per Maryland Rule 2-543(b) but the trial court correctly found that "where a request for an auditor is made one month before trial in an action pending in excess of one year, such a referral would cause unnecessary delay in the resolution of this case. Furthermore, the Court... finds that the interests of the parties can be properly determined by the Court." Moreover, if Mrs. Creel was so concerned that the accounting rendered by Lilly and Altizer's accountant was incorrect, then she should have immediately hired her own appraiser to review the accountant's work and/or make an independent valuation of Joe's Racing. * * *

Second, we disagree as to Mrs. Creel's argument that the accountant's valuation was in error and that the trial court subsequently arrived at an incorrect distribution of Mr. Creel's interest in the partnership. Mrs. Creel maintains that the only way to ascertain the true value of her deceased husband's interest in Joe's Racing is to liquidate all of its assets but we agree with the trial court, which held:

> The surviving parties under the Code and existing case law had to account for the inventory and pay to the Estate its appropriate share, *but not sell off the assets in a liquidation sale.* (Emphasis added)..

In making his findings, the trial judge looked to paragraph 7(a) of the partnership agreement and also [UPA section 40], which outlines the rules of distribution in settling accounts between partners after dissolution. * * *

Finally, Mrs. Creel contends that the accountant's valuation improperly considered only the book value of the business and not its market value. "Book value" refers to the assets of the business, less its liabilities plus partner contributions or "equity." "Market value" includes the value of such intangibles as goodwill, the value of the business as an ongoing concern, and established vendor and supplier lines, among other factors. Again, we concur with the trial court's findings as to the valuation of Joe's Racing.

In making no finding of goodwill value, for example, the trial court likely considered the fact that Joe's Racing had only been operating a little over a year before the partnership was formed, and after Lilly and Altizer became partners with Mr. Creel the business was only in existence for nine months before Mr. Creel died. On these facts, it is reasonable for the trial court to conclude—without any evidence presented to the contrary—that a small business selling NASCAR memorabilia, which had been operating for barely two years, did not possess any goodwill value.

c.

Our goal in this case, and in cases of a similar nature, is to prevent the disruption and loss that are attendant on a forced sale, while at the same time preserving the right of the deceased partner's estate to be paid his or her fair share of the partnership. With our holding, we believe this delicate balance has been achieved. For the reasons stated, we hold that paragraph 7, subsections (a) and (d), of the partnership agreement should be interpreted as outlining an alternative method of winding-up Joe's Racing and arriving at its true value other than a "fire sale" of all its assets. Even if there were no partnership agreement governing this case, however, we hold that Maryland's UPA—particularly in light of the legislature's recent adoption of RUPA—does not grant the estate of a deceased partner the right to demand liquidation of a partnership where the partnership agreement does not expressly provide for continuation of the partnership and where the estate does not consent to continuation. To hold otherwise vests excessive power and control in the estate of the deceased partner, to the extreme disadvantage of the surviving partners. We further hold that where the surviving partners have in good faith wound up the business and the deceased partner's estate is provided with an accurate accounting allowing for payment of a proportionate share of the business, then a forced sale of all partnership assets is unwarranted.

*   *   *

III. CONCLUSION

We hold that Maryland's UPA does not grant the estate of a deceased partner the right to demand liquidation of a partnership where the partnership agreement does not expressly provide for continuation of the partnership and where the estate does not consent to continuation. Winding up is not always synonymous with liquidation, which can be a harsh and unnecessary measure towards arriving at the true value of the business. A preferred method in a good faith winding up is the one used in this case—the payment to the deceased partner's estate of its proportionate share of the partnership. Thus, we further hold that where the surviving partners have in good faith wound up the business and the deceased partner's estate is provided with an accurate accounting allowing for payment of a proportionate share of the business, then a forced sale of all partnership assets is generally unwarranted. * * *

JUDGMENT OF THE COURT OF SPECIAL APPEALS AFFIRMED. COSTS IN THIS COURT AND THE COURT OF SPECIAL APPEALS TO BE PAID BY PETITIONER.

Notes

1. Under the UPA, the death of a partner dissolves the partnership. UPA § 31(4). As discussed earlier in this Chapter, on dissolution, unless otherwise agreed, each partner has the right to liquidation (the right to have partnership obligations discharged, and the partner's interest in cash). UPA § 38(a). Arguably, the estate of the deceased partner does not have the same right. UPA section 38(a) gives the right to liquidation to *partners*. The estate is only an assignee of the deceased partner's interest in the partnership, but not a partner. UPA § 27. As such, the estate, has only the right to receive the deceased partner's interest and to an accounting. UPA § 27(2).

On the other hand, UPA section 41(3) refers to the continuation of the business of a dissolved partnership "with the consent of... the representative of the estate of the deceased partner". This seems to imply that the business of the partnership cannot be continued without the consent of the "estate."[A] As discussed in *Creel v. Lilly,* many courts have so held.

2. Under the RUPA, the death of a partner results in the *dissociation* of the deceased partner from the partnership. RUPA § 601(7)(I). As discussed in Chapter 15, a withdrawal *by express will* also dissolves the partnership, and triggers a winding up. By contrast, a partner's death results in the dissociation of the deceased partner, RUPA § 601(4), but does not cause a dissolution. RUPA § 801(1). Under RUPA section 603(a), where a partner's dissociation does *not* result in a dissolution and winding up, Article 7 of the RUPA applies. That is, the partnership must purchase (or cause the purchase) of the deceased partner's interest in the partnership. RUPA § 701(a).

> UPA Section 31(4) provides for the dissolution of a partnership upon the death of any partner, although by agreement the remaining partners may continue the partnership business. RUPA Section 601(7)(I), on the other hand, provides for dissociation upon the death of a partner who is an individual, rather than dissolution of the partnership. That changes existing law.... Normally, under RUPA, the deceased partner's transferable interest in the partnership will pass to his estate and be bought out under Article 7.

RUPA § 601 Comment 8.

3. In *Creel v. Lilly,* the court found that, although Paragraph 7 of the partnership agreement was "a crude attempt to draft a 'continuation clause' in the form of a buy-out option".

4. In *Creel v. Lilly,* the court indicated that UPA section 38 requires only a winding up of partnership affairs, but does not require a liquidation. From the opinion in *Creel v. Lilly,* it is not clear that the partners who continued the *business* of the partnership (though under a different name) *discharged* existing partnership obligations. In that connection, note that the partnership's lease did expire. Did the partnership have any outstanding debts or contracts? Would that have made a difference to the court?

5. One of the traditional arguments for avoiding liquidation is that it is too drastic a remedy, that it can destroy the value of an ongoing business. That argument assumes that partnership assets must be sold piecemeal. If the concern is preserving the value of an ongoing business conducted by the partnership, the business can be sold in its entirety? Ongoing businesses are sold often enough to give rise to a class of businesses that specializes in the sale of other businesses — "business brokers." In the context of the sale of a small business, such as the one in *Creel v. Lilly,* who are the most likely buyers of the partnership's business?

6. In valuing the partnership for the purpose of a buy-out of the interest of a deceased partner, how should the value of the partnership be determined?

A. Estate law has its own entity-aggregate dispute. Though the estate is a discrete, segregated fund of assets, it is not considered to be an entity separate from the estate's representative.

a. The traditional view is that value is best determined by the market. In *Creel v. Lilly*, is there any indication that the court considered the fair market value of the partnership's business as a going concern?

b. In *Creel v. Lilly*, the deceased partner's interest was valued primarily at book value, and without any consideration for goodwill. The court affirmed the exclusion of goodwill on the basis that the business was too young to have any goodwill. As discussed later in this Chapter, goodwill is the value of the business as a going concern over the value of its assets. If the value of the business in *Creel v. Lilly* as a going concern was the same as the value of its assets, why would a liquidation of its assets have been "drastic" or "harsh?" Do you think that the partners who continued the business thought it had no value as a going concern? Does it make any difference that they changed the name of the business? Is the name of the business the sole source of goodwill?

7. In *Nicholes v. Hunt*, 273 Or. 255, 541 P.2d 820 (1975) (which was the model for Problem 16.1), both partners were competing for the right to continue the business of a partnership at-will in which there was no agreement giving either the right to continue. The court allowed Hunt, the inventor, to buyout the interest of Nicholes, the investor.

> In the case at bar, payment of creditors is not a problem. The partnership debts had been paid by [Hunt], the managing partner who started the business. A large portion of the assets have been reduced to cash and bank time certificates of deposit. The audit on which the trial court based its distribution of assets included a substantial sum for 'good will.' Although [Nicholes] contributed to the success of the shot manufacturing business there is evidence that [Nicholes] was not always attentive to the business or to the decisions and recommendations of [Hunt], the managing partner.
>
> We conclude, as [Hunt] contends and as the trial court found, that the equities lie with [Hunt] in this case. Further, since there was no evidence regarding the value which the partnership assets might command on the market, it is difficult for us to determine whether a sale would be beneficial or prejudicial to the respective parties. As earlier described, this is a unique, or unusual, business which requires particular knowledge of the remanufacturing process and ability to repair and operate the necessary machinery. [Nicholes] argues that he is entitled to purchase the 50 percent share of [Hunt] but this is no answer to the problem that confronted the trial court. [Hunt] conceived and designed the machinery and the method of operation, which was successfully operated for a number of years before formation of the partnership at will. [Nicholes] is not precluded from engaging in a like or similar business.

541 P.2d at 828. With both partners interested in continuing the business, wouldn't a court-supervised auction of business have been the best way to determine its value?

Hunt was fortunate in that the court gave him "custody" of the partnership business. If you had represented Hunt during the formation of the partnership, what contractual safeguards could you have used to protect his rights?

B. Distributions on Liquidation

1. In General

Problem 16.2
Read Problem 13.3, page 628.

Parker v. Northern Mixing Co.
Read case and following notes, page 629.

Note on Firm Financial Statements
Read Note on Firm Financial Statements, page 633.

Problem 16.3
Read Problem 13.4, page 636.

2. Service Partners

Problem 16.4
Read Problem 13.5, page 636.

Becker v. Killarney
Read case and following notes, page 637.

Parker v. Northern Mixing Co. (Part 2)
Read case and following notes, page 640.

C. Disputes about Partnership Property

Problem 16.5

Sisters X and Y were unemployed until one day in January they decided to start their own business, a neighborhood newspaper. Their only agreement was an informal oral one. X owned a small lot with a vacant garage on it. The sale value of the lot and garage was about $4000, and its rental value was about $100 per month. X offered to let the newspaper operate from the garage as the headquarters and office. Y found a used printing press for sale and purchased it for $3000, and she bought other furniture and supplies costing about $2000. The printing press and furniture and supplies were moved into the garage on February 1, and X and Y worked to sell advertising space and to produce a weekly edition for the next three months. They made enough income for that period of time to pay their operating costs, but no profit was earned. On May 1, X suffered a severe heart attack, and she was incapacitated for the next six months. Y ran the business alone for that six-month period, and $6000 was generated above the business expenses. X died on November 1. The business had remaining furniture and supplies worth about $1000 on November 1. No more business was conducted after November 1, and there were no outstanding claims or obligations against the business. The estate of X claimed one half of the value of the business or $5000 (one half of the $6000 profit, one half of the value of the printing press of $3000, and one half of the value of the supplies and furniture of $1000), as well as ownership of the lot and garage. Y argues as follows: (1) The estate gets nothing because Y contributed both the printing press and furniture and supplies and is entitled to the $6000 as wages, since X did not work for the business for the six months when the $6000 was earned; or (2) If the estate is to share in the assets of the business, then the lot and garage must be included so that Y gets one half of the sale value of the lot and garage. How should the assets be distributed between X's estate and Y? *See Cyrus v. Cyrus,* 242 Minn. 180, 64 N.W. 2d 538 (1954), and *Eckert v. Eckert,* 425 N.W. 2d 914 (N.D. 1988).

In Re Estate of Bolinger (Part 2)
971 P.2d 767, 1998 Mt. 303 (Mont. 1998)

TERRY N. TRIEWEILER, Justice.

[Re-read the facts of the case earlier in this Chapter.]

ISSUE 10

Did the District Court err when it refused to recognize the real property of the ranch as an asset of the partnership?

The District Court concluded that

[I]t was never intended by the [partners] that the land referred to in the Agreement should become an asset of the partnership to be distributed or taken into account on the dissolution of the partnership or death of a partner.

On that basis, it concluded that the partnership did not own the land and consequently made no award to the estate based upon its interest in the real property.

On cross-appeal, the estate contends that it is entitled to a share of the value of the real property. In reliance on § 35-10-203, MCA, it asserts that the land was acquired with partnership assets and therefore became partnership property. In the alternative, it asserts that because equitable principles require the inclusion of the land among the partnership assets, a resulting trust is created for the estate's benefit. Appellants contend in response that the partnership agreement clearly reflects the partners' intent to preserve the real property as solely Hal's property and not to transfer ownership to the partnership.

[RUPA section 204(c)] states:

Property is presumed to be partnership property if purchased with partnership assets even if not acquired in the name of the partnership or of one or more partners with an indication in the instrument transferring title to the property of the person's capacity as a partner or of the existence of a partnership.

As reflected in the statute, property is merely presumed to become property of the partnership if it is acquired with partnership assets. The presumption is rebuttable and may be overcome.

Whether property belongs to the partnership depends primarily on the intent of the partners. The partners' intent may be inferred from a variety of sources, such as their agreement and their conduct, although no single factor is determinative.

Here, the District Court relied primarily on the partnership agreement when it concluded that the partners did not intend that the land become partnership property. The agreement stated in relevant part:

[Hal] will contribute said lands for the use of said partnership and that in consideration thereof said partnership will make the annual payments due on a mortgage indebtedness owing against said lands... and will pay the cost of any necessary repairs or improvements in connection with said lands and all taxes levied against said lands during the term of this agreement.

The agreement also stated that Hal, in whose name title has always been held, reserved "the right to sell any or all of said lands," as well as the right to live in the home on the ranch.

The language of the agreement states that Hal contributed the land for use, and not outright as an asset of the partnership, as evidenced further by his reservation of the right to sell the land. His reserved right to live on the land also indicates that the parties had no intention of turning ownership of the land over to the partnership.

The District Court found that over $700,000 had been paid by the partnership for the use of the land, and it is that payment of funds on which the estate relies for its alleged interest in the land. As suggested above, payment of partnership funds does not by itself cause property to become an asset of the partnership. Nor is use by the partnership sufficient in and of itself to convert a partner's property into property of the partnership. In fact, it is not unusual for property to be used for partnership purposes although it does not belong to the partnership.

The estate offers no authority by which we might conclude that payments made by the partnership in consideration for use of land necessarily establish an intent on behalf of the partners that the property become a partnership asset, or that such payments necessarily alter the nature of ownership in the property. We look instead to the partners' intent, which in this case indicates clearly that Hal would retain ownership of the land.

Accordingly, we conclude that the District Court did not err when it refused to award the estate a share of the value of the land.

Notes

1. *Eckert v. Eckert*, 425 N.W.2d 914 (N.D. 1988), involved a partnership engaged in the business of farming and ranching. In the course of partnership business, one of the partners did business with various farm cooperatives. Be-

cause the cooperatives always dealt with one partner, all patronage credits arising out of partnership business stood in the name of that partner. The court held, that, in settling partnership affairs after the death of one of the partners, the cooperative patronage credits should be included as partnership property:

> Property which is titled in the name of an individual partner may nevertheless be partnership property. The determination whether property held in the name of an individual partner belongs to the partnership is a question of fact. The relevant inquiry is whether the partners intended that the property in question be partnership property or individual property.

*   *   *

The [provisions of UPA section 8] have consistently been construed to create a presumption that property acquired with partnership funds is partnership property. For example, the Court of Civil Appeals of Texas stated in *Conrad v. Judson*, [465 S.W.2d 819, 828 (Tex. Civ. App. 1971)]:

> We think there is a presumption, under the above authorities, and particularly the Texas Uniform Partnership Act, that property purchased with partnership funds is intended to be partnership property; and if one would contend otherwise the burden would be on him or her to offer proof of a different intention and to obtain an affirmative jury finding thereon.

> Cases from other jurisdictions which have adopted the Uniform Partnership Act are in accord. The presumption extends beyond purchases with partnership funds to any acquisition of property derived from partnership labor, materials, or other assets.

> In this state, a presumption shifts the burden of proof to the party against whom it is directed.

Problem 16.6

For nearly 20 years, Dawson was a partner at the Manhattan law firm of White & Case. The firm asked Dawson to withdraw as a partner. When the talks stalled, White & Case voted to dissolve the partnership and re-form without Dawson.

White & Case's financial statements did not show goodwill as an asset of the firm. The White & Case partnership agreement provided that "the Firm name" and goodwill were "deemed to be of no value." Under the partnership agreement, partners being admitted to White & Case paid nothing for goodwill. Moreover, the partnership agreement provided that, in determining the amount to be paid to a withdrawing or a retiring partner, the value of goodwill was to be excluded.

Dawson claims that the firm's goodwill should be included as an asset in valuing his interest. *See, Dawson v. White & Case*, 88 N.Y.2d 666, 672 N.E.2d 589, 649 N.Y.S.2d 364 (1996).

Salinas v. Rafati

948 S.W.2d 286 (Tex. 1997)

OWEN, Justice, delivered the opinion for a unanimous Court.

In this case, we consider whether an award of $1,428,000 to a physician for his interest in a professional partnership upon dissolution is supported by any evidence and whether the intangible assets of the dissolved partnership include the goodwill and individual earning capacities of the former partners. We conclude that goodwill attributable to individual partners is not an asset subject to division upon dissolution and that the evidence does not support the jury's award.

Three radiologists, Drs. S.A. Rafati, Guillermo Salinas, and Abel E. Salazar, were the general partners of Radiology Associates located in Laredo, Texas. Their written partnership agreement addressed the death or withdrawal of a partner and included a noncompetition provision that applied to a withdrawing partner, but the agreement did not specify the duration of the partnership, nor did it address dissolution. The partnership enjoyed considerable financial success for a number of years, but over time the relationship among the three physicians deteriorated. Eventually, there were discussions about Rafati's possible withdrawal, but agreement could not be reached. Ultimately, Salinas notified Rafati by letter that Salinas was dissolving the partnership by his "express will."

At the time of dissolution, the partnership's assets consisted of accounts receivable, cash on hand, office furniture and equipment, utility deposits, and a leased office that was used only for billing. The partnership employed one radiologist on a fixed-salary basis and had several other employees who were highly skilled, although they were not physicians. The partnership had also enjoyed the benefits of a contract between Salinas and Mercy Hospital under which Salinas was the director of the radiology department. The contract permitted his partners and associates to perform the work of the radiology department if the written approval of the Hospital were obtained. The parties dispute whether this contract was personal to Salinas or a partnership asset. The Hospital owned all the medical equipment used by the partners in the practice of radiology, and the physicians saw their patients at the Hospital.

After dissolution of the partnership, the accounts receivable and cash on hand were divided without dispute. However, Salinas and Salazar then formed a new partnership called Associates in Diagnostic Radiology in which Rafati was not included. The new partnership continued the practice of radiology using the same office space and employees as the former partnership, and the contract between Salinas and Mercy Hospital continued in effect.

Rafati and his wife sued Salinas and Salazar alleging breach of fiduciary duty and wrongful dissolution. They further alleged that Rafati had not been fully paid for his share of the partnership, which they contended consisted of more than just the tangible assets and accounts receivable. At trial, the Rafatis' expert placed the value of the partnership between $756,821 and $2,940,000, which was derived by predicting what the partnership's future income would have been. The defendants' expert valued the partnership at approximately $405,000, which was based on the value of tangible assets and approximately $500,000 in accounts receivable, less the cost of collection and partnership liabilities. As already noted, however, the accounts receivable had been divided without dispute upon dissolution.

The jury found that Salinas and Salazar had breached their fiduciary duty to Rafati and had wrongfully dissolved the partnership. Damages were assessed at $400,000 for breach of fiduciary duty, $1,000,000 for wrongful dissolution, and $20,000 in attorneys' fees in connection with the wrongful dissolution claim. The jury also found that Rafati was owed $8,000 for cash advances made to Salazar. Finally, in response to Questions 7 and 8, the jury found that Rafati did not receive payment in full for his interest in the partnership after dissolution and awarded the Rafatis $714,000 from each defendant, for a total of $1,428,000 as the value of Rafati's one-third partnership interest.

Salinas and Salazar moved to set aside the findings on wrongful dissolution and breach of fiduciary duty, and all parties filed motions in connection with Questions 7 and 8. Salinas and Salazar moved to disregard the answers to Questions 7 and 8, arguing that under the [Uniform Partnership Act, § 38(1)], Rafati's interest consisted only of his one-third share of the physical assets of the partnership and that there was no evidence to support the jury's answer to the valuation issue. The jury's answers to these issues presented a problem for the Rafatis even though the findings were very favorable. The jury's award reflected a partnership value of at least $4,284,000, more than twice the amount alleged in the Rafatis' pleadings. The Rafatis moved to amend their pleadings and, in another motion, sought leave to conform the pleadings to the jury's verdict and for judgment on that verdict. At the hearing on the parties' competing motions, the trial court granted the motion of Salinas and Salazar to disregard the jury's findings in Questions 7 and 8, but then rendered judgment for the Rafatis in accordance with the remainder of the verdict. All parties appealed.

The court of appeals held that there was no wrongful dissolution or breach of fiduciary duty as a matter of law and rendered judgment that the Rafatis take nothing regarding those claims. The Rafatis have not sought review of that determination in this Court. The court of appeals also held that some evidence supported the jury's award of $714,000 from each defendant for Rafati's interest in the partnership. Accordingly, the court of appeals held that the trial court should have allowed the Rafatis to amend their pleadings to conform to the verdict, and the court of appeals modified the judgment to award the Rafatis the amount that the jury found in response to Questions 7 and 8. Salinas and Salazar seek review of that judgment.

Although in this Court neither party makes any reference, by citation or otherwise, to the statutes governing partnerships, we note that the dissolution of the partnership between Rafati, Salinas, and Salazar is governed by the Texas Uniform Partnership Act (TUPA). The more recently enacted Texas Revised Partnership Act (TRPA) applies to partnerships formed on or after January 1, 1994 and to those partnerships formed before that date that elect to be governed by the new act. *Id.* art. 6132b-10.03(a). The Rafati, Salinas, Salazar partnership was formed in 1987, and they made no election under TRPA.

The dissolution of a partnership that is not in contravention of the partnership agreement is governed by [UPA] § 38(1). Partners may by agreement provide for a different distribution upon dissolution. However, the only issue presented to us regarding dissolution is whether there is some evidence to support the jury's valuation of this dissolved professional partnership. The principal contention of Salinas and Salazar in this Court is that the ability of the former partners to earn income in the practice of medicine is not evidence of the value of the dissolved partnership.

The jury found that Salinas and Salazar should each pay the Rafatis the amount of $714,000, for a total of $1,428,000 for Rafati's one-third interest in the partnership. This means that the jury valued the partnership as a whole at $4,284,000. There was no evidence from which the jury could find anything approaching this amount. The expert witness called by the Rafatis valued the entire partnership at between $756,821 and $2,940,000. There was no other evidence from which the jury could have concluded that the partnership was worth $4,284,000. A jury must have an evidentiary basis for its findings. Accordingly, the trial court did not err in disregarding the jury's findings in Questions 7 and 8, and the court of appeals erroneously set aside the trial court's determination.

On this basis alone, we must reverse the judgment of the court of appeals. Whether the Rafatis are entitled to a new trial turns on whether some evidence supports the jury's finding that Rafati was not fully compensated for his interest in the partnership. Under the Rafatis' theory of the case, the future earning capacities of former partners can be considered in valuing a professional partnership upon dissolution. The Rafatis offered evidence under this theory and would be entitled to a remand if this were a proper basis for damages. For reasons we discuss below, we conclude that under the facts of this case, the earning capacity of the former partners is personal to each of them and is not a partnership asset divisible upon dissolution.

The dissolution of this professional partnership was not wrongful, and the operation of the partnership as a business ceased. Salinas and Salazar formed a new partnership under a new name. There is no contention nor is there any evidence that the name of the former partnership had goodwill separate and apart from the personal talents and abilities of each of the partners or that any partner had the right or the desire to form a new partnership using the name of the dissolved partnership.

Rather, the Rafatis contend that the value of the dissolved partnership should include the ability the partnership would have had to produce income in the future. Although the Rafatis' expert purported to remove any personal goodwill from his valuation of the partnership, he testified unequivocally that his valuation is based on what Salinas and Salazar could earn over time if they and their employees continued the practice of radiology in Laredo in the same manner as they had done in the past.

Salinas and Salazar contend, and we agree, that the Rafatis treated the partnership upon dissolution as if it were a salable, going concern, when by definition, the partnership ceased to exist after the period of time necessary to wind up outstanding matters. The value that the Rafatis attributed to the partnership was largely based on the talents and abilities of the individual physicians and their ability to generate income in the future. To the extent that the valuation of the dissolved partnership was based on the goodwill attributable to the personal skills and talents of the former partners, it improperly took into account intangibles that were not partnership assets.

Our Court considered the rights of partners upon dissolution in *Rice v. Angell,* 73 Tex. 350, 11 S.W. 338 (1889). Although that decision is of considerable age, its reasoning remains sound today. The Court in *Rice* very thoughtfully explored the boundaries of goodwill when a partnership is dissolved and one or more of its former members continues to engage in the same type of business. The dispute in *Rice* was between two men who had been partners in an insurance agency. The plaintiff had initially purchased an interest in the partnership, but after several years, his colleague dissolved their relationship. This Court recognized in *Rice* and later in *Nail v. Nail,* 486 S.W.2d 761 (Tex.1972), that a distinction must be drawn between the goodwill that attaches to a professional person because of confidence in the skill and ability of the individual and the goodwill of a trade or business that arises from its location or its well-established and well-recognized name. When a trading partnership dissolves, one partner may secure the right to continue the business at "the old stand." *Rice,* 11 S.W. at 340. The probability that customers would resort to the old place of business may be deemed a valuable right.

We contrasted that kind of arrangement, however, with the dissolved partnership in *Rice.* In *Rice,* patronage was not affected by the location of the office, and the success of either individual in controlling the business they once shared depended on the personal capacity of each of the former partners to attract and hold the representation of insurance companies and clients. We observed that the agency relationships that had existed with a number of insurance companies ceased upon dissolution of the partnership and that each of the former partners would have the same opportunity as the other to compete for the right to represent insurance companies. The *Rice* decision was careful to distinguish situations in which the partnership had a generally recognized name, such as the "Galveston Insurance Agency," that would lead patrons to do business with any person or firm using that name, from a partnership name that was not generally recognized, composed of the names of the former partners.

Subsequently, in *Nail,* we recognized that although goodwill can exist as

an incident of a continuing business having locality or name,

the distinction has been drawn that

professional good will is not so much fixed or as localized as the good will of a trade, and attaches to the person of the professional man or woman as a result of confidence in his or her skill and ability.

Nail, 486 S.W.2d at 763. Nevertheless, there may be goodwill in a professional partnership that is separate from the skills or attributes of an individual member. A case illustrating such a situation is *Geesbreght v. Geesbreght,* 570 S.W.2d 427 (Tex.Civ.App.—Fort Worth 1978, *writ dism'd*), in which a physician owned shares in a professional corporation that provided emergency-room physicians to hospitals. The corporation had contracts with several hospitals and employed about fifty to one hundred physicians on a part-time basis and ten on a full-time basis to satisfy those contracts. The court of appeals drew a distinction between the goodwill built up by the physician personally at the hospital at which he practiced and the corporation's goodwill arising from the opportunity under its contracts to provide service to other hospitals at which he did not practice. The court of appeals reasoned that if the physician and other shareholders sold the corporation, the right to do business as that corporation would continue and the goodwill built up by the company would continue for a time.

The ultimate holding in *Geesbreght* was that the corporation had goodwill separate and apart from that of the physician as a professional practitioner. The goodwill of the company, apart from the goodwill associated with the physician himself, could be considered in dividing the community estate upon divorce. *Geesbreght* and *Nail* illustrate the considerations involved in determining whether an estate includes goodwill. Neither establishes an absolute rule.

This is not a case in which the partnership at issue is an ongoing enterprise. The issue is whether there was goodwill attributable to Rafati's former partnership separate and apart from the skills, personalities, and attributes of the professionals themselves and whether such goodwill survived the dissolution. The Rafatis are claiming that an asset of the dissolved partnership, namely goodwill, has been requisitioned by the former partners and is being used in their new partnership.

The Rafatis' expert candidly conceded that the skills of the physicians were the primary asset of the business. Even had he not done so, it is evident that a valuation based on the earnings of the physicians improperly takes into account goodwill that is attributable only to the professionals personally. Rafati's former partnership is indistinguishable from the one at issue in *Rice*. Each of the former partners now has the opportunity to compete for the partnership's former business. Indeed, Rafati opened a radiology practice at a new location in competition with Salinas and Salazar. Rafati's true complaint is that he has not been as successful in that competition as he would have liked.

The Rafatis' attempt to harness the future earning capacity of Salinas and Salazar highlights the incongruity of a rule of law that would allow a partner to recover a share of a former partner's ability to generate income under the guise of goodwill. If the Rafatis' theory were correct, Salinas and Salazar could also seek to recover from Rafati the value of the goodwill he took to his new practice. There would be offsetting claims, with the more successful former partners compensating the less successful ones indefinitely. This would defeat the very purpose of a dissolution of a partnership, which is to sever the ties that bind partners and to terminate the sharing of profits. If we were to accept the Rafatis' arguments, we would be undercutting the right of partners to dissolve their partnership. We would also be engrafting onto the partnership agreement a postdissolution sharing arrangement based on the personal earning capacities of other partners.

The Rafatis point to the fact that Salinas and Salazar continued to do business in the same location, with the same employees, and under the same contract with Mercy Hospital. However, the evidence showed that the office was used only for billing purposes; the doctors performed their services at the Hospital. There was no evidence that any business was directed to the former partnership by virtue of the location of the billing office. The lease covering the office building might have a value divisible on dissolution as a tangible asset, but no evidence was presented to establish its value. All the employees at issue were at-will employees. Upon termination of Radiology Associates, Rafati had the same opportunity to hire them as did the new partnership. In fact, the testimony indicated that he spoke with several of them about that possibility. The employees were not assets of the partnership.

The remaining point of contention is the contract with Mercy Hospital. The Hospital had discussions with Rafati and Salinas that led to the execution of the contract that is at issue. The Hospital sought a single physician to assume the responsibilities of director of the radiology department and would not agree to a contract other than with an individual physician. The Hospital was willing to contract with either Salinas or Rafati, who were partners at that time, but not both. Rafati and Salinas agreed that it should be Salinas since Rafati had no interest in performing administrative functions, which were required by the contract.

The written agreement with the Hospital provided in part:

The Director shall be present in the Hospital and shall be available when needed for consultation...and for performing and reporting radiological examinations as required by patient volume and pre-established schedules and emergency situations. If the approval of the Hospital is obtained in writing, the work of the Radiologist may be done in part [by] such assistant radiologists as may be duly appointed to the medical staff by the Hospital and employed by the Director or associates or partners in practice with the Director who have been appointed to the medical staff. Nothing contained in this paragraph or in this agreement shall be construed to permit assignment by the Director of any rights under this agreement, and such assignment is expressly prohibited.

Thus, the contract provided that the Hospital could allow radiologists who were employees, associates, or partners of Salinas to assist him. However, Salinas could not assign any rights under the contract to anyone, including his partners. Salinas did testify, however, that although the contract was with him and him alone, he in fact had shared the benefits of the contract with his partners.

Although Rafati had in the past benefited from the contract with Mercy Hospital as a partner of Salinas, the provisions of the contract and the facts surrounding its execution lead to the conclusion that it was personal to Salinas and was not a partnership asset. If Salinas had died while the partnership with Rafati was in effect, neither Rafati nor Salazar would have had the right to insist that the Hospital allow one of them to assume the rights and responsibilities of Salinas. The contract with the Hospital would have terminated on the death of Salinas. Or, if the partnership agreement had provided for a definite term and at the end of that term Salinas had chosen not to renew or extend the agreement, neither Salazar nor Rafati would have had the right to assume all or part of the duties of Salinas under the contract or to require the Hospital to allow either of them to work in the radiology department.

Further, it has generally been recognized that the goodwill of a professional partnership cannot be the subject of an involuntary sale or transfer. Rafati could not compel Salinas to perform the contract to satisfy partnership obligations, nor could the contract be sold to other physicians. Unlike tangible property that may be held in the name of one partner for the partnership, such as title to land, the contract between Salinas and Mercy Hospital was one for personal services to be rendered by Salinas. Given the nature of this contract, its value after dissolution should not be considered in determining Rafati's share of the partnership assets.

Notes

1. "Goodwill" has been defined as the reasonable expectation of continued patronage of a business by its clientele. That is, goodwill is the business's ex-

pected future income. Goodwill is based largely on the *reputation* of the business, and depends on several factors, including continuity of location, continuity of name, customer lists, contracts with employees, customers and suppliers, and the like.

2. Conflicts between partners regarding the valuation of a partnership's goodwill often arise after the dissolution of a partnership, particularly where some of the partners wish to continue the partnership's business. Often, the continuing partners wish to minimize the valuation of goodwill. They do so not because they think goodwill is not valuable (or else why do they wish to continue doing business?) but because they do not want to pay the departing partner for his or her share of goodwill. Such conflicts can be avoided at the planning stage by having the partners agree in advance as to the method of valuing goodwill.

3. Professional partnerships—lawyers, doctors—pose special problems in considering the question of goodwill. Until somewhat recently, the common law rule was that partnerships in businesses involving personal skills had no goodwill as a partnership. Because the reputation of the business could not be separated from the *individual* skills and reputations of each partner, not only was there no *partnership* asset of goodwill, even the individual goodwill was inherently unsalable. Most modern courts have rejected this reasoning, and recognize that professional partnerships may have goodwill. See, Gary S. Rosin, *The Hard Heart of the Enterprise: Goodwill and the Role of the Law Firm*, 39 So. Tex. L. Rev. 315 (1998).

4. In *Dawson v. White & Case*, 88 N.Y.2d 666, 672 N.E.2d 589, 649 N.Y.S.2d 364 (1996), on which Problem 16.4 was based, the court explained:

> The first issue is whether White & Case possessed goodwill that was capable of distribution upon dissolution. When applied to law firms, the term "goodwill" refers to the "ability to attract clients as [a] result of [the] firm's name, location, or the reputation of [its] lawyers" (Black's Law Dictionary 695 [6th ed]). We conclude that the Special Referee erred in including goodwill as an asset of White & Case in the partnership accounting.
>
> Analysis begins with the statutory instruction that "[I]n settling accounts between the partners after dissolution,... *subject to any agreement to the contrary* ...[t]he assets of the partnership" include the "partnership property" ([UPA § 40(a)(I) [emphasis added]). By statute, then, the partners are free to exclude particular items from the class of distributable partnership property, and such an agreement will be enforced in an accounting proceeding. Thus, even if a given partnership might be said to possess goodwill, the courts will honor an agreement among partners— whether express or implied—that goodwill not be considered an asset of the firm. Elucidating this principle, Judge Cardozo explained:
>
> > Good will, when it exists as incidental to the business of a partnership, is presumptively an asset to be accounted for like any other by those who liquidate the business.... The course of dealing, however, can stamp it with a different quality. Partners may contract that good will, though it exist, shall not 'be considered as property or as an asset of the co-partnership'.... The contract may 'be expressly made,' or it may 'arise by implication, from other contracts and the acts and conduct of the parties' "

In *Brown,* the issue was whether a brokerage company was obligated to account to a former partner for the company's goodwill even though goodwill was not mentioned in the partnership agreement or in the company's books, incoming members paid nothing for goodwill, and a recently retired partner did not receive compensation for goodwill. The Court concluded that the trier of fact might infer "from the course of dealing between the partners when new members came in and old ones went out that by tacit understanding there was to be no accounting for good will." The same conclusion was reached in the context of a law firm dissolution in the case of *Siddall v Keating* (8 AD2d 44, aff'd 7 NY2d 846).

The pertinent facts of this case are similar to those of Brown and Siddall: new White & Case partners never paid anything for goodwill; departing partners never received a payment for goodwill; and goodwill was not listed as an asset in the firm's financial statements. Indeed, the partners' intention not to credit goodwill is even more apparent in this case than in either Brown or Siddall. The White & Case partnership agreement contained the following provisions:

> It is expressly understood and agreed that no consideration has been or is to be paid for the Firm name or any good will of the partnership, as such items are deemed to be of no value" (art fourth [c]); and

> The computation of the amount with which a Former Partner shall be charged or credited...shall exclude any value for the good will of the partnership or the Firm name, as such items are deemed to be of no value" (art sixth [d]).

Dawson attempts to avoid these provisions by claiming they are inapplicable. He contends that article fourth relates solely to White & Case's 1978 "sale and purchase" arrangement by which the partners reallocated their partnership percentages and that article sixth only applies in the event of a partner's withdrawal, retirement or death, not to this expulsion situation. We disagree and find that the partnership agreement reflects the binding written expression of the terms under which these partners assented to associate with each other and evinces their intention that goodwill be deemed "of no value." Its provisions reinforce our holding that, for purposes of this partnership accounting, White & Case lacks distributable goodwill.

We note that the holding in this case is based on the specific facts presented, and should not be construed as a prohibition against the valuation, in the appropriate case, of law firm goodwill. In addition, the existence of law firm goodwill has been recognized in conjunction with the recent promulgation of Code of Professional Responsibility DR 2-111 (A), which authorizes the sale of "a law practice, including good will," by a "lawyer retiring from a private practice of law, [or] a law firm one or more members of which are retiring from the private practice of law with the firm" (see, 22 NYCRR 1200.15-a [a]).

To the extent that dictum in *Siddall* stands for the proposition that a professional business, as a matter of law, cannot have any goodwill apart from the goodwill of its constituent members, we note that this rationale has been rejected by this Court in a different context and has been superseded by the economic realities of the contemporary practice of law, illustrated by attorney advertising, internationalization of law firms, and other professional developments. In short, the ethical constraints against the sale of a law practice's goodwill by a practicing attorney no longer warrant a blanket prohibition against the valuation of law firm goodwill when those ethical concerns are absent.

D. Right to Wind Up

In addition to the basic question of what procedures are to be followed upon dissolution of a business entity, the equally fundamental question of who may or must represent the firm during its liquidation arises. After all, considerable discretion and judgment may have to be exercised regarding many details of the liquidation, as the business completes contracts that had been entered into prior to dissolution and as the business is reduced to cash. Who is at the helm during the period after dissolution can be very important as well because liabilities for both the firm, and its co-owners in some circumstances, may result. See, UPA §§ 34, 35; RUPA §§ 702, 703, 804, 806; RULPA §§ 608, 801; ULLCA §§ 407, 703, 804.

Questions about rights to control winding up assume even greater significance when you realize that, by the time of liquidation, the honeymoon is over. As the following materials indicate, business break-ups are often as acrimonious and dispute-ridden as are their family counterparts.

Problem 16.7

In 1998, Maria, Naomi and Olga formed an unincorporated firm to operate an arts and crafts retail shop under the trade name "Maria's Maravillas". Maria, Naomi, and Olga are the firm's only owners, and they have equal interests in its capital, profits and losses. The agreement among the owners sets neither any definite term of the firm nor any specific undertaking for which it was organized.

Two years into the operation of the firm, the firm had yet to break even. Maria became disenchanted with the firm's prospects for future success. Maria sent Naomi and Olga a written notice of her withdrawal from the firm, effective immediately.

The owners disagree as to how the firm should be wound up. Naomi and Olga argue that Maria's Maravillas should be continue to operate for a reasonable time to allow for the sale of the business as a going concern. Maria believes that Maria's Maravillas is not sufficiently successful to permit its sale as a going concern, and that continuing to operate the firm risks increasing the firm's losses. Maria demands that the firm's assets be sold piecemeal.

Naomi and Olga have filed suit against Maria in a court of competent jurisdiction. They make the following claims:

I. Maria wrongfully dissociated from the firm.

II. As a result, Maria has no right to participate in its winding up.

III. In any event, as a majority of the owners, Naomi and Olga may continue to operate Maria's Maravillas for a reasonable time while seeking to sell the store as a going concern.

Maria has filed a counter-claim in which she asks for judicial supervision of the winding up of the firm, and the appointment of a receiver.

In answering the following questions, assume that, except as described, the agreement among the owners has no provisions that would affect your answer.

a. If the owners are partners in a partnership under the UPA, how should the court rule on the parties' claims? *See* UPA §§ 31(2), 33, 37 & 38(2).

b. If owners are partners in a partnership under the RUPA, , how should the court rule on the parties' claims? *See* RUPA §§ 601(1), 602(b), 603(b)(1), 801(2), 803 & 804.

c. If the owners are members in a member-managed LLC under the ULLCA, how should the court rule on the parties' claims? *See* ULLCA §§ 601(1), 602(b), 603(b)(1), 801, 803 & 804.

d. If the owners are members in a manager-managed LLC under the ULLCA, with Maria as the manager designated in the operating agreement, how should the court rule on the parties' claims? *See* ULLCA §§ 601(1), 602(b), 603(b)(1), 801, 803 & 804.

e. If the firm is a limited partnership under the RULPA, with Maria as general partner, and Naomi and Olga as limited partners how should the court rule on the parties' claims? *See* RULPA §§ 602, 801(4) & 803.

Problem 16.8

Under the facts of Problem 16.7, suppose that under the applicable agreement among the owners, the firm was for a term of ten years. How, if at all, would that change your answers to the questions in Problem 16.7?

Investcorp, L.P. v. Simpson Investment Company, L.C.
267 Kan. 840, 983 P.2d 265 (Kansas 1999)

SIX, J.:

This summary judgment case involves a family controversy over the dissolution of a Limited Liability Company (LLC). The LLC was organized under the Kansas Limited Liability Company Act (the Act), K.S.A. 17-7601 *et seq.*

The Simpson Investment Company, L.C. (Company) members were deadlocked on important management issues. Several members withdrew to effect dissolution of the Company. The parties dispute whether these withdrawing members may now participate in dissolution, including liquidation of the Company's assets. The issue is control of dissolution. Both family factions rely on the Company's operating agreement to support their positions. The plaintiffs are the withdrawing Simpsons. The defendant Company is comprised of the remaining Simpsons.

* * *

The plaintiffs, as appellants, present three questions for review:

(1) Does the operating agreement allow the withdrawing members to participate in dissolution?

(2) Were the withdrawing members justified in assuming they could participate in the liquidation when they made their decision to withdraw? and

(3) Is the alleged "intransigence and incompetence" of the remaining members a genuine issue of material fact requiring an evidentiary hearing on the appointment of a receiver?

The district court, in entering partial summary judgment for the Company, held that dissolution is properly controlled by the defendant Company and its remaining members. Under the district court's ruling, the withdrawing Simpsons are no longer members of the Company. No finding was made on plaintiffs' contention that the current members of the Company are not competent to control dissolution, and no receiver was appointed.

We recast the three presented questions into the one dominant issue: Who is to control the Company's dissolution? The answer is, the Company. * * *

FACTS

The Company was formed in 1991 by two brothers, Donald and Alfred Simpson, to manage various land holdings of the Simpson family.

The operations of the Company are governed by an Amended and Restated Operating Agreement (operating agreement). Presently, the sole asset of the Company is 104 acres of commercial property in Johnson County. The Simpson family has held this land since 1941. Its worth is estimated at over $10 million. Donald and Alfred created several trusts for the benefit of their respective family members and themselves. These trust entities comprise the membership of the Company. (All members but one, Investcorp, L.P., are trusts.)

The Donald Simpson family (the remaining Simpsons) hold a 50% ownership, and the Alfred Simpson family (the withdrawing Simpsons and the Christopher A. Moran Trust [Moran Trust]) hold the other 50%. The Moran Trust, Mark Simpson, trustee, is aligned with the Alfred Simpson family but did not withdraw. The election of the Moran Trust to remain was strategically significant. Section 9.3 of the operating agreement required unanimous consent of the remaining members to continue the Company when dissolution is initiated by a member's resignation. The Moran Trust did not consent to continue the Company. The result was dissolution.

Each family had contradictory ideas about the disposition of the 104 acres. The plaintiffs claim they attempted to resolve the stalemate, offering, among other things, to divide the property. The operating agreement does not allow partition. It provides:

No member shall have any right to seek or obtain a partition of the Property or other assets of the Company, nor shall any Member have the right to any specific assets of the Company upon the liquidation of or any distribution from the Company.

Family differences were not resolved. Alfred's family (spearheaded by Mark) decided to force dissolution by withdrawing as members. They did so according to the terms of the operating agreement, which directed that any member could resign after giving 6 months' notice. The withdrawing members noticed their resignations on April 10, 1996.

Under the operating agreement, the Company could elect to purchase a withdrawing member's interest. The remaining members (the Donald Simpsons plus the Moran Trust) declined to do so. The Company refused to proceed with dissolution even though the operating agreement required unanimous consent to continue. The withdrawing members then sued the Company seeking dissolution and appointment of Mark Simpson as receiver.

The district court ruled that the Company was dissolved because unanimous consent by the remaining members to continue was not obtained. The Company had argued that the Company was not dissolved because a majority in interest of the remaining members had agreed to continue the business. The district court, in ordering dissolution, relied on the version of K.S.A. 17-7622(a)(3) existing in 1991 when the Company was formed. Under that statute, consent of all remaining members was required to continue the Company unless the articles of organization otherwise provided a right to continue. K.S.A. 17-7622(a)(3) was amended in 1995 to permit an LLC to continue by consent of a majority in interest of the remaining members. L.1995, ch. 245, § 16. The Company contended that the withdrawing members had no right to participate in dissolution because they were no longer members of the Company. The district court agreed.

DISCUSSION

Our primary question is who controls dissolution of the Company.

We first examine the operating agreement. A key section provides:

9.2 Effect of Dissolution. Except as provided in Section 9.3 below, upon the dissolution of the Company, the Members shall proceed to wind up, liquidate and terminate the business and affairs of the Company. In connection with such winding up, the Members shall liquidate and reduce to cash (to the extent necessary or appropriate) the assets of the Company as promptly as is consistent with obtaining a fair value therefore, satisfy and compromise the liabilities of the Company (which may include the establishment of reasonable cash reserves for any contingent or unforeseen liabilities of the Company), make distributions, in cash or in kind, to the Members and do any and all acts and things authorized by, and in accordance with, the Act and other applicable laws for the purpose of winding up and liquidation.

The district court construed Section 9.2 as excluding the withdrawing members from participating in dissolution. The district judge looked to the definition of "Members" in the operating agreement. Members are defined as

those persons who are members of the Company from time to time, including any Substitute Members.

The judge noted that under Kansas law, the phrase "from time to time" has been defined as meaning "at intervals" or "as occasion may arise." He reasoned,

This clearly indicates that the term "Members" as used in Section 9.2 of the Operating Agreement is to be construed as meaning the members of the Company as of the relevant time of examination of the document. That time is now. . . .

The district judge's order granting partial summary judgment to the Company provides insight into the nature of the controversy:

> On May 19, 1997, the Court ruled from the bench that, with respect to the issue of who should control dissolution of the Company, there is no genuine issue of material fact, summary judgment on this issue is proper, and partial summary judgment should be entered in favor of Defendant. The Company and its current Members (excluding Plaintiffs, who have resigned as members) are entitled to control dissolution pursuant to the following findings of fact and conclusions of law.

The conclusions of law included:

> 6. The Members are specifically authorized by this Order to preside over dissolution of the Company; and are specifically required, through the proper managers of the Company or otherwise, and pursuant to Section 9.2 of the Operating Agreement and pursuant to K.S.A. 17-7623 and 17-7624, to do all things and acts in connection with dissolution of the Company, including but not limited to [performing the listed dissolution duties set out in K.S.A. 17-7623, 17-7624(a), (b), (c)(1), (c)(2), (c)(3) and (c)(4); 17-7625; 17-7626; and 17-7627].

The plaintiffs reason anyone who withdrew before them and has no economic interest would not be allowed to participate, but that they should because they caused the dissolution and still have an economic interest. Plaintiffs' economic interest rationale interprets Section 9.2 to include some "former members" but not others.

The plaintiffs advance four arguments of construction that they believe signal an interpretative error by the district court:

> (1) Section 9.2 does not differentiate between "remaining members" and "former members." According to the plaintiffs, if the operating agreement had intended that only "remaining members" could participate in liquidation, the agreement would have said so.

> (2) Section 9.2 uses only the term "Members," thus, the logical context of that word includes all members, current and former, who have an economic interest in Company assets. The plaintiffs suggest this conclusion is borne out by examining the last time the word "members" is used in section 9.2 (in a provision stating distributions will be made to all members).

> (3) The term "remaining members" is used in other sections of the agreement, but was not used in section 9.2. Plaintiffs point to section 9.3 as an example:

>> Continuation. Notwithstanding the provisions of Section 9.1 and 9.2 above, the death, retirement, resignation, expulsion, bankruptcy or dissolution of a Member or the occurrence of any other event which terminates the continued membership of a

Member in the Company, shall not cause the Company to be wound up, liquidated or terminated, in the event all of the remaining Members unanimously consent to the continuation of the Company.

(4) the word "members" is not used anywhere else in the agreement to refer only to members remaining after the withdrawal of some members. The plaintiffs reason that "members" should include all who have a financial interest in the Company. As to the operating agreement's reference to "from time to time" in defining members, plaintiffs assert the relevant time is when they elected to initiate dissolution under the Act.

The Company argues that Section 9.2 does not distinguish between former members and current members because it consistently refers only to current members. Here, dissolution was caused by the withdrawing members and one remaining member who did not consent to the continuation of the Company. According to the Company, upon the dissolution, the plaintiffs were no longer members; thus, at the time of the judicially recognized dissolution, the only "members" left to proceed with liquidation were those who did not withdraw.

The plaintiffs direct us to authority from other jurisdictions and the Uniform Limited Liability Company Act (ULLCA) for guidance. The parties agree that the operating agreement is unambiguous. We are reluctant to agree with those conclusions.

Whether an instrument is ambiguous is a matter of law to be decided by the court. Generally, if the language of a written instrument is clear and can be carried out as written, there is no room for rules of construction. Here, the parties, in concert contend the operating agreement must be enforced as written. The plaintiffs say there is no ambiguity because clearly the agreement means what they say it means. With equal vigor, the Company says there is no ambiguity because clearly the agreement means what they say it means. (Here, "meaning," like beauty, is in the eye and interest of the beholder.)

We find only moderate assistance in resolving the question of who may participate in dissolution (winding up) by looking to either the ULLCA or the law of other states. The ULLCA § 803(a) excludes managers or members who dissolved wrongfully. Kansas does not distinguish between wrongful and rightful dissolving members. Some states take the ULLCA approach; however, there is a lack of consensus on the question and states have chosen different courses. *See e.g.,* Ariz.Rev.Stat. Ann. § 29-707(A) (1998) (treating a resigned member as an assignee); Ga.Code Ann. § 14-11-604(a) (1994) (stating the members or managers in control prior to dissolution may wind up); Md. Corporations and Associations Code Ann. § 4A-904(a) (1998 Supp.) (unless the members have provided otherwise, only "remaining members" may participate in winding up).

Resolution of the Simpson family dispute is fact driven. Each Simpson faction advances a reasonable view of the operating agreement's meaning of "member." However, we are persuaded that the plaintiffs' view should prevail. The use of "remaining Member" in Section 9.3 and also in Section 8.7 is significant in view of the fact that the term "remaining Member" is not found in Section 9.2. Section 8.7 says:

Adjustment of Percentage Interests.

Upon the purchase by the Company of a Selling Member's Interest in accordance with Section 8.5 above, the Percentage Interests of each remaining Member shall be adjusted in accordance with the provisions of this Section effective as of the Valuation Date. The Percentage Interest of each remaining Member shall be adjusted to that percentage determined by dividing the Percentage Interest of such Member prior to such adjustment by the total Percentage Interest of all Members (other than the Selling Member) prior to such adjustment. (Emphasis added.)

We are required by the cardinal rule of contract construction to determine the parties' intent from the four corners of the operating agreement. We are to construe "all provisions together and in harmony with each other rather than by critical analysis of a single or isolated provision." Metropolitan Life Ins. Co. v. Strnad, 255 Kan. 657, 671, 876 P.2d 1362 (1994). The parties did not make use of the word "remaining" in Section 9.2, but they did so elsewhere.

The many references to "member" in the Act when coupled with the operating agreement suggest the better view is that, in dissolution, "member" includes a withdrawing member having a financial interest in the Company's assets. For example, we note that Section 4.1 of the operating agreement, entitled Allocations and Distributions, provides in part:

(b) Liquidation proceeds shall be distributed in the following order of priority:

(I) To the payment of debts and liabilities of the Company (including those to the Members) and the expenses of liquidation; then

(ii) To the Managers in payment of the Manager Additional Contributions (if any) and any return thereon; then

(iii) The remainder to the Members in accordance with their respective positive Capital Account balances." (Emphasis added.)

Withdrawal as a dissolution trigger is contemplated by the operating agreement. Withdrawal here was proper. The operating agreement defined "members" as

those persons who are members of the Company from time to time, including any Substitute Members."

Each plaintiff has a financial interest in the Company. Until dissolution has run its course, plaintiffs are members. The plaintiffs were forced, by the Company's refusal to initiate dissolution, to sue. The Company refused to acknowledge the requirement of its own operating agreement, i.e., upon a member's resignation, the Company could only continue by unanimous consent of all remaining members.

We believe the resolution here is found in the interplay of the Act and the control provisions of the operating agreement. Compensation for all Simpson economic interests is not an issue. The Company does not deny the withdrawing Simpsons their right to be paid once the Company's assets are reduced to cash. The operating agreement places control in "the Managers."

The district court in its June 6, 1997, journal entry ordering dissolution said:

10. . . . [D]efendant is in dissolution within the meaning of the Kansas Limited Liability Company Act, and within the meaning of the Amended and Restated Operating Agreement, and should immediately take the steps set out in K.S.A. 17-7622(b) et seq. to conclude that dissolution, namely:

A. Immediately execute a statement of intent to dissolve in the form prescribed by the Secretary of State;

B. Immediately file such statement with the Secretary of State;

C. Pay all fees and franchise taxes as prescribed in the Kansas Limited Liability Company Act;

D. Upon the filing with the Secretary of State of a statement of intent to dissolve, cease to carry on its business, except insofar as may be necessary for the winding up of its business; and

E. Within 20 days after the Company has filed a statement of intent to dissolve, immediately cause notice thereof to be mailed to each creditor of, and claimant against, the limited liability company.

The court reserves any ruling upon the issue of who shall liquidate defendant's property pending further hearing.

The Company did not appeal from this order. The district court followed on August 18, 1997, with its second partial summary judgment order. Summary judgment placed control of dissolution in the Company and its current members "through the proper managers of the Company or otherwise." Control in the managers is consistent with K.S.A. 17-7627(b), which provides:

The certificate of dissolution shall be returned to the representative of the dissolved limited liability company. Upon the issuance of such certificate of dissolution, the existence of the company shall cease, except for the purpose of suits, other proceedings, and appropriate action as provided in the Kansas limited liability company act. The manager or managers in office at the time of dissolution, or the survivors of such managers, or, if none, the members, shall thereafter be trustees for the members and creditors of the dissolved limited liability company. In such capacity, the trustees shall have authority to distribute any company property discovered after dissolution, to convey real estate and to take such other action as may be necessary on behalf of and in the name of such dissolved limited liability company.

The managers in office at the time of dissolution are responsible for carrying out the acts of dissolution prescribed by the district court. This view is consistent with LLC commentary on the subject. See Callison & Sullivan, Limited Liability Companies, § 10.4, p. 73 (1994); 1 Ribstein & Keatinge on Limited Liability Companies, § 11.08 (1992).

The managers of the Company must dispose of the property and distribute its assets according to K.S.A. 17-7625. The road map for dissolution (the winding up of the Company) has been set by the district court. The managers are to follow that map in a timely manner. The district court did not err by placing control of dissolution in the Company through its managers; however, the plaintiffs, because they have a financial interest in the assets of the Company, are members during dissolution.

The plaintiffs' second issue, that they were justified in assuming they could participate in the liquidation when they made their decision to withdraw, is resolved by our including the plaintiffs as members during dissolution.

The Receiver Issue

The plaintiffs contend the "intransigence and incompetence" of the remaining members of the Company is a genuine issue of material fact. Upon suing the Company, the plaintiffs requested that Mark Simpson be appointed as a receiver to oversee dissolution (and if not Mark, then any qualified person other than a member of Donald's family).

On the question of whether a receiver should be appointed, the district judge ruled:

> The competency of the current members of [the Company] to control dissolution of the Company, including liquidation of the real property of the Company in the time frame previously ordered by the Court, is not an issue before the Court in the present posture of this case.

The district judge, in his second partial order of summary judgment said,

> Therefore, at this time, no receiver shall be appointed to preside over dissolution." (Emphasis added.)

The Act does not contain a statutory procedure for appointing a receiver. We note that other jurisdictions provide for the appointment of a receiver or trustee by the district court upon "cause shown." See e.g., Ga. Code Ann. § 14-11-604(a) (1994); Me. Rev. State. Ann. tit. 31, § 703(1) (1996).

When the district court ordered dissolution, it required the Company, through its managers, to complete dissolution procedures. Among other things, the Company is to liquidate and reduce its assets to cash as promptly as is consistent with obtaining a fair value therefor. Each Simpson faction submitted affidavits relating to the competency of the remaining members to effectively dispose of the 104 acres.

The plaintiffs argue that the district court erred by not holding an evidentiary hearing on the competence of the remaining members to accomplish the liquidation of the 104 acres. In submissions to the district court, Mark Simpson alleged that the remaining members:

> (1) lacked the necessary qualifications to proceed with liquidation; and

> (2) had no incentive to expedite the liquidation.

No other allegations were made, and no one other than Mark Simpson made allegations that the remaining members were unfit to carry out the liquidation. Mark opined,

> [T]he remaining Members are not capable of selling the assets for fair market value within the time frame required by the Operating Agreement.

According to Mark,

> The remaining Members have repeatedly demonstrated a total lack of sophistication, understanding and ability to effectively and responsibly deal with any potential buyer.

Mark insisted the remaining members had rejected commercially reasonable transactions. Mark believed only he had the necessary experience as a real estate broker to efficiently dispose of the property.

Both Donald and Reed (father and son in the faction opposing Mark) related their desire to hire an independent third-party broker to market the property and find a buyer. Donald explained that he and his brother, Alfred, agreed to hold the property together. The idea was to develop one parcel and sell when the surrounding area was in an optimum stage of development. Donald stated they could have sold the property in 20- or 40-acre tracts long ago. They declined to do so because they wished to wait until a planned project for development was in reach. Donald concluded by saying he agreed that the time had come to make serious efforts to sell the land.

Reed described the business sophistication of the Donald Simpson family in a second affidavit. He explained that

[1.] Donald was 69 years old, with 50 years of experience in finance, business, insurance, and real estate.

[2.] Nina Simpson (a co-trustee of several Company trust members) was 37 years old, with a BS in business from Kansas University and a masters in Business Administration from Dartmouth. Her career has been in banking, working at the Federal Reserve in Kansas City, and at MBNA in Baltimore, Maryland, in the area of commercial real estate lending.

[3.] Marshal Simpson (a trust beneficiary) was 39 years of age, with a BA in Economics from the University of Missouri at Kansas City. He made his career as a commercial real estate mortgage broker and is the owner of Union Commercial Mortgage of Kansas City.

[4.] Finally, Reed himself has a BS in Business Administration from the University of Arizona and a Masters degree in architectural management from Kansas University. He explained that his career in business, banking and real estate spanned 20 years. He currently has the responsibility for commercial investment real estate for a brokerage firm in the Kansas City area.

The record reflects that after the district court's order to proceed with dissolution, the Company did engage professional third-party brokers to sell the 104 acres.

The district court heard some evidence on liquidating the real estate after Plaintiffs filed their notice of appeal. Richard Baier, a professional broker with C.B. Richard Ellis, testified he was engaged by the Company to market the property in 1997. According to Baier, the Company timely responded to all offers. John Sweeney, of Terra Venture, Inc., engaged to assist in the retail marketing of the property, also testified. He testified his firm was actively marketing the property both as one parcel and as subparcels and pad sites.

We note the district court, in ruling that the competency of the current members of the Company is not an issue, prudently said:

The Court, by so ruling, does not mean to preclude any future review by this Court or any court of the compliance by the current members of Simpson Investment Company, L.C., with any order of this Court.

The district court did not err by failing to hold a full evidentiary hearing on the issue of the remaining members' alleged "incompetence and intransigence." The plaintiffs' allegations are minor accusations based on the subjective conclusions of Mark alone. Even if proved, Mark's allegations are insufficient to justify the appointment of a receiver. There were neither allegations of fraud, breach of fiduciary duty, or waste, see Browning v. Blair, 169 Kan. 139, 145, 218 P.2d 233 (1950), nor a showing of "good cause." The plaintiffs failed to produce a single compelling or constructive reason for the appointment of a receiver. The district court did not err by refusing to further entertain the plaintiffs' request.

Affirmed in part, reversed in part, and remanded:

(1) The Company through its manager trustees controls dissolution,

(2) the plaintiffs are "members" of the Company during dissolution, and

(3) refusing to appoint a receiver was not error.

On remand, the district court has jurisdiction to:

(a) monitor its previous orders as modified by this opinion,

(b) decide who the managers are to control dissolution, and

(c) consider any appropriate future matters that may arise concerning the Company's dissolution, including the appointment of a receiver, if either the requirements of Browning v. Blair, 169 Kan. 139, 218 P.2d 233 (1950) (fraud, breach of fiduciary duty or waste) or a showing of good cause have been met and the interests of all members will best be protected by the appointment of such receiver.

Notes

1. In *Investcorp, L.P. v. Simpson Investment Company, L.C.*, why does it matter whether the withdrawing Simpsons are "Members" for purposes of Section 9.2 of the LLC's operating agreement? Do you agree with the court's analysis of the operating agreement?

2. Once the court in *Investcorp, L.P. v. Simpson Investment Company, L.C.* decided that the withdrawing Simpsons were "Members," why didn't it apply Section 9.2, which seems to direct the "Members" to wind up the business of the LLC? Would the Court have reached the same result if the LLC had been a manager-managed LLC under the ULLCA? *See* ULLCA §§ 103, 301 & 803.

3. An early version of the Kansas LLC Act applied in *Investcorp, L.P. v. Simpson Investment Company, L.C.* Most modern partnership, limited partnership and LLC acts expressly provide for an owner, and sometimes the representative or transferee of an owner, *for good cause shown,* to petition a court for judicial supervision of the process of winding up. *See, e.g.,* UPA § 37; RUPA § 803; RULPA § 803; ULLCA § 803.

Paciaroni v. Crane
408 A.2d 946 (Del. Ch. 1979)

BROWN, Vice Chancellor.

This case presents the question of what is to be done with a valuable race-horse now that the partnership that owns him has suffered a falling out among the partners. * * *

The animal whose destiny hangs in the balance is Black Ace, a 3-year old, standardbred racehorse. Black Ace is a pacer and is possessed of exceptional speed. He has been raced primarily in 3-year-old stake races. His purse winnings this year, as of this date, are $96,969. He is still eligible to compete in seven other stake races between now and the end of the racing season in early November. These include the prestigious Little Brown Jug in Delaware, Ohio, on September 20, and the Messenger at Roosevelt Raceway, New York, on October 27. The purse money for these remaining stake races totals more than $600,000.

Black Ace has so far distinguished himself as being one of the better 3-year-old pacers in the country. However, he has been unable to beat the two pacers generally rated as the best of the crop, namely, Sonsam and Hot Hitter. Testimony at trial would rank Black Ace presently as perhaps the fourth to sixth best 3-year-old pacer in the country this year. However, while he has yet to win a big one, his performances in the big races, against the top competition, have been credible.

On July 28 at Vernon Downs, a three-quarter mile track, Black Ace finished third to Sonsam and Hot Hitter in 1:54 1/5, a mere 1/5 second off the winning time. All three horses broke the existing track record for 3-year olds by a considerable margin. On August 11, at the Adios Pace in Pittsburgh, in which he was permitted to participate by the Court, Black Ace finished fourth to Hot Hitter and Sonsam in the first heat, and third to Hot Hitter in the second. His times on a five-eighths mile, off track, were 1:57 and 1:57 4/5, in each case being only 5ths of a second off the winning times. On August 26 at the Canadian Prix d'Ete, another event in which he was permitted to participate by the Court while this litigation was ongoing, he placed second in 1:55 4/5 and third to Hot Hitter in 1:54 3/5. Hot Hitter's time of 1:54 established a new world record for a sophomore pacer on a five-eighths mile track. The previous record was 1:54 3/5, the time in which Black Ace traveled the distance.[1]

Thus, it appears that Black Ace has at least the potential on a given night to win a major stake race, a potential that is now enhanced by the fact one nemesis, Sonsam, will race no more this year as the result of an injury. This is significant for the following reason. The testimony at trial places a current value on Black Ace of approximately $500,000. Should he be able to win one or more of the remaining major stakes, he could in all likelihood be syndicated for two to four times that amount. Or so the testimony goes.

Consequently, if he is permitted to complete the racing season, his value could increase substantially. Conversely, should he become injured or should his

---

1. Since the commencement of the drafting of this decision, the Court, again after a hearing and again over the objection of the defendant, permitted Black Ace to race in a less prestigious stake at Scioto Downs on September 8. He won the race in a time of 1:57 3/5.

performances fall off, his value could decrease significantly or perhaps become nil. Such is one of the hazards that goes with the ownership of racehorses. And it is this circumstance which lies at the heart of the present controversy. Having thus set the stage, I turn to the facts and legal principles which must govern the outcome.

The parties to this action are the plaintiffs Richard Paciaroni and James Cassidy, who own a 50 per cent and 25 per cent interest in Black Ace respectively, and the defendant James Crane, who owns the remaining 25 per cent. Crane is also a trainer of standardbred horses who has enjoyed considerable success over his 20 years in the business, particularly with regard to selecting yearlings and developing them into successful racehorses. His most notable success in the selection and development process was the horse Nero, which was syndicated for $3.6 million. There is no question or issue here as to Crane's competence and ability as a trainer. Until the final act on the part of Paciaroni and Cassidy which gave rise to this litigation, Crane has been the sole trainer, as well as the occasional driver, of Black Ace.

The business relationship between the parties came into being during the fall of 1977. Cassidy and Crane were casual acquaintances. It was suggested that they buy a horse together. Cassidy brought Paciaroni and a fourth party into the picture. Crane attended horse sales in both Philadelphia and Lexington, Kentucky, with a view toward purchasing a yearling for the group. Although they bid on at least one, they were unsuccessful. Crane and Cassidy next attended a sale in Harrisburg, Pennsylvania. It was there that Black Ace was selected and bid in at a price of $35,000. The four men each contributed equally to the purchase price. Crane took the horse to his facilities in Aiken, South Carolina, and entered into the breaking and training process. As a 2-year old, Black Ace started nine races, winning three and placing second in three.

As to the nature of the arrangement between the four parties, it was informal at best. There was no written agreement. Each owned a 25 per cent interest. It was understood that Crane was to be the trainer and that he would be in charge of the day-to-day supervision of the horse, including the selection of his equipment, his rigging, his training, etc. It was also understood, although apparently without any formal discussion, that all would be consulted with regard to the selection of drivers, the races in which the horse would be entered and other decisions of major consequence. In practice, this was done with perhaps a minor misunderstanding here and there. All participated in selecting the stake races in which the horse was to be entered, although the recommendations of Crane were apparently followed because of his superior knowledge on the subject. Along the way, Paciaroni bought out the interest of the fourth party to the venture, thus giving him his 50 per cent ownership interest. Prior to the summer of 1979 there is no indication of any type of problem arising that was not worked out amicably between Paciaroni, Cassidy and Crane. In other words, there were no irreconcilable confrontations which had to be decided by the vote of two of the owners over that of the other.

At this point it seems fitting to note that all three parties agree that their relationship with each other was that of a partnership. The business of the partnership was to own and race Black Ace for profit, with the partners to share in the profits or losses in proportion to their ownership interests. As trainer, Crane billed for and was paid for his services. He was also paid for the cost of supplies, equipment, veterinary care, etc. However, as a 25 percent partner, he bore his 25 percent share of these expenses. This was also understood from the outset.

By early 1979 the signs of dissension that inevitably seem to develop between trainer and owners began to appear. The horse apparently has a ring bone condition. He began to manifest problems on the track. Paciaroni and Cassidy felt that he should be examined by veterinarians other than the one relied upon by Crane. Crane was not enthusiastic for this. Eventually, at the insistence of Paciaroni and Cassidy, Crane took the horse to New Bolton Center where he was examined by one of the top horse veterinarians in the East. It was the recommendation of the latter that the angle of the hooves be increased so as to relieve the pressure on the rear part of the hoof. Crane, however, flatly refused to do this. As an alternative, the New Bolton personnel recommended squaring the hooves. Crane agreed with this and did so.

Nonetheless, Paciaroni and Cassidy were obviously soured by Crane's refusal to heed the expert advice. Thereafter, in June, the horse began pulling first on one line and then on the other and was trying to go over the hub rail. As a result the decision was made not to start him at a major stake race at Brandywine Raceway. There was some disharmony between the parties surrounding this. Later, in July, Black Ace fell to his knees in the stretch of a race at the Meadowlands, taking two other horses out of contention along with him. He failed to finish the race and Paciaroni and Cassidy were concerned that they had almost lost him. They apparently attributed this to Crane's refusal to follow the advice of the New Bolton veterinarian.

Following the Meadowlands incident, the parties met and discussed the situation, with Cassidy and Paciaroni showing their displeasure. The meeting concluded with tensions seemingly soothed. However, that same evening, Crane advised that he felt that they should discontinue their business relationship and wind up their mutual affairs. He denies that he gave any indication of surrendering his role as the trainer of Black Ace. In fact, he was still acting as trainer when Black Ace raced at Vernon Downs some two weeks later.

Paciaroni and Cassidy responded by directing Crane, by telegram dated July 26, to turn the horse over to another trainer immediately following the July 28 race at Vernon Downs. Crane refused to deliver him to the first new trainer designated. At the other partners' direction, however, and upon the advice of counsel, he did eventually deliver the horse to James F. Larente, a trainer and driver of some 30 years experience and one whose expertise in the racing business is conceded. In so doing, however, Crane retained the eligibility papers to Black Ace, without which the horse cannot be raced. This suit followed, with Paciaroni and Cassidy seeking injunctive relief to compel Crane to surrender the eligibility papers, and with Crane seeking the appointment of a receiver for the partnership so as to sell the horse and thus liquidate the partnership asset as soon as possible and to control his activities in the meantime.

Since the institution of this suit, the Court has refused to permit Black Ace to race in a stake race at Vernon Downs. I have, however, allowed him to race in the Adios and the Prix d'Ete as noted previously. His efforts in these two events have gained him two seconds, a third and a fourth place finish, winning some $35,000[2] in purse money in the process. Thus, to some extent, it seems that the

---

2. The Scioto Downs venture on September 8 added another $13,750.

Court has been unwittingly acting as an interim receiver insofar as racing decisions are concerned. With seven stake races still remaining, this is a position which must be abdicated with all due haste. Thus do we arrive at the issues and contentions of the parties.

The positions taken by Paciaroni and Cassidy are not totally consistent, although they are not significantly divergent. Paciaroni feels that either the partnership has already been dissolved by act of the partners, or that it should be formally dissolved by order of the Court as part of this proceeding. He considers the sale of the horse to be a necessary result either way. Cassidy takes the position that the partnership has not yet been dissolved. He harbors this view because he feels that the decision of him and Paciaroni to give the horse to a new trainer constituted nothing more than a partnership decision to terminate Crane as trainer, and not one to either voluntarily terminate the partnership relationship or to expel Crane from the partnership business.

Cassidy, like Paciaroni, concedes that the horse must be sold so as to eventually settle affairs between the partners. (This is due to the fact that the partners have been unable to reach any agreement as to one side buying out the interests of the other.) However, both Paciaroni and Cassidy take the position that Black Ace should be permitted to participate in the remaining 1979 stake races for which he is eligible, at least for so long as he is fit and able to race. * * *

As for Crane, he agrees with Paciaroni that a dissolution of the partnership has taken place and that the horse must be sold in order to wind up partnership affairs. However, in the meantime, he strenuously objects to the horse being raced by Paciaroni and Cassidy under the direction of any trainer other than himself. He would prefer to have the horse sold as soon as possible. (In fact, he originally sought to have him sold at auction at a sale held at the Meadowlands on August 28, 1979, an application that was denied, among other reasons, due to the lack of time available to the Court prior to the sale date to thoroughly consider the situation.) At the same time, he is not opposed to having Black Ace continue to race in the scheduled stake races provided that he has some assurance he will not be harmed in the process. (This stems from the fact that Larente, with the approval of Paciaroni and Cassidy, has made adjustments to the horse and his equipment which Crane opposes.) To this end, Crane asks that a receiver be appointed to make all decisions regarding the care, custody, training and entry of Black Ace in the various races until such time as he may be ordered sold by the Court.

In support of his position that Paciaroni and Cassidy have no right to take the horse from him and to race him through another trainer, Crane contends that since it was understood from the beginning, that he, as a partner, would also be the trainer of any horse purchased by the partnership, then it was within the initial contemplation of all that he would be, in effect, the managing partner of the partnership. He has offered testimony designed to show that it is the prevailing custom and practice in the harness racing industry that where a trainer also purchases an ownership interest in a horse from the outset, and particularly with regard to a yearling, it is commonly understood that the trainer-owner has the right to control the horse even though his ownership interest may be less than 50 per cent. * * *

* * *

To begin with, the existence of the partnership is conceded by the parties. There was no written agreement. It was not formed for the purpose of any solitary undertaking. There was no time specified for the duration of the relationship. I therefore conclude that we are dealing with a partnership at will.

* * *

Following their meeting in July after Black Ace fell in the Meadowlands race, Crane made it clear that he wanted their partnership relation as owners of the horse to be terminated. Shortly thereafter, Paciaroni and Cassidy responded with their July 26 telegram to Crane, the content of which was as follows:

MR AND MRS J CASSIDY AND MR AND MRS R PACIARONI TO-GETHER REPRESENTING 75 PERCENT OWNERSHIP OF THE 3 YEAR OLD COLT 'BLACK ACE' HEREBY NOTIFY YOU THAT YOU ARE RELIEVED OF YOUR EMPLOYMENT AS TRAINER OF 'BLACK ACE' EFFECTIVE IMMEDIATELY FOLLOWING THE GAINES PACE AT VERNON DOWNS SATURDAY JULY 28 1979 AND YOU ARE TO TURN OVER CUSTODY OF SAID COLT IN GOOD AND SOUND CONDITION AT THAT TIME ALONG WITH ALL NECESSARY PAPERS AND EQUIPMENT TO PERSON OR PERSONS REPRESENTING CASSIDY'S AND PACIARONI'S

While it might seem that the telegram was carefully worded so as to appear to relieve Crane of his duties as trainer, the fact that it also says that he is to surrender the horse to persons representing Paciaroni and Cassidy clearly indicates, I think, that Paciaroni and Cassidy had decided to go their separate way, without Crane. Nothing that transpired thereafter weakens this conclusion in any way. To the extent that there could be any doubt, it was certainly resolved as of the time that Crane petitioned this Court for the appointment of a receiver to sell the horse. However, I am of the view that the partnership was placed in a state of dissolution by the express will of the partners at least by July 26, 1979.

Having reached this conclusion, where does it leave matters? Obviously, the partnership is now in the winding up stage. [UPA § 30.] But how is it to be accomplished here, given the unusual nature of the primary partnership asset?

All three partners agree that the horse must be sold in order to wind up partnership affairs. The only dispute is as to when he must be sold and what is to be done with him in the meantime.

As noted previously, Paciaroni and Cassidy take the position that since the partnership relation continues until the time of termination and distribution of assets, then as a consequence the will of the majority of the partnership interests should control the manner of winding up. For this they rely on the following provisions of the Uniform Partnership Act found at [UPA § 18]:

[(e)] All partners have equal rights in the management and conduct of the partnership business.

[(h)] Any difference arising as to ordinary matters connected with the partnership business may be decided by a majority of the partners; but no act in contravention of any agreement between the partners may be done rightfully without the consent of all the partners."

In particular, they rely on the first portion of [UPA section 18(h)] as giving them, as the majority, the right to have the horse finish the stake racing season under the guidance of Larente and over the objection of Crane.

However, as I see it, it is the latter portion of [UPA section 18(h)] on which Crane relies. Again, it is his argument that there is a prevailing custom in the harness racing business that a trainer who also owns an interest in a horse, even though it be less than a majority interest, has the right to train and control the racing of the horse so long as his ownership interest continues. He says that this custom forms a part of the oral agreement between him, Paciaroni and Cassidy, and that consequently any attempt by the latter to take charge of the horse by majority vote would be in contravention of the partnership agreement. In other words, he says that under the latter portion of [UPA section 18(h)] he cannot be removed as trainer and the horse given to another trainer without the consent of all three partners and Crane does not give his consent.

Taking these contentions in reverse order, I find on the evidence that Crane has not established an industry custom to the extent that it would permit the Court to make it a part of the partnership agreement between the parties. I stress the fact that I am not necessarily finding that there is no such custom. I simply hold that on the evidence presented it has not been established.

*   *   *

Having thus disposed of Crane's contention that he has an absolute right to control Black Ace during the winding up process by virtue of the partnership agreement, I turn to the argument of Paciaroni and Cassidy that they have a similar right under [UPA section 18(h)] by virtue of constituting the majority interests. This argument I also reject. I do so because [UPA section 18(h)] permits a majority vote to decide any "difference arising as to ordinary matters connected with the partnership business." Under the exceptional circumstances of this case I do not view the difference between the parties to be one which has arisen in the ordinary course of partnership business. Quite the contrary. The partnership is dissolved. Crane is fearful that if the horse is allowed to continue racing with the changes made by Larente as authorized by Paciaroni and Cassidy, he may well suffer injury and decline from his present value before he can be sold, thus jeopardizing Crane's one-fourth interest. Crane is also fearful that his professional reputation will suffer if it becomes general knowledge that the horse he has developed has been taken from him by legal process and is being raced by another. Paciaroni and Cassidy, on the other hand, say that the horse should be raced because his value may well be increased thereby. They say that they have the once-in-a-lifetime opportunity to be the owners of a champion caliber racehorse. They say that they also have the right to seek to obtain the highest possible price for him when he is sold, something that can only be done if he finishes out his stake race season. This difference between the partners is hardly one which has arisen in the ordinary course of partnership business. Accordingly, I conclude that Paciaroni and Cassidy have no statutory right to wind up affairs simply because they can out vote Crane.

Thus, if neither side has a right to control the winding up process under the positions they have taken, where does this leave us? In my view, it throws matters into [UPA section 37]. That statute reads as follows:

Unless otherwise agreed, the partners who have not wrongfully dissolved the partnership or the legal representative of the last surviving partner, not bankrupt, has the right to wind up the partnership affairs; provided, however, that any partner, his legal representative or his assignee, upon cause shown, may obtain winding up by the court." (Emphasis added.)

Since I have found that the partnership was dissolved under [UPA section 31(1)(b)], it follows that the partnership was not wrongfully dissolved. (Regardless of whether or not this is a necessary condition to seek winding up by the Court, I find it to be present here.) On the present status of the matter, then, I conclude that both sides to this controversy have sought a winding up of partnership affairs by the Court[,] Crane by asking for a receiver to control the horse and to bring about his sale, and Paciaroni and Cassidy by seeking authority to race the horse in the remaining seven stake races for which he is eligible in an effort to accumulate additional winnings for the partnership and to hopefully increase his value for purposes of sale in the fall. This being so, what authority does the Court possess?

* * *

[It] is generally accepted that once dissolution occurs, the partnership continues only to the extent necessary to close out affairs and complete transactions begun but not then finished. It is not generally contemplated that new business will be generated or that new contractual commitments will be made. *Compare,* [UPA §§ 33, 35]. This, in principle, would work against permitting the balances due on the various stake payments to be made so as to permit Black Ace to participate in the remaining few races for which he is eligible. However, in Delaware, there have been exceptions to this.

In *Trincia v. Testardi, supra,* because of the acrimonious nature of the dispute between the parties and the complications involved in winding up, the Court found it appropriate to appoint a receiver

> to take control of the business with authority to procure the continued operation of the business until he can recommend an advantageous disposition of the assets.

57 A.2d 645. And in *Hurley v. Hurley,* Del.Ch., 33 Del.Ch. 231, 91 A.2d 674 (1952) the Chancellor found that it was not improper for the two surviving partners to have continued a building supply business for some three years after the death of the third partner where their purpose had been to seek a better price upon liquidation. As stated at 91 A.2d 675:

> I believe that the defendants were entitled to wind up the partnership affairs by liquidating the assets over a period of time rather than by an immediate forced sale. There is no evidence that the defendants took an unreasonably long time in winding up the business. In fact the uncontradicted testimony was to the effect that substantially more was realized by proceeding in the manner indicated rather than by an immediate liquidation.

While the Court in *Hurley* had the benefit of hindsight, it seems that a principle can be drawn from these two decisions, namely, that where, because of the nature of the partnership business, a better price upon final liquidation is likely to be obtained by the temporary continuation of the business, it is permissible, during the winding up process, to have the business continue to the degree necessary to preserve or enhance its value upon liquidation, provided that such continuation is done in good faith with the intent to bring affairs to a conclusion as soon as reasonably possible. And one way to accomplish this is through an application to the Court for a winding up under [UPA section 37], which carries with it the power of the Court to appoint a receiver for that purpose. With this in mind, I briefly review the elements involved in this situation.

The business purpose of the partnership was to own and race Black Ace for profit. The horse was bred to race. He has the ability to be competitive with the top pacers in the country. He is currently "racing fit" according to the evidence. He has at best only seven more races to go over a period of the next six weeks, after which time there are established horse sales at which he can be disposed of to the highest bidder. The purse money for these remaining stake races is substantial. The fact that he could possibly sustain a disabling injury during this six-week period appears to be no greater than it was when the season commenced. Admittedly, an injury could occur at any time. But this is a fact of racing life which all owners and trainers are forced to accept. And the remaining stake races are races in which all three partners originally intended that he would compete, if able.

The alternative to racing on through the remaining stakes would be to turn Black Act out to pasture until he can be placed in a suitable sale. The balance of his three-year-old racing season would be lost and his true potential might never be realized while he is owned by the partnership. While this might go to preserve whatever present value he now has, it would not seem to be the most plausible thing to do when the reason for which the horse exists is measured against the unique opportunities remaining available to him.

Under these circumstances, I conclude that the winding up of the partnership affairs should include the right to race Black Ace in some or all of the remaining 1979 stake races for which he is now eligible. The final question, then, is who shall be in charge of racing him.

On this point, I rule in favor of Paciaroni and Cassidy. They may, on behalf of the partnership, continue to race the horse through Larente, subject, however, to the conditions hereafter set forth. In reaching this decision, I must confess that I have a great deal of sympathy for James Crane. Nor would I be inclined to take this action except for the extraordinary circumstances prevailing and the brief time for which it will endure. Crane is the one who helped select Black Ace and he is the one who got him this far. I have not the slightest doubt that his opinions as to what was best for the horse were sincere. He appears to be a sincere and able person. Nor can I say that his opinions were wrong. But the differences of opinion that, according to Mark Twain, make for good horse races, also breed disputes between trainers and owners. And in this case, I have no doubt that Paciaroni and Cassidy, based on the information available to them, have also acted in what they thought to be the best interests of the horse and the partnership enterprise.

Nonetheless, when such an impasse occurs, someone must come up short regardless of the good intentions that brought it about in the first place. On the facts of this case, it must be Crane. At the same time, he does have a monetary interest in the partnership assets which must be protected if Paciaroni and Cassidy are to be permitted to test the whims of providence in the name of the partnership during the next six weeks. Accordingly, I make the following ruling.

(1) As a part of winding up the affairs of the partnership, Paciaroni and Cassidy may act as the liquidating partners and may cause Black Ace to race in some or all of the seven remaining stake races, provided, however, that they shall first post security or corporate surety in the sum of $100,000 so as to secure to Crane his share of the value of the partnership asset as established by the evidence at trial. This does not mean that Crane's interest in the partnership is established at that figure. There may be other assets and undoubtedly there are liabilities. It is simply to protect Crane against the possibility that during the winding up process that much of his present interest in the value of the partnership property may be lost or diminished by destruction or injury to the horse prior to final liquidation as a result of continuing to race him. This appears no different in principle than the requirement made by statute in some states that surviving partners give bond in favor of the estate of a deceased partner during the period of winding up.

(2) If Paciaroni and Cassidy are unable or unwilling to meet this condition, then they shall forego the right to act as liquidating partners. In that event, each party, within seven days, shall submit to the Court the names of two persons who they feel qualified, and who they know to be willing, to act as receiver for the winding up of partnership affairs, including the supervision and control of the horse for the remainder of this racing season. I shall then consider designating one such person as receiver.

(3) In the event no suitable person can be found to act as receiver, or in the event that the Court should deem it unwise to appoint any person from the names so submitted, then the Court reserves the power to terminate any further racing by the horse and to require that he simply be maintained and cared for until such time as he can be sold as a part of the final liquidation of the partnership.

(4) The Court further reserves jurisdiction to take such further action with regards to the partnership interests as may appear necessary.

As to the rulings hereby set forth, IT IS SO ORDERED AND DECREED.

Notes

1. The court in *Investcorp, L.P. v. Simpson Investment Company, L.C.* indicated that the person appointed by the operating agreement as manager would continue as manager of winding up. The court in *Paciaroni v. Crane* indicated that, under the facts of that case, the dispute as to whether the partners should complete the racing season could not be resolved in the customary manner (by a majority of the partners). That court reasoned, that the dispute was not in the "ordinary course of partnership business".

a. Does the opinion in *Paciaroni v. Crane* stand for the proposition that all disputes among owners as to the course of a winding up must be decided by a court?

b. Does it require that only disputes out of the ordinary course of *winding up* require court resolution? If so, what would be in the ordinary course of winding up firm business? *See, e.g.,* UPA § 33.

Does RUPA section 803(c) resolve the question? Suppose that partners are divided as to whether to continue the business in order to enhance its value on sale. Under RUPA section 803(c), is that a dispute that may be decided by a majority of the partners?

2. In *Paciaroni v. Crane,* when the court decided that the partnership would be wound up in the manner favored by Paciaroni and Cassidy, did the court make its own business judgment as to better course of winding up? What is the difference between what the court did, and the appointment of a receiver to wind up?

3. Given the court's decision to allow Black Ace to complete the remainder of the racing season, was it proper for the court to insulate Crane from the risks attendant to winding up in the manner approved by the court? *See* UPA §§ 30, 33 & 35(1)(a); RUPA §§ 802(a), 804, 806(a) & 807(b) (second sentence).

Problem 16.9

Supposed that, in Problems 16.7 and 16.8, you had represented Maria at the time of the formation of the firm. How could you have drafted the agreement among the owners to avoid the problems in *Investcorp, L.P. v. Simpson Investment Company, L.C.,* page 810, and *Paciaroni v. Crane,* page 820?

E. Fiduciary Duties

Problem 16.10

In April, 1970, Fulton and Baxter formed to sell life, health, and disability insurance, under the name Fulton-Baxter & Associates. The partnership entered into non-exclusive general agency contracts with various insurance companies. In addition to sales made by the partners, policies were sold through the partnership by a number of appointed agents. When these agents sold policies written by insurance companies with which Fulton-Baxter had an agency contract, the partnership was paid an override commission. After 1970, these agents accounted for the bulk of gross sales processed through the partnership.

On or about September 25, 1975, Baxter told Fulton that he wanted to terminate the partnership and divide its assets. Fulton agreed, and suggested that each partner place a value on the partnership assets with one partner to have the option of buying or selling at the stated value. Baxter agreed.

Pursuant to the agreement, both partners prepared separate valuations of the assets. Fulton placed a value of $6,000 on "goodwill," while Baxter listed "goodwill" as an asset having no value. Similarly, Fulton placed a value on the group contracts and override commissions totaling $40,000, while Baxter listed these contracts as assets with no value to the partnership. As a result, the partners were unable to reach a settlement of their differences.

Thereafter, Baxter entered into new general agency contracts with the insurance companies formerly serviced by the partnership. These new contracts were in the name of L. W. Baxter & Associates.

Contracts with Fulton-Baxter, the partnership, were subsequently cancelled, but not before some policies were processed under the L. W. Baxter contract. Baxter had the Yellow Page listing changed from Fulton-Baxter to L. W. Baxter & Associates. Baxter also had the telephone company change its records to show that the telephone number used by the partnership was now to be used by L. W. Baxter & Associates. Baxter instructed the post office not to release partnership mail when Fulton requested it. Baxter continued to occupy the partnership offices and when the lease expired, he renewed it in his own name. In short, all the assets that Baxter had claimed were worthless, ultimately came to be the assets of his new insurance agency.

Did Baxter owe fiduciary duties to the partnership or to Fulton after September 25, 1975? If so, did Baxter breach any such duties? If so, what remedy or remedies should Fulton have? *See Fulton v. Baxter,* 596 P.2d 540 (Okla. 1979).

Rosenfeld, Meyer & Susman v. Cohen
145 Cal. App. 3d 853, 194 Cal. Rptr. 180 (1983)

NEBRON, Associate Justice.

This is an appeal from a judgment on the pleadings, a partial summary judgment.

The issue which underpins all causes of action here involved may be generally stated as follows: Given the facts of this case, does a former partner of a partnership at will owe any fiduciary duty to former partners after dissolving the partnership and subsequently agreeing with former clients of the dissolved partnership to accept and carry on business which was originally a portion of the assets of the dissolved partnership?

Appellant Rosenfeld, Meyer and Susman (hereinafter called RM & S) consists of the 17 former partners of a dissolved at-will law partnership suing in the name of the dissolved RM & S partnership as both winding up partners and in their individual capacities. Respondents Peter R. Cohen and Deborah D. Riordan, as administratrix of the estate of Edward J. Riordan, deceased (hereinafter called C & R), are the two former partners who dissolved that at-will partnership. International Rectifier Corporation (hereinafter called Rectifier) is a former client of the dissolved RM & S partnership.

In late 1968, Rectifier sought attorneys to bring a major patent antitrust action on a contingent fee basis. After considering the proposals of several law firms, Rectifier entered in a written agreement with RM & S in March 1969, employing RM & S to represent Rectifier in that litigation. The agreement provided that RM & S would be paid limited fees of $30 per hour up to a maximum of 1,000 hours per year for five years against one-third of any recovery and that Rectifier would bear all costs and expenses.

Most of the attorney services rendered by RM & S were performed by C & R, the two senior litigators at RM & S, both experienced in antitrust litigation. From March 1969 through April 30, 1974, RM & S attorneys spent in excess of 19,000 hours on the case. Moreover, RM & S also supervised almost 60,000 hours of paralegal and document clerk services. Other than C & R, no partner had anything but a passing acquaintance with the Rectifier case. The Rectifier account substantially increased RM & S's expenses. RM & S was required to rent additional office space, hire additional support personnel for the Rectifier action and employ additional attorneys to handle matters which otherwise would have been attended to by C & R.

[E]ach partner's profit percentage was fixed by a committee and approved by the partnership. Profits were determined only after fees were received by RM & S and then divided among the partners pursuant to their current partnership percentage, regardless of a partner's work on any particular matter. Throughout the five years that C & R handled the Rectifier action, they received approximately $800,000 from RM & S, despite the fact that they produced virtually no income for the firm during this period. The other partners of RM & S expected to share in the fee from the Rectifier action should it eventually materialize.

By late 1973, C & R believed the trial of the Rectifier action would commence in the fall of 1974 and that the case would settle for between $20 million and $50 million, or, if tried, that the judgment would be approximately $100 million before trebling. Sometime in December 1973, or January 1974, C & R demanded that they be allocated double their partnership percentage of the fee to be paid by Rectifier in connection with the Rectifier action. C & R threatened that if RM & S did not agree to change the partnership allocation, they would withdraw from RM & S. Thereafter, RM & S partners negotiated with C & R to avoid their withdrawal or to make arrangements for C & R to complete the Rectifier action should they withdraw from the firm. As these negotiations progressed, C & R made new demands and stated to two of the partners of RM & S that they would never settle the dispute which they had created. As late as March 26th, or 27th, Riordan told a third partner that C & R no longer needed RM & S. Riordan stated his belief that if C & R withdrew from the firm Rectifier would hire C & R to complete the case, and would provide the necessary financing.

On March 28, 1974, RM & S partners and C & R met with Rectifier's president (Lidow) and vice-president/general counsel (Koris). RM & S described the problem at the firm and explained that the firm was willing to make concessions to C & R, but that C & R would not agree. RM & S also assured Rectifier that if C & R withdrew, RM & S would do whatever was necessary to pursue the case, such as assigning other partners to work on the case and/or retaining, at RM & S's expense, skilled antitrust attorneys as co-counsel. Rectifier's officers stated that they wanted C & R to remain on the case and that C & R should do whatever was necessary to achieve that result.

On April 11, 1974, C & R by memorandum to the other partners gave notice of their withdrawal from the firm effective April 30, 1974. During the first week of May 1974, C & R formed the law firm of Cohen and Riordan. At that time Cohen had no prospective clients, but he believed that Rectifier would ultimately discharge RM & S and hire C & R to complete the antitrust action.

On May 14, 1974, Rectifier mailed a letter of discharge to RM & S and on the following day hand delivered a similar letter of discharge to RM & S. On May 16, 1974, Rectifier retained C & R as attorneys in the Rectifier action.

The C & R-Rectifier agreement provided that Rectifier would pay to C & R $250,000 per year and 8 3/4 percent of the recovery in the Rectifier action. The agreement further provided that C & R would indemnify Rectifier against its total attorney's fees (including fees payable to C & R and RM & S) exceeding 1/3 of Rectifier's recovery in the antitrust action, and that the 8 3/4 percentage contingent fee would be held in escrow for C & R until the amount of the total fees was resolved.

The C&R-Rectifier agreement permitted C & R to receive approximately two times their RM & S partnership percentage of the Rectifier fee. The 8 3/4 percent contingent fee provided for equals approximately 26 percent of the fee that Rectifier was obligated to pay RM & S under the RM & S-Rectifier agreement. It is also approximately 2.2 times C & R's claimed 1973 partnership percentage of 12 percent in RM & S's 33 1/3 percent contingent fee. Thus, both C & R and Rectifier were to financially benefit by the new C & R-Rectifier agreement.

Trial of the Rectifier action commenced in November 1974, and in August 1975 the action was settled for $33 million. Pursuant to the C & R-Rectifier agreement, Rectifier paid C & R $337,000 in current compensation for the period May 1974 through August 1975, and placed $2.4 million in escrow as C & R's 8 3/4 percent contingent fee. In October 1975, RM & S commenced the present action.

[RM & S allege] that C & R breached their fiduciary duty as partners of RM & S [(Breach of Fiduciary Duty)] by dissolving RM & S in bad faith to cause Rectifier to discharge RM & S and obtain increased compensation for themselves (Bad Faith Dissolution); further, that the Rectifier action was the unfinished business of the dissolved RM & S partnership and that C & R breached their fiduciary duties by failing to complete the case for the dissolved partnership and that they held the sums received from Rectifier for completing the case as constructive trustees for the dissolved RM & S (Unfinished Business).

The [lower court] denied C & R's motion for summary judgment, but found that the following issues regarding the cause of action for breach of fiduciary duty were without substantial controversy: (a) That RM & S was a partnership at will; (b) that RM & S had failed to state a cause of action because a partner in a partnership at will may exercise his right to dissolve the partnership for any reason and in bad faith; and (c) that Rectifier terminated their agreement with RM & S in mid-May 1974, and that the termination of such agreement precluded RM & S from stating a cause of action against C & R for breach of C & R's fiduciary duty to complete unfinished business.

Appellants claim that such rulings were prejudicial because they were precluded from proving that C & R violated their fiduciary duties to RM & S prior to mid-May by: (a) Formulating a secret plan to let RM & S finance the Rectifier action until C & R believed the case was close to trial and then making a joint demand for an unprecedented division of the contingent fee; (b) making disparaging remarks to Rectifier about RM & S which C & R did not disclose to RM & S; and (c) failing to complete unfinished business before the termination of the RM & S-Rectifier agreement.

Was the Rectifier action the unfinished business of the dissolved RM & S partnership so that C & R breached their fiduciary duties by failing to complete the case for the dissolved partnership and thus held the sums received from Rectifier for completing the case as constructive trustee for the dissolved RM & S?

The concept of unfinished business arises from the rule of law that upon the dissolution of a partnership, the partnership is not terminated but continues to exist for the limited purpose of winding up its affairs and completing all unfinished business. [UPA §§ 29, 30, 33]. Thus, on May 1, 1974, the day following the dissolution of RM & S there existed three entities: C & R (comprised of Cohen and Riordan), a new RM & S (comprised of the partners of RM & S remaining on April 30, 1974), and the dissolved RM & S which had not yet been wound up. Until the dissolved partnership was wound up, the partners of the dissolved RM & S continued to owe fiduciary duties to each other, especially with respect to unfinished business.

Two fiduciary duties are particularly relevant to this appeal:

First, each partner of a dissolved partnership has the duty to wind up and complete the business of the dissolved partnership existing prior to its dissolution (unfinished business). [UPA §§ 30, 33]; *Smith v. Bull*, (1958) 50 Cal. 2d 294, 303-304, 325 P.2d 463 ("As to the 'unfinished business,' a duty to perform services rests on the partnership at the time of dissolution and continues thereafter to rest on the partners or the surviving partner."); *Little v. Caldwell*, (1894) 101 Cal. 553, 558-562, 36 P. 107 ("[T]he surviving partner must complete all executory contracts of a firm which remain in force after the death of a partner.").

Second, a partner of a dissolved partnership may not take any action with respect to unfinished business which leads to purely personal gain.

A partner of a dissolved partnership who violates any one of these fiduciary duties is liable to the other partners for this breach.

Notwithstanding the foregoing, the [lower courts] dismissed RM & S's claim that C & R were liable for such breach, reasoning that Rectifier's discharge of RM & S precluded any liability. The [lower courts] focused on the date of RM & S's discharge rather than the date of RM & S's dissolution to determine the duties of C & R with respect to unfinished business. To determine whether business of a dissolved partnership is unfinished business, the court should look to the circumstances existing on the date of dissolution of the partnership, not to events occurring thereafter. Thus, in *Smith v. Bull*, the court states that *Little v. Caldwell* clearly indicates the line of demarcation between "unfinished business," being business covered by contracts of employment at the time of dissolution, and other matters, not covered by contracts of employment, but which *thereafter* become the subjects of contracts of employment through the goodwill previously existing between the partnership and the clients. As to the "unfinished business," a duty to perform services rests on the partnership at the time of dissolution and continues thereafter to rest on the partners or the surviving partner.

And in *Heywood v. Sooy*, (1941) 45 Cal. App. 2d 423, 426, 114 P.2d 361:

[T]he test of what constitutes 'unfinished business' of a partnership upon dissolution is whether there existed, at the time of the dissolution, any contract of employment between the partnership and the clients for the performance by the partnership of the services thereafter claimed to be "unfinished business."

It is clear, therefore, that the RM & S-Rectifier agreement was unfinished business of RM & S on May 1, 1974, the day following the dissolution of RM & S.

Given the facts of this case, the [lower court's] conclusion that Rectifier's discharge of RM & S in mid-May 1974 precluded a cause of action for C & R's breach of duty to complete the Rectifier action for the dissolved partnership was error. A trier of fact could find that C & R dissolved RM & S for the very purpose of voiding its fiduciary duty to RM & S; that Rectifier's mid-May discharge letter was therefore the result of C & R's breach of duty to complete unfinished business rather than a termination of C & R's duty; that it was because of C & R's breach of duty during the period May 1 to mid-May that the dissolved RM & S was discharged by Rectifier and lost the difference between what it would have received under the RM & S-Rectifier agreement and the quantum meruit recovery less attorneys' fees that RM & S would have received from Rectifier.

The [lower court's] conclusion that Rectifier's discharge of RM & S required dismissal of RM & S's cause of action for breach of C & R's fiduciary duty was also erroneous because a partner of a dissolved partnership who attempts to reap personal gain from the unfinished business of the dissolved partnership is liable to his copartners for breach of fiduciary duty, despite any discharge of the dissolved firm. The existence of the fiduciary duty prohibiting partners of a dissolved partnership from entering into contracts for personal gain in connection with unfinished business of the partnership is well established.

In *Little v. Caldwell*, after the dissolution of a law partnership by the death of one of the partners, the surviving partner entered into a contract with a client of the dissolved partnership to appeal a contingent fee case unsuccessfully tried before dissolution. The new contract altered the existing obligations and rights of the parties by relieving the client from the obligation to pay additional costs and increasing the contingent fee from 15 percent to 60 percent. The surviving partner argued that the client's entry into this agreement with him after the dissolution of the partnership extinguished his obligation to share the fee with the deceased partner. But the court in rejecting this argument stated:

In the discharge of this obligation or duty in relation to the unsettled and unfinished business of the firm, the surviving partner occupies the position of a trustee, and, while he may compromise disputed claims, or modify an existing contract by releasing the other party thereto from some of its obligations, when in the exercise of an honest judgment the best interest of the partnership seems to him to require such action, still, in doing so, he cannot be permitted to make gain for himself at the expense of the estate of the deceased partner, by consenting to the extinguishment of a contract belonging to the partnership, and the substitution therefore of another relating to the same subject matter, and in the profits of which he alone is to participate. Whatever may be the effect of such new or substituted contract as between the immediate parties to it, a court of equity in settling the accounts of the partnership will not treat it as an entire extinguishment of the original contract, or deny the right of the representatives of the deceased partner to an equitable participation in the profits realized from the latter contract, and which may be regarded, so far as concerns the partnership, as only a modification of the former contract.

After *Little v. Caldwell* was retried, the trial court held that the second contract entered into by Caldwell with the client was but a modification of the first. This finding was supported by evidence that the second contract did not provide for a fee of 60 percent but for an additional 45 percent fee and because defendant had asked for a release from plaintiff of plaintiff's rights under the first contract. Since the findings of the trial court were sufficient to dispose of the case, the Supreme Court did not address the consequences which would follow from a so-called termination of the first contract and a substitution of a "new contract." The court did, however, state the trial court was also justified in holding that the contracts were not separate and distinct because

> [t]he consideration moving from the attorneys, that they were to prosecute to a conclusion the litigation in question, always remained; the terms of their compensation and risk in so doing alone were varied.

So in the present case, the consideration moving from C & R—their prosecution of the Rectifier action—continued under the C & R-Rectifier agreement, only the compensation to be paid by Rectifier being varied and this without the acquiescence of RM & S. It is clear that a partner completing unfinished business cannot cut off the rights of the other partners in the dissolved partnership by the tactic of entering into a "new" contract to complete such business.

Given the facts of this case, though Rectifier had a right to terminate the contract with RM & S and hire C & R, C & R could not avoid what was tantamount to a conflict of interest—*i.e.,* the fiduciary duty it owed to RM & S.

Rectifier's purported discharge of RM & S is irrelevant to the issue of C & R's breach of their fiduciary duty to the remaining partners of RM & S. A partner's fiduciary duty to complete unfinished business on behalf of the dissolved partnership arises on the date of dissolution and governs each partner's future conduct regarding this business. Since the Rectifier action remained exactly the same case before and after RM & S's dissolution, C & R's liability for failing to complete the Rectifier case for the dissolved RM & S and for entering into a contract personally to profit from the unfinished business of the dissolved RM & S survived execution of the C & R-Rectifier agreement and Rectifier's discharge of RM & S.

The *Little v. Caldwell* opinions and the other unfinished business cases strike a reasonable balance between a partner's right to pursue his own business after dissolution of a partnership, and his duty of loyalty to his ex-copartners. The partner may take for his own account new business even when emanating from clients of the dissolved partnership and the partner is entitled to the reasonable value of the services in completing the partnership business, but he may not seize for his own account the business which was in existence during the term of the partnership. Clearly, the balance between such competing public policies is upset if a partner may dissolve a partnership to cause a termination of a partnership business, or if a partner may withhold his necessary services from the dissolved partnership to preclude the completion of unfinished business, or if the partner may complete such business and retain the proceeds for himself.

The rulings of the [lower courts] are reversed and the cause is remanded for further proceedings not inconsistent with this opinion.

Notes

1. In *Meehan v. Shaughnessy,* 404 Mass. 419, 535 N.E.2d 1255 (1989), Meehan and Boyle, two partners in the law partnership of Parker Coulter, be-

came dissatisfied and formed their own firm. Before they dissolved the partnership, Meehan and Boyle made arrangements to begin practice in their new firm immediately after dissolution. They leased and furnished new offices. They prepared a list of Parker Coulter clients that they felt would move their business to the new firm. They even approached other Parker Coulter lawyers about leaving with them. When asked if they were planning to leave the firm, they denied it. *After* they announced their departure, Meehan and Boyle refused to identify to the other partners those clients and matters they intended to try to take with them. Although the partnership agreement, as interpreted by the court, permitted them to take partnership clients upon payment of a "fair charge," the court found that Meehan and Boyle had breached their fiduciary duties:

> Parker Coulter argues that the judge's findings compel the conclusion that Meehan and Boyle breached their fiduciary duty not to compete with their partners by secretly setting up a new firm during their tenure at Parker Coulter. We disagree. We have stated that fiduciaries may plan to compete with the entity to which they owe allegiance, "provided that in the course of such arrangement they [do] not otherwise act in violation of their fiduciary duties." *Chelsea Indus. v. Gaffney*, 389 Mass. 1, 10, 11-12, 449 N.E.2d 320 (1983). Here, the judge found that Meehan and Boyle made certain logistical arrangements for the establishment of MBC. These arrangements included executing a lease for MBC's office, preparing lists of clients expected to leave Parker Coulter for MBC, and obtaining financing on the basis of these lists. We believe these logistical arrangements to establish a physical plant for the new firm were permissible under *Chelsea Indus.*, especially in light of the attorneys' obligation to represent adequately any clients who might continue to retain them on their departure from Parker Coulter. There was no error in the judge's determination that this conduct did not violate the partners' fiduciary duty.

> Lastly, Parker Coulter argues that the judge's findings compel the conclusion that Meehan and Boyle breached their fiduciary duties by unfairly acquiring consent from clients to remove cases from Parker Coulter. We agree that Meehan and Boyle, through their preparation for obtaining clients' consent, their secrecy concerning which clients they intended to take, and the substance and method of their communications with clients, obtained an unfair advantage over their former partners in breach of their fiduciary duties.

> A partner has an obligation to "render on demand true and full information of all things affecting the partnership to any partner." [UPA § 20]. On three separate occasions Meehan affirmatively denied to his partners, on their demand, that he had any plans for leaving the partnership. During this period of secrecy, Meehan and Boyle made preparations for obtaining removal authorizations from clients. Meehan traveled to New York to meet with a representative of USAU and interest him in the new firm. Boyle prepared form letters on Parker Coulter's letterhead for authorizations from prospective MBC clients. Thus, they were "ready to move" the instant they gave notice to their partners.

On giving their notice, Meehan and Boyle continued to use their position of trust and confidence to the disadvantage of Parker Coulter. The two immediately began communicating with clients and referring attorneys. Boyle delayed providing his partners with a list of clients he intended to solicit until mid-December, by which time he had obtained authorization from a majority of the clients.

Finally, the content of the letter sent to the clients was unfairly prejudicial to Parker Coulter. The ABA Committee on Ethics and Professional Responsibility, in Informal Opinion 1457 (April 29, 1980), set forth ethical standards for attorneys announcing a change in professional association. Because this standard is intended primarily to protect clients, proof by Parker Coulter of a technical violation of this standard does not aid them in their claims. We will, however, look to this standard for general guidelines as to what partners are entitled to expect from each other concerning their joint clients on the division of their practice. The ethical standard provides that any notice explain to a client that he or she has the right to decide who will continue the representation. Here, the judge found that the notice did not "clearly present to the clients the choice they had between remaining at Parker Coulter or moving to the new firm." By sending a one-sided announcement, on Parker Coulter letterhead, so soon after notice of their departure, Meehan and Boyle excluded their partners from effectively presenting their services as an alternative to those of Meehan and Boyle.

Meehan and Boyle could have foreseen that the news of their departure would cause a certain amount of confusion and disruption among their partners. The speed and preemptive character of their campaign to acquire clients' consent took advantage of their partners' confusion. By engaging in these preemptive tactics, Meehan and Boyle violated the duty of utmost good faith and loyalty which they owed their partners. Therefore, we conclude that the judge erred in deciding that Meehan and Boyle acted properly in acquiring consent to remove cases to MBC.

2. In *Fulton v. Baxter,* 596 P.2d 540 (Okla. 1979), on which problem 16.10 is based, the court stated:

In order to determine whether the jury correctly concluded that defendant appropriated partnership property, this Court must resolve three questions:

(1) What was the extent of defendant's duty relative to partnership property?

(2) Did the defendant breach that duty?

(3) Did the evidence support the amount of damages awarded?

The duty concerning profits derived from a partnership is found at [UPA section 21(1)], which provides:

Every partner must account to the partnership for any benefit, and hold as trustee for it any profits derived by him without the consent of the other partners from any transaction connected with the formation, conduct, or liquidation of the partnership or from any use by him of its property.

AGENCY, PARTNERSHIPS AND LIMITED LIABILITY COMPANIES

[UPA section 21(1)] is unambiguous and imposes an absolute duty. This duty remains undiminished by the fact that a partnership has been dissolved. [UPA section 30] provides that on dissolution of a partnership, the partnership is not terminated, "but continues until the winding up of partnership affairs is completed."

This Court has consistently held that good faith is most especially required where one partner is trying to oust another partner. [T]hroughout the period in question, the defendant was bound to exercise good faith relative to partnership transactions and property.

Evidence in this case shows that defendant purposely brought about the termination of the partnership lease and renewed it in the name of L. W. Baxter. Conduct of this category is not to be permitted in the context of the partnership affiliation. In *Waller v. Henderson*, [135 Okla. 231, 275 P.2d 323 (1929)], we adopted the rule that a partner may not obtain a renewal of a partnership lease for his own purpose to commence after the expiration of the original lease, or after the termination of the partnership without disclosing those facts to his co-partners. The rule is succinctly stated at 60 Am. Jur. 2d *Partnership*, § 127, at 53:

Even after dissolution of the partnership, the equitable expectancy of renewal (of the lease) remains a partnership asset for the purposes of liquidation, to be taken into account and disposed of for the common benefit of the partners, and hence, a renewal after dissolution of the firm, taken by less than all the partners, inures to the benefit of the firm.

We therefore have no difficulty in finding that defendant breached his fiduciary duty and wrongfully appropriated the partnership lease to his own benefit, notwithstanding his insistence that the offices occupied by the partnership were of no value to the partnership.

We are unpersuaded by defendant's argument that the business relationships, overrides, and agency contracts could not be wrongfully appropriated since they were contingent or cancellable at will. We agree with the statement found in *Rowley on Partnerships*, § 21.1, at 544 (1960), which reads:

The same rule which governs the securing of leases applies to other benefits, and if a member of an insurance partnership secures a renewal of agencies in himself and for his own benefit, it is held that he takes them for the use of the firm, and this even though the other partners contemplated going out of business.

In the instant case, the defendant not only renewed the agencies in himself, he processed policies through his own agencies before the partnership contracts were cancelled.

The record reveals sufficient evidence from which the jury could conclude that defendant wrongfully appropriated valuable partnership assets and converted them to his own use.

3. When partners are engaged in transactions between themselves, such as where one partner is purchasing the interest in the partnership of another partner, should the partners owe each other any fiduciary duties? In *Johnson v. Buck*,

540 S.W.2d 393 (Tex. Civ. App. 1976). Johnson and Buck were partners in a real estate development partnership, with Johnson as managing partner. Johnson convinced Buck that they were in danger of losing their entire investment. Johnson misrepresented the financial condition of the partnership and their bank's willingness to renew partnership loans that were coming due. Buck then sold his interest in the partnership to Johnson for substantially less than its true value. In fact, the business was currently making money, and Johnson anticipated it would continue to do so. Not only had the bank not cut off the partnership's credit, it had loaned money to Johnson so he could buy out Buck. The court placed on Johnson the burden of proving that his dealings with Buck were fair, and had little difficulty in finding that Johnson had violated his duty of loyalty. Not only had he failed to make full disclosure of all material facts, he had actively misrepresented the facts. The court found that Buck was entirely justified in relying solely on his partner without any independent verification, especially when the partner relied on was the managing partner.

4. Compare the holding in *Johnson v. Buck* with the holdings in *Walter v. Holiday Inns, Inc.*, 985 F.2d 1232 (3rd Cir. 1993) and *ONG International (U.S.A.) Inc. v. 11th Avenue Corp.*, 850 P.2d 447 (Utah 1993), both of which involved alleged non-disclosures in connection with one partner's purchase of another's interest in the partnership.

a. In *Walter v. Holiday Inns, Inc.*, the defendant argued against any duty of disclosure, on the grounds that the parties were negotiating at arm's length and had equal access to the relevant financial records. 985 F.2d at 1238. Although the court hesitated to embrace that proposition, *id.*, it found that any non-disclosures were *immaterial* because "each of the plaintiffs was a highly sophisticated and experienced investor", *id.* at 1239-40, with complete access to the relevant records. *Id.* at 1239-48.

b. In *ONG International (U.S.A.) Inc. v. 11th Avenue Corp.*, the court reasoned that

> when a relationship becomes adversarial and the partners deal at arm's length, their fiduciary duties to each other may be extinguished

850 P.2d at 454. Nevertheless, under the facts of that case, it upheld the trial court finding of

> a fiduciary relationship and its concomitant duty to disclose", because the defendant managing partner had "controlled and withheld relevant partnership information,

and thus had greater access. *Id.*

Are the holdings in *Johnson v. Buck, Walter v. Holiday Inns, Inc.*, and *ONG International (U.S.A.) Inc. v. 11th Avenue Corp.* consistent with each other? With *Konover Development Corp. v. Zeller*?

F. Obligations Arising before Dissociation or Dissolution

Problem 16.11

Nestle and Ellis were partners in Red Rocks Meat and Deli. The business was conducted on premises Nestle and Ellis leased from Wester & Co. in June 1978. In October 1978, Nestle transferred his interest in Red Rocks Meat and Deli to Herline, who was admitted as a partner instead of Nestle. Ellis and Herline agreed to assume all liabilities of Red Rocks Meat and Deli, and to indemnify Nestle. In January 1980, Nestle and Ellis signed an addendum to the original lease. Under the addendum, Nestle and Ellis leased additional space from Wester & Co. The addendum changed the base rent for the original premises. By May 1980, Nestle and Ellis had defaulted on the lease payments for both premises. Is Nestle liable to Wester & Co. for breach of the lease? Should Nestle have taken any other steps to help protect against the risk of continuing personal liability? What other facts would you like to know in determining Nestle's continuing personal liability? *See Wester & Co. v. Nestle*, 669 P.2d 1046 (Colo. 1983).

Bradford v. First National Bank
932 P2d 256 (Alaska 1997)

FABE, Justice.

I. INTRODUCTION

The First National Bank of Anchorage (First National) brought an action against the 4M 2B Investors partnership (4M 2B) and each of 4M 2B's past and present general partners to collect the unpaid balance of a loan it made to 4M 2B. George H. Bradford and Elizabeth Bradford, two of 4M 2B's eleven original general partners, appeal from the superior court's judgment against them in that action.

II. FACTS AND PROCEEDINGS

The Bradfords, along with four other couples and one individual, formed 4M 2B in 1983 to build, operate, and own the Peninsula Center Mall in Soldotna. To finance this project, the partnership borrowed $3 million from the Alaska Industrial Development Authority (AIDA). AIDA made this loan pursuant to a loan agreement (Loan Agreement) setting forth the general terms of 4M 2B's obligation, a promissory note (1983 Note) stating the interest rate and monthly payments on the loan, and a deed of trust and security agreement providing the shopping center as security for the debt.

AIDA raised the money that it loaned to 4M 2B by issuing a $3 million tax-free revenue bond (1983 Bond). The repayment terms of the 1983 Bond were identical to those of the 1983 Note. Payments on the bond, however, were limited to the loan payments made to AIDA by 4M 2B. AIDA sold the bond to First National and, under a trust indenture (Indenture), also appointed First National trustee of the bond. To provide First National with security for the bond, AIDA transferred its interest in 4M 2B's promissory note and deed of trust to First National. In addition, the individual partners in 4M 2B personally guaranteed the bond debt.

In 1985 the Bradfords and another couple, James C. Benson and Sandra K. Benson, withdrew from the 4M 2B partnership. Under an agreement with the continuing partners (Assumption Agreement), the Bradfords relinquished "their entire interest in the partnership" in consideration of the "distribution to them by the partnership of certain real property." The continuing partners agreed to "assume and . . . satisfy all debts and liabilities of the old partnership" and promised to "indemnify and hold the Retiring Partners harmless from all such debts and liabilities." 4M 2B notified First National of this change in the partnership on July 1, 1985, enclosing a copy of the withdrawal agreement.

In 1986, 4M 2B signed a modification agreement that lowered the interest rate and monthly payments that it was required to make on the loan made to it by AIDA. The continuing partners of 4M 2B signed this modification agreement, but the Bradfords and the Bensons did not. To account for the modified loan repayment terms, AIDA, First National, and 4M 2B agreed to modify the Indenture. Pursuant to the modified Indenture, AIDA cancelled and replaced the 1983 Bond with a "revenue refunding bond" (1986 Bond). The terms of the 1986 Bond reflected the 1986 modification of the interest rate and repayment terms of the loan.

In August 1989 AIDA and First National again agreed with 4M 2B to refinance the loan. The continuing partners in 4M 2B signed a new promissory note (1989 Note), and AIDA issued another revenue refunding bond (1989 Bond) to cancel and replace the 1986 Bond. As part of this refinancing, 4M 2B provided additional real property as security for the new note.

In 1992, four more partners in 4M 2B retired. At the same time, one new partner joined the three remaining partners to continue the partnership.

4M 2B stopped making payments on the loan in February 1994, and in May 1994, First National sent a notice of default to 4M 2B, the three original continuing partners, and the four partners who retired in 1992. The notice declared the outstanding principal and interest to be immediately due and payable and warned that First National would take "steps . . . to enforce the personal liability of the borrower and partners of the borrower and to protect and enforce the interests in property securing payment of the note." On June 13, 1994, First National brought suit against 4M 2B and each past and present partner. First National also joined other defendants with claims against the real property securing the promissory note. In the suit, First National sought judgment for the entire amount of the debt, enforcement of its right in the property securing the loan, and recovery of certain costs.

On September 28, 1994, 4M 2B filed for bankruptcy protection, and on January 9, 1995, three of the four continuing partners and all of the partners who retired in 1992 also filed petitions for bankruptcy. First National moved for summary judgment against the Bradfords, the Bensons, and the one continuing partner who had not filed for bankruptcy. The superior court granted this motion on March 19, 1995. First National then moved for entry of final judgment against the Bradfords and the Bensons under Civil Rule 54(b). After first denying this motion, the court reconsidered and granted the motion, entering judgment against the Bradfords and the Bensons on July 31, 1995.

The court limited execution on the judgment to the amount by which the outstanding balance of the judgment exceeded $1.4 million, the estimated maximum value of the real property securing the loan. The court later adjusted the judgment to reflect the bankruptcy court's conclusion that the value of the real property was only $1,244,578.59.

The Bradfords appeal the superior court's grant of First National's motion for summary judgment and entry of final judgment.

III. DISCUSSION
A. The Bradfords Are Liable as Sureties for 4M 2B's Debt to AIDA.

To resolve the question of the Bradfords' liability for the debt to First National, we focus on the Loan Agreement, on the promissory note between 4M 2B and AIDA, and on the agreement the Bradfords made when they withdrew from the partnership. We conclude from these documents that upon their withdrawal from 4M 2B, the Bradfords became sureties with respect to the partnership's debt. We base this conclusion on the rule that

> [t]he suretyship relation is created where the surety[,] . . . having been one of several principal obligors, one or more of the other co-principals contracts to assume the entire duty of performance.

Restatement of Security § 83(d) (1941). The Restatement's comment on this clause addresses the precise issue before us:

> Two persons, after binding themselves as principals, may subsequently change their relations so that between themselves one has the entire duty of performance, that is, so far as they are concerned, they have become principal and surety. A common situation to which the rule stated in this Clause applies is where a partner retires and the old partners assume all the firm obligations. The retiring partner is a surety in respect of the others.

Id. § 83 cmt. f. A creditor is bound by the suretyship relationship created in this way when it receives notice of the assumption agreement between the continuing and retiring partners. *Id.* § 114 cmt. f.

We applied this rule in *State v. McKinnon*, 667 P.2d 1239, 1241-42 & n. 4 (Alaska 1983). In that case, two half-brothers entered into a partnership and took out a loan from the State of Alaska. When the men dissolved the partnership, they signed a termination agreement providing that the partner continuing the business "agreed to assume the obligation of repaying the loan. . . ." They notified the State of this agreement. We held that the agreement and the notice of the agreement to the creditor changed the withdrawing partner's status from co-obligor to surety.

When the Bradfords withdrew from 4M 2B in 1985, the continuing partners agreed to "assume and . . . satisfy all debts and liabilities of the old partnership" and to "indemnify and hold the Retiring Partners harmless from all such debts and liabilities." 4M 2B notified First National of this agreement. Thus, in light of *McKinnon* and general surety law, we hold that the Bradfords became sureties for 4M 2B's debt upon their withdrawal from the partnership.

The Bradfords argue that they did not "agree to become . . . sureties for the remaining 4M 2B partners' obligation." They assert that, under *McKinnon*, such an agreement on their part is necessary for the creation of suretyship status. This assertion is not correct. While we noted in *McKinnon* that the withdrawing partner agreed to remain personally liable for the debt and that the change in status from co-obligor to surety was "consistent with the intent of the parties," we did not state that such agreement or intent is required to create suretyship status. 667 P.2d at 1242. Indeed, partnership law imposes liability for existing partnership debts on withdrawing partners whether or not they agree to remain personally liable. [UPA § 36(1).] The Assumption Agreement impliedly recognizes this basic rule by providing that the continuing partners will indemnify the Bradfords against their continuing personal liability.

The Bradfords concede that First National did not expressly agree to release them from liability for 4M 2B's note. Instead, they argue that First National impliedly discharged them under [UPA Section 36(2)]. This section provides:

[(2)] A partner is discharged from an existing liability upon dissolution of the partnership by an agreement to that effect between the partner, the partnership creditor and the person or partnership continuing the business. The agreement may be inferred from the course of dealing between the creditor who has knowledge of the dissolution and the person or partnership continuing the business.

The Bradfords argue that First National's failure to notify them of the modifications to the promissory note, to require them to approve those modifications, and to provide them with notice of default supports the inference that First National intended to discharge them. We disagree.

As sureties, the Bradfords ceased to be the principal obligors, but they remained liable for the loan upon default. First National had no right of recourse against the Bradfords until the partnership defaulted. It thus had no obligation or reason to notify them of or secure their approval for the modifications to the loan, nor did it have a duty to give them notice of default. *See McKinnon,* 667 P.2d at 1241, 1244; Restatement of Security § 136 (stating that "the surety's obligation to the creditor is not affected by the creditor's failure to notify him of the principal's default unless such notification is required by the terms of the surety's contract"). First National's course of dealing exclusively with the continuing partners was entirely consistent with the Bradfords' surety status. Therefore, we hold that First National's course of dealing under these circumstances could not as a matter of law support an inference that it intended to discharge the Bradfords.

This conclusion is supported by [UPA § 36(3)]. That subsection provides:

[(3)] Where a person agrees to assume the existing obligations of a dissolved partnership, the partners whose obligations have been assumed are discharged from liability to a creditor of the partnership who, knowing of the agreement, consents to a material alteration in the nature or time of payment of the obligations.

It is this subsection that expressly provides for discharge of a surety. Under this subsection, a surety is discharged only when the creditor

consents to a material alteration in the nature or time of payment of the obligations.

[UPA § 36(3)]. By implication then, a surety is not discharged when the creditor consents to nonmaterial alterations in the nature or time of payment, regardless of whether the surety has notice or approves of the alteration. The Bradfords acknowledge that [UPA section 36(3)] does not release them from liability in this case. Thus, they apparently agree that First National's agreement to lower the interest rate and monthly payment on 4M 2B's loan was not the kind of modification of the partnership's obligation that would discharge them. Accepting the Bradfords' argument would therefore require the conclusion that the same course of dealing that specifically does not discharge the Bradfords under [UPA section 36(3)] does discharge them under [UPA section 36(2)]. Such an interpretation would violate the general rule that this court

> interprets each part or section of a statute with every other part or section, so as to create a harmonious whole.

Rydwell v. Anchorage Sch. Dist., 864 P.2d 526, 528 (Alaska 1993).

* * *

IV. CONCLUSION

For the reasons above, we AFFIRM the superior court's grant of First National's motion for summary judgment and entry of final judgment against the Bradfords. We REVERSE the superior court's award of attorney's fees and REMAND to the superior court for award of the entire amount of the attorney's fees requested by First National.

Notes

1. A dissociating partner remains liable to partnership creditors, UPA § 36(1), except to the extent particular creditors may expressly or impliedly agree otherwise. UPA §§ 36(1), (2). Because the continuing partners have agreed that, *as between them and the dissociating partner*, they will be responsible for obligations to partnership creditors, the dissociating partner's liability is similar to that of a surety. *B-OK, Inc. v. Storey*, 79 Wash. 2d 387, 485 P.2d 987 (1971). Thus, UPA section 36(3) gives the dissociating partner the common law suretyship discharges resulting from a material alteration in the nature or time of payment by a creditor who knows of the dissociating partner's change in status. *See also*, UPA §§ 41, 42.

2. In *Wester & Co. v. Nestle*, 669 P.2d 1046 (Colo. 1983), which is the basis for Problem 16.11, the court found that the partnership creditor had by its actions discharged the former partner, Nestle:

> Following trial on the primary action, the court resolved the factual disputes in Nestle's favor. Finding that the partnership had dissolved when Nestle withdrew, the court applied [UPA § 36(2)] to the facts and concluded, from lessor's knowledge of the situation and the parties' course of dealings, that lessor had consented to Nestle's discharge from liability. It also concluded that provisions in the addendum materially altered the parties' liability on the underlying lease, thereby discharging Nestle from liability by application of [UPA § 36(3)].

> The dissolution of a partnership does not of itself discharge the existing liability of any partner. [UPA § 36(1)]. A partner is discharged from existing liability by an agreement to that effect between the withdrawing partner, the remaining partners, and the partnership creditor, and

>> such agreement may be inferred from the course of dealing between the creditor having knowledge of the dissolution and the person or partnership continuing the business.

[UPA § 36(2)]. Or, under [UPA § 36(3)], a material alteration in an existing liability will discharge from liability a partner whose obligations have been assumed.

The trial court found, on conflicting testimony, that the conditions for discharge from liability under both of these subsections existed, and such factual findings, supported by evidence in the record, may not be disturbed upon appeal.

3. RUPA sections 703(a), (c) and (d) are the RUPA provisions equivalent to UPA section 36.

G. Obligations Arising after Dissociation or Dissolution

Problem 16.12

ABC Construction is a dissolved at-will partnership. Before its dissolution, ABC Construction was engaged in the business of building homes. At the time ABC Construction was dissolved, it had partially built several homes under a contract with MNO Homes. After dissolution of the partnership:

I. Al, one of the partners who knew that the partnership had been dissolved, purchased on open account from XYZ Lumber $2,000 worth of two-by-fours. The lumber was to be used in completing the homes that ABC Construction was building for MNO Homes.

II. Pat, a servant of the partnership, took delivery of the two-by-fours. While she was driving to the job site, she negligently ran a stop sign, and collided with an sports utility vehicle (SUV) driven by Donna Driver. In the collision, Donna was injured, her SUV was totaled, and the two-by-fours were all broken.

ABC Construction has asked you to advise them as to their liability to XYZ Lumber and to Donna.

    a. Under the UPA, are ABC Construction and its partners liable t

        (1) XYZ Lumber for the purchase price of the two-by-fours; or

        (2) Alice for her injuries and the damage to her SUV?

    b. Under the RUPA, are ABC Construction and its partners liable to

        (1) XYZ Lumber for the purchase price of the two-by-fours; or

        (2) Alice for her injuries and the damage to her SUV?

Palomba v. Barish
626 F. Supp. 722 (E.D. Pa. 1985)

JAMES McGIRR KELLY, District Judge.

Presently before this court is defendant Robert C. Daniels' motion [for] summary judgment.

Plaintiffs, a group of seamen, were allegedly injured while the vessel they were on was in navigable waters of the Atlantic Ocean. Plaintiffs engaged the defendant law firm of Adler, Barish, Daniels, Levin & Creskoff (Adler-Barish) to represent them in their action against the ship for damages. Defendant Marvin Barish, a partner of Adler-Barish, was the attorney who handled plaintiffs' claims.

The court which was presiding over the plaintiffs' action against the ship dismissed certain of the plaintiffs' claims (hereinafter "dismissed plaintiffs") because dismissed plaintiffs were not produced for deposition and medical examination and plaintiffs' expert witness medical reports were not furnished for the steamship company as required by an order entered and agreed to by counsel. The remaining plaintiffs' claims (hereinafter "limited plaintiffs") were allowed to proceed to trial as to damages, but a key expert witness was prohibited from testifying...due to the alleged failure of defendant Marvin Barish to make the expert witnesses reports available to the steamship company's counsel.

Plaintiffs here allege they suffered injury due to the alleged malpractice of defendant attorneys who had represented them in their claim against the steamship company.

In Count I of the complaint the dismissed plaintiffs assert that because of the negligence of the defendants in the preparation and handling of their claims, they were prejudiced and lost the right to recover damages against the steamship company.

In Count II of the complaint the limited plaintiffs assert that because of the negligence of the defendants they were injured because they were deprived of putting into evidence material and testimony which would have benefited them in their attempt to establish damages.

Count III of the complaint asserts a claim on behalf of all plaintiffs for punitive damages against the defendants for "continual and flagrant disregard of agreed upon scheduling orders."

I have jurisdiction over plaintiffs' action because of diversity of the parties. Accordingly, I must apply Pennsylvania state law. Pennsylvania law is clear that the negligence of one partner acting in the ordinary course of the business of the partnership will be imputed upon the non-acting partners, making the non-acting partners jointly and severally liable for the negligence. [UPA §§ 13 & 15].

Defendant Daniels has contended that he was forced out of Adler-Barish, thus dissolving the partnership two years prior to the time of the purported negligence which gave rise to plaintiffs' claims. While plaintiffs have alleged negligence on behalf of all defendant attorneys, they assert that defendant Marvin Barish was the firm's representative which they dealt with.

A party who has prior dealings with a partnership and without [actual or constructive] knowledge of a subsequent dissolution of the partnership, and continues to deal with a partner, can hold liable the former partners of the dissolved partnership. [UPA § 35].

Thus, a party who is not given notice of dissolution, but continues to transact business with a "partner," can hold liable the former partnership. It should be noted at this juncture that even after dissolution, a partnership is not terminated but continues to exist until the winding up of partnership affairs is completed and the authority remains to act for the partnership in winding up partnership affairs and complete transactions begun but not yet finished at the time of dissolution.

North Star Coal v. Eddy, 442 Pa. 583, 586, 277 A.2d 154, 156 (1971). The dissolution of a partnership will not relieve an individual partner of a duty under a contract entered into before the partnership was dissolved. Thus, I find the fact that Daniels' withdrawal from Adler-Barish two years prior to the purported negligent act is of little moment to whether or not Daniels can be held liable for the malpractice of his former partners.

An action of malpractice by an attorney can generally be based upon either tort or contract theory. The action brought by plaintiffs here appears to rest upon tort theory for recovery. Generally a tort by one partner occurring subsequent to dissolution of a partnership cannot be imputed upon the former partners, unless the party who committed the tort was winding up the partnership affairs or completing partnership business. A partner who has not, *inter alia*, wrongfully dissolved the partnership has the right to wind up the partnership affairs. [UPA § 37]. Because no pleadings or material submitted to the court have expressed that defendant Barish wrongfully dissolved the partnership, I must assume that Barish had a right to wind up certain former Adler-Barish commitments.

Defendant Daniels has submitted an affidavit of his counsel, Neil Witkes, to support his position that plaintiffs had actual knowledge of the Adler-Barish firm being dissolved, since Daniels' withdrawal from Adler-Barish. Witkes avers that certain correspondence of various plaintiffs which were addressed to the successor firm of Adler-Barish establishes that these plaintiffs had knowledge of the expulsion or absence of defendant Daniels from the firm. It may be permissible, but not advisable, for an attorney to present his own affidavit for a motion for a summary judgment. However, here the more serious problems arise because of possible hearsay and authentication questions of the documents Witkes has submitted as well as inferences such writings convey. Indeed, the fact that plaintiffs addressed letters to a succeeding firm of Adler-Barish does not dispose of all questions of fact as to whether or not the plaintiffs had knowledge that Daniels was no longer with the law firm which represented them. The letters do not preclude an issue of fact in dispute. Because I find in consideration of the letters, an issue of fact still present, I need not rule as to whether the letters should be excluded because they were not properly authenticated or may contain hearsay. Daniels has submitted an affidavit averring that he was expelled from the partnership and was denied access to the client files to which he could have obtained address information of clients so that notice of his leaving Adler-Barish could be made. Conversely, other partners of the former Adler-Barish firm who are defendants in this action have submitted affidavits averring that Daniels withdrew on his own accord and was not forced out of Adler-Barish; additionally, other defendants aver that Daniels was not prohibited from accessing client files. Thus, I cannot rule as to the absence of a factual dispute concerning Daniels leaving the Adler-Barish firm. Moreover, the fact that Daniels' former partners allegedly wrongfully denied him access to the client files does not release Daniels from his duties to plaintiffs.

Daniels' submission of affidavits has not precluded a genuine issue of fact concerning, *inter alia*, whether or not plaintiffs had knowledge of the dissolution of Adler-Barish or that Barish was not charged with winding up Adler-Barish's affairs. Accordingly, I must deny defendant Daniels' motion for summary judgment as to Counts I and II of plaintiffs' complaint.

Last, I turn to defendant Daniels' assertion that the punitive damages claim, Count III of plaintiffs' complaint, is improper because defendant Daniels avers in his affidavit that he was not a partner of Barish when the purported negligence occurred. However, as stated earlier, the fact that a partnership dissolves does not terminate affairs that were current at the time of dissolution; termination of liability occurs once the current matters (at time of dissolution) are resolved or wound up. Moreover, the very fact that Barish was permitted to wind up affairs for the former partnership may in itself be a reckless act. Accordingly, defendant Daniels' motion for summary judgment as to Count III must be denied.

Notes

1. Under UPA section 35(1)(a), after dissolution a partner may bind by partnership by any act appropriate for

  a. winding up partnership affairs or

  b. completing transactions unfinished at dissolution.

How did the court in *Palomba v. Barish* apply that principle? How would it apply to Problem 16.12?

2. The RUPA equivalent to UPA section 35(1)(a) is RUPA section 804(1). That section refers only to acts appropriate to winding up partnership affairs. RUPA section 804(1) omits without comment acts appropriate to completing transactions unfinished at dissolution. Would that change the result in either *Palomba v. Barish* or Problem 16.12?

3. UPA section 35(1)(a) and RUPA section 8704(1) are directed to the power of *partners* to *bind* the partnership.

  a. On what basis could you argue that the partnership is liable for contracts entered into, in the course of winding up or in completing unfinished transactions, by agents of the partnership who are not partners?

  b. On what basis would you argue that the partnership is liable for torts committed by partnership personnel in the course of winding up or in completing unfinished transactions?

How would the court in *Palomba v. Barish* have handled those questions?

Problem 16.13

Under the facts of Problem 16.12, suppose that after dissolution of the ABC Construction, Al (one of the partners) signed a new contract to construct a home.

  a. Under the UPA:

    (1) Are ABC Construction and its partners subject to liability on the new contract?

    (2) What are the rights as between Al and the other partners with respect to the contract?

(3) What steps should the partnership or the partners take to avoid liability on any future such contracts?

b. Under the RUPA:

(1) Are ABC Construction and its partners subject to liability on the new contract?

(2) What are the rights as between Al and the other partners with respect to the contract?

(3) What steps should the partnership or the partners take to avoid liability on any future such contracts?

Problem 16.14

Under the facts of Problem 16.13, suppose that one of the partners, Bob, had withdrawn from the partnership, but that the partnership agreement provided that a partner withdrawal would not dissolve the partnership.

a. *Al* enters into a new contract for the construction of a home.

(1) Is Bob subject to liability on the new contract?

(2) What are the rights as between Bob and the remaining partners with respect to the contract?

(3) What steps should Bob take to avoid liability on any future such contracts?

How do the UPA and the RUPA apply?

b. Assume that Bob left on bad terms with the other partners. After Bob has withdrawn as a partner, *Bob* enters into a new contract in the name of the partnership for the construction of a home.

(1) Are ABC Construction and its partners subject to liability on the new contract?

(2) What are the rights as between Bob and the remaining partners with respect to the contract?

(3) What steps should the partnership or a remaining partner take to avoid liability on any future such contracts?

How do the UPA and the RUPA apply?

Wolfe v. East Texas Seed Co.
583 S.W.2d 481 (Tex. Civ. App. 1979)

DOYLE, Justice.

East Texas Seed Company (appellee) sued Charles R. Wolfe (appellant) and Nick Wolfe, doing business as Wolfe Construction Company, for certain goods and merchandise sold and delivered to the construction company on an open account from February 9, 1974, through September 30, 1974, for a total amount of $6,323.05. Alternatively, appellee sued the partnership of Charles R. Wolfe and Nick Wolfe, doing business under the firm name of Wolfe Construction Company, for the amount of the debt, claiming that appellee had no knowledge of the dissolution of the partnership in 1973, said partnership having been formed in 1971. Appellee further alleged that if it had been aware of said dissolution it would not have extended credit to the construction company. Appellant defended on the grounds that he was without legal capacity to be sued since his partnership with Nick Wolfe had been dissolved in 1973 prior to the inception of debt made the basis of this suit. The trial court awarded appellee judgment against the defendants, jointly and severally, for $5,318.04 with interest. Only Charles R. Wolfe appealed.

[Appellant] allege[s] that the district court erred in rendering judgment for the plaintiff in that there was no evidence of probative value in the record to show that the plaintiff knew of or relied in any way on the individual credit of defendant Charles R. Wolfe as a partner in the company in selling the merchandise or incurring the account, and that the court also erred in rendering judgment for the plaintiff against defendant Charles R. Wolfe in that the evidence of record clearly shows that this defendant received no value or benefit from any of the items made a basis of this suit.

Appellant argues that pursuant to the [UPA], he is not under any duty to tender notice of dissolution of the partnership to creditors and, further, that he is absolved from all partnership liability under [UPA section 35(2)], stating:

(2) The liability of a partner under Paragraph (1b) shall be satisfied out of partnership assets alone when such partner had been prior to dissolution:

(a) Unknown as a partner to the person with whom the contract is made; and

(b) So far unknown and inactive in partnership affairs that the business reputation of the partnership could not be said to have been in any degree due to his connection with it.

Appellant cites no authority for his interpretation of this article.

A fair summary of the testimony concerning the partnership and its dissolution is as follows: Appellee's manager, Mr. Kirby, admits he did not know whether appellant's company was a partnership when it first began doing business with them. He stated that he first became aware of the partnership in 1974 after it had been dissolved. He further explained that if he had known of the dissolution he would have investigated the matter and that it would have made a "whole lot" of difference to his company.

Appellant strongly contends that since the partnership had been terminated before the inception of the debt, he should not be personally liable. As a general rule this would be true where notice of the dissolution has been given to third parties who had dealings with the partnership. On the other hand, absent any notice of dissolution, appellant cannot escape personal liability for the subject debt unless he can show that prior to dissolution, he had been "So far unknown and inactive in partnership affairs that the business reputation of the partnership could not be said to have been in any degree due to his connection with it." [UPA § 35(2)(b)].

The facts before us show that appellee did business with the company prior to the partnership dissolution; that appellant was known as Wolfe Construction Company; that the company was composed of two brothers, Nick and Charles R. Wolfe; that either man had authority to purchase seed; and that both men bought and paid for the seed. Appellant denies receiving any benefit from these transactions personally, but admits the partnership could have purchased the seed and benefited from it. Business was continued by appellant under the same name of Wolfe Construction Company, Nick Wolfe still worked for the company and no notice of partnership dissolution was sent to appellee. Appellant's reputation was relied on in transactions with appellee, and even in the absence of any partnership agreement parties may be bound as partners as to third parties.

The judgment of the trial court is affirmed.

Notes

1. As discussed in *Palomba v. Barish*, page 845, and the following notes, the dissolution of a partnership changes the actual authority of the partners to acts appropriate for winding up or for the completion of unfinished transactions. Under UPA section 35(1)(b), despite dissolution, partners continue to have the power to bind the partnership, by acts that would have bound it prior to dissolution, but only to:

a. persons who had *extended credit* to the partnership prior to dissolution, UPA § 35(1)(b)(I); and

b. others who had known of the partnership prior to dissolution, UPA § 35(1)(b)(II).

As to prior creditors, this "lingering partnership authority," if you will, is cut off only if the creditor had knowledge, UPA § 3(1), or notice, UPA § 3(2), of the dissolution. UPA § 35(1)(b)(I). As to persons who were not prior creditors, lingering partnership authority can be cut off by knowledge or notice, but also by publishing a notice of the partnership's dissolution in a newspaper of general circulation in each place in which partnership business was regularly carried on. UPA § 35(1)(b)(II).

2. Is UPA section 35(1)(b) consistent with the principles of agency law you studied in Chapter 14?

a. Is a partner a person who would have lingering apparent authority?

b. Are prior creditors and persons who had known of the partnership persons that would be protected by lingering apparent authority?

c. Under agency law, are there persons who would be protected by lingering apparent authority, but who are not protected by UPA section 35(1)(b)?

d. Is the difference in the types of notice required to cut off lingering partnership authority consistent with the kinds of notice required to cut off lingering apparent authority?

3. Historically, so-called "silent partners" and "dormant partners" were still partners with full personal liability for the obligations of the partnership, both during its active life and during its winding up. This was even the case for partners who had withdrawn from, or otherwise ceased to be associated with, the partnership, but third parties had not been notified of their departures. See, UPA §§ 33-36, 41-42.

a. UPA section 35(2) limits the liability of certain dormant partners to partnership assets. If partnership creditors cannot reach personal assets of those partners, why would the UPA speak of the partners being liable at all?

b. UPA section 35(2) protects a partner *only* when the third party

(1) did not know that the person was a partner, UPA § 35(2)(a), *but also*

(2) the partner was "[s]o far unknown and inactive in partnership affairs that the business reputation of the partnership could not be said to have been in any degree due to his connection with it." UPA § 35(2)(b).

Why might the drafters of the UPA believed that the first requirement was not adequate to protect persons dealing with the partnership?

4. As to dissolutions, the RUPA provisions analogous to UPA section 35 are RUPA Sections 804 and 805. These sections make several changes from the rules of UPA section 35:

a. Partners have the power to bind the partnership to any person without notice of dissolution, not just to creditors and to persons who had heard of the partnership before dissolution. RUPA § 804.

b. There are two major changes in the manner in which lingering partnership authority terminates:

(1) The RUPA treats all persons without actual notice of a partner's dissociation in the same manner. That is, the RUPA does not distinguish between prior creditors and persons entering into contracts.

(2) Notice by publication in a newspaper of general circulation is no longer effective or required.

(3) Partners' lingering partnership authority terminates 90 days after the filing of a "Statement of Dissolution" under RUPA section 805.

5. For dissociating partners, the RUPA sections analogous to UPA section 35 are RUPA sections 702, 703, and 704. These sections are similar to RUPA section 804 and 805, but with slight adjustments:

a. A *dissociating partner* is not liable for new partnership obligations to persons who did not reasonably believe that the dissociating partner was a partner at the time of the transaction. RUPA § 703(b)(1).

(1) Does this requirement make sense? As a general matter, are partners only liable on partnership obligations to creditors who reasonably believed they were partners? See RUPA § 306.

(2) Would the RUPA have changed the result in *Wolfe v. East Texas Seed Company?*

b. Similarly, the partnership's liability for contracts entered into *by a dissociating partner,* is limited to persons who reasonably believed that the dissociating partner was still a partner. RUPA § 702(a)(1). As a general matter, is the partnership only liable to persons who reasonably believing the partner was a partner? See RUPA § 301(1).

c. The provisions for termination of lingering partnership authority after a partner dissociation are similar to RUPA sections 804 and 805, but with some changes:

(1) Lingering partnership authority terminates *two years* after a dissociation. RUPA §§ 702(a), 703(b).

(2) It also terminates 90 days after the filing of a "Statement of Dissociation" under section 704.

6. As to both partner dissociation and dissolution, the "dormant partner" provision has been eliminated from the RUPA.

7. Regarding the prospect that a dissociating member of a limited liability company might act in such a way as to bind the firm, see ULLCA §§ 703, 804. Section 804 also addresses a manager's post-dissolution actions.

H. Additional Problems

16.15. In January, Art, Ben, and Clark decided to open a very small ice cream shop called ABC Tastee Treat. Art contributed $20,000, Ben contributed $18,000, and Clark (who had no money) contributed nothing. The three men had an oral understanding that they would share the profits equally. They also agreed that if any one of them died, the survivor or survivors had the right to continue the business by paying the deceased's estate one third of the fair market value of the business. The three men operated the restaurant for several months, and it was only moderately successful (it earned a slight profit each month). They spent $500 a month to run an advertisement in the local restaurant/diner's guide called Gourmet Guide. Clark decided to go to Alaska and he left for Alaska to live there permanently on June 1, without telling Art or Ben. Art and Ben continued to operate the business for a few more months. Art and Ben decided to have some remodeling work done in the restaurant by Smith Construction Company, so they contracted to have $5000 worth of work done. It was completed in July, but was not paid for. Art died on September 1. Ben operated the restaurant for a few days alone. On September 10, he signed a contract for $1,000 for the advertisement to run in the October and November issues of Gourmet Guide. However, Ben quickly became tired of running the restaurant alone, and he closed the business on October 1. He sold the entire business on October 1 for $40,500, which was the best price he could obtain in the market under the adverse economic conditions prevailing at the time of the sale. Gourmet Guide claims its right to $1,000. Ben claims a right to $5,000 in compensation ($1,000 a month for each of the months of June, July, and August for his services in running the restaurant plus $1,000 for the period of September 1-30 and $1,000 for the period of October 1-30 in addition to his contribution of $18,000. Smith Construction Company claims $5,000.

a. What are the rights of each of the parties—Art's estate, Ben, Clark, Smith Construction Company, and Gourmet Guide—from the pool of $40,500?

b. If the proceeds from the sale had been inadequate to pay Gourmet Guide and Smith Construction, and if Clark had funds, could Clark be liable to pay for those expenses incurred after he had left the company?

c. What should Clark have done in order to avoid the risk of further personal liability when he left for Alaska?